Principles of

Advertising & IMC

Second Edition

Tom Duncan, Ph.D.

Director, IMC Graduate Program
Daniels College of Business
University of Denver
and
School of Journalism & Mass Communication
University of Colorado at Boulder

McGraw-Hill
Irwin

Boston   Burr Ridge, IL   Dubuque, IA   Madison, WI   New York   San Francisco   St. Louis
Bangkok   Bogotá   Caracas   Kuala Lumpur   Lisbon   London   Madrid   Mexico City
Montreal   New Delhi   Santiago   Seoul   Singapore   Sydney   Taipei   Toronto

**McGraw-Hill
Irwin**

PRINCIPLES OF ADVERTISING & IMC

Published by McGraw-Hill/Irwin, a business unit of The McGraw-Hill Companies, Inc., 1221 Avenue of the Americas, New York, NY, 10020. Copyright © 2005, 2002 by The McGraw-Hill Companies, Inc. All rights reserved. No part of this publication may be reproduced or distributed in any form or by any means, or stored in a database or retrieval system, without the prior written consent of The McGraw-Hill Companies, Inc., including, but not limited to, in any network or other electronic storage or transmission, or broadcast for distance learning.

Some ancillaries, including electronic and print components, may not be available to customers outside the United States.

This book is printed on acid-free paper.

3 4 5 6 7 8 9 0 WCK/WCK 0 9 8 7 6 5

ISBN 0-07-111118-2

www.mhhe.com

Preface

To Professors

Advertising, as you know, is changing. That is why this textbook is about advertising *and* IMC. It includes all the key advertising principles and practices *plus* the integration process that maximizes advertising's effectiveness. IMC—integrated marketing communication—is no magic wand or silver bullet but simply the process of advertising, promotions, and media working together in strategic and effective ways. As the following excerpts attest, integration is no longer just a buzzword. Integration is now the foundation of most major advertising and promotion efforts.

> In a study of 273 major U.S. companies, 43 percent said having one agency that could offer fully integrated services was "very important."
>
> *Advertising Age*, June 10, 2003 (AdAge.com).

> According to the CEO of MVBS, "We needed to get people to buy into the fact that there was a larger idea that was better for everyone . . . The larger idea, of course, is integrated marketing services for clients."
>
> *Advertising Age*, March 16, 2003 (AdAge.com).

> Ogilvy & Mather was named Agency of the Year because it "soared creatively, packed a powerful new-business punch, and excelled at creating integrated programs for a roster of blue-chip clients."
>
> *Advertising Age* Special Report, January 14, 2002, pp. 1, S1.

> According to Don Calhoun, executive VP of marketing for Wendy's: "It is important for us at Wendy's to have all of our resources integrated under one roof . . . integration produces the best results."
>
> *Wall Street Journal*, August 16, 2002, p. B5.

> McCann's newest strategic planning tools "address the marketing landscape shift of the late 1990s, when print ads and TV spots went from being the primary communication channels to being simply two channels among many that also included event marketing, e-marketing, PR, and relationship marketing."
>
> *Advertising Age*, March 18, 2002, p. C26.

> Publicis CEO Maurice Levy "ensures that all [marketing communication] disciplines are combined from the beginning of the process, avoiding the fragmented model we're used to seeing as the end product of poor integration. To put it simply, the brand communication is born of the whole."
>
> *Advertising Age*, March 4, 2002, p. 30.

This text (like every other major textbook written for the introductory course in advertising) includes coverage of industry organization, customers' buying behavior, segmenting and targeting, and positioning, along with explanations of the marketing communication (MC) functions and media. However, to these fundamentals, *Principles of Advertising & IMC* adds a thorough treatment of the practices critical to building customer relationships and brands. Presented here are the IMC concepts and processes used by companies that truly put the customer first. IMC is about integrating *marketing* and *communication*.

If you agree that advertising and promotion should be taught from an integrated perspective, check the subject index of your current textbook to see how much coverage is given to these critical integration practices:

- Brand/customer touch points (intrinsic, unexpected, company-created, customer-created).
- Branding, brand building, and brand equity.
- Customer retention and lifetime customer value.
- Two-way, interactive communication.
- Construction and use of databases.
- Brand messages rather than marketing communication messages.
- Cross-functional organization.
- SWOT analyses (internal <u>s</u>trengths and <u>w</u>eakness, external <u>o</u>pportunities and <u>t</u>hreats).
- Zero-based planning.
- Customer service and its communication role in retaining customers.
- Relationship metrics.

If those topics are not covered in your current textbook (or are mentioned only briefly), your students are receiving only part of the big picture of how advertising is being practiced today.

Content "Quality Control"

In preparation for the development of this revision, the first edition was reviewed by a panel of professors who had adopted and used the text, as well as by a group who had used competing textbooks. At the same time, two groups of students were asked to give their anonymous feedback on the book. In response to the input from both professors and students, the first edition was revised, and the new version was sent to a second panel of professors for review. Because of this *triple set of reviews*, the text you are now holding is as current and accurate as it could possibly be.

As a result of this feedback and rewriting, the new edition differs from its predecessor in many important ways. Key topics are explained in a more clear and concise manner. The discussion of *management issues* has been streamlined, and the number of *visuals and examples* has increased. A discussion of *channel marketing* has been added. More explanation is given to *customer service* and its impact on *customer retention*. More explanation also is given to *personal selling*. *Direct response* appears in its own chapter. And the *IMC model has been simplified*.

Because of the rigorous reviews, we are confident that *Principles of Advertising & IMC* provides the most contemporary textbook discussion of advertising and IMC. Using many examples and cases, the book explains what smart companies and marketing communication agencies are doing to build customer relationships and brands.

Acknowledgments

A book like this is possible only with the help and input of many people. I am indebted most to my wife, friend, and academic colleague, Professor Sandra

Moriarty. Her wisdom and advice over the years have been invaluable to my development of an IMC concept and process. Her patience and understanding during the writing of this book are impossible to repay.

A big thanks to Steve Patterson, the McGraw-Hill/Irwin sponsoring editor who originally signed this book. His confidence and foresight regarding the academic and professional importance of IMC gave birth to the book's production. Thanks to Linda Schreiber, executive editor, who very professionally managed the development and revision of the book along with Sarah Crago, who diligently managed the day-to-day logistics and paid close attention to the many details so necessary in producing a book package of this nature. Thanks to Laura Edwards for editing and giving many suggestions for ways to make the content more accessible to students. Thanks to Kristen Meador for research and editing assistance. Thanks also to the production team at McGraw-Hill: Susanne Riedell, project manager; Matt Baldwin, designer; Jeremy Cheshareck, photo coordinator; and Rose Range, supplement producer. The time and energy they contributed to the production of the second edition are priceless.

Others who made significant contributions, for which I am extremely grateful, are:

Peggy Bronn, Professor of Marketing, BI School of Business, Oslo, Norway.

Clarke Caywood, Former Director, IMC Graduate Program, Northwestern University.

Ed Chambliss, Team Manager, The Phelps Group.

Bob Davies, Vice President, Price/McNabb.

Michelle Fitzgerald, Connection Planner, Fallon.

Mark Goldstein, Fallon's Worldwide Director of Integrated Marketing.

Richard Goode-Allen, Assistant Professor, University of Colorado–Boulder.

Amy Hume, Media VP, Leo Burnett.

David Miln, marketing communication and brand consultant, London.

Marieke de Mooij, international cultural marketing consultant, the Netherlands.

Joe Plummer, Executive Vice President, Director of Brand Strategy and Research, McCann-Erickson World Group.

Don Schultz, founder of Northwestern University's IMC program.

Karl Weiss, President, Marketing Perceptions Inc.

Thanks to the following people who reviewed the first edition or manuscript drafts in various stages and provided insights, commentary, and suggestions that enhanced the quality and usefulness of this text:

Janice Bukovac, Michigan State University

Jerone Christia, Coastal Carolina University

Douglas Allen Cords, California State University

Rama Jayanti, Cleveland State University

Tom Leach, University of New England

Terry Paul, Ohio State University

Carolyn Predmore, Manhattan College

Lopo Rego, University of Iowa

Vicki D. Rostedt, University of Akron

Richard Stafford, University of Kentucky

Sandra H. Utt, University of Memphis

Lara Zwarun, University of Texas

Richard Beltramini, Wayne State University

Newell Chiesl, Indiana State University

Jerry Conover, Northern Arizona University

Stevina Evuleocha, California State University–Hayward

Aron Levin, Northern Kentucky University

Sandy Lueder, Southern Connecticut State University

Esther Page-Wood, Western Michigan University

Corliss Thornton, Georgia State University

Terri Albert, University of Hartford

Tiffany Barnett White, University of Illinois

Leila Collins, University of Maryland

Susan Mudambi, Temple University

Michelle Patrick, University of North Carolina

Eugene Secunda, New York University

Allen Smith, Florida Atlantic University

For Students

You've been doing it . . . and probably never realized it!

If you are like most college students (or just about anybody else), you have been "doing" advertising most of your life. Think about it. When you select your clothes, shoes, car, eyeglass frames, and everything else that's personal, chances are, one of your considerations is how you hope these things will make you look. Your decisions result in messages designed to say something about you to the people around you.

Some of the other "ads" that you have created and sent about yourself include where you work or go to school; the brand of bike, skis, snowboard, tennis racket, or golf clubs you use; how you react in certain situations (laugh, get angry, walk away); the things you do and the places you go to have fun; and the friends you hang around with. All these things, people, and behaviors send messages about you and impact to what extent others notice, like, and accept you.

Do you buy nonbranded things to signal that you are not materialistic and overly brand conscious? If you do, these selections and behaviors also send a message to others, just as traditional advertising does. Face it: From a marketing perspective, you are a brand, with a certain identity and image that is being constantly reinforced or changed by the decisions you make.

Just like you, IBM, McDonald's, Ford, Starbucks, and most other companies want to be liked—and want their products to be liked and accepted. Every day companies make decisions that affect how others perceive them. They pay a lot of attention not only to what their advertising says but also to the messages communicated by the design of their packages, by their employees' uniforms, and even by the design of their places of business. Like you, companies are aware that how they talk to customers and other stakeholders "advertises" something very important about them. They know that *everything* they do, and sometimes what they don't do, can send a powerful brand message.

This book explains how companies develop identities, images, and brands that create customer relationships that in turn produce sales and profits.

What Does "Advertising" Mean?

Several years ago, a global advertising agency, Leo Burnett, showed a sample of consumers a wide range of brand messages—a TV commercial, a magazine and newspaper ad, a direct-mail offer, a coupon, a recording of a telemarketing call, a picture of a sponsored event, a news story that said good things about a company or brand, and a package with an appetizing picture of the product inside. When asked to characterize these brand messages, the majority of consumers said they were all examples of "advertising," things companies use to persuade customers to like them and buy their products. They used *advertising* as an umbrella term referring to a variety of brand messages.

The word *advertising* is used in the same broad way in the title of this book (and many competing textbooks) because the book includes chapters on sales promotion, direct response, public relations, and events and sponsorships. Although consumers may call all persuasive messages "advertising," the umbrella term in this book is not *advertising* but *marketing communication*. Why? Because in the industry, mass media advertising is considered to be just *one* of many marketing communication functions.

What This Book Is All About

Because advertising, public relations, sales promotion, direct marketing, and the other MC functions have become so sophisticated, and the media so fragmented, commercial message clutter has significantly increased. As a result, companies find it extremely challenging to reach prospects and retain current customers. At the same time, emerging communication technologies, especially the internet, have greatly empowered customers by providing them with more ways in which to talk back to companies. Interactive media are available around the globe.

The difference between brand messages and media continue to blur as we see increased use of product placements, events, sponsorships, and brand-driven editorial content. The use of databases and computers to segment and profile customers is becoming more pervasive, easier, and less costly.

As a result of these new ways of communicating, customers have become more business-savvy and have higher expectations than ever before. This has resulted in fierce competition among brands and in top management demanding even greater accountability for how advertising and promotion budgets are spent. This textbook explains advertising and promotional practices within this marketplace environment—the real world.

The old marketplace motto "Caveat emptor" ("Let the buyer beware") has become obsolete. Today, a more accurate axiom is "Let the company beware." Recognizing this change, smart companies intensify their efforts to *integrate* their marketing communications and all other brand messages, because doing so is the most cost-effective way to build brand relationships and brand value.

Every business is unique, so advertising and promotions for every situation will be different. Nevertheless, there are basic principles and practices on which all advertising and promotion planning should be based. The overall objective of this book is to help you understand the various marketing communication functions, the major media alternatives, and the processes for integrating these activities in the most effective and efficient way in order to develop long-term, profitable brand relationships that build brands and create brand equity.

Every major text-book written for the advertising principles course must include the most up-to-date chapters on media planning, public relations, legal and ethical issues, sales, positioning, brand awareness, and international issues. Each book also strives to offer explanations of the major marketing communication functions and media. Principles of Advertising & IMC 2/e by Tom Duncan expertly covers everything you are looking for in a principles textbook and prepares students for the real world of advertising. But if you are looking for all of this and more, turn the page and see what else Tom Duncan's completely updated and revised book has to offer.

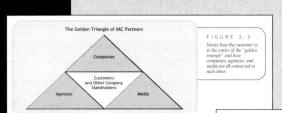

The Golden Triangle of IMC Partners

Companies

Customers
and Other Company
Stakeholders

Agencies

Media

FIGURE 2-3

Notice how the customer is at the center of the "golden triangle" and how companies, agencies, and media are all connected to each other.

ETHICS AND ISSUES

The Strategic Debates behind a Sponsorship

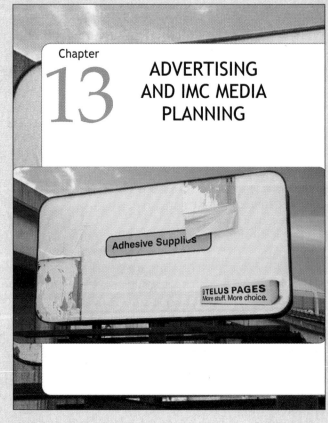

Chapter

13

ADVERTISING AND IMC MEDIA PLANNING

Adhesive Supplies

TELUS PAGES
More stuff. More choice.

CUSTOMERS ARE
AN INVESTMENT.
MAXIMIZE YOUR RETURN.

PeopleSoft

EXHIBIT 16-13
This ad for management software company PeopleSoft explains how its software can help with customer relationship management (CRM) programs.

Key Point Summary

Key Point 1: Personal Selling's Role and Objectives

Personal selling is two-way communication that uncovers and satisfies the needs of prospects, providing mutual, long-term benefits for both parties. Personal selling's primary role is retaining and growing customers, as well as customer acquisition.

Key Point 2: The Personal Selling Process

The process of personal selling, whether for acquiring new customers or selling to current customers, involves generating leads, qualifying leads, making the sales call, identifying and responding to objections, closing the sale, and following up to build and maintain the customer relationship.

Key Point 3: Personal Selling Management

In addition to integration, the two big issues in sales management are measuring the effectiveness of the effort and identifying the appropriate compensation and reward system. Personal selling is most effective when it is supported by other MC functions, such as advertising, public relations, and direct response. IMC programs rely on personal selling because of its strengths, which include the power of personalized, two-way communication, relationship building, accountability, flexibility, and the ability to collect useful information in the process of making a sale.

TABLE 6-6	Pro Forma for Maple Syrup Manufacturer	
Forecasted number of cases that will be sold next year		1,000,000
Sales price per case		$25
Forecasted sales revenue		$25,000,000
	Dollar Allocation per Case	Percentage of Sales
Cost of goods (materials)	$10.00	40%
Labor	2.50	10
Warehousing and distribution	1.25	5
Sales commission	2.50	10
Marketing communication	2.50	10
Administration and overhead	3.75	15
Profit before taxes	2.50	10
Total	$25.00	100%

PRINCIPLES OF ADVERTISING

Media Planning

Industry Organization

Scheduling

International Issues

Public Relations

Segmenting & Targeting

Budgeting

Legal & Ethical Issues

Sponsorship

Positioning

Sales

Brand Awareness

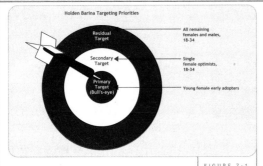

Holden Barina Targeting Priorities

Residual Target

Secondary Target

Primary Target (Bull's-eye)

All remaining females and males, 18-34

Single female optimists, 18-34

Young female early adopters

FIGURE 7-1

"Young female early adopters" were the primary target segment for the Holden Barina "BG" campaign.

Segmenting can be done at different levels of specificity. For example, a manufacturer of bicycles could begin by dividing a market into bike owners and non owners. Bike owners could be further segmented into bike racers, mountain bike riders, leisure riders, children, and parents. An important part of segmenting is specifying the characteristics that successfully predict who will be in the groups.
Segmenting is done to provide a marketer with targeting options. Figure 7-1

What makes Principles of Advertising

Only one book presents the basic advertising principles and practices *within an integration perspective*. Tom Duncan reaches beyond the expectations of the average principles of advertising course to explain in depth the practices that are so critical in integrating marketing communications and media. In addition to the traditional advertising topics, Duncan presents additional IMC topics not covered in other books, such as branding, customer service and retention, cross-functional organization, and a whole lot more. Throughout the text, Duncan also shows students that a company communicates in many other ways besides advertising and promotions, that communication between a company and customers is integrated and on-going.

. . . AND IMC

Media Planning

Industry Organization

Databases

Scheduling

Customer Service

Branding

International Issues

Public Relations

SWOT Analysis

Customer Retention

Cross-functional Organization

Relationship Matrix

Segmenting & Targeting

Budgeting

Legal & Ethical Issues

Two-way Communication

Zero-based Planning

Lifetime Customer Value

Sponsorship

Brand Building

Positioning

Brand Equity

Sales

Brand Awareness

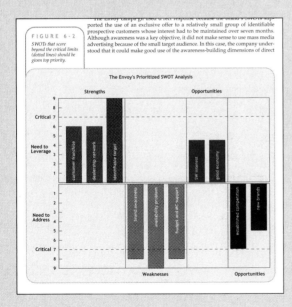

FIGURE 6-2
SWOTs that score beyond the critical limits (dotted lines) should be given top priority.

The Envoy campaign used direct response because the brand's SWOTs supported the use of an exclusive offer to a relatively small group of identifiable prospective customers whose interest had to be maintained over seven months. Although awareness was a key objective, it did not make sense to use mass media advertising because of the small target audience. In this case, the company understood that it could make good use of the awareness-building dimensions of direct

buyers and sellers to enter this new world of beauty and opportunity.

20550771-0.html>; Business, October 2002, <www.respon-service.com/archives/oct2002_issue2/business/internat.htm>.

PERSONAL SELLING: THE PRIMARY TWO-WAY MARKETING COMMUNICATION FUNCTION

Everyone does personal selling. Children sell lemonade, magazine subscriptions, and Girl Scout cookies. Students sell prom tickets and yearbook ads. Doctors "sell" exercise and diet programs to overweight patients. Lawyers "sell" briefs to skeptical judges. The fact is, **personal selling** is person-to-person interactive communication used to ultimately persuade. It is the oldest marketing communication function (see Exhibit 16-2).

A TALE OF TWO COMPANIES

Cross-Functional Planning at MetLife and General Electric

Cross-functional planning alone does not guarantee integration, but the lack of it almost always guarantees disintegration. Metropolitan Life Insurance Company (MetLife), the second largest insurance company in the United States, offers a good example of what can happen when a cross-functional team is not in place or has no authority. For years MetLife agents were allowed to use questionable sales practices, promising more than they could deliver. Because the sales operations was not actively monitored by a cross-functional team, MetLife soon found itself in deep trouble. Over 40 states levied fines, totaling $20 million, against the company. MetLife also faced the issue of making refunds of up to $75 million. After public disclosure of these problems, MetLife sales decreased by 25 percent. Finally, because of the lawsuits and legal problems, the company's credit rating was re-

tions. Pit sessions are held in the main auditorium of GE's Management Development Institute in Crotonville, New York. Staffs are challenged to speak up when problems are spotted. GE CEO Jack Walsh (now retired) said, "The group has to get together and fix the problem . . . You've got to take the responsibility to take the ball and run with it." He empowered employees to intervene in the system in order to provide solutions. From his experience with the Pit, Walsh created a new organizational structure for GE called "Work-Out." The GE workforce was organized into flexible, natural teams that meet frequently to discuss how to improve processes. The objective is more efficiency, less waste.

The secret to GE's innovative management approach is communication. Cross-functional teams with the authority to investigate various work processes

The Instructor's Resource CD includes the Instructor's Manual, Test Bank, and PowerPoint Presentation.

The Instructor's Manual has been completely rewritten, combining the author's classroom and industry knowledge with the expertise of other teachers in the field. The new Instructor's Manual has an array of classroom tools for each chapter: objectives, key points, chapter perspectives, lecture outlines, case discussions, project ideas, video teaching notes, and more.

The Test Bank contains a variety of new questions in the standardized multiple choice, true/false, short answer, and essay questions plus new mini-case application sections which are crafted by the author and unique to this supplement package.

Coke: A Successful User of MC to Build a Brand

In addition to a new, attractive design, the PowerPoint presentation is also completely redesigned with ads and images that can be enlarged within the presentation and extensive speaker's notes to help instructors further enhance their lectures.

The video package is completely updated with new video segments on UPS, Monigle, MINI Cooper, and other well-known and interesting companies. The videos are tied to cases and topics contained within the textbook. The integration of these materials provides great groundwork for compelling classroom discussions.

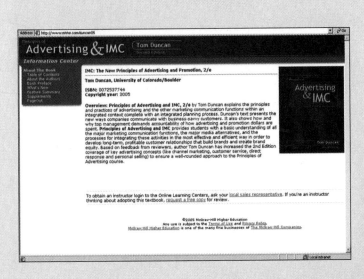

The Online Learning Center houses the Instructor's Manual, PowerPoint slides, and a link to McGraw-Hill's course management system, PageOut, for instructors, and study outlines, quizzes, key terms, career information, and online resources for the student.

Brief Contents

Contents

3 Brands and Stakeholder Relationships 66

Part Two

BASIC MC STRATEGIES FOR BUILDING BRANDS 102

4 How Brand Communication Works 102

7   Segmenting and Targeting 206

**Effectiveness Case: Insights from
Everywhere: McCann-Erickson, Melbourne,
Australia** *208*

**What's the Point of Segmenting and
Targeting?** *210*

Part Three

CREATING, SENDING, AND RECEIVING BRAND MESSAGES 274

12 The Internet and Interactivity 384

Effectiveness Case: BMW's "Films" Makes
Interactivity a Winner *386*

Part Four

THE MARKETING COMMUNICATION FUNCTIONS 460

14 Consumer Sales Promotion and Packaging 460

15 Channel Marketing: Trade Promotion and Co-Marketing **488**

16 Personal Selling **514**

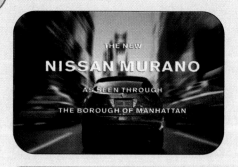

21 International Marketing Communication 666

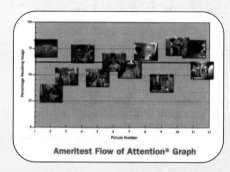

Ameritest Flow of Attention® Graph

22 Measurement, Evaluation, and Effectiveness 696

Chapter

1

Using Advertising and Promotion to Build Brands

Key Points in This Chapter

1. What are the functional areas of marketing communication?
2. How would you explain the IMC concept to someone?
3. What is the IMC process?
4. Why is integration so important in marketing communication?

Chapter Perspective

The Changing World of Advertising and Promotion

No industry is more creative, exciting, rewarding, and challenging than advertising and promotion! This industry is unique because it puts everything it does on stage for the world to see and respond to—loving it, hating it, being moved by it.

Not long ago most client companies and agencies cared only about creating and sending brand messages in order to sell products. Today, companies also engage in dialogue with their customers, and increasingly customers themselves initiate these conversations. Companies realize that building a relationship and trust are more likely to boost sales and profits than is "talking at" customers and prospects. Selling additional products to current customers is significantly less costly than selling to a new customer for the first time.

Another change is the increasing amount of new information and communication technology. New media, such as the internet, cellular phones, and wireless computing, make marketing communication programs ever more complex. That's why it is useful to approach advertising and promotion from the integrated marketing communication (IMC) perspective.

The most important things that you will learn from this chapter are that successful companies use many types of communication, not only to win new customers but also to keep them, and that communication—the sending and receiving of messages—is at the heart of all relationships, including our relationships with our favorite brands.

So, welcome to the new integrated world of advertising and promotion.

AAAAAA-FLAAAAACK!
How Integrated Marketing Communication "Ducked" the Competition

In 1955, three brothers in Columbus, Georgia, pooled $40,000 and decided to sell supplemental cancer insurance. The start-up was slow, and the company was underfunded. Things got so bad at one point that the brothers sold their office furniture to generate money in order to stay in business.

Today, AFLAC is the number-one provider of supplemental insurance, insuring more than 40 million people worldwide. It is a Fortune 500 company with a basketful of accolades for excellence in business environment, earnings, and effectiveness. It has been judged one of the 100 Best Companies to Work For in America (*Fortune* magazine), the Most Admired Company in Life and Health Insurance (*Fortune*), and one of the Best Companies for Minorities (*Fortune*); it also boasts an A+ (superior) rating from Standard and Poor's 500 Index.

One of the things that has made AFLAC so successful is its integrated marketing communication approach to building its brand. Because of the company's creative one-voice, one-look advertising, an ordinary duck has become a memorable company symbol and a pop culture icon. AFLAC has also integrated this creative brand message into extensive sponsorships and specialized media buys to reach its prime customers and prospects. In addition, the company's extraordinary community involvement has generated positive brand publicity.

Those advertising and publicity practices, however, are only one aspect of the company's integrated approach. AFLAC knows it is impossible to have an integrated brand image without being integrated internally. Examples of what this means include keeping employees informed, using information technology to track customer interactions with the company, doing intensive employee training, and providing employee perks and a good working environment in order to keep employee morale high. The result of these practices is top-quality customer service. In other words, AFLAC places as much

EXHIBIT 1-1

emphasis on retaining customers as it does on acquiring them—a basic principle of IMC.

Target Audiences

The AFLAC communication program is targeted at four audiences, every one of which can have an impact on the effectiveness of a campaign:

1. AFLAC employees.

2. Employees of other companies who have insurance but find that their policies do not provide enough coverage.

3. Companies, especially human resource departments, that could offer AFLAC supplemental insurance to their employees.

4. Potential sales representatives. Like most insurance companies, AFLAC has an ongoing effort to expand and support its sales fore.

Marketing Communication Objectives

In 1999, despite $100 million spent on advertising in the previous five years, AFLAC's level of brand awareness was only 14 percent. A market analysis conducted by the company and its advertising agency, the Kaplan Thaler Group, determined that AFLAC's advertising, like that of similar companies, was filled with "boring, scary campaigns cluttered by large spenders and overly sentimental, generic advertising." Although AFLAC was profitable, managers knew it had the potential to be even more so—if it could do a better job of connecting with customers and prospects. This knowledge produced the following objectives:

- Increase brand awareness—among individuals and human resource decision makers—from 14 percent to 50 percent.
- Increase the network of independent sales associates and insurance brokers by 15 percent.
- Increase qualified sales leads by 20 percent.

To meet the objectives, the company and agency agreed that a creative "big idea" was needed— an idea that would connect with consumers and position AFLAC as a friendly, helpful provider of supplemental insurance. It was also agreed that the "big idea" had to have "legs"—that is, it had to work in a variety of marketing communication formats. Above all, it was imperative that the brand messages make the AFLAC name highly memorable.

Advertising and Promotion Strategy

A duck. With an attitude. And with an unflappable commitment to getting the name AFLAC to the humans it encountered, almost always under difficult or goofy circumstances.

The duck debuted in 2000. In the 10 commercials created through 2002, "America's best-known spokes duck" waddles into a variety of situations, trying to supply the right answer—"aaaaa-flaaaaack!"—to questions, comments, or situations pertaining to supplemental insurance. TV spots include "Auto Mechanic," "Yogi Berra at the Barber," "Natural History," "Grand Canyon," "Figure Skaters," "Roller Coaster," "Wrestling," "Bed," "Steam Room," and "Park Bench." The original campaign tag line, "Without it, no insurance is complete," was strengthened with a call-to-action added to more recent spots: "Ask About It At Work."

"The advertising was entertaining and awareness-oriented, but at the same time it sent a strong, relevant message about the need for supplemental insurance," explained Linda Kaplan, CEO of AFLAC's advertising agency.

Media Strategy—Delivering the "Duck" Message

AFLAC's main medium is TV—where the duck can quack in real-life but often frustrating situations. According to Al Johnson, AFLAC's director of corporate communications, TV programs are chosen in which AFLAC can be the dominant insurance advertiser, such as college football, major league baseball, cable programming with select demographics, and network news. The remaining advertising money is spent on websites and promotional brochures and sell-in kits for the sales staff and human resource personnel.

AFLAC's website (www.aflac.com) provides information for all current and potential target audiences. Viewers learn about the company's highly regarded working environment, can watch the much-liked duck commercials, and learn about the company's philosophy and support for community services.

Public Relations through Events and Sponsorships

AFLAC has a corporate policy that encourages employees to participate in community activities during the workday. AFLAC gives special recognition to employees who volunteer, believing that volunteerism "allows employees from various departments to build camaraderie while making a difference in the community." Among the public relations events that employees participate in or that the company sponsors have been the following:

- Employees have spent time on Saturdays completing the painting and landscaping of several homes built by Habitat for Humanity.

- "Christmas is for Kids" is an annual campaign that raises thousands of dollars through the Valley Rescue Mission and the House of Mercy. Employees, including the chairman and CEO, shop for, wrap, and distribute thousands of gifts to 1,000 poor children in the Columbus, Georgia, metro area, home to AFLAC's corporate headquarters.

- John Amos, CEO and one of the three founding brothers, died of lung cancer in 1990. In his honor, AFLAC became a $3 million sponsor in 1995 of Children's Healthcare of Atlanta, one of the largest pediatric cancer centers in the United States, with a specialty in treating patients with sickle cell anemia. AFLAC helped transform the facility into one of the most modern of its kind. In appreciation, the hospital named one of its special centers the AFLAC Cancer Center and Blood Disorders Service. AFLAC employees help patients and their families year-round through volunteer work and fund-raising events. Members of the sales force can elect to have monthly payroll deductions to support the center, fostering friendly competition between territories.

Sales Promotion Premiums Help Keep the Duck Top-of-Mind

To help keep the AFLAC duck flying high in the sky of brand awareness, the company offers the duck as a premium on the AFLAC website. Over 60,000 plush ducks wearing a blue AFLAC bandana and fitted with an AFLAC sound chip that squawks "aaaaaflaaack" have been sold. All the revenue—more than $300,000 to date—goes to the AFLAC Cancer Center. Other duck premiums include T-shirts, golf club head covers, caps, and bobble-head ducks.

Evaluation: Measuring the Success of AFLAC's Integrated Advertising and Promotion Programs

A year-and-a-half after the duck advertising began, 90 percent of AFLAC's target audiences recognized the company's name, far surpassing the objective of 50 percent. Even more important, sales in the United States increased 30 percent. This outcome indicated the company had also achieved its marketing communication objectives of increasing sales leads by 20 percent.

AFLAC CEO Dan Amos: "It's hard to think what things would be like without the duck. The tremendous momentum built in our U.S. organization is due in no small part to the successful duck campaign. The duck continues to strengthen the AFLAC brand and fuel tremendous growth both in the sales of our supplemental coverage and [in] our sales force," where recruiting increased 22 percent over the previous year.

Source: This case was written by Linda Lazier, Ph.D., using information from the AFLAC website (www.aflac.com); Bethany McLean, "Duck and Coverage," Fortune, July 23, 2001, online library; Geoffy Calvin, "Quack Heard 'Round the World," Fortune, Aug. 31, 2001, online library; Advertising and Marketing Effectiveness (AME) award details; AFLAC press releases; and a phone interview with Al Johnson, AFLAC director of corporate communications.

COMMUNICATION: THE BUILDING BLOCKS OF A BRAND

When you think about Nike, Starbucks, or Ben & Jerry's, what comes to mind? If you're like most people, it's a certain image, feeling, or impression. This is because a **brand** is *a perception resulting from experiences with, and information about, a company or a line of products.* What many people fail to understand is that brands live in the heads and hearts of customers—not on the side of a package (the image on a package is a logo; see Chapter 3). What marketing communication (and this book) are all about is how to create, deliver, manage, and evaluate **brand messages**—*all the information and experiences that impact how customers and other stakeholders perceive a brand.*

But creating awareness of a brand name is only one part of building a brand. Customers want to know what to expect from a brand—how they will benefit from using the brand, what the brand stands for, how the brand will make them feel when they use or own it, what recourse they have if they don't like the brand, as well as how much the brand costs and where it can be purchased. The information and feelings that are communicated about a brand, along with how the product performs, help customers form an opinion of a brand—a brand impression—that determines to what extent they will purchase and repurchase it. Generally speaking, the number of customers and how much they buy determines to what extent a brand is successful—and contributes to business profits.

This book will help you understand how brand messages and product experiences—the building blocks of a brand—come together to create an impression about a brand in your mind and in the minds of millions of other people. It will explain strategies and practices used by marketers such as AFLAC to create and deliver brand messages. This book will also explain what you would be doing if you decided to be a marketing or marketing communication professional.

> "McCann's newest strategic planning tools address the marketing landscape shift of the late 1990s, when print ads and TV spots went from being the primary communication channels to being simply two channels among many that also include event marketing, e-marketing, PR, and relationship marketing."
>
> McCann-Erickson CEO James Heekin III

Marketing Communication

If you have taken a marketing course, you are probably familiar with the four Ps of marketing—*product, price, place,* and *promotion.* Although all four say something about a brand (and are discussed in later chapters), promotion contains the marketing communication functions, which, along with media, are the primary focus of this book.

Marketing communication (MC) is *a collective term for all the various types of planned messages used to build a brand*—advertising, public relations, sales promotion, direct marketing, personal selling, packaging, events and sponsorships, and customer service. For decades most of the emphasis was on advertising; however, the 21st century is seeing a shift: more of the marketing communication tools are being used strategically to complement and reinforce one another. The CEO of McCann-Erickson Worldwide explains that the agency's newest strategies are moving from the use of mostly advertising to a wider set of MC tools.

MC functions, however, have little value without **media,** *the vehicles through which marketing communication messages are carried to (and from) target audiences.* The media that marketers use most frequently include TV, radio, newspapers, magazines, outdoor boards, internet, mail, and the telephone.

Building brands is the overall objective of all marketing communication as well as all marketing activities. One of the best brand-building jobs ever has been accomplished by Coca-Cola. Look at Exhibit 1-2. What is being advertised? You probably said "Coke," because the Coke logo is so well

EXHIBIT 1-2

Even though the letter is different, the advertisement still says "Coca-Cola." Why is that so?

Enjoy
Adver-tising

The secret formula, revealed.

Advertising. The way great brands get to be great brands.

www.netaid.org

EXHIBIT 1 - 3

*This NetAid
advertisement introduces
the nonprofit group and
explains how to make
donations to good causes
through the website.*

recognized even when modified. Building a brand is the same as building a business. Generally speaking, the more successful a company is at building its brand or brands, the more profits it will make and the greater its brand equity will be. **Brand equity** is *the intangible value of a brand*—value added to a product or service that derives from a perception in customers' minds (this concept is explained more fully in Chapter 3).

MC functions and media help build a brand by connecting a company with customers. Brand messages also add value to a brand for both customers and the company. Customers gain value by learning about what problems a brand can solve or what opportunities it offers and where it can be purchased, as well as answers to specific questions. In the case of nonprofit organizations, MC messages provide information about how to support a good cause (see Exhibit 1-3). Customers can also gain value when they purchase a brand that is well known and has a good reputation.

As sociologists have pointed out, people (and companies) use brands to help define themselves. Wearing a Rolex watch says something different about a person than does wearing a Swatch watch. Also, buying a well-known brand provides many people with peace of mind from knowing that the product is of good quality and the company will stand behind the product if there is a problem.

The Functional Areas of Marketing Communication

What makes working in marketing communication so exciting and challenging is that there are so many tools from which to choose—such as advertising, sales promotion, direct marketing, publicity, and packaging. Each MC tool is a functional area of communication expertise and specialization. When used creatively, each can significantly impact how customers think about a brand.

One of the important strategic decisions marketers must continually make is what mix of MC functions and media would be best for their brands. A **marketing communication mix** is *the selection of MC functions used at a given time as part of a marketing program.* Besides selecting the mix, marketers must also decide to what extent each function will be used. An MC mix is like a cake that can be made from a variety of ingredients, with the most commonly used ingredients being eggs, salt, milk, sugar, and flour, plus some type of flavoring. Just as the amount of each of these varies from recipe to recipe, the amount of advertising, sales promotion, and other MC functions varies from one MC mix to another.

In this section, eight MC functions are discussed. In addition to providing examples of how each tool can be used, the profiles provide a definition and a summary of each one's primary use in building brands. As you read about what these functions can do, imagine yourself as the marketing communication manager for a major brand. With this responsibility in mind, keep asking yourself this question: *How would I go about determining which MC functions and media I should use to create a promotional campaign for my brand?*

Advertising

One of the greatest uses of advertising in modern times was the launch of the VW Beetle in the 1960s. Auto advertising at that time was bombastic, showing big cars in big settings. The legendary Doyle Dane Bernbach agency presented the Beetle as small and ugly but reliable and fun, using headlines such as "Think Small," "Ugly Is Only Skin Deep," and "Lemon." By recognizing the car's limitations while at the same time dramatizing its quality (Exhibit 1-4), this advertising not only drew attention and created brand awareness, it sold cars. *Advertising Age* selected this campaign as number one in its top 100 ad campaigns of all time. **Advertising** is *nonpersonal, paid announcements by an identified sponsor.* It is used to reach large audiences, create brand awareness, help differentiate a brand from its competitors, and build an image of the brand.

The opening AFLAC case is a modern example of how advertising can quickly increase brand awareness and brand knowledge. As this case points out, the advertising was successful in achieving its objectives because it was creatively done. Unfortunately, much advertising is neither creative nor memorable. Because most advertising is designed to create brand awareness and an image for a brand, its impact is difficult to measure. The American retailer John Wanamaker once said to one of his assistants, "I know half of my advertising is a waste." When the assistant suggested that half of the advertising be canceled so the department store company could save money, Wanamaker responded, "The problem is, I don't know which half it is."

Advertising has historically been the dominant communication choice for many companies; however, that is changing. At Adwatch: Outlook 2002, a meeting of 400 advertising industry executives, much of the conference buzz centered on the use of marketing communication functions other than traditional advertising.[1] Recently the three largest advertising agency conglomerates (companies that own many different types of marketing communication agencies) reported that the *majority* of their revenues now come from providing marketing communication functions other than advertising.[2]

Think small.

EXHIBIT 1-4

Why is this 1960s campaign that introduced the VW Beetle considered one of the all-time great examples of advertising?

Direct Marketing

One of the oldest and most successful retail brands is Sears. It began in the mid-1800s and was built by the use of direct marketing (see Exhibit 1-5). The company's first marketing effort was sending out catalogs containing a selection of watches and jewelry. This direct marketing was so successful that Sears quickly expanded its product offerings to include everything from underwear to houses with preconstructed walls, windows, and doors that could be assembled wherever a customer had a plot of land. As urban areas expanded, Sears opened retail stores but kept its general-merchandise catalog in print until 1993.

What differentiates direct marketing from other MC functions? **Direct marketing** is *an interactive, database-driven MC process that uses a range of media to motivate a response from customers and prospects.* As the name implies, no retailers or other members of the distribution channel are involved in *direct* marketing (although some retailers use this form of selling in addition to retail sales).

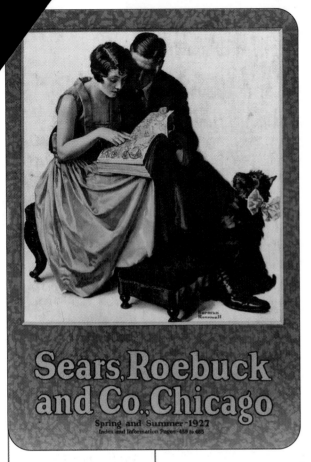

Sears, Roebuck and Co., Chicago
Spring and Summer 1927
Index and Information Pages 459 to 485

EXHIBIT 1-5

Why was the Sears, Roebuck catalog so successful as a marketing communication tool?

Today, Dell Computer Corporation is an example of how direct marketing can be the primary MC function used to build a successful brand. Michael Dell started the company when he was a student at the University of Texas. His strategy was to market directly to customers and build the exact computer that each customer wanted. Today, the primary medium that Dell uses to interact with customers is its website. Go to the Dell website shown in Exhibit 1-6. How quickly can you find a page describing a laptop computer that you would be interested in buying?

Publicity (A Form of Public Relations)

Although the launch of the VW Beetle in the 1960s was extremely successful, the brand eventually lost its cachet, and sales decreased so drastically (for a variety of business reasons) that VW quit manufacturing the car for the U.S. market. Then in 1998 a redesigned car was introduced in the United States as the "New Beetle." The brand was rebuilt primarily by publicity. The Ruder Finn public relations agency introduced the new Beetle with stories showing tie-dyed T-shirts, daisies, and peace symbols, which rekindled nostalgia for the 1960s. The new Bug even came with a bud vase, as did the press kits that Ruder Finn sent out. Because of this creative use of brand publicity, 900 local and national TV news segments featured the new Beetle during the week of its official launch. Matt Lauer introduced it on *The Today Show,* and Harry Smith, on CBS's morning TV show, took a new red Beetle for a spin around Times Square. The car made the cover of *Business Week* (Exhibit 1-7) before it was available in showrooms.

An example of the use of public relations to build a totally new brand is the story of Viagra. How to explain a medicine to treat erectile dysfunction posed a communication challenge. Pfizer, the maker of Viagra, determined that the best MC function to use initially was public relations. The resulting media buzz (brand publicity) and word of mouth generated by the publicity efforts prompted Pfizer to call the public relations effort "something of a cultural phenomenon."[3] Acclaimed as the fastest-selling new drug in history, the brand was launched in 40 countries, and 200,000 physicians wrote 7 million prescriptions for Viagra—all because of the brand-building introductory publicity. Not until a year later did the advertising campaign that featured ex-presidential candidate Bob Dole begin.

The terms *public relations* and *publicity* are often used interchangeably. They are not synonymous, however. **Publicity** is *stories and brand mentions delivered by the mass media without charge.* It is only one aspect of public relations. Tom Harris, former president of the Golin/Harris PR firm, estimated that close to 75 percent of PR firms' revenue comes from brand publicity. According to the Public Relations Society of America, **public relations** are *communication activities that help "an organization and its publics adapt mutually to each other"* in an effort to gain the support and cooperation of those publics.

Because publicity is "unpaid"—the media don't charge for using brand stories as they charge for advertising—it is frequently used to increase brand awareness and make news announcements about brands and companies. Publicity also is used to communicate with hard-to-reach audiences (such as executives who are

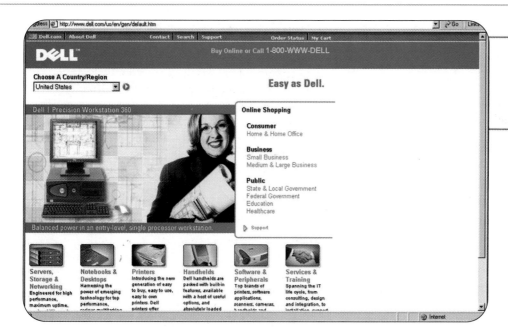

EXHIBIT 1-6

How has Dell Computer made its mark in marketing?

not heavy TV viewers and also who have people screen their mail and calls). One of the most important uses of publicity is to build brand credibility. Why this is possible is explained in Chapter 17 on brand publicity.

Sales Promotion

In the mid-1800s, patent medicines were one of the most widely advertised products. Because so many brands competed for consumers' attention, some brands began using sales promotion to get attention and acquire new customers. Sales promotion works by adding extra value, such as a price discount or a free trial, to an offer to stimulate consumers to try or buy a product (see Exhibit 1-8). A maker of patent medicine by the name of Dr. Kinsman offered a free box of his Heart Tablets to anyone willing to try them. Dr. Kinsman believed that if customers had nothing to lose, they would try his product, find it helpful, and make many repurchases. Another maker of patent medicine, Dr. Pierce, promised $500 to any woman not cured of "female weakness" by his medicine.

Over 100 years later, marketers are still using sales promotion to give customers an extra reason to buy. Pick up any local newspaper and you will find many ads containing coupons and sales promotions offers: "0% Financing on all Ford Explorers." "Buy one pair of shoes and get the second for half price at Famous Footwear." "Stay three nights at a Marriott and get the fourth night FREE." And then there are Coke and Pepsi, constantly trying to outpromote each other with a "2 Liter Bottle for only 99¢" deal. A type of sales promotion that is gaining in popularity is the frequent-buyer or customer loyalty program. Many grocery chains offer their frequent shoppers who have signed up (see Exhibit 1-9) significant discounts each week on selected items.

Because there are so many brands in each product category, and because so many of the products in a category are

EXHIBIT 1-7

Public relations was the marketing communication tool used to launch the new Beetle. Why was it chosen?

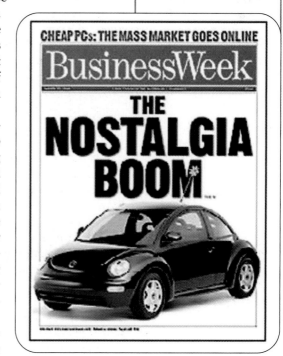

EXHIBIT 1-8

What sales promotion techniques were featured in these early advertisements?

similar, marketers offer customers reduced prices, coupons, small gifts, and other incentives in an effort to get attention and motivate buying. **Sales promotion** is *a short-term, added-value offer designed to motivate an immediate response.* Although generally used to motivate a buying decision, sales promotion is also used to move people through the buying process toward a particular brand. For example, some car dealers give customers free hot dogs and soft drinks just for visiting the dealer's showroom.

Although sales promotion has helped build brands and, even more important, helped brands keep customers from switching to competing brands, the overuse of promotional offers can actually harm a brand. Sales promotion must be combined with other MC functions and used strategically, as discussed in Chapters 14 and 15.

Personal Selling

EXHIBIT 1-9

How are frequent-buyer programs used to build customer relationships?

One of the earliest American brands to be built by personal selling is Fuller Brush, which began in 1906. This company sold a line of brushes and other home products door-to-door. By 1950, it was estimated that 9 out of every 10 U.S. homes had received a visit from the "Fuller Brush man" (a phrase coined by the *Saturday Evening Post*). These salesmen were so popular that they were often depicted in Blondie and Dagwood, Donald Duck, and Mickey Mouse comic strips. In 1948 a comedy, *The Fuller Brush Man* starring Red Skelton, was a box office hit.[4] Personal selling also inspired the now classic play *Death of a Salesman*, by Arthur Miller, which portrayed the less glamorous side of this MC function.

Like all the MC functions, contemporary professional personal selling has become increasingly sophisticated and strategic. For years, IBM was perceived as the number-one computer

company, and much of IBM's success was due to its smart and dedicated sales force, which introduced various businesses to computers and their uses. Although IBM did not invent the computer, it was the industry leader until the 1980s; then its status and fortunes dropped. Many competitors were selling computers of equal or better quality and at lower prices than IBM was charging. What rebuilt the brand was a new CEO, Lou Gerstner, who redefined personal selling at IBM. He insisted that personal selling was a consulting function and that IBM sales reps should help customers determine what hardware and software they needed and then teach them how to use it. Sales representatives also were trained to be not only sources of information but also innovators and designers, problem solvers, and troubleshooters. The turnaround of IBM was due to its Global Services division, whose mission was to sell "customer solutions"—service—rather than just hardware or software.

Personal selling is *interpersonal communication in which a salesperson uncovers and satisfies the needs of a customer to the mutual benefit of both.*[5] Although most of the income of most sales representatives is based on how much they sell, more and more companies are basing compensation on how successful salespeople are at building and maintaining relationships with customers. In many business-to-business (B2B) categories, personal selling is the dominant MC function.

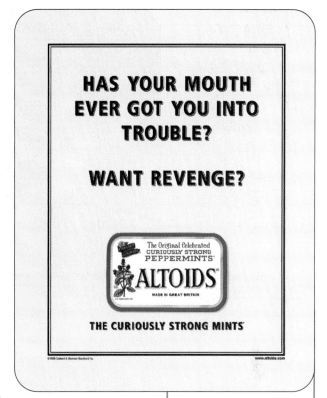

EXHIBIT 1-10

In addition to its "Curiously strong" slogan, what has made the Altoids brand so popular?

Packaging

One of the greatest breakthroughs in marketing came in 1879 when Procter & Gamble launched Ivory soap.[6] It was a breakthrough because Ivory was a branded product inside a distinctive package at a time when soap was a commodity and was sold unbranded out of a barrel or box. Packaging helped build the Ivory brand. The success of Ivory helped create the concept of "packaged goods," which eventually led to the system that P&G designed to manage its many branded products.

A more modern example of the power of creative packaging is Altoids. The brand, which originated in England more than 150 years ago, began a new advertising effort in the 1990s to increase brand awareness, especially among youthful customers. The new advertising emphasized Altoids' unusual package (see Exhibit 1-10). Because the Altoids box is made of metal, unlike the containers of almost all other candy and breath mints, the package is easily remembered and recognized in stores and generates impulse sales. Another benefit of the metal package is that many customers reuse it and even collect Altoids tins. The longer packages are kept around, the longer they work to keep the brand top-of-mind.

Packaging is *a container and conveyor of information.* A package can help in brand building by presenting various kinds of brand information—everything from ingredients to recipes that suggest multiple uses. Like sales promotion, packaging can add value to a product.

Events and Sponsorships

In 1949 Pillsbury held its first Pillsbury Cook-Off contest. Over the years this annual event has provided a fountain of brand publicity and has helped to show

EXHIBIT 1-11

How do Harley-Davidson events help build identification with the brand?

that Pillsbury is a cooking innovator as well as a provider of quality foods and ingredients. Furthermore, the event has enabled Pillsbury to maintain a leadership position in the food industry by publicizing the types of foods and ingredients used by some of the country's best amateur cooks.

Events are *highly targeted brand-associated activities designed to actively engage customers and prospects and generate publicity.* Public relations departments and agencies often use events to generate brand publicity. Harley-Davidson is an internationally recognized brand that has become a cultural icon in part by sponsoring events. When many think of a Harley owner, an image of "outlaw" Hell's Angels bikers wearing chains and black leather jackets often comes to mind. Behind that somewhat distorted image, however, is a subtle brand-building effort that leverages the Harley mystique and camaraderie. The Harley Owners Group, known as HOGs, constitutes a worldwide community of Harley owners; the organization and its events have been strategically nurtured by the Harley-Davidson company over the years.

Local and regional HOGs meet at rallies and annual summer gatherings. A HOG rally is an experience to remember (see Exhibit 1-11). It usually lasts from two to three days. Participants ride, race, and show off their machines (and their apparel). The company provides new bikes and prototypes to try out. HOG members get ideas for new designs for their bikes, tell stories about other meets, and polish their cycles (five different kinds of wax are used for different parts of the motorcycle, and it takes hours to polish a bike to show standards). What's unexpected is that the HOG members represent a wide range of socioeconomic groups and ages, everyone from outcasts to lawyers and professors. Harley-Davidson realizes that by sponsoring these events it is cementing relationships with its customers and making its brand even stronger and more valuable.

Most events are sponsored—that is, they are identified with one or more brands. But sponsorship goes beyond events. **Sponsorship** is *financial support of an organization, person, or activity in exchange for brand publicity and association.* Sponsorship is used not only to increase brand awareness but also to help define a brand through association. Nike sponsors Tiger Woods not only because he can be

EXHIBIT 1-12

Brands build affinity with spectators by sponsoring major events. How does that work?

a walking billboard for the Nike swish but because Nike wants to associate its name and products with Woods's excellent athletic performance.

Sponsorships come in all formats and sizes. The NASCAR stock car shown in Exhibit 1-12 carries the logos of many sponsors. How many can you identify, besides M&M? Although the lesser sponsors' logos are hard to see, especially when the car is traveling close to 200 miles per hour, these sponsors get other benefits (explained in Chapter 19).

Customer Service

For many years, exceptional service was something that customers expected only at expensive restaurants, at high-priced hotels, or while shopping in stores like Neiman Marcus and Tiffany. Good customer service was a product attribute that seemed to be available only to the very rich. But today, customers have a choice of many brands in almost every product category, and how a company treats customers can be the major reason for choosing one brand over others. As you watch TV and read newspapers and magazines, notice how many companies say that they are "customer focused" or "put customers first." Even though their follow-through is often less than desired, these ads show that companies recognize how important customer service is in building brands.

Southwest Airlines has been a consistently profitable airline in the United States, even during economic downturns. Why has Southwest been so successful when competitors have faced bankruptcy? The primary reason is customer service. People who work for Southwest are selected and trained to believe in a philosophy that values both efficiency and fun. This attitude was seeded in the company by long-time CEO Herb Kelleher, who loved to entertain employees and passengers with all sorts of antics (see Exhibit 1-13). Southwest employees, in terminals and on board planes, are known for their jokes and spirited attention to passengers. Serving customers and having fun are part of the Southwest Airlines culture and a primary builder of this remarkable brand.

Customer service is *a company's attitude and behavior during interactions with customers.* At first glance, it may seem strange that customer service is a marketing

EXHIBIT 1-13

What makes Southwest Airlines a profitable airline even in economic downturns? How do its customers relate to the airline?

communication function. The reason it is, is that interactions with customers send some of the most impactful messages that customers receive about a brand. If the interactive experience is positive, it will strengthen the customer relationship. If it is negative, it can weaken or even kill a brand relationship.

The Media of Marketing Communication

Nobody believed Ted Turner in 1980 when he said there was a market for a 24-hour news service. Now CNN News Group (see Exhibit 1-14) is one of the largest and most profitable news and information operations in the world. More than 1 billion people worldwide have access to at least one of CNN's services, which are delivered through eight cable and satellite television networks, two radio networks, 10 websites, and CNN News Source, the world's most widely syndicated news service.[7]

Although TV, radio, newspapers, magazines, outdoor boards, internet, mail, and the telephone are the predominant MC media, marketers have devised other creative ways to deliver brand messages and connect to customers. One of the fastest growing is product placements in movies and TV shows. Another is retail store design.

A recent *Wall Street Journal* article featured what it described as the largest ad display to be constructed in New York City's Times Square.[8] Designed by the Ogilvy & Mather Worldwide agency for Hershey Foods, the 2,500-square-foot "ad" is a storefront facade that rises 15 stories (see Exhibit 1-15). With flashing lights, steam machines, neon lighting, and a message board that can be programmed so consumers can flash personal messages to their loved ones, it is a massive advertisement built in a high-traffic location. It joins other brick-and-mortar "ad" retail properties such as Nike's "retail theater" stores and the General Mills "Cereal Adventure" at Mall of America in Bloomington, Minnesota. These retail environments create a memorable brand experience as they entertain and touch the emotions of those who see them.

Besides the proliferation of media alternatives, there has been a major increase in the use of two-way communication between customers and companies. Brand messages initiated by customers take the form of complaints, inquiries, suggestions, and compliments. The poster child for this interactive, two-way dialogue is, of course, the internet. Amazon.com® has made extraordinary use of this medium to build its brand (see Exhibit 1-16). When used for direct marketing, the internet makes it possible to run a retail operation 24 hours a day, seven days a week. It also extends a company's reach around the world. Because the internet is computer and database driven, companies such as Amazon.com® can remember what customers order and tailor follow-up communication to appeal to individual interests predicted by products previously purchased.

Each of the marketing communication functions and all the media are discussed in greater detail in later chapters. They are introduced here to provide an overview

EXHIBIT 1-14

CNN broke new ground with its 24-hour news service. Why was there a market for this channel?

of the communications that marketers use and to indicate why marketing communication and brand building require a disciplined and strategic approach to choosing and coordinating MC functions and media.

INTEGRATED MARKETING COMMUNICATION (IMC): A CONCEPT AND A PROCESS

Although MC functions and media have been used for decades, how they are selected and used has significantly changed over the years. Recent changes are due to the widespread use of computers, databases, new communication technology (such as the internet and wireless devices), and the wider array of brand choices. Deciding which MC functions to use, and how much of each, is quite a responsibility. Added to this responsibility, however, is the need to manage the creation and delivery of these messages as well as respond to inquiries, complaints, and suggestions from customers and prospects.

Earlier in this chapter you were asked how you would go about determining which MC functions and media to use to build your brand. If you are a smart marketing manager, here is what you would say: *Use an integrated marketing communication (IMC) process.*

Integrated marketing communication (IMC) is *a process for planning, executing, and monitoring the brand messages that create customer relationships.* IMC is about synergy (discussed below) and creativity, integration, and communication. Although many companies have coordinated and focused their marketing communication to a certain extent, one of the best examples of how to do IMC is the story of Saturn.

EXHIBIT 1-15

Even the retail environment can send messages. What do you think this storefront says about the Hershey brand?

A Different Kind of Car Story

The launch of the Saturn line of cars in 1990 shows what IMC is all about. In the late 1980s, General Motors knew it had a problem. Tracking studies by J. D. Power and Associates, the automotive research company, found that an increasing number of consumers were saying that they would not even consider buying a GM car. After several years of losing market share to competitors, particularly efficient small-car manufacturers in Japan, the giant auto company knew it had to move away from its old way of making and marketing cars.

GM's solution was to launch a new brand—Saturn—and purposefully not identify it with General Motors. GM also made the decision to use new manufacturing facilities as well as new marketing practices. A new plant was constructed in tiny Spring Hill, Tennessee, a long way from Detroit with its entrenched way of building and selling cars. Then GM hired San Francisco–based Hal Riney & Partners, a marketing communication agency that wasn't a traditional car advertising agency.

EXHIBIT 1-16

Why is the internet said to be an "interactive" medium?

GM also set up freestanding Saturn dealerships, which sold only Saturns (see Exhibit 1-17).

The Hal Riney agency worked with Saturn from its earliest days. It was involved in planning every brand message—names of models, hang-tags on rearview mirrors, dealer-training programs, the union relations program, and community relations with the town of Spring Hill. Hal Riney & Partners managed a network of agencies to craft a far-reaching communication program for all Saturn **stakeholders**—*individuals and groups that affect or are affected by an organization.* Stakeholder groups included new employees and dealers, vendors and suppliers, the community of Spring Hill and other communities where dealerships would be located, the media including the automotive press, and, of course, potential customers.

Pre-launch advertising and other MC messages focused on relationships with these stakeholders. One was an award-winning video about Spring Hill and what Saturn Corporation was doing to protect its rural small-city atmosphere. Pre-launch ads celebrated Saturn employees. One showed an executive and a union member bonding as they traveled around the world researching new ideas for Saturn cars. Another critical strategic decision that sent a powerful and differentiating message about Saturn was a "no-haggle" pricing policy. Researchers had found that most people said arguing over price made buying a new car an extremely unpleasant experience.

After the launch, advertising featured satisfied owners who recalled in their own words their experiences buying a Saturn. The key message, consistently communicated, was that Saturn Corporation was a new kind of car company. Saturn's slogan was "A different kind of company, a different kind of car." This relationship-focused philosophy distanced Saturn from the rest of General Motors (and competing brands) by celebrating respect for customers and employees, trust, and two-way communication.

IMC is also about managing day-to-day interactions with customers and prospects. Because business is ongoing, brand communication must be too. There are always customers and prospects who have questions, complaints, and suggestions which must be heard and given a timely and satisfying response. Today, building relationships and brands involves much more than just *sending* messages to customers and prospects.

IMC practices that delivered on Saturn's "different kind of company" promise included honest car-buying advice from the sales associates, individual customer care and convenience, no-haggle pricing, and a no-quibble return policy (within a specified period) if buyers were not satisfied with their car. Saturn's car-buying process was designed to be sensitive to customers' styles of decision making. And Saturn's aftermarket practices (maintenance and repair) focused on making customers feel that they remained part of the Saturn family.

Today, many companies and agencies recognize the value of being customer focused, of integrating their marketing efforts, and of no longer depending on traditional advertising. Read the excerpts from *Advertising Age* news stories listed in the IMC in Action box. What changes do they indicate are taking place in marketing communication?

IMC Is an Ongoing Process

Take a look at Figure 1-1. IMC is an ongoing communication process that spins off brand relationships, which when strong produce brand equity, sales, and profits. There is no beginning or end to the IMC process, because brand communication does not stop and start—it is continuous. That is why *evaluating and planning* are in the same box in Figure 1-1. Companies constantly evaluate the impact of brand messages on customer attitudes and responses and adjust their marketing communication plans accordingly. Planning provides direction for creating and delivering brand messages.

The media both deliver the messages and provide ways for customers and prospects to initiate and send messages to the company. As customers receive brand messages and respond to a company (by buying its products, asking questions, having repairs made, and so on), brand experiences are created. Each brand experience either strengthens or weakens the brand relationship. Strengthened relationships result in increased sales and profits, enhancing brand equity. Weakened relationships result in lost sales and lost customers, undermining brand equity.

IMC IN ACTION

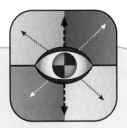

Testimonials about the Need for Integration

- Ogilvy & Mather Worldwide was named *Advertising Age's* U.S. Agency of the Year because the agency "soared creatively, packed a powerful new-business punch, and excelled at creating integrated programs for a roster of blue-chip clients."

  Rich Thomaselli, "Ogilvy Builds on Blue Chips," *Advertising Age*, Special Report, "Agency of the Year," January 14, 2002, pp. 1, S1.

- According to James Heekin, former CEO of McCann-Erickson Worldwide, the agency's mission is "a shared commitment to collaborative [e.g., integrated] solutions for clients . . . One of the toughest things business faces today is the ability to collaborate across [marketing communication] divisions."

  John McDonough, "CEO James Heekin III Talks about McCann's 'Best-in-Class' Mission," *Advertising Age*, March 18, 2002, p. C26.

- Publicis CEO Maurice Levy introduced "La Holistic Difference," a method of integration, to all the Publicis agencies, including Hal Riney. His method "ensures that all disciplines are combined from the beginning of the process, avoiding the fragmented model we're used to seeing as the end product of poor integration. To put it simply, the brand communication is born of the whole."

  Art Zambianchi, letter to the editor, "Many Promote IMC but Don't Grasp It," *Advertising Age*, March 4, 2002, p. 30.

- "The multimillion-dollar 'Play to win' global campaign represents the first time Big Blue has pooled ad dollars of its server, software, storage, and global services businesses to deliver an integrated message."

  "IBM 'Plays to Win' with New Push," *Advertising Age*, April 15, 2002, p. 9.

- After Wendy's was moved from Bates USA to McCann-Erickson, Don Calhoon, executive VP of marketing for Wendy's, said, "It is important for us at Wendy's to have all of our resources integrated under one roof." He explained that "integration produces the best results."

  Vanessa O'Connell, "Wendy's Transfers Ad Business to Unit of Interpublic Group," *Wall Street Journal*, August 16, 2002, p. B5.

- Dan Wieden, cofounder of Wieden & Kennedy and creator of Nike's legendary "Just Do It" campaign, says, "There's a growing clamor to reinvent advertising." According to Wieden, W&K is attempting to push advertising into entirely new territory by merging it with entertainment in the form of films, TV programs, music recordings, stage plays, and even books. "Many in the business, including Wieden, believe that the industry is at an evolutionary crossroads." The reason Nike and other clients approve of this, said Wieden, is that "it enables them to be associated with content that seems more pure, authentic, and desirable than an ad; in the best-case scenario, consumers may actually seek out this content."

  Warren Berger, "Just Do It. Again." *Business 2.0*, September 2002, pp. 76-84.

Integration Produces Synergy

Integrated marketing communication is a concept as well as a process. To understand what *integrated* means in this context, it is useful to think about integration and synergy together. **Integration** is *the combining of separate parts into a unified whole.* One outcome of integration is **synergy,** which is *the interaction of individual parts in a way that makes the integrated whole greater than the sum of its parts.* This interaction is sometimes expressed as $2 + 2 = 5$. When brand messages reinforce each other, synergy is produced. When the messages are all different, they can be

FIGURE 1-1

*What differentiates IMC
from traditional advertising
is that it is an ongoing
process that constantly
impacts relationships with
customers, prospects, and
other stakeholders.*

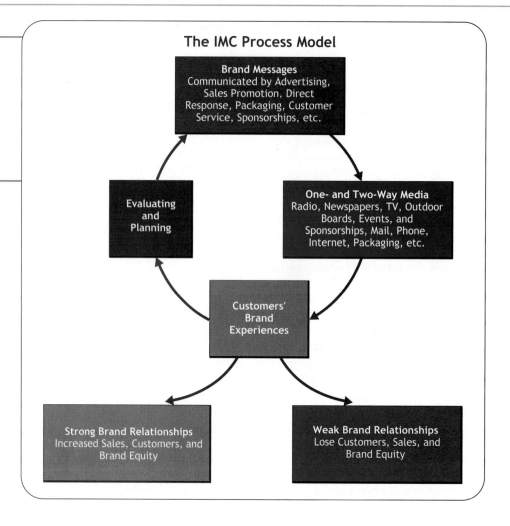

The IMC Process Model

Brand Messages
Communicated by Advertising, Sales Promotion, Direct Response, Packaging, Customer Service, Sponsorships, etc.

Evaluating and Planning

One- and Two-Way Media
Radio, Newspapers, TV, Outdoor Boards, Events, and Sponsorships, Mail, Phone, Internet, Packaging, etc.

Customers' Brand Experiences

Strong Brand Relationships
Increased Sales, Customers, and Brand Equity

Weak Brand Relationships
Lose Customers, Sales, and Brand Equity

confusing and actually distract from a coherent impression of a brand and do not produce synergy.

Achieving integration and synergy, however, requires more than making brand messages look and sound alike, what some call "one voice, one look." Integration needs to occur in all areas where a customer comes in contact with a brand—such as customer service and product performance. Otherwise, the marketing communication messages, no matter how consistent and integrated, will ring hollow.

The fashion retailer Gap understands that everything it does communicates a message and must be integrated. In the early 2000s, Gap saw sales slide after it moved into ultra-trendy clothes. To undo the damage, in 2002 the retailer resumed doing what it had always done well, selling the basics—jeans, khakis, jackets, and classic tops with a new cut, style, or color. To bring that idea to life, and to reach both younger and older customers, Gap announced its new line of products with new advertising that paired oldies but goodies such as Willie Nelson with young hipsters such as Ryan Adams under the campaign slogan "For Every Generation." According to Gap's CEO, however, these ads were only part of the company's

> **"It is a fundamental shift in the role and purpose of marketing, from manipulation of the customer to genuine customer involvement: from telling and selling to communication and sharing of knowledge."**
>
> Regis McKenna, relationship marketing expert

communication program: "[You cannot] separate them from the stores and the merchandise."[9] This broader definition of integration is well stated by Regis McKenna, author of *Relationship Marketing*, who sees a fundamental shift in the direction of marketing communication: "The marketer must be the integrator. Both internally—synthesizing technological capability with market needs—and externally—bringing the customer into the company as a participant in the development and adaptation of goods and services."[10]

Understanding the *concept* of IMC helps a company recognize that it needs to become more integrated. Understanding the *process* tells the company how to begin doing so. Integration is like quality: companies are always striving to improve it, but it is nearly impossible to achieve 100 percent. Many companies, however, are using IMC to become better integrated and thus do a better job of communicating, retaining customers, and building their brands. Another good example is FedEx.

Unless you have been living in a cave, you have seen FedEx trucks with the orange and purple FedEx logo numerous times. This bold, colorful identifier is more than just a logo; it is a design concept that has been integrated into all of FedEx's brand messages—trucks, packaging materials, uniforms, advertising, and company brochures (Exhibit 1-18). This one-look identification program, however, is only one aspect of how FedEx practices integrated communication. To improve customer relationships, the company provides an online tracking system that saves time for customers and the company. It also involves employees in business decision making through its "One-on-On" program, which features appearances by top FedEx executives on the company's closed-circuit television network. This live video conference goes into every FedEx office, and any employee regardless of position, can ask questions or make suggestions of top management.

Ongoing evaluation is another characteristic of IMC. At FedEx customer feedback is captured and summarized for every 24-hour period. A "service quality indicator" shows how the company has performed on 12 customer satisfaction criteria. This report appears on every employee's computer each morning.

EXHIBIT 1-18

FedEx has done a good job of integrating its brand messages. In what other ways does the company bring integration to its marketing communication?

Managers in the marketing department have access to a customer database that identifies and segments customers into "the good, the bad, and the ugly." The good ones are those who are most profitable and the ones marketing works hard to retain. The "bad" ones are those who give the company only a portion of their business and thus need to be nurtured and grown. The "ugly" ones are those on whom the company loses money and therefore works to terminate the relationship.[11]

The concept and practice of integration is not new. Every MC program is integrated to some extent. What is new, however, is how integration is practiced in today's marketplace where there are so many communication choices and players. In most small businesses, integrating brand messages is relatively easy because everything is controlled at one central point. But as companies grow, as MC departments and MC agencies become more specialized, walls go up around the MC functional areas, creating "departmental silos." Generally speaking, the bigger a company is, the more MC silos it has, and the more difficulty it has coordinating and integrating brand messages that help create trust in a brand (see Exhibit 1-19). As Peter Senge, known for his theory of the "learning organization," explains:

Trust is not given. It's earned.

 And EDS earns that trust a million times each day - with systems we created to confidentially process everything from credit card transactions to income tax returns. Across the world, companies and governments trust us to handle vital financial, medical and personal information in a way that builds consumer trust and respects ever-evolving government standards. Shouldn't you? Call 800-566-9337 to learn more, or visit www.eds.com/security_privacy.

EDS
solved.

Functional divisions grow into fiefdoms, and what was once a convenient division of labor mutates into the "stovepipes" [departmental silos] that all but cut off contact between functions. The result: Analysis of the most important problems in a company, the complex issues that cross functional lines, becomes a perilous or nonexistent exercise.[12]

The Benefits of Using IMC

Companies benefit in many ways from integrating their marketing communications. IMC helps brands differentiate themselves from competitors by being more customer focused. It improves accountability because relationships can be tracked in relation to sales and profits. It increases brand trust because emphasis is placed on customer retention rather than on single transactions. It fosters internal coordination and focus. These benefits are explained in detail in later chapters.

A FINAL NOTE: IMC CUTS THROUGH MESSAGE CLUTTER

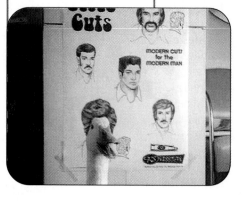

Marketplace confusion arises from the proliferation of brands and products. Forty years ago, the average grocery store carried about 8,000 items, counting all the brands and their different sizes and flavors. Today that number is closer to 30,000. Such proliferation is not limited to items available in food, drug, and mass merchandising stores. The number of services has also grown. When you look in the Yellow Pages, you find dozens of competing companies in most service categories. Consumers suffer from brand-choice overload.

They also suffer from brand communication overload. The average person watches TV four hours a day, has a choice of over 50 channels, and is exposed to 42,000 TV commercials every year, even with zipping and zapping. Factor in commercials on rented videotapes, radio commercials, ads in newspapers and magazines, ads on packages, billboards, direct-mail offers, telemarketing calls, and commercial e-mails, and you have an avalanche of brand messages.

By coordinating marketing communications and fine-tuning message strategies, IMC makes brand messages more relevant, more effective, more sensitive, and less wasteful of media and personal time. An example is the trend in data-driven communication toward self-selection: people in the target audience are encouraged to opt in for messages that interest and concern them, so there is less need for intrusive media that interrupt and irritate consumers.

Key Terms

advertising 9
brand 6
brand equity 8
brand message 6
customer service 15
direct marketing 9
event 14
integrated marketing
   communication (IMC) 17

integration 21
marketing communication
   (MC) 7
marketing communication
   mix 8
media 7
packaging 13
personal selling 13
public relations 10

publicity 10
sales promotion 12
sponsorship 14
stakeholders 19
synergy 21

Key Point Summary

Key Point 1: MC Functions

The key functional areas of marketing communication are advertising, direct marketing, publicity (a form of public relations), sales promotion, personal selling, packaging, events and sponsorships, and customer service.

Key Point 2: Key Elements in the IMC Definition

The concept of IMC is that focusing on customer relationships will result in more sales and profits than focusing only on generating sales transactions.

Key Point 3: IMC Process

IMC is an ongoing process for planning, executing, and evaluating the brand messages that create customer relationships. The basis of the IMC process is ongoing one- and two-way communication. This is in contrast to the traditional linear use of advertising and promotion to do a series of MC campaigns.

Key Point 4: Benefits of IMC

IMC provides greater brand differentiation, accountability, and coordination. It is more effective at cutting through message clutter compared to traditional advertising and promotion. It also increases customer and stakeholder trust.

Lessons Learned

Key Point 1: MC Functions

a. What is advertising, and what is its primary use?
b. What is direct marketing, and how is it used?
c. What is the greatest strength of publicity?
d. Why is sales promotion so important in a marketing program?
e. What is the primary advantage of personal selling?
f. Why is packaging considered a marketing communication tool?
g. What benefits are derived from using events and sponsorships?
h. Why is customer service included in the list of functional areas of marketing communication?
i. What is a marketing communication mix?

Key Point 2: Key Elements in the IMC Definition

a. How is *IMC* defined? What are the key elements in the definition?
b. How do the concept and the process of IMC differ?
c. Explain the difference between a stakeholder and a customer.
d. Why do marketers care about building relationships with their customers?
e. What does *synergy* mean? How does synergy relate to marketing communication?
f. What is a one-voice, one-look strategy?

Key Point 3: IMC Process

a. Why must keeping customers be an ongoing process?
b. What is the relationship between evaluating and planning?
c. What is the difference between one-way and two-way brand messages?
d. Why shouldn't marketers simply focus on creating sales transactions rather than spending time and money building strong relationships with customers?
e. Explain how IMC "spins off" either strong or weak brand relationships.

Key Point 4: Benefits of IMC

a. What has been the impact of brand and product proliferation on marketing communication?
b. In what ways does integration create greater efficiencies in marketing communication?
c. How do integrated communication programs build trust?
d. A focus on departmentalization has what effect on marketing communication?
e. How does IMC cut through message clutter? Choose a major brand, and develop a list of the marketing communication tools it uses in its marketing communication mix. Is the brand using a one-voice, one-look strategy?

Chapter Challenge

Writing Assignment

Identify a product that you think needs to work on its brand image. Look at how each element of the marketing communication mix is delivering a message, and recommend how the effectiveness of the communication could be improved.

Presentation Assignment: AFLAC

Develop a short survey to investigate the effectiveness of the AFLAC campaign. Interview 10 people of different ages and occupations and both genders. Ask whether they have seen the AFLAC commercials, what settings they remember, and whether they like or dislike the commercials and why. Finally, determine whether they understand the product being sold. Prepare for class a presentation that summarizes your findings.

Internet Assignment

Go to the websites for Barnes & Noble (www.barnesandnoble.com) and Amazon.com (www.amazon.com), and compare their operations. Pretend you are going to buy a book, and analyze the differences in the way the two companies handle your transaction and attempt to create a relationship with you.

2

IMC Partners and Industry Organization

Key Points in This Chapter

1. How do different types of agencies perform their services?
2. Why are media important partners in marketing communication?
3. How is the corporate side of marketing communication organized?
4. What issues in agency/client relationships affect IMC?

Chapter Perspective

It's All about Organization

MC professionals often ask why IMC is so hard to do. Integration poses an organizational challenge because so many participants are involved in creating and delivering brand messages—the company, its agencies, the media, distributors and retailers, and the many MC support services. A rigid structure of corporate departmental silos and specialized MC agencies—each working in its own area of expertise—is one of the barriers most brands face when striving for integration.

No company can build relationships externally until it builds them internally and with its MC partners. Thus, IMC requires cross-functional planning and is most successfully practiced in small companies. Nevertheless, large companies that recognize the value of integration are working to become more focused through better internal integration.

This chapter discusses the major players who need to be integrated as partners in brand-relationship building. It closes with a discussion of cross-functional planning and monitoring, tools that managers use to create integration within the organization.

IMC AND WALLBANGERS GO TOGETHER AT THE PHELPS GROUP

Joe Phelps loves playing in a band and doing integrated marketing communication. As strange as it may seem, these two loves overlap in the structure and practices at the Phelps Group, an integrated marketing communication agency in Santa Monica, California, a few blocks from the Pacific Ocean.

One of the important things Joe learned in his band days was the importance of feedback: "All you had to do was look at the audience to know if you were getting through. Whenever we saw the audience drift away, we instantly changed rhythms, music, or did whatever was necessary to get them back."

Appreciating the value of feedback, Joe has institutionalized it in his agency. One of the first things you notice if you visit the Phelps Group is a 30-foot-long wall in the center of the first floor. Pinned to the wall are magazine and newspaper ads, TV scripts and TV photoboards, package designs, PR releases, brand-concept statements, logos—all marketing communication ideas in various stages of development. Looking more closely, you see that on most of these there are a variety of notes in different handwriting. This is the Wall (see the chapter-opening photo)!

The purpose of the Wall is to get feedback on work in progress. Everyone in the agency—from receptionists to Joe Phelps himself—is encouraged to walk past the Wall at least once a day and react to whatever draws his or her attention, offering suggestions as well as compliments (signatures are optional). Gut feedback coming from so many marketing brains makes for better work.

To make sure the Wall remains top-of-mind with everyone, get-togethers called WallBangers are held at 3 P.M. twice a week. Snacks are set out around the Wall, and everyone in the agency is expected to gather around and offer feedback on the posted brand messages (see Exhibit 2-1).

Because feedback drives the agency's work, the Phelps Group has established multiple feedback channels in addition to the Wall. *External feedback* comes from:

- Periodic client surveys of the agency's performance.
- Surveys of service suppliers (production houses, photographers, media representatives, research companies—"whoever sends the agencies invoices").

EXHIBIT 2-1

- Outside classes—those that employees teach and those that they take—in related areas.
- CEO-to-CEO conversations to ensure the agency is contributing to clients' highest needs.

Internal feedback comes from:

- 360-degree performance evaluations—annual surveys of each person by peers, superiors, and subordinates.
- Group surveys—critiques by the agency's employees of the company's overall work and working conditions.
- Spring Advance—an off-site two-day session in which the agency sets goals and creates action plans for the coming year.
- Fall Retreat—an off-site session at which individuals develop and discuss individual performance objectives.
- Monday morning meetings—presentations of agency work and of "educational minutes" (helpful hints that cover all areas of agency work).
- BrainBangers' Ball—an agency-wide brainstorming session each Thursday with lunch provided by the agency. At the balls a team that is having a problem solving a specific problem can ask for input from the whole agency.

Another thing Joe learned playing in bands was the dynamics of self-directed groups or teams. Although different musicians took the lead at different times, band members always played together. Playing as a team, letting each team member lead at certain times, and relying on constant feedback to connect to audiences are some of the basic principles Joe has used to organize and run the Phelps Group.

The agency's offices have an open architecture: no one has a closed office—including Joe, the owner and CEO. There are conference rooms with doors so meetings can be held without disturbing or being disturbed, but five-foot partitions in the rest of the office area encourage interaction.

To provide clients such as Petco, Tahiti Tourism, Whole Foods Markets, Crystal Cruises, and Panasonic with integrated marketing communication, the Phelps Group has become one of the most creative agencies in the United States. Because the agency is relatively small, with around 50 employees, it's able to do things seldom done in larger agencies.

Reflecting Joe Phelps's belief that traditional business hierarchies are counterproductive, the agency is organized in teams around each client. Each team is made up of individuals whose specialization is needed for each client's particular needs. Although the Phelps Group offers IMC, some clients hire the agency to provide only one or two MC services. Each team is self-directed. Rather than being told what to do by some high-ranking person in the agency, the team collectively plans and executes in response to its interaction with the client and to feedback received from the marketplace.

Although teams are the foundation of the Phelps Group's organization, the agency recognizes that individuals are the building blocks of that foundation. Thus, the agency works constantly to balance teamwork and individual achievement and growth. Instead of department heads, there is a coach for each MC area. Whenever particular areas of expertise are needed by a team, coaches are available to support their representatives on the team. They also "coach" (rather than supervise) individuals in their areas of specialization.

To celebrate the success of his agency's horizontal organization, Joe Phelps wrote a book, *Pyramids Are Tombs*. The title refers to the vertical organization of most agencies. The traditional hierarchy, Phelps writes, is similar to a pyramid, "which as we all know, is a tomb."

WHO ARE THE IMC PARTNERS?

The basic players in marketing communication are (1) MC agencies, (2) the media, and (3) the companies and brands behind the marketing communication, which include nonprofit organizations, government bodies, and all other entities that have something to sell. Companies, including nonprofit organizations, can exist only if enough people are persuaded to buy their products and services or, in the case of nonprofits, donate time or money.

To tell customers about their products, services, and causes, most companies hire marketing communication (MC) agencies to create and place brand messages in the media (the exceptions are businesses, mostly quite small, that do everything in-house). The more a company spends on marketing communication, the more it is likely to use one or more MC agencies.

The ad in Exhibit 2-2 shows what can happen when the three players work together as partners. The ad is for the Milk Processors Educational Program, a trade organization of dairy farmers dedicated to increasing the consumption of milk. It was designed by the Bozell advertising agency and placed in a variety of magazines.

Because the lion's share of the revenue earned by most media comes from advertising, the media couldn't exist without advertising. But the media can sell advertising only if they have significant numbers of readers, listeners, or viewers—the more they have, the more they can charge. Clearly, companies,

EXHIBIT 2-2

Advertiser and medium are paired in this ad for the International Dairy Foods Association's Processor Education Program, which is a spin-off from the long-running "Got Milk" campaign created for the Milk Processors Association by the Bozell advertising agency.

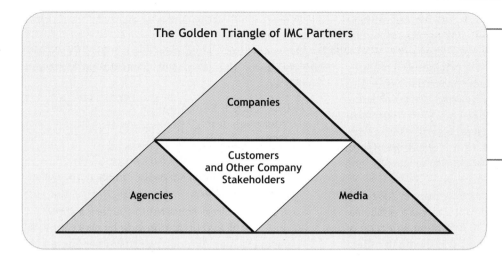

The Golden Triangle of IMC Partners

Companies

Customers
and Other Company
Stakeholders

Agencies

Media

FIGURE 2-1

Notice how the customer is at the center of the "golden triangle" and how companies, agencies, and media are all connected to each other.

agencies, and media are interdependent, coexisting in what is sometimes called marketing's *golden triangle* (see Figure 2-1). The triangle of partners in IMC is shown surrounding customers and other company stakeholders (all those who can affect or be affected by a company or brand) to illustrate the customer-centric nature of IMC.

Every business operates within an industry or product category, such as air travel, pharmaceuticals, high technology, fast food, or agribusiness. If you were a marketing communication manager, whether for a company or for an agency, you would need to become expert in the industry or product category in which your company or client competes. Even retail is a marketing specialty, and even Mall of America depends on marketing communication.

IMC IN ACTION

Mall of Them All Celebrates 10 Years

Mall of America in Bloomington, Minnesota, is the largest shopping and entertainment complex in North America. Covering a space as big as 97 football fields, this quasi-township has over 11,000 employees, plus a university, high school, wedding chapel, medical clinic, and police station. It is Minnesota's top tourist attraction, drawing some 130,000 shoppers on peak days; on any busy weekend, Mall of America becomes the third largest city in Minnesota. It has more than 520 stores, 86 restaurants, and 14 movie screens; it also has its own seven-acre amusement park, called Camp Snoopy, and a 4,000-creature aquarium, called Underwater Adventures.

The marketing communication staff handles media relations, community and government relations, national and international tourism and promotion, and advertising—in addition to managing hundreds of special events and major promotions throughout the

EXHIBIT 2-3

year. The Mall has an in-house marketing department but also uses an outside advertising agency, a media-buying company, and the Weber Shandwick Worldwide public relations agency for additional marketing tasks. Partners who cosponsor promotions are also important to the Mall. Its sponsorship division has co-operative partnership arrangements with Northwest Airlines, PepsiCo, Sam Goody, General Mills, Visa, United States Postal Service, Cruise Holidays, Health Partners (sponsor of the Mall Walk program), QVC, and Xcel Energy, among others.

The Mall celebrated its 10th anniversary in 2002 with a big media splash engineered by its in-house public relations staff. The theme was "Celebrating a Decade of Fun." Marketing efforts played off this theme to reflect on the past 10 years and helped position the Mall for the future. Public relations was the main marketing vehicle—promoting Mall of America's success in the face of detractors and economic downturns and telling the story of how the Mall created a new shopping experience, changing mall shopping from a simple commercial transaction to a recreational event.

The public relations department successfully utilized a satellite media birthday feed to TV stations, a Mall of America 10th-Year Celebration press kit, a national wire release, and live shots from all four major local television stations. Media coverage included hosting one station's weekend morning shows.

In addition to the media coverage, the marketing staff held contests and giveaways featuring new Mall retailers, thus showing how the Mall keeps customers' experiences fresh. Advertising featured the "Decade of Fun" theme in all media messages; and the events department hosted celebrations featuring the stars of *Spy Kids 2*, the Radio City Music Hall Rockettes, country music artist Phil Vassar, and a week of children's characters breakfasts.

The anniversary celebration was a great success, and the results of the promotion included the following highlights:

- *USA Today* featured Mall of America on the front page of its "Life" section (August 9, 2002).
- *CBS Sunday Morning with Charles Osgood* featured Mall of America as its "Sunday Passage" (August 11, 2002).
- Associated Press ran a Mall of America story that was picked up nationwide by over 30 newspapers in markets such as Pittsburgh, Sacramento, Cleveland, Indianapolis, Iowa City, and Columbus.
- The *Los Angeles Times* ran a 10th anniversary front-page story on Sunday, September 15. It was picked up by other media outlets including *Newsday*.
- The *Caroline Rhea Show* taped a segment that aired on the inaugural show, on Tuesday, September 3.
- 75 stories ran on local television stations.
- 28 print stories ran in local print publications.

And a special promotion brought publicity and visibility as Mall of America was recognized with a proclamation from Minnesota's Governor Jesse Ventura declaring August 11, 2002, "Mall of America Day."

Source: Trevor Boulter, public relations coordinator, Mall of America.

At the same time, most marketing communication managers also have their own areas of specialization, such as mass media advertising, direct marketing, sales promotion, and public relations. Each of these functional areas is represented by an association, such as the Public Relations Society of America (PRSA) for public relations practitioners, that provides educational services and information to members. Part IV of this book explores each of the major marketing communication functions. This chapter examines how agencies, media, and companies are organized and are partners in developing brands.

The discussion that follows looks at all three partners. It begins with the most visible element—marketing communication and the agencies that produce these messages. Then it considers the media involved in delivering the messages. It ends with a discussion of the agency's client—the company, brand, or organization paying for the marketing communication.

HOW IS THE AGENCY WORLD ORGANIZED?

Marketing communication used to be dominated by advertising agencies, but that has changed as other marketing communication functions have become more widely used. This change also reflects advertising's search for a wider definition of advertising that includes ways to reach customers in addition to traditional mass media. Hal Riney, former chairman of the Publicis & Hal Riney advertising agency, says clients are looking for new ways to communicate because "the audience easily dismisses most of the messages they see or hear."[1] This need for more effective ways to reach customers has prompted traditional ad agencies to acquire other MC agencies and offer more types of marketing communication services.

How Do Agencies Work?

There are many types of MC agencies. Table 2-1 lists some—not all—of the agencies in the Diversified Advertising Services division of the Omnicom Group holding company. Read the lefthand column of the table and see whether you can describe each agency's function. Check your answer against the righthand column. Also among Omnicom's holdings are BBDO, DDB, and Chiat/Day, three major advertising agencies.

> ". . . more ad clients are abandoning conventional brand advertising in favor of efforts offering more immediate returns, i.e., coupons and price promotions."
>
> Hal Riney, former chairman of Publicis & Hal Riney

TABLE 2-1   Some of the MC Agencies in Omnicom's Diversified Advertising Services Division

MC Function	Agency	Services Provided
Branding and identity consulting	Interbrand	Brand strategy, naming, corporate identity programs, brand valuation
Consumer/corporate advertising	Merkley, Newman Harty	Advertising, strategic planning
Financial BtB advertising	Doremus	Financial advertising, financial printing
Design and image consultancy	The Designory	Graphics, collateral, package design, environmental design
Direct marketing	Rapp Collins	Creative and strategic planning for direct-response marketing, database creation and management, fulfillment, website design
Direct-response TV	SCP Directory Advertising	Strategic planning, response tracking, media management
Directory/Yellow Page advertising	Ketchum Directory Advertising	Market research, creative services
Event marketing	Kaleidoscope	Product launch events, trade shows, lecture bureau, field sampling, sports marketing
Field marketing	CMP International	Merchandising, personal selling
Graphic arts	RC Communications	Desktop publishing, color separations, photo labs, retouching, slide presentations

(continued on page 36)

TABLE 2-1 Some of the MC Agencies in Omnicom's Diversified Advertising Services Division *(continued)*

MC Function	Agency	Services Provided
Health care	Targis Healthcare	Medical/pharmaceutical advertising and public relations
Information technology	Quantum Plus	Marketing process redesign, database development, decision support tools
Media planning/buying	Creative Media	Media planning and buying, direct response, new media, interactive media
Merchandising, POP displays	Schultz International	Design and manufacture of permanent POP display systems
Multiethnic	The Rodd Group	IMC agency for reaching ethnic audiences
Organizational communication	Smythe Dorward Lambert	Internal communications, reputation management, management education and training
Public relations	Porter Novelli	Marketing support, media relations, crisis and employee communication
Sales promotion	Alcone Marketing	Kids' marketing, interactive marketing, premium fulfillment, entertainment marketing, trade marketing
Research	M/A/R/C	Marketing segmentation, sales forecasting, customer satisfaction tracking, customer value analysis
Retail marketing	Integer Group	Retail merchandising, field marketing, consumer and trade promotions.
Sports and event marketing	Millsport	Sponsorships, event administration, travel/hospitality
Telemarketing	Optima Direct	Outbound and inbound telemarketing, database-driven direct marketing

The most common types of agencies are those that specialize in mass media advertising, public relations, direct marketing, sales promotion, and packaging/corporate identity. Most MC agencies have between 20 and 40 clients (also called *accounts*). To avoid conflicts of interest, most agencies handle only one company in a particular product category.

Many large corporations not only work with a variety of MC agencies but also, when the budget is extremely large, use two or more agencies within a specialty area such as advertising. In these cases, the competing agencies handle different brands, product lines, or geographical regions.[2]

Although every agency has its own unique organization, job titles, and departments, there are commonalities among agencies. Some provide a full range of services to clients; others specialize in certain types of work. The single largest number and type of MC agencies, especially in terms of MC dollars handled, are advertising agencies. For this reason, much of the following discussion is about them.

Full-Service Advertising Agencies

A **full-service agency** is *an agency that provides all or most of the services needed in its area of MC specialization.* In advertising, a full-service agency provides research services, creative development of brand messages, media planning and buying, and account management (which involves strategic planning). The term *full-service* does not mean that an agency provides expertise in all the MC functional areas. Also, full-service agencies do not actually make final print and broadcast ads. Instead, they create rough drawings, layouts, and storyboards (for TV commercials), and they write scripts and ad copy. They then oversee the production of the ads and commercials by specialists outside the agency.

Figure 2-2 shows an organization chart for a typical full-service advertising agency. The three main departments are creative services, media, and account or client management. A production department works for the creative services department. Traffic department is responsible for keeping track of the ads as they go through the production process. If an agency has a research department, it works primarily with creative services and account management. In creative services, media, and account management, people are assigned to work for specific clients (also called *accounts*). With the exception of major accounts, most agency people work on two or three accounts at the same time. Here is a brief description of each of these areas.

- *Account management* **Account managers** are *liaisons between an agency and its clients.* Most agencies have a director of client services at the top of the account management hierarchy. Below this person are account management directors, then account supervisors, account executives, and assistant account executives. As in most organizations, the people at the low end of the hierarchy do much of the day-to-day logistical work. The primary responsibility of the account management department (also called *client services* or *account services*) is to identify clients' problems and preferences and help develop communication strategies to address them. Account people usually

FIGURE 2-2

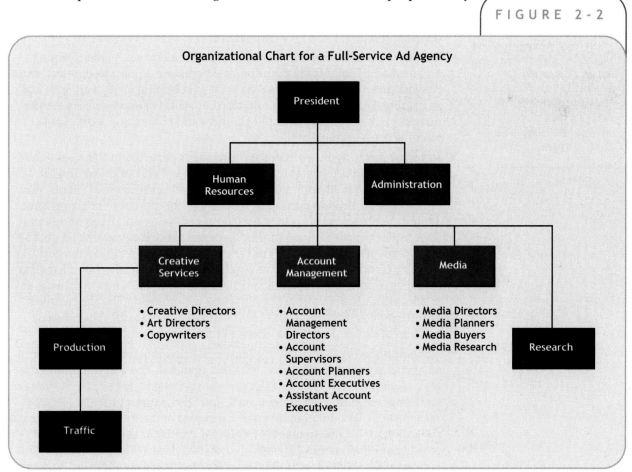

Organizational Chart for a Full-Service Ad Agency

For cooking disasters SOS.

work directly with people at their level in the client's organization. For example, account supervisors talk to directors of marketing, and account executives work with **brand managers,** *executives who manage a company's brand or product line.* Once account managers know what the client needs and wants, they work with the creative services and media departments to see that the clients' advertising needs are met.

Another important task of account managers is to take creative ideas and media plans to clients and persuade them to approve those ideas and plans. If a client is not sold on the ideas presented, the creative services or media people need to do more work.

- *Creative services* The people working in creative services are responsible, in cooperation with account managers, for coming up with the creative ideas that deliver on the agreed-to message strategies (see Exhibit 2-4). Working in this department are **copywriters,** *who develop the verbal brand message (the copy),* and **art directors,** *who develop the visual aspects of brand messages (the design and layout).* They frequently work as a team under the guidance of a **creative director,** *who supervises the development, execution, and production of the creative ideas.* **Producers** are *those who oversee the logistics and costs of producing radio and TV commercials.* A position that links the creative staff with account managers in large ad agencies is the **traffic manager,** *who controls the flow of work through the approval and production process.* Traffic managers track progress of the various MC materials as they are being produced, keep jobs on deadline, and engage outside special services—such as artist, photographers, and typographers—when needed.

- *Media* The media department has two basic objectives: media planning and media buying. **Media planning** is *determining media objectives and strategies for delivering ads to target audiences.* **Media buying** is *negotiating for and purchasing the broadcast time and print space detailed in the media plan.* Media directors oversee the work of the planners and buyers and work closely with the account managers.

- *Research* Large agencies may have a research department that uses quantitative and qualitative research tools to improve their understanding of consumers and to identify the most appropriate audiences for clients' marketing communication messages. Working in this department are research analysts and research directors, each assigned to several different accounts. This department is also used for testing creative strategy ideas and evaluating work at various stages. The latter activity often produces tension between creative services and research. Creatives typically claim that such testing is invalid and can eliminate a good idea. Clients, however, want as much assurance as possible that the ideas recommended by the creatives are attention getting and are persuasive before they invest thousands or millions of dollars to produce them and place them in the media.

- *Account planning* The account-planner position is increasingly popular in ad agencies and in some public relations agencies. The **account planner** *uses research and customer insights to bring a strong consumer focus to the planning of marketing communication.* According to Jon Steel, author of *Truth, Lies, and Advertising,* "Account planning was conceived as a way for agencies to treat the affliction that ails so many American advertising agencies today, by creating and maintaining meaningful relationships with consumers."[3] The account planner has been able to help reduce the tension between research and the creatives by having research take a more proactive, up-front role in creative development. As one expert in this area has stated, "an account planner must have consumer insight"[4] and that insight is expressed in a **creative brief,** *a document that is given to the creative team to help in their planning of the message executions.*

An account planner is responsible for understanding the target audience (using a variety of quantitative and especially qualitative research) and being the customer advocate within the agency. This person's job is to make sure creative ideas and brand-positioning strategies are responsive to customers' wants and needs. The account planner is primarily found in advertising agencies but also in some other marketing communication organizations, such as Porter Novelli, a public relations agency.

- *Other agency departments* Because advertising agencies are businesses, most of the large ones have finance, accounting, human resources, and legal departments. Most advertising agencies strive to generate a 20 percent profit margin. This means that for every $5 an agency earns, after the paying of salaries and all other expenses, $1 is gross profit (before taxes).

In an effort to make sure that work on a large account is as integrated and focused as possible, Foote Cone & Belding and some other agencies pull all the individuals working on a particular account out of their respective departments and physically locate them in the same area. That way, media people who have a question about the creative plan, for example, can simply go to the adjoining office or yell over the partition to get an answer. This proximity reduces misunderstandings, promotes synergy, and produces work faster.

Creative Boutiques and Freelancers

A **creative boutique** is *an agency of creative specialists, usually writers and designers, who work for clients and other agencies.* These organizations are similar to the creative departments in full-service agencies. Creative boutiques usually work on a project basis, turning over finished work to another agency for media placement and buying. Boutiques are often started by creative people, such as a copywriter/art director team, who worked for a full-service agency, did very well, and decided to be their own bosses. To demonstrate how creative they are, agencies promote themselves with brand messages.

Freelancers are *independent creative people who are self-employed and take on assignments from an agency or a marketer on a project-by-project basis.* Freelancers can be considered one-person boutiques; they specialize in copywriting, art direction, photography, or artwork. They usually work for small clients who can't afford an outside agency, or they do work that a client's ad agency would charge too much for doing. They also take assignments from large agencies when these agencies need extra help or when no one at an agency knows how to (or is willing to) do such things as creating a brochure, a menu, or a product directory.

Media Buying Services

As the name implies, **media buying services** are *agencies that specialize in buying time and space—that is, placing brand messages in the media.* Media buying services developed as small and medium-sized companies when advertising agencies realized they were paying a higher price for media because they were buying in relatively small quantities. By buying for many different clients, media buying services can have the same buying clout as the large full-service agencies. Media buying agencies generally receive a commission of 2 to 4 percent of the media dollars they manage. (The idea of media placement is also important in public relations; some companies specialize in distributing publicity materials to the media.)

In recent years several large full-service advertising agencies have spun off their media departments into freestanding media buying services. An example is Zenith Media Worldwide, which grew out of the merger of Bates and Saatchi & Saatchi (and still exists even though Bates and Saatchi & Saatchi have since split up). By making media buying a separate function, these media agencies can attract clients for which their parent agencies don't do creative work.

Among the fastest-growing media agencies are those that handle product placements. **Product placements** are *paid verbal or visual brand exposures in entertainment programming.* Rather than buying time and space for their clients, these agencies negotiate with producers of movies, TV shows, and other entertainment events to have their clients' brands appear or be mentioned in these entertainment products. The price of these placements depends on the extent of a brand's presence and the size of the anticipated audience. Feature This, one of the top product placement agencies, has offices around the world.

Agencies That Specialize

Most of the very large advertising agencies, such as J. Walter Thompson, Leo Burnett, BBDO, and Young & Rubicam, handle primarily consumer products. Medium and small agencies, however, often handle both B2C (business-to-consumer) and B2B (business-to-business) accounts. Poppe Tyson, the agency featured in Exhibit 2-5, specializes in handling high-technology clients. Pharmaceutical companies often hire public relations firms that work mostly in health care and government relations because the health-care industry is so specialized and subject to so many government regulations. Some agencies also specialize in such areas as sports, technology, agribusiness, and financial products.

As the size of ethnic populations has increased in the United States, so has the number of MC agencies that focus on specific ethnic groups. Los Angeles–based Muse Cordero Chen, for example, specializes in reaching Hispanic, African-American, and Asian consumers. Many of the large consumer product companies with multimillion-dollar budgets allocate a certain portion to reach minority audiences. For example, McDonald's has used Burrell Advertising, which specializes in creating and placing advertising for African-American consumers.

In-House Agencies

Some companies feel they can save money and have more control over their marketing communication by doing much of the work themselves. To do this, they set up an **in-house ad agency,** *a department within a company that is responsible for producing some or all of that company's marketing communications.* In-house agencies are commonly used in retail advertising and are found in the headquarters of grocery and drugstore chains that must create new ads every week. The retail in-house agency must work closely with the chain's buyers and store managers to provide promotions within tight deadlines. It also must be aware of quantities of products that have been purchased to ensure that when customers respond to promotional offers, the stores have enough product on hand to satisfy demand.

Upscale marketers such as Calvin Klein, Ralph Lauren, Coach, Guess, and Banana Republic handle their own marketing communication in-house because they believe they can best control the creative effort and bind it closely to their brand image. Marketers use in-house agencies to control both costs and the creative product, eliminate the expensive overhead of external agencies, and take advantage of commissions offered by the media. Also, companies that do not have a large enough budget to attract the interest of outside marketing communication agencies do their own marketing communications, working with freelance copywriters, artists, and publicists. Depending on the type of business, an in-house

EXHIBIT 2-5
Poppe Tyson's ad is designed to differentiate its marketing communication services by explaining how advanced the agency's services are in the area of electronic communication technology.

agency may also do brand publicity, sales promotion, and direct marketing as well as advertising.

Although economies can result from having an in-house agency, there are also shortcomings. First, in-house control is often won at the expense of creativity. Because in-house agency people work on only one account—their company—they don't have the benefit of interacting with, and learning from, people working in other types of businesses. Second, working for an in-house agency instead of for an independent agency is often a second choice for creative professionals, particularly in advertising, so the talent pool lacks depth. Third, because an in-house agency is buying only its own media space and time, it has less bargaining power than an advertising agency that is buying media for dozens of companies and, therefore, its media costs are likely to be higher.

Other MC Agencies and Suppliers

Much of the previous discussion focused on advertising agencies; however, there are also agencies that specialize in other areas of marketing communication. The following list summarizes the wide range of MC services available from these agencies:

- *Direct marketing:* Direct-marketing firms use databases and technology to help clients acquire and build profitable, long-term relationships with their customers. Activities include strategic planning, response management, media buying, and customer management.

  Sample agency: Rapp Collins Worldwide (www.rappcollins.com)

- *Events marketing:* Event-marketing firms specialize in organizing events on behalf of companies and brands. They plan as well as oversee the events, and they provide clients with management of the many details, logistics, and suppliers involved in successfully sponsoring events.

  Sample agency: EventPro (www.eventpro.com)

- *IMC:* Agencies offering IMC manage the strategic use of a variety of marketing communication tools to create strong brand relationships for clients and their customers.

  Sample agency: Phelps Group (www.phelpsgroup.com)

- *Packaging:* Package design is an important part of brand design because it creates the "face" of a brand and establishes the way customers recognize a brand in a store and relate it to other marketing communication messages.

  Sample agency: R.BIRD (www.rbird.com)

- *Public relations:* Public relations firms counsel companies about public opinion and how to manage their relationships with various stakeholder groups to create a platform of trust. Important to IMC, they manage publicity related to creating visibility for a brand (see Exhibit 2-6). Other PR programs focus on corporate communication as well as on employee, community, and financial relations.

  Sample agency: Golin Harris (www.golinharris.com)

- *Relationship marketing:* A company that specializes in relationship marketing helps clients build relationships with their channel partners and employees, as well as customers.

  Sample agency: Carlson Marketing Group

- *Sales promotion:* Promotional marketing uses creative ideas to connect brands with customers through fun, as well as added-value programs, intended to motivate the audience to respond. These agencies design and manage such promotions as premium offers, sweepstakes and contests, and in-store merchandising materials and displays.

  Sample agency: Frankel (www.frankel.com).

In addition to agencies that specialize in different types of marketing communication, the industry also includes **MC suppliers,** *specialists who provide MC*

EXHIBIT 2-6
Golin/Harris is a public relations agency, but its focus is on using MPR to build brands. Notice the firm's slogan used in this ad—"Building Trust Worldwide."

It has come to our attention that the strength and quality of our brand is not nearly as well-known as that of our clients.

We'll take that as a compliment.

For a more client-focused approach to your business, call Rich Jernstedt, @ 312.729.4400.

GOLIN/HARRIS
Building Trust Worldwide
www.golinharris.com

agencies with support services. The following list identifies several types of MC suppliers:

- **Brand strategy and design firms:** These companies create, manage, and value brands (see Exhibit 2-7). Services typically include brand research, designing corporate and brand identity systems (brand naming, logos, packages), brand-positioning strategy and architecture (sub-brands), and brand valuation.

  Sample firms: Interbrand (www.brandchannel.com) and Landor Associates (www.landor.com)

- **Call centers:** Firms that operate banks of telephone operators are used in telemarketing as well as customer service. Most firms handle both inbound calls (from customers) and outbound calls (to customers).

  Sample firms: CALLogistix (www.CALLogistix.com) and MPC Call Centers (www.mpccallcenters.com)

- **Design studios:** These firms offer graphic design services for brands, as well as graphic design for all media forms (advertising, television, packaging, print, corporate identity materials).

  Sample firm: The Designory (www.designory.com)

- **Fulfillment houses:** Fulfillment houses handle the back end of direct marketing and e-commerce and specialize in getting products to the customer.

  Sample firms: Federated Direct (www.federated-fds.com) and National Fulfillment Services (www.nfsrv.com).

- **Internet companies:** These firms specialize in e-commerce and interactive media and can be hired to design websites (see Exhibit 2-8) and manage the response functions. They also specialize in online advertising and leveraging the brand-building capabilities of the internet.

  Sample firm: DoubleClick Inc. (www.doubleclick.net).

- **Production houses:** Advertising agencies usually hire photographers, artists, film directors and producers, costume designers, and music producers, among others. All of these are outside companies that work as suppliers for agencies.

  Sample firm: MFK Productions (www.mfkproductions.com).

- **Research companies:** Research companies conduct market research with consumers and businesses; they also evaluate marketing communication ideas and test their effectiveness.

  Sample firm: m/a/r/c research (www.marcresearch.com).

Not until the 1980s did agencies begin to talk about integration and recognize that their clients needed a way to better manage and coordinate their marketing communications. The agencies, however, didn't know how to satisfy this need. Some of the large agencies offered services such as "Whole Egg"

E X H I B I T   2 - 7

Landor Associates, a leading package-design firm, has expanded its business services into brand consulting.

E X H I B I T   2 - 8

Rod Rodenburg, owner of the internet design firm Ion Design Inc., created this website for PBS for its special on Napoleon.

(Young & Rubicam) and "Orchestration" (Ogilvy & Mather), but these were primarily efforts to obtain a larger portion of their clients' MC assignments rather that efforts to provide a practical process for integrating brand messages and building brands. The services soon faded away.

Those early IMC approaches focused on "one-voice, one-look" advertising and didn't take into consideration the fact that everything a company does has the potential to send a powerful brand message. Only in recent years have advertising agencies made progress in offering IMC services. As several of the quotations listed in the IMC in Action box in Chapter 1 illustrate, agency executives know that integrating marketing communication is a must for the future. They are still experimenting, however, to find the best way to accomplish this for their clients. Interestingly, when a sample of agency and client executives was asked, "Who directs the integration effort?" Seventy-four percent of the agency respondents said agencies do, and 94 percent of the client respondents said clients do.[5] The reality, confirmed in other research studies, is that integration is driven by clients. Because clients pay the bills, they call the shots.

HOW DO MEDIA PARTNERS FIT IN?

A mass medium may be radio, television, newspaper, phone, or some other method of delivering a message. The **mass media** are *broad-based communication systems that reach a large and diverse audience.* In the mass media, advertisements are placed, or bought, by agencies acting on behalf of their clients. Most of the marketing dollars of many consumer and major B2B companies are spent on media. Table 2-2 lists the top 15 media companies in the United States.

T A B L E 2 - 2	Top 15 U.S. Media Companies (*based on 2001 revenues*)
Company	**Net U.S. Revenue** (*in millions*)
AOL Time Warner	$27,205
Viacom	15,211
AT&T Broadband	10,329
Walt Disney Co.	10,288
Cox Enterprises	6,266
NBC TV (General Electric Co.)	6,033
News Corp.	5,914
Clear Channel Communications	5,703
Gannett Co.	5,571
DirecTV (General Motors Corp.)	5,550
Comcast Corp.	5,130
Tribune Co.	5,104
Advance Publications	4,000
Hearst Corp.	3,986
Charter Communications	3,953

Source: Reprinted with permission from the August 19, 2002 issue of *Advertising Age*. Copyright Crain Communications, Inc. 2002.

Media companies are greatly dependent on outside sources for editorial and program content. For example, a newspaper's reporting staff produces only about 15 percent of a newspaper's total content; the remainder comes from advertisers, businesses (in the form of press releases), the community (schedules of events and letters to the editor), news syndicates, and features syndicates (which provide such items as comics and crossword puzzles). The need for content is the reason why NBC is willing to pay the National Collegiate Athletic Association billions of dollars for a multiyear contract to carry NCAA basketball and football games. The TV networks know that if they televise NCAA games, they will have millions of viewers, who become a valuable asset that the networks can "sell" to advertising agencies, which will place their clients' message in these media vehicles.

The way media content is presented has also changed. There is a preference for visuals, especially in newspapers, and for shorter stories. This trend was started, to a great extent, by *USA Today* (see Exhibit 2-9). Its use of color photos, pictorial graphics, and numerous short stories has greatly influenced the look of other newspapers as well as TV news programs and magazines.

EXHIBIT 2-9

First published in 1982, USA Today now has a worldwide circulation of over 2 million. Its exciting and colorful format has influenced many newspapers to become colorful and more appealing to readers.

How Is the Media World Changing?

Several recent changes in media affect how companies communicate with prospects and customers. One is the new communication technologies, such as wireless communications and high-speed internet services, which are changing the look of content as well as delivery systems.

Another change is an increase in media alternatives. With the exception of newspapers, most types of media—such as magazines, cable TV, and radio—have had a significant increase in number. A relatively new type of media is **place-based media,** which are *public venues where brand messages can be displayed.* Brand signage has been visible in public places such as sports arenas and transportation terminals for years, but these messages have gotten much more sophisticated and prolific. Brand messages are now appearing in schools, in senior centers, on in-flight videos, on gas pumps, and even on rest-room doors.

A third change is that media companies recognize that they can add value to their delivery systems by providing potential advertisers not only more in-depth information about their respective audiences but also consumer research findings. For example, media research departments spot trends in product categories, show what other media their audiences receive, and provide case histories of how their media have had certain effects on sales. Even local media are doing more consumer research to help attract more local advertising.

The fourth change came about as a result of the 1996 Telecommunications Act, which allows single ownership of competing media. This law has resulted in larger media conglomerates and a convergence of media services. Disney's merger with ABC, for example, has resulted in a company that can provide marketers a wide range of media alternatives: radio stations, TV networks, cable channels, websites,

EXHIBIT 2-10

This Canadian Magazine Publishers Association ad makes the point that only Canadian magazines give authentic coverage to Canada.

sponsorships (the Mighty Ducks hockey team), magazines, and movies (for product placements).

Finally, because of fragmentation—more media choices—and the consolidation of media ownership, media types and suppliers are trying harder than ever to establish their own identities. As Jack Myers, the author of *Reconnecting with Customers,* states: "The extent to which media companies can tie together program or editorial content, media buys and value-based promotions will dictate their value in the new media age."[6] In 2001, when AOL acquired Time Warner, one of the promised benefits to marketers was integrated offerings of a variety of media channels, as the following excerpt from the company's website promises:

AOL Time Warner Global Marketing Solutions provides tailored, idea-driven, integrated programs to marketing partners by leveraging the breadth of AOL Time Warner's powerful media and entertainment assets . . . Global Marketing Solutions (GMS) is making it easier for advertisers and agencies to do business with AOL Time Warner by serving as an entry point for unique access to AOL Time Warner's wealth of content, media platforms, consumer relationships and marketing infrastructure.[7]

The idea was to combine AOL's internet channels with Time Warner magazines such as *Time,* airtime on the company's TV networks such as CNN, and product placement opportunities in Warner Bros. films and TV shows. The fact that this didn't happen was one reason cited for the decline of the value of AOL Time Warner stock from $75 a share to under $15 in 2002. "Failed Effort to Coordinate Ads Signals Deeper Woes for AOL" was a front-page headline in the *Wall Street Journal.* But more telling was the subhead for this article: "Infighting among Divisions Derails Key Merger Goal."[8] In other words, this new media conglomerate was never able to properly integrate internally in order to offer advertisers attractive and economical media packages.

Most media (newspapers, magazines, radio, television, outdoor, and others) have their own national associations that promote their respective capabilities. The Magazine Publishers Association in both the United States and Canada runs ads such as the one in Exhibit 2-10. The media promote themselves not only collectively through their associations but also individually.

Nontraditional media include such innovative forms as painted buses, hot-air balloons, and signage in novel places such as on sidewalks and the sides of buildings. New media are those that involve computers and telecommunication, such as the internet (World Wide Web), intranets (networked communication systems within companies), extranets (networked communication systems that include external suppliers and agencies), pagers, and wireless devices such as cell phones.

How Can Media Help Make Integration Happen?

Many media companies perform creative work for clients similar to the work provided by agencies, especially at the local level. They help retailers plan and create ads and other promotional materials. The most sophisticated media companies also recommend other media because generally a mix of media is necessary to create and maintain brand relationships. Meredith, a large magazine publisher, for example, can package for a client a promotional effort that combines advertising in its magazines such as *Better Homes & Gardens* with supporting store promotions and direct-mail pieces.

Some companies represent the ultimate in integration because their product consists of both brand messages and media. The merger of Disney and ABC was mentioned as an example of a merged company's role as a media provider. But Disney itself is also a marketer, and the merger has resulted in visual merchandising and a mixture of special events that together have made the Disney brand highly memorable (and profitable). Disney offers an example of *closed-loop marketing*—the medium is the product as well as the message. Disney characters are integrated into Disney movies, television programs, merchandise, and theme parks; any area in which children (and adults) come into contact with these characters may lead them to other Disney offerings. The Disney entertainment media empire includes sports channels (ESPN and ESPN2) and internet services (with ABC Online, which is tied into America Online). Disney purchased the Web search engine Excite!, giving Disney a huge Web presence. Each Disney entity reinforces the others but still offers something slightly different in the area of entertainment; such reinforcement creates synergy.

BEHIND THE MESSAGES AND THE MEDIA ARE THE CLIENTS

If you were to work on the company side of the golden triangle (see Figure 2-1), you would be employed by the "client"—that is, the marketer or advertiser who initiates and pays for the marketing communication. These companies can be anything from an independent coffee shop (Exhibit 2-11) to a global giant such as Unilever, which has thousands of employees working all over the world. The client can also be a nonprofit organization. Many small, local companies use little or no marketing communication other than a listing in the Yellow Pages and a sign out front. At the other extreme, in 2001 General Motors spent $4.3 billion on advertising media, and Unilever spent $4.4 billion.[9] Table 2-3 lists the top 15 U.S. marketers and the top 15 global marketers.

In this book, as in the business world, companies are classified as being business-to-business (B2B) or business-to-consumer (B2C). A B2B company sells to other companies products that help those companies operate or that are used as components in the products they make or the services they provide. Gore-Tex is a good example (see Exhibit 2-12). Gore-Tex does not make coats, gloves, or shoes, but rather makes a branded fabric that it sells to companies that do make coats, gloves, and shoes. Some companies sell to both consumers and businesses. Kraft Foods, for example, sells hundreds of food products to consumers (B2C), as well as to restaurants and the food service industry (B2B customers).

B2C companies, such as Nike, make goods or provide services specifically for consumers (end users). However, it's more complicated than that. Nike sells some of its products directly to consumers in its own stores (B2C) but, for the most part, sells its products to other retailers (B2B), who then sell Nike athletic shoes and apparel in their stores. To further complicate this picture, some manufacturers, such as Johnson & Johnson and Procter & Gamble, sell only through distribution channels: distributors and retailers buy all of their products for resale to consumers. Nevertheless, all of these companies are called B2C because their products are designed for consumer use.

This is why **channel marketing,** *the process manufacturers use to build relationships with members of the distribution channel,* is so important to B2C marketers. They

TABLE 2-3   Top 15 U.S. and Global Marketers Based on Media Spending (*in billions of U.S. dollars*)

Top Spenders in United States[a]		Top Spenders outside of United States[b]	
General Motors	$3.37	Unilever	$2.98
Procter & Gamble	2.54	Procter & Gamble	2.61
Ford	2.41	Nestlé	1.56
PepsiCo	2.21	Toyota	1.35
Pfizer	2.19	Volkswagen	1.29
DaimlerChrysler	1.99	Coca-Cola	1.18
AOL Time Warner	1.89	Ford	1.13
Philip Morris Cos.	1.82	General Motors	1.09
Walt Disney Co.	1.76	PSA Peugeot Citroen	1.00
Johnson & Johnson	1.62	Fiat	.988
Unilever	1.48	Renault	.914
Sears	1.48	L'Oreal	.913
Verizon	1.46	Kao Corp.	.715
Toyota	1.40	McDonald's	.694
AT&T Corp.	1.37	Mars Inc.	.694

[a]Based on estimated media spending plus promotion and direct-marketing spending in 2001.
[b]Based on total measured advertising spending in 2000.

Source: Reprinted with permission from the June 24, 2002 issue of *Advertising Age*. Copyright Crain Communications, Inc. 2002.

are dependent on these channel members not only to buy but also to promote manufacturers' brands to end users. In companies that provide products both for other businesses and for consumers, such as Sprint, separate marketing communication campaigns are used for the two different target customer groups— channel members and end users.

Centralized and Decentralized Organization of Marketing

Very large companies, such as General Electric, that produce many different kinds of goods and services are usually divided into **strategic business units (SBUs),** which are *product, brand, or geographical divisions that operate as individual businesses within the company.* Within a typical company (and SBU) are these departments: finance, operations (in service companies) or production (in manufacturing companies), marketing and sales, research and development (R&D), human resources, and information technology. Marketing is generally organized in one of two ways—centralized or decentralized.

In an organization with **centralized marketing,** *a single authority is responsible for all marketing communication messages* (see Figure 2-3). Centralization is generally used when all products are sold under one brand name, such as Nikon, Caterpillar, and Maytag. In these companies the various marketing functions, such as advertising, marketing services (which includes most of the other marketing communication functions), and marketing research, report to a director or vice president of marketing and sales. If a company has an extensive product line, such as Maytag, a product manager may handle each subgroup of products, such as washers and dryers, refrigerators, ranges and cooktops, and dishwashers. Supporting all product managers are the marketing research and marketing services departments. Marketing services oversees the work of the outside marketing communication professionals and agencies.

Centralized marketing is used by some international companies, such as IBM. Although IBM has a director of marketing and sales in most major countries, the advertising and promotions used by these directors are tightly controlled by IBM's international headquarters and lead agency, Ogilvy & Mather in New York. Local managers can often control the scheduling of their marketing communication programs, but the look and sound of the messages does not differ from country to country. The reason for a centralized organization of marketing activities is to maintain and reinforce brand-message consistency. This organizational strategy is most appropriate for products whose use is not culturally sensitive, such as computers and airline travel.

In an organization with **decentralized marketing,** *management responsibility is assigned by brand or geographical region* (see Figure 2-4). In a company with multiple brands, such as Procter & Gamble and General Mills, each brand has a brand manager who is responsible for administering all aspects of a brand, including its marketing communication. Generally speaking, the more sales a brand has and the more departments and agencies there are working to

EXHIBIT 2-12

Gore-Tex is an "ingredient" brand as its product is used to make other goods.

> "There's nothing worse in business than having departments. Why? Because the people in different departments don't talk to each other."
>
> Jack Welch, retired CEO of General Electric

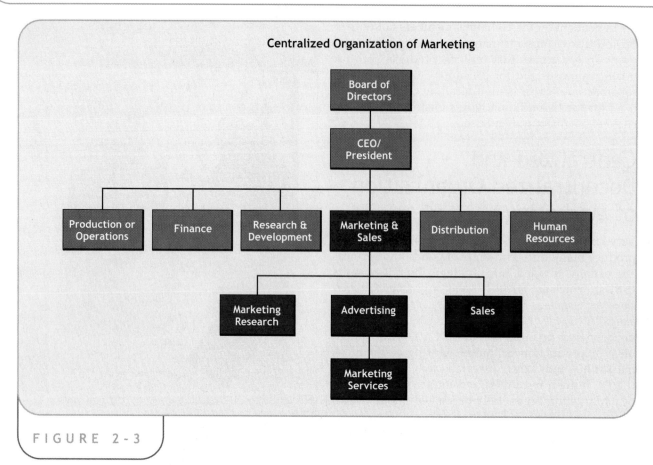

FIGURE 2-3

support the brand, the more daunting is the challenge of integrating all their work. Jack Welch, longtime CEO of General Electric, believed strongly in a "boundary-less" organization in which employees from different divisions are encouraged to talk to one another.[10] IMC provides a process for linking and coordinating departments. IBM also has recognized the problem of compartmentalization and has developed products to help companies overcome it (see Exhibit 2-13).

In an organization with decentralized marketing, each brand has one or more agencies and its own set of brand messages that have little or no relationship to messages about the other company brands. In this type of organization, the company name (for example, Procter & Gamble) is the corporate brand and receives little promotion; the majority of MC dollars are put into the product brands (Crest, Tide, Cheer, Pampers).

Marketing also may be decentralized when a company sells, in more than one country or region, culturally sensitive products such as food or apparel—products that require a localized message. In these cases, each area manager is given responsibility for sales and marketing decisions. Although this approach results in brand messages differing from area to area, most companies insist that the brand name and identifying marks be used consistently (branding strategy is discussed in Chapter 3).

Marketing Services

Although most brand managers are directly responsible for a brand's marketing communications, in many companies a separate department handles day-to-day marketing communication activities (such as marketing research, sales promotions, packaging, and event planning). This department, called **marketing services,** *coordinates the work of internal communication specialists and external*

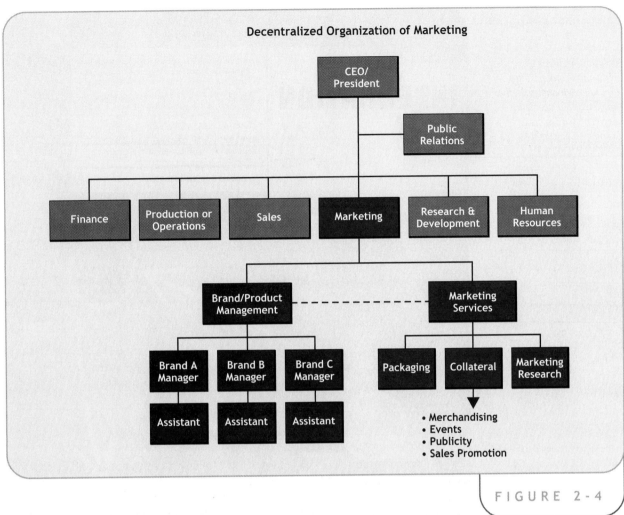

Decentralized Organization of Marketing

FIGURE 2-4

communication agencies other than the brand's advertising agency. Marketing services is a support function for brand managers.

When advertising receives the major portion of a brand's MC budget, the advertising agency generally reports directly to the brand manager or to the director of marketing, not to marketing services. Also, the brand-publicity function may or may not be part of marketing services. Even when it is, those performing that function may still report to the director of public relations. Because public relations, by definition, has skills for building relationships, it is becoming a critical function in companies that are committed to building stronger and longer-lasting customer relationships.

The scope of brand and product managers' authority varies. In some companies they have responsibility and authority for all business decisions affecting their particular brands, including budgeting and profit and loss. In other companies, they have responsibility for integrating all activities affecting their brands, but they don't have final authority for major decisions such as approving new MC campaigns, adding new products, or changing prices—decisions that are made by the head of marketing.

In most cases, a company's sales force does not report to a brand manager but rather reports to a vice president of sales (or sales and marketing). In many companies, especially B2B companies, marketing is seen as support for the sales force. Frequently there is tension between sales and marketing. Marketing generally has a longer-term perspective, desiring to do things to build both the brand and enduring customer relationships. Sales, in contrast, is more interested in

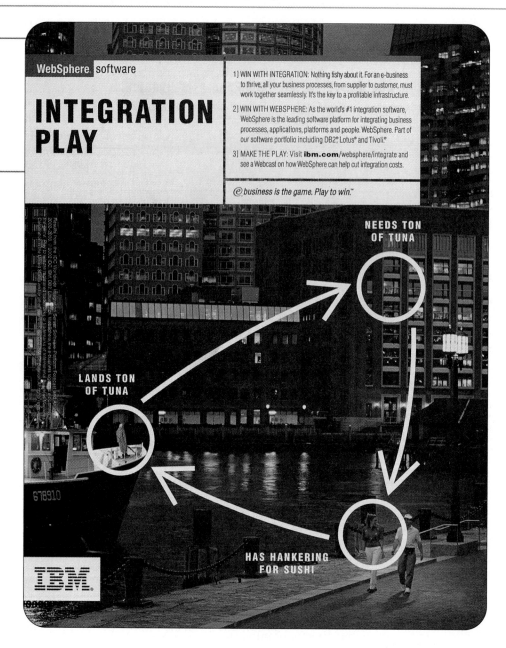

generating transactions in the short term because they constitute the measure of sales people's performance and determine how much they earn. The reality is that companies and brands have both short- and long-term needs that ought to be coordinated.

Marketing Channels

Nearly all manufacturers of consumer package goods, as well as many manufacturers of industrial products, use channels of distribution to move products to end users. Channel members include *distributors, brokers* and *wholesalers,* and *retailers.* In most cases, channel members buy products from manufacturers and then resell them—at a higher price in exchange for transporting and warehousing—to other manufacturers or consumers. If manufacturers cannot convince channel members to carry their products, the manufacturers are forced to go out of business. This is why channel members are an important target audience. They are the gatekeepers for products reaching end users. Manufacturers use MC tools to create and maintain relationships with channel members just as they (manufacturers) do with end users.

Retailers are particularly important and have tremendous influence on the marketing of brands. Wal-Mart, for example, works closely with manufacturers of the products it sells, not only on promotional strategies but also on the design of the products themselves. (For information about some of the partnership programs that manufacturers use to ensure the cooperation of retailers who sell their brands, see Chapter 15.)

Another important organizational consideration for today's retailers is the integration of the various ways in which they sell to customers—online, in stores, and from catalogs. Circuit City, for example, has integrated its brick-and-mortar stores with its online channel, allowing customers to buy in whatever way they prefer. They can go online to browse, make a purchase online, and then go to a store to pick up the merchandise.[11] Such retailing strategies demand a high level of integration in customer messages so that all of a retailer's channels are saying the same thing.

Government and Nonprofits Are Businesses Too

The federal government was the 24th largest marketing communication spender in the United States in 2001, investing slightly over $1 billion.[12] A large portion of this spending was done by the armed forces in their effort to recruit men and women into military service. State and local governments also spend millions to promote various causes and issues. Two of the biggest areas of state MC spending are the promotion of tourism and the promotion of state lotteries.

Nonprofits such as United Way and the Red Cross use marketing communication tools to help raise money and enlist volunteers and members. As nonprofit organizations—such as museums, symphony orchestras, zoos, churches, political parties, and universities, as well as other good causes such as Habitat for Humanity and the Sierra Club—have become more competitive, their marketing and MC efforts have become more sophisticated. The Metropolitan Museum of Art in New York, the Smithsonian Institution in Washington, DC, and other museums not only hold membership drives and fund-raising events but also publish magazines and sell merchandise through catalogs. The primary objectives of nonprofit organizations include recruitment and membership, contributions and fund-raising, and attitude change. The Partnership for a Drug-Free America, for example, sponsors public service campaigns on ways to change attitudes toward drug use, as well as behavior.

HOW DOES THE AGENCY/CLIENT RELATIONSHIP WORK?

In terms of making the golden triangle work, the most difficult issues are found in the relationship between clients and their agencies. Let's look first at agency compensation and evaluation and then consider some of the issues posed by integrated marketing communication, such as cross-functional planning and IMC leadership issues.

Compensation

Agencies are compensated in several ways: commissions, fees, retainers, and markups. The method of payment varies by type of MC agency, by individual client, and often is a mix of these various ways.

IMC IN ACTION

Can You Sell America like Soap?

Charlotte Beers, former head of powerhouse agencies Ogilvy & Mather and J. Walter Thompson, was hired after the September 11, 2001, attacks by Secretary of State Colin Powell to polish America's image abroad, especially among Muslims. Could marketing communication be used effectively to counter the anti-U.S. messages that fundamentalist Muslim schools have been directing to young people for more than half a century? Could America be sold like a brand? Beers, who was given the title "Under Secretary for Public Diplomacy," believed that it could be if the communication plan focused on what the United States stands for. She explained, "We're going to have to communicate the intangible assets of the United States—things like our belief system and our values."

Beers's first act was to find the right U.S. spokesperson. She selected Chris Ross, a former ambassador to Syria and Algeria who speaks fluent Arabic, to help present the U.S. case in the propaganda war that has surrounded the U.S. response to the terrorist attacks. When the Arabic TV station Al-Jazeera first played a tape of Osama bin Laden's post-9/11 comments, there was no one who could respond for the United States. By the time his second tape played, Ross was in Al-Jazeera's Washington studio taking the broadcast apart in fluent Arabic and participating in the analysis of the tape with an international panel of experts.

Other immediate activities for Beers included meeting with prominent Muslim Americans to gauge which messages would be most likely to promote a positive image of the United States. She also used marketing research to determine how best to connect with younger Muslims, and she initiated better training for embassy public relations staffs.

Beers's most tangible project, however, was a 24-page booklet that hammered home the grisly imagery of the September 11 carnage. Using Bin Laden's own words, the brochure showcased his masterminding of the attacks. Made available in print and on the internet, the brochure was produced in 14 languages and distributed in Mideast countries, sometimes as a supplement in newspapers. Knowing that part of this mission was educational, Beers also proposed university programs, with computer training, to teach English in Mideast universities, a neutral site for beginning the dialogue with young Muslims. Another project was using the advertising industry's public service arm, the Ad Council, to create a poster to plaster all over Arab countries announcing that the $5 million reward for information leading to the arrest of the "Most Wanted Terrorist" was being raised to $25 million.

Of course, getting the word out in countries where the media are controlled and hostile was another problem. To support that effort, Beers convinced Congress to allocate $30 million to create a new radio network, Radio Sawa, an Arab-language rock network that is a younger, modern version of Voice of America.

In her travels Beers found that many Muslims were concerned about the lives of Muslims in the United States, so a $10 million international ad campaign by McCann-Erickson was produced. However, after about a year on the air, the commercials were pulled—for various reasons. According to the U.S. State Department, the campaign needed to place more emphasis on public relations. According to the *Wall Street Journal*, several of the targeted countries, among them Egypt and Jordan, were refusing to use the spots on their government-owned TV stations.

In March 2003 Colin Powell announced that Charlotte Beers had resigned her post "for health reasons." Criticism of Beers' work seemed to have peeked when several Arab countries refused to air her "Shared Values" TV campaign which had been created to run in

EXHIBIT 2-14

Muslim-dominated countries. Where the campaign did run it seemed to have little impact. An article in London's *Financial Times* quoted an Egyptian "moderate cleric" who lectures in Islamic universities as saying: "So far I haven't seen any warm response [to the videos] from the Muslim community here." According to CNN, some government officals felt Beers "did not understand her target audience." Other observers questioned why the government chose an advertising rather than a public relations solution. What do you think?

Think About It

Do you think the campaign will make any difference? If you were in charge of this campaign, what else would you recommend doing?

Source: Adapted from Ira Teinowitz, "Beers Draws Mixed Review after One Year," September 23, 2002, pp. 3, 57; Margaret Carlson, "Can Charlotte Beers Sell Uncle Sam?" and Alexandra Starr, "Charlotte Beers' Toughest Sell," from <www.businessweek.com/magazine/content/01_51/b3762098.html>; Charlotte Beers, keynote address at the annual meeting of the National Council for International Visitors, Washington, DC, March 14, 2002 <www.state.gov/r/us/9509.html>; Shawn Donnan, "Muslims far from sold on TV campaign to rebrand America," *Financial Times*, November 2–3, 2002 (weekend edition), p. 22.

Commissions

For years, most full-service ad agencies did all their work in return for a 15 percent **commission,** *a payment that represents a percentage of a client's total media spending.* Suppose a client spends $5 million a year on media. Over the course of the year, the agency would bill the client $5 million but pay only 85 percent of that amount ($4.25 million) to the media, keeping 15 percent, or $750,000 ($5,000,000 × 15% = $750,000). The commission system originated when agencies first began because their primary purpose was to act as sales representatives for the media. But the agencies soon found that many companies didn't know how to create ads and thus were reluctant to buy advertising space. Seeing an opportunity to sell more space, the ad agencies began offering to do the ads for free for companies that agreed to buy advertising space. The more space the agencies sold, the more creative work they were willing to do for a client.

This system continued until the 1980s, when media costs began increasing at a faster rate than inflation. This meant that clients were paying agencies more for the same amount of work. Under pressure for more profits, clients began to renegotiate contracts, forcing agency commissions down to between 8 and 12 percent, depending on the size of their media budgets. The larger a budget was, the lower the percentage rate. Today, not only has the traditional 15 percent commission been lowered for many clients, but clients are continually exploring alternative ways to compensate their agencies.

Fees and Retainers

Public relations firms and many other MC agencies are fully or partially compensated by fee or retainer. Also, advertising agencies that handle accounts that spend less than about $2 million a year on media often work on a fee or retainer basis (because their media spending doesn't generate enough commission, even at 15 percent, to cover agency costs). A **fee** is *a fixed payment based on a standardized hourly charge.* To pay for all the time it takes to create and execute a publicity program (in which the idea is to place stories in the media without charge), a PR agency needs to be paid in some way other than a commission. Therefore, PR executives (and MC managers in other functional areas as well) typically sit down with a client, discuss the client's needs for the year or for a project, and then set a monthly fee.

An annual **retainer** is *an arrangement in which a client contracts to work with an agency for a year or more and pay that agency a certain amount*. The agency is "retained" by the client to work on its account. As it does with the fee approach, the agency keeps track of employee hours to determine whether the retainer is adequate. All employees of public relations firms are required to keep track of their hours and expenses and charge them to the appropriate clients.

The amount of a fee or retainer is estimated by taking the hourly wage of each person assigned to an account and multiplying that by an overhead and profit factor. Suppose an account supervisor's time is billed at the rate of $150 an hour. One-third of that amount ($50) would go for the account supervisor's salary and benefits (insurance, retirement fund, bonuses). The remaining two-thirds ($100) would go for the firm's overhead (administrative and support staff salaries, rent, utilities) and for profit.

Markups

Another source of income for agencies is the marking up of services that the agency buys for clients from another company. For example, when a direct-marketing agency designs a direct-mail piece, the printing, envelope addressing, and envelope stuffing are done by outside companies that specialize in each of these tasks. The printer and the letter shop (and any other suppliers) bill the direct-marketing agency for their services, and the agency marks up each bill by a certain percentage to cover the cost of administering the project. Suppose a printer charges $50,000. The agency may add a 20 percent markup (20% × $50,000 = $10,000) and send the client a bill for $60,000. When the client pays the direct-marketing agency, the agency keeps $10,000 and sends the remaining $50,000 to the printer. Markups cover the cost of the agency's dealing with outside companies.

Performance-Based Compensation

As clients have focused more on accountability, advertising agencies in particular have seen an erosion of client budgets.[13] In response, some agencies and their clients have worked out a performance-based compensation plan. In most cases performance compensation is only a portion of the total amount a client pays (the remainder is commissions or fees). Performance compensation is determined by the extent to which marketing communication objectives are achieved. Suppose campaign objectives are to (1) increase brand awareness by 10 percentage points, (2) increase trial by 25 percent among new users, and (3) generate 25,000 requests for additional information. The agency would be paid according to how many of these objectives were achieved within a set period of time.

Bonus payments may be built in for results that exceed objectives (how these objectives are measured is discussed in Chapter 22). For an example of a creative approach to agency incentives, consider how the bonus is determined for Crispin Porter & Bogusky, the agency handling the BMW Mini launch. The 70 Mini dealers vote on how effective the agency has been in developing the brand. Their votes determine the bonus that Mini pays the agency.[14]

From a client's perspective, the ideal arrangement would be to tie agency compensation directly to the client company's sales and profits. This approach, however, works better in theory than in practice, because so many variables (in addition to MC) affect sales and profits. Among them are product performance, distribution, competitive activity, customer service, and the effectiveness of the sales force. This is why most measures of MC performance are based on awareness and other communication measures. Public relations is the exception. It is considered unethical to base compensation on the number of stories that appear as a result of a PR firm's efforts for a client, because final decisions about what appears in the media are out of the PR firm's control.

In general, compensation is an area that is going through a great deal of change, and agency/client contracts are as individualized as the products they promote. A study by the Association of National Advertisers found that, as a percentage of the overall compensation to MC agencies, pure commission-based compensation was only used by about one-third of all clients. At the same time, the use of fee-based compensation has been significantly increasing.[15]

There is no longer only one set way to compensate agencies. As the president of a major ad agency said to this author, "The way we are compensated today varies by the number of clients we have. We have a different contract with each one because no two clients have the same needs or the same level of media spending."

Agency Evaluation

Companies should conduct periodic reviews of all agencies with which they have an ongoing relationship. This needs to be done for the same reason companies evaluate employees, departments, and other suppliers.

There are two basic types of agency evaluations: quantitative and qualitative. For agencies that are paid a fee (hourly or otherwise), a client can do a *quantitative audit* of an agency's records to determine whether the hours and expenses for which the company has been billed are correct. In a *qualitative survey*, employees who have frequent contact with an agency rate the agency in areas such as responsiveness, thoroughness, meeting deadlines, cooperativeness, level of initiative, source of new ideas, and creative abilities. When budgets are quite large, a client company sometimes conducts separate evaluations of the agency's creative department, media department, and account service area. The more money an agency handles for a company, regardless of the type of agency, the more critical are the periodic evaluations.

Evaluations are beneficial for several reasons. Foremost, they help a company determine whether it is getting its money's worth. Unless the evaluation is based on performance measures, this is a subjective call and should reflect the thinking of not just one or two people. Second, most people like feedback. Real professionals even appreciate negative feedback, as long as it is constructive and objective, because they realize it will help them improve. Most agencies would rather be criticized and given a chance to improve their performance than simply fired. The primary purpose of agency evaluations should not be to determine whether the company should continue working with an agency (just as every employee evaluation is not about whether to fire someone), but rather should be to determine how the agency and company can work better together.

Some client companies ask their agencies to evaluate them. How are the company's people performing? Do they give clear directions? Are they competent? Are their critiques of the agency's work insightful, objective, and helpful? One of the most helpful pieces of information a company can receive is how its MC people compare to those working for the agency's other clients.

How Does Cross-Functional Planning Work?

Integration is an organizational challenge to both the company and its agencies. Marketing must compete for its budget with all the other departments in a company. Production wants money for new equipment, distribution wants new trucks, and human resources wants more training programs and greater employee benefits. And, of course, marketing wants more money so it can do more advertising and promotion. Consequently, when top management divides up the corporate budget, these departments can become aggressive competitors. Turf wars in many companies make it difficult to plan and monitor comprehensive communication programs, and these disputes can be solved only by programs that are designed to get people talking and working together and reward them for doing so.

Complicating things is the fact that once marketing gets its budget, all the groups within marketing (sales, advertising, sales promotion, and others) find that they must then compete for their share. This competition may seem self-serving, but it is often the result of managers' genuine beliefs in the power of their respective MC areas to best serve the brand. Also driving some of these budget battles is the fact that in most companies, the larger a manager's staff and budget are, the larger is the manager's salary.

To lessen the negative effects of departmental silos and budget battles, companies are increasingly using cross-functional planning to manage their marketing communications. Egos and silos should not be allowed to get in the way of creating and retaining customers. **Cross-functional planning** is *a process for planning and monitoring brand relationships that involves all departments that directly or indirectly "touch" the customer.* Cross-functional planning helps increase consistency in all brand messages, ensures that the big creative idea is integrated in all messages, and facilitates coordination of the timing and scheduling of the various MC programs (see Exhibit 2-15). Cross-functional planning provides a mechanism, when necessary, to reallocate portions of the MC budget in order to address problems or take advantage of opportunities.

An example of the benefits of a cross-functional approach to planning comes from Hallmark Cards, Inc. The company significantly decreased its time-to-market by integrating its organizational structure for developing and introducing a new line of cards. According to a Hallmark executive, after setting up a cross-functional team, the company was able to develop a new line of cards in nearly half the time it took before:

> We grouped people together who had been separated by disciplines, departments, floors, and even buildings to cut down on the queue time, spur creativity, and end the throw-it-over-the-wall-it's-their-problem attitude. This [integrated team approach] worked so well that half of the line hit the stores . . . eight months ahead of schedule

EXHIBIT 2-15

The objective of cross-functional planning is to get all the employees who are involved in a marketing communication program "in the same boat and rowing in the same direction." Siebel has an employee relationship software program that is designed to enhance this coordination.

. . . We think the team worked because by bringing a group of people together like that, they got focused and [had] direct communication linkages.[16]

Cross-functional management experiences expose prospective managers to a wide variety of business operations. Cross-functional planning helps broaden managers' understanding of the business by acquainting them with the objectives, strategies, strengths, and weaknesses of the different divisions within a company as well as with a variety of marketing programs and functional areas. Once people are involved in cross-functional planning and in the monitoring of customer relationships, rigid organizational silos that keep people from sharing information and coordinating programs are broken down.

Unfortunately, many companies have been slow to develop cross-functional systems. As Prensky, McCarty, and Lucas have concluded about integrated marketing, "at present, marketing organizations are behind in developing the content of communication programs and the process of coordinating such programs."[17] Consulting companies and software manufacturers, however, are moving into this gap (see Exhibit 2-15).

Cross-functional planning helps employees become less short-sighted. People in an organization who know and care about only their own positions and departments have little concern or sense of responsibility for the organization's collective results, as the MetLife experience demonstrates (see the Tale of Two Companies box). Such isolation is epitomized in the often-heard comment "It's not my problem!"

How Do Agencies and Clients Work Together on IMC?

Other than small retailers, most companies use one or more marketing communication agencies. Smart companies include these agencies on their cross-functional teams because the agencies provide the expertise for creating and delivering brand messages. These agencies provide specialized MC services that a company can't or doesn't want to provide itself, but they also make the coordination problem more difficult.

In integration-driven companies the trend is to pare down the number of agencies in order to get more consistency into MC programs. The problem with using multiple agencies is coordinating their work. 3M Company, for example, moved from having 34 agencies in 23 countries to one agency, Grey Worldwide. Many agencies are trying to position themselves as experts in IMC. Major advertising agencies that have handled integrated campaigns for various clients include BBDO, DDB, Leo Burnett, Ogilvy & Mather, and Young & Rubicam. The large agencies, however, still emphasize their creative advertising work despite their talk about how important integration is. Truly integrated agencies are more commonly found among mid-sized agencies such as Cramer-Krasselt and Fallon Worldwide. Several agencies, such as The Phelps Group and Price/McNabb, have reinvented themselves as IMC agencies. Other firms with IMC capabilities are Trinity Creative Communications, Tucker-Knapp, InterOne Marketing Group, and the Gage Marketing Group.

Agency Networks

Because the MC agency industry has been steadily growing and is quite profitable, there have been many mergers and acquisitions, which have consolidated most of the major global agencies into one of five MC networks. Table 2-4 shows the top 5 of these holding companies and ranks them by worldwide gross revenues and takes into account income from the advertising, public relations, sales

A TALE OF TWO COMPANIES

Cross-Functional Planning at MetLife and General Electric

Cross-functional planning alone does not guarantee integration, but the lack of it almost always guarantees *dis*integration. Metropolitan Life Insurance Company (MetLife), the second largest insurance company in the United States, offers a good example of what can happen when a cross-functional team is not in place or has no authority. For years MetLife agents were allowed to use questionable sales practices, promising more than they could deliver. Because the sales operations was not actively monitored by a cross-functional team, MetLife soon found itself in deep trouble. Over 40 states levied fines, totaling $20 million, against the company. MetLife also faced the issue of making refunds of up to $75 million. After public disclosure of these problems, MetLife sales decreased by 25 percent. Finally, because of the lawsuits and legal problems, the company's credit rating was reduced (its relationship with the financial community had also been damaged).

According to a MetLife spokesperson, the company had failed to enforce stated policies for sales messages. The MetLife auditors "would give a warning, lawyers would go down there [to Florida, where much of the trouble was centered] and say 'This has to stop,' but there wasn't follow-through." The internal pressure for sales performance overwhelmed the wiser voices. If a cross-functional management team had been in place, perhaps the voices of those concerned with the long-term impact on brand relationships and reputation would have been heard. Regardless of who was to blame, MetLife faced a marketing communication nightmare both internally and externally.

In contrast, General Electric created a forum dubbed "Pit" where, every two weeks or so, visiting GE employees gather to spot problems and argue for solutions. Pit sessions are held in the main auditorium of GE's Management Development Institute in Crotonville, New York. Staffs are challenged to speak up when problems are spotted. GE CEO Jack Welch (now retired) said, "The group has to get together and fix the problem . . . You've got to take the responsibility to take the ball and run with it." He empowered employees to intervene in the system in order to provide solutions. From his experience with the Pit, Welch created a new organizational structure for GE called "Work-Out." The GE workforce was organized into flexible, natural teams that meet frequently to discuss how to improve processes. The objective is more efficiency, less waste.

The secret to GE's innovative management approach is communication. Cross-functional teams with the authority to investigate various work processes come up with recommendations that managers must address on the spot and then implement. Such an approach not only opens up innovation but also protects a company against the kinds of problems faced by MetLife.

Think About It

What was the reason for MetLife's problems? What can you learn from GE's approach to management that applies to a marketing communication program?

Source: Adapted from Mark Suchecki, "Integrated Marketing: Making it Pay," *Direct*, October 1993, pp. 43–49; Weld Royal, "Scapegoat," *Sales & Marketing Management*, January 1995, p. 62; Judy Quinn, "What a Work-Out," *Performance*, November 1994, pp. 60–63; Marshall Loeb, "Jack Welch Lets Fly on Budgets, Bonuses, and Buddy Boards," *Fortune*, May 29, 1995, pp. 145–46.

promotion, direct-marketing, and other nonadvertising companies owned by each conglomerate.

In the three largest networks—Omnicom, Interpublic, and WPP—revenue from advertising is now less than half of their respective total revenues. That means the other marketing communication areas are providing the majority of revenues. These huge MC conglomerates serve as a good industry barometer, showing how clients are allocating their MC dollars and, according to *Advertising Age*, reflect an industrywide trend.[18]

T A B L E 2 - 4	World's Top MC Agency Groups (based on 2002 world revenues)	
Agency	**Group Headquarters**	**Revenue (in millions)**
WPP Group	New York	$8,165.0
Interpublic Group	New York	7,981.4
Omnicom Group	New York	7,404.2
Publicis/Bcom3	Paris	4,769.9
Dentsu	Tokyo	2,795.5

Source: Reprinted with permission from the April 22, 2002 issue of *Advertising Age.* Copyright Crain Communications, Inc. 2002.

The Role of the Client in IMC Leadership

Most marketing experts agree that clients drive integration. Casey Jones, president of Grey Worldwide, San Francisco, advocates that clients' CEOs should appoint a chief marketing or communication officer who has absolute control over the brand. This person should send the message to employees that they must "integrate or die," says Jones.[19]

The problem with implementing IMC is that many companies haven't set themselves up for integration. David Sable, president of the Wunderman agency, says that "Because clients' marketing departments are separated into different centers of responsibility . . . they don't approach their customers holistically, so neither can their agencies."[20] In 2002, IBM took steps to bring integration to its varied business enterprises by pooling its marketing communication dollars for its servers, software, storage, and global services units in order to deliver an integrated message under the theme "Play to Win."[21]

Agency Integration Issues

It is up to the client to ensure that brand communication is integrated; but if agencies are to be partners, they too must be organized to make integration work. According to Philip Geier Jr., long-time CEO of the Interpublic Group of Companies, more and more ad agencies and other specialized agencies are recognizing the need for integration and are taking steps to become more IMC focused and less dependent on advertising.[22]

There are organizational problems on the agency side of integration, as well as on the client side. Typically, all the media people are in one area, all the creatives in another, and all the account management people in yet another. Although they attend planning meetings, often their primary allegiance is to their respective departments. Progressive agencies that recognize the value of IMC, such as the Phelps Group, often bring all members of a client team together. Nevertheless, integration problems occur even in progressive agencies when other MC functions are involved.

Studies indicate that ad agencies in particular are reluctant to integrate other marketing communication agencies into cross-functional planning. According to one study, ad agencies "prefer to ignore the other communication channels or to operate independent firms under a corporate umbrella that offers full service but little integration."[23] But the integration problem is not restricted to advertising. Many nonadvertising agencies realize that they are always competing with ad agencies for budget allocations and are often considered second-class MC players by both ad agencies and clients. A few public relations academics even speak disparagingly of IMC as "marketing imperialism" and see it as a ploy for marketing and advertising to take over public relations. Such an attitude is nonproductive and the opposite of what IMC is all about.

Three strategies that agencies can use to organize themselves in order to offer integrated services are (1) adding on other MC functions, (2) reinventing themselves, and (3) operating as a lead agency with a team of supporting agencies. With the add-on functions approach, an agency that specializes in one area (such as advertising or public relations) adds departments so that clients do not have to go elsewhere for specialized services. Several years ago FCB Worldwide added a sales promotion and a direct-marketing department to its full-service advertising agency to better serve its clients.

Sometimes an agency buys or partners with specialist agencies, although that strategy can be problematic if there is no mandate to integrate the two at the strategic-planning level. Specialist departments can also be "grown" internally. When the Leo Burnett agency wanted to add direct-marketing services for its clients, it simply went out and hired people with direct-marketing experience.

A FINAL NOTE: IMC PARTNERS BENEFIT BY WORKING TOGETHER

The extent to which a client trusts and respects the expertise of its MC agencies can significantly affect the quality of the agencies' work, not to mention the smoothness of the working relationship between client and agencies. In good relationships (as in good relationship marketing), neither party is taken for granted. What often determines the level of trust and respect is the client's attitude toward its agencies. Does the client see each agency as a supplier or a partner? The answer is a major concern to agencies.

In one of the largest account moves in advertising history, IBM consolidated its $500 million global account at Ogilvy & Mather Worldwide, dropping about 70 other agencies, believing that centralized marketing creates the best path to achieving integration. At the same time, all of IBM's U.S. marketing communication disciplines were consolidated under a single management group, Marketing Services & Communications, which includes advertising, media relations, executive communications, direct marketing, trade shows, publications, employee communications, and more. The greater the psychological distance is between agency and client, and the more agencies that are involved, the harder it is to integrate programs. IBM's action is an important recognition of the need for a close and positive agency/client relationship.

Key Terms

account manager 37
account planner 38
art director 38
brand manager 38
centralized marketing 49
channel marketing 47
commission 55
copywriter 38
creative boutique 39
creative brief 39

creative director 38
cross-functional planning 58
decentralized marketing 49
fee 55
freelancer 39
full-service agency 36
in-house ad agency 40
marketing services 50
mass media 44
MC suppliers 42

media buying 38
media buying services 39
media planning 38
place-based media 45
producer 38
product placement 40
retainer 56
strategic business unit (SBU) 49
traffic manager 38

Key Point Summary

EXHIBIT 2-16

To make brand champions of its employees around the world and integrate them into the delivery of the brand message, GM created BrandZone, an internal intranet tool that communicates the essence of the brand by empowering employees to live and give voice to the new brand promise.

Key Point 1: Agencies

Full-service agencies in the various areas of marketing communication provide a basic set of services that can be supplemented by MC suppliers such as creative boutiques, freelancers, and media buying services. Agencies sometimes specialize by industry, and sometimes they are partners in networks of agencies. Compensation is usually through commission, fee or retainer, or markups. Performance-based compensation is becoming more prevalent. Agencies serve their clients in many different ways; the nature of the service affects how they are staffed and compensated. The type of agency/client relationship also determines the degree to which agencies are able to support their clients with cross-functional planning. Agencies use several different organizational approaches—adding functions, reinvention, and acting as a lead agency—to manage cross-functional planning.

Key Point 2: Media

Recent changes that have affected how media companies work with agencies and their clients include the development of new communication technologies, an increase in media alternatives, the provision of information about target awareness, the legalization of single ownership of competing media, and attempts by media companies to establish their own identities.

Key Point 3: The Corporate Side

On the corporate side, marketers of all types direct the management of marketing communication. A cross-functional IMC team on the corporate side ensures consistency in all brand messages and coordinates the timing and scheduling of MC programs. It does this by linking specialized departments, making each department that is involved with brand relationship aware of what the others are doing, and making sure that programs are not redundant, counterproductive, or in some other way at cross-purposes with each other.

Key Point 4: The Agency/Client Relationship

The agency/client relationship is impacted by issues involving compensation and evaluation of the agency's work. The organizational tool that both agencies and clients use to coordinate IMC programs is cross-functional planning. IMC works best when the client takes leadership; however, agencies have to solve internal organizational problems in order to be able to provide integrated services.

Lessons Learned

Key Point 1: Agencies

a. What is a full-service agency? How does a full-service agency differ from a creative boutique?
b. What is an agency network?
c. In what ways do agencies specialize?
d. What is an in-house agency? In what situations is one used?
e. What kinds of suppliers do agencies use? What services do they provide?
f. How do commissions and fees differ?
g. Why are companies increasingly implementing performance-based compensation plans for MC agencies?
h. Which of all the agency jobs described in the staffing discussion most appeals to you? What skills and abilities do you have that might make this job a career for you?
i. Describe three approaches that agencies use to manage cross-functional planning.

Key Point 2: Media

a. What recent changes in the media world have affected the operation of MC programs?
b. What are place-based media, and how do they work?
c. Why should media consider themselves to be brands?

Key Point 3: The Corporate Side

a. Identify the departments commonly found within a company.
b. Why are there departmental silos and turf war problems in traditional organizations?
c. Define *cross-functional planning*.
d. Why is cross-functional planning a necessary ingredient of integrated marketing communication?
e. Find the organizational chart of a company with which you are familiar. Analyze the structure of the company, and explain how it organizes marketing and marketing communication functions.

Key Point 4: The Agency/Client Relationship

a. What are the four main ways in which agencies get compensated? How do they differ?
b. Explain how cross-functional planning would work on both the client and the agency sides of the business.
c. Why do experts recommend that the client take the lead in driving integration?
d. What changes do agencies have to make in order to offer integrated services?

Chapter Challenge

Writing Assignment

Identify an MC agency about which you would like to know more. Look up the agency in the trade press (conduct an electronic search in your business school library), contact the agency's PR department and request copies of brochures it has produced, and look up the agency on the Web. Analyze the following:

1. What is the agency's area of business (its marketing communication specialty)?
2. How is the agency organized? What departments does it include? Is it part of a network?
3. What is the agency's philosophy of business?

Presentation Assignment

Partner with someone in your class. Take turns conducting mock interviews for a job in an MC agency. Present your interviews to the class.

Internet Assignment

Choose one of the agencies mentioned in this chapter, and go to its website. From what you find on that site, develop a profile of the agency addressing the following points:

1. What is the agency's focus, specialty, or area of business? What services does it provide its clients?
2. What is the agency's philosophy of business?
3. How is the agency organized?

Chapter

3

Brands and Stakeholder Relationships

Key Points in This Chapter

1. What does it mean to say that a brand is more than a product?
2. Explain the three steps in building a brand.
3. What are the key factors in creating brand relationships?
4. What is brand equity, and how is it affected by brand relationships?

Chapter Perspective

Companies Make Products, but They Sell Brands

In many companies, the number-one marketing priority is to create customers. As management consultant Peter Drucker explained many decades ago, when this effort succeeds, the company is rewarded by making sales. According to Drucker, building **customer relationships**—*a series of interactions between customers and a company over time*—will produce more sales and profits than will focusing on sales transactions alone. This is why more companies are placing greater emphasis on retaining customers.

IMC is a process; it is a means to an end. That end is brands and stakeholder relationships. IMC seeks to maximize the positive messages and minimize the negative messages that are communicated about a brand, with the objective of creating and sustaining brand relationships. But that's only one reason why companies practice IMC. When used to build long-term relationships, IMC also builds and strengthens the brand itself. The stronger a brand is, the more value it has. Positive brand relationships generate profits.

Understanding how brands are built and managed requires an understanding of how relationship-building communications are created and managed. This chapter explains what a brand is, describes how brands are created, and looks at the characteristics of brand–customer relationships.

THE BRAND-BUILDING BUSINESS
Siegel & Gale

With over thirty years experience as a brand identity and brand consulting company, Siegel & Gale understands that a great brand is much more than a flashy logo and clever advertising. A great brand is built on a solid foundation—a compelling brand promise that defines and decommoditizes a company's value to both internal and external audiences. A brand promise is based upon a clear, penetrating, ownable idea. It evolves from the core truths of an organization and helps a company transform perceptions of itself.

Siegel & Gale believes building must go beyond the development of a promise and the standardization of marketing communication and graphics. Great brands obsess not only with unifying the brand's expression across all media, but also with aligning all behavior and all operations around the delivery of the brand promise.

"Great companies and brands share an unwavering organizational commitment to a common purpose that creates uncommon value," explains Siegel & Gale managing director, Noah Manduke. "These world-class organizations meticulously align their behavior and communications around more than just a promise. They pursue an ideal. The resulting brands don't just build a business, they create a cause with powerful emotional underpinnings."

The world's most recognizable brands—such as Disney, Harley-Davidson, Tiffany, Nike, Lexus, and Apple—enjoy enduring emotional connections with consumers because they have each captured a high ground in their respective categories. They don't just make a promise; they make THE promise (in their product category) and consistently deliver upon it.

These brands are built on an underlying singular idea that drives each organization's communications and behavior across all channels, from the inside out. This enables all brand communication to be consistent. The new interactive media create new kinds of brand identity challenges and experiences that must be taken into consideration such as how companies respond to customer-initiated contacts.

Siegel & Gale's brand building process begins with research that uncovers, interprets, and expresses a company's unique qualities and hidden values. This information comes from in-depth interviews with the company's employees and from a close analysis

EXHIBIT 3-1

of the company's evolution and strategic developments. The objective of this analysis is to harvest and articulate a compelling, inspirational, and transformational idea for the brand—a promise the company can rally behind and deliver upon.

Another service offered by Siegel & Gale is showing clients how to integrate the brand promise into every point of contact with key internal and external stakeholders. A brand project for Lehman Brothers, for example, began by unifying Lehman's diverse global organization through communication programs for clients, investors, and prospective employees based on the brand positioning line: "Lehman Brothers—Where vision gets built." The CEO of Lehman Brothers summed up the communication process when he said: "In many ways, each of us is a Lehman Brothers brand manager. We have the responsibility to fulfill the unique promise of our brand for everyone encountering it. Individually and collectively, we need to ensure that we remain the Firm 'Where vision gets built.'"

One of Siegel & Gale's clients, Tom's of Maine, originally built its brand selling a natural toothpaste. It then found it needed to expand its brand and positioning to include more products if the company was to continue to grow. Siegel & Gale helped Tom's of Maine reposition itself as a "Natural Care" company. This was accomplished with a redesigned logo and packaging system that maintained the brand's roots, while at the same time opening the door to new business opportunities that leverage the core brand values that Tom's of Maine had built over the years.

Caterpillar, a manufacturer of heavy equipment with 69,000 worldwide employees and plants in 12 countries, provides a more extended example of Siegel & Gale's approach to brand building. This was a 10-year effort in which Siegel & Gale helped transform not only Caterpillar's brand positioning and identity but also its corporate culture.

In the early 1990s, it was clear the Caterpillar brand needed to be refocused following a massive reorganization, which resulted in decentralized services and often, ineffective brand messages. Siegel & Gale began by helping the company reposition itself, providing the foundation for a new corporate identity. The new corporate positioning was an honest statement of Caterpillar's purpose summed up in the line, "It's not only what we make that makes us proud—it's what we make possible."

The new brand positioning shifted from a focus on product features to an emphasis on product benefits. Rather than MC messages making the Caterpillar machines the heroes in their advertising, the new MC messages focused on the remarkable things that customers accomplished with Caterpillar equipment. The new brand identity was built on a distinctive character and personality relevant to both internal and external audiences, which helped to tell the story of Caterpillar's new positioning strategy in its marketing communication programs.

An internal marketing campaign used the corporate magazine and a flagship brochure to bring this message to employees. Rather than showing pictures of strip mines and big earth-moving equipment, there were images of everything from building bridges and dams to tearing down the Berlin Wall and putting out oil fires in Kuwait. Employee and dealer/customer materials were developed to carry this message, and it was also included in the company's annual reports and corporate videos. Brand training programs included *The Corporate Voice* book, which was given to all communication managers. A customized training program with supplemental course books and an interactive training "game" was designed to make sure that the new philosophy was widely understood and adopted by all employees.

The same message was then taken public through TV commercials to reach customers and prospects. Sales materials were redesigned and simplified using a standardized format for Cat's "specalogs" that showed how to use the new positioning materials when doing personal selling. Even business documents were streamlined and simplified. Invoices, for example, were transformed into multipurpose, customer-focused documents that also acted as a complete record of a customer's account. Recently, the Cat Rental Stores, an independent sub-brand, were included in the new brand repositioning through a unified visual identity system that created distinctive brand contact touch points.

Over the 10-year period of Siegel & Gale's relationship with Caterpillar, this unified approach to integrating communications *and* behavior has become a part of Caterpillar's corporate culture. It has permeated the company and created a sense of global identity and pride across all of the company's business lines and has contributed directly to Caterpillar's stability and growth.

Source: Siegel & Gale corporate brochure and Noah Manduke, Siegel & Gale managing director.

WHAT "BRAND" MEANS

When tobacco giant Philip Morris acquired Kraft Foods several years ago, it paid six times the value of Kraft's physical net assets. The Philip Morris CEO said his company needed a portfolio of brands with strong customer relationships that could be leveraged to enable the tobacco company to diversify itself, especially in the retail food industry.[1] Philip Morris was willing to pay billions of dollars for a set of customer and trade brand relationships. Likewise, the former CEO of automaker Chrysler once explained that the future success of his company was not determined by its past sales and profits but rather by Chrysler's brand relationships with its dealers and customers.

So what is a brand? In chapter 1, *brand* is defined as "a perception resulting from experiences with, and information about, a company or a line of products." According to Interbrand, one of the top brand consulting firms in the world, a brand is "a mixture of tangible and intangible attributes, symbolized in a trademark, which, if properly managed, creates influence and generates value."[2]

Why does one brand have twice the share of another when there is no difference in product attributes or performance and both brands sell for the same price? The answer is—a difference in perceptions. A brand is basically a perception, not a logo on the side of a package. A brand exists only in people's heads and hearts. In the marketplace, perceptions are the collective result of everything a customer or other stakeholder sees, hears, reads, or experiences about a company and its brands. A perception can be influenced through positive (and negative) communication experiences, but not controlled. According to a creative director for Chrysler's in-house MC agency, the auto industry has a lot of *parity products* (products with few distinguishing features). In such a situation, perceptions become very important: "Practically the only difference that's left is the perception of what the car feels like and how it's gonna make you feel when you drive it."[3] IMC helps guard against a perception virus—message misunderstanding that infects and weakens brand messages and ultimately kills relationships.

A brand differentiates a product from its competitors and makes a promise to its customers. From a corporate perspective, a company's brand (or brands) should drive the corporate strategy, according to Jeff Smith, director of a leading brand consultancy.[4] To determine what this means operationally, says Smith, a company must answer this question: "What are all of the ways that one of our customers or potential customers can form an impression of our brand, our company, or our products?" Since company–customer contact can happen almost anywhere, anytime, the brand must be the driving, unifying force directing all functional areas on an ongoing basis, as the IMC process model in Chapter 1 demonstrates.

Table 3-1 lists the top 50 brands in the world according to Interbrand. (Rankings were based on financial performance, role of branding in these companies, and each brand's strength as determined by a proprietary Interbrand formula.) As you look through this list, how well do you think each brand matches the preceding descriptions of a brand?

A brand is more than just a product. Cars, checking accounts, candy bars, shoe repair, computers, and medical care are all products. What differentiates one car or one checking account from another, however, is the brand. Take universities. In their most basic form they all offer the same product—education. They all have instructors, courses, and students, and most have classrooms and buildings. Yet despite this list of commonalities, there are major differences among them. These differences are determined by the type and quality of instructors, variety of course offerings, location, number and types of students, success of athletic teams, quality of facilities, and size of endowments, among other things.

T A B L E   3 - 1   Top 50 of the World's Most Valuable Brands

1. Coca-Cola, U.S.	18. Gillette, U.S.	35. Volkswagen, Germany
2. Microsoft, U.S.	19. Merrill Lynch, U.S.	36. Ericsson, Sweden
3. IBM, U.S.	20. Sony, Japan	37. Heinz, U.S.
4. General Electric, U.S.	21. Honda, Japan	38. Louis Vuitton, France
5. Nokia, Finland	22. BMW, Germany	39. Kellogg, U.S.
6. Intel, U.S.	23. Nescafé, Switzerland	40. MTV, U.S.
7. Disney, U.S.	24. Compaq, U.S.	41. Canon, Japan
8. Ford, U.S.	25. Oracle, U.S.	42. Samsung, Korea
9. McDonald's, U.S.	26. Budweiser, U.S.	43. SAP, Germany
10. AT&T, U.S.	27. Kodak, U.S.	44. Pepsi-Cola, U.S.
11. Marlboro, U.S.	28. Merck, U.S.	45. Xerox, U.S., and British Petroleum, U.K.
12. Mercedes, Germany	29. Nintendo, Japan	46. IKEA, Sweden
13. Citibank, U.S.	30. Pfizer, U.S.	47. Pizza Hut, U.S.
14. Toyota, Japan	31. Gap, U.S.	48. Harley-Davidson, U.S.
15. Hewlett-Packard, U.S.	32. Dell, U.S.	49. Apple, U.S.
16. Cisco Systems, U.S.	33. Goldman Sachs, U.S.	50. Gucci, Italy
17. American Express, U.S.	34. Nike, U.S	

Source: Reprinted from the August 2, 2002 issue of *Business Week* by permission. Copyright the McGraw-Hill Companies.

Branding, *the process of creating a brand image that engages the hearts and minds of customers*, is what separates similar products from each other. What comes to mind when you think of each of the following: Notre Dame, MIT, Bryn Mawr, and St. Olaf? You probably don't think about classrooms, students, and faculty. Instead, you think about things such as football, academics, and Catholicism (Notre Dame), high technology (MIT), women's elite education (Bryn Mawr), and a small, liberal arts college (St. Olaf College). Look at how the names of these universities are presented in Exhibit 3-2. How well do you think the "look" of each college logo matches up with the image you have of each school?

What you see in Exhibit 3-2 are **logos,** which are *distinctive graphic designs used to communicate a product, company, or organization identity*. Brand identity tells the source of a product and often suggests a personality for the brand. Keep in mind that both companies and products have identities and images that differentiate them from competitors, so in this book the word *brand* is used in discussions of both products and companies. Furthermore, you should remember that brands are just as important in B2B and nonprofit marketing as they are in marketing consumer products.

Customers and prospects are influenced by a wide variety of messages that are sent by both the tangible and the intangible attributes of a brand. *Tangible* attributes are characteristics you can observe or touch, such as a product's design, performance, ingredients/components, size, shape, and price (see Table 3-2). Although brand mangers have input on the messages sent by these tangible attributes, brand managers' primary responsibility is to influence a brand's *intangible* attributes, such as its perceived value, its image, memories associated with the brand, and even the perceptions and impressions of those who use the brand. Intangibles are important in brand building for two reasons: they are hard for

Notre Dame
Football, academics, Catholicism

MIT
High technology

Bryn Mawr
Women's elite education

St. Olaf
Small, liberal arts

competitors to copy, and they are more likely than tangible attributes to involve consumers emotionally.

The ad for the Range Rover in Exhibit 3-3 illustrates how an ad can communicate an emotional as well as a rational message. What intangible and tangible attributes differentiate the Range Rover from other SUVs?

Brands Live in Heads and Hearts

Although a company may own a brand name and logo, and greatly influence what people think about its brands, the actual brand meaning that influences behavior resides in the heads and hearts of customers and other stakeholders. If no one were aware of a brand, the brand would have no value because it would have no impact on anyone's buying decision. Of course, you don't know or care about the brands of some of the products you buy—low-risk purchases such as a broom, milk, or matches. But you can be sure that the retailers who decided to buy and resell these items cared very much about the brands they selected for their stores to sell.

TABLE 3-2	Brand Characteristics
Tangible Attributes	**Intangible Attributes**
Design	Value
Performance	Brand image
Ingredients/components	Image of stores where sold
Size/shape	Perceptions of users of the brand
Price	
Marketing communication	

Keep in mind that brands operate at different levels and have different meanings at different stages in the distribution chain along which products move from manufacturers to end users, and with different customers. Just as you make a different impression on the people you meet at school, at work, or on an athletic field, the impression a brand makes depends on the point where customers come into contact with the brand. A brand image is the sum total of all these brand impressions.

Brand Experiences

Ultimately the meaning of a brand is based on customers' experiences with the brand, either positive or negative. An experience with a brand's television commercial, its appearance in a store, or its telemarketing can create a positive or negative experience. These experiences lead to customer satisfaction or dissatisfaction. It has been estimated that when customers switch brands, three out of four times the switch has nothing to do with product performance but rather is a response to customer service and other aspects of the brand experience that customers believed were less than satisfactory.[5]

According to Daniel Morel, CEO of the direct-response agency Wonderman, "customer experience has more to do with brand building than anything else." He maintains that "brands are 'lived' and adapted by each customer according to their own individual experiences with them."[6] Positive brand experiences are created by relevance and by offering value through the brand relationship. Starbucks Coffee, for example, invests in building its brand by ensuring that customers have a "consistent, positive, enveloping experience [each time they enter one of its stores], leading to loyalty and strong word-of-mouth among friends."[7]

The British have always driven on the wrong side of the road.

It's not that we can't get it right. We simply have our own way of doing things.

While other automobiles are either unusually rugged, or extravagantly civilized, we've made the one luxury car that isn't dependent on the luxury of a road.

Short of going across endangered terrain, there are very few places you won't see it.

With its massive chassis, and permanent 4-wheel drive, a Range Rover can go through anything from a desert

to a snowstorm. In fact, it can even go through time, gracefully.

Range Rovers in their third decade are still performing automotive impossibilities from the Serengeti to the Himalayas.

RANGE ROVER

Lest we remain complacent, though, we always manage to make improvements that improve even a Range Rover.

The 1991, for example, has a quieter ride, along with a larger fuel tank for increased touring range.

Why not call 1-800-FINE 4WD for a dealer near you? Obviously, at around $42,400, a Range Rover isn't inexpensive.

But it's an investment you'll feel quite comfortable with.

Whichever side of the road you're on.

EXHIBIT 3-3
How does Range Rover position itself in terms of its tangible attributes and intangible associations?

Brands Transform Products

A basic principle of branding is that a brand transforms products—goods as well as services—into something larger than the products themselves. A pair of Wrangler jeans is different from a pair of Levi's jeans, even if they are both made of denim. Wrangler and Levi's have different personalities because of brand images created primarily by marketing communication messages.

Suppose you give your father a Gucci watch. This watch is more than a timepiece. It is a message that you

> " . . . customer experience has more to do with brand building than anything else."
>
> Daniel Morel, CEO, Wonderman

EXHIBIT 3-4

This ad extends the Halls brand (which has been well received over the years) to a line of sugar-free cough drops. It promises consumers they can expect the same level of throat-soothing performance, plus—no sugar!

care and willingly paid a lot of money as testament to that caring.

How powerful is branding? A brand and what it represents can affect what people are willing to pay for a product. In blind taste tests, respondents were asked which of two samples of cornflakes tasted better. Unbeknownst to respondents, the samples were identical, yet the number of those who chose sample A over sample B increased from 47 to 59 percent when respondents were told that sample A was Kellogg's (sample B was not given a recognizable brand name). People *perceived* the "brand cereal" as tasting better even though both the cereals were identical. Another study found that when identical TV sets were sold, customers were willing to pay $75 more for those branded Hitachi than for those branded GE.[8]

Branding has such impact on consumer perception that retailers, rather than relying solely on manufacturers' (or name) brands, have worked to create their own brands. A **store brand** (also called a house brand or private label) is *a brand used exclusively by one chain of stores for a line of products made to the chain's specifications*. For many years store brands were generally lower in price and quality than name brands. Eventually, however, chain stores realized that linking their names directly to low-quality merchandise was transforming the overall perception of their stores in the wrong direction. In recent years, the quality of store brands has greatly increased along with positive perceptions of those brands.

Brands Make Promises and Set Expectations

In terms of consumer purchases, the essence of a brand is a promise. This promise sets expectations for what a person considers likely to occur when using a product. French branding expert Jean-Noël Kapferer explains that "a brand is also a contract, albeit a virtual one, between a company and a customer."[9] Knowledge of what a brand stands for and past experiences with the brand allow customers to make a quick and easy decision. That's what a promise means—you know what to expect.

Consistency, a fundamental principle of IMC, is critical to the establishment of a brand promise. Hayes Roth of the brand design and consulting firm Landor Associates, explains that a "clear and compelling brand promise consistently communicated at all points of touch is the principal benefit of branding."[10] Promises mean little, however, if the product fails to meet expectations. Marketing communication has been used for years to make promises in order to generate sales. Unfortunately, too many businesses do more promising than delivering when managing their brand relationships, because they fail to consider that what they are really doing is setting *unrealistic* customer expectations. But when a promise is strong and the product delivers, as when Halls Cough Drops promise and deliver relief of throat irritation (Exhibit 3-4), the promise becomes a platform for helping build a long-term relationship with satisfied customers. This is why it is important to create brand messages that make realistic promises—ones the brand can deliver.

Generally, brands fail to meet expectations for one of two reasons. The first is that expectations are raised too high, usually in overzealous advertising. The second is that products or supporting services are defective. Companies must constantly monitor customer expectations and product performance to make sure there is no gap between them—or that there is a *positive* gap and the product surprises customers by delivering more than they expected. When a *negative* gap exists, either the brand promises need to be restrained, or the managers responsible for product performance need to be made aware that their products are not meeting expectations. (For a detailed discussion of the measurement and evaluation of effectiveness, see Chapter 22.)

HOW BRANDS ARE CREATED AND MAINTAINED

Building a successful brand, whether for a company or for a new product, requires strategic planning and a major investment. When electronics manufacturer Hewlett-Packard spun off one of its divisions, coming up with a new brand name—Agilent—took many months. The new company then spent millions of dollars to create awareness and position the new brand. How is such a branding program undertaken? Three steps lead to successful brand strategies: (1) selecting the desired brand position, (2) developing the brand's identification, and (3) creating the brand image. Once a company has more than one brand, it then needs a system for managing how the brands interrelate.

1. Selecting the Desired Brand Position

When the United States Marine Corps warns "We don't promise you a rose garden," and supports that idea with the slogan "The Marines are looking for a few good men," the Corps is staking out a leading position among the various U.S. military organizations (see Exhibit 3-5).

Brand position is *the standing of a brand in comparison with its competitors in the minds of customers, prospects, and other stakeholders*. The positioning concept was developed by Al Ries and Jack Trout over 20 years ago.[11] According to Ries and Trout, customers who are aware of several brands in a product category automatically compare and rank those brands according to the differences they perceive among them. For example, when people think of cars, they might think of Volvo as the safest, Corvette as the sportiest, and Ford as the most practical.

Although brand positions, like brands themselves, exist in people's heads and hearts, a company's marketing communication can greatly influence how customers perceive a brand in relation to competition. The challenge is to select a position that can be realistically supported by the product, the company, and the marketing communication—and that can be appreciated by customers and prospects.

Consider the athletic shoe category. Rockport has positioned itself as "the leader of the walking fitness movement." Rockport designs shoes for comfort and distributes its products to stores that cater to older customers (who are more interested in walking than competing). Its marketing communication visually and verbally says "comfort" and speaks to the older

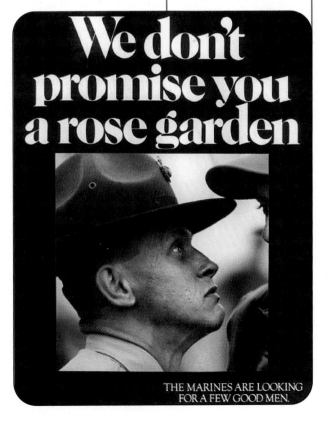

E X H I B I T   3 - 5
When it says, "We don't promise you a rose garden," the Marine Corps is positioning itself as a military organization looking for tough recruits who aren't afraid to tackle difficult assignments.

We don't promise you a rose garden

THE MARINES ARE LOOKING FOR A FEW GOOD MEN.

wearer of athletic shoes. In contrast, Nike has positioned itself as the "performance and personal success" shoe, and LA Gear has positioned itself as the high-fashion athletic shoe.

Because brand position hinges on a brand's meaning, changing a brand's meaning can allow a company to move or enlarge its brand position. Disney, for example, is trying to expand the meaning of "Disney movie," which for many years has meant "classic animated characters that appeal to children." Not wanting to be pigeonholed as a kiddie-flick company, Disney managers are beginning to release some action-and-adventure films—such as *Pirates of the Caribbean* (starring Johnny Depp and Hidalgo)—as Disney-branded movies instead of marketing them under the company's sister brand, Touchstone Pictures.[12] The question remains how far the meaning of the Disney brand can be stretched.

Positioning Strategies

A positioning strategy is generally based on one of several variables: category, image, unique product feature, or benefit. Following is an explanation of positioning strategies along with an example that illustrates how each is used.

Category Positioning This type of positioning is possible anytime a brand defines, creates, or owns a category or subproduct category. Rockport "owns" the walking-shoe category because it was first to successfully take advantage of the movement in the 1990s toward walking, an exercise favored by people not interested in participating in active sports. Similar to category positioning is **preemptive positioning,** *brand positioning based on a generic feature that competitors have not talked about.* Pre-emptive positioning is often used by **commodity products,** *goods and services that have very minor or no distinguishing differences.* A good example is peanut butter. The Jif brand positions itself as the peanut butter with "Fresh roasted peanut taste." However, all major brands of peanut butter are the result of roasting and then processing peanuts into a creamy consistency, so any brand could say it has a "fresh roasted peanut taste." But because Jif first used this product feature to differentiate itself, other brands don't use it because they don't want to risk being confused with Jif.

Image Positioning This type of positioning differentiates on the basis of a *created association*. It is similar to pre-emptive positioning in that any brand can attempt to create a differentiating image for itself. Often these attempts fail, however, because the image is not realistic, not creatively constructed, or not used long enough to actually build up an association between the brand and the desired image. A very successful example, however, is Marlboro. At one time, advertising for Winston cigarettes showed cowboys doing what cowboys do—herding cattle, branding them, and eating beans around a campfire. Nothing really imaginative. The creative people at the Leo Burnett advertising agency in the 1950s, however, decided they could take this attempt at "cowboy" positioning and make it distinctive and inspirational. To do this, they used a solitary cowboy as a symbol of independence, put a tattoo on his arm, and always showed him isolated in dramatic western settings. As a result, Marlboro became one of the most popular and well-recognized brands in the world.

Unique Product Feature Positioning This type of positioning is based on an element that is unique to the product or company. **Product features** are *tangible and intangible attributes of a good or service,* and they provide a basis for positioning. Price and how it translates into value is an intangible feature that is the basis of Wal-Mart's position as the low-price leader in mass merchandising. Wal-Mart's slogan is "Always low prices." The company once said it had the "lowest prices," but legal challenges from competitors forced Wal-Mart to revise its slogan, which it did while still maintaining the perception of being the low-price place to shop.

Another example of unique feature positioning is the low-price airline JetBlue which describes itself as "Fashionably simple and efficient" (Exhibit 3-6). JetBlue knew it could not differentiate itself from other low-price airlines on price, so its positioning is based on tangible features. The airline cut costs in areas where it knew it could not differentiate itself, such as food service, while investing in areas that make a more lasting impression: leather seats, individual video screens at every seat, and highly fashionable yet functional flight attendant uniforms. Well-done IMC ensures that JetBlue's website reflects the simple but efficient look and feel of the airline (www.jetblue.com). After the 9/11 attacks, JetBlue was the first airline to install bulletproof, double dead-bolt cockpit doors.[13] This prompt action created favorable PR among nervous travelers and allowed the airline to further differentiate itself from competitors. When it was only five years old, JetBlue was rated the number-two domestic airline (after Midwest Express) by both *Condé Nast Traveler* and *Zagat*.

EXHIBIT 3-6
Low price airline JetBlue has uniquely positioned itself in order to be a viable contender in the airline industry.

Benefit Positioning This type of positioning is based on **benefits,** *advantages that allow a product to satisfy customers' needs, wants, or desires.* Crest, for example, is positioned as the cavity-fighting toothpaste. Most benefits are experiential, functional, or symbolic, any of which can be the basis for brand positioning. An example of experiential benefit positioning is a video game that promises a new type of challenge. Symbolic benefits, such as belonging to a certain country club, make people feel a certain way through achievements, associations, or attitude.

Managing a Brand's Position

Marketing managers may develop positioning statements, such as Rockport's "Leader in walking fitness." But such statements don't really mean anything if they're not in customers' minds. To determine how customers perceive a brand and its competitors, one thing market researchers do is ask a sample of customers to participate in perceptual mapping. **Perceptual mapping** is *a visualization technique that indicates how customers perceive competing brands in terms of various criteria.* Figure 3-1 is a hypothetical perceptual map for Nike, Rockport, and LA Gear shoes. Maps like this indicate how a sample of customers ranked each brand, from low to high, on selected criteria, which for athletic shoes could be comfort, performance, quality, price, or style. Numerical rankings for each criterion are averaged and plotted. The map enables brand managers to quickly see how their brands compare, in the minds of consumers, with competing brands.

Repositioning a Brand

Sometimes brands need to be repositioned because their original position no longer fits the modern-day culture. The IMC in Action box describes the dramatic change from positioning based on a product feature to positioning based on image by Dr. Scholl's sandals.

FIGURE 3-1

A Perceptual Map

This perceptual map indicates how Nike's position might compare with the positions of two other competitors. Where would you place Reebok on this map?

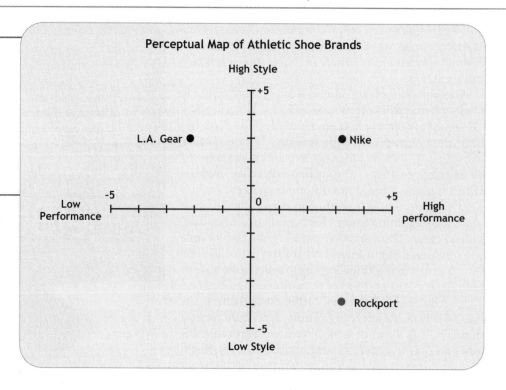

FIGURE 3-1

A Perceptual Map

This perceptual map indicates how Nike's position might compare with the positions of two other competitors. Where would you place Reebok on this map?

Repositioning may also be used when a brand extends its product line and needs to redefine itself in terms of its new goods or services. For example, H&R Block, long known as a tax expert serving middle-class American taxpayers, began expanding its offerings into a wider portfolio of financial services designed to meet all the financial needs of its clients. One way to signal that the brand had a new position was to replace the blue and white H&R Block logo, which the company had used for many years. Landor Associates recommended a new logo and brand-identity system anchored by a green "block," symbolizing strength and confidence. The vibrant color green represents growth. Exhibit 3-7 shows how the new logo has been applied across various publications that present H&R Block's new range of services.

2. Developing Brand Identification

The brand name and symbol chosen to represent a brand need to reflect the position of the brand, and they must work as identification cues. Names and brand symbols are what customers look for when shopping, whether in stores, in catalogs, on the internet, or, in the case of B2B products, at trade shows and exhibits. The more memorable and relevant the brand name and symbol are, the faster and less costly it will be to create awareness of a brand, position it in customers' minds, and develop an image for it. Making it easy to find and repurchase a brand is an important factor in customer retention. Thus the more specific and less ambiguous brand-identity cues are, the more they help customers save time looking for a product, which adds value to the brand.

A good example of the impact a brand name can have on sales was demonstrated by a study of mutual funds that changed their names strictly for marketing purposes (no change in product offerings) to strengthen the distinctiveness of the identification cues. Funds that changed their names attracted "22% more new money than funds of similar size [and] investment style" which made no changes.[14]

IMC IN ACTION

Dr. Scholl's Takes a Step Forward

Who would have thought that 1960s-style pedal-pushers, cat-eye glasses, and Dr. Scholl's wooden sandals would come back in style?

Is it retro? Is it nostalgia? Or is it just a down economy? For whatever reason, Dr. Scholl's stodgy exercise sandals found their way onto Sarah Jessica Parker's feet on the hit TV show *Sex and the City*. After the actress wore a pair of hot-pink Dr. Scholl's on-screen, sales of the clunky sandals skyrocketed.

The Dr. Scholl's brand dates back to the early 1900s, when foot pain was considered inevitable. Dr. William Mathias Scholl, a young Chicago doctor, earned his way through medical school as an apprentice shoe repairer and as a shoe sales clerk which began a lifetime study of foot relief. After graduating from medical school, he started a company to manufacture orthopedic foot products. The wooden-sole sandal made its appearance in 1968 and quickly became the favorite shoe of the Earth Day set.

In the 1970s, Dr. Scholl's were known as exercise sandals that not only made your feet feel better but also gave you sturdy calves. The leather strap design with the gold buckle became an icon for shapely lower legs. To reinforce the "healthy exercise" positioning strategy, however, the wooden flip-flops were placed in the pharmacy aisle in drugstores.

Dr. Scholl's marketing managers, jubilant about the *Sex and the City* product placement, sensed an opportunity to change the brand position of the sandals from a fitness line to a fashion line. The 125-year-old Brown Shoe company, which makes other dowdy but comfortable lines, such as Naturalizer and Buster Brown, hired designers to turn the clunky sandals into a fashion statement. The result? A revamped product line in pastel and hot fashion colors, leopard and camouflage prints, metallics, and frayed denim. Other brand extensions include high-heeled models and, "Heaven," a new rubber-soled version with padded leather insoles.

Should you expect to find Dr. Scholl's in drugstores? Not anymore. The sandals have moved into trendy shoe stores as well as online stores, such as Shoe.com. These stores even carry gold name-plate necklaces to further the brand identity.

The brand's repositioning took another step forward when independent designers started buying, repainting, and reselling the shoes with hand-painted flowers and patchwork designs. Now you can buy a $34 pair of stylishly decorated Dr. Scholl's for as much as $145 in boutiques in Manhattan. The website kissmyfeet.com offers 10 hand-painted themes, including zebra stripes and cherries, all priced at $169 a pair.

If you don't want to pay the price, you can take a plain pair home and paint them yourself, because many of the stores selling the older traditional styles also hand out ideas on how to personalize them.

Think About It

In what way was the Dr. Scholl's brand repositioned? How did repositioning happen? Do you feel the change is permanent or just a fad?

Source: Sally Beatty, "Sales of Dr. Scholl's Oldie Are Stepping Up," *Wall Street Journal*, February 14, 2003, p. B1; Kathy Cano-Murillo, "Dr. Scholl's Sandals Are Back, and All Dressed Up," *Arizona Republic*, August 17, 2002, <www.azcentral.com/home/crafty/0817crafty17.html>.

Brand Names

Although choosing a memorable name is more art than science, successful brand names generally are the result of extensive research. For example, when Lucent Technologies spun off its enterprise communication division , marketers wanted a name that would break away from the traditional sound of telecommunication company names. Landor Associates came up with Avaya, inspired by an ancient word for "unity." In market research, customers commented that the name felt energetic, positive, and "smooth." Landor recommended adding the corporate descriptor "communication" to emphasize the human aspect of Avaya's business. The name and descriptor together reinforce perceptions of a company whose

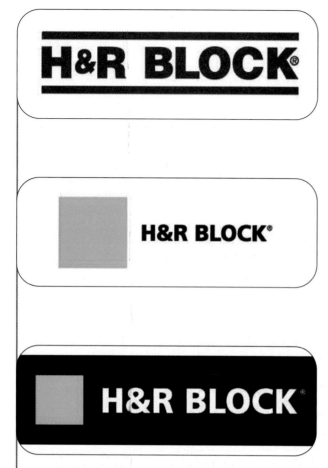

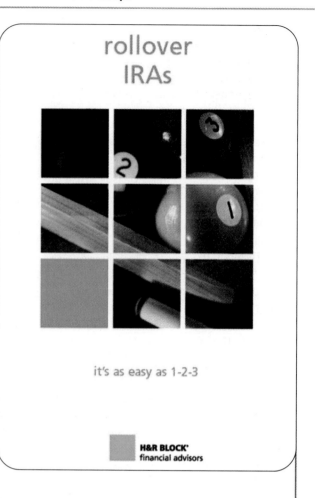

rollover
IRAs

it's as easy as 1-2-3

EXHIBIT 3-7

Landor Associates revitalized the H&R Block brand-identity system by moving from the familiar blue-and-white logo to a green block logo that is more adaptable for the company's new portfolio of services.

employees are united around a common goal of helping businesses develop strong and seamless relationships with their customers.

Successful brand names share several characteristics that help make them memorable. A good brand name usually communicates one or more of the following characteristics:

- *Benefit:* Slim-Fast promises weight loss (Slim) and promises it immediately (Fast). As for Head & Shoulders, the name says this product is for people who worry about ugly dandruff falling onto their shoulders.

- *Association:* Hewlett-Packard chose the name Agilent for a high-tech spin-off because it conveyed a positive, relevant meaning—namely, agility, which is a good characteristic to have in the fast-changing technology industry. Subaru chose Outback as the name for its rugged off-road SUV, hoping it would evoke the fun and adventure of the Australian wilderness.

- *Distinctiveness:* One way to communicate distinctiveness is to use a simple word that is completely unrelated to the product, such as Apple (computers) or Charlie (perfume). A distinctive name suggests a distinctive product and ensures that there are no similar brand names with which the product will be confused. The internet employment service Monster.com (see Exhibit 3-8) stands out from Jobs.com and JobFinder.com because of its name.

- *Simplicity:* Names that are difficult to say or spell are not likely to be remembered. That is why many brand names are short and phonetically easy: Tide, Bic, Allstate, Saturn. Pronounceability is thus a consideration in choosing a brand name. Because of the increase in multinational marketing, it is also

important that names properly translate into other languages. When the phenomenally successful Harry Potter series of children's books was introduced to China, the lead publisher, Scholastic, translated the character's name phonetically as "Ha-li Bo-te" so that Chinese readers would find it easy to say. Some companies have been embarrassed by brand-name translations, however. When Clairol introduced its curling iron Mist Stick into Germany, it didn't realize that the German word *mist* means manure.[15]

For a good overview of brand naming, visit the website of Cintara, an agency that specializes in corporate identity and branding (www.cintara.com/naming).

Brand Symbols

We live in a visual world. Having a symbol for a brand can greatly increase a brand's recognition. Cattle, for example, are branded with a unique symbol in order to show which ones belong to which ranchers. In the realm of products and companies, a distinctive *logo* is used to indicate a product's source or ownership. Corporate logos range from a simple name (Coca-Cola in its distinctive Spencerian script) to abstract designs (see Exhibit 3-9).

A trademark is similar to but broader than a logo. A **trademark** is *an element, word, or design that differentiates one brand from another.* The hourglass design of a Coke bottle and AT&T's four-note jingle are trademarks. The literal meaning of *trademark* is "mark of a trade." Some of the first trademarks were initials and other

symbols that silversmiths punched into their products. A company has exclusive use of a trademark by using it first and consistently, and by registering it with a government agency. A problem can arise, however, if a trademarked name, such as Kleenex, becomes commonly used for a product category. Though a hallmark of successful branding, the generic use of a brand name may cause the company to lose its exclusive right to the name as a legally protected trademark. This has happened to some brand names. Refrigerator, originally a brand name, is now a category label.

In order for logos and trademarks to do their job, they should be distinctive, simple, and consistent with the desired image and positioning of the brand. Notice how the bold, square-cornered typeface used in the logo for Sears's line of Craftsman tools (see Exhibit 3-10) connotes "masculine" and "strong" and helps reinforce the brand position.

Brand logos usually are enduring symbols, but they may change as the brand matures. The Betty Crocker image has been updated many times over the decades. Apple Computer's original logo—an apple with rainbow colors—was long considered a classic design because it was not only brightly colored and youthful (the early image of Apple computers) but also distinctive, simple, eye-catching, and memorable. Recently Apple revised the logo, giving it a solid color to appear more modern.

3. Creating a Brand Image

Giving a brand an identity and a position is not enough to make the brand come alive and connect with customers. Think of people you have met. Simply knowing their names, physical traits, and occupation doesn't tell you much about their personalities. What tells you more are the images of these people you have in your mind. A **brand image** is *an impression created by brand messages and experiences and assimilated into a perception or impression of the brand.* For an example of brand image, look at the Marine Corps ad in Exhibit 3-5 with its tough-guy image.

An image makes a statement about a brand's personality. Harley-Davidson's spread-winged eagle symbol represents more than just a motorcycle. Harley-Davidson has a brand personality that appeals to black-leather-clad, devil-may-care individuals who want (permanently or temporarily) to be nonconformists. An image adds value to a brand because the image can communicate something about the buyer to other people. As Dutch branding experts Giep Franzen and Freek Holzhauer have explained, "the products you wear, drive, or subscribe to can tell others what you think is important."[16] Harley-Davidson ads have an attitude that shapes the personality of the brand and reflects its "outlaw" positioning. People who buy and ride Harley-Davidsons want to identify with that image.

> " . . . the products you wear, drive, or subscribe to can tell others what you think is important."
>
> Giep Franzen and Freek Holzhauer, branding experts

Managing a System of Brands

As companies grow and expand the number of products they make, they not only extend their brands to these products but often give these products separate brand names. **Multi-tier branding** is *the use of two or more brands (all owned by the same company) in the identification of a product.* Examples include IBM ThinkPad and Kellogg's Corn Flakes. In these examples, there are two tiers: corporate names— IBM and Kellogg's—are *corporate* brand names, and ThinkPad and Corn Flakes are *product* brand names (Exhibit 3-11). A corporate brand name is the mother brand, or umbrella brand. A product brand name identifies a specific product or line of products. A third tier would be a *model brand name*. An example of three-tier branding is Chrysler's (mother brand) Jeep Cherokee (product brand) Laredo (model brand).

Use of the corporate brand is intended to communicate trust and quality, because the company itself usually has been in existence longer than the product line and has established perceptions of trust and quality. The role of the product brand is to communicate such benefits as performance, reliability, and image. Take Kellogg's Special K, for example. The name Kellogg's says the cereal is well made, well packaged, and fresh—product features that customers have come to associate with Kellogg's products. The brand name Special K is designed to identify the product as a healthy cereal. In three-level branding strategy, the model brand communicates an even more specific level of performance and sometimes price (such as "the low-priced model of the Jeep Cherokee").

Multi-tier branding is used for several reasons. One is to take advantage of the value of the corporate name. Another is to strengthen the corporate brand by connecting it with a successful product line. A third is that a product brand helps differentiate the offering from other products sold by the company, as well as from competing products. Multi-tier branding basically combines two (or more) sets of brand perceptions with the idea that two (or more) brands are stronger and more attractive than a single brand.

Multi-tier branding creates strategic challenges for brand messages. When doing multi-tier branding, MC managers must decide how much emphasis to give each brand. In a print ad for Special K, for example, how much space should be devoted to talking about Kellogg's and how much to Special K's specific product features and benefits? The answer reflects input from customers and prospects. If customers express more concerns about product quality than about the healthy aspect of the product, then Kellogg's, the corporate brand, should be given more emphasis. In the case of Special K, the product name dominates.

HOW BRAND RELATIONSHIPS ARE CREATED AND MAINTAINED

According to Regis McKenna, "A successful brand is nothing more than a special relationship."[17] Brand success depends on retaining customers, and good customer relationships lead to retention. A customer relationship program that builds a brand must be a long-term effort to develop trust, not merely a traditional advertising and promotion campaign that focuses on short-term transactions.

Strategies that focus only getting sales can be dangerous. When customers are persuaded or manipulated into buying something they don't need or want, a company risks several undesirable outcomes. First, customers who have been overpromised will ultimately be less satisfied than those who haven't been and thus will be more likely to bring back a product or demand special handling, both of which increase operating costs. Second, disappointed customers become negative spokespersons for the brand. Third, disappointed customers are less likely to buy again; so the sale becomes a one-time transaction rather than the beginning of a relationship, and the investment made to get that first (and only) sale is lost.

> "A successful brand is nothing more than a special relationship."
>
> Regis McKenna, relationship marketing expert

Customer Bill of Rights in an Interactive Age

1. Customers have the right to contact the company 24 hours a day, 7 days a week and at least be able to leave a message.

2. Customers have the right to select how to contact a company (phone, mail, fax, e-mail).

3. Customers have the right (e.g., option) to talk to a human being without being subjected to multiple levels of an automated voice-response system.

4. Customers have the right to talk to a company representative with enough knowledge to answer any reasonable question or complaint.

5. Customers have the right to talk to a company representative with enough authority to make a decision.

6. Customers have the right to privacy regarding their transactions (e.g., the option to control the selling of their names to other companies).

7. Customers have the right to a timely response relative to typical use of the product (e.g., if the product is used 24 hours a day, then response should be available 24 hours a day).

8. Customers have the right to be rewarded in proportion to their support of the company (e.g., buying, referring others, following procedures).

9. Customers have the right to avoid intrusive phone calls, junk mail, and spam e-mail.

10. Customers are right 98 percent of the time. The other 2 percent they have the right to a sensitive and empathetic explanation of why they're not right.

If overpromising is not a good strategy for building customer relationships, then what is? A better approach is to commit to a customer-centric philosophy that values employees' who in turn support the policies that keep customers satisfied. The "Customer Bill of Rights" (as shown in Figure 3-2) sets forth a customer-centric philosophy that drives a retention strategy.

The Importance of a Customer-Centered Approach

Obviously, how a product performs, its price, and the places in which it is distributed affect to what extent a customer buys and re-buys a brand. But these three Ps—performance, price, and place—often are not the deciding criteria. Performance, price, and place are often so similar among competing brands that repeat purchases and a customer's share of category spending are determined by "behavior" variables such as the following:

- *Consistency:* Consistency is communicated by product uniformity as well as by uniformity in the way a company positions itself and responds to situations. A brand needs to deliver the same message and present the same image in all brand messages. This consistency is the objective of IMC programs. When you go into a McDonald's restaurant, no matter where it is, you expect certain menu items, reasonable prices, and a clean eating area

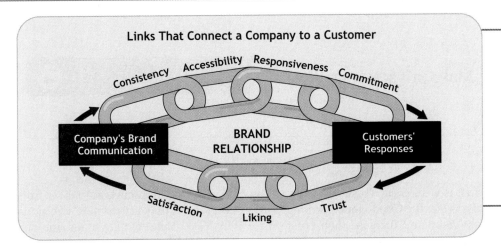

Links That Connect a Company to a Customer

Consistency   Accessibility   Responsiveness   Commitment

Company's Brand Communication

BRAND RELATIONSHIP

Customers' Responses

Satisfaction   Liking   Trust

FIGURE 3-3

Why are these behavior variables important?

Adapted from Richard Cross and Janet Smith, *Customer Bonding: Pathway to Lasting Customer Loyalty*, Lincolnwood, IL: NTC, 1994, p. 54–55. Reprinted with permission from The McGraw-Hill Companies.

because these are the benefits you experienced in the past at McDonald's. If things are not as expected, customer trust is reduced.

- *Accessibility:* When there is a problem, customers want to feel they have recourse, such as the ability to quickly contact someone and have the problem fixed.

- *Responsiveness:* When questions, inquiries, and complaints are quickly and thoroughly handled, customers not only are more satisfied but feel the company really cares about and appreciates their business. Responsiveness can overcome negative feelings a customer may have about a brand. For example, when a company responds immediately to customer complaints, the quick response itself has motivated customers to give the brand another chance.

- *Commitment:* Customers want to feel that a company has their best interests at heart and won't do and say anything simply to make a sale. When a sales clerk tells you the store doesn't carry your size but says you might find it at one of the store's competitors, you feel that the store is committed to helping you and not just itself. This is the ultimate in customer-centric service.

A company that excels in consistency, accessibility, responsiveness, and commitment is likely to satisfy and be liked and trusted by customers (see Figure 3-3).

Satisfaction results from inputs such as positive product performance, beneficial brand attributes not offered by competitors, knowledge that others are using and happy with the brand, and the company's quick response to complaints or inquiries. Unsatisfied customers—who may increase the customer-service workload, switch to another brand, and say bad things about the brand to their friends and family—cost the company money.

Liking something is often a reason for testimony. Most people talk about their positive experiences and things they like, and they influence prospective customers. But if a brand's or company's commercials are irritating, its receptionist is snobbish, its manufacturing plants pollute the air and water, or its products break easily, then word may get around that this company or brand is not likable. Dislike is a strong reason to switch brands.

The primary consideration when selecting a brand is *trust.* Can a customer trust a brand to provide the benefits promised? If the brand does not perform properly, can the company be trusted to stand behind its product? The reason most often given for making a particular brand choice is that the brand is trusted more than competing brands. When brand messages promise more than products deliver,

Make privacy your choice.™

trust is weakened. This is why managing customer expectations is so critical. Emblems like the Good Housekeeping Seal are intended to make customers' decisions less risky and increase their trust. Since 1909, *Good Housekeeping* magazine has guaranteed that if a product bearing the seal is defective (within two years of purchase), the magazine will replace the product or refund the purchase price. An organization dedicated to helping build trust in brands of websites is TRUSTe (see Exhibit 3-12), which has an emblem that can be posted on websites that meet TRUSTe standards for safety and security practices.

Trust and a good reputation must be earned. Like a person's reputation, trust in a company builds over time and through a series of interactions. Companies must always strive to gain and keep customers' trust and remain aware of the fact that trust is a product of both reality (what a company says and does) and perception (what customers *think about* what a company says and does).

The Importance of Customer Retention

The importance of brand relationships to customer retention was illustrated several years ago when Coca-Cola was accused of distributing contaminated products in Europe and taking too long to respond to the problem. Six months after the news broke—and after Coke's stock had lost nearly one-third of its value—a headline on the front page of the *Wall Street Journal* read: "To Fix Coca-Cola, Daft Sets Out to Get Relationships Right." Coke's then-CEO Douglas Daft was quoted as saying, "Every problem we had can be traced to a singular cause: We neglected our relationships." Daft admitted the company had failed to adequately communicate with its European customers and other stakeholders—European Union bottlers, government regulators, and the media.[18] The result? Coca-Cola customers heard and read a lot of negative messages about Coke before the company finally explained the problem and what was being done to fix it. Coke lost the trust of many customers (both consumers and business customers), as well as other stakeholders.

Brand relationships have bottom-line results, as the Coca-Cola story demonstrates. Because relationships cost money to create and maintain, they had best result in sales or in reduced costs of doing business. Even nonprofit associations have to be sensitive to costs and to their relationships with supporters regarding fund-raising, membership dues, and volunteerism. Unless an organization's brand relationships are profitable, the organization will soon be out of business.

Another important principle of brand relationships is that stakeholders overlap. Although brand messages are aimed at customers, companies must assume that other stakeholder groups will be exposed to those messages as well. For example, employees as well as suppliers can be customers or investors in a company—another reason why message consistency is so important.

A number of principles in addition to bottom-line impact and stakeholder overlap guide the creation of brand relationships. One is the need for managers to shift their mind-set from customer acquisition to customer retention.

Balancing Customer Acquisition and Customer Retention Efforts

Although much of the discussion in this chapter focuses on the creation of new brands, most brand communication involves existing brands and focuses on building long-term relationships with customers. Brand relationships connect customers and brands beyond the first purchase and keep customers coming back. According to Siebel, the leading information technology marketing-support company, repeat sales account for 70 percent of the average company's total revenue.[19] As the Learning International ad in Exhibit 3-13 illustrates, a successful customer relationship program—almost by definition—has to be customer-centric.

New companies—or companies launching new products—must focus on acquiring new customers. But as the shift from acquisition to retention occurs, both the message strategy and the media of communication change. For example, brand acquisition is often seen as a responsibility of advertising and mass media communication, which are good at creating awareness. A retention strategy, however, relies on more personal forms of communication, such as personal sales, direct marketing, customer service, and the internet. It opens the door for the customer-initiated messages you would expect in a conversation or dialogue.

Do you really put your customers first?

Check:

☐ *Top down and bottom up, your people can articulate the organization's service strategy.*

☐ *Customer expectations are understood—and shared—at all levels.*

☐ *Skills that build customer loyalty are upgraded regularly.*

☐ *Customers view your service providers as resources, not obstacles.*

☐ *Service providers can—and do—make decisions on the spot to ensure customer satisfaction.*

Check more than three statements and your organization already has made quality a strategic priority.

But check three or fewer statements and your competitive edge could be eroding day by day.

Learning International knows how to help organizations turn a service vision into action. We offer training designed to improve the quality of *every* service interaction. To benchmark your organization's service performance, write or call for information on a new research study, *Lessons From Top Service Providers*, and its self-scoring Assessment Tools.

Learning International
225 High Ridge Road,
Stamford, CT 06905
1-800-456-9390, ext. 57

Learning INTERNATIONAL

Circle No. 120 on Reader Service Card

EXHIBIT 3-13

Learning International is a B2B company that helps companies learn how to provide better customer service by putting the customer first.

Making a sale to a current customer is far less expensive than making a sale to a new customer. Thus a company that builds strong relationships with customers will retain these customers, and the result will be more sales and profits than the company would have experienced from focusing mainly on getting new customers. This is the leaky bucket theory. Suppose you have a bucket, and your job is to keep it filled with water. If the bucket has holes, there are two ways to keep it filled—by constantly adding water or by plugging the holes. Your job will be easier if you plug the holes. The same principle applies to business. Stopping current customers from leaving will result in more sales and profits than will investing the same amount in acquiring new customers.

Customer retention is the topic of numerous articles in the marketing press; nevertheless, most companies do not manage it well. One survey of 200 companies found that the vast majority were doing little to create and manage customer relationships. Despite pledges to be customer driven, most were cost driven and on average were losing 20 percent of their customers each year.[20] The percentage of such loss differs by product category, brand, and company. In the automotive field, for example, over 55 percent of new-car buyers don't re-buy the nameplate

A TALE OF TWO COMPANIES

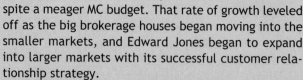

Edward Jones and Prudential

The success of the Edward Jones brokerage company offers an example of the positive results of focusing on relationships rather than on transactions. Concentrating on towns outside the reach of major cities, Jones is the Wal-Mart of brokerage houses. Jones closely monitors its salespeople to make sure they are sending messages that create trust among customers and potential customers. To this end, Jones designed a compensation system to encourage its brokers to put the interests of their customers first and sales second. Salespeople are continually reminded that they are selling mostly to people who are not experienced investors in the stock market, and therefore brokers should steer customers away from especially risky investments. And to make sure customers aren't being motivated to buy and sell unwisely just to generate commissions for the broker, Edward Jones has a system to identify accounts that show excessive trading.

The company's success has resulted from the strategy of acquiring customers for the long term and providing them with the services they need in order to retain them. As a result, Edward Jones customers hold their funds nearly three times longer than the industry average. The company, with over 3,350 offices,

watched its revenue nearly triple in the first half of the 1990s, despite a meager MC budget. That rate of growth leveled off as the big brokerage houses began moving into the smaller markets, and Edward Jones began to expand into larger markets with its successful customer relationship strategy.

Compare the Edward Jones way with the messages that Prudential Securities (formerly Prudential-Bache Securities) used in building (or destroying) many of its relationships. In 1994, Prudential was forced to pay $1.4 billion to settle state and federal securities fraud charges that it had supplied its brokers with misleading promotional literature. According to a *New York Times* investigation, one of the primary reasons for the misleading promotional material was Prudential's corporate culture, which emphasized transactions—short-term sales—over long-term relationships with customers. Unlike Edward Jones, Prudential Securities, according to one observer of the situation, had "utter disregard for the ultimate harm it might do to the customer."

Think About It

How can an emphasis on relationships instead of on transactions help a company's business? What exactly did the Jones brokerage do to create long-term positive relationships with its customers? *Source:* Greg Burns, "Can It Play out of Peoria?" *Business Week,* August 7, 1995, p. 58; excerpt from Kurt Eichenwalk's *Serpent on the Rock,* in *Sales and Marketing Management,* September 1995, p. 83.

EXHIBIT 3-14

Edward**Jones**
Serving Individual Investors Since 1871

they are replacing. Saturn, however, loses only 45 percent, and Infiniti loses only 30 percent. Both companies are known for being focused more on relationships than on sales. The Tale of Two Companies box illustrates the difference between a transaction-focused and a relationship-focused way of doing business.

Not All Relationships Are Equal

Just as there are different levels of intensity in personal relationships, so are there different levels of intensity in commercial relationships. The intensity of a brand relationship varies for each customer and product category (see Exhibit 3-15). The success of the Grateful Dead provides an example of the benefits of strong brand intensity. The group's popularity has lasted 30 years even though the group never had a number-one hit (and had only one top 10 song). The reason for the band's longevity is the loyalty of its followers. Unlike most bands, which perform only one show in each city they tour, the Grateful Dead often gives several performances in each city and the same fans attend them all.

Customers have strong emotional feelings for some brands but see other brands as strictly utilitarian. A dedicated Pepsi loyalist would not be caught drinking Coke. Someone who regularly uses a particular shampoo is not going to feel comfortable using another brand. The same Pepsi or shampoo fan, however, may not have a commitment to a particular brand of milk or laundry detergent. To successfully communicate with customers, a company needs to know the level of intensity that customers feel for its brand and for the product category.

Assume that brand relationships vary from "no loyalty" to "intense loyalty." Customers at the "no loyalty" end of the range are brand-switchers; those at the "intense loyalty" end consistently buy a particular brand. The marketing goal, of course, is to move as many customers as possible to the "intense" end of the range. Not only are the loyal customer relationships cheaper to maintain, but loyal customers also speak the praises of the brand, making positive contributions to the brand's marketing communication efforts.

Knowing customers' level of **brand loyalty,** *the degree of attachment that customers have to a brand as expressed by repeat purchases,* helps companies customize brand messages. One strategy for strengthening brand relationships is to encourage the "connected" customers (see Figure 3-3)—through invitations and rewards—to join a brand-user group, thus increasing the intensity of their relationship with the brand. IBM, Microsoft, Apple, and many other computer companies have set up user groups. The Harley Owners Group (HOG), mentioned in Chapter 1, is a club created not by the Harley-Davidson company but by Harley owners themselves, although the company supports the club as much as possible.

Such groups constitute **brand communities,** *collections of customers who own the same brand and enjoy talking to each other, learning from each other, and sharing new ways of using their products, as well as getting help in solving brand related problems.* Internet chat rooms likewise create brand communities for a vast array of products. Members of brand communities, like other loyal brand users, often become advocates for the brand, moving to the highest level of brand loyalty.

GRILL SEEKS LONG-TERM RELATIONSHIP. SERIOUS INQUIRIES ONLY.

With enough head-turning features to keep things really interesting, this grill is built to last a lifetime. Broilmaster Premium Gas Grills come with the most durable features known to man. Our adjustable, cast iron cooking grids are porcelain coated. The extra-thick, cast aluminum grill heads faithfully maintain the heat. And Broilmaster's stainless steel bow-tie burner system with infinite control levels is even patented. All this, plus an extensive industry-leading warranty that ensures the honeymoon never ends. Begin your love affair today. For your free brochure and recipe booklet, call 1-800-851-3153.

BROILMASTER PREMIUM GAS GRILLS

THE MOST DURABLE GRILL KNOWN TO MAN

EXHIBIT 3-15
This ad demonstrates that a customer can have a strong, even intense, relationship with a product.

Loyalty Is the Relationship Reward

In most product categories a small number of heavy users account for a large percentage of a brand's sales and profits, even though these customers may not be totally loyal to the brand. **Heavy users** are *customers who buy an above-average amount of a given brand.* The exact definition differs by category. Heavy users are sometimes identified as the top quintile (the top 20 percent) of customers based on volume. According to the **Pareto rule,** a marketing rule of thumb named after

Italian economist Vilfredo Pareto, *80 percent of a brand's sales come from 20 percent of its customers*. Although the precise ratio varies for every company, the majority of sales and profits almost always come from a minority of a company's customers.

Companies prize brand loyalty, but it is not the only measure of a "good" customer. Some customers who are loyal to one brand only are light users—their total purchases are relatively small. Medium and heavy users, even those who regularly buy two or three brands in a category, can actually be more valuable as customers. This is why companies think in terms of **share of wallet,** *the percentage of a customer's spending in a product category for one particular brand*. Because few companies can capture 100 percent of a customer's share of wallet, heavy users are particularly important. A study of 83 grocery chains determined that the top 10 percent of customers, who were members of the chains' frequent-buyer programs, spent twice as much per week as the next 10 percent spent. The study also found that the "top 30 percent of shopping-card holders [frequent buyers] account for approximately 75 percent of a store's total sales, versus only 2 percent for the bottom 30 percent."[21]

Pfizer, the world's largest drug manufacturer, has promoted its own discount-drug card to Medicare recipients. The idea is to make it possible for senior citizens and disabled people who are eligible for Medicare to get Pfizer drugs at a discount. The strategy is: The discount card is both a reminder and a rationale for seniors to make repeat purchases of Pfizer drugs. Some critics, however, worry about the ethics of signing up these vulnerable groups for a loyalty program.[22]

Word-of-Mouth Advocacy

One of the benefits of loyal customers, such as those depicted in the Broilmaster ad in Exhibit 3-15, is that these people are likely to say good things about the company or brand. Advocates for a brand tend to communicate positively with prospects and thereby generate referrals for the company. Word-of-mouth on behalf of a brand is highly persuasive.

Brand advocacy is the top rung on a model of relationship intensity developed by Richard Cross and Janet Smith in *Customer Bonding: Pathway to Lasting Customer Loyalty*.[23] The steps leading to advocacy begin with awareness and move through identifying with the brand, feeling connected and in communication with the brand, and being part of a brand community, to, finally, being an advocate for a brand (see Figure 3-4). Businesses usually have a segment of customers at each level. For most brands, the higher a level of relationship intensity is, the fewer customers there are at that level.

Customer Relationship Management

An increasingly popular term used to describe a company's approach to customer-focused marketing is *customer relationship management*. Defined narrowly, **customer relationship management (CRM)** is *a type of database software for tracking customers* (see Chapter 8 for a detailed discussion of data-driven communications). Ruth Stevens, a professor and consultant, says CRM is "a combination of retention marketing and customer service."[24] A much broader definition describes it as being similar to IMC:

> Total Customer Relationship Management is the optimization of all customer contacts through the distribution and application of customer information. Simply stated, it is your promise, that no matter how your customers interact with you, you will always recognize who they are. Total CRM requires the cooperation of all departments and divisions within an organization around this concept.[25]

The heart of a CRM program is information technology and database systems, and the objective is to keep the company in touch with the relationship history of its own customers. The CRM consulting firm Front Line Solutions has a free website (www.crmguru.com) that features the latest CRM practices and

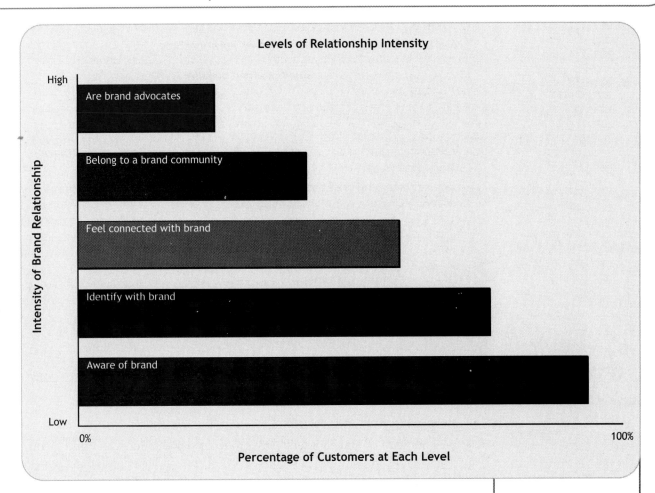

FIGURE 3-4

Customers who are brand advocates are a small percentage of total customers. Why do you think this is so?

Source: Adapted from Richard Cross and Janet Smith, "The Customer Value Chain," *Marketing Tools*, January–February, 1997.

applications. Other major CRM consulting services are Avaya, Siebel, the SAS Institute, and German-based SAP, which will custom-design a firm's CRM system. SAP is also using the Web to provide customer service by providing a free online database of CRM problems and solutions that customers and prospects can search and apply to their own situations.

An important thing to remember about CRM is that most customers don't want to be "managed." However, they usually appreciate a relationship program that delivers something of value, and relationship programs do deliver benefits to both customers and the company (see Table 3-3).

An example of using CRM to benefit the customer as well as the company comes from the automotive field. Most automotive dealers understand the importance of maintaining contact with their customers, but few do much more than send notices and perhaps a magazine. Daewoo, however, added value to its relationships with its British customers by building a helpful experience around regular servicing. Daewoo offered courtesy loaner cars, flexible scheduling, and follow-ups.[26] Daewoo's program also helped customers maintain the value of their cars through regular servicing; at the same time its relationship program brought a positive aura to the brand, a result that is usually rewarded with higher levels of customer loyalty and advocacy.

Relationship Building Applies to All Stakeholders

Although a marketer's job is to build relationships with customers, he must be aware that marketing is part of a company and that the entire company must build

TABLE 3-3   Benefits of Brand Relationships

Benefits to the Company

Impact on Costs

- Selling to current customers costs less than attracting new customers
- Relationships spread the costs of acquisition
- Loyal customers are brand advocates, reducing MC costs
- Satisfied customers require less hand-holding

Impact on Sales/Profits

- Loyal customers buy more
- Loyalty increases long-term customer value
- Fewer defections increase sales

Benefits to the Customer

- Less risk
- Fewer decisions
- Fewer switching costs
- Greater buying efficiency
- Increased association, self-identification

relationships with *all* stakeholders. Any group of stakeholders can affect a company's sales and profits, and therefore every group of stakeholders should be taken into consideration when brand messages are created and sent. What a company does affects them, and what they do can affect the company.

From a marketing perspective, the most important group is customers (end users), followed by employees (Figure 3-5). Then come all the other groups whose relative importance varies by industry and by situation: suppliers, the media, MC agencies (for those companies that use agencies), government regulators, the communities in which a business is located, the financial community and investors, and special-interest groups.

Customers are so important because they create sales. Employees are important because they produce (or acquire) the goods and services a company sells, and because those who interact directly with customers are perceived by customers as "being the company." Some executives, especially in the service industry, believe that employees, not customers, should be a company's number-one priority. The rationale is that unless employees know their jobs, feel they are being treated fairly by the company, feel they are members of a team, and find meaning in their work, they are not going to provide excellent service to customers. Employees' treatment of customers is one of the most critical brand messages that can be sent. As one management consultant said: "It's impossible to build a loyal book of customers without a loyal employee base."[27]

As companies increasingly encourage and facilitate customer interactivity, more customers will be talking with more people in a company, and companies that ignore employees will pay a heavy cost. A study conducted by the Food Marketing Institute found that 46 percent of employees in the companies surveyed argued with customers, 22 percent did slow or sloppy work on purpose, 20 percent came to work hung over, and 11 percent damaged property while horsing around.[28] IMC uses internal marketing to help keep employees informed of marketing programs and to boost employee moral and involvement in MC programs.

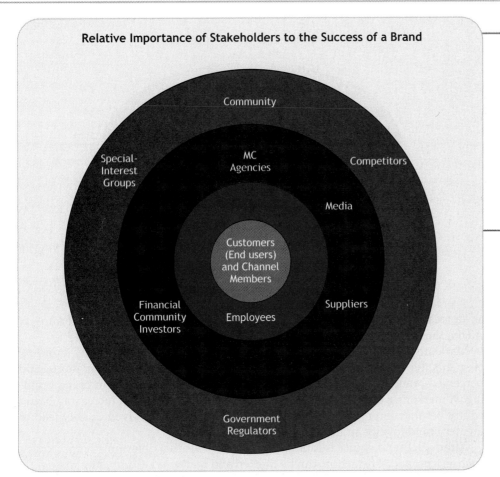

Relative Importance of Stakeholders to the Success of a Brand

FIGURE 3-5

Why are customers in the center?

Adapted with the permission of The Free Press, a Division of Simon & Schuster Adult Publishing Group, from MANAGING BRAND EQUITY: Capitalizing on the Value of a Brand by David A. Aaker. Copyright © 1991 by David A. Aaker. All rights reserved.

HOW BRANDS CREATE EQUITY

Recall from the beginning of this chapter that Philip Morris was willing to pay billions of dollars for Kraft Foods' customer and trade relationships. What helped create those relationships was awareness and the image of the Kraft brand name and of other brand names owned by Kraft.

Two basic components determine a company's or brand's value. One is physical assets, such as plants, equipment, and land. The other is **brand equity,** which is *the intangible value of a company beyond the value of its physical assets.* (Brand equity is sometimes called **goodwill.**) FedEx and Disney and other companies that have built strong brands over many years have tremendous brand equity. In fact, the average value of all American-based, publicly owned companies is 70 percent greater than the replacement cost of their physical assets. This additional 70 percent shows the value of branding.[29]

The importance of brand equity is increasing for most companies. In a study of senior managers, 84 percent said their company's focus on brand equity had increased in the last two to three years (only 3 percent said it had decreased). The main reasons given for this increase were "product commoditization" (all products being essentially identical) and "increased competition."[30] David Aaker, a recognized brand authority, identified five elements of brand equity (see Figure 3-6): brand-name awareness, brand associations, perceived brand quality, proprietary brand assets (such as patents and trademarks), and brand loyalty, which he defines

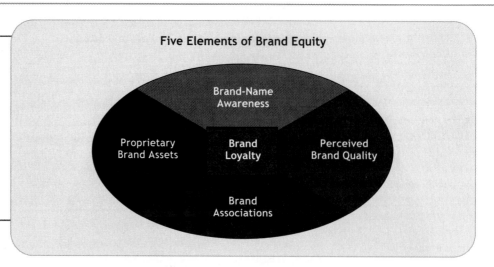

FIGURE 3-6

Note in Aaker's list of brand equity elements, brand loyalty is at the center of these. Why do you think this is?

Source: Adapted from David A. Aaker, *Managing Brand Equity: Capitalizing on the Value of a Brand Name* (New York: Free Press, 1991).

Five Elements of Brand Equity

Brand-Name Awareness

Proprietary Brand Assets

Brand Loyalty

Perceived Brand Quality

Brand Associations

as "a measure of the attachment that a customer has to a brand."[31] According to Aaker, the first four elements strongly influence the fifth, brand loyalty.

Marketing communication directly impacts three of the brand equity–building elements that Aaker identified: brand-name awareness, brand associations, and perceived brand quality. So it's easy to see the critical role of MC in brand building. A marketing communication strategy is often successful in increasing brand equity because improved awareness, associations, and perceived quality lead to greater brand loyalty and trust (see Exhibit 3-16).

Although brand equity is intangible, the elements that determine brand equity, such as trust and satisfaction, can be tracked and measured. Companies frequently conduct studies to determine levels of brand awareness, levels of perceived brand quality, and the nature and quality of brand associations. They also measure brand loyalty by determining the percentage of a customer's category purchases and repeat purchases. How many times do you buy a Snickers bar when you buy a candy bar? If it's one out of every four times, then Snickers has a 25 percent share of wallet for your candy bar purchases. Brand loyalty accumulates (or dissipates) as customers' buying experiences are tested against the expectations created by brand messages.

How Brand Equity Is Leveraged

Increasing brand awareness and acceptance means not only selling more products but also finding opportunities to sell even more products by leveraging the equity in the brand. Consider Coleman, the long-time maker of camping equipment. The company decided to expand into the home outdoor grill category. After considering a variety of new grill designs, it decided to go with a traditional design but differentiate the new product from other grills by coloring it in Coleman's "signature green." To outdoor enthusiasts, this color is almost as well known as the Coleman name. The use of the green immediately communicates that a product is "a Coleman." Because of the brand equity inherent in the new grill, it got immediate distribution in Sears and Home Depot, among other retailers, and captured a 5 percent share of the outdoor grill market in its first year.[32]

A variety of strategies allow marketers to take advantage of brand equity. Among them are adding new distribution channels, extending the product line sold under the brand name, co-branding with another brand, and licensing the brand to other manufacturers to use on their products.

Broadening Distribution

Avon cosmetics, long sold only door-to-door, are now available in J.C. Penney stores under the sub-brand Avon "beComing." Boston Market, the chain offering roasted chicken and meatloaf dinners, was able to expand many of its food offerings into the frozen section of grocery stores. Starbucks now sells its whole coffee beans in grocery stores. Tupperware, for years sold only at home parties, is now available at Target stores. Getting mass merchandiser and grocery chain distribution is extremely difficult and expensive for most brands. But when a brand has developed strong customer loyalty, these types of stores are eager to carry them.

Brand Extensions

Another way to leverage brand equity is **brand extension,** which is *the application of an established brand name to new product offerings.* Brand extension is generally most successful when it involves similar products. Within the last few years, for example, premium car manufacturers such as BMW, Lexus, and Mercedes-Benz have extended their brands to SUVs, a product category long dominated by Ford, Chevrolet, Nissan, and Toyota.

There are advantages and disadvantages to extending a successful brand to other products. The advantages are savings in time and money when a company introduces new products because the brand is already known and instantly communicates a certain level of trust (if the brand already has that perception). One disadvantage is the danger of diluting the power and meaning of the brand. If customers associate the brand with a certain product, such as laundry detergent, and suddenly the association is extended to apparel or writing instruments, sales of the laundry detergent could suffer. To be successful, brand extension should result in a compatible fit with the established brand. Another disadvantage is that if the new product fails, for whatever reason, that failure could reflect negatively on the brand's original products if any strong association developed with the failed product.

TRUST. THE UNIVERSAL LANGUAGE FOR SUCCESSFUL PARTNERSHIPS.

The partnerships you formed in childhood have contributed to your success today. When you're exploring real estate opportunities 12 time zones away, global partnerships based on trust are crucial.

At Cushman & Wakefield, we're relationship-oriented, not just transaction-driven. That's why we've established a worldwide real estate services organization that offers the same standard of excellence on a global basis that distinguishes us in the U.S.

Today we provide real estate solutions tailored to our clients' specific needs in more than 30 countries, in the major business centers of the world.

Now that you're bigger, the world is even smaller. To put us to work for you call 1-800-346-6789.

CUSHMAN & WAKEFIELD.

Improving your place in the world."

www.cushwake.com   CUSHMAN & WAKEFIELD WORLDWIDE

EXHIBIT 3-16
How does this Cushman & Wakefield ad communicate the idea that trust is important in successful brand relationships that link a company to its customers?

Co-branding

Like multi-tier branding, **co-branding** is *a strategy that capitalizes on using two brand names (owned by separate companies) and provides customers value from both brands.* Co-branding helps companies that sell commodity products, such as credit cards and air travel, to differentiate themselves. Co-branding involves a contractual relationship between two marketing partners, such as Visa and the United Airlines Mileage Plus program.

Brand Licensing

A strong brand can be licensed. In essence, **brand licensing** is *renting the brand equity to another company, which benefits from the association.* The beauty of brand licensing is that the company owning the brand can continue to use it while also collecting a fee for the brand's use by another company. An example that most

EXHIBIT 3-17

Why is it important for other brands to use the Gore-Tex brand in their advertising?

students are familiar with is the licensing of their university's name, logo, and mascot to apparel makers. Well-known universities generate hundreds of thousands of dollars from licensing. It has become such an important source of income that most large schools have licensing managers. Although licensing is a good way to generate extra revenue from a brand, it is a concern for brand managers because it allows a company's brand to be used by marketers who may not keep the brand's best interests in mind. Consequently, monitoring brand licensing is critical to maintain a consistent brand image.

Ingredient Branding

Another way to add value to a brand (and to a brand message) is through **ingredient branding**—*using the brand name of a product component in the promotion of another company's product*. The "Intel Inside" message used by various computer hardware manufacturers is a good example. The manufacturers hope to reinforce the quality of their finished products by featuring the maker of the most important component in the computer: the processing chip. Another example is Gore-Tex. Gore-Tex doesn't make gloves, shoes, coats, or jackets, but rather makes a lightweight, warm, and water-resistant fabric from which these items are made. Gore-Tex fabric, however, has become so well known and respected, and has been promoted so prominently (often even more than the apparel brands), that many customers ask for a "Gore-Tex jacket" even though no such brand of jacket exists. Ingredient branding is also used by food products manufacturers. Some dessert mixes, for example, promote the fact they contain Hershey's chocolate chips or NutraSweet.

For ingredient branding to be successful, the ingredient brand must have a high level of brand awareness. When it does, an ingredient brand adds value to the products in which it is used. Manufacturers who use such ingredient branding have found that they can sell their products at premium prices (Exhibit 3-17).

A FINAL NOTE: A BRAND IS A RELATIONSHIP

One of the most important effects of using IMC is the building of trust in brands. Remember that a brand is nothing more than a special relationship, and that communication is what drives relationships. The St. Paul Company recognizes this and makes it a focus of its advertising (see Exhibit 3-18). Trust is essential for creating the brand relationships that make successful brands. These relationships, however, must provide added value for customers; otherwise, the relationships will soon dissolve. How a company makes its goods or performs its primary services is no longer the number-one factor in establishing a brand's value. The new priority is communication—how a company controls or influences the communication dimensions of everything it does, as well as how it manages the exchange of information between it and its customers and other stakeholders. Brand communication greatly affects the quantity and quality of brand relationships, not only with customers but with all stakeholders.

EXHIBIT 3-18

Key Terms

Key Point Summary

This chapter focuses on the notion that a brand is a special relationship and that brand value is determined by a brand's stakeholder relationships.

Key Point 1: More Than a Product

A brand's value can be greater than value of goods and services when its image is positive. The financial community measures this support in terms of brand equity, which represents the goodwill that accrues to a brand from its brand relationships. Brand equity reflects a brand's intangible attributes and is driven by marketing communication.

Key Point 2: Brand-Building Steps

(1) Position the brand to differentiate it from competing brands. (2) Develop brand identification by selecting a name and symbol to represent the company or product. (3) Create a brand image to help further differentiate the brand and to make it easier for customers to recognize and recall.

Key Point 3: Brand Relationship Characteristics

(1) To create a brand relationship, shift from a customer acquisition strategy to a customer retention strategy. (2) Remember that not all relationships are equal, because some are more profitable than others. (3) Be aware that other stakeholder relationships can be as important as customer relationships. (4) Stakeholders overlap, so take care to maintain consistency across all marketing communication messages. (5) Remember that customer loyalty leads to other benefits, such as brand advocacy by customers.

Key Point 4: Brand Relationships and Brand Equity

Brand relationships are created from all the interactions and transactions that customers and other stakeholders have with the brand. Brand relationships are the net sum of stakeholder support that creates value for the brand.

Lessons Learned

Key Point 1: More Than a Product

a. What is a brand? Why is a brand more than just a product?
b. Explain how brands work to transform products.
c. Explain how brands work to create expectations.
d. Define *brand equity*. Explain how brand equity relates to brand relationships.
e. How do the tangible and the intangible components of brand equity differ? Why is the intangible side becoming a more important factor in estimating brand equity?
f. Analyze your brand relationships. Do you buy any brands consistently? Are there product categories in which you choose from a set of brands, any one of which is acceptable to you? Are there product categories in which you have no brand preferences at all? Explain the differences among these three types of categories.

Key Point 2: Brand-Building Steps

a. List and explain the brand-building steps.
b. What is a brand position?
c. In choosing a brand name, what's the difference between using a benefit description strategy and an association strategy?
d. What is a trademark? What is the role of a trademark in a brand-identity program?
e. What is a brand image?
f. Using the perceptual map below, plot the relative positions of three universities you considered attending in terms of "Academics" and " Fun." Rate each university on each factor from 1 to 10; then plot the schools' locations on the map. What other factors affected your choice of school?

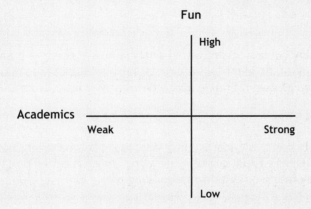

Key Point 3: Brand Relationship Characteristics

a. What are the key characteristics of a successful band relationship program?
b. Describe the company and customer sides of a brand relationship, and describe the links that forge the relationship.
c. Why do managers need to think about both customer acquisition and customer retention strategies? Is it more expensive to make a first sale or a repeat sale? Why?
d. Have you ever been exceptionally disappointed (or exceptionally pleased) by a brand? Describe the five levels of relationship intensity.
e. Explain the concept of "share of wallet."
f. Why are employees a key stakeholder group?
g. Why is loyalty important, and what rewards does a brand reap from loyal customers?
h. What needs to happen to turn stakeholders into brand advocates?
i. Why are all stakeholders important? What problem is created when the interests of all stakeholders are not considered in brand relationship programs?
j. Describe a personal experience you have had as a customer. Explain your feelings about that experience. From the list of brand characteristics, identify the ones that seem to be the most fragile in your brand experience.

Key Point 4: Brand Relationships and Brand Equity

a. Explain how the support of each stakeholder group affects brand equity.
b. Why is brand extension used? What does it contribute to a brand from an IMC perspective?
c. How do multi-tier branding, co-branding, and ingredient branding differ?
d. What key problem does brand licensing create for IMC programs?
e. If you were responsible for a chain of fast-food restaurants, what relationship policies would you establish for your employees? What suggestions would you make to better motivate the employees and increase the positive aspect of this contact point with customers?

Chapter Challenge

Writing Assignment

Pick a company, and identify what things it does or does not do to help build and maintain a good relationship with customers. Make recommendations for improving the company's relationship-building practices.

Presentation Assignment

Select a successful brand, and identify all the elements that help make it a good brand. Chart these, indicating visually which are the most important.

Internet Assignment

Visit the Amazon.com and Barnesandnoble.com websites. Analyze how these two brands are presented on their sites. Is there a strong sense of brand identity? What relationship-building techniques do they use with their customers? Write a report on dot-com branding based on what you learn from these two companies.

Case Assignment

Pick a store that you frequent that uses loyalty cards. Interview the store manager, and write up a case describing the role of the loyalty card in the retail chain's marketing communication program. Explain how the store could make the card a more effective relationship-building tool.

Part II

Chapter 4
How Brand Communication Works

Inbound by InfoCision

Always the right call...

Key Points in This Chapter

1. How do the elements of the basic communication model relate to marketing communication?
2. What are the six components of communication, and how do they relate to marketing communication?
3. What are the four types of brand-customer touch points?

Chapter Perspective

Every Touch Point Communicates

The marketplace is a social system in which customers, companies, and media interact. Communication involves the sending and receiving of messages. A company or brand can communicate with, or "touch," customers, prospects, and other stakeholders in many different ways. What many companies overlook and fail to leverage are opportunities for dialogue with customers and prospects.

Companies sometimes believe that if they don't say anything or don't respond to a customer, they have avoided sending a brand message. Wrong! A company CEO who responds to a question from the media with "No comment," actually communicates a great deal. What most people "hear" is that the CEO is scared to give the right answer or doesn't know the answer, both of which are bad messages to send. A company that chooses not to respond to a customer's complaint communicates loudly and clearly that it doesn't care about its customers and is not willing to stand behind its products.

Every thing and every person and every message that touches a customer communicates something positive or negative about the organization. The appearance of a service employee, whether neat or sloppy, says something about the company's pride in its work. The design of a product and package says modern, juvenile, feminine, old-fashioned, expensive, dull, or something else. The tone of voice on the phone or the attitude of a clerk or customer-service representative all speak to the personality and friendliness of the organization.

A company and a brand cannot *not* communicate. The challenge, then, is *how* to manage brand communication in order to accomplish business and marketing objectives cost-effectively. To answer this question requires understanding how communication—and marketing communication—work, which is what this chapter is about.

LOVE AND ICE CREAM: THE HB STORY
McCann-Erickson, Dublin, Ireland

Marketing communication consists of the messages companies send and receive and the media involved. It's also about perceptions, how customers interpret the many messages they receive about a brand. In the late 1990s, HB Ice Cream, Ireland's number-one ice-cream brand, decided to change its stodgy brand perception. This is the story about how that message was communicated at every possible point of contact with the brand.

With increasing competition facing its ice cream, HB's parent company, Unilever, decided to introduce a new brand identity for HB across Europe. McCann-Erickson Dublin was asked to develop a communication program to launch the new HB brand identity and test it in Ireland. McCann's communication effort was so successful that it not only achieved high awareness scores in a highly competitive product category but also was a winner in the Advertising and Marketing Effectiveness (AME) international award program.

The Marketing Challenge

Traditionally a "poor relation" on the fringe of Europe, the Republic of Ireland earned the tag "Celtic Tiger" through a sustained level of high economic growth during the 1990s. As unemployment rates, stubbornly high for many years, eased downward, larger numbers of Irish young people (18 to 34 years old) opted to stay home rather than emigrate, creating the youngest population profile in western Europe.

Because of its long heritage in the Irish market (since 1926), HB is regarded with great affection by Irish consumers as "our ice cream." It dominates the market despite being bought in 1973 by global marketer Unilever. The HB brand name acts as an umbrella for a wide range of products—three take-home ice-cream brands and five impulse brands (bars and cones bought out of a freezer in a store).

The challenge? Because HB already had a leading share of the Irish ice-cream market, the business objective was to grow the *category* by increasing ice-cream consumption.

Campaign Strategy

HB planned to fight for a share of the market in the bigger category of refreshment, using its impulse brands. HB's consumer research had determined that

EXHIBIT 4-1

the key target audience for the HB take-home brands consisted of housewives with children, and that the target for the impulse was young adults aged 15 to 34. However, McCann decided that the strategy needed to move beyond these two audiences. Executives wanted a new brand identity with a more contemporary brand perception, especially for the younger people in the HB market. Given HB's ubiquity and broad acceptance, the identity effort could be aimed at *everyone* in the Irish market.

The Brand Message

For 30 years the HB logo, with its initials (from the original founders, the Hughes Brothers) in script mounted in an oval and printed over four bars, had been a familiar symbol in the Irish media, on signs in the streets, and in shops. The brand also had a high pan-European advertising presence on TV and on billboards. Irish consumers came in contact with HB brands everywhere. It was impossible to walk down an Irish street without seeing HB signage, point-of-purchase displays, branded litter bins, or window stickers on the local corner shop. HB branded freezer cabinets were a prominent feature in shops.

The original logo was appropriate to a relatively undeveloped market in both ice-cream consumption and other refreshments. However, competition had recently become much fiercer as the lines had started to blur between ice cream, carbonated soft drinks, confectionery, and yogurt categories. The time had come to recognize consumers' greater familiarity with ice cream.

EXHIBIT 4-2

The communication effort needed to touch the emotions of the audience. The new design continued to use the familiar HB initials (see Exhibit 4-2) but replaced the oval with a heart shape. The design sought to communicate the values of natural togetherness and love. "Natural togetherness" provided a key emotional benefit by focusing on people enjoying ice cream in a social, interactive environment.

The message strategy utilized a major public event to spearhead the campaign and involve the audience. The big idea was to capitalize on the new heart-shaped logo by using St. Valentine's Day weekend as a launch platform to create rapid and widespread awareness, excitement, and recognition of the new HB identity. The event would be supported by advertising so that when consumers saw on-pack and in-store changes, they would understand what was happening to the familiar HB brand.

Delivering the Message

Fitting a brand of HB's stature and ubiquity with a new identity was clearly a task that needed to go far beyond advertising to engage all possible contact points. Changing all HB's packaging, shop-front signage, point-of-purchase, and freezer cabinet brand messages in every supermarket and grocery store in the country was a logistical challenge.

Rather than relying on a TV commercial to announce the logo, the McCann team felt strongly that the communication should include new media and contact points where appropriate. The core media idea was to create Ireland's first-ever themed weekend on Irish TV. St. Valentine's weekend was dubbed "The Love Weekend," and themed television programming sponsored by HB included movies such as *Sleepless in Seattle*, *Truly Madly Deeply*, and *Brief Encounter*; romantic episodes of *The Simpsons*, *Friends*, and *Golden Girls*; and a special called *An Intimate Evening with Michael Bolton*. In addition, a local television network created a phone-in music video request show called *Cupid's Corner*.

McCann's event-based plan allowed the agency to put in place a completely integrated communication strategy. That meant combining the three elements—the TV spot, a local media launch event, and on-the-street promotional activity—so that consumers were involved with a 360-degree communication program for the new brand identity. In addition to traditional media time and space placements, the campaign also used sponsorship "stings," short TV spots that announced HB's sponsorship of the Love Weekend. The networks also ran tie-in promotional teasers for the programs. In newspapers, the TV listings were printed over color watermarks of the heart logo.

A key element of HB's strategy to compete against the major refreshment brands was to establish a strong street presence in the main urban centers. To get the new HB logo on the street, McCann teamed up with a Dublin film-production company to project video images on large outdoor screens or walls. The Love Weekend TV reminder ads were also projected on large walls at city center locations on St. Valentine's night in Dublin, Cork, and Belfast. If the event didn't quite cause national gridlock, it did manage to slow Saturday-night traffic near the light projections. McCann also had "hit squads" at each location distributing HB "Passion Test" cards, short questionnaires that tested the passion in one's life.

In an effort to further bring the event alive, McCann placed a color ad leading into the TV listings that offered people the chance to win a family holiday. This strengthened HB's ownership of the weekend's TV listings while at the same time the contest generated excitement and enthusiasm.

Evaluation of the HB Campaign

Market research conducted two weeks after the Love Weekend but prior to any signage or point-of-

purchase changes found that nearly half of all Irish recognized the new symbol. Furthermore, 70 percent of the 15 to 24 age group were aware of the logo, and 75 percent of these immediately associated the logo with HB Ice Cream.

Ice-cream sales in Ireland are seasonally biased to the summer months, so another objective was to stretch the impulse ice-cream season so that it starts earlier. Given the success of the Love Weekend with increasing sales in February, it is now part of HB's strategy to launch the new impulse season each year with a St. Valentine's weekend themed TV event.

Unilever managers were so impressed with the Irish campaign and the results it achieved that they decided to replicate the strategy in all their ice-cream markets. McCann's video of the whole campaign has become the template for similar launch activity in other markets.

Source: This case was adapted with permission from the Advertising and Marketing Effectiveness (AME) brief for the HB brand-identity campaign prepared by McCann-Erickson Dublin.

HOW DOES COMMUNICATION WORK?

Conceptually, communication is a fairly simple process: someone—a person or an organization—creates and sends a message to an individual or organization. In every commercial communication situation, companies (or their agencies) that create brand messages do so with certain objectives in mind—to inform, impress, persuade, and/or generate a response. If you have taken a psychology or marketing course you are probably familiar with the traditional sender–receiver communication model. This model has been adapted to show how brand communication works (see Figure 4-1). A good understanding of this model will enable you to understand all the various aspects of marketing communication that are discussed in the remainder of this book.

Once a company decides what it wants to say, it starts the communication process, thus becoming the **source,** or **sender**—the *initiator of a message.* The creation of an organization's brand messages is generally done by one or more MC agencies. In the basic model of communication, this *process of creating a brand message to convey an intended meaning and elicit a certain type of response* is called **encoding.**

A **message** is *an idea encoded in a combination of words, pictures, actions, symbols, and/or events.* The encoding challenge is to use words, pictures, and other cues whose meanings are shared by members of the intended audience. An **MC message** is *anything that talks about a brand, such as newspaper ads, radio commercials, direct-mail pieces, sales clerks, or customer service* (see Exhibit 4-3). A communication **channel,** or **media vehicle,** is *the means by which a message is delivered—letter, e-mail, radio, television, newspaper, telephone, an event.*

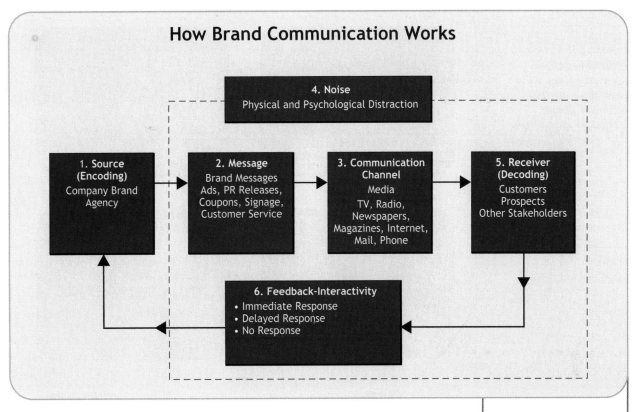

How Brand Communication Works

4. Noise
Physical and Psychological Distraction

1. Source (Encoding)
Company Brand
Agency

2. Message
Brand Messages
Ads, PR Releases,
Coupons, Signage,
Customer Service

3. Communication Channel
Media
TV, Radio,
Newspapers,
Magazines, Internet,
Mail, Phone

5. Receiver (Decoding)
Customers
Prospects
Other Stakeholders

6. Feedback-Interactivity
• Immediate Response
• Delayed Response
• No Response

FIGURE 4-1

A good understanding of this model is necessary in order to understand all the various aspects of marketing communication.

The **receiver** is *anyone who is exposed to a message*. Once receivers, usually customers and prospects, receive a message, they must decode it. **Decoding** is the *process of interpreting what a message means*. After customers decode a message, they respond in some way, indicating to what extent the message was received, properly decoded, and persuasive. This response is called **feedback,** which is *a response that conveys a message back to the source*.

The communication process occurs in a context or environment where other things are going on—competitive brand messages, people walking by, a telephone ringing, as well as thoughts inside customers' heads. These "other things" are called **noise**—*interferences or distractions that can negatively affect the transmission and reception of a message*. Companies and their MC agencies go to great lengths to create brand messages that have impact—that are attention getting as well as memorable.

HOW DOES MARKETING COMMUNICATION WORK?

Now let's reinterpret the basic communication model as a model of how marketing communication works. The numbers 1 through 6 in the subheads refer to numbers on Figure 4-1.

1. The Source and Encoding

Because companies and other organizations have something they want to sell, most marketing communication starts with them and their agencies. They are the source (customers also can be sources, as will be explained later). And it is their

E X H I B I T   4 - 3

This Dunkin' Donuts commercial opens with a young boy with a box of Dunkin' Donuts Munchkins watching an older man feeding ducks in a park. The boy tosses a Munchkin to the ground. It is picked up not by a duck but by a man in business suit, who eats it and walks on.

"Ducks" :30
SFX: Outdoor sounds.
(Open on a young boy with a box of Dunkin' Donuts Munchkins watching an older man feeding the ducks in the park. The boy then takes a Munchkin and tosses it at the ground, hoping for the same result. Instead, we see a man in a business suit nonchalantly pick up the Munchkin, eat it, and walk on)
Anncr. (VO): There's just something about Dunkin' Donuts.
Logo and tagline

corporate or brand name that appears in these messages identifying them as the sender of the MC messages.

Publicity, of course, is an exception. Although a company or its PR agency often provides the information and ideas for a publicity story, and these stories include the company (or brand) name, the perceived source of these MC messages are third parties—the media. Unless a story is negative, a credible third-party source brings integrity to the company's message. An important factor in customers decoding a message and forming attitudes about a brand is the perceived integrity of the sender. *The extent to which a message sender is believable* is called **source credibility.**

Several years ago the scientist and cosmologist Carl Sagan was asked what one invention he would most like to see created. He answered: "A baloney detection kit so that every citizen can tell when he or she is being lied to."[1] Although Sagan was expressing concern about government sources, many customers feel the same way about advertising (and other MC) messages—always wondering what parts of ads are true and what parts are hype. Why do customers feel this way? They know that the sources of advertising are companies that are trying to sell them something. This does not mean customers don't believe anything they see in ads, but rather that they decode ads with caution.

This natural consumer skepticism is the reason why building brand trust is so important. The more customers and prospects trust a company and brand, the more likely are customers and prospects to decode advertising with less skepticism. One way companies can help overcome source skepticism is by providing multiple "proof" points, or reasons why a brand will deliver on its promise. Another way is for companies to be good corporate citizens and refrain from doing things that negatively affect their reputations.

The encoding step is generally the responsibility of MC agencies. Once the brand position and target audiences have been agreed upon, agencies create MC messages. Agencies must have a thorough understanding of the target audiences to ensure that the words, pictures, and other communication cues used in messages will be decoded with the meanings intended. (Encoding methods are explained in Chapters 9 and 10.)

2. Brand Messages: Everything Communicates

When most people hear the term *brand message,* they think of such things as magazine and TV ads, coupons, publicity releases, and packaging. Those, however, are only one type of brand message—namely, MC messages. Remember from Chapter 1 that a **brand message** is *all the information and experiences that impact how customers and other stakeholders perceive a brand.* A brand message can originate from anywhere inside or outside a company. A company's behavior, the design and maintenance of its physical facilities, its hiring practices, its stock price, what others say or write about the company, as well as its MC messages, all say something about a brand or company.

The corporate headquarters of Transamerica Corporation in San Francisco was designed to be more than just a structure to house corporate offices. The insurance company wanted the building to be a strong brand message by being unique and memorable—a message in steel and concrete that instantly said "Transamerica." This objective was achieved, and today the "Pyramid" is part of Transamerica's logo (see Exhibit 4-4) and, like the Golden Gate Bridge, is a symbol of the city of San Francisco.

Although marketing people are not responsible for all brand messages sent by a company, they must constantly monitor what messages customers and prospects are receiving as part of the total communication program of the organization. When a negative non-MC message is sent, hundreds of positive MC messages may be negated. In most cases these negative messages are unintentional; those responsible for them simply didn't realize what the impact of

their words or actions would be. Stephen Manes, a technology columnist for *Forbes*, points out that what a receiver receives may not be what the source intended. Manes is particularly concerned with technological glitches, such as those that sometimes reformat e-mail: "The idea that what you transmit may not be what your correspondent receives—even before allowing for misinterpretation—hasn't yet managed to penetrate the corporate psyche."[2]

> "You can never be sure how your message will look or sound to someone at the other end."
>
> Stephen Manes, *Forbes* technology columnist

An example of the impact of unexpected negative brand messages comes from the telecommunication company Qwest (formerly US West). In 1995 it consolidated its customer-service centers going from 530 to 26 offices.[3] As a result, customers who called with problems and questions had long waits or got busy signals. Customers got so angry that they called their states' public utilities commissions and complained. After issuing several warnings, the public utilities commissions started fining the company millions of dollars. Besides having to pay these fines, the company also had to endure a lot of negative publicity as the media ran major stories discussing the fines and the bad service that generated them. Because this company's total communication was not integrated, the company suffered.

What makes this story tragic from an integration perspective is what was going on in Quest's marketing during this time. Although customer service was understaffed and underperforming, marketing was spending approximately $50 million a year on MC messages (heavy TV and newspaper advertising). Ironically, one of the products being advertised was a special phone service offer to help small businesses improve their customer service.[4] Quest could have received a much better return on its MC investment if it had moved some of its advertising dollars over to its customer-service department. The company not only could have provided customers with better service, but it could also have avoided a lot of unexpected, negative publicity, all of which overwhelmed the advertising messages.

This example indicates why building brand relationships requires managing a brand's *total* communication effort. This does not mean that marketing communication people are responsible for everything in a company, but rather that they are responsible for identifying when negative or inconsistent brand messages are being sent. When such messages are found, they need to be brought to management's attention and, through the use of cross-functional planning (← Chapter 2), eliminated.

A basic principle of integrated marketing communication is that *everything a company does, and sometimes what it doesn't do, can send a powerful brand message.* Think for a minute about the 4 Ps of marketing: product, price, place, and promotion. Although the 4 Ps concept is useful for explaining marketing, it is somewhat misleading because it implies that communication occurs only in one of the Ps, promotion. It is true that "promotion" refers to marketing communication, which is responsible for many of the brand messages; but each of the other three Ps has a strong communication dimension as well (see Figure 4-2). Following are examples of the brand messages sent by product, price, and place (points of distribution).

Product Brand Messages

United Parcel Service (UPS) makes a point of washing its delivery trucks every evening, knowing that a clean truck sends a message of professionalism and says, "This company takes pride in its work." Also operating on the principle that if something looks good it must be good, companies in the auto industry have always maintained staffs of industrial designers to style cars. The same principle also operates in other industries. In computers and appliances, industrial designers are important members of the product development team. When Apple

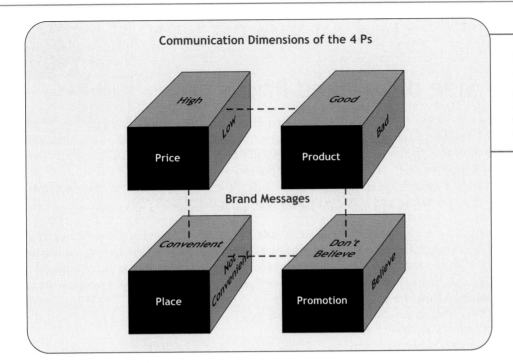

Communication Dimensions of the 4 Ps

Price · High · Low

Product · Good · Bad

Brand Messages

Place · Convenient · Not Convenient

Promotion · Don't Believe · Believe

F I G U R E   4 - 2

The light blue sections of each of the 4 Ps boxes represent the communication of each "P."

Computer introduced the iMac, the new computer attracted the attention of computer users and shook up the entire computer industry and its approach to product design (see Exhibit 4-5). The appearance of the iMac sent a powerful brand message. The beautiful *design* of this computer reflected positively on Apple's association with creativity.

Price Brand Messages

The price that is charged for a particular brand is a message indicating how the brand compares with competing brands in quality and status. That is why price is often used to differentiate brands. Other aspects of pricing also send strong messages. The frequency and the extent of brand promotions, for example, say something about a brand. The more a brand is on sale and the more it is discounted, the more ordinary it is perceived to be. When McDonald's unveiled its plan to sell Big Macs and Egg McMuffins for 55 cents (to help commemorate its 55 years of being in business), the company soon found it was sending a negative message. The price cut made some customers perceive the products as cheap and resulted in the financial community's slicing a big chunk off the company's share price. One financial analyst commented, "They have transformed one of the great brands in American business into a commodity."[5] Pricing messages, like all others, must be strategically integrated with all other brand messages in order to send customers and other stakeholders a coherent, meaningful message. The IMC in Action box discusses the issue of demand pricing. What kinds of messages does this practice send?

Place (Distribution) Brand Messages

The places where products are distributed can send brand messages. There's a big perceived difference, for example, between cosmetics sold at Wal-Mart and those sold at Nordstrom, even when they are the same product or the same brand. The fact they are sold in a "discount" store says they must be a "discount" product.

E X H I B I T   4 - 5

The bright colors and streamlined curves of the iMac dramatize Apple's slogan "Think Different."

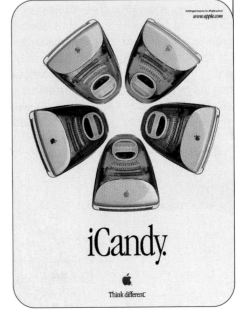

www.apple.com

iCandy.

Think different.

IMC IN ACTION

The Customer Side of Demand Pricing

What brand message is being sent when prices suddenly change? Computers and databases have enabled companies to use variations in price to help manage capacity and inventories. This strategy is called *demand pricing*. When capacities decrease, prices are raised to maximize revenue return on products being sold. Oil and gas prices are good examples of demand pricing.

Airlines have been using demand pricing for years. As the date of a scheduled flight comes closer, the airlines' computers automatically raise or lower prices in response to how many seats for that flight remain unsold. Using a database of historical sales, the airlines have good estimates of how many seats should be sold one week out, two weeks out, and so on. When seats for a particular flight are being sold faster than normal, the airlines raise the price for the remaining seats (and vice versa when sales are slower than expected). This is one reason why, for any given flight, the ticket prices paid by passengers on board greatly vary.

Using the same strategy, Coca-Cola is testing vending machines that raise and lower prices in response to changes in the outside temperature. Because more people buy soft drinks on hot days than on cold days, machines are programmed to charge more for a can of Coke when temperatures go up. It is also possible to program vending machines to increase prices when sales significantly increase in a short period of time (for example, during a special event), in part to prevent the machine from running out before its regularly scheduled restocking.

Demand pricing may help Coke maximize its profits on vending machines, but it may also send a negative brand message to people who regularly use the vending machine. One day a can of Coke may cost 75 cents, and the next day, when the temperature goes up, a can may cost a dollar. Will customers think they are getting ripped off? Will customers look for a Pepsi machine, where they know the price doesn't change?

Will demand pricing make them switch from Coke to another brand the next time they go to the store and stock up on soft drinks?

Think About It

What is demand pricing? How might it send negative messages to customers? Why is demand pricing less of a problem for airlines than for soft-drink companies?

EXHIBIT 4-6

Another "place message" is communicated by where products are displayed within a store. Brands on the bottom shelf are often perceived as being not very popular.

When the European pen company Mont Blanc decided to reposition itself as an upscale brand several years ago, one of the first things the company did was stop distributing its products in stationery stores that sold cheap pencils, pens, and paper along with paperback books and magazines. The company said those stores did not project the type of image with which it wanted the Mont Blanc brand to be associated.

Promotion (Marketing Communication) Brand Messages

Promotion is about marketing communication messages. What must be kept in mind, however, is that *how* a company communicates sends a message in addition to the actual words and content. How an MC message is designed and what media carry the message add to or subtract from the intended meaning. Most of the remainder of this book is about how to create and send MC messages.

3. Media Channels: Connecting Companies and Customers

Media are the channels that connect companies with customers. Most MC messages are carried by TV, radio, newspapers, magazines, internet, mail, and outdoor boards. Most of these types of media can be used to reach not only mass audiences but smaller, specialized markets, as Exhibit 4-7 illustrates.

Nontraditional media—including buildings and sports stadiums that have electronic billboards and signage, faxes, kiosks, movies and TV shows (which have product placements), packaging, and even sidewalks—are carrying an increasing number of MC messages. And buzz, the word of mouth that happens when people talk about a product, is also the focus of some nontraditional strategies. Some movies, like the *The Hours* and *Chicago*, are released in limited venues in order to heighten the anticipation generated by buzz.[6]

For many years media were considered primarily as vehicles or delivery systems. However, they should be thought of as channels that link companies and customers psychologically as well as physically. Psychologically, media can add to (or subtract from) the intended meaning of a MC message and campaign. Each medium has an image just as every brand has. A message in *Forbes* has a different significance than a message in *Playboy*, *Cosmopolitan*, or *Rolling Stone*. The more positive and relevant the image of a medium is to a brand, the more the medium can enhance that brand's messages. For example, B2B companies like to advertise in magazines such as *Business Week* and *Fortune,* which are seen as prestigious business publications and thus provide a prestigious editorial environment for ads. In a way, media are the stage on which a brand message "performs."

EXHIBIT 4-7
Traditional media are usually thought of as mass media that reach large audiences. However, a niche market such as Hispanic consumers in the United States can be reached with media such as the Spanish Broadcasting System.

4. Noise: The Clutter That Derails Communication

In 2003, companies such as Honda and Toyota pulled their TV commercials during the first days of Operation Iraqi Freedom even though they knew viewership would be up.[7] These companies believed war reports could stir up tremendous emotional feelings that would make thinking about a new-car purchase seem irrelevant. From the marketers' point of view, the TV's editorial content was likely

TABLE 4-1	Types and Sources of Noise	
	Noise from a Brand's Communication Process	**Noise from outside a Brand's Communication Process**
Physical noise	• Poor print reproduction	• Distracting sights and sounds in the environment
	• Distorted sound or visuals (electronic messages)	• Recipient's multi-tasking
	• Bad timing of messages	• Competitive messages
Psychological noise	• Mixed meanings of words or visuals	• Irrelevance to recipient's wants and needs
	• Dislike for or distrust of message source	• Satisfaction with competitive brand
	• Confusion resulting from inconsistent messages about brand promise	

to be noise drowning out the companies' messages intended for customers and prospects.

All communication, including marketing communication, takes place within an environment that contains distractions. Noise can be physical or psychological, and it can come from within or outside the intended communication effort (see Table 4-1). Although zero-defect communication is impossible to obtain, marketers must constantly work to minimize noise.

One of the most troublesome sources of psychological noise is inconsistent brand messages. A past advertising campaign for a popular American beer provides an example. A content analysis of the TV commercials found three different selling strategies. Some of the commercials were selling "good taste," others "fun with friends," and still others "high quality." It was not realistic to expect customers to remember all these product claims, but customers who did remember them probably were confused about what this beer was really all about.

One type of noise of particular concern to marketers is **clutter,** which is *competition among commercial messages.* Clutter is evident when you open a newspaper and a bunch of ads stares you in the face. Clutter makes it difficult for a particular brand message to get attention. It is important, therefore, to know what competitors are saying, as well as when and where they are delivering their messages. Marketers compete not only *with* brands but also *for* the attention of customers and prospects, as well as other stakeholders, as Exhibit 4-8 shows.

TV commercial breaks, for example, often contain up to 10 commercials. Magazines' and newspapers' content is 50 to 70 percent ads. Primacy and recency theories say that the first thing and the last thing you see, hear, or read (in any situation) are more likely to be remembered than all the messages in the middle. Knowing this, agencies negotiate for the first or last place in a print publication or broadcast commercial break, to improve the odds that their messages will be remembered.

EXHIBIT 4-8

In this type of visual-heavy environment, every brand message is surrounded by a lot of visual noise that is distracting.

5. The Receiver and Decoding

In marketing communication, the intended receiver is the **target audience,** which is *a group that has* *significant potential to respond positively to a brand message*. There are two types of responses to messages. One is physical. When you look through a magazine or have the TV on, you physically receive many ads. But even though these ads may register on your senses, you probably only *really* read, watch, or listen to a small percentage of them. The other type of response is psychological. In this more advanced manner of decoding, the receiver selects messages to pay attention to, understand, and, if the marketer is lucky, remember.

Decoding is basically the reverse of encoding. Symbols sent by the source must be reconstructed into the original idea or into something close to it. For decoding to be successful, there needs to be shared meaning between the source and receiver. Otherwise, the receiver (the customer) will not correctly understand what the source (the company) is saying about the brand. Shared understanding of symbols is the result of common fields of experience between encoders and the intended audience.

Receivers' **fields of experience** determined by past activities and observations create the "codebook" used to find meaning in all messages, including brand messages. Fields of experience directly affect how receivers decode messages. They can make an audience more (or less) receptive to a brand message. Suppose your company designs boats and market research indicates that the target market in the United States for yachts tends to be Republicans. You might not want to sub-brand your newest 42-foot sloop *The Clintonian*. The decoding process is also influenced by the receiver's immediate needs, wants, and concerns. If you're hungry, you will likely respond differently to a sign for pizza than you would if you had just eaten.

Marketers can help ensure that messages are decoded as intended by having a thorough understanding of customers, empathizing with them, and speaking their "literal and emotional language."[8] Even then, the potential for misinterpretation often still exists. For example, when a brand is advertised as selling for half price, the message can be decoded as "a good value" or as "a cheap, low-quality product." To clarify MC messages, companies use **strategic redundancy,** which means *saying the same thing in several different ways*, so that receivers will have several chances to get the message. One of the big advantages of an IMC program is that it is designed to build in strategic redundancy by coordinating all the messages delivered by the various MC functional areas so they reinforce one another. Look at the ad in Exhibit 4-9. Notice that the headline, illustration, and body copy all "say" that communication systems need to work together as a team. To help ensure that messages are decoded as intended, companies need to be aware of their target audience's field of experiences.[9]

Another technique to help ensure proper decoding is keeping messages simple. An old rule of thumb in advertising says, "Be single-minded." This means that there should be only one main idea in a brand message. A variation on that principle is KISS— "Keep it simple, stupid"—which recognizes that the simpler the message thought and execution, the easier it is for receivers to get the main point.

IMC helps close the gap between intended and perceived messages and thus minimizes the miscommunication, misperception, and misunderstanding that results from inadequate brand communication. It

EXHIBIT 4-9
The Novell ad says that communication systems need to work as a team. It says that visually by showing dogs running wild, then showing them as part of a dogsled team. It also says it in the headline "Team up all" and in the body copy, ". . . they can all be harnessed as one Net."

team up all
your different networks to run as
one Net.

In today's economy, companies are struggling with the complexities of the Net. Trying to make intranets, extranets, the Internet and multiple software platforms work together. Well now, with Net services software from Novell, they can all be harnessed as one Net. So employees, partners, suppliers and customers will have the freedom to connect—securely and reliably. And companies will have the power to change their eBusiness as fast as the Net economy. Find out how to get all your Nets working as one at www.novell.com

Novell.
the power to change

does this by being responsible for the way messages set expectations, and by monitoring what perceptions customers have about the brand. When expectations rise too high, a company must either work to bring its product performance up to that level or create MC messages that make more realistic promises.

A company can use two-way communication to give a brand a more positive perception. One way to do this is to invite customers to ask questions. Caring for a new baby, for example, may sound like a simple thing, but new parents often encounter unexpected difficulties. The baby-food company Gerber has a toll-free telephone number that parents can call with questions about feeding and raising a baby. The company does not give medical advice, but its representatives do answer thousands of questions each month from new parents. Merely knowing that there is a place where they can call and get answers is a tremendous added value to these parents and leads them to perceive Gerber as an especially caring company.

Because a perception is the result of communication, a perception provides a window on the success of a message strategy. In other words, tracking customer perceptions is an important source of feedback and the first step in evaluating the success of brand messages.

6. Feedback and Interactivity

In an attempt to convince 250,000 potential customers to try its Olay Daily Facials product, Olay launched a pilot program that used the telephone to get prospective customers to respond. In exchange for limited personal information, consumers could obtain a free sample of the new product simply by calling 1-800-TRY-OLAY and interacting with a speech recognition system. Consumers who called in were also given the option to join Club Olay, a relationship program that provides consumers with free samples, newsletters, and other benefits. This is an example of how companies are striving to create interactivity with their customers by building a promotional program around feedback.[10] Feedback indicates that customers, prospects, and other stakeholders have been "touched" by a brand message. There are three types of feedback: immediate, delayed, and no feedback at all.

Immediate feedback is ordering or buying, asking questions, sampling, or interacting in some other way with a brand soon after a brand message is received. Immediate feedback is especially valuable to those doing direct-response marketing (direct mail and telemarketing), which is designed to get the audience to respond immediately with a purchase or some other action. The same is true for most retail advertising, such as grocery and department store ads that include special prices. Other types of immediate response include queries and requests for information, visits to a store, trying a product or using a sample, or repeating the purchase of a product previously tried. Business-to-business marketing often uses feedback to generate leads for personal sales.

Delayed feedback is a response given at a later time. The delay doesn't mean that a message has had no impact. Image advertising, for example, is designed to work over time, creating and maintaining brand awareness and a positive feeling about a brand. The message impact of advertising comes at the point when the consumer is contemplating a purchase and a message impression from the advertising stimulates the selection of the advertised brand. Both B2C and B2B customers remember numerous advertising messages about a brand; then when a need arises or they find themselves in a position to take advantage of an opportunity offered by a brand, they respond by making a purchase, asking for more information, visiting a store, sampling the product, or taking some other action. When feedback does occur, it is often in response to multiple brand messages. Brand messages are also designed to reinforce brand choice—in other words, to keep current customers satisfied with their brand choice and confirm the wisdom of their choice.

This is particularly important for major purchases, such as automobiles.

No feedback is rarely a desired response, but it is meaningful and important. When there is no feedback, a company needs to find out why, because it may indicate a negative impact. If the message was never received, the wrong media may have been used or the message may have been sent to the wrong place or at the wrong time. A nonresponse could also indicate that there was too much clutter or other noise, or simply that the message was not relevant or persuasive enough to move the target audience to respond. It could also mean that the consumer is not in the market for the product or is loyal to some other brand.

> "The promotional monologue of advertising at the seller's convenience is being replaced by dialogue at the customer's convenience."
>
> Anders Gronstedt, author of
> *The Customer Century*

If a message is received but misinterpreted, the message may have been poorly encoded. If a message was received and properly decoded but there still is no response, the message may not have been persuasive enough, or receivers may not have been potential customers. When the latter is found to be the case, the company should not waste money designing and sending further messages to this target audience, or the company should significantly change the message to appeal to the target audience's needs or interests.

Occasionally, very useful feedback comes from brand messages that were not initiated by the brand itself. Some companies, for example, monitor category-related chat rooms on the Internet to see what people are saying about the company and brand. And eBay, the giant online auction company, uses customer feedback as its primary tool in protecting its users from scam artists. Its famous "Feedback Forum," a rating system that records the reputation of all eBay members, both buyers and sellers, is designed to create trust for its online transactions.[11]

BRAND-CUSTOMER TOUCH POINTS

A survey by the Pew Charitable Trusts found that 46 percent of customers had walked out of a store because of bad service.[12] This type of contact between a customer and a company is the contact point where customer frustration is most visible.

Any situation in which a customer comes into contact with a brand or company is a **brand–customer touch point.** The touch-point concept suggests that there are many kinds of brand messages besides MC messages, and that media are not the only means by which customers come in contact with a brand message. Understanding how touch points affect customers is critical to managing the customer expectations that drive brand relationships. As the HB Ice Cream story in the opening case illustrates, every touch point contributes to customers' impressions of a brand.

The concept of touch points was first popularized by Jan Carlson, former chairman of Scandinavian Airlines System (SAS). During the time he managed this world-class company, Carlson realized that certain company–customer interactions (touch points) had a significant impact on whether customers chose SAS the next time they flew. He called these touch points "moments of truth." They included on-time departures and arrivals, careful handling of luggage, and courteous interactions with airline personnel.[13] He also discovered that messages delivered at these touch points were often more powerful than anything SAS could say in its marketing communication.

To manage touch points, a company must first identify them. Next, it must prioritize them based on the following criteria: (1) impact on brand loyalty, (2) ability

EXHIBIT 4-10

Touch points are all the different ways customer come in contact with a company. Gateway makes sure its "cow" imagery is used on everything from retail buildings to packaging.

of the company to influence the touch-point experience, (3) cost of making each contact a positive experience, (4) extent to which contacts can be used to gather customer data, and (5) extent to which contacts are appropriate for carrying additional brand messages. Finally, touch points must be integrated to ensure message consistency as the Gateway pictures point out (see Exhibit 4-10). Every touch point, to some extent, strengthens, maintains, or weakens the relationship between a brand and a customer. The four basic categories of customer touch points are company created, intrinsic, unexpected, and customer initiated (see Figure 4-3).

Company-Created Touch Points

Company-created touch points are *planned MC messages, such as ads, news releases, brochures, packages, and store decor.* When Lexus or its agency, for example, creates and places an ad in *Time* magazine, it is creating a contact point with the magazine's readers and using the magazine to connect with its target audience. The Gateway building and packaging with Gateway's black-and-white cow graphics

FIGURE 4-3

IMC Brand Touch Points

How would you rank the importance of these?

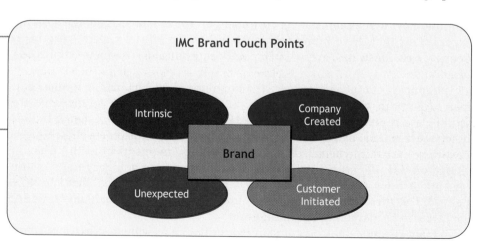

IMC Brand Touch Points

Intrinsic   Company Created

Brand

Unexpected   Customer Initiated

IMC IN ACTION

Coffee with Car to Go

The Volvo Conservatory in Manila, the capital city of the Philippines, is an airy, sparkling-white showroom for Volvo cars that bears no resemblance to any other car showroom you have ever seen. It offers a coffee shop, a bank, music concerts, and art exhibits, as well as lectures on values and on the environment.

The Volvo Conservatory has taken the concept of an entertaining location to an extreme. Except for a display of three Volvo models and one auto accessory shop, there is no obvious sign that this is a car dealer's showroom. The Coffee Beanery, a chic local café, serves customers all day at one end of the showroom; at the opposite end sits a branch of the Urban Bank. People come to the Conservatory to use these facilities, so Volvo becomes part of their daily lives. Many Filipino coffee drinkers become Volvo buyers because of this subtle marketing approach.

The owner of the dealership, Selene Yu, has created a unique culture that appeals to Philippine sensitivities. He explains that the name Conservatory, which suggests an English greenhouse, is relevant because he views the business as a place to nurture the four values that Volvo wants to impart: safety, protection of the environment, social values, and support for the arts. All of these have broad appeal in the Philippines.

In addition to selling cars, the Volvo Conservatory holds concerts by local bands to convey the message that the car is not only for middle-aged executives but for young people as well. It sponsors environmental films to send the message that the Scandinavian automaker is committed to preserving nature. It sends car experts to colleges to educate students on car safety and responsible driving. Volvo brochures are passed around during all these events. The Conservatory works—and sells cars—because it appeals to the values of its Filipino customers.

Think About It

What is a touch point? Why should MC managers be concerned with touch points other than traditional marketing communication? In what ways does the Volvo Conservatory create unusual and effective customer touch points?

are also company-created brand statements. Another creative way of touching customers is described in the IMC in Action box.

One of the advantages of company-created touch points is that, for the most part, they can be highly controlled. The other three touch points—intrinsic, unexpected, and customer-initiated—cannot be controlled, but marketing communicators can do many things to influence them.

Intrinsic Touch Points

Before investing in company-created touch points (which cost money), a brand should identify and examine its **intrinsic touch points**, which are *interactions with a brand required during the process of buying or using that brand*. Because these contacts are inherent to the buying or using of a brand, these touch points are always sending messages, especially to current customers. Here is a list of intrinsic touch points for most car rental businesses; it is impossible for a person to rent and use a car without these interactions:

- Company representative who answers toll-free reservation number or clerk at rental counter.
- Driver of van to the car holding area.
- Attendant who checks car out of the car holding area.

- Signage and directions.
- Appearance of the car lot and cleanliness of the van and rental office lobby.
- The rental car itself—how clean it is, how well it runs, and its brand name.
- Attendant at car return area.

For years, renting a car meant standing in line at a rental office and then filling out a lot of paperwork. Recognizing that this was not a pleasant customer experience (i.e., an intrinsic, negative brand message), rental car companies introduced a special service for heavy users. Hertz's Gold Card service, for example, requires members to provide all their personal information, including credit-card number, only once. From then on, Gold Car members are taken directly to the car holding area where a sign displays members' names and the slots in which their cars are waiting with keys in the ignition and trunks open waiting for luggage. All a Gold Card customer is required to do is show a valid driver's license and the rental agreement (which is hanging on the review mirror) when exiting the Hertz lot. This type of service sends a positive message to Hertz heavy users: "Hertz cares about you, knows your time is valuable, and will do a little more work on our end to ensure that your experience is hassle free."

Most intrinsic touch points are connected with customer service. They send powerful messages because they are generally personal and occur in real time. Because these touch points are so important, companies such as Virgin Atlantic (see Exhibit 4-11) use ads to promote their customer service.

Although marketing is often not directly responsible for many of the intrinsic touch points, such as managing service personnel, marketing can make suggestions about how to improve these interactions with customers in order to send a positive brand message. How quickly does a company reply to customer inquiries and complaints? A response seems more positive, regardless of its content, if it is given sooner rather than later. A timely response "says" that the company is concerned and has made the customer's problem a top priority.

In the case of packaged goods, the package itself, such as a jar of Smuckers jelly, is an intrinsic touch point. How easy it is to open, to reseal, and to dispose of all send messages about the brand. Because intrinsic touch points are inherent in the buying or using of a brand, they have the attention of the customer at least for a brief period of time. Recognizing this, companies can use these touch points to deliver a company-created brand message. For example, on the Smuckers jar can be printed a dessert recipe that calls for Smuckers jelly, or the jar can contain a peel-off coupon good on the next purchase. In the case of Hertz, promotional signs can be displayed and brochures distributed at the checkout and check-in touch points, as well as in the car. Unfortunately, some companies over exploit touch points, as explained in the Technology in Action box.

As you can see, intrinsic touch points not only send messages, but often provide the opportunity to deliver company-created messages. And because intrinsic touch points, by definition, involve current customers, the messages sent at these touch points are some of the most critical in retaining customers.

EXHIBIT 4-11

Virgin Atlantic is well known for the excellent service it provides its customers. This ad, directed to B2B customers, promises the same good service even when handling commercial cargo.

For a refreshingly good service with no bitter aftertaste, give us a call.

Now, doesn't that sound a-peel-ing?

www.virgin.com/cargo · Telephone 1 800 828 6822   virgin atlantic cargo

TECHNOLOGY IN ACTION

Touch-Point Sore Point

By over exploiting the opportunity to send a company-initiated message, some companies turn what could be a good brand experience into a negative one. Some intrinsic touch points are emotionally loaded interactions, such as calling a company with a complaint or trying to figure out how to do a certain transaction on an automated teller machine. When a company-created message is placed at these touch points, interfering with what the customer is interested in trying to accomplish, the message can cause an emotional response that may have an enduring negative impact on the brand or company.

Consider what Bank of America did when it sold commercial "time" on its ATMs. Five- to seven-second mini-TV commercials run on the ATMs while customers approach the machines. The commercials stop when customers key in their requests, then resume while the transactions are being processed. In response to customer complaints, a Bank of America spokesperson said that research indicated that customers will tolerate commercials for products in which the customers are interested.

Think About It

What is the flaw in the bank's thinking? If marketers at the bank know that commercials irritate customers, why do they have them on the bank's ATMs? How can they know whether customers are interested in the products being advertised when they walk up to the ATM? What other communication might be offered at this touch point that would be more positive for the company and less irritating to customers?

Source: "Bank of America Puts Ads on ATMs," by Sally Beatty. Copyright 2002 by Dow Jones & Co., Inc. Reprinted by permission of Dow Jones & Co., Inc. via the Copyright Clearance Center.

EXHIBIT 4-12

Unexpected Touch Points

As their name suggests, **unexpected touch points** are *unanticipated references to a brand that are beyond the control of the company.* They can be either positive or negative. One of the most powerful types is **word-of-mouth brand messages,** or *personal communication between customers or other stakeholders about a brand,* particularly when it is from a dissatisfied customer. A face-to-face personal message from someone you know can be more persuasive than ads and other MC messages, particularly if the point is supported by solid reasons. This kind of personal word of mouth has the power of **third-party credibility,** the believability of *people who are not affiliated with a brand and have nothing to gain or lose from its success or failure.* Third parties are often more believable than company sources because they have no vested interest in a brand.

Other stakeholders—investors and analysts, employees, suppliers, distributors, and government officials—can also be sources of unexpected messages. Although negative comments can be the most damaging messages a brand faces, unexpected positive word-of-mouth messages from any of these sources can be powerful testimony on behalf of the brand.

The media also produce unexpected touch points by writing about a brand or company. In almost all product categories today—from cooking to computers—there are experts who write and talk about products. Publicity releases generate brand touch points, but companies have no control over what stories these releases inspire the media to produce. A good example is a major utility company that announced it was requesting a multimillion-dollar rate increase and later sent out a press release saying it was going to spend $25 million sponsoring the Olympics. The Olympic sponsorship release appeared the day after the rate increase announcement and resulted in dozens of angry letters to the editor from customers. Because of the timing, many customers thought the rate increase was going to pay for the sponsorship, which made them very unhappy—a major unexpected touch point for this company. As will be explained in Chapter 17 on PR and publicity, although companies cannot control unexpected touch points, there are things they can do to anticipate and influence them.

Customer-Initiated Touch Points

A communication area that marketing departments often overlook is the **customer-initiated touch point,** *an interaction that occurs whenever a customer or prospect contacts a company.* As the communication model in Figure 4-4 shows, customers and prospects can be the source of brand messages in the same way as a company and its MC agencies. In other words, marketing communication can be two-way communication as well as one way. At first glance, the customer-initiated touch-point model may look similar to the MC model shown in Figure 4-1. A close look, however, reveals the differences. The major difference is that the source is now the customer or stakeholder, rather than the brand, which becomes the receiver. Likewise, the messages and the channels of communication are different.

Managing the response to customer-initiated touch points is a critical part of IMC because these contacts, like intrinsic brand contacts, occur primarily with current customers and thus significantly impact customer retention. Most customer-initiated touch points involve complaints or inquiries about product usage. Contacts are made by angry or frustrated customers who may stop using the

FIGURE 4-4

This is a basic communication model transformed to depict customer-initiated brand communication.

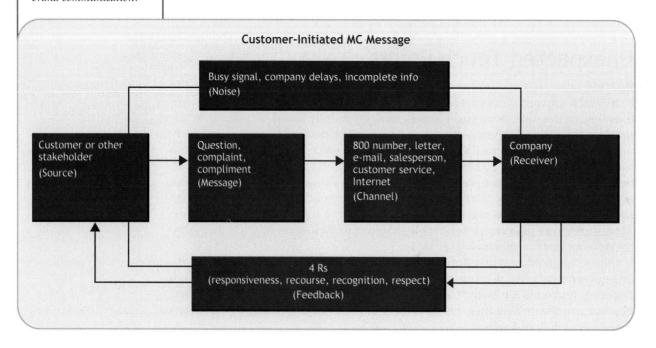

brand if they aren't satisfied. How a company responds can significantly impact the repurchase decisions of these customers.

The new communication technologies make it easier for customers to contact a company. At the same time, to show they are customer focused, more and more companies are inviting customers and prospects to contact them by advertising their 800 numbers and e-mail and website addresses on packages and in many of their other MC messages. Many companies, however, do a poor job of responding to customer-initiated messages. Studies on e-mail and phone contacts have found that the majority of company responses are rated only fair or poor.[14] One of the main problems facing companies today is how to cost-effectively interact with, and have a purposeful dialogue with, customers.

Interactivity

To create long-term, profitable relationships, integrated MC programs use **interactivity,** or *two-way communication that sends and receives messages from customers and other stakeholders.* IMC interactivity does *not* mean merely collecting the names and addresses of customers and potential customers in order to send them more and more brand messages. It *does* mean learning about customers in order to have a **purposeful dialogue** with them, *communication that is mutually beneficial for the customer and the company.*

Companies talk a great deal about creating a dialogue with customers. But in too many cases their brand communication is intrusive and irritating and thus perceived as self-serving and providing no added value for the customer. Marketers obviously want to tell customers about products and persuade them to buy. For the communication to be mutually useful, however, the customer must want to hear about the products and must choose to be exposed to this information, as the FM Global ad in Exhibit 4-13 demonstrates.

Companies should not stimulate and facilitate interactivity indiscriminately. The gathering of feedback should be done selectively, for not all brand relationships are equal, and having a dialogue with stakeholders always costs money. One of the early mistakes made by companies using the internet was inviting everyone to talk to them. Many responders were not customers or potential customers but merely people surfing the internet looking for something to do. Few companies can afford unproductive interactivity.

An easy and useful thing that a marketer can do to ensure that customers perceive the dialogue to be purposeful is

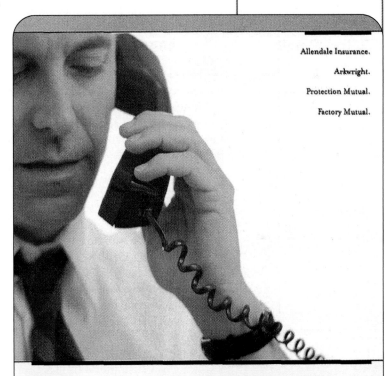

EXHIBIT 4-13

In purposeful communication, companies listen as well as speak to customers. Think about the last time you contacted a company. Was the company a good listener?

Allendale Insurance.

Arkwright.

Protection Mutual.

Factory Mutual.

IT'S AMAZING WHAT CAN HAPPEN WHEN YOU LISTEN TO YOUR CUSTOMERS.

Here's what you told us. You want a business partner with outstanding global resources and unmatched flexibility to solve your particular issues. With loss control engineering that can impact the bottom line. Streamlined communications, expanded capacity and responsive claim support. And here's how we responded. FM Global. The merged company of Allendale, Arkwright, Protection Mutual and Factory Mutual. Four organizations have converged to form one truly remarkable company. **Securing the future of your business.**

FM Global

www.fmglobal.com or 800-343-7722.

to ask customers what information they want about a brand, when and where they want it, and in what form. This is especially true for B2B marketers selling complex goods and services in which there are many product variations. Some customers prefer receiving brand information by mail, others electronically; some wish to meet with sales representatives only on certain days. Unless a marketer asks for this information and makes it available to everyone in the company who has contact with these customers, customers will not perceive companies as being respectful of their time.

The Four Rs of Purposeful Dialogue

To be successful, purposeful dialogue must embody the four Rs of interactivity that customers are looking for: *recourse, recognition, responsiveness,* and *respect.*

- *Recourse* A major concern of most customers is how to avoid risk when buying a product. What are their options after buying—that is, what recourse do they have if they don't like the product, if it doesn't work properly, or if it breaks? **Recourse** is *easy access to someone who can solve a problem.* How companies handle complaints, for example, affects repeat purchases. This aspect of marketing communication is second only to product quality in building customer loyalty. The easier it is for customers to get questions answered and problems dealt with, the more likely they are to develop good relationships with a company. The Bombay Company, a furniture manufacturer and retailer, has a no-questions-asked policy. Says President and CEO Robert Nourse, "We'll take the thing back with no hassle, no questions, no guff about 'Where's the receipt?' The cost of that is peanuts compared with what you gain in customer loyalty."[15]

- *Recognition* Customers and other stakeholders like to be personally recognized; that is one of the first steps in a relationship. In IMC, **customer recognition** means *company acknowledgment of purchases and of the customer's interaction history with the company.* You remember conversations you have had with friends. For a brand relationship to be effective, there must be some way to nurture that same kind of memory. This applies to product categories in which customer names are automatically collected in the course of doing business, such as most services, most B2B categories, and most major consumer purchases (cars, appliances, insurance, mortgages). Collecting such information makes it possible to develop a personalized message strategy, one that is more welcome than the usual anonymous mass media ad.[16]

  An even better type of recognition occurs when a company not only knows a customer's transaction history but incorporates references to it (when appropriate) into future communications with that customer: customers who are frequent buyers receive special recognition, and customers who had problems with the company receive empathetic attention. Consumers, however, will see through insincere recognition. In direct-mail solicitations, for instance, companies often address a potential customer by name. If the company has had no relationship with the customer, the person being contacted will recognize this familiarity as a ploy.

- *Responsiveness* Merely providing customers a toll-free number or an e-mail address so they can easily reach the company is not being responsive. Responsiveness occurs when a company representative listens to a customer and stays with the customer until the problem is solved or next steps are agreed to. In other words, **responsiveness** is *a reaction that produces customer satisfaction after a customer-initiated company contact.* The amount of time elapsing between when a product is ordered and when it is received, or between when a complaint is made and when a reply is received, sends a strong message. The shorter the elapsed time, the more responsive a company is seen to be. Texas Instruments receives approximately 200,000 inquiries a year. Over 95 percent are answered within 2 hours and nearly all within 24 hours.[17]

- *Respect* Howard Gossage, a partner in a San Francisco advertising agency in the 1950s and 1960s, has gone down in advertising history as one of the most insightful and intelligent people to work in advertising.[18] Among his many insights was the idea that a marketer's audience is more important than the product or brand. Gossage preached that, without respect for the audience, a company's advertising is sure to be a waste of money. **Respect** means *consideration* and not hammering customers with advertisements and other messages in which they have little interest.

EXHIBIT 4-14

High tech customers generally have a good feeling when they see this logo. One reason is because the company is very responsive.

Focusing on customers does not mean smothering them with brand contacts. Customers aren't interested in interrupting their lives to receive brand messages, in idly chatting with marketers, or in continually being offered a product or line extension that they don't need. Typical B2B customers, for example, receive between 20 and 60 pieces of mail each business day—the last thing they want is more "junk" mail. They resent intrusive messages and are creating more and more defense mechanisms against them. They will be more willing to be part of a commercial relationship if it is clear that the company respects them and their time.

In a focus group of business customers of a major computer company that had recently discovered database marketing, group members were quick to say how intrusive this company's brand messages had become. The company had been bombarding customers with sales calls, customer satisfaction surveys, new-product information, and "courtesy calls." When the company was mentioned, one of the respondents said he used the firm's software and

> "People read what interests them. Sometimes it's advertising."
>
> Howard Gossage, *The Book of Gossage*

hardware but if he received one more disruptive call from the company he would switch to a different brand, no matter how much the cost. He was tired, he said, of being bothered by this company.

Fifteen minutes later in this same discussion, group members were asked if they would attend a half-day seminar sponsored by this computer company. One of the first people to say "yes" was the person who had threatened to drop the company. When asked why the change in attitude, he explained that he could schedule the seminar at his convenience. In other words, he was willing to give the company a half-day of his time on *his* schedule but not two minutes on *the company's* schedule.

Companies that have a purposeful dialogue with their customers listen and respond to customers and do not constantly bombard them with "sales" messages. Herb Kelleher, CEO of Southwest Airlines, explains in one sentence why Southwest is known for great customer service: "We don't have a Marketing Department, we have a Customer Department." Southwest's emphasis on the people part of its marketing effort has created a 360-degree view of the whole brand, one that creates a total brand experience based on all brand messages, through all channels, and at all touch points.[19] Southwest understands the importance of company-customer touch points.

A FINAL NOTE: CREATING STICKY COMMUNICATION

A website is "sticky" if the site keeps the attention of a visitor for a longer-than-average period of time. Sticky communication gets attention and gets remembered. Communication is also sticky if it contributes to relationship building and creates customer loyalty over time. How can you know whether your messages are sticky? The answer is by using real-time feedback to monitor communication.

In the past, feedback that could be used to track the impact of marketing communication was limited to periodic customer-tracking studies and ad hoc market research surveys. Today, the concept and processes of acquiring feedback include ongoing responses through dialogue and customer-initiated communication. As you will learn in Chapter 5, in most buying situations there are numerous steps, and at each step it is possible to involve customers and get feedback in order to know what customers are thinking and planning to do. Also, brand relationships encourage interactions and dialogue, each of which creates a feedback opportunity for brand messages.

New telecommunication and computer technologies have made it more cost-effective to listen to customers, record their comments, and facilitate their questions, complaints, and concerns. They have also made it possible for customers and other stakeholders to initiate conversations with companies. Because of this two-way communication, the interaction between companies and their customers and stakeholders is more important than ever before.

Key Terms

brand-customer touch point 117
brand message 109
channel 106
clutter 114
company-created touch
 point 118
customer-initiated touch
 point 122
customer recognition 124
decoding 107
encoding 106

feedback 107
fields of experience 115
interactivity 123
intrinsic touch point 119
MC message 106
media vehicle 106
message 106
noise 107
purposeful dialogue 123
receiver 107
recourse 124

respect 125
responsiveness 124
sender 106
source 106
source credibility 109
strategic redundancy 115
target audience 114
third-party credibility 121
unexpected touch point 121
word-of-mouth brand
 messages 121

Key Point Summary

This chapter explains the basic source/message/media/receiver/feedback communication model and how it changes to accommodate the interactive dimensions of IMC.

Key Point 1: The Basic Communication Model

The basic communication model begins with a source (company/brand, agency), encoding (MC agencies) a message (ad), which is transmitted through media (media). Amid noise (physical and psychological distortion), a message is received then decoded (perceived and interpreted), which prompts some type of response (feedback).

Key Point 2: The Six Components of Marketing Communication

Each of the four Ps has a communication dimension and delivers messages on behalf of a brand. Media are the channels of communication that deliver the messages to the receiver, usually a customer or prospective customer, who must decode the message and interpret it. Noise includes all the distractions that might get in the way of the message delivery or the audience's reception of the message. Feedback is the response sent back to the company that sent the message. It is also the pivotal step in changing from a one-way communication approach to a two-way approach that invites dialogue between the company and customer.

Key Point 3: Brand–Customer Touch Points

Every exposure that a customer or other stakeholder has to a company or brand, no matter the nature or extent of the exposure, is a brand-customer touch point. These touch points may be created by the company or they may be intrinsic to the process of doing business with the company or brand. Some of them are unexpected and uncontrolled. The often overlooked customer-initiated touch point is particularly important in creating customer dialogue.

EXHIBIT 4-15
Target builds its touch points on its strong brand identity.

Lessons Learned

Key Point 1: The Basic Communication Model

a. List the key elements in a basic communication model and the order in which they occur.
b. What is the difference between encoding and decoding?
c. Using the communication-based model of marketing, analyze the opening case, and explain how the various elements in the case fit into the model.

Key Point 2: The Six Components of Marketing Communication

a. Explain the statement "Everything a company does, and sometimes what it doesn't do, can send a powerful brand message."
b. How do product, price, and place brand messages differ? Identify your favorite brand, and give an example of how each type of message impacts on your perception of that brand.

c. Develop a list of products for which your perception of *value* is the most important decision factor influencing your decision to buy them. Then create a list of products that you buy because of their *price* and another because of *perceived quality*. What are the differences among the three lists? What do these lists say about your personality and values?

d. How are messages delivered in an IMC program?

e. Give an example of a nontraditional media opportunity that you have experienced. Was it effective in commanding your attention?

f. In one of the magazines you read, find an advertisement that you think is confusing. Explain why decoding the meaning of this ad gave you problems.

g. Explain how perception works. What does it mean to say that perception is reality?

h. What role does purposeful dialogue have in building a brand? What brand-customer touch points offer the greatest opportunity for purposeful dialogue?

i. Does interactivity strengthen or weaken a brand relationship? Explain.

Key Point 3: Brand-Customer Touch Points

a. Define the term *brand-customer touch point*. Explain the differences among the four types of touch points. Analyze the HB Ice Cream case for examples of touch points. If one or more is not discussed explicitly in the case, then recommend a way to introduce that element into next year's campaign.

b. Working in a small group, develop for your college or university a list of touch points that a potential student might encounter. Analyze the messages delivered at those points, and prioritize them in terms of their importance to prospective students.

c. Explain what happened when you or a friend called a company to complain about a product. Did the company make use of this touch point to get additional feedback from you?

Chapter Challenge

Writing Assignment

You have been asked to advise a club on how to manage its communication program. Develop for the club its own communication model, and explain how the model can help the club identify its communication problems and develop better communication programs and activities.

Presentation Assignment

For a small retail business, develop a presentation that shows how understanding the communication model can help the retailer improve communication with customers and prospects. In an outline, list the key points you want to present. Give the presentation to your class or record it on videotape (audiotape is also an option) to turn in to your instructor, along with the outline.

Internet Assignment

Have you ever had a bad experience when traveling by air? Or a good experience? Did you make an effort to complain to or compliment the company? A number of websites handle complaints on behalf of travelers for a fee, particularly complaints that can result in ticket refunds. The U.S. Department of Transportation has an electronic in-basket for complaints about two particular topics: airline pricing and overbooking (www.oig.dot.gov). The Better Business Bureau of New York also compiles complaints from its site (www.newyork.bbb.org) and relays them to the Department of Transportation. The travel agency One-Travel.com has set up a website (www.1travel.com) with complaint channels and consumer-affairs materials. Consult two of these websites, and compile their advice and your own ideas about how to write a complaint letter and a compliment letter.

Chapter

5

Consumer Response

Key Points in This Chapter

1. Who are these people called consumers?
2. How do consumers respond to marketing communication?
3. How does the consumer's brand decision making work?
4. How do MC messages affect that decision-making process?

Chapter Perspective

Reactions, Responses, and Decisions

Imagine you were at a party last weekend and you heard a new CD. Your friend mentioned it was by a great new group and she really likes their music. Two days later as you were leafing through *Rolling Stone,* you saw a review of this CD and the group. Next day you were in a record store and you saw a poster announcing the group's new CD release. A marketer would be interested to know about the various types of messages you received about this group and its new CD, but what the marketer *really* wants to know is *how you responded* to those messages.

Your response might go something like this: The CD caught your attention when you heard it at the party and sparked your curiosity about the group. When your friend said the new group was great, that made you even more interested because you respect your friend's opinion. Seeing the

Rolling Stone review heightened your interest, as you remembered you liked the sound. Finally, seeing the poster in the record store brought your positive impressions of this CD back to mind and motivated you to at least listen to it again in the store and possibly buy it.

The previous chapter outlined the communication process, a process that ends with a response or feedback. Even though much of the reaction to marketing communication messages is internalized and hard to dig out through formal research, we know that these responses occur and that they drive people's decision making. However, before you can understand how MC messages work to impact consumer attitudes and behaviors that lead to a particular brand choice, you need a more general understanding of how consumers go about making brand decisions.

CUSTOMERS LOVE THE STARBUCKS EXPERIENCE

EFFECTIVENESS CASE

Besides home, school, and work, where do people gather to meet friends and relax in a comfortable environment? Seattle-based Starbucks Coffee has made that place a Starbucks coffee shop for some 22 million customers a week.

Starbucks is now a global brand. With more than 6,400 stores, including 1,400 in 30 countries outside North America, Starbucks has become a major player in the coffee market. On a fast growth track, the company hopes to have 10,000 stores by the end of 2005.

Starbucks sells hot and cold coffees, espressos, mochas, lattes, au laits, cappuccinos, frappucinos (a frozen coffee blended with a variety of flavors), and even Chai and Tazo tea, as well as pastries, coffee beans, espresso machines, and other gift items. The product line varies with the location and the climate. But the constant focus is on customer service and on the quality of the coffee—the beans, how they are roasted, how they are mixed and flavored, as well as how the coffee is rotated out and kept fresh in the stores. All brewed coffee is less than an hour old when it is served. The emphasis on a quality coffee experience makes it possible for the company to charge more than two dollars for what used to be seen as a commodity product—a cup of "joe."

Who Are These Starbuck Customers?

Starbucks originally targeted young college-age people typical of the Seattle coffeehouse culture.

EXHIBIT 5-1

Then those people grew up and became young, upwardly mobile executives. Yuppies and baby boomers—another group that connects with the Starbucks experience—like to celebrate their affluence with little treats like gourmet coffee. Both groups are less interested in the bar scene and more attracted to environments where they can hang out, listen to music, and visit with friends. Both groups value Starbucks as much for the coffee shop experience as for the coffee itself.

How Do People Decide to Go to Starbucks?

Buying a fancy gourmet coffee drink is definitely not a basic need but rather an expressive choice that reflects customers' aspirations as well as their desire for a relaxing social experience. Starbucks has almost single-handedly upgraded the tired image of the 1960s smoky coffeehouse into a cozy French sidewalk café or Italian espresso bar. In the United States it has created a small cultural revolution in people's social behavior.

Starbucks also makes the decision to choose Starbucks easy by having lots of convenient locations. The master plan calls for a Starbucks on every corner—or nearly. In New York City, for example, there are more than 300 Starbucks coffee shops. The location of that corner, however, is very important as the company seeks to make convenience part of the Starbucks mystique. You can also find Starbucks at airports, bookstores, and hotels through alliances with such companies as Barnes & Noble, Sheraton and Westin hotels, and United Airlines. And the Starbuck's frappuccino beverage is sold in supermarkets, as well as the coffee shops.

Starbucks Appeals to the Head and Heart

The Starbucks attraction is partly head and partly heart. On the cognitive level (head), Starbucks has transformed customers' preferences by teaching them what good coffee tastes like. Starbucks has established a worldwide standard for great coffee, and its customers simply know that its coffee tastes better. It has also profited from the growing market for gourmet coffee, which has made traditional coffee from long-time coffee brands such as Maxwell House and Folgers seem less desirable.

Customers also choose Starbucks because they like the company's community focus and social responsibility platform. To quickly build a customer base for each new store, a store connects with a local charity and gives free drinks and donates tips and other funds to that organization. The strategy of connecting immediately with a local cause helps overcome the image of Starbucks as a large, impersonal global chain.

Another reason customers choose to visit Starbucks is the staff. Starbucks employees are called *baristas*, Italian for bar server (somewhat like a sommelier in a fancy French restaurant who helps you choose your wine). The company believes that every dollar invested in employees shows up in customer satisfaction and, ultimately, on the bottom line. The company's generous employee benefits packages include health care, dental care, stock options, training and motivational programs, career counseling, and product discounts for all workers, full-time as well as part-time. Employees also are encouraged to play an active role in the environment movement, as well as in other local communities causes, and are given time off for these activities.

In line with the environmental awareness of both of its target audiences (boomers and yuppies), Starbucks donates money to the Earth Day Network ($50,000 in 2003) and has in-store promotions for local Earth Day activities. Its customized cup sleeve carries an environmental message and the Earth Day Network website. Starbucks' director of environmental affairs explained that the company tries "to reduce its impact on the planet" through programs such as giving away coffee grounds for garden compost. In 2003, hundreds of Starbucks partners were involved in Earth Day activities, such as

- Teaming up with Earth Fest in Dallas in a downtown area beautification project.
- Joining with Denver Urban Gardens in an effort to beautify the city's parks.
- Partnering with Friends of Morningside Park, the Columbia University Earth Coalition, and the New York City Parks Department on the seventh annual Morningside Park cleanup project.

Problems in Java Heaven?

International success can bring headaches. In some countries, anti-U.S. protesters of Operation Iraqi Freedom made Starbucks a target. Although most of its domestic stores are company owned, its international strategy uses joint ventures or licenses to other companies, which own and operate the local stores. This strategy is designed to make the chain responsive to local concerns. Even Arab-owned stores, however, were closed for awhile because of anti-U.S. protests over the Iraq and Palestine situations.

Because Starbucks has become a cultural corporate icon, it also attracts critics of large corporations. There is a website entitled "Ihatestarbucks.com." Naomi Klein's book *No Logo* is critical of Starbucks for its coffee-harvesting conditions and some of its employee practices.[1]

The Bottom Line

Starbucks started as a six-store Seattle coffee-bean retailer. But the vision of its chairman and CEO, Howard Schultz, was to follow in McDonald's footsteps. Schultz has built the Starbucks brand, on a minuscule budget and with little advertising, from a small business to a global corporation with some $4 billion in annual revenues. The company's messages—the ones with the most impact on customers—are delivered in customer service and by employees who operate like ambassadors, creating strong personal relationships with their regular customers. The response by satisfied customers is keeping Starbucks on a roll on Main Streets around the world.

Source: Helen Jung, "Starbucks' Growth Risks Backlash in War Protests," The Detroit News, April 22, 2003, <www.detnews.com/2003/busines/0304/22/b04-143736.htm>; "Starbucks Coffee Celebrates Earth Day with $50,000 Commitment," April 17, 2003, CSR Wire, <www.csrwire.com/article.cgi/ 1758.html>; Rick Aristotle Munarriz, "Krispy Kreme vs. Starbucks," The Motley Fool, <www.Fool.com>, April 22, 2003; Jack Sirard, "Starbucks Has a Way of Beating Pessimists," The Sacramento Bee, April 22, 2003, <www.sacbee.com/content/business/v-print/story/6497865p-74>; "Making Customers Come Back for More," Fortune, March 16, 1998, pp. 156–157.

PROSPECTS AND CUSTOMERS, CONSUMERS AND BUSINESS BUYERS

The phrase *consumer behavior* is used to refer to how people and organizations think about, buy, and use products. (Companies *consume* just as individuals do, however, the word consumer generally refers to individuals.) Marketing communication managers are particularly interested in how consumers' thoughts and behaviors develop *as a response to MC messages*. For marketers to design brand messages that elicit responses and impact someone's decision-making process, they first need to understand to whom they are talking—current customers or prospects, consumers or businesses—and how those audiences respond to MC messages. Different types of consumers respond to MC messages in different ways, and MC managers must recognize these differences, as well as understand the reasons behind them.

Prospects versus Current Customers

The brand decision-making process of a person who is considering a brand for the first time is different from the process of someone who has purchased that brand before. A **prospect** is *a person who has never bought a brand but might be interested in it*. A **customer** is *a person who has purchased a brand at least once within a designated period*.

From a company perspective, motivating a prospect to buy for the first time is the process of acquiring a customer and thus requires an *acquisition strategy*, an important objective of which is creating brand awareness. Motivating a customer to make repeat purchases is a *retention strategy*. Here, rather than focusing marketing communication on brand awareness (since it has already been achieved to some extent), MC messages keep the brand top-of-mind and motivate more frequent purchases.

One of the biggest mistakes a company can make is to take for granted that current customers will continue to make repeat purchases. Acquisition and retention call for different types of message strategies because prospects and customers use different pathways in making a brand decision. Persuading current customers to make repeat purchases is easier and less costly than motivating a prospect to buy for the first time, but it still requires some strategic marketing communication effort.

Consumers versus Business Buyers

Prospects and customers exist in both the B2B and the B2C markets. In B2B communication, the buying decisions of prospects or current customers call for levels of involvement and cognitive processing different from those in typical B2C communication. Most business decisions makers, for example, do more research and analysis than do consumers, and they use more of a cognitive approach than an emotional approach. The BASF ad in Exhibit 5-2 illustrate a B2B marketing communication campaign that uses a cognitive (problem-solution) message. Other differences between consumer and business decision making include the following:

- Business buying decisions generally involve inputs from more than one person. The larger the decision is, the more people and departments are involved. Some businesspeople have buying authority; others can greatly influence the buying decision. Technical people such as engineers may not actually purchase equipment, but a company's high-tech buyer probably consults them before choosing computer and software systems. Identifying who has the buying authority is usually not as difficult as determining who influences the buying decision. To maximize sales, B2B marketers need to target brand messages to both buyers and influencers.

- Most businesses buy goods in larger quantities than consumers do, so the average business transaction is generally worth considerably more than the average consumer transaction. In B2B marketing, the high cost of personal selling—the most expensive MC function—can be justified with other forms of MC messages used to support these personal selling efforts.

- Large business transactions often affect other activities within a company; therefore, business buying carries higher risk than consumer buying. Minimizing risk is always an objective of business buyers and something that B2B marketers must keep in mind when creating brand messages.

- Many business buying decisions are based on responses to requests-for-proposals (RFPs). A business that wants to make a major purchase invites companies to bid on satisfying a stated need. The internet makes it possible for companies to send their RFPs to more bidders and makes the response process faster than ever before. RFPs form a common business platform on the internet and have even moved into B2C marketing with the success of such companies as Priceline.com.

Create a new world where lightweight plastics can outfly metals.

Aerospace designers are limited by their materials, not their dreams.

At BASF, we looked at the design limitations of metals and saw the need for a radically new generation of materials. The result: strong, lightweight, carbon fiber reinforced plastics. These Advanced Composite Materials will enable future designs to carry more, faster, farther.

In one industry after another, from aerospace to automotive, our broad-based technologies help us create new worlds by seeing in new ways.

The Spirit of Innovation

BASF

EXHIBIT 5-2
Knowing that manufacturers often can choose either metal or plastic for certain products, this brand message created by the chemical products company BASF urges adoption of its "radically new generation of materials."

What Impacts Decision Making?

Customers and prospects are influenced by a number of cultural and social forces, as well as personal factors. All of these combine to establish the context within which marketing communication is delivered and the way people respond to the messages.

The Sociocultural Context

Culture—*group values based on traditions and distinctive history*—includes such things as sets of common beliefs, attitudes, and values. Cultural values that relate to clothing, music, food, and drink can determine the appropriateness (or inappropriateness) of marketing certain types of products. For example, marketing bikinis and alcoholic beverages might not be appropriate in Muslim societies, no matter what the brand message. **Society** is *a group of people who live together and organize their lives as a community*. Relationships result from intimate bonds, such as family ties, but they are also a product of a sense of community. IMC programs attempt to build commercial relationships through messages that connect people with a brand and with a community of other brand users.

Companionship is another aspect of the social context that affects how people respond to a message. We know that people respond to, and value, what their family and friends say about brands. For example, in the opening story about the CD, an important message came from a friend who knew the group and liked its music. Word-of-mouth messages can be extremely influential on someone considering a purchase decision, especially if they come from a person who is better informed or more experienced with the brand or product.

Social class is *a ranking of people in a society by factors such as family history, occupation, education, and income.* Some societies, such as India, are highly stratified with clearly defined social classes. Other societies, such as the United States, are more fluid, and to some extent people can move up as a result of their own initiative and accomplishments—and most expect to do so. In the United States, therefore, aspirational messages—those that present an image or product associated with a group to which the customer *wishes* to belong—usually strike a chord, especially among people roughly identified as being in the middle class. The following list identifies the most common social classes in the United States and indicates their estimated size:[2]

- *Upper upper* (1 percent of the population): The highest class, usually represented by "old money" and well-known families.
- *Upper* (about 2 percent): Professionals and businesspeople who have achieved financial success.
- *Middle* (about 43 percent): Professionals, small-business owners, and corporate managers with comfortable incomes.
- *Working class* (about 38 percent): Lower-middle class or blue-collar workers who earn an average pay.
- *Upper lower* (about 9 percent): The "working poor," who perform unskilled labor and menial work for minimal wages.
- *Lower* (about 7 percent): People who dwell in poverty and are often unemployed and on welfare.

Some of the most powerful motivating forces in brand decision making are the people who influence customers' decision making. Sociologists use the term **reference group** to indicate *the associations and organizations with which people identify or to which they belong and which influence their attitudes and behaviors.* For customers, reference groups include family, friends, fellow workers, recognized category experts, as well as well-known people such as athletes, entertainers, and politicians. For businesses, reference groups include professional associations, brand leaders in their product category, consultants, and important customers. Messages from these people, particularly word-of-mouth testimonials, can be an extremely persuasive form of communication. Hallmark often depicts reference groups such as family and friends in their advertising (see Exhibit 5-3).

Reference groups can be grouped into five categories: personal, membership, experts, aspirational, and disassociative:

Reference Group Categories

Personal	Family, friends, co-workers
Membership	Clubs, churches, schools
Experts	Opinion leaders, consultants, leading professionals in category
Aspirational	Famous entertainers, athletes, politicians
Disassociative	Counterculture, gangs, antisocial people

That last group is a *negative* reference group: most people generally want to do and buy the *opposite* of what members of a disassociative group do and buy.

E X H I B I T   5 - 3

This Hallmark commercial opens on a birthday party for grandpa, a curmudgeon who isn't happy with anything until his 7-year-old granddaughter recites a poem and then hands him a Hallmark card. The words of the poem, which we later realize are the words in the card, bring a shocked silence to the family who anticipate a bad reaction from grandpa. Instead, the words of the card bring a smile to grandpa's face. "It's your birthday and you're 75, some people wonder how you're still alive . . . Even though I know it's not your grumpy style, Happy Birthday. Would it kill you to smile."

Marketing communication often situates a message in a social context that uses the reference group as a cue. For example, a country club or a sports team may connect with an audience's sense of affiliation, the message being, "I want to be like them." Research has shown that reference groups play a big role in the decision to purchase products that are publicly used or consumed—such as clothes, cars, watches, golf clubs, skis, rental cars. That is why celebrities and other highly visible people are used in marketing communication for these products. Even disassociative groups can be used effectively in marketing, as in the gross-out behavior of characters in some antismoking campaigns (see the IMC in Action box p. 160).

Personal Factors

In addition to age, gender, and education—other personal factors—needs and wants, attitudes, opinions and beliefs, personality, and motivation—affect how people approach a buying decision. Some people are experimenters and rush to try something new; others are risk averse and hold back until a new product has a track record. Because every person is an individual, the closer a marketing communication can speak to a person as an individual, the more likely is the message to ring true. Here are some of the key personal factors that affect how people respond to MC messages.

Needs and Wants   A recent Blondie comic strip opened with Blondie saying to Dagwood, "Dear, I think we need new carpets and drapes in the living room." He responded, "What we need is a bigger bank account!" She answered, "Dagwood . . . There you go again . . . confusing something we need with something YOU want (see Figure 5-1)."[3] Demand for goods and services is motivated by human **needs and wants,** which are *biological and psychological motivations that drive actions.* While both biological needs (such as for food or shelter) and psychological ones (such as for love or respect) require more immediate response, wants

F I G U R E   5 - 1

How many of your buying decisions are driven by needs vs. wants?

Reprinted with Special Permission of KING FEATURES Syndicate.

F I G U R E   5 - 2

This model lists some marketing insights derived from Maslow's hierarchy of needs.

Source: Michael Soloman, *Consumer Behavior* (Upper Saddle River, NJ: Prentice-Hall, 2002), p. 77.

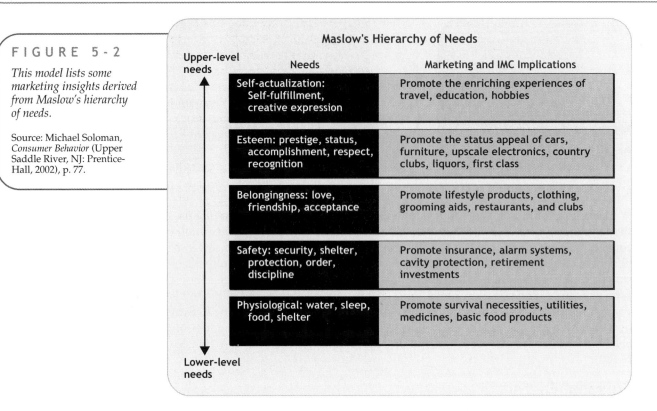

command a lot of attention in consumers' minds. Needs are what we feel we *must* have; wants are what we would *like* to have.

Marketing communicators have found the **hierarchy of needs** described by the psychologist Abraham Maslow to be a help in analyzing the strength of these needs and wants (see Figure 5-2).[4] **Maslow's hierarchy of needs** is *an arrangement of human needs and wants listed in the order in which, according to Maslow, people satisfy them.* According to Maslow, only when basic, low-level needs are satisfied can people consider wants at higher levels in the hierarchy. At the base are physiological needs for water, food, clothing, and shelter. Above them are needs for safety, followed by psychological wants for belongingness, esteem, and self-actualization (finding challenge in new ideas and creative impulses).

Marketers must understand needs and wants because the marketing concept is based on the notion that companies should sell products designed to meet customers' needs and wants, not whatever is easiest for the company to produce. The next personal factors are important because they guide brand responses:

Attitudes, Opinions, and Beliefs An **attitude** is *a general disposition or orientation toward objects, people, and ideas usually accompanied by negative or positive judgments.* An **opinion** is *a specific judgment that is emotionally neutral.* A **belief** is *a thought or idea based on knowledge.* Unlike attitudes, which are charged with emotion, opinions and beliefs are more cognitively based and tend to be emotionally neutral. Attitudes, opinions, and beliefs reflect a philosophy of life, and marketing communications may be designed to align with various philosophies in order to be relevant to specific types of consumers, who may then respond favorably to the brand message. Changing consumers' attitudes—especially turning a negative attitude about a brand to a more positive view—is a challenging task for marketers, but many campaigns do achieve this result.

There is a social dimension to opinion, as the opening CD story demonstrated when the friend made a comment about the new music group. Sociologists refer to **opinion leaders** as *people to whom others turn for advice or information.* Lawrence Feick and Linda Price developed the concept of "market maven" to describe people who are actively involved in passing on marketplace information,[5] particularly about trends such as new fashions, music groups, and computer programs and games. MC programs are sometimes designed to reach these people specifically, because marketers know that they will influence others.

Motivations   The response to an MC message also depends on a person's **motivations,** which are *internal impulses that when stimulated initiate some type of response.* Some motivations are transient—as when you secure a job interview and are motivated at that moment to purchase a new suit to impress your prospective employer. Other motivations are constant. Most people, for example, are consistently motivated by the desire to save money on purchases. That is why MC sales promotion offers such as "Save 25%" and "Free brush when you buy a large bottle of X shampoo" can motivate consumers.

HOW BRAND DECISION MAKERS RESPOND TO MC MESSAGES

If people rushed out and bought a product every time marketing managers ran a MC message, those managers would be thrilled. Alas, the world is not so simple. In fact, marketers struggle to figure out *which* MC messages, among the many customers receive, truly influenced customers' purchase decisions. People respond to marketing communication in a variety of ways, and sometimes it's difficult to make the connection between the message and the purchase. The task of evaluating the effectiveness of brand messages and the media used is easier in direct marketing because there are few variables between the message and the response. A number of factors, however, impact the response to advertising and public relations.

One problem in connecting a purchase to an MC message is that other marketing-mix factors may either improve or decrease the chance for a positive response. For example, the price may be too high, or the brand a customer usually prefers may *not* be carried in the store where the customer is shopping.

Hierarchy-of-Effects Models: The AIDA Sequence

The ability of advertising, public relations, and other marketing communication to generate a purchase may be moderated by intermediate responses. The idea that there are levels of communication response is presented as a *hierarchy of effects.* A **hierarchy-of-effects model** is *a description of a series of stages of response that brand decision makers move through.*

A classic hierarchy-of-effects model of message response is the AIDA sequence. **AIDA** is *an acronym identifying four persuasive steps or desired effects that a brand message might have on customers and prospects: attention, interest, desire, action.* The first effect is a brand message attracting the *attention* of a prospect (see Exhibit 5-4). The next effect is *interest* in the brand, and the third is *desire* for the brand. The final effect is *action,* which may be one of several responses in addition to an actual purchase, such as seeking more information, talking to others who have used the brand, visiting a store, or making a trial use (such as test driving a car) or sampling the product (such as tasting food in a supermarket).

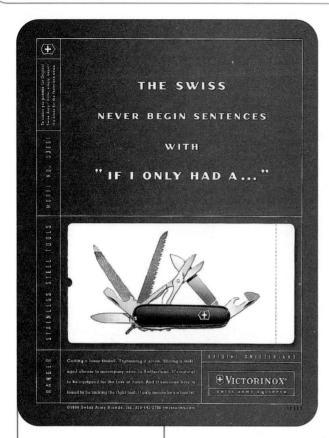

THE SWISS

NEVER BEGIN SENTENCES

WITH

"IF I ONLY HAD A..."

Cutting a loose thread. Tightening a screw. Slicing a well-aged cheese to accompany wine. In Switzerland, it's natural to be equipped for the task at hand. And if someone here is found to be lacking the right tool, it only means he's a tourist.

ORIGIN: SWITZERLAND

✚ VICTORINOX®
SWISS ARMY EQUIPPED

©1998 Swiss Army Brands, Inc. 800-442-2706 swissarmy.com

EXHIBIT 5-4

The headline of this ad for a Swiss knife is designed to capture attention and create interest by inviting readers to finish the sentence. The copy is designed to intensify desire, and the toll-free number is provided to stimulate action.

Effective marketing communication depends on brand messages that attract people's attention. Creative ideas like the AFLAC duck and the nonstop Energizer bunny build awareness because they help a brand message stand out. Marketers often use kittens, puppies, and babies in advertising because most people are drawn to them and they spark interest. Using a celebrity whom a brand's target audience finds compelling, such as the various people featured in the long-running "Got Milk" campaign, can also increase the interest and desire of prospects and customers. Sales promotion offers are particularly good at intensifying the action response.

Think/Feel/Do Models

Although the AIDA sequence appears to be linear, brand decision making is not always that predictable. More recent theories about buying behavior show that buyers don't always take the decision steps in a specific order. Another model (see Figure 5-3) identifies three general kinds of responses—thinking, feeling, and doing—and their components.[6] The order of think/feel/do responses, for example, varies by product category, type of buyer (business or consumer, customer or prospect), and buying situation, but most of all by level of *involvement*—the degree of personal relevance a product or message has for a decision maker.

Levels of Involvement

Products such as food staples (milk, bread, butter) and utility products (brooms, batteries, detergents, toilet tissue, gasoline) are perceived as **low-involvement products** (see Exhibit 5-5), *products that are relatively cheap, are bought frequently without much consideration, and are perceived as low risk.* In contrast, **high-involvement products,** such as cars and computers, are *products for which people perceive differences among brands and are willing to invest prepurchase decision-making energy.* Typically, such purchases are more expensive and have greater social consequences, and as such are perceived as high risk.

Most people approach *high*-involvement purchase decisions by "thinking" about them first. In contrast, the first response when considering a *low*-involvement product, such as a convenience or an impulse product, is likely to be "feeling" or even "doing." You buy a package of gum, for example, because you *feel* like having some gum. Or you see a magazine next to the cash register as you're checking out at a food store, and you reach over on an impulse and grab it without really thinking or feeling strongly about the decision.

Like decision making, messages can also be described as commanding different degrees of attention, concentration, and involvement. Messages for high-involvement products are likely to be detailed, quality assuring, and so on—if they link a brand promise to important personal goals, such as getting the highest-quality computer or the best price on a car. In contrast, messages for low-involvement products are often designed to stimulate impulsive purchase decisions for products like chewing gum and candy. Such messages are likely to emphasize "fun" or "convenience."

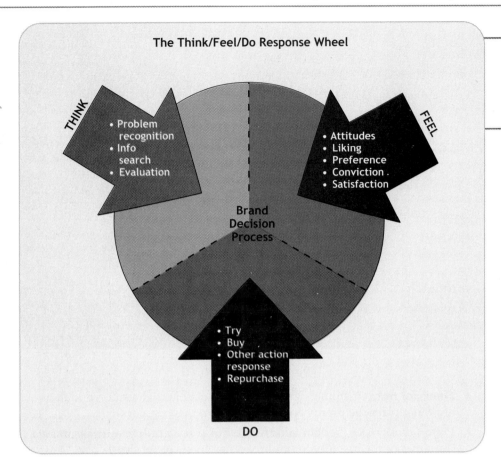

The Think/Feel/Do Response Wheel

THINK
- Problem recognition
- Info search
- Evaluation

FEEL
- Attitudes
- Liking
- Preference
- Conviction
- Satisfaction

Brand Decision Process

DO
- Try
- Buy
- Other action response
- Repurchase

FIGURE 5-3

What can cause the order of think/feel/do responses to vary?

Relevance   The key to determining the level of involvement is **relevance,** *the extent to which a product or its message is pertinent and connects with a customer's personal interests.* For example, Bally Total fitness offers samples of health and wellness products in its locker rooms and its instructors sometimes promote the products before and after classes. The products are provided by its promotion partners, such as Kraft, Colgate, Stouffer's Lean Cuisine, and Dove. Although the samples are designed to maximize the relevance of health and fitness products, some critics worry that Bally's program is too intrusive and question whether it may be negatively affecting consumer perceptions of not only the gym, but also the products.[7]

If you need a new pair of glasses, you will be more receptive to brand messages in this goods and service category than you otherwise would be. You'll want to make sure that the optometrist you select can competently provide glasses that match your prescription. You may also be concerned about the look of the glasses and picking out frames of the right style. The brand name on the frame is, for some, an important fashion statement. Personal relevance makes a new pair of glasses a high-involvement purchase. Message planners find these points of relevance by acquiring **customer insight,** which is *understanding how customers see themselves, the world around them, and the products and brands they use.*

Risk   High-involvement products, and the MC messages that communicate about them, represent above-average risk and expense. The risk factor, particularly for B2B and expensive consumer products, motivates customers to carefully evaluate brand choices. There are risks that both consumers and businesses try to minimize:[8]

No One Can Resist A Sunkist® Orange.

- *Financial risk:* Customers lose money when a brand doesn't work; they have to replace the product or spend extra to make it work.
- *Performance risk:* Product failures can cause other failures such as missed deadlines or the inability to produce other goods or services.
- *Physical risk:* The brand may hurt or injure those who use it.
- *Psychological risk:* The brand may not fit in well with the consumer's or company's self-image or corporate culture.
- *Social risk:* The brand may negatively affect the way others think of the customer.

By recognizing (through research) which of those risks apply to a company's product categories, marketers can design brand messages to minimize the perceived risk. For example, car manufacturers often emphasize the duration of their warranties. By knowing what types of risks most concern customers, companies can relate their brands' features and benefits to these risks and improve their chances of being purchased. The 3 Musketeers ad in Exhibit 5-6 reduces the risk of trying a reformulated version of this favorite old candy bar.

Shifts in Decision Making because of Involvement Not all brand decision-making situations motivate people to move through a hierarchy in the same way. To better understand how the order of thinking, feeling, and doing can vary, see whether you can determine which order of think/feel/do has been used in each of three scenarios (answers are at the end of the scenarios):

- **Scenario 1:** Bradley stopped at the drugstore on the way home from work to have a prescription filled. While checking out, he bought on impulse a copy of *Time* magazine. When he got home, he found himself reading the magazine rather than watching his favorite Thursday-night TV show. The next day he picked up from the floor one of the subscription cards that had fallen out of the magazine. After looking at the price and recalling that his checking account was in pretty good shape, he realized that subscribing to

EXHIBIT 5-6

The long-time favorite 3 Musketeers candy bar is changing its texture (fluffy) and the quality of its chocolate. To reassure loyal customers and minimize their risk in trying something new, this ad includes a coupon for a free candy bar.

the magazine would be cheaper in the long run than buying it from a store each week.

- **Scenario 2:** Liz and Mike needed an apartment in Atlanta, Georgia, where Mike was being transferred by his company. To make the decision on an apartment, the couple first determined how much they could spend each month on rent, then how much room they needed, and finally the part of town in which they wanted to live. Next they began looking at what was available that met their criteria. As they went through six different apartment units, they could tell that some were more comfortable and pleasing than others. Finally, after settling on the one that was second-closest to Mike's new office, they signed a contract and made a damage deposit.

- **Scenario 3:** Lindsay was very frugal with the money she earned. She had a credit card, for example, but made a point of paying off the balance every month to avoid finance charges. But for some time, she had been walking on her lunch hour past a store window close to her office. In the window was a beautiful leather jacket. One day, she was having lunch with a friend and pointed out the jacket. Her friend said she had one similar to it. That did it: Lindsay walked in, handed the clerk her credit card, and pointed to the jacket in the window. That evening, when she took the jacket out of its box, the first thing she saw was the price tag. She spent the rest of the evening trying to figure out how she was going to pay the credit-card bill that would come in two weeks and include the cost of the jacket.

(Answers: Scenario 1, do, feel, think. Scenario 2, think, feel, do. Scenario 3, feel, do, think.)

The think/feel/do model sets up several different message responses that can lead to a brand decision. The route taken depends, to a large extent, on involvement and the degree to which people find themselves elaborating on the message.

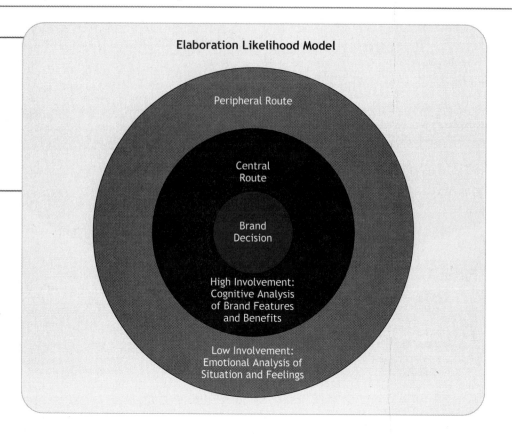

Elaboration Likelihood Model

The Elaboration Factor

It's been technically possible to have videophones since the 1960s. However, manufacturers of videophones for years were unable to create a market for these products. Why? We can answer that question by understanding how a persuasion model based on involvement—the elaboration likelihood model (ELM)—is used to help analyze customer behavior (see Figure 5-4).

In this context, **elaboration** refers to *the degree to which customers think about a message and relate the information to their own lives as they make purchase decisions.* Similar to the head and heart approaches, ELM proposes two paths that customers use in processing information about a product. They follow the *central route* when they are highly involved in the decision and the product is highly relevant. They follow the *peripheral route* when they are less involved and the product has a lower level of personal relevance.[8, 9]

In the case of videophones, manufacturers never explained these products in a way that was relevant to consumers and appealed to either the central or the peripheral routes of message processing. There was even a negative message associated with being unexpectedly "on camera." Today, however, wireless videophones are becoming popular items. Not surprising, they are being advertised to young people in ways that appeal to both their central and their peripheral processing routes. Ads emphasize the phones' mobility, which makes them more relevant than home-bound videophones. The phones are also shown as offering ways to have multiple interactions with friends (via virtual games and e-mail messages, as well as sending and receiving video pictures). Finally, the videophone is presented as a luxury item or status symbol, in contrast with the basic cellular phone, which has become a utility item.

Peripheral-route processing is based on message factors such as imagery, emotion, associations, celebrity spokespeople, and music—all of which can create

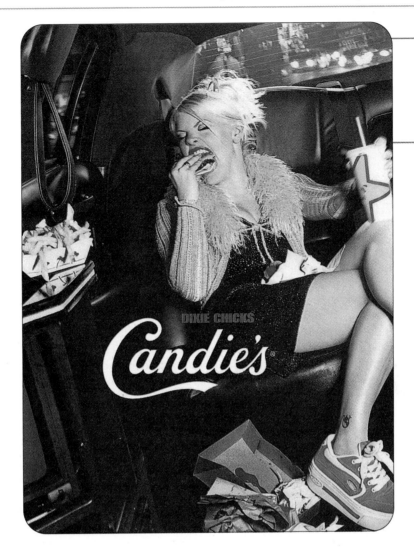

EXHIBIT 5-7
This strong image ad associates Candie's shoes with a specific lifestyle and type of celebrity.

interest in a message even if there is little interest in the product itself. In other words, the decision to like, buy, or try a product is based on factors peripheral to the product and its features. You usually don't think about product features, for example, when buying a soft drink. It may even be a totally impulsive purchase. Peripheral-route decisions are more passive and are often responses to emotional appeals, as well as to image and lifestyle advertising.

Event marketing, trade shows, and retailing use experiences and the environment to attract and focus people's attention, eliciting a type of peripheral processing similar to image and lifestyle advertising. MC messages directed at peripheral processing are designed to stimulate the senses without necessarily being informative. **Image messages,** for example, are *messages that deliver a desired representation or perception of a brand* (see Exhibit 5-7). This type of message operates through association cues. The message triggers an association between a quality (such as sexiness, speed, or strength) and the brand.[10]

Although buying a videophone may seem to involve mostly central-route processing, you may find something else in the back of your mind nagging at you as you mull over such a decision. What if you're having a bad-hair day when the phone rings? What if you aren't dressed when the phone rings? These peripheral thoughts have been found to be resistance points to be overcome by marketers intent on creating demand for videophones.

HOW BRAND DECISION MAKING WORKS

People do not make brand decisions in a vacuum, nor does everyone act in the same way. People move through a four-step decision process (see Figure 5-5). First they recognize a problem or an opportunity. Then they evaluate brand alternatives. Next, they decide what action to take. Finally, they evaluate the purchase decision or other action taken. Each of these steps is explained below.

Step 1: Recognizing a Problem or an Opportunity

Purchase decision-making begins with recognizing a problem that creates a need (or want) or recognizing an opportunity that will provide a benefit not previously thought of or considered possible. The first of the following two examples shows how a brand message is used to make prospects aware of an opportunity; the second shows how a brand message can intervene in problem solving.

How do you take and use class notes? If you are like most students, you see note-taking not as a problem but rather as a common, necessary task. You know how to do it and are satisfied with the results. Then you read an article in your campus paper about a new software product that promises to make note-taking easier and to help improve your grades. The brand message in the article (which resulted from a publicity release sent from Easy-Notes software company) presents an *opportunity*. Easy-Notes placed the article in campus newspapers because it knew its brand message would reach the readers who are most likely to buy its product. Because Easy-Notes offered an opportunity that is relevant to you, you suddenly find yourself in a decision-making situation.

Unlike you, some of your friends are getting lower grades than they would like to achieve because of poor note-taking. *Problem recognition* motivates them to respond to a brand message that promises to improve their note-taking skills. The perception of a need heightens their awareness and receptivity to messages about

FIGURE   5-5

The last time you bought something, which decision path did you follow?

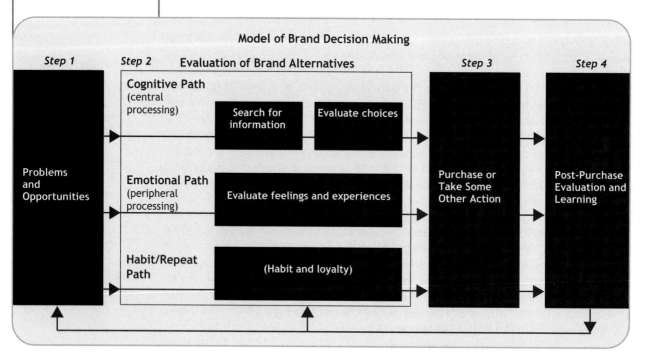

Model of Brand Decision Making

better note-taking. Thus, when Easy-Notes runs an ad in the campus newspaper, these students are likely to notice it. Because Easy-Notes has smart marketers, it's brand messages talk about both better grades and better note-taking. The company is using two complementary brand messages—one that presents an opportunity and the other that offers a solution to a problem.

Marketers use Maslow's hierarchy of needs to analyze and determine which levels of needs or wants their brands are most likely to satisfy. As the two examples demonstrate, brand messages focus on needs and wants to set up both *opportunities* for a brand purchase and *problems* that can be solved by the brand. The Clif Bar Challenge ad in Exhibit 5-8 demonstrates a problem-solution message. The basic physiological needs—for food, water, and so on—are easily recognized and prompt an immediate response to an opportunity. Even some basic needs may have a psychological dimension. You need shoes, for example, but you may desire Nikes or Doc Martens.

Psychological needs are more considered than basic physiological and safety needs and may be driven by problems as well as opportunities. Perhaps you need a new book to read on a trip (the problem), and the opportunity to get one comes when you are walking through the airport and see a collection of top selling books for sale in one of the shops. Furthermore, psychological needs—for belongingness, esteem, and self-actualization—can motivate you to aspire to a higher level of education or motivate you to want status or luxury products. Aspiration, status, and luxury are themes frequently used in marketing communication.

EXHIBIT 5-8
This ad visually and creatively demonstrates that when you need energy, you can get a boost from a Clif Bar.

In industrialized societies, most people are able to satisfy their physiological and safety needs, so selling strategies focus mainly on the wants at higher levels in Maslow's hierarchy—belongingness, self-esteem, and self-actualization. However, marketers are also able to leverage basic needs such as safety. A good example comes from competition for market share among two products: roller skates and in-line skates. In the 1990s, U.S. sales of roller skates plunged from $100 million to $30 million a year while sales of in-line skates surged. Knowing that some three dozen deaths occurred after in-line skates became popular, roller-skate manufacturers began to call attention to the hazards of in-line skating in their brand messages. As a result, roller skates were able to take sales away from in-line skate brands, revitalizing the traditional roller-skate category.[11] This was accomplished by brand messages that made skaters think about their own safety, addressing a basic need.

Step 2: Evaluating Brand Alternatives

Once people become aware of a problem or opportunity, they look for ways to solve the problem or take advantage of the opportunity. In this step of brand decision making, customers and prospects begin their search for brand information and develop feelings about various brands.

It is impossible for a brand to be considered if prospects are not aware of that brand. **Awareness** is *getting a message past the senses—the point of initial exposure—and into consciousness.* But consideration of the product usually requires some kind of knowledge. **Brand knowledge** is *understanding of a brand and its benefits.* Obviously, the greater brand awareness and brand knowledge are, the more presence a brand will have in a person's information search. That is why a common MC objective is to maintain or increase brand awareness and brand knowledge in the target audience.

Recognition and Recall

There are two levels of brand awareness as measured through memory—recognition and recall. **Recognition** is *identifying something and remembering that you saw or heard of it earlier.* **Recall,** a higher level of awareness, is *bringing something back from memory.* Generally speaking, the greater brand knowledge is, the more easily a brand can be recalled.

Think about the last time you were walking across campus and saw two people whom you *recognized* as individuals you met recently at a party. Although you recognized both, you could *recall* the name of only one of them. The reason you recall that person's name was that the two of you discussed traveling in Europe, a special interest of yours. This person had a characteristic that had *relevance* for you—international travel. What this little scenario demonstrates is that recognizing something is easier than recalling it from memory. From a marketer's perspective, however, brand recall is preferable to brand recognition. To stimulate brand recall, the marketer must identify the brand and relate it to a customer or prospect in some meaningful way (see Exhibit 5-9).

Knowing that recall is more difficult to achieve than recognition, marketers often design messages that focus primarily on recognition. For example, for years the main character in TV commercials for StarKist tuna has been Charlie the Tuna. Although Charlie himself is not good enough for StarKist—"Sorry, Charlie"—he is still integrated into the StarKist label to help customers recognize this brand when standing in the tuna section of a store.

If brand recognition or recall does not give customers enough information to make a purchase decision, they are likely to look elsewhere—to past experiences, to personal sources such as reference groups, to other marketing communication (such as packaging, displays, and salespeople), to public sources (mass media, organizations, and *Consumer Reports*), or to product examination and trial (test drives, free samples). Each of these sources of information requires a different amount of effort and carries a different amount of believability (see Table 5-1).

Evoked Sets

Brand awareness and brand knowledge don't guarantee that a brand will be selected. During the evaluation step of brand decision making, people narrow brand choices from all those they are aware of (*awareness set*) and have considered (*consideration set*), to the ones they have previously evaluated as "okay" to purchase (*evoked set*). Marketers want their brands included in the **evoked set,** which is *a group of brands that comes to mind when a person thinks of a product category because the person has judged those brands to be acceptable.* This judgment results from prior use of the brand or from brand knowledge gained in some other way (such as from ads, publicity, or word-of-mouth). Figure 5-6 illustrates the alternatives for someone considering a snack; it depicts categories as well as competitive brands in each category.

Most businesses use something similar to an evoked set—namely, *authorized* brands or suppliers that have

EXHIBIT 5 - 9
The Dunkin' Donuts ad illustrates the idea that when you crave a donut and coffee, you can't wait. The idea is creatively expressed, and the product is presented front and center to intensify the brand memorability.

Coffee so good
you just can't wait.

TABLE 5-1	A Comparison of Information Sources	
Source	**Effort Required**	**Believability**
Past experiences	Low	High
Personal sources (e.g., friends)	Low	High
Marketing communications	Medium	Low
Public sources (e.g., media)	Low	High
Product examination and trial	High	High

Source: Adapted from Paul Peter and Jerry Olson, *Consumer Behavior and Marketing Strategy* (Burr Ridge, IL: Irwin, 1996), p. 311. Reprinted with permission from The McGraw-Hill Companies.

been approved to do business with the company. Unlike consumers who casually build their evoked sets over time, most businesses have committees with an ongoing responsibility to evaluate all the different brands and suppliers that provide products to the company. For marketers selling to businesses, the challenge is to have their brands "authorized." This is done through personal selling, ads and articles in trade magazines, and booths at trade shows. The more visible and integrated these messages are in design and timing, the more successful marketers are at getting their brands authorized.

Because most customers use evoked sets, it is no surprise that a study conducted by Grey Worldwide determined that pure brand loyalty is rare.[12] Grey found that customers in the United States, the United Kingdom, and Australia routinely make their choices from a group of brands they consider acceptable—the evoked set. Other research has found this to be true in nearly every product category, which is why striving for complete brand loyalty is not realistic. More appropriate marketing objectives call for getting a brand into more customers' evoked sets (and authorized lists) and increasing the brand's share of customers' category spending (increasing share of wallet).

The Three Paths to a Decision

The evaluation step proceeds along one of three paths, or over a combination of these paths, to a decision. Think about the different ways people approach buying a car. If they choose the *habit/repeat path*, they simply buy the brand that they bought before. Satisfied with the car they are now driving, they have no motivation to change brands. This is the easiest and quickest path to take to a brand decision. Other people choose the *cognitive path*. They search for information about various brand alternatives and then analyze this information before making a decision. Still others prefer the *emotional path*. They look at the styling of various cars, and imagine how each car would make them feel; then they make their decision.

Many scholars, as well as message planners, have considered brand decision making as primarily a cognitive activity. But as Michael Solomon points out, the information-processing model has been overemphasized.[13] In addition, the cognitive and emotional approaches are not mutually exclusive. Most brand decisions are partly rational and partly emotional and are made with both the head and the heart (see Figure 5-7).

". . . many in the [consumer behavior] field are now beginning to embrace the experiential paradigm, which stresses the subjective, nonrational aspects of consumption as well as cultural influences on customer behavior."

Michael Solomon, *Consumer Behavior*

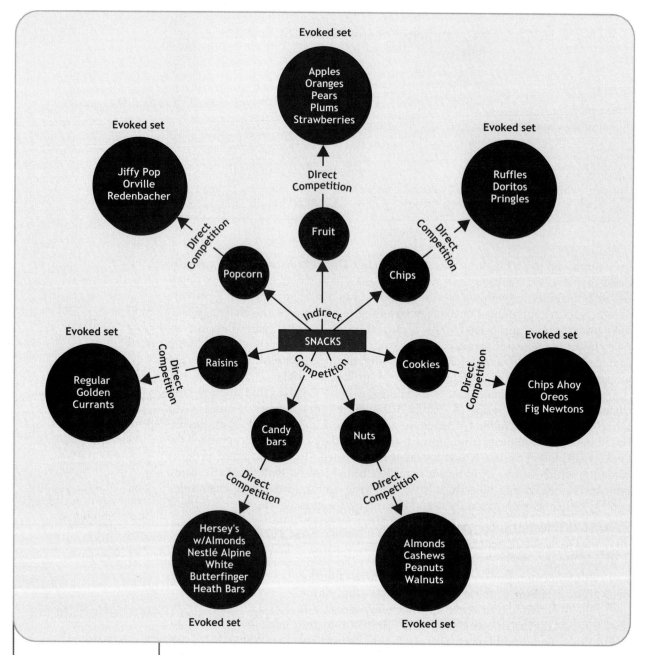

FIGURE 5-6

This model shows how there is both direct and indirect competition. Direct competition are the brands in the evoked set.

Source: Warren Keegan, Sandra Moriarity, and Tom Duncan, *Marketing*, Prentice-Hall, 1995, p. 288.

The Habit/Repeat Path   Habit or repeat-purchase decision making occurs when a brand meets or exceeds expectations and people buy it again (see Figure 5-8). When a customer recognizes a problem or opportunity similar to the one that prompted the original purchase, there is no searching for information or evaluating alternatives, only recall that the brand previously selected has been meeting expectations and thus can automatically be repurchased.

Here is an example in B2B buying. A utility company that operates a fleet of service trucks uses a cognitive model to find a brand of gasoline that will provide the best performance and the best price and will offer extended credit. Once the utility company makes a brand decision and the brand's performance meets or exceeds expectations, drivers are told to always buy that brand of gasoline. If the drivers begin reporting that some of the gasoline stations are sometimes out of gas, or if there are billing problems, the brand selection will be reviewed.

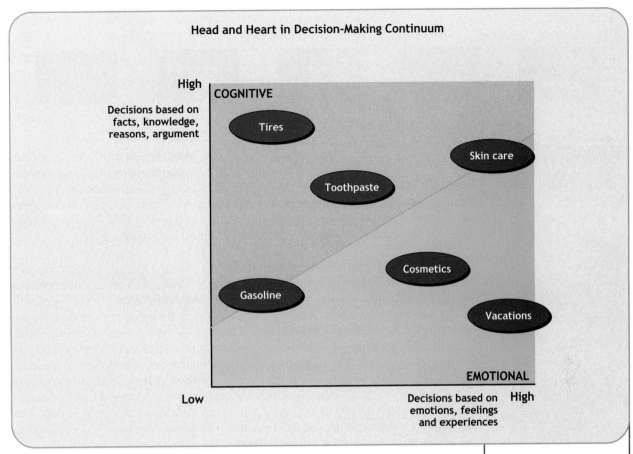

Head and Heart in Decision-Making Continuum

FIGURE 5-7

Where on this chart would you place athletic shoes and fast-food categories?

If the gasoline company the utility is using is smart, it will use MC functions such as direct mail and personal selling to motivate the utility company to buy not only gasoline but motor oil from the gasoline company. It could also integrate a reward program that sends premiums to the utility company when its total purchases reach a certain level. This tactic would strengthen the customer relationship and reinforce the utility's decision to remain faithful to the gasoline brand even when there are occasional billing and/or supply problems.

The habit/repeat path is an extremely important model because it is the decision-making model that drives customer retention. This "shorthand" decision making turns brand selection into a habit and creates loyal customers. If you ask your parents or friends why they always buy a certain brand, they likely will tell you, "I've always bought that brand and never been disappointed." Most of the time they can't remember why they first started buying it. Marketing communication for habit/repeat customers primarily focuses on brand reminders. Some messages, such as those that car dealers send after a purchase, may also be designed to confirm the wisdom of a customer's decision.

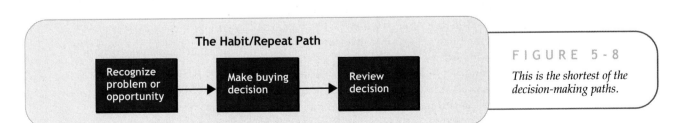

The Habit/Repeat Path

Recognize problem or opportunity → Make buying decision → Review decision

FIGURE 5-8

This is the shortest of the decision-making paths.

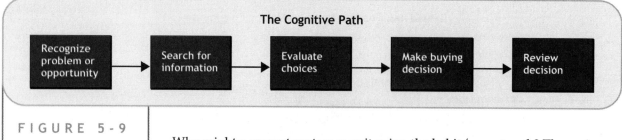

The Cognitive Path

Recognize problem or opportunity → Search for information → Evaluate choices → Make buying decision → Review decision

FIGURE 5-9

What was the last brand you bought using this decision-making path?

Why might a current customer quit using the habit/repeat path? The main reasons are that the brand is not available or the post-purchase evaluation (Step 4 in brand decision-making) shows the brand no longer meets expectations. An unsatisfactory evaluation can result from such things as a price increase, a change in performance or quality, or the recognition of a better way to solve the problem (usually the result of a successful competitve brand message).

The Cognitive Path Customers choose this path in situations where involvement is high and there is a significant element of risk, such as for an expensive product (car, insurance policy, computer, furniture, international travel); an unfamiliar product category (medicine, legal counsel, financial services); an infrequently purchased product (kitchen appliances, an audio system, exotic foods, rodent extermination services); or a high-involvement product category (pets, education, clothing, a CD from a new group) (see Figure 5-9). Customers in these situations are aware of possible consequences of their actions and are concerned about making a "good" decision. They are more inclined to spend time to become informed and think carefully about the alternatives before taking any action. That is why such purchases are sometimes called *considered purchases*. The psychological dimensions of cognitive decision making are summarized in Table 5-2.

TABLE 5-2   Cognitive Decision Making

Step	Psychological Dimensions
1. Problem/opportunity recognition	Needs and wants
	Attention
	Selective perception
2. Information search	Awareness
	Brand knowledge
	Central/peripheral processing
	Active and passing processing
3. Evaluation of choices	Cognitive/affective response
	Evoked sets
	Preference and conviction
	Likability
	Source credibility
4. Behavior, action	Sample, visit, try/buy
5. Review of buying decision, repeat buy	Cognitive and conditioned learning
	Learning from satisfaction and dissatisfaction
	Cognitive dissonance

A person who chooses the cognitive path is thinking about a problem or opportunity. This **cognitive response** is *a response driven by reasoning, judgment, or knowledge.* Types of cognitive responses include asking questions, elaborating on the message by reinterpreting it in terms of one's own life and needs, and making associations with other products and ideas. These are ways people respond to a brand message and, in the process, acquire brand knowledge, as in the TABASCO ad in Exhibit 5-10.

Knowing that some people choose the cognitive path when buying a car, one selling strategy used by Saturn is to equip sales associates with information about competitors' cars (as well as Saturn cars). The idea is not to argue against competing models but rather to give prospects as much information as possible. Saturn recognizes that buying a car is a cognitive decision for most people and believes that customers will respect Saturn for providing objective information they can use in such a decision.

Because people taking this path usually focus on brand differences, marketers appeal to them by using side-by-side product demonstrations or by explaining unique product features. A study of 1,000 television commercials found that the most persuasive ones included a brand-differentiating message. In other words, the commercials that helped customers distinguish one brand from another were the most effective.[14]

EXHIBIT 5-10
This ad makes the point that TABASCO sauce is hot but it also builds the argument that you will want more no matter how badly you "got burned." It is a creative ad, one that uses the distinctive package for maximum brand recognition, but it also delivers a compelling visual and message that you have to think about.

To motivate prospects to give their brands more consideration during the evaluation step, many companies include sales promotions in their IMC programs. By offering samples or price reductions, prospects are given more reasons to purchase. Also a sales promotion offer, along with additional brand information, can reduce cognitive dissonance which is discussed next.

Cognitive Dissonance Marketers need to be aware of and address the postpurchase evaluation element that psychologists term **cognitive dissonance,** which is *the uneasiness that results when two or more beliefs or behaviors are inconsistent with one another.* When such dissonance occurs during the evaluation of choices, customers generally search for more information or look more deeply into their feelings. An example is having to decide between going skiing over spring break or staying on campus to write a research paper due the week after spring break. The tension this decision creates can lead to dissatisfaction with the ski destination as it becomes associated with guilt. The Covenant House commercial in Exhibit 5-11 uses dissonance to compel people to respond with donations.

When marketers know that cognitive dissonance may occur, they can create messages designed to lessen the tension. For example, the company trying to sell you the spring-break ski trip could emphasize students' need for a mental break in order to think smarter and more creatively later. The ski resort could explain that it provides quiet rooms for study early each morning and late each afternoon. Such messages can help alleviate cognitive dissonance.

The Emotional Path People who choose the emotional path are driven by feelings and emotions. Although marketers have known for years that buying decisions are influenced by both the head and the heart, they assumed the head consistently played a much more important role.[15] Recently, companies have

Sadly, it's our 20th anniversary

COVENANT ⬥ HOUSE
No kid should be homeless

EXHIBIT 5-11

The commercial juxtaposes a birthday cake with 20 burning candles and a street kid warming her hands over a candle. The message— "Sadly, it's our 20th anniversary"—contrasts with the birthday imagery to create a sense of guilt and inspire people to contact the shelter and make a donation.

discovered an important role in marketing communication for messages that stimulate feelings. Such feelings are an **affective response,** which is *a feeling or attitude resulting from emotional processing* (see Figure 5-10). (Psychologists use the noun *affect* to refer to an overall emotional state; it is not the same thing as an *effect*.)

The opening story demonstrated that some aspects of Starbucks customers' decision making are driven by facts and information—customers know that Starbucks consistently makes a high-quality cup of coffee. But other important aspects of their decision making are emotional and experiential—people like the decor, the social aspect, and the friendly service.

Prospects and customers who prefer the emotional path to brand decision making, recognize problems and opportunities just as cognitive-path decision makers do. But how they respond is different. Rather than searching for information that they then rationally analyze, they focus on their *feelings* about their alternatives. When a person no longer feels good about wearing a particular suit, for example, the experience of "no longer feeling good" can kick in when the person sees a suit ad. Not only will the person be motivated to attend to the ad, but will do so by asking himself or herself: "How would I look in that suit?"

Recognizing that emotional responses drive many brand decisions, marketers are emphasizing the experiential aspect of their brands. As Joseph Pine and James Gilmore explain in *The Experience Economy,* marketers are increasingly using experiences to transform commodity goods and services into brands that engage customers in personal ways and create brand relationships.[16] An involving buying experience, according to Pine and Gilmore, is based on the concept of "marketing as theater." That's why theme restaurants such as Planet Hollywood and Rainforest Café and department stores such as Bloomingdale's and Nordstrom focus on creating an exciting retail environment that elicits a positive affective response. The retail store becomes a place in which customers are participants in the "staging of the shopping play."

Pine and Gilmore emphasize that the more customers are engaged, the more likely they are to begin and then maintain a relationship with a brand. Although companies can use an experience-based approach to acquire customers, it is also a way to reach and reinforce the relationship with current customers.

Another reason why the emotional path is being used more is the increase in service products and the importance of service in all kinds of product categories. Because services (which by nature are experiential) account for over three-fourths of the U.S. economy, brand experiences are becoming an increasingly important MC strategy and tactic. Even goods have experiential brand touch points when you consider events and sampling.

Because decisions reflect both emotional and cognitive inputs, marketers should give customers and prospects

> **"Staging brand experiences is not just about entertaining customers but rather about engaging them."**
>
> M. Joseph Pine II and James H. Gilmore, *The Experience Economy*

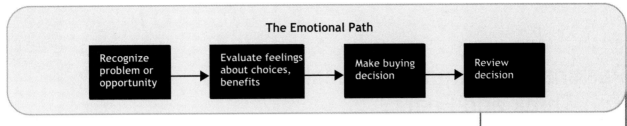

reasons to buy that are emotional as well as rational: they should speak to the heart as well as the head. This is especially true for low-involvement products.

The "Real Victims" campaign, described in the IMC in Action box, used a combination of emotional and cognitive messages designed to touch the feelings as well as the thinking of Parkinson's disease victims in order to convince them to take action.

Notice that the three paths to brand decision making relate to the think/feel/do model discussed earlier (see Table 5-3). The habit/repeat approach usually starts with "doing"; the cognitive approach usually starts with "thinking"; and the emotional path starts with "feeling."

Step 3: Deciding What Action to Take

The evaluation step leads to some kind of response. Most marketers hope that the response is some kind of behavior or action. Customers, however, may be confident in their brand choice but remain undecided about the purchase, asking themselves questions such as these: Can I really afford this? Will I be disappointed with the product after I buy it? Can I find the product someplace else for less money? To respond to these questions and motivate action, companies offer money-back guarantees, free samples, and other incentives. AOL, for example, mails CDs that offer hours of free online connection to motivate people to sign up.

At one time, marketers cared only about generating one type of behavior—a purchase. However, they learned that other behaviors can be just as important. An example comes from the automotive industry. Ninety percent of new-car buyers visit a dealership an average of three times before they buy. Each visit is a behavior, the result of a decision to visit or not to visit. Once prospects decide on the brand of car in which they are most interested, they must then decide on a dealer, then which model to buy, what options to select, and what form of financing to use. Smart dealers use an integrated set of messages to encourage prospects to move through this decision process.

TABLE 5-3	Three Paths to a Brand Decision	
Type of Decision Making	**Route**	**Products**
Cognitive processing	Think/feel/do	Car, major appliances, high-involvement and new products
Experiential processing; impulse, experiences	Do/feel/think and	Snacks, beverages, cigarettes, small household items featured at the checkout stand
	Feel/do/think	Restaurants, sporting events, trade shows, new products where sampling and demonstration are important
Habit/repeat processing	Do/think/feel	B2B supplies; routine purchases, repeat purchases leading to brand loyalty

IMC IN ACTION

Parkinson's Commercial Makes You Think and Feel

The Parkinson Coalition of Houston wanted to expand its reach to minorities afflicted with Parkinson's disease, a progressive disorder of the nervous system marked by shaking limbs, muscle weakness, and difficulty in walking. Because awareness and interest among racial and ethnic minority groups about Parkinson's were low, this campaign was designed to create a change in the attitudes and behaviors of minorities.

As market research discovered, three factors often kept these people who suffered Parkinson's from seeking help and made the development of this campaign a challenge: (1) skepticism about the helpfulness of the Parkinson's organizations (an emotional barrier), (2) embarrassment among those with the disease (an emotional barrier), and (3) an overall lack of knowledge of the disease (a rational barrier). This is why in order to connect with the target audience, the Parkinson Coalition needed to establish trust and credibility.

The McCann-Erickson team identified its primary target audience in Houston as African Americans and Hispanics 50 years of age or older who were afflicted with Parkinson's disease. The broader secondary target audience included all adults 50 or older with Parkinson's disease.

The communication strategy was to inspire and connect with the primary and secondary target audiences on an emotional level by focusing on people who had the disease but were hiding it. These people were identified sympathetically as the "real victims." The ads used the general theme "how I once was versus how I am now," which was designed to connect with the target audiences as well as evoke empathy. Demonstration of the disease's most common symptom (trembling) was used to distinguish Parkinson's from other diseases.

The Parkinson Coalition's "Real Victims" campaign used television exclusively because it was the only medium that could visually show the key symptom, and it provided the best opportunity to create an emotional response among viewers. The campaign planners felt that an emotional response was necessary to maximize contact with the coalition. There were two television commercials:

- A commercial targeted to the African-American audience used a blues guitar player who was having trouble getting his fingers to cooperate in the way they used to. The key line in this spot was "Living life in slow motion."

EXHIBIT 5-12

The blurred image of a man with Parkinson's disease helps to emotionally illustrate the confused world in which these patients live. The closing shot provides a phone number so anyone who is interested can call for more information.

- A commercial targeted to Hispanics featured an older Hispanic man trying to tie his shoes with trembling hands. He said that he felt that he was getting old before his time and that his body seemed to have a mind of its own. A key visual effect showed the lead character moving in and out of focus, the blurring creating a visual metaphor for the loss of control that haunts men and women with Parkinson's disease.

The result? A sizable portion of minorities with the disease responded to the commercials by contacting the Parkinson Coalition. The "Real Victims" campaign was effective because it touched the hearts and minds of minority populations with empathetic and believable messages.

Source: This case was adapted with permission from the Advertising and Marketing Effectiveness (AME) award-winning brief for the Parkinson Coalition of Houston, Texas, prepared by McCann-Erickson Southwest.

The objective of most automotive-related brand messages in the mass media is to get prospects to visit a dealer's showroom. Once prospects come to a showroom, it's obvious they are in the information-seeking and evaluation stages. Auto dealers satisfy customers' needs at this point with brochures and well-trained sales representatives. After the initial visit, a smart dealership will send the prospect a thank-you mailing and offer a small premium (such as a pen flashlight, a can of compressed air for inflating a flat tire, or an emergency flasher) in exchange for making a return visit and taking a test drive. The repeat visit, the result of several brand messages, moves prospects closer to making a buying decision.

Step 4: Evaluating the Purchase Decision or Other Action

The last step in brand decision making is brand evaluation by the buyer. After making a purchase, customers consciously or subconsciously evaluate their decision and arrive at some level of satisfaction or dissatisfaction. Did the brand meet expectation; "Did I make the right decision?" The answer to that question leads either to a repeat purchase or to a return to the evaluation step to search for a different brand for the next purchase in that product category.

Every company wants prospects to buy once and then move onto the habit/repeat path. For that to happen, however, buyers must be satisfied. Thus a company must follow up a sale, when economically feasible, to make sure the buyer is completely satisfied. Follow-up messages, such as postcards or phone calls from a dealer after a car has been purchased, for example, can provide reinforcement for the decision. They also provide an opportunity for feedback. One way companies get feedback at this critical stage is to use customer surveys such as the one shown in Exhibit 5-13.

Learning

The product review process involves **learning,** which is *a change in what a person knows that comes from exposure to new information or experiences.* Psychologists have two basic theories about how most people learn. These theories shed light on the post-purchase evaluation and correspond to the cognitive and emotional decision-making models we have been discussing. **Cognitive learning theory** is *a view of learning as a mental process involving thinking, reasoning, and understanding.* According to this theory, we think by comparing new information to what we already know—that is, to thoughts and information filed away in memory. **Conditioned learning theory** (also called *stimulus–response theory*) is *a view of learning as a trial-and-error process.* We confront a new situation, respond in a certain way, and something happens. If what happens is good, we are likely to develop a positive feeling

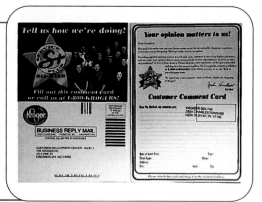

about it and respond the same way the next time we are in that situation. If the experience is bad, we are likely to change our response and try something else. Such patterns of behavior represent the way customers and B2B buyers manage their brand selections.

Learning also intersects with involvement: cognitive learning is especially active in the purchase of high-involvement products; conditioned learning, in the purchase of low-involvement products. Reinforcement advertising is used to remind people of their good brand experiences. Personal two-way communication is used to counter negative reviews when customers complain to a company.

HOW MC MESSAGES INFLUENCE CONSUMER DECISIONS

Because the role of marketing communications is to ignite responses or intervene in the decision process, brand messages must be persuasive. **Persuasion** is *the act of creating changes in attitudes and behaviors.* Persuasive MC messages are designed to get customers and prospects to think and feel positive about a brand, and to make that brand their choice when they select a product. MC managers focus on a number of factors—attitude formation and change strategies, brand likability, credibility and trust, and believable arguments—to trigger the desired consumer response.

Attitude Formation and Attitude Change

Whether they are consciously aware of it or not, most customers and prospects have attitudes about many brands. These attitudes are based on what they have seen, heard, experienced, and learned about brands in the process of evaluating brand choices. Marketers seek to understand and influence these attitudes because they are an important underlying factor in a brand getting into a customer's evoked set and ultimately becoming the customer's brand choice.

Public opinion surveys and other types of customer surveys attempt to identify underlying customer attitudes that often affect behavior. For example, a study by *Glamour* magazine investigated how women aged 18 to 54 perceived "value." The study found that product performance was at the top of the list (mentioned by 92 percent), followed by "getting my money's worth" (90 percent). The next most important factors in determining value were "durable/stays in style" (74 percent), "makes me feel good about using/owning it" (63 percent), on sale or had a coupon (50 percent), and impresses others (22 percent).[17] Compare these findings with your own attitudes toward product value. How would you rank each factor if you were buying a new suit?

Attitudes have two dimensions—direction and degree of conviction. *Attitude direction* is whether the feeling is positive or negative. *Degree of conviction* is how sure customers are about their attitudes, how strong their feeling are—slightly positive, very positive, slightly negative, very negative. Marketing messages can reinforce or confront and change strong and negative attitudes. They can overcome negative, weak attitudes. The most common consumer responses that originate with MC messages are shown in Figure 5-11.

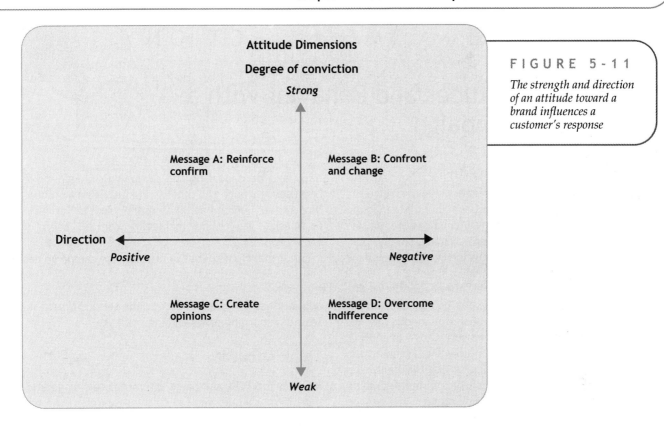

FIGURE 5-11

The strength and direction of an attitude toward a brand influences a customer's response

Four attitude and belief change strategies used in marketing communication are as described here in the selling of ice cream:[18]

1. *Changing beliefs about the consequences of behavior.* Customers might be persuaded that a new ice cream isn't as fattening as they think it is.

2. *Changing evaluations of consequences.* Customers might be persuaded that eating a new ice cream is okay, even if it is fattening.

3. *Changing beliefs about the perceptions of others.* Customers might be persuaded that it's okay to eat a new ice cream because a friend says it's really good.

4. *Strengthening motivations to comply.* Customers might be persuaded to eat a new ice cream because everyone else is eating it.

The IMC in Action box describes an antismoking campaign that works to reinforce the opinion that smoking is unhealthy and change the attitudes of teens who think smoking is "cool."

Brand Likability

A brand's likability can be a critical factor in consumer decision making. If you dislike a brand's advertising—many customers disliked Benetton's controversial social issue advertising—then you may refuse to even put that brand in your evoked set. Likability is an appeal to the heart. But as the Benetton ads illustrated, sometimes the liking response can be driven by cognitive messages, as well as emotional ones.

There are two dimensions to liking: *liking the brand* and *liking the message.* In an IMC program, care is taken to integrate these two so that liking the message is a halo that reflects positively on the brand. Some advertising managers argue that *liking* a brand message is not important as long as customers *remember* the brand. They say that irritating ads may even attract more attention and stay in memory

IMC IN ACTION

Changing Attitudes and Behavior with a Gross-out Campaign

Since 1996, the Arizona Tobacco Education and Prevention Program (TEPP) has been seeking to change the attitudes and ultimately the behaviors of teenagers. The strategy of the campaign—which uses the tag line "Tobacco: tumor-causing, teeth-staining, smelly, puking habit"—is to speak to teens in their own language and use gross humor to get their attention.

In one television commercial, a teenager sitting in a movie theater with his date spits gooey, chewed tobacco into a cup. His date absentmindedly reaches over and takes a drink from the cup. Gross! In another commercial, the mad doctor creating Frankenstein chastises an assistant for bringing him the lungs of a smoker. In yet another (which has stimulated some complaints from adults), a smoking teen tries to be cool by telling a story about how smart dogs are. "I mean, dogs got, like, giant brains. They know when things suck," the boy says as the dog lifts his hind leg and extinguishes the cigarette in his master's hand.

Did the message reach teens? Within weeks of the campaign's first appearance, Arizona teens were repeating the slogan and mimicking lines from the ads. In addition, more than 300,000 items—such as T-shirts,

hats, and pens bearing the campaign's slogan—have been sold through the Smelly, Puking Habit Merchandise Center, which has taken orders from as far away as Alaska. Its online marketing can be seen at www.tepp.org.

Since making its debut in Arizona, the campaign has been distributed in other states by the U.S. Centers for Disease Control and Prevention. The ABC television network has run the ads as a public service during its Saturday-morning programming.

Think About It

How has the TEPP campaign attempted to change attitudes? What would you say to the researcher who observed that teens' awareness of the slogan doesn't prove the ads are working? Can such a campaign lead to behavior change?

Source: Adapted from Barbara Martinez, "Antismoking Ads Aim to Gross Out Teens," *Wall Street Journal*, March 31, 1997, p. B1; Amy Silverman, "Mrs. Good Retch," *Phoenix New Times*, April 24, 1997; Millie Takaki, "Arizona Anti-Smoking Ads Gain National Momentum," *Shoot*, April 18, 1997, p. 7.

longer than appealing messages. Research, however, has found a positive correlation between liking the message and liking the brand.[19] Ultimately, the development of a long-term brand relationship depends on customers' liking how a brand presents itself. One reason for Land Rover's success is its advertising (see Exhibit 5-14), which, like the vehicle itself, is engaging and helps create trust in the brand. Customers typically like the ads as much they like the car!

Credibility and Trust

Another important factor influencing customers' responses is whether customers find a message to be believable. Marketing programs use public relations because articles in the news media generally have higher levels of credibility than do sponsored messages such as advertising. A factor influencing believability is the perceived credibility of the source, which relates to the trust factor in relationships. Unfortunately customers are increasingly less trustful of marketing communication messages. A survey of 1,100 customers by the Porter Novelli public relations agency found that Americans are increasingly cynical about *all* sources of information—political ads and election coverage, media (one-third say the media are

FREELANDER

THE LAND ROVER EXPERIENCE   LAND-ROVER

losing credibility), and corporations (44 percent say companies are less credible). Only 20 percent believe companies are completely truthful during a corporate crisis; more than a third think corporations withhold negative information.[20] Whom did these respondents say they trust? Customer advocacy groups such as Consumers Unions ranked highest; the media were a distant second.

To help make messages more believable and counter this lack of trust, companies sometimes use opinion leaders. Such people are generally credible sources, as well as outgoing, likable, and with higher-than-average social status. Knowing that opinion leaders are credible and trusted, and therefore can influence purchase decisions, companies hire or work with them to support the company's brands.

Believable Arguments and Reasons

A study by the Cummings Center for Advertising Studies at the University of Illinois found that, although Americans report that they do not generally trust advertising, they do have more confidence in cognitive ad claims than in ads that try to create an emotional response.[21] Companies that create messages in which arguments and reasons are used appeal to people following the cognitive path to a decision.

When Johnson & Johnson launched its Acuvue disposable contact lenses, it first communicated with eye care specialists, sending them information about the product so they could have informed discussions with potential customers. Only after these experts and opinion leaders had a chance to assimilate the brand information—talking with their patients and writing about it in their columns, newsletters, and trade journals— did the company begin sending brand messages to prospects.

Another communication strategy that provides a believable argument is a product demonstration. When a brand's benefit can be demonstrated, customers are not only told what the brand will do but are shown. The result is a more trustworthy message because seeing is believing.

Information that strengthens the credibility of a message is called a **support argument.** *Information that challenges the credibility of a message* is called a **counterargument.** Studies have shown that the opinions of highly credible sources may outweigh customers' initial opposition to messages. Johnson & Johnson educated eye care specialists about Acuvue in order to overcome customers' fear of, or resistance to, the idea (new at that time) of leaving contact lenses in overnight. Through the eye care professionals, Johnson & Johnson used support arguments to defend against potential counterarguments from prospective customers.[22]

A FINAL NOTE: PERSUADING PEOPLE TO PERSUADE THEMSELVES

This chapter opened with a story about you hearing a CD by an unknown group and how your curiosity and interest might lead you to buy the CD. You were responding to MC messages and, in effect, persuading yourself to try the CD, because the messages you received touched the right buttons at the right moments in your brand decision process. In a sense, marketing communication is a type of intervention in a personal brand decision process.

Customer-behavior researcher Lisa Fortini-Campbell explains, in *Hitting the Sweet Spot: The Customer Insight Workbook,* that marketing communication has to be customer focused if it is to have any impact on people's attitudes and behaviors. She says, "Think how good it feels when someone really understands us and speaks to us with a genuine understanding of who we are."[23] She says that such understanding touches our "sweet spot." We all want someone (a friend, a company) to speak to us honestly, "not as some statistical model, or something to be manipulated like a marionette in the marketplace, but from one living breathing human being to another—with caring, understanding, and shared values." As Fortini-Campbell explains, when marketing communication is sensitive to individuals, "You don't persuade people. They persuade themselves."

Key Terms

affective response 154
AIDA 139
attitude 138
awareness 147
belief 138
brand knowledge 147
cognitive dissonance 153
cognitive learning theory 157
cognitive response 153
conditioned learning theory 157
counterargument 161
culture 135

customer 134
customer insight 141
elaboration 144
evoked set 148
hierarchy-of-effects model 139
high-involvement products 140
image messages 145
learning 157
low-involvement products 140
Maslow's hierarchy of needs 138
motivations 139
needs and wants 137

opinion 138
opinion leader 139
persuasion 158
prospect 134
recall 148
recognition 148
reference group 136
relevance 141
social class 136
society 135
support argument 161

Key Point 1: Who Are These People?

People who respond to brand messages are prospects or current customers; they also may be consumers or business buyers. These people make brand decisions in the context of social, cultural, and personal influences.

Key Point 2: How Do Consumers Respond to Marketing Communication?

Responses to marketing communication are analyzed in terms of two types of models. Hierarchy-of-effects models, such as the AIDA sequence (attention, interest, desire, action), summarize the types of impact a brand message has on a prospect or customer. Think/feel/do models move away from the idea of a hierarchy and introduce the idea that several different paths lead to a decision, and the choice of a path depends on the buying-behavior situation. According to think/feel/do models, the response to a brand message is governed by the degree to which involvement is high or low, and the level of involvement reflects perceptions of relevance and risk.

Point 3: How Does Brand Decision Making Work?

The four brand decision steps are (1) recognizing a problem or an opportunity; (2) evaluating brand alternatives; (3) deciding what action to take; and (4) evaluating the purchase decision or other action taken.

EXHIBIT 5-15
Customers are likely to become more loyal when they like what a brand stands for.

Key Point 4: How Do MC Messages Affect That Decision-Making Process?

Effective MC messages are persuasive. They result in attitude formation and change, which can lead to behavior change. Factors affecting persuasiveness of MC messages include likability, message credibility, and trust.

Key Point 1: Who Are These People?

a. How do prospects and customers differ? How do MC messages need to be adjusted for these two groups?
b. How do consumers and business buyers differ? How do MC messages need to be adjusted for these two groups?
c. Give an example of how society and culture affect someone's decision to buy a product.
d. What is a reference group? Identify a reference group to which you belong, and explain how that group influenced some buying decision that you have made.
e. How do a need and a want differ? Give an example of a purchasing decision that you have made in which the distinction between a need and a want is apparent.

Key Point 2: How Do Consumers Respond to Marketing Communication?

a. What does AIDA stand for? Why is the AIDA sequence referred to as a hierarchy-of-effects model?

b. How does the think/feel/do model differ from the AIDA model?

c. Why do hierarchy-of-effects models shed more light on the decision making of new buyers than on the decision making of repeat buyers?

d. Find ads or other types of marketing communication that illustrate the think/feel/do variations. Analyze how they work. Also analyze how they deliver or cue the AIDA effects.

e. Explain the difference between low involvement and high involvement. Is the difference determined by the product, the consumer, or the communication?

f. Explain the relationship between relevance and levels of involvement? Give an example showing how relevance affected a buying decision that you have made.

g. Explain how the concept of elaboration affects the way you make brand decisions. Give an example from your own experience.

Key Point 3: How Does Brand Decision Making Work?

a. How does a problem differ from an opportunity? Find an ad that uses the problem approach and another that focuses on opportunities. Explain how the messages work.

b. Distinguish between needs and wants, and between problems and opportunities. Give an example of each that might motivate the purchase of a product.

c. Find an article in the business press about consumer trends. Brainstorm with others in your class to come up with ideas for new products that would address these consumer needs and wants.

d. What are the three paths to a brand decision? Describe each one, and give an example of each.

e. Why are there fewer steps in the habit/repeat approach than in the cognitive or emotional approaches?

f. Contrast cognitive learning theory and conditioned learning theory.

Key Point 4: How Do MC Messages Affect That Decision-Making Process?

a. Explain the role of persuasion in marketing communication.

b. What are the two dimensions of attitude? Choose a product category, and describe the dimensions of your own attitude about that category.

c. Describe the four attitude and belief change strategies. Pick a high-involvement product that you are interested in buying, and explain how you might respond to MC messages using each of the four change strategies.

d. What is the difference between liking the brand and liking the ad? Find an example in which the two likability factors are working at cross-purposes (you like the brand but not the ad, or vice versa).

e. Collect cigarette ads that seem to be aimed at young people. Analyze how they affect attitudes in their attempt to sell cigarettes. Compare these ads with those in the Arizona "gross-out" campaign and other antismoking campaigns. Which ones do you feel are most effective? Why?

Chapter Challenge

Writing Assignment

The Parkinson's Coalition case in the IMC in Action box provides an example of customers using both the head and the heart to make a decision. Explain how these different styles of reasoning work and how marketing communication can influence them. From what you have learned about customer decision-making processes, what would you recommend to the Parkinson's Coalition for next year's campaign?

Presentation Assignment

A local coffeehouse has hired you to analyze its customers' behavior. But first the manager wants you to give the organization's employees a crash course in the basics of brand decision making. Go back through this chapter, and list all the information you can find that seems relevant to using marketing communication to effectively relate to retail customers in a coffeehouse. Prepare a presentation to the store owner and manager on those factors that you think are most important for them to consider. What factors that would influence the purchase of coffee drinks and other products sold in the store do you believe their marketing communication should address? Develop an outline of the key points you want to present. Give the presentation to your class, or record it on videotape (audiotape is also an option) to turn in to your instructor, along with the outline.

Internet Assignment

Browse the Motley Fool website (www.fool.com), and find a discussion that relates to consumer behavior. Write a report on this topic, explaining it in terms of the consumer responses and brand decision making described in this chapter.

Research Assignment

Consult those articles and books and others that you find in the library that relate to consumer behavior, and explain how advertising and other forms of marketing communication are successful (or not successful) in influencing the consumer decision process. Develop a marketing communications plan for the introduction of a new product of your choice that makes the most effective use of marketing communication to influence the brand decision making of your target audience.

Chapter

6

IMC Planning

Follow Andrew as he takes the ENVOY on the ultimate ROAD TRIP

Key Points in This Chapter

1. How does IMC campaign planning work, and how does it use zero-based planning?
2. What are the six steps in the IMC planning process?
3. Why is internal marketing important in IMC planning?

Chapter Perspective

Knowing the Score

Integrated marketing communication is often compared to an orchestra. Just as an orchestra's performance is guided by a musical score, an IMC campaign must have a written score, or plan. This plan details which marketing communication functions and which media are to be used at which times and to what extent.

An IMC campaign plan is a written document. It can be as minimal as a set of organized notes by a person running a small retail business or as complex as a 100-page document for a multimillion-dollar brand campaign. But all good plans, regardless of size, have six basic elements: targeting (designated customers and prospects), SWOT analysis, objectives, strategies and tactics, a budget, and evaluation. The plan-

ning process begins with the selection of the desired audience for the brand message. Research then determines the strengths and weaknesses of a company or brand from the perspective of customers and prospects. Planning also takes into consideration marketplace opportunities and threats—the things that companies cannot control but can leverage or address to their advantage.

This chapter explains the differences between objectives, strategies, and tactics and describes the six steps in the planning process. The chapter ends with a discussion of internal marketing, because companies cannot properly execute an IMC plan without the full knowledge and cooperation of all their members.

TRAVELING WITH AN ENVOY
McCann-Erickson Relationship Marketing, New York

If you ask 10 different people what an envoy is, you'll probably get 10 different answers—including a diplomat who ranks slightly below an ambassador and a messenger or representative. GMC, General Motors' truck division, asked McCann-Erickson's Relationship Marketing office in New York to get people excited about the launch of the GMC Envoy, a midsize, luxury sport-utility vehicle (SUV) and to inspire them to test-drive one. The challenge was to build interest even though the car wouldn't be available for seven months. In essence, GMC was asking McCann to start from a base of zero and build an identity and consumer demand for a vehicle nobody could yet see, touch, or drive. It was a difficult challenge, but the McCann team came up with a plan that made the GMC Envoy ready to hit the road and ultimately contributed to Envoy's being named SUV of the Year in 2002 by *Motor Trend*s magazine.

Target

McCann determined that the target audience consisted of three segments: current GMC Jimmy owners, current competitive SUV owners, and current luxury-car owners with a high likelihood of purchasing an SUV. McCann chose this upscale audience because these people were the most likely to be interested in purchasing the Envoy.

The Envoy campaign used direct-response media (specifically, a series of mailings to the target audience) because the company could obtain names and addresses of the people to whom it was targeting this exclusive offer. Like most MC clients, GMC did not want to spend a lot of money—in fact, the budget was quite small for a new-car launch—but it did want to make a big impact. In order to announce the car and prevent the target audience from purchasing other SUVs before the Envoy became available, the campaign had to create interest, intrigue, a brand position, and a brand identity almost immediately.

The Marketing Challenge

The GMC Envoy was scheduled for release in the late spring of 1998. Market research indicated that the SUV product category was extremely competitive. GMC therefore had concerns that potential customers would purchase competitors' models before

EXHIBIT 6-1

the Envoy hit showrooms. Obviously, the company wanted to prevent this from happening, but doing so wouldn't be easy for a number of reasons:

- No Envoys would be available for consumers to test-drive or even look at for seven months.
- Consumers were not aware of the Envoy (because it was a new brand).
- There was no budget for a regular introductory campaign until early summer (four months after the beginning of the peak SUV-buying period).
- Many SUV brands were already well established.
- Several new SUV brands were scheduled to come into the market at the same time as the Envoy.
- There would be competition between the Envoy and GMC's already-existing compact SUV, the Jimmy.

Although the Envoy had those things working against it, research also showed that the brand had several conditions working in its favor:

- The manufacturer, GMC, had a good reputation.
- GMC had a good dealer network.
- SUV prospects were fairly easy to identify.
- The demand for SUVs was strong and growing.
- The economy was healthy and growing, which meant that consumers had a reasonable amount of disposable income.

By combining traditional direct-marketing and sales-promotion tactics with some very creative advertising elements, the McCann team created an award-winning IMC campaign that excited prospects' interest and kept them waiting to learn more about the new Envoy.

MC Objectives

A critical element of the IMC plan for the Envoy was to track interim responses to know who was interested, who visited showrooms, and who placed orders for the car. In addition, the McCann team set forth several specific communication and behavioral objectives:

1. Create awareness of the Envoy launch among 50 percent of the target audience.
2. Keep the target audience from buying another brand of SUV before the Envoy was available.

3. Motivate 10 percent of the target audience to visit a showroom and ask for the Envoy by name.
4. Create a brand identity and position for the Envoy as an SUV that combines both luxury and technology.
5. Generate sales of 3,500 units within the first three months of the Envoy's launch.

Creative Strategy

The overall communication strategy was to *position* the Envoy as an upscale, sophisticated SUV. The McCann team believed it could get the attention of the targeted upscale audience by playing up the fact they were being given the "inside track" on Envoy.

Because no Envoys were available to test-drive, the *big idea* was to invite prospects on a vicarious test drive described by a fictitious American diplomatic envoy and his brother who worked for GMC. A critical creative element of the big idea was to have the test-drive story take place in Europe, because the audience had a propensity for international travel.

McCann planned a set of direct-mail pieces featuring two brothers (see Exhibit 6-1). Their pictures were included in one of the mailings; each brother represented an aspect of the Envoy. In developing these characters, the McCann team went so far as to create their biographies, complete with education, marital status, and favorite foods, music, and drink. The first brother was Steven Bank, the director of GMC's Envoy development. The fictitious Steven was the brain behind the Envoy. He talked in "marketing speak." A left-brain character, he embodied the rational reason for buying this vehicle. His brother, Andrew, was a right-brain person. An American diplomat stationed overseas, Andrew provided the emotional reasons for owning the Envoy. He described the Envoy as if he were describing a friend. Together, Steven and Andrew presented two perspectives on why buying a GMC Envoy was a smart decision—and they were so "real" to prospective customers that they received 40 proposals of marriage!

Media Strategies

Direct mail was the primary medium used in the GMC Envoy launch, and brand messages were targeted to a select, upscale audience. To get the attention of these sophisticated people (who receive many direct-mail offers), the Envoy campaign letters were mailed from Europe. The envelopes had fictitious hotel return addresses, foreign stamps, real cancellation marks, and no GMC branding.

McCann chose these elements to create impact and ensure the mailings were opened.

There were six mailings. Timing was important. If the mailings arrived too close together, prospects wouldn't have time to really begin thinking seriously about purchasing an Envoy. If they arrived too far apart, recipients would lose track of the travel story and the mailings would lose their synergy. McCann decided that intervals of 10 to 14 days would be optimum.

In two of the later mailings, targets were asked if they would like to visit a GMC showroom to see the new Envoy. This helped maintain an ongoing dialogue between the prospects and the two characters who embodied the Envoy brand. The direct-mail campaign also made it possible for the agency and GMC to instantly track results so that they would know who was interested and to what extent.

EXHIBIT 6-2

Envoy mailing with sweepstakes entry form and postcards.

Promotional Strategy

A sweepstakes with the opportunity to win a free two-year Envoy lease was part of the third direct mailing (see Exhibit 6-2). It was included to motivate a higher level of response and find out who the real prospects were. The sweepstakes entry form asked five questions regarding interest in buying a new SUV and interest in the Envoy. A postage-paid business reply envelope was included to make it easy for prospects to respond. Those who responded were immediately sent more information about the Envoy, and their contact information was sent on to the GMC dealership nearest them. Dealers then made further follow-ups, letting prospects know when the Envoy would be available for a real test drive.

Evaluation of the Envoy Campaign

By closely analyzing its target audience, taking advantage of the strengths of direct mail, and using an engaging, creative message strategy, GMC and McCann were able to introduce the Envoy with a great impact but without a huge budget. The dueling letters from the dueling brothers were able to sustain the target audience's interest over a seven-month period. Because of the high level of interest, the campaign created an instant brand identity and image for the Envoy.

GMC believes these results are noteworthy for the automotive and relationship marketing industries because they show that (1) consumers can be motivated to purchase a $33,000 vehicle through direct-mail brand messages without the benefit of costly broadcast and print mass media advertising or traditional "cash-back" offers, and (2) the Envoy's targeting approach was able to identify the very best prospects for the direct-response campaign. And being named SUV of the Year by *Motor Trends* is even more recognition of the effectiveness of the Envoy launch.

Source: This case was adapted with permission from the award-winning Advertising and Marketing Effectiveness (AME) brief for the launch of the GMC Envoy prepared by the McCann-Erickson Relationship Marketing office in New York.

STARTING AT ZERO WITH IMC CAMPAIGN PLANNING

Although managing the acquisition and retention of customers is an ongoing process, most companies once a year do a major analysis to determine what changes need to be made in their marketing communication efforts during the coming year. Each

EXHIBIT 6-3
*Planning for new products
always starts from zero, but
that's also a good approach
for established brands that
need to be sensitive to
changes in the competitive
marketplace. This postcard
showing Nantucket was
used in the Envoy launch.*

Greetings from Nantucket

review should start with a clean sheet, as marketers consider how various tools and budgets are used. This process, which is called **zero-based planning,** *determines objectives and strategies based on current brand and marketplace conditions, which are considered the zero point.* That's particularly true when a new product, such as the GMC Envoy (see Exhibit 6-3), is being launched.

A formal campaign plan is done for several reasons. First, it provides a rational process for identifying the most important communication issues on which the company should focus over the next 12 months—that is, to determine how best to use marketing communication to help the company achieve its sales and profit objectives. Second, it informs everyone involved with MC, including outside MC agencies, what is expected of them. Third, it helps ensure that the MC effort is integrated and focused on the most important communication issues. Fourth, a MC plan tells top management how and why MC dollars will be spent and what the company can expect in return for the dollars it is investing in marketing communications. Finally, the plan provides a standard against which progress and final results can be measured.

In most cases, the annual plan takes the form of a **campaign,** which is *a set of MC messages with a common theme that runs for a specified period of time to achieve certain MC objectives.* The larger the MC budget, generally speaking, the more pieces and parts a MC plan will have, such as a number of different customer segments being targeted and a number of different MC functions being used.

Planning throughout the Organization

Zero-based campaign planning occurs at multiple levels within an organization. At the corporate level, it means revising the business plan, which is the company's overall strategy of operating, in order to maximize profits and shareholder value. The business plan is concerned primarily with profit, brand equity, and the company's share price (if the company is publicly owned).

Below the corporate business plan are the plans of individual departments— operations/production, human resources, financial, marketing, and sales. In the case of marketing, the analysis and planning focus primarily on goals for sales and

EXHIBIT 6-4

EXHIBIT 6-4

A company may decide to target a variety of users and broaden its market, as Motorola hoped to do for its cell phones.

share of market, which can be met through such strategies as launching a new product, a line extension, or expanding the market (see Exhibit 6-4).

The level below the department level is where analysis and planning take place for marketing communication that focuses on customer relationships (acquisition and retention), brand awareness, brand knowledge, trial, repeat purchase, and overall customer satisfaction. In very large companies with very large MC budgets, the final level of planning is done by each of the major MC functions—advertising, publicity, sales promotion, events and sponsorships, and direct response.

This chapter discusses a typical planning process (see Table 6-1) used for an overall MC plan. Planners focus on target audiences, objectives, strategies and rationales, the budget, and the scheduling of MC activities. The plan also describes what ongoing market testing will be done and specifies what measurement methods will be used to determine the effectiveness of the plan once it has been executed. MC managers working with the people in their departments and with the director of marketing are responsible for putting the MC plan together. Companies that have a good relationship with their MC agencies may ask members of the agency for their ideas and suggestions.

Applying Zero-Based Planning

For years most companies conducted MC planning by looking at a few market research studies and then making some slight adjustments to the plan that had been used the year before. Today this approach is being replaced with the more sophisticated zero-based approach. The "zero" means that planning starts with no preconceived notions about what MC functions or media are needed.[1] Rather than starting with last year's plan, planners select functions and media in light of current marketplace and brand conditions. For example, advertising may have been heavily used in the preceding year to increase awareness, but now awareness

TABLE 6-1	**Zero-Based Campaign Planning**
Step	**Description**
1. Identify target audiences	Analyze the various customer and prospect segments, and determine which to target and to what extent.
2. Analyze SWOTs	Summarize internal (strengths, weaknesses) and external (opportunities, threats) brand-related conditions; determine the success of the MC functions and media used in preceding year.
3. Determine MC objectives	Decide what marketing communication programs should accomplish.
4. Develop strategies and tactics	Determine which MC functions should be used and to what extent. Choose brand messages and means of delivery. Support each strategy with a rationale. Decide when each MC program will begin and end.
5. Determine the budget	Decide what the overall MC budget will be and then how money will be divided among the selected MC functions.
6. Evaluate effectiveness	Conduct ongoing MC tests in an effort to find more effective ways to do IMC. Monitor and evaluate all the IMC efforts to determine effectiveness and accountability.

TABLE 6-2   Zero-Based Plan for Envoy

Key SWOTs	MC Objectives	Best MC Function	Rationale
Identifiable target	Create 50% awareness among target audience	Direct marketing	Small audience; contact information available
Availability problem	Motivate 10% to visit showroom when available	Direct marketing	Build curiosity; draw out interest over a longer period of time
Low budget and little MC support	Sell 3,500 units in advance of availability	Direct marketing	Use personal contact medium to presell target

levels are fine and a more important concern is getting trial, which means using more sales promotion and less advertising during the coming year.

Zero-based planning makes sense because competitors and distribution channels are constantly changing, as are customers' wants and needs. With the increase in interactivity and tracking of customer interactions, companies now have more data on which to base MC and media decisions. Table 6-2 from the Envoy campaign is an example of how this planning is conducted.

Merely because this planning process starts from "zero" does *not* mean, however, that a company won't continue to do some of the things it has done before. Obviously, if there is still need for a promotional effort or an advertising strategy that was used successfully in the preceding year, it should be repeated. One aspect of corporate learning is keeping track of what worked and didn't work. Such learning should help guide annual campaign planning.

THE IMC PLANNING PROCESS

This six-step planning process is equally applicable to B2C and B2B companies; to companies of every size, from the smallest retailer to the largest global brand; to service providers as well as manufacturers; and to nonprofit organizations. Each medium and each MC function has its own unique strength. An organization can determine the right mix of media and MC functions only after it has targeted its audience. The first step in zero-based planning, therefore, is to identify key customer and prospect segments.

Step 1: Identifying Target Audiences

To advertise and promote a product to everyone would be a waste of money because there is no single product that everyone wants or can afford to buy. An analysis of the consumer behavior and the customer-response factors (discussed in Chapter 5) will lead to a better understanding of the people and companies most likely to be in the market for the product. Therefore, companies (both B2C and B2B) segment customers into groups based on certain characteristics and the likelihood that group members will buy the product; then companies target messages specifically to these key audiences. The term **segmenting** means *grouping customers or prospects according to common characteristics, needs, wants, or desires.* **Targeting** refers to *analyzing, evaluating, and prioritizing the market segments deemed most profitable to pursue.* (For a detailed discussion of segmenting and targeting, see Chapter 7.)

Targeting focuses the MC effort on (1) current customers who are most likely to repurchase or influence purchases; (2) customers and prospects who need special attention for whatever reason (they may have slowed their frequency of purchase, have had a serious customer-service problem, have had a dialogue with the brand but have not yet purchased); and (3) prospects who have never bought the brand but might buy it, given their profiles. Other stakeholders who affect or influence these three categories of customers and prospects may also be targeted. Because of its emphasis on consumer insights, account planning helps companies identify and understand their target audiences (← Chapter 2).

Because it is expensive to send out brand messages, the more precise the targeting is, the less the media waste. Also, only by knowing whom to target can a brand do a SWOT analysis (explained next) and develop objectives and strategies that are relevant and persuasive.

Step 2: Analyzing SWOTs

Many marketing plans in the United States are based on an annual **situation analysis,** which is *an analysis of marketplace conditions.* The problem with this type of analysis is that it doesn't categorize and prioritize findings from a strategic viewpoint, which is what a SWOT analysis does. A **SWOT analysis** is *a structured evaluation of internal strengths and weaknesses and external opportunities and threats that can help or hurt a brand.* SWOT is an acronym for Strengths, Weaknesses, Opportunities, and Threats.

Strengths and weaknesses are internal factors under a company's control (see Figure 6-1). Strengths and weaknesses are determined by asking customers and prospects—the target audiences identified in step 1 of the IMC planning process—not merely by asking colleagues within the company, as often happens. Opportunities and threats are external elements—the company has little or no control over them though on occasion can influence them.

Recognizing Internal Strengths and Weaknesses

A company's strengths and weaknesses form the most important planning input from a SWOT analysis because the company has control over these elements. Strengths are competitive advantages; weaknesses are competitive disadvantages. Strengths should be leveraged and weaknesses fixed. GMC had successfully marketed its Jimmy SUV model; this was a strength that could be leveraged when the company launched the new upscale Envoy.

Strengths and weaknesses include such things as how customers and prospects perceive a brand's innovativeness, the convenience of finding and buying the brand (distribution), its pricing compared to competition, the expertise and helpfulness of its sales force, the condition of its physical facilities, and its overall

FIGURE 6-1
SWOT Analysis Categories

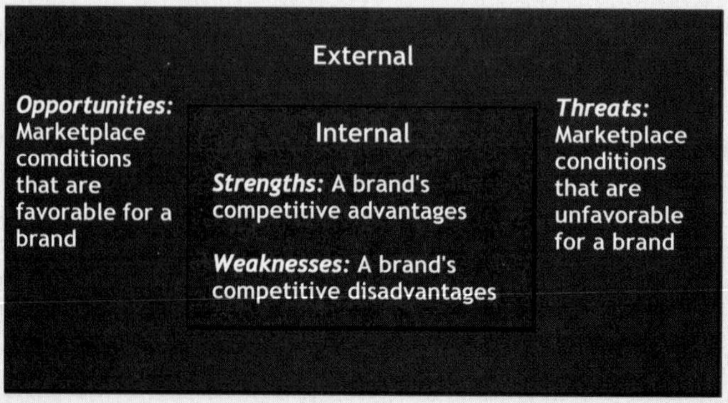

External

Opportunities: Marketplace comditions that are favorable for a brand

Internal

Strengths: A brand's competitive advantages

Weaknesses: A brand's competitive disadvantages

Threats: Marketplace conditions that are unfavorable for a brand

financial strength. Brand image, brand positioning, corporate culture, and core values can also be either strengths or weaknesses. (Although brand images and reputations live in customers' minds, they are considered internal controllable elements because the company can make changes in the 4 Ps [including MC messages] that will in turn affect how these are perceived.)

To determine strengths and weaknesses of *customer relationships*, research can have customers rate a brand and its competitors on the following characteristics, or *relationship constructs*, which are dimensions of brand relationships (⬅ Chapter 3):

1. *Trust* the brand.
2. Are *satisfied* with the brand.
3. Perceive the company as *consistent* in its dealings and product performance.
4. Perceive the company as *accessible*.
5. Perceive the company as *responsive*.
6. Feel the company is *committed* to customers and puts them first.
7. Have an *affinity* for the company and its other customers.
8. *Like* the company and enjoy doing business with it.

To determine the strengths and weaknesses of a brand's *communications*, a SWOT analysis should also include how the brand compares to its competitors in each of these areas among the target audience(s):

- Top-of-mind awareness.
- Overall brand awareness.
- Percentage who have tried the brand.
- Percentage who have repeated.
- Share of customer's category spending on the brand.
- Percentage of customers who have repeated and then quit buying (churn rate).

Keep in mind that other things also affect each of these measures, such as price, places of distribution, and product performance. MC obviously has more impact on awareness, for example, than on repeat purchase, which is mostly affected by product performance. However, even repeat purchases can be influenced by sales-promotion offers and other MC efforts.

Just as important as *how* a brand scores on these relationship constructs is *why* it scores high or low. For example, if a brand scores low on trust, the first thing a company must do is determine the source of the distrust (among the possibilities are poor customer service, overpromising in planned messages, and poor product performance). Negative performance messages can make millions of dollars in marketing communication a wasted investment.

An example of the benefits provided by relationship analysis comes from athletic-shoe manufacturer Nike's early experiences of selling to women. In the early 1990s, women made up only about 5 percent of Nike's customer base. When Nike did some customer research, it discovered that women did not find advertising that featured Michael Jordan and other male athletes relevant; these messages didn't talk to women. As a result, the company created a separate women's campaign with advertising copy that addressed how women felt about their bodies and themselves. The ads included lines such as "Did you ever wish you were a boy?" "You were born a daughter," and "A woman is often measured by the things she cannot control." Soon after this campaign, women accounted for 15 percent of Nike's sales.[2] Such success is what led Nike to move further into the women's market, reaching the market niches of girls and young women (see Exhibit 6-5).

A company can also learn of its strengths and weaknesses by analyzing service calls, interviewing the sales force and front-line retail employees, doing observation studies of customers shopping, maintaining customer advisory boards, reviewing what the trade press and the popular press are saying about the company and brand, and doing formal or informal surveys of the brand's suppliers and channel members.

Recognizing External Opportunities and Threats

External factors that companies must live with are a mixture of opportunities and threats. Threats are marketplace conditions that reduce the perceived value or attractiveness of a product or that result in its being more costly to make or provide. For example, GMC could see the level of competition building in the upscale SUV category and was worried that prospects would purchase competitors' models before Envoy was in showrooms. By definition, threats can't be controlled, but sometimes a company can lessen their impact. The idea is to anticipate them and make efforts to counteract them. Exhibit 6-6 is an ad that addresses a threat to Shell, an oil company that many say exploits the environment.

EXHIBIT 6-6
The problem of environmental impacts affects oil company exploration. This ad positions Shell as being sensitive to the issue of the destruction of rain forests.

Opportunities are social and economic conditions and situations in the marketplace that can positively alter customers' attitudes about and behavior toward a company's products. Smart companies identify and leverage opportunities. GMC, for example, determined that there was an opportunity to extend its market appeal into the upscale SUV category because of the growth in the overall upscale-car category. Other examples of where opportunities and threats can come from are competitive activities, laws and regulations, technological innovations, industry trends, and socioeconomic conditions.

Prioritizing SWOTS

Once the SWOTs have been identified, they need to be prioritized. Although many things can be taken into consideration when prioritizing SWOTs, the following criteria can be used for most product categories:

1. *Realistic damage* to brand relationships and brand equity if a weakness or threat is not addressed (i.e., anticipated and counteracted).
2. *Realistic benefit* if a strength or opportunity is leveraged (i.e., used to its full potential).
3. *Cost* of addressing or leveraging each SWOT.
4. The *time frame* in which the company has to address or leverage each SWOT.

Each criterion should be weighted for importance, reflecting the product category and the company's long-term objectives. Table 6-3 shows how the GMC Envoy's SWOTs, as outlined in the opening case, could be evaluated and given priority scores.

TABLE 6-3   Prioritizing the GMC Envoy's SWOTs

Ranking of each SWOT item from 1 to 3 according to its importance to the company's objectives (with 3 being the most important).

	Damage If Not Addressed	Benefit If Leveraged	Cost of Addressing or Leveraging	Window of Time	Total*
Strengths					
• Strong GMC consumer franchise	—	2	3	1	6
• Good dealership network	—	2	3	1	6
• Identifiable target	—	3	3	3	9
Weaknesses					
• No Envoy brand awareness	3	—	2	3	8
• Not available until spring	3	—	3	3	9
• Small budget, no major MC support until spring	3	—	2	3	8
Opportunities					
• Increasing interest in SUVs	—	2	1	2	5
• Good economy	—	2	1	2	5
Threats					
• Established competitive brands	3	—	3	1	7
• New brands coming into market	2	—	2	1	5

*The higher the number, the higher the priority.

Once the SWOTs have been scored, the scores can be graphed as in Figure 6-2, which shows the key SWOTs more clearly than does Table 6-3. Notice that strengths and opportunities, which need to be leveraged, are charted above the middle line and that weaknesses and threats, which need to be addressed, are below the middle line. SWOTs that extend beyond the dotted "critical" lines are deemed to be most in need of being either leveraged or addressed. A company determines the critical lines based on past experience. As you can see, there were four key SWOTs on which the Envoy campaign needed to act.

After the company has prioritized the SWOTs, it must use them to set objectives. No company has the time or resources to address and leverage all its SWOT findings, but the prioritization can help IMC planners determine where to focus their attention. A prioritized SWOT analysis also leads to decisions about which marketing communication tools to use.

The Envoy campaign used direct response because the brand's SWOTs supported the use of an exclusive offer to a relatively small group of identifiable prospective customers whose interest had to be maintained over seven months. Although awareness was a key objective, it did not make sense to use mass media advertising because of the small target audience. In this case, the company understood that it could make good use of the awareness-building dimensions of direct

FIGURE 6-2

SWOTs that score beyond the critical limits (dotted lines) should be given top priority.

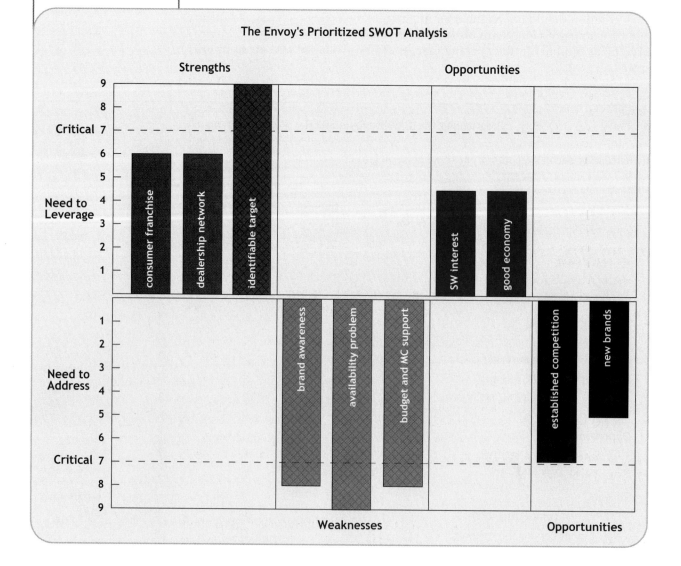

TABLE 6-4   Examples of Envoy's Measurable Objectives

Key SWOTs	MC Objectives	Best MC Function	Rationale
No brand awareness	Create 50% awareness among target	Advertising	Not appropriate because of small audience, product availability, and small budget
Identifiable target	Create 50% awareness among target	Direct marketing	Small audience; contact information available
Availability problem	Get 10% to visit showroom when available	Direct marketing	Build curiosity and draw out interest over a longer period of time
Low budget and little MC support	Sell 3,500 units in advance of availability	Direct marketing	Use personal contact medium to presell target

response. Somewhat unusual in the Envoy example is the fact that just one MC function, direct response, was used to achieve the four main MC objectives, which can be seen in Table 6-4.

Step 3: Determining Marketing Communication Objectives

The primary purpose of setting objectives is to state what is to be accomplished in order to direct an organization's efforts and allow the organization to evaluate effectiveness. **Objectives** are *what marketers want to accomplish with marketing communication.* They should be measurable if marketers truly want to prove that an MC plan was effective. "Measurable" means that numbers are assigned to the objectives, such as "Increase awareness by 10 percent" or "Motivate 70 percent to buy the brand again."

Prioritized SWOT Findings Determine Objectives

An example of how a SWOT analysis was used to set an objective comes from the wine industry. Retailing in the wine and liquor industry has moved from small family stores to large self-service stores. Because of this change, customers must make their own selections with little or no help from informed salesclerks. For years, winemaker Robert Mondavi depended on the retail sales staff to explain and sell the Mondavi brand. The loss of this support has become an increasing threat to the brand. It is an external threat because it is a situation over which Mondavi has no control.

To make this condition even worse for Mondavi, the number of wine choices has significantly increased (another external threat), making it even more difficult for a single brand to be noticed and selected. To address these two external threats, Mondavi and its agency, Ketchum, San Francisco, agreed that one of the company's primary MC objectives would be to increase direct contact with customers and prospects, regardless of where they buy their wine (see Exhibit 6-7). To make this objective measurable, Mondavi stated its objective as follows: "Generate 500,000 unique website visits and 150,000 customer-initiated calls to customer-service center by year-end."

What Makes a Good Objective?

Because a marketing plan defines the target audience at the outset, objectives do not have to mention the target. Only when the target audience is different from the

EXHIBIT 6-7
Newsletters can be designed to increase opportunities for direct contact with customers.

EXHIBIT 6-8
When something is measurable, you know exactly what to expect. This is important in any kind of strategic planning.

Numbers don't lie.

Take goats, for example.
How many Mongolian goats do you think it takes to get enough fleece to make a single Lands' End® Cashmere Sweater? The answer: anywhere from 2½ to 4 goats.

And guess how many feet of cotton yarn go into our men's Pinpoint Oxford shirts? 64,306 feet. That's a little over *12 miles* of cotton – in each shirt.

Fact is, we use lots and lots of cotton. Our Stonewashed Jeans are a tough 13½ oz. cotton denim: a fine, honest fabric. Know how much denim we used in our jeans last year? Enough to fill *19* railroad boxcars.

Now, we're not just playing with numbers here. Numbers tell a lot about Lands' End.

Like the more than *400* crofters – cottage weavers in Scotland–who hand weave the fabric for our Harris Tweed jackets.

Or the *115* inspectors who work full time trying to make sure everything that wears a Lands' End label deserves it.

In fact, when you figure what all the numbers say about Lands' End – our *passion* to get things right for our customers – doesn't it make you want to see a copy of our catalog?

We'd be happy to send you the latest number.

© 1998 Lands' End, Inc.

For a free catalog, call anytime
1-800-388-7941 [154]   *Guaranteed. Period.®*

Name _____
Address _____ Apt. _____
City _____ State _____ Zip _____
Phone ( ) _____ Day/Night (circle one)
Mail to: 1 Lands' End Lane, Dodgeville, WI 53595. **www.landsend.com/catalogs/154**

stated one is it necessary to define it in an objective. Also, it is assumed that each objective listed must be achieved within the year for which the plan is designed. As with the target audience, the time period is stated only when it differs from the overall plan—for example, "Within the first three months, obtain 75 percent awareness among the retail trade of the brand's new, improved formula."

Well-written objectives pass the SMAC test. They are

Specific.

Measurable.

Achievable.

Challenging.

The more *specific* an objective is, the better it is. The objective "Increase brand knowledge by 15 percent" is less specific than "Increase knowledge of the brand's superior warranty by 15 percent."

When objectives are *measurable,* it is easy to determine whether they have been achieved (see Exhibit 6-8). Many companies make the mistake of having *directional objectives* such as "Increase brand awareness." The problem with directional objectives is that it is difficult to tell when they have been achieved. For example, does a 1 percent increase in brand awareness achieve the objective "Increase brand awareness"? Technically speaking it does, but in most situations a 1 percent increase is seldom significant enough to satisfy management. When the objective is stated in measurable terms, such as "Increase awareness 10 percent," the organization can tell when the objective has been achieved (assuming, too, that the plan defines *awareness* and proposes a valid means of measuring it).

In order to set a realistic and measurable objective, a company first needs a *quantifiable measure of the current situation.* This measure is called the **baseline** or **benchmark.** For example, if you want to set a share-increase objective, you first need to know what the current share is. If the current share is 10 percent and you want to increase it to 12 percent, then you are proposing a change of 2 share points. This is a 20 percent increase (2/10 = 20%). But herein lies a problem for most companies: they are not willing to spend the money required to determine the necessary benchmarks. Unless a company knows what percentage of its target audience is aware of its brand, has tried it, has made repeat purchases, and so on, there is little or no basis for setting measurable objectives.

Unless objectives are *achievable,* those responsible for meeting them will not take them seriously. Some managers set objectives too high, hoping to maximize the effort of those involved. Because meeting objectives gives employees a sense of satisfaction, employees are likely to resent managers who consistently set unreachable objectives. Yet objectives should be *challenging* in order to push employees to be creative and do their best work. Admittedly, the line between challenging and unachievable may be thin, and it takes experience to know where that line is.

Communication Objectives versus Marketing Objectives

Because building and managing brand relationships requires influencing the attitudes and behavior of customers, IMC objectives are of two types. *Communication objectives* focus on attitudes. *Marketing objectives* focus on behaviors, what companies want customers and prospects to "do." In general, the most-desired objectives are to have customers buy the brand, make repeat purchases, and increase their amount of usage. However, having prospects request more information, visit a showroom, or sample the brand, and having customers refer the brand to others, are also desired behaviors. Objectives for each of those examples could be written like this:

Behavior Desired	*Measurable ("Do") Objectives*
• Request information	Receive 10,000 requests a month for new product brochure.
• Sample product	Distribute samples to 35 percent of target households.
• Visit showroom	Motivate 50 or more visits to showroom each week during promotion period.
• Make brand referrals	Generate 20,000 applications in which applicants indicate they were referred by a current customer.
• Make multiple purchases	Have 20 percent of all brand purchases be multiple purchases.
• Buy more frequently	Increase average rate of purchase from 2 times a month to 2.5 times a month.

All marketing communication should have a positive impact on either attitudes or behavior. Increasing the credibility of claims and reinforcing or changing brand positioning are examples of *communication* effects that can be tied to customer attitudes. Increasing trial, sales, and requests for information are examples of *marketing* effects on behavior. Both types of objectives are needed because customers and prospects can't be expected to "behave" in the desired way without being convinced that to do so is in their best interests.

Using Consumer Behavior Models to Set Objectives

As explained in Chapter 5, hierarchy-of-effects models explain how brand messages affect the brand decision-making process. Companies use the steps in these models to guide them in setting MC objectives. The AIDA sequence—awareness, interest, desire, action—for example, suggests that a brand have *communication*

EXHIBIT 6-9

Understanding the frustration of drivers who are driving in urban traffic leads to an objective for Minneapolis Metro Transit that seeks to move people out of their cars and onto mass transit.

objectives for achieving certain levels of brand awareness, certain levels of interest, and so on. Action, the last step in the AIDA sequence, is a *marketing* (behavioral) objective (see Exhibit 6-9).

In the case of B2B products and high-priced consumer products, MC objectives may address where customers are in their buying process. An insurance company may set an MC objective for its sales representatives as follows: "All customers who request a quote on their home and automobile insurance policies will be contacted personally within 72 hours of their quote requests." This objective would relate directly to customers at the interest step in the AIDA decision-making hierarchy.

Figure 6-3 shows that the percentage of the target audience affected at each hierarchical step gets smaller as customers move toward the last step, action. This illustration gives hypothetical response rates to demonstrate how drastically the percentage of customers affected drops as customers move through this series of effects. Drop-off happens because making people aware of a brand is much easier than persuading them to buy a brand or take some other action. The level of expected impact obviously varies with the product category, the brand, and the strength of the brand messages.

FIGURE 6-3

Achieving communication objectives is easier than achieving marketing (behavioral) objectives.

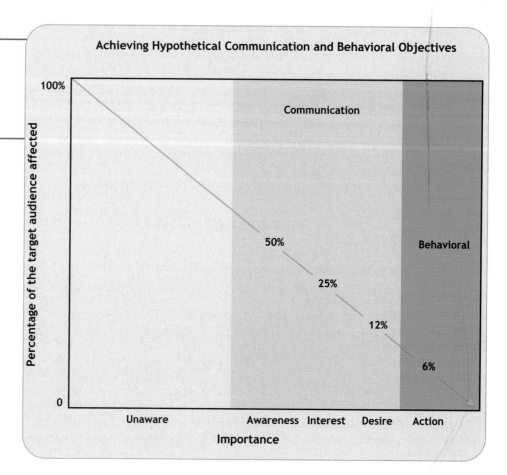

Achieving Hypothetical Communication and Behavioral Objectives

MC objectives can also be based on the think/feel/do model (◀ Chapter 5). Once a company decides what a target audience should think and feel about a brand, it can determine a desired percentage for thinking and feeling. Examples of "do" objectives were given earlier. Here are examples of "think" and "feel" communication objectives:

"Think" Objectives

- Convince 50 percent of the target audience that Brand X is the most durable.
- Make 35 percent of the target audience aware that Brand X has the longest warranty.

"Feel" Objectives

- Have 40 percent of the target audience rate Brand X as the brand "easiest to do business with."
- Convince 55 percent of the target audience that Brand X is the most prestigious of all brands in its category.

The quantitative aspect of an objective—the percentage or raw number to be achieved—often depends on the brand's past performance and how much MC support is available. The more research that has been done on the results of past MC efforts, the more educated the current estimate can be. For example, if customers' measured interest in the brand is generally half of their measured awareness of the brand, and their action is half of their desire for the brand, it would be realistic to set an awareness objective of 80 percent, an interest objective of 40 percent, and a desire objective of 20 percent in order to justify increasing the action objective to 10 percent.

Setting Customer-Focused Objectives

MC objectives should also be set for one or more of the eight relationship constructs listed earlier in this chapter. Knowing that trust, for example, is the most important relationship component, a brand would be smart to have a trust objective, such as "Determine that at least 85 percent of current customers *trust* our brand more than any other." Other such communication objectives could include the following:

- "75 percent say our brand is the most *responsive*."
- "80 percent say our brand is the most *consistent* in its dealings with customers."
- "90 percent say our company is more *accessible* than any other competing company."

Some marketers don't focus too much on attitudinal objectives because, they argue, there is no absolute link between achieving them and achieving behavioral objectives. Although it is true that increases in awareness, trust, and other pure communication measures do not guarantee increases in sales, common sense says that if no one is aware of a brand, or if those who are aware of a brand don't trust it, the chances of it selling well are small. The exact relationship between attitudes and behavior differs by brand and over time as marketplace conditions change, but there is always some level of relationship. This is why it is imperative that brands conduct ongoing evaluations of customer perceptions and behavior.

Once the objectives have been written in terms of leveraging or addressing the key SWOTS, the next step in zero-based planning is figuring out how to achieve the objectives.

Step 4: Developing Strategies and Tactics

Every objective should be supported by one or more strategies. **Strategies** are *ideas about how to accomplish objectives*. In the Envoy case at the beginning of the chapter, the strategy was to take audience members on a virtual Envoy tour of Europe. To accomplish this, various tactics were used. **Tactics** are *specific actions to be taken to execute a strategy*. They are the executional details that bring a strategic idea to life. In the Envoy case, the foreign-addressed envelopes, the pictures of the brothers and of other European scenes, and the details of the sweepstakes were tactics.

The MC agencies are generally responsible for tactics as well as strategies. Artists, writers, producers, and creative directors make the strategic ideas come to life in the form of commercials, brochures, and merchandising kits. Notice how both strategies and tactics are discussed in the Snapple case in the IMC in Action box. (Chapter 9 discusses message strategies in more detail; Chapter 10 covers tactics).

Phases of Strategy Development

The strategic development of an MC plan generally goes through two phases. The first is determining *which* MC functions and which media to use. This is generally obvious from the SWOT findings, as previously explained. The second phase is the more creatively challenging and is the reason why companies hire MC agencies. In this phase, ideas must be created for *how* each MC function and medium will be used. (Phase three is selling the creative ideas to management.)

Phase 1: Selecting the Marketing Communication and Media Mixes
Most marketing communication plans use a mix of MC functions because there are always several SWOT-identified areas that need to be addressed or leveraged. A **marketing communication mix** is *the selection of MC functions used at a given time as part of a marketing program* (see Exhibit 6-11). Deciding which MC functions can most efficiently and effectively help achieve the MC objectives is not too difficult if marketers stop and think about what each MC function does best. For example, to help achieve the objective "Increase belief of brand claims by 15 percent," publicity would be used because it has relatively high credibility. If the objective is "Increase trial by 25 percent," then sales promotion may be the best MC tool because sales promotion adds tangible value to a brand offering. The larger the MC budget is, the deeper a company can go in addressing and leveraging SWOTs; often the result is the use of several of the major MC functions.

The challenge of determining an MC mix is not only deciding which functions to use but determining how much of each. One MC function may take the lead while one or more of the others are used for support. It may be decided, for example, that an event, such as exhibiting at trade shows, is the major MC function to be used. This is the case with ProTeam, a B2B company that makes and sells industrial vacuum cleaners. ProTeam uses some advertising in trade magazines, but over 75 percent of its marketing communication budget goes into exhibiting at trade shows. This MC mix reflects the company learning that, while trade magazine advertising helps keep the ProTeam brand top-of-mind, it was more cost-effective to convert prospects into buyers and to maintain relationships with customer by exhibiting at more trade shows.

In the Envoy case, a SWOT analysis determined that one of the main objectives should be to create awareness of the new Envoy among 50 percent of the target audience. The first strategic decision to be made, therefore, was to identify the best MC functions and media to use. Envoy's limited budget made mass media advertising (often used to create awareness) not an option. What made the most sense was direct marketing and the medium of regular mail. As Table 6-5 indicates, the

IMC IN ACTION

Snapple Ups and Downs

The Snapple brand of fruit and tea beverages started in Brooklyn in 1972 and became a huge marketing success in the 1980s. Its relationship with its customers created a cult-like devotion that even involved customers sending in ideas for new flavors. Wendy, the "Snapple lady," was the star of marketing communication that featured her as epitomizing the brand's personality. Originally a receptionist for Snapple, Wendy was shown opening the mail and reading letters from enthusiastically satisfied customers. Because of her success in this role and the strength of this idea as a campaign theme, Wendy eventually became head of a six-person customer-service department that handled an average of 2,000 letters a week.

Despite its successful customer relationships, Snapple had problems expanding its distribution beyond the mom-and-pop stores that had been its loyal supporters in the beginning. Larger retail chains simply would not carry the brand. Enter Quaker (the giant packaged-foods company), which had solved a similar problem when it took over Gatorade.

Investors believed that Snapple had grown as much as it could as an independent and needed the marketplace power of a large company like Quaker to solve its distribution problems. Unfortunately, Quaker's pressure on retailers to stock the full line of Snapple beverages irritated these retailers and left many of the brand's loyal distributors out in the cold. Furthermore, Quaker seemed not to understand the magic of the marketing communication that had created the Snapple cult; instead, it moved toward more traditional image-oriented campaigns.

Quaker's major marketing effort became an ambitious sampling

EXHIBIT 6-10

program in the summer of 1996 that was intended to expand Snapple's market and reach consumers at every possible point of contact from beaches to parks to Little League games to office buildings. Unfortunately the "Snapple Sample Guys" didn't connect with enough consumers to rebuild the Snapple franchise. In 1997 Quaker sold Snapple to Triarc Companies, taking an estimated $1.4 billion loss. Triarc focused on the youth market and increased Snapple's distribution before selling the brand to Cadbury Schweppes in October 2000.

Cadbury Schweppes continued the focus on the younger demographic with a wacky campaign that featured fruit ripening into maturity and encountering fruit sex. A little racy, perhaps, but the fruit-love spoofs continued to push sales growth after Snapple turned its fortunes around and became profitable once again.

And now Snapple has launched a clever website called "Snappleton," which is a virtual community that contains museums, movie houses, and post offices, as well as interactive stories about the interconnected lives of the people you find in these places. Snapple has also produced TV commercials that animate their beverage jars (see Exhibit 6-10).

Think About It

What was the source of Snapple's success in its early days? What caused Snapple sales to tumble? Could that problem have been solved with a new or different marketing communication program? Does targeting a younger audience make sense? Will the "fruit love" idea or the Snappleton website re-create the customer bonds of the original campaign?

Source: "Snapple Launches Clever Site Called 'Snappleton,'" *URLwire,* May 20, 2002; Apryl Duncan, "Snapple Gets Sexy," *Advertising About,* April 30, 2002, <http://advertising.about. com/library/weekly/aa050101a.html>; "Phyllis Berman, "Juicing It Up," *Forbes,* May 18, 1998, pp. 134–36; Cliff Edwards, "Quaker Oats Co. Sells Snapple at $1.4 Billion Loss," *Daily Camera,* March 28, 1997, p. 6b; Greg Gattuso, "Drinking It in Communication Is Key to Snapple's Customer Loyalty," *Direct Marketing,* October 1995, pp. 26–29.

EXHIBIT 6-11

Companies often use a mix of marketing communication functions in a campaign such as was used by the Canadian Egg Association.

direct-response function uses many different types of media. The Envoy plan relied on regular mail because it enabled the use of foreign stamps and exotic return addresses, which got the target audience's attention.

Selecting the right media mix is just as important as selecting the right MC mix. A **media mix** is *a selection of media channels used to deliver brand messages.* Media mix

186

TABLE 6-5   Extent of Media Usage by Each Major MC Function

MC Functions	TV	Radio	Newspaper	Magazine	Mail	Int	
Advertising	XXX	XXX	XXX	XXX	X	XXX	
Publicity	XXX	XXX	XXX	XXX		XXX	
Sales promotion	X	X	XXX	XXX	XX	XX	
Events			X	X	X	X	
Direct response	XX	X	X	XX	XXX	XXX	
Sponsorships	XXX	XX		XX		XX	X
Personal selling					XX	XX	

Note: The number of X's represents to what extent each MC function makes use of each medium: XXX = frequently used; XX = occasionally used; X = rarely used.

strategies and creative message strategies are interdependent and ideally are developed in parallel. For each target audience, a strategic media mix is determined. In any given campaign, different types of media can be used at different times and to different extents to deliver specific types of messages to specific audiences (media mix is discussed in detail in Chapters 11 through 13). As you can see in Table 6-5, most media are used by most of the MC functions but to varying degrees. For example, sales-promotion offers are most often delivered by mail, magazines, and newspapers, and very seldom by radio and TV (infomercials and home shopping channels are direct-marketing activities). This is why the MC mix and the media mix must be integrated.

The media strategy of the Robert Mondavi winery, discussed earlier, included not only advertising in specialty magazines (a medium Mondavi had used rarely over the years) but also a newsletter and direct-mail pieces sent to people who visited the Mondavi winery or its internet site (which receives about 5,000 visits a month).[3] By using personalized direct mail aimed at customers who initiated contact with the brand, Mondavi's strategy was to replace the personal attention consumers once received in the family-owned stores.

Phase 2: Selecting the Creative Idea Inexperienced marketers often mistakenly think that selecting a particular MC function or medium constitutes a strategy. But for the Envoy launch, simply sending standard direct-mail pieces would likely have been ineffective. The big creative idea—to take the audience on a virtual test drive—made the strategy succeed. Once direct mail was selected as the primary medium for delivering the introductory messages for Envoy, the next step was to come up with a creative way to use the direct-mail messages to achieve the agreed-upon objectives.

The creative strategy was a virtual tour with two fictitious brothers, one of them a diplomatic envoy. The creative strategy and media strategy worked because together they were able to get attention and involve and motivate the targeted prospects to respond.

The media strategy was a series of mailings, to the target audience, of engaging letters that the two brothers had written to each other. The strategy called for the mailings to look noncommercial (see Exhibit 6-12). In one letter, Andrew refers to

EXHIBIT 6-12

Mailing from England with cocktail-napkin sketch

the Envoy's high-intensity discharge headlamps, calling them "some new-generation thingamajig." In the next letter, Steven gives technical reasons to explain why this "thingamajig" is so revolutionary. The letters were written in a personal and often humorous manner and contained enclosures such as a paper cocktail napkin that had a sketch of Andrew.

Let's compare a weak, incomplete strategy with a good, complete strategy. "Use sales promotion": this is a weak, incomplete strategy because it doesn't contain an *idea* about how to use the MC tool. "Use a team of doctors to conduct a media tour explaining the breakthrough qualities of the brand in curing the common cold": this is a much better strategy. Tactical decisions would involve selecting the towns, such as the top 10 markets, for the media tour. This strategy not only implies a MC function—publicity—but states an idea for *getting* publicity.

Another good example is the strategy used by Michelin, a manufacturer of premium-priced automobile tires. One of Michelin's communication objectives is to convince car owners that Michelin tires are the most durable and safest tires on the market. A weak strategy to accomplish this objective would have been "Use television advertising." Instead, Michelin devised a strong, creative strategy: "Associate the Michelin brand name with protecting families by showing babies sitting on or in Michelin tires." This strategy links Michelin tires to babies (who, everyone knows, are precious and have to be protected); the message is "Michelin is a safe tire—it protects."

For more on the development of creative ideas, see Chapters 9 and 10. In addition, each of the chapters in Part IV, on the major MC functions, gives examples of creative strategies.

Phase 3: Selling the Strategy with a Strong Rationale The last component in developing strategies is to explain why the strategy ideas are sound. Executing ideas, particularly the production and media placements of brand messages—costs money, and managers responsible for approving expenditures want to be given reasons why the strategic ideas being presented will work. If the agency or department recommending strategies cannot provide a convincing rationale, the ideas probably are not very good.

GMC's rationale for using direct mail was that the audience was small, the contact information was available, and a more general mass media campaign would be inefficient. The rationale for the creative strategy—the two-brothers-in-Europe virtual tour—was that (1) the target audience was sophisticated world travelers, so the foreign stamps and return addresses of upscale European hotels would be attention getting and enticing; (2) the upscale direct mailing was strategically consistent with the image objective for the new Envoy; and (3) the postcards would build curiosity and extend interest over a longer period of time because they would break through the typical "junk mail" clutter.

Strategy Involves Timing and Scheduling

An important aspect of MC strategy is timing and scheduling—determining which media placements, promotional programs, and other MC activities should happen first or last or in between. For example, most brands have seasonal buying patterns—sales are higher during some months and lower during others. Most swimsuits in the United States, for example, are sold in late spring and early summer. Strategic planners must decide how far in advance of the buying season to start sending out brand messages and how late into the buying season to maintain marketing communication support.

There is no magic formula for timing promotional programs. Normally each product category has its own seasonal pattern. Companies can apply some logic, however. Most promotional support for swimsuits, for example, begins in late winter and early spring. This is when people begin to tire of cold weather and begin thinking about the pleasures of summer. During this time, people are most receptive to swimsuit brand messages. Another factor is when retail stores begin displaying the suits. When stores set out new merchandise, they expect manufacturers to have marketing communication programs running that will help generate sales.

Another timing concern is when the other MC functions are to be used. For a direct-response campaign that uses mass media advertising, direct mail, and telemarketing, timing is extremely important. The mass media advertising should run two to three weeks before the direct mail is sent out. Two to three days after the direct mail hits, the telemarketing should be done. The mass media advertising urges the target audience to look for the direct-mail offer, which helps take it out of the junk-mail category. But if the telemarketing starts too early, before the direct mail hits, the response will be significantly less because the target audience's awareness of the brand and offer is still weak or nonexistent. If the telemarketing starts a week or more after the direct mail has hit, the impact of the direct mail will have been lost and again the response rate will be less.

Timing is also important when publicity is part of an MC campaign. Where the publicity angle has news value (for example, a new product or a significant improvement to an old product), it is better to do the brand publicity before advertising. This way, the information is still news and editors will be more likely to run the stories.

A challenge often faced by both B2C and B2B companies is coordinating the timing between marketing, production, and sales. Each of these areas needs lead times of several months (sometimes even more). Once a new product has been given the go-ahead for production, three to six months may elapse before the first product is actually manufactured. At the same time, sales is making calls and presenting the new product so that when production starts, finished goods will not have to sit in a warehouse for long. To support the sales effort, marketing communication materials—ads, direct-mail pieces, special events, trade-show exhibits—need to be produced, which can take several months. In the case of some consumer products, media time and space need to be bought three to six months ahead to guarantee the best rates and placement.

If any of these departments—production, sales, marketing communication—fails to perform as planned, then the company begins to lose money, top management starts asking embarrassing questions, and customers become disillusioned because things didn't happen as they had been promised. When timing fails, relationships both internally and externally can be hurt.

In the case of new consumer products, most companies don't like to begin marketing communication support for a product until it has at least a 60 percent "all commodity volume" (ACV) level of distribution. In other words, until the product is on display and available for consumer purchase in stores that account for 60 percent of all retail sales in the product category, a company feels it is wasting its marketing communication dollars. And even with 60 percent ACV, this means only 6 out of 10 consumers who see the marketing communication and then look for the product will find it.

Timing and coordination go together. They are both critical elements of integration. The best way to ensure right timing is to discuss individual department plans in cross-functional meetings, letting everyone know what everyone else is planning to do and when they are planning to do it.

Step 5: Setting the Budget

Marketing and marketing communication departments (and their campaigns) are allocated *a fixed amount of money for a fixed period of time*—in other words, a **budget.**

EXHIBIT 6-13
The pieces in an MC mix can include ads, brochures, and direct-mail pieces. All of these pieces, and the departments that created them, fight for a share of the MC budget.

Marketing competes with all other corporate departments (such as finance, production, and human resources) for its share of the total corporate budget. Each department brings in a budget along with a projection of what the spending will do to contribute to the company's profits. Management then allocates a portion of the overall corporate budget to each department based on what management feels is the best combination of spending to maximize profits.

In a perfect world, these allocations would be done objectively and rationally. The reality is, however, that allocating corporate funds can be highly political. The more political power certain managers or departments have, the more likely they are to receive more than their objective share. That's why cross-functional management is important. The more others in the company, especially top management, know what the marketing department does and accomplishes, the more political support it is likely to have.

Once marketing receives its budget, it then needs to allocate the money to the various MC functional areas (see Exhibit 6-13), which, like the departments, compete among themselves for what they feel is necessary to run their programs. A universal curse of planning is that no one ever has a large enough budget to do everything that needs to be done. This means adjustments need to be made in plans. In the case of marketing communications planning, this adjustment can be made fairly easily if the plan is based on prioritized SWOTs. Managers simply go back to the plan and take out the lowest-priority objective or two—whatever it takes to stay in budget. The remaining objectives and supporting strategies then determine how much money will be allocated to each MC function and to major types of media.

Cost or Investment?

From an accounting perspective, MC spending is an expense—one of the many costs necessary to run a business. Most marketers, however, prefer to think of MC spending as an investment. The difference in these two philosophical perspectives is that "costs" are necessary evils but "investments" provide something called a *return on investment (ROI)*. The better the investment is—the smarter marketers and their agencies are about how MC dollars are spent—the greater is the return on the MC investment.

The problem with considering MC spending as an investment is that so many other things besides ads and promotions affect sales. Some of these other variables are support received from channel members, what competitors do regarding making product improvements or changing prices, new government regulations that affect producing or selling the company's product, and social and economic trends that affect how consumers spend their money. Even weather can affect sales: above-average number of storms can shut down airports, or a cold spring can reduce swimsuit sales. Consequently, although marketers promise that they can create a certain level of sales, top management knows that these promises are subject to many unknown and uncontrollable factors.

When a company's top executives consider MC a cost rather than an investment (as most of them do), they are much more likely to cut MC spending when business becomes weak. They argue that by cutting costs, they can maintain profits (profits are what is left after costs are subtracted from total sales revenue). Marketers argue back that reducing MC spending will result in sales being reduced even more. The problem with both arguments is that they can be proved only after the fact—after costs have been cut or after a plan is allowed to run without being cut.

The best support that marketers can have for getting larger marketing budgets and protecting these budgets from midyear cuts is history. As mentioned in Chapter 1, companies today have the ability to track sales and closely measure what effects MC programs have on sales. Unfortunately, such tracking is often a low priority and therefore is seldom done.

Determining How Much to Spend on MC

Many factors, both internal and external, can affect sales and how customers respond to MC. Nevertheless, most marketers agree that the relationship between MC spending and sales roughly follows an S curve, as shown in Figure 6-4. The relationship between MC spending and sales is not linear—that is, increases in

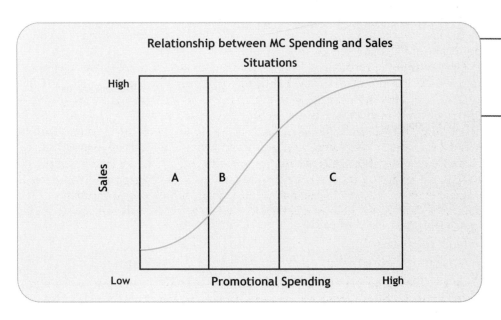

FIGURE 6-4

Why is Situation B the ideal spending range?

dollars spent do not generate a constant increase in sales. The S curve shows that when a company underspends (situation A), there is little impact on sales. Underspending is relative to competitors' MC spending and means the brand's advertising and promotion are not enough to have a presence and therefore have little impact. Like a choir with too few members, too little spending can hardly be heard. The middle part of the S curve (situation B) is the ideal spending range: incremental spending produces incremental sales. At the top of the S curve (situation C), the return from additional spending has a decreasing affect on increasing sales. Situation C often indicates that the market has been saturated. Everyone who is likely to respond to brand messages has been reached and persuaded to buy. Those who are still not customers would require so much persuading that it would not be cost-effective to do so.

Determining the spending level that will correspond with situation B, in which the company gets the best return on the MC dollars spent, is challenging, because the "right amount" of spending varies by product category and even by brand. Once again, a brand's MC and sales history is the best information that a company has to go on. The more accurate a company is in tracking its sales in relation to its MC spending, the better are its chances of arriving at the most cost-effective level of MC spending.

Companies use several different budgeting methods to determine how much money to allocate to MC. Recognizing the difficulty of predicting sales results, most companies use a combination of four types of budgeting: percent-of-sales, return-on-investment, objective-and-task, and share-of-voice.

Percent-of-Sales Budgeting This method is based on the sales forecast for the coming year and the costs for making and selling the product. This percentage is found in a brand's financial **pro forma**, which is *a breakdown of forecasted sales on a per unit basis*, as shown in Table 6-6.

To budget for MC, a marketer looks at all the costs involved in making and selling a product, as well as a desired (and realistic) profit. Each area (production, MC, distribution, and so on) estimates how much money it will need to do its job. These amounts are added up, and a total cost per unit is determined. The company

TABLE 6-6   Pro Forma for Maple Syrup Manufacturer

Forecasted number of cases that will be sold next year		1,000,000
Sales price per case		$25
Forecasted sales revenue		$25,000,000
	Dollar Allocation per Case	**Percentage of Sales**
Cost of goods (materials)	$10.00	40%
Labor	2.50	10
Warehousing and distribution	1.25	5
Sales commission	2.50	10
Marketing communication	**2.50**	**10**
Administration and overhead	3.75	15
Profit before taxes	2.50	10
Total	$25.00	100%

then estimates, by looking at competition and examining its own competitive advantages, what it believes is a reasonable selling price per unit. It then subtracts all the costs from this selling price to determine whether enough profit is left to meet desired profit objectives. If there is not, then all the various areas must see where they can reduce costs. Also, the selling price may have to be adjusted as well as the desired profit objectives. Cross-functional management can be helpful in this process.

Marketers have found they can help themselves in these budget negotiations with on-going internal messages about the role of MC in strengthening brand–customer relationships and selling products. This is called *internal marketing,* which is "the application of marketing inside the organization to instill customer-focused values."[4] Internal marketing is critical in making the planning process run smoothly and keeping employees and departments informed of MC plans and is explained in more detail later in this chapter.

Once budget adjustments have been resolved, all operating areas (of which MC is one) know how much money they have to spend. To illustrate how a pro forma is used in budgeting, we'll look at how a manufacturer of maple syrup goes about budgeting. The manufacturer of maple syrup (see Table 6-6) estimates that at $25 a case, it can sell 1 million cases in a year. It then figures how much it will cost to make and sell this many cases and how much profit it needs to make. As the table indicates, $2.50 per case is the allocation for MC, which is 10 percent of sales. To determine the *total* MC budget, multiply the number of cases that the company expects to sell (1,000,000) by $2.50, which comes to $2,500,000.

A critical element of a pro forma is the sales forecast. Suppose the maple syrup company didn't make its sales forecast and sold only 800,000 cases. If it still spent $2.5 million on marketing communication, it would have spent 12.5 percent rather than 10 percent of sales (800,000 × $25 = $20,000,000; then $2,500,000 ÷ $20,000,000 = 12.5%) on marketing communications. This extra 2.5 percentage points (which equals $500,000) must come out of profit, which would make top management very upset! Typically, if a company sees midyear that it's not going to make its sales forecast, it will cancel some of the marketing communication programs to avoid hurting profits. (Although that is not always a smart thing to do, it is done frequently.)

In most companies, the percentage of sales spent on marketing communication is similar from year to year. Many companies that use this budgeting method also keep their MC and media allocations nearly the same from year to year, as well. For example, if 50 percent of the MC budget was spent on TV and magazine advertising last year, that is the percentage of the MC budget that will be allocated to TV and magazine advertising this year. As you might imagine, merely repeating the previous year's spending mix, regardless of changes in the marketplace, is the easiest but not always the smartest way to budget. What is smart is to analyze what last year's budget was able to produce, and to determine which MC functions and media provided the greatest return. These findings, along with an analysis of what it will cost to accomplish specific objectives, should determine how much to spend on MC.

Another drawback to the percent-of-sales method is that it assumes that the creative strategy and execution, as well as the MC functions used, are the same from year to year. The reality is, if a company and its MC agencies are able to come up with a creative idea that is very attention getting, memorable, and persuasive, the company may actually be able to cut back on spending because the brand messages are working harder than normal. (Some would argue that when such a successful campaign is developed, spending should be increased in order to fully leverage its impact. This is an especially strong argument for a brand that has a relatively small share of market and thus a lot of opportunity for growth.)

ROI Budgeting **Return-on-investment (ROI)** is *a ratio of income to spending.* Top management likes this method because it comes closest to telling to what extent the company will profit from the dollars allocated. There's an old saying: "You have to spend money to make money." To be profitable, however, a company must make *more* money than it spends. If it spends $100, it had better make back more than $100. This is called a positive ROI and is necessary to stay in business. One of top management's major responsibilities is to *maximize* the return on the monies the company spends. Therefore, the more an MC department can promise AND support a high level of return, the more likely it is to receive the budget it requests.

ROI budgeting is also used to help determine whether *extra* MC spending is a good investment. Suppose the maple syrup company has an opportunity to sponsor 10 major festivals in New England during October when the leaves are at their peak of fall colors. The cost of the sponsorships is $200,000. Money for this sponsorship was not included in the budget, so the sponsorships must produce sales in addition to the 1 million cases already budgeted for. The question that marketing must answer is: How many additional cases must be sold to pay for this sponsorship—that is, to make it worth doing?

To answer this question, it is necessary to do a **breakeven analysis,** which is *a formula for determining the point at which the cost of selling equals the revenue.* The formula is: Promotion cost divided by the dollars per case available. We know that the promotion cost is ($200,000). But what are the "dollars per case available" to pay for this? To find this, we go back to the company's pro forma (see Table 6-6). At first glance, we might say the dollars available are $2.50, which is the amount per case allocated to MC. But there is actually more money available. We can add to the MC $2.50 the monies allocated to "administration and overhead" ($3.75) and the "profit before taxes" ($2.50), because "administration and overhead" is a fixed cost and the $2.50 per case for profit was to generate $2.5 million, which is all the company is expecting in profit. Fixed costs, such as electricity, heating, and employee salaries, are those that do not change even with slight sales variations.

Dollars Available per *Extra* Case Sold

Regular MC allocation	$2.50
Administration and overhead	3.75
Profit before taxes	2.50
Total per extra case	$8.75

We can now determine how many extra cases must be sold as a direct result of the festival sponsorship. We divide $200,000 by $8.75, which equals 22,857 cases, which is the minimum ROI (number of cases needed to be sold to break even on an investment of $200,000):

$$\frac{\text{Cost of sponsorship}}{\text{Cost available per case}} = \text{Number of cases necessary to break even}$$

$$\frac{\$200,000}{\$8.75} = 22,875 \text{ cases}$$

Once the company's marketing and sales force know how many extra cases have to be sold, a judgment call must be made. If they feel confident that the festivals will be able to generate that amount or, better yet, *more* than that amount, then the sponsorship would be considered a good investment, particularly if the Northeast is an area where the company wants to increase its market share.

ROI also can be used to evaluate two different MC programs. An insurance company did this when it wanted to test the idea of adding telemarketing to its media mix. In this case, ROI is the cost per sale generated by each of the two plans.

TABLE 6-7

	Traditional Allocation		Test Allocation	
Advertising	70%	$175,000	10%	$25,000
Direct mail	30	75,000	25	62,500
Telemarketing	–	–	65	162,000
Total		$250,000		$250,000

Both plans spent the same amount of money, but the allocations (how the monies were spent) varied. Traditionally, when introducing a new product, the company used advertising (TV and newspaper) and direct mail. Table 6-7 is a breakdown of the regular mix and the test mix, the leads generated, and, most important, the average cost per sale.

Table 6-8 shows the results. The objective was to generate quality sales leads that could be converted into transactions. As the two ROIs in the table demonstrate, the test plan produced 563 sales with a cost-per-sale of $444, while the regular MC plan cost-per-sale was $6,250. In other words, the ROI of the test plan was 14 times better than the ROI of the regular MC plan.

Objective-and-Task Budgeting This method starts with zero-based planning which determines the marketing communication objectives and the "tasks" that need to be done to accomplish each objective. An **objective-and-task budget** is *an estimate of the cost of each MC task identified by zero-based planning.* Suppose one objective is "To increase customer retention 10 percent," and it's decided that the most cost-effective way to do this is to send each customer a New Year's thank-you basket of fruit and candy. This cost can be easily estimated. If this or a similar program has been used before, *and* if the company kept a record of these programs and their results, the costs and results can be more accurately predicted.

MC agencies often have useful information about the cost to achieve certain objectives, particularly if they used similar programs with other clients and know the costs and results. (Of course, it must be kept in mind that agencies are eager to sell

TABLE 6-8

	Leads Generated	
	Regular Plan	Test Plan
Advertising	438	375
Direct mail	812	750
Telemarketing	–	2,625
Leads generated	1,250	3,750
Cost per lead	$\dfrac{\$250,000}{1,250} = \$200$	$\dfrac{\$250,000}{3,750} = \$67$
Conversions (sales made)	40	563
ROI—Cost per sale	$\dfrac{\$250,000}{40} = \$6,250$	$\dfrac{\$250,000}{536} = \$444$

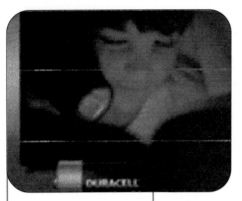

EXHIBIT 6-14

Companies that produce competing products frequently become locked in a battle where sales are thought to depend on share-of-voice media spending.

their programs and thus will sometimes select the most positive results to share with clients.)

The limitation of objective-and-task budgeting is the difficulty of accurately predicting how much spending is needed to accomplish each objective. What worked last year may not work this year.

Share-of-Voice Budgeting Share-of-voice spending is *a brand's portion of total media spending in that brand's product category.* Many marketers assume that share-of-voice spending should be fairly close to a brand's share of market. Thus, if total media spending in the small-battery category is $300 million a year, and Duracell is spending $100 million, then Duracell's share-of-voice spending should be around 33 percent. If Duracell's share of market is 45 percent, most advertising agencies would say that the brand is underspending (see Exhibit 6-14). If such a difference existed, Duracell's marketing managers would have a strong argument for asking top management for a larger budget. If a brand wants to significantly increase its share of market, it must be prepared for share-of-voice spending to be greater than its current share of market.

Like other methods, share-of-voice spending has its shortcomings. Like percent-of-sales budgeting, it fails to take into consideration the quality of the creative messages. Share-of-voice spending also doesn't allow for reacting to changes in the marketplace other than competitors' increases or decreases in their MC spending. For example, if a major competitor gets into profit trouble and greatly reduces its MC spending, share-of-voice budgeting would have all the other brands also reducing their spending levels, when in fact this may be the best time to increase spending and take advantage of a major competitor's weakness.

MC Budget Allocations

Once the marketing department is told by top management how much the marketing budget will be, marketing must decide how this money will be spent. The first allocation decision is by target market. How will money be divided between efforts to acquire targeted customers and efforts to retain current customers and get a larger share of their category spending? This decision is based on return on spending—in other words, the sales revenue that will result from spending $100 to get new customers versus the amount that will result from spending $100 to retain current customers.

The final allocation is based on geography. Because most companies have different levels of distribution and different shares of market from city to city, the amount of advertising and promotion effort often differs from market to market. An example of a strategy that can be used for geographical budget allocations comes from Eckrich, a processed meat company.

Eckrich divided its markets into three groups: mature, introductory, and growth. The mature markets were those where Eckrich's share was over 25 percent; introductory markets were those where market share was below 10 percent, and growth markets were those in which share was 10 to 25 percent. As a result of discussions with the company's MC agency it was decided to use the mature market allocation as a benchmark. Introductory markets would be allocated only 50 percent of what the mature markets were allocated, and growth markets would be allocated 150 percent. These allocations are summarized below:

Market	Share	Allocation
Introductory	<10%	50%
Growth	10-25%	150%
Mature	>25%	100%

To determine the 100 percent weight, the MC agency determined the media costs in all the markets. This calculation in turn enabled it to come up with what an equal or 100 percent weight would be for all markets. The rationale for this allocation strategy was that distribution and share were so low in the introductory markets that there were not enough sales to justify a lot of spending. In the case of growth markets, the rationale was that there was now enough distribution in the market to risk investment spending to build a strong consumer base. As for the mature markets, the benchmark spending was the level needed to defend against competitors and maintain share.

Step 6: Evaluating Effectiveness

Sometimes marketing communication is great: you remember the ad and the brand, the promotion draws people into the store, and the store display motivates people to try the product. Sometimes marketing communication doesn't work: the ad is forgettable or the point is unclear, no one remembers the promotion, and the direct-mail piece gets thrown away without being opened. Rance Crain, editor in chief of *Advertising Age*, wonders why it comes as a shock to companies when their advertising doesn't work. After mentioning a couple of examples of ads and promotional pieces that didn't work, he observed that "Companies don't realize the implications of their ads because the managers all think the same." He concludes that "They need to spend more time with ordinary people."[5] In other words, marketing and agency people need to do a better job of research on the effectiveness of their creative ideas as they are developing them.

Market Testing

Because the marketplace changes constantly, the only way to know whether something will work is to try it. Good annual plans have some type of testing built in. Procter & Gamble, for example, is always testing new advertising approaches. For most of its major brands, it has three different creative campaigns in the works. One is the national campaign. The second is a campaign that has beaten the national campaign in a laboratory test and is now running in a few test markets to determine whether it does, in fact, produce better results than the national campaign in the "real world." The third campaign is the one being developed to beat the campaign that is in test market.

Another important planning element marketers should test constantly is the level of media spending. How much media spending is too much? How much is too little? Many brands select two or three markets and increase media spending (and other marketing communication support) to see whether sales increase enough to pay for the extra spending and earn the company extra profits. At the same time, companies are always trying to determine the minimal level of spending necessary to maintain their brands' market share.

When a company is considering major changes in marketing communication strategies—such as repositioning, changing the brand name, changing an advertising theme that has been successful for several years—a market test can help determine whether these major changes can be cost-justified.

The downside of test marketing is that it is time-consuming and costly. A test market requires customizing the changes to be tested and then isolating and monitoring these markets to ensure the test is conducted without bias. Most market tests must last at least six months before results are valid. Finally, by the time a test market is conducted and analyzed and changes suggested by the findings are incorporated into the whole marketing process, from one to two years have gone by. Because the marketplace is constantly changing, the findings and implied changes may no longer be as relevant as they would have been two years before. Chapter 22 goes into greater depth about the various test methods that companies and

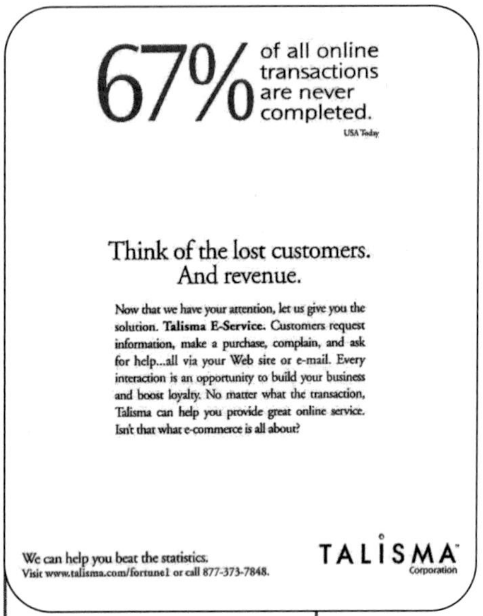

EXHIBIT 6-15

One typical objective for Web marketers is to decrease the percentage of shoppers who drop out before completing a purchase, a problem alluded to in this ad for Talisma.

agencies use to help prevent costly mistakes as well as provide ideas for improving MC efforts.

Campaign Effectiveness

The effectiveness of a campaign is evaluated according to how well the effort meets its objectives. This is why a company should clearly define its objectives in measurable terms (see Exhibit 6-15) and specify a time frame within which each objective is to be achieved.

Companies can obtain information regarding the effectiveness of their MC campaigns from corporate and industry reports, as well as by conducting primary research. Evaluation of MC spending must also include measures of relationship strengths in addition to the usual sales, share, and awareness measures. Sales and share are historical measures, but relationship strengths are predictors of future sales. Chapter 22 discusses evaluation in detail and presents some methods for evaluating the effectiveness of marketing communication in brand-relationship building.

In the Envoy launch campaign, the direct-mail campaign had a response rate of 10.5 percent, considerably higher than the usual rate of 1 to 2 percent. Of those who responded, there was a conversion rate (a commitment to buy) of 19 percent. The cost per response was $19.21, and the cost per conversion (actual sale made) was $184. This $184 investment was only one-fifth of the automotive industry's normal MC allocation per car, which meant that this campaign was highly cost-effective. GMC tracked and attributed 4,162 unit sales to this campaign—including sales made to people who came to dealerships in response to the Envoy campaign but ended up buying other GMC models instead.

The Role of Feedback

One aspect of IMC that is different from traditional marketing communication is the emphasis on continuous feedback. Current, shared information is critical for decision making by the cross-functional teams. That means companies must have ways of listening to customers wherever contacts with customers occur—particularly contacts with front-line employees. The overnight delivery company Federal Express, for example, tracks performance measures that are distributed daily. In addition, it tracks monthly indicators for all areas, including public relations, and conducts an online employee survey every three months. Managers use the results for discussions with employees and act on the survey information immediately wherever change is needed. Senior managers are required to spend a few days every year in a given sales district to get close to both customers and the front line of the sales and marketing efforts.[6] Continuous feedback programs help the company become a *learning organization.*

INTERNAL MARKETING

One of the primary responsibilities for marketing departments is to interpret the needs of the customer and the marketplace and bring that information to all departments. To complete this task, marketing needs input from the very people—employees—it is working to motivate and keep informed. Managing this two-way flow of information is an important objective of **internal marketing,** which is *an ongoing effort to involve employees in the planning process and then communicate the* *finalized plan back to them to get their buy-in and support.* As one marketer said: "You can't expect people to play from the same score if they don't have access to the same music."

Employees, especially those "touching the customer," should be thought of as customers—and, in fact, employees often are customers, too. The more employees are informed and made to feel a part of the company's effort to build customer relationships, the more they will satisfy customers. Companies can increase morale and productivity by keeping employees informed so they aren't embarrassed when asked about certain programs, for example. Also, giving employees a sneak preview of advertising and promotional materials before they begin running makes them feel that they really are members of the "team." Internal marketing can also enhance employee loyalty. Reducing employee turnover means lower training costs and an overall increase in experience throughout the company. A study of employee loyalty found that it is possible to generate commitment among employees with good communication, opportunities for personal growth, and workplace flexibility.[7] Most important, however, internal marketing can help create internal understanding of, and respect for, the company's core values, which are the essence of its brands.

Like external marketing, internal marketing is dependent on communication and problems arise when employees are not kept informed. There are three basic aspects of internal marketing communication: informing employees, empowering them, and listening to them.

Informing Employees

In a survey of internal communication of U.S. companies, half of the managers and front-line supervisors surveyed cited inadequate interdepartmental communication as the number-one problem behind poor customer service. According to the marketing manager of a major bank with hundreds of branches, making employees aware of current marketing programs is an ongoing challenge: "We're doing well if 80 percent of our tellers are aware of a new promotion when it begins."

Just as a company uses many different MC functions and media to communicate with customers, it should also use a variety of messages and channels of communication to reach employees. Like customers, employees have their preferred methods of receiving information. For this reason, good internal marketing makes use of company intranets, newsletters, e-mail, voice mail, bulletin boards, and face-to-face meetings with employees. An **intranet** is a *computer network that is accessible only to employees and contains proprietary information.* Intranets facilitate communication (e-mail, messaging), collaboration (shared databases, conferencing), and the coordination of work flow (work-flow applications integrate messaging and databases). Extranets are another valuable "internal" communication channel as they help keep outside MC agencies informed. An **extranet** is a *limited-access website that links suppliers, distributors, and MC agencies to the company.*

Empowering Employees

Because internal marketing provides employees with information, it enhances **employee empowerment,** which means *giving employees the resources to make decisions about problems that affect customer relationships.* As companies downsize and shift responsibility to lower levels, service employees on the front line of customer contact are making more decisions that affect customer relations. Generally, the more information these employees have, the better the decisions they will make.

Empowerment programs must be supported by training and information about company policies—a communication challenge. Automaker Nissan requires all dealer employees (including clerks and receptionists) for its Infinity models to attend six-day training programs designed to teach employees how to recognize and address legitimate customer problems. A support program with the objective of creating empowered and responsive employees has these goals:

- To inform employees about their role in satisfying customers.
- To inform employees about their role in the company's success.
- To reward employees on the basis of their individual performance and the company's overall performance.
- To listen to employees when they have ideas about how to better serve customers—even when the ideas involve other areas of operations.
- To give employees easy access to customer information files and other databases that enable them to make quick and knowledgeable responses.

Listening to Employees

Like external marketing, internal marketing depends on two-way communication. If an internal marketing program only sends messages, employees will see the program as propaganda. If company messages are going to have integrity, internal marketing must encourage and facilitate employee feedback, which will let managers know whether employees understand and agree with the internal marketing messages and are willing to support the various MC programs.

Even more important, listening to employees can provide valuable real-time customer research that helps in budgeting, planning, and adjusting MC plans. A justified criticism of some MC plans is that they are made in corporate office "ivory towers." Such plans don't address the real problems and opportunities in the marketplace. Customer-contact employees can be a valuable source of competitive and product performance information.

Customer-contact employees vary from industry to industry. In some industries, such as office machines and automobiles, service personnel are the employees most likely to have ongoing contact with customers. The people who deliver grocery products—soft drinks, snacks, processed meats, dairy products—directly to the stores are important contact points. They often are responsible for shelving the products or setting up merchandising materials, so they are constantly in the stores mingling with ultimate customers. These delivery people are often the first employees to be aware of product or marketing communication problems or other customer concerns. As the IMC in Action box illustrates, internal marketing that facilitates employee input about customers' needs can improve MC planning.

An example of internal communication gone wrong comes from Wild Oats, a chain of natural foods stores known for social responsibility and sensitivity to employees. Customers, employees, and the media were amazed when they one day learned that the Wild Oats CEO had ordered managers to search employees' bags twice a day as part of an antitheft policy. Several managers resigned in protest, and negative stories appeared in the local media. In response, the CEO wrote a letter to the local newspaper admitting that the store's "infamous loss-control memo was not well thought out, impossible to enforce, and, in retrospect, just plain Dilbertesque." (The latter is a reference to the well-known comic strip "Dilbert," which lampoons poor management practices.) The CEO concluded that the ruckus had caused the company to conduct "a comprehensive internal review of how we communicate to our staff members and the need to think more completely about the consequences of our actions."[8] This company learned the hard way that everything it does and says, including in-house staff policies, sends a brand message to all its stakeholders—and to customers in particular.

IMC IN ACTION

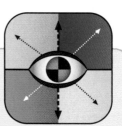

Using Employee Input in MC Planning

For its SoftBench Suite, a Unix application program sold to businesses, Hewlett-Packard (HP) developed a marketing communication program based on defining customers' needs. The division began its planning with a product-positioning workshop that defined customers' dilemmas with Unix and identified HP resources that could be used to address these dilemmas.

One result of this customer-focused approach was that planners determined that each HP department—sales, product marketing, engineering, customer support—understood a different aspect of customers' needs. According to a HP marketing manager, "By integrating all perspectives, we were able to think constructively about how our product addressed those

dilemmas. Out of all this, we developed a creative strategy focused on customer need."

The creative strategy used the theme "We understand" to emphasize HP's understanding of the issues, pressures, and constraints that software developers and software development managers faced, such as unrealistic deadlines, hidden code errors, simultaneous development of multiple application versions, and transition problems in moving to object-oriented programming. This theme was launched in a print advertising campaign, reinforced in three direct-mail pieces and a trade-show handout, showcased on the company's website, and then later picked up in another division's direct-marketing campaign promoting a product bundled with SoftBench.

As HP managers discovered, true integration goes beyond coordinating graphic designs and key messages. Entire divisions or companies need to adopt an integrated attitude to implement an effective marketing communication program. HP used that approach so that customers would be greeted at all levels with the idea that HP understood their dilemmas. For example, in speaking to customers, all HP employees—from customer-service representatives to sales associates to product marketing engineers—focused on the same thing: understanding and solving the customer's problem.

Integration as a process makes everyone in the company a salesperson. Integration as an attitude allows employees to offer solutions, not just programmed responses, to customers.

Think About It

Why is it important to use a customer focus in planning an IMC program? How was this done in HP's SoftBench Suite campaign planning? In what way were cross-functional teams needed to plan, implement, and monitor the "We understand" campaign?

Source: Adapted from Lindell, P. Griffith, "Lining Up Your Marketing Ducks: Integrated Marketing Communications," *Marketing Computers*, October 1996, p. 27.

EXHIBIT 6-16

A FINAL NOTE: PLAYING FROM THE SAME SCORE

An IMC campaign plan defines the way a company does business by creating a customer focus rather than department-focused programs that can work at cross-purposes and send mixed messages. The more focused a company is on transactions rather than on building long-term relationships, the weaker its relationships with customers will be. The successful launch of the GMC Envoy demonstrates how effective an integrated, single-minded effort can be when it is designed to build relationships over time.

In order to create this customer focus throughout the company, it is necessary that everyone play from the same score: an integration-driven marketing communication plan. This plan also demands internal marketing in order to deliver messages with consistency from everyone who touches a customer. The less inconsistent the messages are at these brand–customer touch points, the less integrated the brand positioning will be in the minds of customers and other stakeholders.

Integration planning and execution are not easy to accomplish. As more stakeholders are taken into consideration, as more functional areas are used, as more different media are used, planning and executing in a consistent manner become very complex. The biggest barriers to integration, however, are egos and turf battles.[9] Because the pay of most managers and executives is proportional to the size of their staffs and budgets, it is only natural for them to want the largest staffs and budgets that they can get. Consequently, the decision to reallocate MC and media monies to where they can do the most good is often hampered by executives who stand to lose out personally. To overcome this barrier, companies and agencies are beginning to design compensation and reward systems in such a way that people are not penalized when their budgets are temporarily reduced. Although integrated planning isn't easy, it is essential for companies that want to compete in the 21st century.

Key Terms

baseline 180
benchmark 180
breakeven analysis 194
budget 189
campaign 171
employee empowerment 199
extranet 199
internal marketing 198

intranet 199
marketing communication
  mix 184
media mix 186
objectives 179
objective-and-task budget 195
pro forma 192
return on investment (ROI) 194

segmenting 173
share-of-voice spending 196
situation analysis 174
strategies 184
SWOT analysis 174
tactics 184
targeting 173
zero-based planning 171

Key Point Summary

Key Point 1: IMC Zero-Based Planning

A marketing plan is governed by the company's overall business plan and gives direction to the marketing communication plan. Zero-based planning (which starts from current conditions rather than from past or expected future conditions) is used to identify the appropriate MC area that can best deliver on the objectives.

Key Point 2: The IMC Planning Process

The six steps of IMC planning are: (1) identifying the target audience, (2) analyzing SWOTs, (3) determining the MC objectives, (4) developing strategies and tactics, (5) setting the budget, and (6) evaluating the effectiveness of the IMC program.

Key Point 3: Internal Marketing

Internal marketing is the process of involving other employees in the planning process and then communicating the plan back to them to get their buy-in and support.

EXHIBIT 6-17

The objective of this ad is to dramatize the need for people to support wildlife, which is a cognitive objective, but it does so in an emotional way, so it also tends to touch peoples emotions. Finally it asks for supporters to order a free Action Kit, so it also motivates a behavioral response.

Lessons Learned

Key Point 1: IMC Zero-Based Planning

a. What is zero-based planning? What assumption does it challenge?
b. How do strategies, objectives, and tactics differ?
c. How did Hewlett-Packard use strategic planning in its SoftBench Suite campaign?
d. What are objectives and strategies? What does it mean to make integration an attitude?

Key Point 2: The IMC Planning Process

a. Using the six-step planning process, reconstruct the key planning decisions behind the GMC Envoy campaign.
b. Why is SWOT analysis the first step in zero-based planning?
c. What internal and external factors are involved in a SWOT analysis? Give an example of each from the Snapple case, and explain how they were addressed or leveraged.
d. Convert the six "tasks" that McCann-Erickson faced in the GMC Envoy case into measurable objectives.
e. Explain the four different ways to develop a marketing communication budget.
f. How do marketers know whether an IMC campaign is effective?

Key Point 3: Internal Marketing

a. Define *internal marketing*.
b. What is the role played by communication in internal marketing?
c. Analyze the HP SoftBench Suite campaign in terms of its internal marketing dimensions. What was done? What other activities and programs would you recommend?

Chapter Challenge

Writing Assignment

Using the six planning steps, create a model that visualizes these steps, showing what other things influence each step. Apply your model to your favorite apparel brand. From information that you find out about the brand from research and from your own personal experience and knowledge of the brand, explain how the brand's marketing communication program works. Write up your analysis, and use your model to explain your analysis.

Presentation Assignment

Research Snapple. What has happened most recently to turn around this troubled brand? What objectives and strategies would you recommend to Snapple's current manager to build on the brand's history? Using the six-step IMC planning process, develop a marketing communication plan for Snapple for next year. Present your plan to the class.

Internet Assignment

Consult the website for the John W. Hartman Center for Sales, Advertising, and Marketing History at Duke University (http://scriptorium.lib.duke.edu/adaccess). The site contains more than 7,000 print advertisements produced between 1911 and 1955. To demonstrate that the basics remain the same, find an ad in the collection that demonstrates one of the following: (1) leveraging an opportunity, (2) addressing a threat, (3) leveraging a strength, or (4) addressing a weakness.

Chapter 7

Segmenting and Targeting

Members of Surfrider Foundation, California. www.jockey.com

Just the bros sportin' the comfies

Let 'em know you're
JOCKEY
boxers

Key Points in This Chapter

1. How and why are companies moving away from mass marketing to smaller yet more profitable customer segments?
2. Why is segmenting to find your most profitable customers important?
3. What characteristics can companies use to identify different types of customer segments?
4. How does targeting work to implement segmentation strategies?

Chapter Perspective

Carving Up the Market

Some marketers believe that it is important to reach as many potential customers as possible; they don't want to pass up a single one. Although this goal might seem to make sense, it ignores the factor of cost efficiency. Reaching "everyone" costs money and sends lots of unwanted messages to people who aren't customers (and are unlikely to ever be customers). It makes more sense to narrow the audience to people who are most likely to buy.

Segmenting identifies those groups of customers and prospects who are most likely to respond to marketing communication messages. One segmentation strategy used by marketers looking for new customers is to profile a brand's current profitable customers, then look for those that are similar. Targeting prioritizes the identified segments and selects segment characteristics that can help in creating MC messages and selecting media to reach the targeted segments. A segment that should always be targeted is current customers because it costs significantly less to create a transaction with them than with prospects.

Progress in marketing research and database technology has allowed companies to learn more about current customers and the differences among them. Now companies are able to track which consumers purchase what products, how often, and in what quantities. Companies can often track which messages customers heard or saw, what else their customers are buying, and who they are—how old they are, where they live, and other profile information. Most important, companies can determine which customers are profitable and which are not.

INSIGHTS FROM EVERYWHERE
McCann-Erickson, Melbourne, Australia

Holden Ltd. is Australia's premier automaker. The Barina—Holden's smallest model and one of the oldest models in the Australian market—had been a success in the small-car market for many years. However, in recent years, it became clear that the model had lost its way and was on a decline. This situation raised a number of questions for Holden: How do you get a small car back on track and design a marketing communication program that will help it finish ahead of the competition? Who should be involved in planning the turnaround? Is there a pricing problem? A targeting or positioning problem? A promotional problem? Where do you start?

The McCann-Erickson office in Melbourne saw it as a research problem, one that called for a better understanding of the car's target market in order to create a more on-target creative strategy and communication mix.

The Marketing Challenge

The Barina was originally launched in the Australian market with an advertising campaign called "Beep, Beep," which used the Road Runner character from the old Warner Bros. cartoon series. This campaign transcended the memorable limits of most advertising and became part of the Australian vernacular. The car was soon affectionately referred to as the "Beep Beep Barina." Even when Holden abandoned the Road Runner visual, the "Beep, Beep" was maintained as an advertising sign-off and a powerful mnemonic device.

However, in the 1990s, the Barina's sales declined by 16 percent and then by an alarming 43 percent. There were a number of reasons for this, including an increase in small-car brand alternatives and greater price competition. The most critical change, however, was the decline in interest by the traditional small-car target market—young women.

Segmenting and Targeting

McCann-Erickson Melbourne formed a cross-functional task force to gather information about trends important to the Barina's key target market. This task force included personnel from advertising, market research, public relations, and promotions, as well as innovators from other consumer categories such as music producers, magazine publishers, and clothing marketers.

From the research, the McCann task force determined that the primary target audience would be a subsegment of young women—those in their early 20s who were also characterized as "early adopters," that is, the first to try something and then influence the opinions of others. The broader target audience was identified as "single, female optimists" aged 18 to 34. The third most important segment was all remaining 18- to 34-year-olds, male and female.

The research was also designed to determine why young women had abandoned the Barina. Knowing the *why* is what enables a company to create brand messages relevant to a targeted segment. The McCann task force found that safety was not particularly relevant to young women. Further, Barina's image, which was still associated with the dated "Beep, Beep" campaign, did not match the segment's aspirations—it was considered too young and "girlie." This research also revealed that young women have a great affinity with their cars—they see their car as an "accomplice" in their life. Therefore, a car's image and personality are important to this group. And the car must suit their lifestyle. McCann also found that this segment considered traditional car advertising dull, uninspiring, and unengaging. What scored high with this segment was unexpected advertising conveyed with wit.

To convince "young female early adopters" that Barina was "cool," the McCann team first had to understand what this group considered cool in general and then anticipate the next trend. To do this, the team conducted innovative multidisciplinary research designed to monitor the lifestyle and attitude trends of this group. This research unearthed two key facts: (1) The target needs to identify with the brand, by identifying with a projected brand user who represents someone she would like to be. (2) The target was interested in Japanese *manga* (a highly identifiable style of comics and animated cartoons), which if translated into advertising could potentially be a very original and unique communication device for Barina (see Exhibit 7-1).

EXHIBIT 7-1

The BG character was created to appeal to the segment of females in their 20s who were "early adopters" of fashion and trends.

Objectives and Strategies

McCann determined that the Barina campaign's communication objectives were

- To create a "cool" image of the Barina among 75 percent of the target audience.
- To have 75 percent of the target audience associate Barina with two or more of the following attributes: fun, smart, independent, outrageous, and stylish.

The consumer research and resultant understanding of the key target audience indicated that if the McCann team was going to change perceptions of Barina and leave "Beep, Beep" behind, a radically different creative approach was critical. Barina needed to break the rules of traditional car advertising, in terms of both medium and message. The resulting communication strategy recommendation were

- To develop a character who reflected the identified lifestyle aspirations of the target audience.
- To develop a sense of intrigue and consumer involvement. (The target audience needed to discover Barina for itself, not be told.)
- To build the brand in a consistent supporting manner across all communication expressions.

Message and Media Strategy

The Japanese cartoon style provided an approach that was fresh and original and in tune with the early adopters' aspirations. The result was an animated character called "BG"—Barina Girl—which represented the target audience's lifestyle, aspirations, and personality. The story lines described BG as handling life's highs and lows with intelligence, wit, and spunk. For example, a "Bad Hair Day" commercial was inspired by discussions in a focus-group session.

In this commercial, BG uses her Barina to deal with her bad-hair problem in an imaginative way.

McCann repositioned Barina as a hip brand by building a strategic street presence prior to the launch of the multimedia campaign. This was accomplished by creating a BG Roller Blading Team, which appeared at selected trendy festivals and gave away premiums branded "BG." Recipients had no way at that point of knowing what "BG" meant, and the simple "BG" logo was reminiscent of a secret underground nightclub symbol. The BG premiums included T-shirts, sun cream, backpacks, stickers, and key rings. Posters designed to look like those for underground bands were hung in selected inner-city areas.

The agency then launched a multimedia advertising campaign that capitalized on the broader target's unique relationship with each medium. The BG commercials appeared only in a select list of television programs and movies considered to be leading-edge, must-see programs among the target. The character BG was given her own weekly radio program on a key radio network. McCann developed new adventures each week to keep the campaign fresh, maintain consumer involvement, and capitalize on topical issues.

A half-page comic strip appeared in another popular medium for the target, a weekly magazine (see Exhibit 7-2). The strip cartoons were supplemented with full-page color ads themed around the magazine's special issues such as most beautiful people, celebrity weddings, best and worst dressed, and best bodies.

Evaluation of the BG Campaign

Quantitative testing of the BG campaign was positive: 97 percent of targeted respondents liked the manga-style animation. Findings from ongoing qual-

EXHIBIT 7-2

The cartoon style of this ad and the message about BG getting an exclusive interview with an American basketball team were designed to get the attention of young single women—the Holden Barina's primary target audience.

itative tracking studies found that the targeted segment was shifting its perceptions of the Barina and its manufacturer, Holden. In approximately 20 focus groups, the campaign was discussed spontaneously and enthusiastically. In terms of the behavioral objectives, the campaign had a positive impact on sales. Since the BG campaign launch in 1998, the Barina sales decline has been reversed and sales have grown by 30 percent. This case demonstrates the importance of segmenting a market, identifying a target, and then learning as much as possible about that target in order to create messages and select media that will have an impact.

Source: This case was adapted with permission from the award-winning Advertising and Marketing Effectiveness (AME) brief submitted by McCann-Erickson Melbourne.

WHAT'S THE POINT OF SEGMENTING AND TARGETING?

Suppose you have been hired by a bicycle company to help plan its marketing strategy. The first thing you have to do is figure out who might be in the market for your line of bikes. Segmenting and targeting are processes that companies use to determine whom they want to reach in order to build brand relationships. Recall from Chapter 6 that **segmenting** is *grouping customers or prospects according to common characteristics, needs, wants, or desires,* and **targeting** is *analyzing, evaluating, and prioritizing the market segments deemed most profitable to pursue.*

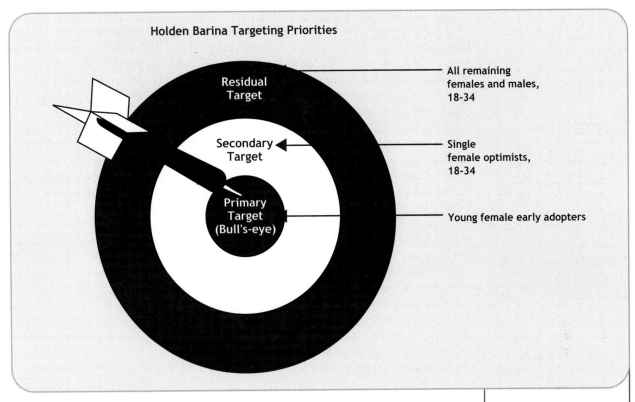

Holden Barina Targeting Priorities

Residual Target

Secondary Target

Primary Target (Bull's-eye)

All remaining females and males, 18-34

Single female optimists, 18-34

Young female early adopters

FIGURE 7-1

"Young female early adopters" were the primary target segment for the Holden Barina "BG" campaign.

Segmenting can be done at different levels of specificity. For example, a manufacturer of bicycles could begin by dividing a market into bike owners and non-owners. Bike owners could be further segmented into bike racers, mountain bike riders, leisure riders, children, and parents. An important part of segmenting is specifying the characteristics that successfully predict who will be in the groups.

Segmenting is done to provide a marketer with targeting options. Figure 7-1 illustrates the Barina targeting decision. Barina identified "young female early adopters" as being the most responsive and profitable segment and thus the center of the target. McCann also realized it had to reach beyond this initial segment. Its next most important targets were "single, female optimists" aged 18- to 34, followed by all remaining 18- to 34-year-olds, male and female. Compared with those in the center, those farther from the middle of the target are less likely to respond and are therefore less profitable. Targeting thus allows companies to focus their MC efforts on segments that promise the greatest potential return on investment (ROI).

Moving Away from Mass Marketing

Segmentation is not a new concept. Soon after Henry Ford became successful selling his mass-produced Model T, which was introduced in 1908 and came in one color only (black), Alfred Sloan, then head of General Motors, realized his company would have to do something different to compete with Ford. The more Sloan learned about who bought cars, the more he realized that different segments of customers wanted different types of cars. He also figured out that once he got a customer, he could keep that customer if he could provide different cars to match customers' changing needs for cars as customers grew older and more financially secure and moved from one lifestyle segment to another.

General Motors became one of the first companies to offer a range of models for each customer segment, from the low-priced Chevrolet; through Pontiac,

Oldsmobile, and Buick; to the most expensive family car (at that time), the Cadillac. Sloan figured that as his Chevrolet customers advanced in life and could afford a better car, his company could still target them, but with a different car and message. In this way, GM could retain those customers. Sloan also realized that cars allowed the more successful people to show they were different from the middle class or the less successful. Early segmentation efforts allowed General Motors to beat out Ford for first place in the automotive industry by the late 1920s.

Along with the rapid growth of mass media in the United States, mass marketing became the norm in the middle of the twentieth century. In the late twentieth century, media technologies changed marketing yet again. Segmentation took on more and more importance as marketing moved away from mass marketing. Marketing today is, in the name of efficiency and effectiveness, becoming more focused on smaller but more profitable segments of the market.

Mass marketing is an attempt to sell the same thing to a wide range of customers. Little effort is made to tightly target messages to certain groups. The obvious problem with mass marketing is it wastes a lot of money reaching people who have no interest in the product. Yet, despite pronouncements by some in the MC industry who say that mass marketing is dead, the reality is that many companies still sell to a broad range of customers.

Target, Wal-Mart, Kroger, Safeway, Walgreen, and other large retailers advertise heavily in mass media, especially in newspapers and supplements, yet are quite successful, because they have redefined mass marketing by offering a variety of products and brands in most product categories. In this way, they are able to satisfy many different customer segments. In their shampoo sections, for example, there are shampoos for regular, dry, and oily hair, for dandruff control, and for babies, as well as shampoos with built-in conditioners. In essence, these mass marketers *are* practicing multiple segmentation because they are offering products and brands that appeal to different customer segments. In a move toward more narrow targeting, individual stores in national chains are increasingly being encouraged to customize their merchandise mix to best suit customers in their geographic area.

Focusing on Niche Segments

Niche markets are defined by a *distinct commonality shared by those making up a segment.* Take for example deep-sea fishing. Those who enjoy this activity are a subsegment (or niche) of people who like to fish. Like many niche segments, those who like deep-sea fishing have special equipment, special clothing, and specialized media, especially magazines. The Coricidin advertisement in Exhibit 7-3 shows a product (CoricidinHBP) that has been reformulated for a simple niche market: people with colds who also have high blood pressure.

Although niche markets, by definition, are smaller than mass markets, they can still include millions of customers. *Modern Maturity* magazine—sent only to those seniors who are members of the American Association of Retired Persons (AARP)—is considered a niche publication, yet it is one of the largest circulation publications in the United States, reaching over 20 million readers.

In recent years, companies have been dividing their markets into smaller and smaller segments. For example, all the people who buy cars can be divided into segments according to such factors as the size of car, styling and handling, price tag, and engineering. Some customers are willing to pay more for engineering (BMW), others for styling (Corvette), and others for

EXHIBIT 7-3
The headline in this ad is designed to attract the attention of that segment of consumers who have a cold and also suffer from high blood pressure.

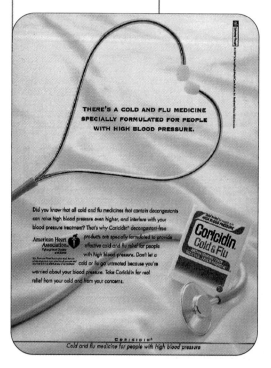

size and functionality (SUVs). Every buyer may want a little something different, but it is not cost-effective for car manufacturers to create a unique car for *each* individual (although customization is being done to a greater degree than ever before, and the costs are coming down). Manufacturers and service providers are still interested in taking advantage of economies of scale whenever they can, but they are doing so by targeting smaller segments and niche markets rather than providing just one product for all customers in the category.

In business-to-business marketing, there are also niches in most product categories. Take printing presses, for example. The niche market for high-end, specialty-color presses includes companies such as Hallmark Cards, which demands very sophisticated, high-quality performance. At the other end of the printing-press market is the niche for "job printers," who use small printing presses that are only a step above a photocopy machine in their level of quality.

Segments of One and Mass Customization of Products

Along with the increase in niche marketing has come an emphasis on **one-to-one marketing,** which means *customizing products and marketing communication according to individual needs.* One reason for this is that services, which by definition are customized to a certain extent, account for over 75 percent of business activities today. A popular marketing book that came out in the mid-1990s, *The One to One Future,* predicts that this type of marketing will be increasingly used as companies become more technologically sophisticated in their manufacturing and marketing.[1] Nevertheless, one-to-one marketing is today generally affordable only for higher-priced consumer and B2B products—with one important exception: one-to-one messages can and should be used in responding to complaints and inquiries regardless of a brand's price point.

Also being more widely used is mass customization of products, which is somewhat similar to one-to-one marketing but economically more feasible. **Mass customization of products** is *a manufacturing process that is programmed to choose ingredients/parts to produce custom-designed goods.* (This is accomplished through computer-aided design and computer-aided manufacturing—CAD/CAM.) A good example is Dell Computer, which has built a multibillion-dollar brand by customizing computers for individuals and companies. Stores such as Office Depot and Staples are now cutting back on their in-store selection of computers, replacing this inventory with a computer terminal that customers use to configure their own computers. They pay for the computers in the store, the orders are sent in, and the computers are built and shipped directly to customers' homes or offices. For marketers this trend means more brand communication to explain the mass customization process in order to help customers get exactly what they want. Companies doing mass customization of products must be prepared to handle even more two-way communication, because customization generates more questions than does simply selling a product off the shelf.

HOW ARE SEGMENTATION STRATEGIES DETERMINED?

Segmentation and targeting are used in both consumer and in business-to-business marketing. The more diverse a company's line of products is, generally the more customer segments the company will have. For companies already doing business, there are seven basic steps in segmenting and targeting (see Figure 7-2). (New companies or those going into a totally new product category would use

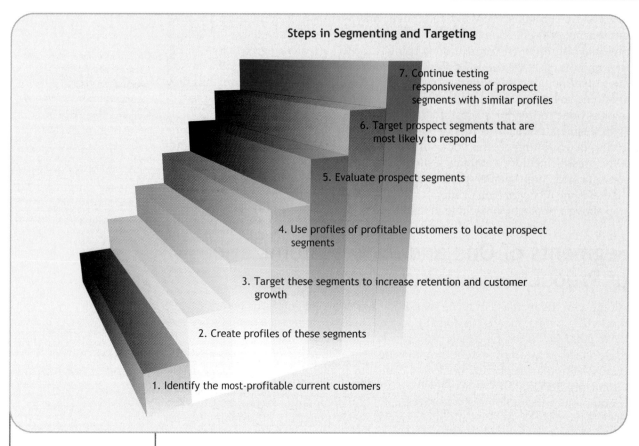

Steps in Segmenting and Targeting

7. Continue testing responsiveness of prospect segments with similar profiles

6. Target prospect segments that are most likely to respond

5. Evaluate prospect segments

4. Use profiles of profitable customers to locate prospect segments

3. Target these segments to increase retention and customer growth

2. Create profiles of these segments

1. Identify the most-profitable current customers

FIGURE 7-2

Why is customer segmentation so important?

only the last three steps.) The first three steps concern current customers; the last four, prospects.

How Are Current Customers Segmented?

A key principle of IMC is "Know thy customers." Segmentation makes this knowledge possible by identifying and profiling current customers. The segmenting process begins by setting up a system for identifying customers, usually by assigning each one an identification number. Various aspects of each customer's transactions and personal profile data are then recorded. These data are analyzed for certain shared characteristics that can be used to form segments such as new customers, high-profit customers, and short-term customers (collecting customer data is discussed in detail in Chapter 8).

Three benefits result from knowing customer profiles. First, it costs less to sell additional products to current customers than it does to sell the first product to new customers. Current customers don't have to be "brand-educated" on each transaction as first-time buyers do. The cost per sale for current customers (assuming they have been satisfied with their prior purchases) is estimated to be 5 to 10 times less than for selling to a new customer.

Second, some customers are more profitable than others. These customers need to be identified and made a top priority in customer-retention efforts. Not all current customers are equally valuable because in nearly every company the Pareto (80/20) rule holds true (⇐ Chapter 3). A close examination of customer transactions and profitability will show that a minority of customers generate the majority of business. Although this ratio varies by company, the high-profit segment of customers should be satisfied before all others.

E X H I B I T   7 - 4
Home redecorating and remodeling is an important consumer trend addressed in this humorous ad.

the great indoors® The store for those who love to decorate, redecorate and remodel.

The third benefit of segmenting current customers is that once the most profitable ones are identified and profiled, the profile can be used to find new customers. SRDS, a service which collects pricing and audience data from media providers, has profiles of the audiences of most communication media. Thus magazines (and other media) can be selected on the basis of how closely their audience profiles match the profitable-customer profile, as is illustrated in the Great Indoors ad in Exhibit 7-4.

Current customers should not be taken for granted. Past purchases do not guarantee future ones. Customers' only reason to continue buying a brand is to receive superior satisfaction in product performance and customer service. Although ensuring satisfaction is costly, it is far less expensive than acquiring new customers to replace unsatisfied ones. That is why a company should think first about how best to retain customers before investing in new ones. Furthermore, because most current customers do not give any single brand 100 percent of their category purchases, companies encourage current customers to increase their percent of category spending on the company's brand(s).

What Is the Difference between Buyers and Users?

In some product categories, the person making the brand decision—the person doing the shopping—may not be the primary user of the brand. In such cases, a company must decide to what extent it should target the buyer instead of the user. Before this decision can be made, a company needs to fully understand the role that the user plays in influencing the brand decision. Consider the following example.

Before beginning an MC campaign, a processed-meat company used market research to determine that most hot dogs are eaten by children but purchased by mothers. The company then conducted focus groups to better understand the dynamics of these two key segments—buyers and users. Moms said they made the brand decision but their children had veto power over the brand choice. What they meant was that when children refused to eat a certain brand, the mothers would no longer buy that brand. As one mother put it: "Buying something that I have to throw away because they won't eat it is a waste of money." At the same time, mothers also said they paid little attention to brands requested by their children.

The meat company decided that the best strategy was to target moms with a message that showed children enjoying the brand. The strategy was quite successful.[2]

Segmenting Based on Profitability

Effective segmenting is based on overall business and marketing objectives. When a company wants to expand by reaching a new segment of customers, it must weigh the *benefits* of doing so (growth potential, market dominance) against the *costs* of doing so (expanding beyond its area of expertise, diluting its focus by serving too many diverse customer groups). Creating and sending brand messages and listening and responding to customers all represent expenses, so segmenting and targeting decisions ultimately affect profits.

One approach to profitable targeting begins with analyzing the size of customer segments. The primary question to answer is: Is each segment large enough to generate enough revenue to cost-justify a customized marketing effort? An example of a company that did this analysis was Midas, which offers repairs on auto brakes and exhaust pipes (among other services) with no appointment required (see the IMC in Action box).

In addition to segment size, customers can be classified by their spending patterns and by their relationship maintenance costs.[3] This suggests four classifications of customers (unprofitable low-volume, unprofitable high-volume, profitable low-volume, and profitable high-volume) and corresponding strategies; these are outlined in Table 7-1.

One way to maintain a good relationship with high-volume customers is to reward them for their brand loyalty. One of the best examples of doing this is the airline frequent-flyer programs. The more miles a customer travels a year, the

T A B L E 7 - 1   Profitability Segments

Classification	Strategy	Example
Unprofitable or Marginally Profitable Customers		
Low-Volume: Customers who do little business with the company and who cost more to service than the company receives in profit from them; a drain on resources	Charge them for extra services	A credit-card company may install a service charge for customers who charge less than *x* dollars each month
High-volume: Customers who buy in large quantities and therefore demand discounts and a high level of service	Use a graduated level of discounts and charge for certain services	An office supply company may charge for delivery of orders that amount to less than *x* dollars
Profitable Customers		
Low-volume: Customers who are generally happy but do the bulk of their business elsewhere	Design marketing programs to increase brand's share-of-wallet	A retail store may set up a frequent-buyer program
High-volume: Customers who buy in large quantities and generate the majority of profit; the company's best customers	Reward and recognize them	A department store may send high-volume customers "exclusive invitations" to special sales

IMC IN ACTION

Midas Turns Segments into Gold

In the past, the main market segments for the auto service chain Midas were believed to derive from three criteria: age of car (the older the car, the more likely it is to need repairs); size of car (repairs on big cars are expensive for customers but profitable for Midas); and driver (women offer more potential for cross-selling). Although this was the conventional wisdom of the day, Midas did not know for certain whether these segments were real and, if real, whether they were profitable.

When Midas conducted research into customer-service expectations and satisfaction, it became clear there were only two segments: the car lover and the utilitarian. Both segments were sizable enough to be profitable, and both wanted fast, reliable, no-surprise, one-time repair. However, their preferences about the way the service was delivered were different, so the messages delivered by the service, as well as the marketing communication messages, had to change for the two groups.

Knowing these service segments exist, the question for Midas became: Is it economical to serve both the utilitarian and the car lover? A quantitative check of the economics in this particular case revealed that about 50 percent of Midas customers fell in each segment, making the creation of different relationship programs to serve each viable.

For the car lover, Midas designed brand messages to talk specifically about the car, offering to check on maintenance and service items (wash wheels when brakes have been changed) and call every six months or yearly to inform the customer it is time for a checkup. These messages also stressed that Midas allows customers to watch the repair process and to see old parts and the packaging from the new ones.

For the utilitarian segment, Midas used a different strategy. People in this group didn't want to feel they were wasting time, so the brand messages emphasized that Midas shops would give them a newspaper or a game to play while they waited (so the time didn't seem so long), offer to call a taxi, or, better still, provide a replacement car. Further, the messages explained that at the end of the repair Midas employees would reassure them that the work was well done, that the bill would be in line with the estimate (no surprises), and that they should be able to drive their car for a certain number of miles without any problems.

What this example demonstrates is that segmenting requires, above all, a customer orientation. Company managers must put themselves in the shoes of the different customer segments and not be limited by traditional company practices.

Think About It

How did Midas change its segmentation strategy? How did Midas know that changing would be a profitable strategy?

EXHIBIT 7-5

more benefits and privileges that passenger receives, such as first choice on seating and coupons for free upgrades.

Low-volume customers, in contrast, can sometimes cost too much to retain. For example, GE Capital charges credit-card holders who pay off their balances every month an annual $25 fee. The company realizes this fee may motivate some customers to switch to another credit-card brand, but GE Capital would rather lose these customers than continue to lose money by providing them services for little in return. In contrast, some of GE Capital's credit-card customers who pay off their monthly balance have an extremely high level of charges; GE Capital makes money off them via the 2 to 4 percent the company charges retailers for handling transactions. GE Capital uses specially written software programs to identify this profitable but small customer segment—early-pay high-spenders.

Another consideration in segmenting on the basis of profitability, especially with B2B customers, is that today's marginally profitable customers can become tomorrow's profitable customers as their businesses grow. In the 1980s and early 1990s, some of the large computer companies screened and rejected prospective customers if they spent below a certain amount each year on computer software and hardware. IBM, for example, rejected prospects spending under $40,000 a year. What IBM came to realize, however, was that when these companies grew and began spending much more than $40,000, they remembered IBM's rebuff and consequently gave their business to IBM's competitors. (IBM has changed this screening strategy.) The bottom line? When using profitability as a segmentation factor, it is important also to analyze prospects' potential for growth.

Recency, Frequency, and Monetary Estimates: RFM Segmenting

Information about customers' purchase behavior is particularly useful in identifying which ones are most likely to respond to a new offer. What we have learned from direct-response marketers (the companies that send you all those catalogs) is that the customers who are most likely to respond to a new offer are those who have bought most *recently* and most *frequently*, and who have spent an above-average amount (*monetary*) over a designated period of time. **Recency (R)** is *a measure of how long ago a customer purchased from a specific company*. Those who purchased in the last 60 days, for example, are more likely to buy again than those who purchased months or years before. **Frequency (F)** is *a measure of how often, within a given period, a customer purchased a specific brand*. Frequency is somewhat less valuable as an indicator than recency because new customers obviously will not have had time to make repeat purchases. **Monetary (M)** is *a measure of the amount a customer spent with a specific company over a given period*. Each of these measures, of course, varies by product category. For automobiles, average recency can be two years, but for ice cream, it is more likely 30 days.

RFM segmenting can be applied to a company's current customers as well as to prospects. In the case of prospects, the RFM analysis is based on prospects' total product category purchases. Prospects may have been buying from competitors, but if these prospects rate high on RFM, they are more likely to become new customers than are others who rate low.

How Are Prospects Segmented?

Segmentation strategies for prospects start with current customers. Marketers use the profiles of their most-profitable customers to select media whose audiences have similar profiles. The theory is pretty simple: Similar people respond to similar messages. Exhibit 7-6 is an ad for Fox Sports that tries to reach a male audience with a humorous message about sports fans.

EXHIBIT 7-6
The Fox Sports TV commercial shows how a product may be defective (like the steering on this boat) if made when workers are distracted by the baseball playoffs on Fox TV. This is aimed at male sports fans.

Self-selection is *a method of segmenting prospects by motivating potential customers to respond in some way and identify themselves as being interested in the brand.* In this "raise your hand" strategy, mass and niche media are initially used to reach a broad range of prospects with a brand offering. Brand messages invite those interested in the brand to respond by sending back a form, calling a toll-free number, sending an e-mail, visiting a store, or responding in some other way. Frequently, companies use incentives to increase response. Companies must be careful, however, to make sure that the incentives are not the sole motivation for responding. In most cases, especially with B2B products, if prospects are not willing to invest some effort in order to learn more about a new brand, then they probably are not valuable prospects.

Procter & Gamble used self-selection when it introduced Cheer Free, a detergent without perfumes created especially for those who are allergic to such additives. Not knowing who these allergy-sensitive customers were, Cheer ran mass media ads that offered a free sample to people allergic to detergent perfumes. In this way, Cheer was able to aggregate high-potential customers and build a segment based on self-identification. For the most part, those responding to this free offer identified themselves (or someone they knew) as being in need of the product. At that point, the company was able to switch to more highly targeted direct mail.

Another benefit of self-selection is that it is respectful of customers' privacy and avoids the wastefulness that comes from overdependence on intrusive forms of brand-message delivery. Prospective customers are increasingly resistant to what one British advertising executive has called "stab 'em in the heart till they buy" selling strategies. The technique frequently used to facilitate self-selection is the "opt-in" option often found in e-mail, website, and direct-mail offers.

To help get past customers' defense mechanisms against commercial messages, some companies use **permission marketing,** *a method of segmenting in which prospects are persuaded to volunteer their attention to brand messages.* Yoyodyne Entertainment and other companies use sweepstakes, contests, and games to persuade people to agree to be exposed to brand messages. When H&R Block wanted to introduce a new service called "Premium Tax," it hired Yoyodyne to design and place online billboards that said "H&R Block: We'll pay your taxes sweepstake." When people clicked on this billboard, they were told they could participate in this sweepstakes by agreeing to receive three e-mails a week for ten weeks. Each e-mail contained information about H&R Block's new service offering. The more e-mails participants opened, the greater chance they had to win. Organizers of the sweepstakes claim that of the 50,000 who initially responded, the average number who opened each e-mail was 40 percent.[4]

TYPES OF SEGMENTATION

The factors that influence brand decision making identified in Chapter 5—such as involvement level—can be used to identify segments. On the surface, segmentation may seem easy to do. A company that sells fishing rods, for example, should send brand messages to people who fish. But unfortunately, it's not that simple. There are many kinds of fishing, as mentioned earlier, such as deep-sea fishing, fly fishing, trout fishing, and ice fishing. Each of these fishing activities requires different kinds of fishing gear and attracts different types of people. Therefore, it is necessary to look at the distinguishing commonalities of each fishing segment.

Taken together, the commonalities create a *profile* of each segment. The more detailed a profile is, the more useful it is in creating relevant brand messages and selecting media to reach audiences who are most likely to respond. The most commonly used characteristics, or variables, for profiling are behavior (usage/benefits), demographics, psychographics, and level of brand relationship (see Figure 7-3). Most companies use more than one set of characteristics for each profile. With the exception of psychographics, these sets of characteristics can be used for profiling both consumer and B2B segments.

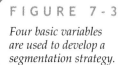

FIGURE 7-3

Four basic variables are used to develop a segmentation strategy.

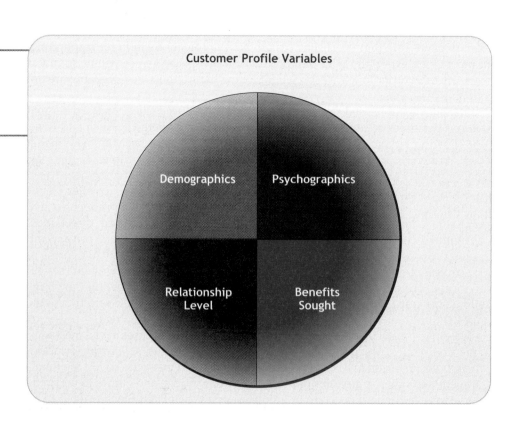

Customer Profile Variables

Demographics

Psychographics

Relationship Level

Benefits Sought

Behaviorial and Benefit Segments

Behavioral segmenting is *segmenting based on product usage and product-related behavior* (see Exhibit 7-7). In every product category there are variations in usage: heavy users, medium users, light users, and nonusers. The criteria for placing customers in each group vary for each product category. For example, a person who buys a new car every year is a heavy user, but a person who buys laundry soap only once a year is a light user.

To identify usage groups for a given product, the company must determine what amount the *average* customer purchases per year. Customers who purchase above-average amounts of the product can be placed in the heavy-user group, and so on down the line. For example, if the average buyer of shampoo buys four bottles a year, the shampoo industry may consider those who buy six or more bottles a year heavy users, those who buy three to five bottles a year medium users, and those who buy one to two bottles a year light users.

Current customers can be further segmented by what and where they buy. For example, some customers buy most of their clothes from discount stores, and others prefer better service and greater selection and therefore buy most of their clothes from department or specialty stores. A similar type of segmentation can be done on the basis of what type, flavor, model, or style of a product customers buy. Students who buy mostly T-shirts and jeans may be labeled the "casual segment"; executives who buy mostly suits may be labeled the "business segment."

Patrons of fast-food restaurants can be segmented not only by how frequently they visit a fast-food restaurant but also by meal occasion: breakfast, lunch, dinner, or snack. Knowing who makes up these meal segments allows a fast-food chain to (1) design for each meal segment messages that reinforce usage of that meal occasion and (2) cross-sells other meal occasions. For example, if Burger King can identify heavy breakfast users, it can offer them a frequent-buyer incentive (to retain them) and also offer them an incentive to come in for lunch or dinner. This type of **cross-selling,** or *using the sale of one product to promote the sale of related products*, is one way to "grow" customers and get more of their fast-food dollar. A related concept, **up-selling,** means *encouraging customers to buy a more expensive product than they had in mind*. For example, car dealers frequently offer accessories or low financing rates in order to motivate customers to buy a more expensive model car than they would otherwise choose.

Benefit segmenting is *segmenting a market according to the benefits customers seek as the result of using a brand*. Consider how benefit-segmented the lodging industry has become. OAG's HotelDisk, a directory of North American hotels, segments hotels into 30 categories, including hotels that offer "star chefs in the dining room," state-of-the-art fitness centers, and in-room faxes and computer printers. There is even a group of hotels with special rooms designed to fight the effects of jet lag. Customers can pick a hotel that offers the specific benefits they want to receive.

Another example of a strategy developed from a benefit perspective comes from the airport food service industry. Restaurant managers were asked to identify their customer segments. These managers initially came up with four segments: business travelers, tourists, local airport employees, and travel groups. Like Midas's first guesstimate of their customer segments (in the preceding IMC in Action box), the airport restaurants' segments seemed obvious but turned out to be a myth. What the managers quickly learned when a survey was done is that people who eat at airport restaurants could be grouped into one of two

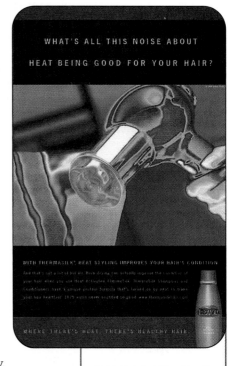

WHAT'S ALL THIS NOISE ABOUT HEAT BEING GOOD FOR YOUR HAIR?

E X H I B I T   7 - 7

This Thermasilk ad is directed at a specfic user segment—shampoo users who use a hair dryer.

segments—"in a hurry" and "not in a hurry." One half of "airport eaters" is looking for a quiet place and relaxation; the other half is in a hurry and wants a fast meal. The action resulting from this segmentation finding was to train the restaurant wait staff to identify which segment customers were in and then serve them accordingly, either with a quiet corner or with fast service.

Demographic Segments

Once a segment is identified by its behavior characteristics, the next step is to segment and profile each segment according to its **demographics,** which are *definable statistical measures, such as age, gender, and ethnicity.* Credit-card companies, for example, use age in their demographic segmenting. People most likely to sign up for their first credit card are in the age category 16 to 19. The following list shows the most commonly used demographic measures:

Age	Family size
Education	Family life stage
Income	Residence type
Gender	Ethnicity
Occupation	Religion
Geography	Nationality

A good source of basic demographic information is census data, which are available in most industrialized countries. The year 2000 U.S. census, for example, collected 220 different pieces of demographic information on households and compiled them by residential block.

For many brands, demographics are often the best predictors of consumer behavior and therefore the primary means of segmentation. What customers buy often reflects how old they are, how much money they make, and how well educated they are. Certain demographic characteristics often correlate with certain product and brand choices. A highly paid executive is more likely to buy a Mercedes than is someone who just graduated from high school.

One of the challenges a company faces in maintaining brand relationships is that individual customers, over time, experience changes in age, income, education, and other factors. These changes cause changes in wants, needs, and desires. A company must decide whether to expand its product offerings to meet these changing needs (doing so might confuse brand identity) or implement an ongoing customer-replacement strategy.

Age, Life Stage, and Generational Cohorts

Age is an indicator of purchasing power, as well as the type of products purchased. Senior citizens control a great deal of the wealth in the United States; in Asian countries they have a great deal of the population's respect, so they have a great deal of influence on family purchases. Mostly born before or during World War II, this "gray market" includes young seniors (ages 60–74) and older seniors (75-plus). This is a huge market; there are over 68 million U.S. seniors alone, more than the population of France, Canada, Italy, or the United Kingdom. This is also one of the wealthiest retired generations.[5] And with baby boomers currently heading into their 50s and early 60s, the market size of the senior segment is going to get even bigger and more economically important relative to the rest of the population.

Young people in the United States are also a significant economic segment. Teens and "tweens" have significant discretionary income and spend it on clothes, music, food, and entertainment. Teenage Research Unlimited has estimated that the 31.6 million U.S. teens (ages 12 to 19) each week spend, on average, $66 of their own money (from jobs and allowances) and $27 of their parents' money.[6]

The term **life stages** refers to *the different periods in life of an individual or family.* Life stages include "single," "young family," "single-parent family," "family with older children," and "empty-nesters" (couples whose children have grown and left home). People have certain needs and wants at different stages in their lives. People in the "young family" segment, for example, are more interested in furnishing their homes and buying children's products than are "empty-nesters," who are more interested in travel and luxury items that they can better afford now that their children are gone.

Cohorts are *groups of individuals from the same generation.* Though they may be approximately the same age and may likely be in the same life stage, cohorts are more likely to be bound by common experiences such as going through the Great Depression or the Vietnam War. The unusually large number of births after World War II created a bulge in the U.S. population statistics. Baby boomers, most of whom are now in late middle-age, comprise some 38.4 percent of U.S. households but control 49 percent of all dollars spent each year, which is why companies want to reach this segment. Other interesting labels for cohorts, such as "baby boomers" (people born between 1946 and 1964), "baby busters" (the generations that followed boomers), and "echo boomers" (the children of baby busters), have been coined to describe people in terms of their age and life stage.

"Generation X" identifies the group whose 45 million members were born between 1965 and 1979. "Gen Xers" grew up on television and computers and are described as independent-minded and cynical because of the economic and social problems present when they were young (such as the AIDS epidemic, an economic recession, corporate downsizing, and a doubling of the U.S. divorce rate). They have also been found to be skeptical of advertising and other promotional activities. An interesting campaign conducted by the wine industry targeted this segment by using the slogan "Forget the rules! Enjoy the wine," an iconoclastic appeal to people who were presumed not to be concerned about traditions such as matching the right kinds of wine to meat and fish.

"Generation Y," individuals born after 1980, has a spending power of $150 billion per year. Gen Y, in contrast to Gen X, is generally thought to be more optimistic and entrepreneurial because of being raised in a more nurturing style amid an economic boom. Many marketers are trying to reach this group, but it is an elusive target with far greater diversity than any other lifestyle group. Toyota, for example, targeted the new Scion microminivans to this millennium generation and unveiled them with hip hop music in the background and dance-music CD giveaways. Toyota's usually staid sales staff was dressed in jeans, camouflage Puma sneakers, and T-shirts.[7]

Gen Y has also been called the "Digital Generation" (Generation D) because it has grown up with the internet and other computer technologies. It has been described as better informed, more empowered, and more cause oriented than preceding generations. The 1999 Cone/Roper Cause-Related Teen Survey found that social issues would motivate 55 percent of teens to switch brands and that 90 percent want to factor a company's cause-related activities into their buying decisions.[8] The newest generation, sometimes dubbed the "Millennium Generation," has not been profiled very well yet by marketers, but demographers have predicted that it will be an even larger group than the boomer market.

Ethnic Segments

Demographic segments based on ethnicity are increasingly important in the United States, where ethnic markets include such segments as African Americans, Asians, and Latinos or Hispanics. In the United States, the disposable income of

EXHIBIT 7-8

*As this ad illustrates,
the question is no longer
whether information
is available about
ethnic segments but
how thorough the
information is.*

ethnic segments is increasing faster than that of the total U.S. market. The Hispanic share of U.S. spending, for example, rose from 5.2 to 6.2 percent between 1990 and 1997, an amount estimated at $348 billion. The African-American share of spending in the same period rose to 9 percent, an estimated $469 billion.[9] The year 2000 U.S. census found over 35.3 million Hispanic persons, an increase of 58 percent over the 1990 total, making this group 12.5 percent of the U.S. population. Based on the 2000 census, Hispanic people are projected to be 15 percent of the U.S. population by 2020 and 25 percent by 2050. At the same time, Hispanic household incomes are projected to grow from 77 percent of the national average in 2000 to 82 percent by 2020.[10]

The Donnelley Marketing ad in Exhibit 7-8 illustrates how demographics relating to ethnicity and location can be used. Note that even within an ethnic segment, there are differences in age, education, income, and other important product-usage predictor factors.

The U.S. market is particularly diverse; many ethnic segments bring a variety of national and cultural differences. Kenny Irby at the Poynter Institute, a media school in St. Petersburg, Florida, for working journalists, has developed a diversity wheel (see Figure 7-4) to explain the implications of one's own background on understanding people of different backgrounds, which is a critical skill for marketing communicators.

But it's not just in the United States that ethnic marketing is an important strategy. Consider Malaysia, for example. The Malay population is large and politically powerful. The Chinese segment is nearly as large and very important in the business sector. There is also an Indian segment, which is smaller but still important in the business sector.

In some cases, brands are designed specifically for an ethnic group. In other cases, mainstream brands have marketing communication campaigns tailored to specific ethnic cultures and values. Both of these approaches can have unexpected negative consequences if the targeting is not handled with sensitivity, but they can work quite well if it is. One of the first ethnic segmentation and targeting examples comes from the 1940s, when Pepsi-Cola developed a sales team to market its soft drinks to African Americans, a group that showed high loyalty to Pepsi.[11] Pepsi did this in order to protect this loyalty and build on it, which it was able to do simply by giving special attention to this special group of customers.

An ongoing industry question is whether marketers are doing a good job targeting ethnic groups, given their market growth. Critics note that companies spend a disproportionately small amount of money for advertising in ethnic media. A study of radio, for example, found that stations targeting minority listeners earn about 29 percent less than stations that offer more general programming.[12]

Geodemographic Segments

Another important way to describe a segment is to look at geographical information. **Geodemographic segmenting** is *segmenting that combines geographic and demographic data to identify residents of a particular area with certain demographic traits.*

Geographic descriptions of a segment consider such factors as international, national, region, state, city, climate, topography, and urban/suburban/rural.

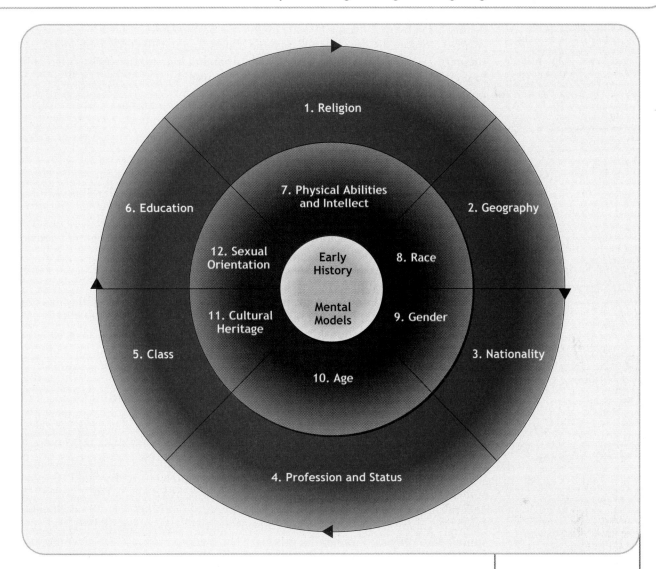

1. Religion
6. Education
7. Physical Abilities and Intellect
2. Geography
12. Sexual Orientation
Early History
8. Race
11. Cultural Heritage
Mental Models
9. Gender
5. Class
3. Nationality
10. Age
4. Profession and Status

Pharmaceutical manufacturers, for example, know that different allergies appear in different geographic areas, and they market their over-the-counter remedies accordingly: in Indiana, it's ragweed; in California, it's grass; in the Northeast, it's trees. In the car category, four-wheel drive vehicles are marketed more to people living in the Rocky Mountain states than to people in Chicago because of obvious geographic differences.

A number of business information programs, such as ClusterPLUS (Donnelley Marketing) and Claritas PRIZM, are able to insert census data (down to zip codes and blocks) into mapping software that companies can then use to chart where their best customers are located. Demographic information can also be input from companies that compile lists of driver's licenses and auto registrations. With all this information, ClusterPLUS and PRIZM have created 40 to 50 lifestyle profiles based on where consumers live and their purchase behaviors. The programs then assign each neighborhood, defined by zip codes, to one of the profiles. The underlying assumption is that customers who live close to each other have similar wants and needs. Once brands develop a profile of their customers, they use PRIZM or ClusterPLUS to create segments they want to target by grouping zip codes that best match their profiles.

Keeping up with the changing tastes of segments requires creative research techniques. To keep track of the urban youth market, one company used "Street

FIGURE 7·4

According to this model of diversity, our inner core, our early history, supplies mental models that shape our ability to understand people of different backgrounds. The middle and outer circles may change over time but still are critical demographic and psychographic variables shaping our views.

Source: Used by permission of Kenny Irby and The Poynter Institute.

Teams," a network of some 80 kids in 28 cities in the United States. These teams roamed clubs, malls, sports fields, playing courts, and record stores looking for the urban buzz *before* it started buzzing. Such urban intelligence networks, often able to predict trends for the global teen market, are used by global marketers such as Nike and Tommy Hilfiger.

Psychographic Segments

The problem with using only demographics to segment markets is that, although they provide a great deal of factual information, they do not explain what people like, think, and believe. This is why many companies also use **psychographics,** which are *measures that classify customers in terms of their attitudes, interests, and opinions as well as their lifestyle activities.* Typical lifestyle activities that are used include hobbies, club and organization memberships, types of entertainment and music enjoyed, shopping habits, vacations taken, and sports participation.

Certain consumer decisions are driven more by psychological needs and wants than by physical realities. Hallmark Cards, for example, places more emphasis on psychographics than on demographics when segmenting and targeting its customers. A writer for the card company explained: "To reach consumers, we consider the states of a relationship rather than an age. Whether you're 25 or 65, you have the same feelings—that giddy uncertainty in the beginning, the bottomless thrill of falling in love. Targeting a 40-year-old makes no sense because that 40-year-old may feel like a teenager."[13]

Psychographic segmentation groups customers by lifestyle. That is the focus of L. L. Bean marketing (see Exhibit 7-9). The word **lifestyle** refers to *the way people choose to spend their money, time, and energy.* SRI Consulting Business Intelligence (SRIC-BI), a research company that specializes in developing personality and lifestyle classification information, produces a research product called Values and Lifestyles (VALS). The company's original segmentation study divided U.S. consumers into nine groups based on Maslow's hierarchy of needs (◄ Chapter 5) and the inner-directed/outer-directed dichotomy described by the sociologist David Reisman. It was criticized because it tended to place the majority of consumers into only a couple of the groups. The current version, VALS 2, combines demographics and lifestyle data gathered from two national surveys of 2,500 consumers who responded to 43 lifestyle questions. It now places people into one of

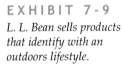

EXHIBIT 7-9
L. L. Bean sells products that identify with an outdoors lifestyle.

DON'T MISTAKE
A Street Address
For Where You Actually
LIVE.

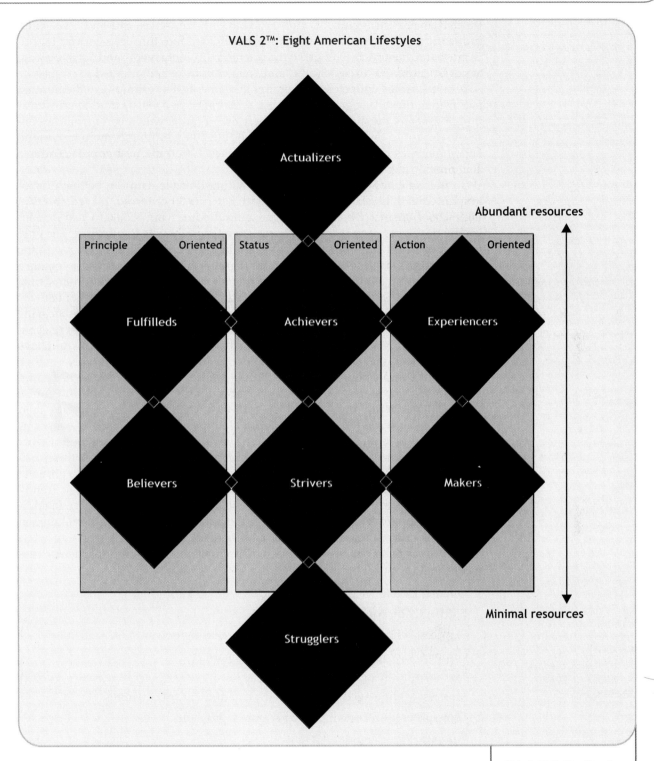

VALS 2™: Eight American Lifestyles

Actualizers

Abundant resources

Principle   Oriented   Status   Oriented   Action   Oriented

Fulfilleds   Achievers   Experiencers

Believers   Strivers   Makers

Minimal resources

Strugglers

eight groups. (For more information on VALS, go to its website: www.future. sri.com/vals.)

In Figure 7-5, the eight VALS 2 groups are arranged in a rectangle. The vertical dimension represents resources (income, education, self-confidence, health, intelligence, energy level, eagerness to buy); the horizontal dimension represents self-orientation (principles, status, and action). Each group orients itself to its world and social environment differently and displays distinct decision-making patterns, product usage rates, and media behaviors. At the top of the figure are "actualizers," people with abundant resources and a great deal of self-confidence. At

FIGURE 7-5

Lifestyles are used to segment and prioritize customers and prospects. In which of these boxes would you put yourself; in which would you place your parents?

the bottom are "strugglers," people who have few resources and find it challenging just to get by. In between are six groups divided into three categories: (1) "fulfilleds" and "believers" are principle oriented; (2) "achievers" and "strivers" are status oriented; (3) "experiencers" and "makers" are action oriented.

Lifestyles often cut across demographic segments. For example, in the hunting and fishing lifestyle segment, there is a wide range of ages, incomes, and education. Marketers must determine for their own brands which commonalities are most relevant to their products. Sometimes lifestyle profiling is more important, and sometimes demographics take precedence. Often the best approach uses a combination of both.

To illustrate how much more discriminating lifestyle data can be than demographic data, think about Harry and Todd. Both are 33 years old, played sports in high school, are married and have two young children, earn $55,000 a year in managerial positions, go to the same church, and generally vote Republican. The only real difference is that Harry is a dedicated family man, always playing with the kids when he has time and really helpful around the house, but Todd spends a minimal amount of time at home, preferring to play cards with his buddies, drink, and, whenever he can, golf or go fishing with "the guys." If you were going to try to sell Harry and Todd a life insurance policy, would you use the same message strategy for both? For Harry, the life insurance benefit that would be most relevant would be making sure that his family is taken care of. For Todd, you would have better luck stressing the savings benefit of a life insurance policy.

One of the most famous lifestyle terms—*yuppies*—was used in the 1980s and 1990s to describe young urban professionals who aspired to a good life. Yuppies (young, upperwardly mobile professionals) were characterized as driven by their desire to be upwardly mobile and accumulate possessions. As status-conscious adults, yuppies tended to marry later than average, then had "yuppie puppies" or "gourmet babies," recognizable by their expensive status-brand clothing. Although you don't hear much about yuppies today, their babies are still a growing market for designer products. It's not just OshKosh B'Gosh in the closet. Trendy children's brands also include Versace, Moschino, Hermès, and Kenzo.[14] In addition, yuppie parents seriously planned their infants' intellectual development around educational toys, developmental experiences, and tests.

Recently, a slew of lifestyle terms has been coined to identify particular segments of the population.

Dinkies: Double income young couples with no kids.

Biddies: Baby boomers in debt.

Skippies: Schoolkids with income and purchasing power.

Guppies: Gay upwardly mobile professionals.

Maffies: Middle-aged affluent folks.

Mossies: Middle-aged, overstressed, semi-affluent suburbanites.

Dimps: Dual-income couples with money problems.

Woopies: Well-off older persons.

Relationship Segments

Companies that understand the importance of creating long-term relationships with customers base their segmentation strategies on customers' perceptions of their relationships with a company and customers' behavior within that relationship. Four loyalty segments indicate the types of relationships customers have with a brand.[15] Not all customer relationship segments are equal. Recognizing differences between them can be helpful in targeting the most important groups, as well as designing messages to address their interests. The typical loyalty segments are defined as follows:

- **No loyalty:** Customers feel little attachment to the brand and are not likely to make repeat purchases, so there is little return to be expected from these switches or nonusers. This is seldom a targeted segment.

- **Inertia loyalty:** Customers feel little attachment to the brand but make repeat purchases out of habit. The best strategy to use for this group is to make the purchase as easy as possible. Frequent-purchase clubs, like those that send women's hosiery to members on a regular schedule, exemplify the strategy for this segment.

- **Latent loyalty:** Customers feel strong attachment to the brand but make few repeat purchases. Latent loyalty is particularly true for major purchases, such as cars and large appliances. A customer may purchase a washing machine only once every 20 years or so, but Maytag wants this person's loyalty when the time comes to replace that machine. Maytag also wants this person as an advocate who testifies on the brand's behalf to family and friends, to maximize the power of word-of-mouth advertising. Reminder marketing communication, reward programs, and programs to stimulate word-of-mouth testimonials are important strategies for this segment.

- **Premium loyalty:** Customers feel strong attachment to the brand and make frequent repeat purchases. Abercrombie & Fitch is determined to retain the loyalty of youthful customers who wear the label as a badge to impress friends. A strategy for this segment involves developing a sense of belonging to a special club, either in spirit (Abercrombie shoppers, Saturn owners) or in actuality, such as the self-organized Harley Owners Group (HOG).

AT&T has invested in a future customer segment (no loyalty yet) by giving over $150 million worth of telecommunications equipment and services to elementary and secondary schools. The company is hoping that its donations will make the AT&T brand familiar to young people, who are already buying cell phones and eventually will be moving into their own homes.

Segmenting for New Products: The "Adopter" Segment

The term *new product* can refer to a product that is new in the market or one that is new to the prospect. Because customers adopt new brands at different rates, information about these adoption patterns can also be used to segment prospects, as the opening case on Holden Barina illustrated. In that case, the young women coming into the market were making their first new-car purchase. Even though the Barina had been around, it was a new-product purchase for this group. In the Barina case, females were segmented by age and type of "adopter" (early versus late). The campaign capitalized on early adopter's profiles by using the internet: BG was given her own highly successful and constantly changing interactive website: www.bg.com.au.

Adoption segments reflect the fact that some people are more willing than others to take a risk. Think about internet users. Who was the first person you knew to get online and explore the Web? Would you identify that person as an innovator? Do you know any people who still have not learned to use the internet? As Table 7-2 shows, customers can be divided into five categories: innovators, early adopters, early majority, late majority, and laggards. These categories are frequently used in marketing communication strategies, particularly to define the target audience for the introduction of new products.

T A B L E   7 - 2   Categories of Adopters

Category	Percentage of Population	Characteristics	MC Strategy
Innovators	2.5%	Risk-takers, cosmopolitan; often affluent and well educated	Use publicity releases and the internet; retention is extremely important, because innovators influence early adopters.
Early adopters	13.5	Leaders in their communities and a source of information about new things; above average in income and education	Use the internet, direct-response, events, and advertising that lets them raise their hands to try; retention also very important, because early adopters influence early majority.
Early majority	34.0	Take their lead from the early adopters and wait for them to be satisfied first; slightly above average in age and education	Use advertising emphasizing "new" and "better," with case histories/demonstrations, comparisons with competition.
Late majority	34.0	Older than average and less well educated; tend to be skeptics and more comfortable with old values	Use sales promotion and guarantees/warranties to reduce risk; advertising should focus on demonstrations.
Laggards	16.0	Suspicious of innovation and its source; have little education, low income; often are social outsiders	Use advertising as brand reminder; use price-oriented sales promotion.

Source: Adapted with the permission of The Free Press, a Division of Simon & Schuster Adult Publishing Group, from DIFFUSION OF INNOVATIONS, Fifth Edition by Everett M. Rogers. Copyright © 1995, 2003 by Everett M. Rogers. Copyright © 1962, 1971, 1983 by The Free Press. All rights reserved.

Understanding differences in people's attitudes toward innovation is important in identifying audiences to target with different kinds of messages about new products or product changes. For example, innovators and adopters are most likely to be attracted by messages stressing a product's newness; the late majority are most likely to be attracted by a message that stresses that the product has been well tested and well received. These different segments, like other segments, vary by product category.

HOW DOES TARGETING DELIVER ON SEGMENTATION STRATEGIES?

Once the segments have been selected, the next step is to prioritize the segments on the basis of a combination of business and marketing objectives and profit potential. This prioritization is the first step in targeting. Targeting is the process used to identify which segments MC messages should be designed to reach, and to determine how much MC spending should be used to reach each segment. Making sure the MC message is "on target" is a key issue in strategic planning.

To begin to answer these questions, marketers look at their marketing objectives, at their budgets, and at the estimated sales and profit returns that could be expected from each segment. At the least, most companies target current customers, prospects, and channel members (assuming products go through distribution channels). Companies that practice IMC also target internal departments and employees (← Chapter 6) to help ensure that customer audiences receive a consistent brand message from everyone within the organization.

Targeting decisions also consider timing—how and when customers make brand-buying decisions. In B2B marketing, for example, buyers often go through several steps before making a brand selection. These buyers can be targeted at the various steps in their decision making (← Chapter 5). In the consumer market, couples who get married are targeted right away by real-estate agents and home furnishing stores, knowing that newly marrieds are prime prospects for houses and furnishings.

Frequently the major targets are further broken down. For example, a manufacturer of children's clothing may target both parents and children (presenting obviously different messages to each but maintaining a consistent look across all brand messages). The primary target may be parents, because they make the purchase, and the secondary target may be children, who can influence the purchase decision. Targeting implementation also means developing media and message strategies to reach each selected segment.

Message Targeting

Targeting starts by using the profile characteristics of each segment to find commonalities of needs and wants to which brand messages can be related. Segmentation characteristics, such as demographics and psychographics, can be used to predict how customers will respond to certain message strategies. As shown in Figure 7-6, the more characteristics that are used to qualify and define a target, the smaller that targeted segment will become. A question that always faces marketers is how narrowly to target.

Once the target characteristics are known, message and media strategies can be developed. The primary elements in a message—such as the headline in an ad or the cover on a brochure—should speak directly to an identified interest of the target audience, thus separating that audience from all others. Reaching numerous target audiences is a central strategy of many businesses. Xerox cleverly makes good use of that fact in its B2B advertising for its copiers (see Exhibit 7-10). The IMC in Action box explains how different companies have targeted certain youth segments.

To target market segments, companies select media whose audiences most closely match the brand's target audience. Here are the types of media that a pharmaceutical company such as Eli Lilly might choose to reach four important targets:

- *Primary care physicians:* medical journals (which carry articles about clinical test of drugs) and field representatives (who make personal calls on doctors).

- *Insurance companies/HMOs:* Direct mail, e-mail.

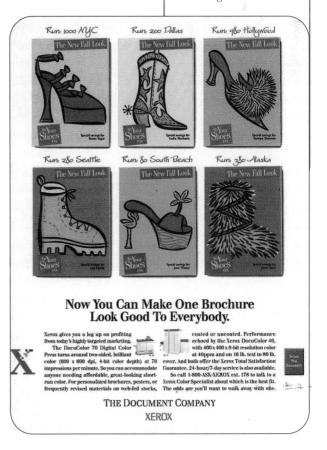

Now You Can Make One Brochure Look Good To Everybody.

THE DOCUMENT COMPANY
XEROX

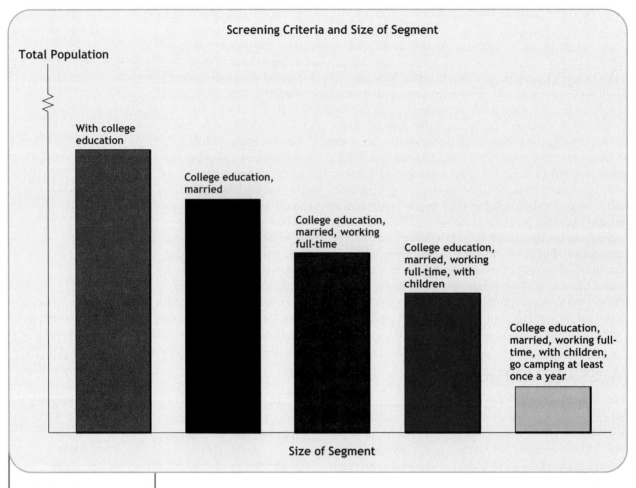

Screening Criteria and Size of Segment

Total Population

With college education

College education, married

College education, married, working full-time

College education, married, working full-time, with children

College education, married, working full-time, with children, go camping at least once a year

Size of Segment

FIGURE 7-6

The more the screening, the smaller the segment.

- *Hospital administrators:* Exhibits at the administrators' national conferences.
- *Patients:* TV and magazine ads.

One of the benefits of the internet is that it enables companies to practice narrow targeting as direct mail does but at a much lower cost. And of course the internet can be used to reach many different audiences.

Profitability Targeting

One question companies must ask themselves is how fast do they want to grow and how much are they willing to invest in acquiring new customers in anticipation of future profits. One of the principles of IMC is to strategically balance MC efforts between current and prospective customers. The extent to which current customers should be targeted differs for every brand. The main deciding factor is how much it costs to generate a sale from current customers versus the cost per sale for new customers. The greater the difference is, the more one segment should be targeted over another. However, just because new customers cost more to acquire doesn't mean that the investment won't pay off in the long term.

To help determine the cost of targeting a segment (and therefore a segment's potential for profitability), ask to what extent the target is[16]

- **Measurable:** Can customers in the segment be identified and counted? A company may know that redheads like its brands. However, unless there are ways of identifying where redheads live and work, or what media they consume, the segment is too nebulous to work with other than through a self-selection strategy.

IMC IN ACTION

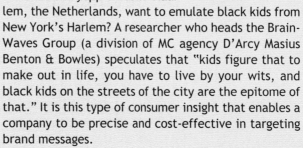

Hip-Hop and the 'Hood

Fila USA started as a sportswear marketer that made tennis togs for the country-club set. So why did it run edgy, dark ads against graffiti-filled inner-city playground walls with a chorus of clanging garbage cans in the background? Fashion designer Tommy Hilfiger has made a fortune selling preppie wardrobes to well-bred suburbanites. So why did he give away wardrobes to rap stars, send rappers down his fashion runway, and add athletic shoes to his brand's lineup? The answer is that the funky street culture that embraces rap and hip-hop has become a fashion statement among teenagers, sort of a universal youth badge. Even white kids in Kansas wear the flamboyant fashions of the inner city—baggy jeans, green hair, camouflage T-shirts, vintage lambskin-lined flight jackets, metallic sweatshirts, and, of course, Nike shoes.

Mistic Beverages, the many-flavored soft-drink brand, used Dennis Rodman's parti-colored hair in a "Show Your Colors" promotion. And Sprite, Coca-Cola's spirited lemon-lime drink, pitted rappers MC Shan and KRS One against each other in a verbal duel that became an ad. Sprite also inked a deal with Shabazz Brothers Urbanwear to give away $1 million worth of the clothing with a mean street attitude in a bottle-top promotion. Riding on the popularity of black street culture, Sprite's volume jumped almost 18 percent, three times as big an increase as the next most successful soft drink.

Shabazz Fuller, owner of Urbanwear, explains why these major corporations are looking to "the 'hood" (the neighborhood) for inspiration: "They want to piggyback on our brand equity, which caused us concern at first, but it's cool. They're supporting the whole rap community."

Why does the kid from Kansas, or the Euro-yuppie from Haarlem, the Netherlands, want to emulate black kids from New York's Harlem? A researcher who heads the BrainWaves Group (a division of MC agency D'Arcy Masius Benton & Bowles) speculates that "kids figure that to make out in life, you have to live by your wits, and black kids on the streets of the city are the epitome of that." It is this type of consumer insight that enables a company to be precise and cost-effective in targeting brand messages.

But most of all it's about brands. The African-American market, with its $325 billion in spending power, cares intensely about brand names. A rapper called Q-Tip sends that message in a song that starts with Tommy Hilfiger and then goes on to list a dozen other brand names such as Tanqueray, Lexus, Donna Karan, and BMW. As *Brandweek* observed, "street certification in a rap song is a marketer's dream come true."

Think About It

How does this box explain or relate to niche marketing, and how does niche marketing differ from mass marketing? Why would marketers want to mimic the styles of the urban streets in marketing their products to young people?

Source: Adapted from Joshua Levine, "Badass Sells," *Forbes,* April 21, 1997, pp. 142–48; Nicole Crawford, "The Worm Proves Mistical," *Promo,* July 1997, p. 8; and Sarah Van Boven, "Toeing the Designer Line," *Newsweek,* November 17, 1997, p. 77.

- **Accessible:** Can customers in the segment be reached with the product and brand messages? A segment of prospects that live outside a brand's area of distribution may not be attractive because expanding distribution may cost more than the new sales would justify.

- **Substantial:** How many customers or businesses make up the segment? Unless the segment has enough critical mass—in terms of size or dollars to spend—it may not be worth singling out. Segment sizes differ by product category: convenience goods need large segments; manufacturers of airplane carriers may need only one customer.

- **Differential:** Does the segment have commonalities that distinguish it from other segments? Customers within a segment need to have certain needs, wants, or desires that will motivate them to respond to certain messages and offers.

- **Actionable:** Can the segment be served? The company must have the capacity to make enough product to serve the segment, enough salespeople to reach the segment, and enough marketing communication budget to send messages to the segment.

Segmenting and Targeting B2B Customers

As important as segmenting and targeting profitable customers is in consumer marketing, it is even more so in B2B marketing. The average B2B customer spends more and costs more to acquire than the average consumer. Like consumers, most companies don't give one company 100 percent of their category spending, so there is always the opportunity to increase the spending of these customers. Although this chapter discusses segmenting mostly in terms of consumer marketing, most of the segmenting concepts, such as customer profitability, are also applicable to B2B marketing. However, you should be aware of some different terms and special considerations in B2B segmenting and targeting.

In North America, businesses have been segmented by the government according to the North American Industry Classification System (NAICS), which provides multilevel segmentation by industry. The U.S., Canada, and Mexico agencies responsible for this classification system are now developing a complementary system that will be called NAPCS (North American Product Classification System). It will focus more on services that are not based on industry of origin.

The sample listing in Figure 7-7 shows how NAICS works for one particular industry—fabricated metals. A manufacturer of pliers is assigned the code

FIGURE 7-7

What is the similarity between this figure and Figure 7-6?

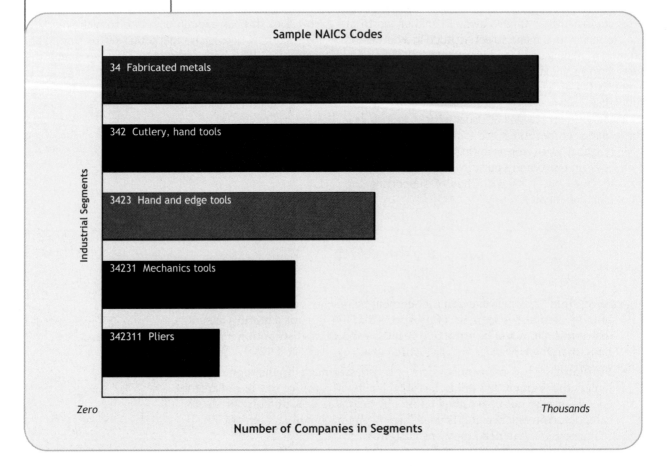

Sample NAICS Codes

34 Fabricated metals

342 Cutlery, hand tools

3423 Hand and edge tools

34231 Mechanics tools

342311 Pliers

Industrial Segments

Zero   Thousands

Number of Companies in Segments

number 342311. The "34" indicates that the company falls within the broad category of "fabricated metals." As you can see, a company that sells a product that appeals to makers of "cutlery and hand tools" has a much bigger target audience than does a company that has a product relevant only to manufacturers of "pliers." The value of this classification system for B2B marketing communication is that it provides a company with a quick way to identify companies that are in a particular industry.

NAICS codes are helpful for a company selling products like computers, which have applications in many different kinds of industries. IBM, for example, frequently puts together marketing communication programs aimed at certain NAICS codes, such as companies involved in distribution, manufacturing, or service industries. Segmenting on the basis of these well-defined sets of criteria lets everyone involved in marketing at IBM know exactly which types of companies are being targeted, because of the code numbers.

Other common B2B segments are based on company size, which is determined by total sales or number of employees. Companies also can be segmented by characteristics similar to those used in consumer marketing:

- *Purchase behavior:* large or small volume; level of price sensitivity; average order size, order frequency.
- *Benefits:* special needs, level of service required.
- *Demographics:* company size; type of firm, organization, or industry.
- *Credit rating:* companies with a low credit rating are higher-risk customers.
- *Geographics:* areas in which a company is located or does business.
- *Psychographics:* corporate culture, level of risk taking.
- *Relationship level:* loyalty of customers, percentage of customers' category spending received by the company/brand.

Targeting and Ethical Issues

Some criticism of marketing and marketing communication arises from controversial targeting of special groups. Many people feel, for example, that children shouldn't be targeted for certain kinds of products, such as sweetened cereals and violent video games. Ethnic groups resent what they see as a bombardment of "sin product" ads, such as those for liquor and cigarettes. As the Ethics and Issues box discusses, companies need to consider ethics when targeting certain segments.

ETHICS AND ISSUES

Offensive Targeting

For some food manufacturers, particularly those that sell candy and sugared cereals, running ads for food products on Saturday-morning cartoon shows and before child-oriented feature films is targeting at its best. They can economically transmit their sales messages to a demographically perfect audience. But to opponents of advertising to kids, such targeting is another example of socially irresponsible marketing.

Critics warn that advertising directed toward children may be contributing to alcohol abuse, violence, childhood obesity, an increasing level of childhood diabetes, and compulsive buying by young adults.

There are other reasons why targeting can raise hackles. Credit-card companies are criticized for targeting college students who have little income. Critics charge that cartoon characters such as Joe Camel and the Budweiser frogs entice young people to buy cigarettes and beer. Although the tobacco company R. J. Reynolds claimed that the Joe Camel campaign was not directed at children, it was compelled to abandon the cartoon image in all of its marketing. In 1998, an agreement was reached between 46 states and several tobacco companies to settle lawsuits filed by the states. Part of the agreement was that the companies would not advertise in media whose audiences had more than 15 percent in the 12 to 17 age range. However, two studies done in 2000, one by the Massachusetts Department of Health and the other by the American Legacy Foundation, determined that tobacco companies had actually increased their levels of advertising in magazines reaching this youth audience.

Similarly, in Britain, Bass PLC has marketed low-alcohol drinks that critics say encourage underage drinking. With a sugary flavor, offbeat packaging, and quirky names such as Hooper's Hooch and Stunn Potent Passion, these "alco-pop" drinks have been denounced by the government and consumer groups that claim that their makers are inappropriately targeting young people.

Other critics focus on the targeting of alcohol and tobacco products to racial and ethnic minority groups. The use of billboards for such ads is a particularly sensitive issue in urban areas where ethnic groups feel they are being massively targeted for these products. The products that generated the greatest criticism included Uptown, a low-menthol cigarette formulated for African Americans; Dakota cigarettes, targeted to young, poorly educated, blue-collar women; and PowerMaster malt liquor, a high-alcohol beer marketed to young black men that in its advertising emphasized getting a fast buzz.

PowerMaster's maker, G. Heilman, subsequently got in trouble with the U.S. Bureau of Alcohol, Tobacco, and Firearms (BATF) when it introduced a line extension called Colt 45 Premium, which the BATF felt was really PowerMaster in a new package. Although packaging may contain information about alcohol content, the BATF doesn't permit brewers to *advertise* alcohol strength.

Target marketing of such products raises the paradox of "good marketing but bad ethics." A study of such practices found that people believe that a targeting strategy is unethical if it involves targets perceived as vulnerable and products perceived as harmful. These concerns can cause an uproar leading to protests, bad publicity, and costly legal battles.

The Code of Ethics of the American Marketing Association states, among other things, that (1) products should be safe and fit for their intended use, (2) communication about products should not be deceptive, (3) companies should disclose risks associated with products, and (4) companies should not use false and misleading marketing communications.

Think About It

What issues are associated with the targeting efforts described here? Why are people critical of such practices? Consult a general-interest magazine and find an ad for a product that you think needs to be reconsidered in light of the American Marketing Association's Code of Ethics. Explain why you question the ethics of the marketing of this product.

Source: Joan Lowy, "Kidblitz: Do Advertisers Rob Cradle?" *Daily Camera,* December 11, 1999, p. D1; Nancy Millman, "Tonning Up Kids," *Chicago Tribune,* January 9, 1997, p. 3-1; "Cigarette Billboards Draw Heat, Fire over Tasteless Message," *Daily Camera,* July 9, 1998, p. 7C; Ernest Beck, "Bass to Reformulate Low-Alcohol Drink to Address Criticism," *Wall Street Journal,* September 11, 1997, p. B4; N. Craig Smith and Elizabeth Cooper-Martin, "Ethics and Target Marketing: The Role of Product Harm and Consumer Vulnerability," *Journal of Marketing* 61 (July 1997), pp. 1–20; and "Tobacco Ads Targeting Teens, Study Says, " *Daytona Beach News Journal,* May 5, 2000, p. 2A.

A FINAL NOTE: BALANCING ACQUISITION AND RETENTION

Good marketing communication emphasizes the importance of knowing and targeting current customers. Most companies seldom strike a proper balance between targeting current customers (for retention) and targeting prospective customers (for acquisition). Because of the traditional emphasis on transactions rather than relationships, and on acquiring new customers rather than retaining and growing the current ones, many marketing programs are not as cost-effective as they could be.

A survey conducted by *Direct* magazine, for example, found that marketers are more likely to use their direct-marketing budgets to gain new customers rather than to retain current ones.[17] Obviously, a real strength of targeting with direct-marketing messages and media is the ability to individualize and customize messages. Current customers should be the first target of this type of marketing communication. Strategic segmenting and targeting allow a company to use marketing communication tools efficiently. They are an essential part of zero-based planning (◀ Chapter 6).

In the opening case, Holden made a major effort to retain its current customers—young women in the small-car market—by repositioning its Barina model. It was also essential for Holden to reach young women as they came into the market. The BG campaign was designed both to retain the interest of current customers and to reach new prospects as they matured. In most cases, segmenting and targeting call for a careful balancing of the two objectives of acquisition and retention.

Key Terms

behavioral segmenting 221	life stages 223	permission marketing 219
benefit segmenting 221	lifestyle 226	psychographics 226
cohorts 223	mass customization of	recency 218
cross-selling 221	products 213	segmenting 210
demographics 222	monetary 218	self-selection 219
frequency 218	niche markets 212	targeting 210
geodemographic segmenting 224	one-to-one marketing 213	up-selling 221

Key Point Summary

Key Point 1: Moving Away from Mass Marketing

Because there are few real mass market products, marketers are targeting ever smaller and more profitable segments for the sake of message efficiency and effectiveness. The segmentation process involves identifying the types of customers in the market, analyzing them for their common characteristics and profitability, and then targeting those who are most likely to respond when motivated by MC messages.

Key Point 2: Profitability

Segmentation identifies and prioritizes groups of customers with common characteristics in order to target the most profitable groups and develop retention programs for them. Segmentation starts with the identification of characteristics of current customers. After the segments have been identified, the next step is to target the customers who offer the most profit potential by analyzing their recency, frequency, and monetary characteristics.

Key Point 3: Types of Segments

Segments are defined in terms of such characteristics as behavior and desired benefits, demographics (including ethnic segments and geodemographics), psychographics, relationship levels, and adopter status. These variables can be used to match a segment with current high-profitability customers.

Key Point 4: Targeting

Targeting is the process of selecting high-priority segments that are most likely to respond to marketing communication programs. Self-selection, which lets customers aggregate themselves as a target market, locates the most interested and responsive target.

Lessons Learned

Key Point 1: Moving Away from Mass Marketing

a. Distinguish between segmenting and targeting.
b. List and describe the steps in the segmentation process.
c. Explain why there has been a move away from mass marketing and toward segmented marketing.
d. What is a market niche?
e. What is one-to-one marketing? How is it different from mass marketing?
f. Define *self-selection*. Why is self-selection considered to be the technique that locates the most interested and most responsive target audience?
g. Find an advertisement for a product that you think is marketed to a niche. (*Hint:* Look in special-interest magazines.) Explain the characteristics of those who make up the niche, and analyze how the message is designed to speak their interests.

Key Point 2: Profitability

a. Why should companies start with current customers when developing a segmentation and targeting strategy?
b. What is the difference between buyers and users?
c. What is profitability segmentation?
d. What does *RFM* stand for? How are these factors used to ensure customer profitability?

Key Point 3: Types of Segments

a. What are the five types of customer segmentation discussed in this chapter? Give an example of each.
b. Distinguish between demographics and psychographics, and explain the role of each in segmentation.
c. Explain how a company can develop segmentation strategies based on a knowledge of relationship factors.
d. Working in teams, consult the diversity wheel (Figure 7-4). For each section of the middle and outer circles, write a specific insight about yourself and about the other person. When you have completed the list, identify all the points of similarity and all the points of difference.

Key Point 4: Targeting

a. How does business-to-business segmenting and targeting differ from consumer segmenting and targeting? How are they similar?
b. Analyze the contents of your closet or medicine cabinet. Find one brand that you think was targeted to you. Explain why and how that brand's targeting works in general, and tell how it speaks to you personally with its brand messages.
c. Explore the ethics of targeting children who watch Saturday-morning cartoon programs. Suppose you were working on the advertising for a sugar-laden cereal, can you think of any socially responsible way to advertise it on Saturday-morning cartoon shows? What would be your personal opinion about this assignment?

Chapter Challenge

Writing Assignment

The Australian automaker Holden wants to market its Barina model to young women. Review this chapter on segmenting and targeting and Chapter 5 on the brand decision process. How many ideas from these two chapters would you recommend that the Holden marketing manager consider in developing next year's marketing plan? List all the principles and strategies that you think might be useful in developing this strategy.

Presentation Assignment

Develop a class presentation on the use of stars as campaign spokespersons. Choose from Dennis Rodman, Tiger Woods, Michelle Kwan, or some other star with whom you are familiar and who has appeared in advertising for a client. Analyze the effectiveness of this star in reaching either mass or niche audiences. How does the use of stars assist in the segmenting and targeting of a campaign? Develop an outline of the key points you want to present. Give the presentation to your class, or record it on a videotape (audio tape is also an option) to turn in to your instructor, along with the outline.

Internet Assignment

Go to the SRI Consulting Business Intelligence's VALS website (www.future.sri.com/vals), and click on "survey." Match your lifestyle with the VALS typology. Where would you be located, and how well do you think that designation fits you?

Chapter

8

Data-Driven Communication

When precise marketing unites you with your customers...

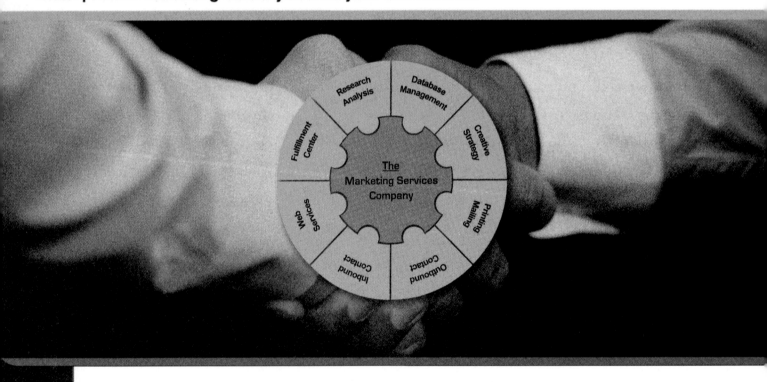

Key Points in This Chapter

1. What is data-driven communication, and why is it used?
2. How are customer data collected, converted into information, and integrated into the IMC process?
3. What privacy and security issues are associated with building relationships with customers?
4. How do companies use databases to manage customer relationships and to customize MC messages?

Chapter Perspective

Learning about Customers

Companies collect data to learn about customers in order to target messages accurately and make marketing communication relevant to target audiences. Knowing how customers respond to offers, what they buy and don't buy, why they buy and don't buy, how much they buy, when they buy, and which ones are profitable and which are not is all valuable information. It also offers the potential to make marketing communication more personal and more relevant to customers.

In days gone by, the mom-and-pop grocery store used to know its customers; the grocer could relate to them as individuals. Today's sophisticated information technology (IT) systems are making it possible for companies once again to "know" their customers and have a memory of past interactions with them. Such systems allow companies to cost-effectively collect, analyze, and use such data in planning marketing communication.

Databases and IT are also the engines that drive integration and interactivity. Because of IT, large numbers of employees have access to current customer data, which is a must in cost-effective IMC. Finally, IT allows faster and broader evaluation of IMC programs, and as a result marketing people are more accountable than ever before.

This chapter introduces components of data-driven communication, discusses privacy and security issues related to data collection and use, and explores the management and use of customer databases in IMC programs.

BRITISH AIRWAYS TAKES OFF WITH RELATIONSHIP MARKETING
Carlson Marketing Group, London, England

Traditionally known as an airline for business travelers, British Airways (BA) recognized a huge growth opportunity in the leisure travel market—one of the fastest-growing travel sectors. The question was, How could BA best penetrate this market? BA used TV and magazine advertising, but still felt its MC efforts weren't having the impact they should have against the leisure travel segment.

After conducting extensive research, BA identified the type of offering that would be most suited to this segment of travelers, and decided to create the Travel Service, a one-stop service for leisure travelers, which was designed and launched by the London branch of the Carlson Marketing Group. The resulting campaign was unique in that it matched product offerings to members' interests (see Exhibit 8-1). Furthermore, it used a database to profile BA's most profitable customers in order to identify high-profit prospects.

The Personalized Strategy

At the time British Airways was developing its program, a number of competitors were already offering consumers "travel services." These consisted of travel agents offering customers the convenience of electronic or phone sales service, and banks and credit-card companies extending their product offerings. However, these services used blanket communications that were neither personalized nor specific. BA believed its Travel Service would better meet the needs of individual leisure travelers by using more personalized brand messages.

The British Airways Travel Service proactively mailed members "inside information" on the latest offers and holiday destinations from BA and its partners, relevant to members' interests and lifestyles. It provided members with new ideas and suggestions about when and where to go, where to stay, and what to do at each destination. Where possible, it matched the offering to specific details provided by members on their "preference forms." The product offering included flights, holidays, accommodations, car rental, and foreign currency exchange—the full travel experience.

Campaign Strategy

The Carlson Marketing Group designed the launch campaign for the Travel Service to recruit high-value members who fit the profit profile and would generate new revenue opportunities for British Airways. The campaign's marketing communication strategies were

- To drive additional in-store traffic and encourage enrollment at point of purchase.

EXHIBIT 8-1

An introductory mailing announces British Airways' new database-driven Travel Service program

New ideas to keep you in the know

- To develop a distinct set of brand values that complemented British Airways' master brand while still permitting the Travel Service to stand alone.
- To create a consistent approach to all aspects of marketing communication.

The target audience was identified as two key groups:

"Dinkies": dual income, no kids; young independents, 25 to 35 years of age, affluent; sophisticated and ambitious when making travel arrangements; plenty of spontaneity and spare income to match.

"Global Greys": 45-plus years of age, affluent; children have left home, plenty of time to enjoy newfound freedom; enough financial resources to travel.

The campaign consisted of three parts. First, a self-selection recruitment strategy used direct mail, posters, and point-of-purchase materials to encourage prospects to raise their hands and sign up. Second, the agency chose an activation strategy using direct mail to maximize the relationship with members after recruitment; the objective was to encourage members to book and repeat-book. Third, Carlson established a training program (internal marketing) to educate British Airways staff about the program and their role in the recruitment process and ongoing service delivery.

Due to the highly targeted nature of the program, the success of the effort depended on building a solid database. BA generated the database from prospects identified as having an appropriate profile for a BA leisure offering. The airline selected data from existing databases consisting of customers who had previously purchased direct from BA. Prospects were sent a "recruitment pack" containing the preference form, which generated additional information for the database, such as frequency of travel, travel plans, types of offers of interest, travel partners, annual household spending on travel, and particular interests while on holiday. This database enabled the company to generate highly targeted, personalized direct-mail communications on an ongoing basis.

The strategy behind the Travel Service and its launch campaign was that by gathering data from customers and developing relationships with them, BA could better understand their needs, aspirations, and travel desires in order to proactively target them with the latest, most relevant offers and destinations on an ongoing basis. This would increase members' propensity to make leisure bookings with BA. Hence, BA created its Matching Service to enable the Travel Service to deliver to members details of offers that matched their preferences. The benefit to members was twofold: inside information on the latest offers from BA and its partners, along with a degree of being proactive that no other travel service provider could equal.

The creative proposition driving the campaign was based on the concept of "inside information": "Only the British Airways Travel Service proactively sends you the 'inside information' on the latest offers and destinations that are relevant to you . . . so you never miss out."

By targeting prospects from current BA databases and setting up a separate Travel Service database to record the additional information obtained from the campaign's responders, the Travel Service was able to match members' interests and behavior with BA. Through the Travel Service, BA was able to develop strong, personalized relationships with its leisure customers.

The British Airways Travel Service launch campaign, driven by a customer database and a multistage direct-mail program, met its key performance objectives and successfully recruited a critical mass of 170,000 members into the program by the end of year one. It also reached incremental and gross revenue targets. Finally, it won a Gold Medallion in the international Advertising and Marketing Effectiveness award competition.

Source: This case was adapted with permission from the Advertising and Marketing Effectiveness (AME) award-winning brief for British Airways prepared by the Carlson Marketing Group agency in London.

USING DATABASES TO BUILD RELATIONSHIPS

John McGarver, 48, has a 350-acre farm that's located an hour's drive northwest of Des Moines, Iowa. He runs about 200 head of cattle and plants about 150 acres of corn each year. There have been some tough times, but overall he has been fairly successful. One reason is his ongoing interest in new and better ways to run his farm. He subscribes to three farm magazines (*Farm Industry News, Farm Journal,* and *Successful Farming*), is a member of his local Farm Bureau Federation, and attends the Iowa State Fair every year.

On one of his many trips to the local grain elevator, John glanced through an issue of *Successful Farming* that had just come out. An article that caught his attention gave the pros and cons of a new weed management product, Soil Saver. Before he could finish the article, however, his turn came to have his corn weighed and transferred to the holding silo, and he pretty much forgot about Soil Saver. A week later, however, he received a flyer in the mail about Soil Saver. The more he read the direct-mail piece, the more interesting this new product seemed—until he got to the section on how much it cost. Although the product offered some new benefits, John felt the price was out of line and threw the flyer away. Soil Saver was pushed to the back of his mind once again. Then at the end of the week he got a phone call from a clerk at the local farm co-op. John learned that the co-op was now handling Soil Saver and had a special promotion for the first ten farmers in his area who agreed to try the product in the coming planting season. After ten minutes of discussion, John signed up to become a Soil Saver customer.

John's three encounters with Soil Saver brand messages may seem coincidental. But don't be fooled. All were data driven to create synergy and impact prospects. The ad in *Successful Farming* was placed because the magazine's reader profile, constructed from its database of subscribers, indicated the magazine reached a high percentage of farmers who planted corn, wheat, and soy beans. In addition, the collective data on the magazine's readers was helpful to Soil Saver's agency when it created the ad for the new product. The direct-mail flyer was sent to John because his name was in a database of Midwest farms with over 100 acres of tillable ground. Finally, John received the phone call because he was in the local farm co-op store's database of customers who had purchased fertilizer and weed control products within the last 12 months. Soil Saver had paid the co-op store a special promotional allowance to make personal phone calls (tightly targeted telemarketing) to likely prospects who had indicated they wanted to be made aware of new product information.

As explained in Chapter 1, IMC does three things more effectively and efficiently than traditional marketing: acquiring, retaining, and growing profitable customers. IMC achieves all three in part by using prospect and customer information compiled in databases. A **database** is *a collection of related information that is stored and organized in a way that allows access and analysis.*[1] That's how British Airways was able to match a product offering—its new Travel Service (see Exhibit 8-2)—to its customers' interests and how Soil Saver was able to acquire John as a new user.

Companies use many other types of databases to add value to brands and help them communicate with customers. For example, by putting product offerings, price lists, and inventory reports into online databases, companies can provide information to customers and other stakeholders much more quickly and much less expensively than they can by printing and distributing paper catalogs and brochures. Making timely and accurate information easy to access not only saves the company money but adds value for customers. Also, these increases in operating efficiency can lead to more competitive pricing. Companies have become so reliant on databases that if suddenly they all disappeared, most companies would not be able to function. This chapter explains how to collect and manage data in order to make marketing communications work more effectively.

Digitization Makes Brand Information More Available

A database can hold anything that can be **digitized,** that is, *converted into numerical form by means of a binary system of 1s and 0s.* Everything you see on a computer

EXHIBIT 8-2
The British Airways Travel Service mailing focused on ideas for holiday vacations. Included in the package were inserts that described various destinations and provided important information for travel planning.

monitor, including everything on the internet, has been digitized so a computer can store or find information and provide it when you want it. Words, pictures (both moving and still), and sounds can all be converted from their normal analog form into a digital form. Thus, databases can contain text, videos, graphics, music, and, of course, plain old numbers.

Digitization allows us to collect, store, retrieve, analyze, and transmit data quickly and cost-effectively. One of the most important benefits of digitization is its accuracy in reproduction. For years, digitization and databases have been used in the production of printed information—magazines, newspapers, reports, and catalogs. Magazines are now electronically produced (using dozens of databases and computers) until the very last step, when ink is applied to paper. It is relatively easy to think about internet delivery of magazines and newspapers someday overtaking their printed versions.

What Is a Customer Database?

A customer database can be as simple as a shoe box full of index cards containing the names and addresses of customers. In the case of the Speedy Car Wash, featured in the IMC in Action box, the company database is a list of license plate numbers.

Although some small retailers are quite successful with lists or shoe-box databases, most companies use computerized databases. A company's customer database is a strong competitive tool because no competitor knows what a company knows about its own customers. This proprietary (privately owned, exclusive) information can provide a company with a strong competitive advantage when dealing with its own customers. Keep in mind, however, that customer data alone are not too helpful. A company must make sure the collected data are accurate and relevant. Once this is achieved, the data must be properly analyzed to create useful information. Unfortunately many companies are much better at collecting than at analyzing data.

IMC IN ACTION

Cleaning Up on License Plates

Jimmy Branch, the owner of the Speedy Car Wash in Panama City, Florida, uses his customers' license plates to track the frequency of their purchases. With such information, he was able to determine that two-thirds of his customers came in only once or twice a year. What's more, he found that the remaining customers—those who washed their cars at Speedy three or more times a year—were responsible for two-thirds of his revenues.

He used this information to revamp how he markets his car wash business. He created discounts to encourage the lower-frequency customers to come in more often. For example, someone who has a car washed receives a coupon for $3 off another car wash if it's used within two weeks. Frequent customers receive special recognition and efforts to persuade them to buy extra services, such as a wax or undercarriage wash, when they visit. If they respond to some short questions about their car-service needs—and thereby help Branch keep his computer information updated—they qualify for a few dollars off the cost of the extra services.

Tracking customers by license plate number has also helped Speedy's salespeople individualize customer contact. When a customer pulls in, a salesperson at the front counter enters the customer's plate number into the computer. Repeat customers' names come up on the screen, so the salesperson can greet each of them personally. This kind of recognition and response creates effective brand relationships.

Think About It

Branch learned about the frequency with which his customers visited his car wash. How did he learn that information? How does this information help his staff build customer relationships?

Source: Laura M. Litvan, "Increasing Revenue with Repeat Sales," *Nation's Business*, January 1996, p. 36. Reprint by permission, *Nation's Business*, February 1996. Copyright 1996, U.S. Chamber of Commerce.

Database marketing helps companies manage brand relationships in a variety of ways:[2]

- Understanding customers and prospects.
- Managing customer service.
- Understanding the competition.
- Managing the sales operation.
- Managing the marketing and marketing communication campaigns.
- Communicating with customers.
- Providing information resources to customers.

Occasionally you will hear people talk about *database marketing* being the same thing as *direct-response marketing*. It is not. Direct marketing is just one of the marketing communication functions. **Database marketing** is *marketing that is managed through a database system that gives the company interaction memory*. It can and should be used with all marketing communication functions and in the selection of media. Another term for this is **data-driven communication**. A company's first objective in using a customer database is to identify who its customers are. That information is what the Speedy Car Wash captured with its list of license plates. Surprisingly, many retail businesses have only a vague notion of who buys the products they offer. Some companies use a loyalty card to keep track of their regular customers.

Even B2B companies often don't know who their end users are, because their products are sold through distributors and retailers. As explained in Chapter 4, it is difficult to have a meaningful dialogue with someone about whom a company knows nothing, and it is nearly impossible to design goods and services that will satisfy the needs of "unknown" customers.

An important reason for capturing customer-behavior information in databases is to determine how effective the company's various marketing programs are. For years, marketing departments have been criticized for their inability to show how their spending has affected sales and the building of long-term brand relationships. By using databases to track how customers respond to campaigns and promotional offers, marketers are better able to show cause and effect and to calculate the return on a marketing program investment.

Customer identification and accountability are only two uses of customer databases. The Database Application Checklist (see Table 8-1), developed by the advertising agency Saatchi & Saatchi, provides examples of many business and marketing questions that customer database systems can help answer and address.

How Information Technology Supports IMC

A database by itself just sits there. It takes an information system to make a database useful. The department responsible for managing an organization's hardware (computers), software (programs), and databases (information) has one of several

---

T A B L E 8 - 1   Database Application Checklist

To help its clients increase the efficiency of their marketing communications, Saatchi & Saatchi asks them the following questions to see to what extent they are maximizing the use of their databases for strategic planning and managing their brand relationships.

- Do you know how much promotional money you can afford to spend to attract a new customer?
- When you undertake sales promotion or other direct-response activities, do you keep in contact with the respondents?
- What resources does your company have at present to capture data on your customers and prospects?
- Do you know what proportion of your sales comes from what proportion of your customers?
- Can you identify existing customers of one brand who might be receptive to promotion and cross-selling of another?
- Do you know if your number of accounts is the same as your number of customers?
- Can you determine the lifestyles of your customers?
- Can you quickly and inexpensively identify actual customers of your product for inclusion in focus group panels or for other research purposes?
- Do you know if your sales representatives call on all your potential B2B customers?
- If you could differentiate between your high-, medium-, and low-value customers, would you spend your marketing money the way you do today?
- Have you monitored the relationship between various media schedules with brand awareness and sales across countries?
- Do you regularly test different uses of media across brands and countries?

Source: Adapted from *The Total Communications Audit* (London: Saatchi & Saatchi), pp. 6–7.

Lenny Melman.
Became Lana Melman on December 21st.
Is she in your database?

Now there's a data company with a singular focus — data.

Not sales consulting. Not IT services. Not product bundling.

Just the most complete, accurate and current name, address and phone data possible.

Every record is updated with telco-verified data.

And delivered to our customers at least 3 months sooner than the industry average.

With over 120 million records changing each year, those 3 months can make quite a difference.

To give your database more focus, visit amacai.com or call 1-800-434-1565.

AMACAI

EXHIBIT 8-3

A great challenge of data-driven communication is keeping up with customer changes—addresses, names, deaths, and so forth as humorously presented in this ad for Amacai.

names, depending on the company—data processing, information systems (IS), information technology systems (ITS), or information technology (IT). The last is the most common.

A company's IT department usually operates a **database management system (DBMS),** which, among many other things, *records customer information, tracks customer interactions, and links customer databases that are already in existence* (such as product orders, accounting records, service and repair records, and customer service). A good DBMS allows users to look up the status of customers' orders (which are in one database) and compare it to customers' order histories (which are often in a separate database). A good DBMS is updated regularly to keep track of customer changes, as illustrated in Exhibit 8-3.

Database management systems improve the ability of customer-service representatives to communicate with customers. The service reps can find out what customers ordered in the past and what problems they experienced. Such knowledge helps them to be empathetic toward customers, which in turn increases customer retention. Some technology experts, such as John O'Connor and Eamonn Galvin, feel that a database is the greatest single application of information technology available to companies.[3] Figure 8-1 indicates how widespread the use of customer databases is within organizations.

Marketing communication managers do not need to be information technology experts, but they do need a basic understanding of how IT operates and what IT can do to improve MC planning. Unless marketing people know what information exists within the company's systems and in what forms it can be provided, they will find working with IT people extremely frustrating. One of the most important things marketing managers can do is to build a strong working relationship with one or more people in the IT department. This is not just smart organizational politics but also a move to make sure all employees can get support when they need it—for the good of all the company's stakeholders. Even more than other departments, most corporate IT departments have an ongoing backload of work. Marketing competes with many other departments for getting help and must remember that among the goals of internal marketing (← Chapter 6) are getting buy-in and support from other departments such as IT.

How Corporate Learning Makes IMC More Effective

Databases are the institutional memory of an organization. Before the widespread use of database management systems—and still in companies that do not use them—customer responses to MC programs and other important pieces of customer relationship dealings often resided only in the heads of individual employees. When those employees left a department or company, that information went with them. Capturing responses to marketing programs and customer feedback makes it possible for companies to record and learn from their past experiences and thus create a "learning organization."

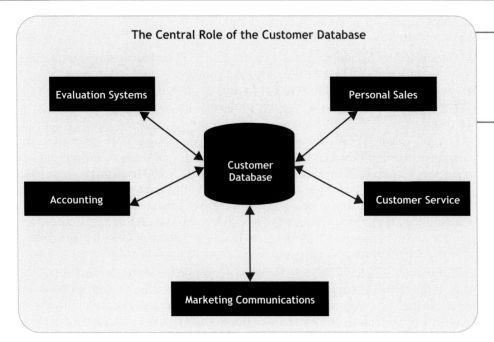

The Central Role of the Customer Database

Evaluation Systems

Personal Sales

Customer Database

Accounting

Customer Service

Marketing Communications

FIGURE 8-1

The use of customer databases is widespread within organizations.

A learning organization has a feedback program that involves four activities: (1) ongoing data collection, (2) continuous aggregation of data, (3) periodic trend analysis (looking for a "critical mass" of comments or behaviors suggesting problems or opportunities), and (4) making information available to individuals who need it to do their jobs. Capturing, analyzing, and sharing customer feedback not only increases corporate learning but also communicates to employees that such learning is a top priority. A database of competitive information and activity that is made available to employees can also be valuable. By integrating this external information into MC and other business planning, a company will become more competitive.

Data-driven marketing and corporate learning are organizational issues because they demand that information systems be set up so that information can be shared. As Ron Kahan, president of a Denver database company, explains, "The knowledge gleaned from a marketing database must fuel a corporate culture of service. It should act as a strategic hub with spokes permeating every business unit within the enterprise."[4]

The following list summarizes four important ways in which customer databases contribute to organizational learning.

1. *Databases record customer history.* Capturing and making available information about customers ensures that relationships extend beyond individual sales or customer-service interactions. An important added value to customers when interacting with a company (by phone or e-mail) is realized when a company has, as part of its database management system, a "single customer view." This means that once customers identify themselves, their profiles come up and are visible to whomever in the company these customers talk to. Customers do not need to repeat their phone numbers, for example, or special membership numbers every time they are passed along to another person or department. Because this single view

> "The knowledge gleaned from a marketing database must fuel a corporate culture of service. It should act as a strategic hub with spokes permeating every business unit within the enterprise."
>
> Ron Kahan, president of a Denver database company

includes customers' past interactions, company representatives can personalize their conversations with customers.

2. **_Databases are the source of insights._** By collecting and analyzing information on how consumers use products, companies can gain insight into consumer behavior. Complaints, compliments, and inquiries, properly quantified, can help companies design new products, solve problems, and develop brand-message strategies.

3. **_Databases uncover market changes._** If a company is constantly monitoring its customers, it will pick up on their changing interests and tastes. The Mervyn's department store chain captures conversations with 50,000 to 70,000 customers a year. An example of how Mervyn's benefited from this data collection effort comes from one of its Texas stores during a recent Christmas season. When shoppers said they had started listening to a certain radio station that had changed to country-and-western music, Mervyn's was able to instantly revise its radio buy to include this station and more effectively drive its Christmas business.

4. **_Databases help the sales staff._** Databases compiled from retail checkouts, allow retail chains to supply manufacturers with timely information, giving them the opportunity to change their presentations to match rapidly developing markets. This is particularly important for sales to channel members. Del Monte, known for its canned fruits and vegetables, maintains a database of nearly 55,000 food stores, drugstores, and mass merchandisers that carry its products. It can analyze the buying patterns at each store and provide a profile of each store's most frequent customers. This information is then passed along to the Del Monte sales force to help them target stores with specific products and also to share information with the stores to build relationships with the trade.

Another important aspect of customer databases is that they are valuable assets. Because the primary purpose of business is to create customers, the databases that contain profiles of these customers in some cases are more valuable than land, labor, and capital. When Pan American World Airways declared bankruptcy, United Airlines bought the company's South American routes—primarily to acquire Pan Am's frequent-flyer database. Because United was already servicing South America, the list of Pan Am's best customers for flights in that region was all the more valuable. United could contact Pan Am customers directly and motivate them to switch to United.

SETTING UP A CUSTOMER DATABASE

The more information a company captures and stores in a database, the more expensive the database is to construct and maintain. Also, as a database increases in complexity, it becomes increasingly difficult to use. One of the most important considerations is to design a database management system that all the various people who need access to customer information can easily use. This task should be carried out by a cross-functional team so that all departments have input into what data to capture, what role they will play in capturing and using the data, and how the data will be configured for easiest retrieval by each user group. The Sun Microsystems ad in Exhibit 8-4 dramatizes this point.

Because tracking and capturing customer information is costly, the database setup must be clearly thought out ahead of time. The more complex a company's MC programs and aftermarket service (service provided after a product has been purchased), the more demands will be made of the database and the more important it is to consider the following six questions before investing in a database system.

1. **What data are needed?** *How much does the company need to know about prospects and current customers? What specific pieces of information are actionable?* Deciding what data to collect is one of the biggest challenges. Companies can be just like people who go through a cafeteria line and select much more than they can consume. What they can't use goes to waste. The challenge is to be realistic about what data will be used to make strategic decisions and what data would simply satisfy curiosity.

2. **How will the data be collected?** *From whom will data be collected? What are the least costly ways to obtain the desired data? How much can the company spend to collect customer data?* Although the cost of collecting data depends on the amount collected, data collection is definitely an expense. The way to minimize the cost is to have the data provider (whether an information company or a customer group) do as much of the data entry as possible. United Airlines, for example, does an annual survey of its high-volume flyers. If these customers respond to the survey online, they are rewarded with 2,000 frequent-flyer miles. If they choose to respond to a paper-and-pencil survey, they receive only 1,000 miles. The difference in the rewards reflects the fact that it costs United money to input the answers from the paper survey into a database, whereas online survey answers go directly into the database.

EXHIBIT 8-4
As this Sun Microsystems ad argues, technology is supposed to make things easier rather than harder.

3. **How will the data be stored?** *How much data can the system process and at what speed?* Data storage is conceptually similar to inventory storage. Both require a warehouse whose architecture determines its efficiency for various functions such as storing, assimilating, and keeping track of contents. Database designs are heavily influenced by financial needs, production needs, or sales needs. The more manipulation that must occur to satisfy these needs, the more costly and time-consuming database management is. Therefore, it is important that marketing be involved in database planning to make sure that its information needs can be met.

4. **How will the data be used?** *What kinds of analyses will be conducted? What kinds of decisions will be based on the results? What reports will be prepared directly from the database?* Marketing uses database information to determine lifetime customer value, calculate customer profitability, measure the extent of cross-category buying, profile heavy buyers, and track frequency of complaints, inquiries, and compliments. Since 1990, Levi Strauss & Co. has been building a database of its customers. Through various direct-response techniques, such as toll-free numbers and sweepstakes, the company has created customer profiles. According to P. J. Santoro, the company's former database marketing specialist, "Everything we find out about customers is being put on the database. It helps us identify where our customers live, their spending habits throughout their life cycles, finances, value of their home, and kind of car they drive."[5] The information has generated 50 different psychographic profiles. Levi Strauss uses this segmented list to do cooperative promotions with retailers.

5. **Who will manage the database?** *Will the marketing department or information systems management be in charge? How easy to use must the system be? What*

> "Power used to mean that you controlled information. Now, power comes from providing greater access to the information."
>
> Robert M. Howe, IBM

individuals and departments will have access to what information? Who will be able to add and delete information? "Power used to mean that you controlled information. Now, power comes from providing greater access to the information," says Robert M. Howe, head of IBM's consulting business.[6] A survey of business-to-business marketers found that the marketing department handles the databases in 44 percent of companies, the information technology department in 15 percent, and both departments together in 26 percent of companies.[7] At Kao, Japan's largest packaged-goods company, all marketing and sales managers have access to a database that contains shipping, point-of-purchase, market share, product cost, and qualitative consumer feedback information.

A major question every company must deal with is who will be allowed to add, delete, and change data in the database. The more people there are within a company who interact with customers, the more there are who need authority to change data. At the same time, the more people who are making changes to the database, the more opportunities there are for errors.

6. *How accurate and secure does the database need to be? How frequently does the information need to be updated? How confidential are the data?* Maintaining data integrity is an ongoing challenge. A survey found that 61 percent of the respondents in one customer database had changed either their name, title, company affiliation, address, or phone number within the past year.[8] Because databases are becoming so valuable as corporate assets, security is also a major issue. Companies set up "firewalls" to prevent people from outside the company from getting into company databases. Inside the company, people are given passwords that allow them to access certain databases on the basis of job need.

Collecting Customer Data

Building a good customer database is easier for some companies than for others. Most B2B companies automatically record customer names, addresses, and phone numbers and maintain a history of transactions as a regular part of doing business. In many consumer product categories, especially services, customer data are automatically collected in the course of doing business. Inter-Continental Hotels and Resorts, for example, compiles valuable data every time a customer reserves a room or checks in. However, Inter-Continental discovered that its customer information database was cumbersome and difficult to access for marketing purposes. To correct this, the company designed a global marketing initiative designed to provide a standard procedure for creating and managing its customer database. Customer information is now captured from 80-plus hotels all over the world and is transferred electronically every week to Inter-Continental's central customer database. For a recent five-year period, the database processed over 5.9 million stays, aggregated this data, and developed customer profiles and interaction history for 2.9 million guests.[9]

Scanner Data

Often the most important customer information is derived from the sale itself by capturing **scanner data,** *point-of-purchase (also called point-of-sale) information gathered at the retail level by chains that have frequent-buyer programs.* Most retail chains encourage customers to have a frequent-buyer card scanned each time they shop at one of the chain's stores. To get a card, consumers fill out an application that requires them to provide demographic and lifestyle information. This information is then cross-listed with each customer's purchases.

Companies motivate customers to use their cards by offering them frequent promotional deals (available only to cardholders) or rewards when they reach certain levels of spending within a specified time period. Retailers not only use scanner-built databases for their own marketing efforts but also sell the data to manufacturers. Kraft Foods, for example, collects demographic and product-buying information for customers from over 30,000 food stores. For many years, Radio Shack has asked customers for basic information—address and phone number—as the sale is made. Other means of gathering information as part of a transaction include the following:

- *Proprietary credit cards:* Many retailers have long offered their own credit cards, primarily to capture reliable information about customer purchasing patterns.

- *Membership programs with ID cards:* Online computer equipment retailer and auctioneer Egghead.com tracks sales through the use of a scanner card. Each time a customer uses the Egghead card, he or she receives an automatic 5 percent discount on purchases. The company has issued over 1 million cards; to obtain one, a customer has to fill out an extensive questionnaire. This information, in turn, is used to develop customized quarterly newsletters. Exhibit 8-5 shows the questionnaire that British Airways uses to collect customer data from those who join its Travel Service.

- *Credit bureau appending services:* A retailer that does not have its own frequent-buyer card can build a customer database by taking names from credit-card and check purchases. However, doing so requires a great deal of manual labor. Credit-card charges must be sent to a credit bureau, which

EXHIBIT 8-5

British Airways Travel Service used a questionnaire to gather information about new customers. To motivate people to respond, the questionnaire was supported with a drawing for free travel for two from London to New York.

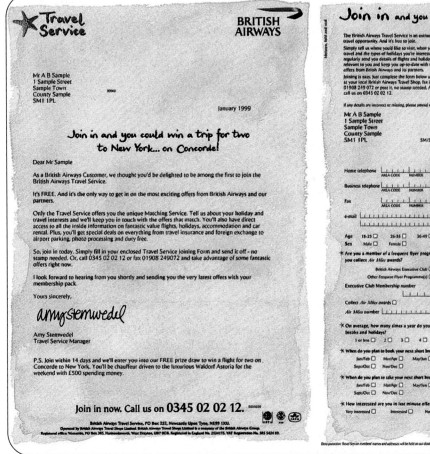

can use the charge-card number and name to find the customer's address. Although there are no laws against doing this data building in-house, the practice of using a credit bureau to "append" addresses and phone numbers to names has been heavily criticized as an invasion of privacy.

Data Gathering from Marketing Communication Programs

These examples show how interactive marketing communication programs not only deliver messages but also build customer relationships.

Permission Marketing

As explained in Chapter 7, permission marketing involves motivating customers and prospects to agree to receive MC messages. The Asthma ad in Exhibit 8-6, for example, invites asthma sufferers to call a toll-free number or visit the association's website. The benefit of building databases in this way is that receivers of subsequent MC messages are more likely to be receptive to them and not view them as intrusive. The downside of permission marketing is that many consumers give false mailing addresses and other inaccurate information (they merely respond to receive the promotional incentive). Also, according to one survey, 40 percent of responders change their e-mail addresses each year and less than a third of these inform companies of the change.[10]

Coupons, Sweepstakes, and Promotional Offers

Modern printing technology allows identification numbers to be placed on coupons and address labels. Thus, companies that distribute coupons through the mail know which households respond to which coupons. Multibrand companies that send out a selection of product coupons use the ID numbers to determine which households are redeeming coupons for baby products, dog food, diet foods, snack foods, and other products. This information gives a company opportunities for cross-selling (⬅ Chapter 7) additional products and to eliminate those who are not prospects. For example, households that are heavy consumers of diet foods are likely to be poor prospects for snack items; a company can thus save money by not sending coupons for snack foods to those households.

Promotional offers should be designed to identify potential customers, not only those interested in getting free merchandise. Responses that request informational pamphlets on product-related subjects, for example, identify serious prospects. Crayon and marker manufacturer Crayola generated names by running a sweepstakes in its first free-standing insert (FSI), a manufacturer-produced flyer inserted into a newspaper. Parents could enter by filling in a coupon with their children's names, birthdates, addresses, and phone numbers. In return, each child received two free Crayola markers. The company received approximately 400,000 coupons—that is, 400,000 names of current and prospective customers.[11]

Warranty Cards

Many new products, particularly electronics and appliances, come with **warranty cards,** which are cards that ask *where the product was purchased, the price, whether it was on sale, whether it was a gift, plus several demographic and psychographic questions.* Most warranty cards also contain a few questions that relate directly to the brand and product bought. These cards are mailed back to database companies that compile and maintain records for subscribing companies. The information is used to contact customers about product changes, updates, and recalls, but also the data are often compiled into larger lists and sold to direct marketers. Gates Energy

No bar or bolt can keep this attack out of the home. Asthma.

AMERICAN LUNG ASSOCIATION

Asthma fears nothing. It has already reached 26 million. To stop the epidemic, call 1-800-LUNG-USA or visit www.lungusa.org

EXHIBIT 8-6
The Asthma association uses a mass media ad to find asthma sufferers who are then invited to contact the association by calling a toll-free number or through the website.

Products, for example, offered $20 rebate coupons to encourage consumers to return product registration cards when it introduced its new rechargeable batteries. The company used this information to market its products directly to customers, thus bypassing retailers.

Membership and Frequent-Buyer Clubs

Many large retailers use frequent-buyer clubs (see Exhibit 8-7) or membership programs to identify their customers and, if they are making use of good database programs, to track their purchases in order to customize promotional offers.

Toymaker Mattel has been gathering names through its Magic Nursery line. After purchasing or receiving a doll, the child (usually a girl) sends in the name

Introducing a Better Way to Save.

The Quick and Easy Way to Instant Savings...

✓ Complete your application and bring it to the customer service counter.

✓ You'll instantly receive your Preferred Savings Card and two keytags.

✓ Don't want the hassle of carrying a card? You can use your phone number instead! (Allow 4 weeks to process.)

About Privacy: Fact is, if you are uncomfortable giving out personal information, we'll still give you an Albertsons Preferred Savings Card. But we hope you'll share a little about yourself. Why? To reward you for shopping with us. Your name and address allows us to contact you for sweepstakes, to return lost keys and to send you exclusive Preferred Savings Card offers. And remember, Albertsons will never disclose your personal information to any other party for their use. Ever.*

*Except when compelled by law.

Sign up today & save with your Albertsons Preferred Savings Card.

△ Albertsons

EXHIBIT 8-7

Albertson's and most other large grocery chains use frequent-buyer clubs to motivate their customers to sign up for a preferred-customer card. Sometimes the card only makes customers eligible for discounts, but the card also can be used to track purchases and customize promotions.

she gave it, her own address and age, and the store where it was purchased. In return, the child receives a Mother's Day card signed with the baby's name and a coupon. When Mattel introduced another doll into the product line, children living in areas where the doll was available received an announcement. Mattel has also used the list, containing approximately 100,000 names, to mail out coupons for its Barbie line.

In 1993 the Swiss watchmaker Swatch started a collectors club, which is promoted in more than 500 designated "collector" stores in Europe. In return for approximately $80 a year for membership, collectors receive special privileges: a Swatch watch produced exclusively for club members; a catalog of every Swatch watch ever produced; special offers on collectible watches and accessories such as T-shirts and artwork; invitations to attend at least six special events a year, including special travel and hotel arrangements; VIP seating at Swatch-sponsored music concerts, some of them held exclusively for members; and the quarterly *Swatch World Journal* with information on all new-product launches and styles. The club boasts more than 100,000 members in seven European countries and the United States. Ten thousand of them showed up for an exclusive rock concert in Italy.

Catalogs

Bloomingdale's, a New York–based department store, produces approximately 300 different catalogs and promotional mailings per year. Customer purchases are tracked to determine who receives which offers. Someone who bought a men's suit would receive notice about a sale on men's accessories.

Little Tykes, which makes a large variety of toys for young children, uses its mailing list to send a catalog twice a year, although customers cannot purchase directly from the catalog but must go to retail stores. The catalog is sent to people who call the company's toll-free number (featured in all advertising and on all packaging) and ask to be added to the mailing list—a list that contains over 1 million names. When customers call, the company collects information on the ages of the children and whether the caller is a parent or grandparent. In addition, mini-catalogs are placed in all toy packaging along with information about how to join the mailing list.

Toll-Free Numbers

A **toll-free number** is *a phone number that companies use to make it possible for their customers to call them without paying a long-distance charge.* Health Valley Foods was able to expand its distribution from health food stores to grocery stores by tracking consumers. The company collected names from letters and calls to a toll-free number. Once a loyal customer base was established, the company was able to show supermarkets that its products would sell.

E-Mail and Websites

Many companies have websites, chat rooms, user groups, and Web communities for users of their products or for people wanting information. These are excellent vehicles for collecting data as well as interacting with customers. Airlines, for example, frequently send their frequent flyers announcements of special vacation packages. A ski resort in Colorado, Copper Mountain, sends e-mails to a database of past customers when a major snowfall is forecast (avid skiers like to ski on fresh powder).

Surveys

Our Own Hardware, a 24-state chain, uses an electronic survey box in each of its 1,200 stores. In return for sharing their names, addresses, preferences, and purchasing information, customers receive on-the-spot discounts and coupons.

As companies go about building their customer databases, they must constantly be sensitive to privacy issues. In the next section is a discussion of how to collect personal customer data and at the same time respect and protect the privacy of customers and prospects.

HOW DATA GATHERING AFFECTS PRIVACY AND SECURITY ISSUES

In the battle of profits versus privacy, companies have to decide how important their customer relationships are in the long term and whether they can afford the potential of alienating customers by tracking their shopping behaviors—with, or especially without, their knowledge. A poll on privacy by Harris Interactive found that the top three consumer concerns were "that companies they patronize will provide their information to other companies without permission (75%), that their transactions may not be secure (70%), and that hackers could steal their personal data (69%)."[12]

Whenever consumers learn about the misuse of personal information, they become wary of all information gathering, even by reputable companies. Customers worry that their personal information, such as credit-card numbers, will be stolen while they are placing an order through some form of direct or internet marketing. The security of database information is even more important to companies. This issue is addressed in the B2B ad in Exhibit 8-8.

Collecting Personal Data

Privacy issues directly impact the heart of relationship building—trust. Thus, how companies collect data and use that data is an important aspect of IMC. Collection of personal data has been attacked in recent years by consumer watchdog groups as an invasion of privacy. A company that buys customer data from other companies, compiles the lists, and from them develops a customer profile to send out personalized brand messages can be seen as crossing the privacy line. Many customers do not understand list brokerage and thus cannot figure out how the company acquired such information. Another consumer concern is that companies will link individuals' names with incorrect data (such as false information on credit reports, internet reading patterns based on an accidental visit to a porn site, and so forth).

The Direct Marketing Association (DMA), composed of a group of companies particularly interested in database marketing, has developed data collection

Think of us as information bodyguards.

In today's digital world, trust is everything. That's why EDS provides the most innovative security and privacy solutions. From network protection to customer information. We help you evaluate and mitigate risk, and implement a comprehensive security and privacy strategy that builds trust and keeps your business safe and sound. To find out more, visit us online at www.eds.com/security_privacy, or call 800-566-9337.

EXHIBIT 8-8

In this ad, the information technology company EDS calls attention to its privacy and security systems. The ad delivers a message of trust to business customers that rely on EDS to manage their information systems.

guidelines for its members. In 1998 the FTC (Federal Trade Commission) passed the Children's Online Privacy Protection Act, which in essence stated: "It is unlawful for an operator of a website or online service directed to children, or any operator that has actual knowledge that it is collecting personal information from a child, to collect personal information from a child in a manner that violates the regulations prescribed" by the FTC.[13] For more information on privacy issues and practices, go to the website of the Center for Democracy in Technology, www.cdt.org.

When consumers find out that their purchases and lifestyles have been or are being monitored, particularly for commercial purposes, they become concerned. Consumers are more likely to be receptive to personal data collection if these conditions exist:

1. They know the data are being collected.
2. They gave permission for data to be collected.
3. The information being asked for is relevant to buying or using the product.
4. The use of the information will benefit them and not just the company—for example, it speeds up the delivery time of the goods and services they want, or alerts them to information they want, or shields them from information they do not want.
5. They feel they have control over what is done with the information.

Some people know that credit-card companies have been collecting data on their purchase behavior for years and that grocery stores are now able to collect very specific information about their purchases. Customers who use a frequent-buyer card may protest when they realize what information is being collected and how that information is used. One woman canceled her food-store loyalty card when she received a personal letter reminding her it was probably time to buy more tampons.[14]

Privacy Is Situational

When British Airways asks its customers about their travel plans (see Exhibit 8-9), or when your doctor asks you questions about your personal health, you are not likely to consider these questions an invasion of privacy. However, if your doctor asks you what your annual income is and what shares of stock you own, you may rightly feel that he or she has crossed the privacy line. And when you are talking to your stockbroker, questions about your diet and sedentary lifestyle are likely to seem out of line.

Privacy is situational. When a company asks questions that are not relevant to its products or business dealings, customers become suspicious. Suspicion weakens trust, which is the foundation of relationships. The feeling that a company has violated privacy can cancel out the positive impact of dozens of expensive MC messages. That is why privacy practices must be integrated into all MC activities.

Because medical records are moving from paper files in doctors' offices to electronic files, the possibility of a national health-record network exists. That will be great if you are traveling and need medical attention. It will not be great if your family secret about alcoholism, abortion, or venereal disease comes to light and you are sent unsolicited product offers relating to one or more of these conditions. The Ethics and Issues box asks you to analyze the ethics of different data-collecting situations.

Ethical Data Use in IMC

Companies are becoming more sensitive to the ethics of customer privacy. For example, Experian Information Solutions (formerly a unit of TRW), which maintains credit records on some 180 million Americans, spent over $30 million in the last few years updating its computer network and launching programs to soothe customers' privacy concerns. This policy was partially a response to laws passed in several states requiring credit-reporting agencies (which provide credit checks of individuals for companies) to provide consumers a free copy

How the Travel Service benefits you

Here at the Travel Service we're always striving to look after you and offer you the ultimate travel experience. That's why we offer you a number of benefits:

★ The Travel Service gives you the inside information on the latest flights and holidays from British Airways and partners including exclusive offers and advance notice of exciting travel promotions.

★ Our unique Matching Service enables us to bring you the latest offers relevant to your travel interests.

★ Our specially trained Travel Consultants can give you all the advice you need to plan and book your holiday.

★ We bring you new and inspirational holiday ideas and in depth destination information.

★ Together with our partners, we can fly you to over 240 destinations worldwide.

★ We work with over 20 travel partners, specifically chosen for the quality of products and service they offer.

★ We're there for you seven days a week, 8.30am - 8pm Monday to Friday and 9am - 5pm at weekends.

★ We're operated by British Airways, bringing you worldclass expertise and an unparalleled level of service - all your meals and drinks free on board our aircraft, a complimentary overnight bag on longhaul flights and free headphones for our award winning in-flight entertainment.

Surfing With British Airways Travel Service

We intend that the Travel Service should always make the most of today's technology for the benefit of our members, which is why we've enhanced and improved our web site. Simply log on and you can get full details about any of the holidays we've featured in this pack - plus much more information about our many inspirational travel opportunities. There's page after page of ideas - it's the innovative way to plan your next holiday!

You can find our web site at www.britishairways.com/travel-service. Once on line, you can explore at your leisure.

EXHIBIT 8-9

The British Airways Travel Service mailer contains a number of inserts. This one focuses on the benefits of membership and reflects the type of traveler the customer is and the information that customer has provided the company.

of their credit record and information about the companies that have asked for checks on them. TRW's efforts led to an 80 percent reduction in mix-ups on financial data from people with similar names. "Consumers have interests in economic choices and privacy," says Martin E. Abrams, director of the former TRW's privacy and consumer policy. "Our job is to find an equilibrium between the two."[15]

Nike used a direct approach to addressing customers' feelings about privacy when it gave each purchaser of its All Conditions Gear a survey card. The headline, in large, bold print, asks, "Would you like to receive Nike publications?" Then several questions with "yes" or "no" replies are listed—for instance, "If Nike makes its mailing list available to other companies, do you wish to be included?" The options are immediately visible and well explained, giving the consumer the feeling that participation is his or her own choice.

Major information companies such as Equifax even bank on the fact that companies will pay to know which customers do *not* want to hear from them. They compile lists of customers according to whether or not they wish to receive mail offers for different categories of products and services. This information is then sold to direct marketers so they can be more effective in their targeting.

Companies that want to respect their customers' privacy, build trust, and thus strengthen brand relationships need to have and put into practice a privacy policy. According to the FTC, there are five core principles that such a policy should contain:[16]

1. *Notice:* Consumers should be given notice of an entity's information practices.
2. *Choice:* Consumers should be given choice with respect to the use and dissemination of information collected from or about them.
3. *Access:* Consumers should be given access to information about them collected and stored by an entity.

ETHICS AND ISSUES

How Much Is Too Much?

Where should the line be drawn to limit the collecting of customer data? Here are some examples of company activities that caused customers and consumer watchdog groups to complain. Keep in mind that when a brand is accused of violating the privacy of its customers, not only are relationships weakened but resulting negative publicity may weaken all of a brand's stakeholder relationships. How would you react in each of these situations?

- A researcher developed a watch that could be activated by a microchip embedded in a magazine page. The watch could monitor how long a person looks at the page. The inventor proposed that the device be given to a sample of a brand's customers and prospective customers. To get as objective a measurement as possible, the company would not tell the customers about the watch's dual function.

- Porsche stirred up a storm when it sent a direct-mail piece to its typical upscale owners. The copy in the mailing identified the prospects in terms of sensitive demographic information such as job title and income level.

- Blockbuster Video announced that it was planning to sell information about its customers' viewing habits. Thousands of customers protested in angry letters.

- A little-noticed section of the Health Care Portability and Accountability Act, passed by

Congress in 1996, could make it easier for all kinds of strangers to find out if you've ever had a heart attack, an abortion, medically treated depression, or a positive HIV test. A number of companies are already compiling information from consumers' medical records.

An entire industry collects data on millions of people from public and private sources. Information brokers dig through public records—birth certificates, court records, driver's licenses, real-estate deeds, and change-of-address forms—to compile lists that they sell to direct-mail firms, retailers, insurers, lawyers, and private investigators. One of these vendors offers a service that searches more than 100 million records and can return with a person's Social Security number and other information that scam artists can use to set up phony bank and credit-card accounts, a crime known as "identity theft."

Think About It

What privacy issues do sensitive marketers who use database information have to consider? What practices do many consumers find particularly irritating?
Source: Tom McNichol, "The New Privacy Wars," *USA Weekend*, May 16, 1996, pp. 16–17. Used by permission; Ellyn E. Spragins and Mary Hager, "Naked Before the World." From *Newsweek*, May 16 © 1996 Newsweek, Inc. All rights reserved. Reprinted by permission.

4. *Security:* Data collectors should take appropriate steps to ensure the security and integrity of information collected.
5. *Redress:* Enforcement mechanisms, through self-regulation, government regulation, or other means, should be available to ensure compliance.

Once customer databases have been built and privacy concerns taken into consideration, it is time to manage the use of the databases.

BUILDING RELATIONSHIPS THROUGH DATA MANAGEMENT

Although most companies have IT departments, marketing communicators need to know and understand enough about database management systems to know what they can and should not expect from IT. Databases are the primary tool used in managing customer relationships, an activity or program sometimes referred to as *customer relationship management* (◀ Chapter 3). CRM programs started out as tools to help the sales force keep track of customers and prospects but are becoming more strategic and more customer focused. All customer relationships, however, are based on information, such as knowledge about customers' interests and purchasing behavior, as well as information about the company's previous customer interactions.

Tracking is easier to do in some product categories than in others. That is an important consideration in the decision to invest in expensive database systems. Product categories in which tracking customer interactions is easy and categories in which it is more difficult are as follows:

Easy-to-Track Product Categories

Financial institutions: banks, brokers, insurance.

Monopolies: public utilities.

Contractual services: club memberships, trash removal, lawn care.

Personalized services: doctor, dentist, lawyer, hair care, car repair.

Big-ticket goods: real estate, cars.

Retail stores with their own charge cards: department and specialty stores.

Rental agencies: video, car, hotel, sporting equipment.

Direct-response companies: mail order, telemarketing, online services.

Business-to-business companies.

Difficult-to-Track Product Categories

Packaged goods and consumer durables.

Retail stores: food, drug, discount stores (that do not have frequent buyer programs).

Retail services: restaurants, movie theaters, dry cleaners.

Products bought in bulk by a company that are then passed out to employees—for example, cell phones, laptop computers, company cars, uniforms.

When a company's primary customers are distributors or retailers, the company must make special efforts to gather information about the end users of its products. One way to do this is through establishing partnerships with retailers. Motorola, for example, rewards its dealers with points for acquiring new customers. To get reward points, dealers must supply Motorola with information on these new customers. The company not only puts this information into its customer database but also sends the new customers $100 certificates that they can redeem at their local dealer when they refer a new customer to that dealer. In this partnership effort, Motorola owns the database, and the retailers benefit from a customer-acquisition incentive program.

Some manufacturers of packaged goods say that they cannot justify the cost of building a database of end users. What they overlook is that it is not necessary to track every single customer, rather only the most profitable ones. Because a relatively small percentage of customers accounts for the majority of sales and profits, these manufacturers should begin by identifying their heavy users. The Coke Card shown in Exhibit 8-10 rewards customers with discounts from Coke's marketing partners. This is the first step in Coke's effort to build a database of its loyal users.

Consider a mass marketer like Colgate-Palmolive. Although it cannot justify individually capturing and responding to every purchase of its many product varieties, the company can use retail store scanner data to identify and respond to heavy-user households of its bar soaps, toothpaste, shaving lotions, and so on. Collective sales can amount to as much as $400 a year per household. With this type of customer information, it becomes cost-effective for Colgate-Palmolive to mass-customize and reward brand-loyal customers for their past business (with special high-value coupons, for example), and to motivate them to buy even more of the company's brands. Manufacturers of consumer products can also create affinity clubs, which are manufacturer-sponsored clubs like the one Procter & Gamble has for parents who buy Pampers.

Enhancing Customer Data with Data Overlays

It is not always necessary for a company to invest in gathering *all* the desired customer-profile information, especially for consumer packaged goods. Often this additional data can be rented from outside sources such as Equifax. The new data are then overlaid on a company's customer database. **Data overlay** means *enriching one database by adding another to it.*

EXHIBIT 8-10

Marketed to college students, this Coke Card promotion contains a list of partner businesses—restaurants, clothing stores, movies and video rental stores, e-commerce companies, and many more—where the Coke Card delivers discounts.

For example, the Polk Company, which specializes in gathering information related to the automotive industry, captures new-car purchase information. Equifax collects and processes data from warranty cards—the cards you get when you purchase appliances and other consumer goods. Companies such as Samsonite and Canon hire companies such as Equifax to tabulate and analyze their warranty cards. All of the data collected are given back to the respective companies, including responses to any specialized questions. The company then uses the demographic and psychographic data to expand and update its national household database—that is, it overlays the new data.

Using Data Mining to Provide Customer Insights

As the Paine Webber story in the next IMC in Action box illustrates, companies too often do not make use of data they already have that could improve their customer communications. Completed warranty cards, for example, are often filed away and never used as a source of vital data for customer profiling. After rebate offers are fulfilled, the forms are often destroyed and thus vital customer information is lost.

Data mining is a useful metaphor for *sifting and sorting the information warehoused in a company's database.* The purpose of data mining is to spot trends, relationships—for example, heavy users buy less frequently than the average customer but in larger quantities—and other nuggets of information and customer insights in order to make better marketing communication decisions. Data mining can help marketers accomplish one of their most important responsibilities: customer segmentation.

IMC IN ACTION

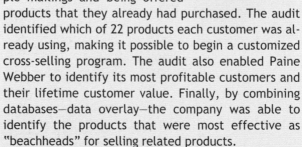

The Data Gold Mine

The full-service brokerage firm Paine Webber learned the value of customer databases when, with the help of its advertising agency, Saatchi & Saatchi, it did a communication audit of its customers (using the Database Application Checklist shown in Table 8-1, page 247). Paine Webber knew how many *accounts* it had but did not know how many *actual customers* it had, because it didn't know which customers had more than one account. It also didn't know the characteristics of the customers who had more than one account. Consequently, it was not able to communicate efficiently with its current customers.

Like many other companies, Paine Webber was ignoring the fact that the data already in its possession could be extremely valuable for developing more profitable business strategies. It preferred to market each of its products to the "average customer," overlooking the fact that many of these people were already buying more than one of its products.

Saatchi's audit discovered that Paine Webber's 1.8 million accounts were held by 717,000 individual customers. This revelation resulted in significant savings in the company's marketing communication, not to mention the reduction in customer aggravation from continually receiving multiple mailings and being offered products that they already had purchased. The audit identified which of 22 products each customer was already using, making it possible to begin a customized cross-selling program. The audit also enabled Paine Webber to identify its most profitable customers and their lifetime customer value. Finally, by combining databases—data overlay—the company was able to identify the products that were most effective as "beachheads" for selling related products.

As a result of the customer audit, Paine Webber's marketing communication strategies became better focused and its targeting more precise. The analysis involved data that were already captured but not fully utilized by the company's marketing department. Paine Webber only needed to mine its own gold.

Think About It

How did Paine Webber change the way it analyzes and uses the data it collected? How was Saatchi able to use the information from its audit to help Paine Webber turn data into communication strategies?

Using Databases to Customize Brand Communication

Having good customer databases is one thing. Fully utilizing them is something else. A survey of B2B marketers found that 85 percent used their marketing databases only for building and using customer and prospect mailing lists.[17] A survey of 179 companies found that less than a third were using their databases to profile and segment customers according to their buying habits. What accounts for this underutilization? Many databases are not designed with marketing in mind. Many marketing people do not take the time to learn how to use databases. Some databases are not properly managed and contain inaccurate and out-of-date data. And in some companies marketing is not allowed to access the databases in a meaningful way.

Customer databases can be used at each stage of a brand relationship: acquisition of customers, retention, growth, and reacquisition (recovery of lost customers). Generally a single database can contain all the information that is needed for developing strategies and tactics for each stage. Information consultants such as SAS Institute help companies develop databases that will help improve their communication with customers (see Exhibit 8-11).

EXHIBIT 8-11
SAS Institute offers CRM programs that offer a number of features, including profiling customers and calculating marketing return on investment.

Customer Acquisition

What is the first thing a company should do when putting together a data-driven customer-acquisition program? It should examine the profiles of its most profitable and use these characteristics to find prospective customers. A practice called **prospecting**—*using data to identify prospective customer types*—works in both consumer and B2B marketing. Once a company has found commonalities among profitable customers, it can go to a list broker for help in finding lists that most closely match.

The *Evansville (Indiana) Courier and Press* used this data-driven technique to determine how to attract new subscribers. The newspaper identified three distinct profiles of current subscribers. The *Courier and Press* then sent a promotional offer to 1,000 prospective households matching up with each of the three profiles. All were offered a 30-day trial subscription. The lowest response rate was 24 percent, the highest 82 percent. As a result of that test, the newspaper decided to concentrate its marketing efforts on nonsubscribers who matched the highest-response segment's profile.

Using Data to Help Retain Customers

In retention programs, listening to customers is as important, if not more important, than talking to them. Some B2B companies are now making a special effort to ask customers when and how they would like to be contacted by the company. This information is placed in the customer database so it is readily accessible for one-to-one messaging. This practice shows respect for loyal customers' time and schedules and allows companies to direct the brand communication in a way that is personally appropriate.

But listening isn't enough. Companies must respond and in some cases make changes when what they hear indicates problems or opportunities. Figure 8-2 shows how a customer database can be used for doing *exception analyses*. This type of analysis uses a special software program to periodically scan a customer database and indicate when an above-average number of complaints, inquiries, or compliments have been received within a certain period. The critical number will vary depending on the size of the customer base and product category. Note that the customer database captures all interactions, not just sales, receiving input from customer contacts handled by marketing, sales, and customer service.

Excessive inquiries about a product or subject—such as "How do I eject a disk without turning off my computer?" or "Have my parts been shipped yet?"—indicate either that more information needs to be made available to customers or that the product needs to be redesigned so that it stimulates fewer questions about its use. NEC, a manufacturer of computers and monitors, ran an exception analysis of its customer database and found that it was receiving 1,500 calls a month from customers saying they couldn't get their CD-ROM to read the CD disk they were trying to use. As it turned out, in nearly every case, the caller had forgotten to insert the CD into the disk drive. Each customer service call cost NEC about $20 to handle. After discussions with its research and development team, NEC decided to add to the front of the monitors a small digital display panel that indicated whether a disk had been inserted. This change nearly eliminated calls for

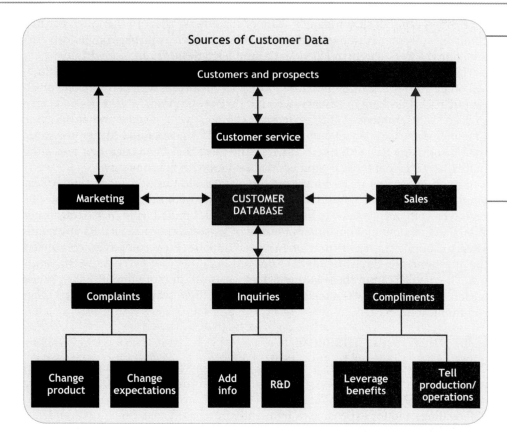

Sources of Customer Data

Customers and prospects

Customer service

Marketing ← → CUSTOMER DATABASE ← → Sales

Complaints   Inquiries   Compliments

Change product / Change expectations   Add info / R&D   Leverage benefits / Tell production/ operations

FIGURE 8-2

Customer databases have many uses.

Source: Tom Duncan and Sandra Moriarity, *Driving Brand Value: Using Integrated Marketing to Manage Profitable Stakeholder Relationships* (New York: McGraw-Hill, 1997), p. 216.

this problem, saving the company approximately $360,000 a year, far more than the cost of the minor product modification.[18]

When above-average numbers of compliments are recorded in a given period, the company should examine them to see whether they relate to some benefit of the product that could be further leveraged in the brand's marketing communication messages. Compliments should also be forwarded to the production department and people as a way of recognizing good work and praising employees. Morale boosting improves customer service and lowers the number of product defects.

All companies, no matter how good they are, receive complaints. What is critical, however, is to note when too many are being received about a particular good or service. Negative exception reports act as an early warning system. Complaints indicate either that the company's products or methods of handling customers are faulty or that customers' expectations are not being properly managed. As explained in Chapter 2, managing expectations is one of the primary responsibilities of marketing communications.

Here is an example: Soon after putting a new fleet of cars into service, a national car rental company sees that customer complaints about the lack of certain features are increasing month to month. The company can decide whether the cars need to be upgraded or the MC messages need to be changed to lower customers' expectations about the cars' features. One possibility would be an MC campaign stressing that economy cars mean economy rates.

Customer Growth

Growth programs encourage current customers to give a brand a greater share of their category spending. Consumer panel data, collected by independent information companies, can show a company's share of customers' category spending. For B2B companies, average customer category spending is often available from industry associations as well as from independent research studies.

California First Federal bank has a good customer database and uses it to cross-sell other products. Banks often lose money on customers who use only one product such as a checking or savings account. By cross-selling, Cal Fed has been able to decrease its number of single-service customers by 11 percent and at the same time increase customer retention by 58 percent.[19] As explained earlier, the more links a company has with its customers—the more services a customer uses—the more likely it is that those customers will remain with the company.

Growth programs are also important in business-to-business marketing. An example is Meridian, a $100-million-a-year subsidiary of Northern Telecom that sells high-tech software systems to businesses. Meridian pulled from its B2B customer database five potential customers for one of its software products. Each was invited to complete a needs-assessment questionnaire. Four companies completed the questionnaire, three attended a sales presentation, and two bought the product. The payback from these two contacts was sales of more than $75,000.[20] One reason this program was such a success is that there was almost no marketing communication waste.

Customer Reacquisition

Customers leave a brand for any number of reasons. Reacquisition programs can minimize the ultimate loss. Because these programs must be customized, they are relatively expensive to administer. Therefore, they are often more appropriate in B2B dealings and for expensive or frequently purchased consumer goods and services. Recognizing how critical this area is, Ford Motor Company–Mexico, has a Director of Customer Recovery. Some former customers are impossible to reacquire, such as those who moved out of the shopping area or, in the case of a B2B, went out of business. But most customers who quit buying switched to another brand or to another company because they either were dissatisfied or were convinced to try something different.

The first step in customer recovery is to determine as quickly as possible when a customer is no longer a customer. The longer customers stay away from a business, the less likely they are to return. Because customer databases capture purchases, computers can be programmed to periodically examine transaction frequencies and create a list of all customers who have not made a purchase within a set number of days, weeks, or months. Also, because each customer generally has a certain purchase frequency, software can be used to determine when each customer's purchase frequency has been broken. After a certain nonbuying period, these customers' files should be flagged.

Once lapsed customers are identified, the next step is to contact them to determine why they have stopped buying. In some cases, the mere act of contacting lost customers and showing an interest in them is enough to bring them back. Those who are no longer in the product category can be forgotten. But for that majority who have had a bad brand experience, the next step is to determine why this occurred. Competing long-distance phone companies, for example, find that perceived or actual cost savings cause some customers to switch carriers, so the companies offer lost customers up to $100 for switching back.

Reasons for leaving need to be captured into the database and periodically analyzed. As with other complaints, when a particular reason appears more frequently than expected, it is time for the relevant operational, manufacturing, or customer-service procedures to be reexamined and revised or brought back up to standards. Even though recovery programs are relatively expensive, many companies have found that recovered customers are more loyal and profitable than are average customers who never left.

Personalizing the Message

Once a company has mined and analyzed its customer and prospect data, the next step, especially for B2B and certain consumer goods and service companies, is to design and execute marketing communication efforts that include personalized brand messages. Have you received phone calls and mailings in which your name is inserted into what is obviously a form message? Although you probably recognized right away that this message is not really personal, the technique, which uses a database to match names to phone numbers and addresses, can significantly increase the level of response. Nevertheless, it remains the lowest level of message personalization (see Figure 8-3).

At the second level, personalized brand messages refer to some aspect of a customer's interaction with a company, such as a previous transaction, complaint, or inquiry. Clothing retailer Gap, for example, captures transaction information for all charge-card purchases. The chain can then program its computers to find data such as all customers who purchased sportswear in early spring in the last three years. A computer-written but personalized letter can be sent to each of these, noting their habit of buying sportswear each spring and even referring to specific items purchased. The primary purpose of the letter may be to invite these customers to a special showing of this year's newly arrived spring sportswear or to make some other special offer.

In Chapter 7, mass customization of products was explained. In IMC, there is also **mass customization of MC messages,** which is *the large-scale personalizing of customer interactions with a company.* Standardized MC letters, e-mails, and telemarketing calls can be personalized not only by adding a person's or company's name but also by referring to customer-specific information that can be automatically pulled from a customer database and does not threaten customers' privacy. Mass-customized messages that are perceived as personalized can also be created by grouping customers with like behavior (buying each spring), by referring to specific items purchased (coats bought last winter), and by making a special offer to current customers ("You're invited to a special preview of our new fall fashions.").

At the third and highest level of personalization, the messages address an individual customer's specific problem. Such personalization is common in B2B messaging when salespeople know enough about their customers and prospects to formulate a solution to a particular company's problem or to point out an

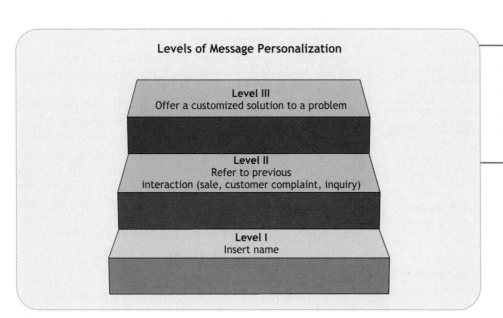

Levels of Message Personalization

Level III
Offer a customized solution to a problem

Level II
Refer to previous
interaction (sale, customer complaint, inquiry)

Level I
Insert name

FIGURE 8-3

Message personalization starts with simply inserting a name and moves to a customized solution to a customer's problem.

overlooked opportunity. High-level personalization can also be used for some consumer products. For example, the insurance company USAA keeps an up-to-date database of all its policyholders, including names and birthdates of children. When a policyholder's child turns 16, the insurance company automatically sends a computer-generated letter offering car insurance for the new driver in the family. The policyholder sees this as a personal letter (even though it was computer generated) and welcomes the reminder. Customized brand messages are also seen as less intrusive than run-of-the-mill junk mail.

Southern California Gas Company used its database to identify customers experiencing large differences in their summer and winter utility bills. These customers were targeted for a "leveling" payment plan that took their total annual cost and averaged it out into 12 equal monthly payments. By allowing customers to level out their monthly payments, the company was able to add value to its service. Personalization of the communication ensured a high response rate for the payment-plan program.

Customer Recognition and Reward

When a company is able to recognize customers by remembering who they are and how they have interacted with the company, it adds value to its brands. Both B2B customers and individuals appreciate being remembered and recognized. Harris Bank's emphasis on collecting customer information and using that information to provide personalized communication and services, for example, has resulted in an average customer relationship of 20 years versus the industry average of only 4 years.[21]

Domino's Pizza provides another example. Domino's installed a caller ID system in all of its 700 company-owned-and-operated stores and in close to half of its franchised stores. The system is tied in to a customer database so that the order histories of repeat customers immediately come up on a screen along with their addresses and phone numbers. Those in a hurry have only to say "The usual" before they hang up because the screen has all the necessary information. Domino's can have the name and address of a first-time caller on the screen in less than four rings (as long as the caller has a listed phone number).

Databases also allow companies to do more than merely recognize their customers. Companies that surprise and delight their high-profit customers with reward programs are more likely to keep these customers for the long term. British Airways Travel Service, for example, provides discounts to its best customers (see Exhibit 8-12).

Department store chain Neiman Marcus discovered that even affluent customers appreciate recognition and rewards. The retailer annually rewards its most important customers with a free airline trip for two around the world plus a lunch with the local store manager. In its ongoing customer-satisfaction research with these big spenders, the lunch, not the trip, is usually mentioned as being the more appreciated reward; having the store manager sit across the table and call them by name is much more valuable to these customers than a free around-the-world trip.

Traditional retailer Sears has used a simple, low-cost method to strengthen brand relationships with top customers. It identified and sent top customers a small, pressure-

EXHIBIT 8-12

In this mailing, British Airways Travel Service offered select customers a 10 percent saving on travel costs.

sensitive "Best Customer" label to put on their Sears charge cards. Employees were instructed to give these customers special attention, such as personally introducing the customers to the department or store manager or making a special effort to point out items on sale.

A FINAL NOTE: RELATIONSHIP MEMORY

In data-driven communication, the proper focus is not on information technology and information systems but rather on the integration of these systems into marketing communication activities. The British Airways campaign described in the opening case was successful because it created bonds with BA customers. The Travel Services program made it possible for the airline to target messages to its customers' personal interests and track BA's interactions with them.

In a similar vein, several members of a company's sales force may call on the same clients. Without a common database, one sales rep cannot know what another sales rep promised and sold, and all of them may find they are competing with each other or wasting customers' time by making duplicate presentations. Customer-information files create interaction memory for the company and thus minimize duplication.

Consumers' brand perceptions and experiences are recorded in their memories; they learn something new with each new experience. Likewise, businesses can learn about their customers if transactions and interactions are recorded in their institutional memory. In order for there to be a successful relationship between a company and its customers, there needs to be a relationship memory on the company's side similar to the customer's memory.

Key Terms

data mining 262	database marketing 246	prospecting 264
data overlay 262	data-driven communication 246	scanner data 252
database 244	digitized 244	toll-free number 256
database management system (DBMS) 248	mass customization of MC messages 267	warranty cards 254

Key Point Summary

Identifying profitable customers and knowing how, when, and in what way they have interacted and want to interact with a company depends on collecting information in an accessible database.

Key Point 1: Data-Driven Communication

A customer information system compiled as a database is the institutional memory system used by companies to become smarter in order to better meet the needs of customers. Such an information system records, stores, aggregates, and shares customer and other stakeholder information throughout an organization. Using customer databases, a company can track and segment customers in order to make its marketing communication more efficient and effective. Capturing customer information makes it possible for companies to become learning organizations.

Key Point 2: Setting Up Databases

Managing databases involves setting up systems, collecting data, and manipulating the databases. The hardware and software known as a database management system (DBMS) tracks customer interactions and links customer databases that are already in existence. Customer information is collected automatically at the point of purchase and through customer-initiated communication. Data overlay and data mining are techniques used to make the data more useful.

Key Point 3: Privacy and Security

Companies gather customer-profile data in order to personalize their interactions with customers. Misuse of this personal data constitutes an invasion of privacy. Customers may worry that a company will either cross the privacy line or link their names with inaccurate data.

Key Point 4: Managing Customer Relationships

New customers are obtained in acquisition programs through prospecting, which profiles heavy users to find potential new customers with matching characteristics. Retention programs identify ways to please current customers. Reacquisition programs seek to lure back those who have defected. Growth programs increase the purchase activity of regular customers and identify unprofitable customers. By tracking the behavior of current customers, companies can personalize messages and responses to inquiries when talking to them.

EXHIBIT 8-13

This announcement of a new car wash was mailed to nearby homes and used a "free wash" promotion to encourage neighbors to try the service.

Key Point 1: Data-Driven Communication

a. What do the initials *IS* and *IT* stand for? Why are IS and IT important to a data-driven communication program?
b. What is a database?
c. Define the term *learning organization* and give an example of a company that fits the definitions.
d. Explain how a "learning organization" uses databases.
e. Explain how large and small companies might use databases in an IMC program.

Key Point 2: Setting Up Databases

a. Why is a cross-functional team needed for designing a database system?
b. What six questions need to be answered before a database system is set up?
c. Explain two ways customer data can be collected, and give examples of each.
d. What is the purpose of data mining? Give an example of how it can be used to develop better marketing communication strategies.
e. If you were designing a membership recognition program for an association to which you belong, how would you go about setting up a database system?
f. You have been asked to build a database of friends and supporters of your school or department. What types of databases might be available to you? How would you go about combining them, and what would you need to do to make the new list as efficient and effective as possible?

Key Point 3: Privacy and Security

a. What are two major consumer concerns about privacy?
b. Why is privacy situational?
c. What is "identity theft," and how does it tie in to database management?
d. What can a company do to make sure its database program is responsive to privacy issues?

Key Point 4: Managing Customer Relationships

a. What four types of programs are used to customize brand communications, and how do they work?
b. Explain how prospecting works.
c. What is cross-selling? How is it used in growth programs?
d. How and why are profitable customers identified?
e. Have you (or has someone you know) been targeted by an acquisition or retention program? How did the program operate? How did you respond?
f. What is mass customization of MC messages? How do companies use it to create brand messages?
g. A local store has asked you to help design a customer recognition program. What techniques might you recommend?

Writing Assignment

Use the Database Application Checklist (Table 8-1) to develop a mini-audit that you can refer to when you interview a local company about how it collects and uses customer data.

Presentation Assignment

Assume that you have a new job or an internship. You have been asked to prepare a presentation for a marketing staff training program on the strategic use of databases. Develop an outline of the key points you want to present. Give the presentation to your class or record it on videotape (audiotape is also an option) to turn in to your instructor, along with the outline.

Internet Assignment

Visit www.CRMguru.com for an in-depth understanding of the latest CRM practices and applications. This website is open to students for free. Analyze the materials and discussion items on this site, and identify a problem or debate that is engaging the CRM community. Explain the problem and the differing viewpoints in a written report to your instructor.

Chapter 9

Creative Message Strategies

THE ORIGINAL
ARIZONA
JEAN COMPANY

Key Points in This Chapter

1. What information needs to be considered in planning message strategies?
2. What are the key elements in an IMC message strategy brief?
3. How does the creative process work to develop big ideas?

Chapter Perspective

The Creative "ROI"

To paraphrase the words of Keith Reinhard, long-time CEO of DDB Worldwide: Today, more than ever, if marketing communication is not *relevant*, it has no purpose. If it is not *original*, it will attract no attention. If it does not strike with *impact*, it will make no lasting impression. In the DDB approach to developing message strategies, the initials *ROI* (for relevant, original, impact) are equated with the financial investment made by clients in marketing communication. To be effective, the message strategies must also deliver bottom-line ROI (return on investment).

Relevant messages that speak to the head and the heart connect with the target audience on a personal level. The message strategies that really ignite consumer responses, however, contain the big O—the *originality*

dimension in Reinhard's ROI formula. The originality factor first springs to life in the "big idea." How this creative concept is developed and executed determines to a great extent how effective the ultimate brand messages stemming from the message strategies will be in having an impact.

Linda Kaplan Thaler, head of the Kaplan Thaler Group, explains, "Advertising awards are nice, but the real victory is making a dent in the culture—part of what we call our Big Bang philosophy. It's why our AFLAC duck is an answer in the *Times* crossword puzzle, there's a greeting card about our Herbal Essences organic experiences, and *Saturday Night Live* does send-ups of both of them."[1]

MASTERCARD'S "PRICELESS" CAMPAIGN IS PRICELESS

"I wish I had done that one." That's the typical response to a great creative idea. That's also how MC professionals look at the MasterCard "Priceless" campaign, which has been running since 1997 and has won innumerable awards, as well as moved the brand into a more competitive position against market leaders Visa and American Express.

The first "Priceless" ad told the story of a father who took his son to a baseball game for the first time. The format is one that everyone has come to know, starting with items that you can put a price on and ending with some intangible that can't be measured in dollars. For example, a more recent commercial opens with two young men cruising in a Volkswagen van as they try to visit most of the major baseball parks. The passenger clutches a baseball as the voiceover breaks into the familiar rhythm: "U.S. road maps, $11. Ballpark guide, $22. Opening day tickets, $18. One stadium down, 29 to go: Priceless." The commercial ends with the slogan, "The best things in life are free. For everything else there's MasterCard."

Background

MasterCard International is a portfolio of credit-card companies including Cirrus and Maestro, along with MasterCard. It serves consumers and businesses in 210 countries and territories. With 30 million acceptance locations, 25,000 business partners, and 820,000 ATM locations around the world, MasterCard is the most widely accepted global payment card in the world.

The campaign challenge began when the McCann-Erickson agency was given the charge to turn around the floundering MasterCard brand, which had come to be perceived as an everyday, ordinary credit card—the *other* card you keep in your wallet behind Visa and American Express. The award-winning "Priceless" advertising campaign that resulted can be seen in 45 languages in 96 countries.

The Breadth of the Campaign

A variety of involving experiences such as sponsorships, sweepstakes, and other consumer and channel marketing programs have been set up to support the campaign. For example, MasterCard has been a long-time supporter of international soccer and is the key sponsor of the sport's five most prestigious events, including the FIFA World Cup™. As sponsor, it gains exclusivity as the official payment system for these events. It also has the right to use the official marks and logos on its advertising, promotions, and merchandising and receives guaranteed on-field perimeter signage.

MasterCard also sponsors soccer great Pelé, who has made more than 150 appearances worldwide on behalf of the company. In a related co-branding effort, more than 2 million World Cup-themed affinity cards have been issued bearing his likeness. (An affinity card carries the image of a particular

EXHIBIT 9-1

dinner (blind date): $63

coffee, dessert (another blind date): $16

movie, popcorn, soda (yet another blind date): $24

finding someone you want a second date with:

priceless

Dating's not easy, but paying for it is. MasterCard® is accepted at over 15 million locations. Don't forget your breath mints.

there are some things money can't buy. for everything else there's MasterCard.™

MasterCard.
5912 3956 7890 1234
J. CHEISH

organization or individual with which people want to identify, such as a university or the World Cup competition.) MasterCard and its sponsoring financial institutions have used Pelé's photo on over 20 million cardholder inserts, mailings, and collateral promotional materials.

To promote its international image, MasterCard used its "Priceless" advertising in the award-winning "Swap" commercial, which featured the tradition of opposing soccer players "swapping" their jerseys following a match as a sign of mutual respect. The commercial was shot in three countries—Prague, Czech Republic; Cape Town, South Africa; and Tokyo, Japan—using a total of 10 locations with 26 actors and more than 200 local extras. More than 30 different "swaps" were filmed with actors representing different nationalities so each region had the option of using a version that best represented its market.

Debra Coughlin, senior VP of Global Brand Building, explained that "[t]he message of true sportsmanship in relation to the FIFA World Cup rings true to our brand position and has broader meaning in relation to the current events of the world." The commercial was shown in more than 50 countries, which leads Coughlin to observe, "We believe the core message communicated in 'Swap' resonates with consumers around the world—regardless of country or nationality." To ensure that the message would work for a global audience, Coughlin's global brand building team worked closely with each local country "to ensure the important nuances of the respective cultures and countries were respected, captured, and communicated."

In another partnership agreement, MasterCard and Universal Entertainment announced in 2003 a multiyear marketing alliance that made MasterCard the preferred card for Universal's theme parks and resorts, its Universal Pictures theatrical and home entertainment releases, its Universal music operations, and its internet properties, such as mp3.com, mp4.com, e-music.com, and rollingstone.com.

Supporting the Universal sponsorship agreement, MasterCard created a television commercial using the "Priceless" theme. The new ad, filmed on location at Universal Studios Theme Park in Orlando, features a family experiencing Universal's "Hulk" Roller Coaster as part of a "Priceless" day at the park.

In another co-branding effort, MasterCard, the Chase bank, and Universal teamed to launch the Universal Entertainment MasterCard, which offers consumers world-class rewards linked to Universal's movies, television, music, theme parks, and interactive games.

Alliances like the ones with the FIFA World Cup and Universal Entertainment also benefit the finan-cial institutions, merchants, and other business partners affiliated with MasterCard. In explaining the Universal partnership, Larry Flanagan, MasterCard International's chief marketing officer, explained that the alliance illustrates "MasterCard's ongoing commitment to creating business-building opportunities for our members and merchant partners by aligning the brand with the world's premier properties."

Special promotions also support the "Priceless" theme. For the baseball stadium journey commercial, for example, MasterCard joined with 15 baseball teams to offer a Grand Slam Ticket Pack, which includes four game tickets and vouchers for concessions. Another special promotion, the "Priceless Night on the Town" sweepstakes, was launched in March 2003. MasterCard customers are automatically entered for a chance to win a night on the town anywhere in the United States when they use their debit MasterCards.

Promotions have been equally effective in MasterCard's international marketing. A Puerto Rico promotion won a gold at the 2002 Cannes Film Festival for the way the campaign was integrated into a broadcast of *Titanic*. On-screen captions referred to film elements as "Jack's tuxedo: $900" and "Rose's evening gown: $1,500." The last line was: "A reserved space on the lifeboat . . . priceless." In a Malaysian creativity contest, a 23-year-old man won a new Lotus Elise car when his entry on loyalty beat 70,000 other entries. His design featured the word "Priceless" in India ink and Chinese calligraphy with a red hand-drawn signature stamp resembling the MasterCard logo.

Another example of how the "Priceless" campaign has been extended is found on MasterCard's website, www.MasterCard.com/internship, where it is used as the theme for MasterCard's "Priceless Edge Internship Experience." The internship program offers "priceless" experiences in music and sports careers. In addition to the actual internships, the website also offers a series of short courses in both music and sports marketing.

Effectiveness of the "Priceless" Campaign

The success of the "Priceless" campaign has helped MasterCard improve its competitive position. The card has gained market share for five years running. MasterCard's chief marketing officer credits the campaign with helping narrow the gap between MasterCard and Visa. "Five years ago, we had a weak brand . . . We now have a strong brand." A *Brandweek* commentator observed that the campaign has "galvanized the brand, providing energy and vitality within the credit-card association and its constituencies of member banks, merchants, and consumers."

Some charge the campaign theme with having outlived its effectiveness, but the MasterCard executive believes it still has some life left in it. The "Priceless" campaign travels well and has now been used in some 30 countries outside the United States, including Germany, the United Kingdom, France, Japan, and other countries in Asia and Latin America. In the United States, a Spanish-language campaign aimed at the Hispanic market was easily adapted by focusing on family. In "Fatherhood," a father diapers an infant, then takes her out in a stroller, illustrating the idea that fatherhood is priceless. Another spot, "Grandma," shows a grandmother and granddaughter shopping for ingredients for a family recipe. At the end, the two share the dish, another "priceless" moment.

The campaign works because of its soft-spoken creative message, which invokes the basic needs of life and puts MasterCard at the heart of the emotional response to the things that give our lives meaning. It works because of its insight into basic human values, which brings a wandering brand back to consumer relevance. The judges at the Effie Awards said the campaign helped "define a new aspiration that was in tune with emerging consumer values."

Source: Business editors, "MasterCard Launches Debit MasterCard 'Priceless Night on the Town' Sweepstakes," Business Wire, March 4, 2003, <www.businesswire.com/ cgi-bin/cb_headline.cgi?&story_file=...>; "MasterCard International and Universal Announce Multi-Year Marketing Alliance," February 13, 2002, and "MasterCard Launches Global "Swap" Advertising Execution in Support of 2002 FIFA World Cup™ Sponsorship," May 13, 2002, MasterCard International News Release, <www.MasterCardintl.com/cgi-bin/newsroom.cgi?id=681>; Business editors, "MasterCard Announces Extension of Unprecedented Commitment to Soccer's Five Most Prestigious Events," March 12, 2003, Business Wire, <www.businesswire.com/cgi-bin/cb_headline .cgi?&story_file=...>; Vanessa O'Connell, "MasterCard 'Priceless' Ads Grow Old," Wall Street Journal, September 30, 2002, p. B8.

HOW TO DEVELOP A CREATIVE MESSAGE STRATEGY

Anyone can put together an ad, publicity release, sales-promotion offer, event, or any other type of MC message. The challenge is to make these messages creative enough to be noticed, read (or listened to), and acted upon. To do this requires a message strategy, which is one of the primary areas of expertise offered by MC agencies. There are two main steps in producing successful MC messages. The first is developing a creative message strategy, and the second is executing that strategy in the form of ads, publicity releases, sales-promotion offers, events, and all the other MC forms.

This chapter focuses on developing marketing communication strategic ideas—in particular, "creative briefs" that drive the creation of the big ideas that in turn motivate responses. Chapters 9 and 10 go together. This chapter explains why message strategy is important. It focuses on the ideas behind creative messages—*what* to say and why. The next chapter focuses on *how* to say it—the execution of creative message strategies.

A **message strategy** is *an idea about how to creatively and persuasively communicate a brand message to a target audience.* Generally, such strategies blend rational and emotional thinking and integrate them in a creative way. The message strategy for Michelin tires is to associate the brand with protecting babies. All parents can strongly relate to the responsibility of protecting their children. Consequently, showing that Michelin is good enough to protect parents' most precious possessions—their children—makes this message strategy successful.

A successful message strategy also makes the brand relevant to customers. For example, some years ago, a campaign for V8 showed people hitting themselves on their foreheads and saying, "I could have had a V8." V8's marketing challenge was that people didn't drink vegetable juice when they were thirsty. Why didn't they?

No reason, market researchers learned—they simply *didn't think of it*. Connecting with this reality about customers allowed the brand to develop the strategic idea: it's a dumb mistake *not* to consider V8 when you're thirsty. The idea of suddenly remembering something—and wishing you had thought of it earlier—is an experience everyone can relate to. Tying that common forehead-hitting gesture with the V8 brand brilliantly reminded customers of a beverage choice that they would regret forgetting.

The appeal of a message establishes an emotional or rational link (or both) between the customer and the brand. An **appeal** is *an idea that motivates an audience to respond*. Aspiration, comfort, convenience, economy, efficiency, reduction of fear, love, nostalgia, pride, health, luxury, patriotism, sex, and safety are ideas that engage the minds and touch the hearts of the target audience, and ultimately motivate a response.

In their ongoing competitive war, Coke and Pepsi have searched for strategic ideas that would differentiate the brands in a way that customers would find relevant. Both have had winning ideas, such as "The Real Thing" for Coke and "The Pepsi Generation" for Pepsi, but both continue to search for new appeals to reach new consumers. Recently Coke has tried to portray itself as natural and relevant, using the "Coca Cola . . . Real" slogan. In one commercial, movie star Penelope Cruz is shown drinking a bottle of Coke in front of a diner packed with men and then accidentally belching. A Coke spokesman said the commercial brings the "natural" strategy to life because it "reflects genuine, authentic moments in life." [2]

The MC industry is constantly searching for creative ideas that are attention getting and relevant, such as the ad in Exhibit 9-2. While major global corporations like Coca-Cola and Pepsi spend millions of dollars annually duking it out in the "cola wars," smaller companies too must make their marketing messages compelling. Why is creative message strategy so important? Brands need to break through the clutter of commercial messages. Bob St. Julian, managing director of Lowe Hunt, says to ask yourself why you remember so few ads—and what makes those rare ones that you do remember stand out. His answer: "They were the ones that broke new ground. They told a relevant brand truth in a fresh and original way." [3]

> **"They told a relevant brand truth in a fresh and original way."**
>
> Bob St. Julian, Lowe Hunt

THE IMC MESSAGE STRATEGY BRIEF

When MC agencies create brand messages—whether ads, publicity releases, packaging, or sales-promotion offers—the development of these messages is guided by a document known as the: creative brief, creative platform, creative plan or workplan, creative strategy, or copy strategy. This book uses **message strategy brief** to refer to this document, which consists of *statements about a brand that summarize the research and insights for the creative team*. This helps team members identify the direction and focus for their creative and media ideas.

Over the years, many advertising agencies have customized the elements that make up their message strategy briefs. Table 9-1 lists the elements in the message strategy briefs of seven major agencies. Although each list contains slightly different elements, there are many similarities. The terms used in these lists, if unfamiliar to you now, will make sense as you go through this chapter.

One technique used to summarize a message strategy in a single sentence is to complete the following statement:

EXHIBIT 9-2
What makes this ad for Madeline Shoes so attention getting and interesting?

Obsessively shoe obsessed   Madeline

The purpose of this MC message is to convince _____ [target audience] _____ that _____ [brand] _____ will _____ [benefit] _____ because _____ [proof]. The tone of the message should be _____ [description of message personality] _____.

The strategy for the MasterCard "Priceless" campaign could be expressed as follows:

The purpose of the MasterCard "Priceless" campaign is to connect emotionally with customers and convince them that they will benefit by using their MasterCards because it lets them enjoy things—most of them intangibles—that you can't put a price on, such as family time. The tone of the message is thoughtful and nostalgic.

TABLE 9-1   Elements of Seven Agencies' Message Strategy Briefs

Ogilvy & Mather	DDB Worldwide	Young & Rubicam
1. Product	Marketing Objective	Key Fact
2. Key Issue/Problem	Competitive Advantage	Consumer Problem
3. The Promise	Advertising Objective	Advertising Objective
4. The Support	Action by Target	Creative Strategy
5. Competition	Key Insight	1. Prospect Definition
6. Target	Reward/Support	a. Product Use
a. Demographics	Brand Personality/Tone	b. Demographics
b. Psychographics	Position	c. Psychographics
7. Desired Behavior	Media	2. Competition
8. Target's Net Impression		3. Consumer Benefit
9. Tone & Manner		4. Reason Why

Tracy-Locke	Leo Burnett	Campbell Mithun
1. Target	Target	Business Goal
2. Brand Promise	Desired Belief	Consumer Profile
3. Reason Why	Reasons Why	Current Attitudes
4. Brand Character	Tone	Desired Attitudes
5. Focus of Sale		Desired Action
6. Tone		Selling Proposition

Citigate Cunningham

Value Propositions

(for each proposition):

   Key Messages

   Proof Point

   Sound Bite

Compare the Citigate Cunningham message brief outline to the other message strategy briefs summarized in Table 9-1. How do they differ in structure? How are they alike? Citigate Cunningham applied the brief shown in Figure 9-1 to the analysis of Freshwater Software. The analysis determined Freshwater's key value propositions, which were found to lie in three areas: "eBusiness growth" (the Freshwater system is a key to its clients' growth in e-business); "rapid, global scalability" (easy-to-add global customers); and "brand integrity" (the Freshwater system is recognized as trustworthy). Under each of those three propositions are a key message—what the proposition means and what it is all about—proof for the proposition, and a sound bite that restates the proposition in customer-focused language.

Although message strategies should be the foundation of *all* MC messages, the reality is that advertising agencies make greater use of this aspect of brand communications than do other MC agencies.

In genuine IMC, message strategies are broad enough to be executed by *each* of the major MC areas. Coming up with a clever headline that works only in advertising is generally not a good strategy. Michelin's message strategy, previously

Positioning Statement	Mercury Interactive is the leading provider of comprehensive Internet growth solutions for eBusiness		
Value Propositions	eBusiness growth	Rapid, global scalability	Brand integrity
Key Messages	Our services, technologies and expertise are critical enablers of eBusiness growth	We help companies scale their Internet businesses quickly and globally	We create trust in our customers' Internet brands
Sample Proof Point	2,500 growing businesses outsource website monitoring to Freshwater	Freshwater measures website availability from 11 global networks	Freshwater helps meet unique eBusiness brand requirements, including 24-hour availability
Sample Sound Bite	"We have time and resources to build other areas of our business when Freshwater monitors our Web environment."	"As we add customers around the world, Freshwater makes sure they can reliably complete transactions on our website."	"Freshwater makes sure my website is available 24 hours a day, seven days a week, so it can support my overall business brand."

FIGURE 9-1

Citigate Cunningham's "Positioning Platform" identifies the message strategy for Mercury Interactive.

mentioned, is considered broad because it can be applied to other MC areas such as publicity (with stories about child safety and automobiles), sales promotion (by offering child and auto-related premiums like car seats), and direct response (in e-mails and regular mail offers that show babies and Michelin tires).

The three basic steps in developing a message strategy brief are shown in Figure 9-2: (1) determining the MC communication objectives, (2) finding about customers insights, and (3) selecting a selling strategy. But the creative planning is not over once the marketing manager has developed a message strategy brief. Sometimes finding a creative way to *present* the strategy for approval—either to agency managers or to clients—is as important as the creative message strategy itself.

Step 1: Determining Communication Objectives: What Type of Impact Does the Message Need to Achieve?

How do you sell a massive SUV like a Hummer when there are consumer concerns about safety, gas mileage, and environmental impact and car sales have dried up? That problem worried GM planners when they unveiled the Hummer H2, a luxury version of the Gulf War driving machine. The objective of the marketing communication was to change consumer perceptions of the Hummer as a macho military machine to a car you can drive around town. The rationale for the repositioning strategy was that women would see the H2 as a safe vehicle, rather than a macho one.[4] However, GM also discovered that the macho image of the Hummer is appealing. This is why some ads for the brand have headlines such as "Slip into Something a Little More Metal" and "Threaten Men in a Whole New Way."

The impact of the Hummer H2 repositioning message strategy is measured against the message objectives. Therefore, stating appropriate message objectives is an important factor in determining the desired impact. For that reason,

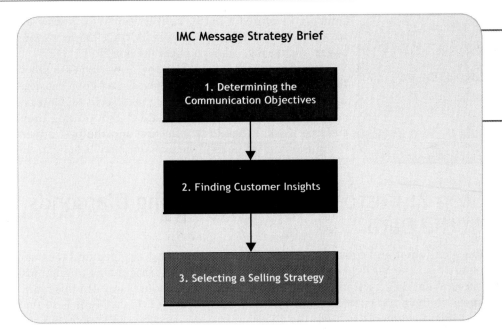

FIGURE 9-2

There are three basic steps in developing a message strategy brief.

marketers often base message objectives on a hierarchy-of-effects model. Recall from Chapter 5 that the AIDA model identifies four consumer decision points (attention, interest, desire, and action) where a message can have an impact. A communication objective can state any of those decision points.

Chapter 5 also discussed consumer decision making in terms of three paths to a consumer response: cognitive, affective, and behavior or action—the think/feel/do model. These paths also can be used to craft message objectives for the various functional areas. The list that follows shows typical MC objectives that relate to the three paths to a consumer response. Because these are *types* of MC objectives, they are not stated in measurable terms; this can be done only when objectives are applied to a specific brand situation. Notice also that these objectives are phrased in terms of consumer response or the effect of the messages on the target audience.

Sample Marketing Communication Objectives[5]

Cognitive path: Create awareness of brand or opportunity to use or buy it; educate about brand use, explain how it can solve a consumer problem; create or increase brand knowledge and understanding.

Affective path: Create or change a brand image or personality; create or change attitudes and brand liking; ignite a desire or need; create or strengthen an association; strike an emotional chord. (This was the focus of the Master-Card "Priceless" campaign.)

Behavioral path: Increase trial; increase purchase and repeat purchasing; inspire customers to tell others about brand; inspire visiting a showroom, visiting a website, returning a card, or inquiring about the brand.

Remember, we are talking about communication and persuasion objectives, not marketing objectives (sales, share of market, and so forth). Communication objectives focus on the impact that can be delivered through a message that creates shared meaning. Persuasion goes a step further and stimulates impact that leads to attitude formation and change, as well as behavior.

An example of behavioral impact designed to achieve MC objectives is Verizon's "Can you hear me now?" campaign which generated a flood of new business for the cell phone service. Verizon's message strategy was to "demonstrate the brand's extensive coverage by using exotic locations for conducting conversations." The

> ". . . we believe in the effectiveness of great creative ideas."
>
> Tony Granger, Creative Director, Bozell

campaign featured a nerdy Verizon employee testing for blank spots in Verizon's coverage by traveling to various places and asking, "Can you hear me now?"

Tony Granger, creative director at Verizon's agency, Bozell, reported the campaign generated a 34 percent sign-up rate, well beyond the campaign's objectives. Granger says that even though he is fanatical about doing great creative work, it has to be effective and the best advertising is both. "At Bozell," he explains, "we believe in the effectiveness of great creative ideas."[6]

Step 2: Customer Insight: Finding Diamonds in the Data

Once customer and prospect segments are identified and targeted and message objectives have been determined, agencies must closely analyze the target audiences. What do they want to hear? What do they care about? How can this brand speak to their wants, needs, and desires? The purpose of this analysis is to find customer insights that enable the choosing of a strategy that will relate and resonate with those targeted.

Customer insight is *below-the-surface attitudes and beliefs that influence customers' behavior.* Ogilvy and Mather's Emma Cookson, strategic planning director, describes the search for customer insight as a process of discovering creative gems hidden in the research, or "diamonds in the data."[7] An example is understanding how women consider beauty to be as much inside as outside, as illustrated in the Freeman skin care product ad in Exhibit 9-3. The message strategy was to connect with the things that are important to young women. The execution of this strategy used the actual "insights" as copy on the T-shirt to show that Freeman really understands what young women consider important.

Back in the 1950s Leo Burnett came up with the idea of associating Marlboro cigarettes with rugged, masculine cowboys working in the wide-open spaces of the West. The reason for this association, however, was not that cowboys were the primary target. Leo Burnett had the insight that young and middle-aged men fantasize about the freedom and macho independence enjoyed by cowboys. By offering a cigarette that symbolized this romantic idea, maker Philip Morris allowed men to escape into this fantasy each time they lit up. Leo Burnett's simple insight made Marlboro one of the top brands in the world.

In *The Consumer Insight Handbook*, Lisa Fortini-Campbell gives another example of customer insight. She says the following is the reason why the movie *Pretty Woman* was so successful with the female audience: "[I]t touched a dream [that every woman has] always harbored . . . if we're in the right spot at the right time, someone rich, handsome, sophisticated and kind will see us for who we really are and carry us off on his white horse. Or in his white limousine. And we'll live happily ever after."[8]

Another example of a campaign built on a customer insight is the "Unboring" campaign for Swedish furniture giant, IKEA, which is featured in the IMC in Action

EXHIBIT 9-3

A soft spot for dad, burgers, kids, and the guy downstairs. That's how the "Beauty inside" theme is related to an inside glimpse of a young woman's personal values.

IMC IN ACTION

IKEA's "Unboring" Campaign Slams Furniture Puritans

In a campaign titled "Unboring," Swedish-owned furnishings retailer IKEA took potshots at the American penchant for holding onto old furniture. The effort by the Miami agency Crispin Porter+Bogusky explores the reasons why people keep furniture even when it's tacky, disliked, or unfashionable. Furniture industry studies have found, for example, that Americans tend to keep sofas . . . forever. And even when sofas are moved "out," they are usually relegated to some other use—moved into the family room or given to a kid in college. Bedroom furniture stays around for 16 to 20 years, and formal dining-room furniture has an average life span of 20 years. IKEA's ad manager calls it "furniture gravity" and says, "Get over it."

To overcome the somewhat irrational reasons for holding onto things we secretly want to replace, CPB developed mini-soap operas about people getting rid of their stuff. Aggressively questioning the customer's taste may seem like a strange way to sell a product, but the ads are fun and engaging and deliver the message that Americans are stuck with housefuls of stuff that they would like to replace.

For example, in one ad, an old desk lamp no longer loved by its owner is carried out to the curb. Viewers see the spiffy replacement glowing in the window through the eyes of the old lamp while sad music plays and rain falls. Then a man with a Swedish accent ap-

pears before the camera and says, "Many of you are feeling bad for this lamp. That is because you are crazy. This lamp has no feelings. And the new one is better."

In another ad, an unattractive creamer in the form of a cow sits on a table with two table settings. As a man and woman passionately embrace off-camera, they rattle the china and knock everything over, including the moo-cow pitcher, which falls to the floor. The camera focuses on the broken cow lying in a pool of its own milk. A Swedish guy passing by glances in the window and says, "Right now, you feel sad for the moo-cow milker. That is because you are crazy. This woman knows tacky items can easily be replaced with something better at IKEA."

In addition to the television commercials and a catalog, the "Unboring" campaign includes an interactive element with a dedicated website, www.unboring.com that provides room configurations and self-help tools to assist customers with their "old furniture attachment."

Source: "Can the New Ad Campaign from IKEA Convince Americans to Have More Dining Room Tables Than Spouses?" IKEA press release, September 26, 2002, <www.ikeausa.com/about_idea/pres_room/press_release_int.asp?pr?_id=696>.

---

box. Creatives at the Miami agency Crispin Porter+Bogusky realized that people hold onto furniture almost forever—sometimes even furniture that they hate but can't bring themselves to get rid of. The CPB campaign was designed to give people permission to unload all that stuff—and replace it with furniture that they like.

Finding customer insights for a brand is the responsibility of the account planner, who is considered to be the "voice of the customer." **Account planning** means *using research and brand insights to bring a strong consumer focus to the planning of marketing communication*. As explained in Chapter 2, an account planner is a researcher and a strategic thinker whose mission is to see the brand through the customer's eyes and write up those insights for the message strategy brief. The insights uncovered by account planners can reflect or expand on the customer analysis obtained through a SWOT analysis (◄ Chapter 6).

The objective of a message strategy is to connect with the customer in a meaningful way. The challenge is to identify the harbor in the customer's heart or mind where the brand can throw out an anchor. The MasterCard "Priceless" campaign, for example, is anchored by the idea that there is value in the little things in life that we buy, but we can't put a price on the intangibles—relationships, experiences, emotions—that these things represent.

A good account planner uses observational research and in-depth probing to see how and why customers think and behave as they do. Creative director Michael Drazen says he gets exceptional ideas by listening to his family and neighbors, as well as strangers and heroes (his are Bob Dylan and Pablo Picasso). He used one of these everyday insights to develop a message strategy for an early Volvo ad that defined the car's ownership of the safety position—"a father tells his daughter's prom date, 'take my Volvo' because there was a thunderstorm. That was the beginning of the shift to sell cars, particularly Volvo, on safety." [9]

As Drazen explains, good ads and other MC messages are about relationships and real life. When a message is exceptional, it talks to people in ways they find engaging. He says target audiences should laugh or feel good when they are exposed to MC messages, not think "what are they trying to sell to me?"[10]

Account planning is used primarily in advertising agencies but also in other marketing communication agencies. In advertising, Abbott Mead Vickers BBDO (AMV) in the United Kingdom and Goodby, Silverstein & Partners and TBWA Chiat/Day in the United States are agencies that have pioneered the use of account planning. Porter Novelli, a public relations agency, also has used account planning to develop publicity strategies.

Unfortunately, most definitions of account planning say little or nothing about creating and managing either a dialogue or an ongoing relationship with customers. This will change, however, as more agencies and companies adopt IMC, for the two concepts—IMC and account planning—complement each other. Account planning insights can be tremendously useful in planning relationship-focused message strategies.

Step 3: Selecting a Selling Strategy

Over the years, agencies and their clients have developed a variety of selling strategies that are basically strategic templates. One of the most widely used focuses on a brand's main **benefit,** *how a product satisfies customers' needs, wants, and desires.* Most brands offer several benefits, but the one that should be used is the one that is the basis of the brand's positioning strategy (◄ Chapter 3). Inherent in a good position is a promised benefit. A brand's position is how it differs, in a positive and beneficial way, from competing brands (see Exhibit 9-4).

A benefit-selling strategy can appeal to the head or heart, either of which can experience a benefit from buying and using the brand. People buy cars for both rational and emotional reasons. They like a car's attributes (gas mileage, price, handling, and so forth), but they also may like its looks and the way the car's image reflects their own self-image.

Consider again the MasterCard "Priceless" campaign. It focuses on a benefit, an emotional benefit. To analyze the benefit strategy of that campaign, complete the following sentence: If I

EXHIBIT 9-4

This ad attempts to portray Target not as an average discount store but as a store that offers quality merchandise at a value price.

use _____(product)_____, I will _____(benefit)_____.
Your wording will probably read something like: "If
I use my MasterCard, I will have a memorable
experience."

Sometimes the benefit is referred to as a **promise,** *a
statement describing what good things will happen if a person uses a product:* If you buy _____(brand)_____,
then _____(this is what will happen)_____.
Sometimes the promise implies something negative
may happen if you *do* or *do not* behave in a certain way.
This *fear appeal* is used often in public service announcements. For example, in the aftermath of the
September 11 attacks, a White House Drug Control
Office ad during the 2002 Super Bowl said: If you
buy drugs, you may be subsidizing terrorists. *Advertising Age's* Bob Garfield observes that such a proposition is "a dramatic way to counter the 'victimless
crime' argument."[11]

Because sometimes a promise may stretch believability, the focus of the selling strategy may need to
give more weight to the **reason why,** which is *support
or proof points that explain why a product will provide the
promised benefit.* Generally, "reasons why" refer to important product features (see Exhibit 9-5).

Another similar selling strategy focuses on the **features** of a brand, which are *attributes that give a product
a distinctive difference,* such as its design or engineering.
Although customers buy products for the benefit they receive, sometimes talking
about a feature that strongly *suggests* a benefit is more persuasive because it helps
answer the question "How can this product benefit me?" An example of a category
that frequently uses a *feature-selling strategy* is disposable diapers. When you tell a
new mother that Pampers is the most absorbent disposable, that mother knows
right away that absorbency (a feature) means dryness for her baby's little bottom.
A dry baby is a happy baby, a state that mothers and babies prefer.

One particularly common feature-selling strategy focuses on price (a feature).
This strategy, *value pricing,* is used by Wal-Mart and other discount retailers to
make the point that the store offers the best-quality product you can buy *for that
price.* Notice that "best quality" is qualified—the quality is best for that price; there
may be better-quality products, but they would cost more.

Although price is a feature and an absolute, value is not. **Value** is *a perception of
what something is worth in terms of quality and price.* A selling strategy for value often
uses a comparison to put value into perspective. An example of how even the perception of a high price can be recast as a good value comes from the gasoline industry. To show that a gallon of gas is a good value at $1.50 or $1.60 per gallon,
compare it to other products such as a pint bottle of Evian, which can sell for as
much as $1.49. There are eight pints in a gallon, so the price of a gallon of Evian
(when purchased in pints) would be $1.49 × 8 = $11.92 for a gallon of water!

A **unique selling proposition (USP)** is *a selling strategy based on a product's most
distinctive difference from competitive products.* This is another strategy that directly
reflects the brand's position. An example is the USP for Colgate's Total, which
states that the toothpaste is *the only one* that offers 12-hour protection.

For most selling strategies, it is important to identify the **support,** which is
reason or proof points on which a claim, benefit, or proposition rests. The formula for
analyzing support is: If I use _____(product)_____, I will _____(benefit)_____
because _____(support)_____.

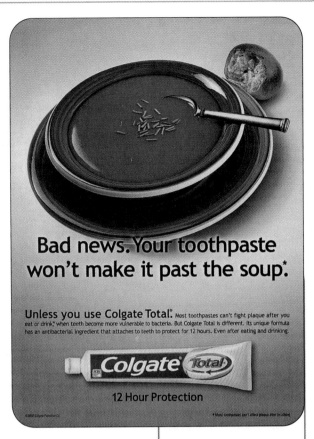

**Bad news. Your toothpaste
won't make it past the soup.***

Unless you use Colgate Total. Most toothpastes can't fight plaque after you
eat or drink,* when teeth become more vulnerable to bacteria. But Colgate Total is different. Its unique formula
has an antibacterial ingredient that attaches to teeth to protect for 12 hours. Even after eating and drinking.

Colgate *Total*

12 Hour Protection

EXHIBIT 9-5
*Does your toothpaste
just wash off? This ad
dramatizes Colgate
Total's claim of 12-hour
protection. The ad
promises that the
toothpaste continues to
fight plaque after you eat
something. The reason
why is that Total has a
"unique formula [that]
has an antibacterial
ingredient that attaches
to teeth to protect for
12 hours."*

1 Now you don't.   2 Now you see it.

With 3M microreplication technology, a single 50 watt bulb can turn 100 feet of

curving Alpine guard rail into 100 feet of *guide* rail. The 3M™ Lighted Guidance Tube is

one more shining result of our unique culture — a free exchange of ideas, a willingness

to take risks — that lets us make the leap *from need to...*

3M *Innovation*

For more information, call 1-800-3M-HELPS, or Internet: http://www.mmm.com

EXHIBIT 9-6
*Why would 3M choose
an informational strategy
over other strategies?*

In some industries, such as pharmaceuticals and food, any health claims, as well as any other statements of superiority, have to be supported by research. For emotional selling approaches, the support may come in the imagery. For example, the appeal of the Marlboro cowboy—the independence and manliness of cowboys— is communicated in the western landscape, the cowboy's horse, and his dress and mannerisms, all of which can be reflected in a consumer's self-image. Saturn has maintained its position as a customer-focused car brand and supported that message by pointing to its excellent customer-service ratings. The IMC in Action box discusses how Saturn's customer-focused position is continuing through a change in its agency.

Other selling strategies include the following:

- *Generic:* A **generic strategy** *stresses a basic feature or benefit of a product that is not brand specific.* For a long time Campbell Soup used a slogan that said "soup is good for you." Any maker of soup could say the same thing. Campbell Soup, however, has over 70 percent of the soup market, so it can afford to sell the soup category because it knows it will get 7 out of 10 soup purchases. A generic strategy is primarily used in monopolistic or brand-dominant situations.

- *Pre-emptive:* A **pre-emptive strategy** *focuses on an attribute or benefit that any other product in the category could have claimed but did not.* This strategy is used in categories with little product differentiation and in new-product categories. In the Verizon "Can you hear me now?" campaign, the strategy was basically pre-emptive. Most companies offering wireless service have technicians on the road testing for dead spots in their service. By being the first to use that feature and doing so in such a highly memorable way, Verizon was able to nail down a position as the wireless company that cares about finding the spots where its customers can't get good reception.[12]

- *Informational:* An **informational strategy** is *a selling strategy based on giving the facts about the brand and its attributes.* It's used with new products and products that have distinctive features that are strong points of competitive difference. A demonstration or a comparison can be used to prove the claim (see Exhibit 9-6).

- *Credibility:* A **credibility strategy** *heightens conviction and decreases the perception of risk.* It is particularly useful with major purchases or products that affect security, safety, or health. Publicity releases that appear as news stories, for example, boost credibility because they have been reviewed by objective reporters and editors. An advertisement that uses endorsements, expert testimonials, or demonstrations to deliver a message is designed to build credibility. When Venus and Serena Williams play with Wilson rackets (for which they are handsomely paid), their choice says this brand of tennis racket is one of the best—otherwise, why would the top players in the world be using it?

- *Emotion:* An **emotional strategy** *connects with customers and prospects at the affective level* and moves them to respond with feelings. A number of emotional appeals are used in marketing communication, such as fear, love, and humor. The "Priceless" campaign is built on an emotional appeal based on family warmth and nostalgia.

IMC IN ACTION

Saturn Drives Customer Bonding

Saturn was a star in the General Motors stable because it managed to escape the stodgy GM image by setting itself up as a separate brand with a strong customer relationship position. It's un-carlike advertising used folksiness based on real stories of customers and employees that were appealing to Saturn's primarily female target audience.

Hal Riney & Partners' initial marketing communication program built an image of a caring car company offering personalized customer service and respectful dealer sales tactics. Annual owner surveys from J. D. Power and Associates backed up the positive customer-service claims. In 1994, to celebrate its first five years, the well-publicized Saturn Homecoming brought 44,000 people to Spring Hill, Tennessee, to meet other owners, as well as the people who had built their cars.

The Riney strategy was to turn the Saturn brand and its fairly mediocre design—*Advertising Age* columnist, Bob Garfield, described the car as "a brown shoe on wheels with the performance profile of an anvil and the sex appeal of yeast"—into a brand community of average people who proudly wore their loyalty as "a badge of inconspicuous consumption." Garfield explained that the ads "turned mediocrity into a brand benefit by focusing on the iconoclastic new corporation wholly in sync with the target buyers' Kumbaya mentality. It was a bravely different company selling to a bravely unsuperficial audience and everybody involved was a hero."

But time passes and philosophies change. So in 2002, GM pulled the Saturn brand inside the corporate fold and moved away from the Hal Riney agency and the advertising that had made the fairly average car seem outstanding. The account was awarded to Goodby, Silverstein & Partners, a well-respected creative agency. Goodby's assignment was to create a new brand anthem that would build on the Saturn's reputation and then move into campaigns for new Saturn lines, such as the L-Series and the Ion.

Goodby's brand strategy focused on people without cars to dramatize the idea that Saturn isn't about cars, it's about people. The branding ads show a montage of streets and parking lights and people walking or pretending to drive. A guy in one shot is shown backing out of his driveway, on foot. The voiceover explains: "When we design cars, we don't see sheet metal. We see the people who may someday drive them." Jamie Barrett, creative director at Goodby, explained that not showing the car wasn't a gratuitous trick but rather was a powerful expression of the idea that Saturn puts people first.

As Bob Garfield explained in his critique of the brand ads, the strategy is pre-emptive in that any car company could make that claim. However, Saturn has more credibility than most car companies, given the car's customer-focused legacy. Garfield called the branding commercial "a work of genuine genius."

Source: Jean Halliday, "Goodby creates car ads without the car," *Advertising Age*, August 13, 2002, p. 15; Bob Garfield, "Saturn drivers more like zeros than heroes in new campaign," *Advertising Age*, April 22, 2002, p. 65; Bob Garfield, "Aiming for a wider audience, Saturn makes a right turn," *Advertising Age*, August 19, 2002, p. 33. Reprinted with permission. Copyright, Crain Communications 2002.

- *Association:* An **association strategy** *makes a psychological connection between a brand (its attributes or image characteristics) and its customers and prospects.* Celebrities, for example, are associated with a brand because they lend their glamour to the product and to the user.

- *Lifestyle:* A **lifestyle strategy** is *a type of association strategy that uses situations and symbols of lifestyles that the target audience can identify with or aspire to.* This selling strategy, in which the situation "strikes a chord" or resonates, is used with highly competitive product categories with little differentiation, such as apparel, that rely primarily on images to transform the product into a distinctive brand (see Exhibit 9-7).

EXHIBIT 9-7

Lifestyle messages use an association strategy that links a brand with a way of life, a situation, or a place—in this case, a Caribbean or island lifestyle.

- *Incentive:* An **incentive strategy** is *a selling strategy that creates a sense of immediacy and rewards customers for responding quickly.* It is used in product situations where a quick bump in sales is desired, and as a defensive reaction to counter a competitor's strategy. Sampling and sales promotions, such as AOL's CD mailers offering free hours and price discounts, are a type of incentive.

- *Reminder:* A **reminder strategy** *keeps a brand top-of-mind with the target.* It is used with mature brands that have an established brand identity, and it is designed to jog the customer's memory at a point of purchase. Most of the classic Coca-Cola advertising is not focused on attributes or features but rather is designed to keep the Coke brand top-of-mind.

- *Interactive:* The **interactive strategy** is *creating two-way communication in order to open up communication with customers and capture their feedback.* This strategy is used with any product when it makes sense for customers to contact a company.

How do MC managers choose which strategies to use when conceptualizing a message strategy brief? First of all, they recognize that different strategies achieve different objectives. Notice the relationship between the objectives and strategies in Table 9-2, which groups strategies according to the type of consumer response that the objective is trying to elicit.

The work that goes into planning a brief comes together as a statement describing the primary messages to be delivered. Here is a summary of the message strategy for the "Make Sense of Our Times" campaign, developed by Bozell/New York for the *New York Times* after the September 11 tragedy:[13]

> Since the tragic events of September 11, there has been a significant increase in the number of people picking up *The New York Times* at the newsstand. In an effort to maintain these individuals as readers, *The Times* would like to create a campaign running inside the newspaper and entice these single-copy purchasers to keep coming back. *The New York Times'* daily coverage of events since September 11 will help readers understand the impact it has had on all of our lives.
>
> We want to connect with individuals who recently picked up the paper for the first time (or for the first time in a long time) to learn more about the circumstances surrounding the events of September 11. The situation left these people in need of true insight and thoroughness in order to gain a deeper understanding of what happened and its consequences around the world. **We want to make them feel like they'll be missing out if they don't continue to pick it up on a daily basis.**

With the message strategy brief in place, the next step is coming up with the big idea that is the hallmark of successful MC messages.

TABLE 9-2	Objectives and strategies that drive responses	
Type of Response	**Message Objectives**	**Message Strategies**
Think (cognitive)	Awareness, brand knowledge, understanding, conviction	Information, generic, pre-emptive, credibility
Feel (emotional)	Brand image and personality, liking, desire, self identify	Emotion, association, lifestyle
Do (action, behavior)	Buy, try, repeat, visit, contact, tell others	Incentive, reminder, interactive

THE BIG IDEA TAKES A CREATIVE LEAP

As the chapter opening indicates, ROI is about not only a financial return on investment but also "relevance, originality, and impact." A big creative idea is *original* because it hasn't been used before and therefore gets attention. It is *relevant* so that it can hold people's attention. And it has *impact* because it affects attitudes or behavior. Part of being original and attracting attention is being unexpected, clever, and often humorous. Consider the commercial for Osteo Bi-Flex, which shows Frankenstein looking at scenes from his old films and calling himself "a stiff." He then extols the product benefits that have helped him "loosen up."[14]

A good creative idea takes the dull language of the strategy statement and transforms it into an exciting, attention-getting, and memorable message. Consider the strategy behind the long-running "Got Milk" campaign, which is designed to remind adults that milk is good for them (see Exhibit 9-8). The big idea is to use celebrities to catch attention and build an association between successful and admired people and drinking milk.

The move from the business language of strategy to ideas that engage attention has been called the "creative leap" by advertising legend James Webb Young, founder of Young and Rubicam. It's also called **concepting,** which means *finding the creative concept that will bring a selling strategy to life.*

Concepting is a challenge. Even products that seem dull to customers deserve the investment of creative talent. Stacy Wall, a well-known copywriter and creative director, worked on Nike and other prestigious accounts before starting his own business. One of Wall's first directing tasks was for a pesticide from the FMC Corporation—not a glamorous assignment, but it gave him a chance to test his wings as a director and to prove that he could bring creativity to even the dullest of products. The campaign direction came from the not-too-exciting question "Why don't we give our corn to the rootworms?" Wall's idea was to work with other rhetorical, almost absurd, questions such as "Why don't we give our ice cream to the flies and our sidewalks to the gum?" He brought this strange and big idea to life with interpretive imagery that was as visually interesting as the idea of abandoning a sidewalk to chewing gum.[15]

The Magic of a Big Idea

The big idea synthesizes the purposes of the strategy; joins the product benefit with consumer desire in a fresh, involving way; brings the subject to life; and makes the reader or the audience stop, look, and listen. In IMC, a big idea translates the strategy into a catchy umbrella theme that unites all the various brand messages and contributes consistency to the various brand messages. That's the business person's way of explaining a creative idea.

For most creative people, getting an original idea is like magic, although it is a product of hard work in backgrounding and becoming informed about the product and its category. Generally, big ideas come to mind after you have immersed yourself in a problem until it dominates your thoughts. As John O'Toole, former president of the American Association of Advertising Agencies, has noted, big ideas are not necessarily products of thought but rather of inspiration.

The Simplicity of a Big Idea

A big idea is often one that communicates a simple idea in a simple way, like the campaign for V8 that used the theme "I can't believe I could have had a V8" accompanied by a "whack on the side of the head" gesture. David Ogilvy, a founder of the highly successful agency Ogilvy & Mather, pointed out that campaigns that

Grow Moore.

About 15% of your
height is added during your
teen years, and milk can help.
What more can you ask for?

got milk?

EXHIBIT 9-8

The "milk mustache" is the visual that represents the creative leap from the idea of reminding people about a common, well-known product.

run five years or more are the superstars; they keep on producing results and memorability because of the strength and simplicity of their big ideas. Superstar campaigns have run for Dove soap (33 percent cleansing cream), Ivory soap (99 44/100 percent pure), Perdue chickens ("It takes a tough man to make a tender chicken"), and the U.S. Army ("Be all that you can be"). Some of these campaigns have run for as long as 30 years. That's the staying power of a big idea!

An effective big idea is often one that takes a simple idea and plays it to its extreme. Nike's "Tag" commercial, for example, which won the Grand Prix at Cannes in 2002, is based on the idea of all the people in a dense urban area involving themselves in a citywide game of tag. Kash Sree, the copywriter for the "Tag" commercial, explains that the idea originated in those curious, copy-heavy print ads that instruct people on the finer details of playing various games. "It sounds really silly but we just thought, OK, let's do a TV ad off of it, and we wrote it in literally half an hour."[16]

A Good Idea Has "Legs"

When professionals say an idea has "legs," they mean that it can be used for different audiences, in different media, in different versions, and over an extended period of time. Having "legs" is particularly important in IMC, because big ideas have to stretch across several functional areas.

The big idea is usually associated with advertising, but big ideas can spring from, and are used in, other MC functional areas as well. For example, a Scandinavian campaign for Black Gold beer was unusual because of its use of a big idea for an event that would attract a younger audience and reposition the beer as hip. This particular big idea—a film noire festival, which reflected back to the beer's name—demanded both artistic vision and insight into the target audience's interest in participating in such an event.

Although a big campaign idea can come from any MC function, it is logical to search for it primarily within the MC function that is most appropriate to address or leverage the situation. Once the creative team determines what the lead MC function will be, it must select other MC functions to round out the support.

How Do You Get a Big Creative Idea?

To be effective, marketing communication has to blend rational strategy with inspired and engaging creative ideas. A leading creative person puts it this way: "We always celebrate the intuitive right side of the brain, but the analytical left side is just as important. After all, great advertising isn't about creativity for its own sake. It has to work."[17]

Inspired big ideas are the product of creative thinking. To *create* means to originate—to conceive a thing or idea that did not exist before. Typically, creative thinking involves taking two or more previously unconnected objects or ideas and combining or arranging them to form something new (see Exhibit 9-9).

Where does creativity come from? Can it be developed? Is it a gift that only special people have? Although most people believe that creativity springs directly from human intuition, creativity is very much a way of thinking that can be learned or at least strengthened. Some people exhibit more creativity than others, but creativity lives within all of us. If humans weren't creative as a species, we wouldn't have discovered how to harness fire, domesticate animals, irrigate fields, or manufacture tools. And as individuals, we use our natural creativity every time we select clothes from out of the wardrobe in the morning, contrive an excuse, cook a meal, or choose a costume for a party.

> ". . . great advertising isn't about creativity for its own sake. It has to work."
>
> Linda Kaplan Thaler,
> president of her own agency

FairytaleClassic

EXHIBIT 9-9

What makes a classic shoe? A glass slipper? A running shoe that has been around forever? Reebok uses the juxtaposition of a well-loved running shoe with Cinderella's glass slipper to bring a novel twist to the concept of a classic.

Getting started is the hardest part. Kara Goodrich, creative director at the Arnold agency in Boston, says that she starts with the brief and goes "directly to the part that says 'point of the ad.' It's not that I don't find research useful—it's just that I don't need to pore through tons of it." She looks for what she calls "the cogent points." She explains that she's a believer in intuitive thinking. "I believe that a lot of people in the ad business are smart people to begin with—and they have a pretty good working knowledge of a lot of things, including all kinds of trivia. " But getting a great creative idea also involves more than research and information. She says, "a lot of the skill in what we do involves empathy—so it's not so much a matter of reading research on parents as empathizing with being a parent."[18]

In business, the **creative process** is recognized as *a formal procedure for increasing productivity and innovative output by an individual or a group.* It is used to get ideas and solve problems. Individuals responsible for creating ads, packages, sales promotions, websites, and news releases use various approaches in the development of new ideas. Whatever specific approach you use to get a new idea, the creative process has a fairly predictable set of steps: exploration, insight, execution, and evaluation. Let's look at each step in turn.

Exploration

In the exploration stage, copywriters and art directors begin by assembling the raw materials from which ideas emerge—facts, experiences, history, knowledge, and feelings, plus all the information gathered in the review of the marketing situation that is summarized in the message strategy brief. Brainstorming is useful at this stage. **Brainstorming** is *a formal process in which a small group gathers together for the purpose of generating a multitude of new ideas.* The goal is to record any inspiration that comes into anyone's mind, allowing each new idea an opportunity to stimulate other people's thoughts. Brainstorming is like a series of mini-explosions. One person's idea leads someone else to think of something else.

Brainstorming was developed many years ago by Alex Osborn, one of the founders of the BBDO agency. Although designed as a group activity, the technique can be used in creative teams, usually the copywriter and art director, or even by one person working alone. Arnold's creative director Kara Goodrich explains: "I need to be alone for the vast majority of the time when I am concepting." She works alone until she has some ideas that she is ready to share with her partner. Then they bring their ideas together and sift out the best.

At the exploration stage, quantity is more important than quality. A basic principle of brainstorming is to get as many ideas on the table as possible, because any one idea may ignite someone else's thinking. Another principle is to not be judgmental while discussing ideas. Every idea is valuable because it stokes the creative fire. Evaluation comes later.

According to Sally Hogshead, an agency creative director, the best work comes only if brainstorming produces a lot of ideas. According to her, "If you're lucky, you draw up 100 ideas internally for every 20 that go to the client. You present 20 to the client for every five that get produced. You produce five decent ideas for every one that's great. If you're lucky."

Another exploration approach is based on **lateral thinking,** which means *bouncing from one thought to another in free association.*[19] Playing with metaphors is a good way to jump-start lateral thinking. Ask yourself, "What is this product like?" And then, like a dog digging for a bone, search for the craziest possible metaphors. That's how the long-running Absolut Vodka campaign has kept itself fresh. The shape of the bottle, used as a visual metaphor, has been compared to everything from high-rise buildings to freeways.

Edward De Bono, an expert on creativity, has described his method of getting ideas as the Six Hats (see Table 9-3). In De Bono's workshops, people are assigned a hat to wear and are asked to respond to a creative problem using the viewpoint that the hat represents.[20]

Whichever creative thinking technique is used, the aha! experience that comes from lighting on a great idea is similar to the way a compelling idea ignites a thought in a customer's mind. In both cases, something magical happens as the idea takes on a life of its own. Creativity expert Roger Von Oech describes it as "a whack on the side of the head."[21]

During the exploration stage, you hope for inspiration. Some people take a walk through shops, thumb through magazines, or look at award show books. Kara Goodrich says she looks at other people's work, not for specific ideas but rather "at how they solved a problem, their thought process." She goes on to say that "you might be able to apply the way they thought about their problem to the way you're thinking about your problem. It can sometimes help to jar you, creatively."[22]

Insight

In the second step of the creative process, insights are extrapolated through the tedious task of reviewing all the pertinent information, analyzing the problem, identifying patterns, and searching for a key verbal or visual concept to communicate

---

TABLE 9-3   De Bono's Six Hats

White hat: Facts, data, and information. "What info do we have? What is missing? What information would we like to have? How can we get it?"

Red hat: Feelings, intuitions, hunches, emotions, and gut feelings. "Here's how I feel . . . ."

Yellow hat: Optimism, the logical positive view of things; focus on benefits. "This might work if . . . ; The benefit would come from . . . ."

Green hat: New ideas, alternatives, possibilities. "We need some new ideas here— are there any other alternatives? Could we do this in a different way? Is there another explanation?"

Blue hat: Analysis of the process being used, priorities, agendas. "We have spent too much time looking for something/one to blame; Let's figure out the priorities; Let's try some green-hat thinking to get some more new ideas."

Black hat: Cautions and critical judgements. "The regulations say . . . ; When we did it before . . . ; It would be a mistake to . . . ."

Source: From SIX THINKING HATS by Edward De Bono. Copyright © 1985, 1999 by MICA Management Resources, Inc. By permission of Little, Brown and Company, (Inc.).

what needs to be said. This is the stage at which the search for the big idea—that flash of insight—takes place. It may come all at once, but sometimes it doesn't come until the creative team lets the information stew and simmer for a while.

Techniques that creative people use to stimulate this insight include the following:

- Changing patterns—unexpected juxtaposition.
- Looking at things in different ways—making the strange familiar, and the familiar strange.
- Adaptation—changing the context.
- Imagining—asking "What if?"
- Reversal—looking for the opposite.
- Connection—joining two unrelated ideas.
- Comparison—building a metaphor.
- Elimination—subtracting something or breaking rules.
- Parody—fooling around, making fun of something, looking for the humor.

An example of how a twist can be applied to an otherwise routine idea is the Visa campaign that features well-known people in predictable situations. The Bob Dole commercial—a Super Bowl favorite and a Cannes International Advertising Festival winner—showed the former senator and (unsuccessful) presidential candidate returning home to Kansas, where he is known to everyone as "Bob." His rousing welcome turns sour when a local store owner refuses to accept his check without an ID. With deadpan humor, Dole quips, "I just can't win." In another commercial, actor and New Age spiritual writer Shirley MacLaine, too, is asked to show ID, even though the cashier claims to have known her in past lives.

Execution

In the third step of the creative process, the creative team focuses on the execution of the idea, which is sometimes as important as the idea itself. To get a sense of the importance of message execution (the subject of Chapter 10), consider the ads in Exhibit 9-10.

> "How well you sell ideas is as important as how good those ideas are."
>
> Bruce Bendinger, *The Copy Workshop*

One aspect of execution that MC managers don't always think much about is presentation—the selling of ideas. Ideas don't sell themselves; how they deliver on the strategy has to be explained. In a workbook for copywriters, Bruce Bendinger says, "How well you sell ideas is as important as how good those ideas are."[23] To get the big idea approved, creative people may have to convince not only the client but others within the agency. Winning over the members of the agency account team, for example, can turn them into valuable partners in the presentation to the client. Developing a creative strategy that clearly delivers on the message strategy brief, as well as on the overall marketing communication strategy, will always help.

Evaluation and Copytesting

In the last step of the creative process, creative people use both judgment and research to evaluate their big ideas. In part, the evaluation is based on the intuition of professionals who serve as creative directors or on an agency's in-house review board. Here is how the creative director of the award-winning *New York Times* "Makes Sense of Our Times" campaign pushed his creative team: "The guys sweated blood on this . . . They [would] keep coming up with ideas and I [would]

just keep sending it back, sending it back. It's difficult, it's really, really difficult." His point is that a great idea is difficult to find and shape. "It's much harder to come up with a great idea. It takes more time. It's harder to create, and it's normally harder to sell."[24]

For clients, evaluating a big idea is almost as difficult as coming up with one. When the agency (or the advertising department in an in-house agency) presents creative concepts, the client is suddenly in the role of a judge—without having gone through the other steps in the creative process. And the problem with a truly creative idea is that no one has done it before, so it appears risky. David Ogilvy recommended that clients ask themselves five questions when evaluating new work:[25]

1. Did it make me gasp when I first saw it?
2. Do I wish I had thought of it myself?
3. Is it unique?
4. Does it fit the strategy to perfection?
5. Could it be used for 30 years?

Evaluation for big-budget MC efforts also may rely on **copytesting,** which is *testing the effectiveness of a brand message, a creative concept, or elements such as a headline, slogan, or visual for creative impact and understandability.* Testing can be conducted at all points during the development of the creative strategy and executions, and even after the completed materials are in use.

A well-known example of the use of testing to determine the power of alternative creative elements comes from John Caples, a pioneer in the direct-response area. For *Reader's Digest*, Caples determined which articles would be the most popular, both to feature in the magazine and in promotional copy, by writing small ads offering many different articles for free and placing them in a daily newspaper. Readers selected the ones they wanted, and this "vote" gave Caples information about the popularity of the article titles.

Time and money constraints mean that not every idea can be tested. Even though some agencies conduct research to test ideas, a lot of marketing communication go/no-go decisions are based on the judgment of the creative team and the client's marketing staff. They ask themselves questions such as: What's wrong/right with this idea? What if it fails? And, most important, does this idea achieve the message and MC objectives?

Creative Ideas, Ethics, and Sensitivity

Ideas that at first glance seem brilliant sometimes generate criticism for being tasteless, sexist, or racist after given a second thought. In 1999, an ad on the Super Bowl for Just for Feet showed a barefoot Kenyan runner who is tracked down by four white hunters who drug him, tag him, and release him with Nike shoes that he tries to shake off but cannot. The wild animal metaphor, which the agency undoubtedly thought was funny, was widely criticized for its insensitivity and racism.

John Eighmey, a former advertising executive who teaches at Iowa State University, wonders why no one saw the offensiveness. He observes that advertising ideas have many possible starting points as well as reviewers—the writer, art director, account person, or the client. "But somewhere along the way at Saatchi & Saatchi [or the client, or the network], someone should have said, 'Time out.'" He concludes, "Advertising is about truth. It is about the relationship between a company and its customers." From a bigger perspective, he says, "As a dominant form of voice in American culture, it should be about the expression of values and aspirations that move us ahead."[26]

Great creative ideas should be culturally sensitive in order to add to the integrity of the brand, rather than tarnish it. In recognition of that responsibility, the American Association of Advertising Agencies adopted a standards of practice that include a Creative Code. In addition to insensitivity, the code also forbids misleading statements and unsupported claims (see Figure 9-3).

A FINAL NOTE: THE BALANCING ACT

The real art in planning for the creative IMC message lies in balancing the big idea and the selling strategy so they work together. When the creative message overpowers the strategy, the message may be remembered but the brand identification may be forgotten. If the strategy overpowers the creative idea, the message will be dull and never get attention, let alone be remembered. "The agencies that are really great and amazing are those that have some kind of balance," said Tony Granger. "There are agencies that are too creative department–led where the insight is sometimes lacking. There are agencies that are account men–dominated that are full of boring work. The real magic comes when there's a balance."[27]

The stories we tell and remember are the ones that intersect in personal ways with our lives. Achieving that effect calls for both strategic thinking and creative thinking. Brand stories achieve it when they are based on nuggets of insight into how customers feel and think about a brand. Chapter 10 explains how creative and strategic brand stories are brought to life, and how the ideas are executed in words and visuals that grab and stick.

FIGURE 9-3

The Standards of Practice of
the American Association
of Advertising includes a
creative code.

Reprinted with permission
from The American
Association of Advertising
Agencies.

Standards of Practice of the American Association of Advertising Agencies

FIRST ADOPTED OCTOBER 16, 1924—MOST RECENTLY REVISED SEPTEMBER 18, 1990

We hold that a responsibility of advertising agencies is to be a constructive force in business.

We hold that, to discharge this responsibility, advertising agencies must recognize an obligation, not only to their clients, but to the public, the media they employ, and to each other. As a business, the advertising agency must operate within the framework of competition. It is recognized that keen and vigorous competition, honestly conducted, is necessary to the growth and the health of American business. However, unethical competitive practices in the advertising agency business lead to financial waste, dilution of service, diversion of manpower, loss of prestige, and tend to weaken public confidence both in advertisements and in the institution of advertising.

We hold that the advertising agency should compete on merit and not by attempts at discrediting or disparaging a competitor agency, or its work, directly or by inference, or by circulating harmful rumors about another agency, or by making unwarranted claims of particular skill in judging or prejudging advertising copy.

To these ends, the American Association of Advertising Agencies has adopted the following *Creative Code* as being in the best interests of the public, the advertisers, the media, and the agencies themselves. The AAAA believes the Code's provisions serve as a guide to the kind of agency conduct that experience has shown to be wise, foresighted, and constructive. In accepting membership, an agency agrees to follow it.

Creative Code

We, the members of the American Association of Advertising Agencies, in addition to supporting and obeying the laws and legal regulations pertaining to advertising, undertake to extend and broaden the application of high ethical standards. Specifically, we will not knowingly create advertising that contains:

a. False or misleading statements or exaggerations, visual or verbal

b. Testimonials that do not reflect the real opinion of the individual(s) involved

c. Price claims that are misleading

d. Claims insufficiently supported or that distort the true meaning or practicable application of statements made by professional or scientific authority

e. Statements, suggestions, or pictures offensive to public decency or minority segments of the population.

We recognize that there are areas that are subject to honestly different interpretations and judgment. Nevertheless, we agree not to recommend to an advertiser, and to discourage the use of, advertising that is in poor or questionable taste or that is deliberately irritating through aural or visual content or presentation.

Comparative advertising shall be governed by the same standards of truthfulness, claim substantiation, tastefulness, etc., as apply to other types of advertising.

These Standards of Practice of the American Association of Advertising Agencies come from the belief that sound and ethical practice is good business. Confidence and respect are indispensable to success in a business embracing the many intangibles of agency service and involving relationships so dependent upon good faith.

Clear and willful violations of these Standards of Practice may be referred to the Board of Directors of the American Association of Advertising Agencies for appropriate action, including possible annulment of membership as provided by Article IV, Section 5, of the Constitution and By-Laws.

Copyright 1990
American Association of Advertising Agencies

Key Terms

account planning 285
appeal 279
association strategy 289
benefit 286
brainstorming 294
concepting 291

copytesting 297
creative process 294
credibility strategy 288
customer insight 284
emotional strategy 288
features 287

generic strategy 288
incentive strategy 290
informational strategy 288
interactive strategy 290
lateral thinking 295
lifestyle strategy 289

Key Point Summary

pressure-treated redwood:
$715

radial saw:
$320

15 boxes of nails:
$40

always knowing where your kids are:
priceless

©2001 MasterCard International Incorporated

Wouldn't it be great if you could build their college and first apartment in your backyard too?
We'll get you $10 off any purchase of $50 or more at outdoordecor.com when you use MasterCard.®
Sign up with MasterCard Exclusives Online™ at mastercard.com

there are some things money can't buy. **MasterCard**. for everything else there's MasterCard.™

EXHIBIT 9-11

*Another magical moment
in the long-running
MasterCard "Priceless"
campaign.*

Key Point 1: A Creative Message Strategy

A message strategy is an idea about how to creatively and persuasively communicate a brand message to a target audience. It is generally a blend of rational and emotional thinking that connects with members of a target audience in a creative way because it is relevant to them.

Key Point 2: The Message Strategy Brief

The IMC message strategy brief is developed by determining 1) communication objectives, 2) insights about customers, and 3) selling strategies.

Key Point 3: The Creative Process

The creative process is a four-step procedure that people use to discover original ideas: (1) exploration, understanding all the background information and research findings; (2) insight, using the background information and research to create a big idea; (3) execution, taking the big idea into all the various brand messages and producing MC pieces; and (4) evaluation, stepping back and considering whether the big idea is on target.

Lessons Learned

Key Point 1: A Creative Message Strategy

a. What is a message strategy? How is a message strategy used in marketing communication?
b. Why is relevance an important dimension of a creative message strategy?
c. What is an appeal? Choose one of the ads in this chapter or in earlier chapters, and explain its appeal strategy.
d. Why does a message strategy need to be creative?

Key Point 2: The Message Strategy Brief

a. What are the three main steps in developing a message strategy brief?
b. Study the seven agency briefs in Table 9-1. What elements appear most consistently in them? What elements appear infrequently? If you were asked to develop your own outline for a message strategy brief, what would you include?
c. What is a key customer insight? Give an example of what customer insights contribute to the development of message strategy.
d. Find an example in ads elsewhere in this book of a claim, a benefit statement, a reason why, and a USP. Explain the logic behind each one.
e. Write the benefit statements for one of the ads that you like from this chapter. Use the following formula: If I use _____(product)_____, I will _____(benefit)_____ because _____(support)_____.
f. How does the MasterCard story in the opening case exemplify a message strategy brief? Analyze the "Treehouse" ad (see Exhibit 9-11) in the MasterCard "Priceless" campaign, and construct a message strategy brief for it.

Key Point 3: The Creative Process

a. Define *creativity*. What are the key characteristics of creativity?
b. What are the four steps of the creative process? Describe an experience you have had in coming up with a creative idea. How was your experience similar to or different from the process described in this chapter?
c. Set up a brainstorming session with some of your friends. Ask them to come up with a new idea for an Absolut ad. Experiment with the brainstorming techniques. Which approach generated the most ideas?

d. Find a marketing communication execution that you believe is highly creative and a similar one for a related product that you feel isn't creative. Critique both pieces, and give reasons for your evaluation. Are both on strategy as best you can figure out from the message you see expressed in the materials?

Chapter Challenge

Writing Assignment

Find an article in the trade press that describes a new marketing communication campaign or program. Critique the message strategy, using the information given in the article. What is missing? If you were working on this account as a planner, how would you develop the message strategy brief? Write a memo to your instructor describing the approach you would take.

Presentation Assignment

Collect all the MC materials you can find for one of your favorite brands; then re-create what you believe the message strategy brief is for this brand. Analyze the creative idea. Is it a big idea that both grabs and sticks? Is the creative idea on strategy?

Internet Assignment

Look up the website for any of the brands mentioned in this chapter. Find a site that presents the company's brand strategy. Summarize what you find there in terms of the message strategy decisions, and explain how that strategy is made visible on the website.

Chapter

10 Message Execution

The 845 Stripe. For higher, longer shots. *Tommy Armour*

Key Points in This Chapter

1. How are brand-message executions planned?
2. How is copy written for MC messages?
3. What is art direction, and what is its role in MC messages?
4. Why is message consistency important?

Chapter Perspective

Telling a Brand Story

Why is Nike such a strong brand? Nike's brand story is known around the world. Peak performance—that's the essence of the Nike brand and the underlying aspiration of Nike customers. The idea comes to life in any number of executions that show athletic superstars nailing the race, the basket, the home run, the hole in one.

A strong brand has a good story; brand communication is all about the telling of the story. The stories we tell and remember are the ones that intersect in personal ways with our lives. Brand stories do that when they are based on nuggets of insight into how customers feel and think about a brand. Figuring that out is the role of the strategies that you read about in Chapter 9. The *execu-*

tion of a strategy is the presentation of those insights in stories that ring true with the target audience.

There are essentially two sets of decisions to make in executing a brand message: what elements to use in the brand story and how to structure those elements. The execution elements include all the bits and bytes of a brand message—the words, the sounds and music, the photos and illustrations, the costumes and settings, the lighting—all the many physical details of a production. The structure is the way these elements are combined—the layout, the flow, the form of the message—how everything comes together to deliver the story.

A SWEET ROMANCE
Bates Advertising, Auckland, New Zealand

Arnott's is an Australian biscuit (cookie) and cracker manufacturer that has successfully expanded its market to many areas of the Pacific region. In neighboring New Zealand, however, Arnott's was seen as an "Aussie interloper" and was having a tough time competing against locally entrenched New Zealand brands. If you were assigned to develop a meaningful relationship between Arnott's and current and potential customers in New Zealand, what would you recommend? That was the challenge given to Auckland's Bates Advertising, which created a moving, award-winning campaign for Arnott's. Using IMC, a great creative idea, and an engaging story, Bates was able to involve New Zealand consumers with the brand in an emotional way.

The Marketing Situation

Arnott's had been in the New Zealand marketplace since 1983 and by the early 1990s had nearly a 30 percent market share. However, by the mid-1990s, growth had begun to stagnate. Increased competition for shelf space was threatening the profitability and market share of established brands.

EXHIBIT 10-1

Arnott's developed a romantic lead character, Michael, to appeal to its largely female target audience. The creative idea demonstrates the need for and power of a special relationship.

The biscuit category is characterized by low consumer loyalty. Focus-group research found that consumers had a large repertoire of favorite brands and saw few points of difference among the product offerings.

In addition to the core consumer target market, which Arnott's identified as household shoppers aged 18 to 49 with children, the brand also needed to focus attention on the retail trade target. Competitor Griffin's had come to own the category's primary values (warmth, approachability, trust, caring, everydayness, and friendliness). Arnott's had a perception problem. The company's own research found that the brand was seen as cold and inaccessible and thus at odds with the overall "warmth" of the biscuit category.

Message Strategy and Execution

Bates decided that the message strategy for Arnott's was to create an emotional connection to the brand. The communication objectives were (1) to improve the brand positioning on key biscuit values (caring and friendly); (2) to increase perceptions of the brand's modernity, quality, and relevance to New Zealand; and (3) to increase trust with the business-to-business audience.

Arnott's was a brand looking for a relationship with the New Zealand consumer. The big idea was to create soap-opera format commercials that featured Michael, an attractive young man, and his search for a meaningful relationship. For two years, the entwined stories of Michael and the Arnott's brand unfolded in the style of a long-running television series, an approach very different from traditional marketing communication in this category. Together Arnott's and Michael won the hearts of New Zealanders.

Bates introduced Michael to the target audience in a lonely-hearts advertisement. In the commercials, his words struck a chord with New Zealand women, thousands of whom responded to his plea for "old-fashioned love." As the campaign evolved, New Zealanders joined Michael in his search for happiness. Arnott's products were featured as integral components of each commercial, providing occasions for meeting and sharing.

The series had three phases. The first phase focused on Michael's experiences as he dated the array of women who answered his advertisement, the second on the development of a significant relationship, and the third on its outcome. The third phase used an interactive approach that involved customers in the campaign. Arnott's biscuits were at the heart of every commercial episode.

In the second phase of the series, Michael bumps into his perfect match in the supermarket parking lot. Not only does he get her name—Jessica—but he also manages to get her phone number. Their relationship begins. During the ensuing episodes, Michael falls hopelessly in love. But for Jessica, Michael's ardor is too much, too soon. Like most divorced women living in the modern world, she has a lot to juggle: her commitment to her son Billy, the challenges and opportunities of her career, and the possibilities that a more independent life can bring. There's also Billy's dad—how does he fit into all of this? Phase two concludes with a cliffhanger: Jessica's ex turns up at the local park, and tension mounts as Jessica seems to be following Billy straight back to his daddy's arms.

The conclusion used an innovative interactive television commercial that allowed viewers to vote on Michael's fate. They were offered four possible conclusions to Michael's search for old-fashioned love:

1. Jessica returns to Billy's dad.
2. Jessica chooses neither man.
3. Michael wakes up to discover that the whole thing was a dream.
4. Jessica chooses Michael, and the two get married and live happily ever after.

These alternative scenarios were launched on television, and the voting forms were available on point-of-sale posters and in magazines. A combination of public relations and an "advertorial" in a women's magazine then took over to build further interest in the outcome.

The winner: a wedding! More than 15,500 consumers participated in this campaign by voting for one of the options. The greatest number of votes was tallied for the wedding. And in a break from convention, Arnott's announced and staged the wedding in a joint venture with the women's weekly magazine. A front cover and an "editorialized" photo spread reported on the event. The wedding took on a life of its own, as New Zealand consumers identified with the fictional Michael and Jessica.

Evaluation of the Arnott's Campaign

This highly successful campaign stopped Arnott's share-of-market erosion and changed consumers' perceptions of the brand. Results show that in the space of two years, Arnott's moved from being a brand without meaning or relevance to the New Zealand consumer to being a favorite brand, closing the "preference gap" between itself and competitor Griffin's. Even more important, Arnott's protected its market share while at the same time increasing its average price to 10 percent above the category average. Finally, as an unusual test of its emotional strength, the campaign was voted "Most Romantic" television commercial by the Romance Writers Guild.

Source: This case was adapted with permission from the Advertising and Marketing Effectiveness (AME) award-winning brief for Arnott's prepared by Bates Advertising agency in Auckland, New Zealand.

BRAND-MESSAGE EXECUTIONS

For Arnott's, the integrated campaign told the story of a meaningful relationship and built a caring image for the brand. The strategy of building an emotional connection was executed by using a soap-opera format, attractive stars, an involving brand interaction, and a classic sweet ending. All those executional decisions made the creative idea—romantic "cookie moments"—an award-winning and effective MC campaign.

A big part of the magic of a great idea lies in the way it is executed—and a big part of execution involves creating the right image (see Exhibit 10-2). A **message execution** is *the format of a completed MC message, such as an advertisement, brochure, or package label.* There is no magic formula for producing good message executions.

EXHIBIT 10-2
The rough style of the type, the outdoorsy visuals, and the survival attitude of the message all work together to create an image for the state of Nevada.

Five decision areas are key for people on the creative side of marketing communication—writers, designers, and producers—as they seek to bring a big idea alive in an attention-getting and memorable message:

- Message storytelling
- Tone and style
- Words (copywriting)
- Pictures (art direction)
- Consistency

Message Storytelling

The Arnott's campaign works because it tells an involving and fun story. As Bob St. Julian, managing director of the Lowe Hunt[1] agency explains, "To be remembered you have to create wonderful advertising that people love. It doesn't matter how strategically sound your ad is if you can't stand out. No one is going to notice your very well-researched, correct message. Don't just settle for ticking the boxes on the brief."

The first step in the execution of a brand message is to identify the best way to present the message or tell the brand's story. Experienced creative people look for the technique and style with the greatest persuasive appeal for the idea being presented.

For example, Gateway launched its Profile PC by going head-to-head with rival Apple in a comparative advertising story. Gateway's ads show the Profile PC alongside Apple's iMac, associating the new Profile with iMac's breakthrough design. Gateway used the slogan "Think Smarter," a takeoff on Apple's "Think Different" slogan. Making a direct comparison with a rival is always risky, but Gateway is betting that its advantages in performance, software selection, and price will outweigh the dangers of promoting a competitor.[2]

Execution strategies may be described, in a general way, as either lectures or dramas, which correspond to the head and heart approaches. Execution strategy specifies the format or approach to be used to tell the brand story. Some message formats are referred to as "formulas" because they are frequently used. The following list describes common message story formats:

1. *News announcement:* Uses a straightforward, factual presentation and emphasizes a news angle; used for press releases in publicity and as a straight-sell approach in advertising that emphasizes an appeal to reason; useful for new products or products with a new formulation or use. *Example:* Colgate Total (see Exhibit 9-5).

2. *Inherent drama:* Finds a characteristic of a brand that can be dramatized in storytelling or mythmaking that sets the brand apart from competitors; used in categories with little product differentiation. *Example:* Metro Transit (see Exhibit 6-9).

3. *Testimonial/endorsement:* Uses celebrities, experts, or typical users to deliver a message endorsing a product; used in categories where there is product differentiation or where credibility is important (see Exhibit 6-5). Endorsements can work if the person or group is right for the product. Research supports the power of Oprah Winfrey or *Consumer Reports* to make people who have no opinion of a product suddenly see it as top of the line.[3] *Example:* Luxuryfinder.com.

4. *Talking head:* Lets a spokesperson tell a story in his or her own words using dialogue, monologue, or interview techniques; generally found in low budget TV and radio commercials. *Example:* Coopers & Lybrand (see Exhibit 10-7).

5. *Lifestyle:* Focuses on associations, particularly those related to the life of the user; for example, beer and soft-drink advertisers like Mountain Dew frequently target their messages to active, outdoorsy young people, focusing on who drinks the brand rather than on specific product advantages. *Example:* Arizona jeans.

6. *Problem/solution:* Identifies a problem that the product can solve—often the premise of "soap opera" commercials; used to dramatize product differentiation and entertain at the same time. *Example:* Verizon TV commercials—"Can you hear me now?"

7. *Demonstration:* Invites audience members to believe the evidence of their own eyes; for highly persuasive communication, "Don't just say it, show it"; used with products that have a demonstrable point of difference. *Example:* 3M (see Exhibit 9-6).

8. *Comparison:* Where the objective is to showcase a competitive advantage, then a comparative approach may be used, which names the competitor and proves

that the sponsoring brand performs better in some kind of test. *Example:* the classic "Pepsi challenge" campaign showing people preferring Pepsi in a blind taste test.

9. *Picture caption:* In print, this tells a story with illustrations and captions; particularly useful for products that have a number of different uses or come in a variety of styles or designs; a comic-strip panel approach also can deliver this type of story. *Example:* Crest Whitestrips (see Exhibit 10-3).

10. *Jingle:* Uses music and catchy words to entertain and remind the audience of brand values (see IMC in Action: Hijacking the Soundtrack of Our Lives, later in this chapter); used for products with little product differentiation and for brand-image messages; an old maxim in advertising is "If you can't say it, sing it."

11. *Humor:* Entertains, dispels negative images, and creates a fun, likable personality for undifferentiated products. Note: Humor is subjective and can distract from the product; it should be used with caution—watch for issues of questionable taste. *Example:* Great Indoors (see Exhibit 7-4).

12. *Animation/cartoons:* Uses drawings, puppets, and claymation characters (made of clay but filmed like puppets, movement by movement) for their entertainment value as well as for communicating difficult messages and reaching specialized markets. *Example:* Snapple (see Exhibit 6-10).

Because using one of those common formats produces a predictable message, some creative people start with an idea for one format and then twist the idea into something that unexpectedly violates or parodies the format. That's one way to take a predictable idea and turn it into a creative one through the execution.

Alex Bogusky, creative partner at Miami's Crispin Porter + Bogusky, described the success of his agency's "Truth" campaign for the antismoking Legacy Foundation as a "fresh, guerrilla-like feel that was quite unlike anything else around."[4] The ads are targeted at young people in the 18 to 24 age group and appeal to their skepticism about big business and adults who tell them what to do. In one soap-opera-ish commercial called "Secrets of a Tobacco Executive," on-screen words reveal that "He had a terrible secret," and viewers see the executive's daughter confronting him and hostile neighbors pounding on his car. The secret is revealed at the end when he is seen addressing a group of fellow tobacco executives about targeting young people because they are the industry's future.[5] In another commercial, one that won many awards, a documentary style shows body bags being dumped on the New York street in front of Philip Morris headquarters, and a tag line says, "Every day 1,200 people die from tobacco."

Tone and Style

In marketing communication, **tone** refers to the *general atmosphere or manner of expression.* The tone is a cue about the nature of the message and the personality of the brand. Tone of voice—businesslike, solemn, angry, happy, cheering, fearful, sympathetic, frustrated—signals the appropriate emotional response. The ad in Exhibit 3-5, for example, uses a threatening tone for the familiar line "We never

EXHIBIT 10-3

The "Whiten while you . . ." line communicates the idea that teeth whitening is easy and can be done anytime. The use of the three panels demonstrates the daily activities that can be conducted as you are whitening your teeth.

WHITEN WHILE YOU...

WHITEN WHILE YOU...

WHITEN WHILE YOU...

EASY, HUH?

YOU DON'T HAVE TO MAKE TIME TO WHITEN YOUR TEETH. YOU'VE ALREADY GOT THE TIME—WITH CREST WHITESTRIPS. THEY WORK ANYTIME WHILE YOU DO ALMOST ANYTHING. JUST THIRTY MINUTES TWICE A DAY FOR TWO WEEKS. YOU EVEN WHILE READING THIS MAGAZINE. SIMPLY BEAUTIFUL.

REVEAL YOUR WHITER SMILE.

promised you a rose garden" to dramatize the tough-guy mentality of the United States Marines. Tone can also imply conversation—an important dimension of relationship-focused communication.

The personality of the brand speaks through the planned messages, but the style of the language also signals the target audience. Ads with an "attitude," for example, are frequently targeted to young people, particularly the Generation X group, presumed to be anti-advertising. The tone surrounds the message and sets up audience expectations about the brand relationship.

Something to remember when setting the tone of a brand message is that the typical marketing language of the strategy statements is rarely appropriate for a consumer audience. In *Creative Advertising*, Sandra Moriarty warns against "strategy hypnosis."[6] She says that creative people have to understand the strategy, then move beyond it.

Some styles—pedantry, preachiness, and pomposity—don't work very well in marketing communication. Creative teams also try to avoid messages using the corporate "we" when it occurs in so-called brag-and-boast approaches. Negative messages, particularly those that patronize or put down the audience, are also ineffective. Another problem is insensitive or stereotyped images, such as those discussed in the Ethics and Issues box.

The Diesel and Club 18-30 Holiday ads discussed in the Ethics and Issues box also used humor as part of their message strategy. They demonstrate message designers' greatest problem with humor: it is tricky to use—what is funny to one person may not be funny to another. And if it fails as humor, then it tends to fail as a message.

Another problem with humor is that if it succeeds it may steal attention away from the product. A "Blondie" comic strip, for example, shows Dagwood laughing his head off about a commercial. He goes through a long explanation of the story line until Blondie asks him what the commercial was about. Dagwood responds: "I don't think they said." Marketers can think of numerous examples of humorous commercials that people can remember even though they can't remember the product.

Humor can also be insensitive. A Metamucil fiber supplement ad shows a National Park Service ranger pouring a glass of Metamucil into Old Faithful at Yellowstone National Park and announcing that the product is what keeps the famous geyser "regular." The creative team thought the idea was so outrageously funny that everyone would see the humor. The Yellowstone park superintendent, however, complained that the ad undermines National Park Service efforts to discourage people from putting any foreign objects into geysers.[7]

Slang is another problem when targeting a younger audience. Remember "ill" or "sick" for *good*; "phat," which became "that's butter"; or "that's gravy" for *luscious, rich,* or *big*?[8] It is hard for ad folks—even if they are young—to get the nuances right when using slang in a commercial, but the biggest problem is that teen and urban street slang changes so fast that it is often out-of-date by the time the commercial is produced and runs.

Should humor and slang be avoided? Both can be appropriate if used with sensitivity and tested carefully. Budweiser made slang work with its "Whassup?" line. Humor, in particular, scores well with audiences when they like the joke and can remember the brand. The search for funny ideas, as *New York Times* advertising columnist Stuart Elliott observes, "is indicative of the increasing role that humor plays in advertising for routine products and services because of its ability to reach skeptical, jaded consumers who may be turned off by more hard-selling tactics."[9]

The Synergy of Words and Pictures

Words and pictures play different roles in the logic of a brand message. Pictures— or, more broadly, *visuals*—are usually designed to catch attention and to move the reader into the copy. To get the point of the ad in Exhibit 10-4, you have to read the

ETHICS AND ISSUES

Is It Fun, Tasteless, or over the Top?

Reaching a youthful audience is not easy for middle-class, middle-aged MC executives. Consequently the brand messages targeted to this group are turned over to young creative people who can talk the language of the target market. But sometimes these people, who may be right on target in terms of the tone of voice and attitude, may turn off folks who question the appropriateness or even the ethics of the approach. That's a problem for IMC managers aware that stakeholders overlap and that what is appropriate for one group may alienate others who see the message.

Benetton is the classic example of a company that has used provocative social statements in its messages, presumably to connect with the unorthodox views of its Gen-X and Gen-Y customers. Diesel is also well known for its outrageous and provocative imagery. Diesel's objective seems to be to position its brand as outside or beyond the predictable, and its ads turn convention upside down. In one ad, a takeoff on an old western, the good-looking young hero, who is first seen putting on his jeans, kisses his beautiful wife and cute baby good-bye. In the next scene, a grubby old nasty guy is seen waking up in bed next to an ugly woman. He sneers at her, kicks a dog on the steps outside the saloon, and generally behaves abominably. A gunfight between him and the young hero takes place in the street, and the nasty guy wins. The gunfight scene closes with him picking his nose.

In another example, a racy campaign for Club 18-30 Holidays raised eyebrows at the 2002 Cannes Film Festival, where it received the Grand Prix award. The print campaign featured pictures of vacationing young people that, on careful inspection, suggested erotic scenes. As described by one industry leader, the winning ads "cleverly but vulgarly juxtapose models to mimic sex acts, including bestiality."

The print ads were intricately composed and art-directed in order to create the illusion of the "sex plays." In one, a man on a beach blanket has both hands in the air. Behind him and facing him is a woman in a bikini. Through careful composition and the tricks of photography, it looks as though the man's hands are fondling the woman's breasts.

Supporters of the ad, created by London-based Saatchi & Saatchi, say it is clever in the way it leads its twenty-something target audience to concentrate on the ad in order to spot the visual tricks. The uproar that the ad sparked was attributed by some to differences in American and European cultures: Europeans are believed to be more open than Americans to sexual innuendo.

An Ogilvy & Mather creative director who was a member of the Cannes print jury was quoted as hating the Club 18-30 ad. She explained in a letter to the *AdAge.com* editor that, although the sexual theme is probably spot-on for the target and is a clever strategy, she felt the ad was "a cheap pee-wee joke" that didn't deserve to be titled "the best print ad in the world." And Kirk Carr, advertising director for the *Wall Street Journal* and past chairman of the Business Marketing Association, called the ad a setback for the ad business. He said, "The award helps accelerate a downward spiral in taste that alienates the public and erodes audience receptivity to all advertising."

A year earlier, a Cannes jury over which Keith Reinhard, Chairman of DDB Worldwide, had presided had disqualified an entry because of its offensive content. Reinhard had affirmed the American Association of Advertising Agencies' code with its admonition to avoid content "offensive to public decency," and he had urged judges of ad competitions to disqualify works violating these industry standards. The 2002 Cannes judges soundly rejected his advice.

Think About It

Is it okay to be offensive to broader social views if the message speaks to the interests of your target audience? If you were handing the account for Club 18-30 Holidays and your agency brought you an ad that you knew some people would feel is vulgar and tasteless, would you approve it? Is it okay to abandon any sense of responsibility for taste and decency because you think the audience will like the idea?

Source: "What's New Portfolio," *Adweek,* December 22, 1997, p. 24; Jim Hanas, "Saatchi London Sex Ads Win Cannes Grand Prix," June 18, 2002, *AdAge.com,*: <www.adage.com/news.cms?newsid=35101>; Nancy Volk, letter to the editor, "Second Lions Jury Member Slams Press Award," *adage.com,* June 26, 2002, <www.adage.com/news.cms?newsid=35128>; Kirk Carr, "The Advertising Standards We Honor," *adage.com,* <www.adage.com/news.cms?newsid=35829>.

copy. The words and the picture work together to deliver the concept.

Figure 10-1 is a hierarchy-of-effects model of creative elements. As the figure indicates, in print messages the visuals and headline attract attention. Subheads and the lead (first) paragraph of body copy spark interest. Body copy and other elaboration devices such as boxes and supporting visuals help build credibility and stimulate desire. The closing paragraph and reminder information such as slogans and tag lines at the end of the piece prompt action. The closing may sometimes include a last line that functions as a call to action—it tells the target audience what to do or gives helpful information such as where the product might be found. Other action items at the end—the logo, slogan, tag line, signature—provide brand identity and reinforce the brand position.

EXHIBIT 10-4
The angry-looking metal shavings in the visual contrast with the smooth silken surface of the shell. The point—that Dove deodorant has a moisturizer that smoothes razor-burned armpits—is clear only if the visual attracts you to read the copy.

Although it is important that the words and pictures work together in creative messages, it helps if the visual adds something to the words and the words extend the idea presented in the visual. If the visual is a literal translation of the words, the concept may be rather predictable, perhaps even boring. But a unique conjunction or juxtaposition of words and pictures results in synergy and creates a richer meaning than either element carries by itself.

COPYWRITING

Whether copywriters apply their skills to a variety of MC functions or specialize in only one, they need to understand the similarities and differences in writing for print media and writing for electronic media. Writing publicity messages (whether print or electronic) presents special challenges to copywriters.

The goal is to present the strategic idea in words that cajole and inspire—but most of all in words that get attention and linger in memory. One memorability device is a **slogan,** which is *a clever phrase that serves as a reminder of a brand, company image, or campaign theme.* A headline-getting change in slogans occurred when General Electric unplugged its long-time slogan "We bring good things to life" and moved to "Imagination at Work." In use since the late 1970s, the "good things" slogan was recognized as one of the truly great corporate slogans of modern times. Harvard professor Stephen Greyser said its strength came from its double meaning. He acknowledged that the new slogan also has a double meaning—"imagination when we are at work" and "imagination at work for

FIGURE 10-1

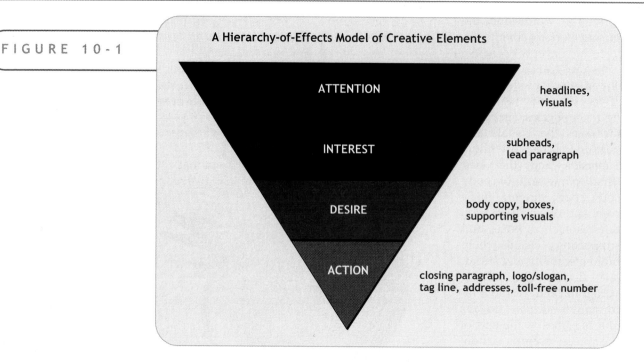

A Hierarchy-of-Effects Model of Creative Elements

you"—and said that only time will tell if the new line has the staying power of the "good things" slogan.[10]

Slogans, headlines, and other MC writing use catchy phrases. Catchy phrases are often humorous or clever. However, although humor can be desirable in copywriting, copywriters should be careful not to be *too* funny—that is, not to cross over any line that may make the ad offensive or sound too much like a punch line. Consider the following list, which appeared on the internet, of funny parodies of good slogans:

On a septic tank truck sign: "We're #1 in the #2 business."

On a plumbers' truck: "We repair what your husband fixed."

On an electrician's truck: "Let us remove your shorts."

On a maternity room door: "Push. Push. Push."

At an optometrist's office: "If you don't see what you're looking for, you've come to the right place."

In a restaurant window: "Don't stand there and be hungry. Come on in and get fed up."

At a truck stop: "Eat here and get gas."

In the front yard of a funeral home: "Drive carefully. We'll wait."

At a radiator shop: "Best place in town to take a leak."

Writing for Print

Print text is usually described as either display or body copy. **Body copy** is *the text of the brand message.* **Display copy** is *copy in a type size larger than that of the body copy and meant to entice readers into reading the body copy.* The terminology is the same for brochures and direct-mail pieces as for advertisements. In addition to the **headline,** which is *a line set in large type to get readers' attention and lead into the body copy,* other display copy includes picture captions and subheads, as well as underlines and overlines that either lead into the headline or expand on it, and slogans or tag lines that wrap up the creative idea at the end of the message. In general, the objectives in writing display copy are to grab attention, excite interest, build curiosity and get readers to spend time with the message.

To be effective, a headline must serve a set of purposes. Attracting attention is the foremost, but it must also engage the audience, explain the visual, lead the audience into the body copy, and cue the selling message. The average MC message has only a couple of seconds to capture a reader's attention. In a print piece like the Gillette ad in Exhibit 10-5, the selling premise—"Three Revolutionary Blades"—is introduced in the headline.

Ideally, headlines present a complete selling idea. Research has found that, on average, three to five times as many people read the headline as read the body

copy. So if the selling premise isn't clear in the headline, the message may be wasting the client's money. In outdoor posters or billboards, the headline is the only copy, so it has to communicate, along with the visual, the entire message. The difficulty is that the headline needs to be short and succinct. The traditional notion is that short, one-line headlines are best but a second line is acceptable. In one study of over 2,000 ads, most headlines averaged about eight words in length.[11]

Publicity writers also pay close attention to creating provocative, newsworthy headlines. The headline will determine how much attention an editor pays to the publicity release. If the editor doesn't find the headline interesting and engaging, the article is not likely to make it into print.

Finally, headlines, particularly in publicity writing, are used to showcase news. Consumers look for new products, new uses for old products, or improvements on old products. "Power words" that imply newness—such as *new, improved,* and *redesigned*—can increase readership and should be employed whenever applicable.

We're in a period of declining emphasis on copy in print ads. Copy-heavy ads are hard to find, even in newspaper ads for newspapers themselves. Tony Granger, award-winning creative director at Bozell, explains the philosophy behind the *New York Times*' "Makes Sense of Our Times" campaign. "We have a fundamental belief that people do not read print advertising any more. You don't spend time doing that." He explains, "Gone are the days when consumers waited with bated breath to read your ads. Give me the message, let me get in and out very quickly."[12]

Captions are *verbal explanations of visuals.* **Call-outs** are *mini-captions positioned around an illustration to help explain or emphasize certain elements in an illustration or picture.* Call-outs are used throughout this textbook to call attention to important quotes. In Exhibit 10-5 call-outs point to the various parts of the product—specially positioned blades, comfort edges, lubricating strip, springs, pivot design, contour grip, single-point docking, and flexible microfins.

At the end of a printed piece may be found a **tag line,** which provides either a call to action—for example, instructions on how to respond—or a slogan that serves as a brand or campaign reminder cue. A tag line is often used to summarize, in a catchy way, a campaign's big idea. The Gillette tag line in Exhibit 10-5 is "The Closest Shave in Fewer Strokes with Less Irritation." Also at the end of an ad are facilitators, which include the information that makes an inquiry or purchase easier, such as a map, a toll-free number, or an e-mail or website address. In the Gillette ad, a website address is listed: www.MACH3.com.

Brand identification information is typically showcased at the bottom of the piece, usually in a distinctive logo or a **signature** (*a distinctive way of printing the brand name*). A signature can also be a logo, as in the case of Coca-Cola, whose familiar brand name appears in all planned messages in a distinctive Spencerian script.

Writing for Electronic Media

Some of the rules that pertain to writing for print media hold true for radio and for television and other types of video. Yet electronic media have special dictates. A broadcast message, whether designed for television or radio, uses a script to outline the critical elements and the structure of the brand message. At the top of the script is information about the client and product, the title of the piece, the date, the writer's name, the length of the segment, and other identification information, such as a script number. An audio script, such as the one in Exhibit 10-6 for a radio commercial, contains the auditory descriptions that help identify the source and content of the message. Typically the source is identified on the left side in capital letters (the person speaking, music, or sound effects). The text on the right contains the dialogue.

Washington Apple Commission
Washington Apples
They're As Good As You've Heard.
C. Kram
Radio :30
WAC-3

(SFX):	a telephone rings; the cradle lifts
MAN:	(an avuncular voice) Hello.
CALLER:	Oh. I'm sorry. I was looking for another number.
MAN:	976-EDEN?
CALLER:	Well. . . yeah.
MAN:	You got it.
CALLER:	The flyer said to ask for Eve.
MAN:	Yeah, well, she's not here. I can help you.
CALLER:	Oh. . . no. That's okay. I'll just. . .
MAN:	Hold on, hold on. Let me get the apple.
CALLER:	The apple?
MAN:	You ready? Here goes. . .
(SFX):	crunch
CALLER:	That's. . . you're eating an apple. That's the "little bit of paradise" you advertised?
MAN:	Well, that's a little *bite* of paradise. The printer made a mistake.
CALLER:	I'm supposed to sit here and listen to you eat an apple?
MAN:	Well, it is a Washington Apple. . .
(SFX):	crunch
CALLER:	Look, I'm not going to pay three dollars a minute just to sit here while you. . .
MAN:	Nice, big, Red Delicious Washington Apple. . .
(SFX):	crunch
CALLER:	. . . eat an apple. . . it does sound good.
MAN:	It is nice and crisp, you know.
CALLER:	Sounds good. . .
MAN:	Kinda sweet.
CALLER:	Uh-huh. . .
MAN:	Fresh. . .
CALLER:	I shouldn't. . . this is silly. . .
(SFX):	crunch
CALLER:	What are you wearing?
MAN:	Well, a flannel shirt and paisley ascot.
CALLER:	Oh. Describe the apple again.
MAN:	Mmmm-hmmm
V.O.:	Washington Apples
(SFX):	crunch
V.O.:	They're As Good As You've Heard.

EXHIBIT 10-6
This is an example of a radio script used to guide the taping of the commercial.

Audio Copy

Radio provides entertainment and news to listeners who are generally busy doing something else—driving, washing dishes, reading the paper, or even studying. To be heard, a message must be catchy and interesting. Radio listeners usually decide within seconds if they're going to pay attention. Therefore, to attract and hold listeners' attention, radio copy must be designed to break through the clutter of other environmental stimuli. To do this, radio copy also uses recognizable sounds—such as the sound of a pop tab opening, then the sound of pouring a drink over ice—to add aural imagery to the message. But keep in mind: intrusive, yes; offensive, no. An insensitive choice of words, an overzealous effort to attract listeners with irritating sounds (car horns, alarm clocks, screeching tires), or a character that sounds too exotic, odd, or dumb can cause listener resentment and ultimately inattention.

Radio and other audio copy has to be clearer than any other kind of copy. The listener can't reread to find the antecedent of a pronoun, so what the pronoun refers to has to be immediately clear. The English language is so full of homonyms (words that sound alike) that listeners can easily confuse the meaning of a word that does not have a clear or sufficient context. Think of the confusion that can result if a listener can't tell whether a radio commercial is using *cereal* or *serial*.

One of the challenges of writing for broadcast media is making the script fit the time slot. The copywriter may type the script on a normal page and then count the lines, allowing approximately five seconds for each 80-character line. However, the delivery changes for different types of messages, so writers must read the script aloud for timing. With electronic compression, recorded radio ads can include 10 to 30 percent more copy than text that is read live.

There is more to audio than just TV and radio commercials. Think about how a company answers the phone. How does that "brand voice" differ from the voices you hear when you call its competitors? Advanced speech recognition technology is making it possible for a customer to have a personal, yet still automated, conversation with a company. Companies strive to make sure that the automated voice reflects the personality of the brand and that the voice system recognizes the emotional dimensions of conversations with customers.

If you call E*Trade's customer-service line, you may forget you're talking to a computer because the voice is so lifelike. E*Trade's voice system was designed to sound like "a man in his thirties who seems trustworthy and knowledgeable." The company recognizes that the voice delivers a powerful branding message—this is a good trading service run by reliable professionals who know all about the perils of making a stock trade.[13] E*Trade's marketing team spent hundreds of hours on creating the right nuances and inflections, because the conversation with the automated line is the closest that many customers will ever get to the company.

United Airlines has used voice branding on its customer-services line. Passengers can track down lost luggage by talking to a computer. UAL hopes that the soothing and apologetic female voice at the other end of the line—considerate, willing to stop at nothing to find customers' bags—will help repair the customer relationship damaged by the lost luggage. UAL struck exactly the right note in the flight information voice, which is so smooth and engaging that callers have asked if they can take the guy to dinner.

Music

Another type of audio element is music, which is used in both radio and television commercials, as well as in corporate videos and the "hold music" you hear when you phone a company. When music is used as a background, its purpose is to help create an emotional tone for the message. Another way music is used is in **jingles,** which are *short songs that deliver a brand story in an easy-to-sing format.* Jingles are highly memorable, and they offer copywriters a way to repeat a line in a nonirritating way.

An example of a visually interesting television commercial that uses music to sing the praises of its pants is a series of commercials for clothing retailer Gap. The "Khakis swing" ad featured Louis Prima and energetic swing dancers wearing khaki pants; the "Khakis rock" spot has skaters dancing to an electronic beat. Clearly, the copywriters who created these ads understood the power of music.

Well-known songs can be used to associate a brand with a musical style or period. For example, Alana Davis sang a version of the classic Crosby, Stills, Nash & Young song "Carry On" at the 2003 Super Bowl.[14] Music was part of a Sony commercial about a "zoomer" (Sony's word for active baby boomers) who spends his life savings to fly in a Russian space capsule. The ad referred viewers to a Sony website where the song could be downloaded for 99 cents and where it took off as a single on its own. Ads often use well-known music, but this was one of the few times when a song originally recorded for an ad became a hit single. Procter & Gamble had a similar experience with a song titled "Always (Thinking about You)," performed by Canadian singer Lisa Dalbello and featured in a

IMC IN ACTION

Hijacking the Soundtrack of Our Lives

Telecom giant Verizon announced in 2002 that it would be rolling out a new campaign to introduce its bundled and discounted local, long-distance, wireless, and broadband products. The television and radio commercials used the Beatles' 1968 hit "All Together Now" to promote Verizon's new "Veriations All" package.

General Motors' ad agency, Campbell-Ewald, checked the rock-and-roll archives, found more than 200 songs that mentioned Chevrolet or Chevy products, such as Corvette or Camaro, and used the songs as the basis for a campaign featuring music from the Ramones to the Beach Boys, Don McLean, Elton John, and Prince. The campaign was inspired by a billboard that bragged, "They don't write songs about Volvos."

Why build a commercial around a popular, albeit dated, song? The Verizon marketing communication director explained, "We couldn't find a better fit with our 'Veriations All' plan than that Beatles song. Not only is the title a great match, but the tone of the song is upbeat and festive. And that's the takeaway we want for customers when they hear about 'Veriations All.'"

So it sounds like a great idea for the execution of the Veriations theme, right?

Wrong, says Ken McConnellogue, who voiced an audio essay on NPR about songs that have been hijacked to hawk products. He points to the use of the Beatles song "Revolution" in a commercial for Nike shoes. That particular song, he points out, rails against capitalist society, so it was ironic that the song was co-opted by a "capitalist machine." His main point, however, is that some songs "become part of the soundtrack of our lives. They evoke a special meaning about a place or a time or a person," and says McConnellogue, "it stinks" to put these songs on par with common jingles.

It's not just the Beatles. Toyota uses the Who's "Baba O'Reilly." Steve Miller's "Fly like an Eagle" promotes the U.S. Postal Service. Creedence Clearwater Revival's "Fortunate Son" sells Wrangler jeans. The Band's "The Weight" is used in a Budweiser commercial. "Should I Stay or Should I Go" by the Clash is the theme for a malt beverage. McConnellogue points to Cadillac's use of Led Zepplin's "Rock n' Roll" as particularly incongruous, as well as commercially exploitative.

Think About It

Is it okay to build a creative strategy around a favorite piece of music? If one of your favorite songs is used to promote shoes or beer, will you care? Is there a trust dimension between a band and its fans that is violated when a commercial links the song to a product?

Source: Vanessa O'Connell, "GM to Sing the Songs Chevy Inspired," *Wall Street Journal*, October 1, 2002, p. B10; Christopher Saunders, "New Verizon Ads to Promote Service Bundle," *Internetnews.com*, August 6, 2002, <www.google.com/search?q=verizon+ads&btnG=GoogleSearch&hl=en&ie=ISO-8859-1>; Ken McConnellogue, "Revolution," KUNC Local, November 12, 2002, <www.publicbroadcasting.net/kunc/news/news.newsmain/action=article&ARTICLE_ID=416741>.

Cheer commercial.[15] Another example is the classic "I'd Like to Teach the World to Sing," which was written for Coca-Cola and then became a pop song. The IMC in Action box raises some questions about the way familiar music is used in some advertisements.

Video Copy

Video uses the standard techniques of audio; however, its visuals can attract attention and describe something better than words—by showing it. Video copywriters use action, music, sound effects, settings, casting, and special effects, all of which can add an element of drama to the message.

To illustrate some basic principles of writing video copy, let's describe a commercial in detail. Champagne producers have tried to persuade people to drink champagne at times other than New Year's Eve. How would you break through this wall, knowing that people may like the festiveness associated with champagne more than they like the taste? A campaign for Moët & Chandon by the agency Kirshenbaum Bond & Partners uses the distinctive pop of the cork to announce times for small celebrations. Rather than focusing on holidays, the campaign shows two intriguing women lying on their backs in a field, an amorous couple in a dark café, a woman rising from a bathtub, and a woman and two men in a rowboat. All the characters become alert as they hear a sound—though the audience doesn't hear it (a technique designed to pique the viewers' interest—"What did those people all hear?"). The ad then uses a voice-over (the sound of an unseen narrator speaking) in which a woman asks in a sultry tone, "Is it possible for one sound to do more than break the silence?" The voice-over continues: "Can one sound be inherently French, yet transcend every language?" The spot ends with a visual of a Moët cork being shot toward the viewer, accompanied by an unmistakable popping sound. The copywriter wrote only two sentences; the challenge came in matching those sentences, in style and tone, to the visuals and sounds.

A video script is more complex than an audio script because it contains both audio and video instructions. In order to illustrate the visual ideas, a storyboard is used to provide a pictorial diagram of the scenes. A **storyboard** is *a series of key visuals and accompanying dialogue that explains a TV commercial.* The storyboard coordinates the action with the dialogue by showing key frames with their associated audio track underneath the various scenes. Once a TV commercial is produced, photoboards are often made as shown in Exhibit 10-7. Photoboards are

EXHIBIT 10-7
*This is an example of a
:30 TV photoboard.*

Coopers & Lybrand

NOT JUST KNOWLEDGE. KNOW HOW.

"Best of Times"   30 Seconds

(MUSIC THROUGHOUT)
ANNCR: (VO) It's a whole new world facing
today's chief executive.

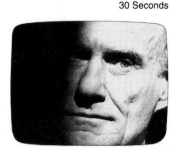

The economy is global. Competition is fierce.

Financial pressures are unrelenting.

But, there is one firm that can help CEO's make
the difference between the worst of times

... and the best of times. (CROWD APPLAUDS)

Coopers & Lybrand.
Not just knowledge. Know how.

similar to storyboards, the only difference being the use of photos of actual scenes rather than drawings of them.

ART DIRECTION

In most MC messages, the visual elements—the "look" of the piece—are supposed to attract attention and communicate something about the brand or company. The appearance of an annual report, for example, can create a positive (or a negative) impression that stays with a potential investor and helps (or hinders) his or her acceptance of the written message.

The creative team must be sure that the various elements in a piece of marketing communication flow logically. To have a sense of how creatives do that, we need to understand how visual elements are selected and assembled. As noted in Chapter 9, the art director is responsible for photos, illustrations, filming, logos, and so on—anything that has to do with the look of the brand message (see Exhibit 10-8).

Visualizing the Big Idea

Art directors and other graphic artists must decide on a theme and then translate that concept into visual elements. This process, known as **visualization,** is *the first step in expressing the big idea visually.* Both copywriters and art directors are imaginative, and they put their imagination to work in the four-step creative process (exploration, insight, execution, and evaluation) outlined in Chapter 9.

An example of an art director's creativity comes from an advertisement for Amica, which specializes in automobile insurance. The ad shows a car on a dark road, beneath a headline that says to hold the ad up to the light. When you do, you can see a huge truck bearing down on the car. The truck and the Amica logo and copy block are all printed on the back side of the page and can be seen and read only when light shines through the page.

Another dimension of visualization is deciding how the message elements—words, pictures, and sounds—will be presented and ordered to best communicate the big idea. The "shark" theme in Accenture's "Masters of Design" campaign was effectively brought to life in an interactive brochure, as the IMC in Action box explains.

The Role of Visuals

The word *visual* refers to any kind of art. In print advertising, the art usually consists of a photograph, a computer-generated image, or a hand-drawn illustration. In video, the art element may be live-action film, still photos, or animation. The Heinz ad in Exhibit 10-8 puts the product front and center, a technique sometimes referred to as "product as hero."

The style of the art is also important. An intimate style uses a soft focus and closeup views. A documentary style portrays the scene without pictorial enhancements such as fancy editing. A dramatic style features unusual angles, distorted color, fast-paced cuts, or blurred action images. Photos can also smack you right in the eyes or leave you laughing or crying, as Exhibit 10-9 (page 323) illustrates.

A powerful visual tool that is sometimes overlooked is *white space,* which is the area in an ad, brochure, or other printed piece in which there are no words or visuals. The next time you are looking at a newspaper, compare the ads. The ads with the most white space are likely to be for

EXHIBIT 10-8

This ad was carefully designed by the art director. The shot of the Heinz bottles with their familiar labels fills the entire ad; the body copy appears in the label of the middle bottle.

IMC IN ACTION

How a Shark Swims past the Secretary

Accenture, formerly called Andersen Consulting, is the world's largest consulting company and, in Germany, one of the most important. Decisions on hiring a business consulting firm of this caliber are made at the CEO level. The problem Accenture faced was how to get a message about Accenture consulting services onto CEOs' desks. It's hard to reach chief executives via traditional media, and their mail is filtered by executive secretaries who function as gatekeepers. Accenture in Germany gave the assignment—to develop a direct-mail message that would get past the secretary—to the Frankfurt office of MC agency Wunderman Cato Johnson, now called Impiric.

To achieve this objective, Accenture had to ensure that the execution of the message would be so interesting that the secretary would pass it on and the CEO would take the piece home. The creative director explained, "If the CEO takes our mailing home and reads it to his [or her] children or grandchildren, then we've surpassed our objectives."

The "Master of Design" campaign, which carried the message that Accenture was a partner in a company's business reengineering, used television commercials and a print campaign that included airport posters. A long-running advertising campaign using a "school of fish" theme had been used by Accenture for the past several years. The evolution followed the company's shift from being a solutions provider on a project basis to being a consulting service that provides ongoing guidance to continuously strengthen clients' business performance.

The key element of the "Master of Design" campaign came to be known as the "Shark" mailing. It was built on a short fairy tale about a school of goldfish living in an undisturbed and peaceful world where they happily perform their work. Suddenly enemies enter the marketplace. Another fish—the Master of Design—becomes the goldfish's consultant and redesigns the loosely grouped school of fish into a new, more powerful organization with the profile of a shark.

The Shark mailing, which was much more than a brochure, invited the reader to take an active part in the story development. The story could be read at several levels—as a simple fairy tale for children or as a sophisticated metaphor for business executives. It was presented in a blue box with a laser graphic of a fish on its cover that appeared to be moving in water. When the lid was opened, water sounds and music could be heard. The first page showed a school of fish swimming through the streets of a city, many wearing homburg hats. Some of the fish were mounted on magnets, which gave a three-dimensional effect and invited readers to move them around as they progressed through the story.

Evaluation

Accenture initially sent 140 pieces to its narrow target audience. The mailing generated a 20 percent response, far above the average. Another important aspect of the Shark mailing was that it integrated into the ongoing "Master of Design" campaign, which successfully repositioned Accenture as a leader in reengineering consulting services.

Think About It

Why do you think this execution was so successful? What elements of the execution separated it from most other direct mailing offers?

Source: This case was adapted with permission from the Advertising and Marketing Effectiveness (AME) award-winning brief for Accenture prepared by the Wunderman Cato Johnson agency in Frankfurt, Germany

luxurious brands or upscale retail stores. White space is a MC message luxury that communicates just that.

Typography—the typeface used to present the words in the message—has a design dimension and contributes to the style of the message. When artfully designed and crafted, a **typeface**—*a set of letters and numbers with a distinguishing design*—evokes a mood. Thus, as Exhibit 10-2 illustrates, different typefaces convey different tones (formal, funny, regal, casual) and must be integrated with other elements of the brand message.

Sometimes the visual is not determined until the art director or designer actually "lays out" the ad (designs its look and locates its elements). Advertising managers and art directors often keep an extensive file, or morgue, of noteworthy ads, photos, and illustrations—to serve as idea ticklers. Brand messages use many standard subjects for visuals, both product related and image focused.

As an example of the sensory impact a promotional visual for a brand can deliver, consider the 42-foot-high Coke bottle on the rooftop of Atlanta's Turner Field in a public park called the Sky Field.[16] It is made of 983 bats, 79 mitts, and 5,788 baseballs (see Exhibit 10-10). Oversize Adirondack chairs with back slats in the distinctive hourglass shape of the Coke bottle are spread around the Sky Field as well. Such creative visuals signify a new age of architecture and furniture as marketing communication.

Casting and Settings

The look of the people and the places (settings) depicted in the visuals are also important design decisions. One challenge is making the people in the ads match the personality of the product. Advertising for brands such as Donna Karan and Ralph Lauren is all about lifestyle. The imagery of the people in the ads tells a story about the brand personality.

Another approach to celebrities is visible in Gap ads that feature actors with real histories that we know about. One ad shows Dennis Hopper and Christina Ricci, wearing white shirts and khakis pants. He is sitting in some kind of patio chair and she is serving him something. The subtext comes from what we know about each of these actors—Easy Rider meets the Addams Family.[17] Perhaps the message is that they are both outsiders enjoying a life of privilege.

Successful casting and character development—the horn-rim Elvis Costello spectacles and blue Verizon jacket—are what made the Verizon techy nerd who traveled around the country asking "Can you hear me now?" so memorable and so subject to parody.

Print Layout and Design

In print media, the noun **layout** refers to *an orderly arrangement of the elements making up an MC message:* visuals, headlines, subheads, body copy, captions, trademarks, slogans, and signatures. During the layout process the creative team brings coherence to the visual message and uses style to help create meaning.

By creatively arranging elements—for example, surrounding the text with lines, boxes, shades, and colors—and relating elements to one another in size and proportion, the designer can enhance the message. The design principles of balance, proportion, and movement are guides for uniting images, type, colors, and qualities of the medium into a single communication.

In advertising, there are a number of standard layouts. Traditionally, print ads scoring the highest recall have a poster-style format, and a single, dominant visual occupies between 60 and 70 percent of the ad's total area. Some research shows

EXHIBIT 10-9
Commercial photographer Nick Vedros created this offbeat photo. The assignment was to illustrate the message "Dentyne gum is refreshing," which he did by creating a photo of a young couple embracing in a frozen shower that was lined with icicles and had streams of ice cascading from the shower head.

EXHIBIT 10-10

This gigantic Coke bottle at Atlanta's Turner Field is made of bats, balls, and mitts.

that ads scoring in the top third for "stopping power" (getting attention) devote an average of 82 percent of their space to the visual.

The layout also serves as a blueprint for production. It shows the size and placement of each element; it tells the copywriter how much copy to write; it suggests the size and style of the image to the illustrator or photographer; and it helps the art director specify the type. Also, once the production manager knows the dimensions of the piece, the number of photos, the amount of typesetting, and the use of art elements such as color and illustrations, he or she can accurately determine the cost of producing it.

The print design process serves as both a creative and an approval process. In the conceptual phase for print media, the designer uses "rough" art to establish the message's look and feel. The following list describes the evolution of a print message:

- A **thumbnail sketch**—or, simply, thumbnail—is *a small, very rough, rapidly produced drawing used to try out visual ideas.* The artist creates the thumbnail to visualize a number of layout approaches without wasting time on details; the best sketches are approved and developed further.

- A **rough layout** is *a preliminary, hand-drawn arrangement of elements in the actual size of the ad.* Headlines and subheads suggest the final type style; illustrations and photographs are sketched in; and body copy is simulated with lines.

- A **comprehensive layout,** or comp, is *a highly refined representation of the finished piece;* it allows the client to see how the brand message will look. A comp is generally quite elaborate, with colored photos, text hand-lettered or typeset, photostats of subvisuals, and a glossy spray-coat. When the design process reaches the comp stage, all visuals should be final.

- A **dummy** is *a mock-up that shows the actual size, look, and feel of brochures, multipage materials, packages, and point-of-purchase displays.* The artist assembles the dummy by hand, using colored markers and computer proofs, mounting them on sturdy paper, and then cutting and folding them to size. A dummy for a brochure, for example, is put together page by page to look exactly like the finished product and may be as polished as a comp.

- The **mechanical** is *final, camera-ready artwork.* In print production, the type and visuals must be placed into their exact position for reproduction by a printer. Today, most designers do this work on the computer, completely bypassing the need for old-fashioned paste-up. The art goes directly from disk to an output device that makes negatives for the printing process.

At any time during the print design process—until the printing press lays ink on paper—an artist or designer can make changes to the piece. Today, the expense of making changes and corrections in a layout done on the computer with digitized artwork is far less than it used to be.

Video Design

The strength of video is its real-life believability and its cinematic qualities, which come from moving pictures and sound. A humorous example that also demonstrates the shock potential of video comes from London, England, where the Borough of Islington ran a public service commercial reminding dog owners to pick up after their pets. The commercial shows a man outside a Georgian home squatting in front of its wrought-iron fence with his pants down. The next shot shows a standard Islington street sign with the words "You Wouldn't." Next is a shot of the man pulling up his pants as a neighbor in a business suit walks by. Then comes a shot of street sign that reads "Don't Let Your Dog."

Action and motion, as well as sound and music, are also important tools in video design. Nike's 90-second Olympic commercial "Move," for example, was praised for its beautifully synchronized celebration of sport and motion. One critique described it as "better than the Olympic opening ceremony that it interrupted."[18]

Another strength of video that emerges in design and production is special effects. The power of the computer to create fantastic images is opening up new kinds of imagery for film, MTV, and commercials. Steve Jobs's Pixar Animation Studios in Emeryville, California, is a leader in this area, working on movies as well as commercials. The German company Mental Images has won praise for the realistic images it created for *The Matrix* and the Levi Strauss ad featuring 600 stampeding buffalo. Called "mental rays," the technique bounces light off many virtual surfaces creating depth, shadow, and highly reflective surface images.[19]

An award-winning series of commercials for Fox Sports by Cliff Freeman & Partners is a product of imaginative editing and computer manipulation of images (see Exhibit 10-11). The idea was to insert two trash-talking, pasty white guys named Alan and Jerome into an NBA game. The editor and agency producer sifted through hundreds of hours of NBA footage to find shots that worked with the scripts, each of which centered on a particular play, such as making a jump shot or driving to the basket. If, for example, Jerome was doing offense, then the creative team looked for defenders. Everyone else was removed, and footage was shot of Jerome synchronized with the original action. A composite technique was used to superimpose Jerome's footage on the original footage so it looked as though he was playing in the game. At the end, it looked as though Alan and Jerome were part of the action in real NBA games.[20]

The creative process for a radio or TV commercial, a sales video, or a webpage is similar to the process for print materials, but the planning pieces are different. The first step in print is to develop a layout; in video, the art director works with a storyboard. The completed storyboard presents all the design decisions in such areas as scene, setting, characters, action, lighting, props, camera movements, and film editing techniques.

In video, the art director is very much involved in artistic development and determining the look of the scene. Using the script, the art director draws a series of frames on a storyboard to present the look of the image and the flow of the action sequences, or shots. The art director sketches the video image scene by scene and establishes the nature of the action. He or she carefully designs how each scene should appear, arranging actors, scenery, props, lighting, and camera angles to maximize impact, beauty, and mood.

EXHIBIT 10-11

This commercial for Fox Sports was built from composite images that were shot and then combined in the editing process.

The storyboard is the guide for filming. Upon approval of the storyboard, the commercial is ready for production, a process that involves preproduction planning, the production shoot, and postproduction editing. In the production stage, art directors must be able to work with a variety of professionals—producers, directors, lighting technicians, and set designers—to successfully develop and produce a commercial.

Online Design

According to one study a majority of business executives said the primary objectives for their companies' websites were to "build brand awareness" and "provide information." These objectives, which are primarily about one-way communication, illustrate the lack of emphasis on one of the major relationship-building characteristics of a website: interactivity. A printed brochure can build brand awareness and supply marketing information, but a website can also engage customers and other stakeholders in valuable dialogues. Unless a website is interactive, a major portion of its value goes unused.

Every element of interactive design should be done with the customer in mind. Building a website that meets the needs of the target audience is difficult, but research is there to help, as Table 10-1 demonstrates. The figures, compiled by Forrester Research, indicate that users are most likely to return to sites that have high-quality content, are easy to use, are quick to download, and are updated frequently.

Online design is a hot area of design. On the one hand, it is similar to poster design, and, in fact, that is how designers usually approach online ads or the opening page of a website. It is also similar to video design in that both work with a screen as a frame. On the other hand, the content is entirely different. Video offers all the benefits of cinematic techniques as well as realistic action. Online images are often dominated by words—although this is changing rapidly as the technology improves and makes animation and sound easier to integrate into website design.

T A B L E 1 0 - 1	Factors Driving Repeat Site Visits
Factor	Percentage of Respondents Citing This Factor as Important
High-quality content	75%
Ease of use	66
Quick to download	58
Updated frequently	54
Coupons and incentives	14
Favorite brands	13
Cutting-edge technology	12
Games	12
Purchasing capabilities	11
Customizable content	10
Chat rooms	10
Other	6

Source: Heather McLatchie, "E-Business Essentials," *clipwebzine*, August 23, 1999, <www.clipwebzine.com/article.cfm?storyid5163>.

Because of the magic of digitizing, web design can combine images from all different sources, such as photographs, type, film, sound, and games. The art can be illustrations or photographs that, through animation, can move. Any illustration can be scanned and manipulated through such art programs as PhotoShop and Flash. Sites should load quickly and be viewable on a variety of browsers. Ease of access is determined by the complexity of the design and the use of animation and multimedia formats.

There are two basic types of online formats. One is online advertising, usually presented as a banner. The other is a website, essentially an online brochure that gives information about a company, as well as details about its products, brands, and services, and contact information. More complex is a website that is interactive, allowing customers to contact the company with questions, shop online, and link to other products and services, such as chat rooms and product-related reference information.

Online Advertising

The first format of web design is the **banner,** which is *a small ad on some other company's web page.* These mini ads function like outdoor boards: they have to grab attention quickly with highly condensed information and interesting animation. Buttons on banners that you can click on take the internet user to the sponsor's website. The function of banner advertising is to tease the viewer into investigating the company behind the banner, and the success of banners is usually measured in terms of their click-through rate. Exhibit 10-12 shows some banners that represent good online design.

Online display ads look more like small space ads in newspapers and magazines. The same design principles apply: use a headline to catch attention and convey an interesting idea, and keep the body copy (if any) simple. The visual impact usually lies in the overall design of the ad. Art may be used, but, graphics consume memory and may be problematic given viewers' various levels of computer and software sophistication. The fancier the art and the animation effects, the harder it will be for users with simple systems to view the graphics.

Website Design

The first step in creating a successful website is to set objectives. What is the purpose of the site? There are a multitude of possible answers, including education, conversation and dialogue, feedback and research, entertainment, and sales. The

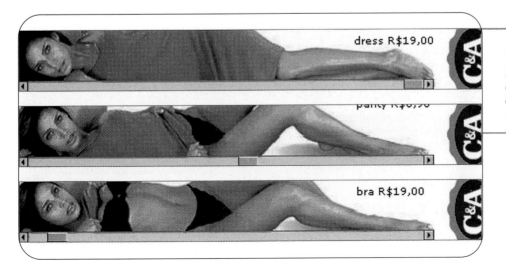

EXHIBIT 10-12

How important of a role do you think banner advertising will play in the future?

next step is to identify the target audience: Who are they? How long have they been online? What kinds of browsers and computers will they be using? What languages do they speak? Why will they come to the site and with what expectations? How often will they come to the site? Will they want to download, print, or e-mail website information? What are their product needs?

Web-page design begins with an outline of the content and a flow chart that shows how the site will be navigated and how the links will perform. The first page is called the **home page,** and that is *the place where viewers begin looking at a website.* Usually, the home page offers the viewer a number of options that can be accessed by clicking on a graphic or type element. Most web pages have **hyperlinks** which are *buttons or other sensitive areas on the page that, when clicked on, move the viewer to another page or site.* Hyperlinks, which have to be plotted into the design, add an interactive or customer-guided element unavailable in any other form of marketing communication.

What complicates online design is **navigation**—*the process by which people access a website, find the information they want, and move around within the site and to other related sites.* Websites are not designed for the linear reading of one page after another. People jump around when they are visiting a site. Therefore, routes have to be mapped that represent typical viewers' patterns of information processing. It should be easy for viewers to go in whatever way they want to go, whenever they want to go there, and easily get back to the home page or other areas in the website.

In the early days of the Web, sites were overloaded with every new graphic trick designers could find. The new credo in website design is to make pages user-friendly. As business columnist Paul Tulenko has observed, the goal is to "get the basics out there quickly with a bit of class."[21] Stephen Wildstrom, a *Business Week* technology writer, took several big companies—United Airlines (www.ual.com), Hertz (www.hertz.com), and Microsoft (www.microsoft.com)—to task for their difficult designs. He observed that it is faster to make a reservation or get a question answered by phone than it is to use these sites.[22]

Websites can be designed from the very simple to the very complex. Figure 10-2 illustrates the range of complexity a website design can have. Designers worry about adding complicated audio and animation effects that consumers do not want. For example, REI, an outdoor-products retailer, reported that when users were given the option to choose either a multimedia format or a text-and-photos-only format, most chose the latter. However, those who chose to look at the video presentations bought significantly more than those who chose not to.[23] The following list contains guidelines for creating websites that work:

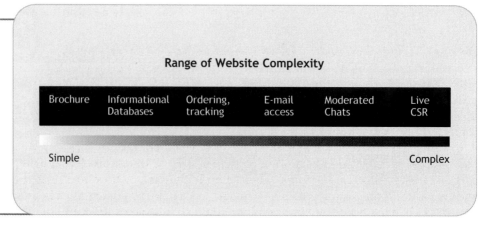

FIGURE 10-2

Think about the last website you visited. Where would it fall on this continuum?

Note: For examples of a listing of good B2B websites go to <www.netb2b.com> and click on "The NetMarketing 200" minibanner; the site is owned by *Advertising Age* magazine. Another site that offers advice on web marketing and online design is <www.ClickZ.com>.

Range of Website Complexity

Brochure	Informational Databases	Ordering, tracking	E-mail access	Moderated Chats	Live CSR

Simple   Complex

- Make the home page work hard to establish your identity and tell what you do.
- Make the interface intuitive. People shouldn't need training in order to use the site; all operations should be obvious.
- Make content prominent. Don't bury the content under a lot of graphics, ads, or complicated site design.
- Make navigation user-friendly.
- Don't create too many levels.
- Make sure menu options are complete.
- Give users a way to return to the main menu.
- Use links rather than long periods of scrolling.
- Put navigation aids at both the top and the bottom of the page.
- Provide a site map.

Contact information is particularly important in this day of interactivity—yet it is also highly problematic. A study of Fortune 100 companies found that 50 percent did not have a simple e-mail link on their websites. Instead, visitors had to click four or more times and then fill out extensive forms with personal information. Ten companies had no e-mail links at all.[24]

A good example of a website that is simple yet involving and invites interactivity is one for Purina's Tidy Cats brand of cat-litter products, www.tidycats.com. The home page has five main elements: a brief description of the product line, a picture of a package of Tidy Cats crystals, a listing of website categories (which are link buttons), and a bold linking banner that says, "See the Product Demo." The product demo link brings up a screen from which a cartoon demo can be downloaded. Viewers are told approximately how long the download will take. The animated demo is both informative and fun to watch. Check it out.

The fifth element on the Tidy Cats home page is a website Feedback button that links to a page titled "Tell Us What You Think" (see Exhibit 10-13). The company uses data gathered from this page to continually refine the website. An even more important link on the home page is one of the website categories: "Contact Us." This further encourages customers to ask questions, complain, or make suggestions.

Other MC Design Areas

Art directors are engaged with design problems that contribute to the consistency of a brand image in a number of ways besides advertising.

Brand Identity

One area of design that is particularly important in IMC is corporate or brand-image design. The term **brand identity** refers to *the design of the public face or distinctive visual appearance of an organization or brand* (◀ Chapter 3). This "look" provides the elements needed to recognize the brand. The pieces of a corporate identity program include logos, trademarks, distinctive colors, typography, brand characters, and graphic styles.

Companies successful at maintaining a consistent brand identity, such as FedEx and Intel, have established a set of graphic standards for the use of all brand and corporate identification elements. These standards explain how to use logos and other brand marks and colors on signage, truck side panels, letterheads, ads, and so on. Having and enforcing graphic standards also helps to legally protect

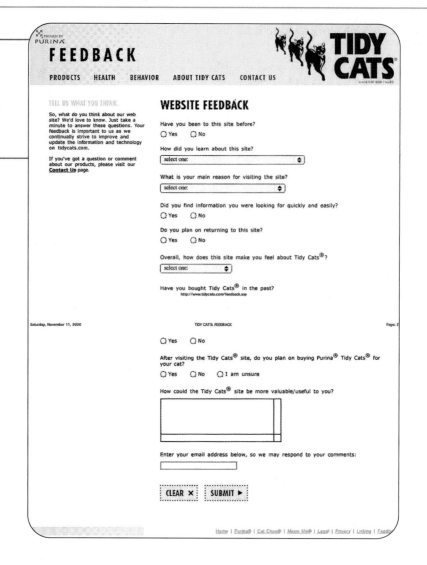

FEEDBACK

PRODUCTS   HEALTH   BEHAVIOR   ABOUT TIDY CATS   CONTACT US

TELL US WHAT YOU THINK.

So, what do you think about our web site? We'd love to know. Just take a minute to answer these questions. Your feedback is important to us as we continually strive to improve and update the information and technology on tidycats.com.

If you've got a question or comment about our products, please visit our **Contact Us** page.

WEBSITE FEEDBACK

Have you been to this site before?
○ Yes   ○ No

How did you learn about this site?
[select one: ⬍]

What is your main reason for visiting the site?
[select one: ⬍]

Did you find information you were looking for quickly and easily?
○ Yes   ○ No

Do you plan on returning to this site?
○ Yes   ○ No

Overall, how does this site make you feel about Tidy Cats®?
[select one: ⬍]

Have you bought Tidy Cats® in the past?
http://www.tidycats.com/feedback.asp

Saturday, November 11, 2000   TIDY CATS: FEEDBACK   Page: 2

○ Yes   ○ No

After visiting the Tidy Cats® site, do you plan on buying Purina® Tidy Cats® for your cat?
○ Yes   ○ No   ○ I am unsure

How could the Tidy Cats® site be more valuable/useful to you?
[   ]

Enter your email address below, so we may respond to your comments:
[   ]

[CLEAR ✕]   [SUBMIT ►]

Home | Purina® | Cat Chow® | Meow Mix® | Legal | Privacy | Linking | Feedb...

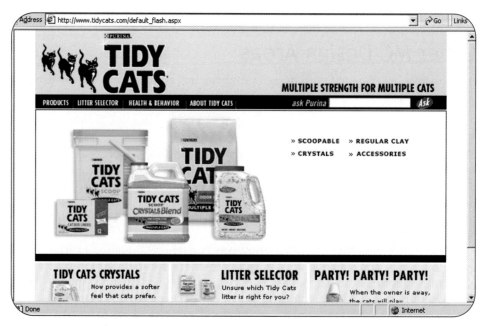

Address [🔹 http://www.tidycats.com/default_flash.aspx   ▼] ⟳ Go | Links

PURINA

TIDY CATS®

MULTIPLE STRENGTH FOR MULTIPLE CATS

PRODUCTS   LITTER SELECTOR   HEALTH & BEHAVIOR   ABOUT TIDY CATS   *ask Purina* [   ] *Ask*

» SCOOPABLE   » REGULAR CLAY
» CRYSTALS   » ACCESSORIES

TIDY CATS CRYSTALS
Now provides a softer feel that cats prefer.

LITTER SELECTOR
Unsure which Tidy Cats litter is right for you?

PARTY! PARTY! PARTY!
When the owner is away, the cats will play

Done   🌐 Internet

trademarks and logos. The graphic standards (often printed in a book or manual) need to be in the hands of every department and agency that develops materials bearing the brand name, trademark, or logo. These standards ensure consistency in corporate and brand identity.

To help maintain graphic consistency, there are software programs for warehousing digitized logos, trademarks, promotional illustrations of products, and so on. By having these centrally controlled and updated, a global company can have brochures, ads, and other brand messages produced around the world but maintain visual consistency because there is a single source for the visual elements.

Exhibits

Exhibits, displays, and booths—particularly those used for trade shows—are exciting, visually intensive, three-dimensional formats requiring the creation of a much more complicated design concept than a two-dimensional print ad. All the brand-identity information needs to be easily observable, but exhibit designers may also have to worry about traffic patterns as people move through the space and within and around the designed environment. Trade show exhibits are complicated by the inclusion of message sources such as video screens and computer systems, as well as people staffing and visiting the booth. Most exhibits go beyond sending messages in words and pictures by allowing for actual product demonstration. Models, mock-ups, and actual product demonstrations are showcased to the extent space permits. It's very much a hands-on environment, and the messages are enhanced by the credibility that comes from face-to-face communication (see Exhibit 10-14).

Packaging

A package, especially for consumer goods, is an important communication vehicle. Its front panel or label defines the product category, identifies the brand, delivers short copy points, and functions as the "last ad a customer sees" before making a purchase decision. A package is more than just a physical container for a product. It

EXHIBIT 10-14
Because trade shows are a major B2B marketing communication function, booths are often elaborately designed.

EXHIBIT 10-15
The distinctive design of Celestial Seasonings boxes is an important part of the herbal tea's brand image.

reflects the brand image and delivers visual impact. The objective is to generate nearly instantaneous and universal recognition. Consistency of design—between the package design and other brand-design elements—delivers a key visual message. Coca-Cola's hourglass-shaped bottle remained as a brand icon even when the company switched from glass to plastic bottles. Other classic packaging examples include the Mrs. Butterworth's syrup bottle, the L'eggs egg-shaped hosiery containers, and the artful boxes that hold Celestial Seasonings herbal teas (see Exhibit 10-15).

THE CONSISTENCY CHALLENGE

A challenge in brand communication is to develop MC messages that are strategically consistent with the brand position and image. The more MC messages there are, the harder it is to keep the messages consistent. There are two levels of consistency. *One-voice, one-look consistency* applies primarily to campaigns. *Strategic consistency* applies to all brand messages, not just MC messages.

Executional Consistency: One Voice, One Look

One-voice, one-look consistency is *the type of consistency that occurs when all advertising, sales promotion, sponsorships, publicity, direct response, packaging, and other MC messages have the same look, sound, and feel.* One-voice, one-look consistency indicates that everything is integrated at the execution level. For example, when Levi Strauss broke a new campaign for its Dockers khakis, it relied on a Dockers-dedicated team at agency Foote, Cone & Belding (FCB) in San Francisco to create messages using the Dockers "Nice pants" line for everything from posters to bus shelters to the Dockers.com website. All of these messages had the same look and personality and conveyed the same message, although some messages were more abbreviated than others.

Consistency can be created in an IMC campaign by mirroring the style of a message from one execution to another or from one medium to another. Some of the practices that marketers use to achieve one voice and one look include the following:

- *Visual connections:* a similar format in layout and art style (Absolut vodka ads, Pepperidge Farm packages), or colors (Tiffany package), as well as the key visual element (Maytag's "lonely repairman").

- *Verbal connections:* words, such as slogans, tag lines, and jingles, that can be repeated over and over (De Beers's "Diamonds are forever," American Express's "Don't leave home without it").
- *Audio connections:* sounds that work like words to anchor an association, such as the Jolly Green Giant's "Ho, Ho, Ho."
- *Continuing characters:* the same characters (Arnott's) or a continuing spokesperson (Bill Cosby for Jell-O) or a spokes character (Jolly Green Giant, Ronald McDonald).
- *Symbols and logos:* McDonald's Golden Arches, Nike's "Swoosh".
- *Continuity in settings:* the place in which a brand story is set—for example, the Western imagery in the Marlboro campaign.
- *Emotional connections:* Hallmark and Kodak messages, for example, usually focus on imagery and situations that tug at the heart; Arnott's also used emotion as a link among its various executions from ads to magazine stories.
- *Thematic continuity:* Wal-Mart is a friendly place—notice the happy faces, the smiling symbol in Wal-Mart ads and the smiling greeters at the door—where you feel good about what you buy because you always get low prices.

One-voice, one-look consistency is difficult to achieve when a lot of different departments and MC agencies are creating MC messages about a brand. For example, an IMC brand audit of a major beverage brand with a marketing communication budget of $150 million found that the marketing services and brand managers were working against 10 different MC objectives. Not surprisingly, a content analysis of a year's worth of planned brand messages found some messages promising quality, some refreshment, and others fun. Because the messages to the same audience were so inconsistent, customers and prospects did not know what to expect from the brand (and poor sales was a result).

A research study[25] into the integration between print advertising and websites looked at message strategy (the objective, promise, or most important message) and at executional consistency (visible in logo, copy and support, product picture, colors, key visual, slogan, and spokesperson). The authors found less integration at the strategy level: only 39 percent of the 186 brands studied showed consistency in the objectives and the promise between the print ads and the website. There was more integration, however, at the executional level: 83 percent of the 186 brands consistently displayed the logo in both print ads and the website.

One of the main things a company can do to achieve "one voice, one look" is to have a cross-functional team of MC managers agree on message standards and then periodically do a content analysis of all the company's MC messages recently produced. The easiest way to do a content analysis is to post all the recent MC messages on a wall and simply step back and see to what extent they are similar.

Strategic Consistency

Because companies must communicate with a variety of stakeholders besides customers, it is important to use **strategic consistency,**[26] which is *the type of conistency that occurs when MC messages differ but every message contains certain core elements.* No matter who the audience is, the brand name and logo should be integrated into all messages to leverage the brand identity the company has created for itself. For example, in selling educational toys, the message to parents will be different from the one aimed at the kids. This does not mean, however, that there can't be certain consistencies in both sets of messages. The brand's personality, positioning, and identification cues, for example, should be consistent, but the individualized

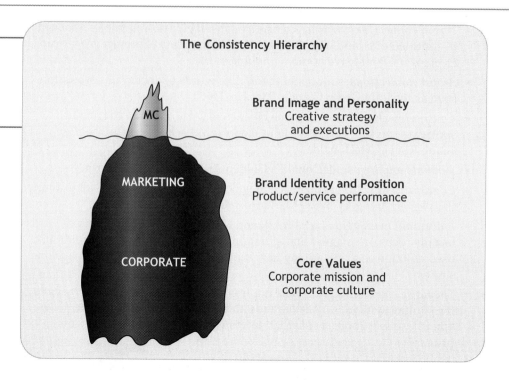

FIGURE 10-3

Consistency in marketing communication is only the tip of the iceberg.

selling propositions may differ—for kids: "exciting fun"; for parents: "they learn while playing."

Changing the packaging or even the slogan of a brand over time always creates a consistency dilemma. On the one hand, companies want to have their brands easily recognized and leverage the identity cues they have established. On the other hand, to avoid appearing "old-fashioned" often requires changing the looks of the brand name and its logo.

To achieve strategic consistency, marketers must walk a fine line between tailoring different messages to various target audiences and maintaining a consistent brand image and position. A McDonald's exterior is reasonably easy to recognize worldwide; however, the company uses its interiors to connect with local communities. In Peru, Indiana, which used to be the winter quarters for several circuses, the interior of the McDonald's has a circus motif and many pictures of the old circus days in the city. In Germany, McDonald's serves beer; in Japan, sushi. But everywhere, there is no mistaking McDonald's for any other brand. Why? McDonald's consistently offers a basic standard menu, in spite of the regional additions, and the cost–value ratio of its offerings is predictably always very good.

As Figure 10-3 illustrates, consistency in MC message executions is only the tip of the consistency iceberg. The deeper you go in analyzing the brand and corporate strategies, the more important consistency becomes throughout the organization's operations. The foundation on which all communication is built is corporate culture, mission, and core values. What comes next are the various marketing elements of brand strategy: product and service performance, brand identity, and brand position.

Corporate culture is *the shared values and beliefs that structure the way an organization's employees work and interact with each other and with other stakeholders*—or, less formally, "the way we do business around here." A **corporate mission** is *what a company stands for and represents*. A corporate mission is a critical integrative element because coming up with a consistent message is impossible if no one in the company knows what the company stands for. At the marketing level, consistency is signaled by the way the marketing communication reflects the product and service performance messages.

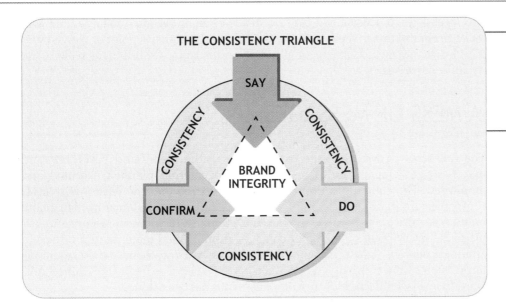

FIGURE 10-4

Gaps in the consistency triangle are red flags for marketing communication planners.

IMC recognizes there is more to integration than just having all the pieces in a campaign look alike. IMC impacts a company's total business operations, not just its marketing communication messages. Nebraska-based Omaha Steaks, for example, bases all of its operations, as well as its marketing communication, on the idea of quality. The president of the family-owned business explained the family's view of quality control: "We're control freaks." And that attitude comes through not only in the company's emphasis on using only the finest USDA-approved corn-fed beef but also in its direct marketing, its internet operation, and its caring employees.

The Consistency Triangle

The consistency triangle shown in Figure 10-4 provides a simple way to analyze how all of a company's brand messages relate to each other. Strategic consistency exists when a brand does what it says, from the customer's perspective, and when what the brand says and does are reinforced by what others say about it. In terms of Figure 10-4,

- *"Say" messages* are MC messages that set expectations.
- *"Do" messages* are messages delivered by the company's product and service messages. They are conveyed by how products actually perform, what they actually cost, how convenient they are to get and use, and the brand's supporting services.
- *"Confirm" messages* are messages from other people who either criticize or praise the brand or company. Personal and positive third-party communication is considerably more persuasive than most MC brand messages.

The "say" messages delivered by marketing communication must be consistent with the "do" messages about how products and services perform, as well as with what others "confirm" about the brand. Gaps between any of these message types threaten brand relationships.

When an airline puts "special handling" tags on the bags of its frequent flyers, it seems to be promising these customers that they will be the first ones to receive their luggage upon landing. If frequent flyers find that their tagged bags arrive no sooner than anyone else's on the flight, then there is a gap between the "say" and "do" messages. If consistency gaps occur too often or become too large, they will make the brand image seem unfocused. From the customer's point of view, strategic consistency means easy recognition of, and trust in, the brand, as well as "no negative surprises."

A FINAL NOTE: A MESS OF MESSAGES

The full array of MC message executions—all the pieces and parts, bits and bytes—creates a mess of messages if they are not carefully planned, executed, and monitored. The communication complexity involved and the reason why most companies are fighting to maintain some measure of consistency in their many brand messages are easy to see. As the chief strategist for General Motors once explained: "Every point of customer contact—from printed material to products to after-sale service—must present the customer with a clear and harmonious impression of the company, its products, and its services. And this unified outward image is a reflection of the company's internal consistency."

Consistency is a means to an end. That end is positive brand relationships. Success at creating this level of consistency is what made the Arnott's campaign an effective message strategy across a variety of executions. The integrated campaign worked because it told a brand story about a meaningful relationship that contributed to building an image for Arnott's as a caring brand. A creative campaign that successfully develops a memorable product image not only can build a new brand but can turn around a troubled brand.

Key Terms

banner 327
body copy 314
brand identity 329
call-outs 316
captions 316
comprehensive layout 324
corporate culture 334
corporate mission 334
display copy 314
dummy 324

headline 314
home page 328
hyperlinks 328
jingles 318
layout 323
mechanical 324
message execution 307
navigation 328
one-voice, one-look
    consistency 332

rough layout 324
signature 316
slogan 313
storyboard 320
strategic consistency 333
tag line 316
thumbnail sketch 324
tone 310
typeface 322
visualization 321

Key Point Summary

Key Point 1: Message Executions

A message execution is the format of a completed MC message. People on the creative side of marketing communication focus on storytelling, tone and style, words, pictures, and consistency.

Key Point 2: Copywriting

Copywriters strive to produce copy that attracts attention and is remembered. Headlines grab attention, subheads and the lead paragraph spark interest, body copy builds credibility and stimulates desire, and the closing paragraph and reminder information such as slogans and tag lines prompt action. Audio messages must be catchy, interesting, unforgettable, and intrusive enough to attract and hold listeners' attention. Video copywriters use action, music, sound effects, setting, casting, and special effects to add drama to the message.

Key Point 3: Art Direction

Visualization is the first step in expressing the big idea in MC message development. Art direction involves choosing the message elements—words, pictures, sounds—and deciding how to present and order them to best communicate the big idea.

Key Point 4: Message Consistency

One-voice, one-look consistency means that MC messages have a consistent look, sound, and feel across a variety of media and functional areas; it results from a unified, well-integrated creative strategy. Strategic consistency means that messages may vary with the needs of the audience, but every message maintains brand consistency by presenting certain core elements. Strategic consistency also means coordinating all types of messages (product, service, and unplanned, as well as planned messages) in order to guarantee that there are no gaps between the "say," "do," and "confirm" messages.

EXHIBIT 10-16

This ad comically shows a man protecting himself from falling debris with a Samsonite suitcase to prove the product's durability.

Lessons Learned

Key Point 1: Message Executions

a. What are the five key decision areas?
b. Find an ad that illustrates one of the 13 common message story formats. Explain how it works.
c. How do tone and style differ? Find an ad that you think illustrates a distinctive tone and another one that demonstrates a distinctive style. Explain how they work.

d. Do you want a visual element to be a literal representation of the thought expressed in a headline? What is gained and what is lost with such an approach?

Key Point 2: Copywriting

a. What is the purpose of a headline?
b. How do display copy and body copy differ?
c. Find a copy-heavy print ad. Make a copy of it, and on the copy in red ink identify the headline and the body copy. If any of the following elements appear in the ad, identify them as well: captions, subheads, overlines, underlines, tag lines, call-out quotes. Finally, circle the brand-identification elements, and label them as a logo or signature.
d. What is a script? How do scripts for audio and video media differ?
e. Describe a broadcast announcement that you think is particularly intrusive. Why is it irritating? What might be done to soften the irritation yet keep the message on strategy?
f. Find an ad that you think is particularly well written and one that isn't. Compare the two, and explain your evaluation.

Key Point 3: Art Direction

a. What is art direction? Explain the role of an art director.
b. What is visualization?
c. What is a layout? What information does a layout provide?
d. What is a storyboard? What information does a storyboard provide?

Key Point 4: Message Consistency

a. What is one-voice, one-look consistency? How does it differ from strategic consistency?
b. Collect all the communication materials you can find from a local bank. Analyze them and your experiences with the bank in terms of the consistency triangle. Can you identify any gaps between the "say," "do," and "confirm" messages?
c. Find a product or service that demonstrates inconsistency in the materials developed by the various marketing communication areas. Redesign the materials using a one-voice, one-look approach to create more consistency in these planned messages. Explain your changes.

Chapter Challenge

Writing Assignment

Collect all the MC messages you can find for one of your favorite brands. Analyze their creativity, big idea, writing, and design. How is the brand image expressed in these pieces? What might be done to strengthen the presentation of the brand image and personality? Present your analysis to your classmates.

Presentation Assignment

Adopt a local client—a store, a manufacturer, or a nonprofit organization. Analyze the strategy behind your client's marketing communication messages. Next, examine all the MC messages this company has produced over the last 12 months. Using the consistency triangle (Figure 10-4), identify any gaps in consistency among these various messages. Prepare your analysis for presentation to your client.

Chapter
11

Media Characteristics

Key Points in This Chapter

1. What are media, and how are they classified?
2. What are the important characteristics of print media?
3. What do media planners need to know about broadcast media?
4. Why are out-of-home media useful in a media plan?

Chapter Perspective

Connecting with Customers

Over the years the word *media* has become tightly associated with the word *advertising*, leading many to think that media are used only for advertising. Nothing could be further from the truth! All marketing communication messages are carried by some form of media. Brand publicity, sales-promotion offers, direct-response offers, and sponsorships all use various media to deliver messages to customers. These media include not only the obvious and traditional advertising media—radio, TV, outdoor boards and posters, newspapers, and magazines—but also the internet, telephone, mail services, coffee mugs, signs, company trucks and cars, package labels, Yellow Pages, company stationery and business cards, pens, T-shirts, and matchbook covers. These are all *created touch points* (◀ Chapter 1), and they offer a marketer the most control over the way the message connects with the customer.

Another myth is that the media's only job is to provide opportunity for message exposure. The reality is that companies are not satisfied just to have their messages sent or shown to target audiences. They demand that media add value to messages by increasing their impact on attitudes and behaviors; and this can happen only when media are viewed as touch points that create connections with customers.

In IMC the role of media is not only to deliver brand messages but also to help create, sustain, and strengthen brand relationships by connecting companies and customers. The difference between delivery and connection is significant. *To deliver* means "to take something to a person or place"; *to connect* means "to join together." Delivery is only the first step in connecting: it opens the door to touching a customer in a meaningful way with a brand message.

JUMBO, LARGE, MEDIUM, SMALL, MINI

Unconventional—that's the story of the revival of the popular British brand. Now owned by the BMW Group, the MINI Cooper has its roots in the Swinging England of the 1960s. The tiny car is surprisingly roomy and fun to drive, with agile handling that reflects its long history of Monte Carlo race victories. Its reemergence took the car market as well as the advertising industry for a ride, summed up in the campaign's communication claim, "LET'S MOTOR."

Consumer Insights

Its quirky image was mirrored in its unconventional strategy for its U.S. launch in March 2002. Kerri Martin, the Marketing Communications Director and Guardian of the Brand Soul, knew that potential buyers were, opinion leaders, risk takers, and technologically savy. The MINI customer profile was based on psychographics—phrased as the MINI Mindset—rather than the usual age- and gender-focused demographics.

Because of this insight into the target market, Martin instructed the MINI's agency, Miami-based Crispin Porter+Bogusky (CP+B), to move away from traditional advertising and use novel promotional tactics to create buzz about the brand. CP+B creative partner Alex Bogusky explains that the campaign was successful because it wasn't about ads, but about the long-term vision making the brand an icon. He explains, "The communication claim, 'LET'S MOTOR' is an invitation to exhilaration and an emotional attachment to a different way of thinking about a different kind of car." The engaging brand story is evident in the "Let's get acquainted" web commercial, in which a bulldog surprisingly finds himself attracted to a MINI, and also in the Cooper S, "Unauthorized Owner's Manual." This direct-mail piece to new owners tells them things like where to wedge CDs or how to store a bicycle. It encourages motorers not to worry about scratches or getting the car dirty or putting miles on the experience-o-meter, aka the odometer. It also asks them to be kind to cyclists.

The campaign fit the brand personality perfectly and captured the soul of the MINI. Its success led it to be named the Innovative Campaign winner of the year by *Business 2.0.*

Unconventional Media for an Unconventional Car

Of course, the budget for the launch was as tiny as the car, and that also forced the agency to come up with a very clever brand-differentiating idea that made maximum use of nontraditional media, such as

EXHIBIT 11-1

touring the country with a MINI mounted on the top of an SUV. To extend the MINI brand experience into showrooms, MINI supported a global corporate identity design that uniquely positioned the brand in the automotive category.

A month before the launch the advertising began with billboards and a teaser campaign. With no cars present, the billboards had lines that proclaimed the cars' point of difference, "The SUV backlash begins now," "Goliath Lost," and "XXL-XL-L-M-S-MINI." The billboards also included the car's Web address, MINIUSA.com encouraging consumer discovery.

Using guerrilla marketing to announce the launch, CP+B created buzz by mounting MINIs on top of Ford Excursion SUVs and sending them to national auto shows and a tour of 21 major cities. Potential customers were also invited to experience the "MINI Ride," which was an innovative display that uses an actual MINI set up like a children's coin-operated ride. The sign announces, "Rides $16,850. Quarters only, Please."

CP+B also exhibited the MINI during sporting events in major stadiums around the country. At these events, consumers received cards inviting them to "Sip Not Gulp," which referred to the car's stingy fuel usage, and visit MINIUSA.com, where they could design and customize their own MINI and sign up to become a MINI leader.

In keeping with the MINI marketing director's instructions to avoid conventional advertising, CP+B came up with the idea of running the ads along the margins of magazine editorial pages. The edge-of-the-page ads feature the car, and the slogan "Nothing corners like a MINI. LET'S MOTOR." In *Rolling Stone* an ad used orange staples in its binding to resemble a road on which the MINI was motoring. Even the more conventional magazine ads were quirky. In order to suggest that the MINI was speedy with great handling, one print ad that showed a car driving up a spiral ramp also included a real air-sickness bag in case the passenger found the G forces to be too great.

Rather than buy time on television, the campaign used four 60-second cinema spots. Jim Poh, VP of Creative Content Distribution at Crispin Porter + Bogusky, explained that the attentiveness level is better for theater commercials than TV, plus the cinema spots can be better targeted to reach MINI's target audience. The unconventional campaign also benefited from a high level of publicity, and more than 75 percent of buyers report that they saw either an ad or a story about the ads. Other creative ideas included a "MINI Parking Only" stencil mailed to buyers after they put down a deposit on a car and the MINI Owners Lounge allowed them to follow their own car's production online. The sales delivery

process was also enhanced with customers finding a mint on their seat and a steering wheel wrap stating, "Your MINI has been thoroughly inspected from boot to bonnet. FYI; Boot is the British term for trunk and a bonnet is the hood."

The campaign was also supported by the MINIUSA.com website, which features a car configurator, features and specs, screensaver downloads, photo gallery, and historical timeline but also sells MINI MotoringGear and Motoring Accessories that reinforce the idea of motoring. An innovative Internet promotion that supported the launch featured a crew traveling around the country shooting footage for a promotional video for point of sale. The route was unplanned, to celebrate the MINI's free-wheeling motoring spirit, and MINI enthusiasts were invited to suggest places to visit. MINI sent e-mails to hand-raisers—people who had identified themselves as interested in the MINI—and a day later the company had 800 responses with location suggestions.

A MINI Success Story

The innovative campaign was a hit with consumers who signed up on a waiting list to get their MINI cars. In the six months preceding the launch, the website registered more than 210,000 leads. In the seven weeks of the launch period, MINIUSA.com registered nearly that many visitors, which testifies to the effectiveness of the outdoor advertising. More than 55,000 Web visitors signed up to receive the e-mail newsletter.

Jack Pitney, MINI's General Manager, reported that in just nine months the MINI went from zero to 25 percent brand awareness, which he says is far beyond the original objectives. By June of 2003 MINI enjoyed a 67% awareness. The original 2002 sales goal of 20,000 was exceeded in the first nine months with 24,590 cars sold. Pitney expects that the new annual goal will be 30,000 units. However, sales are limited because there are only 78 dealerships nationwide.

Source: Suzanne Vranica and Vanessa O'Connell, "2002 Ads: Cheer Up!" Wall Street Journal, December 19, 2002, p. B1; "Mini Marketing Chief Proves Them Wrong. A Marketer of the Year Helps Car Surpass Sales Expectations," Automotive News, *January 13, 2003; Jean Halliday, " 'Let's Motor' Mini Cooper Campaign Gets in Gear," and "BMW's Mini Returns with Interactive Promotion,"* AdAge.com, *November 19, 2001, <www.adage.com/news. cms?newsId=35066>; John Gaffney, "Most Innovative Campaign,"* Business 2.0, *May 2002, <www.business2.com/articles/mag/print/0,1643, 39313,FF.html>; Stefano Hatfield, "Sunshine Supermen," April 1, 2002,* Creativity Magazine, *<www.adcritic.com/ news/creativity/detail/?q=35188>.*

THE MEDIA BUSINESS

The selection and use of media can be just as creative as the writing of a publicity release or the creating of a magazine ad, as the story about the launch of the redesigned BMW Mini Cooper demonstrates. Media planners used to be subservient to the creative team. In IMC, however, media people work alongside the creative people in developing campaigns. The media not only deliver brand messages but can influence a brand's image because they operate as a created touch point. This is the difference between simply delivering a MC message and facilitating the connection of the brand, both emotionally and cognitively, with customers and prospects. Status and luxury brands, for example, often place ads in such magazines as *Architectural Digest* and *Gourmet*. Marketers hope that the upscale editorial environment will reinforce the brands' own upscale images, and they believe that the high production quality of magazine advertising sends an appropriate message.

Intel has used TV not only because it reaches a broad audience but also because TV's audio dimension has enabled Intel to establish an audio brand identity—the four tones that play when the "Intel inside" logo is shown. Signage, another type of media, has become a brand signature and popular brand identifier for McDonald's and many other companies. The point is, media can add to or subtract from a brand message, depending on which media are used and in what way.

One of the primary ways in which brands are built is through **media exposure,** which refers to *the number of people who see, read, or hear a medium.* Through magazine and television exposure, Martha Stewart, the subject of the IMC in Action box, became a household name and built her own media empire based on the cultivated brand image of her name. The fact that her involvement in a questionable stock-trading incident was big news in 2003 was a testament to the fact she had become a major celebrity brand.

Media exposure, however, does not guarantee *message* exposure. While media planners try to gain the most cost-effective media exposure they can for a brand, it is up to the individual brand messages to attract attention, change attitudes, and motivate behavior. As shown in Figure 11-1, most brand messages generate a

FIGURE 11-1

This chart shows the hypothetical relationship between levels of message involvement and responses to messages.

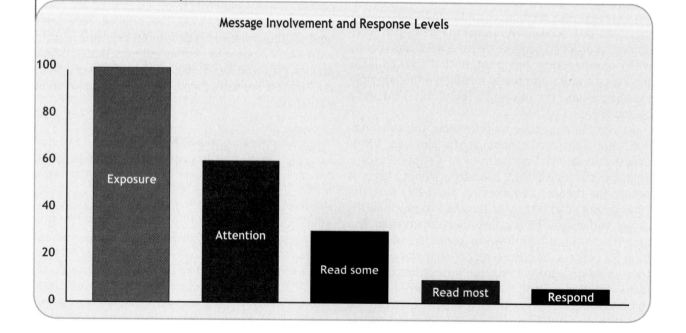

IMC IN ACTION

The Rise and Fall of Martha Stewart's Omnimedia Empire

Although Martha Stewart became known for her color-coordinated bedrooms and bathrooms, her recent notoriety resulted from accusations that she participated in insider trading. From a media perspective, however, Martha Stewart is a special story because of how she creatively turned her personal brand into a media company, Martha Stewart Living Omnimedia, Inc.

The multimedia empire started in 1982 with Stewart's landmark book, *Entertaining*, which has sold more than 500,000 copies. The company's book line has continued to grow, with dozens of titles for cooking, weddings, decorating, and so on. In 1989, Stewart developed the prototype for an upscale how-to magazine, *Martha Stewart Living*, which was published by Time Warner. In 1997, she bought control of her "crown jewel" from Time Warner, and it joins her other magazines: *Martha Stewart Weddings, Entertaining,* and *Clotheskeeping.* She visualizes her typical reader as a supremely confident 40-year-old woman with a family and a part-time job, living in a nice house in the suburbs. Rather than running articles about getting a man, dieting, or the latest hairstyles, Stewart aims her how-to content at this audience's sense of self-reliance.

Martha Stewart produces and owns rights to her daily TV show and radio program, plus TV specials, such as her holiday special in 1999, which reached 7.8 million households. She also makes regular appearances on other TV programs. She writes a syndicated weekly newspaper column, "Ask Martha." Altogether, her media properties reach 88 million people a month. Because of the quality demographics of her audience, her media command premium ad rates. The books and magazines generate 65 percent of the company's sales; TV and radio account for another 12 percent.

Her Web entries include MarthaStewart.com, which, with its 1 million registered users, is a hit with advertisers as well as consumers, who actively participate in its chat rooms. Stewart's internet and catalog sales accounted for roughly 13 percent of the company's revenues. The secret to Stewart's media success is her ability to create original, high-quality content (stories and programs) for media networks that are strategically consistent and that can cascade through various media, retail outlets, and the Web. The shared costs and cross-promotions ultimately lead to higher revenues and earnings.

The fact that Martha Stewart is the walking, talking personification of her brand was originally a major plus in developing an impactful brand image. However, when a brand is driven by one person and that person becomes embroiled in scandal, it negatively affects the whole company. In 2002 advertising revenues were down dramatically, and Martha Stewart Omnimedia's profits fell far short of what Wall Street was expecting. In June 2003 Stewart was indicted.

This negative brand message once again impacted shareholder value as the stock lost 15 percent of its value the day of the indictment. A sub-headline in the *Wall Street Journal* read: "Branding Experts Suggest Company Distance Itself from Celebrity Founder."[1] CBS.MarketWatch.com's story on the indictment opened with this paragraph: "There's no getting around it: Martha Stewart, the woman, is analogous with Martha Stewart, the brand. But when Stewart faces a jury of her peers, will her trademark—and, ultimately, the fate of her company—be on trial as well?"[2]

Think About It

How many different media are involved in the Martha Stewart Omnimedia empire? What made the Martha Stewart media brand so powerful? In light of the negative publicity about Martha Stewart's stock-trading activities, if you had been advertising in some of Stewart's media vehicles, would you continue to do so? Why or why not? If you were an advertising manager for one of her media properties, how would you explain the negative publicity to potential advertisers?

Source: Diane Brady, "Inside the Growing Empire of America's Queen," *Business Week,* January 17, 2000, p. 63; Lisa Singhania, Brian Steinberg, and Suzanne Vranica, "Martha Stewart Firm Needs Space," *Wall Street Journal,* June 4, 2003, p. B4; Jennifer Waters, "Martha Stewart: The Woman, the Brand," *CBS MarketWatch.com,* June 4, 2003.

EXHIBIT 11-2

Advertising on coffee sleeves is a way to slip under the radar and make an impression in an unexpected setting.

response from only a small percentage of those who are exposed to the message. The challenge is to find media whose audiences are most likely to respond and thus narrow the difference between the number exposed (which is what media prices are based on) and the number who respond (which is the return on the media investment).

One of the biggest changes in marketing communication over the last two decades has been media fragmentation and proliferation. They have been a mixed blessing, giving marketers and their agencies more choices in how to reach customers but, at the same time, spreading customers' attention over so many different media that it is much more of a challenge for a company to reach all of its targeted prospects and customers. Despite the increase in media options, however, it is important to note that four media—TV, newspapers, direct mail, and telemarketing—account for over two-thirds of media spending.

Another problem is media clutter. So many brand messages are being delivered by so many different types of message delivery systems that media planners are being more and more creative in trying to find unusual ways to reach their target audiences, such as the coffee sleeve advertising illustrated in Exhibit 11-2. Such innovative media ideas are referred to as "under the radar" techniques by agency owners Jonathan Bond and Richard Kirshenbaum, who wrote a book of that name.[3]

Media Classifications

The plural noun *media* is an umbrella term for all types of print, broadcast, out-of-home, and interactive communication (see Figure 11-2). The singular noun *medium* refers to each specific type (TV is a medium, radio is a medium, newspapers are a medium, and so on). A specific publication, TV channel, or radio station is a *media vehicle*. Examples of media vehicles are the *New York Times,* MTV, *Newsweek,* and the America Online portal on the internet. When a company "buys media," it is really buying access to the audiences of specific media vehicles.

Another way to classify media is by reach and characteristic of media. Here, media planners use such terms as *mass media, niche media, addressable media,* and *interactive media.*[4]

FIGURE 11-2

This chart shows media classification levels and groupings.

Mass Media and Niche Media

Mass media are communication channels through which messages may be sent to the "masses"—large, diverse audiences. Niche media are communication channels

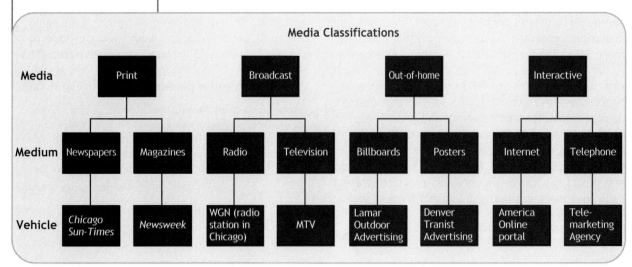

Media Classifications

Media	Print		Broadcast		Out-of-home		Interactive	
Medium	Newspapers	Magazines	Radio	Television	Billboards	Posters	Internet	Telephone
Vehicle	*Chicago Sun-Times*	*Newsweek*	WGN (radio station in Chicago)	MTV	Lamar Outdoor Advertising	Denver Transit Advertising	America Online portal	Telemarketing Agency

through which messages are sent to audiences with a distinct commonality. Channel One is a niche medium that reaches teenagers while in school.

The distinction between mass and niche media is not always easy to make. Recall from Chapter 7 that *Modern Maturity* magazine is considered to be a niche medium, but it has a circulation of over 20 million people who are very diverse except for one factor—they are 55 or older. Similarly, millions of people worldwide watch soccer's World Cup playoffs. Like *Modern Maturity* subscribers, the World Cup audience is extremely large and diverse, yet the soccer fans are younger than the world population in general. Even so, most would argue that the World Cup coverage, like the coverage of most major sporting events, has a mass rather than a niche audience.

Thus, a media planner's primary concern should not be how a medium is labeled but rather to what extent its audience would be interested in what a brand has to offer. Subject, content, and distribution patterns are indicators of an audience's interests.

Addressable Media and Interactive Media

Media that carry messages to identifiable customers or prospects are referred to as **addressable media** because all can be used to send brand messages to specific geographic and electronic addresses. Addressable media include the internet (see Chapter 12), postal mail, and the telephone (see Chapter 18). Addressable media are used primarily to communicate with current customers or with carefully selected prospects.

Two-way media allowing both companies and customers to send and receive messages are called **interactive media.** The benefit of interactive media such as the telephone, the internet, and personal salespeople is that they allow an instant exchange of information to take place. More important, they make it possible for a customer to contact a company.

Media Intrusiveness

Because of the high level of commercial message clutter, companies need all the help they can get in attracting attention to their messages. Media planners know that media vary in their degree of intrusiveness (see Figure 11-3). The most intrusive medium is personal selling because the sales representative's presence

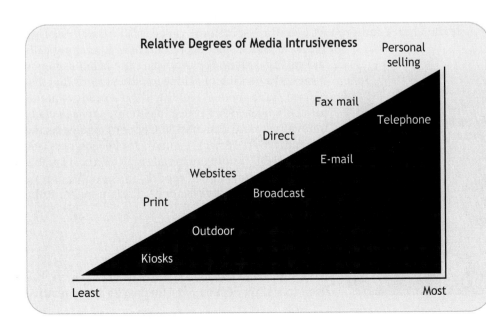

Relative Degrees of Media Intrusiveness

Personal selling

Fax mail

Telephone

Direct

E-mail

Websites

Broadcast

Print

Outdoor

Kiosks

Least   Most

FIGURE 11-3

Generally the more personal or addressable a medium is, the more intrusive it is.

demands attention. The least intrusive media are print—newspapers, outdoor boards, magazines—because users choose when and to what extent to use these media. The more intrusive a medium is, generally speaking, the more it can be personalized, but also the more costly it is to use.

Admittedly, the word *intrusive* has negative connotations. If a message is too disruptive, it is not exactly something that helps build brand relationships. Companies often find themselves in an awkward position. They know it is to their advantage to get brand messages to customers and prospects, but they also know that many of these messages may not be welcome. There are several ways to minimize intrusiveness. One is to choose media whose target audience is interested in the product category. Research has shown that one of the benefits of specialized magazines is that readers enjoy learning about new products from the advertising. To help get attention and not be intrusive is one of the reasons why events, sponsorships, and product placements in movies and TV shows have become so popular. Also, giving customers the option to opt-in for receiving brand information means that when MC messages are sent, they are not unexpected and therefore not seen as intrusive.

Media Strengths and Weaknesses

The strengths and weaknesses of each medium are relevant to any type of brand messages they carry, regardless of the type of marketing communication message—everything from traditional advertising to publicity resulting from a news release. Table 11-1 summarizes the strengths and weaknesses of each medium discussed in this chapter and the next. Terms that may be unfamiliar to you are defined in each discussion. The information summarized in Table 11-1 is the most important of all the information in the three media chapters (Chapters 11 through 13).

PRINT MEDIA

The print media include newspapers and magazines, directories, mail, brochures, packaging, and all other forms of message delivery that are produced by printing words or images on paper or some other material, such as balloons, T-shirts, caps, and pens. Print messages are relatively permanent compared to broadcast messages, which are fleeting. In this case, *permanence* means that the message can be kept (clipped and saved, for example) and revisited.

EXHIBIT 11-3

UNAUTHORIZED OWNER'S MANUAL

Sales brochures and product literature (sometimes called *collateral materials*) are designed to assist sales representatives in making calls and taking orders. For example, the MINI's agency designed a vending machine for showrooms that dispensed (for a modest fee) the MINI's product literature, as well as other collectible items.[5] An especially innovative piece in the MINI Cooper launch was the "unauthorized owner's manual" for new owners (see Exhibit 11-3). Training materials may also be available in printed form. Annual reports are a good example of more elaborate publications that are meant to be kept, at least for a year.

Newspapers

Although readership of U.S. daily newspapers has been in a slow decline over the last 25 years relative

TABLE 11-1   Strengths and Weaknesses of Major Media

Medium	Strengths	Weaknesses
Newspapers	• Reader education and income • Tangible • Reader habit, loyalty, involvement • Short lead time • Low production cost • High one-time reach • Good for detailed copy	• Poor reproduction, especially color • Decreasing readership • Clutter • Media waste (mass audience)
Magazines	• Audience selectivity • Expertise environment • High-quality reproduction • Long life • High credibility	• Long lead time • Low "mass" reach • Costly production • Low frequency (weekly, monthly, or quarterly)
Television	• Impact: sight, sound, motion • Good builder of reach • Local and national • Targeted cable channels	• Broad audience • High production cost • Intrusive • Messages short lived
Radio	• Audience selectivity • "Theater of the mind" • Frequency builder • Relatively low product cost	• Background (low attention) • Low reach • Sound only • Messages short-lived
Outdoor	• Localized • Frequency builder • Directional signage	• Low attention • Short exposure time • Poor reputation (visual pollution) • Zoning restrictions
Direct mail*	• Highly selective • Measurable results • Can be personalized • Demands attention	• Clutter/junk-mail perception • High cost per message • Long lead time
Telemarketing*	• Personalized • Real-time interaction • Attention getting • Measurable results	• Costly • Ugly image • Intrusive
Internet*	• Mass and addressable • Can be personalized • Extremely low cost • Can be interactive	• Clutter • Limited reach • Limited creative options

*The internet is discussed in Chapter 12, direct mail and telemarketing in Chapter 18.

to population increases, newspapers are still a major medium, especially for carrying local advertising. In fact, 45 percent of all local advertising is carried by daily newspapers. While daily newspaper circulation has been declining, there has been growth in weekly, alternative, and ethnic newspapers. Active urban singles are particularly interested in alternative papers, usually given away at newsstands and in busy spots such as coffee shops and restaurants. The *Chicago Reader* and the *Denver Westword*, for example, offer extensive coverage of popular culture and local entertainment and dining. Mostly targeted at twenty-somethings who find the local daily newspaper to be largely irrelevant to their lives, these Gen-X newspapers are beginning to attract national advertising from companies who long to reach this group.

Although newspapers are primarily a local medium, in the United States there are two national daily newspapers—*USA Today* and the *Wall Street Journal*. An example of a niche national newspaper is *Women's Wear Daily*. Although national newspapers carry only an extremely small percentage of U.S. newspaper advertising, this is not true in some other countries. In Japan and Korea, for example, the major newspapers that most people read are national rather than local. The same is true in some of the smaller European countries.

Hispanic newspapers in the United States are growing much faster than the Hispanic population itself. In 1990, there were 355 Hispanic newspapers and 177 Hispanic magazines. By the end of 2003, there were 550 Hispanic newspapers and 352 Hispanic magazines.[6]

To fight the readership decline and competition from other media, many daily newspapers have invested heavily in redesign, in the addition of special-topic sections, and in equipment that delivers better production values. Also, all major U.S. papers now have websites that contain past stories as well as news updates throughout the day.

Formats and Features

Newspapers come in two basic sizes. **Broadsheets** are *newspapers with full-size pages,* such as the *New York Times* and *Chicago Tribune*. **Tabloids** are *newspapers whose pages are half the size of broadsheets.* Examples of tabloids are the *New York Daily News* and the *Chicago Sun-Times*. Traditionally, tabloids have been perceived as more sensational than broadsheets and aimed at a more blue-collar audience, although this stereotype doesn't fit all tabloids.

Most medium- and large-circulation newspapers divide their content into topic sections such as sports, entertainment, lifestyle/fashion, finance/business, and food, in addition to the local/national/international news section that usually fronts the paper. Many of the special-interest sections rely heavily on news releases provided by public relations departments and agencies. Companies can quasi-target their paid brand messages by asking the newspaper to place their advertisements in the most relevant section (leisure-oriented brands in the sports section, food items in the food section, personal care brands in the lifestyle/fashion section).

Classified Ads, Display Ads, and Inserts

Newspapers offer three basic types of advertising: classified, display, and supplement inserts. Approximately one-third of a newspaper's advertising revenue comes from its classified section. **Classified ads** are *small-space, words-only ads presented in a clearly labeled section with no surrounding editorial content.* Classifieds ads are organized by category (items for sale, automobiles, apartments for rent, help wanted), which helps readers quickly find what they are looking for. They are priced according to word count, generally run multiple times, and are used primarily by consumers and small, local businesses.

In recent years, there has been an increase in **classified display ads,** which are *ads in the classified section that include graphics and larger sizes of type.* These are used primarily by local businesses such as car dealers and real-estate firms. Most major newspapers have their classifieds online for wider access.

The majority of a newspaper's advertising space is filled with **display ads,** which are *ads that generally contain more graphics and white space than copy and appear next to editorial content.* Unlike consumers and small business that buy space in the classified ad section, where readers seek out certain goods and service providers, most users of display advertising assume that customers and prospects will not specifically search out their ads. Thus, they depend on the editorial content to pull readers through the paper, providing exposure to their ads.

Display ad space is sold either by the column inch or by the standard advertising unit (SAU). A **column inch** is *a space that is one column wide and one inch tall.* (Most columns are approximately 2 inches wide.) A space that is four columns wide and 10 inches tall occupies 40 column inches (4 columns × 10 inches). The **standard advertising unit (SAU)** is *a set of predetermined spaces that are constant in size in every newspaper that has adopted SAU standards* (see Figure 11-4). These standards were set up in response to complaints from national advertisers that using local newspapers was too costly because every paper had its own dimensions, which meant that separate ads had to be produced for each paper used. Now, a national brand that wants to buy newspaper space can have its agency create an ad that conforms to one of the SAU sizes and know that the ad will be acceptable at most papers. (The SAU system, however, has not encouraged many national advertisers to use newspaper advertising, for reasons explained later in this chapter.)

Supplement inserts, the third way to advertise in newspapers, are *inserts that are preprinted by an advertiser and enclosed with the newspaper.* These inserts are usually 100 percent advertising, and often each one is for a separate company. Retailers such as Target, Walgreen's, and Home Depot commonly use inserts. *Supplements that contain ads, most with coupons, for a variety of national brands* are called **free-standing inserts (FSIs)** and are sold primarily by two national sales-promotion companies, ADVO and Valassis Communications. Companies using supplements and FSIs supply their own printed materials, but papers charge an insert fee based on the size of the insert and the paper's circulation.

Coverage and Audience Measurement

Because newspapers are primarily a local medium in the United States, they are probably the most personal of all the mass media. Most people think of their hometown paper as *their* paper. The strength of this feeling is evident each

FIGURE 11-4

Why was having a standard set of ad sizes important to advertisers?

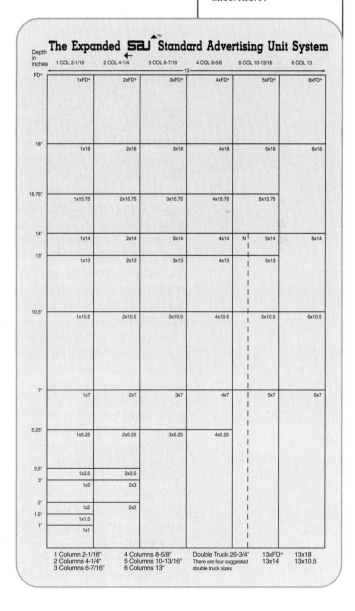

time a paper redesigns its format. Such changes always generate letters from readers asking "How dare you change *my* paper!" Because readers identify so closely with their newspaper, this medium is especially good for creating connectivity.

National advertisers generally use newspapers only on a market-by-market basis to add extra media weight in places where competition may be extremely strong or the brand is having trouble building its consumer franchise. Newspaper penetration—that is, the percentage of population reached by a paper—in large metro areas is 25 to 35 percent by the major dailies; in smaller cities the penetration may be as high as 75 percent. Newspaper readership is highest in middle- and upper-income neighborhoods and lowest among teenagers (regardless of socio-economic status). Large metro papers often divide their metro areas into zones and have a separate section of the paper for each zone. This allows the paper to carry more local content (neighborhood news and features) and sell advertising at a much lower rate to businesses in each zone (because their ads are carried in only one or two zones, not in the newspaper's full circulation area).

Sales and Pricing

Newspaper representatives sell advertising space and promotions, such as event sponsorships or special editions. These people generally work totally or partially on commission. Besides local sales reps who work directly for a newspaper full-time, there are national "rep firms" that represent many different newspapers across the country. These firms sell to regional and national brands that want to buy newspaper space in more than one city. A major benefit to ad agencies from using rep firms is receiving only one invoice for all the space bought in several different papers.

Standard Rate and Data Services (SRDS) provides media profiles, production requirements, and advertising rates (in both hard-copy and online formats) to subscribers. This service is used by advertising agencies for their local and national clients. The most widely used SRDS services are for magazines and newspapers. In addition, most newspapers (and magazines) publish a **rate card,** which is *a list of advertising space costs and discounts.* For local retailers, newspapers have discounts based on the amount of space a retailer buys during a year—the greater the volume, the lower the rate. For very large accounts (usually retailers that place one or more full pages of advertising each week), advertisers may negotiate an annual rate that is lower than anything shown on the rate card. Newspaper rates are determined by circulation and the amount of space a brand uses. There are also extra charges for the use of color and sometimes for placement in special locations within the paper.

Newspapers charge national brands as much as 50 percent more than they charge local advertisers. They justify these higher rates by claiming that it costs more to do business with national advertisers than with local retailers. Unlike for locally placed advertising, newspapers have to pay a commission (15 percent) to agencies that place ads for national and regional brands. Because of the increased cost and the necessity of dealing with many different newspapers, many national companies seldom use newspapers as part of their media mix, except to add extra weight as previously explained.

One way national brands can advertise at local rates is to have their local franchisees (such as Avis, Kentucky Fried Chicken, H&R Block) place and pay for the ads. Often franchisees form local co-op groups that pool their marketing communication dollars and hire an agency to handle their promotional efforts. In automotive marketing, for example, dealer groups often organize to create and place advertising within a metropolitan area or region.

Many manufacturers offer **cooperative advertising,** *a system in which a manufacturer pays a portion (normally half) of the cost when a local retailer advertises the manu-*

facturer's brand. Many newspapers keep track of which manufacturers are offering co-op ad programs. Because some retailers, particularly small ones, often are unaware of or forget about these funds, the newspaper provides a service to its retail customers and, at the same time, sells more ad space by making the retailer aware of co-op allowances.

Strengths and Weaknesses of Newspapers

Newspapers boast a number of strengths. They reach a mass local audience, between 25 and 75 percent of households in their metro area. Generally speaking, however, the greater the metro population, the lower the percentage of households reached. Like magazine readers, newspaper readers are above average in education and income. The fact that newspapers are tangible allows customers and prospects to be exposed to brand messages when and where they prefer, and to read and reread ads at their own pace for better comprehension.

Because most newspaper circulation is daily, frequency can be quickly built among those who regularly read the newspaper. The average newspaper reader spends 29 minutes a day reading a weekday edition, slightly more reading a Sunday edition.[7] The newspaper has a designated place in subscribers' daily routines. The fact that newspapers offer a constant supply of information and entertainment means that most subscribers have an emotional involvement with their daily newspaper, which is a benefit to advertisers. Finally, daily newspapers provide marketers with flexibility and short lead time. Newspapers have a quick production process, which allows a company to change the content of its advertising up to 24 or 48 hours (depending on the newspaper) before the paper is published. Interestingly, research has shown that newspaper readers often consider advertising to be news, too.

Newspapers have several weaknesses. Their average life span is only one day. They are printed on low-quality porous paper (called newsprint). Consequently, when ink is applied, it spreads, which is why newspapers have relatively poor reproduction qualities for any kind of graphics. Clutter is also a problem in newspapers. Not only does a brand message compete with other ads for attention, but it must also compete with all the editorial content. Perhaps the most serious weakness, from an IMC perspective, is that newspapers are a mass medium. Even though an advertiser can quasi-target a message by requesting that it appear in a special-topic section (such as sports or food), the cost of the space is based on the paper's total circulation. This means that there can be a high percentage of media waste.

Magazines

Most magazines won't permit unconventional media buys, but as part of its campaign, MINI Cooper convinced a few to print ads in innovative and eye-catching new ways. See Exhibits 11-4a and Exhibit 11-4b for examples.

Magazines are classified by frequency of publication (weekly, monthly, bimonthly, quarterly) and by type of audience (consumer, business, trade, and professional). Magazines are also classified by how they are distributed. *Magazines that sell subscriptions* are classified as **paid-circulation publications.** Even these publications, though, receive approximately three-fourths of their income from advertising sales. In contrast, **controlled-circulation publications** are *trade, industrial, and organizational magazines that are distributed free to those working in a given subject area or affiliated with a given organization.* These magazines make up for the lack of subscription income by selling ads, selling their

EXHIBIT 11-4A

One of many innovative ideas in the launch of the MINI Cooper was the ad that ran in the margin of the magazines with the slogan "Nothing corners like a MINI. LET'S MOTOR."

EXHIBIT 11-4B

Another in a line of MINI Cooper's successful magazine ads, Rolling Stone printed this ad and used orange staples in its binding as part of the road the MINI Cooper is motoring on.

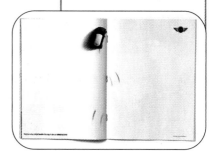

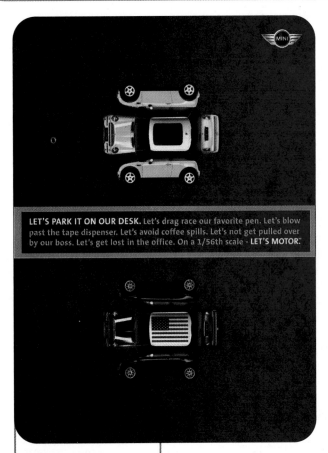

LET'S PARK IT ON OUR DESK. Let's drag race our favorite pen. Let's blow past the tape dispenser. Let's avoid coffee spills. Let's not get pulled over by our boss. Let's get lost in the office. On a 1/56th scale - **LET'S MOTOR.**

EXHIBIT 11-5

This ad on heavier-than-normal stock was bound into magazines. It features two scale models of the MINI that readers could punch out and fold to make their own desk model.

database of subscribers, and in some cases sponsoring annual trade shows.

Although there are some good controlled-circulation publications, most media planners prefer buying space in paid-circulation magazines. Logic tells us that people are more likely to spend more time reading a magazine they have paid for than one they have received for free.

Formats and Features

Unlike newspapers, which strive to provide news and information coverage of a geographical area, most magazines focus their content coverage on a particular subject. Professional and trade journals often take either a horizontal or a vertical approach to a subject. An example of a *horizontally focused* magazine is *Chain Store Age*, which discusses the operation of chain retail stores (drug, food, mass merchandisers, sporting goods, hobby shops) regardless of the type of merchandise being sold. An example of a *vertically focused* magazine is *Supermarket News*, which discusses issues related to just one industry, selling products in food stores.

Another characteristic that differentiates magazines from newspapers is production quality. Because magazines are printed on higher-quality paper than newspapers, photographs reproduce particularly well (the ink doesn't run as it does on newsprint paper).

In an effort to strengthen relationships with current customers, some large companies publish their own magazines (see Exhibit 11-6). On first glance, these look like most other magazines with full-color pictures and interesting layouts. However, the subjects discussed are all related in some way to the company's products. Some of these customer-focused magazines have ads only for company brands; others sell space to noncompeting brands. A somewhat similar magazine concept is used by TV celebrities who have their own magazine such as *O*, by Oprah Winfrey and *Rosie*, which was a joint venture between Rosie O'Donnell and the Gruner + Jahr publishing company. Although *Rosie* reached a circulation of 3.6 million in 2002, the magazine ceased publication when O'Donnell claimed she no longer had the editorial control promised to her by the publisher.

Magazines offer a wider range of ways to present brand messages than newspapers do, although both are print media. The following are types of advertising specific to magazines:

- *Gatefolds:* Two or more oversize pages that fold out from the magazine.

- *Preprinted ads* called **tip-ins:** *Ads that are bound or glued into the magazine but are printed on heavier paper than the rest of the magazine.* Tip-ins attract attention when people are thumbing through. A version of the Mini's "unofficial driver's manual" was distributed as a tip-in glued into *Fast Company* and other magazines.

- *Business reply cards (BRCs):* Postcard-size cards that are (a) slipped between the pages (so they easily fall out when the magazine is read), (b) tipped into the binding so they are easily seen but held in place, or (c) stuck onto an ad. BRCs provide a good way to begin a customer dialogue or to measure to what extent an ad has generated a response.

EXHIBIT 11-6
mMode *is a controlled-circulation magazine published by AT&T Wireless and sent free to customers.*

- *Pop-up ads:* Three-dimensional ads that stand up when the magazine is opened to the page on which they appear.
- *Scent strips:* Patches that readers can scratch or pull off to elicit a smell (used for perfumes, air fresheners, and foods).

Some magazines, such as *People,* have the capability, using an ink-jet printer, to imprint the names of individual subscribers in ads inside the magazine. This is a good technique to call a reader's attention to the ad, but it significantly increases the cost of the ad space.

All of those options help attract attention to a brand message. They also can greatly increase the price of advertising in a magazine. The media planner must determine that the increased cost will be justified by increases in message exposure and customer response.

Coverage and Audience Measurement

SRDS publishes two main magazine directories—one for consumer magazines and one for business publications. In the business and industrial product categories, there are magazines for nearly any type of service and manufacturing area imaginable. The business directory has over 7,500 listings divided into 186 market classifications ranging from architecture to woodworking. Because magazines' rates, specifications, circulation, and printing options periodically change, SRDS publishes a new directory each month. It also has an online edition that is constantly being updated. The consumer directory has 86 category listings for over 3,000 magazines, including 380 international magazines and 300 farm magazines.

Although most magazines (both consumer and B2B) have national distribution, several consumer magazines are targeted regionally and locally. Major metro areas have their own magazines, such as *Tampa Bay Life* and *San Francisco Focus;* examples of regional magazines are *Sunset* and *Yankee,* which serve the Southwest and Northeast, respectively. Large-circulation magazines such as *Sports Illustrated* and *Business Week* also have regional and even metro editions. Like zone editions of newspapers, these local and regional editions of magazines provide area companies the prestige of using national publications but charge advertising rates based on the circulation in their trading area.

When buying space in regional or local editions, media planners must remember that even a large-circulation magazine like *Time,* which reaches about 4 percent of U.S. households, will reach only a proportional percentage of households in a local market. The good news for *Time* is that many of the households in its 4 percent local reach are desirable ones, those whose income, education, and professional levels are above average. Some magazines also have demographic editions. *Newsweek,* for example, prints a special edition for female executives; Exhibit 11-7 shows how this special edition reaches adult women with above-average demographics.

EXHIBIT 11-7

Newsweek, like many other large-circulation magazines, has special editions that go to specific audiences. Marketers can buy in just this edition, thus minimizing media waste.

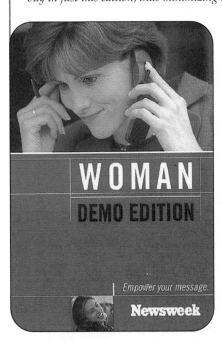

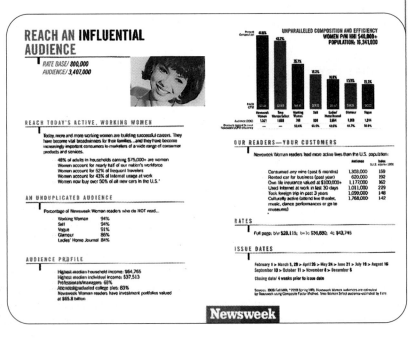

Another way to think about magazine coverage is from a product category or subject area perspective. A media planner wants to know what percentage of homeowners *House and Garden* reaches, because homeowners make up the magazine's target audience. For a trade magazine serving the institutional food service industry, it would be important to know what percentage of food service managers the magazine reaches.

Because circulation is a major factor determining how much a magazine charges for advertising space, agencies and marketers do not simply take the magazine's word about readership; they use third-party research services to verify circulation. The Audit Bureau of Circulation is the primary verification service for consumer magazines. Besides certifying circulation, this bureau also gives a geographical breakdown of the circulation and indicates the amount of paid circulation (magazines sold at newsstands and by subscription) versus the number of copies that are given away. The circulation of business and professional magazines is monitored by the Business Publication Audit service. Magazines pay to have their circulation audited and the findings published.

Circulation figures, however, do not tell the whole story. Compared to newspapers, most magazines have a higher **pass-along rate**, that is, *the number of people who read the magazine in addition to subscribers or buyers of the magazine.* Business and professional magazines, especially, have high pass-along readership because they are often routed to different people within an organization and are kept in the company library. *Newsweek's* edition sent to female executives, for example, has a circulation of 800,000 but an audience of 3 million. This means, on average, each copy is read by more than four women (the number is determined through readership surveys). Pass-along rates, of course, are estimates based on interviewing customers about their reading habits and the source of their reading materials. Media planners must keep in mind that circulation and readership can vary significantly from one magazine to another.

Sales and Pricing

Magazine space is sold in portions of a page—quarter-, half-, and full-page ads, as well as **double-page spreads,** which are *ads printed across two facing pages.* There are also custom space buys, such as "islands," which are spaces in the middle of editorial content. As with newspapers, the more magazine space a brand buys, the lower the rate. Four-color ads cost more than black-and-white ads. *Ads with graphics that go to the edge of the page,* called **bleed ads,** also cost more but attract more attention

Magazine space is sold by salespeople working directly for the magazine and by media representatives who sell space in a variety of magazines. Magazines also have rate cards, as newspapers do, but are known to do more negotiating on rates: most space sales are for bigger dollars, which allows more room for negotiation. When comparing magazine ad rates, cost per reader reached is more informative than costs based on circulation.

Strengths and Weaknesses of Magazines

As mentioned earlier, an advantage of magazines is their high-quality reproduction. These higher production values, however, mean that production takes longer than in newspapers, so more lead time is required to place ads in a magazine (one to three months depending on the magazine).

Because most magazines are subject specific, one of their greatest strengths is their audience selectivity. Although there are a few general-interest magazines—*Time, Newsweek, Reader's Digest*—the vast majority of magazines focus on one area. Not surprisingly, Cuisinart, which makes food processors, advertises in *Gourmet* and *Better Homes & Gardens* because these magazines often run stories that attract readers interested in learning about new and better ways of preparing food. Such readers are high-potential prospects for Cuisinart. Subject-specific magazines are seen as being authorities on their respective subject areas. Therefore, brands that advertise in them can benefit from this expertise halo, an added value for a brand message.

Like newspapers, magazines are tangible and thus allow readers to read them at their own pace. Magazines also have strong reader involvement because readers (of paid-circulation magazines) have selected and paid for their magazines, a strong indication that they are interested in a magazine's subject and will spend time with the magazine. Magazines are even more permanent than newspapers because they are kept much longer and are frequently picked up and read more than once, providing additional opportunities for a brand message to be seen, read, and have an effect.

A feature of magazines that many marketers particularly like is the ability to do a **split run,** *a process in which a marketer places one ad in one half of a magazine's circulation and a different ad in the other half.* This allows marketers to test one offer, headline, or creative approach against another. The only thing that is required is that both ads contain a response device such as a toll-free number, coupon, or order form that is coded so that the marketer can tell which ad produced a higher response.

Magazines, too, have weaknesses that concern advertisers. Although highly targeted, most magazines have relatively limited reach of a brand's target audience. This is more true of consumer than of B2B magazines. Magazines also have a long lead time, which means the **closing date,** *the date by which advertising materials must reach the publisher,* is up to three months before publication. Consequently, magazines do not offer the scheduling flexibility of newspapers and some other media. Another drawback is their lack of frequency. Many appear only once a month or even less often; especially industry magazines and trade journals. Finally, magazine ads are more costly to produce than newspaper ads (but far less expensive than TV commercials).

Directories

To many people, directories sound pretty boring. But for many B2B companies, as well as many retailers, they are often one of the most important media vehicles used. The most widely used and known directory is the Yellow Pages, either a section within a phone book or (in large cities) a separate book that contains listings of businesses by product category. No one company owns the name "Yellow Pages," so many of the 2,000-plus publishers of telephone directories across the United States use the term.

All businesses that have a telephone are listed in the Yellow Pages; however, a business must pay extra for a display ad. Yellow Pages display ads not only repeat (from the one-line listing) the business's phone number and address but may also provide a locator map, business hours, a list of services or brands carried, number of years in business, and other claims to help differentiate the business from its competitors. Display space is contracted annually but paid for monthly in a fee added to the business's phone bill. As with magazines, space is sold by portions of a page—full, half, quarter, eighth.

A directory is both a reference source and an advertising medium. Customers go to the Yellow Pages not only to look up telephone numbers but also to see which businesses offer a certain product, what their hours are, and where they are located. The amount of information, its arrangement, and its accuracy can send a brand message—positive or negative. What makes a Yellow Pages brand message valuable is that the people who see it are seeking information about the product category. In other words, customers reached by Yellow Pages ads are generally in the second or third step of the AIDA sequence described in Chapter 5—they are *interested* in a product (see Exhibit 11-8).

A weakness of the Yellow Pages is that they are printed only once a year. This means that new businesses that begin mid-year must wait to be listed (unless they plan far ahead). It also means that any changes in contact information, hours of operation, and so on cannot be made until the next directory is published. To help circumvent this weakness, most Yellow Pages are also now available online (see the Technology in Action box).

Thousands of other directories are published by trade associations, industrial groups, and special-interest groups—and most of them accept advertising. Whether aimed at B2B customers or consumers, directories facilitate customer dialogue, steering people to places where they are most likely to get their questions answered.

TECHNOLOGY IN ACTION

Directories Go Electronic

You can now use your personal computer to find all the restaurants within driving distance that serve Mexican food at moderate prices. You probably can read their menus online and see photos of their dining rooms. Then, when you choose one to go to, your computer can plot a route from your home to its door.

The electronic directories (e-directories) that are coming online can do all of this. Yellow Pages publishers, as well as independent directories, are developing these new e-directories as supplements to the familiar printed directory. They aggregate business listings, just like a regular printed directory, and accept paid advertising. There are more than 600 directories of this type. (A complete listing of Internet Yellow Pages is maintained by the Kelsey Group at www.kelseygroup.com.)

Electronic Yellow Pages have advantages for both companies and consumers. Companies can continu-

ously update their listings—the Mexican restaurant, for example, can add new menu specialties or change its prices. E-directories can also provide in-depth information to customers by setting up links to other sections or websites. This feature is particularly useful for banks and other companies that offer complex product packages. E-directories thus give customers and prospects instantaneous access to searchable information that may not be available in any other format.

Think About It

When might you want to consult an electronic directory? Go to the Kelsey Group directory of electronic directories and see how close it comes to providing information you might use in your city or town.

BROADCAST MEDIA

As broadcast media, radio and television have several characteristics in common. On average, people spend 85 percent of their media time with broadcast media and only 15 percent with print media.[8] This statistic might seem to indicate that broadcast is the best place for brand messages. Keep in mind, however, that people do other things while listening to radio and watching TV, especially when commercials are on.

As noted in Chapter 10, both radio and television accept news releases; video news releases, especially, can be effective in generating brand publicity. Local stations often cover special events—such as a grand opening of a store or a sports event—by doing on-site broadcasts; thus broadcast media can be helpful in supporting event marketing programs. Compared to print messages, however, broadcast messages are fleeting. Once a message appears, it is gone until it runs again. (People rarely record commercials in order to watch them over and over.) The fleeting nature of broadcast media is one reason why cable news channels like CNN, sports channels like ESPN, and the Weather Channel have been so successful—they can provide programming 24 hours a day for people who want to tune in for a short while to catch the latest update (see Exhibit 11-9).

Broadcast commercials are more intrusive than brand messages in print media. Programming and commercials are presented in a stream, one after another. Readers of print media can select stories and ads in whatever order they want and completely ignore whole sections. With broadcast media, this is difficult to do. The remote control and VCR make it possible to time-shift programs and zip past commercials; but the presentation form is still linear, and viewers and listeners have to attend to information in the order in which it is presented.

EXHIBIT 11-9

One of the advantages of cable broadcasting has been the introduction of full-time news, sports, and weather channels. This ad identifies the number of cable subscribers who turn to the Weather Channel.

Audience Measurement

Exposure to broadcast media is measured in rating points. A **rating point** is *1 percent of a communication vehicle's coverage area that has been exposed to a broadcast program.* If the Super Bowl is said to have had a 40 national rating, this means that during an average 15-minute segment of the Super Bowl program, 40 percent of all U.S. households were tuned in. At the local level, a radio or TV program that has, for example, 3 percent of the households in its market tuned in is said to have a 3 rating (in that broadcast coverage area).

Broadcast ratings are based on a communication vehicle's coverage area, or **marketing universe,** which is *a specified target profile within a geographical area.* This universe can be defined however a marketer wants to define it: all households in the Detroit metro area, adults nationwide, or women aged 25 to 49 in the Northwest.

Although the price charged for broadcast time is based on ratings, media planners must remember that ratings tell only what percentage of households within a metro area are tuned to a certain TV or radio program. Ratings are not a measure of the number of people paying attention to commercials. Media exposure does not equal message exposure. For broadcast media, actual message exposure is only 25 to 50 percent of program exposure.[9]

A broadcast term related to a rating is **share,** *the percentage of persons using a radio or TV at a particular time who are tuned to a particular station.* For example, during the evening hours, about one-half of U.S. households have their TVs on. This number, called *households using TV (HUT),* is the base number on which share is figured. In the preceding Super Bowl example, if 60 percent of all U.S. households had one or more TV sets on while the Super Bowl was being broadcast, the Super Bowl's share would be 67. This number is calculated by dividing the Super Bowl rating of 40 by 60, the percentage of sets turned on ($40 \div 60 = 67\%$). A program's share is always larger than its rating because there is never a time when every household is listening to radio or watching TV. Stations that have relatively low ratings sometimes talk about their share rather than their rating, because share numbers are larger.

TV audiences are measured by companies such as Nielsen Media Research, which provides the ratings on which television networks and stations base the cost of their airtime. Ratings for radio are determined by Arbitron. These audience measurements are taken four times a year in periods known as "sweeps." During the sweeps periods, networks run special programming and stations heavy-up their self-promotions. The idea is to maximize viewing and thus create higher ratings, which then allow networks and stations to increase their prices for commercial time.

Nielsen does its research in 210 television markets, where it asks a sample of the population to record their viewing behaviors in diaries. Nielsen also uses "people meters," boxes wired to TV sets in a sample of homes in 47 markets. The meters track daily viewing data and automatically relay this data to a central location for analysis.[10] One of Nielsen's newer measurements is a share-of-viewing report that separates the TV audience into the following categories: network, syndication, cable, PBS, pay cable, and local/other. This breakdown makes it possible for companies to compare network, syndication, and cable viewing patterns for 32 time periods. Another company that collects TV viewing data, along with demographic and lifestyle data, is Mediamark Research Inc. (MRI).

Because ratings are a major factor in determining what advertising rates broadcasters can charge for their various programs, the major TV networks have been complaining for years that the Nielsen ratings understate the size of their audiences. Consequently, these networks (CBS, ABC, NBC, and Fox) have formed a joint venture with Statistical Research Inc., creating a rating service called Systems for Measuring and Reporting Television (SMART). One of the primary objectives of SMART is to include out-of-home viewing (at, for example, barber shops, transportation terminals, bars, and restaurants), which Nielsen does not include in its research.

Sales and Pricing

Broadcast time is sold in units. Stations often quote prices in 30- and 60-second units (written as :30 and :60). Of course, costs vary not only by the amount of time but also by the estimated size of the audience. For example, station A charges $1,000 for a :60 commercial while station B charges only $800. If station A's audience is twice as large as station B's, then station A's unit is a much better value even though its unit cost is $200 more. Pricing is also done on a per point (rating point) basis, which is discussed in more detail in Chapter 13.

Although audience size is important, other audience characteristics, such as income and lifestyle, also are important in putting a price on a program or channel's

ahh...the rich aroma
of success...

Food Network is proud to say that our viewers are some of the most desirable consumers in the world. They're people who believe that "the good life" has as much to do with knowing the right Beaujolais as it does choosing a new car. As a matter of fact, Food Network viewers are more likely to buy or lease new cars, own 3 plus credit cards and belong to more than 2 frequent flyer programs than average cable viewers.*

These financially full-bodied consumers turn to Food Network because our original programming makes life more flavorful in one of the areas they care about most.

To reach more active, upscale consumers, call:

Karen Grinthal   Jim Dowdle   Colleen Griffin   John Poruch
New York   Chicago   Los Angeles   Detroit
212.398.8836   312.606.8836   310.858.8191   248.740.0341

food NETWORK.
www.foodtv.com
aol keyword: food

EXHIBIT 11-10

This ad brags that Food Network viewers are "some of the most desirable consumers in the world." That's because the upscale audience believes that "the good life" depends on making the right food choices, as well as choices about other products.

time. The ad in Exhibit 11-10 for the Food Network promises potential advertisers an upscale audience.

Ad rates for broadcast media are much more negotiable than rates for print media because broadcast commercial time is both fixed and perishable. Subtract programming time from 24 hours in a day, and the remaining time is what is available for commercials. The only way to get more commercial time is to cut back on programming, which most stations are reluctant to do because it is the programming (not the commercials) that attracts audiences. Print media can increase or reduce the number of pages in each edition in response to how many pages of advertising were sold. Broadcasters, however, cannot increase or decrease the number of hours in a day. Therefore, when there is an above-average demand for commercial time, stations increase their prices, and when the demand is below average, stations decrease their prices to attract more buyers. In other words, broadcast pricing is based on supply and demand.

Broadcast time is said to be perishable because when a unit of time goes unsold, then it is simply gone. You cannot sell a time slot that is in the past. Another reason why broadcast rates are negotiable is that a station's cost of operation remains the same whether some, all, or none of the commercial time is sold. A station may choose to cut its rates rather than to get nothing at all for a given unit of time.

Another pricing characteristic common to both radio and TV is that rates vary according to how much guarantee an advertiser wants that a scheduled commercial will actually run. Because stations never know how much demand they will have for commercial time, they have what is called a **pre-emptible rate.** This is *a relatively low rate that doesn't guarantee a given commercial will run at a given time.* If another advertiser is willing to pay more for the time, the station can pre-empt the advertiser that accepted the low rate. If a retailer is buying time to support a grand opening or a special event, it is not a good idea to buy pre-emptible time because the promotional support may not be there. On the other hand, this is a money-saving choice for reminder and image messages that can run anytime.

Another overall difference between print and broadcast media is that broadcast audiences constantly fluctuate, whereas print audiences stay fairly constant from issue to issue. The size of a station's audience varies significantly by time of day and program offering.

Radio

Today in the United States there are more than 10,000 commercial radio stations, split about evenly between AM and FM. Signals from AM stations can travel up to 600 miles (depending on atmospheric conditions); the range of FM signals is only 40 to 50 miles. There are also noncommercial stations, many of which are affiliates of the nonprofit National Public Radio (NPR) network. Although NPR stations are referred to as noncommercial, they do carry brand messages, and these have in fact slowly expanded from simple "sponsored by" lines to soft-sell commercials.

(Nonprofit stations are not allowed to make direct offers.) Online radio stations—both commercial and noncommercial—are also beginning to build audiences.

In addition to radio, marketing communicators may also consider various types of audio formats for brand messages and brand reinforcement. For example, CDs are often used by brands or in support of brand events—as when McDonald's used CDs by pop icons Britney Spears and 'N Sync as premiums (giveaways). Custom CDs, such as Wrangler Jeans's "Country Christmas," are assembled specifically for the brand's use. Sometimes these efforts represent several partners in addition to the product sponsor. One recent promotion by bootmaker Doc Martens also had the support of Warner Bros. Records, American Eagle Outfitters, and *Spin* magazine. Such a promotion can cost over a million dollars, depending on the amount of support in the form of advertising or publicity.[11]

Adding to media fragmentation is satellite radio, which is being introduced in the United States by two companies—Sirius and XM Satellite Radio. The benefit over conventional AM and FM radio stations is that satellite companies promise national coverage, digital sound, over one hundred channels from which to choose, and fewer commercials. Listening to satellite radio, however, requires special custom receivers, which cost around $250. Because each satellite broadcast company has its own receiver standards, two receivers are needed if a person wants to listen to both companies' broadcasts. There is also a monthly subscription cost, and because satellite broadcasts are national, there is no way to get local news and weather. Until these costs and limitations are significantly reduced, some argue, satellite radio will not become a major medium.

Formats and Features

Research has shown that radio is a background medium: it is often on while people are doing other things (multitasking). Listeners tune in and out as something catches or loses their attention. Because people get used to having radio in the background, brand messages must break through to get and retain attention. In spite of the background nature of radio, however, radio programs and stations generally have loyal audiences.

Radio listening can be an intimate and personal experience, as the ad in Exhibit 11-11 demonstrates. The effectiveness of radio as an advertising medium comes from its ability to use programming to target audience interests. Like readers of local newspapers, radio listeners generally have a favorite radio station, which they call *their* station because of its format and on-air personalities. These preferences help counterbalance the "background" nature of radio and enable it to connect with loyal listeners. Radio also offers **image transfer,** *a process by which members of a target audience exposed to the sights and sounds of a brand's TV message recall the visual elements of the message when they are exposed to a similar soundtrack on radio.* In other words, radio can support, reinforce, or remind listeners of a message that they saw on television that had strong visual impact.

Although radio is a broadcast medium, it differs in several significant ways from television.

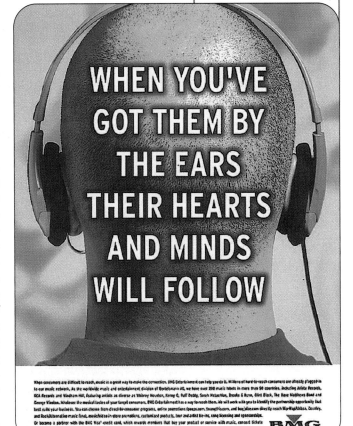

EXHIBIT 11-11

Radio reaches its audience at the personal level and has the potential to deliver a very powerful impact because of the relationship between listeners and the stations they love to listen to.

WHEN YOU'VE GOT THEM BY THE EARS THEIR HEARTS AND MINDS WILL FOLLOW

BMG

First and most obvious, it provides only sound. Second, whereas TV viewers select programs, most radio listeners select stations, so radio stations command more brand loyalty than do TV stations and networks. Third, the majority of television advertising is national, and the majority of radio advertising is local. Most national advertising that radio stations do receive comes as spot buys from national brands that want to have extra weight in certain markets. Fourth, networks play a major role in TV but a minor one in radio.

Probably the most significant feature of radio is that each station has one specific kind of programming, called a *format*. Most stations provide news and weather to some degree, and the lion's share of all their other programming comes in one of the formats listed in Table 11-2. The four most popular radio formats are country, adult contemporary, religion/gospel, and Top 40. Because each format attracts a different type of audience, planners can easily match station and brand audience profiles. Talk radio is another format, and programs with Rush Limbaugh and Howard Stern have dedicated listeners.

Most stations using a music format buy their programming from syndicators. These companies record and distribute the various music formats either by satellite or by CD, so all a station has to do is plug in and play. These computer-driven

TABLE 11-2   Radio Formats

Format	Description
Top 40	Contemporary hit rock songs
Album-oriented rock	Recent or current rock music, usually with a driving beat and often with electric sound
Alternative or progressive rock	Various types of music, especially those not found on conventional music stations, such as avant-garde rock
Classic rock	Like album-oriented rock, but emphasizing music from the 1960s, 70s, and 80s
Adult contemporary	Soft, light vocals and instrumental music with a jazzy or soft rock sound
Urban contemporary	Upbeat, usually current dance or rap music
Blues	Music with its roots in rural black America used to communicate the trials and tribulations of life, especially in the delta area of the Deep South
Rhythm and blues	Soul music with a mellow beat and rich vocals—more traditional than urban
Country	Ballads, contemporary, and classic songs with a traditional, rural American influence
Jazz	Vocals or instrumentals, ranging from blues ballads of the 1930s and 40s to the electronic sounds of the 1990s
New Age	Soft instrumental music or soft jazz; also known as "fusion"
Easy listening	Light instrumental and vocal music largely from the 1940s through the 1970s
Oldies	Popular vocal or instrumental music from the 1950s through the 1980s
Classical	Symphonic, chamber, operatic, and show music
Spanish	Music, news, and information programming in the Spanish language
Talk	Topical programming on a wide range of subjects, from personal to political, often in the form of interview or call-in shows with a dynamic host
Religious	Music, information, or teaching; music may include Christian rock, gospel, choral, or instrumental

format packages come complete with automated commercial breaks and station breaks, during which the correct time is announced along with the local station's call letters. If a station wants to have its own live news reports periodically throughout the day, that time is automatically scheduled in. The format packages also contain a few national commercials that the syndicate has presold. Most radio stations run between 15 and 20 minutes of commercials an hour, the majority of which are local. Syndicated programs, both music and talk, are sold to only one station in a market.

There are a couple of dozen national radio networks, but only about 5 percent of the average local station's advertising revenue comes from them. Most of the national networks supply news segments throughout the day. There are also special networks such as the National Black Network, which is carried by about 100 stations. Certain programs, such as those hosted by Paul Harvey and Rush Limbaugh, are sold to stations on a market-by-market basis. Such popular programs, which can be heard in almost every radio market in the country, also carry national commercials.

In radio, the on-air personalities (talk-show and music-format hosts) are often "brands," and listeners often relate more to them than to the station. To leverage these radio personalities, some advertisers do not run prerecorded commercials. Instead, they supply the on-air personalities with a list of their brand's attributes. The hosts then talk about the products for 30 or 60 seconds in their own words, making sure to include a majority of the brand's selling points. In one case, a manufacturer of breakfast sausage used radio advertising in several markets during morning drive time. The company chose stations with live DJs. Company sales representatives took electric skillets into each station and helped the DJs fry the sausage on-air, talking about the brand while periodically holding the mike near the skillets so listeners could hear the delicious sizzling sound of the sausage being prepared. Not only was the brand message delivered but the selling points were given greater credibility because the DJs were known and respected by their listeners. The risk of using such a strategy, however, is that there is no guarantee the DJs will cover the important brand points. Also, not all on-air personalities have large, loyal audiences or are willing to do "live" commercials.

Another unique radio feature is the remote broadcast from a retailer's place of business. Most stations will agree to do a remote broadcast when a retailer buys a certain amount of airtime, and usually such buys are used for special promotional events like store openings or major sales. Remote broadcasts are especially effective when the on-air program host is well known and listeners are promised hot dogs and soft drinks or other premiums for visiting the business during a certain period.

Another way a brand can get extra airtime for little cost is to provide stations with the brand's products, which can be given away. Radio stations are always doing things to encourage more listeners to tune in. Frequently used incentives are quizzes and drawings. Brands that donate merchandise to be used as prizes get their names and key brand claims mentioned every time listeners are told about the prizes that can be won in a drawing or contest.

Radio stations also sponsor events to help create a closer relationship with their listening audiences and to provide their advertisers another way to reach customers. A good example is END radio station 107.7 in Seattle, Washington. One of its recent events, "E4: A Modern Midway of Music and Machine," had exhibits of new music technology, video games, and demonstrations of new interactive electronics along with extreme sports exhibitions and several bands (X-ecutioners, Custom, and Alien Crime Syndicate). These events are designed to attract youths (ages 15 to 29) and thus attract advertisers such as Levi's, Doc Martens, and SoBe.

Coverage and Audiences

Because radio is primarily a local, consumer medium, it is seldom used for B2B brand messages. Radio is considered the most pervasive medium because it can be listened to anytime, anywhere. According to the Radio Advertising Bureau, the average person listens to radio about three and a half hours a day, and in the course of a week, 96 percent of Americans 12 and over listen to radio at least once.

Most radio stations can be received easily throughout a metro area and even farther afield if they are AM stations. An average station, however, reaches (is listened to), at any given time, only 1 to 3 percent of the local audience because there are so many stations. For this reason, most marketers who use radio use more than one station and use radio along with other media buys. It is difficult to get a high level of audience reach unless heavy schedules are bought on the majority of stations, which is generally cost-prohibitive. For this reason, radio sales representatives often sell the image-transfer qualities of radio as a supporting media buy. Because radio is often less expensive than TV, radio can be a cost-effective way to build message frequency and extend the impact and length of a TV campaign. When a company buys radio time, the buy includes a number of commercial units. Buying radio is like eating potato chips—no one thinks of just one. Because the average radio exposure is so small, repetition is important.

Radio listening varies by time of day, as Figure 11-5 shows. The term **daypart** refers *to a block of time identified by a station for the purpose of setting ad rates*. The "morning drive-time" daypart has the largest radio audience, reaching 50 percent of adults aged 18 and older. During these hours people are getting dressed, fixing and eating breakfast, or commuting—activities that can be done without too much concentration, which facilitates radio listening.

Audience Measurement

Several companies measure radio audiences: Arbitron, RADAR, and Birch/Scarborough. RADAR and Birch do their research by phone, calling a sample of listeners each day for seven consecutive days and asking which stations they listened to and at what times, on the previous day. Arbitron, the most widely used service, recruits samples of households in each major U.S. metropolitan area. Respondents are sent a diary in which they are asked to record, on a quarter-hour basis, the stations they listen to over seven days. Arbitron then collects the diaries and tabulates the data to show each station's ratings and share at each quarter hour for selected demographic groups. Other important figures from the diaries are daypart and station cumulative (called "cume" for short) ratings. The cume is the number of different people who are reached within each daypart, day, and week.

Sales and Pricing

Radio time is sold in units of 10, 30, and 60 seconds. The most common length for a radio commercial is 60 seconds. Few 30-second commercials are used because they are often the same price as 60-second commercials; thus a brand can have 60 sec-

FIGURE 11-5

Radio listening varies significantly by time of day.

Radio's Daily Reach by Daypart for Adults 18+				
6–10 a.m.	10 a.m.–3 p.m.	3–7 p.m.	7 p.m.–Midnight	Midnight–6 a.m.
50%	43%	43%	23%	16%

onds of exposure for the price of 30 seconds (or slightly more, because the longer commercial costs a little more to produce).[12] Because radio is a background medium, more time allows the advertiser a greater chance to gain attention and exposure.

Some people think radio is an "inexpensive" medium because the cost of one commercial unit is considerably less than the cost of a newspaper ad or a TV commercial unit (within the same market). The reality, however, is that radio's costs can be nearly the same as spots on TV and newspaper placements *when you consider the size of the audiences reached by each medium.* Also, the impact of a radio spot is, on average, less than that of a TV spot because radio is dealing with only one of the senses—hearing.

Radio rates are determined by a station's ratings, which vary by time of day, and by audience demographics. If a media planner wants a schedule of commercials to run only in morning drive-time, the cost will be higher than if the schedule is for "run-of-station," which means the spots would be spread throughout the various dayparts. Audience demographics affect rates because some audiences are more valuable to brands than others. A station with an audience that skews high on women aged 18 to 49, for example, is able to charge more than a station with an audience of teens or adults 55 and over.

Strengths and Weaknesses of Radio

Radio is called "theater of the mind" because listeners must provide their own mental visuals for the words, sound effects, and music they hear. Listeners create mental pictures not only for programming content but also for commercials. Such a high level of mental involvement happens, however, only when the programming or commercial messages are attention getting and the words and sounds are rich in imagery.

Station programming formats provide radio with its most important strength—selectivity. As with magazines, when an audience has a common interest, it is relatively easy for media planners to match the audience to a brand's audience profile. For example, the audience for a golden-oldies station is much older than the audience for a Top 40 station and has different wants and needs. All-news and classical formats have audiences that skew higher in education and income than most other formats.

As with newspapers, there is a short lead time for preparing and running a low-budget radio commercial. A radio spot can be written and produced in a couple of days and placed into a station's schedule in less than a week. Radio spots with custom-written music, special sound effects, and well-known talent, however, can take a couple of months to arrange and produce.

Like TV, radio is intrusive, which is both a strength and a weakness. On the one hand, intrusiveness is a strength because radio presents brand messages whether the audience wants to hear them or not. On the other hand, some people find offensive the fact that radio does this, and many have conditioned themselves to ignore the messages.

Radio's other limitations are that it has no visuals and is fleeting. Another serious limitation is the fact that radio is used as background entertainment by people who are doing other things. Finally, even with sophisticated audience measurement techniques, it is difficult to determine what percentage of brand messages are actually heard.

Television

Television has the broadest exposure of any medium. In the United States, almost 99 percent of homes have TV, the average home has 2.2 sets, and one or more sets is on an average of 7 hours and 26 minutes a day, according to Nielsen Media

Research. Because television reaches a large audience and can deliver messages with highly dramatic effects, both consumer and B2B companies use TV. Many large companies, both consumer and B2B, also recognize TV's potential for keeping their brand top-of-mind with stakeholders other than customers—with investors, employees and prospective employees, suppliers, and the financial community.

Although the television medium offers broad exposure, the audience is fragmented because of the many channels available to watch. An often-heard criticism is that television reaches such a wide and diverse audience that most brands that use it are paying to reach many who are neither customers nor prospects (see Chapter 13 for a more thorough discussion of media waste). This criticism was more true 20 years ago than it is today with dozens of specialized network and cable channels. Although the average TV program audience is significantly smaller than in the past, many of these audiences have specific commonalities that can now more easily be matched to a brand's target audience.

Most people have little interest in or knowledge of the organizational structure of television. To viewers, TV is simply a bunch of channels with programs and commercials. Media planners, however, need to understand this structure, especially now, because more media dollars are spent on television than on any other medium. The major growth area in TV spending is cable, where budgets increased by over 400 percent in the last 10 years. Television spending has five classifications: national TV networks, national spots, local spots, syndicated programming, and cable stations (see Table 11-3).

Spot buys are *purchases of TV time in certain markets by regional or national companies.* Spot buys are used by national advertisers to react to certain local market situations or to leverage an opportunity such as gaining new distribution or responding to seasonal changes. For example, in the northern part of the United States, when the weather turns cold, it's a good time to begin promoting antifreeze and snow tires.

Network TV is made up of six national networks: ABC, CBS, NBC, Warner Bros. (WB), Fox, and UPN. Each network has **affiliates,** which are *local market stations that agree to carry programming and commercials provided by a network.* In Denver, for example, KDVR is the Fox affiliate and KCNC is the NBC affiliate. Local affiliates often co-brand themselves by building awareness of their own call letters, as well as the name of their network. Networks originate programming and sell commercial time to national brands that appear on all affiliate stations. (Occasionally an affiliate pre-empts network programming to broadcast a local event, such as a weather service announcement.) Networks supply program content throughout the day but not continuously, allowing time for local news shows, syndicated programs, and locally produced programs. During the time periods when content

TABLE 11-3	TV Spending (estimated for 2004)
Spending Classification	**Amount ($ in billions)**
National network	$17.6
National and local spots	23.3
Syndication	2.9
Network and local cable	20.3
Total	$64.1

Source: Jack Meyers Report, "Myers Ad Spending Revised Forecast: 2003 Growth Slows to 3.1%; 2004 Will Be Up a Robust 5.3%,"<www.jackmyers.com>, May 12, 2003. Jack Meyers Report. Used with permission.

is supplied by the networks, local stations have only a few minutes per hour for local advertising.

Syndicated programs such as *Oprah, Wheel of Fortune,* and *Jerry Springer* are created and sold to stations by independent producers. Initially, stations paid a fee for these shows and then recovered their costs by selling time within the shows. Today, however, stations seldom pay for syndicated programming because the syndicators have already sold most of the commercial time to national brands, leaving few unsold time slots for stations to sell locally. The syndicators try to have their shows carried in as many markets as possible (though on only one station in a market), because the more households a show reaches, the more the syndicators can charge for spots within the show. Local stations like syndicated shows because they provide programming for free.

In many markets there are independent stations that don't belong to any network. The vast majority of their content is syndicated programs and network re-runs (a form of syndication). Because the cost of producing original programming has become so high, especially when the shows have high-priced talent, networks lose money if they cannot sell reruns.

Formats and Features

Television is frequently referred to as either *broadcast* or *cable*. This distinction can be confusing because viewers who have cable receive *both* cable and broadcast channels from their cable service. But the distinction remains because the networks for many years were received—that is, broadcast—only over the air. At one time, three networks (ABC, CBS, NBC) dominated TV viewing in the United States. However, cable channels have been making steady inroads. In the last 10 years, according to Nielsen reports, sets tuned to cable channels have more than doubled, going from about 1.5 to 3.5 hours a day, leaving the major networks with only half of the total viewing audience.

Today, slightly over two-thirds of U.S. households have cable, one-third subscribe to pay TV, and about 10 percent subscribe to a direct-broadcast satellite provider, according to the Television Bureau of Advertising. Because the majority of U.S. homes receive TV signals by cable, a new channel that wants to gain distribution of its programming has to buy its way into the marketplace. What this demonstrates is that the subscriber base of cable companies (and, increasingly, of direct-broadcasting satellite companies) is a collection of audiences that can be "sold" to channels that want to reach these subscribers.

Households that do not have cable or a satellite dish can receive only local, over-the-air channels. Up until 1999, direct-broadcast satellite companies such as DirecTV and EchoStar could not transmit local stations, which put them at a competitive disadvantage with local cable operators. The change allowing satellite companies to carry local stations has resulted in more rapid growth of satellite TV.

Breaking down hours of viewing according to demographic categories shows that adult women are heaviest viewers of TV, followed by adult men (see Table 11-4). The networks claim that they can still reach every corner of the country, something that cable companies can't do. NBC, for instance, says it reaches 59 percent of all adults under the age of 50 in a single week. That is 21 percent more than the top 10 cable networks combined. NBC also boasts that it reaches 32 percent more upper-income viewers—those with more than $75,000 in household income—than the top 10 cable channels combined.[13] The fact that cable TV is made up of dozens of channels is both good and bad for marketers. The good aspect is that it allows marketers to select channels with audiences that have a common interest in such areas as cooking, gardening, and home repair. But companies selling mass-marketed products are forced to buy many different cable channels in order to have broad reach.

T A B L E   1 1 - 4   Average Hours Spent Viewing TV per Day

Category	Hours and Minutes Spent Watching per Day
Women	4:51
Men	4:19
Teens	3:04
Children	3:12

Source: Used with permission of Television Bureau of Advertising and Nielsen Media Research.

Sales and Pricing

In the early days of TV, the most frequently used commercial lengths were one minute and two minutes. As TV time has become more expensive, the average length of commercials has significantly shortened. In 1999, 60 percent of all network TV commercials were 30 seconds, 31 percent were 15 seconds, and only 6 percent were 60 seconds.

In television, as in radio, marketers buy time in dayparts (such as morning, prime time, late night) or in specific programs whose audiences are most likely to match a brand's target profile. Television's eight dayparts vary significantly in price (see Table 11-5). There are approximately 100 million households in the United States, so 1 point (or 1 percent) represents 1 million households (on a national buy). The cost per point (CPP) or the cost of reaching 1 million households with a 30-second commercial, for example, is nearly four times as much during prime time ($27,000) as during early morning ($7,300) and daytime ($7,400).

There are several reasons for this extreme difference in costs. First, viewers pay more attention during prime time viewing than they do during other parts of the day. Thus, commercials during prime time have a better opportunity to *connect* with listeners. Second, prime-time audiences are generally the most desired daypart audience. A much higher percentage of those who watch TV during early morning, daytime, and early and late fringe dayparts are low-wage earners or are

T A B L E   1 1 - 5   Total U.S. Household Cost per Point (CPP) by TV Daypart

Daypart	CPP for :30 Commercial
Early morning	$ 7,300
Daytime	7,400
Early fringe	10,100
Early news	12,900
Prime access	16,500
Prime time	27,000
Late news	18,600
Late fringe	12,500

Source: SQAD June 2002 issue, 2nd quarter 2002 average spot televisions CPPs for 210 US markets. Reprinted with permission.

retired, unemployed, or chronically ill—not the ideal target audience for most brands. Finally, most marketers feel that prime time has a certain prestige environment, and being part of that environment adds prestige to their brands.

A major portion of network TV time is sold each spring during the "up-front" selling period, when networks preview their fall line-ups for agencies and their clients. The prices that networks are able to get during this up-front period are a predictor of what TV prices will be for the coming year. Although TV networks sell time directly to agencies (and companies), national spot buys are sold by national "rep" firms, companies that represent a group of local stations. A company that wants to advertise in only the top 25 markets, for example, is likely to negotiate with a TV rep firm.

As explained earlier, TV advertising rates are based not only on ratings but also on how much inventory (time) is available. If a station is 80 percent sold out for the next two weeks, rates for the remaining time will be higher than they would be if the station were only 60 percent sold out. When buying commercial time on TV, media people seldom depend on a rate card. Instead, they call stations or their representatives, explain how many rating points they are interested in buying, and then ask for a price.

Syndicated programs are sold by the syndicators or their representatives. Each cable channel, such as ESPN or Discovery, has its own sales force, along with national sales firms that represent more than one channel. At the local level, each station has its own sales force that calls on retailers and other local organizations.

Strengths and Weaknesses of Television

Because TV is so dynamic (due to its ability to carry sound and moving visuals), it is often considered the prestige medium for marketing communication. When retailers consider taking on a new line of products, they often want to know to what extent this line will be promoted on TV.

A major limitation of using TV, especially for small brands, is high production costs. The average cost of making a national 30-second spot is over $350,000. (Spots produced by a local TV station cost far less but often look far less professional.) Another limitation of TV is clutter. Almost one-third of prime time, for example, is now being used for nonprogram content (commercials, station and network identification, and promos for upcoming programs). A **commercial pod,** which is *the commercial break in a TV program,* can carry 10 or more different brand messages. Nevertheless, according to the Television Advertising Bureau, 76 percent of viewers feel commercials are "a fair price to pay for being able to watch TV." Lead times for TV can also be a limitation, especially at the national level. The best programs and time slots are often sold four to six months in advance.

Infomercials

Besides traditional commercials, another way to deliver a brand message using TV is with an **infomercial.** This is generally *a 30-minute commercial "program" that demonstrates a product, presents testimonials from satisfied users, and offers viewers one or more ways to buy the product direct (toll-free number, website address, mailing address).* Infomercials typically feature complicated products that need demonstration—everything from sophisticated consumer electronics to exercise and body-shaping equipment.

A company using infomercials must be concerned about the handling of responses to the infomercial. Some call centers have better trained and more professional representatives than others. The more complex a product offer is, the more important it is for representatives answering the phone to be well trained. A company needs to supply the call center with its infomercial media schedule, for incoming calls significantly increase every time an infomercial airs. By knowing this schedule ahead of time, the call center can staff up and reduce the number of callers who respond but hang up because they have been on hold too long.

For products sold only through an infomercial, companies need to generate roughly $3 in sales for every $1 spent on TV time. If the product is also available in retail stores or on the brand's website, the ratio is only about $2 to $1 because the infomercial helps drive retail store sales as well as direct purchases.

Interactive TV

The convergence of computers, television, and the internet is referred to as **interactive TV,** a technology that allows viewers to respond directly to TV commercials with a click of the remote control or a remote keyboard. Viewers can order movies instantly, for example, rather than having to make a phone call. By clicking on a website address in a commercial, a viewer can go directly to the site to get further brand information or place an order. Interactive TV also allows viewers to obtain information while watching a program. For example, while watching a baseball game, a viewer can bring a player's profile on-screen as the player is coming to bat. The work to make television a two-way medium has been going on for several decades. Although the technology now exists for interactive TV, customers have been slow to embrace it; many are not yet convinced of its value.

OUT-OF-HOME MEDIA

In addition to print and broadcast, another large group of media are the **out-of-home media.** A more specific term, *place-based media,* was defined in Chapter 2 as public venues where brand messages can be displayed. Billboards (also called *outdoor boards*) and transit posters are two of the most common categories of out-of-home media. Others include theater and video ads, product placements in movies, aerial advertising (see Exhibit 11-12), electronic kiosks; ads in elevators or bathroom stalls; banner displays on automated teller machines (ATMs), chalk-and-stencil sidewalk messages, placards on shopping carts—the list could go on and on. Posters and small digital screens are making it possible to reach people almost anywhere they go, and particularly in situations where they have nothing else to do, as when they are riding on a bus.

Outdoor Advertising

Outdoor advertising dates back at least to the Roman Empire, when commercial signs were painted on city walls. In modern times, as cars and highways took over the landscape, large signs along highways and streets became message-delivery points. A classic example is the "See Rock City" campaign, which began appearing on barn roofs in 1936. Since then, the Lookout Mountain rock formations in Tennessee have been promoted on some 900 barns in 19 states from Michigan to Florida. Although many of the barns have disappeared, the remaining ones are celebrated as pieces of pop culture.[14] Today the outdoor advertising industry remains strong and profitable; annual expenditures are estimated to be $4.8 billion.[15]

Modern outdoor advertising comes in three standard forms: bulletins, 30-sheet posters, and 8-sheet posters. A nonstandard form, called a *spectacular,* is used for extra attention-getting power (see Table 11-6). The most widely used is the 30-sheet poster. (The "30" once referred to the number of sheets of paper that were pasted together to form a message on a single board. Although individual sheets are larger today, requiring fewer per board, the industry continues to use the term.) Whereas 30-sheet posters are purchased for only a month or two, the contracts for spectaculars often run for several years. Spectaculars are generally permanent, lighted, and often animated in some way. They are extremely expensive compared to other outdoor forms. Times Square in New York City has a number of spectacular boards, including ones that carry live TV broadcasts. As the name suggests, these boards are visually stunning and often quite memorable. Design of spectaculars in recent years has included images that extend beyond the traditional rectangular borders to include pop-outs that make the boards three-dimensional.

Signs and Posters

Exploiting the concept of creating effective brand contact points, out-of-home message delivery includes a wide range of locations where brand messages can be posted. Besides traditional outdoor boards, outside signage includes signs on trucks and shopping bags; even uniforms serve as vehicles for brand messages. These are the media we encounter as we go about our daily business (see Exhibit 11-14, page 375).

Advertisers commonly purchase space from public transit authorities. Posters appear on (and inside) buses, subway trains, and taxis, as well as in bus shelters and subway stations. Other place-based media include malls, stores, health clubs, and libraries, as well as community, student, and senior centers. Posters inside a conveyance or waiting place generally have a captive audience that can spend some time with a message, so those posters are designed to deliver more complex messages.

One of the newest attempts to attract attention to advertising posters (such as those found at bus stops and in subways) is to arm them with sound tracks that deliver short brand messages and atomizers that spray brand-related scents. Proctor & Gamble, for example, used posters to advertise its new Head & Shoulders shampoo, which is billed as "citrus fresh." Pushing a button on the poster activates a whiff of the citrus fresh scent.[16] The benefit of these posters is greater message

EXHIBIT 11-12
This ad for the Aviad company, which creates and delivers aerial advertising, targets high-tech and dot-com companies.

TABLE 11-6   Outdoor Advertising Forms

- *Bulletins*: 14 by 48 feet; either painted or printed panels; usually created for a local marketer in the outdoor company's shop and then assembled on the billboard structure.

- *30-sheet posters*: 12 by 25 feet; the basic outdoor format for national and local marketers; printed on large sheets in multiple copies and then distributed to local outdoor companies, which mount the sheets on the outdoor board.

- *8-sheet panels* (also called *junior panels*): 5 by 11 feet; good with pedestrian traffic; often used by food-product manufacturers as a reminder near a grocery store.

- *Spectaculars*: nonstandard; used in busy metro areas such as New York, Hong Kong, London, and Las Vegas; electronic signs with movement, color, and flashing lights designed to grab attention in high-traffic areas.

IMC IN ACTION

The Outdoor Roots of Wall Drug

In 1931 Dorothy and Ted Husteads bought a drugstore in Wall, South Dakota, population 800. Ted had just graduated from University of Nebraska's School of Pharmacy. From day one, things were tough for the Husteads. They had four children, and the Great Depression was under way.

In 1936 things looked bleak. The store had few customers. Wall was on the main highway leading into the Black Hills, which attracted thousands of tourists each year, especially during the summer. Travelers coming from the east drove right by the little drugstore, but few stopped. Dorothy Husteads knew that if there was some way to motivate these tourists to stop, the store had a chance of making it.

In 1936 cars had no air conditioning, and the drive across South Dakota was a hot and dusty trip. Knowing how these tourists felt as they drove through Wall, Dorothy realized that they all must be very thirsty. This customer insight gave her an idea. Offer these potential customers free ice water!

Getting the message to the passing tourist, however, was a media challenge. Newspapers and magazines were of no value because the travelers came from everywhere. Even more critical was the fact that the Husteads had no money for advertising. Dorothy and Ted knew they had to reach the tourists as they approached Wall—and do so in a way that cost very little. The solution was roadside signs: outdoor advertising. The Husteads made up signs that read "FREE Ice Water, Wall Drug Store," and placed them several miles apart on both sides of the highways leading into Wall. This simple media strategy not only turned the drugstore into a very profitable venture but also made it known around the world and a popular tourist attraction.

The idea of "free ice water" was not only relevant to passing tourists but also humorous. Realizing how people enjoyed talking about the "free ice water" at Wall Drug, the Husteads began placing the outdoor signs farther and farther away from Wall, South Dakota. Today you can find Wall Drug Store signs not only throughout the United States but also in Europe and even in Greenland! Many of the signs state how many miles it is to Wall Drug, such as the ones in the underground metro system in London: "5,160 Miles to Wall Drug." The London tube campaign not only generated several dozen letters a day to the drugstore but produced several publicity stories in London media, including a 10-minute BBC interview with Ted Husteads, one of the founders' sons.

Today, during the summer, Wall Drug Store (www.walldrug.com) gives away up to 20,000 glasses of ice water in one day. The small drugstore has been expanded. It now takes up nearly a whole city block and looks like a mini-mall: many different shops sell everything from T-shirts to expensive sculptures thanks to creative outdoor advertising.

Think About it

How exactly did Wall Drug Store build such national, even international, visibility? If you were in charge of media for Wall Drug Store, what other message delivery ideas might you suggest?

EXHIBIT 11-13

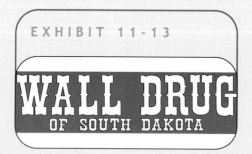

involvement and, at least for a while, more word-of-mouth discussion. The downside is the cost, which is nearly fives times as much as that for a regular poster.

Nontraditional posters have appeared in chalk on city streets, as well as on the sides of buildings. Some buildings have been wrapped with huge preprinted vinyl images. The old Burma-Shave signs that used to adorn highways with little limericks about the shaving cream have inspired modern advertisers to use this low-tech form. In order to reach dot-com companies, the owner of Bostonhire.com, a job-posting site, screwed all-weather poster-boards with the company's name to trees along Route 128, Massachusetts's high-tech corridor. The owner reported lots of calls from his $500 investment. A similar scheme in northern California uses tall billboards mounted on barges in San Francisco Bay to reach people traveling on Route 101 south from San Francisco. The signs are so tall they can be seen from the San Francisco–Oakland Bay Bridge, 10 miles north. The "barge boards" are attractive to marketers because the traditional billboards along Route 101 are sold out for years in advance.

Audience Measurement

Outdoor advertising reaches people as they travel by the sign's site. The advertiser is interested in the percentage of the population of the total market (based on car or pedestrian counts) who, within a 24-hour period, are exposed to one or more boards carrying the brand message.

The basic units of sale for outdoor advertising are called **showings.** Showings are estimated percentages—25, 50, or 100 percent—of population coverage. A brand message appears on as many panels as needed to provide the desired level of exposure—25, 50, or 100 percent of a market's total population. A 50 showing means that 50 percent of the market's population was exposed to one or more of the outdoor brand messages in one day. Outdoor space is sold in sets of boards spaced throughout a market to deliver the desired 25, 50, or 100 showing. Although this medium receives only about 2 percent of all media dollars spent in the United States, in some countries, especially developing countries, it is one of the most widely used to deliver brand messages.

EXHIBIT 11-14
This sand sculpture was turned into an 11-by-15-foot painted wall on the boardwalk of California's Venice Beach.

Strengths and Weakness of Outdoor Advertising

Using outdoor boards in a local market is a good way to extend reach and, even more so, extend frequency of a brand message. Outdoor boards also provide geographical flexibility for targeting. Outdoor boards are sometimes used for teaser campaigns, particularly in support of a new-product launch, as the BMW Mini story illustrates.

Another advantage of outdoor media is that they can attract people with certain commonalties. People attending baseball games obviously have an interest in sports. People in airline terminals are more likely than the average population to be businesspeople or vacation travelers. When advertisers use transit media, the challenge is to select communication vehicles whose audience demographics most closely match those of the brand's target audience. Outdoor boards are used to keep established brands top-of-mind, and their primary function is as a brand reminder. They are also widely used to provide directions—"Shell at next exit" and "KFC two blocks ahead." For the most part, outdoor boards are used for consumer brands.

Limitations of outdoor boards are several. Outdoor boards have "passing" exposure: most people who are exposed are passing by, often at fairly high speeds! This fact, plus the fact that outdoor boards must fight for attention with all the other visual stimuli that surround them, means they must carry simple yet highly

ETHICS AND ISSUES

The Unmaking of Highway Beautification

The Highway Beautification Act (1965) was designed to control the clutter of billboards on our national highways, right? And after nearly 40 years, the act has substantially reduced the number of billboards, right? And the act has been effective at removing unsightly billboards, right?

Wrong. The act has become little more than a billboard protection program. On average, new billboards are twice as big as they were in 1965, and there are 50 percent more of them. The procedures for eliminating billboards that do not meet HBA standards have been gutted. Nationwide, 73,000 billboards do not conform with HBA standards, but few of them will be removed. Some states even allow billboard companies to cut down trees on public rights-of-way to improve the view of private billboards.

Despite the original intent of the law, most rural and scenic areas are not protected from billboards. Congress derailed the program and actually protects billboards from community efforts to remove them. In 1978 Congress amended the law to require communities to pay cash compensation for removing billboards—even nonconforming ones—on federally aided highways and then stopped providing any money at all for the removal of nonconforming billboards.

The industry defends the present lack of regulation by pointing out that billboards are necessary for travelers. Although that may be true for directional and services information, alcohol and cigarette advertising is a big part of outdoor messages. Some critics believe that the cigarette industry is pouring so much money into billboards because they offer an unregulated way to reach young people.

Given these developments, it is no wonder that the billboard industry strongly supports the Highway Beautification Act.

Think About It

Congress will soon reauthorize the nation's transportation law and will have an opportunity to improve or restore the Highway Beautification Act. Do you think there should be more control over billboards on federal highways, or is government control over this advertising inappropriate?

Source: Environmental Working Group & Scenic America, "The Highway Beautification Act: A Broken Law," 1998. Available at http://www.ewg.org/reports/billboards/billboards.html. Reprinted with permission.

---

attention-getting messages. The more visual the message is, the more impact an outdoor board is likely to have. Another limitation is that, when used extensively, the messages may suffer from wear out, as customers ignore boards they have seen several times before.

Outdoor's biggest limitation is its negative perception. Many people consider billboards as nothing more than visual clutter. Environmentalists have referred to outdoor advertising as "visual pollution on a stick." Some states (Maine, Vermont, Hawaii, and Alaska), as well as some communities, have outlawed or greatly restricted the use of outdoor boards. Many metro areas now have restrictions on the heights and placements of billboards.

The Highway Beautification Act of 1965 controls outdoor advertising on U.S. interstate highways. The act was originally designed to prevent "visual pollution" along 300,000 miles of federal highways. As the Ethics and Issues box explains, however, it may have had the opposite effect.

In this day of marketing accountability, another limitation is the difficulty of measuring the effectiveness of outdoor boards. Most outdoor campaigns are part of larger media plans, and it is next to impossible to break out the incremental impact of outdoor messages. Many people passing by in cars never see or read the posted messages. Most companies that sell outdoor advertising keep detailed case histories showing impact on sales. Media planners must interpret these cases carefully, though, before assuming that the results for one brand will transfer to another brand and marketing situation.

Cinema and Video

Besides selling tickets and food, movie theaters can generate revenue by running commercials before movies, called **trailers.** Yet these communication vehicles have some inherent problems. Targeting other than by type of movie—G or PG movies, comedies or dramas—is difficult. Also, people do not readily accept brand messages that accompany movies. Commercials that people see for free at home are especially irritating to people who paid $7 or $8 for a movie ticket.[17] Feeling that commercials detract from the main feature, Disney refuses to distribute its movies to cinemas that run commercials for anything other than upcoming movies.

The advantages of movie-theater commercials include the captive audience and the lack of clutter. A half-dozen or so commercials presented within a two-hour period in a movie theater encounter far less clutter than 60 or more messages appearing within the same time period on television. Moviegoers in the United Kingdom may sit through as much as 20 minutes of advertising before the feature film starts.

The cost of cinema advertising is based on monthly attendance. The cost per person exposed goes down as more and more theaters show a commercial. Generally, though, the cost of in-theater commercials is around $22 per thousand people reached, which is equivalent to the cost of a 30-second prime-time TV spot.

There are other ways to reach people who are going to movies. AMC allows advertising on popcorn bags in its 104 movie theaters. Lighted lobby signs also carry ads and are among nontraditional media chosen types. Some theaters also allow kiosk and parking-lot exhibits. Monster.com pushes its employment search site with trailers that turn into exhibits.

Videocassette producers have found that commercials on rented movies can reach a mass audience. Video is playing an increasingly important role in message delivery for both consumer and B2B brands. Unlike movie theaters, which still tend primarily to run brand messages for movies only—previews or trailers—rental videos are carrying more and more messages for nonmovie products. According to one study, two-thirds of the people who rent videos resent the presence of commercials, yet over half reported they watched the commercials.[18]

Another type of video advertising is the product video produced by a company as an individual infomercial. Nearly every major brand in the United States has a product video, a video catalog, or a CD-ROM to augment the efforts of its sales staff and to use for prospecting. Many car manufacturers, for example, produce videos of new models that let people take virtual test drives on their televisions at home. These test-drive videos are advertised in the conventional way and then sent to individuals who request them. Their overall cost is extremely high when production and distribution are added together. Yet their impact is much greater than that of a typical television commercial, and the high cost may be justified by the positive reactions of high-potential prospects. Payout, or impact on sales, can be easily determined because there is a record of those who received the videos.

Promotional video networks are *companies that use videos or satellite transmission to distribute programs and commercial messages.* Such companies (for example, the Airport Channel, the Medical News Network, the Truck Stop Channel) supply various organizations (airports, hospitals, truck stops) with programming that carries brand messages. The Kmart in-store channel, for example, is sent by satellite to 2,300 stores, and Wal-Mart has set up an ad network that plays brand messages on those long rows of television sets lined up for sale in the chain's 1,950 stores nationwide.

The Greatest Thing Since...

Welcome to Primetime.

PRIMETIME MEDIA

NEW YORK - LONDON - DUBLIN - 60 MARKETS THROUGHOUT THE U.S. AND U.K.
W W W . T D I W O R L D W I D E . C O M   ©CBS

EXHIBIT 11-15

An entire bus wrapped with a supersized poster is an example of a nontraditional medium.

Nontraditional Media

Nontraditional media—hot-air balloons, sidewalk painting, toilet-stall doors in public restrooms, painted buses and cars (see Exhibit 11-15), disposable coffee-cup holders (java jackets), mousepads, ATM screens, race cars, rolling billboards pulled through city streets are increasingly attracting the attention of media people. A company in Paris places ads on the small tables used by sidewalk cafés and bars. The company provides the tables for free, making its money from selling the advertising space. Here is a list of some more nontraditional media:

- Actor Jim Carrey's face appeared on one-inch-high peel-off stickers attached to 12 million California apples to promote the home video release of *Liar Liar.*
- Virtual reality entertainment centers are used in malls to promote merchandise from goods to hit science-fiction movies such as *Star Wars.*
- Buick used packages of airplane peanuts and cookies to market its new Regal sedan. The packages were wrapped in plastic covered with Buick and Regal emblems. Inside, along with the snacks, were photos of the Regal and a chart comparing the car to its competition.
- The Body Shop, an upscale seller of personal care items, has had good luck building awareness with its mobile truck program. The company transformed the vehicle into a source of revenue by linking the traveling display to its growing catalog business.
- Advent Advertising Corporation announced plans to begin selling space on airplane overhead storage bins.
- Otis Elevators and IBM joined together to use flat-panel computer screens to display news and brand messages in elevators.
- When Seattle-based Millstone Coffee moved into the Denver market, it used a technology called the Mobile-Image Projector to beam images of 300-foot-tall cups of coffee and bags of beans on buildings.
- Multinational brands are embossed on the sails of feluccas, the traditional sailboats that travel up and down the Nile River in Egypt.

Nontraditional media are frequently used in **guerrilla marketing,** *a marketing approach that reaches people in unconventional ways—in the streets or in other unexpected places* (see Exhibit 11-16). The idea behind this in-your-face marketing is to extend the impact by creating buzz; the creative delivery of the message has talk value. Motorola used the launch of the *Austin Powers in Goldmember* movie to send teams of demonstrators dressed in outrageous 1970s attire to visit 1,000 theaters where they demonstrated Motorola's T193 mobile phone in the lobbies.[19]

The past decade has seen an increase in message delivery systems as video shopping carts, in-store video networks[20] and **audiotext,** which is *a recorded message that provides information (such as the weather or sports scores) via a toll-free (800) or toll (900) number.* This system can handle thousands of calls at a time, but it is expensive to install.

EXHIBIT 11-16
Actors dressed as butterflies skated around the streets of New York as part of an MSN.com special promotion.

Although nontraditional media may never achieve the status of major media forms, they should be considered for use in narrowly targeted programs. The challenge is to use nontraditional media when they strategically fit into a media mix and not merely because they are different. According to the director of out-of-home and nontraditional media at BBDO, these media have several limitations: lack of audience measurement, equipment failure (such as breakdowns of recorders supplying video messages in elevators), and high production and operating costs.[21]

Product Placement

In Steven Spielberg's 1993 movie *Jurassic Park,* there were more than 1,000 marketing and product tie-ins. **Product placement** is *paid verbal or visual brand exposure in entertainment programming.* For years, movie producers took care not to show brand names on the screen. As times changed, both marketers and producers realized that product placement could be an effective means of sending brand messages. Many moviegoers remained unaware of the practice for some time— a situation that may have been changed by the prominent use of Reese's Pieces candy in Spielberg's 1982 hit *E.T.—the Extra-Terrestrial.* Although product placement is often associated with movies, the biggest showcase for placements is actually popular TV sitcoms.

Product placements are of two types. One type is the incidental inclusion of a brand, such as when a car drives past an Amoco gas station or a bottle of Bayer aspirin sits on a bedside table. Producers of some movies agree to place the actors in cars made by only one manufacturer. The exposure of brand names in these situations is subtle. The other type of placement results in prominent exposure. In the James Bond movie *The World Is Not Enough,* the BMW sports car model Z28 was launched with a starring role. Several scenes had close-ups of Bond driving the car, leaving no question as to the brand. *Austin Powers in Goldmember* has the unlikely product placement of Preparation H.

Product placement offers marketers a unique way to reach mass markets. It does, however, have its limits. Last-minute editing can play havoc with promotional plans. For example, when a Reebok ad was cut from the movie *Jerry*

Maguire, the sneaker company sued Sony for violating the terms of the product placement agreement. The placement had been the centerpiece of a planned Reebok retail promotion that subsequently had to be dumped.[22]

A FINAL NOTE: CONNECTIVITY AND CREATIVITY

Media are used to create a connection between an audience and a brand. But it is also important to use this touch point with the audience in a way that reinforces the brand's image. The unconventional launch campaign for the redesigned BMW MINI fit the brand personality perfectly and captured the "soul" of the MINI. The campaign was a success and an award winner because of its innovative use of media, which proves the point that creative ideas are as important on the message-delivery side of brand communication as on the message-creation side.

The MINI campaign also demonstrates the importance of integration, as does the Verizon "Can you hear me now?" campaign, described in Chapter 9. The nerdy guy driving around the country talking into his cell phone made the question a national catchphrase. How did that happen? The success came from using message placements in the right media. For example, to extend the reach, the campaign benefited from mentions by Jay Leno on *The Tonight Show.* Then it moved to the political arena when Israeli prime minister Ariel Sharon unexpectedly asked U.S. president George Bush, "Can you hear me now?" Tony Granger, creative director at Bozell, says that media and promotional ideas that work "break into the culture"[23] and develop their own momentum.

In the past, media planners were concerned primarily with delivering messages to customers and prospects. This mostly one-way communication told customers what the company wanted them to know. A media mix that connects companies and customers not only informs and persuades but also paves the way for invaluable two-way communication and feedback.

Key Terms

addressable media 347
affiliates 368
audiotext 378
bleed ads 357
broadsheets 350
classified ads 350
classified display ads 351
closing date 358
column inch 351
commercial pod 371
controlled-circulation
  publications 353
cooperative advertising 352
daypart 366

display ads 351
double-page spreads 357
free-standing inserts (FSIs) 351
guerrilla marketing 378
image transfer 363
infomercial 371
interactive media 347
interactive TV 372
marketing universe 360
media exposure 344
out-of-home media 372
paid-circulation publications 353
pass-along rate 357
pre-emptible rate 362

product placement 379
promotional video network 377
rate card 352
rating point 360
share 361
showings 375
split run 358
spot buys 368
standard advertising unit
  (SAU) 351
supplement inserts 351
tabloids 350
tip-ins 354
trailers 377

Key Point Summary

Key Point 1: Media Classifications

How marketers choose to connect a brand with prospects and customers can influence the brand's image. Media carry messages to or from a target audience and can add meaning to these messages. Four general types of media are print, broadcast, out-of-home, and interactive. Media are also classified by audience orientation: mass, niche, addressable, and interactive. When a company "buys media," it is really buying access to the audiences of specific media vehicles.

Key Point 2: Print Media

Print media include newspapers, magazines, brochures, directories, packaging, and all other forms of message delivery that are produced by printing on paper or on some other material and are relatively permanent. Their permanence means they can be kept, filed, or revisited.

EXHIBIT 11-17
As part of its guerrilla marketing effort, the MINI campaign included a MINI mounted on top of a Ford Excursion that visited sporting and other special events where people congregated to demonstrate that the fun stuff always goes on top—your skis, your camping gear, your mountain bike, even your MINI Cooper.

Key Point 3: Broadcast Media

Broadcast media include radio and television. Their messages are more fleeting and more intrusive than print messages. They have great reach and high levels of involvement and impact.

Key Point 4: Out-of-Home Media

Out-of-home media are media that members of the target audience see when they are away from home. The most common are outdoor boards, transit posters, commercials in movie theaters, various nontraditional media, and product placements in films and TV shows.

Lessons Learned

Key Point 1: Media Classifications

a. What are the four general types of media?
b. Explain what the following sentence means: "Media exposure does not guarantee message exposure."
c. What does each of the different types of media sell? On which media do advertisers spend the most money?
d. Explain the difference between a mass medium and a media vehicle. Give examples of each.
e. What is the difference between mass media and niche media? Between mass media and addressable media? Between addressable media and interactive media?
f. Why is intrusiveness a problem for some one-way media? Give an example from your own experience of a highly intrusive message, and describe your response to it.

Key Point 2: Print Media

a. List the various forms of print media.
b. Find examples of classified and display advertising, and explain how they differ.
c. How do newspapers and magazines set their advertising rates?
d. Compare the strengths and weaknesses of newspapers and magazines.
e. What are some of the advantages and disadvantages of advertising in the Yellow Pages?
f. You are designing a marketing communication program for a restaurant near your campus. Would you recommend any print media in your advertising plan? Why or why not?

Key Point 3: Broadcast Media

a. What is a rating point? How do ratings and share differ?
b. What are some of the most popular radio formats? What types of products might be advertised effectively on each?
c. Explain the concept of image transfer. Give an example of a brand message that you have heard that benefits from image transfer.
d. What is a daypart? In which radio dayparts is advertising most expensive? In which television dayparts is it most expensive? Explain the differences.
e. Compare the strengths and weaknesses of radio and television.
f. What is a spot buy? Give an example.
g. You are designing a marketing communication program for a restaurant near your campus. Would you recommend using any broadcast media? Why or why not?

Key Point 4: Out-of-Home Media

a. Describe the different forms of outdoor boards.
b. What is a showing?
c. What are the greatest strengths and weaknesses of outdoor boards?
d. What problems are associated with cinema- and video-related commercial messages?
e. List and describe some of the nontraditional media, and discuss their role in an overall MC campaign.
f. Explain product placement and what it brings to a brand.
g. You are designing a marketing communication program for a restaurant near your campus. Would you recommend any out-of-home media? Why or why not?

Chapter Challenge

Writing Assignment

Refer to Table 11-3, "Radio Formats." Describe what you think the audience profile would be for three of the formats listed there. Why and to what extent do you think the audiences of these three formats overlap?

Presentation Assignment

Choose two college-age friends, and develop a media diary for each one. Take them through a typical day, and ask them what they see, read, view, watch, or listen to. Then consult with your parents or two other adults, and develop media diaries for them. Compare and contrast the two sets of diaries. Develop a presentation for your classmates that explains how the media usage habits of these two groups of people differ.

Internet Assignment

Check out www.MarthaStewart.com. Compare this site with Stewart's section on the Kmart website, www.BlueLight.com. Are the brand images identical, or have there been any changes to adapt to the Kmart audience? Do you feel this branding strategy is effective? Why or why not?

The Internet and Interactivity

Key Points in This Chapter

1. What are the important aspects of interactivity in IMC?
2. In what ways has the internet affected marketing communication efforts?
3. How can a company integrate the internet into building brands and customer relationships?
4. What are the key customer concerns about online marketing?

Chapter Perspective

Adding Two-Way to One-Way Media

The majority of most companies' sales and an even greater proportion of their profits come from current customers with whom the company has established a connection. To motivate repeat purchases, companies need to continually connect and reconnect with customers. The media most suited for doing this are those that are addressable and interactive. The importance of interactive media is reflected in the fact that 39 percent of U.S. media dollars in 2000 were spent on phone, mail, and the internet. This does not include face-to-face personal selling, which some say is the most powerful interactive medium of all (and is discussed in Chapter 16).

One-way media are used most often for creating brand awareness, helping position a brand, and keeping the brand top-of-mind with customers and prospects. In contrast, interactive media are used not only for generating repeat purchases but also for communicating with prospects who have expressed interest in a brand. Interactive media are extremely valuable in building brand relationships because they enable companies and customers to get to know and trust each other.

This chapter explains the value of interactivity and how the internet can be integrated into the overall relationship-building efforts. From a general discussion of communication and technology, it moves to an analysis of the internet and e-commerce. The final section touches on internet privacy issues.

BMW'S "FILMS" MAKES INTERACTIVITY A WINNER

The big debate at the international Cannes Film Festival in 2002 was whether to include BMW's *Hire* film series in the advertising award competition. Although the innovative campaign was already a winner of the sales-promotion industry's Reggie Awards and the advertising industry's Clios and the One Show, the Cannes advertising folks simply didn't know what to do with it. Was it advertising or wasn't it?

That debate showcases a trend in marketing communication. Advertising is seeking to redefine itself as marketers use more promotional tools, including the interactive dimensions of the internet, in innovative ways to strike the right chord with target audiences.

In the bmwfilms.com series, the automaker used a series of online films starring British actor Clive Owen, who, in his role as the mysterious Driver, tackles a host of dangerous situations in his finely tuned, smoothly performing BMW. The high-quality digital "advertainment" was designed specifically for the internet.

BMW's marketing research had found that the traditional BMW customer was a middle-age male with a median income of about $150,000. Managers knew that to grow the market, they needed to reach a younger but equally affluent audience. What made the members of BMW's target market different from the customers of other upscale competitors, such as Mercedes, Lexus, or Infiniti, was their active

"Ambush" :30 trailer
"On a dark freeway, a van swerves close to the driver and the door slides open. From inside, masked gunmen threaten to fire unless the driver stops and surrenders his passenger, a seemingly harmless man they accuse of smuggling diamonds. It's a simple choice: Do or die. Legendary director John Frankenheimer and star Clive Owen combine talents to create a dramatic chase with some unexpected twists."

EXHIBIT 12-1

EFFECTIVENESS CASE

lifestyle. They were engaged in sports as part of their daily routine, not as spectators. They also loved driving and appreciated technology. Their technological orientation was apparent in their high level of internet use, the highest among all buyers of various upscale makes and models.

With a small marketing budget comparable to the budgets of its competition, BMW had found success in alternative media strategies such as the product placement that featured the new Z3 roadster in a cameo appearance in the James Bond film *GoldenEye*. A second Bond film, *Tomorrow Never Dies*, featured the 7 series and BMW's new cruiser motorcycle.

To further combat a slowdown in sales, BMW marketing executives brainstormed with the company's agency, Minneapolis-based Fallon Worldwide, in search of a new marketing communication approach. Two ideas surfaced: (1) to create a series of short films running from five to seven minutes and (2) to incorporate the internet to reach BMW's Web-savvy market. These two ideas were merged and became a series of short films for the internet. Jim McDowell, VP of marketing for BMW North America, explained the justification for moving away from traditional advertising: "What we lost in terms of audience size could be made up for in terms of involvement. In other words, our goal was to produce the most exciting, fun thing people had ever seen come out of their computer."

The story lines all involved a mysterious person who is a professional driver and helps people out of difficult situations. The driver, hired for his superb driving skills and unshakeable poise, encounters unexpected obstacles that test his abilities as well as the various types of BMWs he drives.

The Fallon team found directors were more than willing to sign up for the experimental films because the scripts had gripping and creative story lines that blurred the line between cinema and advertising. The BMW 740i sedan, for example, starred in "Ambush," in which a van swerves close to the driver and the door slides open showing masked gunmen who are threatening to fire unless the driver stops and surrenders his passenger. In a dramatic chase with some unexpected twists, the driver and his car save the passenger (see Exhibit 12-1).

The three films in the most recent series were co-directed by various well-known directors including John Frankenheimer (*The Manchurian Candidate* and *Grand Prix*), Ang Lee (*Crouching Tiger, Hidden Dragon*), Guy Ritchie (*Lock, Stock and Two Smoking Barrels*), Ridley Scott (*Bladerunner* and the Apple Macintosh "1984" launch commercial), Tony Scott

(*Top Gun*), and David Fincher (*Seven*). In contrast to the usual practice in filming commercials, these directors were given free rein to direct the content and action as they saw fit.

Since the debut of the five films in the series in 2001 and three more in the second series, more than 20 million viewers have logged on to the streaming video website. The films can be seen only on www.bmwfilms.com. However, 30-second commercials were developed from them for television commercials designed to work like movie trailers. TV audiences thought the commercials were announcing a movie until the title at the end displayed the BMWFilms logo and directed viewers to the website.

Jarvis Mak, a senior analyst at NetRatings, explained that BMW's goal was to rebuild a brand image and develop a relationship with customers while entertaining them. He said that BMW did that effectively while at the same time garnering a lot of attention for the brand and the film series, particularly among its upscale target market. Mak says that not only did the series create a lot of buzz—with stories in *The New York Times, Time* magazine, *Entertainment Week, USA Today*, the *Village Voice, WiredNews*, and *Variety*, among other publications—but the films also hit the target: more than half of the visitors to bmwfilms.com were males, had broadband access, and fell into BMW's traditional upscale target market with incomes of $75,000 and higher. As a measure of the "stickiness" of the website, the visitors spent more than six minutes at the site on average.

Some of the 2002 films were underscored by subplots that left more questions than answers, an ideal technique for creating intrigue. In addition to the plot and subplots, the films contained real phone numbers and websites. In one promotion, time and place information was given for viewers to assemble to participate in a BMWFilms live-action experience. For example, New Yorkers who called 212-529-9458 heard a disguised voice say, "I have the information you are looking for. Meet me on the corner of Madison and 23rd on August 23rd at 7 P.M. I'll be wearing a tan trenchcoat with a red rose in the lapel. Don't be late."

Those who showed up on August 23 found a bullet-ridden 740I BMW from the *Ambush* film parked on the street. As early as 3:30 on the appointed day, which turned out to include a downpour, people started assembling. McKenna says he approached one guy and explained that the car was used in the bmwfilms.com short film *Ambush*. McKenna told him that he was early—"You're not supposed to be here until seven"—and then was astonished when he found out the guy had come all the way from Orlando, Florida, for the event. By seven, along with locals, the crowd included hundreds of people from as far away as Chicago, San Francisco, Philadelphia, Boston, and Greensboro. All had come to ask the man in the trench coat about the "information."

The BMW films were so effective because the idea was creative, attention getting, and intriguing. It also redefined advertising as it moved the genre into the new world of interactive communication. McDowell explained, "*The Hire* was an unprecedented example of media convergence that both pushed and crossed boundaries."

The Cannes judges finally decided the campaign belonged in the interactive division, where it walked away with the Gold Lion. But that still begs the question of whether *The Hire* film series is good advertising as well. Randall Rothenberg, who critiques

advertising for *Fast Company* magazine, answers the question when he says the series reinvents the genre of advertising: "The BMW Films advertisements show that creative life remains within advertising."

Source: Youngme Moon and Kerry Herman, "BMWFilms," Harvard Business School case, N9-502, 046, January 11, 2002; Randall Rothenberg, "Ad of the Month," Fast Company, *March 2003, p. 40; Patrick McKenna, "The Long Way to Madison and 23rd,"* Promo, *May 1, 2002, <www.industryclick.com/magazinearticle.asp?magazinearticleid=147314&>; Peter Breen, "Hire Education,"* Promo, *May 1, 2002, <industryclick.com/magazinearticle.asp?magzineid=122&releaseid=>; Barbara Gengler, "BMW Back in Showbiz,"* The Australian IT, *June 29, 2002 "Tune Up Web Film Campaign,"* CNET News.com, *June 7, 2002, <www.news.com.com/2100-1023-934052.html>; "BMW to Reprise Web Film Effort,"* June 7, 2002, *<www.internetnews.com/IAR/article.php/1355321>.*

COMMUNICATION AND TECHNOLOGY

J. Crew was originally a catalog company. As its success grew, it expanded into regular retail stores, then expanded again to selling online at www.jcrew.com (see Exhibit 12-2). Although this evolution is not unusual for many businesses today, what is unusual is that in 2002 J. Crew's online sales surpassed sales from its long-established catalog division.[1] This shows that when the internet is properly integrated, it can be a powerful medium that successfully drives e-commerce (electronic commerce). Despite all the dot-com failures a few years ago, examples of online companies that are now operating profitably include eBay, Amazon.com, Yahoo!, Expedia, E*Trade, MarketWatch.com, Ask Jeeves, LookSmart, and Autobytel.[2] The internet is definitely alive and well!

E-business (electronic business) is sometimes confused with e-commerce but is actually much more encompassing. **E-commerce,** *online business transactions and interactions,* is the focus of this chapter. E-business is how all business operations (accounting, production, distribution, as well as marketing and sales) are driven by computer hardware and software that use the internet as a data communication platform.

Integrating Interactivity into Relationship Building

One of the major changes in today's marketplace is the increased communication between companies and customers. According to an article in *The Economist,* the marketing world was much simpler when all that companies did was *send* brand messages.[3] The increasing use of interactive technology leads customers to expect two-way communication with companies—that is, better customer service. They want to ask questions, place orders, and register complaints 24/7.

Driving this increase in interactivity is increasing access to and use of the internet. Consumer and business use of the internet is expanding rapidly because the internet is both inexpensive and easy to use. But the rapid growth has created a

E X H I B I T   1 2 - 2

J. Crew started as a catalog company but is now doing most of its business online.

problem for many companies, namely, how to handle and manage the increase in interactivity. In an attempt to better manage and make use of internet-facilitated interactivity, intranets and extranets have been set up, broadband has been greatly expanded, and companies are experimenting to discover how best to integrate wireless communication into their MC operations.

Different "Nets" for Different Uses

There have been important advances in communication technology throughout history, but from a growth perspective, the most phenomenal is the **internet,** which is *a worldwide system of linked computer networks.* According to a recent survey by UCLA, the internet "has surpassed all other media as the leading source of information" (TV ranked first for *entertainment* but fourth as an information source).[4] A Gallup poll found that 95 percent of those who have used the internet have done so to obtain information, 89 percent to send or receive e-mail, 45 percent to shop, and 21 percent to visit in chat rooms.[5] Approximately 10 percent of internet users have visited online brokerages, banking services, or auction houses.

The internet's greatest characteristic (from a marketing perspective) is being a relatively inexpensive, interactive communication medium. It helps companies connect and build stronger brand relationships with customers, employees, and other stakeholders by increasing the power of two-way communication. The internet has also become a major internal medium for companies that have set up **intranets.** Companies also use **extranets,** which connect employees with all key external stakeholders such as MC agencies, suppliers, and distributors (◀ Ch. 6). As a medium of marketing communications, the internet combines the characteristics of many other media—newspapers, magazines, catalogs, TV, and directories.

But the internet is a two-edged sword. Today, a major problem with a brand can be communicated around the world within minutes by dissatisfied customers. The greater the problem, the faster the word will spread. Intel found this out several years ago when a user discovered a problem with an Intel chip. In a matter of days, the faulty chip became a discussion topic in dozens of high-tech chat rooms, and the issue was soon picked up by offline mass media and further publicized.

Television, cable, computer, and phone companies all are scrambling to take leadership positions in the new world of **convergence,** which is *the combining of*

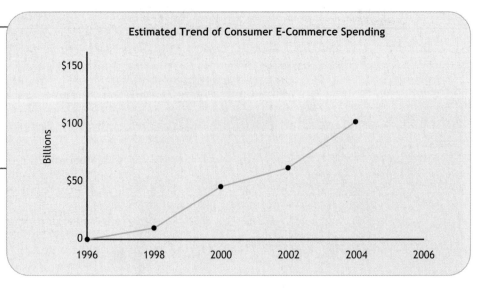

telephone, computer, and TV into one interactive communication device. An example of communication convergence is online streaming video that has the ability to carry live, two-way audio between customers and companies. The primary factor limiting the application of convergence is lack of bandwidth.

Bandwidth *governs the amount of digital information or data that can be sent from one place to another in a given time.* Limited bandwidth is a particular problem for exchanging large data files that contain graphic and video elements. Fortunately, the speed of technological evolution is providing greater and greater data-transmission capacities. This means that as more consumers buy faster computers and have access to more bandwidth through cable and satellite services, companies can deliver more complex brand messages than ever before.

Currently, the internet accounts for only 2 percent of all media spending. This statistic, however, is a bit misleading as to the importance of the role that the internet increasingly plays in acquiring and retaining customers, because the internet is far less costly to use than most other media. A few million dollars (a very small percentage of major MC budgets) can produce a great deal of online exposure and interactivity with customers and prospects. Jupiter Research estimates that 90 percent of U.S. households will be online by 2007 and over a third of these will be connected by high-speed broadband (which allows faster downloading).[6] But even better news for marketers is the estimated increase in online consumer spending (see Figure 12-1).

Using sophisticated software, companies can target brand messages to individuals and quickly alter message content with customized images and appeals. The same information can be used to make a company more responsive to its customers by providing easy access to information. Real-time, targeted, personalized, and interactive brand messages—that's one of the major differences in marketing communication created by the internet. And it's a powerful tool in building customer relationships.

Although the dot-com bust at the turn of the millennium put a dark cloud over e-commerce and the internet, the internet continues to play an important role in marketing communications. In 2001, for example, one study found that 62 percent of new-car buyers spent an average of six hours online gathering information about which brand of car to buy (Exhibit 12-3).[7] Although the internet is

> "Information technology and relationship building are two sides of the same coin in today's service-driven economy . . ."
>
> Siebel e-business self-published report, February 2001

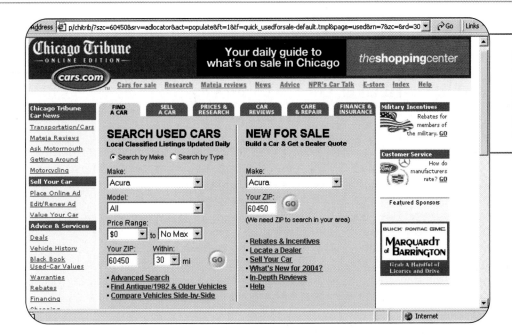

EXHIBIT 12-3
Websites such as cars.com provide information about availability, features, and prices of both used and new cars.

still a minor advertising medium and buying channel, it plays a critical role in many consumers' and B2B customers' brand decision making by . . .

1. *Shifting power from companies to customers by offering them more choices.* Customers can do comparative shopping and learn more about brands, not only from the brands' websites but also from third parties, more quickly and easily than ever before.

2. *Being accessible to the majority of the population.* Individuals who do not have access at home can go online at work or public locations such as libraries, schools, and internet cafés.

3. *Providing an extensive range of information.* Internet users have access to a wealth of information on companies, brands, and nearly every subject there is.

4. *Allowing for unsurpassed speed and coverage.* Especially since the advent of high-speed connection services, information travels across the internet almost instantaneously in most parts of the world.

5. *Reducing the cost of entry.* Opening a business online is far less costly than opening a traditional brick-and-mortar business.

6. *Reducing operating costs.* Selling online is less costly than operating a brick-and-mortar facility.

Wireless Communication

Wireless transmission of data and information is likely to be the single most significant change in media technology during the first decade of the new millennium. China, India, and other developing countries that don't have enough telephone and cable lines to support all the new media are investing heavily in wireless communication, leapfrogging the in-ground stage of communication infrastructure. Customers are now able to access the internet to send and receive e-mail with cellular phones, another indication of the growth of wireless. Although many companies are getting into the wireless business, most marketers of consumer and B2B goods are still waiting to see how viable it is to send brand messages to cellular phones.

TECHNOLOGY IN ACTION

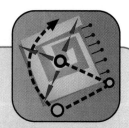

M-commerce Is the Future of Interactive Media

One of the most rapidly advancing types of interactive media is wireless digital communication. Its application to business is referred to as *m-commerce* (*m* for "mobile"). Devices for using this medium include cell phones, some personal digital assistants (PDAs), and global positioning systems (GPSs). The first generation of wireless devices consisted of analog cellular phones. The second generation consisted of digital cellular phones. The third generation can transmit voice, data, and video. Since 2001, wireless phones have been equipped with wireless application protocol (WAP), an industry standard that allows these phones to receive content from the internet.

In some countries, such as Finland and Japan, wireless-phone subscribers already outnumber fixed-line subscribers. The owners use their phones not only to talk to each other but also to send e-mail messages back and forth, pay for small-ticket items such as soft drinks, and subscribe to text messages such as horoscopes and jokes. And the uses are fast expanding. According to one observer, "People will be accustomed to getting up-to-the-minute personal and customized news, from traffic and weather to sports;

stock quotes; and even when movies are playing." Such use, if it becomes widespread, will make wireless communication a particularly attractive way to deliver brand messages.

Retail marketers are excited about the prospect of tying messages to location. A shopper in a mall will be able to request on-the-spot information concerning sales in the mall. A shopper in a grocery store will be able to obtain electronic coupons. A tourist walking past a restaurant can be alerted to a lunch special.

Think About It

What types of brand messages—from what types of businesses—seem the most logical choices for transmission by means of wireless devices? Will the proliferation of brand messages sent by wireless media finally cause customers to revolt against commercial messaging?

Source: Brad Applegate, "From 'Appointment Viewing' to 'News on Demand,'" posted on *MediaPost Monitor*, July 18, 2000, <www.masha@mediapost.com>. Used by permission.

London-based Ovum, a research and consulting firm, estimates that $16 billion will be spent on wireless advertising by 2005. Marketers will be attracted to wireless advertising for several reasons: (1) customers are increasingly mobile, (2) messages can be targeted not only by individual cellular phone number but also by time and location of targeted customers, and (3) wireless provides one more way to reinforce brand awareness and motivate customers to respond (see the Technology in Action box). It is expected that wireless messages will be most successful when used to redirect customers to certain websites and to sponsor web pages that are likely to be accessed with cellular devices, and for "click-and-dial." An example of "click-and-dial" is a message that would appear on your mobile phone's message screen asking whether a birthday or special occasion is near and, if so, would flowers be an appropriate gift. The message would allow you to click through to an online florist to place an order.[8]

Addressable Media and Interactive Media

Addressable and interactive media are reshaping brand relationships. Besides serving as communication vehicles for product offers to customers, addressable media—e-mail, mail, phone, and fax—can deliver messages asking research questions about level of brand satisfaction, further purchase intentions, and reactions

Why is our company tagline a question?

In part, it is meant to be an invitation to you.

In part, it's a question because we really need to know. We don't have all the answers. We just make software and then we watch you use it. And we've noticed you tend to do some pretty amazing things, some things we never would've imagined. We do a lot of our best work trying to keep up with your imagination.

So, for us, this isn't just a slogan; it's an honest question, and how you answer makes all the difference. So we'll ask it again: Where do you want to go today?

Where do you want to go today?

Microsoft
www.microsoft.com

EXHIBIT 12-4

This ad explains Microsoft's tag line, "Where do you want to go today?" as an invitation for customers to interact with the company. (The problem with this ad is it doesn't give an e-mail address or phone number which customers can use to respond!)

to new promotional offers. With the right messages, these media can help retain current customers and increase a brand's share of their category spending. For major-purchase goods and services, it can often be cost-justified to use addressable media to reach targeted prospects.

Even cable television operators now have digital systems with addressable capabilities, so they can send a customized selection of programs and brand messages to a particular subscriber's cable address. A recent deal between TCI and Kraft Foods, for example, experimented with sending different ads to different televisions within the same home. This means that in the near future, a TV in the kitchen could receive an ad for Kraft Singles cheese, while the TV in the basement workshop could receive an ad for a Black & Decker power tool—at the same time.

Interactive media take a step beyond the ability of addressable media in making more intimate the relationship between brands and customers. Companies have traditionally asked, "How can *we* best send messages to our customers and prospects?" They are now beginning to recognize that another question is just as important: "How can *our customers* easily send messages to us?" Companies that sincerely want customers and prospects to talk to them need to provide options for communicating with the company—fax, phone, e-mail, a website, or mail. The more flexibility there is to interact with a company, the more consumers are likely to do so. Microsoft's ad in Exhibit 12-4 invites customers to interact with the company. Something is missing from this ad, however. Can you tell what it is? (The answer is in the cutline for the ad.)

Interactive media include many of the addressable media previously described. The difference between interactive and addressable media is simply in how they are used. As mentioned earlier, the internet can be used as a mass medium (banner ads), an addressable medium (e-mail), or an interactive medium (live chat). From a customer's perspective, interactivity means *accessibility*, *recognition*, and *responsiveness*—all the things people require in a relationship, whether personal or commercial. From a brand perspective, interactivity means the ability to listen as well as speak and then modify corporate behavior as a result of customer feedback.

Four characteristics set interactive media apart from mass media: (1) they can target individuals as well as customer segments; (2) they can be used by customers

Information you need, from the sources you trust. Now on the Web.

Aviation Week Group
A Division of The McGraw-Hill Companies

EXHIBIT 12-5

This ad is designed to pull interested readers to Aviation Week's *website, where more interactive information is available.*

and prospects to talk to a company; (3) they are more measurable and accountable than mass media; and (4) they can demand more attention than mass media because of the personalized brand messages they can carry. The ability to deliver tight targeting is a particularly important benefit.

Interactivity can be either active or passive. *Active interactivity* occurs when a company and a customer talk to each other in real time (by means of the telephone or live chat). *Passive interactivity* involves a time delay—that is, it is asynchronous. A customer may get a fax on demand or use a company-sponsored kiosk or website to ask questions, retrieve information, and request information that arrives later by mail, fax, or e-mail.

Interactivity allows companies to integrate customers into a company. Customers can and should contribute to product planning and development, as well as to distribution and marketing decisions. Indeed, interactivity is increasingly seen as a customer's "right." If customers can easily ask one company a question or voice a complaint, they expect to be able to do so with every company with which they do business. Companies that don't facilitate customer interactivity risk sending a message that they are antiquated and don't care about customers (see Exhibit 12-5).

Although phone and mail are the most widely used interactive media in terms of MC spending, the fastest-growing and -changing media are commercial e-mail and company websites. E-mail and websites depend on different technologies and are used differently by both customers and businesses. For these reasons they are discussed here as different media, although both travel over the internet.

E-mail Marketing

The popularity of e-mail is supported by facts: 60 percent of U.S. adults surveyed said they preferred e-mail to reading traditional mail, and 34 percent said they preferred it to phone calls.[9] This is good news for marketers because e-mail is a less expensive form of one-to-one communication than either regular mail or long-distance telephone calls. E-mail has become a popular and effective way to reach customers because it is so simple and inexpensive to use.[10] Although unsolicited e-mail has become a source of customer irritation, some internet service providers, such as Hotmail, provide customers with free e-mail and internet services in return for their agreeing to view advertising.

Opt-in and Opt-out Strategies

Customer receptivity is an important consideration in the proper use of e-mail campaigns. This is why permission marketing (⬅ Chapters 7 and 8) is increasingly used. Customers who **opt-in,** *give permission for e-mail from a particular company or brand to be sent to them,* and they do not perceive those messages as **spam,** *unsolicited e-mail whose purpose is to sell a product or service.* Spam is not only bothersome to consumers but also a growing concern for businesses and government regulators. In the online environment, spamming has generated a lot of protests. According to *Internet News,* it was estimated that in 2002 businesses spent $8.9 billion to deal with spam (based on lost production time and IT costs).[11] Most major portals screen out mass e-mailings, and consumer groups have been formed to fight spamming. In Seattle, Washington, for example, a group of online users called the Forum for Responsible and Ethical E-mail (FREE) picketed a car dealer that tried to attract customers by bombarding them with unsolicited e-mails.[12] The

Direct Marketing Association originally argued for self-regulation of spam but finally admitted that it is so bad—41 percent of all e-mail is spam—that some form of government enforcement is needed. DMA guidelines say that e-mail should be used only:[13]

1. To solicit current customers.
2. To contact individuals (or companies) who have opted-in.
3. To contact individuals who have not opted-out after being given the opportunity to do so.
4. By marketers who have assurance from list brokers that names supplied conform to one or more of the above.

To motivate customers to opt-in, companies often use sweepstakes, games, or the promise of some type of reward. An example of a motivational offer for opting-in is free online planning calendars with e-mail reminders of key occasions so marked. This is done in exchange for personal data, which can be used to drive customized e-mail ads. Opt-in strategies have two benefits. First, they qualify the person (or company) as being interested in the product category. Second, when customers do sign up, smart companies ask profile questions so they have a better idea of their customers' demographics and lifestyles, which can in turn be used to anticipate needs and wants.

A step below spamming is **opt-out email,** which is *a series of messages that a company sends automatically until notified to stop.* For example, when you sign up for an online newsletter, the web page will often have a box, *already checked*, that says something like "Please send me news about special offers." Unless you uncheck the box (opt-out), the company will send you brand messages at regular intervals. This technique, used for years by book and record clubs, means that unless you tell the company not to send next month's selection, you will receive it. Some customers finds this practice a bit tricky and resent it. The strategy that is most respectful of customers is opt-in e-mail.

Much stricter e-mail regulations in Europe than in the United States have made it better for consumers but in some ways more difficult for marketers. In Germany, Austria, Italy, Denmark, and Sweden, laws require that customers opt-in before they can be sent any promotional e-mails. EU regulations require that "marketers must tell consumers what data they will collect and retain, exactly how it will be used in the future and then give them the option of opting in or out of the process . . . [If] a consumer . . . moves or changes any of the initial information given, the whole process starts over." Such rigid rules for collecting consumer information make marketing databases more difficult to create. But there is good news for marketers: once databases are created in this way, they are more effective, with return rates up to 40 percent![14]

Amazon.com sends out e-mails over its president's signature announcing new products and services to customers and prospects who have already signed up with the company. For example, e-mails were used to announce that Amazon was offering apparel online. Companies use both online and offline messages to invite those interested to "raise their hands" and sign up to be contacted.

E-mail Formats

E-mail marketing can be done in a variety of formats, such as ads, discussion lists, newsletters, and publicity. Which format is best depends on the marketing communication objectives that need to be achieved.

- *Ads.* Companies can send out e-mail advertising as plain text or as **rich media,** which is *e-mail that features audio and/or video.* Rich media e-mails, like those designed by the RadicalMail company, use technology that permits streaming video, among other special effects, to be distributed within an e-mail message rather than in an attachment. They can be extremely effective in attracting people to a company's website. For example, when Warner Bros. sent potential licensees an e-mail message featuring a trailer for an upcoming film, the response rates were exceptionally high.[15]

- *Discussion lists.* E-mail discussion lists (listservs) can include hundreds or thousands of people. Advertisers can add marketing messages at the bottom of each message sent out to the list, which allows them to continually send messages to a targeted group of people.

- *Newsletters.* Marketers send mass e-mailings set up as newsletters on brand-related topics. Unlike members of discussion lists, newsletter recipients can't communicate directly back to the marketer or to other recipients.

- *Publicity.* News releases are being distributed online not only to editors but also to others who need to know about a company's announcements.

Although distributing e-mail costs relatively little in space, time, or postage, the software and hardware required for handling large e-mail distributions can cost millions of dollars. Also, there is the cost of collecting e-mail addresses or renting address lists, as well as creating the messages to be sent. Nevertheless, the cost is still low compared to the cost of using other media. This is why nearly all companies using e-mail hire services such as MessageMedia and Yesmail, which specialize in helping a brand put together an effective e-mail program. When the cost of the service is included, it is possible to estimate opt-in e-mail at about $2 per sale. In contrast, banner ads (discussed later in this chapter) have an average cost per sale of $100; direct mail, approximately $71.[16]

Strengths and Limitations of E-mail Marketing

Research has shown that e-mail is the most effective form of online marketing because it can be personalized and is relatively inexpensive.[17] It is a particularly effective way to retain customers. In a study done by the DMA, 63 percent of companies surveyed said e-mail was their most effective customer retention tool.[18]

Most e-mail ads are designed to encourage **click-through,** *the act of responding by clicking on a link to go directly to a particular website.* Users are 3 to 10 times more likely to click through to a company's website from an e-mail than from a banner ad. One study found that of those who visited a site, 63 percent responded to e-mail campaigns, compared to 29 percent for offline advertising.[19]

Another advantage of e-mail is that once a message has been produced, it has a relatively small distribution cost. Neither the size of the audience nor the size of the message greatly affects the cost. As with direct mail, however, there is the cost of acquiring addresses of other-than-current customers, producing the message, and handling responses. E-mail campaigns also allow for easy testing of offers and how they are presented. Offers and messages that work best can quickly replace those that generate only average or below-average results.

Judging the effectiveness of e-mail is relatively straightforward: costs are balanced against revenues. Marketers must remember, though, that it is the sale that is important, not the number of e-mails opened or the number of responses achieved. For example, consider three different e-mails—all of them sending 1,000 messages—and the responses they elicited:

	E-mail A	E-mail B	E-mail C
E-mail opened	300	400	500
Click-throughs	30	45	40
Sales	5	4	3

Note that e-mail C was the most frequently opened and that B attracted the most visitors to the website. E-mail A, however, produced the most sales.[20]

A major limitation of e-mail campaigns, even when customers have opted-in, is clutter. Internet research companies forecast that clutter will only get worse. In response, an increasing number of anti-spam software systems, which screen out unsolicited e-mails, are being used by both individuals and companies. Another challenge many companies face is responding to e-mails in a timely manner. According to a Jupiter Research study, one-third of customers who contact a company by e-mail expect a response within six hours, and nearly all expect a response within 48 hours.[21] Few companies meet these expectations.

Website Marketing

Most of the major MC functions use the internet, along with the other major media, to connect with customers and prospects. The internet, and particularly websites, are brand-message *expanders.* In other words, MC messages such as ads, publicity releases, packaging labels, and even events can direct customers and prospects to a brand's website for more information about the brand. Offering this level of brand knowledge was simply not possible before the internet was integrated into the MC and media mixes.

Users report spending about one-fourth of their online time gathering information. This is good news for companies. It indicates that an increasing number of customers and prospects are getting used to gathering information online, and it suggests that the internet is an economical medium for distributing brand information.

Websites provide unique brand–customer touch points with online communities and chat rooms. A creatively designed website that is interactive and fun to visit will not only attract visitors but will extend their stay. The website designed for Lexus, for example, is filled with lifestyle information that appeals to Lexus owners and prospects, such as descriptions of luxury hotels, where the best farmers' markets are located, and what a really high-tech home includes. The website plays jazz and "new luxury" music that is heard in Lexus commercials. It also has links to news sites such as MSNBC as well as links to Lexus commercials for visitors who want to learn more about the product.[22]

The most important step for directing customers and prospects to a website is to register it with as many search engines as possible in order to gain visibility and site visits. **Search engines** are *internet tools that use keywords to find websites.* Exhibit 12-6 is an ad for a company that registers the keywords people might use in a Web search. Web marketers often use common keywords to structure their websites in order to maximize how often the sites turn up in searches.

Online Brand Communities

A valuable aspect of a website is the ability to bring together customers and prospects to share ideas on how to use a company's products. **Virtual communities** are *groups of people who focus on certain online activities and establish relationships with one another.* Many major league athletic teams, for example, have websites where their fans congregate and communicate with the team as well as with each other. These fans constitute a virtual community based on team loyalty.

Adobe offers, for each of its products, user-to-user forums that operate like bulletin boards where customers can post and read notes. At the Kraft Foods website, there is a bulletin board called the "Wisdom of Moms Exchange" where people can post such things as recipes and Mother's Day memories. Such sites not only allow loyal users to share tips with each other but also reinforce their commitment to the sponsoring brand. Also available on some corporate sites are chat rooms that allow people to talk to one another in real time.

EXHIBIT 12-6
No matter how beautiful the site, if people can't find it, they won't become customers. The internet keywords service helps companies reach customers by merging the Web address and the product name.

What are the marketing benefits of collecting internet users into like-minded groups? It aggregates people into addressable target markets. It creates bonds, which may deliver goodwill to community sponsors, and it allows the company to listen to its customers, providing a type of real-time research.

Online Customer Service

Responding to customers is a critical management responsibility and another area in which a website can add value to a brand or company. James Daly, editor of *Business 2.0,* predicted that customer service would separate the winners from the losers in the dot-com shakeout that began in 2000 with the devaluation of Web stocks. He points out that customer service is not the last rung on the ladder at the end of the sale, but rather the first—it begins the moment someone arrives on a website.[23] There are three necessary elements for delivering good customer service online:

1. *Thorough and easy-to-use information at the website.* Simple sites may employ a frequently asked questions (FAQ) list, which supplies the answers to commonly asked questions. More sophisticated sites usually offer an index or search engine, which allows users to find help by typing in keywords.

2. *Customizable products and services.* More and more companies are creating websites that allow customers to design the products and services they want. Computer manufacturer Gateway, for example, allows both individuals and businesses to design computers to order. Customers are presented with an extensive menu of features, and their computers are built to the specifications they choose. Similarly, Nike allows some of its website visitors to order custom-made shoes.

3. *Human interaction.* Rarely does a site provide answers to all possible questions. Often there is still a need for a user to communicate with a real person. Companies should provide toll-free numbers so that online users know where to call. They should also allow for easy use of e-mail, although this option should not be provided if the response rate is going to be slow. No online consumer should have to wait more than 24 hours for an answer by e-mail. A quicker solution is a direct online link to a customer-service representative.

The user is able to type in questions and receive immediate responses. Another variation allows a user to type in a question and then receive an immediate telephone call back from a customer-service rep.

A number of products have been designed to help meet online customer-service needs. For example, eGain is an online customer communication company that provides "integrated multichannel solutions" including e-mail management, interactive Web and voice collaboration, intelligent self-help agents, and proactive online marketing. Another company, eTetra.com, offers software that allows a site visitor to click an icon that brings him or her directly to a real person. The program collects information about the site visit and then finds the right person to assist with whatever the customer needs.

A DMA mystery shopping study designed to evaluate online customer service found that the following companies have the best: Nordstrom.com, JCPenney.com, LandsEnd.com, Kmart.com, Amazon.com, CDNow.com, drugstore.com, KBtoys.com, SmithandHawken.com, and TheSportsAuthority.com. Among the key factors in the ratings were checkout processes, ease of communication with a company, and the overall shopping experience.[24]

Customers who want to check out a website or a particular company can go to www.BizRate.com, www.ePinion.com, and www.PlanetFeedback.com to read postings from customers. As you might expect, most of the postings are complaints. From a company's perspective, however, these sites can be of value. A higher-than-average number of complaints will identify a brand weakness. Recognizing that this information is of value to companies, PlanetFeedback provides a monitoring service that provides companies with periodic summaries of complaints about their brands.

E-COMMERCE: ADDING ONLINE TO CLICK-AND-BRICK SHOPPING

At first it seemed that online companies would dominate e-commerce; however, brick-and-mortar companies are increasingly integrating the internet into their marketing operations (thus becoming click-and-brick companies). More than three-fourths of successful online businesses are offshoots of traditional retailers. Some of the reasons for this evolution are that these retailers are established brands, have marketing experience, and have installed information technology systems.[25]

From a customer's perspective, online shopping is fast, convenient, and easy. Originally most online shoppers and computer users were male. However, AOL reported in 2002 that 65 percent of AOL shoppers were female, which is similar to the pattern in offline retailing.[26]

A study by McKinsey (management consultants) found that online companies have done a fairly good job of attracting customers to their websites (see Exhibit 12-7). They have been less successful at retaining customers, however; the retention rate overall is actually decreasing.[27] One reason for the disappointing level of retention is the fact that more than half of online retailers don't make use of the internet's interactive technology.[28]

The product categories with the highest volume of online sales are electronics, books, CDs, computer software, apparel, and toys and games. Online ticketing is another growing category. People have found they can print out tickets for air travel, sports events, and so on from their home printers, along with other information that wouldn't fit on conventional printed tickets, such as schedules and maps. In order to make sure tickets are not counterfeited, a supporting B2B business has been developed that sells encryption and bar code technology to online ticketmasters.

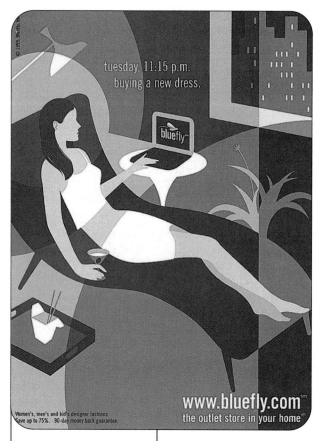

tuesday, 11:15 p.m.
buying a new dress.

bluefly

Women's, men's and kid's designer fashions.
Save up to 75%.   90-day money back guarantee.

www.bluefly.com℠
the outlet store in your home℠

EXHIBIT 12-7

Bluefly is an online designer fashion store that survived the millennium meltdown experienced by many dot-com companies.

Reasons for Using E-Commerce

Small Business Association members who do business through e-commerce say that 50 percent of their online sales are coming from new customers, demonstrating the reach of the internet. The following list shows the main marketing reasons why businesses use e-commerce. Note that the first six have to do with marketing communications:

- To reach worldwide audiences.
- To have a cost-effective dialogue with customers and prospects.
- To aggregate niche audiences in order to reach a critical mass of customers.
- To provide frequently updated prices and other important product information.
- To improve customer service by providing company access 24 hours a day, seven days a week.
- To collect instant feedback and conduct market research, which can be interactive and immediately tallied.
- To provide alternative channels of distribution.
- To provide an extremely cost-effective way to distribute brand information.

For all those reasons, e-commerce is proving to be a viable way to generate sales. For example, after General Motors' Saturn website transformed itself from a passive site (featuring only car information, data comparisons, and dealer referrals) to an active selling tool (featuring an online order form, a lease-price calculator, and an interactive design shop for choosing car options), site visits tripled. A major portion of Saturn's customer leads now originate from the brand's website.[29]

Internet Barriers and Concerns

Although most people agree that e-commerce has great potential, they also know that several barriers must be overcome. The internet has become an information jungle that is cluttered and difficult to navigate. For companies using e-commerce, the marketing communication challenge is to make the company's website easy to find amid this clutter and, once found, easy to navigate.

Another weakness of e-commerce is that only about half the population in developed countries has easy access to the internet (the figure is much lower in developing countries). Even among those who have access, the majority are still using narrowband telephone lines, which can make downloading web pages slow and torturous. When it comes to buying online, there is still a segment of customers who are unwilling to submit their credit-card numbers. According to one study, consumers remain leery of online businesses. When asked "Whom do you trust?" two-thirds said small businesses, and only one-third said online businesses. Interestingly, the trust level for big businesses was no better than for online businesses—just one-third of respondents.[30]

Concerns about the internet include how it will be used, who will control it, and whether it will make businesses even more impersonal than they already are. One organization created as a result of these concerns is Cluetrain, which is devoted to warning businesses that the internet enables people to network and build coalitions that can be more powerful than businesses themselves. Founders of the organization published a book, *The Cluetrain Manifesto: The End of Business as Usual*, and set up a website, www.cluetrain.com, that lists the group's 95 "theses" regarding customer rights.

Figure 12-2 is a "Customer's Bill of Rights in an Interactive Age." Judging from your own buying experiences, to what extent do you think most companies respect these rights?

Offline Advertising for Online Businesses

Originally, online companies tended to place their brand messages only on other websites, on the assumption that marketing offline was too expensive (Exhibit 12-8). If you want to reach only people who have internet access, why advertise elsewhere? Internet companies soon realized, however, that offline advertising, properly targeted, could be cost-effective. The most economical way to advertise is to do joint links and off-line cross-promotions with sites whose audiences are similar or related.

Another realization was that people often surf the Web and watch television simultaneously. During a recent Super Bowl, 22 percent of internet users who watched the game were also online during the broadcast. Twelve percent said they

Customer Bill of Rights in an Interactive Age

1. Customers have the right to contact the company 24 hours a day, 7 days a week and at least be able to leave a message.

2. Customers have the right to select how to contact a company (phone, mail, fax, e-mail).

3. Customers have the right (e.g., option) to talk to a human being without being subjected to multiple levels of an automated voice-response system.

4. Customers have the right to talk to a company representative with enough knowledge to answer any reasonable question or complaint.

5. Customers have the right to talk to a company representative with enough authority to make a decision.

6. Customers have the right to privacy regarding their transactions (e.g., the option to control the selling of their names to other companies).

7. Customers have the right to a timely response relative to typical use of the product (e.g., if the product is used 24 hours a day, then response should be available 24 hours a day).

8. Customers have the right to be rewarded in proportion to their support of the company (e.g., buying, referring others, following procedures).

9. Customers have the right to avoid intrusive phone calls, junk mail, and spam e-mail.

10. Customers are right 98 percent of the time. The other 2 percent they have the right to a sensitive and empathetic explanation of why they're not right.

FIGURE 12-2

Which of these do you think is most important?

Copyright 2001 Tom Duncan, Ph.D. This figure may be reproduced with attribution (tduncan@du.edu).

navigated to an advertiser's website during or after the game.[31] Bud Light took advantage of that connection with its "Making Faces" campaign, which allowed individuals to star in their own Bud Light ads.

Brand building is just as important for online companies as it is for other companies. For new online companies, marketing costs account for 40 percent of Web development budgets.[32] On average, online companies spend $25 million per year on marketing communication aimed at building their brands. It is estimated between 2000 and 2003 online companies spent about $3 billion in advertising.[33]

INTEGRATING ONLINE BRAND COMMUNICATION

As the surviving online businesses mature, marketing is becoming more important. New online companies now spend 25 to 50 percent of their total budgets on marketing communications. Unfortunately, many of the first online companies paid little attention to building their brands and paid the price—bankruptcy. They focused only on technology, building an organization, and creating brand awareness but not on brand knowledge and respect.

Brand building is especially important for online companies for two reasons. First, the internet lowers barriers to entry: starting a company online is easier than setting up a traditional brick-and-mortar retail operation. A company now has a smaller window of time than ever before to establish itself before competitors appear. Second, the internet makes it possible to build brands incredibly fast. Amazon.com did it in less than five years.[34] An organization that helps companies make better use of the internet medium is the not-for-profit Internet Advertising Bureau (www.iab.net).

Online Advertising Growing Fast

Although still a fraction of total media spending, online advertising is growing faster than any other type of advertising. DoubleClick, which refers to itself as a global internet advertising solutions company, places more than 1.5 billion ads on the internet each day. Advertising online offers a number of advantages:

- *Interactivity:* Companies and customers can engage in dialogue.

- *Flexibility:* Brand messages can be instantly changed/revised if not producing desired results.

- *Precise targeting:* People who come to a website are interested in that site's topic, product category, or brand and therefore are more likely to respond.

- *Quick results*: Because people are online 24/7, as soon as an offer is placed online, it has a potential audience that can immediately reply.

- *Measurable*: Hits, click-throughs, and purchases can easily be tracked.

Online advertising comes from online companies as well as from offline retailers who want customers and prospects to visit their websites (Exhibit 12-9). Ad spending on the internet is still increasing despite the dot-com crash of 2001. Spending is estimated to be $16.5 billion by 2005.[35] As online advertising has become more common, however, users have learned to ignore it. Thus agencies are always searching for new and better ways to attract attention. Often, the results is increasingly intrusive online advertising. It's difficult to find the right balance between attraction and irritation.

Once a company decides to advertise online, it must decide on which sites to place its ads. Some common guidelines are used to select these sites: (1) visitors to the sites must match the company's customer profile; (2) the site must have good viability (it is established and promises to be around for a while); (3) the site's privacy policy must be similar to your company's; (4) site content must be compatible with the image of your company; and (5) the site must have performed well for you or other similar companies in the past. Hewlett-Packard spends approximately 75 percent of its online advertising budget on sites that have produced results and the remaining 25 percent on sites that were not used before but meet the other criteria listed above. This strategy is an ongoing process of finding and using sites that produce the best results (as measured by whatever objectives have been established).[36]

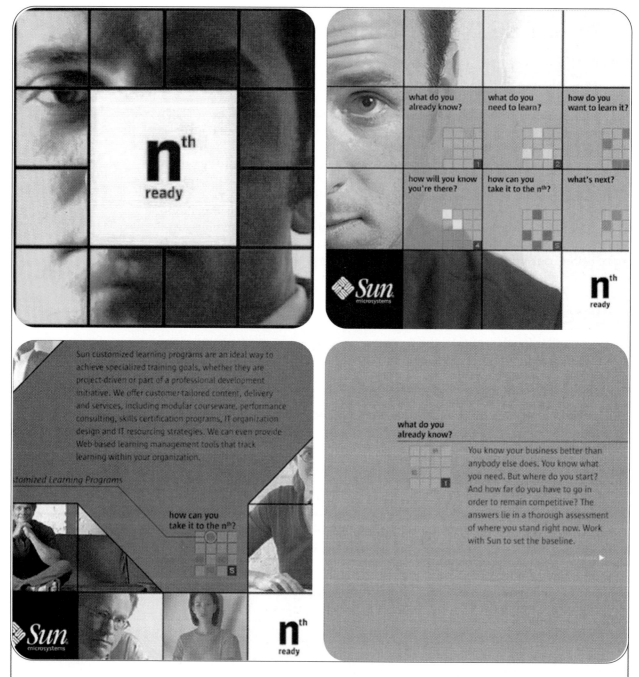

EXHIBIT 12-9

Sun Microsystem's Educational Services division designed an interactive business card for its sales representatives to use with their prospects and customers, as part of a Web-enabled contact management application.

Types of Online Ads

The creativity of the message design is an important factor in attracting attention to a web ad. As an example of the power of a well-designed ad, Scott Kurnit, CEO of iVillage Inc., told this story: "Just the other day I was going through a food site and saw an unbelievable ad for Coca-Cola. I had to use my mouse to take a bottle of Coke and pour it into an empty glass. Then I added ice cubes and a straw. I was so fascinated by it I kept doing it over and over. I spent several minutes of my precious time with this one brand."[37]

Another way to attract attention is with frequency. Some Web advertisers are turning out as many as 850 new online ads a day, or 6,000 per week. Although the average number of online ads created for a company's use is about 8 (and almost half of all companies are using fewer than 2), the 10 largest Web advertisers have averaged 290 different ads. Amazon.com has the most, with some 360 different ads in its portfolio. Production and placement costs in traditional media make such volume prohibitive, but on the Web creating a variety of messages is an important (and less costly) strategy.

Marketers are sure to come up with new ways to deliver brand messages online, but currently the most prevalent types of online advertisements (besides e-mail) include the following:

- **Banner ads.** Banners are configured so that users can click on the ad and be taken to a brand's website. Tracking technology can now be used to instantly identify website visitors and select from a variety of banners to display, depending on the visitor's profile. Two people may view the same page at exactly the same time. One can be shown an ad for financial services, the other an ad for an online bookstore. Banner ads that appear vertically on a screen are known as "skyscrapers."

- **Interstitials.** Similar to a banner ad but more intrusive, an **interstitial** is *an ad that pops up in a separate frame on a screen page.* The user has to stop reading and click on interstitial to eliminate them.

- **Pop-ups and pop-unders.** One step below interstitials in intrusiveness, **pop-ups and pop-unders** are *ads that appear when a viewer closes a page or site.*

Interstitials and pop-ups and pop-unders have become highly controversial because they are so irritating. Viewers hate them; media buyers say the intrusiveness is needed. A class-action suit has been filed against America Online by members who feel that because they pay an hourly fee to use the service, they shouldn't have to deal with such annoyances. According to a study by Grey/ASI, interstitials provoked the greatest irritation of all Web advertising (15 percent). Some interstitials treat you to several minutes of full-screen movies whether you want to watch or not. Barb Palser, of Internet Broadcasting Systems, describes such ads in terms normally reserved for predators.[38]

Customization may be the answer to the intrusiveness problem. Marketing companies such as Be Free, LinkShare, Phase2Media, and SmartAge create advertising for a network of sites that attract users with similar interests. Engage Technologies, with its click-through data on 42 million Web surfers and their visits to some 900 websites, is another company that provides this service to advertisers. When Engage-profiled shoppers, many of whom aren't even aware that Engage is watching them, visit an electronic retailer (e-tailer), that site gets their profiles instantly and can then use the profiles to tailor its offerings and ads. Engage does hide shoppers' identification information, providing only the serial number of their profiles to the retailer. Engage claims that Web users are 50 percent more likely to click on web ads picked by its profiling technique than on ads placed to fit a page's content.

One of the first Web advertising design considerations is deciding how intrusive a banner ad should be. Do you need to attract attention, even if that means "clicking off" a few surfers in the process? Or are you concerned about building a brand relationship with your users? According to a presentation cosponsored by three major online advertising companies, there are five "Golden Rules of Online Branding" regarding banner ads:[39]

- Keep banner simple—the more creative elements (graphics and words), the less ability a banner has to raise brand awareness.

- Maximize size of logo—the bigger the logo, the more likely the banner will send a clear message to customers.

- Maximize size of banner—just as with print ads, the larger the size, the greater impact it has.

- Use frequency—the optimal frequency number differs by product category and banner design, but overall, research findings indicate that a frequency of five impressions is the most efficient.

- Include a human face—the presence of a human face was found to increase attention more than other design elements.

Clearly, not all Web advertisers follow these rules. Some of the new techniques that use a click-or-die strategy can only be described as obnoxious. The idea is to design a site that is "sticky" enough to keep viewers "glued" to it. Web gremlins have been created that hijack your cursor and won't release it until you click on its mother site.

Because business is driven by customers' wants and needs, it is not surprising that ad-blocking software has been developed. AdKiller, Junkbuster Proxy, and AdSubtract are some of the software programs that do this. What especially concerns DoubleClick and other companies that sell online advertising is that some of this ad-blocking software is being installed in modems. If ad-blocking becomes pervasive, many internet service providers will be forced to increase their fees because advertising revenue will be greatly reduced or even eliminated.[40]

Costs and Response Rates

The cost of banner ads is determined by either the number of ad views (impressions) or the number of click-throughs. In 2003, Advertising.com, one of the companies that provides placement of banners and skyscrapers, was charging $1 for each 1,000 impressions of a banner ad or $.55 per click-through. For pop-up ads, the cost for 1,000 impressions was $3.85, nearly four times the cost of a static banner ad. The reason for the increased cost was that pop-ups, though much more attention getting, cannot be used as frequently as banners.

Some companies barter advertising space—that is, they trade space on each other's sites rather than exchanging money. Competition among sites, along with the fact that banner ads are not generating the click-through rates they once did, has caused the cost of online advertising to fall in recent years.

Response rates for banner ads are lower than those for direct mail. The average click-through rate is between three-tenths and five-tenths of 1 percent (3 to 5 responses for every 1,000 people who see the ad).[41] Of those who do click through, only about 1 percent make a purchase. Assuming a click-through rate of five-tenths of 1 percent, this means that only 1 person out of the 20,000 people who see the average banner ad actually ends up responding (20,000 people × .005 who click through ×.01 who respond = 1 response out of 20,000). And this rate continues to decrease despite new audio and visual techniques designed to make ads more attention getting. Not surprisingly, customers interested in high-involvement products are more likely to click through than are those interested in low-involvement products. What is a surprise is that larger banner ads and animation can increase the click-through rate for low-involvement products but not for high-involvement products, according to one study.[42]

Classified Advertising

The ease with which consumers can use keywords to search for only those ads pertinent to them makes online classified advertising a particularly attractive proposition. In addition, online classified advertising can deliver far more than print classified ads. For example, compared to a page in a newspaper, a website provides far more space for photos and can offer multimedia enhancements, such as interactive video tours of homes. Further, the internet is global, unlike traditional classified advertising outlets, such as local newspapers.

Online Ad Targeting

Early online advertising simply targeted the broad Web audience. As technology has grown more sophisticated, businesses are increasingly able to place specifically targeted advertisements online. Online targeting strategies can be divided into three types:[43]

- *Editorial*. Banners are targeted by site or by page topic. For example, advertisers on the Yahoo! search engine can place ads on any of the more than 100,000 categories featured in Yahoo's Web directory.

- *Filtered*. In the most popular form of professional Web advertising today, advertisers can specify targeting parameters, such as the user's operating system or browser software, time period, country, or even internet service provider. The selection mechanism on the service provider's server analyzes the request and selects for placement only the sites that match the ad's specifications.

- *Personalized*. Next-generation systems will use neural networks and other proprietary learning methods to allow personalized content and advertisement selection based on the browsing and interaction history of a particular user, as well as other demographic information. *Ad servers* (computers that control the ad placements) are often run by a company such as DoubleClick, which is neither the advertiser nor the content website. These computers can be programmed so that they fine-tune ad placement to reflect response rates.

Integrating the Internet and Public Relations

For online companies (and offline companies that use e-commerce), home pages are similar to corporate or brand brochures. They are designed to succinctly summarize a company's business, reinforce the corporate or brand identity, and provide a site map so visitors can easily navigate the website. Some good examples of corporate home pages can be found at the following URLs: www.altoids.com, www.apple.com, www.crayola.com, and www.saturncars.com.

Because websites can contain a vast array of information, they can be designed to be useful to all of a company's stakeholders. For media relations, a site can contain a description of a company's business operations, a listing of all its brands and products, a listing of all executives, and, most important, company contact information. Some sites, such as that of AirTran, also carry selected photos that media representatives can easily retrieve and use (www.airtran.com). Most companies post their press releases on their websites and maintain a file of them for a certain period of time. The human resources department often uses the company website to publicize job openings and provide prospective employees easy access to the company.

The websites of public companies can be important sources of information for the financial community. For example, after the story broke regarding defective Firestone tires on Ford Explorers, which were blamed for dozens of rollover accidents, Ford's stock price declined. To address the concerns of the financial community and other Ford stakeholders, Ford put on the opening page of its corporate website a special button that said: "For official Ford News on the Firestone recall, click here." This link took online users to a listing of news releases and other information that Ford had made public about the recall and the company's future use of Firestone tires.

Integrating the Internet into Sponsorship Programs

Rather than simply placing ads on sites, some companies prefer to sponsor entire sites. The site's content may come from a nonprofit association, but it is specifically created to attract target audiences for the corporate sponsor and to promote that sponsor's products. Online educational seminars (just like in-person seminars) represent one of the most common sponsorship opportunities. Other sponsors attempt to create a "halo effect" for their brand by associating it with something positive. An example is the Women's Auto Center sponsored by Ford Motor Company on iVillage, a network of women's sites. Sponsorships are more about building customer relationships long-term than about driving sales short-term.

The importance of sponsorships is increasing. In 1998, banner advertising accounted for 52 percent of online advertising dollars; sponsorships, for 40 percent. For 2001, it was expected that banners would receive only 26 percent of online ad dollars and sponsorships 58 percent.[44] Online events are also being used to attract audiences for a brand. Music sites such as CDnow and CD Universe sponsor online concerts. Among other things, these events reward regular customers and allow them to sample new music.

Some of these internet sponsorships take advantage of the unique character of the internet to maintain a relationship with customers. For example, Levi Strauss & Co. has a series of computer games on its site (www.us.levi.com), all of which are built around the iconic elements of its products (see Exhibit 12-10).

Measuring Online Marketing Communication

The first step in measuring the effectiveness of online marketing communication programs is to identify primary target audiences. Visa, for example, has three primary targets—customers, merchants who accept Visa cards, and banks that process credit-card transactions. Visa wants to see an increase in the number of

EXHIBIT 12-10

Levi's® Games

A group of five games are featured in this section of the Levi® brand website. Most of them use advanced computer graphic plug-ins, which are available on the site, and they attempt to emulate the sticking power of computer games as they make the brand a hero in this entertaining format.

banks that use its for-banks-only website to get answers to frequently asked questions, thus reducing the number of calls to Visa customer service, where each contact is very expensive. A similar objective exists for merchants. In the case of Visa customers, objectives relate to card sign-ups, card usage, and perception of Visa. To determine how well its website is performing, Visa uses the following measurements, which are fairly standard in the industry:

- *Lift:* How many additional transactions were made by Visa cardholders who visited Visa's website?

- *Conversion rate:* What percentage of non-Visa cardholders who visited the site signed up for a Visa card?

- *Brand knowledge and perception:* What percentage of site visitors report knowing more about Visa and thinking more positively about Visa compared to those who did not visit the site?

- *Number of visits:* This commonly used measurement is only of value if the majority of visitors are customers or prospective customers. If people are motivated to visit only for a chance to win a prize, for example, and for no other reason, most visitors may not be prospects.

- *Length of time on site:* The longer people stay on a site, the more likely they are to purchase or learn more about the brand.

- *Number and types of inquiries:* The more a company can engage customers in a dialogue, the stronger the brand relationship should be.[45]

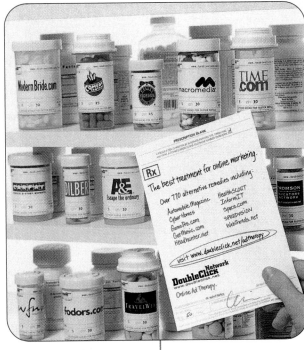

EXHIBIT 12-11
Services like DoubleClick track the behavior of online customers and provide e-tailers with information about online consumer behavior.

One advantage of using the internet for advertising, sending e-mail, and posting a website is the measurability of hits and click-throughs (see Exhibit 12-11). Jupiter Media Metrix, one of the premier media research firms, says, however, that such measures can be misleading. For example, Jupiter points out that although the average click-through on banners is far below 1 percent, these banners are still creating brand awareness, increasing average customer lifetime value, and, if banners are done creatively, helping to reinforce brand image. According to Jupiter, "the actual number of customers that internet advertising generates is often several multiples above what is tracked."[46]

INTERNET PRIVACY ISSUES

As internet use has grown, privacy has become an increasing concern. Georgia Institute of Technology's Visualization and Usability Center did a study of 10,000 Web users and found that 71 percent thought that privacy laws should govern the use of online personal data. Over four-fifths of the respondents objected to companies selling customers' personal data to other companies.[47] In the United States, privacy is protected by judicial interpretation of the Fourth Amendment to the Constitution (see call-out on next page). To what degree the government should pass specific privacy legislation is a topic of ongoing debate. An example of an industry-specific regulation is the GLB (Gramm-Leach-Bliley) Financial Services Modernization Act (1999). It requires financial services firms to inform customers

"The right of the people to be secure in their persons, houses, papers, and effects, against unreasonable searches and seizures, shall not be violated . . . "

Fourth Amendment to the U.S. Constitution

of the firms' privacy policies and give customers the option to opt-out of the companies' name-sharing activities. It also puts financial services firms' privacy policies under closer federal government scrutiny.

In a survey that asked online users if they want targeted advertising and content, the majority of respondents said "yes." When people realize, however, how much information is being gathered about them and the fact that it might be shared with other companies, most express reservations, a fact discovered in a study done by the Pew Foundation. According to this study of 1,017 internet users, 86 percent were in favor of companies asking permission to use personal data (an opt-in policy). About half (52 percent) said that tracking online activities is an invasion of privacy. The study found that 54 percent of respondents had provided personal data to online companies but 27 percent said they never would. The study also found that approximately one-fourth of online users use false identities. When asked about the placing of *an online tracking tool*—a **cookie**—on their computers, 56 percent said they didn't know how to tell whether this had been done (see the Ethics and Issues box). Although computers can be set to reject cookies, only 1 in 10 online users has done so.[48]

According to research done by the University of Pennsylvania's Wharton School of Business, many people who have backed away from online shopping have done so because of privacy concerns. According to the study, concern about "monitoring by third parties" was the highest predictor of not purchasing online, and unwillingness to "trust the business with private data" was another question that scored high.[49] The "privacy" ad in Exhibit 12-12 (page 412) illustrates the seriousness with which marketing communication companies approach this problem.

Privacy Policies

Understanding a company's offline privacy policy and giving permission for certain kinds of data to be collected are the most important elements in an online privacy policy. In internet marketing, that means posting a highly visible link to the company's privacy policy on the opening page. In addition, companies that are sensitive to their customers' privacy concerns may also register with a program like TRUSTe. The TRUSTe icon functions like the Good Housekeeping Seal to monitor companies' privacy performance. Other such services include Pricewaterhousecoopers' BetterWeb, Good Housekeeping's Web Site Certification, and the Better Business Bureau's privacy guarantees.

In the United States, the Federal Trade Commission (FTC) has been carefully watching the development of the Web privacy issue. It released a report in 2000 that found that only 20 percent of sites with 39,000 or more unique visitors per month adequately protect their consumers' privacy. To help companies address the privacy concerns of citizens, the FTC recommends practices for industry self-regulation:[50]

Fair Information Practices

- *Notice.* Give clear and conspicuous notice of what information is collected and how it will be used.
- *Choice.* Let consumers choose whether their information can be used for any purpose besides fulfilling the transaction.
- *Reasonable access.* Consumers should be able to access the information collected about them and have a reasonable opportunity to correct any errors or delete the data.

ETHICS AND ISSUES

The Cookie Monster

When you are browsing the Web or participating in a chat room, you are hiding behind the anonymity of your clever user name. You may not realize the extent to which internet bugs can track your private interests as recorded by your click-throughs called cookies. A cookie issued by a company that has a presence at hundreds of websites can capture customers' comings and goings all over the Web. Cookies may simplify site registration, but they can also leave a trail of the sites you check.

In a "Cathy" cartoon strip, Cathy is confronting old boyfriend and computer guru Irving about what he has found out about her from his online snooping. He reports that she browsed four diet websites, downloaded flea remedies, clicked on "European Airlines," and cruised the personals. He observed that the next time she logged on, she would receive banner ads for "singles weight-loss spas in Italy that allow dogs."

Mirroring Cathy's expression of horror was the public outcry that arose in 2000 when it was revealed that the Federal Trade Commission was investigating DoubleClick for possibly deceptive data collection and data sharing. Complaints arose when DoubleClick revealed that it planned to amass and sell to advertisers personal information about internet users' habits and identities—the type of activity that traditional direct-marketing companies have been engaging in for a long time.

Consumer activists who follow this issue provide some of the best information about cookies and online profiling. Did you know that when you buy a new computer and transfer your files to it, the cookies transfer along with the other data? Did you realize that most computers can be set up to not accept and store cookies? If you want to learn more, check out the privacy watchdog site Junkbusters (www.junkbusters.com) and the U.S. government's Electronic Privacy Information Center (www.epic.org). Webwasher.com or your internet service provider can help you eliminate cookies.

Think About It

What are cookies? What are the good and bad sides of cookies? Do you care whether a site you visit installs a cookie? How can companies use cookies in a way that's sensitive to privacy issues?

Source: Jane Bryant Quinn, "Fighting the Cookie Monster," *Newsweek*, February 28, 2000, p. 63; "Bad Cookies," *Newsweek*, February 28, 2000, p. 12; Andrea Petersen, "A Privacy Firestorm at DoubleClick," *Wall Street Journal*, February 23, 2000, p. B1; Andrea Petersen, "DoubleClick Reverses Course after Privacy Outcry," *Wall Street Journal*, March 3, 2000, p. B1.

- *Adequate security.* Companies should ensure proper handling of consumer information to prevent unauthorized access or identity theft.

America Online (AOL) is in a tricky position regarding privacy issues. It keeps records on more than 21 million subscribers, including names, addresses, and credit-card numbers. AOL says it has never sold data about its members' movements within its systems, which are tracked by AOL's proprietary service. The company believes that its privacy policy is one of the best in the industry. It does, however, sell names and addresses of subscribers to direct mailers, a practice it admits in its privacy policy, and it also buys information about its members from outside suppliers and uses that information to target brand messages to its new subscribers.

Amazon.com has come under attack by two privacy groups. The Electronic Privacy Information Center (EPIC), a Washington-based advocacy group that was part of Amazon's affiliates program, decided to end its partnership with Amazon. Likewise, Jason Catlett, of the private advocacy firm Junkbusters, pulled out of the program, saying that Amazon.com's new privacy policy is "unacceptably weak."[51] Amazon.com's problem arose when it stopped letting customers opt-out of having their personal information shared with other marketing companies and with Amazon.com's retail partners. It also told customers that it considered customer information to be a company asset that can be sold if Amazon.com goes out of business.

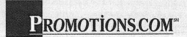
A question that remains unanswered is to what extent the internet industry will regulate itself on the privacy issue. When the Federal Trade Commission surveyed 1,400 websites, it found that a year after having warned businesses to adopt privacy guidelines or face government regulations, 92 percent collected personal information but only 14 percent disclosed how the information would be used.[52] A study done by the University of Massachusetts for the Direct Marketing Association found that only 38 percent of DMA members informed site visitors that they were collecting information on them and only a third sought permission to use this information.[53]

Marketing to children on the internet has warranted special attention. The FTC found that 89 percent of the children's sites surveyed collected personal information. Of those, only 23 percent told children to seek parental permission, less than 10 percent provided parents a way to control the collection and use of information, and only 7 percent said they would notify parents about information-gathering practices. Some sites even used promotions, games, and cartoons to encourage children to provide personal information.[54]

Internet Security Issues

The security of financial transactions is a major concern of online consumers. According to a Gallup poll, slightly over half (55 percent) of all internet users did not feel confident or totally secure that their credit-card information would remain secure.[55]

When the Web-design firm InteractionArchitect was researching security issues for a major European airline, it discovered "that people's perception of security when doing online transactions depends on the simplicity of the site and on the availability of user support." The company suggested that to increase a sense of security, an online transaction site should be comprehensible, predictable, flexible, and adaptable.[56] In other words, perception of security may extend beyond actual security and reassurances of security. Privacy and ease of use are two issues, but payment is of most concern.[57] Without security, a customer relationship is weakened.

A FINAL NOTE: HYPERCHARGED BRAND COMMUNICATION

The internet and its ability to provide information and shopping opportunities 24/7 has created a hypercharged marketplace. Old businesses are transformed, new businesses are created, and competitors come and go—all faster than the blink of an eye.

Interest in the internet first focused on portals, then on B2C retailing, and now on e-business. Companies use the internet for internal communication and managing their many databases and software programs as well as interacting with customers. The problem is, improvements in software and hardware make it expensive for companies to keep current.

To meet these challenges, more and more companies are outsourcing their internet management functions. Staffs can be expanded and contracted as necessary and specialized skills can be acquired as needed. The "virtual corporation," which brings together people around the world to work on a project-to-project basis, has made the distinction between employee and contractor much less significant, increased the need for intranets and extranets, and increased dependency on the internet for e-business and e-commerce. This practice also raises questions about communication consistency and gaps. With increased opportunities come increased communication challenges.

Key Terms

bandwidth 390
click-through 396
convergence 389
cookie 410
e-commerce 388
extranet 389

internet 389
interstitial 405
intranet 389
opt-in 394
opt-out e-mail 395
pop-ups and pop-unders 405

rich media 395
search engine 397
spam 394
virtual communities 397

Key Point Summary

Key Point 1: Addressable and Interactive Media

Addressable media, such as mail, phone, fax, and e-mail, have made one-to-one communication more feasible for many companies. The internet has made customer-initiated communication much easier and put companies in the position of needing to listen and respond. Besides serving as communication vehicles for product offers to customers, addressable media can deliver messages asking research questions about level of brand satisfaction, further purchase intentions, and reactions to new promotional offers.

Key Point 2: Internet-Based Marketing Communication

Most of the MC functions (advertising, sponsorship, events, and others) use the internet. The internet's primary characteristic, inexpensive two-way communication, makes it especially important in IMC and relationship building.

Key Point 3: Websites

The internet can be used as a medium for nearly all the MC functions and is especially helpful in building brand relationships because it makes interactivity so much easier for both customers and companies.

Key Point 4: Consumer Concerns

Consumers using the internet for business and shopping feel more confident about their transactions if they know the company provides an efficient customer-service program should something go wrong with an order. They also worry about privacy and security. Companies can enhance their level of trust by posting their privacy policies and ensuring the security of customer transactions.

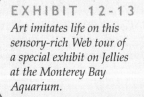

EXHIBIT 12-13
Art imitates life on this sensory-rich Web tour of a special exhibit on Jellies at the Monterey Bay Aquarium.

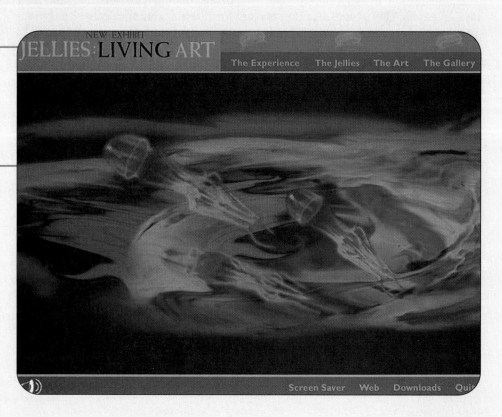

Lessons Learned

Key Point 1: Addressable and Interactive Media

a. How do addressable and interactive media differ? Why is their use increasing?
b. How do interactive media and mass media advertising differ?
c. How do opt-in and opt-out e-mail differ?
d. Is it accurate to say that there is no cost to e-mail campaigns? Explain.

Key Point 2: Internet-Based Marketing Communication

a. How can a company make its website more visible in order to attract more visitors?
b. Explain the attraction-versus-irritation problem with online advertising.
c. How effective are banner ads? How is their effectiveness determined?
d. Why have Web-based companies turned to offline advertising? Find an example, and analyze its effectiveness.
e. Explain how online communities, forums, and chat rooms can be used in marketing programs. On the Web, find a product-related forum or chat room, and explain what you learned at that site.
f. What are two methods of delivering customized messages on the Web?
g. Go to the BMW "Films" website (www.bmwfilms.com), and view one of the feature films. Do you think this is an effective marketing communication tool? Why or why not?

Key Point 3: Websites

a. What is the first step in creating a website?
b. What are three things to think about when you set up a website?
c. What is the most important consideration in website design? What is the biggest problem?
d. What is a webmaster? What are his or her responsibilities?
e. In what two areas of customer service do online companies tend to fall short?
f. Why is infrastructure an issue in customer service?
g. Visit the following sites, which were listed in *Business Week*'s "Favorite Clicks" column. Then pick one, and analyze it using the guidelines listed on page 398:

www.ragingbull.com (a stock market site).

www.zagat.com (a restaurant site).

www.guild.com (a high-end art-and-crafts site).

www.bizrate.com (a place to check out other people's experiences with online stores).

Key Point 4: Customer Concerns

a. Why is online customer service important?
b. What are the three elements needed for delivering good online customer service?
c. Why should privacy be a major issue for Web marketers?
d. What is the relationship between targeting and privacy?
e. What does the TRUSTe icon stand for?
f. What four privacy practices does the Federal Trade Commission recommend?
g. What can an online marketer do to increase customers' sense of security?

Chapter Challenge

Writing Assignment

To analyze the advertising of dot-com companies, find three examples in magazines and three examples of broadcast ads. Videotape TV ads or consult www.superbowl-ads.com, which compiles the ads from the Super Bowl. Analyze (1) the purpose of each ad, (2) the effectiveness of the product explanations, and (3) marketers' brand-building efforts. Write up your analysis in a report for your instructor.

Presentation Assignment

Pick a local company that does Web marketing. Interview its webmaster and analyze its website. Identify its other uses of the internet. Does it sell products both online and offline? What is its privacy policy? How might this company's internet use be improved? Prepare a presentation on what you have found out to give to your classmates.

Internet Assignment

Consult the Cluetrain website (www.cluetrain.com). Write a report for your instructor on the founders' viewpoint and concerns about the use of the internet for business. Draft a set of guidelines for responsible online marketing communication that address the issues raised by Cluetrain.

Exercise idea: This is for the whole class. Ask every student to put a couple of dollars into a fund. Then use this fund to buy fun food products online. Stretch the fund as far as possible so you maximize the number of different companies you buy from. Try to buy the same product from several different companies. Make up an evaluation sheet, based on the interactivity criteria presented in this chapter, so you can evaluate how well each company responds. Note the price differences for the same product and how the response times vary. Follow up and contact the companies that responded poorly. Ask them why they didn't perform as well as their competitors. Then have a party and eat all the goodies! (Another product category is music CDs, which is even better because you can order identical products from many different companies. Since you can't divide up the CDs and share them equally, you can have a drawing or donate them to a children's home at the end of the exercise.)

ADVERTISING AND IMC MEDIA PLANNING

Key Points in This Chapter

1. What are the steps in media planning?
2. What is the difference between reach and frequency?
3. How do you determine a media mix?
4. What role does cost play in selecting media?
5. What are the factors involved in scheduling media buys?

Chapter Perspective

Planning Media Connections

Media are the bridges that carry messages back and forth between companies and customers. In essence, these bridges are opportunities to create customer contact points. As media choices continue to increase, media planning becomes more precise but also more challenging. And because media are a major expense, there is constant tension between maximizing the delivery of brand messages while minimizing the cost. But media are about more than just delivering a message. Media are *how* customer contacts are created—the media used can enhance or detract from the impact and meaning of brand messages. As a result, media planning can be as creative as designing an ad or event.

In this chapter, the focus is on the tools and the process of media planning. This chapter explains why selecting the right media enables companies to deliver brand messages effectively and to connect to their customers and prospects.

USING MEDIA TO HELP REVIVE A GOOD OLD BRAND
Lee Jeans Campaign by Fallon, Minneapolis, Minnesota

Background: Why Buddy Lee Was Revived

Lee Jeans faced a critical brand problem. Males and females ages 17 to 22, at the heart of the jeans market, were saying Lee Jeans were "not for me." They said Lee was "outdated," "boring," and "my mother's jeans." Fallon and Lee decided to reverse perceptions of the 105-year-old brand among these consumers by introducing a new sub-brand, Lee Dungarees, and reviving a diamond-in-the-rough icon uncovered in Lee's archives: Buddy Lee, the brand's vintage "spokes doll" from the 1920s (see Exhibit 13-1).

Lee's goal was to snap younger consumers' heads back and affect significant increases in key attribute measures including "brand for me" and "brand becoming more popular." In addition, Lee wanted to increase sales among young men and juniors. The strategies? Guide fickle consumers down a path of discovery, allowing them to participate in discerning the meaning of the icon and the brand values. Fully integrate the positioning "jeans that won't hold you back" in all communications. Don't try too hard or risk rejection. And use Buddy Lee to create a new definition of cool.

Stage I: Who Is That Cool Guy?

Fallon designed a "discovery" stage to create interest in Buddy Lee and imbue him with coolness. The agency started by creating buzz locally and somewhat "underground." Using guerrilla tactics, brand communication was slightly ahead of the primary target, reaching leaders and influencers first. In these messages, neither jeans nor the brand was ever mentioned. Consumers saw a phantom campaign of otherwise unidentified images of Buddy Lee "wild posted" on walls bordering construction sites and other unusual places on the streets of trendy areas in 15 major cities. Influential hipsters found random, small-space tune-in invitations to watch *The Buddy Lee Story* in music zines, alternative weeklies, and a CD-ROM, as Buddy became a fixture in the new music area. An underground network of web zines linked to the unbranded Buddy Lee website, which told his story but did not link to leejeans.com. The Buddy Lee site was interactive: consumers could submit questions about Buddy, and they were answered directly.

After bar-hopping and clubbing, the target came home and watched *The Buddy Lee Story* between *South Park* episodes. The story ran as a two-part series of three-minute short films on late-night cable. Next, the target saw nonbranded "Coming Soon" trailers on ESPN's Summer X Games' TV coverage. On-site X Games participants and spectators were the first to see the connection between Buddy Lee and Lee Dungarees.

Stage II: Hey, Those Jeans Are Cool!

The brand maintained legitimacy among the "in" circle while moving from the narrowly targeted "discovery" stage to a broader "launch" stage. Ongoing proprietary trend-model and "cool meter" data, which Fallon derived by using account-planning techniques with the target,

EXHIBIT 13-1

EXHIBIT   13-2

helped predict favorite programming among the trend-leader target better than did traditional demographic rating estimates. These measures separated hot from neutral program environments so that the brand connection would be truer—*Buffy the Vampire Slayer*, *Dawson's Creek*, and *Felicity* instead of well-targeted but neutral programs such as *Melrose Place* and *90210*. Fallon customized media schedules on Fox, The WB, ESPN 2, MTV, VH1, E!, and Comedy Central, using consumer-endorsed programming. TV advertising revealed the Buddy Lee–Dungarees connection on messages carried on these channels for the first time. Later TV commercials continued to use Buddy Lee as this cult hero (see Exhibit 13-2).

Results

Buddy Lee became a bona fide pop-culture icon. Visuals of him continue to be modeled on a long list of celebrities (thanks to Fallon's aggressive T-shirt distribution to the young Hollywood elite). The wild postings appear as backdrops on TV (for example, on *NYPD Blue*) and in magazines (such as *Swing* and *Detour*). And the cost of a real Buddy Lee doll has risen from $250 to $1,000, if you can find one.

This campaign created the most significant movement of any Lee brand campaign in the last 12 years. Brand tracking also indicated significant changes in perceptions. Lee as a "brand becoming more popular" moved from 23 percent to 31 percent agreement and "cool to wear" moved from 26 percent to 35 percent agreement. More important, Lee saw a 3 percent growth in market share in a flat-to-down category. Initial sell-in to retailers of Lee Dungarees' original straight leg jeans was 300 percent higher than estimated. Sales grew 281 percent over the previous year among young men and 70 percent (off a larger base) among juniors.

Achieving these goals required intimate understanding of consumers as well as the courage and creativity to use new tools to create a media context. Media selection was based not only on demographics and psychographics but on insight about why and how customers consume media, what they care about, and how they choose brands. The media strategy was anything but vintage.

Source: This case was prepared with the generous help of Mark Goldstein, Fallon's chief marketing officer worldwide; Michelle Fitzgerald, media connection planner; and Bruce Tait, senior account planner.

MEDIA PLANNING: WHAT'S IT ALL ABOUT?

In large companies the media plan is a subpart of the marketing communication plan (which, of course, is a subpart of the marketing plan). **Media planning** is a *process for determining the most cost-effective mix of media for achieving a set of media objectives.* The key is to balance message impact and cost—maximizing impact while minimizing cost. Media are often the largest single cost item in a marketing communication budget, especially for consumer goods and services. General Motors, for example, spends worldwide over $3 billion a year on media. If the selected media do not deliver the brand messages and help them have maximum impact, sales will likely suffer, and much of the media money will have been wasted.

Although media planning is numbers driven, it has a significant creative dimension. Media planners must be creative in analyzing the quantitative aspect while understanding the qualitative dimensions and how people use media. At the Fallon agency, the science and art of how media connect companies and customers is operationalized in the following considerations: the *moment* in which brand messages are delivered, the *mood* of customers or prospects at the time they receive or send brand messages, the *mind-set* of customers and prospects, the *media* that carry the messages, and the *milieu* in which messages are exchanged.[1]

Unless the media budget is extremely small, most companies use more than one medium for several reasons. First, different media have different message delivery features, as explained in Chapters 11 and 12. Second, media strategies, such as the one described in the opening case about Lee Jeans, often call for a variety of media. Finally, a single communication vehicle can seldom reach everyone in a target audience. Figure 13-1 summarizes the variety of media that were used for the Lee Dungarees launch.

The challenge of media planning is becoming greater because the number of ways to send brand messages is increasing. Recognition of this development,

FIGURE 13-1

Lee Dungarees Media Launch Plan

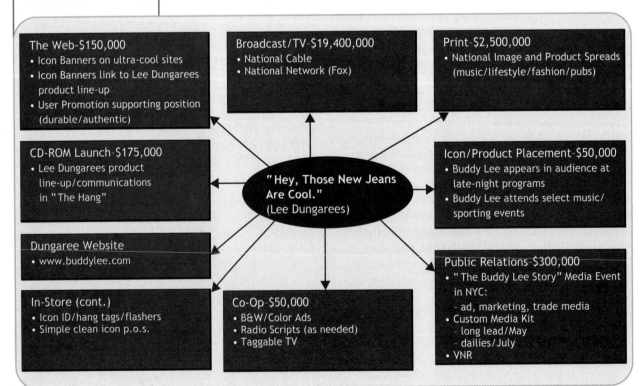

however, has been slow in coming. Not until the late 1980s, for example, did the Advertising Research Association recommend that its 30-year-old model for evaluating media effects be revised to include all marketing communication functions, not just advertising. Fallon Worldwide, which created the award-winning media plan for the Buddy Lee campaign, knows that people come in contact with a brand in a variety of ways and that every contact can be a useful point of interaction. For some time Fallon has used account planners and creative people to design brand messages that emotionally touch the audience. Now the agency is doing the same thing in media by using "connection planners" (results-oriented media planners) to maximize the impact of all types of media that connect with customers.

Recall from Chapters 2 and 3 that there are four kinds of brand touch points: (1) *intrinsic,* which automatically occur during the course of buying or using a brand; (2) *customer-created,* which are initiated by customers and prospects; (3) *unexpected,* which appear in the media and elsewhere unannounced; and (4) *company-created,* which are the marketing communication planned messages. Media are used primarily for the last, although the number of customer-created messages is increasing as companies encourage customers to ask questions, complain, and make suggestions.

Before media planning begins, the brand messages being delivered and received at intrinsic and customer-created touch points should be reviewed. If these messages are negative, they can outweigh any positive effect of company-created MC messages, and the result may be a waste of media dollars (and a poor reflection on the marketing communication department and its agencies). Another reason to identify intrinsic touch points is that they can provide additional "media" opportunities at almost no cost. Intrinsic contacts—such as service delivery, packaging, and repairs—represent opportunities to provide brand information and reinforce brand images. Because these brand touch points automatically demand the attention of customers, especially current customers, they provide a captive audience already interacting with the brand in some way.

The Role of Media Research

Media planners begin their work by doing media research—analyzing both target audiences and media options. The information that must be reviewed includes size and characteristics of the various media's audiences, as well as effectiveness data on how well these media deliver the audiences they promise. Most of the information comes from research companies that compile media statistics and profiles. Mediamark Research Inc. (MRI), for example, provides data on demographic, lifestyle, product usage, and media usage from a sample of 25,000 consumers who are interviewed each year. Information Resources Inc. (IRI) synthesizes the movement of billions of product purchases based on data from retail store scanners.

Media research is also done by agencies. A good example is what the Phelps Group did for its client Western Dental Health (WDH), a network of 130 dental and orthodontic centers throughout California and Arizona that sees nearly 300,000 patients a year. This company's primary advertising medium is TV. Annual spending on TV is approximately $5 million spread over 50 stations. The objective of the TV spots has been to motivate people to call and set up dental appointments.

To find out how cost-effective each TV station was, Phelps did a special media analysis for Western Dental. The agency assigned a separate 800 number to each station (the number was used in the WDH commercials that ran on that station). The WDH central call center was then instructed to keep track of all calls *by the phone number patients used* when they called for an appointment. Using software developed by the agency, WDH obtained a daily record of the number of appointments generated by each TV station.

By dividing the media cost for each station by the number of appointments on each station's assigned 800 number, the agency was able to calculate a cost per appointment for each of the 50 TV stations. After this calculation was done, the agency recommended dropping the lowest-performing stations and using these dollars to buy more time on better-performing stations (those that produced the lowest cost per appointment). The revised media plan (spending the same dollars but on fewer but better performing stations) generated 948 appointments in the first 8 weeks compared to 618 in the previous 8 weeks, a 53 percent increase with no increase in media spending.[2]

The Role of Media Buying

Media buying is *the execution of a media plan.* Media buyers negotiate with publishers, broadcasters, and other media representatives to arrange cost-effective contracts that will satisfy the media objectives. In media buying, it is not the lowest price that is most important but the return on the media investment in terms of effect on the target audience. Media buyers usually do post-buy analyses to make sure the messages were delivered when and to whom as promised.

One trend affecting media buying is the consolidation of media companies into conglomerates (← Chapter 2). Each media conglomerate bundles its various vehicles to offer planners "cross-media buys." Hachette Filipacchi Magazines, for example, offers buyers the chance to use a variety of its vehicles to send "integrated messages." A study commissioned by *Advertising Age* found that half of the companies and agencies surveyed said they had taken advantage of these integrated media packages. The number-one reason given was that they delivered "an integrated marketing message across all [media] platforms."[3]

A Four-Step Planning Process

Although important in its own right, media buying is primarily an execution of, and therefore is driven by, the media plan. This chapter focuses on the tools and process of media planning. Because a nearly unlimited number of media options exists for producing company-created touch points, media planners must sort through a lot of information when developing a good media plan. The task breaks down into four steps: (1) identifying media targets, (2) setting media objectives, (3) determining media strategies, and (4) scheduling media placements. Each step is discussed in this chapter.

Planning Step	Questions to Ask	Tools/Sources for Answers
1. Media targeting	Who is the target audience? Where is the target audience? How big is the target audience? How much does the average target household consume? How is the brand doing in one market in comparison with other markets?	Customer database CDI (category development index) BDI (brand development index) Internal sales data
2. Media objectives	How much reach and targeted reach? How much frequency and effective frequency? What frequency distribution is acceptable? How much media weight (GRPs, TGRPs)?	MRI, Nielsen, and other media data sources Agency computer programs for determining ratings and frequency Past history of campaigns and agency's experience Share data from Nielsen

(continued on page 425)

Planning Step	Questions to Ask	Tools/Sources for Answers
	Should media weight be equal in all markets?	
3. Media strategies	Which media and how much of each in the media mix?	Media kits from each media vehicle being considered (includes rate card)
	What is the best balance of one- and two-way media?	SRDS (Standard Rate and Data Services)
	What is the target customer's buying process?	Personal contact with media sales representative for latest
	When is the best time (aperture) to reach customers and prospects?	costs and availabilities
	How concentrated should the media mix be?	Review past campaigns to see what media weight created what results (must keep in mind other variables)
	How should media be scheduled?	
	Which media are compatible with creative?	
	What media environment is most compatible with the brand's image?	
	What are the best CPMs and CPPs ?	
4. Media schedule	Should media be continuous, flighted, or pulsed?	Budget
	How seasonal is product buying?	Analysis of sales by month, day of week
		Closing dates (when vehicles need to receive ads) from media kits or sales reps

STEP 1: MEDIA TARGETING: FINDING THE TARGET AUDIENCE

The marketing plan identifies the brand's target audiences. The planner's job is to select the communication vehicles and markets whose profiles most closely match those of the target audiences. The greater the match, the better. The extent of the match is determined by looking at how the target audiences differ from the average population. For example, if the target audience is twice as likely as the average population to own a boat, communication vehicles whose audiences are at least twice as likely to own a boat should be considered. Every target market has such **skews,** or *variations from the general population.* The greater the variance from average, the greater the skew. A skew is also sometimes described as an *index.* For example, demographic analysis might reveal that physicians index, or skew, higher on income than does the general population. Skews and indexes indicate to what extent a number—be it a population, an attribute score, or anything else that can be described numerically—differs from the average. Marketers find this information useful because such differences form the basis on which target audiences can be identified and reached.

The size of a target audience also affects media decisions. In general, the smaller the targeted audience is, the more personalized and interactive a message can be. For example, to reach 5,000 households in a city of 100,000, addressable media would be more appropriate than mass media. But if the targeted audience in this same metro area were 50,000, mass media would be more cost-effective.

Similarly, commonality among members of a target group affects media choices. In general, the higher the degree of commonality, the more likely it is that niche media can be found that will reach a high percentage of that target. For example, *Lizzie McGuire,* the Disney Channel program about a junior high school–age girl and her friends, is the top-rated program for reaching the preteen niche market.[4] (Remember, although TV is a mass medium, what matters to marketers is the *program.*) Likewise *Meet the Press,* the dominant Sunday morning TV talk show, gives marketers an opportunity to reach an educated, upscale audience who may not spend much time with other forms of mass media.[5]

When there are few commonalities within a target audience—such as within the target market for chewing gum—mass media are often more cost-effective. But even mass media like TV have programs that reach demographic niche audiences, as a study in 2003 found. In a comparison of the TV-viewing patterns of blacks and whites, only two programs were on the top 10 lists of both: *Monday Night Football* and *CSI: Crime Scene Investigation.* Several of the programs watched by whites, such as *Friends* and *Everybody Loves Raymond,* were low on the list of programs watched by blacks. Likewise, blacks had a number of top 10 shows that didn't appear on the list of favorite programs of white viewers, such as *Cedric the Entertainer Presents, The Bernie Mac Show, One on One, Girlfriends, Half & Half,* and *The Parkers.*[6]

Media Profiles

Many media vehicles profile their audiences in terms of demographics, psychographics (lifestyles), and product usage. That information allows them to analyze their audience in terms of appropriate products to be advertised (see the Ethics and Issues box). However, such detailed information is not always available for many media vehicles, especially those with small audiences. When media vehicles do have audience-profile information, it is generally demographic. Vehicles dealing with particular areas of interest, such as sports, hobbies, or finance, are the ones most likely to have lifestyle and product-usage data in addition to demographic profiles.

Although some media do their own research to profile their audiences, companies often buy these profiles from independent research companies such as Mediamark Research Inc. (MRI) and Gallup & Robinson. Table 13-1 is an example of the types of information available on magazine audiences from MRI. Such information helps media planners understand the audience of a particular vehicle and how it compares to the profile of their brands targeted audiences.

Here's how to read and make use of the information shown in the sample MRI report (Table 13-1). A report such as this would help media planners who are interested in reaching college students (note data is for "College students currently enrolled"). Assuming the decision had been made to use magazines in the media mix, the question then becomes—"Which magazines?" The MRI data shows which magazines are most widely read by college students. Column A is the projected number of college students who have looked into the magazines listed. For Allure, this is 883,000. Column B shows the *percent of a magazine's readers* who are college students. For Allure, 19.19% of its readers are college students, or said another way, four out of five Allure readers are *not* college students. Column C shows what *percentage of college students* read each magazine. According to this report, 5.83% of all college students read Allure. The last column, D, is an index that shows how likely college students are to read a magazine *compared to the total adult population* (18 years+). In the case of Allure, the index is 257 which means college students are roughly 2½ times more likely to read Allure than the average adult. Of all the magazines in Table 13-1, Marie Claire and Maxim have the highest percent of college student readers.

ETHICS AND ISSUES

Lighting Fire under Tobacco Media

In response to increasing government and social pressure for tobacco companies not to promote smoking to children under 18 years of age, cigarette maker Philip Morris announced in 2000 that it would no longer run advertising for Marlboro and its other brands in over 40 magazines that the company had been using. The dropped magazines were *Glamour, Newsweek, Rolling Stone, People, TV Guide*, and others with 15 percent or more of their readers under 18. The levels of youth readership were determined through surveys by Simmons Market Research Bureau and Mediamark Research Inc. (MRI).

That wasn't the first time cigarette media plans were affected by social and legal pressures. In 1997, the U.S. Supreme Court upheld a Baltimore, Maryland, law banning cigarette advertising on billboards and other outdoor locations near schools and other places that attract children. Even in-store point-of-sale racks have come under scrutiny (see Exhibit 13-3). A Camel cigarette display that depicted a yellow-and-purple sports car with a trunk filled with packs of Camel cigarettes was criticized for its appeal to children. Such self-service displays, particularly those attractive to kids, have also been attacked because they make it possible for children to take packs of cigarettes without asking salesclerks for them. The U.S. Food and Drug Administration raised the question of whether these displays are advertisements or merely ways to distribute the product. If they are ads, they come under the jurisdiction of the FDA, with its authority to regulate advertising to children.

EXHIBIT 13-3

Think About It

What is the heart of the issue regarding the advertising and promotion of cigarettes? Does the list of magazines that were deleted from Philip Morris's media plan make sense to you? If 15 percent of the audience profile contains kids, do you feel that is justification for eliminating a magazine from the media buy?

Source: "Magazines Brace for Cigarette Ad Pullout," by Matthew Rose. Copyright 2000 by Dow Jones & Co., Inc. Reprinted by permission of Dow Jones & Co., Inc. via the Copyright Clearance Center.

Trade publications and trade shows make it somewhat easier to select media for B2B targets. Each industry has its own publications and trade shows that attract well-defined product-category audiences. Exhibit 13-4 indicates how a trade publication describes and promotes its audience. Because most B2B brands have smaller customer and prospect universes (compared to consumer brands), better database profiles of these targets, and significantly higher average sales transactions (compared to B2C transactions), they can afford to use more expensive addressable and interactive media.

Determining CDIs and BDIs

A major decision in media planning is how to divide media spending among all the markets in which a brand is being sold. When brands use national advertising, each geographical market receives the same level of advertising. But these brands sometimes "heavy-up" (use more) media spending in regions where household consumption in the brand's product category is significantly above average.

To help make decisions about where to use media to most effectively promote a brand, marketers use a **category development index (CDI),** which is *a numerical indicator of the relative consumption rate in a particular market for a particular product category.* To understand CDIs, remember that 100 is the average index score: anything above 100 is higher than the average, and anything below 100 is lower than

Category	A (000)	B Horiz. %	C Vertical %	D Index
College students, currently enrolled	15,136	7.46	100	100
Men	7,182	7.39	47.45	99
Women	7,954	7.53	52.55	101
Magazines				
Allure	883	19.19	5.83	257
Better Homes & Gardens	2129	5.65	14.07	76
Boating	176	5.88	1.16	79
Bride's	1064	16.64	7.03	223
Family Circle	1068	4.72	7.08	63
Fitness	954	14.38	6.30	193
Glamour	1910	16.09	12.62	216
Good Housekeeping	1238	4.88	8.18	65
Marie Claire	752	23.17	4.97	310
Maxim	2604	26.33	17.20	353
Outdoor Life	460	6.67	3.04	89
Prevention	632	5.85	4.17	78
Reader's Digest	2685	6.27	17.74	84
Shape	1068	18.64	7.05	250
Stock Car Racing	163	4.77	1.07	64
Time	2363	10.31	15.62	138
TV Guide	2330	7.78	15.39	104
Wall Street Journal	364	9.60	2.40	129

TABLE 13-1   MRI Sample Data for Readership of Magazines by College Students

Source: 2002m Doublebase Mediamark Research Inc., extracted from a list of 220 magazines. Used by permission.

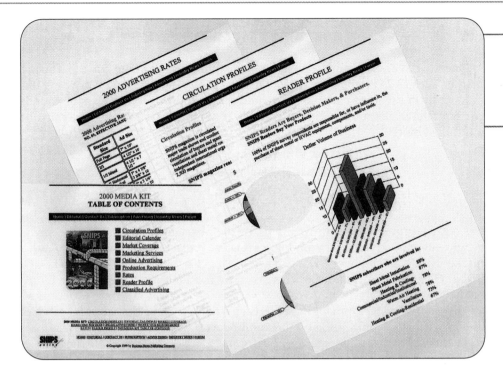

EXHIBIT 13-4

Examples of Information Supplied by Media Companies

the average (the same as in IQ scores). Suppose a city has a CDI of 200 for hot dogs. This means that the average household (HH) in that city consumes twice the national average. If a city has a 50 CDI for hot dogs, that means the average household (HH) in that city consumers only half of the national average. Not surprisingly, companies are generally more interested in markets that have CDIs above 100. Think of the old adage "Fish where the fish are."

To determine a category development index (CDI), you first must determine the average household consumption rate for a marketing universe, such as "total U.S." This "consumption" number becomes the base against which the average household consumption rate of a particular marketing area is compared. Let's look at the processed-meat category and determine the CDI for Milwaukee. First, we must figure the national average consumption. To do this, we take the total amount consumed—1 billion pounds—and divide by the number of U.S. households—100 million households. This shows us that the average U.S. household (HH) consumption is 10 pounds per year:

$$\frac{\text{Total pounds sold in U.S. in a year}}{\text{Total number of households in U.S.}} = \text{Avg. lbs. per HH}$$

$$\frac{1,000,000,000 \text{ pounds sold in U.S.}}{100,000,000 \text{ million households}} = 10 \text{ lbs. per HH}$$

The calculation can be made in whatever unit a category is sold—pounds, cases, jars. It should *not* be made in currency, however, because different brands within a category charge different prices.

Once the average household consumption is determined for the total marketplace, the average household consumption must be determined for the market area in question. To do this, the total number of pounds sold in that market is divided by the total number of households in that market. The following shows the average pounds per household (HH) consumed in Milwaukee:

$$\frac{\text{Total pounds sold in Milwaukee}}{\text{Total households in Milwaukee}} = \text{Avg. lbs. per HH}$$

$$\frac{12,500,000 \text{ pounds sold in Milwaukee}}{500,000 \text{ households in Milwaukee}} = 25 \text{ lbs. per HH}$$

Once the average annual household consumption is known for a particular market, such as 25 pounds for Milwaukee, the CDI is determined by dividing this number by the average national household consumption rate, which is 10 pounds per household. Because 100 is average (by convention), the result here must be multiplied by 100:

$$\text{CDI} = \frac{25 \text{ lbs. in Milwaukee average}}{10 \text{ lbs. national average}} = 2.50 \times 100 = 250$$

This CDI of 250 says that the average Milwaukee household consumes two and a half times as much processed meat as does the average U.S. household. For this reason, processed-meat companies' media plans generally have more media weight—that is, advertising with higher relative impact—in Milwaukee than in a market with a much lower CDI such as Los Angeles (whose processed-meat CDI is about 65). CDIs tell marketers where they are mostly likely to get the best return on their media dollars.

The category development index indicates relative development of a product category by geographic market. The **brand development index (BDI)** is a *numerical indicator of the development of a particular brand within a market relative to all other markets in which the brand is sold.* The higher a city's BDI, the better a brand is doing in that city compared to all the other markets in which the brand is distributed. As with a CDI, a BDI of 100 is average. Let's continue the processed-meat illustration to show how a BDI is determined; the Oscar Mayer (OM) brand is used as an example:

$$\frac{\text{Total pounds of OM sold in U.S.}}{\text{Total number of HH in U.S.}} = \text{Avg. lbs. of OM per HH nationally}$$

$$\frac{500,000,000 \text{ lbs. of OM}}{100,000,000 \text{ HH}} = 5 \text{ lbs. OM sold per HH nationally}$$

$$\frac{3,500,000 \text{ lbs. of OM sold in Milwaukee}}{500,000 \text{ HH in Milwaukee}} = 7 \text{ lbs. OM per HH in Milwaukee}$$

$$\text{Milwaukee BDI} = \frac{7 \text{ lbs. in Milwaukee}}{5 \text{ lbs. nationally}} = 1.40 \times 100 = 140$$

Marketing managers and media planners pay close attention to these numbers in order to track brand performance. One reason for a below-average BDI could be a weak sales force in that particular market. Another possible reason is greater competition, in which case a media planner may opt for more media weight and promotions in that market. However, since all brands in a category use CDIs in their media planning, and all want to "fish where the fish are," high-CDI markets often become promotional battlegrounds in which all the major competitors are buying an above-average amount of media.

STEP 2: SETTING MEDIA OBJECTIVES: WHAT DO YOU WANT TO ACCOMPLISH?

Media objectives reflect what a company wants to accomplish regarding the *delivery* of brand messages. MC objectives describe what a company wants customers to think, feel, and do about its brand (◄━ Chapter 5); media objectives describe how a company will expose customers to brand messages in such a way that the messages *have the opportunity* to impact customers' thinking, feeling, and doing.

In many agencies and companies, creative strategy decisions are made before media objectives are determined. When this happens, a company risks missing some opportunities for connecting with customers. As stated before, *integrating* the media and creative planning (by means of cross-functional organization) produces better media plans, for the following reasons:

- There are now more media alternatives than ever before, and some are much better than others at reaching certain audiences.

- Media planners may be able to suggest new ways to reach target audiences that are just as effective as, but less expensive than, the media a company has always used. Media are a major portion of most MC budgets and therefore should not be an after-thought.

- Some media and programming environments are so specialized or have such strong personalities (such as *Outdoor Living* or the *Wall Street Journal*) that brand messages can have more impact when especially designed to be compatible with them. Reaching a target audience in a media environment with the same "tone" as the brand message enhances communication, as illustrated by the Buddy Lee case (see Exhibit 13-5).

Media objectives explain what needs to be accomplished in order for customers and prospects to be exposed to the MC message. The two media variables that determine this are *reach* and *frequency*. These variables measure the breadth and depth of message delivery. When *reach (R)* and *frequency (F)* are multiplied together, the resulting number is *gross rating points (GRPs)*, which indicates the weight of the media plan. Reach, frequency, and GRPs are explained in the following pages.

Reach

No matter how good an offer is or how creatively a MC message has been designed, it can have no impact until an audience has an opportunity to see or hear

EXHIBIT 13-5
What would you do to make this site reflect the Buddy Lee image even more?

it. MC messages need to reach customers and prospects. In the context of media, the term **reach** refers to *the percentage of an audience that has had the opportunity to be exposed to a media vehicle within a specified period.*

Although reach is a widely used media-planning measure, it is important to keep in mind that it is an *estimate* of communication—almost always an *over*-estimate. Why? Reach is an indication of the *opportunity* for exposure to a brand message; it is not an indicator of how many customers and prospects actually are exposed to a brand message. When you buy a magazine, you may read only a portion of it and not even see half the ads. Nevertheless, you have had an *opportunity* to see the ads, so you are counted as having been reached. (These kinds of estimates make steps 2 and 3 of the media planning as much art as science!)

Reach (R) is expressed as a percentage, although advertisers don't use the percent sign. For example, R = 58 means that 58 percent of an audience in a defined universe had the opportunity to be exposed one or more times to a brand message in a media vehicle. A defined universe can be whatever you want it to be—all households in the United States, all males over 18, all single adults living in Chicago, or whatever.

Calculating Reach

The first step in determining the most effective reach for a message is to select communication vehicles whose audiences most closely match a brand's target audience. This information is available from Mediamark Research Inc., Nielsen, and other research companies. A maker of athletic sportswear, for example, would likely consider tennis, golf, and other sporting magazines rather than cooking and gardening magazines. Next, media planners must know the reach of each vehicle being considered, which is available from each media vehicle (part of its media kit). For example, a chain of dry cleaners in Cleveland, Ohio, thinking of advertising in the *Plain Dealer* would want to know what percentage of households in the newspaper's coverage area regularly reads this publication. Notice the difference between the terms *coverage area* (the geographical area) and *reach* (the percentage of those within the coverage area who are regularly exposed to a vehicle). The *Plain Dealer*'s coverage area is metropolitan Cleveland; its reach is 60 percent, which means 60 percent of households in metro Cleveland regularly read this daily paper.

The coverage area for local TV stations is generally a 50- to 60-mile radius from a city center—the distance most broadcast signals travel. As mentioned in Chapter 11, this *TV broadcast coverage area* is called a **designated marketing area (DMA),** and each is identified by the name of the dominant city in that area. Every county within the United States has been assigned to a DMA. A county is assigned to the city from which 50 percent or more of the county's households receive their TV signals. As shown in Figure 13-2, the Seattle–Tacoma (Washington) DMA includes several counties. Because TV has become such a dominant medium, most marketers now do local-market planning based on DMAs.

A broadcast station may have a wide coverage area but a low reach. Consider, for example, WKMG-TV, whose coverage area is the Orlando, Florida, DMA. Even though all households with TV sets in this DMA *can* receive the station, only a small portion actually has sets on and tuned to WKMG-TV at any one time. In fact, most WKMG-TV programs are seen by fewer than 10 percent of the households. Unlike print media, whose reach is fairly constant (because it is based mostly on subscriptions), the reach of broadcast and cable stations varies program by program.

The way in which reach is calculated varies by medium. The reach of radio and television is indicated by the ratings of particular programs. A program's rating is basically the same as its reach. One rating point equals 1 percent of a broadcast

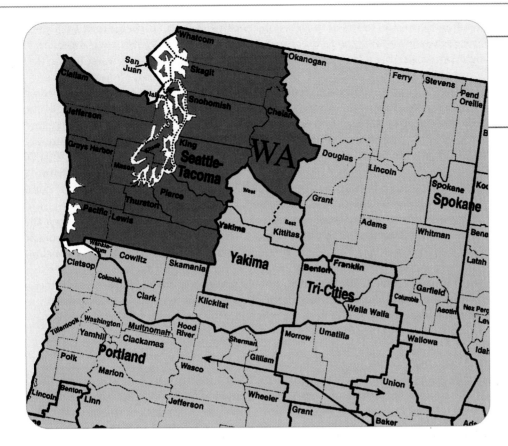

FIGURE 13-2

*Purple shaded area shows
all the counties making up
the Seattle-Tacoma DMA.*

vehicle's coverage area. A rating of 5 means that 5 percent of the households in a station's coverage area were exposed to that particular program. The more households watching or listening to a particular program in a particular DMA, the higher is that program's rating and the higher its reach. Program ratings, which are provided by Nielsen Media Research and by Arbitron, are estimates of average program viewership based on quarter-hour viewing/listening research. The point to remember is that, for radio and TV, *programs* determine ratings, not the stations themselves.

The reach of specialized magazines is based on a universe defined by the category of interest or use, rather than by household in a given geographical area. For example, the universe for the trade publication *Golf Course Management* would be all managers of golf courses.

The reach of outdoor advertising is indicated by the percentage of cars in a metropolitan area that drive by billboards carrying a particular brand message within a 24-hour period. Most companies using outdoor advertising display the brand message on multiple boards at the same time. If a brand message is posted on 10 outdoor boards spread throughout Nashville, Tennessee, for example, the reach is determined by the percentage of cars driving by these boards. If there are 200,000 cars registered in metro Nashville, and traffic counts show that 200,000 cars have driven by one or more of these boards within a 24-hour period, the reach is said to be 100 (100 percent). In outdoor terms, this is known as a "100 showing." (Unfortunately, traffic counts don't recognize the same car driving by more than once, a problem known as *duplication,* described below.)

Another way to determine reach is by the number of message impressions. An **impression** is *one exposure to a brand message.* Media planners sometimes use impressions as a measure of reach when it is difficult to identify a marketing universe (the basis on which a reach percentage can be figured). Internet brand messages are often figured in terms of impressions because it is still difficult to tell who in a target audience has access to the internet. The number of visits to websites carrying a particular brand message determines the number of impressions for that brand message.

In the case of direct mail and telemarketing, the universe base for figuring reach is defined according to the company's identification of its market. For example, the Boston chapter of the Red Cross uses telemarketing in its annual fund drive and can define its universe as all households in the Boston metro area. If there are 400,000 households and 40,000 are called, the reach would be 10 (40,000 ÷ 400,000 = .10). A similar method is used to figure the reach of a direct-mail effort. Simply divide the number of mailings made by the total number of households or companies that make up the defined universe.

Very seldom is a brand lucky enough to find a media vehicle whose reach is 100 percent of the brand's targeted audience. Therefore, most media plans include more than one media vehicle. Yet planners must do their math homework carefully, because adding reach is not always simple. Suppose that in a given coverage area, TV has a reach of 60 percent and newspapers 40 percent. This does not mean that placing brand messages in both media will result in a reach of 100 percent. In fact, when the two are combined, the reach may be well under 100 percent because of duplication. **Duplication** is *the overlapping coverage of two or more vehicles.* If Sprint decided to supplement its *Business Week* advertising by also running ads in the *Wall Street Journal,* in *Inc.* magazine, and on the MSNBC cable channel, many members of the audience would receive the message more than once—there would be a lot of duplication. Some small businesses are exposed to two of these vehicles, some to three, a few to all four (see Figure 13-3). Likewise, the commuter who passes by the same billboard five times a week contributes to duplication in that media. Generally speaking, adding media vehicles increases reach but also increases duplication.

The extent of duplication in a media mix is identified by research—asking people what media they regularly use. Most major media companies conduct such

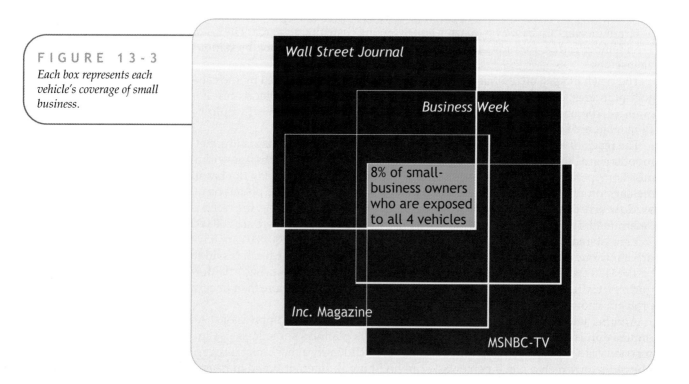

FIGURE 13-3
Each box represents each vehicle's coverage of small business.

surveys themselves or buy the information from independent research companies. Advertising agencies have software programs that compare different mixes of communication vehicles to determine duplication levels, as well as the *undupli-cated reach* of each mix. Duplication is not necessarily negative, because it increases frequency (which can be desirable). Media planners, however, want to know the effective, unduplicated reach of a media mix, because this number represents the actual percentage of a target audience that has the opportunity to be exposed to at least one brand message over a specified period of time.

Targeted Reach

Most marketers, regardless of what they are selling, are not interested in reaching all of the households or businesses in a particular communication vehicle's audience, because some audience members are neither customers nor prospects. This is why it is best to base media planning on **targeted reach,** which is *the portion of a communication vehicle's audience that is in a brand's target market.* Suppose a large lawn-and-garden shop in St. Louis, Missouri, that sells power mowers throughout the city has defined its target audience as metro-area homeowners with lawns. It places an ad in the *St. Louis Post-Dispatch,* which has a 60 percent reach in the St. Louis market. If only half of the households receiving the newspaper have yards, however, then the *targeted reach* is 30 percent of the total metro area—half of the *Post-Dispatch's* reach.

Targeted reach can be determined for any communication vehicle as long as the brand's target audience can be identified within a vehicle's audience. Suppose IBM placed an ad in *Progressive Grocer* in order to create interest in a new inventory managing system. IBM may say it wants to reach managers of stores with annual sales of $3 million or more. Of *Progressive Grocer's* 60,000 readers, however, only 20,000 are managers of these large-volume stores. Therefore, the *targeted reach* for IBM is only one-third (20,000 ÷ 60,000 = 1/3) of the trade magazine's total reach.

Targeted reach is important to calculate because it shows what a company is actually getting for the money it spends on any given media vehicle. Although IBM pays to reach all readers of *Progressive Grocer,* because only a third of them are in IBM's targeted audience, the real cost of using this vehicle is tripled. **Media waste,** which is *reaching people who are neither customers nor prospects,* is a major concern in media planning and buying. Two-thirds of *Progressive Grocer's* circulation are media waste for IBM. Keep in mind that marketers must pay for reaching a vehicle's total audience, regardless of what percentage of that audience is not in the brand's target market.

Media vehicles with 100 percent targeted reach rarely exist, although some companies strive to achieve that goal. Exhibit 13-6 illustrates the pinpointed reach promised by a company that hangs product samples on doorknobs. It must be pointed out, however, that something more important than the percentage of media

EXHIBIT 13-6

Zip codes provide one way to do geographical targeting. However, ImpactMedia, a company that hangs product samples on doorknobs, recommends using its targeting method, which breaks down zip codes into neighborhoods in order to avoid high levels of media waste.

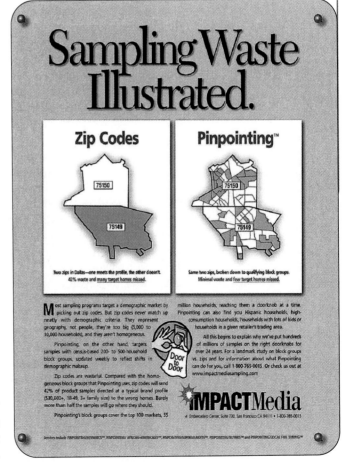

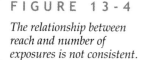

FIGURE 13-4

The relationship between reach and number of exposures is not consistent.

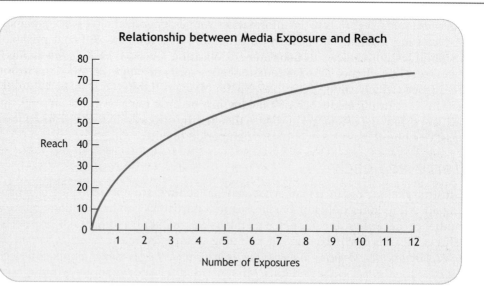

waste is cost per response. A communication vehicle that has a high percentage of media waste may still have a lower cost per response than other vehicles (see Chapter 18).

How Much Reach Is Enough?

In most cases it is cost-prohibitive for a brand to have 100 percent reach of a target market. So the question that must be answered is: How much reach is enough? The answer: The percentage that is most cost-effective to achieve. Media planners determine that percentage by calculating the point at which the cost to reach additional members of a target is more than these customers are worth in revenue. As Figure 13-4 shows, as the number of media exposures increases, the rate of increase in reach diminishes. A certain portion of any target audience is always more expensive to reach than other members because of their lower levels of media usage. Conversely, those who consume the most media are the easiest to reach. There is an old saying in marketing: "Pick the low-hanging fruit first." In other words, don't waste time and money climbing to the top of a tree (to get at those who are hardest to reach) until all the fruit that is easily reached has been picked.

Another factor that helps determine the best level of reach, especially for consumer brands, is where the brand is distributed. If a brand has distribution only in the southwestern part of the United States, for example, then that is the only geographical region that should receive brand messages. Media placement should reflect where the brand is distributed.

When a brand wants to expand into a new geographical area, most retail chains demand to see a media plan before agreeing to begin selling that brand. At the same time, most companies do not want to buy media in an area before they have distribution of their brands in stores doing 60 percent or more of the business in that area. Marketers often face a dilemma. On the one hand, if they promote a brand that has little or no distribution in a market, they are wasting money. On the other hand, if a retailer takes on a new brand and there are no MC messages to make people aware of the brand, it will sit on store shelves and not move. To combat this problem from the retailer side, most major chains charge brands a **slotting fee** for taking on a new brand—*an up-front payment made in exchange for guaranteed shelf space.* If the brand does not sell at an expected level within 90 days, many large chains quit carrying the brand but keep the slotting fee. Therefore, the pressure is on marketers to make sure that when they go into a new area and get distribution, there are enough media messages to create a demand for the brand.

Frequency

In media planning, the word **frequency** refers to *the average number of times those who are reached have an opportunity to be exposed to a brand message within a specified time period.* To understand the difference between reach and frequency, think about this example. Suppose an Atlanta Ford dealer ran an ad in the *Atlanta Journal-Constitution* the same day a news release about the dealership appeared in the newspaper, whose coverage is 65 percent. The combined reach of both brand messages would be 65 because the same households had the opportunity to be exposed to both the ad and the news story. The frequency, however, would be 2 because each household receiving the *Journal-Constitution* had the opportunity to see two brand messages about the Ford dealership. Frequency, then, is the result of message duplication.

To help ensure that a message gets exposed, most media plans call for a frequency greater than 1. Research done by companies such as Roper-Starch, Nielsen Media Research, Gallup & Robinson, and Readex has documented what we intuitively know: exposure to any particular brand message is far less than the exposure to the vehicle carrying that message. This means *message* exposure should be given more attention than *vehicle* exposure.

One study of television viewing behavior found that viewer disinterest plagues commercials twice as frequently as it plagues programs. The primary avoidance technique is doing something else and ignoring the screen (reading, folding laundry, talking on the phone). Another ethnographic study found that when viewers who were actually watching TV encountered a commercial, they changed the channel 52 percent of the time.[7] According to the Nielsen People Meter reports (described in Chapter 11), only 25 to 35 percent of the average TV audience actually sees and pays attention to an average commercial. In the case of radio, only about 20 percent of listeners pay attention to the average commercial. For the average newspaper ad, the percentage is even smaller.[8] What this means is that, in practice, generating at least one *message* exposure among the target audience requires multiple *vehicle* exposures.

A second reason for multiple exposures is to increase the chance that a message will be understood. The more complex the message, the more exposures will be needed in order for the target to fully understand what is being communicated. Finally, and perhaps most obviously, frequency increases the chance that a message will be *remembered.* Recall from the discussion of communication in Chapter 4 that repetition is a major key to memory.

Effective Frequency

As with reach, a media planner must answer a similar question with frequency: How much is enough? An often-quoted guideline is that **effective frequency,** *the number of times a message needs to be seen to make an impression or achieve a specific level of awareness,* is somewhere between 3 and 10. In reality, this is not much of a guideline because the range is so wide. A frequency of 10, for example, requires a media budget over three times as large as that required for a frequency of 3. Most brands do not have this kind of budget flexibility. The "right" level of frequency is that which cost-effectively affects attitudes or behavior. One of the best ways for a company to determine this level is to track customer responses, testing various levels of frequency.

Another reason why the level of effective frequency varies with every brand is that there are so many variables that determine the impact of a brand message. Some of these variables are

1. ***The offer's value and complexity.*** Making prospects understand that a local bank now offers "free checking" does not require nearly as much frequency as

does getting them to understand that the bank offers four different savings-plan options (let alone getting them to remember what those options are and how they differ).

2. *The attention value of the medium itself.* Some media vehicles demand more attention than others, or attention of a different kind. For example, an outdoor board may be startling, but a TV commercial generally commands more sustained attention.

3. *The attention-getting power of the message itself.* The more creative and attention getting a message is, the greater is the likelihood that it will have the desired effect.

4. *The target audience's level of need or desire to learn about a brand.* Some product categories are simply more interesting than others and automatically get attention more easily. Most people, for example, find cars more interesting than laundry detergents. When audience interest is high, less frequency may be needed.

5. *The MC objectives.* If the communication objective is to increase brand awareness rather than to change behavior, probably less frequency is needed.

6. *Personal influences.* Word of mouth can greatly affect the impact of a message. If word of mouth is negative, more frequency is needed to help counter the negative messages.

7. *The amount of competitive brand messages.* Generally, the more frequency competitive brand messages have, the more frequency is needed for your brand. **Share-of-voice spending** is *a brand's portion of total media spending in that brand's product category.* Having a 25 share of voice means that 25 percent of all the media dollars spent in the category within a given time period came from this brand. Most marketers and media planners agree that a brand must maintain a competitive share of voice.

The curves in Figure 13-5 help explain the concept of "effective frequency." Different levels of frequency create difference levels of response. Most media planners agree that there must be a minimum level of frequency before any impact will occur. As frequency continues to increase, however, there comes a time when additional increases have little or no effect. At this point, a marketer's return on the media investment becomes zero or negative. One of two things is generally happening at this point. Either most members of the target audience who are going to respond have done so, or **message wearout**—*brand messages that once attracted attention and motivated the target audience no longer do so*—has occurred.

Another important aspect of frequency response is that it can shift to being more responsive or less responsive. Notice the two response curves in Figure 13-5. The A curve is the more desirable because it generates more response from a lower level of frequency (that is, media spending), so the average cost per response is less than that along the B curve.

Several variables can influence the shape of the frequency response curve. One is the media being used and whether they are reaching the persons most likely to buy. Suppose that response curves A and B are both for an ad offering a McDonald's Big Mac hamburger for 89 cents. The A curve represents a media mix that reached teenagers; the B curve represents a media mix that reached middle-aged and older customers—persons not nearly as interested in the offer as the teens. In this scenario, the A curve represents a better result.

Another variable can be the offer itself. Suppose that McDonald's sent two Big Mac offers to the same teen audience. Offer A advertised Big Macs for 89 cents, and offer B offered them for $1.19. Because the 89-cent offer is more attractive to the target audience, it would generate the higher response represented by the A curve. Media planners must consider these types of variables when evaluating media

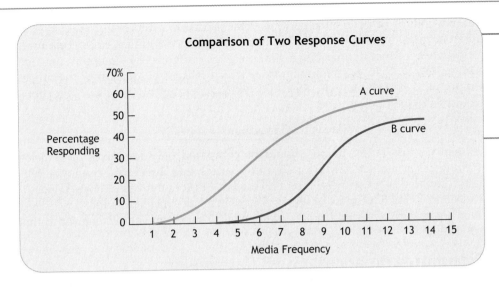

Comparison of Two Response Curves

A curve

B curve

Percentage Responding

Media Frequency

FIGURE 13-5

Response curve A is the more desirable of these two because it requires less frequency.

performance. Sometimes the media cause a difference in response; at other times, a variable other than media affects the level of responses.

Frequency Distribution Analysis

When planning for message frequency, it is important to keep in mind that frequency is an average. For example, when a media plan has a frequency of 7, about half of those reached will be exposed more than seven times and half are exposed less than seven times. For this reason, media planners often do a **frequency distribution analysis** (sometimes referred to as a **quintile analysis**), which is *an analysis that divides a target audience into equal segments and establishes an average frequency for each of these segments* (*quintus* is Latin for "fifth"). For example, a quintile analysis might reveal that the top 20 percent of those reached have an average of 12 exposure opportunities and the bottom 20 percent have an average of only 2 exposure opportunities:

Quintile	Frequency (average number of exposures)
Top 20% of audience	12
Next 20%	9
Next 20%	6
Next 20%	4
Bottom 20%	2

Notice that in this example 60 percent of the target was exposed to the message less than seven times, which was the "average" frequency. What does this tell a media planner? In order to make sure a *majority* of those reached are exposed 7 or more times, the overall average frequency must be greater than 7 (anywhere from 8 to 10, depending on the media vehicles selected).

Reach × Frequency = Gross Rating Points

Reach and frequency are interrelated concepts that when combined produce a measure called *gross rating points*. **Gross rating points (GRPs)** are *a combined measure of reach and frequency indicating the weight of a media plan*. The more GRPs in a plan, the more "weight" the plan is said to have. **Media weight** is *an indication of the relative impact of a media plan*. GRPs are determined by multiplying reach (the percentage of people exposed to vehicles carrying the brand message) by frequency (the number of insertions or units purchased in particular communication vehicles within a specified time period). Suppose 3M Company has five ads in *Modern Office Supplies* magazine, which reaches 50 percent of the office-supply market (3M's target). The total GRPs generated by these five insertions would be 250:

$$50 \text{ reach} \times 5 \text{ insertions} = 250 \text{ GRPs}$$

Ideally, gross rating points should be compared only for mixes of vehicles *within the same medium.* GRPs for TV, newspapers, and direct mail cannot be reliably compared because the different media have different levels of impact. Does a 30-second TV ad have more or less impact than a half-page newspaper ad, an outdoor board, or a 60-second radio commercial? There is no simple answer to this question.

Calculating Broadcast Gross Rating Points

Suppose AT&T wanted to use TV, and the media planners recommended running commercials in four programs, as shown in Table 13-2. In this example, the universe is all TV households in the United States. The reach of each program is determined by its rating. The frequency is the number of times a commercial ran in each program within a four-week period. As you can see, each of the commercials that ran in the *CBS Evening News* had a reach of 6 because the program had a rating of 6. And because the ads ran five times, this portion of the media plan had a frequency of 5. Therefore, 30 GRPs were generated by using *CBS Evening News*.

$$6 \text{ (reach)} \times 5 \text{ (frequency)} = 30 \text{ GRPs}$$

Doing the same calculations for the other three programs and then adding the totals shows that the overall media plan generated 196 GRPs (see Table 13-2).

What the table *literally* means is that 196 percent of U.S. households were reached, which, of course, is mathematically impossible. Just as you can't eat more than 100 percent of a pie, you cannot reach more than 100 percent of an audience. That GRPs often exceed 100 reflects duplication—many households are reached more than once. In this example, some households watching the *CBS Evening News* and *Law & Order* watched each show more than once and therefore had multiple exposures to the ads in these shows. Other households that were reached may have seen more than one *Friends* show, as well as several *Monday Night Football* broadcasts. This is how reach duplication occurs.

To determine the amount of duplication, agencies use computer programs based on audience research done by companies such as Simmons Market Research Bureau (SMRB). For the sake of discussion, suppose that the computer programs showed reach to be 49 in Table 13-2. Once this has been determined, the frequency

TABLE 13-2	GRPs Based on Total U.S. Household Coverage						
Programs	Program Rating		Frequency				GRPs
CBS Evening News	6	×	5	=			30
Friends	10	×	4	=			40
Law & Order	15	×	6	=			90
Monday Night Football	12	×	3	=			36
Total							196

can be found by dividing the total number of GRPs by reach: 196 ÷ 49 = 4. Thus, in this example, 49 percent of U.S. households were exposed, on average, four times to the brand message. In reality, of course, some of the 49 percent were exposed only once or twice, while the very heavy viewing households may have been exposed as many as 18 times (the total number of times the brand message ran).

GRPs indicate the weight of a media plan; the more GRPs, the "heavier" the plan. Comparing media plans to outcomes in the marketplace often gives media planners and account managers a good idea of how much weight should be used to introduce a new product, increase the level of brand awareness, and so on. That is why a typical media objective states a certain number of GRPs: "Support the brand's introduction with 3,000 GRPs within the first three months." Although the media planners are given GRP objectives, however, they still have to make a decision as to the balance of reach and frequency. This is because R × F = GRPs. When you have a set number of GRPs, increasing the reach decreases the frequency, just as increasing the frequency decreases the reach. In the preceding example, if the computer model had said the reach was 63, then the frequency would have been approximately 3 (196 GRPs ÷ 63 reach = 3.1 frequency).

Calculating Targeted Gross Rating Points

When *targeted reach* is applied to a media plan, we talk about **targeted GRPs (TGRPs),** which is *the number of gross rating points delivered against just the targeted audience.* TGRPs provide a more accurate picture of what a brand receives for its media spending. The difference between a plan's GRPs and targeted GRPs is the number of GRPs that are wasted, a number that always needs to be minimized as much as possible. This can be done by selecting the media vehicles that most accurately will reach the targeted audience.

To illustrate how to figure targeted GRPs and see how they differ from GRPs, let's see what happens when the previously described target audience in the AT&T example is changed to *households with incomes of $75,000-plus.* Because only a portion of the households tuned to the four listed shows have incomes of $75,000-plus, the rating numbers are much less (see Table 13-3). Therefore, the *targeted* gross rating points are also significantly less than 196. Notice that the frequency numbers for each program don't change because the number of commercials that ran was the same; only the reach numbers are lower. The targeted reach for *CBS Evening News,* for example, is only 3, indicating that only half of the households tuned to this program had household incomes of $75,000-plus. Given the reduced reach numbers for each program, the targeted GRPs total only 92, less than half of the 196 total household GRPs. Putting the TGRP number into the computer model to determine overall reach would yield a targeted reach of 24. Frequency, however, would continue to be nearly the same: when the 92 TGRP is divided by the new reach of 24, the result is 3.8, the frequency.

TABLE 13-3	TGRPs Based on Households with Incomes of $75,000-plus			
Programs	$75,000-plus HH Rating	Frequency		TGRPs
CBS Evening News	3	× 5	=	15
Friends	5	× 4	=	20
Law & Order	7	× 6	=	42
Monday Night Football	5	× 3	=	15
Total				92

Now that you have some understanding of all the critical media terms, here are some examples of typical media objectives. Like all marketing objectives, media objectives should be measurable, as these are:

- *Reach:* "Have a minimum reach of 65 during each of the first three quarters of the year, and 80 in the last quarter." (This company needs to rid its inventory at year's end, so it needs to advertise special promotions in the fourth quarter.)

- *Frequency:* "Have a minimum frequency of 5 each quarter in markets where share is over 20 percent; have a minimum frequency of 10 in all other markets." (This brand is in a highly competitive and complex category—vitamins—and recognizes that if it is to increase its share of market, it needs to increase brand knowledge, which requires greater repetition of its message.)

- *Target allocation:* "Allocate 50 percent of media dollars to reach current customers and 50 percent to reach prospects." (This brand knows that brand loyalty in its category is very thin so it has to put as much effort against keeping current customers as it does in acquiring new ones.)

- *Timing:* "Have 300 GRPs of advertising support within the month preceding each promotion." (This company has data showing that the higher its brand awareness is during a promotion, the greater is the response to its promotions.)

- *Interactivity:* "Respond to 95 percent of customer/prospect-initiated e-mails within 24 hours." (This company knows that a quick response is an added value to customers because it makes them feel special and important.)

- *Integration:* "Reach 80 percent of targeted media editors/news directors with press releases 30 days prior to start of new-product advertising." (Brand publicity has a much better chance of being used when the story is news. If a company asks for publicity at the same time a new product is being advertised, the news value is diminished by the ads telling the story.)

STEP 3: DETERMINING MEDIA STRATEGIES: HOW WILL YOU ACCOMPLISH THE OBJECTIVES?

Media strategies are ideas about *how* media objectives will be accomplished through the selection of various combinations of media. For every media objective there should be one or more strategies. These strategies describe the media mix—that is, which media should be used and to what extent. Cost is always impacting the selection of strategies. Like every other marketing communication operation, media must operate within a given budget. Because of the large number of media choices, the final decision about which media to use is often influenced by their cost. Media tools used to make objective cost comparisons among media alternatives are cost per thousand (CPM) and cost per point (CPP).

To develop creative cost-effective media-use strategies requires in-depth understanding of each medium's attributes and cost and a thorough understanding of the target audiences. As explained in Chapters 11 and 12, each medium has its own strengths and weaknesses. Table 13-4 is a summary of how major media compare in attributes that marketers take into consideration when deciding which media can best help achieve media objectives.

Media strategies involve more than just identifying which media should be used. "Spend half the money in TV, a fourth in newspapers, and a fourth in

T A B L E   1 3 - 4   Relative Attributes of Major Media

Attribute	Magazine (local)	Newspaper	Outdoor	Television	Radio (local)	Direct mail	Tele-marketing	Internet	Phone	Packaging
Target selectivity	good	poor	poor*	broadcast average/ cable good	good	best	best	good/ best**	best	best
Reach	low	best	high	high	low	low	low	low	low	best
Message impact	average	average	low	average	low	high	high	low	high	high
Geographic flexibility	poor	poor	good	national poor/ local good	good	good	good	low	best	good
Lead time to use	long	short	long	national long/ local short	short	medium	short	short	short	long
Ability to control time of exposure	poor	good	poor	best	best	good	best	best	best	poor
Where vehicles used most	home/ some away	home	out of home	home	home/ car	home/ office	home/ office	home/ office	home/ office/ car	home

*But good geographically.

**E-mail is best.

Source: Based on "General Characteristics of Major Media Forms," in *Media Planning: A Practical Guide*, Jim Surmanek, NTC, 1995. Reprinted with permission from The McGraw-Hill Companies.

outdoor" is not a particularly useful media strategy. A good media strategy states how media can help create a brand experience and engage customers and prospects—that is, how media will create a connection. This requires a good understanding of the brand's customers and targeted prospects, for people's ideas and interests and what it takes to reach them do not remain constant. An example of changing attitudes about the consumer/media vehicle connection is seen in the area of reality TV shows. They originally were considered too edgy for mainstream advertisers; then the broad success of such programs as *Survivor, Joe Millionaire,* and *The Bachelorette* made reality programs acceptable even to conservative advertisers such as Kraft Foods and Procter & Gamble, whose Clairol Herbal Essences sponsored *American Idol.* The most risky program, *Fear Factor,* attracted Dodge Trucks with its aggressive "Grab life by the horns" theme.[9]

Good media strategies require creative selection and use of media.[10] Recall from the opening case the media strategy that Fallon used to help reposition Lee jeans. The strategy was to use media that reached the target audience at unexpected times (such as late, late night) in communication vehicles whose image said nontraditional, off-the-wall, wacky. Another combination creative and media strategy was to use a **teaser campaign**—*a series of messages that carry no brand identification but are designed to create curiosity*—to build interest in later brand messages. It also allowed the target audience, which resents being sold to, an opportunity to "discover" the Buddy Lee story with a more open mind-set.

Another media strategy is used in the entertainment industry to retain customers. Direct-mail offers are sent to past customers prior to the public announcement of an upcoming concert. For example, an entertainment ticketing agency uses its database to find customers who purchased tickets to see rap entertainers and then sends those customers an automated e-mail or phone call to alert them to a just-scheduled Eminem concert. Both the internet and the phone are addressable media that can be used to send brief informational messages to an identifiable target audience. Automated phone calls and e-mails (1) have an extremely low cost, (2) demand attention, and (3) can be narrowly targeted, which significantly increases the level of response.

Media Strategy Factors

An important consideration in determining media strategies is the type of product being promoted. Therefore, when advertising low-involvement products such as detergent, paper towels, or industrial cleaning services, planners should consider the more intrusive media. Another strategy, however, is selecting media whose editorial content creates a more receptive environment. For detergent and paper-towel brands, a "shelter" magazine such as *Better Homes & Gardens* or the Home & Garden television channel provides such an environment. In contrast, high-involvement products such as luxury goods and entertainment offers can make use of print media, where readers select the stories and ads they want to see.

Customers' Buying Decision Process

Media strategies should also be driven by customers' buying decision processes (◄ Chapter 5). For high-involvement products, for example, the buying decision process often follows the AIDA model—attention, interest, desire, action. IBM uses the AIDA model to drive many of its media decisions. Each step in the decision-making process requires a different media strategy. A media strategy for reaching people in the first stage of looking for a laptop computer would be to place image advertisements in business-oriented media such as *Business Week.* For prospects who attended a trade show where they visited an IBM booth and tried a ThinkPad laptop, a media strategy would be to use direct mail to send, immediately after the trade show, an offer for a free 30-day trial (this strategy assumes that names and addresses of booth visitors were captured). An important element of the latter strategy is timing—making sure that prospects receive the offer within a few days of attending the show, before they forget their trial experience.

For mass-consumed products such as computers and cars, a strategy using selected mass media could be useful to create attention and maintain brand awareness and the interest of a broad target audience. However, once a customer enters the desire and action stages for these products, the best media strategy would be to use selected interactive media (mail, e-mail, phone). The closer to the action step, the more personal the message delivery needs to be. The more personal the message and the medium, generally the more impact the two will have (see Figure 13-6). Although interactive and addressable media are expensive, the cost often can be justified because of their ability to motivate behavior.

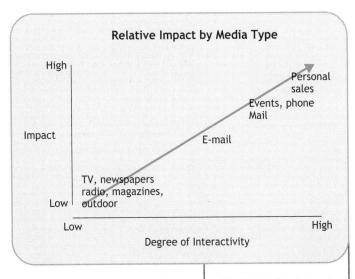

Relative Impact by Media Type

FIGURE 13-6

The more interactive the medium, the more impact it will generally have.

The importance of interactivity during the action stage cannot be overstated. In their early phases, e-business companies such as CDnow and Amazon.com found that people often went to their company websites, filled shopping carts, got ready to check out, then found themselves with a question but no way to get it answered, so they abandoned their shopping carts. That's why many e-commerce companies now make their sites interactive and provide e-mail addresses and phone numbers, as well as hyperlinks to customer service. Making sure that an interested customer can talk to someone in person is vital.

Apertures

A media strategy used by the advertising agency DDB Worldwide demonstrates understanding of customer touch points and of buyer decision processes. This agency uses the word **aperture** (which means "opening") to describe *any situation in which the target audience is highly receptive to a brand message.* Literally, an aperture is the opening in a camera's lens. The wider the lens is open—the wider its aperture—the greater is the amount of light that passes through. Similarly, the more open a person is to receiving a message, the more impact that message can have. A media strategy that is built by following customers through their daily lives tries to identify and take advantage of apertures. A sports stadium, for example, is an aperture in which people are more open to brand messages related to food, drink, and sporting goods than they are to political messages, dietary aids, and life insurance offers.

A new technology called TiVo, however, is playing havoc with the concept of aperture, at least for TV buys. A personal video recorder, TiVo can record up to 80 hours of programming on a hard drive, and viewers can play back the programming on their own time.[11] TiVo makes it possible for viewers to skip the commercials, and that capability has the networks and major advertisers very concerned. TiVo also collects data on viewing habits and can automatically tape shows that it thinks fit a user's profile. TiVo uses that same "profiling" information to deliver customized advertising along with the programs. Some critics of TiVo worry about an erosion of personal privacy. TiVo fans, however, value the control they get from the box that lets them "call the shots regarding when, how, and—soon—even where they watch, as well as what to watch and not to watch."[12]

Response Media

With increasing use of interactive media, companies are beginning to develop media "response" strategies for interacting with customers. In the past, customer service was primarily reactive. With the spread of IMC, however, it is being realized that this important customer touch point can be proactive. To make it so requires a media strategy that ensures that customers have easy access to a company and receive quick and satisfying replies. Companies have the media available to do this (phone, internet, and mail), but most do not have enough personnel to prepare and send replies, especially in a timely fashion (within 24 hours for phone and e-mail contacts).

One of the benefits of websites is that they can contain an unlimited amount of data that can answer customers' and prospects' questions, thereby reducing the demand for a human response. The challenge is to provide navigational guides that make it easy for website visitors to find the information they need. Also, automated answering systems, if properly designed, can take the place of live telephone (⬅ Chapter 12). In banking, for example, customers who want to know how much money they have in their checking accounts can get the answer without talking to a bank employee. Many people call airlines to find out whether planes are departing or arriving on time. Making it easy for them to get this information, by simply asking them to punch in or say a flight number, adds value to the service.

Many companies have found a useful response tool in proprietary software that allows customers to link to a company from their home computers. Print media have effectively been used to distribute promotional CDs. An example is Kinko's File Prep Tool (see Exhibit 13-7), which was included in an issue of the business magazine *Fast Company*. This CD can be used to send documents directly to Kinko's for printing. (The various uses of response media are discussed in more detail in Chapter 18.)

EXHIBIT 13-7

This Kinko service is an example of how a company can use the media (in this case, the internet) to conduct business.

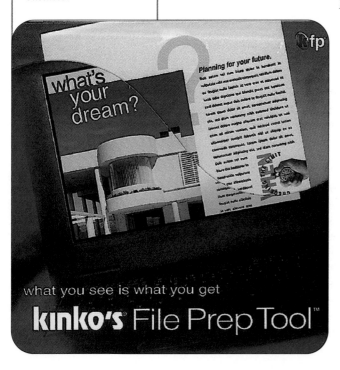

Determining the Media Mix

In the world of media planning and buying, the media selected for a brand constitute a media mix. Determining the media mix is a major strategic challenge that involves two basic decisions: (1) which media to use and (2) how much of each to use. Most media plans call for both one-way and interactive media but are heavy on one-way media.

There is no one best mix. Every brand situation is different, and a mix should be driven by the media and marketing objectives. When the objective is to maximize reach, for example, the more media vehicles used, the faster reach will increase. Table 13-5 shows a hypothetical *unduplicated* reach when two different media are used and one medium has a reach of 45 and the other a reach of 55. In this example, when both media are used, together they produce a reach of 75 (underlined).

Media Weighting

Suppose a product is bought by one segment but the decision is influenced by another segment—

TABLE 13-4   Combined Reach of Two Media

Reach of Second Medium	Reach of One Medium					
	25	35	45	55	65	75
25	46	51	59	66	74	81
35		58	64	71	77	84
45			70	<u>75</u>	81	86
55				80	84	89
65					88	91
75						94

Source: Karsh & Hagan Communication Agency, 2000.

for example, hot dogs (parents buy them but children eat them). A weighting strategy could be 65 percent of media placed to reach parents and 35 percent placed to reach children. Companies also figure media weights for competing brands in order to determine how much weight of their own to use in certain areas. For example, if Harley-Davidson found that Honda (motorcycles) was significantly increasing its media weight to reach 16- to 24-year-olds, it might counter by making a similar increase in media weight for this segment.

Media weights can be figured in terms of media dollars or in terms of reach and frequency. For some brands, media weight is based on dollars determined by a percentage of sales. If Chicago had four times the sales of Indianapolis, for example, then Chicago would be allocated four times as many media dollars. The problem with comparing on the basis of dollars is that media costs vary from market to market. In this case, the cost per thousand for a prime-time TV ad is approximately $30 in Chicago but only $22 in Indianapolis. So even though Chicago would be given four times as many media dollars, the brand would not be able to deliver four times as many messages in Chicago. This is why using gross rating points is so important in determining the relative emphasis on different media schedules in different markets.

Media Concentration

Media mix strategy is influenced by the degree of concentration needed in a plan, which is basically a qualitative decision. A *concentrated* media mix delivers greater frequency (at the expense of reach) than a *broad* media mix. A *concentrated* media mix uses fewer media and communication vehicles than a *broad* media mix. Furthermore, vehicles themselves differ in the concentration of their audiences. Newspapers and magazines provide greater concentration because most are sent repeatedly (by subscription) to the same audience members; broadcast programs have audiences who are not as consistent and usually broader in their characteristics.

Concentrated media mixes are used when an audience can be narrowly defined—for example, "females, 13 to 21, living in major urban areas." Another reason for using a concentrated mix is that it may help build strong relationships with a smaller but more important portion of a target audience, those who represent the heavy users. Such a strategy may be more productive in the long term than building weaker relationships with a large audience, because customers with a strong brand relationship are more likely to respond and more likely to talk positively about the brand to others.

Production costs are another factor in the decision to concentrate media. Using fewer media means that fewer messages need to be produced. If radio, TV, outdoor, and magazines are in a mix, four completely different message formats must be produced. For a small budget, such production can be a major expense. Finally, concentrating media dollars in fewer media can often result in getting more promotional support from these media—and better space and time placements—compared to spreading out the media buy and not being a significant customer for any of the vehicles used.

Finally, some MC executives believe the argument that if three different sources tell you something, the message will have more impact than if you get the message three times from the same source. In this view, a broad mix of media increases message synergy, although empirical evidence is weak to support this belief.

Message Considerations

Creative strategy is a qualitative factor involving the "feel" and complexity of the message. When a message is fairly simple—such as "2 for 1 through Sunday"—a broad mix with a high level of reach (rather than frequency) may be appropriate. But when a brand message is relatively complex, it may require a concentrated mix, because greater frequency gives the target more opportunities to understand the message. Message complexity also suggests considering print rather than broadcast media because, as explained in Chapter 11, print can be read slowly, reread, and even clipped and saved, unlike a broadcast brand message.

Often a combination of media vehicles, each of which relates to different points in the purchase decision process, can be effective. For automakers, such a strategy might be summarized this way: selling the car on TV and selling the deal in newspapers. Cross-over media messages use magazines and Sunday supplements to deliver posters, demonstration CDs, scent sheets for perfumes, greeting cards with the sales message stored on a tiny computer chip, and other special promotions. The *USA Weekend* Sunday supplement, for example, has run movie and other event posters that lift out from the publication and unfold to become decorations for fans' walls (see Exhibit 13-8). The launch of the *Lord of the Rings* movie, for example, included having a magazine feature not only a full-sheet poster but also an article on the poster as a collectible.[13]

Media Environment

Related to message considerations is another qualitative factor, the environment delivered by the medium. Cable channels with specialized content, such as Home & Garden, the Weather Channel, the History Channel, and Arts and Entertainment (A&E), have developed strong brand environments for themselves and their audiences. They have strong relationships with their audiences, who come to the channels with specific expectations. These audiences will be most receptive to product offerings related to program content. A manufacturer of plant fertilizer, for example, would likely do well by buying time on the Home & Garden channel rather than on ESPN.

EXHIBIT 13-8

What other opportunities exist for the use of cross-over media messages when promoting movies?

Another media environment consideration is the compatibility between a media vehicle's image and the brand's image. For some brands, having their messages in the *National Enquirer* and on *The Jerry Springer Show* is no problem. However, these sensational vehicles would not provide a compatible media environment for such status brands as Tiffany and Lexus, or for traditional family brands such as Hershey's chocolate, Kraft mayonnaise, and Johnson & Johnson baby shampoo. A media vehicle's image is determined not only by its content but also by the brands and products whose advertising it carries. The next time you are going through the checkout at your local supermarket, look at copies of the various tabloids to see which brands and products have bought display and classified advertising space in these publications. You'll probably find ads for psychic readers, diet pills, sex aids, and dating services.

Although the practice was more prevalent in the early days of television, you still see on some packages and in some print ads the line "As seen on TV." For little-known brands, advertising on TV—during *any* type of television program—can mean added value for a brand. But for most TV media buys, advertisers want to be associated with a particular program. In the United States, marketers pay two to three times normal rates to advertise during the Super Bowl just to be associated with this spectacular global TV event.

IMC Media Mix Factors

One of the most important considerations in creating an IMC media mix is to choose media that enhance the messages being delivered. As a DDB Worldwide media executive explained, "It is no longer enough to calculate a cost per thousand or other body-count figures. We also need to think about the qualitative benefits that different media vehicles can provide, such as conveying a message with authority or having the ability to be influential."[14]

The selection decisions at this level are based not only on an analysis of various media's abilities to deliver the plan's objectives but also on how media can be integrated to complement one another. In order to develop good media strategies, media planners need to know about more than just the media objectives. The following types of questions must be cross-functionally answered in order to integrate media planning and come up with the most relevant media strategies:

- *What sales promotion offers are being scheduled, at what times, and to whom?* Coupons, for example, are delivered by print media and the internet. If the purpose of these coupons is to attract prospects, an appropriate strategy would be to select media that reach prospects (rather than just current brand users). One way to do this is to find media with audience profiles that are similar to a company's current profitable customers.

- *What direct-response efforts (direct mail and telemarketing) are planned that will need other media support?* As will be explained in Chapter 18, supporting direct-mail and telemarketing offers with other media can increase the response rate ("watch for introductory coupon arriving in the mail soon"). This would suggest a media strategy such as "Begin TV advertising four weeks before direct mail and telemarketing begin."

- *What are the major publicity programs, and to whom should news releases be sent?* A company that advertises in a B2B trade publication may find that publication more willing to accept a news release than one in which the company does not advertise. Local media are also more receptive to press releases from major advertisers. In short, the idea is that "you support us and we'll support you." A media strategy for this situation might be "Select publications that have been receptive to the brand's publicity releases in the past."

- *Are new/improved product introductions planned?* Often, new products are introduced in a regional rollout rather than all at one time nationwide. This strategy allows production to gradually increase its efficiencies, and it enables the MC plan to be tested. Media planners need to be aware of the rollout schedule. An appropriate media strategy in support of rollouts would be "Schedule advertising and promotion to begin four weeks after personal selling begins in each rollout region."

- *To what extent do category sales fluctuate?* Seasonal, day-of-week, and geographical fluctuations are some of the purchasing variables media planners must consider. An appropriate media strategy would be "Allocate 50 percent of annual media support for each selling cycle to run immediately before the cycle begins."

Calculating Media Cost

Another strategic decision relates to how the media budget will be allocated. No brand has an unlimited amount of money to spend on media. Cost is always a consideration in any kind of media decision. Although the costs of time and space are important to know, what is even more important to keep in mind is the cost for creating a lead or a purchase. An easy way to think about most media costs is to think how the post office charges for delivering mail. The more people you send something to, the more money you spend. Also, the bigger the pieces you send, the more each piece costs to mail. The same goes for media: the larger the audience, the greater the cost; and the bigger the message (in length of time or size of ad), the greater the cost. Because media costs are so important, they are discussed at several places in this book (see, for example, Chapters 11 and 12).

Cost per Thousand

Because the number of audience members—customers, households, businesses—is different for every communication vehicle, comparing the cost of a unit of time or space is often misleading. To determine which are the best values among all the many vehicle alternatives that reach the target audience, media planners use a calculation called **cost per thousand (CPM),** *what a communication vehicle charges to deliver a message to 1,000 members of its audience* (the M in the abbreviation is the Roman numeral meaning "1,000"). CPM is found by using the following simple formula:

$$\frac{\text{Cost of ad unit} \times 1,000}{\text{Circulation or audience}} = \text{CPM}$$

Suppose Radio station A charges $500 for a 60-second commercial, and station B charges $1,500. Both stations are in the same designated marketing area (DMA). At first, it seems that station A would be a better buy because it charges $1,000 less for the same amount of time. To determine which is really the better value, however, a planner must know the size of the audience for each station's program in which the commercial would run. In the following calculation, station A's audience is 30,000 and station B's is 120,000:

	Station A	Station B
Cost of a :60 time slot	$500	$1,500
Audience	30,000	120,000
CPM	$\dfrac{\$500 \times 1,000}{30,000} = \$16.66$	$\dfrac{\$1,500 \times 1,000}{120,000} = \$12.50$

As you can see, station B offers greater value, because its CPM is only $12.50, about $4.00 less than station A's CPM ($16.66).

The same CPM formula is used to compare cost efficiencies of different print vehicles. As the following breakdown shows, magazine B offers a better CPM than magazine A, even though A's cost per page is less:

	Magazine A	**Magazine B**
Cost of a full-page ad	$20,000	$30,000
Circulation	800,000	1,500,000
CPM	$\dfrac{\$20,000 \times 1,000}{800,000} = \$25$	$\dfrac{\$30,000 \times 1,000}{1,500,000} = \$20$

The best way to compare similar communication vehicles is to compare targeted reach, which takes into account wasted circulation. The CPM formula applies, except that the targeted reach (in actual numbers) is substituted for the vehicle's total audience. To show how this can change a media decision based on simple CPM, we'll use the magazine A and B in the above example but assume the target is "females with a college education who participate in outdoor sports." Magazine A reaches 200,000 households where the target lives, and magazine B reaches 250,000. As you can see, the targeted cost per thousand (TCPM) is lower for magazine A than for magazine B, even though the opposite was true when the two magazines were compared on the basis of total audience CPMs.

	Magazine A	**Magazine B**
Cost of a full-page ad	$20,000	$30,000
Circulation	200,000	250,000
TCPM	$\dfrac{\$20,000 \times 1,000}{200,000} = \$100$	$\dfrac{\$30,000 \times 1,000}{250,000} = \$120$

Cost per Point and Cost per Response

Similar to cost per thousand is **cost per point (CPP),** *a measure used to compare same-medium broadcast vehicles.* In this use, the word *point* is shorthand for *rating point*, which is 1 percent of a station's coverage area. Because the broadcast coverage area of most TV and radio stations in a market is the designated marketing area, a rating point represents the same number of households for all the market's stations.

You cannot, however, compare the CPP for a broadcast program in one DMA with the CPP in another DMA, because every DMA has a different number of households and thus a different basis for determining what 1 percent (one rating point) is. Again consider Chicago and Indianapolis. One rating point in Indianapolis represents 9,633 households, and one rating point in Chicago represents 32,047 households. When you change the basis on which a percentage is figured, the value of that percentage changes. Which would you rather have, 1 percent of $1,000 or 1 percent of $1 million? There is a significant difference—$10 versus $10,000.

A word of caution: CPPs should not be used to compare two different types of vehicles—such as radio and TV or newspapers and radio—because different media are best compared on the basis of their different strengths (Chapter 11).

The ultimate objective of any marketing communication program is to motivate the target audience to respond in some way. Therefore, the best way (where possible) to compare the cost effectiveness of different vehicles, regardless of their media type, is on the basis of the **cost per response (CPR)** generated by each of the vehicles, which is *the media cost divided by the number of responses generated.* This type of comparison assumes that the message, creative costs, and offer are held constant in all the media used. The desired response needs to be defined in any behavioral way, such as "bought the product," "made a store visit," or "requested more information about the brand or offer." CPR can be determined for media vehicles that have direct and measurable contact with prospects and customers such as e-mail, regular mail, and telephone. When media are used that don't have a built-in tracking mechanism—such as TV, radio, and outdoor—the only way CPR can be determined is by comparing the total cost of the media campaign to all the responses received within a reasonable time period.

Here's one example of how CPR can be used to determine the effectiveness of different media. The Golden Moon, a neighborhood family Chinese restaurant, runs in the local newspaper an ad that costs $810. Every one of the 30,000 households that subscribe to or buy the paper is exposed to the ad. This means that it reaches not only people who live near the restaurant and like Chinese food but also a lot of people who don't live close by as well as all those who don't like Chinese food. Because the circulation is 30,000, and only 5,000 of the homes exposed to the ad are prospects, there is obviously a lot of wasted circulation.

Before the restaurant owner concludes that he shouldn't advertise in the local newspaper again because of the high percentage of wasted reach, there are several questions that he should answer: (1) How many responses did the ad generate? (2) What was the cost of each response? (3) Would any other media vehicle be more cost-effective to use? The answer to the first question is that 90 couples responded. The owner knows this because the ad offered a free dessert to everyone who mentioned the ad. To answer the second question and determine the cost per response (CPR), the restaurant owner divided the cost of the ad ($810) by the number responding (90) and then added the cost ($2) of the promotional premium, the free dessert, to the average cost per response:

Newspaper

Media cost	$810 for the ad
Number of responses	90
Cost per response	$\frac{\$810}{90} = \$9 + \$2 \text{ dessert} = \$11$

To answer the third question—which are the more cost-effective media?—the restaurant owner made the same offer using two other communication vehicles, radio and direct mail. Each was used at a different time but with the same free offer so the owner could determine to which media message customers were responding. (When more than one vehicle is being used at the same time in the same market, one way to track which vehicle is responsible for which set of responses is to use coded coupons. Each ad is given a different code number that refers to a particular vehicle.) The following calculations show the CPR results, including the cost of the free offer when the offer was made by radio and by direct mail:

	Radio	*Direct Mail*
Media cost	$540	$980
Number of responses	30	70
Cost per response	$\frac{\$540}{30} = \$18 + \$2 \text{ drink} = \$20$	$\frac{\$980}{70} = \$14 + \$2 \text{ dessert} = \$16$

As you can see, the newspaper's CPR ($11) was the lowest, even though the cost of the ad ($810) was more than the cost of the radio ad and nearly the same as the direct-mail cost.

The Chinese restaurant example has been kept simple for the sake of explanation. Most brands use a variety of communication vehicles (a media mix), which makes these analyses more complex but, with computers and good planning, still possible to do.

As you can imagine, because media consume a major part of the marketing budget, clients are continuously pressuring their advertising agencies to be as

IMC IN ACTION

Optimizing the Media Buy

Which makes more sense—paying $400,000 for a spot on *Friends* or scattering spots across a dozen or more cable networks and syndicated shows? Savvy media planners know that by using the latter strategy, they can sometimes reach the same number of viewers and save as much as $100,000 on the buy.

In today's age of accountability, clients pressure agencies to prove they are making the most efficient media buys. One way agencies do this is with optimizer programs: computer programs that move beyond analyzing program ratings to factor in various customer data in order to make the decision more precise. Originally devised for European markets, optimizer programs came to the United States when Nielsen Media Research made available data for real-time metered viewing patterns (from People Meters in some 5,000 homes).

Proprietary optimizer models developed by some agencies factor in different types of data. The Bozell agency's optimizer program factors in a TV program's holding power, loyalty, and attentiveness. The media-buying company Media That Works factors in ad clutter. McCann-Erickson's "Media in Mind" program takes into consideration consumers' state of mind (among other things) during media usage. The "Volume Rating Points" program by the Spectra research company adds an equation for sales volume per household using Nielsen's home-scanning program, in which 55,000 people scan their purchases in their home as they unload their shopping bags. Volume rating points indi-cate, for example, whether *ER* viewers purchase more cosmetics, soft drinks, or pain remedies than the viewers of *Frasier*. This is the latest application of single-source data—purchasing data from in-store scanners.

Newer optimizer programs include ratings for other media besides television. J. Walter Thompson's "Thompson Total Marketing" program for its client Ford Motor Company, for example, links Nielsen data with Ford's customer-service database and evaluates print and broadcast for reach. It also includes reach estimates for other marketing communication functions such as events, public relations, product placement, and the Web.

Think About It

If you were asked to develop an optimizer program for a campaign designed to promote the Suzuki method of teaching very young children how to play musical instruments, what target audience features and media characteristics would you include in the optimizer program and why?

Source: David Kiley, "Optimum Target," *Adweek*, May 18, 1998, pp. 39–42; Marc Gunther, "New Software Programs: TV Advertising," *Fortune*, May 11, 1998, pp. 26–27; Verne Gay, "Pumping Up the Volume," *Brandweek*, May 29, 2000, pp. U40–U44.

cost-effective as possible. To help meet this expectation, most MC agencies use an **optimizer program,** *a complex media-planning model that combines Nielsen data with data from in-store scanners and customer-profile databases,* as explained in the IMC in Action box.

STEP 4: DETERMINING THE MEDIA SCHEDULE: WHEN AND WHERE SHOULD MEDIA RUN?

Three commonly used scheduling strategies are flighting, continuous scheduling, and pulsing (see Figure 13-7). **Flighting** is *a scheduling strategy in which planned messages run in intermittent periods.* Clearly, flighting makes good sense for products whose sales fluctuate seasonally. But it is also used when budgets are limited. Why? Media running in flights are presumed to provide sufficient message impact to maintain a brand's presence. With the huge amount of commercial message clutter that exists today, most media planners believe there must be a certain level

FIGURE 13-7

*Most companies use one of
these scheduling strategies.
Which strategy should a
company with a limited
budget use?*

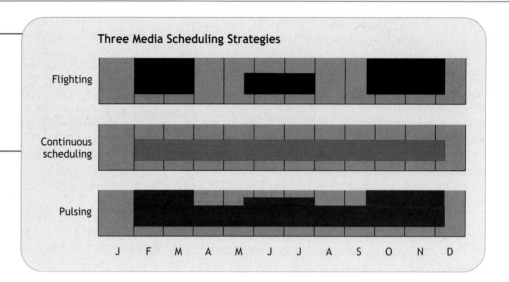

of frequency; otherwise, messages will have little or no impact on the target audience. Flighting can help them achieve frequency without draining the budget.

The opposite of flighting is **continuous scheduling,** *placing media throughout the year with equal weight in each month.* Continuous scheduling is often used by brands with large budgets and fairly constant sales throughout the year. Brands that desire to maintain a certain level of awareness also use this strategy. Another rationale for continuous scheduling is when a product is frequently purchased or, in the case of B2B products, when the brand decision-making process is relatively long and prospects need constant brand reminders.

Pulsing is *a scheduling strategy that provides a "floor" of media support throughout the year and periodic increases* (it basically combines *flighting* and *continous scheduling*). Fast-food and beverage companies with large media budgets often use a pulsing schedule. Once a media schedule is worked out, it is detailed in a flowchart such as the one in Figure 13-8 for Lee Jeans' Buddy Lee campaign.

If a product has *seasonal fluctuations,* media planners schedule their buys with similar fluctuations. However, most MC messages, with the exception of sales promotion and direct response, generally have a lag effect, so the media should precede the season. For example, if tennis racket sales begin increasing in April in the northern part of the United States, then media should begin running in March.

In some categories, such as restaurants and movie theaters, sales vary by day of week, and the majority of sales come on weekends. Media buys supporting these businesses are often scheduled from Thursday to Saturday to reach people when they are making plans for the weekend. Finally, some brands schedule media by time of day. Breakfast foods, for example, may schedule brand messages in the morning to take advantage of an aperture in which customers are thinking "breakfast."

In B2B media planning, *support of events* such as major trade shows requires media support both prior to and during the shows in the markets where the shows are held. B2B media planning is also heavily influenced by introductions of new and improved products. Some companies also schedule media according to when *competitors* begin their brand messages. This is generally true of small brands that feel they must "keep up" with leaders.

Media scheduling can also be influenced by the *type of MC message.* An awareness/image message requires weeks of media to have an effect compared to a promotional offering. A seasonal promotional offer, however, should be made only when the target audience is in a buying mood. Swimsuit manufacturer Jantzen, for

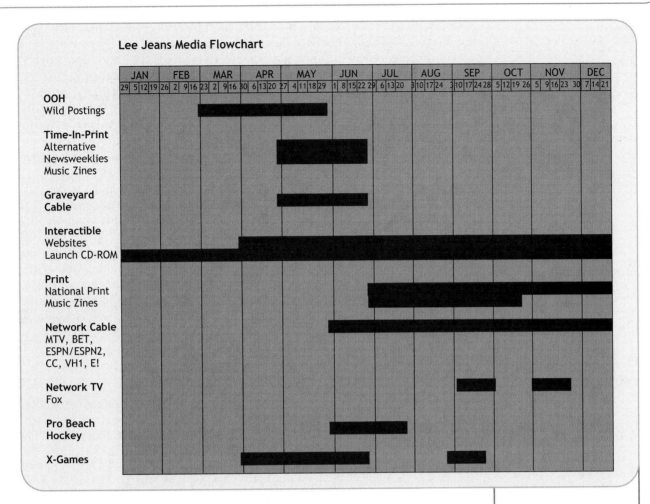

Lee Jeans Media Flowchart

FIGURE 13-8

Bars and their thickness show when the various media are used and to what extent.

example, might start its brand advertising in February but not run any promotional offers until April and May, when the weather has turned nice and people are ready to buy.

Another factor in determining a media schedule is the lead time available. *Lead time* is a calculation of the number of days needed to produce the message and allow the medium time to prepare it for publication or broadcast (magazine lead time can be up to three months). Any sudden changes in the marketing plan, which are more the rule than the exception, generally require changes in the media mix. When media budgets need to be kept flexible, it is best not to depend heavily on national TV and magazines. They demand relatively long lead times; and, once contracts are signed for space and time, it is difficult (though not always impossible) to get out of these commitments.

One way brands attempt to retain customers is to continually make improvements and expand product offers. Each major *new or improved product* needs media support. A new product, for example, may call for an initial media blitz with a heavy concentration of media weight preceding or coinciding with the date of the product's launch. The timing for this support varies. In some introductions, companies wait until the product is in distribution; in others, media placement begins ahead of time to build interest and the desire of customers. In the case of products sold through retail, media buys are sometimes scheduled ahead of the product launch to motivate retailers to stock the new/improved products and also to pull the product through the distribution channel by creating consumer demand. Retailers are more likely to want to stock a new product if customers ask for it.

A *product's purchase cycle* (how often customers buy the product) may also influence media scheduling. The argument is that the more frequently products in a particular category, such as soft drinks, are purchased, the more frequency is needed for brand messages—and vice versa for infrequently purchased products such as refrigerators and cars. This argument would make sense if all the buyers of refrigerators and cars bought them all at one time, say, every three years. In reality, however, there is no major seasonal variation for durable products such as refrigerators and cars; they are constantly being bought. For this reason, you see advertising for major-purchase items year-round because companies cannot know when each prospect will want to buy.

The only solution to this problem is to track customers who make major purchases and then, on a customer-by-customer basis, send out brand messages as each nears the end of a purchase cycle. For example, let's say a manufacturer of fire trucks knows that the average fire district replaces its trucks every five years. This would suggest that four years after a district purchased its fleet of trucks, the manufacturer should begin sending information on its newest models to this district. A company that schedules its individualized message deliveries according to individual purchase cycles must have a good customer database and do customer tracking.

A FINAL NOTE: MEDIA INTEGRATION

Many areas of a company's operations benefit from media scheduling being integrated. The most obvious is the overall marketing plan. When a company introduces a new promotion or product, media support is crucial. But unless the planning is integrated with production and distribution schedules, media may deliver brand messages at the wrong time. A common problem in both B2C and B2B marketing is advertising a product too long before it is available.

Media scheduling and the development of creative materials (such as ads, packaging, and publicity releases) must be integrated so that a company does not miss opportunities for reaching the right audiences, at the right time, in dynamic ways. Media also must be integrated with each of the MC functional programs.

EXHIBIT 13-9

Amazon has leveraged the brand awareness it has created online with its direct mail catalog.

Finally, media scheduling must be integrated into a company's total business operations. A good example is the way in which brick-and-mortar retailers promote their websites, enabling customers to buy online. By integrating the internet medium with the rest of the media effort, businesses have been able to increase sales. Amazon.com has reversed the process, integrating a direct-mail catalog into its predominantly online business. The catalog shown in Exhibit 13-9 is for Amazon.com products other than books.

Key Terms

aperture 445
brand development index
  (BDI) 430
category development index
  (CDI) 428
continuous scheduling 454
cost per point (CPP) 451
cost per response (CPR) 451
cost per thousand (CPM) 450
designated marketing area
  (DMA) 432
duplication 434

effective frequency 437
flighting 453
frequency 437
frequency distribution
  analysis 439
gross rating point (GRP) 439
impression 433
media buying 424
media planning 422
media waste 435
media weight 439
message wearout 438

optimizer program 453
pulsing 454
quintile analysis 439
reach 432
share-of-voice spending 438
skews 425
slotting fee 436
targeted GRPs (TGRPs) 441
targeted reach 435
teaser campaign 444

Key Point Summary

Key Point 1: Media Planning Steps

The process of creating a media plan involves four steps: (1) identifying the target audience, (2) setting the media objectives, (3) determining media strategies, (4) determining the media schedule and timing.

Key Point 2: Media Objectives

There are two primary media objectives: reach and frequency. Reach is the percentage of an audience that has the opportunity to be exposed to a brand message one or more times within a specified period. Frequency is the average number of times those who are reached have an opportunity to be exposed to a brand message within a specified time period.

Key Point 3: Media Mix

The mix of media is planned by analyzing the weight and concentration of various media, as well as message considerations, the media environment surrounding the message, and other factors.

Key Point 4: Media Costs

Media strategies are the decisions intended to deliver the impact called for in the media objectives. These strategies are influenced by customers' buying decision paths, media characteristics, and the calculation of media costs. Media planners compare the CPMs and TCPMs of vehicles in the same medium.

Key Point 5: Media Scheduling

The media schedule is based on considerations of seasonality and timing of the various media mix activities. Lead time is one consideration. Other considerations are factors related to the purchase cycle and to specific strategies, such as the launch of a new product.

Lessons Learned

Key Point 1: Media Planning Steps

a. List and explain the four steps in media planning.
b. What is the difference between media planning and media buying?
c. What is the difference between a media objective and a media strategy? Which comes first?

Key Point 2: Media Objectives

a. What information is included in a set of media objectives?
b. Define *reach* and *frequency*. How do they differ?
c. Explain why duplication and waste are problems for media planners.
d. Marketers ask themselves, "How much reach is enough?" Explain what that question means and how you would answer it. How would you determine how much reach is enough?
e. What is a GRP? How are GRPs computed?
f. What is targeted reach? Why is it important to marketers?
g. What is the difference between a GRP and a TRP?
h. What is effective frequency? What is message wearout? What three factors affect the evaluation of effective frequency and wearout?
i. What is frequency distribution analysis? How is it used in media planning?
j. Find a news article that reports the rating of a recent television program. Is the figure cited in the story a high or a low rating?

Key Point 3: Media Mix

a. Why is a media mix used in media planning?
b. What are three decisions involved in determining the best media mix?
c. What is the difference between a concentrated media mix and a broad media mix? Give an instance in which each approach would be appropriate.
d. How does the media mix reflect the creative strategy?
e. Explain how media weighting decisions affect the way the media budget is allocated.
f. How do you compute a cost per thousand? What does CPM tell you about a medium's audience?
g. What factors did Fallon consider when customizing the media mix for both the discovery and launch stages of the Buddy Lee campaign?

Key Point 4: Media Costs

a. What is a CPM? Why do media planners use calculations such as CPMs in their media plans?
b. Why do media planners compare the cost of a unit of time or space rather than just counting the audience?
c. What is the difference between CPM and TCPM? Between CPP and CPR?

Key Point 5: Media Scheduling

a. In a magazine or newspaper find a print ad that has an obvious seasonality factor. Explain how seasonality drives the media buy.
b. In what ways do the flighting, continuous scheduling, and pulsing strategies differ? How is each used?
c. Give an example of an integration factor that affects scheduling.

Chapter Challenge

Writing Assignment

Reach is the percentage of the target exposed to the vehicle or program, not the percentage exposed to the brand message. In a memo to your instructor, explain this problem, and outline some suggestions about what might be done to make the evaluation of a brand message's reach more reliable.

Presentation Assignment

Interview the advertising manager at a large company or retail store in your community. Summarize that company's media plan and media mix. Explain why the various media were chosen. Present this report to your classmates.

Internet Assignment

Analyze Lee Jeans' Buddy Lee website (www.buddylee.com). Develop a report for your instructor on how the website contributes to the image of the dungarees and speaks to the interests of the brand's target audience. For next year's campaign, what would you recommend doing with this website to make it even more relevant and interesting?

Chapter 14

Consumer Sales Promotion and Packaging

Key Points in This Chapter

1. How do sales promotions add value to a brand offering?
2. What are consumer sales promotions designed to accomplish, and what are their strengths and limitations?
3. What role does packaging play when consumers make brand decisions?

Chapter Perspective

Intensifying the Impact of the Brand Message

Sales promotions are used to intensify a brand contact for customers or prospects, especially when these people are in buying or using situations. Although the primary job of consumer sales promotion is to affect behavior, it can (and should) also heighten awareness and reinforce a brand's image. In major-purchase product categories, where deciding on a brand may take weeks or months, sales promotion can be used to help move prospects and customers through the decision process. Consumer promotional offers provide tangible added value and are generally available for a "limited time only" to create a sense of urgency.

Sales promotions are mostly one-way, nonpersonal messages, although when used in direct-response marketing, they can be personalized. Loyalty programs, a special form of sales promotion, help in retaining customers and attracting a greater share of customers' category spending.

Once consumers arrive in a store, they face three to ten brands in most product categories. The majority of consumers make their brand decisions in-store, so packaging is the last brand message they see before making their brand choice. Packages not only carry an advertising message but can add tangible value to a brand by being reusable, decorative, and sturdy (to protect the product during distribution and over a long period of use), and by containing coupons or premiums to reward purchase.

SNAPPLE'S GOOFY BOTTLES HUNT FOR YARD-SALE TREASURES

Snapple has gotten publicity with its popular campaigns by Deutsch New York, which personalizes Snapple bottles and promotes their antics in unlikely settings, such as a synchronized swim meet and running with the bulls in Spain.

A blowout sales promotion was added to the MC mix in the summer of 2003 when the campaign about the funny personalized bottles was extended to real-life experiences such as an online yard sale (see Exhibit 14-1). To participate in the promotion, customers collected special bottle caps and used them as currency at the Snapple.com website for goods and prizes, such as vintage "Saved by the Bell" T-shirts, foosball tables, and old *Gremlins* lunch boxes. Many brands give away goodies to loyal customers. Deutsch, however, wanted a quirky Snapple-style yard sale: one of the collectibles was a Snapple bottle personified as a chia pet.

The promotion permitted customers to get involved with the brand by "buying" these exclusive yard-sale collectibles and haggling for the best deal, just like at an authentic yard sale. If they bid too low, the website responded with snappy comebacks such as "I wouldn't even sell it to my mother for that."

Label flags and the special bottle caps featured the yard-sale promotion on some 300 million bottles sold in the United States, Canada, Puerto Rico, and the Caribbean. Unusual in-store point-of-purchase displays featured yard-sale-themed cooler boxes, yard-sale signs, and racks with custom-made yard-sale booklets. All customers who participated in the yard sale were invited to register for a "Money can't buy" sweepstakes featuring special dream prizes such as a Nintendo GameCube kiosk, a Piaggio scooter, a Kelly Slater autographed surfboard courtesy of Quicksilver, a surfing trip to Fiji, and a trip to the MTV *Real World Paris*.

In addition to the electronic yard sale, Snapple sponsored two larger-than-life live yard sales in New York City and San Francisco. To bring a touch of the suburbs to the city, these sites were outfitted with a real suburban home facade in a high-traffic location, a backyard BBQ, a lemonade stand, and tables full of yard-sale stuff. The income generated by these real experiences was donated to a national charity. Wendy, the Snapple Lady, made guest appearances at the events and at retail stores in several of Snapple's top markets, where she held her own yard sale.

EFFECTIVENESS CASE

EXHIBIT 14-1

The yard-sale promotion built up Snapple's quirky brand personality by personifying the crudely animated bottles and dressing them up as yard-sale devotees complete with wigs. In the Pamplona bull-running commercial, the bottles confronted guinea pigs with little horns who reenacted the annual bull stampede. In the synchronized-swim commercial, the Snapple bottles sporting goggles and sequined swim caps fluttered around in the swimming pool before performing a grand pyramid routine.

Other media besides TV helped spread the news about the Snapple yard sale promotion, including such surprising vehicles as "Snapple predicts" messages on the back side of fortune-cookie fortunes, napkin dispensers, and individual napkins; pizza boxes and deli bags with printed images of the wacky bottles; a Venice beach wallscape in Califor-

nia; and air banners flown over beaches and other heavily populated summer destinations. Other websites were used to drive Web traffic to the "Yard Sale" promotion. Online ads ran on MTV.com, VH1.com, BET.com, Nick.com, and CMT.com.

On the Snapple.com website were goofy back-stories, the behind-the-scenes stories for each of the ads found on the website. For example, a visit to the "Pamplona" site told the fictional tale of Snapple employees using "Ralph," the guinea pig owned by the sister of a Snapple employee, as the idea for the running-bulls commercial.

The funny promotion and its supporting commercials used an intentionally amateurish style to remind customers of the beverage's early days, when Snapple was seen as a quirky, alternative beverage.

SALES PROMOTION: INTENSIFYING CONSIDERATION

The term *sales promotion* is sometimes misunderstood or confused with advertising, because sales-promotion activities frequently use advertising to create awareness of promotional offers. **Sales promotion,** however, is *a MC function that offers a tangible added value designed to motivate and accelerate a response.* Adding tangible value means that people who respond to the promotion will receive more than just the product and its image. Added value includes a reduction in price (for example, 20 percent off, two for the price of one, no finance charges for a year); extra product (16 ounces of coffee beans for the price of 12 ounces); free samples; premiums (receiving a cosmetic case free with the purchase of $30 worth of cosmetics); and an entry into a sweepstakes. What is the added value promised by the Godiva ad in Exhibit 14-2?

There are two basic types of sales promotions. *Consumer promotions* target end users. *Trade promotions* target members of the distribution channels such as distributors, wholesalers, and retailers. When sales promotions are designed for *consumers,* a marketer is using a **pull strategy,** which is *the use of incentives to motivate end users to purchase a brand and thus pressure retailers to stock that brand.* These promotions result in consumers "pulling" product through the distribution system. When trade promotions are used, marketers are

EVEN IF SHE DOESN'T WIN THE DIAMONDS, YOU'LL STILL LOOK BRILLIANT.

GODIVA
Chocolatier

New York   Paris   Tokyo   Brussels

TABLE 14-1	Allocation of Advertising and Sales-Promotion Spending (based on 2002 spending in the United States)

	Allocation
Consumer promotion	30.6%
Trade promotion	26.6
Advertising	37.6
Other	5.2
Total	100.0%

Source: Allocation of Advertising and Sales Promotion Spending; *PROMO Magazine* supplement, Trends Report 2003, April 2003. © 2003, PRIMEDIA Business Magazines & Media, Inc. All rights reserved.

using a **push strategy,** which is *the use of incentives to motivate the buying and reselling of products.* Trade promotions are discussed in the next chapter.

Many promotional offers last for a "limited time only." They are used to motivate behavior, and having the promotion be short-term creates a sense of immediacy, which, marketers hope, speeds up the brand decision-making process. Furthermore, a price reduction that is not for a limited time is simply a price reduction, not a promotional strategy. The main exception to limited-time promotional offers are loyalty programs, discussed later in this chapter.

Some marketers consider sales promotion a supplement to advertising and personal selling because it can make both more effective. In reality, however, sales promotion is far more than supplementary. A study of marketing communication spending by *PROMO* magazine shows that more money is spent on trade and consumer promotions (combined) than on advertising (see Table 14-1).

HOW CONSUMER SALES PROMOTION WORKS

The primary objective of sales promotion is to motivate consumer behavior—that is, to generate some type of active response such as buying Snapple products in order to get the bottle cap, which serves as currency for an online yard sale. Sales promotion is integrated into the MC mix to provide incentives to act at one or more points in the brand decision-making process. In the case of the Snapple yard-sale promotion, the incentive was designed to encourage purchase of the beverage.

Studies have shown that when sales-promotion tools are used strategically, they can increase sales as much as 400 percent. Keep in mind that the usual grocery-shopping trip takes about 27 minutes.[1] During that time, an average shopper selects only 35 to 40 of the 7,000 products available in the average grocery store (30,000 items if you include different sizes and flavors). Those selections are driven by a customer's previous experience with the brands as well as marketing communication messages, including sales promotion, used to support these brands.

An example of how a sales promotion works is a Maybelline HydraTime lip color direct mail offer. In addition to picturing the product and its shades of color, the card also states selling points (extended-wear, moisturizing), a price reduction offer ("Save $1.00"), and a sample ("Try it now!"). On the back, it gives more information about the shades (their names), information about how the extended-wear feature works ("exclusive ColorBond™"), and a coupon that makes good on the "Save $1.00" offer on the front side.

Advertising creates awareness and interest; sales promotions influence the next steps in buying behavior, such as desire and action. Automobile dealers, for example, offer prospects free drinks and hot dogs just for visiting their showrooms, and companies selling time-share properties offer free dinners and an overnight stay to people willing to listen to a sales pitch. Marketers know that prospects may be aware of and even have some interest in a brand but may not have enough desire to seek out the brand or risk buying it. An extra incentive, however, sometimes moves a prospect into the desire and action stages.

To better understand how sales promotion works, we start with a discussion of the typical objectives that this MC function is used to achieve.

Sales-Promotion Objectives

Sales promotions are intended to intensify consumer response. Unlike many mass media advertising objectives, most of which have to do with awareness and attitudes, sales-promotion objectives are behavior oriented. Consumer sales promotions are designed to do one or more of the following: (1) increase trial and repurchase, (2) increase the frequency or quantity of purchases, (3) counter competitive offers, (4) build customer databases, (5) increase customer retention, (6) cross-sell, (7) extend the use of a brand, and (8) reinforce the brand image and strengthen brand relationships.

Increasing Trial and Repurchase

Packaged-goods brands use sales promotions to encourage trial as well as repurchase. Sales promotions such as special prices and product samples can motivate prospective customers to try something for the first time. America Online's strategy is to offer a limited period of free internet access. Coupons on and inside packages, as well as in other promotional materials such as direct mail, encourage repurchase.

Increasing Frequency and Quantity

Because the majority of the people who take advantage of coupons and price reductions are current customers, a good promotional strategy does more than simply offer current customers a discount. It is designed to increase purchase frequency or purchase quantity at each transaction. This is the reason for "buy one, get one free" offers. If you examine the pricing of these offers, you are likely to find that the price of the item you buy is the maximum retail price and that this price divided in half is close to the normal per package "on sale" price. The "buy one, get one free" strategy is a way of packaging a regular promotion, but with a twist: it motivates the customer to buy *two* items instead of one item at a time.

To increase the frequency of purchases, a company first must calculate the regular purchase frequency, in order to set a goal, and then must design a strategy that will encourage customers to buy the product more often. Suppose market research found that the average user of shampoo buys this product every three months. Knowing this, a company might schedule its promotions two months apart, timing that is intended to increase purchase frequency and convince customers that they should keep the brand on hand.

Countering Competitive Offers

The third objective of consumer sales promotions, countering competitive offers, is used frequently in highly competitive product categories. Airlines, rental car companies, and the manufacturers of soft drinks and breakfast cereals, for example, stay abreast of what competing brands are doing and act frequently to counter

IMC IN ACTION

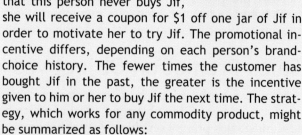

Promotions for Segments of One

Technological advances have created a new type of sales-promotion targeting: promotions sent to "segments of one"—that is, to individual customers. Grocery stores with special computer programs connected to their checkout scanners can print coupons on the back of the sales slips that are generated by each customer's purchases. Catalina, a promotion company that supplies this service, generates instant coupons at checkouts according to whether or not the customer is brand-loyal. Tracking customer purchases over time allows the store to determine, on a given shopping trip, whether the customer is buying a particular brand for the first time or has been buying it regularly.

When a customer buys a jar of Jif peanut butter, for example, the store's computer goes instantly into that customer's history of purchases and shows whether that customer buys Jif regularly. If he does, this information triggers the computer to produce a coupon good for, say, $1 off on a purchase of three jars of Jif. For a different customer, who buys Jif only occasionally, the computer generates a coupon for 50 cents off one jar of Jif in order to increase the customer's frequency and volume of purchases. A third customer comes along and buys Peter Pan peanut butter. If the computer shows that this person never buys Jif, she will receive a coupon for $1 off one jar of Jif in order to motivate her to try Jif. The promotional incentive differs, depending on each person's brand-choice history. The fewer times the customer has bought Jif in the past, the greater is the incentive given to him or her to buy Jif the next time. The strategy, which works for any commodity product, might be summarized as follows:

"Loyal customer" receives $1 off three.
"Switcher" receives 50 cents off one.
"Competitive buyer" receives $1 off one.

Catalina's computer keeps a history of everyone who uses a store card or charge card. This system can also be used for cross-promoting, such as giving a buyer of peanut butter a coupon for a particular brand of jelly.

Think About It

What is a segment of one? Why would a company want to target such a tiny market?

---

these efforts. When Kellogg reduces the price of its brands aimed at children, General Mills soon responds with similar price reductions.

Building Customer Databases and Increasing Customer Retention

Companies that know who their current customers are can use promotions to build databases with customer-contact information. They can then plan programs to reward and retain customers, particularly the most profitable ones. One brokerage firm, for example, sends gifts of exotic candy and prime-cut steaks to customers at year-end; the more trading customers have done during the year, the more expensive are the thank-you premiums they receive. The IMC in Action box describes how supermarkets are using their database information to target promotions to individual customers—known as "segments of one."

Cross-Selling and Extending the Use of a Brand

Cross-selling encourages current customers to try additional goods or services provided by a company (Chapter 7). Because customers already are familiar with the brand and trust it enough to make repeat purchases, selling them on other products under the same brand or made by the same company can be more cost-effective than selling to those unfamiliar with the brand.

Promotions also can be used to extend the use of a brand. An example of a promotional strategy designed to extend a product's uses comes from Nabisco's Grey Poupon mustard. The brand moved from its high-profile "Pardon me" advertising campaign featuring its Rolls-Royce cars and hoity-toity passengers, to a promotional campaign that positions the spicy mustard not just for sandwiches but as a cooking ingredient. Through a coupon redemption program, Nabisco offered promotional products such as measuring spoons and recipe books.[2]

Reinforcing the Brand Image and Strengthening Brand Relationships

Although sales promotions by design add something extra to a brand offering, what is added should not only be compatible with the brand's image but also reinforce that image (see Exhibit 14-3). The Snapple yard sale used goofy animations of bottles to reflect the quirky brand personality that Snapple wants to associate with its brand image. Members of frequent-flyer programs are rewarded on the basis of miles traveled; and the more they travel, the more special they are made to feel. Major airlines, for example, give their frequent flyers a special toll-free number to call for reservations and flight information. Callers to this number are very seldom placed on hold.

How do McDonald's promotions reinforce the image that McDonald's is a kid-friendly place? One way is by offering figurines from the latest Disney movie. One of McDonald's most successful image-building promotions has been its Teenie Beanies offer (small versions of the popular plush toys). Some restaurant owners found eager customers lined up at 5:30 A.M. waiting for the store to open. Many McDonald's restaurants had to set up voice-mail systems to handle inquiries from customers wanting to know which of the toys were available in a particular week.

Sales-Promotion Tools

Many sales-promotion tools exist to accomplish the objectives just described. Table 14-2 indicates the relative use by showing the total spending by U.S. companies on the most widely used consumer sales promotion tools. Notice that price reduction is not included in the table. Although price reduction represents a significant amount of promotional spending, it is impossible to capture industry data for it because of the many different ways in which price reductions are made. Also keep in mind that the allocations in the table should not be interpreted as indicators of how an average company allocates its consumer sales promotion spending; these numbers are national totals.

Each of the major promotion tools is explained in this section. Although these tools are used primarily for consumer promotions, some are also adapted for B2B marketing.

Premiums

In the context of sales promotion, a **premium** is *an item offered free or at a bargain price to reward some type of behavior such as buying, sampling, or testing.* The most effective premiums are those that are instantly available, such as a free toothbrush attached to a type of toothpaste. Premiums can improve a brand's image, gain goodwill, broaden the customer base (by attracting new customers), produce an immediate increase in sales, and reward customers. A premium may be included in the product's package (in-pack

TABLE 14-2   Consumer Sales Promotion Spending, 2002

Promotional Segment	Billions of Dollars	Percentage
Premiums and specialties	$44.1	55%
POP displays	15.5	19
Coupons	6.8	8
Specialty printing	5.8	7
Fulfillment	3.7	5
Internet marketing	1.7	2
Games, contests, sweepstakes	1.8	2
Product sampling	1.3	2
Total	$80.7	100%

Source: Consumer Sales Promotion Spending; Adapted from Promotions Trend Report *PROMO Magazine* supplement, April 2003. © 2003, PRIMEDIA Business Magazines & Media, Inc. All rights reserved.

premium), placed visibly on the package (on-pack premium), handed out in a store or at an event, or sent by mail.

Two major challenges posed by premiums are (1) finding ones that a high percentage of a target audience would want and (2) finding ones that can reinforce a product's brand image. When Starbucks offers a free coffee mug after ten purchases, it wisely includes the chain's logo on the mug as a brand reminder. Because most people enjoy having more than one mug, this offer is motivating, and because the Starbucks mugs are of high quality and contain the Starbucks logo, they reinforce the brand image.

Two types of premiums are often used—consumables and collectibles. Each of them foster customers' desire for more than one. **Consumables** are *products that have a one-time use,* such as movie tickets, gasoline, food, and beverages. **Collectibles** are *items of which consumers enjoy having two or more.* Fast-food chains like to have promotional tie-ins with movies whose main characters can be reproduced in figurines that children (and some adults) eagerly collect. Items for which customers enjoy having many variations, such as caps, T-shirts, and cups, are similar to collectibles and thus also widely used.

Premiums that can be made unique to a brand can also be attractive to customers. One example is a toy replica of a NASCAR race car sponsored by M&Ms. Although miniature toy cars are widely available in stores, the M&M-sponsored car is not (because M&M and NASCAR control the use of that particular car's reproduction).

The cost of a premium should be relatively low compared to the price of the product for which it is being used. If a premium costs as much as the product being sold, the company will lose money on every sale. That is why fast-food chains, such as Burger King, whose average size order is around $5, use premiums that cost less than 50 cents each.

Free is the most powerful sales-promotion word a company can use. Who doesn't like getting something for nothing? When a premium is being given away, the word *free* is strongly emphasized; it not only attracts attention to the brand message but is also a powerful motivator. The premium is only "free," however, when the item it is supporting is purchased (generally at full price).

Selecting the right premium—one that consumers value, is cost-effective, and supports the brand's image— is a challenge. When choosing a premium, marketers should ask themselves the following questions:[3]

1. Does the premium have appeal for the majority of the target audience?

2. Does it have a perceived value?

3. Is it relevant to the product, brand image, or campaign idea?

4. Will customers and the trade easily recognize its value and application?

5. Will it create an immediate behavioral response?

6. Is it a consumable or a collectible (so customers will be attracted even though they already have one or more)?

7. Does it fit into the seasonal/promotional period?

8. Does it have any safety/health concerns?

9. Can it be ordered and quickly reordered in limited quantities (to avoid unused inventories) that are still cost-effective?

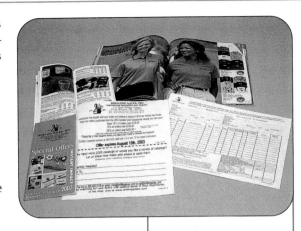

EXHIBIT 14-4
Companies that sell products to be used as specialties promote their products in catalogs and other sales literature.

Specialties

Specialty items do not require any specific behavior. **Specialties** are *items given free to customers and other stakeholders to help keep a brand's name top-of-mind.* Unlike with premiums, no purchase is necessary to get a specialty item. Specialties are generally low-cost items such as calendars, rulers, coffee mugs, T-shirts, and pens (see Exhibit 14-4). B2B marketers may give more costly items, however, such as desk sets, cellular telephones, briefcases, CD players, and watches, to executives or other representatives with whom the company has a relationship.

Spending in the promotional-products category of specialties and premiums is now over $15 billion a year, more than is spent on consumer magazine advertising. All types of businesses, including nonprofit organizations, use specialties for occasions ranging from launching new products and opening new facilities (where creating a new customer base is an important objective), to rewarding current customers and reminding prospects of the brand.

The rationale for using specialty items is the belief that people will think more positively about a brand that gives them something of value—the more added value, the greater the impact. Also, because most specialty items are tangible, recipients are exposed to the brand name multiple times (for example, every time they look at the calendar or drink from the coffee mug), and that exposure helps to keep the brand top-of-mind.

Coupons

A **coupon** is *a certificate with a stated price reduction on a specified item.* Coupons can be used for price reductions or for other merchandise. For example, for some seventy years, General Mills has promoted a Betty Crocker coupon program that permits customers to redeem coupons for a variety of cooking-related merchandise.

Today, over 300 billion coupons are distributed every year in the United States, but only about 2 percent of these are ever redeemed. Coupons have to be distributed through some medium—newspapers or magazines, packages, in-store displays, or direct mail (see Exhibit 14-5). Many reach consumers through colorful **freestanding inserts (FSIs),** which are *newspaper supplements that contain ads, most*

EXHIBIT 14-5

This ad seeks to engage the customer in a taste test. To motivate people to participate by trying Diet Dr Pepper, it includes a coupon for a free two-liter bottle. Note, however, the emphasis on the brand, which is another important objective of this sales-promotion ad.

with coupons. FSIs (← Chapter 11) have a slightly higher redemption rate than regular newspaper and magazine coupons, but coupons on or in packages have the highest redemption levels. Why? They are going to customers of the brand.

Electronic coupons are high-tech coupons distributed instore and online. Online coupons are issued by both individual companies and coupon distribution sites such as Cool Savings (www.coolsavings.com). This site requires that you register and provide a profile of yourself; then it shows you a checklist of lifestyle categories. The company sends coupon offers to you according to the categories you check off. Because customers opt-in and receive offers tailored to their profiles and interests, those coupons are redeemed at a higher rate than are the coupons distributed in newspapers and magazines. Other electronic coupon sites include www. 100hotcoupons.com, www.dealcatcher.com, www.ultimate coupons.com, and www.nocouponclipping.com.

The redemption rate of downloaded coupons is 56 percent, far greater than the average media-delivered coupon rate of 1 to 2 percent. The reason for the high rate of redemption is that customers go to the trouble to get these coupons for products they want to buy.[4] This high redemption rate suggests that companies should try to acquire the names of persons using these coupons and to make sure that the company is not simply discounting sales to current customers.

In-store coupon distribution is handled in several ways: interactive touch-screen video kiosks at the point of purchase, coupons dispensed as a customer walks up to a certain product category, and instant-print coupons issued at the cash register while the customer is checking out as explained earlier in this chapter.

Price Reductions

Short-term price reductions come in various forms: a featured price that is lower than the regular price, on-pack coupons, free goods ("buy one, get one free"), and enlarged packages ("30 more for same price"). Most price reductions are made to "featured brands," which retailers advertise each week to attract shoppers. These items are generally emphasized in a store's local ad, direct-mail flyers, or TV spots. When retailers receive trade promotion allowances (discussed in the next chapter), they generally pass the savings on to customers in the form of price reductions. Sometimes, the retailer even sacrifices some of its own profit margin in order to offer an even lower price on a few featured brands. For a lower price to have meaning, however, it is important that a brand not be price-featured too frequently. For packaged goods, generally featuring a brand not more than one week in every three months will maintain the brand's reference (regular) price.

Another form of price reduction is reduced or extended credit. This incentive is often used with high-priced items such as appliances, furniture, and cars. Typical offers are "No payment till next year" and "Only 0.9% interest." When customers have a strong desire and their only barrier is money, extended-credit offers can be powerful incentives.

When companies advertise price reductions, *how* they do it can send a message about the company. Sometimes the message is in support of a brand strategy, as in the reduced-price offer used for Gillette's launch of the Mach3 razor (see Exhibit 14-6). At other times the price message may undercut or tarnish the brand.

E X H I B I T 1 4 - 6
This brochure announced the launch of the Mach3 razor. To encourage trial, Gillette offered $3 off the price of the razor.

Although the objective is to maximize the return on promotional programs, there are limits to what a company should do in "creatively" announcing these offers. Where the limits are set is often more a question of ethics and relationship building than of what legally can be said. What is your reaction to the offers made in the Ethics and Issues box?

Rebates

Some companies offer customers cash refunds known as **rebates,** which are *a type of price reduction.* Rebates are commonly offered for such items as clothing or household appliances. Large rebates, like those given on cars, are handled by the seller. To receive small rebates, like those given for coffeemakers, the consumer must send the manufacturer proof of purchase (a receipt and a bar-code label) and a completed rebate form. Many people purchase a product because of an advertised rebate but never collect the rebate because they either forget about it or lose the rebate form or the sales receipt. Failure to take advantage of rebates is called *slippage* and is the reason why marketers can offer high-value rebates: people who do not take advantage of the offer essentially cover the costs of those who do. Yet slippage has also led to a decrease in the motivating power of rebates (customers aren't interested in an offer when they feel that getting the rebate is too much trouble).

Sampling

An especially powerful pull strategy, **sampling** consists of *offering prospects the opportunity to try a product before making a buying decision.* Sampling is usually targeted using selected mailing lists or carried out in stores or at events. One of the most costly of all sales promotions, sampling is nonetheless one of the most effective. The proposition is a powerful one: a brand is so good that once people try it they will want to buy it. Sampling offers the greatest credibility of all MC functions because it is based on the product's performance and can instantly move a nonuser to become a customer—if the product lives up to the expectation that has been created for it (see Exhibit 14-7). Sampling is most successful when a product is perceivably different from the competition. Research has

E X H I B I T 1 4 - 7
To launch ThermaCare, a new line of therapeutic heat wraps, marketers mailed the product to homes as a free sample along with a small brochure that explained how it works and the relief that users might expect. This expensive strategy was designed to build credibility and conviction by demonstrating the product's benefits.

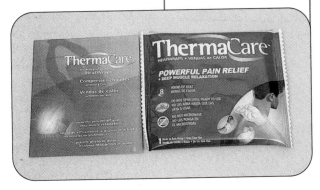

ETHICS AND ISSUES

Creative or Misleading?

With the overall objective of making offers that are perceived as high value but are of minimal cost to marketers, sales promotions sometimes cross ethical boundaries. How ethical do you think each of the following promotional offers is?

1. **"1/2 Price Sale"**: In fine print, the ad says that a customer who buys one pair of shoes at full price can get a second pair of equal or lesser value for half price. Is the headline offer misleading even though the small type explains how the sale works?

2. **End-aisle display of a brand at the regular price**: Shoppers have been conditioned to perceive that products on an end-aisle display are priced below their normal price. Would it be unethical for a retailer to use such a display but price the brand at its regular price?

3. **"Save up to 70%"**: Department stores often run promotions with this headline. The reality is, however, that only a few racks of clothes have been reduced 70 percent; most items that are on sale have been reduced only 20 to 30 percent.

4. **"Fly to NYC for only $149"**: The small print says this price is for a one-way fare and a round-trip

must be purchased in order to get this price. So the cost is actually $298 even if you only want to fly one-way.

5. **"Round Trip to NYC only $299**"**: Another typical airline promotional offer is the low-priced round-trip with a small-print** caveat—limited seats available at this price. The airline is selling only 10 seats on selected flights to New York at this low price, and the rest of the seats are priced several hundred dollars more.

Think About It

Those offers are legal and used frequently. Even so, some consumers are confused and misled by these offers and feel cheated when they find out what the restrictions or conditions are. What is at stake is the trust and respect of customers. Many companies track brand awareness and trial, but few track image and trust. What can a company that uses these types of promotional come-ons do to monitor the damage that might be done to the company's image?

found that the strategy seems to work better with women (73 percent positive response) than with men (57 percent).[5]

Perfume marketers depend heavily on sampling to win customers. Most perfume counters have sampling bottles so users can try the various fragrances. In major department stores at holiday season, there may be as many as 30 competing new fragrance brands, and well-manicured saleswomen armed with spray bottles ask passers-by if they would like a sample spray. To encourage reluctant customers to permit themselves to be sprayed, sellers of Estèe Lauder's Black Cashmere offered hand massages as a promotional incentive for the sampling.[6] "Stink alley," as the perfume aisle is called in Manhattan's flagship Bloomingdale's store, is one place that many customers try to avoid. A more sensitive and less intrusive approach in some stores is to hand out scent cards.

Many in-store sampling programs are tied to a coupon campaign. Sometimes samples are distributed with related items (such as an on-pack sample of hair conditioner given free with the purchase of a shampoo), but this strategy limits distribution to people who buy the other product. A recent innovation in distribution is *polybagging*, hanging samples on doorknobs or delivering them in plastic bags along with the daily newspaper or a monthly magazine (see Exhibit 14-8).

In a practice similar to sampling, food and drug marketers use *combination offers,* such as a razor with a package of blades or a toothbrush with a tube of toothpaste, at a reduced price for the two. For best results, the items should be related. Sometimes, a combination offer may be used to introduce a new brand by tying its purchase to an established brand at a special price.

Sweepstakes, Contests, and Games

A **contest** is *a brand-sponsored competition that requires some form of skill and effort.* A **sweepstakes** is *a form of sales promotion that offers prizes based on a chance drawing of entrants' names.* Contests and sweepstakes gain attention for a brand message and increase store traffic by requiring those who wish to enter to pick up an entry blank at a store or dealership. To encourage a large number of entries, these types of sales promotion should be kept as simple as possible. By law, the prize structure must be clearly stated and rules clearly defined. Because contests, especially, require some effort, the response rate is extremely low. Furthermore, a portion of those who do respond may be "professional" contest entrants who care nothing about the brand sponsoring the contest. "Professional" contest entrants simply enter for the fun of participating and the chance to win. Although sweepstakes and contests don't generate a high rate of response, they are helpful in setting up customer databases (because entrants have to submit their names and addresses and often are asked to answer other questions).

A **game** is *a sales-promotion tool that has the chance element of a sweepstakes but is conducted over a longer time.* Grocery stores may design bingo-type games to build store traffic. The marketing advantage of a game is that customers must make repeat visits to the dealer to continue playing. Brand games have become popular tools to promote brands on the internet.

Sweepstakes, contests, and games all require careful planning and monitoring. Companies must abide by state and federal regulations. For example, although a company can *encourage* entrants to send in a proof of purchase, it cannot *require* a purchase as a condition for entry, because the sweepstakes would become a commercial lottery, which is illegal in most states. The law also requires that the odds of winning the sweepstakes be published on promotional materials.

Contests and sweepstakes must be advertised to be successful, and often they need dealer or retail support. Retailers must be encouraged to build special in-store displays to hold product, help announce a sweepstakes, and provide entry forms. In this way, sweepstakes are used to get off-shelf product display. Some contests and sweepstakes ask the entrant to name the product's local dealer so that the company may award prizes to the retailers who generate the most entries. This policy gives retailers extra incentive to promote the sweepstakes and the brand.

EXHIBIT 14-8
This is a plastic wrapper for delivering newspapers. The bottom contains a pouch in which a free Hallmark card is enclosed. The wrapper itself announces the new line of 99-cent Hallmark cards.

The Media of Consumer Sales Promotion

Every sales promotion needs a vehicle to carry it. It should be clear from the review of the different tools of sales promotion that companies use a broad range of ways to deliver promotional offers. Coupons, for example, appear in mass media advertising, in direct-mail pieces, on packages, and on the back of grocery sales receipts. Contests are announced in ads and at events. Samples are handed out in stores, but they are also mailed to homes and businesses.

Promote

Imagine a scenario where you're able to meet your sales and marketing objectives by making promotional offers tailored specifically to the consumers you want, when you want -- in manageable, measurable increments. Where you can offer prizes, points, premiums or product samples and keep track of the return on your marketing investment as you go.

Imagine being able to locate, identify, qualify and establish one-to-one relationships with a continuously replenished pool of customers, prospects and known category users. Where you can spark and maintain a running dialog with thousands of people ready, willing and able to buy your product because they've chosen to sign on and stay in touch.

Imagine, on a moment's notice, being able to start, stop or change your offer, where you can ramp it up or scale it back according to what's working and what's not. Where you can match the level of promotional activity to the ability of distributors and sales forces to keep up with demand.

To marketers whose experience pre-dates the Internet, this truly is a dream come true. But at Promotions.com -- Internet promotion experts and providers of online promotion solutions since 1996 – it's an everyday reality.

That Internet promotions are an idea whose time has come is underscored by the continued participation of such major marketing clients as Kraft Foods, NBC, The Sharper Image, the William Wrigley Jr. Company, World Wrestling Federation, Compaq Computer and many, many others.

They're discovering what respondents told Forrester Research for a recent special report: that Internet promotions are less expensive, more manageable and more effective---3 to 5 times more, in fact---than offline promotions.

Think about it: the effectiveness of a promotion, the precision of database marketing and the speed, economy, efficiency and measurability of Internet transactions. This win-win-win combo is why expenditures on Internet promotions are expected to grow to $14.4 billion a year by 2005, according to another Forrester Research report.

But don't take our word for it. See for yourself by checking out our Web site. We've designed an Internet promotion for brand, product, agency and account promotion managers just to help you get to know us. Simply log on, opt-in, dialog with us, check out a case history of your choice. You may even win a valuable prize in the process.

So take the first step. Log on to www.promotions.com/brandgame. Making dreams come true for your brand couldn't get any easier.

No purchase necessary. Void where prohibited. Game ends on 9/30/00. Game subject to complete official rules which can be found at www.promotions.com/brandgame. For a chance to win without playing online, hand print your name, complete address, daytime phone number, and email address on a 3 x 5 piece of paper and mail to: Promotions.com Instant Win Game, P.O. Box 5070, Elkoton, FL 34222-5000.

Email promos@promotions.com, Telephone 1-800-976-3831 x166, or visit our Web site at www.promotions.com.

> **Internet promotions are a marketer's dream come true.**
> -Steven H. Krein
> Founding Partner and CEO, Promotions.com
> steven.krein@promotions.com

OUR OPT-IN PRIVACY POLICY
Since its inception, Promotions.com has taken a leadership position in the adoption of a strict Opt-In Privacy Policy as a safeguard to consumer privacy. Full details, which are explicit and available to all respondents, can be found on our Web site, www.promotions.com.

PROMOTIONS.COM™
THE INTERNET PROMOTION EXPERTS

NASDAQ: PRMO © 2000 Promotions.com Inc. All rights reserved.

EXHIBIT 14-9

Internet promotion company Promotions.com explains in this ad how to create effective online promotions.

Many sales promotions, such as displays, are specially constructed and delivered by sales reps or distributors. Sales literature and manuals contain the information that sales reps need about the various types of allowances and discounts they are able to offer customers.

The internet is increasingly being used to deliver sales-promotion offers. Saturn used the internet effectively in its prelaunch efforts to target young buyers for its S-series cars. The automaker ran an online sweepstakes offering the target audience a chance to win a car and, in the process, gathered the names of more than 200,000 potential Saturn buyers.

Publishers Clearing House (PCH), famous for its multimillion-dollar direct-mail sweepstakes, has launched a Web company that represents an entirely new e-commerce business model. The company will leverage the promotion, marketing, and database resources of PCH to create a new customer experience. Site visitors will find a game-playing experience that exposes them to "winning deals" on a variety of merchandise and magazine offers. As site visitors play a game and become interested in brand offerings, they can simply click on the brand mentioned and find out more information and how to order. Because of the game involvement, visitors are motivated to stay at the site longer than they would stay at sites simply offering a catalog of products.

Likewise, packaged-goods marketers are developing free-sample sites that provide them with customer feedback, in addition to an opportunity for customers to try a new product. Two sites offering this service are FreeSamples.com and StartSampling.com. B2B marketer Promotions.com provides businesses with tools for running online promotions, as well as permission-based direct marketing and targeted e-mail campaigns (see Exhibit 14-9).

Promotional efforts are sneaking onto electronic shopping carts as well. A software program from iChoose Inc. searches its database of coupons and deals to find savings on the exact items customers put in their virtual shopping carts. Fickle shoppers can be teased away with the promise of a 10 percent saving or a cheaper shipping fee.[7]

DETERMINING CONSUMER SALES PROMOTION STRATEGIES

Because most consumer sales promotions can show a more direct impact on sales than does advertising, sales promotion has a tendency to be overused or misused. Some argue that sales promotions are simply a way to "buy sales" as opposed to convincing people that a brand is a good value and moving them strategically through a buying process. Marketers of Coke, Pepsi, P&G, and Nike have discovered that traditional retail support in the form of price promotions and coupons drives immediate sales but also can encourage consumers to buy on price—and therefore to switch brands as soon as a competing brand offers a better price. Marketers today are looking for ways to use promotions that will build brand equity, develop long-term customer loyalty, and drive store traffic without being overly dependent on price reductions just to get a short-term increase in sales.

Peter Breen, editor of *PROMO* magazine, stated that marketers need to "forget all that nonsense about consumer promotion being the ugly stepchild of advertising"[8] and focus on its strengths. To that end, the promotion industry is making efforts to become more strategic and less tactical—using promotions to build brands and move customers and prospects through the decision-making process, rather than just reducing the price to move more items (see Exhibit 14-10). As one marketer stated in responding to a survey on sales-promotion activities: "Increasingly, the gimmicks are gone. We must all step up to the challenge of adding real, brand-building value with promotions—the kind that sparks genuine consumer, retailer, and client interest."[9]

Driving Motivation through Partnership Strategies

The challenge is to develop sales-promotion strategies that motivate people to respond in ways identified in the objectives, and at the same time to maintain a commitment to the larger marketing objective of strengthening the brand's perceived value. Sales-promotion strategies use partnership programs, such as cross-promotion and tie-in promotions, to enhance the brand's value to consumers.

Tie-in promotions and cross-promotions are examples of strategies that marry two brands or products in order to enhance the image, and the sales, of both. By combining efforts, companies hope to increase customer response because both products share in the image power and attractiveness of two brands. They also share the costs, which make such arrangements good for both brands' budgets.

Cross promotion is *the promotion of two or more products together*, such as cheese and crackers. The difference between a cross-promotion and a combination offer (mentioned in the discussion of sampling) is that the two brands in a cross-promotion are not packaged together. To obtain the offered savings or premiums, customers must purchase both brands at the same time. This allows two brands to share promotional costs and benefit from each other's image. Exhibit 14-11 is an example of a different type of cross-promotion, one between CBS and Campbell Soup.

A **tie-in promotion** is *the linking of two products in advertising and in-store merchandising promotion*, such as promoting movies and their characters in fast-food restaurants. One of the largest promotional deals brought tie-in promotions for the three *Lord of the Rings* movies into 10,000 Burger King restaurants. Likewise, electronics marketer JVC signed a deal as the exclusive electronics sponsor for the trilogy. Co-branded DVD players and VCR packages by JVC are packaged with movie trailers and behind-the-scenes footage.[10]

Driving Retention through Loyalty Strategies

Sales promotion is one of the most powerful MC functions for helping retain customers and increasing a brand's share of customers' category spending. *Using promotions specifically designed for customer retention*

EXHIBIT 14-12

Marriott rewards its loyal frequent travelers with a variety of gifts, something for everyone (who gives Marriott a lot of business).

is called **loyalty (or frequency) marketing.** In a loyalty promotion, a company offers premiums or other incentives when a customer makes multiple purchases over time. The most simple of these is the coffee or gasoline punch card that allows a person a free coffee or a fill-up after a set number of purchases ("buy 10 and get the 11th one free").

A loyalty program represents a strategy for minimizing customer defections and increasing a brand's share of wallet (see Exhibit 14-12). United Airlines, for example, sends out free upgrades periodically to reward its "Premier Executives"—those who fly more than 50,000 miles a year on United. Retail stores often have exclusive showings and sales for their credit-card customers. Relationship marketing talks about moving beyond customer satisfaction and "delighting" customers, which can be done with the strategic use of sales promotions, such as United's upgrades.

Most loyalty programs have been built on discounts and impersonal gifts (toasters, fishing rods, golf clubs, dinnerware, jewelry). However, as Richard Barlow, former chairman and CEO of Frequency Marketing Inc. notes, after a decade of a hot economy, what people value now is not more stuff but more satisfying personal experiences.[11] Frequent-flyer programs are so successful because they translate into trips and memories, a phenomenon being described as "the experience economy."

How Loyalty Programs Work

Loyalty programs work best when brands have high fixed costs and low variable costs. Probably one of the best examples, again, is airlines.[12] When a plane goes from New York to London, the fixed costs associated with the trip are relatively high: gasoline, crew wages, amortized cost of the airplane, airport fees, and marketing costs. These costs are incurred on the trip even if the plane flies empty. The costs of adding additional passengers, therefore, are quite low: basically the cost of beverages and food given inflight to these additional passengers. Entertainment venues and cable and telephone companies are other types of businesses with high fixed and low variable costs. When such businesses have empty seats and extra capacity, providing their own product (trips, admissions, calls) free as a reward for being a loyal customer costs the brand relatively little. On the other hand, the customer perceives the reward as being of high value; thus, it is very motivational. In other words, unused services and goods become "promotional currency," which can be given to customers for being loyal.

This kind of deal can be a tiebreaker for customers trying to choose between competing brands. The average hotel, for example, sells only about 70 percent of its rooms each night. This means 30 percent of the rooms sit vacant. If these vacant rooms are used to reward customers, a company can greatly increase the impact of its sales-promotion programs with a minimal increase in its IMC budget.

Opportunities to join loyalty programs are delivered through mass media advertising, direct mail, and program literature at brand-contact points, such as airline counters. The Safeway brochure shown in Exhibit 14-13 announces the Safeway Club program for a Spanish-speaking audience. The e-commerce company RagingBull.com, which serves individual investors, wanted a way to retain and reward its loyal internet customer base. It turned to Perks.com, an internet business that provides loyalty programs for online customers, including an incentive-based website, a catalog of rewards, research, data tracking, customer profiling, and customer service.

The best loyalty programs are strategic—that is, they are designed to achieve a certain objective, and they contain an idea for doing so. Because a loyalty program is designed to retain customers and increase a customer's share of category spending, the first step is to determine why customers are leaving the brand or are not giving the brand more of their business. Suppose a bank finds that the major reason why customers are leaving is poor service. In this case, the bank should set up a loyalty program for employees rather than customers. Employees or branches of the bank can then be rewarded for reducing the percentage of closed accounts.

When the airlines found that most frequent flyers belonged to three or more frequent-flyer programs, they began providing larger rewards to those who flew the most. United Airlines, for example, gives its "Premier Executives" double rewards for all flights.

An example of good loyalty objective is "To increase average customer lifetime from 8 to 10 years" or "To decrease the defection rate to 5 percent or less." A rather useless objective would be "To begin a loyalty program." Clearly, a company must set standards for measurement and, more important, provide specific guidelines for what the loyalty program should be designed to do.

Managing a Loyalty Program

When beginning a loyalty program, a company must decide how customers become members. Will all those who make a purchase automatically become members, or do they need to sign up? Generally, having customers opt-in through their own effort ensures better results. Most of these types of programs require prospective members to fill out an application form that asks for customer-profile information. This information becomes valuable not only to employees managing the loyalty program but also to those in sales, those managing direct-response programs, and those in customer service.

Once a program is up and running, a company must be sensitive to how many brand messages it sends to members. Loyalty programs that become intrusive and too aggressive in selling and cross-selling can be counterproductive because customers come to resent being pestered. The primary way to determine when this line is crossed is by listening to customers and asking for their feedback about the amount of brand messages they are receiving. Asking customers up front what product lines and types of brand information they are interested in receiving can also minimize negative effects.

Minimizing the cost of running a loyalty program is critical. Although an airline may use empty seats for rewards, it must ensure that it does not give away seats during periods of heavy demand. Movie theaters often restrict the use of free passes to weeknights and weekend matinees. Similarly, rewards should be designed to increase sales. A free movie pass may be good only when used along with a purchased ticket.

Large companies such as P&G and Kraft Foods create their own multibrand loyalty programs; smaller companies with only one or two brands may not be able

¡Hágase Miembro del Club Safeway Instantáneamente!

SAFEWAY CLUB

Inscríbase Ahora. ¡Empiece a Ahorrar Hoy Mismo!

Ahora los Ahorros están en la Tarjeta

EXHIBIT 14-13
Targeted to a Hispanic audience, this brochure, available at the checkout counter, explains in Spanish how the Safeway Club card program works.

to afford to do so. However, smaller brands can join www.upromise.com, which is a multibrand loyalty program. Smaller brands benefit by being part of a group of brands that is sufficient in size to build and maintain awareness of the loyalty program.

A loyalty program strategy should be set up so that customers remain in the program even after they redeem a reward. Rewards that are given out should have an expiration date, because outstanding rewards are a financial liability. Also, when a loyalty program is designed, a company should have an "exit strategy"—how it will end the program if it is not profitable or no longer fits into the brand's overall marketing strategy. More than almost anything else a marketing communication program does, a loyalty program sets specific expectations for its customers. A company should consider how these expectations can be changed when it's time for the program to end.

Strengths and Weaknesses of Loyalty Programs

The main strength of a loyalty program is increased customer retention. This not only boosts sales but also lowers selling costs because selling to current customers requires less MC spending (Chapter 3). A related benefit is the customer-profile information that loyalty programs generate. Another benefit is that a good loyalty promotion can help differentiate a brand. Differentiation is especially important in a commodity category, where so many brands are similar in performance and price that customers must look hard to find differences among them. A reward for loyalty may be the only thing that sets one brand apart from another. Rewards make customers feel good, and this feeling can motivate them to become brand ambassadors and to make brand referrals.

> "SkyMiles is an affinity brand that insulates and protects Delta from consumer wrath and brand defections."
>
> Mike Capizzi, "Insulating the Brand"

Rewards can also overcome negative experiences. Even though flying, for example, is often trying (late flights, lost luggage), customers who have had bad experiences keep coming back to their chosen airline because it offers free miles. Mike Capizzi, in an editorial in the loyalty program magazine *Colloquy*, pointed to "the ability of a well-designed loyalty program to shield the core brand from a negative experience."[13]

Limitations of loyalty programs are that they can overshadow the brand and managing and running them require more resources than do other forms of marketing communication used by the brand. Also, it's difficult to determine whether such programs are truly cost-effective, especially when competitors offer similar programs. Do they cost more to administer than they are worth in increased revenue? Many companies do not have a clear answer to this question.

Strengths and Limitations of Sales Promotion Overall

The earlier discussion of sales-promotion objectives identified the primary strengths of consumer sales promotions as driving sales (increasing trial and repurchase, increasing frequency and quantity of purchase, cross-selling, and extending the uses of a brand), strengthening customer relationships, and reinforcing brand image. Sales promotion clearly has value in a marketing mix; but, of course, it also has limitations.

Although sales promotions can increase sales, the critical decision of whether to use promotions should be based on their cost-effectiveness. Using a process called **payout planning** or **breakeven analysis** (see Exhibit 14-14; also Chapter 6), planners can evaluate the costs of sales promotions versus the revenue they

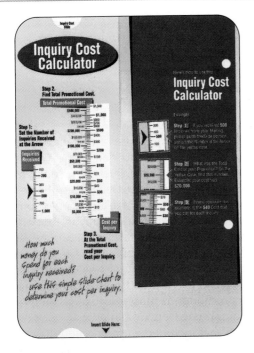 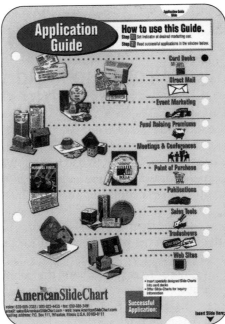

EXHIBIT 14-14

*This Inquiry Cost
Calculator is designed to
give planners a quick
estimate of the cost of a
promotion versus the
revenue returned. The
estimate is based on the
number of responses or
inquiries that the promotion
generates.*

generate. In many cases, promotions are not cost-effective, although they may deliver on other objectives, such as raising the visibility of the brand. One analysis showed that only 16 percent of customer promotions were profitable. In other words, in 84 percent of the promotions, companies spent more than $1 to generate an extra $1 of profits.

Sales promotions are sometimes criticized for attracting customers who are searching for the best deal, not for a long-term brand relationship. These are customers who always try to buy what is on sale and are not loyal to any brand. In automotive marketing, for example, companies have had mixed experiences with online promotions that have brought masses of unqualified consumers into dealerships to enter sweepstakes and win prizes. Once again, targeting is a critical element.

Another limitation of sales promotion is that as soon as one brand in a category has a successful program, competitors soon follow suit. This copycatting usually negates the added-value advantage and transforms the cost of the program into just another cost of doing business. Another concern is that overuse of promotional offers will negatively reposition the brand. A brand that is always on sale or always offering premiums will soon be known as the "price brand" or "deal brand," an image that most brands don't want to have. Most companies limit discounts, not only to protect the profitability of the brand but also to protect the retail price. In the soft-drink category, because Coke and Pepsi frequently run sales of 99 cents or less for a two-liter bottle, many customers refuse to buy until the price is reduced to this level (and then they stock up). For these people, 99 cents has become the regular price.

Two challenges for loyalty programs are keeping an accurate accounting of customer rewards and managing their disbursement. These programs can become so much a part of a brand's offering that if there is a problem with the reward program, the brand relationship can be weakened by the very program that was designed to strengthen it.

Targeting promotional offers is a sound strategy, but it needs to be done in a way that does not anger some customers. For example, in an attempt to attract new customers, some companies, such as Sprint, have offered $50 off to new subscribers. This strategy can attract new customers, but current customers who were never offered this value may feel cheated. When these kinds of new-customer offers are made, it is best to use personalized media so that only noncustomers are exposed to the offers.

Sales Promotion and the Marketing Communication Mix

For a decade, advertising and sales promotion have engaged in a budget battle, and marketing managers and academics have struggled to determine which works best and when to use various MC mixes. A seven-year study by Procter & Gamble, for example, found that price deals and coupons increased penetration—the number of people buying the brand—but had less effect on customer retention. According to the study, advertising also increased penetration, but its impact was weaker than the sales-promotion tools. The study also found that although advertising was more beneficial for small brands, large brands benefited more from promotion.[14]

As more is learned about the relative merits of various types of marketing communication, it remains clear that sales promotion is most effective when it is integrated into the overall marketing program. When General Motors launched its new Aurora model, it used an IMC program that included a direct-mail effort to invite luxury-car owners in 10 cities to events where they could drive and compare the Aurora with Lexus, Infiniti, and Mercedes models. The promotion brought dealers together on one day and consumers together on the next. The auto manufacturer's lead agency, Leo Burnett, worked closely with Frankel & Company, a sales-promotion agency, to manage all of the promotional activities involved with this launch as well as the anniversary festivities.

One of the major challenges of integrated marketing communication is to get the MC mix right. On the one hand, if too much of the communication mix is allocated to advertising, the brand may gain a high-quality, differentiated image but not enough volume to be a market leader. On the other hand, as Larry Light, Director of Marketing for McDonald's, says, "Too much promotion, and the brand will have high volume but low profitability."[15] Some say that a decline in brand loyalty has been the result of increased sales-promotion spending, which has conditioned customers to focus more on prices than on brands and thus become less loyal. It is possible, however, to use sales promotion effectively to build a brand and reinforce its image, as Exhibit 14-15 demonstrates.

What is the appropriate balance between sales promotion and brand-building functions such as media advertising and publicity? Extensive research by the Coalition for Brand Equity shows that overemphasis of sales promotions has a negative impact on a brand. The coalition compiled the following findings:[16]

1. Excessive promotion at the expense of advertising may hurt profits. In the consumer packaged-goods field, experts caution that trade and consumer promotion should not exceed 60 percent of the marketing communication budget. (This can vary from category to category.)

2. A higher ratio of advertising (relative to sales promotion) typically increases profits.

3. A high level of trade and consumer promotion, relative to advertising, has a positive effect on short-term market share but a negative effect on brand attitudes and long-term market share.

EXHIBIT 14-15

This promotion for the Millstone brand of whole-bean coffee is contained in a direct-mail piece sent to the home. It includes a brochure describing the brand's various coffee lines, a sign-up card to receive a free monthly electronic newsletter containing recipes and tips, and a coffee bag with a coupon worth one dollar.

4. Without an effective advertising effort to emphasize brand image and quality, customers become deal-prone rather than brand-loyal.

5. Overemphasis on low prices eventually destroys brand equity.

PACKAGING: THE LAST AD SEEN

The retail environment is a critical brand touch point that delivers brand messages to consumers about package goods and service offerings, not only through sales-promotion efforts but also through product packaging. It is estimated that 60 to 70 percent of brand decisions about packaged goods are not made until consumers are inside retail stores. Thus MC programs that reach consumers and drive them into stores have a direct impact on sales only when the two come together in the place where customers make brand decisions. The package delivers the final message that brings the entire message-and-response process to completion.

As the self-service concept in retailing has expanded, the package has become a particularly important brand message for consumer brands—in effect, replacing the salesperson. As shoppers move through heavily stocked stores, they scan shelves at the rate of 300 items a minute. Amid all this clutter, a package's job is to attract attention and communicate brand information (see Exhibit 14-16).

Packaging is not only the last message but also an important part of a brand's identity, particularly for **consumer packaged goods,** which are *products that are usually sold in food, discount, and drug stores in small packages and have a low unit price.* Outside the United States, these are often referred to as **fast-moving consumer goods (FMCGs).** These products are purchased frequently, and their brand identity is conveyed by their packages or labels. In fact, the package is often the only brand message that distinguishes a branded product from a generic one.

A great example of **proprietary packaging** (*a package design that is patented to prevent any other brand from using it*) is the hourglass shape of the Coca-Cola bottle. It took Coke years to figure out how to replicate this shape in plastic. As a result of that success, Coke introduced a 20-ounce contour plastic bottle. Now it is working on a design for a 20-ounce plastic cup in clear or green plastic, in the famous hourglass shape, that will compete with Pepsi's popular Twist 'n Go cup.[17]

A package is, first of all, a container. But it is more than that. A package delivers a complex message about the product category and the brand's selling points, as well as the brand's identity and image. Just as a store's design sends a strong message about the store, the design and labels on a package communicate important messages about the product it contains. A package is an intrinsic brand message.

EXHIBIT 14-16
In the highly competitive cereal market, marketers rely on the design of their packages to make their brands visible and easy to find.

A person cannot buy (in the store) or use (in the home or workplace) a packaged product without coming into contact with the package. A package, in other words, is a medium for carrying a company-created brand message.

Like merchandising and point-of-purchase materials, a package plays a critical role in brand decision making at the point of sale. There are close links between merchandising and packaging, for both add to, or subtract from, the experience that surrounds a purchase decision.

Objectives of Packaging

An important responsibility of package design is to link the product to other brand messages to which the customer has been exposed. One way to do this is through the use of flags on the front of the package that call attention to product features and present reminder messages that tie in with other MC efforts, such as advertising campaigns and special promotional offers.

Brand-message transfer is strongest when package designers make sure the package is shown in all packaged-goods advertising so that customers know what to look for. Message transfer is also conveyed through the stylistics of the package's artwork. Celestial Seasonings' packaging, for example, uses delicate illustrations, soft colors, and quotations about life to reinforce the product's positioning as a New Age, natural, herbal tea (◄ Exhibit 10-16).

In addition to establishing brand-identity links, package design has specific attention-getting objectives. To determine which colors, typography, and layout styles will attract the attention of busy shoppers, package designers study which items consumers notice and which ones they actually place in their shopping carts. One of the biggest success stories in packaging has been Pepsi's 32-ounce Twist 'n Go container, introduced in 1999. It is spill-resistant, resealable, and designed to fit most car cup holders.

Although packages are most often thought of in conjunction with consumer packaged goods, the packaging concept also applies to services. The service "package" is the environment in which a service is delivered. How many times have you based the selection or rejection of a restaurant on its exterior or interior appearance? Likewise, the uniforms worn by and the vehicles driven by service personnel operating away from their place of business are elements of the service "package."

The Package Is a Free Medium

Although seldom discussed as such, packaging is a major communication vehicle that companies can use to deliver whatever brand message they wish. Unfortunately, many manufacturers of packaged goods still consider a package only as a container. If you think of a package as a communication opportunity, however, the media cost is zero because the package is "already there."

The number of people who walk down food store, drugstore, and mass merchandiser aisles everyday is in the millions—far more than the number who watch an average prime-time TV show. What this means is that a brand's package is like a miniature outdoor board with millions of potential exposures each day. Pepperidge Farm understands this billboarding function and masses its packages to create easy recognition and visual impact.

Companies that fail to make their packages attention getting and appealing miss a communication opportunity. The design cost to improve and modernize a package label, when spread over millions of exposures, not to mention purchases, is one of the best bargains in marketing communication. A good company is a company that produced a line of thin-sliced lunchmeat that was sold in four-ounce plastic pouches. Because this line of six different meats had sales of only

$25 million a year, the company could not cost-justify producing and running print or broadcast advertising for the line. The fact that it carried the corporate brand name, as did all the other 150 different products, was the only MC support the line had, which is why its sales increases were minimal year after year. Then, working with a packaging design firm and spending less than $100,000, the company redesigned the packaging, giving the line much more attention-getting power and appetite appeal. The result was a nearly $7 million increase in sales (a 27 percent increase) the first year after the new package was introduced. The return on the investment (ROI) paid for the cost of the redesign many, many times over.

New technology is bringing innovations to packaging, as well. An Israeli company, Power Paper, is using an ultra-thin flexible battery that can be "printed" on a package like ink to add attention-getting features like music on a compact disc or a tiny video demonstration on a technical product. Such packaging innovations can be educational, as well as attention getting.[18]

The fact that the package is the last brand message that a prospective customer sees before making a brand choice is another strong reason for making package design an important part of an IMC program. This is particularly true for brands and product lines that have little or no other marketing communication support. Techniques like hangtags are used to provide an additional on-product advertisement.

Strengths and Limitations of Packaging

Packages both protect a product and facilitate its transport. But beyond those functional objectives, packages can also be used to make a strong visual statement that brings the brand personality to life, ties in with other marketing communication efforts, and delivers low-cost brand information and reminders in the critical "buy zone" in a store. Furthermore, a package continues to communicate after the buyer leaves the store. The package can provide important decision information, such as nutrition facts, product claims like "caffeine free," and additional information about the product (see Exhibit 14-17). It can also showcase promotions with flags like "Official sponsor of the Olympics," or "Free toy inside."

Sometimes the package itself can be a source of added value, particularly when it is designed for convenience. Aseptic juice packages—juice boxes—for example, created an entirely new category in the beverage market because they are not only portable and lightweight but don't have to be refrigerated. Bottles with a special nondrip spout provide added value for products like syrup and laundry detergent. Packages can even function as a premium when they become collectibles, such as Avon bottles, special holiday liquor bottles, and designer cans used to package teas, cookies, or crackers.

One limitation of packaging is that it is subject to copycat marketing. Suave, for example, is a brand whose positioning strategy is to market copycat products at low prices. The brand's position is signaled by its packaging. Suave's Performance shampoo is similar to Pantene's Pro-V shampoo, which comes in a pale pearlescent bottle. Suave's Fruit Energy line is similar to L'Oréal SA's Garnier Fructis line, which comes in a bright green bottle. For its new products, Suave systematically creates what it calls a "microcosm" of a new hot product, which includes a similar package and similar ingredients.[19]

The biggest weakness of packaging is its potential for clogging up landfills. The long box often used to package CDs is one example of what many consider to be overpackaging. The aseptic beverage box used for milk and juices turned out to

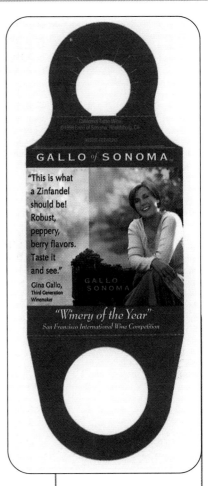

EXHIBIT 14-17
Tags like this can be used to add information to the product's packaging. This tag explains a type of wine and uses a representative of the wine-making family as an authority figure to establish credibility for the brand.

be a nightmare for environmentalists because the thin layers of paper and plastic and the aluminum-foil lining are hard to separate. A number of companies are redesigning their packages in order to make them more disposable. Carnation has converted its pet food cans to recyclable aluminum. Heinz has replaced its perennial dump filler, the squeezable ketchup bottle, with a bottle that can be more easily recycled.

A FINAL NOTE: THE POWER OF CREATIVITY

All areas of sales promotion and packaging use creativity to deliver their messages. People working in sales promotion (who admittedly are biased) say it is the most inventive area in all of marketing communication. One company, for example, mailed pieces of a short-wave radio to engineers with instructions on how to assemble the gadget. Once the engineers received their last piece, they were told where to tune in to receive the promotional message. The promotion was highly effective because the engineers were so intrigued by the inventiveness of the idea.

Today's customers, both consumer and B2B, are extremely value conscious. Therefore, when a brand has a tangible added value (cents off, a premium, a rebate), it helps call attention to the brand and also provides an extra reason to choose that brand. The same is true of packaging. The more value added it offers—through appearance, functionality, or reusability—the more influence it will have on the brand decision-making process.

Key Terms

breakeven analysis 478
collectibles 468
consumables 468
consumer packaged goods 481
contest 473
coupon 469
cross-promotion 475
fast-moving consumer goods (FMCGs) 481

freestanding inserts (FSIs) 469
frequency marketing 476
game 473
loyalty marketing 476
payout planning 478
premium 467
proprietary packaging 481
pull strategy 463
push strategy 464

rebate 471
sales promotion 463
sampling 471
specialties 469
sweepstakes 473
tie-in promotion 475

Key Point Summary

Key Point 1: Consumer Sales Promotions

Consumer sales promotions add incentives to buy or participate, accelerating a product's movement from producer to consumer. Sales promotion drives an immediate response by adding something to the offer that is of tangible value to the consumer, such as lower price, a premium, or a specialty advertising gift.

Key Point 2: How Consumer Sales Promotion Works

Consumer sales promotion, often part of a pull strategy, adds value to a transaction by motivating a response in the "buy zone"—that critical point at which consumers are considering a purchase. Marketers use loyalty programs to retain customers and increase the brand's share of wallet. Limitations of loyalty programs include lowering the value of the brand, attracting customers who are interested only in a deal, and fostering a dependence on a lower price and thus negatively repositioning the brand on a price image.

Key Point 3: Packaging

More than a container, a package is a communication vehicle that delivers a complex brand message (identification cues, image, and selling points), ties in with other marketing communication, and delivers low-cost reminder information about a brand.

Lessons Learned

Key Point 1: Consumer Sales Promotion

a. Why is sales promotion referred to as a sales accelerator? Give examples of how sales promotion might work at different points in a consumer's brand decision making.
b. List at least three objectives that you might have in designing a consumer sales promotion program.
c. Do an aisle check in your favorite drugstore. What products could profit most by identifying segments of one?
d. Define *sales promotion*. Explain how sales promotion adds value to a brand offering.
e. How do coupons and rebates differ?
f. How do sweepstakes and contests differ? Find an example of one or the other, and explain how it works.
g. How do specialties deliver brand-reminder messages?
h. How many different sales-promotion tools and techniques does Snapple use in promoting its brand and beverage? Create a list of the brand's promotional efforts that you find on the Snapple website, www.snapple.com.

Key Point 2: How Consumer Sales Promotion Works

a. What are the key strengths and limitations of consumer sales promotions?
b. Explain how cross-promotions and tie-ins work. Why are they used?
c. Find a cross-promotion involving a movie. Explain why the two brands are in partnership and what they gain from the partnership. In your estimate, is the partnership effective?
d. How do loyalty programs work? What objectives do they accomplish?
e. What are the strengths and limitations of loyalty programs?
f. Loyalty programs work best when a brand has high fixed costs and low variable costs. Explain what that statement means.
g. Check your medicine cabinet, and pick one of your favorite products. How many different sales promotions can you identify as being used in support of this product? Consider not only the product's package but also any other marketing communication you can find that promotes this brand.

Key Point 3: Packaging

a. What communication functions does a package perform?
b. What does it mean to say that packages have a billboard function?
c. Visit your local grocery store, and identify the brand that has the most "shelf facings" (packages that face you as you stand in the aisle). Explain how this brand benefits from the billboard effect.
d. What are the key strengths and limitations of packaging design?
e. List and explain at least three objectives that you might set for your packaging.

Chapter Challenge

Writing Assignment

Introduce yourself to the manager of a local store, and ask his or her permission to do an MC analysis of the store's promotional activities. Then walk through the store and analyze the use of sales promotions and design. Is a distinctive image and personality presented in these materials and activities? What would you recommend to help the store tighten up its promotional program and create even greater impact?

Presentation Assignment

Using *Advertising Age, Brandweek, PROMO* magazine, and other sources, read everything you can find about a special promotion used by one of the major fast-food chains such as McDonald's, Burger King, or Taco Bell. Explain the objectives of the promotion, how it was set up, and how it worked. Describe all the materials, events, and other MC supporting efforts. Prepare a presentation for your class that summarizes your analysis.

Internet Assignment

Check the music section of Amazon.com and the CDnow website. Identify and compare the sales-promotion efforts at both sites. Which one is more effective in its use of consumer sales promotions? Explain why it is so effective.

Chapter

15 Channel Marketing: Trade Promotion and Co-Marketing

Key Points in This Chapter

1. What is trade promotion, and how does it fit into channel marketing?
2. How do trade promotion's strategies and practices operate?
3. What is co-marketing, and why is it an "integrating" practice?

Chapter Perspective

Communicating with the *Real* Customers

When advertising and marketing people talk about the "customer," most of the time, whether in B2C or in B2B, they are referring to the ultimate consumer, or end user—the person or household that actually consumes the final good or service. What is often overlooked is that the real customer for manufacturers of goods are members of the distribution channels, especially retailers. If these people don't buy, end users never have a chance to do so (other than through direct marketing).

Channel marketing is the process by which manufacturers build relationships with members of the distribution channel in order to get their products to end users. Modern-day channel marketing consists of three activities: trade promotion, co-marketing, and personal selling. The first two are the subjects of this chapter; personal selling is discussed in Chapter 16.

For many years manufacturers alone determined what products they would make and what promotions retailers would use. With the growth of powerful retail chains such as Wal-Mart, however, much of the control over product lines, as well as the movement of products through the distribution channel, has passed to the retailers.

Retailers carry only brands that sell well and increasingly are focusing on building relationships between their stores and their customers rather than between their customers and manufacturers' brands. As a result, manufacturers are struggling in this new retail environment to protect their brands, as well as get what they feel is their fair share of promotional support from retailers, which is what this chapter describes.

NIKE AT THE FINISH LINE

Nike understands that the retail store is a vital link in reaching consumers at the precise time and place where they are making brand-purchasing decisions. As Russ Ortiz, Nike's director of market place management, puts it, "Over 90 percent of our sales are in the hands of our retail partners; our brand and our products live in their house, they carry our messages. We build retail marketing programs as part of our communications mix to ensure delivery of more consistent messages about the Nike brand and our products to the consumer. By establishing an emotional brand connection and delivering product information to consumers at the point of purchase, we can help retailers increase sales. By helping build our retailers' business, we are building our own business."

Like many marketers, Nike provides retailers with an annual co-op fund and seasonal co-op kits. The co-op kit contains preproduced print ads and radio spots that are consistent with the Nike brand image and can be tagged with the retailer's name. Also included in the co-op kit are store fixtures and point-of-sale materials that retailers can order, plus a graphic standards guide to ensure that the Nike brand is communicated consistently by the many retailers that sell Nike products.

Finish Line, a mall-based retail chain, has over 500 stores nationwide. Although Finish Line carries a wide variety of name-brand athletic shoes and apparel, Nike often accounts for more than 50 percent of Finish Line's product mix. Finish Line's target consumers are 19-year-old action-addicted collegiate males and females, who are role models not only for teenagers but for maturing adults wistfully recalling their college days.

According to Matt Georgi, director of advertising for Finish Line, "We have a tremendous partnership with Nike—we are in this together, we rely on their marketing team as much as they rely on ours. No retailer wants to look like every other retailer in the mall. That's why we value the custom programs from Nike that help differentiate us, it makes us feel better about putting our marketing dollars behind this brand."

Nike is just as positive about its relationship with Finish Line. Says Jim Beeman, Nike's senior marketing manager, National Strategic Account Groups, "Nike is committed to supporting retailers like Finish Line who feel the same way about our brand as we do, because they help reinforce our brand's premium position in the market place."

This partnership was evident in Finish Line's selection of an agency of record. After a lengthy search, Finish Line hired Cinco Design, a Portland-based firm recommended by Nike (and founded by a former Nike employee). Finish Line's mission is "To provide the best selection of sport-inspired footwear, apparel and accessories to fit the fast culture of action-addicted individuals." Using this mission statement as a foundation, Cinco created a co-marketing campaign that captured the essence of Finish Line and Nike's vital role in Finish Line's business and marketing.

Co-Marketing Objectives

Finish Line, Nike, and Cinco established the following co-marketing objectives* to meet the needs of both partners:

1. Support Nike's brand perceptions as the leader in exciting, stylish, innovative, aggressive, and high-performance footwear, apparel, and accessories for young, athletic consumers among 65 percent of Finish Line customers.

2. Create a competitive advantage for Finish Line by establishing Finish Line as the destination for Nike products among 85 percent of target consumers.

3. Increase retail store traffic and Web traffic for Finish Line by 20 percent during each seasonal campaign.

4. Increase sales of Nike brand products through Finish Line by 15 percent in one year, by highlighting specific products each season.

Strategies

Finish Line, Nike, and Cinco worked together to develop a long-term creative theme, as well as seasonal strategies. Nike and Finish Line jointly approved all MC materials to ensure that they supported both the Nike brand and Finish Line's image and objectives. The integrated campaign was designed to have a long-term sustainable theme and message that tied uniquely to Finish Line while focusing on the selection of Nike products. The campaign needed to be active, fun, energetic, and athletic while keeping Nike products and the Finish Line selection story front and center.

The Finish Line campaign theme was "Choose to Play." The following co-marketing elements delivered this Nike/Finish Line message to consumers:

- In-store fixtures and point-of-purchase displays.
- 30-second TV spots that ran on MTV, Comedy Central, BET, VH1, ESPN, and local market buys around *American Idol*.
- Finish Line Women's print campaign in *Seventeen, Teen People, YM, Shape,* and *Sports Illustrated for Women*.
- www.finishline.com and an e-mail campaign featuring the "Choose to Play" theme.
- Direct mail targeted at current Finish Line customers.
- Nike stories, athletes, and advertisements were featured in *Finish Line Magazine*, targeted to FL's 1.5 million customers in the "Winners Circle" customer loyalty program. *Finish Line Magazine* began in 1997 and is a "magalog": an image builder, with feature articles on athletes such as Michael Jordan, Mia Hamm, and Derek Jeter, plus a direct-sales catalog featuring the new styles available each season.
- Nike ensures consistent execution of in-store fixture and point-of-sale materials as well as training of sales associates on new products and marketing programs using Nike's corps of "Ekins" (*Ekin* is *Nike* spelled backward). Ekins are retail ambassadors for the Nike brand who interact with store sales associates and managers, providing in-store retailer support and education on the Nike brand and Nike products for all Nike strategic partners. (The word *Ekin* is a marketing message itself. Like the colloquial term *wonk*—as in "policy wonk"—*Ekin* is intended to convey the idea that Nike associates know their subject backwards and forwards.)
- Nike and Finish Line committed additional marketing dollars to implement the program above and beyond FL's co-op funding.

Results

The initial campaign resulted in double-digit increases in Finish Line's "buy-in"—the amount of Nike product ordered in anticipation of the customer demand that will be created by a promotional campaign. Finish Line also had a corresponding overall increase in retail "sell-through"—the amount of product bought for the campaign product and sold by Finish Line during the first year. According to Jim Beeman, "As future iterations roll out to consumers, Finish Line and Nike have continued to partner on product, marketing, in-store display, and business initiatives, resulting in increased store traffic for Finish Line and increased profits for both parties." The "Choose to Play" campaign results* are as follows:

- Overall sales of Nike brand products through Finish Line stores increased 20 percent during the first year.
- Calls to the Finish Line store locator increased 200 percent-plus following the first run of print advertising.
- Retail traffic increased by 17 percent.
- Web traffic to finishline.com increased by 30 to 40 percent during each seasonal campaign.
- During the women's national print campaign, total women's sales were up 20 percent over the same selling period in the previous year.
- FL customer tracking study showed that the percentage of FL customers who see FL as the best destination for Nike products increased from 20 to 62 percent after one year.

Furthermore, the "Choose to Play" campaign won the Retail Advertising and Marketing Association's 2002 RAC award, given for best retail broadcast and print advertising campaigns.

The Nike and Finish Line co-marketing program met or exceeded objectives. For confidentiality reasons, however, this case writeup includes altered numbers in the "Objectives" and "Results" sections.

Source: Russ Ortiz, Jim Beeman, Scott Reames, and Slate Olsen from Nike; Matt Georgi from Finish Line. Special thanks to marketing consultant Marla Showfer for writing this case.

COMMUNICATING WITH DISTRIBUTION CHANNELS

To get their brands to end users, manufacturers battle against competing manufacturers for the attention and support of members of the distribution channels. For years this goal was accomplished through **trade promotions,** which are *discounts and premiums offered to retailers in exchange for their promotional support.* In recent years, however, companies have taken the more integrated, relationship-building approach known as channel marketing. **Channel marketing** is *an integrated process that combines personal selling, trade promotions, and co-marketing programs to build relationships with retailers and other members of the distribution channel.*

Members of the distribution channel are called different names depending on their place in the distribution system and the types of products being distributed. The most common distribution channel members are

- *Wholesalers: companies that specialize in moving goods from manufacturers to retailers;* they buy large quantities of a product and then break the quantity down to smaller lots that they then sell to many different retailers.
- *Bottlers:* as in the soft-drink industry, *local companies that buy ingredients in large quantities—for example, the concentrate made by Coke from its famous secret recipe—and then mix them, bottle them, and sell beverages to local stores.*
- *Dealers:* as in the automotive industry, *local companies that buy an inventory of products—for example, cars from General Motors or appliances from Maytag—from a manufacturer and assemble a mix of models for sale in their stores or showrooms.*
- *Retailers: food stores, drugstores, mass merchandisers, and other specialty stores that sell products and services to consumers.* Sometimes retailers are owned by manufacturers (Coach, Nike), but more often they are independently owned or are members of large chains such as Wal-Mart, Safeway, Nordstrom, and CompUSA. In independent stores and chains, manufacturers compete fiercely to have their brands on store shelves and featured in retailers' ads. Most major retail chains have their own brands—*store brands*—which compete with *manufacturers' brands* for shelf space and promotional support.

All distribution-channel relationships are important, but the key relationship for B2C manufacturers is the one with retailers because the retail store is the place where consumers buy products. Retailers are powerful: they control which brands are sold in their stores, where in a store each brand is displayed, how much floor space or shelf space is allocated to each brand, what in-store signage and promotions are used to promote each brand, and which brands are featured in the store's advertising and promotional programs. Not surprisingly, the majority of trade-promotion dollars are spent on retailers.

Consumers are motivated to shop in retail stores by advertising and promotions co-financed by manufacturers and retailers, as the IMC in Action box explains.

TRADE PROMOTIONS: THE FOUNDATION OF CHANNEL MARKETING

Moving products from manufacturers to retailers is a complex process that involves warehousing and distribution logistics. The real challenges, however, are:

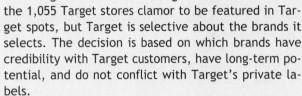

IMC IN ACTION

Target's Bull's-Eye

Target spends over $300 million a year on brand-image and promotional advertising. The retailer has been a major player in the discount retailing market since the 1990s, when it launched an offbeat repositioning campaign. The ads featured a little bull terrier with a bull's-eye, a graphic trick that played off Target's brand logo. The cute character emphasized the chain's mix of everyday items with more stylish offerings.

The Minneapolis-based chain continues to set a standard for the retail world with its award-winning ads and local community sponsorships. For the seventh year in a row, Target won the Heineman trophy for "Best in Show" at the Retail Advertising Marketing Association's (RAMA) annual Retail Advertising Conference.

Target's advertising has been successful in building a unique positioning for its brand, but its ads are often co-branded to include national brands such as Windex, M&M's, and Pringles. Target's 2002 RAMA winner was a 30-second spot called "Pop Art," which featured flood pants and Tide Detergent. Target pays for these spots in part through its co-op funds from manufacturers.

National brands that want to drive big-volume sales through the 1,055 Target stores clamor to be featured in Target spots, but Target is selective about the brands it selects. The decision is based on which brands have credibility with Target customers, have long-term potential, and do not conflict with Target's private labels.

Although being featured in Target advertising drives sales volume for brands, critics on the brand management side feel that Target's own brand message and focus on low prices can overpower the equity message of manufacturer brands.

(1) persuading retailers to **authorize a brand,** which means to *agree to carry a brand,* and (2) persuading retailers to display the product in a positive manner and aggressively promote it to consumers. The majority of trade-promotion spending is used for the latter. However, this is not possible until a brand has been authorized and, therefore, is displayed on retail store shelves.

Trade Promotions for New Products

The first step in getting authorization of a new brand or of a product line extension is using advertising and publicity to create awareness of the new offering among channel members. Advertising in trade magazines and demonstrating products at appropriate trade shows can accomplish this. In the trade ad shown in Exhibit 15-1, what benefit is being promised for the new DVD?

Once trade awareness has been created, the next step is to get authorization by making presentations to retail buyers. Every retail operation, whether an independent store or a chain, has one or more people responsible for buying. A **buyer** is *a person who purchases products for resale and selects which manufacturers' promotions to use.* Before most big chains take on a new brand or a major line extension, a buyer must first be convinced the brand is worth considering; then he or she presents the brand to the chain's buying committee. This committee is made up of senior buyers and other chain executives. Why so complicated? Taking on new products requires changes in the retailer's operations (as explained later in the discussion of slotting allowances). In large chains there are several buyers, each of whom handles several product categories.

YOUR WEDDING DAY
IN PERFECT DETAIL.
RIGHT DOWN TO THAT
PASSING GLANCE
AT THE BRIDESMAID.

EXHIBIT 15-1
New products have to be "sold" to the trade, as well as to consumers. This ad appeared in a specialty magazine for the home theater industry. The retailer will see it there and know the marketer is making an attempt to create consumer demand, which makes it easier for the retailer to decide to stock the product.

If a brand and its manufacturer are new to the marketplace, a new-products presentation begins with a profile of the manufacturer that includes such things as the location of its offices and plants, the company's history, its business track record, and the backgrounds of key executives. The rest of the presentation is the same for old as well as new companies and includes these items:

- *Marketing communication plan:* One of the first things retailers want to know is to what extent a manufacturer is investing in creating consumer awareness and motivation to buy. This means an explanation of the national advertising that has (or will) run along with any additional local advertising and promotion efforts in the store's designated marketing area (⬅ Chapter 13).

- *Special offers:* These include price reductions and other promotional allowances (explained later in this chapter).

- *Sampling the product:* This taste test of food and beverages or demonstration of nonfood products is intended to persuade retailers that the brand is good.

- *Research findings:* This information shows how consumers compare the new brand to competitors and how the brand meets consumers' needs and wants.

- *Profit projections:* This section shows how much the retailer can make, based on purchases of certain quantities being sold at certain prices.

- *Shelf-management diagram:* When a manufacturer asks for more shelf space, it is necessary to recommend to the retailer how the category shelf space could be rearranged to accommodate the manufacturer's recommendation.

If a store is interested in a new product or in a line extension, it requires the manufacturer to pay a **slotting allowance,** which is *a one-time, up-front payment for agreeing to stock a product.* Because the demand for retail shelf space is so great, these fees at large chains can run into the hundreds of thousands of dollars and are considered a major trade-promotion expense. Retailers justify this charge because taking on a new brand requires them to allocate one or more "slots" (spaces) in their warehouses, enter the new brand items into their computer and scanning programs, and rearrange shelf space within their stores where the new brand will be displayed. Because all stores have a finite amount of shelf space, taking on a new brand generally means dropping or greatly reducing space allotted to a current brand. Some large chains give new products 90 days to prove themselves. If sales do not meet expectations, the products are dropped, and all of the manufacturer's investment with that chain is lost.

Slotting allowances are controversial. Manufacturers say the charges are far greater than what it costs retailers to take on a new brand. Also, these high fees often prevent new brands, especially those not belonging to large companies, from getting distribution in major chains—thereby, opponents suggest, suppressing competition. The federal government periodically reconsiders the legality of such allowances but so far has passed no laws against their use.

When Unilever, Procter & Gamble, General Mills, Mars (candy), and other well-established companies introduce new products, retailers are generally receptive because they know these companies have the knowledge and budgets to create consumer awareness and demand. But usually even these companies must pay slotting allowances. An exception is made only when a brand has achieved such high consumer awareness and demand that the retailer taking on the brand assumes little or no risk. A good example is the introduction of Starbucks to grocery stores. Starbucks was so popular and widespread in the United States that retailers were eager to carry the brand. This is a good example of the value of strong brand equity (◂ Chapter 3).

Getting authorization—with or without slotting fees—does not guarantee a brand's success. It's only the first hurdle. The second challenge, persuading retailers to promote the marketer's brand, helps guarantee success—if success means getting ongoing retailer promotional support that complements the brand's national MC effort. This calls for a separate trade-promotion campaign, in addition to the launch campaign aimed at consumers. Such an effort involves setting channel marketing and promotion objectives and the strategies to deliver on them.

Trade Promotions for Authorized Brands

As the following table shows, manufacturers have been moving money from consumer promotions (such as coupons) to trade promotions. Between 1997 and 2000, the percentage of the average marketing budget allocated to couponing dropped from 24 percent to 15 percent; the majority of this money moved over to trade promotions.[1] The table also shows that media advertising picked up one percentage point but trade promotions increased 8 percentage points.

	Advertising	Coupons	Retail Trade Promotion	Total
1997	23%	24%	53%	100%
2001	24%	15%	61%	100%

The increasing use of trade promotions is partially the result of the growing number of brand offerings, which has made the fight for shelf space in grocery, drug, and discount stores brutal. As more and more brands ask for distribution and shelf space, retail chains are happy to play one brand against another to maximize the sales-promotion support they get from manufacturers.

Trade-Promotion Objectives

For brands that have been authorized by a retailer, the primary trade-promotion objectives are to (1) increase distribution, (2) balance demand, (3) control inventory levels, (4) respond to competitive programs, and (5) elicit promotional support by channel members. Before consumers can buy a retail product, it must be available on store shelves. Thus marketers use channel marketing to gain new distribution and motivate the retailers that carry the brand to promote locally.

The most typical trade-promotion objective is to move more product through the channels of distribution (see Exhibit 15-2). These promotions *increase distribution* by lowering the risk for distributors and retailers to buy in greater quantities than normal. What members of the distribution channel fear most is buying product that they cannot resell. By providing them with special selling materials and promotional discounts and allowances (explained later in the chapter), manufacturers reduce the risk of buying in large quantities.

Knowing how important it is to have products available when customers want them, most manufacturers work hard to make sure product is always available at retail. Service companies, similarly, staff up for traditionally busy times of the day, week, or year. When companies find they have too many goods on hand or service

EXHIBIT 15-2

This merchandising poster for the cheese industry's "Ahh, the power of cheese," campaign, illustrates how the Meijer's retail chain uses one of the cheese association supplied posters for in-store support for the campaign.

Snacks made with cheese cause cheesy grins.
Another reason to love cheese from Meijer.

Ahh, the power of Cheese.

personnel who are not being kept busy, they use promotions to *balance demand* and *control inventory levels*. Rental car companies sometimes offer "three days for the price of two" on Friday-through-Monday rentals because this is a low-demand period. For products that have irregular purchase cycles, an objective of sales promotion can be to help level out the sales peaks and valleys.

Trade promotion can also help a brand *respond to competitive offerings*. To counter the introduction of a new competing brand, for example, a company can use a "loading" promotion, in which retailers are given incentives to buy in larger quantities than usual (to load up on a product). This reduces space and demand for the new brand, making it more difficult for the new brand to get and keep distribution. In the high-tech industry, companies continually introduce improved hardware and software. A company that is behind may offer special pricing or product extras in order to prevent current customers from switching to the newer competitive offerings.

Examples of specific trade-promotion objectives, which are determined by SWOT analysis findings (⬅ Chapter 6), are the following (in a plan, these objectives would be stated in measurable terms based on the status of the brand and other relevant marketing input):

- To gain *more* shelf space.
- To gain *better* shelf space. The best shelf space is at eye level and near the beginning of the product category. "Beginning" is defined by the direction from which the majority of customers enter a section—the flow pattern of store traffic.
- To gain *extra* brand displays such as end-aisle displays and complementary product displays, an example of which is having a display of hot dog buns placed above the section of the meat case containing hot dogs.

To help you understand trade-promotion strategies, we next look at the major trade-promotion tools and then discuss trade-promotion strategies.

Trade-Promotion Tools

The essence of most trade promotions is a reduction in price. Price reductions come in many forms, as the following descriptions of promotional allowances illustrate.

Off-Invoice Allowances

An **off-invoice allowance** is *a reduction in the wholesale price, with no restrictions, for a limited period*. It is the simplest of all trade promotions and the one that channel members desire most (see Exhibit 15-3). During the designated promotion period, often 30 days, a brand is discounted a certain percentage, generally between 5 and 20 percent. Much of the discount, the manufacture hopes, will be passed on to the consumer, although the retailer is not required to pass it on. Manufacturers use this tool to maintain their share of retail shelf space and to enable retailers to price these brands competitively. A problem with off-invoice allowances is that some retailers do "forward buying." Near the end of the promotion period, they buy another month's worth of the product, causing the manufacturer to lose two months of selling products at the full wholesale price.

Volume Discounts

As the name implies, a volume discount is based on the amount a retailer buys. The more a retailer buys at a time, the greater the discount. This allowance is designed to motivate retailers to buy more than they normally would. Because retailers have limited warehousing space, manufacturers know that retailers will make a special effort to sell products bought in volume.

Performance Allowances

Performance allowances, which can range from $2 to $5, are *price reductions given to retailers in exchange for the retailer agreeing to feature the brand in its advertising or in other promotional programs*. Exhibit 15-4 highlights a promotion in which clothing maker Savane provided a special allowance to Dillard's department stores for featuring Savane products and agreeing to help collect used Savane-labeled clothing for charity.

EXHIBIT 15-4
Clothing manufacturer Savane offered Dillard's a special allowance in exchange for Dillard's running the special trade-in ad, which collected used clothing for charity.

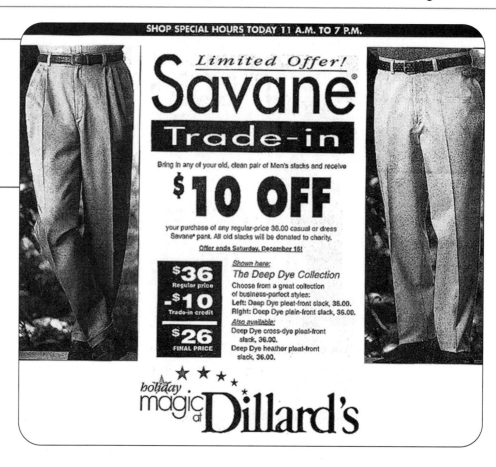

To receive such allowances, a retailer must submit proof of performance—copies of a newspaper ad or affidavits of performance from radio or TV stations, along with invoices from these media. Most major brands provide retailers with prepared advertising materials—ads, glossy photos, sample radio and TV commercials—insisting that they use one or more of these materials in order to qualify for the allowances.

Display Allowances

Another type of performance allowance is an **off-shelf display allowance,** which is *a price reduction for locating an additional quantity of a brand in a high-traffic area such as the end of an aisle.* In exchange for this allowance, retailers agree to give the brand off-shelf display, which automatically attracts more customer attention and increases sales.

Knowing that most retail stores are always trying to reduce labor costs, some brands periodically use shipper displays in order to get off-shelf display, as illustrated in Exhibit 15-5. **Shipper displays** are *specially designed shipping cartons that when opened become display units complete with signage and a quantity of products ready for sale.* Shipper displays demand little extra labor by retailers. Flaps from the carton stand up to help call attention to the display and carry a brand message. Like end-aisle displays, shipper displays are attention getting and can move several times the amount of product that normally moves from the brand's allotted shelf display. The downside for retailers is that they take up floor space, which in most stores is already being used to the maximum.

Dealer Loaders

A **dealer loader** is *a high-value premium given to a retailer in exchange for the purchase of a special product assortment or a specified dollar volume.* An example is a cooler used to stock soft drinks. After the promotion period, the premium belongs to the retailer, who may raffle it off to employees in each store.

Buy-Back Allowances

When introducing a new product, manufacturers sometimes offer a **buy-back allowance,** which is *a payment to buy back the current stock of a brand and replace it with a featured new product.* To further persuade retailers to take on products, some manufacturers guarantee protection from risk by offering to buy back any of their own brand not sold within a specified period.

Dealer Contests

To motivate retail dealers and their salespeople to reach specific sales goals or to stock a certain product, companies offer **dealer contests,** *competitions awarding dealers special prizes and gifts when sales reach a predetermined volume or a stated percentage increase of last year's sales.* Travel-related contests are especially popular. Many chains require that these types of rewards be made to the chain's headquarters and not to individual buyers, so that buyers do not make buying and promotion decisions that are not in the best interest of the chain. The chain then uses the rewards to stage its own internal competitions. On business items such as office supplies, cleaning supplies, and printed forms, sellers sometimes offer trips or other expensive premiums for certain-size orders or multiyear contracts.

In-Store Demonstrations

Manufacturers of food and beverages, especially new or improved products, use **in-store demonstrations,** which means *hiring a person to hand out product samples in-store.* Often, in addition to sampling products, these people hand out cents-off coupons to further encourage purchase of the product being sampled. In-store demonstrations not only move many more cases in a day than average but also introduce the product to customers who are not regular users.

Sales Training

In many high-tech and other specialty stores, sales clerks assist customers by explaining a brand's features and benefits and demonstrating its use. Clerks can do this, however, only if a manufacturer provides the store and its sales staff with brand educational materials or, in some cases, holds special training sessions on how to sell the brand. The extent to which sales clerks are motivated to share their knowledge or sell a brand's features and benefits is also a function of the incentives provided by the manufacturer and the retailer. A sale is much more likely to be made when a consumer is approached by a knowledgeable salesperson who is trained about the product's benefits and features and enthusiastically tries to sell the product to the consumer because of how well it meets the consumer's needs. The enthusiasm of sales clerks can be intensified if they are accruing points from a manufacturer to win, say, $500 worth of free merchandise or a trip to Hawaii as part of a special trade sales promotion.

Co-op Advertising Allowances

Many manufacturers have **cooperative (co-op) advertising allowances** in which *a certain percentage of everything a retailer buys is put into a special "co-op" fund* (see Exhibit 15-6; also ◄ Chapter 11). A co-op fund is typically based on 1 to 2 percent of annual sales to each retailer. The more the retailer buys, the bigger the retailer's co-op fund is. If, for example, Kohl's department stores purchases $50 million in annual wholesale shipments of Nike product, Nike would put $1 million that year in a co-op account for Kohl's to advertise Nike products. When the retailer advertises the brand in newspapers, on radio, on TV, or in some other way, from

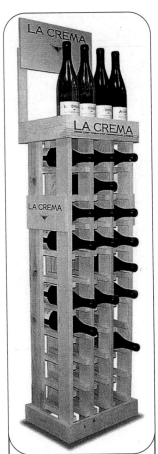

E X H I B I T   1 5 - 5
The La Crema line of wine is distributed in a furniture-quality shipping case rack.

50 to 100 percent of the cost is paid for out of that retailer's co-op fund. Such funds allow retailers to promote a brand on their own schedule rather than just during the manufacturer's promotional periods.

Point-of-Purchase Displays

Point-of-purchase (POP) displays are *in-store advertising displays featuring a product.* If the POP materials are properly integrated, they have the same look and feel as the brand's other advertising and reinforce the brand positioning. POP materials that have a busy design and are located in a cluttered environment may get lost (see Exhibit 15-7).

Retailers sometimes refer to *in-store promotion activities* as **merchandising.** Some manufacturers use field merchandisers to go into stores and make sure the manufacturer's brand is being properly displayed, that POP displays are up and current (where allowed by the retailer), that perishable products are not beyond the "sell by" dates, and that retailers are providing the in-store support that they have been paid to provide.

It is estimated that marketers spent over $15.5 billion on POP materials in 2002[2]—just slightly less than what was spent on consumer magazine advertising. Merchandising and POP materials provided by manufacturers (or for franchised stores by corporate headquarters) give the retailer ready-made, professionally designed brand messages. These materials include banners, signs, window posters, counter stands, floor stands, TV monitors, audiotapes for playing over the store's public-address system, shelf signs, end-cap (end-of-aisle) displays, and special display racks. Retail chains typically create many of their own merchandising materials.

Some agencies specialize in designing POP displays as well as permanent store interiors. If, for example, a store wanted to use a wine-and-cheese theme for a promotion, or even for a store design, then Propaganda, a retail environment design agency based in San Francisco, might suggest such props as picnic baskets, deck chairs, picnic blankets, and photo posters of the countryside. Propaganda's CEO Keith Walton calls that "romancing the customer" with visual merchandising.[3]

The more investment and creativity a retail chain puts into the design and ambiance of its stores, the less receptive it is to POP materials from manufacturers. The argument is that most POP materials are strategically inconsistent with retailers' own messages—an argument that is difficult to refute. Increasingly, companies are recognizing that if in-store merchandising is to have a significant effect on sales, the materials have to be designed extremely well.

The greatest strength of merchandising and POP displays is that they direct attention to a brand at the point of sale. In doing so, they increase customer consideration, positively affecting sales, especially for impulse items. Most important, they can nudge customers from a state of interest or desire to action—making a purchase. An American Dairy Association in-store promotion supported by POP materials increased sales by approximately one-third.[4] When POP materials were used to support a candy and gum promotion, sales increased nearly 400 percent in comparison with stores in which the POP display was not used.[5] POP displays can affect sales in all product categories but are especially powerful when used for impulse items.

The second most important strength of these MC functions is that they integrate the out-of-store MC messages that customers have been exposed to and the in-store shopping experience. These trade-promotion tools also get the attention of the store's personnel and can inspire employees to support a special promotion.

The biggest limitations of POP materials are the retailer's resistance to using them and salespeople's failure to promote their use where they are acceptable. Because display materials can significantly affect sales and are relatively inexpensive to use, most brands prepare them. Consequently, retailers are inundated with them and are forced to be selective. Many retailers are so pressed for time and personnel that roughly half of the promotional materials remain in the stock room, unused and unassembled. Also, because a POP display is place-based—it generally appears in only one location—customers must come to or walk past it in order to be exposed to it. It is estimated that in drugstores and discount stores, only about 20 percent of store visitors browse most of the aisles.[6]

EXHIBIT 15-7
In many stores, clutter is created by the presence of too many in-store promotional messages.

Trade-Promotion Strategies

The strategic challenge is to come up with a mix of promotional ideas that minimizes costs to the manufacturer but maximizes support for the retailer. The right mix differs for each retail chain and can be arrived at only by having in-depth knowledge of a retailer's business. The way to determine the right mix is to look at what allowances will best help retailers' meet their objectives, what competitors are offering, what the company can afford, and how retailers have responded to various promotional offers in the past.

One of the first strategic decisions a company must make is how much of its sales volume will be sold on promotion. A brand is either off or on promotion. **On promotion** means *for sale at a reduced price through incentives offered to channel members.* Generally, premium-priced brands are on promotion less than low-cost brands, which sell primarily on price.

Push and Pull Strategies

Consumer sales promotions are pull strategies because they create consumer demand and thereby "pull" the product through the distribution channel. Push strategies use marketing communication to motivate the trade to buy and make extra efforts to resell products. These efforts thus "push" products through the distribution channels by giving special incentives to get products on retailers' shelves and included in retailers' advertising, special displays, and other in-store merchandising activities.

Manufacturers know that once a retailer purchases several truckloads of a product, the retailer will work hard to make sure the product sells in order to recoup the cost of the product and make a profit on it. An old saying in the produce and meat business sums up the concept of the push strategy: "Sell it or smell it."

Most trade buyers can estimate how much pull will be created by certain kinds of promotions. Before the Contadina ad in Exhibit 15-8 ran, buyers for the chains carrying Contadina were shown copies of the ad by Contadina sales representatives. Buyers were told which media vehicles would be carrying the ad and when, and they were told the specific number of coupons that would be distributed in

their trading areas. Using this information, a buyer would estimate, for example, that the Contadina coupon and advertising during the promotion period would increase Contadina sales by 25 percent. That buyer would then order 25 percent more cases than usual.

Most sales-promotion programs integrate push and pull strategies, using both consumer and trade promotions. The challenge is to integrate both in regards to timing and theme. For example, when Procter & Gamble and other packaged-goods companies introduce a new or improved product, trade-promotion (push) offers precede consumer-promotion (pull) offers such as coupons. This helps ensure that products will be on the shelves when the consumer promotion takes place.

Although push and pull are most frequently discussed in relation to consumer packaged goods, these strategies are also used in selling B2B, service, and considered-purchase products (durable goods). In the case of B2B, often the end users of products are not the same as those who make the buying decisions. Thus the users become the consumers, and the buyers become the "retailers." Having an integrated promotion program designed for both can be strategically sound. Buyers can be given certain incentives for buying, and end users can be given incentives to try new or improved brands or to attend training sessions so that their use of the brand will be more satisfying and productive.

In the case of service products, such as insurance, banking, and transportation, companies often use push incentives to motivate their frontline employees to focus on certain products. Banks, for example, often have competitions among their branches, using premiums to reward those generating the most sales for new-product offerings.

Here are three common strategies used to achieve trade-promotion objectives.

- *Complementing consumer promotions:* For seasonal products, such as lemonade and bathing suits, manufacturers time their promotional offerings to slightly precede the peak selling periods, thereby ensuring that stores have inventory on hand when consumer demand peaks. The Kendall-Jackson story in the next IMC in Action box illustrates a holiday season cross-promotion with Hormel.

IMC IN ACTION

Kendall-Jackson Keeps Its Wine in Mind

From 2000 to 2001, California wine shipments to all markets were up just 2 percent; at the same time, however, Kendall-Jackson's shipments were up 24 percent. That year the company recorded the largest revenue gain among all California wineries. K-J believes one of the reasons for this great performance was its relationship with its distributors. While Robert Mondavi, E & J Gallo, and other brands were spending millions of dollars on television commercials, K-J was spending nothing on broadcast media or mass circulation consumer print media. What it did spend money on, with the objective of building relationships with retailers, restaurants, and hotels, was targeted trade publications.

In 2001, K-J set up a "channel marketing" team with a handful of members. The goal was to win retail aisle space, as well as the hearts, minds, and wallets of consumers. K-J marketing director John Grant explains: "Most consumers walk into the store with no particular brand of wine in mind, and only 25 percent of consumers walk down the wine aisle in markets. Trying to create consumer pull through advertising is ill advised; it's better to try to influence the consumer at the point of purchase. The key to success is to merchandise your product beyond the liquor aisle, through cross-promotions with other brands throughout the store." During the holiday season, Kendall-Jackson uses hangtags on its bottles, as well as brochures, to promote chicken and ham recipes. The ham connection is a cross-promotion with Hormel.

In addition to retail programs, the channel marketing team at K-J develops staff training programs and promotions with restaurants such as Red Lobster and Olive Garden and hotels such as Hyatt.

According to John Maxwell, K-J's director of channel marketing, Kendall-Jackson "provides information and training on all channel marketing programs to their sales force through quarterly sales meetings and through two sales force publications, 'NOW' ('News on Wine') for retail programs and 'By the Glass' for programs with their hotel, restaurant and

bar partners. K-J field sales reps and distributors can be kept up to date on brand developments, get information for all channel marketing programs, and order POP materials, images, ads and other channel communications materials on line at K-Jsales.com."

Source: Adapted from Peter Simon, Chronicle Staff Writer, "What a Difference a Year Makes, Kendall-Jackson Posts Big Sales Gain to Lead States Wineries," *San Francisco Chronicle,* December 30, 2001, p. G3. Reprinted by permission of *San Francisco Chronicle.*

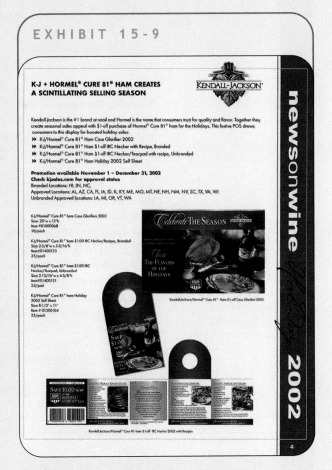

EXHIBIT 15-9

To have a major impact on sales, trade promotions often run when a brand increases its advertising. This strategy is used when brands are being repositioned, have a new advertising campaign, or are entering a peak selling season. Notice how much advertising and how many retail features there are for electric shavers prior to Christmas. Norelco, for example, spends a major portion of its trade-promotion and consumer advertising budget during the last quarter of the year, knowing that electric shavers are a popular gift item. Having stores feature the brand while consumer advertising is running generates increased sales over what would result from trade-only promotions.

- *Countering new competitive introductions:* When a new competitor enters the market or a current competitor introduces brand extensions, most leading brands counter with special promotional offers. The objective is to discourage retailers from taking on the new products or, if they do, to minimize the advertising and display support the new entries receive.

- *Motivating trade support with a mix of allowances:* The primary channel strategy is to create a mix of promotional allowances that are offered to a particular retailer to motivate the retailer's support of the brand. These allowances are used to help achieve specific objectives such as increasing share of shelf space, increasing immediate sales, or strengthening relationships with retailers. Here's an example of a typical packaged-goods trade allowance mix:

  - $2 per case promotional allowance.
  - $1 per case display allowance.
  - Both allowances good for the month of March.
  - In-store demonstrations paid for by the manufacturer during March.

When brands are featured in retailers' weekly advertising or are given off-shelf displays, the sales of these brands (for that week) can increase as much as 400 percent, depending on the prominence of the feature and display and the size of the price reductions. In addition to increasing sales, manufacturers also hope these promotions attract some new users. This is why getting retailer support is so important to manufacturers—and why they are willing to do just about whatever it takes to obtain this support. The Kendall-Jackson story in the IMC in Action box illustrates how a manufacturer works with its retailers.

Manufacturers can customize promotional mixes by accounts, but promotions must be offered on an equal basis to all retailers that compete against each other. According to the federal Robinson-Patman Act (1936), just because a manufacturer has a better relationship with chain A than it has with all of chain A's competitors, it cannot offer chain A a more valuable trade promotion than it offers chain B, chain C, and so on. It is legal, however, to offer varying discount levels based on quantities purchased. The more a store or chain buys, the larger the dollar discount can be.

How Retail Buyers Evaluate Promotional Offers

An increasing number of retail chains analyze sales by brand, by product category, and by store. Scanner checkout systems enable buyers to know which stores are selling what brands at what rate (see Exhibit 15-10). Buyers use this information when evaluating new products and manufacturers' promotions.

Scanner data also let retail chains focus on product *category* promotions. Instead of just looking at the sales of each brand (for example Fritos corn chips) within a product category, chains closely analyze sales of each category as a whole (for example, salty snacks). They then experiment to determine the best mix of brands within each category and the best use of that category's shelf space. They then try to find the optimum emphasis for that category in the chain's advertising. For example, Target's weekly promotional supplement reflects decisions that were made about how much space to give apparel, small appliances, toys, and so on. Obviously the amount of space changes by season, but it also can be influenced by the amount of promotional money Target receives from manufacturers. When buyers

EXHIBIT 15-10

The first digit in a UPC tells what type of code is being used (there are now five different codes around the world), the next five digits identify the manufacturer, the next five identify the product, and the last digit is an "integrity" check, which is determined by a mathematical formula applied to the other numbers in the code.

0   37000 80051   4

are presented with trade promotions, they typically use these criteria to evaluate the offers:

- How much per case is the promotion actually worth?
- How profitable will the promotion be for the retailer?
- How much effort must the retailer put forth to receive the promotion? The more work that is involved (such as setting up off-shelf displays, reallocating shelf displays, featuring the brand in the retailer's ad), the less attractive is the offer.
- Does the offer violate any store policies? For example, some chains do not permit contests in which individual employees receive premiums or rewards from a manufacturer.
- How much consumer advertising and promotion support will the brand provide to complement the trade offer? The more, the better, from the retailer's perspective.
- Will the promotion require the authorization of new products not already being carried? Will it require accepting different package configurations? Any changes in packaging configurations mean more work for the retailer and therefore makes the promotion less attractive.
- What is the promotional period—how long will the retailer be able to buy at the promotional price?
- How flexible is the required performance? Will a store be compensated for putting up window banners or having an in-store display rather than running a newspaper ad that mentions the brand?
- Are the terms and timing of the promotional offer compatible with promotional offers from other brands within the product category?

To increase the chances that store-level programs are approved, marketers should create channel programs that are turn-key and easy for the retailer to execute, or marketers should provide field support to execute programs at the store level. Such assistance may include shipping turn-key floor displays, sending in a merchandising team to set up displays and keep them stocked, setting up and managing in-store sampling programs for retailers, and educating the store sales associates about their products and getting them excited about pushing the products. Field personnel should work on building relationships with local store managers, department managers, and sales associates to gain cooperation for local execution.

CO-MARKETING INTEGRATES MANUFACTURERS AND RETAILERS

In addition to personal selling (discussed in the next chapter) and trade promotions, manufacturers use co-marketing to protect their brand images and still maintain retailer cooperation. **Co-marketing** is *a customized joint effort by a manufacturer and a retailer to establish a mutually satisfying balance between price and image in local promotion of the manufacturer's brands.*

The growing power of retailers has complicated local brand promotions. Target, Albertson's, Walgreen's, and many other large retailers are now in the driver's seat and wield power over their suppliers (the manufacturers) when it comes to delivering brand messages. Retailers often produce their own ads that emphasize their own store brands and feature only the special price of certain product brands. This type of retail advertising not only says nothing about the benefits and image of name-brand products but sometimes features competing brands! In these ads, the

TABLE 15-1   The Biggest Brand Advertisers in the United States, 2001

Rank	Megabrand	2001 Ad Spending*
1	AT&T	$996.6 million
2	Verizon	$824.4
3	Chevrolet	$780.4
4	Ford	$655.9
5	McDonald's	$635.1
6	Sprint	$620.4
7	Toyota	$568.3
8	**Sears Department Stores**	**$511.5**
9	Dodge	$499.2
10	Chrysler	$474.4
11	Honda	$452.5
12	Nissan	$428.1
13	Cingular Wireless	$411.4
14	**Macy's Department Stores**	**$381.0**
16	**Home Depot Building Supply**	**$347.3**
17	**Kmart**	**$338.1**
18	**Wal-Mart**	**$329.9**
19	**Target**	**$313.4**
20	**J. C. Penney**	**$308.4**

*Spending in newspapers, radio, magazines, outdoor, broadcast and cable TV, and radio.

Source:"The 2002 Megabrand Report," *Advertising Age*. Reprinted with permission from the July 22, 2002 issue of *Advertising Age*. Copyright, Crain Communications Inc., 2002.

only thing differentiating the brands is price—and sometimes even the prices are the same, as in ads that often feature Coke and Pepsi price promotions.

Here is an indication of the communication power of retailers: in 2002, several retailers were among the top 20 spenders on mass media advertising in the United States. This means that Sears, Macy's, Home Depot, Kmart, Wal-Mart, Target, and J. C. Penney, have a significantly higher share of voice than *any* of the product brands they sell.[7] In Table 15-1, how many of the biggest brand advertisers in the United States were retailers (they are highlighted in boldface type)?

Objectives of Co-Marketing Communication

Most trade-promotion efforts in the past were designed to help manufacturers drive channel and retailer support with price deals. Co-marketing integrates the manufacturer's needs for brand messages with the retailer's needs, which are primarily focused on pricing strategies and traffic-building promotions. In co-marketing programs, manufacturers and retailers together create promotions to satisfy both sets of objectives. This co-marketing dimension of channel marketing can persuade retailers to use advertising and other forms of marketing communication not only to announce price specials but also to reinforce brand image and positioning.

Building Traffic

Retailers love popular brands because they attract consumers to their stores. Therefore, retailers frequently use leading national brands as **loss leaders,** which are *brands promoted at or below their cost to the retailer in order to draw consumers into stores.* For manufacturers of these brands, the loss-leader role creates a dilemma. On the one hand, they like the extra sales volume that these low-price features generate. On the other hand, they do not like to see their brands sold just on price, because this can cheapen a brand's image and train consumers to be overly price sensitive.

Maintaining Brand Consistency

Although co-marketing gives manufacturers some say in how their brands are presented in retailer advertising and promotional materials, this is not always easy to do. This is because manufacturers and retailers have different objectives, limitations, and selling situations that are sometimes in conflict. Retailers, especially the large chains, are concerned about the following:

- Building their store brand.
- Generating store traffic by carrying and featuring the brands their customers want.
- Maximizing their overall profitability by carrying and promoting the brands that have the highest margins or sales per square foot, thus eliminating from their stores the brands that have low margins and low sales per square foot.
- Enhancing their brand image by selling brands that they can price lower than can competing retailers, or brands from marketers that offer strong marketing support.
- Promoting entire categories—such as jeans, shoes, or laptops—which means including multiple brands and not favoring one brand over another.

To try to counter the potential dilution of a brand image, manufacturers produce a selection of retail print, radio, direct-mail, and television ads for retailers to use. The Nike case at the beginning of this chapter is a good example of a co-marketing program, and the ads in Exhibit 15-11 show Nike brand-image advertising that can be used in Finish Line's "Choose to Play" retail ads and in magazine article layouts. These ads communicate the brand's image while leaving room for retailers to add a featured price and their own logos. To encourage retailers to use these manufacturer-produced retail ads, manufacturers such as Nike, Levi Strauss, and Motorola reimburse retailers 100 percent from co-op funds when they use these ads. When retailers produce their own ads and focus just on price, the reimbursement is much less than 100 percent.

Trade-promotion managers who work for companies that sell their own products through their own stores, such as the Gap, Pottery Barn, and Hertz, have a much easier time executing and controlling image consistency in in-store programs. Because top management has control over these stores through ownership or franchise contracts, the marketing departments can be sure, for example, that key seasonal promotional pieces are displayed prominently in retail stores and that sales associates are aware of new products and their features and benefits.

Integration and Customization

Financed through manufacturers' promotional dollars and monies from retailers, co-marketing programs generally include an integrated mix of trade-promotion elements plus a lot of customization. Having the retailer pay a portion of these expenses increases the likelihood that both parties will be invested in the successful execution of a program.

EXHIBIT 15-11

The image of the woman running for Nike's Air Vamoose line was provided to Finish Line for its "Choose to Play" advertising campaign. The Landon Donovan photo in the Nike shirt was also provided for Finish Line's use in its magazine.

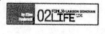

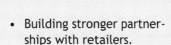

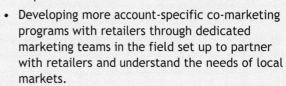

P&G Leads the Way

Procter & Gamble was one of the first leading marketers to shift significant amounts of consumer and trade-promotion dollars toward co-marketing with retailers. For decades the company spent millions of dollars to build equity for P&G brands, primarily through mass media. At the same time, P&G provided millions of dollars in co-op money to retailers that ran ads and offered coupons in freestanding inserts in the Sunday newspapers. While P&G was spending millions to tell consumers that Crest offered the best protection against cavities, for example, retailers were spending P&G's co-op money to tell consumers that Crest was cheap and on sale.

Because customers were being conditioned to buy on price, they bought Crest when it was on sale; then they bought Colgate the following month when it was on sale. To help remedy this situation, P&G in 1999 initiated Organization 2005, which devised several promotional strategies to keep P&G sales strong and increase loyalty to Crest and to the company's many other brands. These strategies included:

- Eliminating or cutting back on promotions such as coupons, refund offers, and premiums, and lowering the everyday price of products across the board.

- Conducting more research to better understand and respond to consumers' needs.

- Building stronger partnerships with retailers.

- Developing more account-specific co-marketing programs with retailers through dedicated marketing teams in the field set up to partner with retailers and understand the needs of local markets.

To support its co-marketing efforts, P&G earmarked $100 million annually for retailer-specific and local promotional efforts—about 6 percent of its $1.7 billion marketing communication budget.

P&G's co-marketing programs with Wal-Mart are two years ahead of its relationships with the rest of the retail world and continue to serve as the model for joint marketing programs among other leading marketers. "Retailers have to decide who they want to work with," says Jim Bechtold, who sets retail strategy for P&G. "We won't do this with every retailer. This requires retailers who aggressively think of their stores as a brand, who are willing to make systemic changes in their business focus, store design, employee training. They have to value research and believe that equity builds over time."

Co-marketing becomes an organizational challenge when a manufacturer, such as Procter & Gamble, has customized programs with dozens of chains that, like Wal-Mart, have hundreds of stores across the country and sometimes abroad. From a retailer's perspective, co-marketing is equally challenging, because many different manufacturers are constantly offering competing programs. The co-marketing strategies of Procter & Gamble are described in the IMC in Action box.

Besides account-specific print and broadcast advertising, manufacturers may also provide special packaging, in-store sampling, and events such as cooking classes or, in department stores, fashion shows. Co-marketing programs can also provide in-store fixtures and displays, incentive programs for sales associates, and loyalty programs (featuring the marketer's products) that retailers can use with their customer database. Manufacturers that bring innovative and exciting co-marketing programs to retailers can differentiate themselves from competitors and strengthen relationships with their retailers—by building business for retailers and for themselves as well.

Why Co-Marketing Is Important

The last decade has seen an increase in money spent on co-marketing, often at the expense of traditional consumer promotions and advertising. Here are some of the reasons why this is happening:

- Some marketers believe that traditional mass media are losing effectiveness as consumers are exposed to an increasing number of traditional advertising messages.

- The economic downturn at the beginning of the 21st century forced marketing managers to be more accountable for results, and co-marketing efforts are easier to measure than, for example, mass media advertising.

- An increase in competitive brands, including store brands, has created cutthroat competition for retail shelf space and floor space. Co-marketing programs help manufacturers negotiate premium floor space and gain additional store marketing support.

- Retailers are reluctant to share customer purchase data with manufacturers unless manufacturers offer them enough promotional support to make it worthwhile. Retailers view their customer information as proprietary and don't want to breach the trust of their customers by widespread use of the data.

- Due to retail consolidation and the proliferation of mega-stores, there has been a power shift from manufacturers to retailers. Today in the United States, for example, five supermarket chains account for approximately 50 percent of grocery sales, three mass merchandisers generate 75 percent of sales in this retail category, and four drugstore chains account for 75 percent of the volume in this retail category.[8]

A FINAL NOTE: THE GREAT PUSH AND PULL

"Sounds interesting, but we'll wait to see just how much customer demand we get before taking the product on." In this often-heard response to a new-product sales presentation, the buyer is challenging the manufacturer's sales pitch and promotion program and is saying in essence, "I'll believe your MC program works only when our customers start asking for your brand." Customer requests would be an indication of the success of a marketer's pull strategy generated by its marketer's advertising and consumer promotion programs.

This common response poses a real dilemma for manufacturers. Most manufacturers don't want to start advertising in a market until they have at least 60 percent distribution (◀ Chapter 13). Also, one of the things that helps a brand to get established is consumers seeing the brand on retail shelves and hearing people who have bought it talk about it. As the old saying goes: "You can't sell from an empty wagon."

Many college students face a similar dilemma when they graduate and begin looking for a job. Many employers say they want only people with experience. But how can new graduates get experience if no one will hire them? Many times it's the same in marketing. How can packaged goods be sold if they have little or no distribution?

From a strategic standpoint, marketers need to understand push *and* pull, and they must design promotional programs that drive consumer demand *and* elicit trade support. This is especially true when launching any new product, but it's also important in maintaining the presence and visibility of established brands.

authorization 493
bottlers 492
buy-back allowance 499
buyer 493
channel marketing 492
co-marketing 505
cooperative (co-op) advertising
    allowances 499
dealers 492

dealer contests 499
dealer loader 498
in-store demonstration 499
loss leaders 507
merchandising 500
off-invoice allowance 497
off-shelf display allowance 498
on promotion 501
performance allowances 497

point-of-purchase (POP)
    displays 500
retailers 492
shipper displays 498
slotting allowance 494
trade promotions 492
wholesalers 492

Key Point Summary

EXHIBIT 15-12

What elements in this website help reinforce Nike's brand image?

Key Point 1: Trade Promotion and Channel Marketing

Trade promotion is used to persuade distributors and retailers to buy a manufacturer's brand for resale to their customers. It is becoming more important because mass media advertising is less effective at creating demand and pulling products through the distribution channel. Channel marketing combines trade promotions and co-marketing with personal selling. It is used because retailers have become such a powerful force. In the current retail environment it is important for marketers to work closely with retailers in promotion programs.

Key Point 2: Trade Promotion's Objectives, Strategies, and Practices

Primarily a push strategy, trade promotions are designed to get the support of channel members. Objectives include (1) increasing distribution, (2) balancing demand, (3) controlling inventory levels, (4) responding to competitive programs, and (5) eliciting promotional support by channel members. Manufacturers use a variety of trade promotions to get authorization for a brand and to encourage the cooperation of retailers in the promotion of the brand.

Key Point 3: Co-Marketing

Because of the increasing power of retailers, most major manufacturers have moved to co-marketing, which is a partnership approach to the development of customer promotional efforts. Co-marketing enables manufacturers to better control how their brands are presented in retailer advertising and promotional materials by partnering with the retailer to protect brand image as well as store image.

Lessons Learned

Key Point 1: Trade Promotion and Channel Marketing

a. How does trade promotion differ from channel marketing?
b. Why are channel marketing and trade promotion increasing at the expense of advertising and other marketing communication functions?
c. In what way is Nike using channel marketing in its dealings with retailers such as Finish Line?

Key Point 2: Trade Promotion's Objectives, Strategies, and Practices

a. How do push and pull strategies differ? Use one of the brands discussed in this chapter in your answer.
b. In what way is channel marketing engaged in creating a push strategy?
c. Explain the main objectives of trade promotions.
d. What is co-op advertising? How does it work?
e. In addition to co-op advertising allowances, explain four other types of allowances used in trade-promotion programs.
f. What is a slotting allowance? Why do slotting allowances complicate marketing strategies?
g. Explain how price promotions are coordinated between a marketer and a retailer.
h. How do retailers evaluate promotions to decide whether to use them?

Key Point 3: Co-Marketing

a. Explain marketers' and retailers' different perspectives on brand communication.
b. What is co-marketing? How does it differ from other types of channel marketing?
c. What has caused the power shift from manufacturers to retailers? What are the implications of that shift for marketing communication?
d. How does the shift to co-marketing affect IMC programs?
e. What is the role of co-marketing in protecting brand images?

Chapter Challenge

Writing Assignment

Interview a manager of a local major store that is part of a national chain. Question the manager about the ways in which Coke, Kellogg's, and another major brand (your choice) work with the retail chain to create promotions that benefit the chain and the individual brands. Write up your findings.

Presentation Assignment

Interview a manager of a local major store that is part of a national chain. Ask for examples of in-store POP materials that have been given to the store but the store has chosen not to use. Find out from the store manager why the materials were never used. Bring the examples to class and explain why the materials were never used.

Internet Assignment

Using one of the search engines, find sources that talk about and give examples of channel marketing activities. Write up two mini-case histories that you find and compare them to the discussion of channel marketing in this chapter.

Chapter

16 Personal Selling

2003

ADA® CHEESE RETAIL SALES VIDEO

•Program Overview •Custom TV & Radio

Ahh, the power of Cheese.
©2003 America's Dairy Farmers™

Key Points in This Chapter

1. How does personal selling work, and what are its objectives?
2. What is the personal selling process?
3. How is personal selling managed, and how does it relate to an IMC program?

Chapter Perspective

Lessons from High-Powered Salespeople

When you look back through history, you see many significant changes brought about by individuals such as social activists Mahatma Gandhi, Susan B. Anthony, and Martin Luther King Jr.; spiritual leaders such as Mother Teresa; and political leaders such as Abraham Lincoln, Nelson Mandela, and Winston Churchill. All of these individuals were great communicators who knew how to motivate others and change behavior. In the highest sense, they were doing "personal selling."

Some historians might say that calling these historical figures "salespeople" is insulting because they "sold" ideas rather than goods and services. Nevertheless, selling an idea—getting volunteers, votes, and donations—is a form of high-powered personal sales. It is personal because the success of the sales effort often depends on personal one-to-one contact, and such efforts are almost always enhanced by an individual's integrity, credibility, and passion.

Unfortunately, over the years the personal selling of goods and services has become associated with manipulation and high-pressure tactics. Although some people still use these practices, today's professional salesperson usually realizes that partnering with customers and prospects in a way that creates a win–win situation is the most effective personal selling strategy.

Although the historical figures mentioned above didn't "sell" for financial gain (as most salespeople do), their success stemmed from their passion for what they believed in, their ability to understand their audiences, and their ability to communicate and persuade. That passion and those abilities lead to the successful selling of goods and services, as well as causes.

AVON'S MARK MIXES BRAINS AND BEAUTY

"Ding Dong! Avon Calling." Avon's famous slogan is now reaching a new and younger audience. The world's largest personal seller of beauty products, Avon, has long been identified with middle-age women and homemakers. Avon's newest MC objective, however, is to tap into the booming market of younger women and teens with a new line of "Mark" makeup.

The Mark line—marketed separately from the regular Avon line to maintain the Avon brand for its loyal customers—strives for a hip, modern image, one that can compete with and appear more sophisticated than Cover Girl. The line is priced a little higher than the regular Avon products but is still competitive with drugstore brands. The name Mark refers to the brand's position as a product designed to help young women "make their mark" in the world. In addition to cosmetics and skin-care products, the line includes bath and body products, fragrances, fashion jewelry, and accessories in sophisticated packaging.

Avon's biggest problem in reaching this target audience is its own dated image, associated with mom and grandma, which is a real turn-off for hip young teens. Indeed, the Mark line might not be able to escape the image of its famous parent brand.

The Mark Education

To sell Mark and educate a new generation of sales representatives, Avon has created a new personal selling program for young women ages 16 to 24. Partnering with the University of Phoenix, Avon has integrated an innovative sales force training program into the launch of the Mark line. New Avon salespeople who complete an online sales training course will receive college credit from the UoP, which specializes in providing practical education for working adults. By positioning Mark as an educational experience, Avon helps to allay parents' concerns about their daughters abandoning their studies in order to "play around with makeup."

Avon says 13,000 young women initially contacted the company about enrolling in the Mark sales training program. The company hopes eventually to enroll some 500,000 young sales reps in the United States. About 17 million young women in the United States are in that 16- to 24-year-old demographic,

and Avon's research has found they spend more than $24 billion annually on beauty-related products.

Avon's research has also found that a typical Mark representative has an average of 13 to 21 young women friends. That means the immediate target audience through the direct-selling channel for the first year would be around 10.5 million.

Mark's Selling Tools

The primary MC tool is the *meet mark* catalog, with graphics, format, and magazine-style articles designed to reflect the brand's spirited and goal-oriented personality. Like the traditional "Avon ladies," Mark sales representatives hand out catalogs when they make a sales call, rather than mailing them. Avon publishes some 10 million of the large-format catalogs in English and Spanish every six weeks. This makes *meet mark*, described as a "megalog," the largest publication reaching this young female audience. In comparison, *Seventeen*, the biggest magazine aimed at teens, reaches only 2.4 million.

Avon hopes its new sales force will sell the products among groups of friends at slumber parties and other informal gatherings. Beauty rituals such as shopping and learning how to apply cosmetics have long been an important way that teenage girls relate to one another. Avon believes the allure of the products, plus the fun of the parties, will make selling Mark a more attractive opportunity for female teenagers than working behind a fast-food counter. Said Deborah Fine, the former publisher of *Glamour* magazine who was tapped by Avon to launch the Mark line and run the new Avon Future division, "It's lip gloss with an earnings opportunity."

The Mark line will be supported not only by personal sales calls but by advertising that will run on youth networks including MTV and WB and in beauty magazines such as *Allure*. Avon is also creating partnership programs with automakers and telecommunication and entertainment companies that will distribute samples and advertise in the Mark catalog. For other forms of interactivity, the effort is facilitated by a toll-free number (1-800-meetmark) and a website (www.meetmark.com).

An integrated recruitment campaign targeted to young women at colleges, high schools, shopping malls, and other youth-oriented venues was used to recruit Mark's initial sales force. In addition to events, the recruitment effort used advertising and other forms of direct marketing to young women. Mark representatives also receive incentives for recruiting other young women.

Mark's Vision

Deborah Fine explains that "Our vision for 'Mark' is to provide young women with an engaging product line, a direct-selling opportunity, and a unique brand experience that engages them in a world of community, participation, and empowerment." The phrase "Meet Mark," will be the invitation to both buyers and sellers to enter this new world of beauty and opportunity.

Mark has another educational mission: to teach financial responsibility to the young businesswomen. Instead of buying the product line on credit in advance of sales, as regular Avon salespeople do, Mark representatives will be encouraged to sell the products and solicit the money from friends in advance. They then place their orders online, using their personal credit cards; they won't be extended credit. Avon says the arrangement is intended to keep the process simple; however, it is also designed to teach

account balancing and to prevent novices from getting into trouble by ordering more products than they can sell.

The Mark line will eventually join the regular Avon product line as part of Avon's global effort. Avon is marketed in 143 countries through 3.5 million independent sales representatives who produce approximately $6.0 billion in annual revenues. Andrea Jung, Avon CEO, said, "Around the world, the name 'Avon' stands for aspiration and empowerment. We look forward to engaging young women on a global scale with the Avon earnings opportunity." The effort also will take this innovative integration of education and sales force training around the world.

Source: "Mark Is What You Make It," Avon Mark website, <www.meetmark.com>; Sally Beatty, "Avon Tries Knocking on Dorm Doors," Wall Street Journal, March 28, 2003, p. B2; "Avon Makes Its Mark," Fashion Windows, March 30, 2003, <www.fashionwindows.com/beauty/2003B/ avon.asp>; "Avon Unveils New Brand, Strategy for Global Business Reaching Young Women," October 17, 2002, News.Com; "Avon Creates Line It Hopes Teens Will Buy and Sell," <www.cnet.com/investor/news/newsitem/0-9900-1028-20550771-0.html>; Business, October 2002, <www.responservice.com/archives/oct2002_issue2/business/internat.htm>.

PERSONAL SELLING: THE PRIMARY TWO-WAY MARKETING COMMUNICATION FUNCTION

Everyone does personal selling. Children sell lemonade, magazine subscriptions, and Girl Scout cookies. Students sell prom tickets and yearbook ads. Doctors "sell" exercise and diet programs to overweight patients. Lawyers "sell" briefs to skeptical judges. The fact is, **personal selling** is person-to-person interactive communication used to ultimately persuade. It is the oldest marketing communication function (see Exhibit 16-1).

The role of personal selling varies by type of business and industry, by the nature of the product or service, and by the business strategy. In B2B product categories, personal selling is one of the most important communication functions. In B2C business, it is often the primary MC function used for high-ticket goods and services such as cars, insurance, real estate, and financial services. Personal selling is also used in some retail stores, such as in department stores' cosmetic departments.

Total spending on personal selling is estimated to be close to the amount spent for all media advertising—over $200 billion.[1] Because personal selling is such an important function, salespeople are often some of the highest-paid employees in a company.

Today's professional salesperson is supported by information technology and the understanding that creating a good relationship will result in more sales than will the manipulative, hard-sell

EXHIBIT 16-1

Do you think personal selling will become more or less important in the future? Why?

TABLE 16-1	Evolution of Personal Selling		
	Sales Era, before 1960	*Marketing Era, 1960-1990*	*Partnering Era, after 1990*
Communication objective	Making transactions	Satisfying needs	Building relationships
Communication strategy	Persuade	Solve problem	Create value

Source: Barton Weitz, Stephen Castleberry, and John Tanner, *Selling* (Burr Ridge, IL: McGraw-Hill/Irwin, 1995), p. 12. Reprinted by permission from The McGraw-Hill Companies.

techniques of the past. Two-way communication, the essence of personal selling, is used to uncover customers' needs and wants and address misunderstandings and objections. In addition, good personal selling today provides product expertise and follow-up service to a transaction and, most important, helps customers to be more successful—that is, it creates value for them. As Table 16-1 shows, personal selling has evolved over the years from focusing on persuasion to creating value through partnering with customers.

Professional salespeople represent one aspect of a total marketing communication organization, and they therefore must conduct themselves in a way that is strategically consistent with all the other brand messages. Where personal selling is used extensively, the salesperson *is* the company in the eyes of customers and prospects.

How Personal Selling Works

Personal selling's primary role is customizing brand messages. Generally speaking, MC functions such as advertising, events and sponsorships, and brand publicity can create brand awareness and knowledge. But personal selling, integrated into the MC mix, can customize brand messages on a customer-by-customer basis.

In personal selling, a salesperson asks many questions of a prospective customer in an effort to understand how a product could benefit that customer. During the dialogue, the salesperson can gauge how the customer is reacting to a product offering. If there are misunderstandings, the salesperson can immediately clear them up. If the prospect does not like certain aspects of the product offering (price, credit terms, delivery schedule), the salesperson can address these concerns and perhaps negotiate a solution. This two-way interaction—and the instant customer gratification it can bring—is what makes personal selling the most powerful MC function a company can use.

Acquiring New Customers

Average annual customer turnover rates are approximately 15 to 20 percent, so salespeople must work constantly to acquire new customers to replace those lost. Acquiring new customers at a faster rate than the rate at which current ones leave the brand is one way to increase overall sales. The problem with acquisition, however, is that more time must be spent *locating potential new customers* (or prospects), (e.g., **prospecting**), than actually making the sale. Sometimes a salesperson may rely on a list (members of organizations, for example). Other marketing communication efforts, such as direct response or advertising, may be used to locate prospects and motivate them to raise their hands as being in the market for a product by contacting the company in some way. A **sales lead** is *a person or organization identified as being a prospect—someone able to benefit from the brand being sold.*

However, in many situations prospective customers don't contact the company. Instead, the salesperson must contact them—either acting on some information that identifies individuals as prospects or making contact simply because people's names appear on some list. That's what door-to-door salespeople do when they sell a product or service in a neighborhood, and it's what telemarketers do when they make their phone calls. *A sales call to a prospect who is not known by the sales rep and has not expressed any particular interest in the company or brand* is known as a **cold call.** Cold-calling is one of the most difficult forms of personal selling because there is no reason to believe the prospect is in the market for the product and the prospect may resent or be hostile about the intrusion.

Retaining Current Customers

A company's current customers must not be taken for granted. Just because they have been buying from a company for years, there is no guarantee they will buy from the company next week. As noted, from 15 to 20 percent of customers turn over each year—that is, they leave one brand for another.

Unfortunately, many businesses overemphasize acquiring new customers at the expense of servicing current ones. Marketing communication agencies themselves do this. Top managers—those most responsible for building their agencies—often spend the majority of their time doing personal selling to get new accounts. Once they sell a company on becoming a client, however, they assign other people in the agency to work with the new client, and they (top managers) go off to do more personal selling. (They are likely to work on a current account only when the client is dissatisfied and threatening to switch agencies.)

Because customer retention is at the heart of a brand relationship, salespeople must do things that not only create but maintain the relationship. A salesperson's number-one personal objective should be to create trust. He or she accomplishes this by demonstrating dependability, competence, a customer orientation, honesty, and likability.[2] Some sales managers say that current customers should always be treated as new customers—receiving the same level of attention and care as prospects (see Exhibit 16-2).

As in all areas of IMC, salespeople must create and manage customers' expectations—expectations not only of product performance but of all the services in support of a brand. After closing a sale, the salesperson should make sure the product arrives on time, that invoicing is properly handled, and that the customer knows how to use the product in the proper way. In B2B situations, the salesperson should be analyzing the customer's business to see in what ways the brand can further improve the customer's processes, sales, and profit. Salespeople are often invaluable information resources to their clients. Because they know how other companies use their products, salespeople have a much broader perspective on the product's applications than any single customer can have. They can add value by not letting customers repeat mistakes made by other customers, as well as by sharing ideas that work (as long as those ideas are not proprietary).

EXHIBIT 16-2
SAS sells software that helps companies manage their customer databases. How can a database help retain customers?

Personal Selling Objectives

You might think that when it comes to setting objectives for personal selling, the main objective would be quite simple: to sell all that you can. After all, the bottom line of personal selling is sales. Though hard to argue with, this objective doesn't give much direction from a communication standpoint to help ensure that the selling effort is focused and cost-effective. In personal selling as in every other MC function, specific objectives are needed that reflect the salesperson's efforts at every step in the selling process, and these objectives should be driven by a SWOT analysis (← Chapter 6).

Avon's personal selling objectives for the Mark line were:

- To broaden the Avon market by reaching a younger female audience.
- To create a hip brand identity for the new Mark line.
- To sign up a core group of young saleswomen.
- To identify prospective customers (and additional sales staff) from within the sales representatives' pool of friends.

Other typical and more measurable objectives for personal selling are:

- To increase distribution to 75 percent ACV (all commodity volume).
- To make sales calls on x number of prospective customers each month.
- To identify y qualified sales leads.
- To call on z current customers each month.
- To increase current customers' business by 5 percent.
- To have product featured in major retail accounts' advertising four times a year.
- To have each account (retailer) that carries the brand carry at least three or more varieties.

Personal Selling Strategies

One of the most successful personal selling strategies is *helping customers solve problems or take advantage of opportunities,* which is called **solution selling** or **enterprise selling** (see Exhibit 16-3). Too often, salespeople—by nature outgoing, gregarious, and aggressive—become so focused on making a sale that all they talk about is their product's features and benefits. The best salespeople, however, motivate prospects to talk about their businesses and the problems they are having or the opportunities they have not yet been able to take advantage of. **Needs assessment,** *asking a lot of questions about how a business operates,* accomplishes this.

The solution approach to selling focuses on the customer's needs and problems, then shows how a company's product can meet those needs and provide a solution for those problems. In high-tech industries, solution selling often involves integrating the sales and engineering functions to come up with new systems or customizing software to fit the customer's needs. Another personal selling strategy is to work with prospects and customers as business partners.

A partnering strategy requires that salespeople learn as much about their customers' businesses as they know about their own. A good example of this was Ed, a salesperson with whom this author once worked. Ed was a salesman for a processed meat company and was responsible for selling to a division of Kroger. He often frustrated the company's marketing department because he refused to present all of the promotions that the department developed. He presented some, but not every one, because he understood Kroger's needs and objectives so well

EXHIBIT 16-3
In this ad, the engineering firm Black & Veatch promotes its ability to help its client companies solve problems relating to water and energy.

that he knew what was good for Kroger and what was not. He didn't waste the chain's (or his own) time by trying to sell products and promotions that didn't fit Kroger's business plan. As a result, Kroger trusted Ed so much that he was often invited to review *competitive presentations* being made to Kroger. He had developed a partnering relationship based on trust. In the end, Ed was one of the top salespeople in the company.

A partnership starts with a working relationship between senior managers on both the marketer's and the retailer's sides. Dedicated retail marketing teams (located close to key retail accounts in the field) become focused on understanding and meeting the marketing objectives, strategies, and challenges of these key retail accounts. Major marketers, such as Kraft Foods, Procter & Gamble, Levi's, and Nike, operate this way.

Often a field marketing team supports the sales force by developing marketing communication plans tailored specifically for major retailer customers. These plans include account-specific sales and communication objectives as well as strategies for product mix, on-floor merchandising and POP displays, retail advertising, and tie-in events between the manufacturer and the retail chain.

Good salespeople function as a liaison between a company and its customers. Often they sell as hard inside their own company as they do outside, to convince their company to make product and process changes that would best serve their customers. Evidence of such customer focus may result in company executives asking salespeople, "Who are you working for, us or the customer?" The correct answer is "Both."

An important relationship strategy in the sales area, particularly in B2B product categories, is entertainment. This is another instance in which personal selling and trade promotions come together. In addition to sales representatives taking customers to dinner, to baseball games, and on other outings, many large companies have lodges and yachts in which customers and prospects are entertained. The budget for personal selling of one major packaged goods manufacturer, for example, includes $3 million for entertainment and $2 million for gifts.

As discussed in more detail in Chapter 19, one reason why companies sponsor race cars, golf and tennis tournaments, and other events is that these provide a special entertainment opportunity to reward good customers and motivate prospects to become customers. Companies that are sponsors can take customers behind the scenes of these events to meet the celebrities, which is a special privilege.

An increasingly important personal selling strategy involves knowing a customer's history of interactions with a company. The use of this strategy is greatly enhanced by technology—specifically by customer relationship management software (← Chapter 3).

Customer Relationship Management and Personal Selling

One of the technologies widely used by sales forces is customer relationship management. CRM is helpful in personal selling in two specific areas. First, it provides individual salespeople with an automated system for organizing sales leads, developing sales presentations, making sales presentations, processing orders, and recording customers' concerns and agreed-upon next steps. Second, having all this information in databases means that it can be easily shared with appropriate departments in the company (production, distribution, marketing, customer service, and accounting) and that customers are *integrated* into the company and customer data are integrated into the MC process. How customers respond to sales offers, their questions and concerns, and what they buy and don't buy are three examples of the valuable information that helps companies communicate with customers.

A survey that asked U.S. marketing executives how they would spend the majority of their MC budget if it were unlimited reveals the importance of CRM. The highest response was for CRM (28 percent), followed by mass media advertising (22 percent); sales promotion and public relations tied at 12 percent.[3]

Because speed is so important in business today, a sale is easily lost if a company spends too much time putting together an offer. Providing salespeople with laptops and modems to access relevant databases can significantly improve the efficiency and effectiveness of the typical sales call. In essence, CRM makes salespeople more productive communicators (see Exhibit 16-4). A salesperson using CRM can sit in a customer's office with a laptop computer, input that customer's needs, and, with a modem, access company databases to determine product design alternatives, product availability, prices, discounts available based on this customer's past volume, the customer's line of credit, and delivery schedules, among other things. Before leaving the customer's office, the salesperson is able to configure a customized product offering. Being able to do this type of communication quickly and accurately is an added value to customers and therefore a way to be more competitive.

IBM, a major provider of CRM software that provides this capability, has gone so far as to reposition itself as the "eBusiness" company (e-business should not be confused with e-commerce, which is more narrow and relates primarily to online selling). As IBM's ad explains, "eBusiness" integrates many operations.

CRM can also manage customer leads and allow sales force managers to make sure salespeople are doing their jobs. By tracking leads and sales calls, and by keeping customer and prospect profiles complete and up-to-date, CRM enables a company to[4]

EXHIBIT 16-4
In this ad, SalesLogix touts its CRM solutions designed for midsize B2B marketers.

- Know which leads were followed up and when, and what the results were.

- Give the leads that were not followed up to other salespeople, if appropriate.

- Determine why sales were not made (for example, a better competitive offer, dissatisfaction with a brand's current products or services, delivery not soon enough).

- Determine who within the prospect company has influence on the brand decision.

- Keep track of buyers who leave one company and go to another.

THE PERSONAL SELLING PROCESS

Personal selling, whether to acquire new customers or to sell additional products to current customers, involves generating and qualifying leads, making sales calls, identifying and responding to objections, closing the sale, and following up to build and maintain the customer relationship.

Generating and Qualifying Leads

Through generating and qualifying sales leads, a personal selling operation can segment and target its market. Sales leads may come from a company's direct-response advertising or from publicity about the company or its brands. They include individuals who call in for information or return a business reply card from a direct-mail piece or a "bingo" card from a trade or special-interest magazine (see Exhibit 16-5). Leads may also come from referrals—satisfied customers, employees, even competitors who feel a prospect is either too big or too small for them to handle.

SEND FOR
FREE INFORMATION
▼ FROM ADVERTISERS IN THIS SECTION ▼

Circle the numbers on the reply card that correspond to this list of companies:

OUTSOURCING

1. ADP
2. Arthur Andersen
3. AchieveGlobal
4. AT&T Solutions
5. Centrobe, An EDS Company
6. Compass America, Inc.
7. Consolidated Market Response
8. Corporate Project Resources, Inc.
9. Exelon
10. Express Personnel Services
11. Fusion Software Engineering Pvt. Ltd.
12. GE Information Services
13. Haas Corporation
14. Keane, Inc.
15. Lockheed Martin
16. Mastek Limited
17. Penske
18. PW Financial Solutions
19. Ryder Transportation Services
20. Sodexho Marriott Services
21. SOFTBANK Services Group
22. Wang Global

VARIABLE ANNUITIES

23. Aetna Retirement Services
24. Conseco
25. Golden American Life Insurance Company
26. Keyport Life Insurance Company
27. Lincoln Financial Group
28. Massachusetts Mutual Life Insurance Company
29. Nationwide/The BEST of AMERICA
30. Northwestern Mutual Life
31. Pacific Life
32. TIAA - CREF
33. Travelers Life & Annuity
34. VALIC

To receive information, circle the numbers below corresponding to numbers and companies listed above. Please type or print all information below.

Name

Title

Company

Address

City   State   Zip

Phone

Electronic Mail Address

1	2	3	4	5	6	7
8	9	10	11	12	13	14
15	16	17	18	19	20	21
22	23	24	25	26	27	28
29	30	31	32	33	34	

1. Title:
A. ☐ Chairman, President, CEO
B. ☐ Vice President
C. ☐ Financial Officer
D. ☐ CIO, MIS Executive
E. ☐ Other Company Officer
F. ☐ Owner/Partner
G. ☐ Middle Management
H. ☐ Professional (Doctor/Lawyer)
I. ☐ Non-Management
J. ☐ Other

2. Type of Firm
A. ☐ Manufacturing
B. ☐ Transportation, Communications, Public Utilities
C. ☐ Construction, Engineering, Mining, Oil/Gas
D. ☐ Information Technology
E. ☐ Other Industry
F. ☐ Banking/Finance
G. ☐ Wholesale/Retail Trade
H. ☐ Service
I. ☐ Government
J. ☐ Other

3. Number of employees in your company worldwide:
A. ☐ Small Office/Home Office
B. ☐ 5-49   D. ☐ 100-999
C. ☐ 50-99   E. ☐ 1,000 or more

S/T   Offer expires September 22, 1998   July 20, 1998   NA

EXHIBIT 16-5

This is a "bingo" card. Readers of the magazine in which the card appears can mark the products and brands they would like to know more about and send the card to the magazine, which forwards the sales leads to the respective companies.

"Our conversion-to-lead ratio was extraordinarily high because we were talking to the right people with the right message."[6]

An HP marketing specialist

When Hewlett-Packard (HP) wanted to motivate corporate customers to upgrade their equipment, the company segmented them by the volume of their previous purchases and then by the job description of the buyers for each of the companies. Specialized mailings were sent to people in each segment, who were then contacted by phone. The calls determined who was most likely to upgrade; those leads were sent to regional sales offices for personal follow-up.

Another way to generate leads is by getting prospects to self-select, as described in Chapter 7. When a customer takes the initiative in expressing interest in a product and providing profile information, that behavior can be highly predictive of future buying, as shown in Table 16-2. Sending brand messages by means of mass media and niche media motivates those interested to identify themselves. Offering premiums can encourage prospects to provide profile information so that a salesperson can decide whether they are *true* prospects.

Managing lead generation sometimes requires mediating the interaction of salespeople and marketing departments, because these two groups often disagree about leads.[5] Marketing often sees a lead as anyone who inquires about the product, while sales defines a lead as someone ready to buy. Marketing people complain that salespeople don't follow up on their leads, and salespeople reply that many marketing-generated leads aren't worth following up. The heart of the problem is that each department wants the other to *qualify* the leads (see Table 16-2).

Once leads are generated, they need to be qualified to determine whether they are genuine prospects. **Qualified leads** are *prospects who seem most likely to buy because of some information that is known about them.* Qualified leads are persons who (1) have a real need or opportunity that the brand can address, (2) have the ability to pay for the good or service, (3) have the authority to buy, and (4) are approachable. A company or person who buys infrequently or demands an unreasonably high level of service may not be a good lead. In the case of estate planning, for example, marketers try to qualify incoming leads by including in the invitation to a seminar a line such as "If your household income is more than $125,000 a year, you can benefit from estate planning." They hope that people who may think they want or need estate planning but don't have the wealth to justify it will not waste the time of the company offering the seminar.

When General Motors introduced its first electric car, it required all potential customers to fill out a customer-profile application before a sales representative would meet with them. GM wanted to target those who were environmentally conscious, already owned at least two gasoline-powered cars, and had a household income over $120,000 a year. Not all products are for all people, and potential customers should be assisted in deciding whether a particular product or brand is for them. Exhibit 16-6 is an

TABLE 16-2   Making Strategic Use of Customer Contacts

According to research:

    60 percent of all inquirers purchase something within a year.

    20 percent of inquirers have an immediate need.

    10 percent are hot leads.

    60 percent of inquirers also contact your competitors.

    50 percent of all new business starts as an inquiry.

But most companies do not take advantage of these inquiries:

    20 percent of inquirers never receive information.

    40 percent of inquirers receive information too late to use it.

    70 percent of inquirers are never contacted by a sales representative.

Source: Arthur M. Hughes, *The Complete Database Marketer* (Burr Ridge, IL: McGraw-Hill/Irwin, 1996), p. 390. Reprinted with permission from The McGraw-Hill Companies.

ad with a return-mail card whose purpose is to generate leads that can be contacted and further qualified.

Qualifying sales leads is so important because the cost of a personal sales call exceeds the cost of most other company-initiated brand contacts. Although the number varies greatly by product category, the average B2B sales call costs about $500. This figure includes the costs of getting to and from each customer (hotel, meals, entertainment, and transportation) plus salary and commission. In some product categories, such as local media sales, a salesperson can visit a half dozen customers a day, making the average cost per call about $50. But a person selling

EXHIBIT 16-6

In this magazine ad, Ryder Transportation Services explains how the company's services are being used by Ace Hardware. A reply card is tipped in (glued) to the ad to make response easy. When the cards come in, they are used to qualify the sales leads for Ryder's sales force.

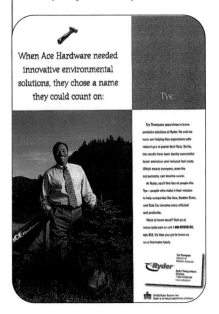

airport radar systems may travel halfway around the world to make one sales call, which could cost the company $10,000. Because the average sales call is so much more costly than using advertising or even direct-response marketing media, it is seldom cost-effective for salespeople to make cold calls. Even when a company has a new product, the company's current customers—who are usually the first group of prospects because they already know the company—must be qualified in order to avoid wasting personal selling time.

In B2B marketing, qualifying leads is especially important. The fact that it takes between three and seven personal sales contacts before a major B2B sale is made[7] means a salesperson may have to make several expensive sales calls before closing a deal. The higher the quality of a lead is, the fewer the visits that are required before a prospect responds. The quicker the response rate is, the lower is the cost per sale.

Making the Sales Call

The sales call occurs when the sale presentation is made. The extent and formality of this presentation varies greatly, depending on the offer itself and the relationship between the salesperson and the prospect. Sales presentations can occur during a visit to a prospect's home or office, or during a group meeting, such as the Avon Mark parties. Generally speaking, the more expensive the product offer is, the lengthier and more formal the presentation will be.

In some situations, personal sales calls are made by phone by a company's inside sales force. (This type of selling is different from telemarketing, explained in the next chapter, because these are not cold calls.) **Inside sales** are *salespeople who regularly call on accounts whose average size orders are not large enough to cost-justify an in-person sales call.* The initial sales call on these accounts may be made by a personal sales rep, or the prospect may respond to an ad or direct-mail piece. The follow-up calls are made by the inside sales department. In some cases members of an inside sales force call on the same customers for years and become very good friends although they never meet face-to-face.

Providing current customers and prospects with an appropriate and accurate sales presentation is critical. Successful salespeople script and practice their presentations to make sure they have the key information on the tip of their tongues. *Companies often provide* **sales literature,** *such as the cheese sales kit in Exhibit 16-7, to help the sales rep make the presentation. Sales literature may include videos, charts with data and documentation, planning forms to work through with the customer, catalogs, and demonstration materials.* Inside salespeople often refer their customers to the company's website for pictures and other visual demonstrations of a product. Good presentations are interesting, keep the attention of prospective customers, and lead them through their decision process to the point at which they are ready to buy.

In solution selling, the sales representative explains how the brand can help the prospect either solve a problem or take advantage of an opportunity. The presentation should be as much about the prospect as about the brand being sold. All of the details of the offer—such as price, delivery schedule, credit terms, and guarantees—are

EXHIBIT 16-7

This sales kit for the American Dairy Farmers' retail marketing program includes a welcoming letter, a sales video, a CD with TV and radio ads, as well as logos and other photographs and graphics. In the pocket on the left is a program overview with promotional dates, reminder postcards, and a plastic newspaper wrapper that includes a cheese description "slide rule."

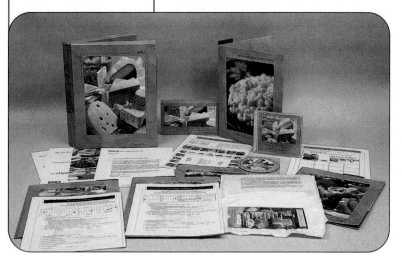

in the presentation. The end of the formal presentation "asks for the order." Asking for the order means asking the prospect to take action. In most situations, before prospects will agree to make a transaction, they have many questions and objections—reasons for not buying.

Handling Objections

If the only thing salespeople had to do was make a presentation and then take an order, they would not be paid very much. Getting a prospect to move through a decision-making process and say "yes" takes a great deal of skill and perseverance. An important skill is getting prospects to voice their objections—that is, to admit the real reason why they aren't convinced or why they don't want to buy now—and then responding to the objections. Understanding objections is key to understanding customers. In the best-case scenario, a sales rep learns what the prospect's objections are, is able to satisfactorily address the prospect's objections during the presentation, and goes on to close the sale. In the worst case, a prospect's unknown objections are not addressed, and a sale is lost. A sales rep who has no idea why a prospect didn't buy will fail to learn anything valuable that could be passed on to company management or avoided in the next call.

For example, a frequent response to a sales presentation is: "You have a good product and we could really use it, but we just can't afford it now." Good salespeople respond to this type of objection in one of several ways. One way is to offer the prospect credit terms that do not require payment for several months. Another is to point out how the product can reduce costs and therefore pay for itself in x number of months. Good salespeople anticipate objections and have answers ready, often in the form of information-filled charts and graphs.

Closing and Following Up the Sale

Once objections have been successfully addressed, the next step is **closing the sale,** which means *finalizing the terms of the transaction and getting the prospect's agreement to those terms,* followed by issuing a purchase order or signing a contract. Moving a customer to this point of commitment, to actually sign on the dotted line, is the goal of the entire selling process.

Once a sale is made, it is important to keep in contact with customers to make sure all of their expectations have been met. Was the product delivered on time? Was it in good shape? Was the billing correct? Is the customer aware of the next promotional opportunities? Making sure the customer is satisfied requires following up in person or by phone, e-mail, or regular mail (see Exhibit 16-8).

Some salespeople are reluctant to follow up, believing that doing so is asking for trouble, because when a customer tells about a problem, the result is extra work for the salesperson. Finding out what went wrong, finding the right people in the company to address the problem, and then making arrangements for the problem to be addressed take time for which a salesperson is not paid anything extra. But avoiding follow-up is a sign of short-sighted thinking. A customer who has a problem that isn't quickly addressed and solved is not likely to remain a customer. Also, follow-ups provide a legitimate excuse for contacting a customer and introducing new products, especially if the customer is satisfied with the first purchase.

EXHIBIT 16-8

This set of four postcards can be used by a salesperson to remind retailers about the campaign and its three promotional cycles and their themes.

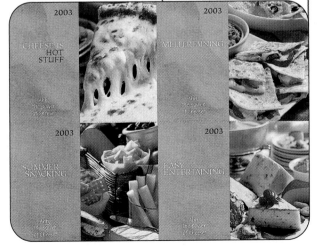

MANAGING THE PERSONAL SELLING FUNCTION

Managing personal selling involves recruiting, training, tracking, compensating, and rewarding sales reps, as well as managing budgets and divvying up accounts. How best to integrate personal selling into the company's overall marketing communication program is also a management concern. Two management issues especially relevant to IMC are (1) how to measure the effects of IMC on sales and (2) how to compensate and reward salespeople. The former interfaces with some of the sales-promotion tools; the latter is similar to spending money on advertising media.

Measuring Personal Selling Efforts

A number of measurements can be used to evaluate personal selling. A *cost per call* is calculated by comparing a salesperson's total costs (salary, commission, expenses) to the number of calls made in a specified period of time (generally one year). A *sales-call-to-close ratio* can be determined by comparing the total number of sales calls made to the number of prospects and customers who actually bought.

Tracking these measurements helps ensure the sales effort is going in the right direction. For example, if the overall company call-to-sale ratio is 5-to-1 this year (meaning one sale was made for every five sales calls), steps should be taken to reduce that ratio to, say, 4.5-to-1 for the following year. Such ratios can be used to evaluate individual sales representatives, as well. If the company call-to-sale ratio for the average salesperson is 6-to-1, for example, a salesperson with an 11-to-1 ratio may well be advised to go work for the competition! Here are examples of how to figure some of these measurements:

$$\text{Cost per call} = \frac{\text{Total sales costs}}{\text{Number of calls made}} = \frac{\$2,500,000}{8,500} = \$294$$

$$\text{Call/sales ratio} = \frac{\text{Number of calls made}}{\text{Number of sales made}} = \frac{8,500}{1,700} = 5$$

$$\text{Sales cost per sale} = \frac{\text{Total sales costs}}{\text{Number of sales made}} = \frac{\$2,500,000}{1,700} = \$1,470$$

For IMC, several other important measures of how well a salesperson performs are (1) the average length of time an individual's accounts have been buying from the company, (2) the average annual sales and profitability of these accounts, and (3) the number of referrals made by these accounts. Because a primary IMC objective is to retain customers, the average customer lifetime should continue to increase if a salesperson is doing a good job. Also, current customers should be motivated to increase the quantity of their purchases from year to year. Finally, customers who have a good relationship with a salesperson and a brand will be more likely to recommend that person and brand to other companies which means the number of these referrals should be tracked.

Over time, determining how many of a salesperson's customers remain with the company and how many have been lost is relatively easy, as is determining how many sales each salesperson has generated. Sophisticated accounting software can now tell the overall profitability of each salesperson's customers. Using discounts, premiums, and other considerations can make a sale fairly easy, but the best salespeople are those who generate sales without making so many concessions that the company makes little or no profit on the transactions.

Compensation and Rewards

Compensation systems are changing in personal selling. Traditionally, compensation was based totally or primarily on sales volume. Some companies still have salespeople work solely on **commission** (which is *a percentage of the sales price paid to a salesperson for each transaction*). Often, top salespeople who work on 100 percent commission are some of the highest-paid people in a company. The problem with commissions being the major compensation factor is that they reward transactions rather than long-term relationships.

To have a customer relationship focus, companies must balance how they reward salespeople, because people respond to what is measured and rewarded. This is why salespeople are increasingly being evaluated and rewarded not only for sales but also for how long customers have been buying from the company (retention), how much customers are increasing their purchase quantities (customer growth), and how much customers are helped by the salesperson to solve their problems and increase their productivity (customer satisfaction).

Special prizes, such as trips and other high-value premiums, are frequently used to increase sales in the short term. For a new-product introduction, for example, salespeople may receive an extra incentive if 65 percent or more of their customers buy the new product within the first 90 days of its availability.

In addition to evaluating salespeople according to set objectives, companies nowadays also ask customers to rate the salespeople who call on them. Because the success of personal selling can be so dependent on working with other people in an organization, some companies even ask people in their distribution, accounting, and customer-service departments to rate salespeople. It is critical that the salesperson's performance be consistent with the firm's positioning and reinforce the firm's other marketing communications. What the salesperson says and does will either confirm or contradict the company's other brand messages.

Integrating Personal Selling and Other Marketing Communication Functions

The primary criterion for determining when personal selling should be integrated into the MC mix is whether the margin on each transaction is large enough to cover the high cost of personal selling. Procter & Gamble can't cost-justify having a sales representative sell its Tide and Ivory soap to individual consumers because the selling cost would be many times the average purchase price of a few dollars. Personal selling is used when a product is complex and the purchase will require assistance to use and maintain the product, such as enterprise software systems, medical imaging devices, and automotive diagnostic equipment sold to auto repair shops. Also, personal selling is integrated into the MC mix when there are a limited number of customers, such as in the beverage can industry, which has only a few dozen major customers (primarily manufacturers of soft drinks and beer).

Personal Selling and Advertising

In B2C selling, advertising is used by retailers such as car dealers and home furnishing stores to get consumers in the door. These retailers know that the products they sell are major purchases for which advertising can at best only create interest. Most buyers of cars and furniture ask many questions during the information-gathering stage of decision making. Once the prospect is in the store, a salesperson is the best resource for responding to these questions, which can be done while customers closely examine the products being considered.

EXHIBIT 16-9

EXHIBIT 16-10

The State Farm ad is directed to small-business owners and invites them to call a sales rep or visit the company's website.
The Fidelity ad describes the services a Fidelity sales rep can provide and invites interested readers to call a toll-free number.

In B2B selling, advertising's brand awareness and brand knowledge do a certain amount of preselling (see Exhibit 16-9). Advertising can be used to communicate information about the company behind a product as well as key product benefits. Mass media advertising can reach a wide range of prospective customers for far less than it would cost for a salesperson to contact the same number and ask whether they were interested in the brand (see Exhibit 16-10). Nevertheless, most B2B decision makers have many questions. Complex products, for example, may need to be demonstrated.

Another aspect of advertising that is integrated into the personal selling process is the designing and production of brochures, sales kits, and other materials that salespeople use during sales calls. These sales kits can be anything from a simple set of price sheets, to a fancy glossy binder, to an elaborate box of varied materials. The American Dairy Association's Cheese Retail Sales Kit (see Exhibit 16-8) was prepared to support and tie into the association's "Ahh, the power of cheese" advertising campaign. These types of sales kits usually include sections on product selection and pricing, merchandising ideas, retailer advertising aids available, consumer advertising schedules, public relations efforts, consumer promotions, market research, and ways to customize these sales materials for individual retail stores.

Personal Selling and Public Relations

Like advertising, brand publicity in the form of press and video releases can help create brand awareness that makes a salesperson's job easier, as it saves time explaining who the company is and what it stands for. In addition, public relations is especially helpful to the sales force in selling innovative and complex products, particularly when a company's brand is endorsed by a third party such as an industry writer or consultant.

The sales force not only benefits from public relations but also *does* public relations. Salespeople are often the most pervasive public face of the company. Because a salesperson is usually the only person from the company who customers ever see and talk to face-to-face, the salesperson *is the company*. If the salesperson is responsive and helpful, the company is perceived as being responsive and helpful. This is why most companies that provide cars or trucks for their sales force insist that these vehicles be kept clean, because they are constantly seen by thousands of people every day (many different stakeholders).

Personal Selling and Direct Response

Direct response is frequently used to generate leads for sales representatives. It may also be used for follow-up contact with current customers. IBM has embarked on several integrated, database-driven pilot campaigns that have generated three times as many qualified leads as did previous campaigns. A key component of these programs is asking customers what they are looking for in products and services and how they like to be contacted by the company—by mail, e-mail, phone, fax, brochures, salesperson's visit, or not at all.

Personal Selling and Sales Promotion

A number of sales-promotion tools and techniques can be incorporated into personal selling to strengthen the salesperson's presentation and help close the deal. For example, a sales kit may include free samples, discounts and coupons, or product-related gifts. Trade promotion (◀ Chapter 15) is an important aspect of channel marketing, which relies heavily on personal selling. Finally, sales reps themselves are the target for incentive programs that are designed to increase their enthusiasm for a product and encourage them to push the product more and sell harder.

Strengths of Personal Selling

The primary objective of personal selling is building trusting relationships (that result in sales). Any brochure or ad can describe the benefits of a brand, but a personal sales call can humanize a brand and a company, particularly when that interaction is supported by CRM.

The greatest strength of personal selling, therefore, is customized two-way communication, which is the ultimate way to integrate a product and its features with customers' wants, needs, and opportunities. Two-way communication is the most powerful form of persuasion—not only to encourage someone to buy but, more important, to encourage that person to remain a customer. By using face-to-face communication, a skilled salesperson can observe a prospect's body language and encourage him or her to express objections. The one-to-one situation facilitates instant feedback to objections (which a good salesperson should anticipate and be prepared to address). Once a relationship is established, motivating sales becomes much easier.

Accountability and measurability, further strengths of personal selling, mean that this aspect of IMC is highly numbers-driven. In most cases, a company can

EXHIBIT 16-11

In this ad for Agillion, a Web-based business software company, personalized customer interaction is supported by an electronic database. The message is that the company can maintain the personalization even if the salesperson is on vacation.

easily measure the sales that each salesperson generates in a specified period. Because most companies use commission-based compensation plans for their sales forces, both companies and salespeople are concerned about how salespeople spend their time and what their selling efforts produce.

Personal selling is the most flexible IMC element. It allows sales messages to be tailored to each customer and prospect, allowing instant changes in a sales presentation as the situation requires. Negotiation is a vital aspect of this flexibility. Personal communication makes it much easier to find the terms that best suit the buyer's needs and to adjust the offer accordingly. If a buyer is primarily concerned with an earlier delivery date, for example, a salesperson may absorb the cost required to meet this date by getting the customer to either buy an additional amount or pay for the merchandise sooner.

Because good salespeople are in constant contact with their customers and know their customers' business, they can collect information and build valuable customer databases. A rich customer database offers vital information to marketing people, allowing them to prepare personalized, targeted messages. Such databases also become very valuable when a customer is assigned to a different salesperson. The Agillion ad in Exhibit 16-11 illustrates how database systems are being used to support customized sales programs.

Limitations of Personal Selling

Like all other MC functions, personal selling has some limitations. The most important limitation is its high cost. Maintaining a sales force is costly because it requires not only salaries (or commissions) but also sales call expenses, recruitment, training, and other internal support functions. Because it is basically a one-to-one medium, there are few economies of scale. In fact, two or three salespeople sometimes go to a single important customer's office to make a presentation or make multiple presentations if they represent different product lines. In personal selling, companies don't even think about cost per thousand (it would give most executives a heart attack). As previously mentioned, a single personal sales call can run into the hundreds of dollars.

Another limitation is that some salespeople overemphasize making a quick sale and lack the patience to build relationships based on promising long-term leads. A study of 40,000 buyers found that only 11 percent of those who made purchases did so within three months of their first contact with the company. The study concluded: "It's important to put a relationship marketing program in place to nurture long-term leads."[8] This limitation, however, is not always the fault of salespeople. Compensation based on commissions fosters the emphasis on transactions at the expense of relationships. Salespeople should be rewarded for generating sales, but when volume is the major portion of their focus, there is a tendency to overpromise in order to make a sale.

The human connection that was described as a strength can also create a dilemma: customers may develop loyalty to salespeople rather than to the company or the brand. As a result, when salespeople change jobs, their customers may move with them. A partial solution to the problem is for the company to maintain a comprehensive database of customer interactions with the company. The database enables a new salesperson to immediately step up and work with each customer intelligently because each customer's history with the company is available.

One of the strengths of personal selling is flexibility, but the flip side of flexibility is often strategic inconsistency. When salespeople begin to craft customer-specific sales deals, they may create and deliver brand messages that are at odds with the overall brand strategy. An upscale, status brand positioning will not be reinforced if a salesperson continually encourages retailers to run sales.

Just as direct-response advertising is seen as intrusive and often in poor taste, personal selling has developed an image problem over the decades because of so much high-pressure selling and less-than-ethical practices. Thus, a common jibe is that someone who seems sleazy is like a "used-car salesman." Many companies today give salespeople euphemistic titles such as marketing associate, marketing representative, admissions coordinator, clinical liaison, professional services representative, or program manager. The idea is to counteract the rejection associated with the word *salesperson*.

A study of college students in the United States, Britain, and Thailand found that students from these diverse geographical areas all had a very low impression of sales as a career opportunity. Although 72 percent agreed with the statement "The financial rewards from selling are excellent," 40 percent said a salesperson's job security is poor. Another sign of the reputation problem comes from a Mesa, Arizona, electrical wiring firm that got almost no response to ads in college papers that said, "Looking for entry-level salespeople." When the same company instead ran an ad for marketing people, résumés poured in.[9]

Regardless of the image that personal selling has, this marketing communication function is a huge industry. For many, it offers an entry-level position into marketing; for others, it provides a lifetime career that brings many financial and personal rewards.

A FINAL NOTE: HIGHEST COST, GREATEST IMPACT

Personal selling is the 900-pound gorilla of marketing communication. It costs a lot to feed and care for this beast, but when used for good, its muscle and impact are generally far greater than any of the other MC functions. Integrating personal selling into the MC mix must always be cost-justified, because the cost is significant compared to the cost per sale of all the other ways to reach customers and prospects. When personal selling is the number-one MC function used, efforts should constantly be made to see where less expensive MC functions and media could be used to help salespeople do their jobs, allowing reps to use their time to do only what personal selling does best—engaging in one-to-one dialogue that permits an instant response to the individual questions and concerns of customers and prospects.

Key Terms

closing the sale 527
cold call 519
commission 529
enterprise selling 520

inside sales 526
needs assessment 520
personal selling 517
prospecting 518

qualified leads 524
sales lead 518
sales literature 526
solution selling 520

Key Point Summary

EXHIBIT 16-12

This ad for management software company PeopleSoft explains how its software can help with customer relationship management (CRM) programs.

Key Point 1: Personal Selling's Role and Objectives

Personal selling is two-way communication that uncovers and satisfies the needs of prospects, providing mutual, long-term benefits for both parties. Personal selling's primary role is retaining and growing customers, as well as customer acquisition. When this is accomplished, sales are made.

Key Point 2: The Personal Selling Process

The process of personal selling, whether for acquiring new customers or selling to current customers, involves generating leads, qualifying leads, making the sales call, identifying and responding to objections, closing the sale, and following up to build and maintain the customer relationship.

Key Point 3: Personal Selling Management

In addition to integration, the two big issues in sales management are measuring the effectiveness of the effort and identifying the appropriate compensation and reward system. Personal selling is most effective when it is supported by other MC functions, such as advertising, public relations, and direct response. IMC programs rely on personal selling because of its strengths, which include the power of personalized, two-way communication, relationship building, accountability, flexibility, and the ability to collect useful information in the process of making a sale.

Lessons Learned

Key Point 1: Personal Selling's Role and Objectives

a. Why is the personal nature of personal selling its greatest strength?
b. Define *personal selling*. What is meant by the statement "Personal selling is more than making a sale."
c. Explain the evolution of personal selling. How has the focus of the effort changed over time?
d. Explain how personal selling occurs at various points in the marketing process. What roles do sales representatives typically play at each point?
e. Sales calls should be treated like planned communication. What does that mean to a sales rep getting ready to make a call?
f. How is personal selling used to acquire and to retain customers?
g. What is the salesperson's number-one personal objective? Why is it so important?
h. Explain solution selling and its enterprise dimension.
i. What is CRM? Why is it important in personal selling?

Key Point 2: The Personal Selling Process

a. What are the four steps in the personal selling process?
b. What is a lead? Why is it important to qualify a lead?
c. What is inside sales? How might it be used by your college or university?
d. What is involved in closing a sale?
e. Why is it important to address objections during a sales call?
f. Explain the importance of follow-up for a salesperson.

Key Point 3: Personal Selling Management

a. Differentiate between the cost per call and call/sales calculations, and explain how they are used.
b. Identify one personal selling measurement that is particularly relevant to IMC managers, and explain why it is important.
c. What is the problem with rewarding salespeople through commissions? What can be done to solve that problem?
d. Give an example of how personal selling can be integrated with these MC functions: (1) advertising, (2) public relations, (3) direct response, and (4) sales promotion.
e. How might Avon use MC functions other than personal selling in support of the Mark selling strategy?

Chapter Challenge

Writing Assignment

Visit a local store that has sales clerks on the floor. Analyze how they (1) greet a customer, (2) try to identify the customer's needs and match the needs to merchandise, (3) up-sell, (4) close the sale, and (5) make an effort to build a relationship with the customer. Are their efforts effective? Write a memo to the store's manager explaining what he or she could do to improve the performance of the sales clerks.

Presentation Assignment

Assume you are explaining one of the following to the new Avon Mark sales force:

- The personal selling process.
- How to identify and qualify sales leads.
- How to make a sales call.
- How to close a sale.
- How to follow up on a sale.

Prepare a presentation on this topic as if you were addressing a group of new young saleswomen for the Mark line, and present it to your class.

Internet Assignment

Go to the website for The Journals of Personal Selling & Sales Management. Click on "Table of Contents." You will then be given a choice of issues. Keep selecting issues and looking at the recaps of major stories in each until you have found at least two that discuss how personal selling ties in with the rest of a company's marketing communication effort. What were the main point(s) in these stories (as explained in the stories' abstracts)?

Chapter 17

Public Relations and Brand Publicity

Key Points in This Chapter

1. What is public relations, and how does it relate to IMC?
2. What are the strengths and limitations of brand publicity?
3. What are the brand-publicity tools?
4. Why is corporate communication important to IMC programs?

Chapter Perspective

The Relationships in Public Relations

Public relations professionals have always understood the concept of relationships—after all, the word *relations* is part of their job title. Unfortunately, many marketing people in the past did not always recognize or appreciate the value of public relations.

Some major steps toward bringing marketing and public relations departments closer came in the early 1990s with the development of a concept called *relationship marketing*, pioneered by PR consultant Regis McKenna.[1] At the same time, courses devoted to relationship marketing began to develop in business schools around the world. Although McKenna's background is public relations, he challenged the marketing industry to become more "customer-centric" and to better understand customer relationships.

"Advertising, promotion, and market-share thinking are dead," wrote McKenna, "and what counts are the relationships a company develops with its customers, suppliers, partners, distributors—even its competitors."

IMC is helping introduce to marketing practitioners some of the concepts that public relations professionals have known about for years, such as the importance of stakeholder relationships. Marketing people are discovering the power and value of marketing public relations—that is, brand publicity—to deliver highly effective, cost-efficient messages. At the same time, public relations people are learning more about marketing and are using marketing concepts such as branding and positioning to build corporate communication strategies.

ORKIN'S INSECT SAFARI PUTS BUGS ON WHEELS

Okay, you got the worst assignment in the world— bugs. Rather, how to get rid of bugs. How can you do anything creative to publicize pest control?

That's probably what you would be thinking if you were assigned to the Orkin Pest Control account. The creative folks at the Ketchum public relations agency, however, saw bugs as a wonderful opportunity for increasing brand visibility and getting people more involved with pest control. Here's the rest of the story.

For 100 years, Orkin Pest Control has been a leader in getting rid of unwanted bugs (the kinds with legs). However, business was off for Orkin in 2001. Sales leads were down, and traditional advertising did not seem to work anymore. More worrisome, people had more trust in local exterminators than they did in a national franchise.

In spite of these problems, consumers still saw Orkin as "the leader in technology" and an educator in insect-world information. Its sponsorship of the Insect Zoo at the Smithsonian Institution's National Museum of Natural History was an important factor in establishing the brand's reputation. The Insect Zoo, which first opened in 1976, was renamed the O. Orkin Insect Zoo when it was refurbished in 1993 with extensive renovations supported by a generous gift from the Orkin Company. According to the Smithsonian's annual report, the 40 docent educators who volunteer to be tour guides at the Orkin Insect Zoo greet more than a million visitors a year.

Ketchum's solution to Orkin's sales problems was to leverage Orkin's Smithsonian connection and its brand position by taking the Insect Zoo idea to local markets. The "Smithsonian O. Orkin Insect Safari" campaign was supported through local publicity, grassroots marketing programs, and online communication. Its objectives were (1) to increase sales leads in its top markets and (2) to reach more consumers directly through the "Insect Safari" exhibit and indirectly through a website.

The campaign's strategy involved creating a free traveling exhibit contained in a 53-foot truck that would visit schools across the country with a multimedia educational program on bugs. The innovative program included a hands-on science exhibit with 3-D models, cross-curricular educational materials that could be tied in with classroom activities, and engaging interactive presentations that combined science, art, and storytelling. Orkin also partnered with local schools, museums, teachers, and entomologists, who connected with the local target audience indirectly through children. Other Safari partners included the Bayer Corporation and CNN/ Turner Learning.

EFFECTIVENESS CASE

EXHIBIT 17-1

The imaginative "Insect Safari" exhibit was unveiled at the Smithsonian. There and at the local exhibits, entomologists taught schoolchildren about insects, and teachers were provided with pre- and post-lessons to reinforce the learning. Students were also given an activity book to use at home with their parents. Publicity was provided through newsletters by the local museums and schools.

A website, www.insectsafari.com, was created to inform people of the exhibit, provide the truck route, and give background information on insects. It also presented a popular Orkin video, *The World's Most Dangerous Pests*, as well as an interactive teaching program titled *Fred's Bugalizer Studio*. In addition, the site offered a virtual tour of the O. Orkin Insect Zoo at the Smithsonian. Teachers' lessons and classroom posters were also available online through this site.

The "Insect Safari" campaign was a great success, producing an increase in sales leads in 70 percent of the markets visited by the tour. Teachers, volunteers, and students who visited the exhibit rated it high in quality, well researched, and interestingly presented. Kids sent thank-you notes, and teachers said they would host the Safari again and use the in-class materials.

In terms of publicity, Ketchum counted 512 stories in the media, including eight hours of television coverage and 41 morning-show interviews. Ketchum's planners estimated the reach at 66 million impressions. All the stories mentioned Orkin as the sponsor. The response was so positive that the "Insect Safari" received a Silver Anvil Award from the Public Relations Society of America (PRSA).

Source: Sara Gulbas, "The Silver Anvil Award," December 2002. Used by permission; Insect Safari website, <www.insectsafari.com/home.asp>.

THE PRACTICE OF PUBLIC RELATIONS

Public relations covers a wide variety of activities designed to affect both public opinion and the opinion of specific stakeholders whose support a company needs. Public relations can be a concept, a profession, and a management function, as well as a practice. Its objective is to create goodwill and understanding—positive relationships—between an organization and its stakeholders. The "Insect Safari" is a good example of a campaign designed to reach a number of stakeholders and create a more positive image for its sponsor (see Exhibit 17-2).

The interests of public relations and marketing overlap, but in many organizations public relations operates separately from marketing and has different goals. One PR professional explains the difference between the two areas this way: "whereas marketing and sales have as their primary objective selling an organization's products, public relations attempts to sell the organization itself."[2]

Public relations strategy can be focused on the corporate brand or on a product brand. Public relations departments generally have responsibility for managing the corporate image. Marketing is generally responsible for managing the image of product brands. The distinction between the two is sometimes fuzzy, especially when the corporate name is the same as the brand name (Nike, Disney) and when both the corporate and the product brand names are used to identify a product (Sony Walkman).

This chapter begins with an overview of the public relations industry and the types of activities it includes. It then explores brand publicity, whose primary objective from an IMC perspective is building a brand's overall credibility. The third main section is devoted to corporate communication—building a company's image and reputation and other corporate public relations areas that are particularly important to IMC, such as employee and financial relations and crisis communication.

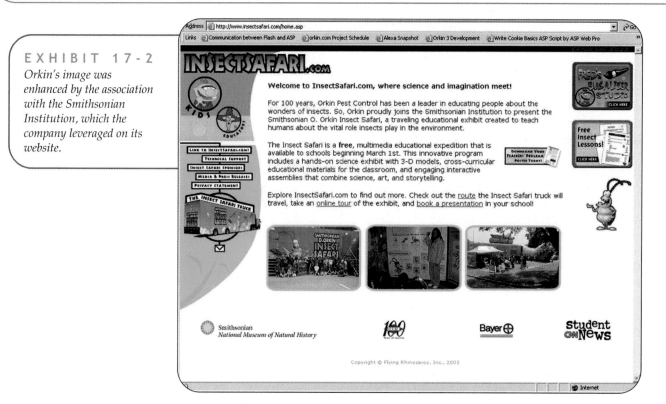

Defining Public Relations

Public relations, as introduced in Chapter 1, is *a communication function used to promote mutual understanding between an organization and its various stakeholder groups.* Here is a list of responsibilities and functions of a public relations department:[3]

- To serve as the central source of information about the organization, and as the official channel of communication between the organization and the public.
- To bring to public attention, through appropriate media, significant facts, opinions, and interpretations that will serve to keep the public aware of the organization's policies and actions.
- To coordinate activities that affect the organization's relations with the general public or with other stakeholder groups
- To collect and analyze information on the changing attitudes of key public groups and stakeholders toward the organization.
- To plan and administer informational programs designed to fulfill most effectively the responsibilities listed above.
- To coordinate the public relations activities with other marketing communication efforts within the organization and to bring a relationship perspective to those areas.

The Public Relations Industry

Public relations is one of the fastest growing of all the communication functions used in IMC. Like most of the other functions, it suffered a downturn following the bad economic news of 2001 and the September 11 tragedy. Industry revenues fell 2.7 percent in 2001, but the industry had experienced a healthy 220 percent growth during the previous decade.[4] Although some of this growth was the result of mergers and acquisitions and the dot-com boom, the trend indicates a healthy industry. Public relations is growing because it has the power to cut through message clutter.[5]

Compared to dollars spent on mass media advertising, public relations spending is relatively minor because public relations triggers little or no media cost, which consumes the major portion of an advertising budget. The major public relations expenditures are for personnel and the production of events, newsletters, brochures, annual reports, and corporate advertising.

Types of Public Relations Activities

In an effort to maintain good relationships with all of an organization's important stakeholders, public relations programs include various "relational," programs, as Exhibit 17-3 shows in an ad for a public relations agency. Table 17-1 indicates the range of "publics," or stakeholder audiences, that are targeted by different kinds of public relations activities, from government officials to employees, the financial community, and the media. These areas of expertise may be developed internally within a company, but they are also available from PR agencies. Some public relations agencies provide a full range of programs, and almost all do publicity and media relations. Some specialize in certain communication areas such as marketing public relations and government relations. Agencies may also focus on specific industries, such as pharmaceuticals, agriculture, or high technology. This chapter discusses these areas, beginning with marketing public relations, commonly known as *brand publicity.*

EXHIBIT 17-3
A house ad for Barkley Evergreen & Partners identifies the agency's areas of specialty as crisis communication, cause marketing, internal communication, media relations, and reputation management.

BRAND PUBLICITY

From an IMC perspective, one of the most important activities in PR is **brand publicity,** *the use of nonpaid media messages to deliver brand information designed to positively influence customers and prospects.* It is estimated that up to 70 percent of the average public relations firm's revenues comes from doing brand publicity.[6] Another indication of the importance of brand publicity is that 13 of the 15 largest public relations firms in the United States have been acquired by advertising agency conglomerates, which recognize the importance of this function in the MC mix.[7]

With the growing interest in relationship marketing, companies are beginning to learn more about relationship management from a public relations viewpoint. To create "more symmetrical relationships," a term used in public relations to describe interactivity, public relations communication must become more data-driven, a point Sandra Moriarty made in *Public Relations Quarterly:*[8]

T A B L E   1 7 - 1   Public Relations Activities and Their Audiences

Activity	Description
Publicity	Programs that support product and brand communication and promotion (brand publicity), and that are directed primarily at customers and prospects.
Media relations	Activities that distribute information to the media creating publicity for an organization; activities that cultivate relationships of trust with key reporters and editors.
Corporate communication	Managed by senior-level counselors, such programs focus on corporate identity, reputation management, and strategic counseling for top management. Responsibilities that are sometimes found in corporate relations include • *Issues management*: functions that monitor public opinion and advise senior management, particularly in companies in sensitive or controversial industries such as pharmaceuticals, liquor, and cigarettes. • *Community relations*: programs that involve members of the local community and address their concerns. • *Government relations (public affairs)*: information programs for legislators, government bodies, and regulatory agencies. • *Industry relations*: activities that address the concerns of the industry in which the company competes.
Employee relations	Internal communication programs that keep employees informed and build their morale (can also be part of internal marketing programs); employee relations can also include labor relations programs.
Financial or investor relations	Information programs for the financial community—investors, analysts, and the financial press.
Crisis management	A general plan designed to manage how a company responds when disaster strikes. It addresses all relevant stakeholders—the general public, employees, the community, media, investors.

As PR people become more proficient with databases and interactive technologies, two-way communication with stakeholders will continue to increase. As it does, there will need to be some serious creative thinking about what it means to participate in communication initiated by a wide range of stakeholders.

As noted earlier, many companies separate marketing and public relations. Public relations managers, particularly those who track issues and public opinions, typically report to the president of the organization. Meanwhile, advertising managers usually report to a vice president of marketing. Where there is no cross-functional organization, advertising managers may have little or no contact with their counterparts in public relations.

An example of the mixed messages this situation can create was demonstrated in a recent edition of the *Wall Street Journal*. On one page was a full-page ad for the high-tech firm Bay Networks extolling the virtues of the company's electronic communication routing and switching capabilities. On the very next page, the lead news story highlighted Bay Networks' disappointing sales, an indication that the company was not satisfying as many customers as it intended.[9] If the company's advertising and public relations departments had talked, perhaps they could have avoided having these two conflicting messages appear at the same time. A negative news story can more than cancel out the effects of a typical "brag and boast" ad.

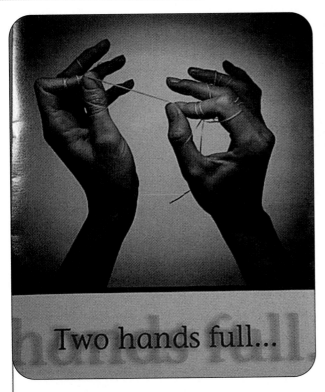

EXHIBIT 17-4
This award-winning news kit was developed to announce the Water Pik Flosser. To get the attention of gatekeepers—the editors and writers who decide what news is worth covering—the packet was designed with a toothbrush doll figure held together with dental floss.

Turf battles and philosophical differences between marketing and public relations have been referred to as "marketing imperialism." This term reflects the views of some public relations managers and PR professors who fear that, in IMC, public relations will become subordinate to marketing. Although this tension seems to be decreasing, it can still be found in some companies and universities. Some PR professionals and academics argue that if any changes are made, marketing should report to public relations, given the latter's traditional role in managing stakeholder relationships and its emphasis on listening as well as talking to stakeholders. However, as long as marketing has a much larger budget than PR, as is the case in most companies, this is not likely to occur.

Although advertising gets a lot of credit for creativity, original ideas are just as prized by the public relations industry, which has its own creativity award, the Silver Anvil, sponsored by the Public Relations Society of America (www.prsa.org).[10] An example comes from Baltimore-based McCormick & Company, which makes spices. Since 1977, the company has been printing its annual report with a scent that smells like one of its spices. Each year, the spice is kept a secret, and the business section of the Baltimore *Sun* runs a pool whose participants guess which scent is being used. The annual report not only gets attention for its novel aroma but also generates media coverage. Another example of publicity creativity is Water Pik's "Two Hands Full" news kit, shown in Exhibit 17-4.

Planning Brand Publicity

Like all marketing communication, an effective publicity effort is guided by a plan. The planning steps are similar to those for other forms of marketing and MC planning: (1) reviewing the situation, (2) setting objectives, (3) developing strategies and tactics, and (4) evaluation (which is covered in Chapter 22).

Reviewing the Situation

Reviewing the situation involves background research, which includes finding the traditional information about the company, the marketplace and competitors, the product or service, and consumers. As with advertising, attitude research is particularly important because most publicity programs hope to affect people's opinions. Attitude research also helps identify key internal strengths and weaknesses and the external problems and opportunities that the publicity program needs to leverage or address. This step is part of the overall SWOT analysis (◄ Chapter 6).

Setting Objectives

Objectives for a public relations plan are similar to advertising objectives in that they seek to build awareness and brand knowledge. However, publicity can also be used to

- Create or increase brand awareness (visibility).
- Increase knowledge.
- Create or change attitudes.
- Create buzz (word of mouth).
- Influence opinion leaders.
- Stimulate referrals and advocacy.
- Generate a sense of involvement.

In some brand-publicity programs, the objective is to get the brand name mentioned in the mass media in as many different ways, times, and places as possible. The assumption is that the more mentions there are in the press, the more top-of-mind awareness the brand will gain. This shotgun strategy may not be cost-effective because, like advertising, publicity should be targeted as much as possible to reach audiences that will be interested in the brand.

Publicity can often create a deeper level of brand knowledge than advertising because it uses media messages (news releases, brochures, events) that can provide more information than can be put into an ad. Publicity is also used to create positive attitudes, as Exhibit 17-5 illustrates. In fact, creating a positive impression of a brand is equally as important as creating awareness.

One of the objectives of the "Insect Safari" campaign was to get people talking about Orkin. Brand publicity can drive the kind of positive word-of-mouth comments among friends, family, and associates that creates **buzz**, a term that refers to *excited talk about a brand*. In particular, public relations seeks to reach and affect **influentials**, *opinion leaders and early adopters who influence other people*. For Orkin, the important opinion leaders were the teachers who influenced the children who then influenced their parents. From buzz come referrals and advocacy on behalf of

EXHIBIT 17-5
In a campaign to position itself as supporting responsible drinking behavior, Anheuser-Busch runs ads helping parents deal with underage drinking.

the brand by customers and other stakeholders, such as dealers and suppliers. Special events planned as part of a public relations program can elicit a high level of brand involvement between a customer and a brand (← Chapter 5).

Buzz is a product of word of mouth. When a brand competes in a crowded and cluttered category, some companies are finding that it might be better—and cheaper—to let customers discover cool new products themselves and talk about those products among themselves. Word of mouth is a powerful tool because of its high level of credibility, and if a topic is hot, it can spread around the world in hours. A recent example was the instant internet discussing and trading on eBay of the U.S. government's "Most Wanted Terrorists" playing cards.

Word-of-mouth strategies currently go by several different names: *guerrilla marketing,* which applies to edgy, unconventional campaigns that generate word of mouth (← Chapter 11), and *viral marketing,* which is online marketing that refers to the way communication spreads on the internet (← Chapter 12). Whatever it's called, word of mouth is low cost because it doesn't rely on expensive media buys. It can be initiated and reinforced by media stories, which is where public relations comes in.[11] Because of its word-of-mouth expertise, the PR department is sometimes responsible for creating both guerrilla and viral communication activities.

Developing Strategies and Tactics

Publicity is used to help create visibility for a brand, build brand credibility, launch products, position the brand as a category leader, and reach hard-to-reach target audiences with articles in special-interest and trade publications. In an IMC program, monitoring and influencing unexpected messages (← Chapter 4) is also an important responsibility of public relations.

Brand publicity is particularly useful in launching new products. Some successful new-product launches have used *only* brand publicity, which takes advantage of the news value of the new product. Breathe Right nasal strips and Gatorade both relied on the on-camera use of the brand by athletes. Publicity can do it alone, however, only when the marketplace isn't too crowded and the product is unique. In a more competitive new-product launch, media coverage in consumer and business media are used to build customer awareness and provide information, as Maytag did when it launched the Neptune washer (see the IMC in Action box).

The internet has changed the brand-publicity process and the way public relations departments operate.[12] The internet can be used to bypass the media when they choose not to carry a news release or they say something negative about a brand or company. Corporate websites, in particular, have become very important sources of public information, providing a profile of the company, its products, its employees, and its business philosophy. E-mail allows PR departments and firms to instantaneously communicate with the media and reach critical stakeholder groups (employees, consumer groups, investment community).

Other aspects of brand-publicity strategy include scheduling and budgeting. The budget is derived from the overall marketing communication budget, but the publicity plan also allocates various amounts to various tactical programs. For example, to support the launch of a new product, a series of news releases on the breakthrough engineering of a new razor were written; a press conference was held in conjunction with a launch party for media and industry influentials; the launch was supported with an extensive news kit; and a series of local news releases were prepared as the product rolled out nationally. A cost analysis was then prepared for each activity to determine whether the original budget was sufficient.

Scheduling and timing can make or break a publicity campaign. Publicity, when it has to do with a news announcement about a brand, is timed to precede advertising and other marketing communication functions. This is especially true for

IMC IN ACTION

Maytag Takes a Spin with Public Relations

When appliance manufacturer Maytag launched its new Neptune, a revolutionary, high-efficiency front-loading washer, into a market dominated by top-loaders, it depended on public relations to get the story out. To get attention and visibility, Maytag and the public relations arm of its advertising agency, Leo Burnett, unveiled the product to the trade and media at a New York launch party hosted by Ol' Lonely, the Maytag Repairman. The event featured famous boomer-era television moms Barbara Billingsley (*Leave It to Beaver*), June Lockhart (*Lassie* and *Lost in Space*), Florence Henderson (*The Brady Bunch*), and Isabel Sanford (*The Jeffersons*).

But Maytag needed more than visibility to support its high-efficiency claim. To drive home that message, Maytag worked with the U.S. Department of Energy (DOE) to conduct a live water-conservation test in Bern, Kansas (pop. 204). After replacing half of the small town's washers with Neptunes for six weeks, the DOE computed a 38 percent savings in overall water use. The successful demonstration was widely covered by the media, which gave even more visibility to the new washer.

The Neptune launch was driven by public relations with very limited advertising. Maytag claims it was the most successful product launch in the company's history because it convinced consumers to trade for a new washer instead of waiting for theirs to wear out.

The raves of other stakeholders, such as financial analysts who were impressed by the company's innovative new product, also drove the Maytag stock price up 100 percent in a relatively short period.

Think About It

What was Maytag's primary selling message? Why did it elect to deliver that message with public relations rather than advertising?

---

new-product introductions, whose news value is good for only a short time. Once the advertising begins, news editors reject the product introduction release because it is no longer "news." The challenge is to continue to find different story angles to keep the brand visible and top-of-mind even after its introduction.

Media Relations

An important aspect of publicity is **media relations,** which refers to *maintaining a positive professional relationship with the media.* The people who manage the flow of information through the media channels are called *gatekeepers.* **Gatekeepers** are *editors and reporters who select (or reject) stories for their publications or stations based on what they think will interest their audiences*—and they are an important target for media relations programs. The objective of media relations is to get these gatekeepers to run a story about an organization or to cover—attend and write about—an organization's activities.

Media relations professionals become adept at "placing" stories in the media by developing good contacts in the media. They cultivate these key media relationships by helping reporters, providing them with information, and making themselves and the executives of their companies available to answer questions.

The relationship between journalists and public relations people can be prickly. In most cases, organizations have legitimate news stories with strong news values. However, if the PR person is seen as simply trying to manipulate the media into providing coverage of dubious news value, there may be problems with the media relationship. To create a positive and effective media relations program, public relations professionals must know their media outlets, understand what the media consider to be news, be able to suggest good story ideas, and be available to answer journalists' questions honestly and openly. Media relations works only when both the channel and the source are open to honest communication.

Strengths of Brand Publicity

In addition to being able to help create brand awareness and knowledge, publicity's other strengths include (1) building a climate of acceptance for a company and its brands, (2) increasing the credibility and believability of brand claims, (3) breaking through commercial message clutter, (4) reaching hard-to-reach audiences, and (5) doing all these things in a very cost-effective way.

Building Acceptance

Positive acceptance is a direct outgrowth of corporate or brand reputation. When people think positively about a company or a brand, they are more likely to accept its claims and point of view—that is, they tend to agree with the communication they hear from the company. More important, they agree that the company or brand is essentially good and trustworthy. Even when problems arise, such as a product failure, customers may be more inclined to agree that it is a good product and give the brand a second chance because of their previous positive experiences. Acceptance leads to trust, and trust is a powerful reason to overcome an occasional disappointment. Public relations programs use ongoing research to track acceptance, as well as reputation and the level of trust and positive attitudes toward an organization or brand.

Increasing Credibility

Probably the most important objective of public relations lies in the area of credibility. The media stories that result from publicity efforts benefit from and seem more believable because of **third-party endorsement,** which is *the perspective presented by a reputable media source that has no personal interest in the success or failure of the product being endorsed.* Public relations messages that are carried in the news media are often seen as more believable than ads. Reporters and editors review news stories based on information provided by public relations offices. If the decision is made to use the information, the objectivity of the news medium enhances the credibility of the story. The third-party endorsement strategy with its built-in credibility is the basis for passing out reprints of articles about the brand or a company's executives.

An example of the effective use of third-party endorsements comes from Steve Jobs's reshaping of Apple. Rather than relying on product claims in Apple advertisements, the publicity team relied almost exclusively on comments from industry analysts. Apple provided them with a steady flow of quotes and research data and created chat rooms and user sites on the internet to generate buzz, which the analysts noted.[13] Another technique is to prepare and distribute an interview with one of the company's top executives (see Exhibit 17-6).

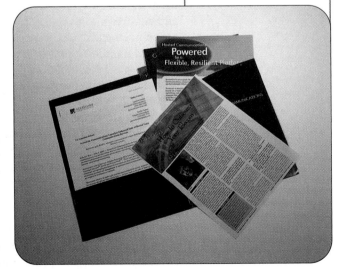

Clutter Busting

All brand messages compete for attention in a very cluttered commercial message environment.

Publicity can break through the clutter of other commercial messages when information is delivered in a creative way, such as at an event that features a personal appearance by a celebrity and important company officials.

A brand message is intrinsically more attention getting, interesting, and believable when it has news value or appeals to human interest. Its power to capture attention can be considerably higher than that of an advertising message. For example, H. J. Heinz Company once made the "world's largest salad" by filling a portable swimming pool with salad makings and then pouring on gallons of a new Heinz salad dressing. Both TV and print editors ran human interest stories on the event, giving Heinz brand exposure and awareness among millions of potential customers.

Reaching the Hard to Reach

Another strength of publicity is its ability to reach audiences that are difficult to reach with advertising and other brand messages. For example, upscale and well-educated audiences, such as business executives, spend less time with television, radio, and popular magazines than other groups do and therefore have limited exposure to traditional advertising. Because this group *does* tend to read newspapers, special-interest magazines, and industry publications, publicity helps reach them and get past the institutionalized communication roadblocks (secretaries and answering machines) that often block sales calls and other direct marketing messages.

Cost-Effectiveness

Although it costs money to have someone write a press release and distribute it, there is no charge for the time and space such messages occupy in the mass media. That makes publicity considerably less expensive than mass media advertising and most other forms of mass communication. Given the impact of a news story, brand publicity becomes a very cost-effective MC tool. The internet has made publicity efforts even more cost-effective, a fact reflected in a survey of brand managers, 42 percent of whom said public relations is the best discipline for brand building on the internet, as opposed to 32 percent who preferred advertising.[14]

Limitations of Brand Publicity

Although marketers control most MC messages to ensure their content, reach, and impact against a targeted audience, they have much less control over brand publicity because the messages are filtered through media gatekeepers—the editors and reporters who make the decision to run the story or not. As with image advertising, the impact of brand publicity is not easily measured because most of it is focused on affecting attitudes and opinions, changes that are difficult to attribute to messages from just one kind of MC function. In public relations, most measurement consists of counting the number of mentions, column inches, or the amount of time a brand or company story receives in the media. It is difficult, however, to link these measures to behaviors and to the bottom line.

Another limitation is that public relations, by its very nature, can go only so far. Editors will not run stories about the same company or brand too frequently (otherwise the communication vehicle loses its own credibility). Consequently, it is more difficult for public relations programs to create a frequency of mention in the same media vehicle. So, although public relations may offer greater credibility, advertising offers greater control and produces the awareness that comes from repetition. Another problem, and one that drives to the heart of its greatest strength, is public relations' own image, a credibility problem that is discussed in the Ethics and Issues box later in this chapter.

Tool or Activity	Description
TABLE 17-2	**Brand-Publicity Tools**
News release (press release)	Any form of print, visual, or broadcast announcement that an organization makes available to the media about its activities; includes video news releases.
News kit (press kit)	A packet of information that includes photographs and drawings, maps, histories, background facts, stories on different aspects of the product or event, speeches, test results, along with the name of the person to contact for more information.
Press conference	A press event in which corporate officials meet with media representatives to inform them about some major company-related story.
Media tour	A series of visits by a spokesperson for a firm to selected cities for meetings with as many local media representatives as possible. The ideal tour includes live appearances on broadcast media.
Media event	A special event, such as a groundbreaking or grand opening, designed to gain media coverage, as well as create an involvement opportunity for stakeholders.
Speeches	Public statements, often ghostwritten by PR staff. Reporters are invited to cover the speech, and clips (for broadcast) or quotes are provided to the media.
Pitch letter	A letter, either regular mail or e-mail, written by a PR person proposing a story idea to an editor or reporter. In close working relationships, the pitch may be made by phone.
Fact sheet	A listing of information about a company or brand that provides background data the media can use when doing a story on the company or brand.

Brand-Publicity Tools

Media relations experts help reporters and editors identify ideas for stories, provide background information, suggest or "pitch" story ideas to key reporters and editors, and, in some cases, provide the story. This practice is referred to as "placing" a story. A good media relations program has a media database with addresses and fax numbers for a variety of media outlets, as well as a contact list with phone numbers and e-mail addresses of key reporters and editors who cover the organization or industry.

Media tools and activities that media relations professionals use to gain publicity are listed in Table 17-2. Even programs that don't directly involve mass media, such as speeches, are designed to get media coverage. To understand how media relations experts handle story ideas, let's look at each form more closely.

News Releases

A self-serving news or human interest story created by an organization or its PR firm and given to the media to generate brand publicity is known as a **news release** or **press release** (see Exhibit 17-7). A news release can appear in both print and video forms.

To be accepted and used, a news release must be professionally created and delivered and meet the basic standards of newsworthiness. Central to an editor's decision to use a publicity release or news tip is the extent to which it has a **news peg** (*an announcement of something that is new*) for a news story or a **human interest angle** (*a story idea that appeals to people for reasons other than news*) for a feature story. Once a story idea has been identified, it must be written up in a form that editors can use with a minimum of editing. Here is a list of pointers for writing news releases:[15]

ACCESSLINE
communications
WWW.ACCESSLINE.COM

Media Contacts:
Lambert Jemley
AccessLine Communications
(206) 686-1096
ljemley@accessline.com

Laura Engle
Citigate Cunningham
(512) 652-2712
lengle@cunningham.com

For Immediate Release

AccessLine Enhances Peoplesoft's Flexible Working Environment Through Hosted Communication Services

Two-Thousand Consultants Are Added to AccessLine Services

BELLEVUE, Wash. — April 5, 2000 — AccessLine Communications, the leader in hosted communications and voice services, has significantly expanded its relationship with PeopleSoft, a world leader in enterprise application software for eBusinesses, by providing more effective communications for an additional 2,000 of PeopleSoft's highly mobile staff and consultants. PeopleSoft initially selected AccessLine for its sales staff, who are constantly on the road and need voice services that convert remote locations — customer sites, hotels, homes — into connected and productive office environments.

PeopleSoft has completed rollout of AccessLine services to 2,000 employees of its world-class consulting division, thereby allowing them easy and efficient communications — no matter where they are. Through wireless technology and AccessLine's hosted services, PeopleSoft has provided its consulting employees the mobility and communications flexibility they need for their jobs.

"Previously, our communications systems couldn't provide a flexible working environment for our mobile employees," said Neil Hennessy, vice president of Engineering at PeopleSoft. "Now through AccessLine, we are able to offer our employees cutting-edge communication tools for a truly mobile environment. They are finding themselves more productive and more empowered in their relationships with our customers, their fellow employees and their families."

AccessLine's regard for high-quality customer service is also key to the success of PeopleSoft's rapid implementation. AccessLine provided PeopleSoft employees with a "high touch environment." Employees were given one-on-one, virtual training and support during every aspect of installation — set up of service, a walk-through of options, step-by-step instructions — all in an extremely short period of time.

(more)

11201 SE 8th St. Suite 200 Bellevue WA 98004   Phone/Fax: 206 621 3500   Toll Free: 1 877 500 LINE

EXHIBIT 17-7

This press release was written to show how AccessLine, a leader in hosted communications and voice services, has been adopted by Peoplesoft. Each time a well-known new client signs up, it provides a news opportunity for AccessLine to promote its telecommunication services.

News Release Checklist

- Ask who, what, why, where, and when, and be sure that these questions are answered in the release.

- Organize paragraphs so that the most news-worthy points are at the top. Get the main news point into the first paragraph and preferably into the first sentence.

- Use short paragraphs with only one point per paragraph.

- Write stories to match the publication's and its audience's interest.

- Keep the copy tight and concise. Draft, redraft, edit, polish, and cut everything superfluous out of the copy.

- Use journalistic style: short sentences, active verbs. Avoid long and inverted clauses, superlatives, pompous phrases, and jargon.

- Be accurate and factual. Never fudge an issue, exaggerate, or create a misleading impression.

- Substantiate any claims; document the facts; quote from reliable sources.

- If it is a news story, is the news angle obvious? Is it timely?

- If it is a feature story, is the human interest angle obvious?

- Can you simplify complex ideas? Is there an example that would help illustrate the idea?

- If you are explaining a process, can you take it apart and describe it one step at a time?

- If the medium uses a style guide, is the story written to that style?

PR Newswire (see Exhibit 17-8), is a service that, for free, distributes news releases to the media, delivers video, print, and audio news releases through a variety of media, including satellite and the internet.

Video news releases (VNRs) are *television news releases, or packages, produced by a company to feature a product or service and designed to run from 30 to 90 seconds on a news program.* They are most effective when a story has a strong visual impact. A VNR produced by Golin/Harris Communications to announce the introduction of McDonald's Arch Deluxe sandwich depicted the unveiling of a foam version of the sandwich built over the famed Cinerama Dome on Hollywood's Sunset Boulevard. The videotape of the event reached some 233 million people (unfortunately, the product didn't meet customer expectations as much as the company wanted).

VNRs are usually sent to television stations along with a script. VNRs can be distributed by videotape, satellite, or the internet. Because VNRs are expensive to produce (budgets can range from $5,000 to $100,000), the following factors should be considered by a company deciding whether to use a VNR:[16]

- Does the story have a strong visual impact?
- Does the video clarify or provide a new perspective on a news story or issue?
- Will the video help a news department create a better story?
- Can the video be used as background footage while a station's reporter discusses the pertinent news copy?

- Can the organization provide unusual visual footage, or an interview, that stations can't get?

Although news releases can be distributed by the company itself, many companies and PR firms use Business Wire, which electronically transmits these releases to a list of media (newspapers, radio, television, and trade journals) selected by the company or PR firm. Business Wire charges about $400 for each press release distributed. Similar services are offered by Feature Photo (www.feature photo.com), which distributes photos; MediaMap (www.media map.com), which has a database of media addresses; West Glen communications (www.westglen.com), which produces and distributes VNRs, as well as PR Newswire.

Fact Sheets, Pitch Letters, and News Kits

Sometimes sending a news release may not be appropriate. Many reporters want an exclusive story. In such a situation, a **fact sheet,** which is *a summary of key information,* can be provided to the reporter, who then writes the story.

A **pitch letter** is *a story proposal sent to a reporter or editor.* Its purpose is to sell a story idea to a journalist who would then follow up and write the story if it's deemed to be of interest to the medium's audience. Often used with a feature story idea, the pitch can be made by regular mail, by e-mail, or (when there is a working relationship between the PR person and the journalist) by phone. Exhibit 17-9a shows an e-mail pitch letter written to a newspaper staff reporter who writes

EXHIBIT 17-8
PR Newswire works for both PR firms and companies. Its expertise is distribution of publicity stories.

EXHIBIT 17-9A
This e-mail pitch letter generated the excellent brand story shown in Exhibit 17-9b. Why do you think this e-mail was so successful?

Chris,
I received your name from Matt Branaugh and met you with Matt at our store in August. I understand you do product reviews, and I want to send you information on our UL Down Inner Jacket, which I thought might be a great product for your Thursday review section.

The jacket weighs approximately 7.5 ounces in size medium, making it one of the lightest down jackets on the market. It has a 15 denier nylon shell and liner, and is filled with 725 fill power goose down. It has a snap front to save weight, and it stuffs into its own sack. The retail price is $129. The jacket comes in unisex sizing SM-XL. Colors are Ink Blue, Red, and Black.

I can bring you a sample and more information.

Jim Heiden
MontBell America, Inc.
303 555 7681 tel; 303 555 5707 fax

EXHIBIT 17-9B

The pitch letter aroused the curiosity of the reporter, who then tried out the product and wrote this article about it. Notice how the reporter personalized the story and made it more than just a standard product review.

COOL GEAR

Mont-Bell weighs in warm with ultra-light down jacket

By Chris Barge
Camera Staff Writer

My mom is the coldest person on Earth.

I was reminded of this fact recently when she came to visit and turned the car heat past boiling all the way up to Loveland Ski Resort. My attempts at breathing a whisper of fresh air were met with fierce demands to roll up the cracked window.

Just like growing up.

When we pulled into the parking lot, I got out, gasped for air, and handed her the new UL Down Inner Jacket the people at Mont-Bell had loaned me to try out.

I would recommend that anyone who values fresh air keep one of these 7.5-ounce babies in the glove compartment in case of similar clashes with cold-blooded passengers. The thing is surprisingly warm for its weight, and it packs down into its own tiny stuff sack.

Best of all, my mom reports it kept her warm on the chair lift all day.

It has a 15-denier nylon shell and liner and is filled with 725-fill power goose down. The front snaps to save the weight of zippers.

"It's quite amazingly light," said John Harlin, northwest field editor for Backpacker Magazine. "I just love pulling it out and showing it to people. They ooh and ahh."

In designing the jacket, which is available at the new

Photo courtesy Mont-Bell America

Light and warm: Mont-Bell's new UL Down Inner Jacket weighs 7.5 ounces and retails for $129.

Mont-Bell store on Pearl Street, designers had one goal.

"The whole deal was to get the lightest down jacket possible," said Jim Heiden, vice president of Mont-Bell America. "I haven't see anything like this. Not in down."

The jacket is perfect on its own for those in-between weather days. It makes a great under layer for when it's freezing out. And it's a smart, space-efficient choice to bring along and wear at the picnic

midway through a winter hike.

The only disadvantage I could see is that it's not very breathable. So if you're planning on working up a sweat in the backcountry, you might just take it along in your pack.

Or leave it with your mom in the car.

The Mont-Bell UL Inner Down Jacket is $129 and comes in ink blue, red and black.

Contact Chris Barge at (303) 473-1389 or barge-c@dailycamera.com.

product reviews for an outdoors column. The product was a new lightweight jacket carried by a local sporting goods store. The article that resulted from the pitch appears in Exhibit 17-9b.

A **news kit,** or **press kit,** is *a packet of information provided by the PR staff to journalists covering a major story such as a special event or a press conference* (see Exhibit 17-4). The kit includes background information, such as biographies, historical information, maps, drawings and photos, speeches, quotes, contact information, website addresses, and any other supplemental material that might help the journalist cover the event and write the story.

News Values

What constitutes "news"? Media relations practitioners are guided by journalism standards for determining what makes a good news story—timely, relevant, topical, accurate, comprehensive, substantiated, concise, unbiased, and, ideally, exclusive, or at least having a special angle that an editor can use to make it a one-of-a-kind story.[17] The following list summarizes the factors that editors and other media gatekeepers use when deciding whether to respond to a pitch letter or to cover an event:

Factors Influencing the Selection of News and Feature Stories

- *Impact:* What is the magnitude (past or potential) of the action or event?
- *Timeliness:* Is it a breaking news story or the latest development?
- *Proximity:* How local is the story angle?
- *Prominence:* To whom does the story happen? Who is involved? How important are they?
- *Conflict:* Is tension or drama created by warring viewpoints?
- *Human interest:* How fun, entertaining, or emotionally engaging is the story idea? Does it touch a chord?
- *Novelty:* Is the story unusual or unpredictable?

Publicists are perfectly legitimate in creating news—that is, doing, finding, or creating something that is the first, biggest, shortest, most expensive, oldest, longest, highest, or most unusual. Special events and special promotions such as the Pillsbury Bake-Off, Tide's Dirtiest Kid contest, Saturn's "Homecoming," and the M&M new colors contest were all specifically created to be news events. Such events are often more important for the publicity they generate than for the number of people directly involved, because the event usually involves a relatively small number of customers (and other stakeholders) but the publicity can reach millions. Heinz made its package a news story when it used three different labels designed by kids on 10 million bottles of ketchup. The publicity resulted in numerous print and broadcast stories that reached millions of ketchup users.

In an IMC program, public relations staff must work closely with sales promotion and event sponsorship planners. For example, Unilever's Sunlight dishwashing detergent partnered with Whirlpool on an innovative way to build brand awareness and make news at the same time. The idea was to find America's messiest kitchen. The contest was promoted through a broad media relations campaign aimed at women's home, lifestyle, and feature editors. A "spring cleaning" press kit mailing, which targeted these editors at newspapers in the top 100 markets and 10,000 local suburban weekly newspapers, generated nearly 125 stories and thousands of entries. Nearly 50 million impressions were delivered, with 100 percent of the stories communicating the fact that the contest was created by Unilever and its Sunlight brand.[18]

Advertising versus Editorial

As with journalists and PR professionals, the relationship between the editorial and the advertising sides of the media is sometimes prickly, and for similar reasons. Advertisers—the companies providing news releases—sometimes feel that a newspaper should use their releases and give them favorable coverage because they spend a lot of money on ads (see the Ethics and Issues box). Even though most media in the United States are supported primarily by advertising, editors and reporters strive to maintain their detachment from the advertising department in order to make news judgments based solely on newsworthiness, rather than on advertiser pressure.

CORPORATE COMMUNICATION

A corporate communication network can be the conduit through which information is disseminated, discussed, debated, and ultimately incorporated into constructive action and long-term knowledge. Calls to action, goal setting, unifying behind a common mission—a company can carry out none of these activities without an effective communication plan.

Public relations carried out by senior executives who advise top management on how the organization presents itself is called **corporate communication.** These executives, and the public relations agencies that advise them, are very much focused on maintaining the corporate brand and corporate reputation. Another term for the work they do is **corporate relations** because it involves creating and maintaining relationships with key stakeholders who can affect the organization's business, such as government officials and regulators.

Corporate communication executives also focus on public opinion and issues management. Because of the powerful effect of public opinion, organizations of all kinds must consider the public impact of their actions and decisions, as well as how changing public opinion can affect the organization's business opportunities. This is especially true in times of crisis, emergency, or disaster, but it also holds true for major policy decisions. Changes in management or pricing, labor negotiations, new-product offerings, changes in distribution methods, and the closing or opening of plants can all affect a community and hence public opinion about the company. Each decision affects different stakeholder groups in different ways. Through effective public relations, managers hope to channel stakeholder opinions toward better understanding of issues and create more positive attitudes, or at least better understanding of the company's actions.

In addition to news releases, the tools used in corporate communications include newsletters and corporate magazines, and communication that affects corporate image and reputation, such as corporate identity programs and corporate advertising.

Corporate Image and Reputation

The difference between an *image* and a *reputation* is sometimes confusing because the two are somewhat related. An **image** is more of a facade or *a representation of a brand or organization derived from planned communication, such as advertising and brand publicity.* Reputation reflects how a company behaves, and it is based on what others say about the company. **Reputation** is *the esteem that a company or brand has in the eyes of its stakeholders.* Reputation depends on the organization's behaviors and is reflected in word of mouth and confirmatory statements by others, as well as in personal experiences with a company or brand. Image can be created; a reputation is earned.

According to Paul Holmes, editor of *Reputation Management,* a brand image is what a company believes about its products, and reputation is the brand plus behavior.[19] Both brand image and brand reputation are important; ideally, they merge to create brand integrity. In Chapter 1, a brand was defined as the net sum

ETHICS AND ISSUES

Should Advertisers Influence the News?

The relationship between the editorial or news side and advertising of a medium relates to publicity. Although many readers of newspapers and magazines, and viewers of television, have little sense of the difference between ads and publicity stories, editors and advertisers are very conscious of the difference.

Because most media in the United States are supported mainly by advertising, an important role of the media is to deliver an audience for advertisers. Cyrus Curtis, founder of *Ladies' Home Journal*, made this point in a speech to business executives in the late 1800s:

> The editor of the *Ladies' Home Journal* thinks we publish it for the benefit of American women. This is an illusion, but a very proper one for him to have. The real reason, the publisher's reason, is to give you who manufacture things American women want, a chance to tell them about your products.

What Curtis was pointing out was that news media must maintain their integrity as a creator and distributor of objective news, because this is what attracts an audience. When this objectivity is violated, a news vehicle risks losing the confidence, and thus the attention, of its audience. The *Los Angeles Times* created problems for itself when it lost sight of this principle. In an attempt to increase short-term profits, it published a special Sunday magazine supplement that was all about the city's new multisport arena, the Staples Center. What was not made public until after the fact was that the *Times* was sharing advertising revenue generated by the supplement with the Staples Center. The supplement looked like a regular editorial section of the paper but was really an advertising supplement. The *Times*'s own reporters were incensed when they found out that they were writing stories for a promotional piece, and their protests brought a great deal of negative publicity to the paper.

Because of their central role in supporting the media bottom line, companies have been known to pull ads out of media that write negative stories about them. According to *Editor & Publisher* magazine, 97 percent of newspaper publishers say that an advertiser has pulled ads because of a story it opposed.[20] Yet such a practice is unprofessional, if not naive, because the news media are not likely to respond to pressure from advertisers. Nor would advertisers really want them to do so. As *Inside PR* magazine has noted, if a media company loses its objectivity, it may also lose its audience.[21]

An example of a more enlightened response comes from Shell. The giant oil company has been criticized fiercely by the magazine *Mother Jones*, most notably for its support of the Nigerian government, which some feel is one of the most abusive in the world. In spite of that, Shell runs banner ads on the MoJo Wire, the website of *Mother Jones*. An editor's note on the site makes it clear that the ads have not bought more favorable coverage and provides links to almost every unfavorable story the magazine has written about Shell. Both were cited in *Reputation Management*: MoJo Wire for accepting the ads, despite reader criticism, and Shell for reaching out to its critics to provide both sides of a complicated issue.[22]

Think About It

What do you think should be the relationship between advertising and the editorial side of a newspaper? Should editors' story decisions be influenced by advertisers?

---

of its relationships. Another way of describing a corporate brand, then, is that it is the net sum of its image and reputation. These two elements together drive brand relationships. An example of a company that understands brand integrity is Sara Lee, which recently offered its controversial cut-tobacco unit for sale. The division, though highly profitable, seemed to undercut the meaning of the company's slogan, "Nobody doesn't like Sara Lee."

A recent Harris poll identified the organization most admired by Americans as the 100-year-old company best known for its baby powder and shampoo—Johnson & Johnson (J&J).[23] One reason J&J has maintained its high level of public esteem is that it puts customers first. Its business credo, written in 1943, begins,

EXHIBIT 17-10

Johnson & Johnson's corporate slogan, "Caring for Generations," is brought to life in this ad that reports on J&J's Management Fellows Program and its involvement with Head Start.

"We believe our first responsibility is to the doctors, nurses and patients, to mothers and fathers, and all others who use our products and services." J&J puts that philosophy into action in its support of programs like Head Start. The ad in Exhibit 17-10, promotes Head Start as a program supported by J&J's Management Fellows Program, which provides business leadership and training for such organizations.

Corporate branding is *the practice of managing the identity and image of a corporate organization.* In addition to J&J and Sara Lee, Sony, Hallmark Cards, and Kraft Foods are companies that work very hard to maintain a strong corporate brand. The corporate brand may be important even if a company has separate brands for some of its product lines, such as Kraft's Maxwell House, Kool-Aid, Tang, Oscar Mayer, and Velveeta. A strong positive corporate reputation is also a key ingredient in brand equity.

An indication of the need for marketing and public relations to work closely together in managing corporate reputation comes from a reputation question in Thomas L. Harris's study of Fortune 500 companies.[24] Harris found that when corporate public relations managers were asked how involved other executives were in managing the reputation of the firm, marketing and advertising managers were third on the list, behind public relations/public affairs managers and CEOs (see Table 17-3).

Corporate Advertising and PSAs

Public relations uses two kinds of advertising. **Public service announcements (PSAs)** are *ads for nonprofit organizations that run on time and space donated by the media.* **Corporate advertising** is *an ad program designed to build awareness of a company and explain what it does or believes.* Both public service and corporate advertising are different from product or brand advertising that focuses on the product and is targeted exclusively to customers and potential customers.

Public service announcements usually promote good causes, such as the Partnership for a Drug Free America. Nonprofit organizations use a variety of other promotional tools but rely on PSAs in particular. They reach a wide audience, and they are cost-effective because the broadcast media in the United States are

TABLE 17-3	Importance of Reputation Management
Type of Manager	**Percentage of Respondents Who Cited Reputation Management as Important**
Public relations/public affairs	60%
The CEO of the firm	51
Marketing/advertising	39
CFO/investor relations	27
Other top management	24
Middle management	11

Source: Thomas L. Harris/Impulse Research, "Corporate Communications Spending and Reputations of Fortune 500 Companies" (Los Angeles: Impulse Research Corp., June 4, 1999), p. 16.

required to provide airtime for public service radio and television commercials. The Ad Council (www.adcouncil.org) is a national organization that uses public communication to stimulate action on significant public issues. Its membership includes advertising and public relations agencies and media. The longest-running PSA campaign in U.S. history features Smokey Bear and the warning "Only You Can Prevent Wildfires." The Ruder Finn agency recently updated the campaign as part of redesigning its educational website www. smokeybear.com for adults as well as children.

Corporate advertising is most frequently used by large, multiproduct companies and by new companies that result from mergers or acquisitions and want to establish a new corporate identity. Firms that specialize in developing corporate identity programs and marketing communication campaigns claim that these efforts have a positive impact on employees, investors, and other members of the financial community, help attract high-quality employees, and increase sales. Sometimes companies engage in **advocacy advertising,** *advertising that takes a stand on an issue or advocates a certain viewpoint.* An example is the ad in Exhibit 17-5, sponsored by Anheuser-Busch and intended to position the company as an advocate of responsible drinking. For another example of advertising that shows a company trying to be socially responsible, see Exhibit 17-11.

An example of a corporate advertising campaign used to reposition a corporate image comes from Cargill, the largest privately held company in the United States. Several years ago, the company began a corporate campaign that sought to change its "invisible giant" image. One commercial featured a rancher saddling his horse while his partner, who is sitting on a fence reading a newspaper, points to the headline "Cargill Develops Technology to Process Beef More Safely." The first man replies, "Yup. And look what they did with it," as the second man turns the page and finds another headline, which proclaims that Cargill will share its innovation with the entire industry. The ad is remarkable, according to *Reputation Management* magazine, not only because it calls attention to Cargill but also because of its offer to share technologies that are good for the consumer, putting customers ahead of private gain. The campaign's theme—"It's not just what we do. It's how we do it"—is designed to emphasize that the company's values are what set it apart from the competition.[25]

EXHIBIT 17-11
Target uses advertising to announce support for local community good causes.

Mission and Cause Marketing

A **mission** is *the task or objective that a company is striving to accomplish, and it reflects the core values of the company or brand.* A central mission can be an important part of an IMC program and become the central focus of integrated communication.[26] The mission statement sets forth the corporate purpose above and beyond making money; it indicates the company's raison d'être. Here are three mission statements that energize stakeholders of their respective companies:[27]

- Merck, the pharmaceutical company: "Preserving and improving human life."
- Johnson & Johnson: "To alleviate pain and disease."
- General Electric: "Improving the quality of life through technology and innovation."

Both marketing and PR should not only be involved in setting a corporate mission but also should be responsible for promoting it.

Mission Marketing

The missions of some companies reflect core values of social responsibility. For example, Ben & Jerry's, Tom's of Maine, and Newman's Own base their business platforms on environmentally sound business practices, emphasizing local community involvement and sourcing their ingredients to support the environment. Generally, such companies engage in **mission marketing** *which is using the company's mission as a selling strategy in order to differentiate and add value to a brand.*[28] The company's socially responsible mission drives all of its business decisions. It is also a platform on which an integrated marketing program can be built.

A mission doesn't have to be as overtly philanthropic as Tom's of Maine's mission, which is to contribute 10 percent of profits to support environmental causes. Nike's mission is to offer well-engineered athletic shoes (and clothes) that help people achieve their peak performance, and that objective drives everything the company does. Apple Computer's original mission, to be "the computer for the rest of us," unlocked computer literacy for children and for millions of adults who had no interest in learning programming language. Although Apple lost much of its momentum through management problems in the 1990s, it still has a devoted following of customers who believe passionately in the company because of its mission and the easy-to-use products that support its business platform.

To *market* its mission, a company selects sponsorship opportunities that tie the mission with a larger public interest, and builds on the connection for the long term. An example is the furniture company Homestead House's support of Habitat for Humanity. Homestead House's sponsorship not only made the company's mission more widely known but also conveyed Habitat's housing message to the company's affluent customers, thereby enhancing Homestead House's brand reputation.

The objective of mission marketing is to build a good corporate or brand reputation for the long term. In the discussion of consistency in Chapter 10, the say/do/confirm model was introduced. In the "confirm" step, the goal is to have customers and other stakeholders say good things about a brand. When people believe passionately in a brand's mission, as they do in the case of Apple Computers, they are likely to become advocates for the brand. The mission, however, has to be supported by good practices and tie the company directly to its target audience. McDonald's sponsorship of the Ronald McDonald House for families of children in hospitals reflects and leverages McDonald's tradition of being a family-focused restaurant. Avon's long-time support of breast-cancer research (see the IMC in Action box) relates to an issue of concern to its target market—women.

Because of the increasing number of product choices and the similarity of many products, companies are looking for ways to give their brands an edge. Mission marketing is one way of doing that. Craig Smith explained this concept well in a *Harvard Business Review* article: "For the first time, businesses are backing philanthropic initiatives with real corporate muscle . . . they are funding those initiatives not only with philanthropic budgets but also from business units, such as marketing and human resources."[29] Mission marketing also uses strategic philanthropy to cultivate those points where the company's long-term interest and the public interest intersect.[30]

Cause Marketing

Related to mission marketing is **cause marketing,** *company or brand support for a good cause through donations of a percentage of sales.* Cause marketing requires an agreement between a nonprofit and a for-profit company that seeks to maximize the benefits to each partner.[31] Carol Cone, CEO of Boston-based Cone Inc., a firm that focuses on cause-related brand marketing, says that the integration of social

IMC IN ACTION

Avon Calling: A Campaign for a Cure

Avon, the cosmetics giant, has been waging war against breast cancer since 1992 and has raised more than $250 million in a campaign to find a cure. The money goes to research institutions and health-care organizations. Avon is the largest corporate supporter of breast-cancer research, prevention, and care in the United States and in the world.

Why does Campaign for a Cure make business sense for Avon? It reflects Avon's slogan—"The company for women"—which in four words conveys the company's business philosophy. Before women had the right to vote, they had employment opportunities in sales at Avon, which began in 1886. As the opening case in Chapter 16 explained, Avon is now providing sales training and opportunities for young women.

The Avon Worldwide Fund for Women's Health was established in 1992. When the decision was made to move more vigorously into philanthropy, Avon's managers asked Avon's sales force and customers what cause the company should take on. Kathleen Walas, president of the Avon Foundation, says there was a clear consensus—breast cancer. That made sense, given that breast cancer is the most common form of cancer in women, one of the leading causes of death for women in the prime of life.

What's involved in a fund-raising campaign on this scale? The campaign uses personal sales by members of its in-person sales force, all of whom are fully briefed on the company's efforts. Avon's catalogs and printed materials, as well as its website, also carry the campaign's message. Most of the money comes from two sources: donations of a percentage of the sales of Avon's "Pink Ribbon" product line (the sales force also forgoes commissions on these products) and money raised from a national series of three-day, 60-mile fund-raising walks. In an average year, some 13 endurance walks attract nearly 40,000 participants, all of whom pledge a minimum of $1,900 to participate. The walks in various cities generate from $4 million to $7.5 million in donations per event.

Avon also distributes a Breast Cancer Crusade Pin, and the sales force has distributed more than 100 million brochures designed to raise awareness as well as funds. Other activities include special events, such as the "Kiss Goodbye to Breast Cancer" concert, which featured singers Natalie Cole and R&B star Kelly Price in 2002. Avon combines the concert with an award ceremony honoring five people or organizations that have helped lead the fight against breast cancer. All of these events are newsworthy and garner immense publicity for Avon and its fund, leading to additional donations.

Much of the money is used for research, but the charitable fund also donates money to more than 600 community-based organizations that help women dealing with breast cancer. It also provides information on managing treatment, wigs and prosthetics, and counseling, as well as more daily concerns such as helping with child care and transportation for women undergoing treatment. The fund has a special focus on providing services to low-income, elderly, minority, and other women without adequate health insurance through the AVON Cares Program for Medically Underserved Women.

The impact of the Campaign for a Cure also can be seen in the lives and sales results of Avon sales representatives. One Texas salesperson, for example, started selling Avon as a hobby. When she discovered in 1998 that she had breast cancer, Avon became her full-time job. And along with the product sales she sold the idea of breast-cancer prevention and care to her clients. In 2001 she not only sold $276,000 in products but also handed out thousands of breast-cancer fliers and personally urged hundreds of women to get mammograms.

Think About It

Why is the Campaign for a Cure a good example of mission marketing? In what ways does it anchor Avon's image and reputation? How does it connect with Avon's various stakeholders?

Source: Susan Orenstein, "The Selling of Breast Cancer," *Business 2.0*, February 2003, pp. 88–94; Melba Newsome, "Heroes in Our Time: Avon Calling," *Sky*, May 2002, pp. 66–68; Michelel Fellman, "Cause Marketing Takes a Strategic Turn," *Marketing News*, April 26, 1999, p. 4; Joyceann Cooney-Curran, "Avon Raises Awareness," *Global Cosmetic Industry*, April 2000, p. 11; "Avon Breast Cancer Crusade Reaches Goal of $25 Million in Funds Raised for the Breast Cancer Cause Worldwide," press release, December 3, 2002, <www.avoncompany.com/women/avoncrusade/news/press20021203.html>.

issues and business practices was not a passing fad of the 1990s. Rather it represents "a fundamental shift in how the world's leading companies will use cause associations to position their organizations and brands for the future."[32]

The benefit to the company comes from its association with the good cause, such as fights against hunger or breast cancer. Cause marketing, however, often reflects a shorter-term approach than does mission marketing. Both cause and mission marketing make strong emotional appeals, but mission marketing delves deeper because it rests on a long-term commitment.

Employee and Financial Relations

In many companies employees are the most important audience for PR messages—even more important than customers—because employees are the frontline of the communication system, particularly in service industries. How they interact with customers and prospects speaks more loudly than messages in advertising or news release. **Employee relations** is *an area of public relations that focuses on establishing and maintaining communication systems with employees.* It is sometimes found in, or coordinated with, the human resources department.

IMC planners pay attention to employee relations because employee relations intersects with internal marketing, the effort to explain a promotional effort to employees and get their support (Chapter 6). Employee communication, therefore, may be an essential first step before any IMC campaign moves outside the company. The tools of employee relations include newsletters, bulletin boards, employee meetings, websites, and intranets which are especially important for large companies with multiple offices or plants, particularly if they are located in many different countries.

Financial relations is *an area of public relations that creates communication directed to—and often developed in collaboration with—investors, analysts, stockbrokers, and financial media.* Because this communication focuses on a company's finances, it is usually handled by a PR professional close to senior management and the company's top financial officer. The legal staff may also be involved in approving any financial communication. Annual meetings with shareholders may also be the responsibility of the financial relations staff.

For a public company, initial communication with investors may be through a letter of welcome, a newsletter, or a brochure about the company's products and brands, philosophy, and history. Brochures are usually developed for major public actions, such as stock offerings. The primary formal communication tool is the *annual report,* a document required by the Security and Exchange Commission, which discloses details of a company's financial position (see Exhibit 17-12). Annual reports are also provided by nonprofit organizations as a means of summarizing the activities of the organization over the previous year.

Crisis Communication

A **crisis management plan** is *a plan for managing a company's response when disaster strikes.* Such plans

EXHIBIT 17-12

3M's annual report, like all such reports, is a company-created brand message.

BUILDING AN EVEN STRONGER 3M
2001 Annual Report

3M *Innovation*

designate who will provide what information to media and employees during a crisis. Although the responsibility of the director of public relations, designing and managing a crisis management plan should involve the marketing department because a crisis poses a threat to the company's reputation and brand relationships.

Proactive companies are realistic; they know that bad things happen. A manufacturing accident or product failure that causes serious injury or death may occur when a company least expects it. The larger a company is and the longer it is in business, the greater is the likelihood that it will face a crisis. This was the case with Bridgestone/Firestone and Ford Motor Company when it was widely publicized that certain Firestone tires on Ford Explorers were breaking down and causing deadly accidents.

The crisis ignited when Bridgestone/Firestone's U.S. subsidiary called a press conference to announce that it was voluntarily recalling 6.5 million tires linked to 46 deaths in the United States as well as to 300 other incidents. The announcement had major public relations implications for both Firestone and Ford, and both suffered damage to their reputations. According to an article in *Reputation Management*, Ford handled the crisis responsibly, with CEO Jacques Nasser prominent in the company's communication of concern for customers. Firestone's response, in contrast, failed to inspire confidence. The Japanese-based company was clearly handicapped by its culture, which prompted a closed-mouth posture toward the media and was focused more on supplier and partner relationships than on keeping consumers happy.[33] The result can be seen in Table 17-4, which reports the results of an opinion poll on the public's view of how the two companies handled the crisis.

The Need for Planning

The secret to managing a crisis is to have everything planned ahead of time. Having a crisis plan worked out *before* a crisis breaks ensures that the company is not forced to quickly improvise a response when emotions are high and the media are knocking on the door with cameras and live video, eager to tell the world how bad things are. During a crisis there is no time to sit back and plan. A company has to respond immediately; otherwise, the media, customers, and others will think the company is trying to hide something.

The crisis plan spells out such things as the names of people to be contacted immediately; responsibilities—who works with which stakeholder group and who talks to the press; guidelines on what can be said and what needs to be checked for

TABLE 17-4	Survey Results Regarding the Ford/Firestone Tire Crisis	
The numbers represent the percentage of respondents who rated each company's handling of the crisis as good or excellent.		
	Ford	**Firestone/Bridgestone**
Level of honesty	53%	34%
Helpfulness	60	46
Speed of response	51	34
Source: Paul A. Holmes, "With Friends Like These . . . ," *Reputation Management* 6, no. 7 (July–August 2000), p. 12.		

legal implications; and recommended actions the company might take to deal with different scenarios. Many companies have disaster scenarios that are used to practice the implementation of the plan.

When a crisis does occur, public relations professionals recommend the following responses from company spokespeople: (1) A reaction should be expressed as early as possible. Don't stonewall, and don't say "no comment." (2) Only designated top company executives—who understand the seriousness of the crisis, as well as the legal liability issues—should talk to the media. (3) The designated spokespeople should explain what happened as they understand it, keeping in mind that people are desperate for explanations. (4) The spokespeople should tell what the company is doing to minimize the damage (such as a product recall). (5) The spokespeople should express sympathy and concern for injured parties and their families. The tone should be humble, and the explanations and concern should be expressed with candor.

What spokespeople should not say or suggest in any way is that the company is responsible for what happened. Such an admission of *liability*—without knowledge of all the related facts, which might take weeks or months to gather and analyze—can result in the company's having to pay millions of dollars in compensation. This is not to say that a company should not accept responsibility for its actions, but only that it should take time to accurately determine what its responsibility is. Instead, spokespeople should focus on the company's concern and the actions it is taking to relieve the damage.

Brand Image Crises

After Burger King ran a promotion giving away Pokémon toys packaged inside a plastic ball, the company was shocked when it was reported that a baby suffocated and another child nearly died (half of the ball package had been placed over the mouth and nose of each victim). The company responded by recalling the ball packages (not the toys themselves). To encourage people to act, Burger King gave a free order of fries to each person who returned a ball package. At the time of the recall, the company had distributed over 20 million of the Pokémon toys. The recall, which was announced in a full-page *USA Today* ad, was not only a responsible thing to do but a smart marketing move because it generated considerable publicity and motivated families to visit their local Burger King once again.

A common source of a marketing crisis is a sales-promotion event or an advertisement that goes awry. For example, McDonald's image suffered when a sales promotion that distributed winning "Monopoly" and "Who Wants to Be a Millionaire" prizes turned out to be a multimillion-dollar scam and the subject of an FBI investigation.[34] The trouble was caused by an employee of the company handling the promotion, who was distributing the game pieces to a network of accomplices. McDonald's says that with the help of an expert panel that includes a former U.S. attorney, a former head of the U.S. Labor Department, and a former U.S. deputy attorney general it has developed a tough new security protocol to protect the production and distribution of future promotional games.

The bottom line of crisis communication is damage control. When a major disaster occurs, especially one resulting in death or serious injury, the damage has been done, and the world will soon be told about it. Look at what happened to Intel when a problem with a Pentium chip was discovered. Even before the mass media made it a big business story, it was being discussed on the internet, whose audience is very important to Intel's reputation. When the crisis occurred, Intel's initial denial tarnished its previously stellar image. But Intel did learn and act. It has since hired people to monitor all major high-tech chat rooms and immediately report any negative comments about the brand.

PUBLIC RELATIONS AND IMC

Public relations is an important element in almost all IMC efforts. It is particularly useful for announcing something because of its news angle. An example comes from a successful IMC campaign for AK Steel that was launched with public relations. The campaign, which also used business and trade advertising, direct mail, events, and a Web site, was created to introduce the company's new antimicrobial steel product. The campaign successfully delivered two different messages to both the consumer and trade audiences. One of the most effective parts of the campaign, which won numerous awards for its creativity, was the building of a concept home by AK Steel and partners in Santa Barbara, Calif. The project demonstrated the use of the product throughout the home. The house was featured on television, including NBC's "Today Show," and in print, including *The New York Times* and *Popular Science*, drawing a great deal of attention to the new product.[35]

A FINAL NOTE: REPUTATION AND RELATIONSHIPS

IMC programs that foster positive relationships move beyond image advertising and seek to affect reputation through credible brand messages. According to public relations professional Terrie Williams, putting relationships into public relations is critical because "people are starved for recognition."[36] She referred to psychologist Abraham Maslow's hierarchy of needs (⬅ Chapter 6) in explaining that acknowledgment and recognition are important dimensions of self-actualization. That's why customer recognition is an important factor in an IMC program.

Good citizenship, or social responsibility, is also an important part of a reputation program. Research shows that consumers will change their buying habits to support companies they perceive as being socially responsible—companies that are environmentally responsible, treat their employees fairly, or work to make their communities better places to live.

Key Terms

advocacy advertising 559
brand publicity 543
buzz 546
cause marketing 560
corporate advertising 558
corporate branding 558
corporate communication 556
corporate relations 556
crisis management plan 562
employee relations 562
fact sheet 553

financial relations 562
gatekeepers 548
human interest angle 551
image 556
influentials 546
media relations 548
mission 559
mission marketing 560
news kit 554
news peg 551
news release 551

pitch letter 553
press kit 554
press release 551
public relations 542
public service announcements (PSAs) 558
reputation 556
third-party endorsement 549
video news release (VNR) 552

Key Point Summary

EXHIBIT 17-13

Well-crafted public relations efforts are designed not only to get awareness but also to change the way people think.

Key Point 1: Public Relations

Public relations is an MC function used to manage communication between an organization and its publics and create favorable relationships with different stakeholders who are targeted by the following types of programs: corporate relations (issues management, community relations, government relations, industry relations), marketing public relations, media relations, employee relations, and financial relations.

Key Point 2: Brand Publicity

Brand publicity encourages purchase and consumer satisfaction through credible communication of information that associates companies and their products with the needs, wants, concerns, and interests of consumers. It is used to build brand credibility, make product news announcements, and launch new products. The strengths of publicity include building a climate of acceptance for a company and its brands, increasing brand visibility, increasing the brand's level of credibility and believability, using news to break through MC clutter, and reaching hard-to-reach audiences through articles in special-interest and trade publications. Limitations include the lack of control over publicity, the difficulty in quantifying impact, and the inability of PR to guarantee frequency of exposure to the message over time.

Key Point 3: Brand-Publicity Tools

Like every other MC function, brand publicity has its own unique communication techniques, such as news releases (in both print and video), news kits, press conferences, and special tours and events for media people. Publicists use pitch letters to stimulate a reporter's or editor's interest in a potential story.

Key Point 4: Corporate Communication

Corporate communication manages a full range of stakeholder relationships. Its focus on the corporate brand is most evident in corporate advertising. Corporate communication is built on a solid mission, which is embedded in the corporate culture and reflected in the corporate image and reputation.

Lessons Learned

Key Point 1: Public Relations

a. Why is public relations a growth area in marketing communication?
b. What are the key elements of public relations as given in the definitions appearing in this chapter?
c. Which stakeholders are addressed by public relations programs?
d. Which types of public relations programs listed in Table 17-2 can also be used in IMC programs?
e. Do a search for a story about a new-product launch, like the Maytag Neptune. In addition to the story placement itself, what other public relations tactics were used to introduce this product? What other MC functions were used?

Key Point 2: Brand Publicity

a. Define *brand publicity*. Explain how it differs from public relations in general.
b. Explain how brand publicity can supplement an MC strategy.
c. List five strengths of publicity.
d. In the marketing trade press, find an example of a marketing program that had both brand publicity programs and issues management were included.
e. What is a media gatekeeper? Why does that person create limitations for publicity's effectiveness?
f. What is third-party endorsement? What effect does it have on publicity? Find an example in which a medium lends credibility to a story about a brand. Explain *how* this credibility is enhanced by the medium.

Key Point 3: Brand-Publicity Tools

Give an example (besides the examples given in this chapter) showing how each of these brand-publicity tools can be used to promote a company or brand:

a. News release.
b. News kit.
c. Press conference.
d. Media tour.

Key Point 4: Corporate Communication

a. What is corporate communication?
b. Identify the three main objectives of corporate advertising. Find examples of ads intended to meet each objective, and explain the strategy behind the communication.
c. Why is corporate culture important to corporate communication managers? How does it affect IMC programs?
d. How does a company's image differ from its reputation?
e. In what way is reputation important to an IMC program?
f. How do mission marketing and cause marketing differ? Which one is more relevant for an IMC program? Why?
g. Analyze how the Swiss-based pharmaceutical and agribusiness producer Novartis (www.info.novartis .com) uses the internet to give substance to the company's environmental claims. Do you feel this is a good example of mission marketing? Explain how you arrived at your evaluation.

Chapter Challenge

Writing Assignment

Pick an organization, and interview some members to find an interesting aspect that would be of interest to your local paper. Write a publicity story that meets one or more of the criteria that editors use to decide whether a story should be used.

Presentation Assignment

Analyze your university or college as a brand. How does public relations contribute to the development of the school's brand? Describe the school's identity, image, and reputation. Develop recommendations on what needs to be done to strengthen your school's branding, and present them to your class.

Internet Assignment

The premier job site for the global public relations industry is Workinpr.com (www.workinpr.com). It is a partnership between the two leading U.S. public relations associations—the Public Relations Society of

America (www.prsa.org) and the Council of Public Relations Firms (www.prfirms.org). The Workinpr.com site offers job-search capabilities as well as up-to-date industry research and career information. Explore all three of these sites, and do an analysis of the field of public relations and how it relates to your personal interests and skills. Prepare a sheet with a column on the left in which you list job requirements (what employers are looking for). In the column on the right analyze yourself on these requirements. Write a conclusion that states whether public relations would be a good career option for you.

Direct Marketing: The Dialogue Builder

THE NEW

NISSAN MURANO

AS SEEN THROUGH

THE BOROUGH OF MANHATTAN

Key Points in This Chapter

1. What are the strengths of direct marketing, and what are the major components of a direct-marketing piece?
2. What is the biggest strength of direct mail? The biggest limitation?
3. What are the strengths and weaknesses of telemarketing?
4. How can direct-marketing efforts be evaluated?
5. What major issues and concerns are related to direct marketing?

Chapter Perspective

Making It Personal

One of the main things that differentiates IMC from traditional advertising and sales promotion is the increasing use of interactivity. The more personal this interactivity can be, the more persuasive it is. Direct marketing has been around for decades. However, its use has drastically changed with new communication and information technology. Interacting with customers is easier and less costly now than ever before.

Direct response can be used as the sole business driver or integrated into a MC mix.

Direct marketing allows companies to accurately measure the effectiveness of this marketing communication function. When it is done properly, the profitability of *each* customer can be determined. As companies continue to demand more accountability, direct marketing continues to grow. This chapter explains not only the basic principles of direct mail and telemarketing but also how direct marketing can be used to integrate customers and prospects into a company's operations.

HOW INFOMERCIALS HELPED ORANGE GLO GROW

In the mid-1980s Max Appel came home from his full-time job each day and went to his garage to continue his experimenting. He was determined to create an all-natural household cleaning product. He had a great deal of respect for the environment and was concerned that most household cleaning products on the market contained too many chemicals to be environmentally friendly. Max's first success was an orange oil-based product for cleaning and polishing cabinets, tables, and other wooden surfaces.

Max and family members began selling Orange Glo wood cleaner and polish and his other creations by demonstrating them at state fairs and home shows. Many of the people who bought Orange Glo were so satisfied that they wrote to Max to order more. Demand became so great that he formed Orange Glo International and began signing up distributors throughout the United States who were able to get the product carried in retail stores. At the same time, Max realized that selling the product direct to consumers provided a much bigger profit margin, so he continued to look for cost-effective ways to do direct marketing.

In the mid-1990s home shopping channels were popular, and Orange Glo decided to give this medium a try. Its first on-air direct-selling attempt appeared on the Home Shopping Network. The challenge was to make household cleaning products interesting enough to attract attention and motivate viewers to pick up the phone and place an order. To meet this challenge, the company hired a passionate, animated spokesperson: the bearded Billy Mays. It worked. This single demonstration instantly sold 6,000 bottles and hooked the company on TV direct marketing.

Infomercials Introduced into the MC mix

Today, the company uses 20-minute infomercials for each of its main products (OxiClean, Kaboom, and Orange Glo). Billy Mays continues to be the company's spokesperson. He not only helped make Orange Glo International extremely successful in a relatively short time but became famous from all of the infomercial exposures. When he does personal appearances or walks through an airport, people line up to get his autograph (see Exhibit 18-1).

Because infomercials must be produced and then TV time bought to run each 20-minute program, Max

Appel and his family quickly figured out it was critical for customers who see the program and respond to be satisfied with the products. Otherwise, they would not repurchase—and all of the money invested in getting those new customers would have been wasted. So every time the company develops a new product, it is first demonstrated before live audiences at fairs and home shows. Max says of these market tests: "You know pretty quickly whether you've got a turkey or a winner." Only when the company knows it has a winner does it invest in an infomercial and airtime for the new product. The cost of producing and airing an infomercial can be spread over a large number of sales, greatly reducing the cost per sale, but only if customers are satisfied and repurchase the product.

Not only does the company spend time experimenting in the development of new products, it applies the same creative development to its infomercials. Different ways to demonstrate products, as well as better ways of shooting these demonstrations, are always being tried. The more dramatic and credible an infomercial demonstration is, the more responses it generates.

Results

Orange Glo International is one of the fastest-growing privately held companies in the United States. In

Billy Mays salutes his audience in an infomercial for Orange Glo products, for which he has been the primary spokesperson and on-air sales rep.

less than 20 years the company's sales have grown from zero to over $250 million.

Source: Reprinted with permission from Response Magazine, *December 2001, p. 34.* Response Magazine *is a copy-*righted publication of Advanstar Communications, Inc. All rights reserved; "Billy Mays sales pitch catches people's attention," by Mitch Stacy, December 29, 2002. Reprinted with permission of *The Associated Press.*

PERSONALIZED AND INTERACTIVE COMMUNICATION

When a company wants to be in direct contact with its current customers and prospects, it uses **direct marketing,** which is *an interactive, database-driven MC process that uses a range of media to motivate a response from customers and prospects.* Over two-thirds of U.S. adults order products by mail, phone, or the internet each year.[1] According to a Direct Marketing Association (DMA) study, $1 out of every $17 (nearly 6 percent) in U.S. sales is due to direct marketing.[2] Moreover, the study found that more than half of all ad expenditures include an offer designed to prompt a potential customer to make a direct purchase, inquire for more information, or visit a store or dealership.

Although direct marketing is frequently part of a company's MC mix, it can be the *only* marketing communication function a company uses to generate business, as demonstrated by so-called catalog companies such as Swiss Colony and TravelSmith. Whereas some such businesses are 100 percent direct (they have *no* brick-and-mortar retail presence), other companies such as Eddie Bauer, L. L. Bean, Coldwater Creek, and Victoria's Secret use a combination of retail stores, direct-mail catalogs, and websites.

In direct marketing no distributor, wholesaler, or retailer stands between the company making the offer and the prospect. Direct-marketing operations include not only generating the sale but also handling the delivery of the product or the requested information.

The Interactive Dimension

Direct marketing is considered *interactive* because there is two-way communication between the company and prospect; either can initiate the dialogue. (For that reason, direct marketing is sometimes called *direct-response marketing.*) Although direct marketing is sometimes used to move prospects through the decision-making process—such as motivating a test drive, sampling, or visiting a showroom—most direct-marketing programs are designed to generate a transaction. The U.S. Postal Service ad in Exhibit 18-2 demonstrates the power of direct response to motivate action.

As an all-in-one buying, selling, and distributing operation, direct marketing is a microcosm of the entire marketing process. Figure 18-1 is a model that shows how the DMA describes direct marketing. It begins with a "business organization" and marketing. The direct-marketing function entails research, segmentation, and message creation (called "advertising creation" in the model). As you can see from the model, there is a wide variety of media from which direct marketers can choose to deliver their offers. The last section of the model identifies the response process: transaction, distribution, fulfillment, and follow-up. From this process information is extracted to update the customer database. Other marketing mix functions are also integrated into the response step.

Direct marketing's use of intrusive media, such as telemarketing and spam e-mail, has tainted its public image. Nevertheless, direct marketing has a proven

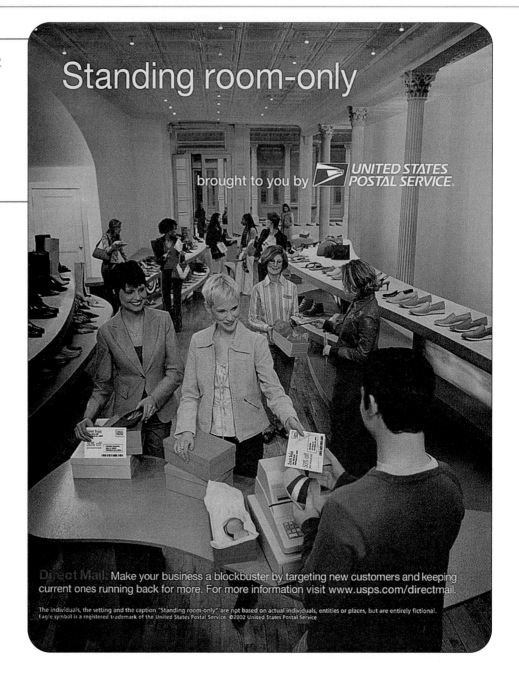

track record and is one of the fastest-growing MC functions. Major social and technological changes over the last several decades are fueling this growth. In the United States, for example, 58 percent of women now work outside the home; in Canada, the figure is 60 percent. This means many families have more income but less time to go shopping. Direct response makes shopping easier and less time-consuming because it can be done from home or office.

The Personal Dimension

With the extensive use of computers and customer databases, companies are able to be more strategic in the use of direct-response programs. When the Fashion Bug chain of clothing stores, for example, installed a new database system, it suddenly

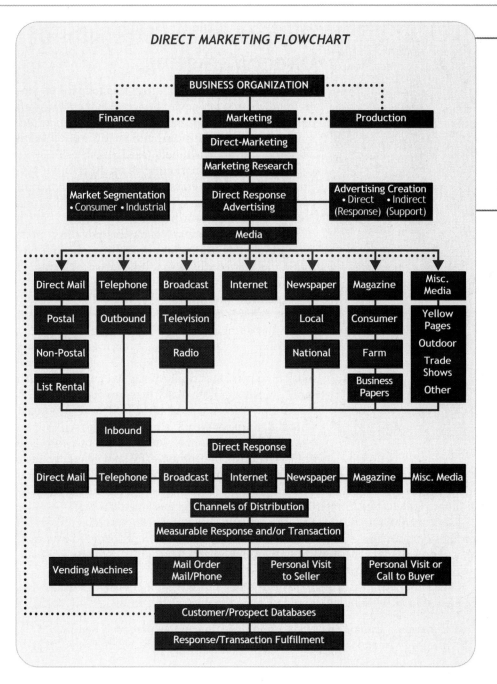

FIGURE 18-1

This is a descriptive model of all the activities and elements that make up direct marketing.

Source: Martin Baier, Henry R. Hoke Jr., and Robert Stone, *Direct Marketing*, October 2000, p. 3.

discovered that 18 percent of its customers made purchases six or more times per year and were the chain's most profitable customers. With this information and the ability to identify these customers, Fashion Bug was able to make customized direct-response offers to these customers that helped retain them as customers.

Cell phones (along with traditional telephones), credit and debit cards, catalogs, and access to the internet have increased opportunities for two-way personal communication between direct marketers and customers and made shopping more convenient. Companies worldwide now provide toll-free numbers so customers can place orders or request information regardless of national boundaries. Toll-free numbers facilitate immediate, direct responses from customers and help companies collect information to create and refine their customer databases.

Your print ad hit him between the eyes.
But why stop there?

closer shave!

Direct Mail can help build the relationship your print ad started.

Your print ad can make a powerful impression with a large audience. Follow it with the personal impression Direct Mail can make. Direct Mail lets you talk to your customers, one-on-one. It puts you on a first-name basis with them. And it's a great way to start a dialogue. Want to start a conversation? Visit us at uspsdirectmail.com. Either way, you'll find a lot of conversation starters.

Fly Like an Eagle.

UNITED STATES POSTAL SERVICE®
An equal opportunity employer

Eagle symbol is a registered trademark of the United States Postal Service. ©2000 United States Postal Service.

EXHIBIT 18-3

In this ad the U.S. Postal Service encourages marketers to use direct mail to support their advertising with a more direct relationship-building contact.

Objectives and Strengths of Direct Marketing

One of the primary uses of direct marketing is to generate new sales. However, because its messages can be personalized and individually targeted, direct marketing is also integrated into an MC mix to retain and grow current customers (see Exhibit 18-3). By its very nature direct marketing is an interactive MC function that creates communication between a company and its customers, which is the foundation of a good relationship (⬅ Chapter 3).

Another reason why managers include direct marketing in the MC mix is accountability. One of direct marketing's strengths is that it is measurable and its likely effectiveness can be gauged through pretesting. As explained later in this chapter, determining the cost of generating a lead or a sale as a result of a direct-marketing program is relatively easy.

Flexibility is another strength of direct marketing: it can be easily adapted to most MC efforts. Direct-marketing messages can be designed and used much more quickly than can many mass media messages. A direct-mail piece can be designed and produced within a couple of weeks; a telemarketing script or an e-mail message can be written and put into use within a few days. In contrast, a TV spot generally takes a couple of months to produce, and the lead time for a magazine ad is several months. Another aspect of direct marketing's flexibility is that the message can be as lengthy as needed, limited only by what the target audience can bear.

When a company needs to produce results quickly, direct marketing, like sales promotion, provides a way to achieve this objective. For offers delivered by e-mail and phone, responses begin coming in immediately; for offers delivered by mail, responses arrive within days.

Direct marketing can help achieve other objectives, including the following (which, if in an actual plan, would be stated in measurable terms):

- *Producing leads:* Direct marketing does this by inexpensively sending messages that ask people to "raise their hands" if they are interested in a particular product.

- *Lead qualification:* Whether leads come from other sources or are produced by a direct-marketing effort, they can be qualified with direct marketing. Prospects are contacted and asked several questions to ensure they are worth spending more money on (through a personal sales contact) to generate a sale.

- *Strengthening brand relationships:* Direct marketing can be used to gather customer-profile data. Customers can be offered a premium or some other incentive in exchange for telling more about their wants, needs, lifestyles, attitudes, and beliefs relevant to the product category. This information in turn is used to create personalized brand messages.

Although most direct-marketing efforts are intended to sell products, direct marketing is also an effective tool of social action. In 2002 a young Nigerian woman, Safiya Husseini, was accused of adultery and sentenced in Nigeria to death by stoning. The story attracted international attention because of the harshness of the sentence. Comunicacion Proximity, a Spanish MC agency, was so moved by the story that it launched a campaign, "Amnesty for Safiya," to collect signatures on a petition protesting the sentence. Having only two weeks in which to work before the sentence was to be carried out, the agency used e-mail and direct mail to collect signatures. The result was over 600,000 signatures sent in by e-mail, 60,000 by mail and fax, and over 40,000 phone calls into a call center set up for this specific purpose. The result was a reprieve for Husseini.[3] (The agency that created this campaign was awarded a Diamond Echo, the top honor in the Direct Marketing Association's annual Echo Awards competition.)

Components and Strategies of Direct Marketing

Direct marketing has what are called front-end and back-end operations. **Front-end strategies** include *the marketing communication and media mix used to explain and deliver an offer.* **Back-end strategies** include *operational decisions about how responses to offers will be received and processed, inventory control, shipping of orders, invoicing, handling of returns, and other customer-service functions.* In essence, the front-end strategies set expectations, and the back-end strategies determine how a company meets (or fails to meet) them. When back-end operations fail to meet expectations, the investment in front-end efforts is wasted. So paying attention to *both* ends is crucial.

The important components of the front end are the offer, the database of targeted prospects, and responses. The most important components of the back end are fulfillment, customer service, and privacy protection. All of these are briefly described below.

The Offer

An **offer** consists of *everything, both tangible and intangible, promised by a company in exchange for money or some other desired behavior.* Besides the product at a particular price, an offer also includes the terms of payment, the guarantee, the time of delivery, and any promised premiums, as well as the image and other intangibles associated with a brand (see Exhibit 18-4).

Offers take a prospect through the AIDA sequence of decision steps—attention, interest, desire, and action. In most cases, the offer is good for only a limited time. This restriction gives the offer a sense of urgency. Direct marketers of consumer goods and services know that if customers don't respond within several weeks, the likelihood of their responding at all decreases significantly. Furthermore, an expiration date limits how long a company needs to maintain an inventory of that particular product.

Does this sound similar to sales-promotion programs? It is. In fact, because the primary objective of a direct-marketing piece is to get current customers and prospects to take some kind of action, sales-promotion devices—premiums, discounts on the product, extended credit terms (◀ Chapter 14)—are common direct-marketing incentives to motivate action. Duplex Products, for instance, sells a prepaid long-distance calling-card package to research firms to help them increase response rates for their surveys. Survey prospects receive a mailing containing the phone card and instructions for responding to a telephone survey. Upon completion, they receive a personal identification number to activate the free long-distance minutes. This offer of an immediate reward produces an average response rate of 18 percent, two to three times higher than comparable research methods.

EXHIBIT 18-4

The Valdoro Mountain Lodge mailing offers recipients a chance to buy in to a new Hilton Grand Vacations Club Resort being built in Breckenridge, Colorado. The package includes a return card (and toll-free number and a website address) to encourage prospects to inquire about buying in to the time-share.

In B2B marketing (⬅ Chapter 15), companies combine direct-marketing offers with sales promotions to stimulate an immediate response in the buying process. For example, an offer might say "Send for more information and receive a free subscription to *Business Week*"; "Visit our booth at the trade show and enter to win a trip to Europe"; or "Try our product for 30 days and receive a discount on your first order."

Database Targeting

Direct-marketing companies live and die according to the quality of their customer and prospect database lists. Because of the costs of creating and printing a piece, obtaining a mailing list, paying postage, and so on, direct marketers seldom make a profit on their first sales to customers. They must capture customers' names, addresses, and other relevant information so they can send out additional offers and transform first-timers into profitable customers. Also, without a database it is almost impossible to tell which offers perform better than others—another critical piece of information necessary for building a successful direct-marketing business. Finally, a database enables a company to personalize an offer. Exhibit 18-5 shows how the author's veterinarian combines a reminder that shots are due for the family's dog with a magazine called *Healthy Pet*.

No matter how creative a direct offer is, it will not be successful if it is sent to the wrong people. The more carefully a database of customers and prospects is constructed, the higher the response rate will be. A brand's database can be compiled from lists of its customers and prospects, as well as from lists compiled by specialized companies called *list brokers*.

Most companies that use direct marketing have someone responsible for *list acquisition*—renting lists from list brokers—as well as managing the company's own house list (database of customers). Three types of customer lists can be rented. **Response lists** are *lists of people who have responded to related direct-marketing offers.*

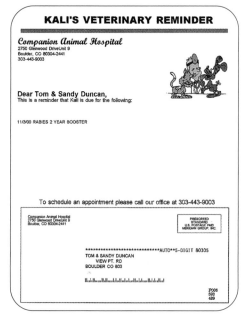

EXHIBIT 18-5

The Companion Animal Hospital mails a free magazine to its customers. The cover is localized with the names of the owner and the pet, as well as reminder information about shots that are due.

Compiled lists are *lists of names and addresses collected from public sources, such as car registrations.* **Subscriber lists** are *lists of subscribers to magazines.* The subscriber lists of magazines that specialize in one subject—such as golf, tennis, travel, or cooking—are especially valuable to brands within the subject category.

A response list should be evaluated on three critical factors: (1) *recency*, how recently the people on the list made a direct-response purchase; (2) *frequency*, how many direct-response purchases they made in the last 12 months; and (3) *money*, how much they spent. (You may remember this as RFM segmenting, described in Chapter 7.) The more recent the purchase, the greater the frequency, and the greater amount spent, the better are the prospects.

List brokers gather names and addresses from a variety of sources—direct-marketing companies, magazines, and companies that collect and process warranty cards. Companies that sell things such as appliances, cameras, luggage, and hair dryers often encourage customers to send in warranty cards that, in addition to purchase date and location, ask about the buyers' interests, hobbies, and ownership of other products. Customers may or may not realize that the information they provide is bought and sold (or rented) by direct marketers. A growing source of lists is e-mail addresses. The most costly e-mail lists include customers who have given their permission to be contacted. Average list rental costs are $250 for 1,000 permission-based B2B names and about $200 for 1,000 permission-based consumer names.[4]

The Response

In direct marketing, a **response** is defined as *something said or done in answer to a marketing communication message.* Like two hands clapping, the response and the offer work together. For example, the value of the offer—including any premiums, awards, or emotional appeals that are promised—is critically important to motivating the customer to respond in the desired way (see Exhibit 18-6). To respond, a prospect or customer can call a toll-free telephone number, visit a showroom, go to a website, send in a contribution to a charity or favorite cause, or become a member.

EXHIBIT 18-6

The Sunset *magazine promotion illustrates the use of a subscription offer that includes a motivation device—a free packet of seeds—and a return card that makes it easy for prospects to subscribe.*

Although the customer must initiate the response, the company must facilitate and handle the response properly to ensure that the response results in the action desired. Customers who respond by using a free phone call should not be put on hold, waiting for a company representative. The longer the hold time, or the more levels of an automated voice menu the customer must go through, the more likely it is that the customer will hang up and a sale will be lost. When a customer does reach a representative, if that rep is not able to answer questions or is rude, the likelihood that the customer will not complete an order increases. Timely fulfillment is also critical to customer satisfaction and retention. According to the DMA, approximately 10 percent of all catalog response orders cannot be immediately filled because the company is out of stock.

Fulfillment

The distribution side of direct marketing is called **fulfillment**—*getting the product or the information requested to the customer in a convenient, cost-effective, and timely fashion.* As noted earlier, this part of direct marketing is often referred to as the *back end* (the term came into use because in many companies the warehouse where products are stored and shipped is in the back end of the building). The fulfillment department is responsible not only for seeing that a product is shipped, but also for managing the inventory, handling the billing, following up on back orders, restocking and issuing credit for returns, and handling exchanges. Another aspect of fulfillment is up-selling or cross-selling.

Time is an important element in fulfillment. U.S. law requires that orders received through direct-marketing solicitation must be filled promptly or the customer must be notified and given the opportunity to cancel the order and receive a full refund. But more important, a customer's desire or need for a product can diminish between the time an order is placed and the time it is received. If the interval is very long, a customer may cancel the order or return the shipped product.

Fulfillment can be handled in-house or outsourced. Some companies use a combination, fulfilling some items themselves and outsourcing others, or they may receive and process orders themselves but outsource the mailing and invoicing. Magazines, for example, often find that receiving and processing orders, generating labels and invoices, preparing statements to certify level of circulation, and managing the subscriber mailing list require more overhead than can be cost-justified. Therefore, they may outsource the handling of fulfillment to such companies as EDS, one of the country's largest fulfillment houses.

As for any company function, there are advantages and disadvantages for outsourcing fulfillment. Because of the volume of work, a fulfillment company knows what works and doesn't work, and it can better afford the latest hardware and software for handling all the logistical details. The downsides are that a company has less control and possibly higher cost (although if a company includes all the equipment and overhead needed to handle fulfillment, outsourcing can actually be cost-effective).

Direct-Marketing Media

Direct marketers deliver their offers using a variety of media including mail, TV, radio, print, catalogs, telephone, and the internet. Marketers often use mass media advertising to encourage people to contact the company—that is, to self-select themselves into the prospect database—and then use direct mail or telemarketing to respond to these prospects. Interested prospects can be identified through a mass media advertising effort for a company-constructed list (see Exhibit 18-7). Catalog direct marketers such as L. L. Bean and Lands' End, home shopping TV channels such as QVC, and online marketers such as Amazon.com are all engaged in direct marketing. The IMC in Action box explains how one such company works.

Direct marketers face a basic communication question: what should be the balance of personal and nonpersonal messages in the marketing communication mix? Varying degrees of message personalization and interactivity are possible (see Table 18-1). At one extreme is real-time interactivity, as in personal selling and telemarketing. Next is delayed-response interactivity: customers must wait, to some degree, to get the information they want. The least interactive media of all are the mass media, which require that customers go to another medium such as the internet, telephone, or fax to respond.

A brand message in any of the mass media that asks the receiver (reader, viewer, or listener) to respond directly to the sender is called **direct-response advertising.** Some people confuse direct-response advertising with direct-mail advertising, incorrectly using the terms interchangeably. Direct-mail advertising is simply one type of direct-response advertising that uses mail rather than other media to deliver a brand offer. The two mostly widely used types of direct-marketing media are the phone and postal mail, which are described below followed by a discussion of another form of direct-response messaging—infomercials. The use of e-mail direct-response marketing is growing fast but still accounts for only a small portion of total direct-response spending compared to direct mail and telemarketing. (E-commerce and e-mail direct marketing are discussed in Chapter 12.)

EXHIBIT 18-7
The Catfish Institute in Mississippi used this attractive ad, which offered a recipe book, to change the image of catfish and encourage consumption. Interested consumers who responded became part of the institute's database.

DIRECT MAIL

Mail may not be as sexy as newer media such as the internet, but it is the third largest medium behind TV and newspapers, accounting for approximately 20 percent of all media spending.[5] The average household receives 18 direct-mail offers a week.[6] People who respond to these offers, and thus find their names on many mailing lists, receive two to three times this number. Mail is a pervasive medium that reaches every U.S. business and household. In the late 1990s, more than half of all U.S. adults placed one or more product orders by mail. Although mail is primarily considered an addressable medium, it is a medium that customers use extensively to communicate with companies. Because most direct-mail offers contain

IMC IN ACTION

Dialing for Flowers

One very successful direct marketer is 1-800-FLOWERS, a pioneer in using direct-response television advertising, telemarketing, and e-commerce to generate sales for local florists. The parent company, Teleway, an innovative relationship marketer, set up a network of 2,500 U.S. retail florists called BloomNet. Teleway creates, schedules, and runs direct-response advertising that generates business for this group.

Teleway receives orders from around the world in one of three telemarketing centers. To send a gift of flowers, you call the 800 number (or visit 1-800-FLOWERS.COM), and a local retailer within the recipient's zip code area delivers the flowers. Each order is transmitted within three minutes to a computer at the florist nearest the recipient's address. The florist makes up the bouquet—using specifications and color photos in Teleway's manual—and delivers the flowers.

In addition to television, the e-commerce company uses direct mail and radio to market its products. Direct-mail catalogs are sent to consumer segments in a file of 1.5 million customers, and radio is used to generate orders from people at work or in their cars. Those who place flower orders may receive a follow-up postcard offering other Teleway products such as gift baskets, candy, or Florida oranges.

A Web pioneer since 1992, the company was named "Top Gift Site on the Web" by ClicksGuide.com. It enlarged its Web presence by buying Greatfood.com and consolidating the gourmet and specialty foods line with the FLOWERS line in an attempt to become the number-one source for thoughtful gifts for all occasions.

Think About It

Why is 1-800-FLOWERS described as a direct marketer? How does such a company differ from other florist companies? How many different marketing communication tools does 1-800-FLOWERS use in its direct-marketing program?

Source: Adapted from William J. McDonald, *Direct Marketing: An Integrated Approach* (Burr Ridge, IL: McGraw-Hill/Irwin, 1998), p. 3. Reprinted with permission from The McGraw-Hill Companies.

EXHIBIT 18-8

800 numbers, website addresses, or business reply cards along with postage-paid, self-addressed envelopes, it is also generally considered an interactive medium.

According to one study, response to direct mail increased significantly between 2001 and 2003. Findings indicate that those "who have responded within the last 30 days to a direct mail offer" increased from 34 percent to 46 percent.[7] The leading mail-order product categories are insurance, financial services, and department stores. Important findings from direct-mail research that should be taken into consideration when direct mail is used include the following:

- Young adults 18 to 21 are more likely than any other demographic group to respond to a direct-mail offer.
- Offers sent in oversized envelopes have higher response rates than those sent in standard letter-size envelopes.
- The average adult receives 22 pieces of mail per week.
- The higher a person's socioeconomic level, the more pieces of mail he or she receives.
- By month, the highest mail volume comes in December, followed by May and June.

TABLE 18-1   The Personalization Continuum of Direct-Response Marketing

Degree of Personalization	Initiation	Interactivity	Response	Message
High	Face-to-face personal selling	Interactive in real time	Personalized communication	Company initiated
	Telemarketing, phone	Interactive in real time	Can be personalized (but often is scripted)	Company or customer initiated
	E-mail, fax	Delayed response	Can be personalized (but often is scripted)	Company or customer initiated
	Electronic kiosks, internet	Instant information retrieval	Mass message	Customer initiated
	Direct mail	Delayed customer response	Can be personalized but usually treated as a mass media message (telephone response can be personal and interactive)	Company initiated
	Catalogs, videos, CDs	Delayed response	Mass messages (telephone response can be personal and interactive)	Company initiated
	Audiotext (900 numbers)	Delayed interaction	Impersonal mass messages; may or may not have a personal company response	Company initiated
Low	Mass media ads	Delayed response	Impersonal, mass message (telephone response can be personal and interactive)	Company initiated

Surprisingly, although direct mail is an addressable medium, the majority of direct-mail offers are impersonal. The labor required to personalize each message is cost-prohibitive for most companies, but there are software programs that can automatically personalize messages to a certain extent. Even so, this software requires a detailed database of customer transactions plus some profile information for each customer—which many companies don't have. Although the trend is for more and more companies to create and maintain better customer databases, the full power of addressable, personalized direct mail has not been the practice.

Formats and Media

Direct-mail advertising comes in a variety of formats. The two most widely used are the catalog and the mail package.

Catalogs

Catalog companies constitute the largest single category of direct marketers. Catalogs describe and usually picture the products offered by a manufacturer, wholesaler, jobber, or retailer. Catalogs are used for both B2B and B2C marketing. Most mail-order companies specialize in certain areas, such as outdoor clothing and equipment (Sierra Trading Post), electronic gadgets (Sharper Image), and gourmet foods (Balducci's). Originally catalogs were a print format and were delivered by mail to a home or office. Since the introduction of the internet, a number of companies use online catalogs either instead of or in support of a print catalog.

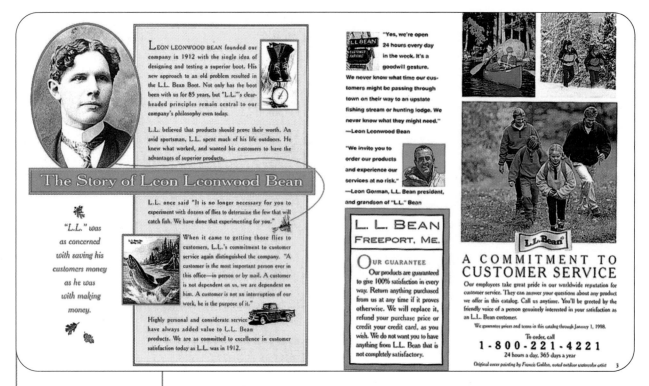

EXHIBIT 18-9

This double-page spread from an L. L. Bean catalog includes a historical feature on the founder, the company's guarantee, and a customer-service commitment statement, along with a toll-free number. The intention of such copy is to lessen the risk people face when they order from a catalog.

The most popular consumer product category making use of catalogs is clothing, followed by home furnishings. This fact reflects the interests of the primary target for consumer catalogs: women.[8] According to the DMA, about 62 percent of adult women buy one or more items a year from catalogs (compared to 48 percent of adult men). Although a catalog itself is impersonal, customers can contact the company through a toll-free number or online, which opens up an opportunity for one-to-one conversation with a sales representative (see Exhibit 18-9).

New media are changing the way catalogs look and perform. Some marketers now have a video brochure or catalog to augment the efforts of the sales staff or to use for prospecting. CDs are increasingly being used to "print" and distribute catalogs, because they are able to store millions of bits of information in a durable yet space-efficient format, can cost less to produce than catalogs, and can feature full-motion sight, sound, color, and music.

Most catalog marketers have adapted their catalogs to work on their websites. Because copy, graphics, and layouts for catalogs—like most advertising messages today—are computer-generated regardless of the medium that will be used, moving these bundles of digital data onto a website is easy. More important, having catalogs on a website allows them to be kept up-to-date, unlike a printed catalog. A company can easily add and subtract items and change prices in response to competitive and other marketplace changes.

Mail Packages

A traditional direct-mail offer—called a mail package—contains more than one item. Although contents vary, the standard package contains five pieces (some of them are illustrated in Exhibit 18-10):

1. *Outer envelope:* The more attention getting and relevant this is, the greater is the chance it will be opened. Tactics proven to increase opening are using colored envelopes and printing a benefit on the envelope.

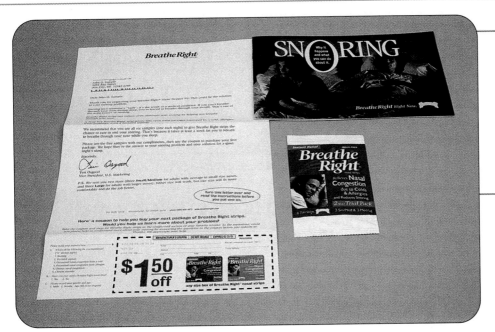

EXHIBIT 18-10
This BreatheRight Snore Stopper Kit is a mailing piece that includes a letter with a combined return card and coupon. It also contains a sample pack and an informational brochure on snoring.

2. *Letter:* Years of research have shown that four pages is the optimum length, enough to explain the offer but not too much for high potential prospects to read.

3. *Brochure or similar selling piece:* Generally this is a heavily visual presentation of the product and its benefits.

4. *Insert:* This odd-size envelope or folded sheet talks about key points of the offer, reinforces the offer, and provides an additional element of involvement.

5. *Business reply card and envelope:* The self-addressed, postage paid envelope makes it easy for customers to respond.

Marketers have found that including several items in a mailing helps attract the recipient's attention and is more involving than using only one piece. The more time a person spends with any brand message, the more likely it is that the message will have an impact and generate a response. Therefore, the more creative and involving a mailer can be, the higher the response rate.

Costs of Direct Mail

In the United States, marketers use any of several classes of mail: express, priority, first class, and third class. (Second-class mail is reserved for authorized publishers and news agents.) The majority of mailings use either first or third class. The U.S. Postal Service does not offer a volume discount on postage. Nevertheless, marketers can do certain things to reduce mailing costs. When there are 500 or more pieces to be delivered, presorting by zip code will reduce the cost per piece. Third-class mail must be presorted and classified by destination and delivered to the post office in bags or on trays.

B2B mailings aimed at top executives are often sent by UPS, FedEx, or some other private carrier—all of which charge more than the U.S. Postal Service. There are two main reasons for using private mail services: packages delivered by private carriers demand more attention and are perceived as being more important than those received by regular mail, and private carriers are more dependable and able to track mailings.

Because a major expense of using direct mail is postage, companies often piggyback their direct-mail offers—that is, they send their offers along with another company's mailing. Piggyback offers, also called *statement stuffers,* appear with utility bills, monthly reports from brokerage firms, periodic frequent-flyer reports to an airline's members, and monthly credit-card statements. Piggyback mailings are seldom as elaborate as single direct mailings.

The cost of an average direct-mail piece (including postage) is $1.68—less than the cost of a B2B or consumer telemarketing call but far more than the cost of an e-mail message.[9] The average response rate for direct mail is higher than for any of the mass media but below that of telemarketing and personal selling.

Strengths and Limitations of Direct Mail

The number-one strength of mail is its addressability. If a company is able to identify its customers and prospects, mail can be a cost-effective medium because it minimizes waste. Addressability also enables a company to personalize its messages. Although a few magazines offer customized messaging (← Chapter 11), newspaper and magazine ads generally deliver exactly the same message to each reader. Marketers that use mail can use their databases to customize messages to customers and prospects. Unfortunately, most companies use this addressable medium to send mass messages that are not personalized.

Addressability allows marketers to measure response rates to direct mailings. Thus mail is a much more accountable medium than most other media. Companies can use mail's addressability to test many different offers and send those that generate the highest response rates to targeted customers and prospects.

Despite the perception of direct mail as junk mail, a piece of mail receives more attention than any *mass* media message, especially when it is well designed and inviting like the Timbuktu flyer in Exhibit 18-11 announcing a special sale for current customers. Few people take things from their mailbox and throw them away without first sorting through them. This fact alone almost guarantees that a direct-mail envelope will be noticed and given some consideration. Unlike ads in newspapers and magazines, direct mail faces no editorial competition for attention (just other direct mail). According to household diary reports, 52 percent of unsolicited mail pieces are opened.[10] The percentage of mass media messages that receive similar attention ranges only between 8 and 35.

Another advantage of direct mail is that the brand message can be of any size or configuration. In general, the more complex and expensive looking it is, the more likely it is to attract attention and be opened—although some marketers have found that small postcards inscribed with a "handwritten" message can cut through mailbox clutter.

As you might guess, any medium that has this many advantages is costly to use, and that is one of mail's major weaknesses. Not only is postage costly, but most mailings are considerably more costly to produce than other types of brand messages (← Chapter 17). A TV commercial may cost $350,000 to produce; but once it is produced, it can be "delivered" to millions of people without any more *production* costs. In contrast, every direct-mail message to be delivered must be produced. Another weakness is long lead time. It can take weeks and even months to create, produce, and send out a mailing. The more complex the piece is, generally the longer the lead time.

TELEMARKETING

Telemarketing is *the practice of using the telephone to deliver a brand message designed to create a sale or sales lead.* The use of telemarketing (including faxed messages,

Grab the girls, head to Timbuktu and get 25% off your entire purchase!!

which come into a home or office through a phone line connected to a fax machine) has been greatly restricted. Telemarketing became so successful that its use increased to the point where the average consumer found it overly annoying. As a result, the U.S. government (following the lead of many state governments) established a national do-not-call registry in 2003. In the first four days, callers registered more than 10 million phone numbers, giving expression to their dislike of telemarketing; the Federal Trade Commission (FTC) expected more than 60 million to register by the end of the registry's first year. Most callers were registered online at www.donotcall.gov or by calling a toll-free number. Companies that call a number on the list are subject to a fine up to $11,000 per call.[11] Excluded from these restrictions are nonprofit organizations, political organizations and candidates, and marketing research companies. The new regulations also allowed companies to make telemarketing calls to current customers through December 2004.

The telemarketing industry is supported by both the Direct Marketing Association and the American Teleservices Association (ATA). ATA says it "represents the call centers, trainers, consultants, and equipment suppliers that initiate, facilitate, and generate telephone, internet, and e-mail sales, service, and support."[12]

In 2002, U.S. organizations spent $80.3 billion on telemarketing—more than was spent on TV advertising.[13] There are several reasons why they did so:

1. A company can accurately estimate its return on investment in a telemarketing program because the results are easy to measure.

2. Telemarketing costs significantly less per customer contact than face-to-face personal selling yet offers many of the benefits of personal selling.

3. Telemarketing is extremely economical for maintaining frequent, personal contact with current customers.

4. Telemarketing by a company that has a customer database is highly targeted.

5. Telephone messages can be personally tailored just as in face-to-face selling.

6. Customers can be reached faster through telemarketing than through most other forms of media.

Phone Formats and Features

Some people have a problem thinking of the telephone as a marketing communication medium. But it definitely must be included when you think back to the definition of *media* as a means of connecting companies and customers. Like mail, **telephony** *(the technical name for the transmission of sound between two points)* is big business. Marketers divide calls into two categories. *Outbound* calls are the ones we refer to when talking about telemarketing. *Inbound* calls are primarily those made by customers responding to direct-marketing offers (in other media) as well as calls made to customer service.

Outbound Calls

Outbound calls are *calls initiated by a marketing organization*. Because it's human participation that makes outbound calls so expensive, some organizations use prerecorded calls, especially to send reminder messages. During the 2002 congressional election, the Republican party used a recorded message from President Bush in its telephone campaign to get out the Republican vote. A chain of oil-change service centers can give its customer database to a telemarketing call center that will script and produce a brief recorded message reminding customers when it is time for their next oil change. The same can be done for any products that are periodically repurchased.

Since 1996, when the Telecommunications Act deregulated telephone service, no phone company has had a monopoly, especially in long-distance service. With the growth of wireless service, telephony has gotten even more competitive. As a result of the competition, phone rates, like most other media rates, can be negotiated—the greater the volume (both inbound and outbound), the lower the rate.

Inbound Calls

Inbound calls are *calls initiated by prospects and customers who are responding to a brand offer or calling with an inquiry, complaint, or request for more information.* Often these come in over a company's 800 number, so they are free for the calling party. Inbound calls are a critical way in which companies connect with customers and will be increasing in importance as customer relationship management (CRM) becomes widely used.

In response to the do-not-call legislation, companies will make more of an effort to motivate customers and prospects to initiate calls. They will do this by making 800 numbers and e-mail addresses more prominent in advertising and on packaging. At the same time, companies are also training customer-service representatives and others who handle inbound calls to make sales offers after callers' questions, complaints, or other reasons for calling have been addressed.

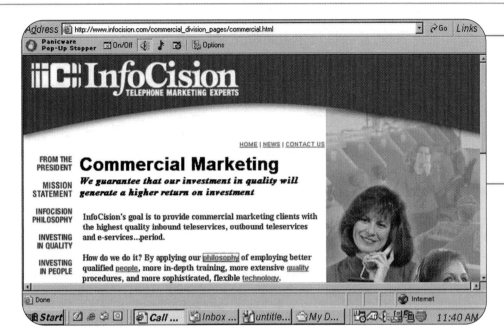

EXHIBIT 18-12
*Why would a company hire
another company such as
InfoCision to handle
customer calls? InfoCision
has the necessary
infrastructure and a staff
of trained responders.*

Inbound calls are one of the most valuable brand–customer touch points because nearly 100 percent come from current customers or from prospects who
want to become customers. As you will recall, a major principle of IMC is that
companies should put at least as much emphasis on customer retention as they do
on customer acquisition. Retention is most likely when a company is good at listening and responding. This is why there are companies that specialize in handling inbound calls for other companies (see Exhibit 18-12).

Most businesses today use some form of automated answering system. Many
people regard such systems as "voice-mail jail." Why do companies use them?
To save money. Such systems can reduce customer-service operating costs by 20 to
50 percent.

Automated systems, however, need not be irritating for a company to save
money. Capital One Finance Corporation, one of the 10 largest credit-card issuers
in the United States, uses an automated answering system that handles customer
calls efficiently and effectively. Capital One receives 1 million calls a week from
customers who want to check their credit-card balances, question a charge on
monthly invoices, ask why their interest rate changed, and so on. As soon as a call
comes in, Capital One's computers (which hold profile data on 17 million customers) go instantly to work. They identify the caller in the customer database
(using the telephone number of the incoming call), analyze that customer's profile
data, predict why the person may be calling, sort through 50 possible internal call
destinations, and even determine what company products may be of greatest
interest to the caller. The computers have been programmed to learn all the numbers from which frequent callers usually call (work, home, cell phone). According
to an article on Capital One's system, "All these steps—the incoming call, the
data review, the analysis, the routing, and the recommending—happen in just 100
milliseconds."[14]

As the Capital One example illustrates, the "old" medium of telephony has
gone high-tech. Because the phone is the primary medium that customers use for
initiating communication with a company, how companies choose to receive
phone calls can affect customer relationships. There is a range of automated answering systems (see Figure 18-2). An automated attendant (AA) offers a recorded
menu from which the caller chooses an appropriate number. An interactive voice

FIGURE 18-2

Companies can choose from a range of automated phone systems.

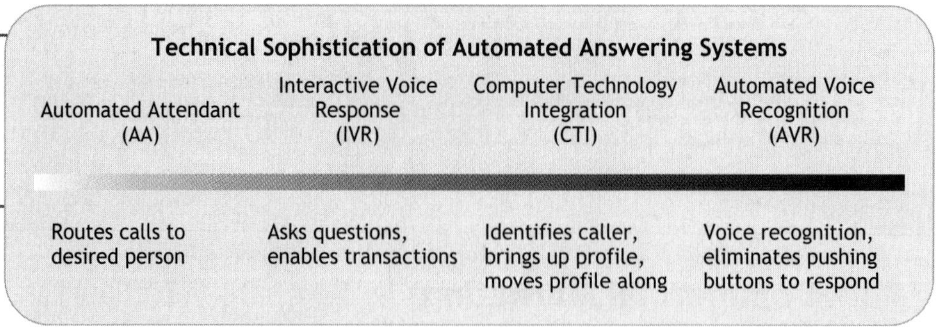

Technical Sophistication of Automated Answering Systems

Automated Attendant (AA)	Interactive Voice Response (IVR)	Computer Technology Integration (CTI)	Automated Voice Recognition (AVR)
Routes calls to desired person	Asks questions, enables transactions	Identifies caller, brings up profile, moves profile along	Voice recognition, eliminates pushing buttons to respond

response (IVR) system does everything an AA does but, in addition, allows callers to interact with the company. For example, a caller can punch in an account number to find out a bank balance or type in a flight number to find out a departure time. The IVR can handle multiple calls at the same time, so callers are rarely put on hold.

When computer technology integration (CTI) is combined with an IVR system, a call can go into the customer database and bring up the caller's profile, as is done at Capital One. This allows customer-service representatives to know who is calling even before the caller speaks (although most callers still are asked for some form of identification). A CTI system also allows the customer-service rep to transfer the caller's profile to another person or department so the customer does not have to repeat any information after a transfer. This technique, called "screen popping," is part of a good CRM system.

The most advanced automated systems are the automated voice recognition (AVR) systems. With these, customers don't have to punch any buttons but simply give oral responses to questions. At the current level of development, most AVR systems pose questions that can be answered with "yes" or "no." Because of accents and different voice levels and manners of speaking, there is still much work to be done in perfecting AVR systems.

Part of a company's media evaluation should be an ongoing monitoring of its automated answering system. After customers learn how to use the system and its shortcuts, its complexity may not seem like a problem for them. But for prospects and new customers, an automated phone system can be intimidating and irritating if not set up with customers' needs in mind.

Integrating Call Centers into the Marketing Communication Mix

Inbound and outbound calls take place in a **call center**—*a bank of telephones staffed by sales representatives whose dialogue is guided by computer-generated scripts* (see Exhibits 18-13 and 18-14). In outbound telemarketing, scripts ensure that all important points are made and that the brand message is consistent. Representatives handling inbound calls have access to scripts with answers to frequently asked questions. Most companies, especially in B2B marketing, also require representatives to make notes of their conversations with customers. Note-taking provides a history of each customer's interaction with the company, which is helpful the next time these customers call.

Although most telemarketing is used for soliciting sales and receiving orders, it can also be used for doing surveys, setting appointments for salespeople, and handling customer service. Companies usually separate customer-service and survey work from solicitations and taking orders, however, because each requires special

Hi! I'm _____ calling from the CLIENT MEMBERSHIP PROGRAM. The CLIENT MEMBERSHIP PROGRAM has developed an industry specific website to promote products like yours in the worldwide market. The website will list company information and product descriptions that support this specific industry.

- [If the company is *not a current member* of the CLIENT MEMBERSHIP PROGRAM, invite them to join the program by]: To best provide you with the tools to develop and support your product, THE CLIENT would like to invite you to review the benefits of joining the CLIENT MEMBERSHIP PROGRAM, a free program, by going to CLIENT MEMBERSHIP PROGRAM WEB SITE. You can then apply at CLIENT MEMBERSHIP PROGRAM WEBSITE.

We show your product [**Product Name Here**] is a potential candidate for the industry specific website. Do you have any other products that might apply to the specific industry Market? Open box needed to print product name/ description/cats/subcats.

I have some questions for you in regard to that/those product/s. Do you have a few minutes that I can ask you some questions?
[Need to be able to record responses for each product listed]:

1) What operating system is this product running on? List versions in check box format.
   - [If their product is *active on Operating System "A"*]: I want to invite you to be featured as part of the CLIENT's Industry Specific Website.
2) Is there a reference site for any of your Client-based installations? Create box for fill-in info on company name, address, phone, web.
3) Do you support an international business opportunity with this product? Y or N
4) Who should be the point of contact for this program? Title? Phone #? E-mail ID? Create fill-in boxes for these fields.

The Industry Specific website information is available on the Web at WEBSITE. I want to thank you [**their name here**] for your time. If you have any questions or need assistance please call us at 800.945.6111, option 1-2. We would be happy to help! Have a great day!

Save info in database and record call in Activity Tracker.

EXHIBIT 18-13
This telemarketing script invites companies to be listed on a website through which they can promote their products.

training. There are exceptions such as Procter & Gamble, whose customer-service representatives sometimes ask a research question after a caller's question or complaint has been addressed.

Strengths and Limitations of Telemarketing

What makes telemarketing a powerful direct-response tool is its addressability and its occurrence in real time. These characteristics make it more personal than mass media messages. Like face-to-face personal selling, telemarketing personalizes sales calls, making it possible to respond immediately to objections and perhaps generate an instant action. Another advantage is that it demands attention. Although some consumers use caller ID and answering machines to screen calls, most people pick up a ringing phone.

Telemarketing's two major weaknesses are cost, especially when calls are being made by a human (rather than a computer), and intrusiveness, which led to the government regulation discussed earlier. Intrusiveness is the dark side of demanding attention. When used for delivering commercial messages, the phone probably has the worst image of all media because of its intrusiveness. An unwanted phone call from a telemarketer can upset even the gentlest, kindest, and most mature of people. According to the president of a telemarketing company, "learning to live with the new limitations may lead telemarketers to develop higher-quality, less-intrusive outbound call practices."[15]

EXHIBIT 18-14

This telemarketing script is used in a sales follow-up to make sure the buyer received the software and was able to install and run it.

Hi! I am _____ calling from CLIENT. Our records indicate your company recently purchased PRODUCT X for software development purposes. I wanted to follow up and talk to you about this purchase.

1. Are you developing software on the hardware system that was recently purchased?
* If yes, continue with the questions.
* If No, ask who is using the equipment (and ask to be transferred to them or get their phone number)
* If transferred, thank this person and repeat from the top with the new contact.

These questions will take approximately 10 minutes of your time. As an incentive, CLIENT would like to send you a complimentary gift [Gift is a size large (only) t-shirt to be sent].

2. Did you receive the box of software included with the hardware system?
_____ Yes   _____ NO
* If Yes, go down to question 3
* If No, ask 2a:
2a. Can you please give me your fax #?

3. Did you remember a brochure included with your subscription?
_____ Yes   _____ NO

4. Have you activated your software subscription?
_____ Yes   _____ NO
* If Yes, go to question 5
* If No, go to question 4A;

4a. Why haven't you activated your software subscription?/Comments: Can you please give me your fax #? _____ Also, I need to know how many machines did you order for which the software subscription has not been activated? [You will need to issue a serial number for *each* machine they ordered from the sheet titled 'serial #s' in the database. Be sure to record next to the serial number in the database what company that number was issued to.] I can fax you a software activation form that you can use to order your software over the Internet OR if you have time, I can walk you through the process right now. Your software will take approximately 1-2 weeks to arrive.

5. Do you find it valuable to include software with your hardware system?
_____ Yes   _____ NO

6. Do you find it valuable to receive automatic software updates (as opposed to single copy)?
_____ Yes   _____ NO

Now, I'm going to ask you a couple of general questions regarding the Hardware offering you received.

OVERALL PROGRAM SATISFACTION

7. How long did it take for your hardware system to arrive after your order was placed?
_____ 1 week or less   _____ 2-4 weeks   _____ 5-8 weeks   _____ More than 8 weeks

8. Overall, are you happy with your purchase?
_____ Yes   _____ NO
Comments:

9. Do you have any comments on what we can do to enhance this offering?
(Possible Answers, <u>DO NOT READ</u>)
_____ Lower the price
_____ Offer more selection
_____ Remove software
_____ Make it easier to purchase
_____ Other

10. Do you have any additional comments I can pass on?
Comments:

Thank you for your time. In order to send you your gift, please give me your name and address.
* Name =
* Company Name =
* Address =

[The size Large (only—no exceptions) T-shirt will be sent out in 1-2 weeks.]. I appreciate your input; have a great day!

INFOMERCIALS

Marketers' use of TV for making direct offers has increased in the last five years, particularly in the area of infomercials, program-length advertisements that may run as long as 30 minutes (← Chapter 11). They are used to entertain and educate viewers about a product or service and then provide information on how to order that product.

The average cost of producing a top-quality 30-minute infomercial (about $200,000) is less than the average cost of producing a quality 30-second national TV spot (about $350,000). Why does an infomercial cost less, despite being 60 times longer? Most infomercials use "talking heads" and only one set, and most 30-second commercials use a variety of sets and actors plus complex production techniques. Here is a list of the major steps and items needed in the production of a typical infomercial:[16]

- A shooting script that includes key selling points and how to respond.
- A set, director, and production crew.
- TelePrompter, lighting, and audio equipment.
- Spokesperson.
- Voice-over for describing details of offer not covered by the spokesperson.
- Original or stock music for background.
- Graphics for visual supers (words that appear on a TV screen over the picture).
- Editing and final mix of visual, audio, and graphics.

Like direct-mail offers, infomercials are tested and revised several times before they are used nationally. According to one infomercial expert, "usually the first test is a failure; two or three tests and re-edits is normal." Airtime for testing an infomercial costs about the same as production—$200,000.[17]

Since most infomercials run on cable stations, often in the middle of the night and during other non-prime-time dayparts, you might think that few if any people actually see them. Research shows, however, that 15 percent of all TV sets are on at 1 A.M. and 66 percent of those who watch cable TV are heavy surfers.[18] Infomercials constantly repeat the important selling points to "catch" surfers who may come across the infomercial and stay for only a minute or two.

EVALUATING DIRECT MARKETING

Measurability is one of the main strengths of direct-response marketing. Although the ability to measure its effectiveness is important, some companies fail to plan far enough ahead to take advantage of this characteristic. Pre-testing takes time, but it can save a company thousands of dollars. Smart companies that use direct marketing make testing and evaluation an ongoing activity. Many elements of a direct-marketing offer can be tested. Every test must specify a benchmark against which the results are judged.

Elements That Can Be Tested

As direct marketing has become more widely used, with some offers being delivered to 10 million or more households, testing has become very sophisticated and complicated, because just one percentage point of difference in rates of response can be worth hundreds of thousands of dollars. Before executing a direct-marketing effort, especially a large-scale one, the following elements should be tested:

- *List:* The lists that are used have been found to be the single most critical factor affecting the rate of response to addressable media (mail, e-mail, telephone, fax). When a company has a list of 1 million people and mails to all of them at the same time, it is not testing but gambling. Before committing to the costs of contacting a large list, the company should send the planned offer to a small sample (5,000 to 10,000 people on the list). If the response rate to this mailing meets or exceeds the planned objective, then the offer can be sent to the entire list with much less risk.

- *Offer:* There are various ways to make an offer. One offer could feature a price of $59.95 along with a free Cross ballpoint pen (which costs the company $5). Another offer could feature a price of $54.95 and no incentive. Both offers would cost the company the same, so the company should use the one that produces a significantly higher response in a test than the other. Each element making up an offer—product, price, credit terms, incentive for responding, guarantee—can be tested. Another opportunity for testing arises when a company decides to change an offer that it has been using for some time. Suppose the product has always had a one-year guarantee and the company decides to change it to three years. The affect of the change on the level of response can be tested.

- *Creative/copy:* An offer can be explained and presented in many different ways. Is a demonstration better than a testimonial? Does a cartoon character work better than a serious, straightforward presentation? Obviously, the creative treatment should be consistent with the overall brand creative strategy. But even within this parameter, there are many alternatives, each of which can affect the response rate.

- *Media mix:* Because different media reach different audiences with different effects, various combinations warrant testing. A company selling a new sun-protection product may test magazines going to three different "outdoor" audiences: hunting and fishing, gardening, and vacationing. Another type of media test is impact. Does a half-page ad generate at least twice the response rate of a quarter-page ad? Unless it does, the company should stick to the quarter-page ad, because a half-page ad costs twice as much.

- *Frequency:* Because current customers are a company's best customers, most companies that use direct marketing send current customers offers throughout the year. Testing the frequency of these offers—how many can profitably be sent within one year—is important. Contacting customers too often not only can be a waste of money (because people stop responding) but also can weaken brand relationships if customers become annoyed.

One basic rule of thumb is used in evaluating direct response: when testing one variable against another, it is critical that the samples for each test be representative of the total target audience. When testing a list, for example, every *n*th name should be chosen, instead of taking the first 5,000 names from two different lists. When testing two different offers in print media, split runs should be used: offer A goes into half of the issues printed and offer B in the other half—that is, each goes into every other issue (← Chapter 11). Making these tests as scientifically pure as possible is a must, because even a quarter of a percent difference in responses can be important (in a mailing of 10 million, for example, a quarter percent represents 25,000 responses).

Evaluation Methodologies

Although direct marketing can be a stand-alone MC function, integrating it into a MC mix is an especially successful strategy in marketing B2B products or consumer considered purchases such as financial services, cars, major appliances, and real estate. In these cases, the direct response that is desired may be a step in the buying process, such as taking a test drive or visiting a showroom.

An example of how direct response and personal selling can be integrated comes from a direct-mail teaser campaign created by Otis Elevator to announce the company's new Odyssey elevator, which is capable of operating in mile-high buildings. Based on a story about Frank Lloyd Wright's conceiving the idea of a mile-high building in 1956 and predicting that an elevator like the Odyssey would make such buildings possible within the next 20 years, the promotion used a letter allegedly written by Wright, in his style, and on his letterhead. The letter was put in an envelope with a three-cent stamp (which was the cost of first-class postage at that time), then inserted in a re-created, lost-in-the-mail envelope, and delivered to difficult-to-reach architects and developers. Some letters were even personalized. For example, the distinguished architect I. M. Pei had almost met Wright once but was scared off by Wright's dogs. A postscript in the letter to Pei expressed regret that the dogs had prevented the meeting. This teaser campaign by Otis drew a 60 percent response rate from the architects and generated $2.5 billion in qualified leads for the sales force.[19]

Evaluating the effectiveness of direct-marketing programs does not require a Ph.D. in mathematics. For example, to determine the response rate, you simply divide the number of responses by the number of mailed offers. If there were 50,000 responses from a mailing of 500,000, that would be a 10 percent response rate:

$$\frac{\text{Number of responses}}{\text{Number of offers mailed}} = \frac{50,000}{500,000} = .10 = 10\% \text{ response rate}$$

Although response rates are always good to know for comparison purposes, the more important measure is cost per sale. The first step in calculating it is adding up all the costs involved in making a direct-marketing offer. This figure is then divided by the number of responses. Suppose the total cost of the mailing was $500,000 and 2,500 responses resulted in sales. The cost of the mailing ($500,000) divided by the number of sales generated (2,500) equals the cost per sale ($200):

Creative development, art and production	$200,000
Mailing lists and computer processing	75,000
Collating and labeling	25,000
Agency fees	50,000
Postage	150,000
Total cost	$500,000
Number of responses resulting in sales	2,500

$$\text{Cost per sale} = \frac{\$500,000 \text{ cost of mailing}}{2,500 \text{ number of sales}} = \$200$$

What determines whether this campaign was a financial success is how much was budgeted for advertising and promotion. If the product was a compact disc player for $399 and only $75 was allocated for advertising and promotion, the campaign was a financial disaster. However, if the campaign was for a high-speed internet service provider that allocated $500 in advertising and promotion for each new customer acquired, then the campaign was a big success, for the cost per sale was $200.

Some marketers naively think that if they use a variety of MC functions and media they are practicing IMC. The challenge to doing IMC, however, is determining the most cost-effective mix of MC functions and media. A good example of how to determine this mix comes from testing done by Ernan Roman Direct Marketing for a manufacturer of telecommunications equipment.[20] This example shows how two different media mixes generate different response rates and different cost per sale numbers.

The objective of the direct-marketing messages in the test campaigns was to generate qualified leads that would result in more sales. Personal selling was used to convert leads into sales. Both campaigns contained mass media advertising and direct mail, but campaign B also included telemarketing. In the more traditional campaign A, the majority of media dollars (70 percent) was spent on television and print advertising. In campaign B, the majority (65 percent) was spent on telemarketing, followed by direct mail (25 percent) and mass media advertising (10 percent). As the following table shows, both campaigns spent the same amount of money: $250,000. Nevertheless, the difference in the number of leads generated by each campaign was dramatic: campaign B generated three times as many leads (3,750) as campaign A (1,250).

Budget Allocations ($ Thousands)

	Campaign A		Campaign B	
TV and print advertising	70%	$175	10%	$ 25
Direct mail	30	75	25	63
Telemarketing	—	—	65	162
Total budget	100%	$250	100%	$250

Leads Generated by Media Mix

	Leads from A		Leads from B	
TV and print advertising	438	35%	375	10%
Direct mail	812	65	750	20
Telemarketing	—	—	2,625	70
Total leads	1,250	100%	3,750	100%

In campaign B, telemarketers contacted all those who received the direct-mail offer. Calls were made within 24 to 72 hours after the direct mail was received. (TV and print began running two weeks before the mailing.) The result was that the cost per lead produced by campaign B ($67) was one-third of that produced by campaign A ($200):

Campaign A	$250,000 ÷ 1,250 = $200 cost per lead
Campaign B	$250,000 ÷ 3,750 = $67 cost per lead

Although knowing the cost per lead is helpful, the most important number is the cost per sale. As the next table shows, campaign B was also more cost-effective on this measure: $444 versus $6,250 cost per sale generated by campaign A. Because the average transaction was $10,000, the MC selling cost for campaign A was over half the price of the transaction—not a good situation to have in most cases.

Cost Per Sale

	Campaign A	Campaign B
Lead follow-ups	400	2,250
Conversion to sale	40	563
Cost per sale	$6,250	$ 444

Only a third (400 of 1,250) of the leads produced by campaign A were followed up, and of those, only 40 (10 percent) were converted into sales. For campaign B these figures were much better: 2,250 of the 3,750 leads (60 percent) were followed up and, of those, 563 (25 percent) were converted into sales. Campaign A produced fewer leads, the leads it did produce were of much lower quality (that is why fewer were followed up), and a lower percentage of those leads resulted in sales.

According to Roman, mass media brand messages often produce lower-quality leads because of the limited amount of information they can carry. Direct mail can carry more information, but even these messages are one-way until someone responds. Those who responded to campaign A versus campaign B didn't have as much information on which to decide whether they were truly interested in the offer. Furthermore, campaign B's use of telemarketing to follow up and add to the information supplied by the mass media advertising and direct mail allowed prospects to learn more about the offer. The better-informed prospects were able to say whether they were really interested. So campaign B generated not only more leads but also higher-quality leads, meaning a higher percentage converted into sales.

CONCERNS RAISED BY DIRECT MARKETING

Direct marketing is criticized for its intrusiveness (phone calls; e-mail and fax spam) and for poor targeting to people who aren't interested in the product. That is why direct mail is sometimes called junk mail. Related to the "junk" concept is spam (⇐ Chapter 12), a term that applies to bulk e-mail and fax messages. The spam wars are discussed in the Ethics and Issues box.

ETHICS AND ISSUES

The Spam Wars

E-mail inboxes and fax machines have become high-tech war zones. The combatants are bulk mailers who send out millions of e-mail and fax messages and the super sleuths who try to shut them down.

What's the problem with getting an unsolicited e-mail or fax? After all, people have been getting unsolicited commercial mail for as long as they have had mailboxes. And don't marketers have a right to distribute their messages to as many potential customers as possible? The First Amendment protects distribution of commercial messages, after all.

And spam is cheap to send, so cheap that a very low response rate is still good enough to make the effort profitable. As few as 100 responses to 10 million messages can make money for the marketer and a commission for the spammer. Internet marketing companies charge $500 to $2,000 for every million addresses, but this cost goes up if the list is more targeted. If the same offer were sent by mail, the costs to buy the list and print and mail the offer would be more than $200,000.

Who uses these services knowing that the delivery system is irritating to almost everyone? Typically, users are companies that are not worried about brand image. They are usually selling credit programs, vitamins and wonder drugs, diet programs, home mortgages, breast enlargement kits, and other dubious products. There are, however, legitimate e-mail marketers who deliver commercial information by e-mail to their customers and to others who signed up to receive the information.

For businesses on the receiving end, the unsolicited spam clogs computer storage, uses up huge amounts of bandwidth, and chokes fax machines. Big internet providers are particularly hurt by the deluge.

Brightmail, which makes spam-filtering software, estimates that spam increased from 16 percent of all e-mail at the beginning of 2002 to 45 percent by early 2003. America Online also reports that spam to its 35 million customers doubled during that period and approaches 2 billion messages a day, more than 70 percent of the total e-mail its customers receive. Some universities are reporting as much as 80 percent of the e-mails in their servers are spam.

Individuals who find endless spam messages in their e-mail inboxes spend endless hours hitting the Delete button. If they are targeted by a fax spammer, they may also find themselves answering endless phone calls that they can't stop, some even coming in the middle of the night. There can also be a financial cost, for the recipient has to pay for the wasted paper gobbled up by unwanted fax messages, and people who receive e-mail or fax calls to their cell phone or pager numbers have to pay for the calls.

So what's the solution? In the cat-and-mouse game of the spammers, companies sell software programs designed to filter out e-mail spam based on recognition of spammer phone numbers or predictable patterns of address. Of course, spammers stay one step ahead by changing their codes. Another anti-spam measure is to sign up on the Remove.Org global do-not-contact list.

Some anti-spam programs are designed to search for secret codes that recognize "web bugs" or "spam beacons" that notify a spammer when a recipient opens a message. There is even a proposal for a new "postal" system that charges a fee to companies that send spam messages to an inbox. But for every new anti-spam device, spammers eventually seem to find a creative way around it. That's the problem built in to an open system like the modern internet.

But remember there are also the legitimate opt-in e-mailers who send messages to customers and others who have given permission to use their e-mail address. However, even that practice has its shady side. Many of these legitimate opt-in e-mail addresses wind up on CD-ROMs that anyone can buy. A New York court ruled that a Niagara Falls, New York, company, MonsterHut, violated antifraud laws for misrepresenting opt-in permission.

Consumers may feel they are losing ground against e-mail spammers, but there is more control over the fax machine. Consumers can register with services like junkfax.org to block unwanted faxes. There is also legislative help with The Telephone Consumer Protection Act (TCPA), which prohibits junk fax advertising that is (1) unsolicited and (2) advertises the commercial availability or quality of property, goods, or services. Press releases from advocacy groups or purely political ads, however, do not count as fax junk. The TCPA makes fax spam illegal in all 50 states and allows recipients to sue businesses that send junk faxes, although consumers may not feel it's worth their time and money to take a case to small claims court for a $500 lawsuit. California has also passed a law that makes spam sent to cell phones illegal.

Similar legislation for e-mail spam is being considered or passed by many state legislatures as well as the U.S. Senate. Most of this legislation aims to provide some basic protection by requiring (1) a subject line that discloses that the message is an ad, (2) a subject line code—ADLT—that announces adult content, (3) accurate information about the sender and routing information, and (4) information about how to remove names from the list. Lawsuits are permitted if these requirements are violated. The anti-spam vigilantes are not hopeful, however, that legislation will be able to win the war against spam.

Think About It

If you were designing an e-mail marketing program for your company, what considerations would make your efforts legitimate and appealing to your customers? What practices would you caution your company against using?

Source: Saul Hansell, "Internet Is Losing Ground in Battle against Spam," *New York Times,* April 22, 2003, <www.nytimes.com/2003/04/22/technology/22SPAM.html>; Jennifer Beauprez, "High-Tech War Pits Sleuth vs. Spammer," *Denver Post,* January 17, 2003, p. K1; Henry Noor, "Spam Isn't Sitting Well with Most," *Boulder Daily Camera,* February 13, 2003, p. 1A; "Commonly Asked Questions about Junk Faxing," <www.junkfax.org/fax/basic_info_qa.html>.

EXHIBIT 18-15

Privacy is another consumer concern that is aroused by some direct-marketing practices. Consumers today are very concerned about their privacy (← Chapter 8). They especially don't like the idea of having their names and other personal information passed around to different types of businesses. As a result, consumers are leery of providing the very information that direct marketers need to segment and target effectively.

While companies must respect and protect consumer information, the good news is that successfully doing so can give a company an edge over its competitors. A study by Kristen Meador found that advertising a privacy policy statement can positively affect brand choice.[21] More important to consumers, however, is how that statement is implemented into a company's business operations. To help companies and the whole marketing industry, the Direct Marketing Association has published a list of 10 things that companies can do to help protect consumer privacy (see Table 18-2). One reason why the DMA is working hard to convince direct-marketing companies to have good privacy practices is to minimize government regulations in this area. Nonetheless, government has stepped in on behalf of beleaguered consumers.

For marketers, the main disadvantage of direct marketing is its relatively high cost per customer or prospect reached. Direct-mail efforts may have costs per thousand (CPMs) up to $400. By comparison, the CPMs of regular mass media advertising range between $15 and $50 (← Chapter 13), but of course they do not have near the rate of return of direct-mail or telemarketing contacts. Because of

---

TABLE 18-2   How Companies Can Protect Customers' Privacy

1. Educate employees about the company's privacy policies, and explain how they are implemented. Train employees how best to respond to questions about their company's handling of customer information.

2. Appoint a chief privacy officer.

3. Conduct periodic audits of the company's online and offline privacy practices, and compare what the company is doing in this area with the policies of other companies in its industry.

4. Refer potential violations of privacy protection (in other companies) to the DMA's Committee on Ethical Business.

5. Actively promote the company's privacy policy.

6. Educate company employees (for their own good) about credit-card fraud and their rights to protection and redress.

7. Promote the Federal Trade Commission's ID Theft affidavit, which helps consumers who have been victims of identity theft.

8. Encourage customers to visit DMA's consumer and privacy websites— www.dmaconsumers.org and www.shopthenet.org—to learn more about consumer privacy rights.

9. Have company managers take a DMA class on how to manage customer data while protecting customers' privacy.

10. For members of DMA: Display the DMA logo in all direct-response messages to show that the company is conforming to a set of nationally recognized privacy standards.

Source: Ways Companies Can Protect Customers' Privacy; Based on a DMA Interactive posting at www.the-dma.org, January 10, 2002. Reprinted with permission of The DMA.

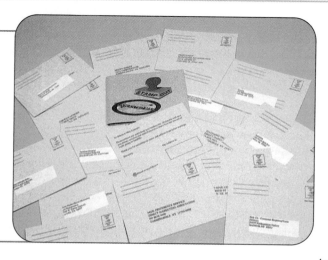

EXHIBIT 18-16

This mailer sponsored by the Boulder Energy Conservation Center, the Governor's Office of Energy Conservation, and the U.S. Environmental Protection Agency contains addressed postcards for a number of major mailing services that will remove a person from mailing and calling lists, as well as DMA addresses.

their relatively high cost, direct-marketing messages must succeed in creating more than an attitudinal response (which can generally be done much more cost-effectively with mass media messages). Correct targeting is also critical because sending messages outside the target audience wastes a significant amount of money. Furthermore, some products simply do not lend themselves to a direct-marketing approach. Certain types of products—such as fresh produce, impulse products (candy bars), and small-ticket, mass-distributed convenience items (toothpicks, ballpoint pens)—have a low profit margin and are therefore not likely to be sold through direct marketing, which must balance the high cost per contact with a high-profit margin on items sold. In addition, consumers are sensitive to the risk that comes from not being able to see, touch, or try on a product before ordering it.

Direct marketing also suffers from clutter. Consumers deluged with junk mail, telemarketing calls, and, increasingly, e-mail are fighting back (see the preceding Ethics box). In addition to inviting potential government oversight, the result of this clutter is an overall decrease in response rates, which means the average cost per response continues to go up. Because of consumer concerns about the increase in number of unsolicited commercial messages, numerous services have sprung up to screen out unsolicited direct-marketing messages (see Exhibit 18-16). Even the Direct Marketing Association offers a Mail, E-mail, Telemarketing Preference Service (P.O. Box 9008, Farmingdale, NY, 11735). Subscribers to DMA are encouraged to use this list and remove the names of people who have requested no unsolicited messages.

A FINAL NOTE: COMMUNICATING WITH INTEGRITY

"Marketing with integrity" was among the issues discussed at a recent national forum of direct marketers. Marketers were told that they must self-regulate, give consumers more control, and treat privacy like a customer-service issue; otherwise, they would risk legislation restricting access to the information they desperately need. They were also warned that the result of neglecting these guidelines would be lower response rates (which are already happening).

Although postage rates continue to go up, direct-mail advertising is still widely used. At the same time the cost of e-mail direct marketing continues to decrease while the number of internet users increases (◄ Chapter 12). All this leads to more and more clutter, thus putting more pressure on creativity in both direct-response message design and knowing when and how to use direct-response media. To find the most cost-effective message and media mix often requires testing several combinations, which is easily done because direct marketing can be easily measured.

back-end strategies 577
call center 590
compiled lists 579
direct marketing 573
direct-response advertising 581

front-end strategies 577
fulfillment 580
inbound calls 588
offer 577
outbound calls 588

response 579
response lists 578
subscriber lists 579
telemarketing 586
telephony 588

Key Point Summary

EXHIBIT 18-17

This is a direct-mail piece by FedEx, complete with a CD that makes it possible for a company to better manage its package delivery. In effect, the CD, which is free, turns a computer into a shipping manager in the FedEx system.

Key Point 1: Strengths and Components of Direct Marketing

The strengths and objectives of direct response include generating immediate sales, as well as increasing customer retention and relationship building. It is valued because it is highly targeted, highly accountable, and cost-effective if the database is good. Direct marketing is personal communication that seeks an immediate action and allows the customer to respond directly to the marketer, bypassing retail stores. Direct-marketing tools offer varying degrees of personalization, from face-to-face direct sales and telemarketing, which are highly personalized; to e-mail, fax, and electronic kiosks, which are less personal although still interactive; to direct mail, catalogs, videos, CDs, and mass-media ads, which are usually not personalized. The elements of a direct-marketing message include the offer, the targeting strategy, the response, fulfillment, customer service, and privacy protection.

Key Point 2: Direct Mail

Mail is a pervasive medium and allows marketers to personalize their messages and make direct contact with customers. It is also interactive in that customers can respond to and initiate contact by mail. Direct-mail formats include catalogs and mail packages. A limitation of mail is its image as junk. Cost is also a limitation when compared to the cost per thousand of mass media–delivered messages. Addressability, the ability to reach a specific person, is its greatest strength.

Key Point 3: Telemarketing

Telemarketing uses have been greatly restricted by the U.S. government, but telemarketing can still be used for contacting current customers and by not-for-profit groups. Outbound calls are initiated by the marketer; inbound calls are initiated by the customer. The biggest limitation of telemarketing is its intrusiveness; however, it is effective because it can be a highly personalized form of contact.

Key Point 4: Evaluating Direct Marketing

One of direct marketing's greatest strengths is that it is measurable. When companies take advantage of this strength by building into the marketing plan enough time to test direct-marketing efforts, hundreds of thousands of dollars can be saved. Direct-marketing evaluation includes the testing of lists, offers, media mixes, and offer frequencies.

Key Point 5: Direct-Marketing Concerns

Targeting people who are not interested in an offer is one of the biggest concerns raised by direct marketing. In telemarketing, the signs of poor targeting are unwanted and intrusive phone calls, as well as junk faxes. In internet marketing, the problem is known as spam. Another major issue for direct marketing is privacy because databases of personal information are used to manage most offers.

Lessons Learned

Key Point 1: Strengths and Components of Direct Marketing

a. Define *direct marketing*.
b. Why do we say that direct marketing is a "microcosm" of the entire marketing process?
c. What are the main strengths of direct marketing? The main limitations?
d. What role do databases play in a direct-marketing program?
e. Explain the role of the primary components of direct marketing.
f. What are front-end and back-end operations? Give examples of each.
g. What media are used in direct marketing?
h. How does an infomercial differ from a traditional TV commercial? What are the elements that make an infomercials effective?
i. Very few people will watch a 30-minute infomercial for the full time. Why is this type of direct-marketing message successful?

Key Point 2: Direct Mail

a. Explain the strengths and limitations of direct mail.
b. How does the cost of mail compare to the cost of other mass media forms? How could you justify using mail?
c. How important is mail as a marketing communication medium?
d. If you were a list manager for a national retail chain, what would be your duties?

Key Point 3: Telemarketing

a. How important is the phone as a marketing communication medium?
b. Compare and contrast outbound and inbound calls in a marketing communication program.
c. What are the key strengths and limitations of telemarketing?

Key Point 4: Evaluating Direct Marketing

a. Why can a direct-marketing message be evaluated more accurately than can a typical TV commercial or publicity release?
b. What elements of a direct-marketing offer can be tested?
c. When in the planning and executing of a marketing plan should direct-marketing offers be tested?

Key Point 5: Direct-Marketing Concerns

a. What is spam? Why is it a problem?
b. Why is protecting customers' privacy an important component of direct marketing? What are companies doing to address the privacy problem?

Chapter Challenge

Case Discussion Questions

1. What did Orange Glo do to make sure that customers made repeat purchases?
2. Explain what needs to be done to make an infomercial attention getting and motivational.
3. What information *not* provided in the case would you need to know in order to recommend other MC functions and media to the marketers of Orange Glo?

Writing Assignment

Take one issue of a magazine, pull out all of the direct-response ads, and separate them into two categories—good examples of direct-response messages and examples that you consider to be weak. Write an analysis of each group, explaining how the good ads differ from the weak ones.

Presentation Assignment

Collect a week's worth of direct mail that comes to your mailbox. Analyze how personalized it is. Prepare a presentation to your class in which you describe the continuum of personalization evident in the direct-mail pieces that you received. Which piece is the most personalized? Which is the least personalized? Where in that range would you put the other pieces?

Internet Assignment

Find the websites of three companies (addresses appear on packages and in brand messages). Contact these companies with an inquiry or complaint, using the response instructions on each website. Keep track of how long it takes each company to respond. Rate each response on how personal it is (was the response personalized or a stock message?). Record to what extent your question was answered or your complaint was addressed. Record to what extent the company made an effort to find out more about you.

Chapter 19

Experiential Contact: Events, Sponsorships, and Customer Service

Key Points in This Chapter

1. What are the major types of events, and what roles can events play in IMC?
2. What types of sponsorship and events do companies use to promote their brands?
3. What are the strengths and weaknesses of events and sponsorships?
4. Why is customer service so important in building brand relationships, and what are its strengths and limitations?

Chapter Perspective

Getting Involved with the Brand

With increasing commercial message clutter and more and more brands from which to choose, brands must work harder not only to get the attention of customers and prospects but to have any impact on their attitudes and behavior. One way to do both is to involve target audiences in a brand experience. People remember little of what they hear, slightly more of what they see, but nearly all of an experience in which they are involved. Therefore, customer involvement in a brand experience can be a valuable part of marketing communication.

The key word here is *involvement*. One of the principles of teamwork is getting people involved so they feel part of what's happening and feel ownership in the results. This is the basic reason for using events and sponsorships. These activities, if properly designed and managed, maximize the positive aspects of customer service by involving customers in positive and memorable ways and sending powerful brand messages based on impactful experiences. Events and sponsorships can work at any point in the brand decision process. Customer service, however, is primarily focused on that key evaluation step after the decision has been made.

JEEP'S SUMMER CAMP FOR ADULTS

Suppose that you sell a common product that can be dangerous and is often misused or underused, and that you want to get your customers together to show them how to use it better. At the same time, you want to stage a fun, family event that's entertaining as well as educational—an experience that drives brand loyalty to the mountaintop. How can you do it?

DaimlerChrysler sponsors an annual owners' gathering, Camp Jeep, that's part vacation and part college. A brilliant marketing scheme, the program invites Jeep owners to pay $300 to attend the week-long event and participate in a memorable brand experience.

Begun in 1995 at Camp Hale, the old World War II 10th Mountain Division ski training camp high in the mountains of Colorado, Camp Jeep teaches people how to handle their cars when they drive off-road. This popular event sells out every summer. Some 55,000 people from 48 states and a number of other countries have gathered to bounce their cars over rocks, crawl through mud, splash across rivers, and grind up mountain trails.

In 1999 Camp Jeep went on the road and moved to other locations, including Nelson County, Virginia, and Branson, Missouri, in the Ozarks. In 2003 the popular summer camp played at two venues: the Blue Ridge Mountains in Virginia and the Santa Ynez Mountains outside Santa Barbara, California. It was held in France in 1999, and the company plans to repeat its European adventures.

Camp Jeep is fun, but it's also informative. Participants, many of whom have never used four-wheel drive for anything other than getting out of their driveways in the snow, are paired with instructors who coach them in the fine art of handling off-the-road and hazardous driving conditions. They learn to negotiate steep downhill grades, riverbanks, large rocks, log-crossings, sand, mud, and other driving obstacles. Once they have mastered the vehicle's capabilities, they can navigate trails of varying levels of difficulty on their own in their own cars.

In addition to the driving experiences, there are numerous discussion groups among Jeep staffers, engineers, and the drivers, such as the "Grand Cherokee Engineering Roundtable." Where else can car aficionados go to talk about gear ratios, transfer cases, and suspension?

Another highlight of the camp is the "World of Jeep" tent, which offers a hands-on tour of the brand's past, present, and future cars. It features Jeeps throughout history, as well as current models and prototypes of new models.

EFFECTIVENESS CASE

EXHIBIT 19-1

But the winning educational experience is Jeep 101, an off-highway course that has proved to be so popular that it now travels to cities across the United States as a separate loyalty program, along with the long-running Jeep Jamborees, which began in the 1950s as the original off-highway vacation.

In addition to the car and driving activities, Camp Jeep features hiking, tubing and whitewater canoeing, rock climbing, archery, Frisbee golf, volleyball, model plane demonstrations, paintball games, and a health and fitness expo. Kids are taken care of with a Crafts Center for Kids, and little ones are propelled around the camp in their own mini-Jeep strollers. A highlight of the camp is a concert celebrating Motown, country, and swing music. The Goodyear blimp has been known to make an appearance, and the fireworks show rivals any Fourth of July display.

The camp is promoted through the Camp Jeep website (www.campjeep.com) and a direct-mail campaign handled by Chicago-based agency FCB Worldwide and its 1-2-1 Marketing unit. But the most important promotion comes from the word-of-mouth testimony of Camp Jeep participants who talk about their experiences to their families and friends. Word of mouth, plus reenrollment, means that typically more than 1,000 attendees register online before the mailings are even sent. An average of 10 to 12 percent of the participants are returnees.

Special promotions include Camp Jeep T-shirts, license plates, and bumper stickers and a Jeep bedroll. Attendees are fiercely loyal to the brand and consider themselves part of an exclusive club. Slogans on these specialties brag "It's a Jeep thing. You wouldn't understand."

The total staff is around 600, which includes the DaimlerChrysler group, as well as about 120 vendor partners who provide products, services, and activities. These marketing partners include 35 magazine sponsors, such as *Southern Living*, which hosted cooking demonstrations, and *National Geographic*, which presented photography seminars. Kawasaki offers free ATV rides and Orvis® gives instruction on fly-fishing.

Camp Jeep is successful not only with its loyal car owners. It has won international recognition as the "Best Program Generating Brand Loyalty" in the Marketing Agency Association (MAA) Worldwide 2002 GLOBES Awards. It won in a similar category for *PROMO Magazine*'s annual PRO Awards in 2002.

Camp Jeep is amazingly successful as an event-oriented sales pitch presented through customer service, education, and fun. As Jeff Bell, vice president of the Jeep Division, observed, "Families come from all over the world to celebrate the Jeep spirit and what it stands for . . . . It's something that only Jeep would do."

Source: Matthew Kinsman, "How I Spent MY Camp Jeep Vacation," PROMO Magazine, October 1, 2000; "Camp Jeep Announces 2003 Dates, Open to Public," Rockcrawler.com December 2002 <www.rockcrawler.com/features/newsshorts/ 02december/camp_jeep_2003.asp>; Matthew Kinsman, "How I Spent My Camp Jeep Vacation," PROMO Magazine, October 1, 2000, <www.promomagazine.com/magazinearticle .asp?magazinearticleid=47900&>; Cliff Gromer, "Over the Hill and through the Wood," <www.popularmechanics.com/ outdoors/outdoors/2001/9/over_the_hill/print/phtml>.

HOW AND WHY EVENT MARKETING WORKS

Some of the most powerful brand messages are those that directly involve customers and other prospects. Recognizing the impact of these types of messages, marketers are becoming smarter about how to create and use the MC functions that produce this type of brand involvement. In this chapter we look at three of these MC functions: events (both created and participation), sponsorships, and customer service.

Event marketing is *a promotional occasion designed to attract and involve a brand's target audience.* According to Claire Rosenzweig, president of the Promotional Marketing Association, "Recent recognition from corporate marketers that event marketing engages consumers with a hands-on, emotionally rewarding brand experience, has caused them to shift budget resources from 'traditional' marketing practices to event marketing, which is the fastest growing practice in the industry."[1] Other reasons for using events are to reach hard-to-reach target audiences, to increase brand awareness, and to provide a platform for brand publicity. According to *PROMO Magazine*, companies spent $132 billion on events in 2002.[2]

Tupperware pioneered the use of an event as a selling tool—the in-home Tupperware party. Door-to-door personal selling had been around for years, but Tupperware creatively turned it into an event that became the cornerstone of the company's marketing and distribution. Sales are driven by lively product demonstrations and socialization. The latter can create peer pressure, as a Morgan Stanley analyst explained: "People at parties do feel a little bit of an obligation to buy."[3] As successful as that approach has been, it is now threatened by online marketing. Some Tupperware sales representatives have set up their own websites, much to the consternation of the Tupperware managers and other sales representatives, who feel the online sales technique will undercut the famous parties. Tupperware has also expanded distribution into some retail stores.

Tupperware parties are unique marketing experiences that represent what has become known as experiential marketing. The basic idea is that a brand can differentiate itself by creating an experience around its product. Instead of selling product performance, companies sell the brand experience.[4]

DaimlerChrysler uses an experience-based strategy with its Jeep Camps, which offer vacation experiences, learning experiences, and social experiences. These experiences help define the brand, producing a strong sense of brand community that borders on evangelism. When the campers return home, they are eager to share their experience with friends and associates, creating brand-advocacy messages through word of mouth.

As Joseph Pine and James Gilmore point out in *The Experience Economy*, for a brand experience to be successful it must offer enjoyment, knowledge, diversion, or beauty. The experience can be passive or active. Passive experiences are those that entertain or provide aesthetic enjoyment, such as visits to museums or demonstrations of a product. Active experiences are ones in which customers participate, such as learning driving skills at Camp Jeep. The key to their success is a "sensory interaction," such as a "tasting" during a tour of a food or beverage plant.

Events can have a major impact because they are *involving*. This characteristic makes an event more memorable and motivating than passive brand messages, such as advertising, because the people attending are participating in and are part of the event. Events can also help position or reposition a brand by associating it with a certain activity, such as the Olympics.

Because most events have a single focus, they attract homogeneous audiences. In most cases, events are selected that attract audiences whose profile matches the brand's current customers. To reach women jeans wearers and reposition Levi's as "youthful, in-style, and sexy," for example, Levi Strauss & Co. sponsored the MTV Video Awards and the Levi's Fuse Tour. The Fuse Tour attracted young females who are prime Levi customers. Brand publicity was used to announce the events and extend the events' awareness-building. These events also became part of Levi's local co-marketing promotions, complete with local TV and print advertising and in-store appearances of the celebrities featured in the events—which generated even more brand publicity.

Because events are individually created, they can and should be designed not only to meet involvement objectives but also to generate brand publicity. Such publicity is likely to reach a larger audience than an event itself will reach. Volvo, for example, estimates that its $4 million investment in tennis events results in over 1.7 billion consumer impressions, an exposure equivalent to an estimated $24 million in advertising dollars.

Companies use events in three ways: they create them, participate in them, and sponsor them.

CREATED EVENTS

Celebrations, concerts, competitions, and other types of happenings are brand-created events. Companies create events to leverage the promotional aspects of such occasions as grand openings, brand or company anniversaries, new-product introductions, and corporate annual meetings. When McDonald's sells a hamburger, it is not an event. But when McDonald's sells its trillionth hamburger, an event can be created—and that is what brand-publicity people get paid to do. Such events can bring people together, but they can also be celebrations designed to attract publicity, such as the 75th anniversary of Kool-Aid, which was held in the summer of 2002.

Internal marketing uses events frequently to build company morale and exchange vital information. Kentucky Fried Chicken, like most franchise companies, has an annual convention to which all franchisees are invited. The objectives of the convention are to introduce new products, procedures, and cooking and store management processes; to provide a forum for franchisees to network and share ideas; and to enable corporate managers to interact with franchisees in a relaxed, pleasant environment. Most corporate meetings, especially those that involve stakeholders such as franchisees who don't have to attend, are held in "vacation" locations to maximize attendance and provide a reward to employees.

Although events attract and involve customers and other stakeholders, those who participate are likely to represent only a small percentage of a brand's target audience. To make an event pay out, the company needs to include elements that will be of interest to the media, thus creating brand publicity as well. Grand openings and the introduction of new products are publicity events (Chapter 14) designed not only to involve customers, prospects, and other stakeholders (such as employees and the financial community) but also to make the six o'clock news or food pages. The more creative, fun, and exciting an event is, and the more people are involved, the more likely it is that the event will generate brand publicity. Baskin-Robbins created an event when it built the world's largest ice-cream cake (5.5 tons) as a tie-in to International Ice Cream Month. Because the cake event was recognized by the *Guinness Book of World Records* and because it attracted hundreds of people, it generated thousands of dollars' worth of brand awareness for Baskin-Robbins (see Exhibit 19-2).

Specialized companies known as *event managers* develop everything from publicity stunts to internal company morale boosters. The Jack Morton Company, which stages all kinds of events for corporations, uses the term *experiential*

EXHIBIT 19-2
Baskin-Robbins created the world's largest ice-cream cake as a tie-in event for International Ice Cream Month.

IMC IN ACTION

How to Turn a Bus into an Event

One of the most competitive consumer product categories is cosmetics. Leading brands such as Cover Girl and Revlon, plus dozens of other brands, are distributed through mass merchandisers. One of these other brands is Rimmel. Made in London, Rimmel products are manufactured by Coty exclusively for Wal-Mart. A top-selling brand in England, Rimmel "reflects London's unique, eclectic culture of music, art and street life," which gives the brand a "sexy, fashion-forward appeal."

When it was decided to give Rimmel an extra promotional push, the brand's marketing team and agency knew they had to come up with something that would reinforce the brand image while at the same time drive sales in Wal-Mart stores. Another objective was to motivate users to visit the Rimmel website so the company could capture e-mail addresses to be used in future promotions. Accomplishing these objectives required communication that would break through competitive clutter, provide a memorable brand experience, and facilitate sampling—a major selling technique in cosmetics marketing. Another objective was to do something that could be localized in order to support Wal-Mart stores throughout the United States.

The strategic solution was a series of mini-events taking place in two London double-decker buses converted into mini London-style discos complete with live DJs and several makeup stations where visitors received beauty makeovers. Inside the buses, alongside the makeup stations, were PCs on which visitors could do their own virtual makeovers. The buses' exteriors carried Rimmel branding that could be easily recognized from over a block away. Scheduled stops on the Rimmel Bus Tour included 300 Wal-Mart stores as well as college campuses. Advertising was used to announce the times and places where the buses would visit.

Collectively, the tours provided close to 21,000 makeovers and distributed 150,000 samples. Sales of Rimmel products in each Wal-Mart store were up an average of 24 percent in the four weeks following a visit.

communication to explain how live events can deliver corporate messages. According to Morton, successful events create an "environment and interactive experience that engage, educate, entertain, and transform" employees, customers, and other stakeholders. When General Motors launched its new Corvette, Morton planned a cross-country "road rally," sending a convoy of 20 brand-new Corvettes along America's historical Route 66, which attracted the attention of Corvette enthusiasts from Chicago to Los Angeles—and generated considerable brand publicity as well.

Event management includes organizing the event and its logistics, staffing it, and marketing it to participants, sponsors, and attendees. Event managers also have to set up and run the event efficiently and safely. In other words, managing an event involves many forms of marketing communication, careful planning, and execution. Imagine the complexity and coordination challenge of the Rimmel Bus Tour described in the IMC in Action box.

TRADE SHOWS AND OTHER PARTICIPATION EVENTS

Rather than creating an event, companies may choose to participate in an event created by someone else. Examples are trade shows, fairs, and exhibits. State and county fairs provide local businesses an opportunity to demonstrate their products for both consumers and local B2B customers. Most major metro areas also have annual auto, boat, and home and garden shows that attract consumers who are especially interested in these product categories. Companies choose to participate in an event according to the type of people it attracts. The more a show's attendees are similar to a brand's target audience, the more sense it makes to participate. Companies rent exhibit space at these type of exhibitions and trade shows. The larger the space and the larger the anticipated attendance, the more exhibit space costs.

The most important participation events for B2B companies are trade shows. Trade shows are second only to personal selling as the most-used tool in B2B marketing communication. Pro-Team, a manufacturer of industrial vacuum cleaners, employs a full-time trade-show coordinator because trade shows are the company's number-one marketing communication function. A **trade show** is *an event at which customers in a particular industry gather to attend training sessions and visit with suppliers and vendors to review their product offerings and innovations.* Suppliers set up booths at which they demonstrate their products, provide information, answer questions, and take orders. The average industry trade show has 10,000 attendees and includes 400 exhibits. Consumer trade shows, which are used to feature new models and products in such categories as cars, boats, and gardening, average from 45,000 to 50,000 attendees and 200 exhibits.[5]

Because of the tremendous importance of trade shows in industries such as electronics and computers, some companies spend hundreds of thousands of dollars each year planning and staging exhibits. One of the largest trade shows, COMDEX, serves the computer industry (see Exhibit 19-3). More than 200,000 computer professionals, corporate buyers, and influencers from 130 countries attend COMDEX. Another 4,000 media and financial analysts attend, making it the best-covered information technology event in the world.[6]

A new type of trade show is the private exhibit arranged by one or several suppliers for a client. Five companies in Indiana, for example, grouped together for a private exhibit held at the Indianapolis Chamber of Commerce. Using an Indy 500 theme, the invitations to exhibit were sound cards that, when opened, produced the high-speed roar of Indy cars. At the show, prospects had to visit all five booths to qualify for a grand prize drawing: two Indy 500 tickets. Of those invited, 27 percent

EXHIBIT 19-3
Booths at trade shows such as the computer industry's COMDEX are extremely elaborate and interactive.

responded, and those who attended produced about 100 new and qualified leads for each of the five sponsors.[7]

An extension of a trade-show exhibit is an online display and demonstration that is highlighted by live chat sessions, a "talk-to-the-company-president session," or some other attraction that would be of interest to customers and prospects. Some companies, for example, offer online corporate seminars that are successful in creating sales leads.

In planning for a trade-show exhibit, a company must decide what products to feature (there is seldom space or time enough to include all products), who will staff the booth, how to screen and qualify visitors to the booth, and how to capture names of qualified prospects. Some of the strategies used to maximize booth attendance are (1) sending out personal invitations a couple of weeks before the show, (2) designing a booth that is aesthetically inviting and pleasant to visit, and (3) using "borrowed interest," such as an entertainer, give-aways, or a drawing for a significant prize, to attract visitors. Table 19-1 contains a checklist for companies planning to have an exhibit at a trade show.

Because trade-show participation is a type of brand communication, the booth should be designed in a way that reinforces the brand/company image and positioning. Some high-tech companies, for example, use laser lights and modern electronic music to help reinforce their position as being on the cutting edge of technology.

Companies participate in trade shows primarily to reinforce relationships with current customers and to create qualified leads for new customers. Trade shows provide opportunities to engage customers in personal communication and

---

TABLE 19-1   Checklist for Exhibiting at a Trade Show

Several Months before the Trade Show

- For each major show, set measurable objectives with a cross-functional team of sales, marketing, customer service, and the trade-show coordinator.
- Design (or update) the exhibit booth, making sure that it is interactive and reinforces the brand image.
- Select products and brands to display in the booth, and determine which ones will be featured (generally the new or improved items).
- Select an incentive to motivate customers and prospects to visit the booth.

Several Weeks before the Trade Show

- Decide who will staff the booth (usually members of sales and marketing).
- Send out personal invitations to current customers and to prospects.
- Train the people who will be staffing the booth, showing them how to screen, qualify, and capture prospects' contact information.

After the Trade Show

- Have the people who staffed the booth fill out an exhibit evaluation form that helps identify changes that need to be made to improve booth productivity.
- Follow up with sales to see which leads have been contacted and how many sales were made.
- Determine the return on investment for the trade-show appearance.

relationship-building activities, such as seminars and receptions. Jim Obermayer, co-author of *Managing Sales Leads*, identifies four reasons why trade shows are so important as a B2B marketing communication tool:[8]

- On average, 83 percent of trade-show attendees have not seen a salesperson from their suppliers within the last 12 months.

- Over 80 percent of those who attend trade shows have buying authority or heavily influence brand choices.

- Two-thirds of trade-show attendees plan to make brand buying decisions at the show.

- Trade-show-created leads cost 70 percent less to close than other leads.

Objectives for trade shows, therefore, should state how many customers and prospects the company wants to see and how many leads it wants to turn into sales. Because of the expense of exhibiting at trade shows, companies need to maximize the number of current customers and prospects that visit their booths in order to cost-justify the participation. The value of participating in a trade show can be determined by several measures: the number of customers and prospects who visit the booth, the amount of orders written at the show, the number of qualified leads obtained, and, most important, the number of sales resulting from these contacts.

SPONSORSHIPS

Sponsorship is *financial support of an organization, person, or activity in exchange for brand publicity and association.* In 2002 companies spent $9.4 billion on sponsorships.[9] Although sponsorships differ from events, the two overlap because many events often have several sponsors. Not surprisingly, many of the use guidelines are the same for each of these marketing communication functions.

Sponsorships both differentiate and add value to brands. Nike, for example, sponsors champion golfer Tiger Woods because Woods is well liked and respected by members of the brand's target audience. The association with Woods helps differentiate Nike from other marketers of sporting goods and also helps increase the status of the Nike brand. If a brand's customers and prospects, for example, enjoy National Association of Stock Car Auto Racing (NASCAR) events, presumably they will like the brands associated with a favorite NASCAR driver.

An important element of a brand is its associations. Sponsorship is one of the main ways in which a brand develops associations. The challenge is to find associations that reinforce the desired image of a brand. If the association is inconsistent with the brand's image and with other MC messages, a sponsorship can do more harm than good—customers will be confused about what and who the brand actually is. Concern about the consistency of image association increasingly flows in two directions; groups and events are becoming increasingly selective about accepting sponsors.

Companies can sponsor a variety of things: media programs, events, individuals, teams, sport categories, cultural organizations, good causes, and so on. It's almost impossible to attend any kind of large function today, such as a rock concert or spring-break beach party, without being inundated by brand banners, posters, and samples. A good example is the annual College Fest in Philadelphia, which attracts up to 10,000 students to its campus convention of music, fashion, games, and social events. During the College Fest, a variety of companies give out coupons and samples at their exhibits.

Companies use the following guidelines when choosing sponsorships:

1. *Target audience:* The audience for what is being sponsored should have the same profile as the brand's target audience(s) within the geographical areas served by the brand.

2. *Brand image reinforcement:* Sponsorships should be used in an environment that is consistent with a brand's positioning and image.

3. *Extendibility:* The more brand exposure a sponsorship can provide, the more beneficial it can be. If the sponsorship is a multiyear relationship, for example, a company may consider promoting the sponsorship on its packaging, as many Olympics sponsors do. Marketers seek brand publicity that extends beyond the publicity directly provided by the event itself.

4. *Brand involvement:* The more privileges a sponsorship provides, the better. Sponsorship of a museum, for example, could include the right to use the museum for a corporate social function, exclusive tours for customers and employees, and invitations to openings of new exhibits.

5. *Cost-effectiveness:* Some sponsorships produce enough brand-message exposure that if the cost of the sponsorship were converted to a cost per thousand (CPM), it would be competitive with other media buys.

6. *Other sponsors:* When a company associates with an event or cause, it does so to enhance its own image and positioning. Because some organizations have many sponsors, a company would be wise to know who the other sponsors are. Most companies expect category exclusivity, which means none of its competitors will be a sponsor.

Sports Sponsorships

Although sponsorships cover a wide range of activities, two-thirds of spending on event sponsorship is sports related. As athletes, sports teams, and leagues at all levels have increasingly recognized the financial benefit of having sponsors—and, in turn, have realized that they can offer added value to brands—companies have found themselves with an increased range of sponsorship opportunities.

The single largest sporting event that attracts sponsors is the Olympic Games. Not only are the Olympics a huge advertising venue, but they also represent a unique sponsorship opportunity. Advertising brings in half of the event's revenue—more than $1.3 billion for the 2000 Summer Games in Sydney—and global sponsorships bring in 21 percent. The lure of the event is its reach: some 3.7 billion people—more than half the world's population—tune in to one or more of the televised games.[10] The 2002 Winter Games in Salt Lake City reached 2.1 billion people in 160 countries. Many of these saw one of the U.S. skaters hand an AT&T cell phone to President Bush so he could say hello to her mother. The brand publicity from video and news shots of the president using this AT&T phone more than paid for what it cost AT&T to give a phone to each of the participating U.S. athletes.

There are many ways to affiliate with the Olympics as a sponsor. There are sponsors for teams and sports, as well as countries. For example, one United States Olympic Committee (USOC) sponsor, General Motors, signed an eight-year contract to support the U.S. team and the Winter Games in Salt Lake City. This gave General Motors exclusive category advertising rights in the United States through 2008: no other automotive brand could have a similar sponsorship association. On a higher level there are worldwide Olympic sponsors, such as Xerox (see Exhibit 19-5), which pays close to $50 million for sponsorship rights, as described in the Global Focus box.

But even minor co-sponsorships can be leveraged if a company is willing to spend the extra money. Husqvarna North America (distributor of outdoor power tools), for example, has been a minor sponsor of NASCAR driver Bobby Labonte, who is on the Joe Gibbs racing team (see Exhibit 19-4). Although Husqvarna's logo on Labonte's car is small and is seldom seen by TV audiences or even by fans attending races, the company has benefited from the sponsorship. One reason Husqvarna chose to sponsor a Joe Gibbs car is that both Husqvarna's North American corporate offices and Joe Gibbs's racing headquarters, where the race cars are built and maintained, are in Charlotte, North Carolina. The sponsorship allows Husqvarna to bring its dealers—that is, its current customers—to Gibbs's headquarters to see the cars being made and to meet Gibbs and hear him talk about NASCAR racing. At the same time, dealers and prospective dealers are frequently invited to Husqvarna's corporate offices for training on how to better sell and repair Husqvarna products.

EXHIBIT 19-4
Tide is a major sponsor of a NASCAR car and of driver Ricky Cravens.

Husqvarna's sponsorship also includes using Joe Gibbs as a spokesperson for the company. He makes TV and radio commercials, and his image is used in collateral print materials. A popular POP piece is a life-size cardboard cutout of Joe Gibbs that dealers can place in their showrooms. To further leverage its NASCAR sponsorship, Husqvarna has an executive suite at Lowe's Motor Speedway, which is also in Charlotte. This provides Husqvarna another way to enrich the visits by dealers and prospective dealers when they are in town on race day.

As the Husqvarna example demonstrates, companies need to spend additional money beyond the sponsorship fee in order to fully leverage a sponsorship. Research has shown that, on average, a sponsor invests approximately two and a

GLOBAL FOCUS

The Olympics Tops the List

On a worldwide level, The Olympic Partners (TOP) is a group of 11 international corporations that join with the International Olympic Committee (IOC) for periods of four years. Each Partner pays an average of $50 million in cash, equipment, and services in order to be a member of the exclusive TOP club. The Olympic Partners support the Olympic movement in exchange for exclusive marketing rights within their categories in every country that is part of the movement, currently 198.

Why bother with an Olympic sponsorship? Companies traditionally capitalize on the natural connection between themselves and the organization—ski manufacturers frequently support World Cup ski events, for example. Most of the sponsors in the TOP club tie into the inherent drama of the Olympic spirit, as well as the worldwide popularity of the event. McDonald's, for example, connects to the good family reputation of the Games, and Coca-Cola celebrates their festive nature (see Exhibit 19-8).

According to a marketing vice president for McDonald's USA, sponsorship support links a brand with identifiable partnerships in a way that makes the brand highly visible to consumers. He said, "We pick and choose our sponsorships very carefully to fit who we are as a brand. It's come down to a couple of key relationships on a global basis, and the Olympics heads the list."

Does it work? Although some companies have found that they have gotten lost amid the clutter, companies that have the financial wherewithal to properly leverage their Olympic connection believe the investment is worthwhile. The Olympics overall remains a positive, powerful, worldwide movement despite bits of negative publicity and occasional drug violations. The Olympic Partners hope some of the gold will rub off, and in most cases it does. One nine-nation study in 1996 found that 93 percent of 4,500 respondents correctly identified the Olympic rings and 74 percent associated them with success and high standards. And research has found that these positive feelings are transferable. Another multinational study found that 62 percent of the respondents view Olympic sponsors as modern and innovative and 59 percent saw them as leaders in their industries. In the United States, these figures were 75 percent and 80 percent, respectively.

When UPS signed on to become one of the worldwide sponsors of the Olympics, it saw that sponsorship as an unusual opportunity to gain global exposure, unify its diverse workforce, establish itself in the Atlanta community (site of the 1996 Summer Games and UPS corporate headquarters), and build long-term business relationships with other Olympic sponsors. In just two years, its research found positive effects in terms of these objectives. Some evidence was particularly compelling, such as a direct-mail promotion that brought in results that were three to four times higher than previous efforts. Another benefit was the impact the sponsorship had on uniting UPS's 38,000 worldwide employees.

Think About It

What reasons do companies give for becoming an Olympic sponsor? How do such sponsorships work? What is required to make an Olympic sponsorship effective?

Source: Reprinted from the paid advertising section, "Why Corporate Support Is Good Business: The Olympic Partnership," prepared for the February 2, 1998 issue of FORTUNE magazine.

half times their sponsorship fee on advertising and promotion designed to make customers aware of the sponsorship and to involve them in some way.

Cause Marketing

Cause marketing and mission marketing, discussed in Chapter 17, are important types of sponsorship that marry philanthropy with marketing. In cause marketing programs, a brand promises to donate money or other types of support to an organization or social activity when a customer buys or uses the brand. (To control their financial liability when promising a contribution for each sales transaction, most brands—in small print—state that donations will be made up to a stated amount of money.) An example is the American Express program to feed the homeless, which has donated two cents to food kitchens for the homeless for each credit-card transaction made by its cardholders. The effort was supported by an advertising campaign stating, "Every time you use the American Express Card, you'll help provide a meal for someone who is hungry." The campaign was estimated to have helped increase AmEx charge-card transactions by 8.4 percent, so in the short term, at least, this promotion was highly successful.

When the internet search engine and navigational portal Lycos found itself struggling to build a brand identity and share of mind among many competitors, it used cause marketing. Following an important principle of cause marketing, Lycos selected to help a nonprofit in a way that leveraged and demonstrated its expertise—searching. Lycos agreed to help the National Center for Missing and Exploited Children. The company learned that the most critical period in finding these children is within the first 72 hours of their disappearance. Because of the short lead time required for using the internet, Lycos developed a system for distributing information and pictures of missing children as soon as their disappearance was reported. Lycos received positive media coverage for its efforts and saw an increase in the number of visits to its portal.[11]

There is no question that such sponsorships can have a significant impact on sales among consumers who appreciate a company's dedication to social responsibility. Exhibit 19-6 shows an ad designed to gain visibility for discount clothing retailer T. J. Maxx's support of the Save the Children organization.

Nonprofit organizations are increasingly offering themselves as a "cause" in order to tap into this type of corporate support. A PROMO Magazine special issue on cause marketing contained six pages of causes looking for corporate sponsors.[12] For a cause to be strategically integrated into a marketing communication program, it must be consistent with a brand's image and needs a bottom-line payout (just as any promotion should do).

The forest products company Weyerhaeuser conducted a study of its contributions to find out whether the company's philanthropic efforts coincided with its objectives. The result was a decision to focus most of the company's contributions on the preservation of forests, countering the negative attitude many have about companies that cut down trees for commercial purposes. By focusing in this way, Weyerhaeuser has been able to get more impact from its contributions while, at the same time, becoming fundamentally more environmentally sensitive. It's a classic win–win situation.

EXHIBIT 19-6
This ad identifies T. J. Maxx as a sponsor of Save the Children.

Evaluating Events

The evaluation of events moves beyond the usual return-on-investment calculations (ROI, comparing revenue generated against the cost of the promotional effort), which are sometimes difficult to derive from an event, to evaluate instead the impact of a brand-event experience on brand image. In other words, the focus is on customer perceptions of a brand and how they may change as a result of a positive experience at an event. Some B2B events, such as exhibits at trade shows, can deliver hard data, such as sales or sales leads. In consumer marketing, however, effective events are more likely to deliver a more positive brand perception, an effect that needs attitude and likeability measures. These perceptions, in turn, can lead to greater customer loyalty, depending on the level of involvement and how positive the experience was.[13] An event, in other words, should be evaluated both as a relationship-building tool in terms of its long-term impact as well as impact on sales in the short term.

Jack Morton, which specializes in event evaluation, measures effectiveness in terms of brand impact and audience engagement.[14] The firm offers pre- and post-event Web-based surveys that track the performance of an event and measure changes in brand awareness and image. If other objectives have been set for an event, these also are measured. In addition to the Web-based tracking studies, the company also uses focus groups, interviews at the event, and surveys.

Strengths and Limitations of Events and Sponsorships

Events and sponsorships enhance a company's or brand's visibility by associating it with something positive, such as a cause or athletic event. Because of the involvement factor, events and sponsorships are also good relationship-building activities that emotionally bind customers to a company or brand, and they can be used to involve a variety of important stakeholders. Sponsors of major events and organizations, such as auto racing, college bowl games, symphonies, and museums, often receive season tickets or passes and other special privileges for their customers and employees.

As sponsorships have grown (currently at about 5 percent per year), so has the need for some way of measuring their impact. Most sponsorships should offer a 150 to 200 percent return on the cost of the sponsorship in terms of advertising and promotional opportunities, not to mention the goodwill and relationships that will arise from the affiliation. The Yankelovich agency's Express Lifestyle Tracking is a new service designed to help companies measure and evaluate the impact of sports and entertainment sponsorships. The system works by distributing survey cards to event attendees to capture data about their behavior and attitude following the event.

The biggest limitation of event sponsorships is that, depending on the scope of the event, they tend to directly involve only a small percentage of a brand's target audience. This is why the return on investment of most event sponsorship is determined not by the event itself but by how well other MC functions leverage the sponsorship. Another problem is the control, or lack thereof, that a company has over the design and management of a sponsored event, as explained in the Ethics and Issues box.

CUSTOMER SERVICE: THE RETENTION DRIVER

> "I hate Sprint and spend way too much time fantasizing about its demise. I have friends who hate Sprint too, and we talk to one another like members of a support group. Whenever I'm in line at Sprint stores, I feel it is my duty to reach out to and dissuade as many prospective customers as I can."
>
> Letter to the editor, *Fortune*

Customer service is *the process of managing customers' interactive experiences with a brand.* It's everything a company does to take care of customers' needs when they buy and use a brand. Customers' needs and wants are important determinants of consumer behavior and consumer response to brand messages (⬅ Chapter 5). Together, customer service, and the customer-focused philosophy that it represents, form the primary personal communication tool used to address these needs.

Customer service is a key reason for adding two-way to traditional one-way marketing communication. By its very nature customer service is interactive, for it involves a response to customer-initiated brand messages. It permits companies to gather real-time feedback that provides insights into the hearts and minds of customers. Every successful business tries to make the customer-contact experience as positive and rewarding as possible. When customer service is good, brand relationships are strengthened; when it is bad, they are weakened or destroyed. Because customer-service experiences are so personal, poor customer service can outweigh a bundle of great ads and money-saving offers. Therefore, service must be strategi-

ETHICS AND ISSUES

The Strategic Debates behind a Sponsorship

How much control should a company that is a major sponsor of an event or cause have over the event or cause? Most organizations make it clear that content and programming are off-limits to sponsors. The more financially secure an organization is, the more it can protect its integrity. The problem is subtle, however, and indirect pressures can influence content or programming.

One community chorale organization provides an interesting example. Like many arts groups, the chorale's financial support came from season-ticket sales and sponsorships. Consequently, when each year's programs were planned, there was always a discussion about how popular the musical selections for each program would be. On the one hand, the true artists argued for more performances of new works and some of the more complicated (and less popular) classical works. On the other hand, those responsible for paying the chorale's bills argued that if the group failed to play to its audience, there soon wouldn't be an audience. The result was always a compromise in which each group felt it had given in too much.

Another ethical issue concerns which events and causes get supported and which do not. Again, be-

cause one of the ways in which sponsors measure the effectiveness of a given effort is by how many people it reaches, this influences where the money goes. Thus most sponsors want to be associated with popular events. As one observer found in a study of sponsorship in Great Britain, "Sponsors favor the performing over the visual arts; the known and the familiar over the novel; prestigious, well-established 'big names' amongst theaters, orchestras and galleries; and London over everywhere else."

Think About It

If a company is truly a good corporate citizen, should it want to influence programming and content? Should it only sponsor the most popular events? Because the company is spending its money, and controls all the other brand messages for which it pays, should it have a say in programming and content?

Source: Anthony Beck, " 'But Where Can We Find Heineken?' Commercial Sponsorship of the Arts," *Political Quarterly* 61, no. 4 (1990), p. 393.

cally integrated into a company's marketing communication programs. And like other types of marketing information, customer service is an added value that helps distinguish a brand or company from its competitors.

Some marketers naively think that if a transaction is handled badly, the cost is simply the loss of a single sale. They do not realize that such a loss may represent the loss of a *lifetime* of transactions from a customer—not to mention the cost of the negative word of mouth that such an unhappy customer might spread. Customer service, whether online or handled in the traditional manner, is, from the customers' perspective, a powerful brand message.[15]

Characteristics of Good Customer Service

The phrase *customer service* suggests a number of things—from a department to an attitude. The attitude is the "umbrella" idea, one that means everything a brand or company does is focused on serving the customer. This service mentality can be seen in four areas, all of which deliver intrinsic brand messages (◄ Chapter 4):

1. *Employee performance* during the delivery of a service, such as when a customer rents a car, takes a plane trip, or has an in-home appliance repaired.

2. *A customer-service department* that handles complaints, inquiries, suggestions and compliments.

3. *Technical support* provided by tech support representatives who answer questions about how to use a product. Tech support reps have product databases with answers to frequently asked questions as well as schematic drawings of products so they can more easily understand how and where customers are having problems. Tech support representatives are generally more highly trained than regular customer-service representatives.

4. *Facilities, operations, and arrangements*, such as extended hours, play areas for children, and signage that helps customers navigate around a store or through a website. Anything that increases convenience for customers can be considered customer service.

According to a study of 2,465 consumers by DDB Worldwide, the top five factors that have a "major influence" on customer retention are (1) product quality/performance (96 percent rated this important), (2) a company's method of handling complaints (85 percent), (3) the way a company handles a crisis in which it is at fault (73 percent), (4) a challenge by a government agency about the safety of a company's products (60 percent), and (5) an accusation of illegal or unethical trading practices (58 percent).[16] Notice that dealing with customer complaints was the second most important factor affecting retention. For this and the following reasons, companies are paying more attention to customer service these days:[17]

1. *Competitive advantage:* Customer service offers a way to differentiate brands, although as more competitors improve their customer-service operations, the competitive advantage becomes an even greater challenge to maintain.

2. *Customers' demands:* As more and more brands compete for customers' business, customers can demand better service.

3. *Customers' expectations:* The promise of good customer service is increasingly highlighted in brand messages. The higher that companies raise the expectation of good service, the more customers will demand it from *all* brands.

4. *Relationship maintenance:* When companies use customer service in a proactive way to maintain contact with customers, customers have fewer reasons to go elsewhere.

5. *Increased technological sophistication of product:* As new technology becomes part of more and more products, customers increasingly need technical support and advice about using these products.

Customer Satisfaction—and Dissatisfaction

Customers don't expect companies to be perfect, but they do expect problems to be corrected quickly. When they are, customers generally stay loyal. When automaker Chrysler issued four recalls in a period of a few months, its market share actually went up. Some observers attributed this rise to the way Chrysler handled the recalls—quickly and honestly. Certain industries—such as airlines, cable television providers, and utility companies—seem to have problems providing good customer service. As an article in the *Wall Street Journal* lamented, "Customer-service woes are now so pervasive in the telecom business that a cottage industry has sprung up to help customers weed through their bills and services. The [customers simply] do not know who to call for services."[18] Stories like this and the ones reported in the IMC in Action box, indicate how complaints can generate publicity that creates negative brand impact extending far beyond the customer's original bad experience.

One reason often cited for poor customer service is that companies try to save money by outsourcing this important customer-handling function. In the words of

IMC IN ACTION

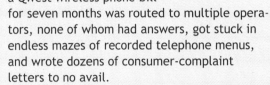

Customer-Service Winners and Losers

Where do you get the best and worst customer service? Some of the winners are Nordstroms, whose retail service is legendary, as well as the Ritz Carlton hotel chain, whose computers even record the types of pillow guests prefer. Home Depot runs home improvement clinics for customers and puts home improvement tips on its website so customers can be informed about what they need before they come into the store.

Some of the worst experiences typically come from airlines, phone companies and cable operators—all of which are in industries where there is little direct competition. Prospects are sometimes won through promotions that over-promise on services as well as rates. Customers may find they have been double-billed or their service has been cut off for some unknown reason. And if they call for repair, they have to be at home for long periods of time and even then the repair person may not come at the scheduled time. Customers who send an email may not get any response, or if they do hear back, the response may be slow, incomplete, or a form note that doesn't answer the customer's question. If customers phone in, they may lose a good chunk of time trying to get through. The problem begins when they find they have to listen to endless menus of options on an automated voice response system. If they get through on the phone, then they may be routed to multiple operators and the operators may not have the right answers. Sometimes they get stuck in endless loops of recorded messages that don't offer an opportunity to escape or return to an earlier menu.

Arguably the worst offender is the telecom industry, which has been battered by economic problems, undigested mergers and acquisitions, and a fast expansion of new products to serve the internet industry and its B2B customers. The Federal Communications Commission received 10,182 complaints from consumers frustrated with wireless and long-distance service in only one quarter of 2002. The headlines and stories in newspapers and magazines are endless:

- How to get a DSL line from Bell Atlantic in 40 easy steps: The *Fortune* magazine writer details "a laborious, enervating process" that took three months, four technician visits, and dozens of phone calls.

- How to get a bill fixed in a seven-month quest for help: A small-business owner fighting a wrongful charge of $220 on a Qwest wireless phone bill for seven months was routed to multiple operators, none of whom had answers, got stuck in endless mazes of recorded telephone menus, and wrote dozens of consumer-complaint letters to no avail.

- How to become the cell phone company people love to hate: According to the *Wall Street Journal*, Sprint PCS gets more complaints per subscriber than any of the other top five carriers.

- How to give up on your company and quit: That was the solution chosen by a salesperson for AT&T who felt she wasn't able to help her clients because company rules prevented her from calling the customer-service lines herself to fix her customers' problems. She says that around her office customer service was referred to as "the customer I don't care center."

- How to get together and sue: Rated as the worst long-distance service provider by the *Wall Street Journal*, WorldCom's MCI has had billing problems ever since it started acquiring smaller phone companies in the late 1990s. In addition to the practice of boosting rates with additional unexpected charges, plus less-than-helpful customer service, MCI WorldCom was sued in a class-action lawsuit by customers who continued to get billed even after they canceled their service.

- How to avoid answering the phone and hearing about the problem: AT&T Broadband revamped its customer service in metro Atlanta, laying off 150 of its 400 call-center workers.

Think About It

What causes the customer-service horror stories? List the practices that tend to generate the most customer-service problems. Analyze them in terms of how they are affected by communication practices.

Source: Carolyn T. Geer, "I Got DSL from Bell Atlantic in 40 Easy Steps!" *Fortune*, April 3, 2000, p. 66. © 2003 Time Inc. All rights reserved. Jennifer Beauprez, "Customer Service on Slippery Slope," *The Denver Post*, November 25, 2001, p. 25A; Bob Parks, "Where the Customer Service Rep is King," *Business 2.0*, June 2003, p. 70-72. © 2003 Time Inc. All rights reserved. Jane Spencer, "The Worst Phone Service in America," *Wall Street Journal*, October 3, 2002, p. D1.

one industry observer who examined customer-service problems in the pay-TV industry: "To cut costs, most pay-TV providers [have] farmed out customer service functions to vast call centers employing thousands of disaffected workers—low-paid, poorly trained, and lacking any real incentive to care about the plight of their faceless customers."[19] One pay-TV company, DirecTV, however, changed this situation by sending its own managers to each of the outsourced call centers, providing the service reps with company information that enables them to answer more questions, providing free satellite TV to reps after they have worked three months, and inviting them to special celebrity events. These perks along with more empowerment to make corrections on customers' bills, decreased DirecTV's "churn rate" one percentage point. This may not seem like much, but it saves the company millions of dollars a year.[20]

Poor customer service, especially in a struggling economy can be factors that affect consumer satisfaction, which is monitored by the American Customer Satisfaction Consumer Index at the University of Michigan Business School. Based on 50,000 consumer interviews and data from 164 companies, the index has fluctuated between a high of 74.5 points (out of a possible 100) in 1994 and a low of 70.7 in 1997, when the dot-com explosion spawned new companies and new employees who paid little attention to customer service. At the end of the 1990s and in the first few years of the new century, however, the score was fairly stable, moving between 72 and 73.[21] Of course, 73 out of 100 points clearly shows that there is much room for improvement in customer satisfaction across all U.S. business sectors.

Some companies are making extra efforts to turn around perceptions of customer service. The phone company Qwest, long criticized for its lack of concern about customer service, increased emphasis on service with the appointment of its new president in 2002, who planned, among other things, to base employees' bonuses on customer-service results rather than on corporate financial goals.[22] The demonstration of customer service then became the primary message of a new Quest advertising campaign. Similarly, the Sheraton hotel chain decided to spruce up its brand by launching the Sheraton Service Promise, a customer-service initiative that awards points, discounts, and cash to hotel guests who find reason to complain, be it about service, the room or other facilities, or even the food.[23]

Objectives and Strategies of Customer Service

The two overriding objectives for customer service are to make customers' interactions with the company a positive experience and to increase customer retention. Stated in measurable terms, these objectives would read something like this:

- To have 97 percent of customers rate their interactions with the company "good" or "very good" (on a five-point scale).
- To reduce to 10 percent (from current 15 percent) the percentage of customers who quit buying from the company each year.

Why is the satisfaction objective not set at 100 percent? The major reasons are that employees are human and will make mistakes and that some customers will never be satisfied. Therefore, if the objective were 100 percent, employees would not strive to accomplish it because they would know it wasn't attainable.

One way the total marketing effort integrates the customer-service function is by having customer-service representatives do some selling once a customer's complaint or question has been addressed. Companies such as Wells Fargo, Verizon, and Citibank are retraining hundreds of their service representatives to offer such products as a DSL line or a home equity loan.[24]

Customer service is also an important tool in a customer relationship management (CRM) program (Chapter 3). While companies continue to spend money on CRM software—a projected $38 billion between 2001 and 2005—customer service seems to be deteriorating. A survey done by Pew Charitable Trusts in spring 2002 found that 46 percent of customers had walked out of a store because of bad service and 81 percent believed that stores were cutting corners on hiring. Jeffrey Pfeffer, a professor of organizational behavior at Stanford University's Graduate School of Business, wonders whether companies are spending money on the wrong thing when buying CRM software. He points out that "before you can manage a relationship, you first need to build it" and if companies can't get customer-service interactions right then "nothing else matters."[25]

Strategies for making interactions a positive experience include being accessible, demonstrating product knowledge, having a positive attitude, being responsive, and collecting feedback. These activities also are sources of powerful brand messages.

Accessibility

When customers have a question or need help finding something in a store, they want to talk to someone. The challenge is to have employees available to respond to customers who come into stores or who contact a company in some other manner. Companies also need to make it as easy as possible for customers to communicate with the company. They can do so by

- Providing free phone numbers in all planned messages (such as ads, invoices, on packages, and service manuals).
- Providing multiple ways for the company to be reached—not only a toll-free number, but also a mailing address, a fax number, and an e-mail address.
- Cross-training customer-service representatives to handle both phone and e-mail contacts, so that when incoming calls peak, employees assigned to handle e-mail contacts can handle phone calls.

A company sends a negative message whenever a customer cannot get through to an employee by phone, fax, or e-mail or cannot find a sales clerk in a retail store. The more difficult it is to reach someone and get an answer, the less satisfying the customer experience is. If a company cannot afford to maintain an adequate staff during peak call times, it should give customers incentives to call during off-peak hours or provide answering machines that ask customers to leave a message, phone number, and the best time to be reached.

Product Knowledge

Knowing how to answer customers' questions is an essential characteristic of good customer service. Representatives need a thorough knowledge of the company's product line and how the products work. This level of knowledge is acquired through a solid training program. Help-desk staffers should be completely familiar with the products before they hit the marketplace. At Roadrunner Sports, a running and sports-shoe catalog company, customer-service representatives are able to help customers buy shoes by phone because they have been trained in how to size and fit shoes and in how to match the right shoe for the right application, all over the phone.

Attitude

How employees think about and approach customers is as important as technical knowledge. Individuals selected for customer contact need to be upbeat and positive types of people. An employee who is able to project a good mood will put a customer into a better mood and make the customer more receptive to what the representative has to say. As Figure 19-1 indicates, tone of voice and, in face-to-face meetings, body language communicate more effectively than words.

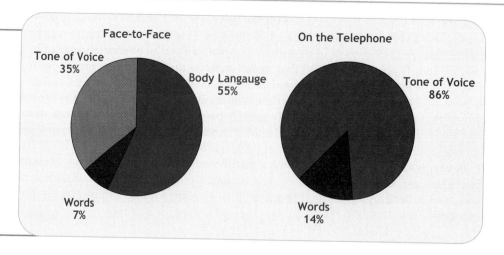

FIGURE 19-1

Ninety-three percent of a message delivered face-to-face is conveyed by the message sender's tone of voice and body language. Eight-six percent of a phone message is conveyed by tone of voice.

Source: Richard Stafford, Marketing Faculty, University of Kentucky. Used by permission.

A company can help employees maintain a positive attitude by making sure employee morale is positive. There are many ways to do this. One way, creating a sense of corporate pride, is described in the AFLAC case at the beginning of Chapter 1. AFLAC doesn't simply make corporate contributions to cancer-fighting organizations, for example, but has companywide fund-raising drives and releases employees to volunteer at local health-care facilities. As a result, AFLAC employees have a sense of community, pride, and positive attitudes about their employer.

Internal marketing (⬅ Chapter 6) presents another opportunity to make employees feel good about their company and job. For example, the director of marketing for Jeno's Pizza had his marketing team give a special presentation of the new Pizza Rolls advertising campaign to employees in the plant where the Pizza Rolls were being made. Because the plant was over 1,000 miles away from the corporate office, these employees had trouble identifying with the company. Seeing the advertising before it went on the air, however, made them feel special and showed them that the products they made were being portrayed as mouthwatering and fun to eat. The comment of one production line worker after seeing the advertising demonstrated its morale-boosting power: "Man, you really spent a lot of money to show people what we make down here!"[26]

Because customer service includes handling complaints from angry customers, representatives can become demoralized or defensive if they do not have a strong positive attitude. The Walt Disney Company, for example, is known for its courteous, enthusiastic staff (even though it does not pay significantly more than other companies). The company excels at profiling, recruiting, and hiring the types of people who can maintain a consistently positive attitude, particularly at its theme parks. Those who are considered good at customer service have the following personality characteristics: professionalism, positive attitude, flexibility, reliability, ability to listen, and empathy.[27] They also receive extensive training.

Responsiveness

A customer bought a VCR at a discount store. The clerk rang up the order incorrectly and then directed the customer to stand in line at the "courtesy" window for a refund, rather than handling the mistake herself.[28] The clerk may have been so unresponsive because she lacked **empowerment**, *the authority to handle customer-relations problems.* Because there cannot be a rule or policy for every imaginable situation, employees must be trained and trusted to respond on the basis of general, rather than specific, guidelines. Employees must be trusted to decide, for example, when taking a short-term loss is likely to result in increasing and extending the lifetime value of a customer—and to differentiate such a situation from a customer's attempt to take advantage of the company.

T A B L E   1 9 - 2   Sources of Customer Information

Source	Percentage
Customer-service departments	90%
Sales force interactions	87
Point of sale	75
Customer user group	64
Inbound telemarketing	53
Outbound telemarketing	52
Other	30
Warranty cards	27

Source: Reprinted by permission of Harvard Business School Press. From Customer Connections by Robert Wayland and Paul Cole. Boston, MA 19997, p. 47. Copyright © 1997 by Robert E. Wayland and Associates, Inc., and Ernst & Young LLP, all rights reserved.

Feedback

The customer-service function is a tool for listening and gathering customer feedback (see Table 19-2). Customer service provides an opportunity to engage in real-time marketing research—but only if a company has in place a system for not only recording customer comments but also asking customers questions. It's a wonderful opportunity to touch the customer's pulse. A common source of feedback is the customer-comment card. But customer-service representatives and other front-line employees, such as drivers and sales clerks, can be empowered to gather feedback in a structured way.

A company must be able to speedily collect, analyze, and report the data back to managers. In all too many cases, however, customer comments—either from the phone or the ubiquitous comment cards—are not retrieved and used. Although some companies are having success addressing consumer issues promptly, proponents of real-time customer-service feedback acknowledge that it raises customer expectations—a significant issue if companies aren't able or willing to truly take action.[29] As Table 19-2 shows, customer service is the number-one gatherer of customer feedback, other than formal market research.

Responding to Customer-Initiated Messages: Complaints and Compliments

The customer-service function is not performed the same way in all companies. In packaged-goods companies, such as Kraft Foods and Procter & Gamble, toll-free numbers and websites are provided to handle consumer questions. High-tech companies have hot lines to answer questions and provide technical support, as well as provide general information about products and services. In small B2B companies, customer service may be the responsibility of sales or even product managers. In large B2B companies, sales representatives are often the first to hear from a customer with a question or complaint, especially if it is something major.

The Research Institute of America did a study for the White House Office of Consumer Affairs and found that 96.7 percent of the people who are dissatisfied with a product or company do not complain to the company, and that 90 percent of those people do not buy again from that company. The study also found that dissatisfied customers talk, on the average, to nine other people about their negative brand experience. Clearly, companies must find ways to encourage unhappy customers to contact the company rather than walk away.

British Airways (BA) found that half of its customers who had a problem with the airline, and who did not let BA know they were dissatisfied, switched to another airline. However, of those who had a problem and discussed it with BA, 87 percent continued as customers.[30] A good customer-service department can generally keep customers from defecting if it has the opportunity to talk to them. The lesson here is that companies should encourage dissatisfied customers to contact the company and should make it easy for them to do so.

Regaining the loyalty of an unhappy customer can sometimes actually result in a stronger brand relationship than existed before a customer had a problem. According to J. W. Marriott, chief executive officer of the Marriott hotel chain, "Sometimes those customers who you make that extra effort to gain back become the most loyal customers that you have."[31]

A customer-service department can be proactive as well as reactive. Proactive policies—such as notifying B2B customers about anticipated shortages, product recalls, or other problems—are important in keeping current customers and minimizing their calls to the company. When a company knows it will be late shipping orders, for example, customers should be notified of the delay.

For years, call centers were notorious for using low-paid, untrained employees. Unfortunately, many top managers saw customer service merely as something the company had to have rather than as an opportunity to better manage customer relationships. With more emphasis on IMC and relationship marketing, this perspective is changing fast. Not only are companies providing higher salaries and more training to their customer-service representatives, but there is also more interaction between customer service and marketing.

Many companies are expanding their customer-service function to their websites. ServiceSuite, a permission-marketing product offered by DoubleClick (which bought Message Media), is designed to handle inbound e-mails, either sorting them by keywords and providing automatic responses or by routing to the proper department e-mails that don't fit into a response category. ServiceSuite also provides real-time live chat with customer-service representatives.

> "In the online world, customers don't see [marketing and customer service] as two separate entities; they see it as one brand."
>
> Larry Jones, MessageMedia

The right communication technology can improve customer-service communication in several ways. It can route a call to the department or representative who talked to the customer before. Computers can be programmed to automatically identify callers (by the number from which they are calling) and transfer them to the last representatives they talked to (if they called before)—all in a fraction of second. Also, having a customer's name, address, and phone number pop up on a screen makes it unnecessary to ask for this information again and avoids recording errors. The right technology allows everyone in the company who touches a customer to provide good customer service.

Evaluating the Customer Service Marketing Communication Function

Two of the most widely used methods for measuring customer service are surveys and mystery shoppers. Some surveys are passive. Target displays a "Guest Comment Card" near the front of its stores (see Exhibit 19-7). Customers can take a card and fill it out whenever they like. Other surveys are done on a periodic basis with an effort to have a representative sample of customers.

Mystery shopping is *evaluative field research into a store's operations conducted by someone who appears to be an average shopper and is not known or recognized by the employees who are being evaluated.* Mystery shopping is provided by a number of companies that can help design and evaluate a study as well as execute it. One important benefit of using a professional mystery shopping service is objectivity. This type of research can be designed to measure whatever performance criteria a company feels are necessary, such as professionalism, product knowledge, compliance to company policy (about what to say and not say), eye contact, and salesmanship.

Surveys and mystery shopping studies are important inputs into a SWOT analysis. They become inputs for designing employee training programs, awarding bonuses, and determining brand-message strategies.

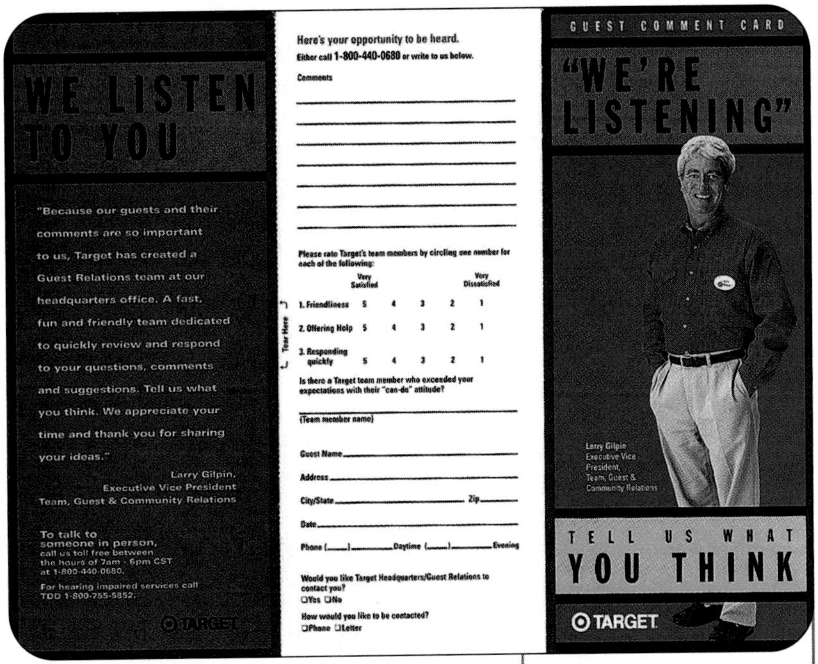

EXHIBIT 19-7
Target takes merchandise back within 90 days without asking questions. Its sensitive approach to customers is evident in its comment card, prominently displayed at checkout counters in Target stores.

Strengths and Limitations of Customer Service

The more complex a product offering is, generally the more critical the role of customer service. For example, a company providing airplane parts and repairs for private aircraft requires more extensive customer service and technical support than does a company making paper clips. Paper clips do not generate a lot of post-purchase questions. Aircraft parts, in contrast, involve unique, project-specific, and sometimes unpredictable situations.

If a company operates with a customer-focused philosophy that permeates the corporate culture and has the commitment of top management, then all of the advantages of two-way communication can be reinforced on the critical customer-service front line. The primary strength of customer service is its contribution to the maintenance of a customer relationship during and after a purchase has been made. Personal encounters, which are more persuasive than mass-media marketing communication, can be used to overcome negative feelings associated with product problems. However, because customer service is rarely managed as part of a marketing program, the communication dimensions of customer service are usually not integrated into the overall marketing communication approach. Furthermore, training people to work in customer service represents a significant expense to the company, especially when turnover in this area is high.

A FINAL NOTE: ADDING EXPERIENCES TO A BRAND RELATIONSHIP

Events, sponsorships, and customer service are critical dimensions of relationship marketing. They provide interactivity, and they create a memorable brand experience. The intensity of involvement that comes from a personal experience is the reason why messages delivered through events and customer service are so powerful. Experiential communication is persuasive because it pumps up the customer's level of attention, interest, and recall of a brand and company.

Marketing communication functions that deliver experiential contact make it possible for a company to develop a positive, highly involving, and memorable link to a brand. They also offer an opportunity to tightly target an audience. Combining the persuasiveness of personal contact with the involvement of experience-focused communication, events, sponsorships, and customer service can be used to create, maintain, and grow more effective brand relationships.

Key Terms

customer service 618

empowerment 624

event marketing 607

mystery shopping 627

sponsorship 613

trade show 611

Key Point Summary

EXHIBIT 19-8

As this picture of the Olympic Park in Sydney, Australia, shows, Coke does an excellent job of leveraging its sponsorship in its presence at the Olympic Games.

Key Point 1: Event Marketing and Sponsorships

Event marketing is the strategic use of an event as part of a marketing program to reach a certain audience. Sponsorships create a positive association in customers' minds between the event and a sponsoring company that underwrites the expenses of the event.

Key Point 2: Types of Events and Sponsorships

Event marketing includes events that are created by a company or organization and participation events, such as a trade show, in which a company is only one of many participants. Cosponsored events, such as the Olympics, are promotional opportunities that allow a company to associate its brand with the event. The primary type of sponsorship is with sports events. Some other types of sponsorships include cause marketing and mission marketing.

Key Point 3: Strengths and Weaknesses of Events and Sponsorships

Events and sponsorships are designed to associate the brand with something positive and create brand likeability, as well as intensify customer relationships by increasing customers' level of involvement with the brand. Their primary limitation is that they involve only a small percentage of a brand's target audience.

Key Point 4: How Customer Service Works

Customer service is both a philosophy of business and a marketing communication function that assumes responsibility for customer satisfaction after the purchase. Customer-service programs are designed to handle complaints, initiate customer contact after the purchase, and elicit customer feedback. Customer service's strength is its use of personal, two-way communication to maintain customer satisfaction after the purchase; its limitations come from the difficulty of training people to effectively manage the problems encountered in these situations and of coordinating marketing and customer-service programs.

Lessons Learned

Key Point 1: Events and Sponsorships

a. What is the relationship between event marketing and sponsorships?
b. Why is event marketing referred to as *experiential communication?* How does it differ from marketing communication methods discussed in earlier chapters?
c. What are the duties most commonly involved in event management?
d. Check out the websites of three of the companies listed in the Global Focus box on page 615. Do they mention their Olympic sponsorship on their websites? Is the sponsorship being effectively used? How would you recommend that these companies better leverage their association with the Olympics on their websites?

Key Point 2: Types of Events and Sponsorships

a. How does a created event differ from a participation event? Give an example of each.
b. What departments or MC functions use events? What do they hope to accomplish with the events?
c. What do events contribute to relationship programs?
d. What is a trade show? Who is its target? What objectives might a company specify for its participation in such an event?
e. How do sports sponsorships work? What are their objectives?
f. Define *cause marketing* and *mission marketing*. Explain how they differ.
g. Find one example of cause marketing and one example of mission marketing. How effective is each at building brand relationships?

Key Point 3: Strengths and Limitations of Event Marketing and Sponsorships

a. What are the strengths and limitations of event marketing and sponsorships?
b. Develop a set of typical objectives (at least three each) for event marketing, sponsorship, and customer-service programs based on the strengths you identify for each area.

Key Point 4: Types of Customer Service

a. Why do we say that customer service drives responsiveness?
b. What are the two meanings of *customer service?*
c. Why is training such an important part of an effective customer-service program?
d. What are the characteristics of a good customer-service program?
e. Have you ever returned a product to a retailer or manufacturer? How was your return handled? What other services did the company's customer-service department offer?
f. What are the strengths and limitations of customer service?
g. Have you ever called a company's toll-free number with a question about a product or service? How well did the help desk or hot line handle your question?

Chapter Challenge

Writing Assignment

Choose a local store or manufacturer in your area. Analyze the effectiveness of its experiential-communication programs. How does it handle events, sponsorships, and customer service? In what ways could the company improve its efforts? Write a report to the marketing manager summarizing and explaining your findings.

Presentation Assignment

Based on your findings in the writing assignment, develop a relationship marketing plan for the company you chose. Identify the key stakeholders, their contact points with the company, and the messages being delivered at those contact points. What might the company do to better manage these relationships? In particular, how can experiential communication be used to grow the company's business with its customers? Prepare a presentation of the marketing plan for your class.

Internet Assignment

Consult one of the following corporate websites, and analyze how the company handles customer interactivity. Look specifically for a toll-free phone number or e-mail address. Ask the customer-service representative a common question to find out how long it takes to get an answer and how satisfactory the answer is. Write a memo to your instructor about the quality of the company's customer service.

www.harley-davidson.com
www.cheerios.com
www.pizzahut.com
www.goodyear.com
www.ual.com (United Airlines)
www.sears.com
www.usmc.mil (Marine Corps)
www.target.com
www.starbucks.com

Part V

Chapter

20

Social, Ethical, and Legal Issues

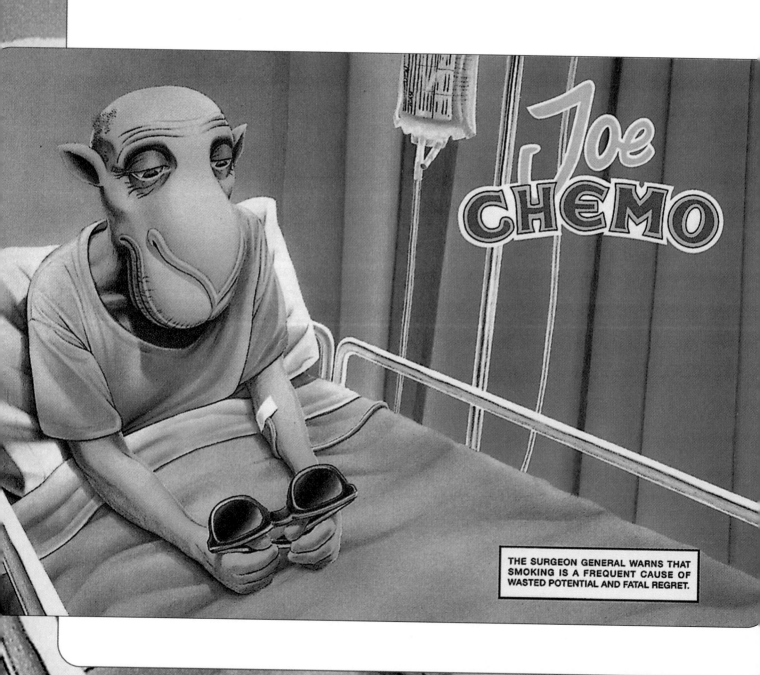

Joe CHEMO

THE SURGEON GENERAL WARNS THAT SMOKING IS A FREQUENT CAUSE OF WASTED POTENTIAL AND FATAL REGRET.

Key Points in This Chapter

1. What issues surround the role of marketing communication in society?
2. What ethical issues relate to marketing communication?
3. What legal issues relate to marketing communication?
4. How is regulation managed in marketing communication?

Chapter Perspective

Managing Marketing Communication with Sensitivity

Because marketing communication is so public by its very nature, it is constantly scrutinized for false promises, misleading statements, and the undermining of social values. In the marketplace of brand messages, constant tension exists among marketers (who want to take advantage of every way they can to persuade people to buy their products), the many laws regulating commercial speech, and the many social mores against which brand messages are measured. Responsible companies want to develop the most effective, attention-grabbing ad campaigns possible, yet they know that if they push beyond acceptable limits—which often are more gray than black and white—they can tarnish their image and risk fines and public humiliation. To make things even more complex, different audiences have different standards against which they evaluate brand messages.

Marketers must continually strive to be competitive while at the same time being legal and ethical in what they say and how they say it. This is why marketing communicators must have a basic understanding of what is and is not socially acceptable, what is legal and illegal, and what is ethical and unethical. This chapter focuses on explaining the issues, standards, guidelines, and regulations that have been put in place by various organizations and government bodies. The chapter's objective is to make you sensitive to the social, ethical, and legal issues that relate to managing the marketing communications that create and sustain customer relationships.

SMOKING IS A FREQUENT CAUSE OF

DO ADVERTISERS HAVE THE RIGHT TO ECONOMICALLY CENSOR THE MEDIA?

A few years ago, CNN was criticized for pulling off the air two ads that warned viewers about global warming. Richard Pollock, spokesperson for the Global Climate Information Project, the lobbying organization that paid for the ads, said, "I think this is totally a censorship issue. This is Ted Turner [CNN founder] pulling views that he personally doesn't like. He has decided to act as an information czar." Steve Haworth, a CNN spokesperson, said the decision had been made not by Turner but by the network's standards and practices committee. Haworth said that it was CNN's policy not to run advocacy ads when an issue is receiving intense news coverage. At the time the ads were first allowed on CNN, the topic was not a major issue. They were pulled, he said, when it "became increasingly apparent that our coverage was intensifying."[1]

It's easy to see how a media owner might be able to manipulate news to advocate a point of view, but can advertisers pressure media? Direct advertiser pressure, particularly on local newspapers, comes in the form of complaints to the editor and publisher, demands that a reporter or columnist be fired or print an apology, and requests that the media bury a story by running it in a less prominent position than its subject might deserve. But the most destructive weapon is an advertising boycott as occurred in the 1980s when the *Los Angeles Herald Examiner* published an investigative report about Southern California grocery stores' practice of shortweighting and overcharging customers. In response, one of the largest grocery chain advertisers canceled its $250,000 contract. Although the report generated a local government investigation, the competing *Los Angeles Times* never ran the story.

In *Advertising Censorship*, Marquette University professor Lawrence Soley examines the issue and presents the results of an in-depth study of the pressures that advertisers exert on the mass media. He reviews the arguments made by the media and other academics that the press, particularly large media, is insulated from pressure applied by disgruntled advertisers. Soley concludes that "there is overwhelming evidence showing that advertisers pressure newspapers to kill or change news stories, and that many large and small newspapers have caved in to the pressure." He also found examples of such pressure being applied to magazines and broadcast media, as well as newspapers, and it happens on the national as well as the local level.

Soley found that much of the pressure comes from the real-estate and automobile industries, as

EXHIBIT 20-1

well as department stores, airlines, and apparel manufacturers. Auto dealers, for example, spend more than $5 billion on advertising, and over half goes to newspapers. In return for their support of the media, dealers expect favorable coverage; otherwise, they withdraw their advertising. For example, after the *San Jose Mercury News* ran an article headlined "A Car Buyer's Guide to Sanity," local dealers demanded a meeting with the publisher, who apologized and offered a page of advertising to compensate them. Members of the local dealer association, however, were not satisfied and canceled their advertising, costing the paper $l million in revenue. The Federal Trade Commission (FTC) cited the group for creating a collective boycott that violated federal antitrust laws, but the FTC also said that *individual* dealers can boycott a media vehicle whenever they choose.

So what's right? Should media be free to make news judgments without pressure from advertisers? What about the rights of advertisers when they feel they are being unfairly attacked by a medium? How should they respond in a responsible and ethical way? Questions such as these are the focus of this chapter as it reviews the social responsibility of marketers, as well as marketing communication ethics and the legal dimensions of marketing communication practice.

Source: David Bauder, "CNN Pulls Two Ads on Global Warming," Boulder Daily Camera, October 5, 1997, p. 14a; Lawrence Soley, Advertising Censorship (Milwaukee: Southshore Press, 2002).

THE ROLE OF MARKETING COMMUNICATION IN SOCIETY

The ad in Exhibit 20-2 shows the power of advertising to sell a socially responsible behavior. Critics ask, however, whether marketing communication has the same kind of power in creating negative social consequences, such as a materialistic consumer culture.

This chapter looks at the various criticisms, ethical issues, and regulatory efforts in order to better understand how marketing communication can perform a useful and positive role in society and operate in a socially responsible way. The intention of this chapter is to represent critical viewpoints that need to be considered and discussed by anyone who is a student of marketing communication.

The goals of an IMC program are to inform, persuade, and listen to all stakeholders. This relationship component gives IMC a platform on which to build a more socially responsible form of marketing communication than some of the past practices in advertising or direct marketing, which look at consumers solely as targets. Unfortunately, many companies are poor listeners. Many are just now setting up the systems and infrastructure needed for commercial listening and responding. For this reason, there is often a gap between social concerns and business practices on issues such as the environment, social values, overpackaging, and designed obsolescence. For example, here is how one marketing communication function—advertising—has been portrayed by a UNESCO critic:

> Regarded as a form of communication, it [advertising] has been criticized for playing on emotions, simplifying real human situations into stereotypes, exploiting anxieties, and employing techniques of intensive persuasion that amount to manipulation. Many social critics have stated that advertising is essentially concerned with exalting the materialistic virtues of consumption by exploiting achievement drives and emulative anxieties, employing tactics of hidden manipulation, playing on emotions, maximizing appeal and minimizing information, trivializing, eliminating objective considerations, contriving illogical situations, and generally reducing men, women, and children to the role of irrational

EXHIBIT 20-2

Marketing communication can be used on behalf of socially responsible causes, such as donations to the poor. Does it also spur people to become overly focused on materialism?

EXHIBIT 20-3
Adbusters is a magazine that is critical of advertising and its role in creating a materialistic culture. These parody ads are typical of the approach used by the publication to make its points.

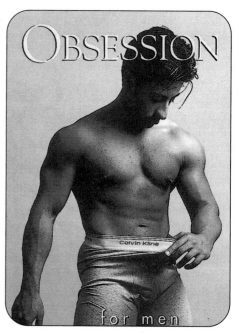

consumer. Criticism expressed in such a way may be overstated, but it cannot be entirely brushed aside.[2]

For an introduction to this world of criticism, go to www.adbusters.org or consult *Adbusters*, a magazine that comments on the social responsibility of advertising and marketing communication—or the perceived lack thereof. The two parody ads in Exhibit 20-3 are from a collection of *Adbusters* postcards.

For the most part, the criticisms made against advertising can be viewed as criticisms made against all forms of marketing communication because the ultimate goal—to influence buying decisions—is the same for each. Most social critics do not make a distinction between marketing communication functions when it comes to charges of over-commercialization and encouraging conspicuous consumption. To them, *any* brand message that directly or indirectly encourages people to consume is manipulative and, thus, suspect.

Does Marketing Communication Mirror or Shape Society?

How much influence does MC have on customers and society as a whole? Critics say that advertising in particular, because of its creative skills and pervasiveness, has created a materialistic culture of conspicuous consumption in which not only are people persuaded to buy goods and services they don't want or need, but brand messages present an idealistic profile of glamor, opulent lifestyles, and happiness that supposedly can be had by buying the right brands. In this way, critics argue, marketers shape how we live.

Defenders of MC say that marketers are given way too much credit for persuasive power. They note, for example, that of the hundreds of brand messages that customers see and hear each day, few are remembered. They point out that 9 out of 10 new-product ideas fail, which wouldn't be the case if marketers were as controlling as critics say they are. They also point out that companies spend billions of dollars on research to find out what customers want. If companies could sell anything they wanted to, then why waste money on customer research?

The reality is that MC and society are intertwined and MC does a little of both—mirroring and shaping. If MC had no impact on customers, why would U.S. marketers spend more than $200 billion dollars a year on various forms of MC? At the same time, the whole marketing concept is based on satisfying customer wants and needs. Environmental issues, for example, became a major social concern in the late 1900s not because environmental responsibility was the subject of a strong MC effort, but rather because of an emerging social consciousness. As a result of this new social concern, many companies began to relate their brand messages to the environment. Even today some marketers still do this, such as the Shell ad in Chapter 6 (Exhibit 6-6, p. 176).

The purpose of MC, its defenders say, is to provide information and to help customers in the brand decision process. They admit that brand messages are designed to be persuasive, but the fact that much effort is made to send these messages only to people already interested in the product category demonstrates that marketers know they can convince only a very small portion of the total population to buy. University of Colorado professor Richard Goode-Allen describes what he calls "adilemmas": On the one hand, he says, critics need to take into consideration that most developed nations are based on a marketplace economy, which requires the production and distribution of goods and services for its existence. On the other hand, marketers must understand that the environment and customers' financial and emotional resources are finite and perishable.

Concerns about Marketing Communication

Thoughts of junk mail, telemarketers calling at dinnertime, spin merchants, and used-car salesmen taint the image of marketing communication. Advertising often ranks at the bottom of many lists of respectable professions. Why is that?

A survey of 1,000 adults conducted by the University of Illinois's Cummings Center for Advertising Studies found that 51 percent of consumers are offended by marketing communication "sometimes or often," that 47 percent believe that most brand messages insult their intelligence, and that 69 percent feel they are occasionally misled by brand messages.[3] The fact that many people have serious misgivings about marketing communication is a result of various perceptions—and sometimes misperceptions. Discussed here are the concerns about MC that are most often heard:

- *MC drives up the cost of products.* Some people feel that MC drives up the cost of goods and services because the cost of marketing is included in the purchase price of products. In other words, customers pay for being sold to. Although it's true that as much as 25 percent of the price customers pay for some cosmetics goes to marketing, marketing costs are a relatively small percentage of the purchase price of most other products. In fact, mass marketing drives prices down and makes products affordable. In the case of cars, marketing costs generally account for 2 to 4 percent of the purchase price. Marketers also point out that often the cost of MC is more than offset by price reductions that result from MC encouraging competition in the marketplace. Howard Morgens, former president of Procter & Gamble, says, "We believe that advertising [i.e., marketing communication] is the most effective and efficient way to sell to the consumer. If we should ever find better methods of selling our type of products to the consumer, we'll leave advertising and turn to these other methods."[4]

- *MC creates a barrier to market entry.* Slotting allowances and the demands of retailers that new products have strong MC campaigns to support new products constitute a barrier for small, entrepreneurial companies trying to enter the market. In addition, customers have been conditioned to buy

EXHIBIT 20-4

What would you say to someone who claimed that MC merchandises too many aspects of our culture?

popular brands. To become a popular brand on a small budget, however, takes either a really unique product or a terrifically creative message, both of which are difficult to achieve.

- *MC merchandises too many aspects of our culture.* In an effort to reach prospects and customers, companies have turned an increasing number of public spaces and activities into conveyors of advertising messages (see Exhibit 20-4). Buses used to carry a sign on their sides; now the whole bus is an ad. Sports arenas now have brand logos on the playing surfaces besides brand messages on walls, the video monitors, and over the public address systems. Grocery carts are now mobile billboards, and the dividers used on the conveyor belts at checkout carry brand messages. Some manufacturers place their labels on the outside of clothes, and others splash their brand name across the fronts of T-shirts and caps—but people pay for the opportunity to wear these branded goods. On some broadcasts of football games, there is a sponsor of the electronic first down line, not to mention logos on uniforms of players and coaches. The idea of seeing brands "everywhere" has made some people concerned about the over-commercialization of every aspect of our lives. But how and where should the line be drawn, and who should draw it?

- *MC sells inferior products.* The criticism that MC encourages people to buy inferior products can be especially true of new products. However, few companies make a profit by selling to a customer just once. And there is no faster way to kill an inferior brand than to convince many people to buy it, only to have them find out that they wasted their money. Not only do customers refuse to make a repeat purchase, they also often tell others about the bad experience (negative word-of-mouth advertising).

- *MC sells unhealthy, dangerous products.* One issue that continues to be discussed is the appropriateness of promoting products that, though legal, may not be good for us, such as tobacco and alcohol. Because marketing is a part of selling, some people say it makes no sense to make it illegal to advertise products that are legal to sell. Nonetheless, companies are viewed as having some social responsibility for the behavior they induce in consumers, be it when executives mislead the public about known harmful effects of smoking or when retailers serve drinks to patrons who then drive drunk. Antismoking advocates continue to push for additional bans on tobacco advertising. The compromise in this case has been to reduce the exposure of tobacco brand messages to children, who cannot legally buy the product. In the case of alcohol, some manufacturers have added socially responsible messages to their advertising. The U.S. Constitution and the Supreme Court support commercial free speech as long as it is factual, substantiated, and not misleading, although there is a continuing debate about how much freedom should be allowed for commercial speech.

  In response to the growing concern of people being overweight, especially children, Kraft Foods has changed some of its marketing practices. The maker of such popular food brands as Oreo cookies, Velveeta cheese, and Oscar Mayer, has reduced the portions in single-serving packages and greatly reduced in-school promotions for Kraft snack items. Kraft has also said it will work to develop more healthy snack foods for children.[5]

- *MC sets unrealistic expectations.* A relatively new concern over MC is the promotion of products to people who may not be allowed to buy them. Regulations concerning pharmaceutical advertising, for example, have been relaxed in recent years so that drug companies can now advertise prescription drugs directly to consumers. In 1997, *Reader's Digest* received $30 million a year from prescription-drug advertising, approximately one-fifth of its annual ad revenue.[6] Yet health insurance companies, trying to rein in spending on drugs, are not always willing to pay for every prescription that a member requests. So while brand messages encourage consumers to ask their doctors for new medicines, doctors are being encouraged (and sometimes forced) by health insurance companies to prescribe alternatives. This conflict between what consumers are told will help them and what they have access to can generate anxiety and frustration.

- *MC is done in bad taste.* In many countries, including the United States, a battle goes on between people who want to establish standards of taste and morality in society and those who feel that open expression must be allowed and defended, even if this means people are sometimes exposed to things they find offensive. Many are concerned about marketers' use of sex and violence to gain attention and sell brands. Even when brand-message content is not offensive to the target audience, it can be offensive to others. The First Amendment to the U.S. Constitution maintains that "Congress shall make no law . . . abridging the freedom of speech, or of the press." Some magazines and newspapers that include ads for X-rated movies, cheap handguns, diet pills, or inflammatory political causes cite the First Amendment when they say they have the right to accept all advertising.[7]

- *MC invites censorship.* The charge against Ted Turner and CNN reported in the opening case is not the first time the issue of media censorship has been raised (see Ethics and Issues box). As long ago as 1935 George Seldes, a reporter and press critic, said that advertisers, not the government, were the principal news censors in the United States. In Seldes's view, the danger lies not with the media editorial decisions but with advertisers who attempt to influence the coverage of news that it is not favorable to their interests.

  Most media strongly protect their right to pick and choose the ads they run. Besides having their own convictions about what messages are and aren't proper, editors and other media gatekeepers are also sensitive to all their advertisers as well as to their audiences. An offense to either side could result in reduced revenue. Although one could debate about the extent to which such practices exist or impact on the publication of news or ads, when the media reject an ad—or a story, for that matter—they are practicing a form of censorship.

- *MC creates visual pollution.* You may recall from Chapter 11's discussion of out-of-home advertising that some people consider the proliferation of outdoor advertising to be "visual pollution" (see Exhibit 20-6). As a result, commercial free speech is sometimes restricted for reasons of aesthetics and, in some cases, safety (restricting the view of drivers, for example). Zoning laws in many states prohibit billboards in certain areas. In newer commercial shopping strips, retail store signage, as well, is often restricted in size and placement.

- *MC pushes one country's culture onto another.* One thing every global or international marketer exports along with its products is its culture. The increased attention given in recent years to this side of global businesses has

ETHICS AND ISSUES

Media Censorship: Who Tells the Other Side of the Story?

The opening case describes CNN's refusal to run ads relating to the global warming issue. CNN has also refused to run ads from the governments of Saudi Arabia, Qatar, and the United Arab Emirates on Arab issues, as well as from a group trying to bolster support for Israel.

And in 2003 MTV refused to run a spot opposing the war in Iraq, citing its policy against using advocacy spots that represent the views of interest groups whose views may not be generally acceptable. An MTV spokesman explained that "The decision was made years ago that we don't accept advocacy advertising because it really opens us up to accepting every point of view on every subject."

The antiwar ad, which was directed by Barbara Kopple, winner of two Academy Awards for her documentaries, featured young people speaking to the camera about their opposition to the war, with scenes from recent antiwar marches interspersed through the spot. Although rejected by MTV, the spots eventually got on air in New York and Los Angeles because backers did an end-run and bought time from local cable providers.

If the decision about what gets heard is the prerogative of editors and producers, how are responsible interest groups supposed to make their point, particularly in a time of crisis or when they are against a government action? A number of groups opposed to government policies allege that television networks and cable channels censor political views by refusing to accept antiwar ads.

The problem seems to lie mostly with television because most networks have similar policies against public advocacy ads. Newspapers are more willing to accept such ads. A group called "Musicians United to Win without War" ran a full-page ad in the *New York Times* signed by Sheryl Crow, Fugazi, and Jay-Z, among other stars.

So what responsibility do the media—particularly television, which reaches the broadest audience and is the most emotional and moving forum for presenting a viewpoint—have to further national debate on major issues? When public debate is essential, do television policies block the views of people who advocate opinions not in line with government policy or with those in power? Is denial of advertising a free-speech issue?

Alex Jones, director of Harvard University's Center on the Press, Politics, and Public Policy, says, "It is irresponsible for news organizations not to accept ads that are controversial on serious issues, assuming they are not scurrilous or in bad taste." He explained, "In the world we live in, with the kind of media concentration we have, the only way that unpopular beliefs can be aired sometimes is if the monopoly vehicle agrees to accept an ad."

Think About It

What are the arguments for and against media's censorship of advocacy ads? What do you believe is a responsible position for the media? For an advocacy group?

Source: Nat Ives, "MTV Refuses Antiwar Commercial," *nytimes.com*, March 13, 2003, <www.nytimes.com/2003/03/13/business/media/13ADCO.html>; Julie Keller, "Blacklisting Martin Sheen?" March 6, 2003, *E! Online News*, <www.eonline.com/News/Items/Pf/0,1527,11391,00.html>; Ira Teinowitz, "Battle Rages over Anti-War TV Commercials," *AdAge.com*, February 24, 2003, <www.adage.com/news.cms?newsId=37202>; Bill O'Reilly Forum, "Antiwar Advertisement Also Anti-America," February 8, 2003, *The O'Reilly Factor*, <members.tripod.com/enMaxwell-ii/00-Edit-News30403/03-BoR-AntiAm-AntiWar-20803nhr.html>.

EXHIBIT 20-5

EXHIBIT 20-6
Some people consider the proliferation of outdoor advertising to be "visual pollution." What do you think?

led to an increase in protests against this "export of culture." In particular, some countries perceive the pervasiveness of American culture and American values as a threat to their own way of life. A writer in the *South China Post* noted: "Whether it is a case of the French going crazy over Jerry Lewis, the Germans channel surfing for *Baywatch*, or Chinese teenagers idolizing Michael Jordan, there is no denying America's role as the supreme exporter of entertainment"[8]—and entertainment is one very powerful aspect of culture.

Many countries have sought to keep American culture out. Conservative Islamic countries have barred American television shows and movies. The Chinese have banned direct selling, forcing Avon, Amway, and other American companies to alter the way they do business in China. The European Union requires all TV channels to carry at least 50 percent European programming. French officials try to limit the number of American films shown in France; some even called the movie *Jurassic Park* a "threat to [French] national identity."[9] In July 1998, there was a two-day meeting of 22 government ministers from around the world to find ways to counter the spread of American culture. What must be sorted out, however, is whether a country is "protecting" its citizens from "corrupting" outside influences or whether it is limiting choices and dictating tastes.

All of these concerns about the effects of marketing communication are legitimate and deserve debate, but debate that acknowledges that there are two sides to most of these issues.

ETHICS AND MARKETING COMMUNICATION

Ivan Preston, a University of Wisconsin professor emeritus who has worked for and testified before courts and regulatory bodies about advertising, makes the point that "Ethics begins where the law ends." Every society has certain **ethics,** *moral and value standards that act as behavioral guidelines.* The ethics of organizations and of individuals within a society form the benchmarks for determining what is right and wrong in different situations. Unlike government laws and regulations,

> **"Ethics begins where the law ends."**
>
> Ivan Preston

which are explicitly stated, ethical codes are generally not written down. Rather, they are held in the social consciousness of an organization or a population, and what constitutes ethical behavior is determined by public attitudes and feelings. Ethics are important in IMC because they provide the basis for the moral choices that individuals and organizations must make in their relationships with each other.

Marketing practices should be guided by an organization's ethics. Marketers should also ask whether brand messages and programs are aligned with the ethics of the brand's stakeholders. If they are not, stakeholder relationships will be weakened. In addition, unethical brand messages can reflect negatively on the MC agencies that create them and the media that distribute them.

Establishing what is or is not ethical is not always easy. For example, various conservative and liberal groups disagree on whether corporate policies that provide benefits (such as insurance coverage) for same-sex partners are ethical. As you will recall from Chapter 1, everything a company does—and sometimes what it *doesn't* do—can send a brand message. The types of policies a company sets down for its employees communicate that company's beliefs to its stakeholders and to the public at large. For years, one reason why Wal-Mart did not offer insurance coverage to the partners of its gay employees was a concern that too many of its customers would think Wal-Mart was "approving" a gay lifestyle. But recently Wal-Mart changed this policy, partially because it became concerned that as social attitudes became more accepting, too many of its customers would think the company was anti-gay if it didn't provide such benefits.

Because ethics are so subjective, some companies simply say that employees must not do anything illegal. In other words, they let the law define their ethics. But even law-abiding companies face ethical issues. Thus companies need to discuss ethical issues and set guidelines for individual and corporate behavior. Just as brand messages should be strategically consistent, corporate behavior should be ethically consistent. A cross-functional group responsible for managing brand relationships should be prepared to deal with ethical issues and allow for open discussion.

The best way to explain the ethical issues marketers face is with examples.

Stereotyping

As our society has become more aware of its diversity, people have become sensitized to cultural, ethnic, gender, and other differences. Although stereotypes sometimes contain grains of truth that may be useful in segmenting a group, the challenge for brands is to develop messages that strike a chord with targeted audiences without reinforcing negative stereotypes. For example, the women's campaigns by Nike reach out to women with messages that strike against the stereotyped images of women presented in some fashion magazines.

Even when using careful planning—for example, testing copy with focus groups comprising members from the targeted audience—companies may still alienate some people. For example, Taco Bell's use of a Spanish-speaking Chihuahua in a series of ads was well received by some Latinos, but others were offended that the Mexican in the ad was a dog.

Sometimes advertisers are able to use messages that can be interpreted favorably by different audiences. Volkswagen created a highly popular television commercial in which two young men drove around town in a VW Golf, stopped to pick up an abandoned chair, then stopped again to dump it off because it smelled. Advertising to a niche market like the Gen-X target in the VW Golf ad can be particularly difficult because appealing to one subset may alienate another. Most viewers saw the two guys as cool Gen-X friends or roommates, but older viewers thought they epitomized the aimless, worthless lifestyle of young people. Meanwhile, gay audiences assumed the two guys were a couple and responded positively.

Advertising to women is particularly challenging. Childless women may not identify with messages directed to mothers. Women who see themselves as overweight may resent messages directed to fitness buffs. Like any demographic group, women are not a monolithic audience and should not be treated as such.

Companies can avoid making some groups uncomfortable or even angry by carefully screening their brand messages and selecting highly targeted media for delivery.

Targeting Vulnerable Groups

As the population as a whole has become more educated about marketing strategies and tactics, concern has been increasing about messages specifically directed to captive audiences, as well as to less educated or unsophisticated consumer groups. A *Wall Street Journal* reporter in 2003 announced the beginning of a new television network, aimed at hospital patients (a captive audience), that would provide programs on health-care topics. The *Journal*'s doubt about the new network's attempts to woo advertisers was evident in the article's headline: "Patient Channel to Blast Ads at Bedridden."[10]

Feeling that companies take "persuasive advantage" of vulnerable or disadvantaged groups, some critics have mounted efforts to ban the promotion of certain types of products from certain media targeted to certain audiences, such as children, the elderly, minorities, and people in developing countries.

Children

Marketing to children is criticized on several grounds. Some critics worry about children being bombarded with consumer images that glorify the buying of products.[11] Parents see children becoming brand savvy at an early age and demanding certain products and brands. Although some might argue that children need to learn consumer skills, the issue raised by this proliferating consumerism is whether children who are too young to have developed the critical skills needed to separate advertising from other types of directions are being unfairly manipulated. In fact, as one education professor reports, young children have trouble distinguishing TV programs from commercials, and most children have little or no understanding of the persuasive intention of commercials, so they are particularly vulnerable to advertising claims and appeals.[12]

Marketing to children has come under question because even the most vigilant parents find it hard to screen all, or even a fraction, of the commercial messages their children see. In general, parents prefer to be the ones to shape their children's buying decisions. But companies are free to advertise in and around schools, during children's programming on television, at sporting events, on product packaging and point-of-purchase displays, on the internet, and in movies and at movie theaters. And parents cannot possibly be on hand to help their children interpret all of these brand messages.

The more children's tastes appear to be shaped by commercial messages rather than by parental influences, the more support there is for regulation. However, groups that want to shield children from commercial messages have found it difficult to collect valid evidence to support their negative views.

The fact that schools are accepting and displaying brand messages in exchange for money, free equipment, and curriculum materials has received strong opposition

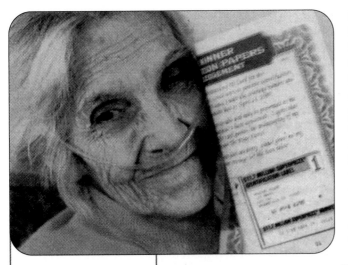

EXHIBIT 20-7
*This newspaper photo
accompanied a story
about an elderly woman
who mistook a direct-
mail solicitation from
Publishers Clearing
House for a notice that
she had actually won the
$1.1 million prize. The
story described how
vulnerable some elderly
people are to certain
marketing techniques.*

from some parent groups. (One of the most controversial is the Channel One Network, described in Chapter 4.) Companies develop lesson plans and classroom videos that some believe are little more than corporate public relations messages aimed at young audiences. Dow Chemical has prepared an instructional video about the benefits of chemicals, and Exxon has one using its 1989 Alaskan oil-spill cleanup as an example of environmental success. Chevron's video on global warming stresses that not all scientists agree that there is a problem.

According to a study by the nonprofit organization Consumers Union, nearly 80 percent of corporate-sponsored school materials contained "biased or incomplete information [that] favors the company or its economic agenda." The study claimed that these materials are full of "self-interested, incomplete or discriminatory points of view [that] basically teach opinion as if it were fact."[13]

Marketers have learned, however, that if their material is too obviously biased, little or none of it will be used. Ron Schmieder, president of the Plastic Bag Association, describes his organization's booklet titled "Don't Let a Good Thing Go to Waste," which is given free to grade school teachers, by saying: "It's good public relations, plus it takes care of a need. We've tried to give a very balanced view of the solid waste issue."[14]

The Elderly

Consumer affairs offices and reporters are often alerted to questionable sales and marketing tactics aimed at the elderly. Some marketers use hard-sell pitches with puzzling details for this target audience (see Exhibit 20-7).

According to Robert Pitofsky, chair of the U.S. Federal Trade Commission (FTC), the elderly are often the targets of telemarketing fraud involving prize promotions, lottery clubs, charity solicitations, and investment offers. Concerned about the problem, the FTC developed the Partnership for Consumer Education to place messages about fraud in catalogs, billing statements, classified advertising, and public transportation to help the elderly and other people be cautious about responding to these offers.[15] Violators of the nationwide do-not-call list launched by the FTC in 2003 are subject to penalties of up to $2,000 per violation, but if the victim is 60 or older, the penalty jumps to $10,000.[16]

Minorities

Commercial messages are often targeted to different ethnic groups. For example, many consumer product companies have developed Cinco de Mayo–themed promotions for Mexican Americans. But when the products being promoted are perceived to be socially unacceptable, concerns arise about exploitation.

Several years ago, R. J. Reynolds announced plans to introduce Uptown, a cigarette designed to appeal to black smokers. The U.S. Secretary of Health and Human Services at that time charged that the company was "cynically" targeting a group already suffering from smoking-related illness.[17] There was similar criticism when G. Heileman Brewing Company planned to introduce a malt liquor called PowerMaster. Because per capita consumption of malt liquor has traditionally been relatively high in African-American communities, this campaign and product drew criticism from anti-alcohol groups and black leaders, who said that the last thing inner-city communities needed was an inexpensive drink with a higher level of alcohol. The Beer Institute countered by saying that it was patronizing for community leaders to suggest that blacks and Hispanics need more protection than the population at large.[18]

Developing Countries

Companies looking to expand business beyond current markets sometimes see opportunities in countries with fewer trade and product restrictions. Tobacco companies come under criticism for using advertising in Asia, eastern Europe, and South America that was long ago banned in the United States and western Europe. Free Cigarettes, a Brazilian subsidiary of the international conglomerate British American Tobacco, has used ads that suggest smoking is an appropriate symbol of teenage rebellion. In one, a teen says, "First we go crazy, then we see what happens."[19]

Pharmaceutical companies have been accused of unethical business practices such as using advertising in developing countries to promote drugs that U.S. regulators have not judged to be safe. Studies have shown that advertisements, as well as labels and package inserts, often overstate benefits and understate risks in countries where government regulations are lacking or are not consistently enforced.[20]

Offensive Brand Messages

To get a feel for different types of commercial messages, imagine a continuum. At one end are straightforward, objective, safe messages. If a company goes overboard in this direction, it can end up with brand messages that are boring or easily forgotten. At the other end of the continuum are attention-grabbing messages. A company that goes too far in this direction can end up with messages that are too controversial and even offensive.

Even marketing communication that is within legal bounds may not be ethical or socially acceptable. As a promotional stunt a British insurance company sent 77 homing pigeons, each in a cage, to reporters in London to announce a new investment product. The reporters were instructed to release the pigeons and were told that the person whose pigeon returned home first would receive a free case of whiskey. Animal rights groups were outraged, and the Royal Pigeon Racing Association wondered "why a responsible organization would send live birds to people without asking them first if they wanted them." The public relations firm that thought up the idea responded, "It just goes to show how sensitive some people are. We think that it was an innovative and clever idea."[21]

When talking about offensive advertising, people often point to sex and social taboos as two areas where brand messages often cross over the line.

Sex

Sexual images are an attention-grabbing device. That is why bikini-clad women have for years appeared in ads for auto parts and nearly every other male-targeted product you can think of. But using sexual images that are unrelated to product claims may be a poor creative decision because these images can overpower the primary brand message. Also, with the attention comes scrutiny and possible protests from audiences (see Exhibit 20-8).

The sexual ads that have drawn the most protest are those that exploit women in general as sex objects and those that use underage models in sexually suggestive ways. However, sexual mores are not the same in all cultures, so it is difficult to develop definitive sexual guidelines. Some ads that are acceptable in European cultures would be considered in poor taste in America. Likewise, some images that work in New York City would draw protests in Muncie, Indiana.

EXHIBIT 20-8
Critics say that advertising uses too much skin and suggestive posturing to sell products. Defenders say that exposed skin and suggestive poses are appropriate for certain products aimed at certain target markets. What do you think?

Taboo Topics

Different segments of the population consider certain products and topics to be inappropriate as the focus of public discussion and commercial messages. Two such products—feminine hygiene items and condoms—were not advertised on American television for many years because stations feared the criticism they would get from their other advertisers and audiences.

In recent years, clothing manufacturer Benetton has generated a great deal of attention and publicity by using images widely considered by some people to be shocking and inappropriate: pictures of human hearts, a man dying of AIDS, and a priest kissing a nun. But just as people who buy sexy underwear aren't generally offended by ads for lingerie, people who are very liberal and often anti-establishment aren't offended by Benetton ads. Companies like Benetton are targeting their current customers and likely prospects; they expect these audiences will accept their ads and are thus inclined to ignore the objections of groups who would likely never buy the product anyway. This can be simplistic reasoning, however, because it overlooks other stakeholders who can affect the profits of a company and brand as much as customers do. Brands don't have to offend others in order to appeal to their target audience. One of the basic creative challenges for marketing communication is to find a way to talk to and persuade customers and prospects that does *not* offend other stakeholders.

Manipulation and Subliminal Advertising

Marketers are expected to influence consumers to purchase goods and services. This influence can take many acceptable forms—product information, pricing, image, and so on. Some individuals and consumer groups suspect that this influence can also assume more insidious forms, akin to mind control and unscrupulous manipulation. Some ads that use strong fear appeals, for example, are criticized for excessive emotional manipulation. Such techniques can result in a negative backlash that turns off the audience.

The most criticized form of manipulative advertising is **subliminal advertising**—*messages that are received subconsciously, below a person's perceptual threshold, causing a desired response.* The topic of subliminal advertising became popular in 1957 when a market researcher, James Vicary, claimed he had increased the sales of Coke and popcorn in a movie theater by inserting into the theater's feature film the phrases "Drink Coke" and "Eat popcorn" every five seconds—but just for a fraction of a second so the words were not consciously seen. Although Vicary's claim caused a major stir in the advertising world, the fact that he refused to disclose the details of his study began to create doubt about the validity of his findings. The marketing community was soon convinced the technique was of no value, and the issue faded.[22]

In the 1970s, interest in subliminal advertising was revived with the publication of several books by Wilson Bryan Key, including *Subliminal Seduction: Ad Media's Manipulation of a Not So Innocent America*. The books, long on anecdotes but short on empirical evidence, have generally been dismissed by researchers who have tried to conduct research that proves such a practice exists or is effective. The topic still receives attention occasionally from some researchers and academics; however, a review of research over the years on subliminal messages shows that they are not considered a viable MC tool because there is no proof that they work.[23]

Some people confuse subliminal advertising with the use of colors, music, typography, and design to create a mood or otherwise set the stage for a consumer response. For example, some believe that patrons in a restaurant that uses earth tones on its walls feel especially relaxed and are inclined to linger and order more food and drinks than they would in a gaudy setting. The "message" imparted by the color of the walls, however, is not subliminal because it is not below

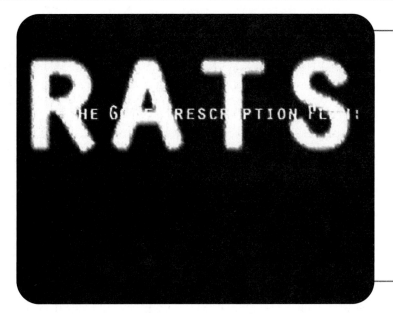

the threshold of awareness. Rather, some people merely find earth tones pleasing and choose to extend their stay to enjoy the ambiance.

During the 2000 U.S. presidential campaign, a TV commercial for Republican candidate George W. Bush reignited the discussion of subliminal advertising. During the commercial, the word *RATS* briefly flashed on the screen when the Democratic Party was being discussed. (The ad's producer said that it was mistakenly left in when a frame containing the word *bureaucrats* was cut from the ad.) Although some media stories called it subliminal advertising, the fact that the word was so obvious took it out of the "subliminal" category (see Exhibit 20-9). Nevertheless, the ad was quickly taken off the air.

There's another very practical reason why most professionals and academics dismiss subliminal advertising. Even if it worked, any company or MC agency that used it would be running the risk of generating negative publicity for itself. People who worked on the ad would talk about it; the story could not be hidden. Who would want to buy from a company accused of secretly manipulating, even brainwashing, its customers?

LEGAL ISSUES RELATED TO MARKETING COMMUNICATION

Public opinion or a marketing manager's opinion may not be enough to determine what is and is not appropriate in marketing communication. Most societies feel that the threat posed by inappropriate or misleading commercial messages is serious enough to warrant the enactment of laws regulating messages and imposing penalties for violations of those laws. In fact, every form of commercial communication in the United States is affected in some way by regulations and watchdog groups that seek to protect consumers and businesses.

Several industry organizations and governmental agencies monitor commercial messages (they are described later in this chapter). They are called on to distinguish between acceptable persuasion, questionable sales pitches, and outright fraud. Responses range from tolerating the messages, to recommending changes, to taking legal action. The following sections discuss the types of legal issues marketers face and describe watchdog organizations' and government agencies' responses to illegal practices.

Commercial Free Speech

The First Amendment of the U.S. Constitution protects free speech, but not until the 1970s was the concept of free speech applied to commercial speech such as advertising. An international cause championed by the International Advertising Association (www.iaaglobal.org), the idea that commercial speech is protected under the First Amendment has its detractors, primarily among groups critical of global marketing and trade, such as ReclaimDemocracy.org and Corpwatch.org.

Commercial free speech, however, is not as "free" as noncommercial speech. For example, a state can regulate advertising for products that are illegal in that state, such as gambling, prostitution, or lotteries. The government also reserves the right to regulate against what it considers to be unfair business practices. In some cases, such as comparative advertising, the regulations extend to advertising. Even signage is regulated, as a restaurant in Kennebunk, Maine, found out when a town official asked the restaurant to cover up the Hebrew National Beef Franks logo on the umbrellas on the restaurant's outdoor patio (see Exhibit 20-10). The local ordinance said that restaurants are limited to three signs. The umbrellas, however, had been in place for more than 20 years advertising Budweiser, Poland Spring, Sam Adams, Coca-Cola, and other products, so the owner brought a lawsuit against the town, charging the questionable restriction limited his right to commercial freedom of speech.[24]

The government also regulates the promotion of categories of products whose manufacture is regulated, such as food products and pharmaceuticals. This area currently generates much debate. The Supreme Court in the early 2000s was split about the amount of regulation necessary; at the same time, the food and drug industries were pushing the Food and Drug Administration to loosen up on FDA restrictions. Pharmaceutical companies, for example, want to see the FDA drop a rule that requires drug makers to list possible side effects in pages of small print in magazine ads. They also want to be able to promote drug uses that have been proven to be effective even if they aren't what the drug was designed to do, a practice called "off-label" promotion. Even press releases that report "encouraging" or "promising" research results for new drugs have been banned by the FDA.[25]

Consumer groups, in contrast, say pharmaceutical promotion—and advertising for prescription drugs in particular—has already gone too far. They point, for example, to a promotion that mailed the prescription drug Prozac to people in southern Florida who didn't ask for it and may not have had a prescription for it.[26] And, as patients become more insistent in asking for expensive brand-name drugs that they have seen advertised,[27] there is the criticism that drug ads are driving up medical costs.

In all cases, however, marketing communication that makes claims about a product's performance must be truthful and not misleading. The Supreme Court uses a two-prong test to determine whether advertising is deceptive: a claim must be factually truthful, and it must be substantiated.[28] If a toothpaste manufacturer says its brand protects teeth from tooth decay, for example, the manufacturer must have on hand valid and reliable research supporting that claim. The FTC policy states: "Many ads contain express or implied statements regarding the amount of support the advertiser has for the product claim. When the substantiation claim is expressed (e.g., 'tests prove,' 'doctors recommend,' and 'studies show'), the Commission expects the firm to have at least the advertised level of substantiation."[29] If substantiation has not been obtained *before* a claim is made, a company is subject to legal action.

Misleading Claims

Although commercial free speech is protected, to a certain extent, by the First Amendment, deceptive commercial speech is not. Factual claims in marketing communication are subject to testing and liable for prosecution if they are determined to be false or misleading. Deceptive advertising has been the focus of many industry and government review actions over the years. According to the FTC's policy statement on deception, "the [Federal Trade] Commission will find deception if there is a representation, omission or practice that is likely to mislead the consumer acting reasonably in the circumstances, to the consumer's detriment."[30]

Generating deliberate consumer confusion is one aspect of deception. In a television commercial called "Mr. Quackers," Duracell promised that its Duracell Coppertop brand would keep its robotic duck quacking long after the other robotic contestants in a "Robotic Fight Club," which were powered by "heavy duty" batteries, failed. The claim was technically correct, but what the ad failed to say was that *all* alkaline batteries—including the Energizers that power the legendary bunny—perform better than the old-fashioned zinc "heavy duty" batteries. Although Energizer wasn't mentioned explicitly in the Duracell commercial, Energizer asked regulators to ban the Duracell ad as "false and misleading" because consumers understood the comparison to be against all other batteries, including Energizer's alkaline batteries. Energizer won, and Duracell had to modify its ad by adding the phrase "excluding alkaline batteries."[31]

Dubious health claims are particularly troublesome. To put a stop to such claims, rival marketers often turn to the National Advertising Review Council (NARC). NARC investigates disputed claims, provides recommendations to the offending companies, and makes its findings public. But it does not fine companies, and compliance by companies is voluntary. NARC gets most of its cases from companies, not from consumers. The number of health-based claims has risen substantially in the past few years, spurred by the increase in prescription-drug marketing. Unlike NARC, the Federal Trade Commission can fine offending companies and seek refunds for customers. Due to the understaffing of the agency, however, the FTC relies on NARC to filter out many potential offenders.[32]

The FTC considers marketing communication deceptive if messages mislead "reasonable consumers" to such an extent that their buying decisions are influenced—that is, they base a decision on deceptive or confusing information. In other words, both explicit and implicit claims must be substantiated. A good example of implicit claims are those that were used by Publishers Clearing House (a direct-marketing company that sells magazine subscriptions) to mislead people (see Exhibit 20-7). Personalized letters that contained phrases such as "winners confirmation form enclosed" and "PCH final notification for tax-free $11,700,000.00 SUPERPRIZE," along with the return address of PCH's "Payments and Disbursements," convinced many recipients that they were winners or could be winners if they bought a bunch of magazines. These misleading messages prompted so many complaints that several dozen state attorneys general filed suit against PCH and eventually won a multimillion-dollar settlement and a promise from PCH to refrain from future use of these practices. When brand messages are found to be deceptive, the offending advertiser is forced to stop the advertising or revise the message, as happened with Duracell. In some cases companies making deceptive claims are subject to fines.

In the last few years juries in several cases have awarded substantial settlements to consumers for questioning potentially false or misleading marketing claims. One example is a case against Ford Motor Company for promoting the Bronco II as "suitable to contemporary life styles" and "appealing to women who may be concerned about driving in snow and ice with their children" yet manufacturing the truck so that it had, among other things, a high center of gravity making it unstable. The commonality in all the cases is "a gap between the product as advertised and marketed and the product as it actually is." Court rulings make it clear that companies would be wise to first show advertisements and marketing campaigns to legal counsel to make sure that the claims don't go too far and leave the company open to liability.[33]

Puffery

Brand messages that are unclear or subject to interpretation are more difficult to regulate. Calling a product the "finest" may be an exaggeration that cannot be proved, but the use of such words is rarely challenged because it is considered to be a legal form of boasting called puffery (see Exhibit 20-11). **Puffery** is *the use of hyperbole or exaggeration to promote a brand*. The Uniform Commercial Code of 1996 maintains that such hype is acceptable—even if it's a lie—unless a buyer can show that such language *was intended* to be interpreted as a fact or a promise.

Wal-Mart, for example, used a tag line that flunked the puffery test. Competitors claimed that Wal-Mart's slogan "Always the low price. Always" implied that Wal-Mart had the *lowest* prices of all retailers. The National Advertising Division of the Council of Better Business Bureaus reviewed the ad and deemed it misleading. Wal-Mart lost an appeal and changed its slogan to "Always low prices. Always Wal-Mart."[34] Why is puffery allowed? The government, and much of the industry, believe that most consumers know that boastful statements by advertisers are harmless exaggerations. Some experts, such as Ivan Preston, disagree and argue that even though the law presumes that people do not believe puffery, research repeatedly finds that consumers actually do believe these claims are true.

EXHIBIT 20-11
Consider this ad for a deodorant. What claims is it making? Is it using puffery? Is it acceptable?

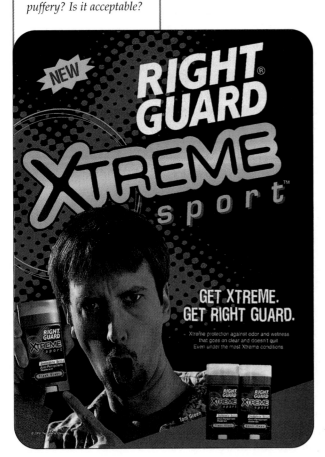

Questionable Business-to-Business Practices

Retailers often charge slotting allowances (⬅ Chapter 15). Some also charge display fees for certain shelf locations (items sitting at eye level are more likely to sell than those displayed higher or lower). Over the years these allowances and fees have escalated so much that small companies cannot afford them. According to an article in the *Journal of Marketing*, "Currently, two schools of thought dominate the debate on these fees. One considers them a tool for improving distribution efficiency, whereas the other proposes that the fees operate as a mechanism for enhancing market power and damaging competition. Managers and public policymakers are uncertain as to the effects of slotting fees and the appropriate strategy to adopt [regarding their use]."[35]

Another example of questionable practices comes from the pharmaceutical industry. Drug manufacturers invite doctors to "continuing education" classes and seminars that sometimes look more like junkets to fancy resorts, golf outings, or cruises. Sales representatives have long provided doctors with product and health information that critics say is too biased toward the sale of the products the reps are selling. Sales reps also provide gifts that some consider to be little more than bribes. Although sales reps play an important role in continuing to inform doctors about advances in the pharmaceutical industry, the question is how best to do the promotion without unduly influencing doctors' decisions on appropriate medical care.

Fraud

More serious in the universe of bad marketing communication practices than any of the previously described questionable tactics is outright fraud at either the consumer or the B2B level. Generally, government agencies aggressively pursue companies that knowingly mislead the public. Companies that have no track record of providing legitimate goods and services are also targeted. Companies engaging in fraud face criminal penalties. One of the most common types of MC fraud is the selling of brand knockoffs—goods that carry a popular brand name but are made by another company and generally are of lesser quality than the brand that has been counterfeited. Most likely to be counterfeited are products that are widely used, such as drugs, cigarettes, sneakers, perfume, and even golf clubs. The International Chamber of Commerce estimates that approximately $375 billion worth of counterfeit goods are sold each year, 8 percent of the world trade.[36]

A widely used advertising fraud is the bait-and-switch offer. An example is advertising a car (the bait) at a very low price, telling prospects who express an interest in it that the advertised car was sold and then showing prospects other, higher priced models (the switch). According to FTC's "Guidelines against Bait Advertising," "No advertisement containing an offer to sell a product should be published when the offer is not a bona fide effort to sell the advertised product."[37]

REGULATORY METHODS AND AGENCIES

A number of different organizations deal with questionable marketing communication messages and practices, including industry self-regulation and government oversight bodies. The following list gives the websites of major organizations and government bodies that set standards and regulations for commercial speech:

ETHICS AND ISSUES

When Is a Puff Not a Puff?

A major two-year government study of diet ads found that many are fake. The study challenged claims made about apple pectin, for example, saying it isn't really an "energized enzyme that can ingest up to 900 times it's [sic] own weight in fat," as ads claimed.

Dubbed "Operation Waistline," the study found that at least 40 percent of the ads for weight-loss products "make at least one representation that is almost certainly false." The study resulted in a series of letters to publications warning them about running ads with false claims—letters that apparently most media chose to ignore, believing that the public already understands that diet pills don't work. And therein lies the problem with puffery.

Technically the diet ads are in violation of deceptive advertising laws. However, they are dismissed by the media because the claims are considered to be so obviously far-fetched that most people can see through them. Some experts disagree and point to research that has found that consumers assume there are facts behind the boasts of puffery.

Ivan Preston, an expert on advertising law, identifies several categories of puffery. Some puffery is simply boasting, which can be legal. Other types of puffery imply claims that, if tested by consumer research, would prove to be deceptive. The problem lies with implied meanings. As Preston says, "Consumers sometimes may not see the falsity as obvious and so possibly take the claim seriously."

Preston, whom the *Wall Street Journal* wryly described in an interview as "the world's greatest expert on 'pure baloney' in advertising," makes the point that any statement based on claims of "better" or "best," though currently allowed by the law, may mislead consumers into believing that a product is better than competitors.

The better/best issue was raised in a legal battle between Papa John's and Pizza Hut. For several years, Papa John's had used the slogan "Better Ingredients, Better Pizza." The puffery crossed the line, however, when Papa John's used the slogan in a commercial that mentioned competitor Pizza Hut. The issue was brought to court. The judge ruled that because the mention of Pizza Hut created a "context," the slogan became an indirect comparison that could not be substantiated and therefore was deceptive.

In an Adforum listserv chat following Preston's interview in the *Wall Street Journal*, one participant with extensive professional experience dismissed Preston's concerns, saying, "It is to be expected that advertisers will make every effort to put the best face possible on the goods and services they offer." He concluded, "short of factually deceptive claims, which I deplore, puffery is the essence of much advertising and is, in my view, perfectly acceptable."

Think About It

What do you think? Should puffery be allowed, or should it be regulated? Is it realistic to assume that consumers see puffery as boasting rather than based on fact? Should claims of "better" and "best" be dealt with differently than exaggerations such as "the finest"? Is puffery, in fact, the essence of advertising?

Source: Joel Stein, "Miracle-Diet Ads Lie? Well, Duh!" *Time,* September 30, 2002, p. 106; Ivan Preston, "A Problem Ignored: Dilution and Negation of Consumer Information by Antifactual Content," *Journal of Consumer Affairs* 36, no. 2 (Winter 2002), pp. 263–83; comments to Adforum listserv by Ivan Preston, Dick Weitz, and Herb Rotfeld, December 31, 2002–February 3, 2003.

Consumer-Protection Websites

Federal Trade Commission	*www.ftc.gov*
FTC "Report on Privacy"	*www.ftc.gov/reports/privacy3/toc.htm*
Online Privacy Alliance	*www.privacyalliance.org*
Commerce Department	*www.doc.gov*
Center for Media Education	*www.cme.org*
Direct Marketing Association	*www.the-dma.org*
Better Business Bureau	*www.bbb.org*

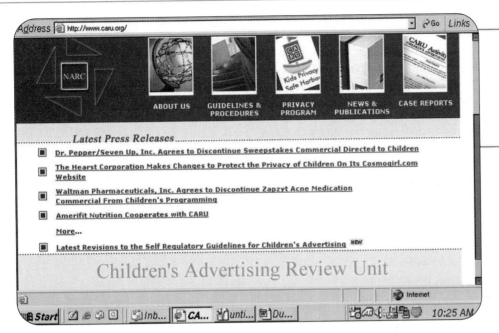

Center for Democracy and Technology	*www.cdt.org*
Electronic Privacy Information Center	*www.epic.org*
TRUSTe	*www.truste.org*
ConsumerAffairs.com	*www.consumeraffairs.com*

In particular, the consumer affairs site at www.consumeraffairs.com is a useful independent source of consumer news, advocacy, and assistance. It provides a form for filing a complaint—that is, a consumer incident report. If you fill out the form, ConsumerAffairs.com will pass your name to legal firms that may contact you about legal actions you might take. Marketing managers should be aware that such sites exist and that there are people monitoring corporate behavior—people who can make life difficult for a company (see Exhibit 20-12).

Self-Regulation

Most of the oversight within the marketing communication industry is handled through self-regulation rather than by government order. It is in the best interest of responsible businesses and trade organizations to maintain high standards, for several reasons. First, the more they do so, the less government interference there should be. Second, industries know from past experience that a few disreputable companies can create suspicion of an entire industry. Finally, the few companies that do not play by the rules may have an unfair competitive advantage, but only in the short term.

Self-regulation occurs by means of a company's own policies, an industry's own standards, and a review of the media delivering brand messages.

Internal Policies

Most companies, marketing communication agencies, and media—not to mention industry associations—have their own professional standards that are used for self-regulating what they do. These standards provide guidelines so employees understand what kinds of messages and interactions with customers are and are not acceptable.

Although marketing communicators are not expected to be lawyers, they should know enough about the laws and government regulations to ask for a legal opinion when programs and practices may have even the slightest chance of being in violation. Most medium and large companies have legal staffs who should be made aware of major marketing communication programs, especially anything new and different. People working in companies without a legal department must make their supervisors aware of anything out of the ordinary that could be in violation. More than one person has lost a marketing job for failure to get legal advice before initiating a program that turned out to be illegal and resulted in negative publicity and costly reputation repairs.

MC agencies sometimes refuse to accept work from certain companies, such as tobacco companies. For the work they do accept, media companies may demand proof of claims, for the agencies themselves are responsible for verifying any claims made by their clients before using those claims in brand messages. Before being distributed publicly, the messages are usually reviewed by agency lawyers. When a claim is found to be misleading, everyone involved—the company making the claim, the agency that produced the ad, and the media running the ad—can face penalties.

Industry Standards

National trade organizations establish guidelines for their members. For example, the Distilled Spirits Council agreed to keep liquor advertising off radio beginning in 1936 and off TV beginning in 1948 (recently some liquor companies started to deviate from that policy). Doctors and lawyers did not advertise until some members challenged the bans enforced by the American Medical Association and the American Bar Association.

Several advertising trade organizations (the American Association of Advertising Agencies, the American Advertising Federation, and the Association of National Advertisers) have their own practice guidelines for their members. More important, they have united to create monitoring groups to deal with questionable advertising practices.

Although many members of trade groups welcome restrictions on marketing tactics as a way to maintain professional standards, some argue that such restrictions are simply a way to preserve the status quo and prevent newcomers from gaining a foothold in the marketplace. And some critics say that the only reason why trade organizations develop codes is to head off government regulations. The Better Business Bureau's Children's Advertising Review Unit (CARU), for example, was set up in reaction to public criticism and government hearings about potential restrictions on advertising to children.[38] As it turned out, however, Congress was not satisfied with industry self-regulation and in 1991 passed limits on televised child-oriented advertising. Table 20-1 summarizes the organizations that are involved in industry self-regulation.

Media Review

The magazine and newspaper trade associations have not set forth advertising guidelines for their members. However, individual media chains and local media outlets often set standards for advertising. Newspapers are more likely than other media to keep out ads that they believe their readers and advertisers might find objectionable.[39] A survey of 321 newspapers found that more than 71 percent asked for verification or substantiation of ad claims.[40] This same survey also indicated that, while 40 percent had a written policy outlining the types of ads they would accept or reject, many chose not to give any such explanations for fear of lawsuits. Rather, they inform advertisers that they reserve the right to reject any advertising. A survey of 184 magazines indicated they were most concerned about "good taste," which generally meant rejecting ads with sexual explicitness.[41]

For the most part, radio and television broadcasters have been highly active in self-regulation. In one area, the U.S. government said that broadcasters actually went too far. The National Association of Broadcasters (NAB) several decades ago

T A B L E   2 0 - 1   Industry Self-Regulation

Organization	Description
Better Business Bureau (BBB)	This well-known national business organization with local chapters keeps files on violators of good business practices and makes these available to the public. Its BBB Code provides guidelines for ethical and responsible advertising, and its monthly publication, *Do's and Don'ts in Advertising Copy*, alerts subscribers to developments in advertising regulations and recent court rulings.
BBB's Children's Advertising Review Unit (CARU)	This unit of the BBB sets forth voluntary television advertising guidelines for makers of children's products.
National Advertising Review Council (NARC)	This organization was established by the Council of Better Business Bureaus and three different ad groups to promote and enforce standards of trust, accuracy, taste, morality, and social responsibility in advertising.
National Advertising Division (NAD)	This is the division of the NARC that monitors advertising and reviews complaints from consumers, consumer groups, competitors, local BBBs, trade associations, and others. Once presented with a complaint, it investigates the issue and asks for claim substantiation, if warranted. Where necessary, it will recommend that the advertiser change the questionable advertising. If the advertiser disagrees with the recommendation, the case can be appealed to the National Advertising Review Board. Since 1973, the NAD has looked at approximately 34,000 cases. As of 1997, only 25 of the advertisers had not agreed to abide by its decisions.
National Advertising Review Board (NARB)	This is the appeals board for NAD decisions. It becomes involved if the advertiser does not want to comply with the NAD recommendations. The NARB panel's decision is final. If the advertiser still does not want to comply, the case is referred to the appropriate government agency.

developed a code for television and radio advertising. One of the guidelines, for example, prevented lingerie commercials from using live models. In 1982, the U.S. Justice Department sued the NAB under antitrust laws.

Government Oversight

Many federal agencies have jurisdiction over one or more aspects of marketing communication. There are so many potential pitfalls in this area that marketers must know the limits of their own expertise and be prepared to consult with people who specialize in keeping up with government rules and regulations. Table 20-2 lists the major federal regulatory agencies in the United States that are involved with marketing communication.

Federal Trade Commission (FTC)

The Federal Trade Commission (see Exhibit 20-13), created by and directly responsible to Congress, has five members, who are appointed by the president and confirmed by the Senate. Since 1914, it has been responsible for regulating interstate commerce and dealing with "unfair trade practices." Recognizing that advertising practices vary by product category, the FTC has established specific guidelines for brand messages in 35 different categories from jewelry to pet products. When there is a problem, the FTC has several tools at its disposal:

- *Affirmative disclosure:* **Affirmative disclosure** is *the FTC requirement that a company provide in its advertising certain information to outline product limitations or conditions.*

TABLE 20-2   Federal Regulatory Agencies Involved with MC

Agency	Description
Federal Trade Commission (FTC)	Charged with monitoring "unfair trade practices," the FTC regulates marketing communication for products sold through interstate commerce.
Federal Communications Commission (FCC)	The FCC oversees the radio, television, telephone, internet, and telegraph industries.
Food and Drug Administration (FDA)	The FDA oversees labeling, packaging, branding, and advertising of packaged foods, medicine (including package inserts and product advertising), and medical devices. The Nutritional Labeling and Education Act established rules for food labels and the use of such terms as *fat free*, *low fat*, *light*, *reduced calories*, and *natural*.
United States Postal Service (USPS)	The USPS has jurisdiction over advertising and promotional messages sent through the U.S. mail. A staff is maintained to review magazines and other publications for deceptive or misleading advertising. The focus has been on health-related products, sweepstakes and game promotions, and pornography.
Bureau of Alcohol, Tobacco, and Firearms (BATF)	The BATF is a branch of the Treasury Department that oversees alcohol, tobacco, and firearm advertising and beer and wine labeling.
Patent and Trademark Office	This office becomes involved in cases involving unauthorized use of trademarks and logos.
U.S. Department of Agriculture	This cabinet-level department's responsibilities include overseeing meat and poultry labeling, and seed and insecticide advertising.
U.S. Department of Transportation (DOT)	The DOT is a cabinet-level department with responsibilities that include overseeing airline advertising and promotions (such as frequent-flyer programs).
U.S. Treasury Department	This cabinet-level department oversees advertising related to currency, coins, and U.S. government bonds.
U.S. Labor Department	This cabinet-level department oversees advertising related to employers and unions.
Securities and Exchange Commission (SEC)	The SEC regulates marketing communication dealing with securities (such as stocks, bonds, mutual funds) and communication to the financial community.
Consumer Products Safety Commission	This government agency can call for corrective advertising for defective products.
Environmental Protection Agency (EPA)	The EPA's responsibilities include defining terms used in "green" advertising and regulating the advertising and labeling of lawn-care chemicals.

- *Advertising substantiation:* **Advertising substantiation** is *the FTC requirement that a company show documentation if there are any challenges to the company's use of safety, performance, efficacy, quality, or competitive price claims.*
- *Consent and cease-and-desist orders:* The FTC can caution a company about questionable advertising. If the company agrees to stop using the ads in question, it signs a *consent order.* If it does not agree, the FTC can issue a **cease-and-desist order,** which is *a demand to stop using the message in question.* In 1995 the FTC ordered New Balance Athletic Shoe company (and all its agencies) to "cease and desist from misrepresenting, in any manner, directly or by implication: That footwear made wholly abroad is made in

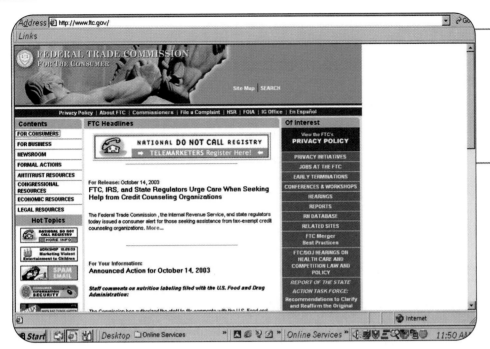

EXHIBIT 20-13
*The Federal Trade
Commission is the primary
government agency
regulating advertising and
other marketing
communication practices.*

the United States."[42] Companies not obeying a cease-and-desist order are subject to civil suits.

- *Corrective advertising:* **Corrective advertising,** is *the FTC requirement that a company must spend a certain percentage of its advertising budget to correct previous false advertising by running advertising explaining that earlier messages were misleading or false.* Corrective advertising is required not only to correct misinformation, but also to punish companies by forcing them to spend money on this effort. In addition, corrective advertising makes public the fact a company has been less than truthful in its brand messages, which does little for its brand image and reputation.

In addition to overseeing advertising, the FTC has issued guidelines concerning coupons, warranties, and sweepstakes. Companies may not run lotteries, which are considered a form of gambling. A promotion would be a lottery if it required "consideration"—if a consumer had to buy something to enter. To get around this rule, companies allow customers to enter a sweepstakes by sending in a card on which they have written the brand's name.

Patent and Trademark Office

The value of a brand—brand equity—is increased when the brand's trademark has been registered (◄ Chapter 3). Attaching a trademark symbol to a brand name or logo is an indication that this is the company or brand's identity. The first company to actively use a name or symbol as an identity mark is generally considered to "own" that mark. Registering a trademark with the Patent and Trademark Office, however, gives a company much more legal protection to exclusively use the mark. Before a name or symbol is registered, a search is made to be sure the mark has not been registered by another company. The symbol ® is a reminder (and warning to those considering using a mark for their own purposes) that the word, phrase, or symbol is legally registered by a company for its *exclusive* use.

Without exclusivity of use, a trademark can lose much of its brand equity. When there is trademark infringement, the owner of the registered trademark can go to court and ask that the court demand that the other company quit using the trademark. The owner can also sue for trademark infringement, because confusion over ownership of a brand obviously damages brand equity. Trademarks are protected through the Lanham Trade-Mark Act of 1947 and updated by a revision of this act in 1988.

Trademarks, service marks, and certification marks can all be protected in the United States. According to David Weinstein, an intellectual property lawyer, the easiest mark to protect legally is one that is a "word, picture, or symbol that conveys little or no information about the nature or features of the products or services with which it is used." Because such a mark is "inherently distinctive," it has a "broader scope of protection than a mark that conveys information or is commonly used."[43] It is advantageous to apply for federal registration as soon as possible in order to thoroughly protect a trademark.

State and Local Regulations

Many state and local governments have agencies that oversee marketing communication within their respective geographical jurisdictions. The National Association of Attorneys General has been particularly proactive in recent years, going after large corporations that individuals and even the federal government cannot afford to fight. Attorneys general from 40 states sued the department store chain Sears, for example, for using misleading tactics to secure payments from bankrupt customers. Fifty attorneys general also sued Zeneca, a British chemicals manufacturer, because the company was using cash rebates connected to price fixing on farm chemicals.

Foreign Regulations

Each country has its own laws concerning commercial messages, and government bodies that enforce such laws. In Quebec, Canada, labels have to be in both French and English because a major portion of the Quebec population is French-speaking. In Puerto Rico, rules for promotions have to be in Spanish as well as English; they also have to be printed in at least one general-circulation newspaper once a week during the promotion; and a notary must be present during the drawing for a prize. In France, alcohol and tobacco advertising is prohibited. That is why Budweiser, a sponsor of the 1998 World Cup, was not allowed to have signs in the stadiums where the soccer matches were held.

One of the responsibilities of the EU (European Union) is to regulate trade practices among member countries. This government body sets standards and lowers trade barriers so that Europe can act as a single continental trading entity, much like the United States. A major topic of debate in the EU, as in the United States, is restrictions on marketing communication.

Companies advertising internationally and on the internet are also subject to foreign regulations. When Virgin Airlines, a British company, advertised prices for its fare between Newark, New Jersey, and London, England, it did not disclose that a $38.91 tax would be added. Although this advertising may have been legal in Britain, the U.S. Department of Transportation fined Virgin $14,000 for the violation.

Consumer Groups

A myriad of special-interest advocacy groups monitor commercial messages related to their causes. They often take their complaints public and organize boycotts when they deem it necessary. Although they have no legal powers, they can pressure companies to change their marketing communication practices.

The Center for Science in the Public Interest is a nonprofit group that monitors the food industry. In 1995, it urged the U.S. Food and Drug Administration to

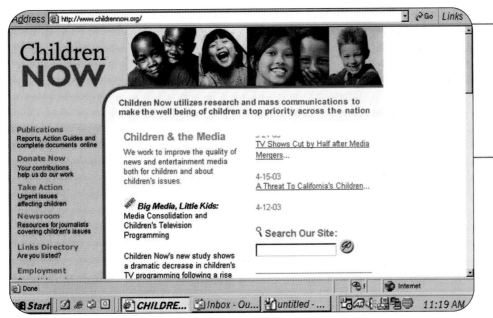

EXHIBIT 20-14
*Children Now's primary
objective is to increase
educational programming
for children on TV. In this
way it is an indirect
"regulator" of TV content.*

revise its food labeling rules. Two examples: General Mills' Berry Berry Kix was deemed mislabeled because the cereal contained no berries and only a minimal amount of fruit products of any kind. The same company's Crispy Wheats 'n Raisins was billed on the package as "lightly sweetened, honey-touched whole wheat flakes and raisins," but the list of ingredients indicated that the cereal was 20 percent sugar by weight.[44]

Action for Children's Television (ACT) was another powerful consumer group. Fortified with grants from major foundations over the years, this group was ultimately responsible for the passage of the Children's Television Act in 1990, which began putting pressure on TV stations to do more educational programming for children. Although ACT was dissolved shortly after this accomplishment—the leaders said it was time for others to do this work—ACT's mission is being carried on by Children Now, found online at www.childrennow.org (see Exhibit 20-14).

MARKETING COMMUNICATION RESPONSIBILITIES

Managing the social, ethical, and legal aspects of marketing communication is a complex task. MC managers need a general understanding of what they can and cannot do from a legal perspective, as well as what they should and should not do from an ethical perspective. They also need to know where to go for expert advice, and they should have some idea about what to do when conflicts arise.

Approval Processes

To minimize legal and other challenges to brand messages requires an approval process with several message checkpoints. The approval steps vary by company, but in large organizations the process generally includes the following steps:

1. Review by the marketing staff.
2. Review by the public relations department from the perspectives of stakeholders other than customers. Are the messages inconsistent with the social, moral, and cultural standards of these other audiences?

3. Copytesting, not only for communication and persuasion but for unintended messages.

4. Review by internal and (in the case of major campaigns) by external legal counsel.

5. Review by the MC agency account team and agency lawyers.

6. Review by the media.

Dealing with Corporate Ethics

To practice ethical behavior, MC professionals must work in an environment where such behavior is encouraged and supported. Not all companies give such encouragement or support; too often, companies do the opposite. A company trying to meet certain financial goals may be tempted to cut corners when testing or labeling ingredients, honoring warranties, and providing the promised after-market service. These companies might also allow (or force) marketing communicators to overpromise in order to increase short-term sales.

All companies should have an ethics statement, and new employees should expect to see it. Lack of an ethics policy may be a red flag alerting a new hire of potential problems in the MC program. Like a crisis plan, an ethics statement should be clearly spelled out and discussed. Problems within the company and incidents outside the company should be used as examples to clarify what is expected of employees. Some companies conduct periodic ethics audits to encourage awareness of various issues that the company is currently facing or might face.

An ethics statement can offer some protection to employees who are being pressured (by middle management) to engage in behavior that the employees believe is wrong. If such behavior has already been identified as unacceptable, the employee can point to the official policy as a reason to refuse to cooperate.

Social Marketing

Some social groups continually criticize marketing communication practices, but others—such as anticigarette and antidrug groups—embrace MC and use it to promote social causes. The same persuasive practices designed to sell products and build brand relationships can be used to help solve social problems or advocate a social-responsible position (see Exhibit 20-15). Public relations expert Bill Novelli, who is president of the Campaign for Tobacco-Free Kids, has said, "[Problem-solving] is what marketing does, because it is a process that forges a close relationship among strategies, audience, and behaviors."[45] The *use of marketing to address societal problems* is called **social marketing.**

Social marketing has proved successful in many cases. Thailand dramatically reduced the number of men becoming infected by HIV (the virus that causes AIDS) by encouraging them to use condoms and reduce their visits to prostitutes. Two years after the government-funded campaign began, the frequency of HIV infection in military recruits had dropped fivefold and the frequency of other sexually transmitted diseases had decreased tenfold.[46]

Social marketing is not without controversy, however. Antidrug campaigns, for example, have been criticized for targeting the wrong problems (focusing on illegal drugs rather than on alcohol abuse); for glamorizing drug use (by combining attractive actors and actresses with violent images); and wasting taxpayer money (by having no effect or, worse, being counterproductive). In 1998, Congress approved an initial budget of $195 million to be spent on antidrug messages on/in television, radio, print, billboard, and interactive media. Said Thomas A. Hedrick, vice chairman of the Partnership for a Drug-Free America, "For the first time we will be able to buy the time slots in the best media vehicles, just like Nike or

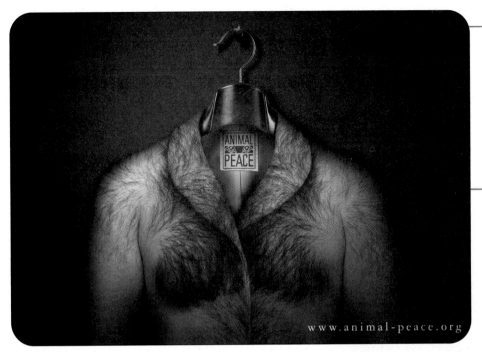

McDonald's or Pepsi does on a regular basis." But Ethan Nadelmann, director of the Lindesmith Center, a drug policy research organization, countered, "For the past 10 years, our nation's kids have been bombarded with anti-drug messages, and it is these same kids who are experimenting with more drugs. While these ads are well intended, this money could be better spent on programs that are proven effective in reducing drug use, such as after-school programs and treatment on demand."[47]

A FINAL NOTE: IS IT THE MESSAGE OR THE MESSENGER?

The critics are right in some ways: marketing communication can be used to promote stereotypes, target vulnerable populations, and use offensive message strategies to sell products. Brand messages can also be misleading and be used to manipulate and deceive consumers. But marketing communication is also a set of tools that can be used for promoting social issues and public debate, as well as for selling soap and soft drinks. Even the promotion of products can contribute in a positive way to social improvement. Selling toothpaste, for example, has cut back dramatically on tooth decay, and selling soap has created higher levels of hygiene around the world. And Apple's promotional efforts have brought computer literacy to technophobic adults, as well as to schoolchildren whose families could never afford computers.

Furthermore, in a broader context, marketing communication enables the vital exchange of commercial information that makes the economy grow, providing jobs and paychecks as well as an astounding range of product choices. MC itself is not inherently good or bad; it is only the messenger. And the message can contribute to social good as easily as it contributes to social problems.

Key Terms

advertising substantiation 656
affirmative disclosure 655
cease-and-desist order 656

corrective advertising 657
ethics 641
puffery 650

social marketing 660
subliminal advertising 646

Key Point Summary

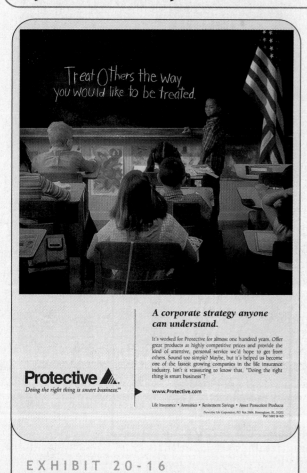

Treat Others the way you would like to be treated.

A corporate strategy anyone can understand.

It's worked for Protective for almost one hundred years. Offer great products at highly competitive prices and provide the kind of attentive, personal service we'd hope to get from others. Sound too simple? Maybe, but it's helped us become one of the fastest growing companies in the life insurance industry. Isn't it reassuring to know that, "Doing the right thing is smart business"?

Protective ▲.
Doing the right thing is smart business.™

www.Protective.com

Life Insurance • Annuities • Retirement Savings • Asset Protection Products
Protective Life Corporation, P.O. Box 2606, Birmingham, AL 35202
PLC-5502 (8-02)

EXHIBIT 20-16

The Protective life insurance company uses this ad to explain why social responsibility is an important corporate philosophy.

Key Point 1: Role in Society

A major debate about marketing communication and its influence on consumers lies in the question of whether it shapes or mirrors consumer opinions and behaviors. Other criticisms center on perceptions of economic, social, or cultural damage created by marketing communication.

Key Point 2: Ethical Issues

Certain standards of right and wrong are applied to commercial messages. Ethical issues include stereotyping, targeting unhealthy products to vulnerable groups, using offensive messages, and manipulating consumers.

Key Point 3: Legal Issues

Marketing communication's primary legal challenges are in the areas of false, incomplete, misleading, and unfair messages. Questionable tactics include practicing bait-and-switch and burying important details in small print. Competitive challenges come from brand and package infringement and pricing promotions. Fraud is the most serious legal issue.

Key Point 4: Regulation

Most MC industries, companies, and media willingly police themselves for potential ethical lapses so that they can maintain high standards and avoid the involvement of government agencies. Markets must comply with an exhaustive number of government rules and regulations at the local, state, national, and international levels. Although no one can know all the rules, each MC planner should know which government body's oversight responsibility is important to the brand and when to seek expert advice.

Lessons Learned

Key Point 1: Role in Society

a. Why is marketing communication a more socially responsible platform than advertising?
b. Explain the two points of view represented in the shape or mirror debate.
c. Choose one of the concerns about MC that you either agree with or disagree with, and research it. Write a two-page report on your findings.
d. Consider the advertiser censorship issue identified in the opening case. Is it fair for advertisers to expect to receive favorable coverage in return for their financial support of the media through advertising? Should editors consider the possible negative response of advertisers or other influential people when making a decision about whether to run a story?

Key Point 2: Ethical Issues

a. How would you define *ethics?*
b. What are sensitive areas in marketing communication? Do you think MC shapes society or mirrors it? Explain your answer.
c. Find an example of a marketing message that offends you or someone you know. Explain why the message seems offensive.
d. Find five examples of cigarette marketing communication, and list the messages they appear to be sending and to whom. What ethical concerns do they raise, if any?
e. Find an example of a social marketing campaign, and analyze how it relates to various stakeholder groups.

Key Point 3: Legal Issues

a. What is the NAD?
b. How do puffery and fraud differ?
c. Find an example of a false or misleading piece of marketing communication, and explain why you believe it has problems.
d. How and in what areas do competitors get involved in challenging a brand's communication?
e. What is your position on commercial free speech? Visit the sites of the International Advertising Association (www.iaaglobal.org) and its critics (www.corpwatch.org) and (www.ReclaimDemocracy.org). Then develop a two-page position statement that outlines the arguments for and against commercial free speech and concludes with your position.

Key Point 4: Regulation

a. What is the main federal agency overseeing advertising in the United States?
b. What is the difference between the FTC's and the FCC's oversight responsibilities for marketing communication in the United States?
c. What is the role of your state's attorney general in overseeing marketing communication?
d. You are planning to launch a new soft drink, first in the United States and then in Europe. List as many regulatory agencies as you can that might factor into the launch, and explain their involvement with this launch.

Chapter Challenge

Writing Assignment

You are the marketing director of a large real-estate company that spends over $1 million a year on advertising in your local metropolitan newspaper. You have just gotten word that the paper is planning a series of investigative articles on the misleading practices used by some real-estate brokers. The story will mention two brokers who work for you, whom you had already disciplined for their out-of-line practices. You thought the matter was taken care of, but it is going to be made public and create an extremely negative impression of your company. You know you have "a million dollars' worth of clout" with the newspaper. You would like to kill any negative reference to your company, but you realize that the newspaper has a social responsibility to its readers. Write a letter to the editor laying out what you would like the paper to do and why.

Presentation Assignment

Pretend you are president of an ad agency who is concerned about your creative department using exploitive illustrations of men and women. Prepare a presentation, using both good and bad examples, that demonstrate what is, and what is not, in good taste and acceptable to do.

Internet Assignment

Visit Junkbusters.com, Epic.org, Privacycouncil.com, and Webwasher.com to determine what they advise you to do about the social, ethical, and legal issues associated with e-commerce.

Chapter 21

International Marketing Communication

ALL THE WORLD LOVES A *Coca-Cola*.

Key Points in This Chapter

1. How is international marketing different from global marketing?
2. How does culture affect marketing communication strategies?
3. How are international markets segmented and targeted?
4. How do marketers plan international message and media strategies?

Chapter Perspective

Marketing to the World

Businesses are experiencing phenomenal opportunities to expand internationally. The ease of doing so, however, depends on which countries they choose to enter, what products they are selling, and what methods they choose to build brand relationships. International marketers face many challenges related to different cultures, languages, and levels of economic development. Adapting brand messages while at the same time maintaining strategic brand consistency requires a delicate balance. Cross-functional planning becomes all the more important when brand messages are being sent across national borders.

Most companies today are "international" even if they don't sell outside their national borders, because some or most of their raw materials or equipment comes from other countries. And even if all of their customers and materials are domestic, their competitors may very easily come from other countries. All companies today must therefore consider international issues when analyzing their competitive position.

This chapter distinguishes between international marketing and global marketing. It discusses cultural factors in international MC, including cultural sensitivity and social responsibility. Segmenting and targeting are special challenges for international marketers, as are message design and delivery.

WHISKAS CREATES A TINY TIGER
BBDO, Düsseldorf, Germany

In the highly competitive cat-food market in the late 1990s, growth rates were nearly zero in most European markets, and all products were seen to perform essentially the same. The Whiskas brand management team at the European office of parent company Mars Inc. decided that the brand needed to differentiate itself and that to do so the emotional core of the brand, on which its relationship with consumers was built, should be emphasized. Enter a brand character: a silver tabby called the Tiny Tiger.

The Marketing Challenge

Revamping this venerable brand was the challenge given to the Düsseldorf, Germany, office of the international MC agency BBDO. A truly international brand sold worldwide, Whiskas had a 14-country European market. It also had many competitors. In addition to Mars's four other European brands, there were also strong entries from Nestlé and Purina. All these brands were fighting for a share of the market, creating a negative trend in 1997 for Whiskas.

Historically, the differentiating factors in the cat-food segment were health, taste, and nutrition. In the late 1990s, all the brands performed essentially the same on these factors. Whiskas had long been successful with the proposition "Whiskas is the preferred food for cats." However, as the competition improved, the Whiskas brand lost its competitive edge.

Campaign Strategy

The objectives of the Whiskas "Tiny Tiger" campaign were to differentiate the Whiskas brand from the competition, to make cat owners feel they had a role in the feeding choice, and to make owners feel good about spending more money for Whiskas. Regardless of country, the target audience for Whiskas is universal: female cat owners between 19 and 65 years of age who are responsible for buying the cat food.

Creative Strategy

The "Tiny Tiger" campaign was designed to give the Whiskas brand a heart by focusing on the brand's core essence, which is "care" (see Exhibit 20-2). The Whiskas brand needed to reflect the core benefit of well-being—"the best way to care for your cat"—a

EXHIBIT 21-1

The small gray tabby cat became the main character of the new Whiskas campaign.

benefit that is universally appreciated across the diverse European market. This strategy allowed the BBDO team to focus on those attributes that are most motivating in each market and determine the balance between the nutrition and enjoyment appeals. Caring is an emotional strategy, but this approach also allowed a degree of rationality.

The creative concept was stated as follows: "With Whiskas you can take the best care of your cat. You can see it and you can hear it. Every day." The creative tactics brought that idea to life with a satisfied cat on the lap framed in the Whiskas mask and the sound effect of a cat's purring. In addition, the silver tabby cat character, Tiny Tiger, was created as the hero of the campaign. These three integrated elements—the cat visual, the purring, and the silver tabby—became the Whiskas key brand signals. The simple graphics of the print ads were designed to showcase these brand-identity elements.

Message Delivery

The "Tiny Tiger" campaign used a full range of marketing communication functions:

- Television, radio, print, and outdoor advertising.
- In-store promotions.
- Point-of-purchase activities.
- Direct marketing.
- A sales video and sales folder for the sales team to use with the trade audience.
- Internet activities, including a website in Germany (www.Whiskas.de).
- Licensed materials (a silver tabby stuffed toy).

For the advertising, the emphasis was placed on television and, to a lesser extent, print and outdoor.

Research determined that cat owners want to see cats in motion, so television provided important visual impact. Print was used in specialized and targeted publications to reach true cat enthusiasts and communicate detailed information about the product. Outdoor offered a unique way to portray the silver tabby cat in a bigger-than-life medium.

Executing an international campaign is always difficult. In this case, the strategy was to use a standardized format with only a change in language for different markets. Because the creative idea was universal, the BBDO team felt that using standardized messages would provide more useful synergy for the brand than attempting to adapt the creative idea to different cultural groups. However, different executions were found to work better in different markets, so the strategy was localized by matching the best-performing executions to each country.

EXHIBIT 21-2

The cover and inside spread from the German Whiskas brochure on kitten care introduce the silver tabby brand character, Tiny Tiger, as a kitten.

The agency created 11 television spots to launch the "Tiny Tiger" campaign. The campaign also introduced a new single-serve pouch, a line of kitten food, and a cat treat (pocket kibble). The spot "Purr," for example, which used all three of the key brand signals—the satisfied cat on the lap, the sound effect of the cat purring, and the silver tabby—showed high involvement of the owner and performed well in all markets. To see how the executions were targeted locally, consider two of the spots, "Cat Shuffle" and "Mmmeat," which were found from tests to do particularly well in France. "Cat Shuffle" succeeded in communicating functional benefits (taste and freshness) as well as emotional benefits (well-being), and "Mmmeat," which created the highest level of brand awareness in that market, focused more on the functional benefits of the best way to care for a cat.

Other Marketing Communication Strategies

To reach the loyal Whiskas user effectively, BBDO designed a promotion to generate new addresses in the Whiskas database. In Germany, the agency elicited huge responses with two promotion strategies: a 15-second tag to the "It's in Your Hands" commercial and a "kitten starter pack," which included various products essential in the care of a new kitten. Of those customers who called the company as a result of the promotions, 70 percent were new additions to the database.

Direct marketing was another important part of the MC mix. Whiskas sponsored a quarterly magazine, kitten brochures in stores, and a shop on the internet site. Other sales promotions included the sampling of dry products and kitten products, and in-store promotions for both the can and the new pouch. Packaging was also part of the mix; a new brand label featuring the silver tabby cat tied the campaign directly to the product on the store shelf.

Evaluation of the Whiskas Campaign

Total European sales results from January to August 1998 showed a significant turnaround from a negative growth rate and drop in share to a positive growth rate. An even larger increase in growth rate and share was noted in 1999. The effort was so successful that the campaign was deemed an award winner at the Advertising and Marketing Effectiveness (AME) international award show. More important, it has launched a brand repositioning that has extended beyond western Europe to other regions such as Poland, Hungary, the Czech Republic, the Baltics, Russia, and the United Kingdom, as well as Brazil and Argentina in South America. Billboards with the silver tabby have also been used in Mexico. And the Tiny Tiger shows up on the new pouch packages in all markets, including the United States. The increasingly widespread use of the brand character shows how a good idea developed in one country (Germany) for a regional market (Europe) can, if successful, evolve into a global theme.

Source: This case was adapted with permission from the Advertising and Marketing Effectiveness (AME) award-winning brief for Whiskas prepared by the BBDO agency in Düsseldorf, Germany.

INTERNATIONAL AND GLOBAL MARKETING

Marketers today realize that they cannot predict where their competition will arise. For example, China's great Olympic gymnast Li Ning (three gold medals in 1984) now competes against Nike in making performance athletic shoes and other sports gear. His Beijing-based Li-Ning Sports Goods Co. sells more sneakers than any other company in the world, including Nike. Determined to turn itself into an international premium brand equal in stature to Nike, Li-Ning now sponsors national sports teams in France, Spain, Russia, and other countries, as well as China. The Li-Ning brand is seen as the vanguard of China's emerging global brands.[1]

Most companies market their products and compete in the countries where their headquarters are located, as Li-Ning did when he first started out in China. *Companies that focus their marketing efforts on their home countries* are called **domestic** (or **national**) **marketers.** A national market, then, is an individual country—such as Germany, Australia, or Mexico—and a national brand is one that is sold in only one country.

Companies that market products in several different countries are said to be **multinational marketers.** Most companies engaged in multinational marketing treat each country as a separate market—and one that is "foreign" from the home country.[2]

Then there are the **global marketers,** *companies that consider their market to be just one—the world.* Generally speaking, brands sold around the world are called *global brands.* A company involved in global marketing focuses on world market opportunities, not limiting itself to individual countries or regions. This does not mean

EXHIBIT 21-3
A Vietnamese woman walks past a Coca-Cola truck in Hanoi.

that global companies have to enter every country in the world; it does mean "widening the company's business horizons to encompass the world when identifying business opportunities."[3] Most companies start locally, expand nationally, move into international marketing, and then, when their brands have proved themselves, become global brands.

One of the best examples of a global marketer is Coca-Cola, whose products are distributed in more than 195 countries (see Exhibit 21-3). Coke is generally recognized as one of the strongest brands in the world. Its enviable global position results in part from the company's willingness to work with local distributors and to support local marketing efforts.[4]

McDonald's has brought the Golden Arches to more than 110 countries, although it saw its franchise tarnished in the 2000s as changing tastes and aging facilities began to hurt its image. The secret to McDonald's global success has been its ability to set up a standardized fast-food restaurant system, with a predictable level of quality, anyplace in the world. Moving to a global stage was a strategic decision for McDonald's after it saw a slowing of growth in the U.S. fast-food industry. By 1997, the number of restaurants outside the United States had reached 23,000, accounting for 49 percent of McDonald's sales. International operations continue to be the area driving growth for McDonald's.[5]

Other major international marketers include Germany's Mercedes-Benz (whose corporate parent is DaimlerChrysler), which is a brand name recognized around the world, and Japan's Toyota and Honda, both of which started out exporting cars from Japan but now invest in manufacturing in numerous countries. The following list identifies the top 25 global marketers and their home countries:[6]

1. Unilever—United Kingdom and the Netherlands.
2. Procter & Gamble—United States.
3. Nestlé—Switzerland.
4. Toyota—Japan.
5. Volkswagen—Germany.
6. Coca-Cola—United States.
7. Ford Motor Company—United States.
8. General Motors—United States.
9. Peugeot—France.
10. Fiat—Italy.
11. Renault—France.
12. L'Oréal—France.

13. Kao Corporation—Japan.
14. McDonald's—United States.
15. Mars—United States.
16. Vodafone—United Kingdom.
17. Nissan—Japan.
18. Henkel—Germany.
19. Ferrero—Germany.
20. Sony—Japan.
21. Philip Morris—United States.
22. Danone—France.
23. France Telecom—France.
24. DaimlerChrysler—Germany and the United States.
25. Telefonica—Spain.

CULTURAL FACTORS

Culture is a major consideration in targeting customers internationally. The word **culture** refers to *the learned behaviors of a people that come from traditions passed on from generation to generation.* It is manifested in how people dress and what they eat, as well as in their music, religion, and entertainment. Culture also includes values and ways of looking at the world—how people act, think, and respond emotionally. It is the glue that binds a group of people together.[7] The question for MC professionals is: How does culture influence customer behavior in response to brand messages?

When planning international marketing communication, companies must assess a country or target group's culture as part of the SWOT analysis. Companies analyze customers' attitudes and beliefs, motivations, and perceptions as they relate to a product category, the brand, and its usage. These culturally embedded traits should affect brand-message strategies differently in each country.

Because culture and communication are closely related, cultural factors are important in planning cross-cultural marketing communication strategies and evaluating their effectiveness. The challenge is to see to what extent there are different response patterns for different cultural groups.

Cultural Differences and Similarities

Marketers planning international brand messages debate how important cultural differences and similarities are. On the one hand are managers who believe that all cultures are different and that brand messages should always be customized for the local culture. On the other hand are managers who believe that universals such as love and happiness can be the basis for cross-cultural campaigns, and that the more specific the target (e.g., computer users) is, the more likely that the target's needs are similar regardless of country or culture. A Procter & Gamble executive explained P&G's approach to the global marketing of its Pampers disposable diapers: "Babies' bottoms are the same everywhere."

In situations of the latter type, brand messages can be standardized around the world (see Exhibit 21-4). If customer segments are homogeneous between countries and across borders, as in the Whiskas example in the opening case, then standardized strategies make sense. But if they are not, there is a need for adaptive strategies, which can result in an incredibly complex international marketing program providing many opportunities for brand inconsistency—obviously a problem for an IMC manager.

Researchers Sak Onkvisit and John Shaw have found, for example, more differences than similarities in consumer responses to marketing efforts. In many product categories, consumer demographics and behavioral responses vary by country. In a review of research studies into cultural differences and similarities, Onkvisit and Shaw concluded: "The evidence is quite overwhelming that consumer/market homogeneity on a global basis does not exist."[8] Some products are definitely "culture bound," such as local food and some types of entertainment.

One principle of IMC is that *the degree of cultural difference is often related to the product category*. Some products, such as medicine, computers, and telecommunication, do not differ much by country; other products, such as food and fashion, may have significant differences. In the Whiskas case, the brand's managers used research to determine that owning and caring for a cat were fairly universal factors (see Exhibit 21-5). Pet-care products represent an unusual challenge, for people in various cultures view pets in different ways. Some cultures (as in France, for example) permit cats or dogs in restaurants, but this practice is not generally accepted in the United States. Thus an ad featuring a pet in a restaurant, for example, would not have the same impact in both cultures—perhaps touching an emotional chord in France and a humor chord in the United States.

Researchers John Quelch and Edward Hoff found that consumer products, established products, and products with simple technologies are the most culturally bound, and industrial products and services, new products, and complex new technologies are the least culturally bound. Not surprisingly, business-to-business brand messages from a variety of countries have been found to be relatively unrelated to cultural differences.[9]

Food products are considered difficult to sell globally because of entrenched national eating habits and tastes. Olive oil sells well in the Mediterranean countries but less well in Scandinavia. Cold cereal with milk is a distinctively North American breakfast, but one that has been slow to catch on in Europe and Asia. For international food marketers, the challenge is whether to develop products suited to local tastes or rather to try to create demand for new "exotic" foods. Many national foods, such as tacos, pita bread, croissants, curry dishes, sushi, gyros, and yogurt, have moved around the world to varying degrees. McDonald's restaurants around the world strike a balance: they offer their standard fare (such as burgers and fries) along with local adaptations such as the McMaharaja (lamb patties) in India and beer in Germany.

So what's an MC manager to do? Obviously the cultural question complicates the practice of one-voice, one-look strategies. Because of the need to plot cultural differences and similarities, international IMC

When money talks, we know better what's saying.

"Makes your tiny tiger purr."

"Every day."

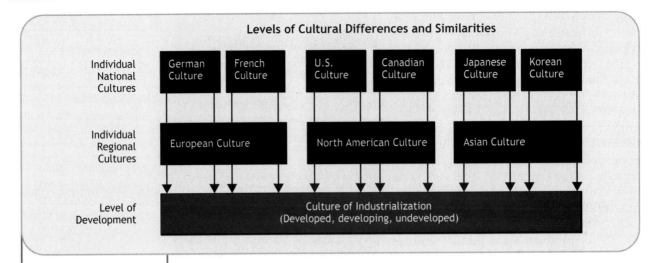

FIGURE 21-1

Cultural differences exist at different levels around the world.

calls for an even more complex plan for strategic consistency than does national IMC. As Figure 21-1 illustrates, the question of cultural differences is complex because culture consists of many different levels. Even within a country, where one might assume there is a great deal of national identity, there may be different cultures, traditions, and languages.

Dimensions of Culture

Studies have found similarities and differences in mass media advertising used in different cultures—including cultures within a country, such as the Hispanic or Asian cultures in the United States. Generally, these studies have found that ads in Eastern cultures tend to be emotional or symbolic and those in Western cultures tend to be practical, utilitarian, hard-sell, or informative.[10]

Hall's High-Context and Low-Context Cultures

Another way of explaining the differences found in cross-cultural studies is in terms of the cultural context surrounding a message. Edward Hall classified countries as being either a high-context culture or a low-context culture. The distinction between "high" and "low" context reflects the extent to which **context**—*the nonverbal elements surrounding a message*—carries meaning and is a significant part of the message in a culture.[11] A **low-context culture** is *a culture in which less emphasis is placed on the social context and more emphasis is placed on words, directness, and time (deadlines and schedules).* A **high-context culture** is *a culture in which meaning is determined by nonverbal cues, social relationships, and indirect communication such as metaphors and aphorisms (statements of principle).*[12]

An informational strategy or hard-sell approach in a brand message is likely to be more successful in low-context cultures, such as the United States, where people rely less on context to interpret the message than they do in Asian cultures. Dramas and imagery are often more appropriate in high-context cultures, such as Japan and France, where there is more dependence on context to signal the appropriate message. This distinction can be summarized as follows:

High-context cultures: Cultures that pay more attention to the physical environment in which the message takes place. Relatively little information is found in the explicit message. People in these cultures are more sensitive to nonverbal cues.

Low-context cultures: Cultures that rely on the explicit message to carry most of the information. There is relatively little reliance on nonverbal cues.

Hofstede's Dimensions of Culture

Another approach used in creating international brand messages is to analyze the components of culture as Geert Hofstede has done. In a study of 50 countries, he identified four basic components of culture:[13]

- Power distance: hierarchical versus egalitarian.
- Uncertainty avoidance: tolerance of risk.
- Collectivism versus individualism.
- Feminine versus masculine.

The differences in business style created by these factors can be major. Augustine Ihator observes that "rugged individualism is essentially an American trait." He explains that the individualistic U.S. business culture values self-determination, achievement, a future orientation, optimism, and problem solving. In contrast, collectivistic cultures, such as Asian countries, value maintenance of the status quo, harmony, and collaboration.[14]

But even in Asia, there are differences in cultural responses to marketing communication. For example, researchers have found that advertising appeals in Taiwan and Hong Kong tend to be dominated more by "Westernized" cultural values than by traditional Chinese values.[15] In these areas, which have evolved somewhat separately from mainland China, Western goods have a certain cachet. The same also holds true for people in many newly developed countries, where the West is sometimes viewed positively as a bastion of power and prestige.

How can an understanding of the work of Hofstede and Hall help in planning IMC? Researchers have found that Hofstede's individualism—collectivism model corresponds to Hall's high-context and low-context cultures: low-context cultures are individualistic; high-context are collectivist.[16] Further, they have identified high-context, collective societies to be mostly Asian and South American—cultures that value social harmony and selflessness. Low-context, individualistic cultures are mostly European and North American; people in these cultures tend to value self-realization and see themselves as independent, self-contained, autonomous. Such an analysis helps to explain why different brand message strategies are needed.

Figure 21-2 adapts Hall's context categories and Hofstede's four factors—each one presented as a continuum—to set up a chart for evaluating the cultural dimensions of a target market. This chart assigns countries to opposite ends of the spectrum in order to demonstrate they differ on these dimensions. In planning a campaign, however, MC managers would need to conduct research to plot the actual positions on these continuums.

Cultural dimensions also can be used to analyze organizations and how people work and communicate within them. In China, for example, business interaction is complex. Gareth Chang, head of Star TV, explained that communication in China "takes a formal and an informal interaction, a balance of the two."[17] A basic principle in most Asian countries is that before a business relationship, such as that between a client and an agency, is cemented, the people who will be working together must get along socially as well as professionally. So in these countries, part of the brand-relationship building, especially for B2B products, often takes place on golf courses and in restaurants.

Culture and Values

Culture functions as a lens that affects how the world is seen, and that lens reflects the values of the people within the culture.[18] **Values** are *enduring points of view that a certain way of thinking and behaving is preferable to a different way of thinking and*

FIGURE 21-2

This chart shows how countries differ on several cultural dimensions.

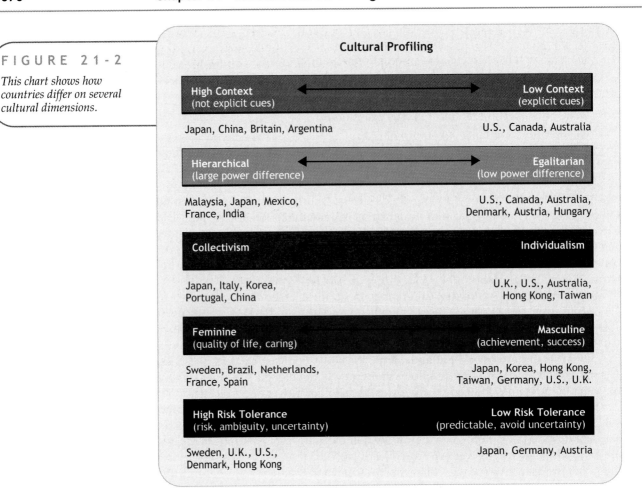

Cultural Profiling

High Context (not explicit cues) ←→ **Low Context** (explicit cues)

Japan, China, Britain, Argentina   U.S., Canada, Australia

Hierarchical (large power difference) ←→ **Egalitarian** (low power difference)

Malaysia, Japan, Mexico, France, India   U.S., Canada, Australia, Denmark, Austria, Hungary

Collectivism   **Individualism**

Japan, Italy, Korea, Portugal, China   U.K., U.S., Australia, Hong Kong, Taiwan

Feminine (quality of life, caring) ← **Masculine** (achievement, success)

Sweden, Brazil, Netherlands, France, Spain   Japan, Korea, Hong Kong, Taiwan, Germany, U.S., U.K.

High Risk Tolerance (risk, ambiguity, uncertainty)   **Low Risk Tolerance** (predictable, avoid uncertainty)

Sweden, U.K., U.S., Denmark, Hong Kong   Japan, Germany, Austria

behaving.[19] Values involve judgments of good or bad, right or wrong. In IMC, it can be an important strategy to link values with a company's mission and understand how culture interacts with brand relationships and a customer-focus philosophy.

Values can affect the way people respond to marketing communication. For example, a study of the differences between Chinese and Hong Kong television commercials found that the five cultural values that dominated Chinese ads were "modernity," "family," "tradition," "technology," and "collectivism." The five dominant values in Hong Kong ads were "quality," "effectiveness," "economy," "enjoyment," and "modernity." The Chinese commercials used more symbolic values; the Hong Kong commercials were more utilitarian.[20]

Values also shape the way companies carry out the actual business of marketing communication. A study of Korean and U.S. agency executives, based on an analysis of Hofstede's dimensions, found differences in how the two groups viewed ethical questions relating to the practice of advertising. For example, a greater orientation to collectivism, hierarchy, and structure contributes to strong company loyalty in Korea more so than in U.S. agencies.[21]

Cultural Sensitivity and Social Responsibility

A critical competency for people managing cross-cultural communication is cultural sensitivity. One way to develop good relations with culturally diverse people is to become aware of communication styles and the problems and misunderstandings they can create.[22] Having cultural awareness—a sense of cultural differences and similarities—is the first step toward becoming culturally sensitive. Flexibility is a second important factor in a manager's relationship proficiency. Both traits are particularly important when international cross-functional teams are assembled.

Media Sensitivity

Global media are magnifying the sensitivity issue. With the development of huge media conglomerates—such as Sony's entertainment division, Columbia TriStar, Time Warner's TV production units, and News Corp.'s Star TV—American and European popular culture spread all over the world. But then something happened: these conglomerates not only discovered local programming but discovered that in many cases audiences *preferred* local shows. So now Columbia TriStar is producing *Chinese Restaurant*, a series in Mandarin Chinese about a young Chinese woman in Los Angeles. The show is carried by 100 Chinese television stations. Columbia TriStar also has become the owner of Super TV, a Mandarin-language channel that reaches 77 percent of the 5.1 million households in Taiwan. Other Columbia TriStar production houses are located in India, Latin America, and several Asian cities. Columbia has also set up shop in Germany to go into foreign-language film production in Europe.

Rupert Murdoch's News Corp. learned a painful lesson about the perils of global marketing when it first expanded into Asia. To gain entry into this large emerging market, News Corp. bought Hong Kong–based Star TV which gave Murdoch a huge broadcast footprint in Asia. A **broadcast footprint** is *the geographical area in which there is reception from a satellite transmission.* The company intended to blanket the region with English-language channels that would be easy to fill with already-produced programming. Star TV soon found, however, that News Corp.'s unwillingness to localize programming was a mistake. Since then, Star's real success story has been its Mandarin-language Phoenix channel. In partnership with two Hong Kong companies, Phoenix reaches some 170 million educated upscale viewers in China, including those in Beijing and the prosperous southern city of Guangzhou.

The model for both television and film is the music industry, where the dominant global companies have discovered two revenue streams by delivering international hits as well as local music. What is emerging is a two-tier production system. English is often the language of international blockbuster films, TV series, CDs, and advertising, but local language hits are equally as important.

The Cultural Imperialism Issue

The headline read: "Brad Pitt car ad is an insult to Asians, says Malaysia."[23] Malaysian authorities were banning a television advertisement that featured Brad Pitt's face in a Toyota ad because they thought the advertisement was humiliating for Asians and represented U.S. propaganda. They saw the use of Western actors and models as an example of cultural imperialism.

The issue of **cultural imperialism** refers to *the impact that a more dominant culture has on another, less dominant culture.* The criticism is based on the notion that American movies, television programs, and especially advertising promote materialism and a culture of consumption. Brand messages and program content from the United States also violate local taboos, such as those of Muslim countries against showing women in bathing suits and other revealing clothing. Opposition to cultural imperialism has led to bans and restrictions on certain brand messages in some countries. In Malaysia, where the Toyota ad with Brad Pitt was banned, all television programs and commercials have to be produced in the country and use local producers and models. In 1998, China allowed only 10 foreign-made films to

EXHIBIT 21-6

Members of an antiwar group in France stage a die-in next to a display of Coca-Cola products in a supermarket in Anglet, France.

be shown in the country; in 1999, it announced that it would ban all unauthorized reception of foreign TV. Both of these policies are nearly impossible to enforce—in any country—because of satellite broadcasting. Nonetheless, various governments, for a number of political, religious, and cultural reasons, are trying to slow the Westernization—specifically, the Americanization—of their cultures.

A related concern for marketers is boycotts based on protests over political policies. When the U.S. and Britain, for example, initiated the war with Iraq in 2003, consumers in a number of countries boycotted American brands. McDonald's and Coca-Cola were particularly vulnerable because they are seen as symbols of America (see Exhibit 21-6).[24] Likewise, a boycott of French products occurred in the United States because the French government did not support the war initiative.

Exploitation

A dimension of cultural sensitivity that focuses on issues of social responsibility is exploitation in the manufacturing of products. Although manufacturing is not marketing communication, when companies are perceived as being exploitive, this sends a negative brand message that can harm a brand's relationship with its customers and other stakeholders. That's why issues that generate protest, such as outsourcing production to third-world countries where wages and living standards are exceptionally low, may lead to the perception that a company is not socially responsible. Nike, among others, has been attacked for such practices, and protests at World Trade Organization meetings have focused on this issue. In contrast, The Body Shop (personal-care products) and Ben & Jerry's (ice cream) are companies committed to protecting the environment and supporting indigenous peoples, goals that each has leverage to build its brands. The Body Shop used the ad in Exhibit 21-7 to separate itself from other international marketers.

Cultural Mistakes

Marketing communication is susceptible to cultural errors if message designers are not sensitive to language and cultural differences. Here are some examples made by various companies:[25]

- In Thailand, a U.S.-designed ad for Listerine was ineffective because it showed a boy and girl being affectionate to each other in public, a relationship display that violated Thai cultural norms.

- In France, Colgate introduced its Cue toothpaste, then found out that *cue* sounds like a certain obscene word in French.

- In Germany, Pepsi's slogan "Come alive, you're in the Pepsi generation" was translated as "Come out of the grave."

- Pepsodent's promise of white teeth backfired in Southeast Asia, where the chewing of betel nuts makes yellow teeth not only common but quite acceptable.

EXHIBIT 21-7
The Body Shop calls attention to the practices of international marketers that outsource manufacturing and use "sweatshop labor," in contrast to its own philosophy of buying ingredients and products from indigenous peoples and supporting their economic development in a positive way.

- The brewer Carlsberg had to add a third elephant to its beer label in Africa, where two elephants are a symbol of bad luck.

The use of color can be a sensitive cultural concern, a fact that can create serious problems for global brands that desire consistency in their brand messages. In Japan, China, and many other Asian countries, the color white is for mourning, as is purple in many Latin American countries. Gold is a strong positive color for Chinese, but not in combination with black, as in the Benson & Hedges cigarette branding. Ikea, an international furniture retailer based in Sweden, uses blue and yellow, the colors of the Swedish flag—but not in Denmark, where that color combination has a negative connotation because of a period of Swedish occupation.[26]

SEGMENTING INTERNATIONAL TARGET MARKETS

There are three ways to classify global or international markets: by geography, by level of market development, and by cohort group. Understanding these distinctions is a first step in the SWOT analysis and in identifying target audiences.

By Geography

The distinctions made earlier in defining different types of international and global marketing also describe geographic markets. The most common geographical classifications are local markets (national or domestic) and international markets, which can be regional or global.

Regional marketing is done in countries that are geographically close, usually within the same continent. In such regions, products are often distributed easily between countries. With the development of alliances such as the EU and NAFTA, regional marketing has gained importance. In Europe, nearly all trade barriers have been eliminated among EU member nations. Similarly, NAFTA was designed to reduce trade barriers between Canada, the United States, and Mexico. In Asia there are several groups of countries with varying degrees of unification. These regional associations and partnerships make it easier for marketers to create and execute MC programs.

EXHIBIT 21-8

Consumers in developed markets are more interested in trying exotic products and unusual foods. These Dutch ads are promoting Tex Mex products and Indian curry sauce.

By Level of Market Development

Another way to segment markets is by the level of development of the country. The **developed markets** in Europe, Scandinavia, North America, Australia, and Japan can be described as *markets in which consumption patterns are focused more on wants and desires than on basic needs.* Consumers in developed countries can easily meet their physical needs (food, clothing, shelter) and thus have money to spend on nonessential goods and services, which include interesting and novel experiences (see Exhibit 21-8). Developed markets are characterized by:

- High levels of literacy.
- A high standard of living.
- A high level of industrialization.
- An infrastructure that supports health care and education.
- A wide variety of media and high rates of media penetration.

Worldwide expenditures on MC media (not including telemarketing and sales promotion) for 2004 have been estimated to be $495.9 billion.[27] Spending on MC in the United States will account for slightly more than half of this figure. For decades, Europe has been the focus of many media and marketing efforts. Switzerland, for example, is home to some of the world's truly multinational corporations, many of which have been dominant in their categories since the beginning of the 20th century.

Although recovering slowly from its 1990's economic slowdown, Japan remains a relatively closed market that is difficult for foreign marketers to enter. Australia is also a difficult market to enter because of fairly tight regulation and its geographic isolation.

Many of the Far East or Pacific Rim countries, such as Thailand, Vietnam, the Philippines, Indonesia, and China, are considered **developing markets.** These are *markets in which the consumption patterns are clearly expanding from necessities to wants and desires.* Mainland China, with a population of 1.2 billion, is the largest market in this category; Malaysia has the fastest-growing economy. Some of the other countries in the Far East region, such as South Korea, Taiwan, Singapore, and Hong Kong, have well-developed economies.

In spite of the Asian economic slowdown in the 1990s, the region is still seen as having great potential, according to Frank Rose, writing in *Fortune* magazine.[28] International companies have again been investing heavily in Asia. With its 3 billion people, Asia comprises about two-fifths of the world's population, as well as some of the most promising markets in the world. China, for example, has some 305 million television households that now can be reached via satellite as well as land-based stations. The country was closed to marketing until 1978, when economic reforms led to sustained growth and a more open market.

> **"[International companies] are placing their biggest bets in Asia, where startup costs are enormous, the regulatory environment is unpredictable, the advertising market is as yet undeveloped and audiences are measured by the billion."**
>
> Frank Rose, "Think Globally, Script Locally"

But doing business in China does involve some adjustments in business practices. Some companies, however, including Danone, Coca-Cola, and Kodak, have made profits there. Danone has become successful by piggybacking off domestic brands and acquiring local companies. Coca-Cola's sales are growing faster in China than anywhere else in the world. Executives have had to come up with creative solutions to rural markets, including promoting the use of returnable bottles and thus lowering cost. Kodak has prospered by opening up nearly 8,000 retail photo stores across China and creating a program by which local Chinese businessmen can run the business. Although success was initially elusive for many companies trying to prosper in China, a study done in August 2002 revealed that 64 percent of about 200 companies surveyed in China reported being profitable.[29]

India, too, is a developing market, and the Middle East is slowly opening its doors to Western thought and trade. Dubai, capital of the United Arab Emirates, is a key city in the southern part of the Mideast region. Riyadh, capital of Saudi Arabia, is also a major center of industrialization. Israel is an exception in this region, of course, because it already has a highly developed economy.

In Africa, Egypt is an expanding economy. Industrialized South Africa offers a stabilized economy and a huge potential for marketers as its African consumer culture emerges. Diverse cultures and closed borders remain in some areas of South America, but strong market opportunities exist in many of the countries, particularly Argentina and Brazil, which means product choice is becoming much more important to consumers.

Undeveloped markets are *markets in which consumption patterns remain focused on basic needs.* Challenges to marketers in these regions include lack of media, a relatively high level of illiteracy, low disposable income, and lack of marketing infrastructure such as distribution systems. Modernization itself within these countries—setting up modern transportation and communication infrastructures (see Exhibit 21-9), as well as distribution channels for adequate health care, education, and food—will provide numerous B2B market opportunities for companies adept at providing these goods and services. And as undeveloped countries do

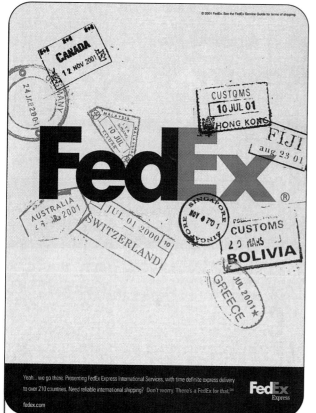

EXHIBIT 21-9

The sign a country is developing occurs when the major international delivery companies, such as FedEx, begin serving that country.

modernize, market opportunities will be created for consumer goods, although the consumer orientation will be more focused on meeting basic needs than on wants for some years to come. Much of Africa, outside the big cities, falls into this category.

By Cultural Cohort Group

A **cultural cohort,** a segmentation concept based on anthropologists' cross-cultural studies, is *a group of people from multiple cultures who share a common characteristic.* From a marketer's perspective, a cohort's common characteristic is (or results in) a specific need, want, or desire. For example, new mothers around the world want their babies to be happy. Thus products such as Pampers disposable diapers can appeal to new mothers regardless of nationality. A cultural cohort can be thought of as a global community with a unifying interest.[30]

The cohort approach to international segmentation uses a stratification method in which customers with similar characteristics, and therefore common wants and needs, can be grouped together despite national boundaries. Examples of cultural cohorts include mothers of infants, business travelers, and cat owners. Recall from the opening case that the target audience for Whiskas was considered universal: female cat owners who are responsible for buying the cat food. Cultural cohorts are particularly noticeable in the high-tech, fashion, and entertainment industries.

The youth market is one of the most distinct global cohort groups and a particularly important global target for many marketers such as Nike, Adidas, Pepsi, and Nokia. But even within this group, there are still segments based on values, personalities, and lifestyles. In a study of more than 27,000 teenagers in 44 countries, the 500-million member group was divided into six distinct value segments (see Figure 21-3). The study found that teens are not necessarily alike worldwide, even within countries; however, some lifestyle characteristics cross national borders.[31]

The music video channel MTV is an example of a powerful worldwide media vehicle that reaches the global youth market. It is also a premier platform for marketers trying to reach a cultural-cohort segment. Although most teens listen to the same kinds of music, MTV has found that there are regional and national differences. The channel's managers learned in MTV's early foray into the European market that the world's youth might all say, "I want my MTV!" but they don't want a copycat version of the U.S. channel. For that reason, MTV now airs 22 different feeds around the world, all tailored for their respective markets. All the channels, however, reflect the familiar, frenetic look and feel of the original MTV.

Viacom, the channel's owner, estimates that every second of every day almost 2 million people are watching MTV, and 1.2 million of them are tuning in from outside the United States. In the early 2000s, MTV reached 116 million homes in Asia—46 million more than in the United States. Since nearly two-thirds of Asia's 3 billion people are under the age of 35, MTV's growth in the region has been explosive, as it attracts those valuable trendsetting early adopters.

To develop relationships with its viewers in the United Kingdom, Russia, and the Philippines, MTV sponsors parties that are showcases for MTV's advertisers such as Nike, Gap, and Levi's. Compaq's European manager attributes a 12 percent increase in profit in Europe to the company's presence on MTV. He explains, "Young people trust MTV, and they trust what is shown on MTV."[32]

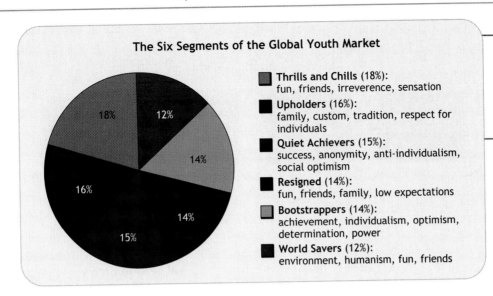

The Six Segments of the Global Youth Market

- **Thrills and Chills** (18%):
  fun, friends, irreverence, sensation
- **Upholders** (16%):
  family, custom, tradition, respect for individuals
- **Quiet Achievers** (15%):
  success, anonymity, anti-individualism, social optimism
- **Resigned** (14%):
  fun, friends, family, low expectations
- **Bootstrappers** (14%):
  achievement, individualism, optimism, determination, power
- **World Savers** (12%):
  environment, humanism, fun, friends

FIGURE 21-3

This is one way to view the global youth market. Notice the special interests of each segment.

MESSAGE DESIGN: THE SAME OR DIFFERENT?

The debate about the best international strategy has been going on since the early 1960s. It became a central issue in the early 1980s when Theodore Levitt in an article in the *Harvard Business Review* said that international companies should use standardized strategies.[33] Research findings consistently show, however, that standardization can be problematic because of differences in national cultures. Nonetheless, corporate managers continue to argue for standardization in the hope of better controlling the presentation of a brand's image, as well as benefiting from the cost efficiencies of a single campaign.

The world may become more nearly a single, homogeneous marketplace, but there will always be economic, geographical, cultural, political, demographic, and technological differences that stand in the way of a truly level playing field. Even if people buy the same products, that doesn't mean they buy them for the same reasons. International marketers are faced with the challenge of taking advantage of new communication technology to reach millions of customers quickly and cost-effectively while ensuring that they are not sacrificing their desired brand image.

Standardize or Localize?

Standardization and localization are the two primary MC strategies used in international marketing communications. A **standardization strategy** (also called a **global strategy**) is *an international MC strategy in which the same basic brand message is used in all countries.* A **localization strategy** is *an international MC strategy in which brand messages are customized to make them compatible with each country's culture and local needs and wants.*

Standardization and localization are at opposite ends of a strategy continuum (see Figure 21-4). Most international MC strategies fall somewhere between these two extremes as marketers aim to "think globally, act locally." A major determinant of whether messages should be standardized or localized is product category as discussed earlier in this chapter.

One problem multinational brands face is that local offices sometimes resent being forced to use global campaigns and make the argument (even when not valid) that the standardized campaign doesn't adequately address the local market. This situation is often addressed by having a global strategy that is locally executed. A

FIGURE 21-4

As this continuum indicates, the balance of localization and standardization can greatly vary.

Source: Adapted from Sandra Moriarty and Tom Duncan, "Global Advertising: Issues and Practices," *Current Issues and Research in Advertising* 13, nos. 1 and 2 (1991), p. 317.

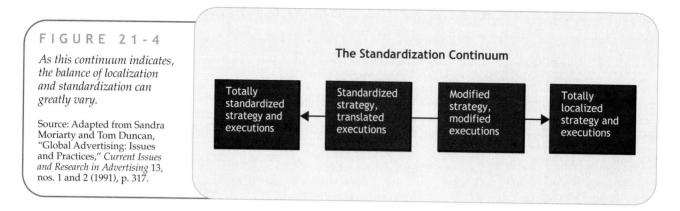

The Standardization Continuum

Totally standardized strategy and executions ← Standardized strategy, translated executions — Modified strategy, modified executions → Totally localized strategy and executions

study of global best practices found that most multinational companies are operating with a combination or two-tier MC strategy: global headquarters determines the broad strategic direction for the brand, and regional or country offices execute the strategy as they see best.[34] Such an approach combines the advantages of both strategies—consistent brand-image development and successful communication accommodating cultural differences.[35]

The Language Factor

Any sort of localization strategy demands that the language of the marketing communication be translated into the language of the countries where the MC materials are used. Automatically that will create some inconsistencies in how the materials are presented. For international products, language may present both a problem and a creative opportunity. The ad in Exhibit 21-10 illustrates how language can become a badge that communicates a product's position.

Online communities are often classified by the languages used as opposed to the geographic region. E-commerce marketers who try to rely on English as an international business language often find that their customers want to do business

EXHIBIT 21-10

The new Beetle communicates its international heritage with this commercial that features the message translated into Russian, Japanese, and Spanish, as well as English.

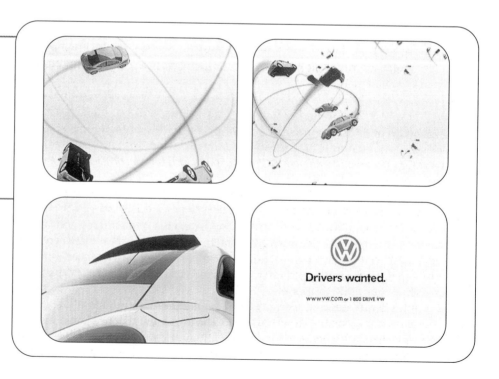

in their own languages. A study completed in June 2000 identified the percentages of online users by language:[36]

Language	Percentage of Internet Users
Dutch	1.8%
Italian	3.0
Korean	3.5
French	3.9
Chinese	5.4
Spanish	5.8
German	5.9
Japanese	8.1
English	51.3

E-commerce companies, such as Amazon.com, eBay, and Bol.com AG (the online unit of the German media giant Bertelsmann AG) are pushing into international business. They are developing local-language sites across Europe and Asia. Amazon.com operates language-specific sites in Germany and France. It has also exported products to customers in 160 other countries where customers access the site in English. Online auctioneer eBay has a dedicated site for the United Kingdom, but its European rival, QXL, is pioneering a different approach. QXL has moved from nation to nation, launching local sites in some and buying established companies in others, and it now operates in 12 different languages with 12 different currencies.

Maintaining Global Brand Consistency

Planning a message strategy for an international brand is more complex, however, than simply deciding whether to standardize or localize the messages. A brand's imagery and logo, for example, are relatively easy to standardize; language is somewhat less so. But consider the models and settings used in an ad. Such aspects of a brand message can be extremely difficult to standardize. Figure 21-5 breaks out 12 dimensions of strategy and gives examples of the elements that need to be considered in the standardization/localization decision.

One survey of 87 multinational companies that market in China, Taiwan, Hong Kong, and Singapore found that 31 percent of the advertising used the same strategy as in the home market, while 68 percent used a different strategy.[37] Robert Hite and Cynthia Fraser found in 1988 that 66 percent of the international companies they surveyed used a combination strategy; only 9 percent used a standardized strategy, and 37 percent used a localized strategy.[38] Ten years later, a major study of advertising in China by Yin found that little had changed: the majority of the international companies surveyed about their practices in China used a combination strategy.[39]

Yin concluded that the majority of the companies surveyed have abandoned standardization. The only exception was the electronics industry, in which no company used a localized strategy, confirming that high-tech markets are less affected by cultural differences than are other types of markets. Furthermore, she observed that even in the emerging markets of developing countries, some degree of localization is a preferred strategy for most companies, rather than the less costly and more efficient standardization approach. Some researchers have found, however, that although global integration can be done with either a standardization or a localization approach, coordination is more difficult with the latter.[40]

The general principle seems to be that it isn't a question of "Think globally" or "Think locally," but rather "Think globally and act locally." Companies wishing to

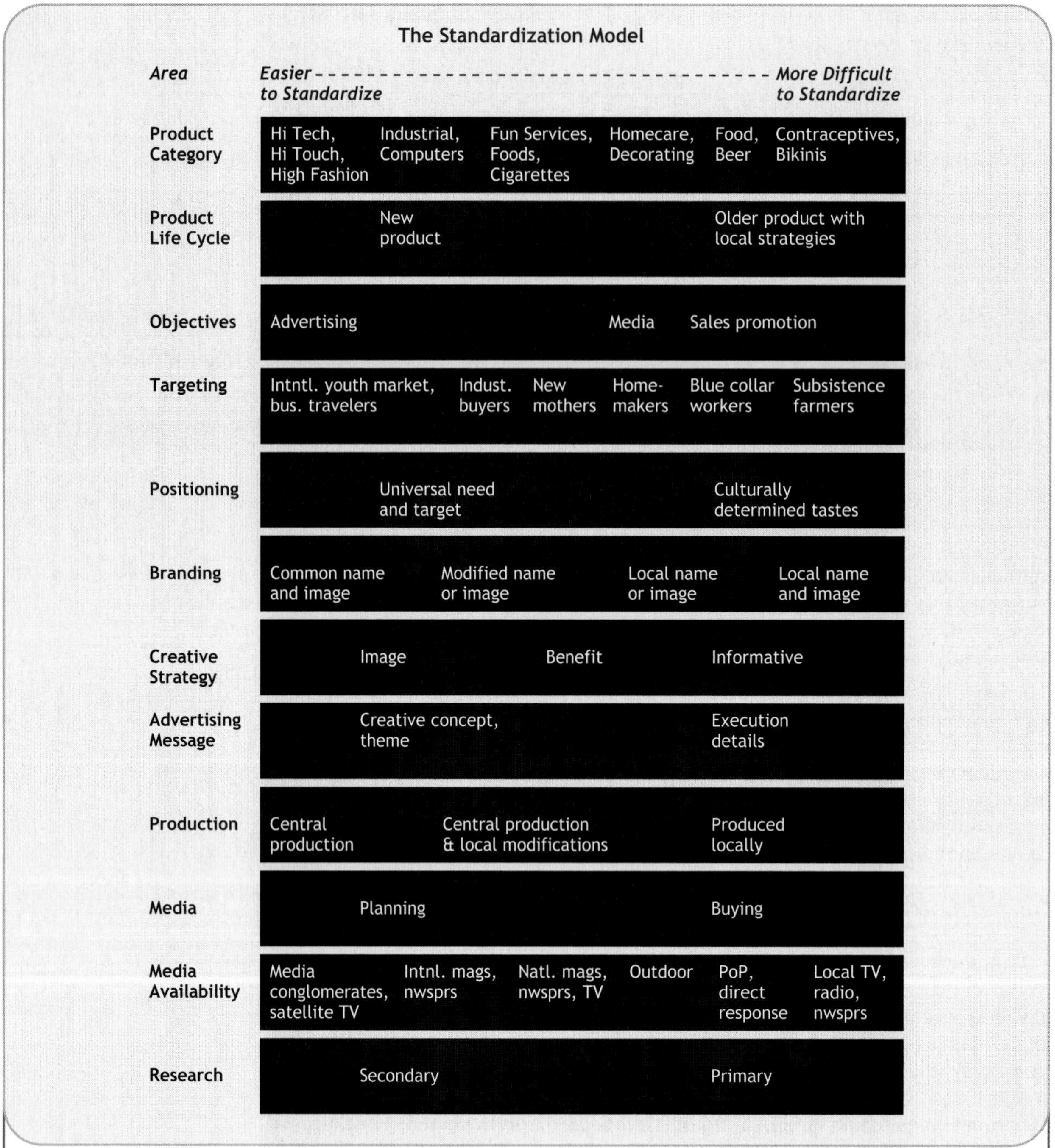

The Standardization Model

Area	Easier to Standardize - More Difficult to Standardize					
Product Category	Hi Tech, Hi Touch, High Fashion	Industrial, Computers	Fun Services, Foods, Cigarettes	Homecare, Decorating	Food, Beer	Contraceptives, Bikinis
Product Life Cycle	New product				Older product with local strategies	
Objectives	Advertising			Media	Sales promotion	
Targeting	Intntl. youth market, bus. travelers	Indust. buyers	New mothers	Home-makers	Blue collar workers	Subsistence farmers
Positioning	Universal need and target				Culturally determined tastes	
Branding	Common name and image	Modified name or image		Local name or image		Local name and image
Creative Strategy	Image		Benefit		Informative	
Advertising Message	Creative concept, theme				Execution details	
Production	Central production		Central production & local modifications		Produced locally	
Media	Planning				Buying	
Media Availability	Media conglomerates, satellite TV	Intnl. mags, nwsprs	Natl. mags, nwsprs, TV	Outdoor	PoP, direct response	Local TV, radio, nwsprs
Research	Secondary				Primary	

FIGURE 21-5

Examples of various levels of standardization and localization applications.

Source: Sandra E. Moriarty and Tom Duncan, "Global Advertising: Issues and Practices," *Current Issues and Research in Advertising* 13, nos. 1 and 2 (1991), pp. 313–41.

launch global marketing campaigns must still play in the local arena of local media, varying government regulations, wide cultural differences, and ever-changing stages of economic and demographic development. Although many of the world's economic and cultural barriers have fallen in recent years, international companies cannot ignore the remaining barriers if they hope to reach their customers on a global scale.

MESSAGE DELIVERY: MEDIA AND TECHNOLOGY

Three basic media strategies allow marketers to reach multinational and global markets. One is to localize media mixes to reflect the mix of media available in each country. Another is to use international publications and satellite TV, whose footprints cover various regions of the world. A third way to deliver media across borders is to participate in programs that have transnational audiences—for example, sporting events such as soccer's World Cup and the Olympics.

Level of Media Development

Print advertising—specifically outdoor, magazines, and newspapers—has historically offered international advertisers the best way to reach cross-cultural markets. *Time, Newsweek, Cosmopolitan,* the *Wall Street Journal,* and many other U.S. publications publish in multiple languages and distribute throughout the world. In developing countries where communication vehicles and literacy are limited, however, radio and posters or billboards dominate the media schedule. In such places, the search is on for nontraditional vehicles and sales promotions that can reach customers in rural villages. The IMC in Action box explains how one marketing entrepreneur is developing methods to reach people in such markets and begin to develop their awareness of brands.

You might not think of outdoor media as being global, but one of the largest outdoor advertising companies in the world, France-based JCDecaux, has nearly half a million display locations spread throughout 1,300 cities in 33 countries. JCDecaux is also the inventor of, and world's largest provider of, "street furniture" (bus benches and shelters) and the world leader in airport and subway posters. In the United States, it is the largest provider of shopping-mall poster displays.

Although print is still the advertising vehicle most often used by international marketers, satellite technology is quickly making television the medium for the masses around the world. China has more than 3,000 TV and radio stations. Ninety-six percent of Chinese urban homes have color television sets. Media growth in China, in general, has been phenomenal as the movement toward a more market-based economy has opened Chinese markets. China has about 2,200 general publications, trade magazines, and newspapers. The fastest-growing development, of course, is occurring with the internet.

Internet: A Truly Global Medium

Marketing communication for many global companies is moving to the internet because it offers an easy solution to global communication. Nike, for example, uses the internet to communicate with its customers worldwide (see Exhibit 21-11).

B2B companies were early users of the internet to interact with suppliers—many of which are in other countries—as well as to communicate with their own international brand offices. As a result, B2B companies are ahead of B2C companies in using the internet to do business internationally. But B2C companies are catching up—particularly in Asia.

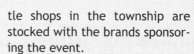

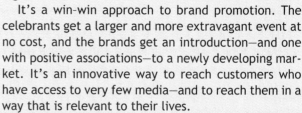

Building Brands in the Bush

Busi Skenjana is pioneering techniques to build brands in the townships of South Africa by using nonconventional media. She is president of Soweto-based IXesha Marketing Focus, a promotions agency that offers packaged-goods brands an entry into township retailing. Her unusual route to building brand awareness takes her not to traditional media but to dirt roads leading to village social and cultural events, such as weddings and funerals.

She has found that entertainment, celebrations, and social and cultural events provide opportunities for visibility for the brands she represents. She brings in all the equipment, furnishings, food, and other accouterments needed to stage the event, such as pans and bowls for food, tents, banners, limos, portable stages, even toilets—all of them branded. For example, a branded bridal limousine carries the message "Here comes the [brand X] bride." After all, the same brand sponsors the Bride of the Year award in local newspapers. And Skenjana makes sure that all the little shops in the township are stocked with the brands sponsoring the event.

It's a win-win approach to brand promotion. The celebrants get a larger and more extravagant event at no cost, and the brands get an introduction—and one with positive associations—to a newly developing market. It's an innovative way to reach customers who have access to very few media—and to reach them in a way that is relevant to their lives.

Think About It

What is the key challenge of reaching customers in undeveloped markets? How does IXesha Marketing Focus reach its target markets?

Source: Busi Skenjana, "Building Brands in a Fragmented Media Society" (paper delivered at the IMM-MASA Conference, Johannesburg, South Africa, March 10, 1998).

E-commerce expanded faster in South Korea than in any other nation between 1998 and 2000. E-commerce is a big business in South Korea, where companies such as E*Trade benefit from the fact that 50 percent of Korean stock trading is now done online. One particular use of the internet that is distinctively Korean is the "PC room," a combination internet café (without the coffee) and game arcade. There are some 15,000 PC rooms in South Korea, complete with Web video cameras and rows of computers jammed in as tightly as they will fit. Although many South Koreans have internet access on home PCs, they come to the PC rooms for souped-up terminals with high-speed links and super graphics, for the camaraderie, and for the help of resident computer geeks who stand by to solve problems instantly. Men tend to spend their time there playing games; women chat online. Computer games also have become a major "sport" marketing arena in South Korea, where at least a thousand professional gamers are sponsored and paid generous salaries by online game manufacturers. The best Korean game players have fan clubs, participate in big game tournaments, and appear on TV shows.

The emerging Web market looks different in Japan than in other countries because of the Japanese fascination with handheld electronic appliances, such as the mobile phone, rather than the computer. A cell-phone company offering a handset that hooks up to the internet signed up 5 million users in its first year. Wireless communication is driving the shape and development of internet marketing in Japan.

Japan's e-commerce works differently, as well. In many parts of Japan, online orders can be placed one day and the goods picked up the next at one of the ubiquitous local convenience stores or even at a gas station. As a result, 7-Eleven, with its 8,000 outlets in Japan, is positioned to be the biggest distributor of e-commerce merchandise.

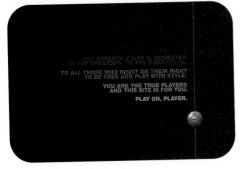

EXHIBIT 21-11

The website <www.nike.com/freestyle> uses the interactivity of the Web to give Nike customers worldwide the opportunity to create personalized messages and participate in improvisational innovation. The images merge street ball players, both football and basketball, with pro players to celebrate the personal styles they bring to their games. The site allows users to create customized screen savers by mixing clips from the Freestyle commercials.

As internet access continues to grow throughout the world, it greatly expands the marketplace for every company that is prepared to do business online. But there are still many traditional barriers such as differences in language. Taxation, money exchange, and making secure delivery of products are also concerns when selling online outside of a company's home country. Another barrier is how and where to resolve legal issues that arise in the course of doing business internationally.

International corporations trying to reach the world's proliferation of internet users must do so in a targeted, constructive manner, just as they would use any other advertising medium. One of the tools now available to international companies is a new global tracking service for advertisers, launched by ACNielsen. Prior to ACNielsen's research service, marketers relied on market measurements that varied by types of information collected, methods used, and level of accuracy. The research company promises consistently gathered information about the number of people and households per country with access to the internet, their online browsing and purchasing habits, and the rates of access at home, work, or other locations.

As internet technology becomes more common throughout the world and more tracking and research services are developed, international advertisers will look to the internet as an integrated brand message vehicle to carry sales-promotion offers, publicity releases, and ad messages. Most important, companies will use the internet to develop an online dialogue with customers.

Media Convergence

Media convergence is *the bringing together of phone, television, and the computer, along with a variety of other new technologies, such as smart cards, pagers, personal digital assistants, and satellite navigational systems.* Brand messages may take on an entirely different shape as wireless communication makes use of all these technologies. This is particularly true in early-adopter countries that pioneered the development of wireless communication, such as the Scandinavian countries and Japan.

Picture a butcher shop in Stockholm, Sweden, where customers are offered a discount for waving their wireless cell phones through an infrared sensor that records the telephone's number. Near closing time on one particular day, the butcher is anxious to move some prime cuts of Argentine beef. Using the store's customer database, he sends out a special offer by an automated phone message to customers who have ordered Argentine beef before—and who happen to be within, say, three blocks of the shop. The mobile phone network finds these customers, pages them, and delivers a message about the special deal, complete with a mouthwatering picture of a sizzling steak. The butcher's wireless company charges a few cents for each message delivered; however, he may recover that cost with the revenue from the Bordeaux ad message delivered at the same time as the beef offer. Customers who buy online get a discount, and the charges are automatically placed on their phone's debit card.

In Japan, Honda is building cybercars that can connect to the internet. The car's internal navigation system uses a computer satellite mapping system, a modem and mobile phone, internet browser capability, and a dashboard-mounted paperback-size screen. It's possible to provide drivers with guides to restaurants, a list of leisure activities, and event schedules.

Media Regulation

Developing an international media plan is not simple—not only because of the varied patterns of local media but also because of the different regulations. Although some media are being privatized in countries as diverse as Israel and Russia, governments around the world still own and control most broadcast media, and many still do not permit advertising. In Norway, there is only one commercial Norwegian TV channel. Other countries limit advertising to a certain number of minutes per hour or per day. European Union guidelines allow only 12 minutes of commercial messages per hour and mandate at least 20 minutes of programming between commercial breaks. Despite individual country regulations barring or limiting TV advertising, however, households in these countries are increasingly being reached with TV commercials carried by satellite broadcasting companies, such as Columbia TriStar and Sky TV. And there are few restrictions on newspapers and magazines.

Many countries also limit or fully prevent the use of certain media such as direct mail and telemarketing. Good information about media use and audience profiles isn't available in every country, especially developing countries. Circulation figures aren't always reliable, audience demographics may be sketchy, ad rates may vary greatly, and mailing lists and phone numbers may not exist in a directory or in a database. And because of costs, the methods used in media research may be considerably different from one market to another, making comparisons almost impossible. Because of the media variations in each country, most international marketers assign national media-planning and -buying responsibilities to in-country media specialists rather than running the risk of faulty, centralized media planning.

INTEGRATION AT THE INTERNATIONAL LEVEL

When companies sell their products outside their home country, IMC practices and principles are even more important than when they sell them domestically. Both international and global marketing call for a complex yet integrated strategy. Building stakeholder relationships with global customers, agencies, media, and channels of distribution can be highly complex and certainly requires cross-functional planning and monitoring. But the same basic integration issues are still driving the strategies.

An example of using an IMC global campaign comes from Microsoft. Its .NET connected software used television, print, and online advertising within a number of countries to showcase studies of how businesses are successfully using .NET software. Because the .NET product line was being promoted globally, Microsoft had to be sensitive to media and global integration issues when adapting the message for other markets. For example, in addition to language, Microsoft also made certain that the examples of .NET use were region specific. For the first half of 2003, the campaign resulted in a 15-point increase in awareness of .NET software among business IT decision makers and a 9-point increase among IT implementers.[41]

The global IMC concept, or GIMC, was developed by Baruch University professors Andreas Grein and Stephen Gould to explain how integration can be managed within a global marketing program. They identified two critical aspects of GIMC planning: *horizontal coordination*, which means coordinating a brand strategy across countries; and *vertical coordination*, which means coordinating a brand message across disciplines. Acknowledging that both standardization and localization are appropriate strategies depending on the product and marketing situation, Grein and Gould then developed a planning model. Table 21-1 identifies the key factors that marketers need to consider when planning a global IMC strategy.[42]

Consistency of branding is the biggest problem for international or global marketers. The English–Dutch global giant Unilever has a vast number of brands in a variety of product categories. In 2003 in an attempt to develop a more cohesive MC strategy for its detergent brands, a campaign was designed that focuses on a universal truth—that kids, no matter where they grow up, think dirt is fun. The "dirt is good" theme is used for Unilver's premium detergent which sells around the world under a variety of brand names, including Wisk in the United States, Skip in parts of Europe, and Omo in many of the company's other markets.[43]

TABLE 21-1   Planning a Global IMC Strategy

Factor	Standardized Strategy	Adapted Strategy
Horizontal Factors		
Target market	Same and mass; global segments	Different segments; regional markets
Market position	Similar market conditions	Different market conditions
Nature of product	Consumer perceives as similar in use, attributes, and positioning	Consumer perceives as different in use, attributes, and positioning
Environment	Similar physical, legal, political, and marketing infrastructure	Different physical, legal, political, and marketing infrastructure
Vertical Factors		
Marketing mix	Same resources allocated	Different resources allocated
Main promotion objective	Build brand equity	Build brand image
Advertising creation	Same theme, appeal, execution	Variations in theme, appeal, execution
Advertising media	Same, possibly global, media use	Different media use; local buys
Sales promotion	Same types and strategies	Different types used
Public relations	Same theme and forms	Variations in theme and forms

Source: Adapted from Andreas Grein and Stephen Gould, "Globally Integrated Marketing Communications," *Journal of Marketing Communications* 2 (1996), pp. 141–58. Visit the Journal at www.tanf.co.uk/journal/routledge/13527266.html. Used by permission.

A FINAL NOTE: THINK GLOBALLY, ACT LOCALLY

The goal of most businesses is to market their products or services to the largest group of potential customers at the lowest possible cost with the greatest possible return on their investment. This strategy would suggest that a company should use a standardized or global message to reach large numbers of customers through international markets, as the Whiskas strategy demonstrated.

This standardized international marketing strategy may work for some brands and may offer various efficiency benefits for a company, but in most cases international businesses need to take local economic, cultural, political, legal, demographic, and media factors into consideration, market by market. And this often means that the marketing communication is better served with a strategy that is adapted to the local market.

Key Terms

broadcast footprint 677
context 674
cultural cohort 682
cultural imperialism 677
culture 672
developed markets 680
developing markets 681

domestic marketers 670
global marketers 671
global strategy 683
high-context culture 674
localization strategy 683
low-context culture 674
media convergence 689

multinational marketers 671
national marketers 670
standardization strategy 683
undeveloped markets 681
values 675

Key Point Summary

Key Point 1: Different Types of International Marketing

National (or domestic) marketing programs are designed for marketing within a country. International marketing programs are for companies that market in a number of different countries. Global marketers sell their products in many countries around the world.

Key Point 2: The Impact of Culture

Cultural differences and similarities reflect people's values. MC planners must be sensitive to these differences. Media sensitivity, cultural imperialism, exploitation, and cultural mistakes are all problem areas that marketers must understand.

Key Point 3: Segmenting International Markets

International markets are segmented by geography, by level of market development, and by cultural cohort group. Understanding these differences is an important part of conducting a SWOT analysis and identifying target audiences.

Key Point 4: Planning International Message and Media Strategies

The big issue in planning international message strategies is deciding how much standardization or localization is appropriate for a particular type of product marketed in various countries. Many companies use a combination strategy. Likewise, in creating a media plan for international markets, a decision has to be made about using local media or media that reach across borders. Such decisions are becoming increasingly complex—yet also hold great potential—because of the growth of the internet and media convergence.

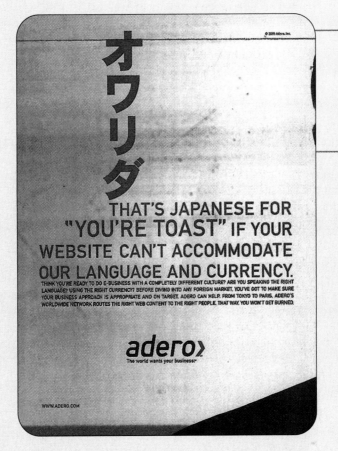

オワリダ

THAT'S JAPANESE FOR "YOU'RE TOAST" IF YOUR WEBSITE CAN'T ACCOMMODATE OUR LANGUAGE AND CURRENCY.

THINK YOU'RE READY TO DO E-BUSINESS WITH A COMPLETELY DIFFERENT CULTURE? ARE YOU SPEAKING THE RIGHT LANGUAGE? USING THE RIGHT CURRENCY? BEFORE DIVING INTO ANY FOREIGN MARKET, YOU'VE GOT TO MAKE SURE YOUR BUSINESS APPROACH IS APPROPRIATE AND ON TARGET. ADERO CAN HELP. FROM TOKYO TO PARIS, ADERO'S WORLDWIDE NETWORK ROUTES THE RIGHT WEB CONTENT TO THE RIGHT PEOPLE. THAT WAY, YOU WON'T GET BURNED.

adero›
The world wants your business™

WWW.ADERO.COM

EXHIBIT 21-12
Using a local language is important in e-commerce, as this ad for an international internet service company illustrates.

Lessons Learned

Key Point 1: Different Types of International Marketing

a. What are the differences between national, international, and global marketing?
b. List three major trends that are driving the move to international marketing. Explain their impact on marketing.

Key Point 2: The Impact of Culture

a. Define *culture*. Explain where in the planning of a marketing communication program culture becomes a factor.
b. Summarize the debate about cultural differences and similarities as they apply to creating and delivering brand messages.
c. If you were to summarize the difference in values between Western and Asian cultures, what would they be?
d. Explain the difference between a high-context culture and a low-context culture. How does context affect marketing communication?
e. Explain the concern that some countries have with Western cultural imperialism. Find an ad that you think might raise the imperialism issue, and explain why you think the ad's strategy might create a problem in an international marketing plan.

Key Point 3: Segmenting International Markets

a. In what three ways can international markets be segmented and targeted? Explain how these factors make a difference in an MC strategy.
b. What are the characteristics of developed markets, developing markets, and undeveloped markets? How does each stage of marked development affect a marketing communication strategy?
c. What is a cultural cohort group? Why is this concept important in international marketing communication? Give an example of such a group.

Key Point 4: Planning International Message and Media Strategies

a. What is meant by *standardization*? By *localization*?
b. What is a combination strategy? How does the standardization continuum (Figure 21-4, p. 684) explain the differences in this approach?
c. What does "Think globally, act locally" mean? How does this advice relate to the IMC principle of being strategically consistent?
d. Describe three media strategies used to reach multinational audiences.
e. What is media convergence? Give an example of it.

Chapter Challenge

Writing Assignment

Identify a product that is sold in your country and in another country. (A good place to start looking is in your school's library in magazines such as *Elle* and *Figaro*.) Collect an ad for the brand in both languages. In a paper, analyze the brand's use of standardization or localization.

Presentation Assignment

Stage a debate between two teams of students. One team supports the idea that standardization is a useful strategy. The other supports the idea that localization is the only way to develop an effective marketing communication plan. Both teams should consider the issue of cultural imperialism in making their arguments.

Internet Assignment

Pick a product category in which you are especially interested. Then go online to find three companies in that category—one in North America , one in Europe, and one in Asia. Compare the three sites, and see to what extent each site reflects the culture of each company's home area.

Chapter

22

Measurement, Evaluation, and Effectiveness

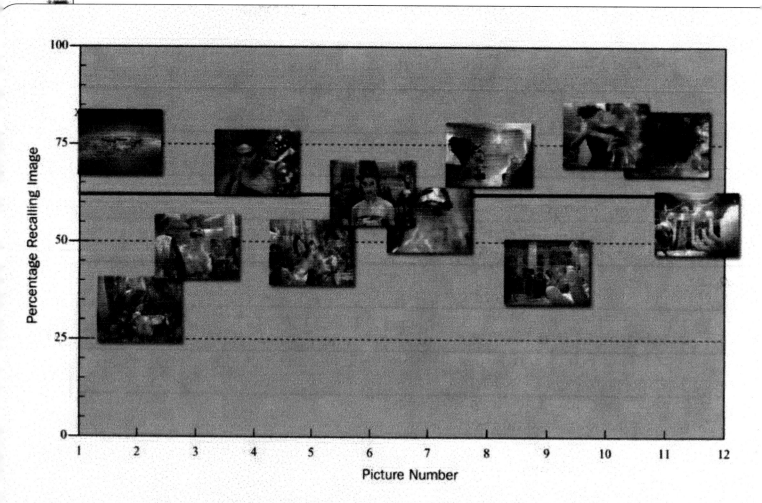

Ameritest Flow of Attention® Graph

Key Points in This Chapter

1. How should the evaluation of brand messages be conducted?
2. What are the common methods used in IMC evaluation?
3. How are IMC processes evaluated?

Chapter Perspective

The Mandate for Accountability

Brand awareness, brand knowledge, customer satisfaction, and many of the other elements that drive brand equity are intangible. Thus measurement is more complicated than simply looking at sales and profits, but a wide range of information-collecting technology that tracks sales and profitability enables companies to evaluate MC efforts. Scanner data, customer databases, and automated customer-service operations generate enormous amounts of marketing data. In many companies, the primary challenge is not collecting more information but finding the time to analyze and make use of the data that already exists.

One of the most important ways to meet this challenge is to measure and evaluate brand messages by monitoring responses from the different brand messages and campaigns that are used. This chapter also discusses two types of IMC audits: the mini-audit and the in-depth audit. It considers evaluation and measurement of brand messages in general before looking at specific methods. It ends with a discussion of the benefits and limitations of evaluation.

HOW MOLSON CANADIAN AND ITS AGENCY USED EVALUATION MEASURES TO MAKE THE BRAND NUMBER ONE

In the mid-1980s Molson Canadian established itself as the number-one brand of beer in Canada. By the late 1990s its chief rival, Labatt's Blue, had increased its marketing effort while several changes were being made in Molson's advertising. The result, a loss of sales and market share, prompted Molson to hire a new agency, Bensimon-Byrne D'Arcy. Molson's new agency was given this objective: "Make Molson Canadian the undisputed #1 beer brand in Canada." To achieve this objective, it was agreed that the brand had to communicate a sense of sociability, quality, and identity—the top three attributes of a leading brand in the mainstream segment of the beer category.

Bensimon-Byrne D'Arcy knew that the new campaign had to be more than a series of cute, attention-getting ads. The campaign had to touch the target audience emotionally and deeply. It was agreed the new message needed to build on the brand's strong heritage of being "Canadian." Past executions had consistently used scenes of patios, cottages, and road trips. They were aesthetically pleasing but lacked the emotional attitude that would motivate the brand's target, LDA (legal drinking age) to 24-year-old males. (Because Canadian provinces have different drinking age limits, one specific age at which drinking becomes legal is not used in marketing planning; instead, marketers refer to the "legal drinking age.")

As with all new major assignments, Bensimon-Byrne D'Arcy used a disciplined research approach for developing and testing new creative ideas. This approach has three steps: (1) exploratory, (2) diagnostic, and (3) evaluative.

Stage 1: Exploratory Research

As Jack Bensimon, president of the agency explained: "In this stage you look for things you don't know you are looking for." To get a good understanding of the target audience—what those young men thought about, what they did in their spare time, what music they liked, what they thought about life, and so on—the agency did on-the-street interviews. Interns and other young agency people were given video cameras and told to find and talk

with members of the target audience. The purpose of these "chats" was to record how this group of consumers thought and talked about a wide range of topics (not just about beer).

As members of the agency team watched hours of video, what they found helpful was not *what* the young men talked about but rather *how* they talked about different subjects—especially about being Canadian. On most topics the dialogue consisted of brief, unemotional comments reflecting typical youthful ambivalence. When topics directly or indirectly related to Canada and nationality, however, respondents became more animated and emotional. Because Canadians, especially young men, are usually reserved when talking about national pride, especially in comparison with Americans, the agency felt it had discovered an interesting customer insight.

Before proceeding, however, the agency knew it needed more confirmation of this finding. Two relevant research studies were found on the internet. A University of Chicago study measuring national pride in 23 countries showed that Canada ranked third (after the United States and Austria). A study by Ekos Research Associates (a Canadian research firm) found "national pride" to be the second most important "attachment in our lives" after family. These two studies helped convince the agency team that what it had seen in the videotapes was not a fluke but deep emotion that could provide the foundation for a long-term brand positioning and creative platform. (Notice that instead of doing costly primary research, the agency made use of secondary research, saving the client thousands of dollars.)

Final confirmation that "Canadian pride" was a solid concept came from a review of current events (another low-cost but productive research effort). The most important of these events was the 30-year anniversary of Woodstock. It took place in upstate New York in 1999 and drew hundreds of thousands of young people for three days of music, fun, and celebration. Because many of the attendees were Canadians, pictures from the gathering proved to be especially informative. Pictures of many participants showed backpack patches, body tattoos, and

T-shirts bearing the slogan "I am Canadian." Conclusion: Young men were proud to be Canadian and were not embarrassed to publicly express their pride. ("I Am Canadian" had been the brand's previous advertising slogan, and though discontinued three years earlier, it had moved into the target audience's vernacular as a form of self-expression.)

Based on these exploratory research findings, the brand's creative positioning was determined to be: "Molson Canadian is the only beer that lets me be as Canadian as I feel." The next challenge was to execute this into compelling brand messages.

Stage 2: Diagnostic Measurements

In this stage, the positioning statement was presented to focus groups of the target audience. Also, first drafts of TV copy were read by the writer (without showing any photos) to focus-group participants to see how well the copy communicated. These focus groups indicated that among this target audience, beer was the only product category that tapped into national pride.

Focus groups were also used to see how advertising messages could be fine-tuned to be more attention getting, involving, and persuasive. Six TV spots were selected to be tested by AdLab. Commercials were made into animatics, which are videos of a series of still photos plus a sound track. (Animatics can be made for about $15,000, less than 5 percent of the cost of a finished commercial.) The animatics were shown to a sample of the target audience. These respondents used a device containing five buttons numbered from 1 to 5 to indicate to what extent they liked or disliked each and every scene (1 = dislike very much; 5 = like very much). Every scene in "Rant," the first commercial tested, received a high rating except for a scene that talked about putting ketchup on macaroni and cheese. It was replaced with a picture and line about the beaver being a "proud and noble animal."

The final copy evaluation was done by mall intercepts in which 150 of the target audience were individually exposed to the animatics test commercials. After viewing, respondents were asked questions about the brand, their intent to purchase, and their anticipated purchase frequency of Molson Canadian. These scores were compared to the average scores of previously tested commercials in the beer and alcohol category. Test commercials scoring significantly better than average were produced and run on-air.

Stage 3: Evaluation

Once the TV commercials and print advertising were developed, the agency made presentations of the campaign to Molson's other MC agencies—packaging, public relations, website development, and channel marketing. This road-show enabled these agencies to coordinate and integrate their work with the advertising, the predominant MC function used by the brand.

Two weeks prior to the television launch, the ad agency coordinated live performances of "Rant" and other commercials, without notice, in movie theaters. This garnered tremendous word of mouth and media coverage.

The public relations agency responded by making the "Rant" commercial come alive in various sports venues. Taking advantage of the National Hockey League's playoff games, which were happening at that time, the agency had "Joe," the spokesperson in the "Rant" commercial, make his speech live before hockey audiences in five major markets. These performances were so well received by the audiences that they began to be covered by the media. As a result, the brand received over four times more exposure from publicity than was generated by the advertising media schedule.

At the same time, the website people put the new commercials on a specially developed brand website and asked site visitors to write their own "I am Canadian" commercials. Over 40,000 did so!

Once the campaign began running, the collective effectiveness of all of Molson's brand messages was measured by changes in brand awareness and market share. Tracking studies were used to determine brand awareness. In this type of research, randomly selected respondents are screened for product usage, and those who qualify are asked with what brands of beer they are familiar. The responses indicate the level of brand awareness for each brand in the beer category.

Results

Twelve months after the beginning of the campaign, the brand's awareness had increased 3 percent. Three percentage points may not seem like much, but they produced an increase of 2.5 market-share points. In the beer category, each share point is worth millions of dollars in sales. What makes these results especially impressive is that during this time Molson reduced its level of spending from the previous year and had a lower share-of-voice than its chief competitor, Labatt's Blue.

Source: Information provided by Jack Bensimon, president of Bensimon-Byrne, Toronto, March 2003.

EVALUATION AND MEASUREMENT OF BRAND MESSAGES

Throughout this book we have talked about the importance of setting objectives. Measurable objectives enable companies to quantify the effectiveness of MC efforts. Measuring and evaluating MC programs is done to see whether objectives have been met and MC programs have been effective. Meeting or exceeding objectives shows that the company's money has been spent wisely.

Accountability is a must in business today. Starting all the way at the top—with the board of directors, who answer to shareholders—and extending down to managers of the smallest departments, there is always someone wanting to know how and why money was spent, how the spending helped generate more sales and profits, and whether the money was spent in the most effective way. Yet according to a study by Accenture management consultants, 70 percent of marketing executives report that they don't really know what kind of return they are getting on their marketing investment.[1] MC managers who lack this knowledge find it very difficult to defend their budgets, let alone justify a budget increase. Keep in mind that marketers are constantly competing internally against all other departments for budget dollars.

Being accountable and knowing whether objectives have been met are not the only reasons to do evaluations and measurements. Just as important is finding out *why* MC efforts worked or didn't work. Evaluation and measurement provide feedback. If questions are constructed in the right way, if the correct observations are done, if the right people (those targeted) are interviewed, marketers will receive diagnostic feedback, a critical component of marketing communication (⬅ Chapter 4). When objectives are or are not met, finding out *why* provides important corporate learning.

Another important reason for measuring MC efforts is to determine the gap between MC expectations and reality. **Gap analysis** is *an analysis of the difference between what customers expect from a brand (based on brand messages) and what they actually experience.* Exhibit 22-1 is a creative depiction of the gap between promise and performance.

An example of the importance of knowing what kind of return a company is getting from its MC budget is demonstrated by Nextel, a provider of cellphone services. When its sales began to decrease, it used data mining (⬅ Chapter 8) to learn which of the MC functions it had been using were producing the best returns. The analysis quickly showed that its Web advertising had been the most cost-effective in producing sales leads. Based on this finding, the MC spending allocation plan was revised. As a result, 100 percent of Nextel's MC budget was spent online—on full-screen pop-ups and special offers. The revised plan not only increased the number of calling plans sold but also reduced the cost per sales lead from $35 to $11.[2]

Completing his term as chairman of the American Association of Advertising Agencies, David Bell remarked, "Nothing remains more critical to the health and rigor of our business than proving what we all know: that advertising [MC] really works; that it works in the ways that are relevant to our clients; and

When packages don't arrive on time things can't get done, people wait, clients leave, customers get angry, reputations get ruined, credibility goes out the window, orders get backed up, jobs get lost, people get demoted, bosses get angry, people are disappointed, stores can't open, assembly lines shut down, factories shut down, accounts go to the competition, money gets lost, meetings are missed, conferences are cancelled, blood pressure goes up, businesses can't open, people can't work, promises are broken, trust is lost, opportunities are missed, deals aren't made, transactions never happen, ideas aren't shared, products don't get made, information is missed, and the person who used the shipping company that messed it up looks really, really, really bad.

When packages do arrive on time the world works just fine.

FedEx
The Way The World Works.™

that it helps drive American business."[3] *Advertising Age* echoed Bell's words, saying that increasingly cost-conscious marketers "are demanding that agencies be held more accountable for their work by demonstrating value for what they charge."[4]

As those two quotes indicate, there is ongoing pressure to evaluate and measure brand communication efforts. Evaluation must include critical areas such as cross-functional planning and monitoring, brand-message creation, media planning and buying, and listening to customers and capturing their complaints, suggestions, and compliments. These are the IMC processes that strengthen the brand relationships that drive profitable brands.

MC evaluation and measurement programs are conducted both during the development of brand-message strategies and after the completion of a campaign. The basic objective is to predict or determine *results*—that is, the changes in behavior or attitudes created by an offer, a promotion, a campaign, a company response, or some other type of brand message. Exhibit 22-2 draws attention to the importance of results in all areas of business. Other objectives of evaluation and measurement include (1) reducing risk, (2) providing direction, (3) determining to what extent marketing communication programs met objectives, and (4) determining to what extent the communication effort proved to be a good investment of the company's money.

EXHIBIT 22-2
Accountability is a big issue in marketing communication, as in other areas of business. In this ad the insurance and financial services company Cigna announces that it accepts responsibility for getting results for its clients.

Important as they are, however, MC measurement and evaluation must be put into perspective. The vast majority of brand messages have never been, and never will be, formally measured or evaluated. Most decisions about whether to use a particular brand message are based on the judgment of a marketing manager (or some other client or agency executive) because there is not enough at risk to justify spending money to evaluate every single message.

Generally speaking, MC evaluation is done primarily when companies (1) have sizable media budgets and (2) stand to suffer significant financial losses if the brand messages fail to achieve the MC objectives. Although some marketing executives feel their personal judgment is sufficient to evaluate brand messages and campaigns, most *smart* executives in these situations prefer to base their use/don't use decisions on some type of objective evaluation.

Although the majority of individual brand messages are never formally evaluated, the selling concept or creative strategy on which a brand message is based may have been rigorously tested. Once an idea for an advertising campaign has been tested and has proved itself, that idea may be executed for a couple of years with no further testing other than tracking studies (explained later in this chapter).

When an evaluation is deemed necessary, several questions need to be answered to justify the expense:

- What should be evaluated?

- What information already exists?

- At what stages should the MC message or campaign be evaluated?

What Should Be Evaluated: The Cost/Value Factor

Evaluation is generally undertaken for critical decisions that involve a lot of money, resources, or staff time, such as changing a logo or launching a year-long campaign. The idea is to determine the probability of success up front, before the money is spent. In particular, marketers want to know whether the level of success will be high enough to justify the program's cost, an analysis that shows the return on investment (ROI). The more that is at risk, the greater the number of developmental evaluations and measurements that should be used.

For example, if Pillsbury were considering replacing its familiar Doughboy with a more modern character, the company would probably spend hundreds of thousands of dollars testing and evaluating alternatives before making such a high-risk decision. After all, hundreds of *millions* of dollars have already been invested in building awareness of the Doughboy as spokesperson for the brand. Switching spokespersons is a big decision that can cost the company dearly if the wrong choice is made.

But if Pillsbury were planning to introduce a new cornbread product using the Doughboy in brand messages related to the launch, spending money to evaluate whether the Doughboy should wear a cowboy bandana in the ads would not be worthwhile. The extent of the bandana's impact on the overall brand message would be so minor that spending time and money researching the question would not be cost-effective.

Evaluation always has costs. Designing and testing questionnaires, conducting interviews or observations, tabulating and coding the findings, and then analyzing these findings are all labor-intensive. When focus groups are used, a company hires research firms to recruit and provide facilities for conducting the focus groups. Focus-group leaders are handsomely paid and today most respondents are paid for participating in focus groups. In the case of mail surveys, there is the cost of printing and mailing questionnaires. The ad in Exhibit 22-3 focuses on this type of cost.

Some MC measurements, however, can be made with very little cost. Recall the explanation of split-runs in Chapter 11. For a few hundred dollars extra, two versions of a print ad can be run in a magazine or newspaper to measure the difference in response for two different offers, headlines, illustrations, or other message components. The same technique can be used in direct mail or with other types of promotional brochures and offers. Although the risk of using one offer versus another may not be great, the cost of measuring is relatively small and thus the cost/value ratio of the measurement is very good.

Evaluations should measure only those things that can be changed. One manufacturing company asked its dealers how satisfied they were with a number of operational areas. Three areas of the business always received low scores, but no changes were made. When the president of the company was asked why not, he explained that making such changes would be too costly. Unfortunately, the company continued to ask the questions, not only consuming time

EXHIBIT 22-3

ePrize is an e-business company that uses a sweepstakes to motivate people to respond to online research.

We get you information about your Web site visitors the old-fashioned way.

We bribe 'em.

That is, we use big prizes to make 'em talk. ePrize can run your company's online sweepstakes from start to finish. In the process, you'll find out who's visiting your site, generate more hits, enlarge your mailing list, and grow your online business. How? Every time someone registers, we compile demographics, purchasing patterns, and other priceless info for you. All at a savings of up to 90% of the cost of doing it yourself. Give us a buzz at 877.837.7493 or visit www.eprize.net

ePrize
eSweepstakes
made easy

and money but also reminding the dealers of things they didn't like about the company.

What Information Already Exists?

Many companies have enormous amounts of data that could be (but have not been) used for evaluative purposes. A good example is a situation that occurred at a public health organization several years ago. When the level of public discussion of acquired immune deficiency syndrome (AIDS) was very high, the organization hired a major advertising agency to conduct focus groups across the United States to see what major questions the average person had about this disease. At the same time, the organization hired a consultant to evaluate the organization's call center, which was set up to answer health questions from medical personnel and the general public. In the course of his audit, the consultant noticed that the representatives made notes on most of the calls they handled. When he asked about the purpose of the notes, he was told they were to help the representatives keep track of the number of calls handled and the subject of the calls so they could do their weekly performance reports. Once the weekly reports were written, the notes were thrown away.

In further observations, the consultant found that the notes often included the questions being asked by the people who called in to the center. Not surprisingly, many of the calls were about AIDS. Those within the organization who had requested the AIDS focus groups did not realize this information was coming in to the organization's call center each day. The problem was that the people who asked for the focus groups were separate from the call center people. Because there was no cross-functional organization involving these two groups, the organization paid thousands of dollars to gather data that it was already collecting.

Similar situations exist in many companies. For example, marketing departments seldom work closely with customer-service departments and consequently have little knowledge of what customers are saying about the brand and company. Also many companies that issue product warranty cards never tabulate those that are returned—and thus never collect the valuable customer-profile information the cards contain. Before a research project is started, it is wise to make sure that the information desired does not already exist.

When Should Evaluation Be Conducted?

Evaluation can be done at several stages during the development and execution of MC campaigns. The first stage is market research into customer perceptions to determine whether the brand's position needs reinforcing, changing, or repositioning. Then, after message ideas have been generated, comes **concept testing,** which consists of *tests that measure the effectiveness of the rough ideas that become brand and campaign themes.* Next is copytesting, which was mentioned in Chapter 9 as a type of research that evaluates brand-message executions in a rough form before they are finally produced. Then there is **concurrent testing,** which is *testing that tracks the performance of messages as they are run* (see Exhibit 22-4). Some companies test at only one stage, others at more than one—depending on how much the company wants to invest in minimizing its risks.

Finally, there is **evaluative testing,** which is *testing that measures the performance of brand messages against their objectives at the conclusion of the program.* The closer a message is to its finished form and the more realistic the testing environment is, the more predictability a measurement generally has, as shown in Figure 22-1. (Some of the terms in this figure may be unfamiliar to you; they are explained later in this chapter.)

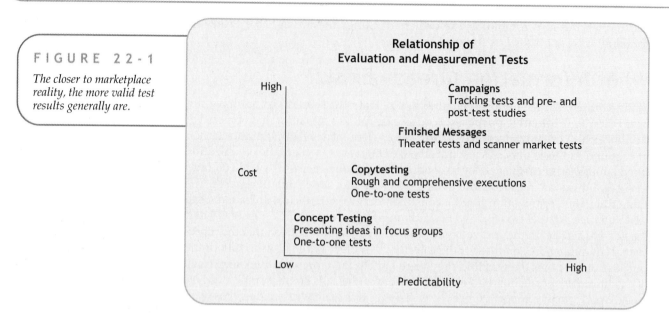

**Relationship of
Evaluation and Measurement Tests**

High

Campaigns
Tracking tests and pre- and
post-test studies

Finished Messages
Theater tests and scanner market tests

Cost

Copytesting
Rough and comprehensive executions
One-to-one tests

Concept Testing
Presenting ideas in focus groups
One-to-one tests

Low   High

Predictability

The Critical Role of Objectives

An effective marketing communication program is one that meets its objectives. MC planners must set measurable objectives. The more closely these objectives can be related to sales and profits, the better they are. But only in the areas of direct marketing and sales promotion is it possible to easily measure message effectiveness by sales.

The problem with using sales results alone to evaluate the impact of all marketing communication efforts is that MC represents only one set of variables that affect sales. Product performance, pricing, distribution, and competition all impact sales, share, and profits. Consequently, in an effort to try to isolate the effectiveness of MC activities, changes in brand awareness, brand knowledge, and attitude change are measured. Although these measures are also influenced by other factors, they are the ones most widely used to evaluate MC efforts. This does not mean that MC departments and agencies have no responsibility for sales and profits. It means that other variables must be taken into consideration when sales and profits are the primary measures (see Exhibit 22-5).

Measuring Objectives

Although every MC plan is different, most plans have communication objectives to increase one or more of the following: level of brand awareness and image (awareness); understanding and recall of brand information (knowledge); the creation of attitude change and preference (persuasion); trial and repeat buying (behavior); and the development of customer acquisition, retention, and growth (relationship building). If an objective calls for a 10 percent increase in brand awareness, for example, then brand awareness should be measured.

If the objectives are behavioral results, such things as requests-for-more information, trial, and showroom visits are the easiest to measure. As explained in Chapters 14 and 18, one of the main strengths of both sales promotion and direct response is their measurability. The number of prospects and customers who respond to a promotion or offer (by buying, sampling, requesting more information, or visiting a store or trade-show booth) can be compared to the targeted population to ascertain a response rate or percentage.

E X H I B I T   2 2 - 5

The Tabasco ad shown in Chapter 5 was so successful that the Magazine Publishers Association featured it in the association's ad. In an attempt to prove the effectiveness of magazine advertising, the MPA reported that Tabasco sales were up 12.4 percent after four weeks of advertising in magazines as part of an overall media mix. What information is missing that would help you determine whether that 12.4 percent is truly an indication of successful marketing communication?

Measuring changes in attitudes and opinions is more difficult because these changes exist only in people's heads. Also, researchers do not agree about whether attitude changes lead to behavior changes—or, if they do, to what extent. Nevertheless, most marketers and academics agree that increases in such things as brand awareness, knowledge, and brand preference are indicators of communication effectiveness and are therefore worth measuring and evaluating.

Baselines

An important factor in setting measurable objectives is knowing the **baseline**— that is, *the beginning point, or where things stand before an MC effort begins.* For example, if you want to increase awareness by 10 percent, you have to know what the current level of awareness is in order to gauge the amount of change—10 percent of what? If 60 percent of the target audience is aware of a brand, and the objective is to increase awareness by 10 percent, then the desired outcome would be an awareness level of 66 percent (60 × .10 = 6, which is added to the base of 60). The objective would be stated like this: "The objective is to increase the awareness level from 60 percent to 66 percent, an increase of 10 percent, within a one-year period."

A tracking study of the launch of the Bella Napoli Pizza product by the Italian food company Buitoni, for example, found that the product had gained a critical level of penetration in its launch period. The communication effectiveness was determined by the following:[5]

- *Awareness:* The 43 percent level of awareness at the pre-launch stage rose to 98 percent two years later, surpassing the main competitor, Findus, which held an 84 percent awareness level during the same period.
- *Brand usership:* Buitoni's penetration went from 11 percent during the pre-launch phase to 59 percent after the launch.

Because of the communication support provided by the launch of Pizza Bella Napoli, Buitoni Pizzas registered a 61 percent growth in sales volume and a 76 percent increase in shareholder value in the following two years.

MEASUREMENT AND EVALUATION METHODS

Advertising and other MC functions are evaluated using a number of different methods. In this section we'll discuss some of the major methods that include determining if the media bought actually ran, concept testing, and pre- and post-copytesting. You will note that the more finished MC messages are and the more real-life the environment is when message effectiveness is measured, the more valid results are likely to be.

Media: Measuring Message Delivery

One focus of MC evaluation is the delivery of the message. If the message is an advertisement, for example, did it run as scheduled? If the message is a public relations message, clients want to know how much "play" the news release received. In both cases, monitoring services can track performance and report back to clients. Press releases are often monitored by the collecting of clips—print and broadcast mentions of the brand or of the news release topic. In addition to simple counts, message exposure is also measured in terms of inches in print and seconds in broadcasts.

Internet services track hits, the number of times a website is visited. Some online monitoring services are able to track a visitor's activity before, during, and after in order to tell the client where visitors came from, what they did while they were visiting the site, and where they went after leaving the site.

Nielsen Media Research is the primary audience service that monitors the play of commercials and estimates consumer viewing patterns based on panels it runs nationwide. A new service offered by the personal video recorder company TiVo is designed to provide advertisers with moment-by-moment reports on the viewing patterns of their customers.[6] Another example of television commercial monitoring comes from a service called Infomercial Monitoring Services, which watches infomercials from some 40 cable channels to make sure the spots run at the right time and on the right channels.[7]

Testing Concepts and Creative Strategies

Advertising concepts and strategies that are supported by large media budgets receive the lion's share of developmental evaluation and measurement. If a company

TABLE 22-1	Measurement and Evaluation Methods	
Element to Be Tested	**Measurement Methods**	**Message-Testing Format**
Concept, creative strategy	Focus groups, intercept surveys, projective tests	Idea statements, visuals on display boards
Awareness, brand knowledge	Surveys	Phone, e-mail, customer-service interactions
Communication and persuasion	Focus groups, one to one, laboratory, e-mail	Rough layouts, comps
Recognition, recall	Magazine portfolio, day-after phone survey, theater	Finished executions, animatics
Physiological responses	Eye tracking, galvanic skin response	Laboratory one to one
Packaging impact	Tachistoscope, observation	Laboratory one to one, in store/aisle
Pilot test	Scanner test-markets	Finished executions
Customer knowledge, attitudes, behavior	Tracking studies	Phone, e-mail
Copytesting (post-test)	Split-run, scanner data, awareness, attitude change, sales	Finished executions

makes three TV commercials, spends $15 million on media time and space, and then finds that the messages are not communicating or persuading, it has wasted the production costs and $15 million. Table 22-1 lists the elements and developmental stages of brand messages most frequently measured, the measuring methods used, and the format in which the evaluations and measurements take place. (Again, terms that may be unfamiliar are explained in the following sections.)

Qualitative research is often used in account planning to find a customer insight that can be addressed with an MC message to deliver on a stated objective. The IMC in Action box explains how such research can be used to develop and refine a message strategy.

The first step in developing a campaign is to identify the most compelling message concept, creative theme, or primary selling proposition. An example of a concept test comes from a U.S.-based frozen-food company. Its food technicians developed a frozen pasta sauce that consumers could make from a package containing chunks of frozen vegetables and a packet of seasoning and thickener. All the consumer had to do was place the ingredients in a skillet, add some water and oil, and cook for 20 minutes. The challenge was to come up with a message concept that accurately described the product and its benefits in a believable and persuasive manner.

The company didn't know whether to focus on the convenience of preparation, the great taste, or the ingredients. Working with its advertising agency, the company wrote the following three concept statements, which were shown to three focus groups of the target audience—women who had families and who liked to cook. Each statement was printed in large letters on poster board. In each focus group, the order in which the three concepts were presented was changed to avoid order bias.

Concept A: Now, in only 20 minutes you can conveniently prepare a delicious-tasting pasta sauce made from flash-frozen vegetables and a secret mix of Italian spices.

Concept B: A rich, thick pasta sauce that is so delicious, your family will not believe you made it yourself.

IMC IN ACTION

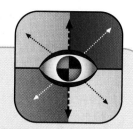

Research Is the Infrastructure behind Creative Ideas

How do you pique the interest of business executives with a message about the infrastructure behind e-business? This was the challenge presented to the IBM WW IMC teams and that was the assignment given to Ogilvy & Mather, IBM's advertising agency. A business-to-business problem, the award winning "E-Business Infrastructure" campaign was built on a solid research foundation led by IBM's WW market intelligence team with contributions from Ameritest Research, The Maya Group, and Perception Research Services.

IBM recognized that a new business opportunity existed in the previously unrecognized area of e-business infrastructure—an opportunity that IBM could address by leveraging its strengths in this area. IBM's objective was to define this new category, generate interest in it, and position IBM as the leader in providing infrastructure solutions.

Ameritest, for example, provided IBM with television advertising research and a strategy loop that resulted in a continual refinement and shaping of the strategy, as well as a consistent focus on meeting the campaign's objectives. Rather than a research "silo," where researchers are brought in to test and report their results, the research team was an on-going integral part of the MC team and their insights were drawn upon to provide ideas, as well as wisdom, in managing the shifting thrusts of the campaign. Two things made this campaign an award winner:

1. The expanded authority that research findings were given in the campaign's development.

2. IBM's insistence that research be used to drive campaign decisions at every step in the development of the campaign.

The initial qualitative exploratory research found that in the post dot-com era, infrastructure was a nebulous subject that many executives didn't think about until they faced a problem or breakdown. Ogilvy & Mather developed a series of TV ads around "Moments of Truth." Copytesting proved the ad's success at dramatizing the problem-solution message. Using an educational strategy, the print campaign delivered information in a textbook format (the "Book of e-Business") to help executives learn more about e-business infrastructure. A visual metaphor, the Leaning Tower of Pisa, demonstrated the importance of a solid structure.

The campaign and the research on which it was based were so effective that the campaign was a winner in the 2003 Grand Ogilvy Research Award competition sponsored by the Advertising Research Foundation. In terms of impact, IBM's unaided association with e-business infrastructure rose to an index of 113 from 100, while its primary competitor's association dropped from 80 to 60. In just over nine months, the campaign exceeded IBM's objectives for new-business generation by 354 percent with more than 1,600 new contracts from sales leads directly attributable to the campaign.

Source: "Ameritest Shares the 2003 Grand Ogilvy Research Award with IBM, along with First-in-Category Win!," <www.ameritest.net> IBM's 2003 Grand Ogilvy Research Award winning case study; e-business Infrastructure campaign. Used by permission. "Spotlight Shines Brightly on IBM Research," April 11, 2003, press release from The Advertising Research Foundation. Used by permission. Amy Shea, "IBM e-business Infrastructure," May 2003, PowerPoint presentation by Ameritest.

Concept C: Because it is a unique blend of flash-frozen Italian tomatoes, onions, celery, peppers, and hearty Italian spices, this is the finest-tasting pasta sauce you will ever make.

After all three concepts were displayed, participants were asked to write down and then discuss which one best described a product they would be most likely to buy and why. The "whys" are the most important aspect of concept testing. The key finding about the pasta sauce was that few focus-group members believed that a great-tasting sauce could be made in only 20 minutes. As a result the final copy promised "a great tasting sauce that you don't have to cook all day."

Creative concepts can be tested in several ways. One is to use an **intercept survey**—*a survey in which people in a mall or at an event are stopped and asked to respond to a short questionnaire.* The questions ask respondents to compare various concepts and comment on them. Intercept surveys are not scientifically reliable studies but rather offer a way to get a quick response for diagnostic purposes. They indicate whether the people being interviewed understand a concept and, if they do, whether they like it.

Focus groups are also used to test creative concepts. A **focus group** is *a group of 8 to 12 members of a brand's target audience who, led by a moderator, discuss some aspect of a brand, product category, or message strategy.* Most focus-group discussions last one to two hours, and participants are paid anywhere from $25 to $200 for participating. The higher fees are for hard-to-recruit participants such as doctors, lawyers, and business executives.

The main benefit of focus-group research is diagnostic. The idea is to learn more about a category, competing brands, and message strategies from the user's perspective, and to "diagnose" any problems. When a participant says that a brand is "not easy to use," a good discussion leader probes to find out why this is so and what could be done to improve the brand's ease of use. Some people call focus groups "red flag" research, signaling their belief that focus groups are a good place to hear about problems. Sometimes when people are working closely on a project, such as a commercial or a set of print ads, they overlook the obvious. Focus groups help catch these oversights.

Focus-group findings should not be projected to a brand's total population because (1) the number of participants is too small, (2) the participants do not represent a randomly selected sample, and (3) quite often two or three "strong" people in a group dominate the discussion, often biasing the expressed views of others. Despite these shortcomings, however, focus groups can provide valuable customer insights.

Copytesting to Predict Communication Effects

Copytesting can be used either while the brand message is in development or after it appears. The ad in Exhibit 22-6 for Insight Express, which is a spin-off of NFO (a panel research company that evaluates campaigns and other brand messages online), illustrates how different people involved in the development of a creative idea may see its potential differently from the audience for whom it is intended.

All brand messages should, to some extent, do two things—communicate and persuade. To make sure these two message objectives are achieved, companies use several different measuring techniques. As explained in Chapter 4, communication happens when the receiver of a message arrives at the meaning intended by the sender who encoded the message. Persuasion takes place when recipients of a message change their attitudes or behavior in the direction desired. Copytesting measures both of these.

Copytesting (Exhibit 22-7) can be used to evaluate several aspects of communication: attention, brand awareness and knowledge, emotional responses, and physiological responses.

Attention

One way to test the attention-getting power of a package, ad, or other brand message is by using a **tachistoscope,** *a device that exposes a brand message briefly to test participants so that researchers can measure how long it takes for a certain message or element to be communicated.* Tests using a tachistoscope are called *t-tests*. Respondents are seated before a screen containing a small hole that they are asked to look

through. Behind the screen, but in complete darkness, is the ad or other stimulus—such as a logo, package, or promotional flag on a package—that is to be tested.

Suppose a company wants to evaluate several package designs. A number of competitive packages and the test package are arranged behind the screen in the way they would be displayed in a store. Respondents are asked to look through the hole and find the brand being tested. Once the light comes on, it stays on until respondents say they see the test brand and can correctly say where it is displayed (upper left, lower right, and so on). This is called a *find-time test*. By testing several different package designs, this test can help marketers determine which package is the most attention getting. Because the average shopper spends only 20 to 30 seconds making a brand selection in most categories, the quicker a package can be spotted, the more likely it is to be purchased.

Brand Awareness and Knowledge

Companies commonly measure two types of brand awareness—recognition and recall (⬅ Chapter 5). *Recognition* is the act of identifying something and remembering that you saw or heard of it earlier. Identifying a person you know within a crowd of people is recognition. *Recall* (or *unaided awareness*) is the more difficult process of bringing something back from memory. You may recognize a person in a crowd, but you may not be able to recall the person's name. Researchers measure recall by asking respondents to name all the brands they can think of in a particular product category. The researchers then give the respondents any brand names they did not mention and ask whether they have heard of those brands (a process called *aided awareness*). As you might expect, aided awareness (recognition) scores are always higher than unaided awareness (recall) scores.

A measure of magazine-ad recall is provided by Gallup & Robinson's Impact Test. Respondents (who have been screened for certain demographic characteristics) are given a magazine to take home and read. The following day the respondents are called and asked to recall as many ads as they can from the magazine. For the ads that are recalled, respondents are asked what brand claims they remember and how likely they are to buy the brand.

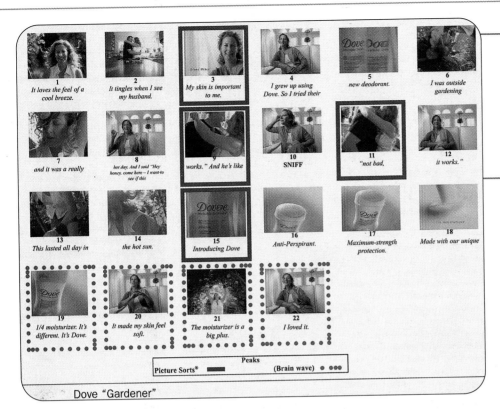

EXHIBIT 22-7

Copytesting is often used to evaluate numerous aspects of communication, including attention, brand awareness and knowledge, emotional responses, and physiological responses.

Recall measurements of TV commercials—called *post-tests* because the commercials have already been made and are on air—are done in a similar way. Respondents are called and asked whether they watched a certain show the day before. If they say yes, they are asked whether they saw a commercial for a product in a particular category (such as hair sprays, cars, brokerage services, computers). If the answer is yes, they are asked what the brand was and what they recall about the commercial. Those who don't recall the particular commercial being studied are then asked whether they remember a commercial for the brand being measured (a recognition question).

Some of the concerns with post-tests are that program content can influence a score, as can the number of competitive commercials running at the same time. And, as with the print tests, there is always a question as to what is actually being remembered—the message execution or the brand claims. It has also been found that well-known brands normally have higher scores than do new and less well-known brands just because of the familiarity factor.

Brand knowledge requires a more in-depth measurement than does brand recall. To measure how much respondents know about a brand and to what extent they see it as different from its competitors, researchers use phone and e-mail surveys. Brand knowledge can also be measured with one-to-one personal interviews, but this expensive method is often not cost-justified. Measurements of brand awareness and brand knowledge are frequently used to evaluate a new or revised campaign effort. Measurements are done as pre- and post-tests—that is, before and after a campaign runs.

Emotional Responses

Recognizing the power of emotions in brand decision making, and also the fact that emotions are difficult for many people to express, MC agency BBDO Worldwide developed a test that measures emotional responses to brand messages. The agency's proprietary Emotional Measurement System lets respondents communicate their emotions by selecting photographs of individuals with various emotional expressions. After respondents are shown a set of brand messages, they are asked to select from dozens of these individual-expression photos (which have been extensively studied and categorized) the images that best illustrate how the brand messages made them feel. The selected photos are used to "emotionally profile" each set of brand messages shown. This allows the agency and client to select the brand message that comes closest to creating the desired emotional response.

An important emotional response that can be measured is likability. Traditionally many MC managers felt that it didn't matter whether customers liked an ad as long as the ad built awareness. More recently, a study by the Advertising Research Foundation of different pre-testing methods found that likability is a powerful predictor of sales success. That's why New York–based Intermedia Advertising Group (IAG), a research company that evaluates television programs and commercials, reports its overall ratings in terms of likability. IAG provides weekly data to *Advertising Age* with the Top 10 commercials identified by their likability score. In addition to likability, the IAG service also reports recall and message understanding. For more about this service, visit the firm's website at www.iagr.net.

The likability of a brand message can be measured along a continuum ranging from "I loved the message" to "I hated the message." Respondents choose a number on the scale (usually from 1 to 5 or from 1 to 7) that best indicates their feeling. Likability tests consider related factors such as these:

- Relevance (personally meaningful).
- Believability, credibility (convincing and true to life).
- Interest (intriguing, fascinating, engaging).
- Enjoyment (entertaining, warm).
- Familiarity (comfortable).
- Surprise (pleasantly surprising).

The likability issue, particularly with advertising, is whether people who like a message will transfer that liking to the brand. In a relationship-focused marketing communication program, likability is presumed to be a key determinant of the continuation of the relationship.

Physiological Responses

Sometimes how we feel emotionally about something affects how we respond to it physically—whether or not we are aware of those responses. According to neurologist Richard Restak, "We have reason to doubt that full awareness of our motives, drives, and other mental activities may be possible."[8] Because people sometimes are not willing to express, or capable of expressing, what they really think or feel about a brand message, measures of physiological responses have been developed. Companies seldom use these tests, so they are described only briefly here. The reason for their limited use is that they are relatively expensive to conduct and the findings are often difficult to interpret.

Probably the most widely discussed physiological test is the *galvanic skin response test*. It uses a galvanometer—the same basic instrument used in lie detectors—to measure minute electrical currents. Marketers use the test to measure to what extent respondents are stimulated or aroused when exposed to a variety of brand messages. Researchers have found that there can be a correlation between level of stimulation and purchase behavior.[9]

Two other tests have to do with eyes—pupil dilation and eye tracking. The *pupil dilation measure* follows the same concept as the galvanic skin response measurement. The more the pupil dilates, the greater is the indication of involvement in the brand message being shown. The *eye-tracking instrument* uses an infrared beam to follow the eye, converting its movement to traces on the ad being tested. Measurements show which ad elements attract the most attention. This information can be helpful in measuring what is known in the MC industry as "vampire creative"—message elements that detract from the purpose of the brand message.

Tools Used to Measure Persuasion

Focus groups, often used to test an ad's communication effects, are not as reliable for testing persuasion. The reason is that there is a low correlation between what people say they will do and what they actually do, especially when it comes to brand selection. "Intend-to-buy" scores—another name for persuasion scores and preference measures—have fooled many companies. Therefore, several levels and methods of persuasion testing have been developed, each providing a little more validity than the one before: (1) theater tests, (2) theater tests with purchases, (3) scanner market tests, and (4) conventional test markets. The more a test simulates real life and includes behavioral responses, the more validity the persuasion score will have.

Theater Tests

After focus groups, companies sometimes use **theater tests,** such as Market Research Inc.'s ASI test (developed by Burke Marketing Research), to measure persuasion effects. These are *tests in which people are invited to a local location for the purpose, they are told, of critiquing a TV program, but actually for the purpose of evaluating their response to a brand message.* Before the showing, participants are asked to complete a questionnaire that asks what brands in certain categories they prefer, and asks as well for some demographic data. Respondents are then shown the program, which contains from six to eight commercials. Three or four are the commercials being tested. After the showing, respondents are asked about the program; they are also asked what commercials they remember seeing (a measure of advertising recall). They are then shown a second program, also containing the test commercials. Following this, they are asked to indicate their preference for brands in a variety of categories similar to the first questionnaire they completed. The difference in the preference scores indicates the level of persuasion.

These laboratory persuasion scores can be given meaning only after they are compared to **norms,** which are *average product category scores accumulated over the years by the research company.* In addition, companies doing this type of research try to get as much follow-up sales data as they can from their clients to correlate lab findings with actual sales results.

Theater Tests with Purchases

The next level of persuasion validity involves forced purchases after the theater showing of a brand message. Instead of having participants complete the second questionnaire described above, respondents are given tokens and taken into a room that is set up as a small store. The shelves are stocked with all the major brands in each of the product categories of the test commercials. Respondents are told to use their tokens to buy whichever brands they want. By recording each person's brand choices and comparing these choices to those indicated on the initial brand-usage questionnaire, researchers can determine how many respondents switched brands. The more who switch, the higher is the persuasion score for the respective test commercial.

One advantage of theater tests is that **animatics** (*rough video footage used in ad testing*) can be used instead of finished commercials. Although finished ads are preferred so they don't look out of place or inferior, animatics save companies a great amount of production costs. A weakness of theater tests is that, because

EXHIBIT 22-8

Checkout scanners can track the purchases of selected households that agree to participate in research studies.

participants are aware they are being tested, they can project intend-to-buy responses that do not necessarily correspond to their normal behavior. Also, forced-purchase decisions provide only directional answers about persuasion (an ad is persuasive or not persuasive); they cannot be used to say that the test commercial would increase sales by any certain percentage.

Test Marketing

Test marketing is probably the most valid persuasion test because it takes place over a longer period in a competitive marketplace. **Test marketing** is *a research design in which an MC campaign is run in two to four markets for anywhere from 6 to 12 months*. Brand sales are compared to sales in similar control markets (those in which the brand has about the same share and is faced with the same major competitors). Three problems are associated with the use of test marketing: (1) It takes a long time. (2) Testing exposes new ideas to competitors. (3) Market tests are expensive. In test marketing, all MC materials must be in finished form, and at least 200 customers need to be interviewed in each of the test and control markets both before and after the market test runs. Scanner market tests and tracking studies are types of test marketing measures.

Scanner Market Tests A **scanner market test** is *a tracking of a household's purchases*. Several major research companies (such as ACNielsen, Information Resources, and SAMI/Burke) provide this type of testing. Each of these companies has made special arrangements with chain stores and local cable operators and newspapers in selected small- to medium-size markets throughout the United States. In each market, researchers have recruited a panel of household members who agree to have a buyer identification card (like a frequent-buyer card) scanned every time they go shopping so that their purchases can be tracked (see Exhibit 22-8). Within each market's panel, participants are divided into two groups, the test group and the control group. The cable company sends the test commercial only to people in the test group. At the same time, newspaper test ads are substituted for regular ads in papers that are delivered to the test households.

Scanner market tests can be used in a short time frame to evaluate sales-promotion offers, which, if successful, generally increase sales within days of running. These tests can also be used for longer-term evaluation of a brand's repositioning or a new campaign theme. One of the benefits of scanner tests is that, by tracking weekly (or even daily) sales, researchers can determine how long it takes for marketing communication to have an effect. The more frequently a product category is purchased, the more telling such a test generally is and the less time it requires. Differences in purchases between test households and control households determine the extent of the promotional impact.

Participating households know they are members of a research panel, but they have no idea what brands are being tested. Because brand selections are made in real stores and respondents use their own money, there is nothing other than the test MC messages to influence the results. Also, results are based on actual sales data, not on scores that have to be translated into sales. Furthermore, this type of test has the advantage of not being obvious to competitors.

There are a couple of shortcomings, however. Scanner market tests have high costs—several times the cost of theater tests. Not only must researchers use finished brand messages, but households must be compensated for participating, stores must be paid for providing scanner data for the test and control groups, and the cable and newspaper media charge a premium for special handling of the test messages. Another limitation is that the percentage of the test panel that makes purchases in the test brand's product category can be relatively small, making projections to a national market difficult.

Tracking Studies Used most frequently by companies that have multimillion-dollar MC budgets, **tracking studies** are *periodic surveys that measure brand awareness, trial, repeat, and customer satisfaction with a brand and its competitors.* Because tracking studies are ongoing, they offer test-and-control as well as pre- and post-test measures of new campaigns and other major changes in the marketing and marketing communication mix. Testing is done by using the materials to be tested in a couple of the markets being tracked, then using the others as control markets.

Tracking studies are one of the best methods for evaluating long-term marketing communication and relationship-building results. Most tracking studies are done by phone (although for brands whose users are also heavy internet users, they can be done online) in several different markets every three to six months. Brands that can afford to do so often track a sample of their strong, weak, and new markets. Unless a company has a database of category users, random dialing is used to find respondents. In the case of service brands, customer-satisfaction tracking studies are often ongoing, with customer interviews being conducted each day or week.

What is asked in a study that tracks awareness, trial, and repeat? Figure 22-2 lists typical questions that a rental car company might ask. To the right of each question is an explanation of the question. Following the screening question, the questions dealing with awareness, trial, and repeat are standard on tracking studies. The remaining questions are customized for each brand and each survey wave (each study is called a *wave*). These diagnostic questions help explain why a brand is growing or declining in sales and share. One processed-meat company conducted a tracking study that always included questions on quality and taste. When it was found that the scores for "tastes great" were falling, the TV advertising (which was the primary MC function) was revised to include more shots of taste satisfaction—close-ups of delicious-looking sandwiches and of people smiling while eating. Within six months after the new advertising began running, taste satisfaction scores began to increase.

Although a tracking study is designed to show trends over time, the results of just one wave of interviews often provide valuable insights into the strengths and weaknesses of a brand's marketing program. Both absolute numbers and the relationship between the various numbers need to be analyzed. Obviously, many brand messages—MC, intrinsic, unintended, and customer created—affect tracking scores. Nevertheless, analyses of tracking studies can often help companies spot MC problem areas.

Table 22-2 is a hypothetical set of tracking scores that could be obtained from the questions in Figure 22-2. The numbers for Brand A are what brand managers dream of—they are very good. The 40 percent top-of-mind is the percentage of respondents who mentioned Brand A first when responding to the recall question: "Please tell me all the brands of rental car brands you can think of." This score is close to the brand's market share and shows that Brand A is by far the number-one car rental brand. The fact that nearly two-thirds of the people aware of Brand A rented at least once in the last 12 months is a good ratio and suggests that there are few, if any, marketing communication concerns. The fact that over half (38/65) rented more than once in this period is also healthy, especially in a competitive category such as rental cars, where actual product differences are minimal.

FIGURE 22-2

Which are recall and which are recognition questions?

Sample Tracking Study Questions

Questions and Answers

Q: Have you rented a car within the last six months?
A: Yes.

Q: Please tell me all the brands of rental cars you can think of.
A: Brand A, Brand B

Q: Which of these brands are you familiar with: Brand C, Brand D, Brand E?
A: Brand C, Brand E.

Q: From which of these companies have you rented a car at least once during the last 12 months?
A: Brand A, Brand B.

Q: From which of these companies have you rented a car **more** than once during the last 12 months?
A: Brand A.

Q: On a scale of 1 to 5, with 5 being the highest rating, how would you rate Brand A's customer service? How would you rate Brand B's?
A: Four for Brand A; two for Brand B.

Q: On a scale of 1 to 5, with 5 being the highest rating, how would you rate the quality of car that you rented from Brand A? From Brand B?
A: Four for Brand A; two for Brand B.

Q: On a scale of 1 to 5, with 5 being the highest rating, how likely would you be to recommend Brand A to someone else? Brand B?
A: Four for Brand A; two for Brand B.

Explanation

Screening question. This question is asked first to make sure the respondent is a category user. If the answer is no, the interview is terminated.

Recall question. The first brand name mentioned is tabulated as the top-of-mind (TOM) brand. There is generally a high correlation between a brand's TOM score and the brand's market share. This is because customers are more likely to mention first the brand they use most. All others mentioned are classified as "unaided" mentions. These are brands that the respondents can recall.

Recognition question. Interviewer asks for each of the brands being measured that the respondent did not mention in the answer to the recall question. The brands with which the respondent is familiar are classified as "aided" mentions. These are the brands that were not recalled but were recognized.

Trial question. The answer to this question indicates which brands the respondent has tried/sampled.

Brand menu question. This answer indicates those brands the respondent feels are OK to use, the ones to which the respondent is loyal.

Here begins the customized questions. This particular one is measuring the perceived level of customer service.

This might be asked to see if the perceived difference in car quality is enough to be used as a copy point in brand messages.

This type of question is generally considered as being the most predictive of brand loyalty. If a customer is very likely to recommend a brand to someone else, that customer is very likely to make a repeat purchase.

* Answers are hypothetical.

T A B L E   2 2 - 2   Tracking Study Scores*

	Brand A	Brand B	Brand C
Top-of-mind (TOM) awareness	40%	20%	15%
Unaided awareness	62	62	38
Aided awareness	90	85	70
Trial	65	65	20
Repeat purchase	38	10	15

*Numbers are hypothetical.

The numbers for Brand B have both good and bad news. The fact that Brand B's top-of-mind awareness is only half of Brand A's suggests that Brand B may need greater brand-message frequency or more memorable brand messages. The conversion from awareness to trial numbers is very good, as nearly three out of four (65/85) of those aware have tried Brand B. That only one out of six (10/65) makes a repeat purchase, however, indicates a severe problem. One explanation is that expectations were set too high and renters were disappointed. Another more likely explanation is that the brand was inferior: long lines, unavailability, or dirty or underperforming cars may account for the product's low repeat-purchase score.

Because Brand C's top three scores are considerably lower than the scores for Brand A and Brand B, it could be that Brand C is not spending enough on marketing communication. If competitive spending reports show that Brand C is, in fact, spending nearly the same as the other two brands, the low scores would indicate that the brand messages are not communicating or not persuading (fewer than one out of three respondents familiar with the brand has even tried it in the last 12 months). The low top-of-mind scores and unaided-awareness scores could also suggest poor media selection—not reaching the target audience. The good news in these scores is that three-fourths of those who tried Brand C repeated, a much higher percentage of conversion than either Brand A's or Brand B's. This suggests that Brand C should also invest much more in promotion in order to motivate trial, because the findings show that once customers try Brand C, the majority make repeat rentals.

Real-Time Tracking

The biggest problem with most traditional customer satisfaction tracking studies is that planning and executing them and analyzing and reporting the findings take so long that the findings are not timely. Who cares what customers were saying three or six months ago? The internet is helping solve that problem because it allows almost instantaneous data reporting. Immediate feedback from a website provides information on a real-time basis that can be used to monitor and change strategies. Karl Weiss, president of Market Perceptions Inc., explains that an "intelligent" online reporting system also can alert managers about customer-satisfaction problems as they develop and point to the sources of these problems.[10]

Weiss uses the following example: The director of customer satisfaction at a large, regional network of three hospitals surveys patients daily. A Real-Time Notification System™ can be set up that allows the director to monitor critical parameters (such as courtesy of attending nurses, patients' involvement in determining care/treatment, courtesy shown to visitors) and compare them to norms for the three-hospital network (aggregate scores) and to norms for each individual hospital. Every time the data-reporting system finds that the results fall below thresholds set for each parameter, an e-mail alert is sent to the director responsible.

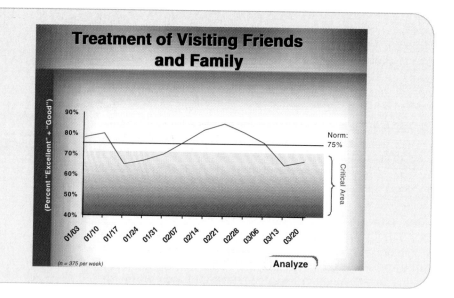

Figure 22-3 illustrates how one parameter—courtesy to visitors—might be monitored. When the percentage of respondents scoring "courtesy of staff to visitors" falls below the organization's norm of 75 percent, a "red flag" e-mail message is automatically generated.

B2B Measurement

Because most B2B marketing communication budgets are not as large as the budgets for consumer brands, B2B companies generally do less copy and media evaluation. Tracking studies, for example, are most typically used for consumer products, although nothing other than cost prevents B2B brands from using them.

Because a much larger portion of most B2B budgets goes into personal selling, B2B companies often use forms of measurement such as advisory boards, customer-evaluation forms, and surveys of industry consultants and members of the trade press. Advisory boards are generally made up of customers (both channel members and end users) but can also include suppliers, consultants, and academics who specialize in relevant areas. The purpose of these groups is to tell companies what they are doing right and what they could be doing better.

IBM ThinkPad, for example, has a marketing advisory board made up of marketing directors from noncompeting companies, suppliers of marketing services, and academics who specialize in marketing and IMC. Each year, for two days, the group is presented with a variety of ideas—everything from marketing plans to special promotions and packaging ideas, to new-product ideas and creative work—and is then asked for reactions and suggestions.

Customer and other types of advisory groups can provide helpful feedback to companies, but there are limitations to this type of MC evaluation. Normally, the customer advisory groups are quite small and not representative of the company's customer base. Also, some members of these groups may have their own agendas and therefore slant their comments to suit their own company needs and desires.

Online Measurement and Evaluation

Online evaluations make sense not only for measuring online marketing efforts but also for replacing or complementing mail and phone surveys. Although online research still accounts for only a small portion of the $6 billion market research industry in the United States, it has been growing. The *rate* of growth has slowed, however, as response rates continue to drop. The two aspects of online research that hold the most promise are *panel surveying* (sending out questionnaires to people who agreed beforehand to participate) and *data delivery* (distributing measurement findings online). Three major benefits of doing online measurements are timeliness, low costs, and narrow targeting—advantages dramatized in the Greenfield Online ad in Exhibit 22-9.

Some MC professionals are concerned that findings from online measurements are not as valid as those from offline phone surveys. Because the majority of consumers are still not active internet users, some argue that samples are not representative of the total population. This suggests that online surveys should be used only when the majority of a product's target audience uses the internet. There is some evidence, however, that online measures can be valid. In one national election, for example, Harris Interactive online polling system correctly predicted the results of 21 out of 22 political races; this success rate was the same as or better than results from several major telephone surveys.[11]

Although most e-commerce companies that undertake MC measurement focus on sales, other meaningful online measurements can be taken. Online tests can measure the

- Number who requested brand information.
- Number who completed a customer profile.
- Number who made complaints.
- Types of people who visit the site.
- Frequency of visits.
- Number who participate in chat sessions.
- Number and quality of website mentions in the media and by other third parties.
- Type and popularity of other sites that request to be linked to the company's site.

Having this type of evaluative information can help companies improve their websites, online offers, and other online relationship-building efforts.

ARE YOU STILL BUYING MARKETING RESEARCH DONE THE OLD-FASHIONED WAY?

Do it better on the internet with the company that pioneered online marketing research.

Our panel of more than one million consumers from all across the internet is the largest of its kind. It produces robust samples of any demographic or lifestyle you choose. You'll get richer, more actionable information quicker than you can say dot com.

Join the Research Revolution!® Contact the world's most experienced internet marketing research company for studies online, on time, on target and on budget.

www.greenfield.com 888.291.9997

Greenfield Online
Leading the Research Revolution®

EXHIBIT 22-9
Online research is speedy, targeted, and inexpensive.

Online Panels versus Spam Surveys

Spam mailings of research questions can quickly generate a large number of responses, but it is difficult to know who responded. It is known that even if respondents are required to provide personal profile data, approximately 25 percent provide false data. Another problem of spam research is that, just as telemarketing has made phone survey work difficult to do (the participation refusal rate is now close to 50 percent), it will make online research more difficult and costly to do. People ignore unsolicited surveys because they either confuse them with sales offers or are annoyed by receiving too much unsolicited e-mail in general.

The concept of permission marketing, mentioned in Chapter 7, applies to doing surveys. The most successful surveys invite people to participate. Not only do people need to give their permission to be sent surveys, but they also must provide personal profiles in order to be in a research panel. This not only ensures a much higher response rate but also provides a database of customer profiles that can be used to match survey respondents to the target audience of a brand for which the research is being done.

America Online (AOL) owns an online research company called DMS, which recruits respondents from AOL's 20-million-plus members. To motivate members to participate, AOL offers various incentives, including credits that reduce AOL membership fees. Other major online research companies (such as Harris and Greenfield) as well as offline research companies (such as NFO and NPD Group) also have sizable pre-recruited panels from which they can select representative brand-audience samples. Recruiting panel members is an ongoing job and requires advertising and tie-in promotions with a variety of websites.

Holding focus-group discussions online offers several advantages, such as saving the cost of renting a research facility and paying high fees for participation. Advertain.com (www.advertain.com) is one of the companies that sets up and runs online focus groups. Operationally, an **online focus group** is *a chat room to which selected people have been invited to meet at a specified time with a moderator.* These groups are most successful when participants are either customers or prospects selected from a highly controlled panel. This helps ensure that participants are who they say they are and are motivated to participate. Because online participants aren't sitting across from each other as in a traditional focus-group setting, the timid are more likely to respond, and people are more likely to challenge and disagree with the more outspoken and aggressive participants. At the same time, there are disadvantages. Face-to-face groups provide a certain amount of body language that is lost online. Online discussions also lack the display of dynamics and emotions that can be a measure of how relevant a certain brand aspect is.

Media Metrix is a company that tracks online media usage of members of a recruited panel. Participants sign up to participate and give permission for their online activities to be recorded. Software for doing the tracking is downloaded by the participants, and their activities are uploaded and sent to Media Metrix for analysis. Such panels provide online marketers a way to measure who is participating and what other online sites attract their customers. Also, changes of website content and presentation or changes in the mix of links with other sites, for example, can be evaluated with Media Metrix findings. In sum, MC planners who intend to use online evaluation should consider the following:

- *Use respondents from a pre-recruited panel.* This provides several advantages: Respondents are known (online users are notorious for disguising their identity). Respondents can be chosen who best match the brand's target profile. The questionnaire is not perceived as intrusive, and respondents feel an obligation to respond.

- *Ensure quick download.* Because respondents are doing the company a favor, the questionnaire should download quickly, and the instructions should be very clear.

- *Limit questionnaire length.* Companies must respect respondents' time. Experts suggest that questionnaires take no more than 15 minutes to complete.[12]

- *Make navigation effortless.* The more work it takes for respondents to complete a survey, the lower the response rate will be.

- *Limit contact frequency.* Because most online surveys are done with panels, if members of the panels are asked to participate too often, they may drop out of the panel. The right frequency depends on the incentives offered, the product category, and the length of the questionnaires. The effect of frequency on response rate is something that can be easily tracked and evaluated. When the response rate begins to decrease and all other conditions are the same, frequency should be reduced.

Advantages and Disadvantages of Online Surveying

Online surveys have both advantages and disadvantages when compared to mail and telephone surveys. Online surveys are faster to prepare and distribute, and responses are received faster—days instead of weeks for the return of mail questionnaires. The number of questionnaires completed in a day is not limited by the number of phone interviewers. Theoretically, thousands of online questionnaires can be completed at the same time because they are self-administered and automatically reported. Online surveys provide more flexibility. They can show not only print messages but also audio and video; offline studies can do so only in certain expensive locations. Unlike mail questionnaires, online surveys can be quickly changed when questions are found to be unclear or misleading. Also, data are cleaned as they are collected. For example, if respondents are asked to do a ranking and they assign the same number to two factors, they are instantly made aware of the error and asked to correct it. Finally, as finished questionnaires are returned, unlike mail questionnaires, they are instantly coded and tabulated without need for entering data manually.[13]

Although most research professionals agree that online research will become more widely used, it does have its limitations. Random sampling produces very low returns. As mentioned earlier, online respondents can hide their identity. Although phone respondents can also do this, area codes and some phone-number prefixes indicate a geographical location for which there are demographic profiles against which respondent profiles can be compared. Also, because respondents can hide their identity, competitors can opt-in to a brand's research panel, hide their identity, and learn what products and ideas the brand is studying. Other concerns are that online samples are not representative and that the research frame (the population from which the respondents are drawn) is not well defined.[14]

EVALUATING THE IMC PROCESS

Processes are more important in IMC than in traditional marketing. IMC requires more interaction with customers and other key stakeholders, more internal sharing of information, and more cross-functional planning for, and monitoring of, brand relationships. These critical processes need to be effectively managed, which can be done only if they are periodically evaluated and monitored.

IMC Audits

An **IMC audit** is *an in-depth research method for evaluating IMC relationship-building practices.*[15] It examines organizational structure, the extent of understanding of MC objectives and strategies within the organization, and the extent to which people agree with those objectives and strategies. It also measures to what extent company-created brand messages are strategically consistent. The IMC mini-audit in Figure 22-4 identifies the various areas covered in a full audit. This mini-audit can be administered to company managers to help them decide whether an in-depth audit is needed.

Brand Metrics

The tracking of a brand's performance occupies a major part of a brand manager's time. Also tracked is the performance of brand communication. Such efforts rely on quantitative and qualitative methods, as well as the tracking and regular reporting of sales, share of market, and costs.

FIGURE 22-4

This 20-question mini-audit is an easy way for an organization to quickly test its level of integration.

IMC Mini-Audit

Circle the number that best describes how your organization operates regarding each of the following statements. If you *don't know* how well your organization is doing for a given item, circle DK (Don't Know). If a question does not apply to your organization, leave it blank.

	Never		Always			

Organizational Infrastructure

1. In our company, the process of managing brand/company reputation and building stakeholder relationships is a cross-functional responsibility that includes departments such as production, operations, sales, finance, and human resources, as well as marketing. — 1 2 3 4 5 DK

2. The people managing our communication programs demonstrate a good understanding of the strengths and weaknesses of ALL major marketing communication tools, such as direct response, public relations, sales promotion, advertising, and packaging, when putting marketing communication plans together. — 1 2 3 4 5 DK

3. We do a good job of internal marketing, informing all areas of the organization about our objectives and marketing programs. — 1 2 3 4 5 DK

4. Our major communication agencies have at least monthly contact with each other regarding our communication programs and activities. — 1 2 3 4 5 DK

Interactivity

5. Our media plan is a strategic balance between mass media and one-to-one media. — 1 2 3 4 5 DK

6. Special programs are in place to facilitate customer inquiries and complaints. — 1 2 3 4 5 DK

7. We use customer databases that capture customer inquiries, complaints, and compliments, as well as sales behavior (e.g., trial, repeat, frequency of purchase, type of purchases). — 1 2 3 4 5 DK

8. Our customer databases are easily accessible (internally) and user-friendly. — 1 2 3 4 5 DK

Mission Marketing

9. Our organization's mission is a key consideration and is evident in our marketing communication plans. — 1 2 3 4 5 DK

10. Our mission provides an additional reason for customers and other key stakeholders to believe our messages and support our company. — 1 2 3 4 5 DK

11. Our corporate philanthropic efforts are concentrated in one specific area or program. — 1 2 3 4 5 DK

Strategic Consistency

12. All of our company-created brand messages (e.g., advertising, sales promotion, PR, packaging) are strategically consistent. — 1 2 3 4 5 DK

13. We periodically review all our brand messages to determine to what extent they are strategically consistent. — 1 2 3 4 5 DK

14. We consciously think about what brand messages are being sent by our pricing, distribution, product performance, and customer-service operations, and by persons and organizations outside the control of the company. — 1 2 3 4 5 DK

15. When doing our marketing communication planning, we use a SWOT analysis to determine the strengths and opportunities we can leverage, and the weaknesses and threats we need to address.	1	2	3	4	5	DK
16. We use a zero-based approach in marketing communication planning.	1	2	3	4	5	DK
17. When doing annual marketing communication planning, we make sure intrinsic brand-contact points are sending positive brand messages and that these contacts are being fully leveraged before we invest in creating new brand-contact points.	1	2	3	4	5	DK
18. Our company uses some type of tracking study to evaluate the strength of our relationships with customers and other key stakeholder groups.	1	2	3	4	5	DK
19. Our marketing strategies maximize the unique strengths of the various marketing communication functions (e.g., public relations, direct response, advertising, event sponsorships, trade promotions, packaging).	1	2	3	4	5	DK
20. The overall objective of our marketing communication program is to create and nourish profitable relationships with customers and other stakeholders by strategically controlling or influencing all messages sent to these groups, and encouraging purposeful dialogue with them.	1	2	3	4	5	DK

Add scores (minus blank items and DKs) and divide by 20.   Score _____

Brand metrics are *measures of brand image and brand impact.*[16] The brand-impact metrics are the usual business measures of sales and brand share. Brand-image metrics measure the following:

- Brand recognition.
- Overall awareness of the brand.
- Understanding of the brand position.
- Brand relevance—how important and meaningful the brand is.
- Whether the brand is delivering on what stakeholders value.
- Brand preference—the level of customer purchase intent.

Brand metrics help companies to develop rich profiles of stakeholders and their relationship to the brand, and that information enables companies to develop appropriate contact points and message strategies.[17]

Relationship Metrics

For the most part, measurements of brand awareness, recall, recognition, trial, and repeat purchases are diagnostics that help explain why brand relationships are strong or weak. To give these findings more meaning, researchers combine them with direct measures of brand relationships, called **relationship metrics.** These are *output controls developed specifically for IMC programs to track the development of brand relationships.*[18] They help explain sales and share trends and provide diagnostic information as a basis for more accurate forecasting.

Some companies feel that brand relationships can be evaluated by simply asking customers whether they are satisfied. Yet more than 70 percent of customers who defect may have been "satisfied." Research by Thomas O. Jones and W. Earl Sasser Jr. found a large gulf between satisfied customers and *completely* satisfied customers. The key to generating superior long-term financial performance is to turn the former into the latter.[19]

In order not to overlook the obvious, companies should continually ask customers whether their wants, needs, and concerns are being addressed. But for several reasons this line of inquiry should not be the extent of measuring "satisfaction," as the Delta Air Lines ad in Exhibit 22-10 illustrates. The idea of asking what customers want and need seldom opens the door to any creative ideas or competitive advantages. Most customers are not trained to be creative in their responses to satisfaction surveys. As one pundit puts it: "The biggest lie in the restaurant business is the answer to the question: 'How was your dinner?'" A company must look for underlying problems, as well as future wants and needs. As a former senior vice president of Hewlett-Packard says, you need to have an "imaginative understanding of the user's needs."[20]

Among the relationship metrics that companies use most successfully are lifetime customer value (LTCV); recency, frequency, and monetary indexes (collectively referred to as RFM analysis); referral index; and share of wallet. Several of these are discussed in previous chapters but are summarized here to allow you to compare and contrast these measures.

- *Lifetime customer value (LTCV):* The purpose of this measure is to show a company what an average customer is worth in revenue. LTCV is determined by multiplying the average number of years customers do business with a company by the average amount they spend each year. This figure is then discounted on the basis of current interest rates to determine "net present value." Once a company knows what an average customer is worth in revenue, it can estimate how much to spend to acquire a new customer and how much to spend each year to retain current customers.

- *LTCV quintile analysis:* Somewhat similar to a customer-profitability measure but with a longer-term perspective, LTCV quintile analysis divides customers into five equal groups based on their lifetime customer value (LTCV). In the top group are the 20 percent with the highest LTCV; in the bottom group, the 20 percent with the lowest LTCV. Tracking the average LTCV of each of the five groups profiles a company's source of revenue. Ideally, the averages in all five groups would continue to increase. A red flag could be an increase in the top group and a decrease in all the other groups, indicating that the basis of support is shrinking even though total revenue may be unchanged or even slightly increasing.

- *Recency, frequency, monetary (RFM) analysis:* As mentioned in Chapter 7, the direct-response industry has discovered that the more recently people have bought, the more often they buy, and the more they spend, the better customers they are. In particular, average purchase frequency—the percentage of customers who purchased within the last 30 days (the period varies depending on product category)—indicates to what extent acquired customers are becoming loyal. Sales could be increasing, but if the average customer is buying less frequently, the support base may be weakening. Similarly, the more a customer spends, the more likely it is that the customer will continue the relationship.

- *Referral index:* This index tracks the percentage of new business resulting from a customer or some other stakeholder recommending the brand. It applies best to large-ticket and service products where it is possible to ask new customers what motivated them to choose the brand. Referrals are confirmation that marketers are doing what they are saying they will do for customers. Because referrals are one of the key behaviors of brand advocates (the highest-level brand relationship), a rising referral index score generally indicates an increase in the number of brand advocates—a good indication that relationship-building practices are working.

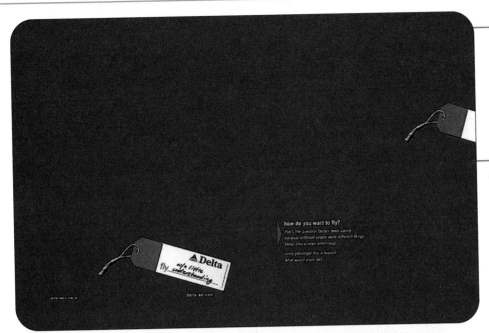

- *Share of wallet:* Because the most profitable customers, especially in packaged-goods categories, buy multiple brands, one brand objective is to get an increasing percentage of these customers' category purchases. Scanner data is helpful in spotting this share trend.

When any of the relationship metrics shows a negative trend, a company needs to find out, first, which areas of the company are sending the messages that are causing the negative trend and, second, what needs to be done to correct these messages. The same diagnostic approach should be used when a trend makes a significant jump. Determining why it jumped may enable a company to leverage certain brand messages still further.

BENEFITS AND LIMITATIONS OF EVALUATION

Evaluating the processes and results of marketing communication has many obvious benefits, but it also has several limitations. In most cases, the point of evaluation is to increase the productivity of brand messages, as Exhibit 22-11 illustrates. Although there are limitations, measuring and evaluating is a good idea overall. Companies, however, will never have the time or money to evaluate everything they do. Awareness of the benefits and limitations helps companies decide when *not* to measure or evaluate.

Benefits

Important benefits of evaluation are that it reduces risk, enriches planning, provides controls, and helps document the contributions of the MC programs and activities:

- *Reducing risks:* One of the ongoing expectations of marketing communication is creativity. By definition, being creative means doing things differently, in new ways. Predicting results, however, is especially difficult when things are done in new ways. But if new creative strategies, media mixes, and brand messages can be evaluated before they are produced or used throughout a brand's marketing area, the risk of failure can be reduced.

- *Enriching planning and managing:* Without information about how a brand is performing, it would be impossible to make intelligent decisions about managing relationships and the communication that drives these relationships. Think about the important role that measurements play in the simple task of driving a car. Imagine trying to drive safely without a speedometer to show how fast you are driving, without a gauge to show how much gasoline is left, or without a temperature gauge to show whether the engine is overheating. The more measurements you have about the status of your car and its performance, the better you can manage the car's performance and upkeep. The same is true of any aspect of business, including marketing communication and brand relationships.

- *Providing controls:* Generally, the larger a brand is, the more people, departments, and outside agencies are involved in its marketing communication activities. The more people involved, the more controls are needed to make sure plans are being properly executed and procedures followed. One of the characteristics that helps build trust is consistency. Through constant evaluation of brand messages and interactions with customers and other key stakeholders, a brand can work to maintain consistency. Tracking studies and audits are important ways to control processes. Scores for awareness, communication, and persuasion are often the basis for agency compensation.

EXHIBIT 22-11
Marketing communication programs that are measurable, such as call centers, are the first step toward improving the productivity of brand messages.

- *Documenting MC contributions:* Because much of what MC does cannot be directly linked to sales and profit, it is necessary to have surrogate measures that can be correlated to sales and profits. For example, by tracking increases in awareness and trial and showing a correlation with increases in sales, an MC department can justify the budget it has been allocated. Often, it can use these findings as a rationale for requesting budget increases.

Limitations

The limitations of evaluative measurements are several: cost, time, validity and projectability, reduced creativity, and overdependence on research and numbers.

- *Cost:* Costs for staff time, along with payments to outside measurement services that operate facilities and equipment and often actually do the measurements, can run into thousands of dollars for the simplest of tests. For companies with multimillion-dollar budgets, these costs are usually not a concern, but for a medium-size or small business, the costs can be prohibitive. This is why most copytesting is done only for national and international advertising TV and print campaigns.

- *Time:* Evaluation takes time. Conducting focus groups in three or four cities can take a couple of months from the time they are first thought of to the analysis of findings. The shortcoming of all evaluation efforts, and especially measurements of marketing communication efforts, is that customers, competitors, and other elements in the marketplace are always changing. So even if an advertising, a publicity, or a promotional program tests well, conditions can change by the time the messages and programs are rolled out to the brand's entire marketing area. When this happens, the results may not turn out as predicted.

- *Validity and projectability:* All measurements are done on *samples* of respondents. Sometimes, getting a sample that is representative of a brand's customers and prospects is difficult. Talking to a mix of customers different from those in the target audience means that the two groups will probably respond differently. If companies try to save money by reducing sample sizes, this can also lower validity. Another danger is looking at sub-sample responses when the total sample size is big enough to project answers only to questions asked of the total sample. For example, findings from a representative sample of 200 teenagers can be projected with a fairly high degree of confidence. However, if a company wants to look at the responses of only the teenagers in that sample who are heavy internet users, this number may be only 70; and statistically speaking, 70 is not large enough to project to all teenagers who are heavy internet users.

- *Reduced creativity:* Some marketers strongly believe that if brand messages are measured on the basis of advertising recall, creatives will work to make the advertising memorable and show little concern about increasing brand knowledge and awareness of brand benefits. Some creatives feel that copytesting, especially when done under laboratory conditions, does not indicate how brand messages would perform in the marketplace. They argue that creative work cannot be reduced to numbers. Consequently, when told that their work needs more brand mentions, more pictures of the package, and so on, they may become discouraged and put in less creative effort.

- *Overdependence on research and numbers:* Too much of a good thing can be bad. A MC department that insists on researching everything, and doing so until the results are exactly what it wants, may lose many opportunities. Just as some managers prefer to make decisions without research, others are so risk-averse that they are afraid to make any major decision without a lot of measurement support. For the latter, calling for more and more measurements to be done can become a way to avoid having to make a decision.

A FINAL NOTE: WHAT IS NOT MEASURED IS NOT MANAGED

Measurement and evaluation involve more than the accumulation of data and the monitoring of sales. If used strategically, evaluation becomes an important source of feedback information used in planning marketing communication efforts as well as making sure they are being executed properly.

To maximize the value of measurements, evaluation information should be as current as possible. Federal Express, for example, compiles its effectiveness indicators on a daily basis. Its evaluation program includes both output and process control information. FedEx also compiles monthly measures for all marketing communication efforts, including advertising and publicity, and it conducts an online employee survey every three months. Managers get the results and immediately take action when measures signal a problem.

It is often said that, for managers making important decisions, it is lonely at the top. But as Anders Gronstedt, who studied the Federal Express communication system, points out, managers with continuous information about communication effectiveness have the information they need to make strategic decisions and never get lonely.[21]

Key Terms

animatics 713
baseline 705
brand metrics 723
concept testing 703
concurrent testing 703
evaluative testing 703

focus group 709
gap analysis 700
IMC audit 721
intercept survey 709
norms 713
online focus group 720

relationship metrics 723
scanner market test 714
tachistoscope 709
test marketing 714
theater test 713
tracking studies 715

Key Point Summary

Key Point 1: Conducting Brand-Message Evaluation

In planning the evaluation of brand messages, the critical questions are: What should be evaluated? What information already exists? When should the evaluation be conducted? Evaluation is conducted to determine whether the MC efforts met or are likely to meet their objectives.

Key Point 2: Methods

The primary categories of measurement are concept testing, copytesting for both communication and persuasion measures, B2B evaluation methods, and online research. MC planners must keep in mind that communication effects (attention, awareness and knowledge, emotional responses, and physiological responses) do not always translate into persuasion effects (actual changes in buying behavior). Tracking studies are important for predicting the latter.

Key Point 3: Evaluating IMC

Process evaluation in an IMC program is conducted using an IMC audit that investigates relationship-building efforts by examining the organization, processes, and strategic consistency of messages being delivered at all contact points. Relationship metrics estimate the value of maintaining relationships.

Lessons Learned

Key Point 1: Brand-Message Research

a. Why is it important to evaluate brand messages before they run?
b. How does evaluation reduce risk?
c. How and why is the cost/value factor important in conducting evaluation research?
d. What role do objectives play in evaluation?

Key Point 2: Methods

a. What is concept testing? Why is it used?
b. When copytesting is used to evaluate the communication impact of a brand message, what kinds of effects are investigated?
c. Describe three tests that evaluate the persuasiveness of a brand message.
d. Explain how online interactions can be used for research purposes.
e. How are awareness and perception studies used in the evaluation of marketing communication?
f. What is the difference between pre- and post-testing?
g. You work as a creative person in an agency. The person sitting next to you works as the marketing manager for a company. Explain how the two of you might differ in your views about copytesting.
h. Explain the debate in the industry about the use of sales and brand share to evaluate the effectiveness of advertising and public relations.

Key Point 3: Evaluating IMC Metrics

a. Why would you want to conduct an IMC audit? What would you learn?
b. How does an IMC audit differ from a communication audit?
c. Explain the underlying logic behind lifetime customer value quintile analysis.
d. What does RFM stand for? What is included in this type of evaluation?

Chapter Challenge

Writing Assignment

Pick a local company, and develop an evaluation program for its marketing communication program. In a two-page memo, outline and explain all the various types of research and evaluation methods that you would recommend.

Presentation Assignment

Develop a program to evaluate relationships for your favorite restaurant. Present to your class a set of relationship metrics. Explain what information they uncover and how that information can be used to develop MC strategies.

Internet Assignment

Visit InsightExpress's website (www.insightexpress.com) for an example of the types of services that online research companies provide. Prepare a report for your instructor on how and when to use the services of this company.

Glossary

A

account manager A liaison between an agency and its clients.

account planner A person who uses research and customer insights to bring a strong consumer focus to the planning of marketing communication.

account planning Using research and brand insights to bring a strong consumer focus to the planning of marketing communication.

addressable media Media that carry messages to identifiable customers or prospects.

advertising Nonpersonal, paid announcements by an identified sponsor.

advertising substantiation The FTC requirement that a company show documentation if there are any challenges to the company's use of safety, performance, efficacy, quality, or competitive price claims.

advocacy advertising Advertising that takes a stand on an issue or advocates a certain viewpoint.

affective response A feeling or attitude resulting from emotional processing.

affiliates Local market broadcast stations that agree to carry programming and commercials provided by a network.

affirmative disclosure The FTC requirement that a company provide in its advertising certain information to outline product limitations or conditions.

AIDA An acronym identifying four persuasive steps or desired effects that a brand message might have on customers and prospects: attention, interest, desire, and action.

animatics Rough video footage used in ad testing.

aperture Any situation in which the target audience is highly receptive to a brand message.

appeal An idea that motivates an audience to respond.

art director A person who develops the visual aspects of brand messages—the design and layout.

association strategy A process that likens a brand to a desired lifestyle, person, place, or other entity.

attitude A general disposition or orientation toward objects, people, and ideas associated with a brand and usually accompanied by negative or positive judgments.

audiotext A recorded message that provides information (such as the weather or sports scores) via a toll-free (800) or toll (900) number.

authorization A retailer's agreement to stock an item.

awareness Getting a message past the senses—the point of initial exposure—and into consciousness.

B

back-end strategies Operational decisions about how responses to direct marketing offers will be handled.

bandwidth What governs the amount of digital information or data that can be sent from one place to another in a given time.

banner A small ad on a web page.

baseline A quantifiable measure of the current situation (also called *benchmark*).

behavioral segmenting Segmenting a market on the basis of product usage or other product-related behavior.

belief A thought or idea based on knowledge.

benchmark See *baseline*.

benefit The favorable result of having or using a product.

benefit segmenting Segmenting a market according to the benefits customers seek as the result of using a product.

benefits Advantages that allow a product to satisfy customers' needs, wants, and desires.

bleed ad An ad with graphics that go to the edge of the page.

body copy The text of a brand message.

bottler A local company that buys ingredients in large quantities and then mixes them, bottles them, and sells beverages to local stores.

brainstorming A formal process in which a small group gather together for the purpose of generating a multitude of new ideas.

brand A perception resulting from experiences with, and information about, a company or a line of products.

brand community A collection of customers who own the same brand and enjoy talking to each other, learning from each other, and sharing new ways of using their products, as well as getting help in solving problems.

brand-customer touch point Any situation in which a customer comes into contact with a brand or company.

brand development index (BDI) A numerical indicator of a particular brand's sales within a market relative to all other markets in which the brand is sold.

brand equity The intangible value of a brand.

brand extension The application of an established brand name to new product offerings.

brand identity The design of the public face or distinctive visual appearance of an organization or brand.

brand image An impression created by brand messages and experiences and assimilated into a perception of the brand.

brand knowledge Understanding a brand and its benefits.

brand licensing Renting the use of a brand to another company.

brand loyalty The degree of attachment that a customer has to a brand as expressed by repeat purchases.

brand manager An executive who manages a company's brand or product line (also called *product manager*).

brand message Information and experiences that impact how customers and other stakeholders perceive a brand.

brand metrics Measures of brand performance.

brand position How a brand compares to its competitors in the minds of customers, prospects, and other stakeholders.

brand publicity The use of nonpaid media messages to deliver brand information designed to positively influence customers and prospects (also called *marketing public relations*).

branding The process of creating a brand image that engages the hearts and minds of customers.

breakeven analysis A process used to evaluate a plan's costs versus the revenue it generates (also called *payout planning*).

broadcast footprint The geographical area in which there is reception from a satellite transmission.

broadsheets Newspapers with full-size pages.

budget A fixed amount of money for a fixed period of time.

buy-back allowance A payment to buy back the current stock of a brand and replace it with a featured new product.

buyer A person who purchases products for resale and selects which manufacturers' promotions to use.

buzz Excited talk about a brand.

C

call center A bank of telephones staffed by sales representatives whose dialogue is guided by computer-generated scripts.

call-out (1) Text positioned around an illustration and pointing to various parts of the visual from the text. (2) A brief passage from the text prominently displayed for impact.

campaign A set of MC messages with a common theme that runs for a specified period of time to achieve certain MC objectives.

caption Text that explains the point of a visual.

category development index (CDI) A numerical indicator of the relative consumption rate in a particular market for a particular product category.

cause marketing Company or brand support for a good cause through donations of a percentage of sales to the cause.

cease and desist order A demand to stop using the message in question.

centralized marketing An organizational arrangement in which a single authority is responsible for all marketing communication messages.

channel The means by which a message is delivered—letter, e-mail, radio, television, newspaper, telephone, or an event (also called *medium* or *media vehicle*).

channel marketing (1) Advertising and promotion efforts directed at members of the distribution channel. (2) An integrated process that combines personal selling, trade promotions, and co-marketing programs to build relationships with retailers and other members of the distribution channel.

classified ads Small-space, words-only ads presented in a clearly labeled section with no surrounding editorial content.

classified display ads Ads in the classified section that include graphics and larger sizes of type.

click-through The act of responding by clicking on a link to go directly to a particular website.

closing the sale Finalizing the terms of the transaction and getting the prospect's agreement to those terms.

closing date The date by which advertising materials must reach the publisher.

clutter Competition among a number of commercial messages.

co-branding A strategy that capitalizes on two brand names (owned by separate companies) and provides customers value from both brands.

cognitive dissonance The uneasiness that results when two or more beliefs or behaviors are inconsistent with each other.

cognitive learning theory A view of learning as a mental process involving thinking, reasoning, and understanding.

cognitive response A response driven by reasoning, judgment, or knowledge.

cohort A group of individuals from the same generation.

cold call A sales call to a prospect who is not known by the sales rep and has not expressed any particular interest in the company or brand.

collectibles Items of which consumers enjoy having two or more.

column inch A space that is one column wide and one inch tall.

co-marketing A customized joint effort by a manufacturer and a retailer to establish a mutually satisfying balance between price and image in local retail advertising of the manufacturer's brands.

commercial pod The commercial break in a TV program.

commission (1) A payment that represents a percentage of a client's total media spending. (2) A percentage of the sales price paid to a salesperson for each transaction.

commodity products Goods and services that have very minor or no distinguishing differences.

company-created touch point A planned MC message delivered by media.

compiled list A list of names and addresses collected from public sources.

comprehensive layout A highly refined facsimile of the finished piece, which allows the client to judge how the brand message will look (also known as a comp).

concept testing Tests that measure the effectiveness of the rough ideas that become brand and campaign themes.

concepting Finding the creative concept that will bring the selling strategy to life.

concurrent testing Testing that tracks the performance of messages as they are run.

conditioned learning theory A view of learning as a trial-and-error process (also called *stimulus-response theory*).

consumables Products that have a one-time use, *such* as movie tickets, gasoline, food, and beverages.

consumer packaged goods See *packaged goods*.

contest A brand-sponsored competition that requires some form of skill and effort.

context The nonverbal elements surrounding a message.

continuous scheduling Placing media throughout the year with equal weight in each month.

controlled-circulation publications Trade, industrial, and organizational magazines that are distributed free to those working in a given subject area or affiliated with a given organization.

convergence The combining of telephone, computer, and TV into one interactive communication device.

cookies Internet bugs that can track private individuals' interests as recorded by their click-throughs.

cooperative advertising A system in which a manufacturer pays a portion (normally half) of the cost when a local retailer advertises the manufacturer's brand.

cooperative (co-op) advertising allowance The practice in which a certain percentage of everything a retailer buys is put into a special "co-op" fund.

copytesting Testing the effectiveness of a brand message, a creative concept, or elements such as a headline, slogan, or visual for creative impact and understandability.

copywriter A person who develops the verbal brand message (the copy).

corporate advertising Ads designed to build awareness of a company and explain what it does or believes.

corporate branding The practice of managing the corporate organization as a brand.

corporate communication Public relations carried out by senior executives who advise top management on how the organization presents itself (also called *corporate relations*).

corporate culture The way business is conducted within a company.

corporate image See *image*.

corporate mission See *mission* (sense 1).

corporate relations See *corporate communication*.

corrective advertising The FTC requirement that a company must spend a certain percentage of its advertising budget to correct previous false advertising by running advertising explaining that earlier messages were misleading or false.

cost per point (CPP) A measure used to compare same-medium broadcast vehicles.

cost per response (CPR) The media cost divided by the number of responses generated.

cost per thousand (CPM) What a communication vehicle charges to deliver a message to 1,000 members of its audience.

counterargument Information that challenges the credibility of a message.

coupon A certificate with a stated price reduction on a specified item.

creative boutique An agency of creative specialists, usually writers and designers, who work for clients and other agencies.

creative brief A document that is given to the creative team to help in their planning of the message executions.

creative director A person who supervises the development, execution, and production of the creative ideas.

creative process A formal procedure for increasing productivity and innovative output by an individual or a group.

credibility strategy A selling strategy that heightens conviction and decreases the perception of risk.

crisis management plan A plan for managing a company's response when disaster strikes.

cross-functional planning A process for planning and monitoring brand relationships that involves all departments that directly or indirectly "touch" the customer.

cross-promotion The promotion of two or more products together.

cross-selling Using the sale of one product to promote the sale of related products.

cultural cohort A group of people from multiple cultures who share a common characteristic.

cultural imperialism The impact that a dominant culture has on another, less dominant culture.

culture (1) The learned behaviors of a people that come from traditions passed on from generation to generation. (2) Group values based on traditions and a distinctive history.

customer A person who has purchased a brand at least once within a designated period.

customer insight (1) Understanding how customers see themselves, the world around them, and the products and brands they use. (2) Below-the-surface attitudes and beliefs that influence customers' behavior.

customer recognition Company acknowledgment of purchases and of the customer's interaction history with the company.

customer relationship management (CRM) A type of database software for tracking customers.

customer relationships A series of interactions between customers and a company over time.

customer service (1) A company's attitude and behavior during interactions with customers. (2) The process of managing customers' interactive experiences with a brand.

customer-initiated touch point An interaction that *occurs* whenever a customer or prospect contacts a company.

D

data mining Sifting and sorting the information warehoused in a company's database.

data overlay Enriching one database by adding another to it.

database A collection of related information that is stored and organized in a way that allows access and analysis.

database management system (DBMS) Software that records customer information, tracks customer interactions, and links customer databases that are already in existence.

database marketing See *data-driven communication*.

data-driven communication Communication that is managed through a database system that gives the company interaction memory.

daypart A block of time identified by a station for the purpose of setting ad rates.

dealers Local companies that buy an inventory of products from a manufacturer and assemble a mix of models for sale in their stores or showrooms.

dealer contest A competition awarding dealers special prizes and gifts when sales reach a predetermined volume or a stated percentage increase of last year's sales.

dealer loader A high-value premium given to a retailer in exchange for the purchase of a special product assortment or a specified dollar volume.

decentralized marketing An organizational arrangement in which management responsibility is assigned by brand or geographical region.

decoding The process of interpreting what a message means.

demographics Definable statistical measures, such as age, gender, and ethnicity.

designated marketing area (DMA) (1) Households in each major U.S. metropolitan area. (2) TV or radio broadcast coverage area.

developed markets Markets in which consumption patterns are focused more on wants and desires than on basic needs.

developing markets Markets in which consumption patterns are clearly expanding from necessities to wants and desires.

digitized Converted into a numerical form, most often by means of a binary system of 1s and 0s.

direct marketing (1) A data-driven marketing approach that combines demand creation with fulfillment. (2) An interactive, database-driven messaging system that uses a range of media to motivate a response from customers and prospects.

direct-response advertising A brand message in any of the mass media that asks the receiver (reader, viewer, or listener) to respond directly to the sender.

display ads Ads that generally contain more graphics and white space than copy and appear next to editorial content.

display copy Copy in a type size larger than that of the text or body copy and meant to entice readers into reading the body copy.

domestic marketers Companies that focus their marketing effort on their home countries (also called *national marketers*).

double-page spread An advertisement printed across two facing pages.

dummy A mock-up that shows the actual size, look, and feel of brochures, multipage materials, packages, and point-of-purchase displays.

duplication The overlapping coverage of two or more vehicles.

E

e-commerce Online business transactions and interactions.

effective frequency The number of times a message needs to be seen to make an impression or achieve a specific level of awareness.

elaboration The degree to which customers think about a message and relate the information to their own lives as they make purchase decisions.

employee relations An area of public relations that focuses on establishing and maintaining communication systems with employees.

employee empowerment Giving front-line employees the resources to make decisions about problems that affect customer relationships.

empowerment The authority to handle customer-relations problems.

encoding The process of creating a brand message to convey an intended meaning and elicit a certain type of response.

ethics Moral and value standards that act as behavioral guidelines.

evaluative testing Testing that measures the performance of brand messages against their objectives at the conclusion of the program.

event marketing A promotional occasion designed to attract and involve a brand's target audience.

event A highly targeted brand-associated activity designed to actively engage customers and prospects and generate publicity.

evoked set A group of brands that comes to mind when a person thinks of a product category because the person has judged those brands to be acceptable.

extranet (1) A limited-access computer network that links suppliers, distributors, and MC agencies to the company. (2) The network that connects employees with all key external stakeholders such as MC agencies, suppliers, and distributors.

F

fact sheet A summary of key information.

fast-moving consumer goods (FMCGs) Heavily promoted products that are usually sold through food and drug stores in small packages and carry a low unit price; in the United States, usually called *packaged goods*.

features Attributes that give a product a distinctive difference.

fee A fixed payment based on a standardized hourly charge.

feedback A response that conveys a message back to the source.

field of experience Interactions receivers have had with an organization or brand, plus the messages they have received about it.

financial relations An area of public relations that creates communication directed to—and often developed in collaboration with—investors, analysts, stockbrokers, and financial media.

flighting A scheduling strategy in which planned messages run in intermittent periods.

focus group A group of 8 to 12 members of a brand's target audience who, led by a moderator, discuss some aspect of a brand, product category, or message strategy.

freelancer An independent creative person who is self-employed and takes on assignments from an agency or a marketer on a project-by-project basis.

freestanding insert (FSI) (1) A supplement that contains ads, most with coupons, for a variety of national brands. (2) A collection of noncompeting brand ads and coupons printed in a newspaper supplement.

frequency A measure of how often, within a given period, a customer purchased a specific brand.

frequency distribution analysis An analysis that divides a target audience into equal segments and establishes an average frequency for each of these segments (also called *quintile analysis*).

frequency marketing See *loyalty marketing*.

front-end strategies The marketing communication and media mix used to explain and deliver an offer.

fulfillment Getting the product or the information requested to the customer in a convenient, cost-effective, and timely fashion.

full-service agency An agency that provides all or most of the services needed in its area of MC specialization.

G

game A sales-promotion tool that has the chance element of a sweepstakes but is conducted over a longer time.

gap analysis An analysis of the difference between what customers expect from a brand (based on brand messages) and what they actually experience.

gatekeepers Editors and writers who decide what news is worth covering.

generic strategy A selling strategy that stresses a basic feature or benefit of a product that is not brand specific.

geodemographic segmenting Segmenting that combines geographic and demographic data to identify residents of a particular area with certain demographic traits.

global marketers Companies that consider their market to be just one—the world.

global strategy See *standardization strategy*.

gross rating point (GRP) A combined measure of reach and frequency indicating the weight of a media plan.

guerrilla marketing A marketing approach that reaches people in unconventional ways—in the streets or in other unexpected places.

H

habit/repeat path The decision path that customers take when a brand meets or exceeds expectations and they buy it again.

headline A line set in large type to get readers' attention and lead into the body copy.

heavy users Customers who buy an above-average amount of a given product.

hierarchy-of-effects model A description of a series of stages of response that brand decision makers move through.

hierarchy of needs See *Maslow's hierarchy of needs*.

high-context culture A culture in which meaning is determined by nonverbal cues, social relationships, and indirect communication such as metaphors and aphorisms (statements of principles).

high-involvement products Products for which people perceive differences among brands and are willing to invest prepurchase decision-making energy.

home page The place where viewers begin looking at a website.

human interest angle A story idea that appeals to people for reasons other than news.

hyperlink Buttons or other sensitive areas on the page that, when clicked on, move the viewer to another page (also called *link*).

I

image A representation derived from planned communication, such as advertising and brand publicity.

image messages Messages that deliver a desired representation or perception of a brand.

image transfer A process by which persons exposed to the sights and sounds of a brand's TV message recall the visual elements of the message when they are exposed to a similar soundtrack on radio.

IMC AUDIT An in-depth research method for evaluating IMC relationship-building practices.

impression One exposure to a brand message.

inbound calls Calls initiated by prospects and customers.

incentive strategy A selling strategy that creates a sense of immediacy and rewards customers for responding quickly.

influentials Opinion leaders and early adopters who, in turn, influence other people.

infomercial A 30-minute commercial "program" that demonstrates a product, presents testimonials from satisfied users, and offers viewers one or more ways to buy the product direct (toll-free telephone number, website address, mailing address).

informational strategy A selling strategy based on facts about the brand and its attributes.

ingredient branding Using the brand name of a product component in the promotion of another company's product.

in-house ad agency A department within a company that is responsible for producing some or all of that company's marketing communications.

inserts Advertisements preprinted by an advertiser and enclosed with the newspaper.

inside sales Calls on accounts whose average-size orders are not large enough to cost-justify an in-person sales call.

in-store demonstration Paying a person to hand out product samples in-store.

integrated marketing communication (IMC) A process for managing the brand messages that impact customer relationships.

integration Uniting and unifying separate parts to create synergy.

interactive media Two-way media allowing both companies and customers to send and receive messages.

interactive strategy A selling strategy that opens two-way communication in order to open up communication with customers and capture their feedback.

interactive TV The convergence of computers, television, and the internet.

interactivity Two-way communication that sends and receives messages from customers and other stakeholders in order to create long-term, profitable relationships.

intercept survey A survey in which people in a mall or at an event are stopped and asked to respond to a short questionnaire.

internal marketing The application of marketing inside the organization to instill customer-focused values.

internet A worldwide system of linked computer networks.

interstitials Ads that pop up in a separate frame on a screen page.

intranet (1) A computer network that is accessible only to employees and contains proprietary information. (2) A walled-off section of the larger internet to which only company employees have access.

intrinsic touch point An interaction with a brand required during the process of buying or using that brand.

J

jingle A short song that delivers a brand story in a easy-to-hum format.

L

lateral thinking Bouncing from one thought to another in free association.

layout An orderly arrangement of the elements making up an MC message.

learning A change in what we know that comes from exposure to new information or experiences.

life stages The different periods in the life of an individual or family.

lifestyle The way people choose to spend their money, time, and energy.

lifestyle strategy An association strategy that uses situations and symbols of lifestyles that the target audience can identify with or aspire to—that is, the situation "strikes a chord" or resonates. See also *association strategy*.

link See *hyperlink*.

localization strategy An international MC strategy in which brand messages are customized to make them compatible with each country's culture and local needs and wants (also called a *multinational strategy*).

logo (1) A distinctive graphic design used to communicate a product, company, or organization identity. (2) A word, phrase, or graphic element used to identify a brand.

loss leaders Brands promoted at or below its cost to the retailer in order to draw customers into a store.

low-context culture A culture in which less emphasis is placed on the social context and more emphasis is placed on words, directness, and time (deadlines and schedules).

low-involvement products Products that are relatively cheap, are bought frequently without much consideration, and are perceived as low risk.

loyalty marketing Using promotions specifically *designed* for customer retention (also called *frequency marketing*).

M

marketing communication (MC) A collective term for all the various types of planned messages used to build a brand.

marketing communication mix The selection of MC functions used at a given time as part of a marketing program.

marketing public relations See *brand publicity*.

marketing services The department that coordinates the work of internal communication specialists and external communication agencies other than the brand's advertising agency.

marketing universe See *universe*.

Maslow's hierarchy of needs An arrangement of human needs listed in the order in which, according to Maslow, people satisfy them (named after American psychologist Abraham Maslow).

mass customization of products A manufacturing process that is programmed to choose ingredients/parts to produce custom-designed goods.

mass customization of MC messages The large-scale personalization of customer interactions with a company.

mass media Broad-based communication systems that reach a large and diverse audience.

MC message Anything that talks about the brand, such as a newspaper ad, radio commercial, direct-mail piece, sales clerk, or the product's package.

MC mix See *marketing communication mix.*

MC suppliers Specialists who supply MC agencies with support services.

mechanical Final camera-ready artwork.

media Means by which the various types of MC messages are sent and received.

media buyers Individuals who negotiate and purchase broadcast time and print space that has been detailed in the media plan.

media buying The execution of a media plan.

media buying services Agencies that specialize in buying time and space.

media convergence The bringing together of phone, television, and the computer, along with a variety of other new technologies, such as smart cards, pagers, personal digital assistants, and satellite navigational systems.

media exposure The number of people who see, read, or hear a medium.

media mix A selection of media channels used to deliver brand messages.

media planners Individuals who determine media objectives and strategies for delivering ads to target audiences.

media planning Determining the most cost-effective mix of media for achieving a set of media objectives.

media relations (1) Activities that distribute information to the media creating publicity for an organization. (2) Activities that cultivate relationships of trust with key reporters and editors.

media vehicle See *channel.*

media waste Reaching people who are neither customers nor prospects.

media weight An indication of the relative impact of a media plan.

medium (plural: media) The means by which a message is delivered—letter, e-mail, radio, television, newspaper, telephone, or an event (also called *channel*).

merchandising In-store promotion activities.

message An idea encoded in a combination of words, pictures, actions, symbols, and events.

message execution The form of a completed MC message, such as an advertisement, brochure, or package label.

message strategy An idea about how to creatively and persuasively communicate a brand message to a target audience.

message strategy brief Statements about a brand that summarize the research and the insights for the creative team, and that help the team identify the direction and focus for their creative (and media) ideas.

message wearout The inability of brand messages that once attracted attention and motivated the target to continue doing so.

mission (1) What a company stands for and represents. (2) What a company is striving to accomplish.

mission marketing A type of marketing communication strategy that uses the company's mission as a selling strategy in order to differentiate and add value to a brand.

monetary A measure of the amount a customer spent with a company over a given period.

motivations Internal impulses that when stimulated initiate some type of response.

multinational marketers Companies that market products in several different countries.

multi-tier branding The use of two or more brands (all owned by the same company) in the identification of a product.

mystery shopping Evaluative field research into a store's operations conducted by someone who appears to be an average shopper and is not known or recognized by the employees who are being evaluated.

N

national marketers See *domestic marketers.*

navigation The process by which people access a website, find the information they want, and move around within the site and to other related sites.

needs and wants Biological and psychological motivations that drive actions.

needs assessment Asking a lot of questions about how a business operates.

news kit A packet of information that includes photographs and drawings, maps, histories, background facts, different stories on different aspects of the product or event, speeches, and test results, along with the name of a person to be contacted for more information (also called *press kit*).

news peg An announcement of something that is new.

news release Any form of print, visual, or broadcast announcement that an organization makes available to the media about its activities; includes video news releases (also called *press release*).

noise Interferences or distractions that can negatively affect a message, its transmission, and its reception.

norms Average product category scores accumulated over the years by the research company.

O

objective-and-task method Budgeting that starts with zero-based planning that determines marketing communication objectives and what "tasks" need to be done to accomplish each objective. Then estimates are made for how much each task will cost.

objectives What you want to accomplish.

offer Everything, both tangible and intangible, promised by a company in exchange for money or some other desired behavior.

off-invoice allowance A reduction in the wholesale price, with no restrictions, for a limited period.

off-shelf display allowance An additional quantity of a brand located in a high-traffic area such as the end of an aisle.

on promotion Selling at a reduced price.

one-to-one marketing Customizing products and marketing communication according to individual needs.

one-voice, one-look consistency Consistency that results when all advertising, sales promotion, sponsorships, publicity, direct response, packaging, and other MC messages have the same look, sound, and feel.

online focus group A chat room to which selected people have been invited to meet at a specified time with a moderator.

opinion A specific judgment that is emotionally neutral.

opinion leaders People to whom others turn for advice or information.

optimizer program A complex media planning mode that combines Nielsen data with other data from in-store scanners and customer-profile databases.

opt-in To agree to receive e-mail from a particular company or brand.

opt-out e-mail A series of messages that a company sends automatically until notified to stop.

outbound calls Calls initiated by a marketing organization.

out-of-home media Communication vehicles that the target audience sees or uses away from home.

P

packaged goods Heavily promoted products that are usually sold through food and drug stores in small packages and carry a low unit price (also called *consumer packaged goods*).

packaging A container and conveyor of information.

paid-circulation publications Magazines that sell subscriptions.

Pareto rule 80 percent of a brand's sales come from 20 percent of its customers (named after Italian economist Vilfredo Pareto).

pass-along rate The number of people who read a magazine in addition to subscribers or buyers of the magazine.

payout planning See *breakeven analysis*.

perceptual mapping A visualization of how customers perceive competing brands on various selection criteria.

performance allowance Price reductions given to retailers in exchange for the retailers agreeing to feature the brand in their advertising or in other promotion programs.

permission marketing A method of segmenting that persuades prospects to volunteer their attention to brand messages.

personal selling (1) Interpersonal communication in which a salesperson uncovers and satisfies the needs of a customer to the mutual benefit of both. (2) Two-way communication that uncovers and satisfies the needs of prospects, providing mutual, long-term benefits for both parties.

personality The distinctive characteristics and traits that make someone a unique individual.

persuasion The act of creating changes in attitudes and behaviors.

pitch letter A letter, either mail or e-mail, written by a PR person proposing a story idea to an editor or reporter. In close working relationships, the pitch may be made by phone.

place-based media Public venues where brand messages can be displayed.

point-of-purchase (POP) displays In-store advertising using displays that feature the product.

pop-ups and pop-unders Ads that appear when a viewer closes a page or site.

pre-emptible rate A relatively low rate that doesn't guarantee a given commercial will run at a given time.

pre-emptive positioning Brand positioning built on a generic feature of the product that competitors have not talked about.

pre-emptive strategy A selling strategy that focuses on an attribute or benefit that any product in the category could claim.

premium An item offered free or at a bargain price to reward some type of behavior.

press kit See *news kit*.

press release See *news release*.

pro forma A breakdown of forecasted sales on a per unit basis.

producer A person who oversees the logistics and costs of producing radio and TV commercials.

product features The elements making up a good or service.

product manager See *brand manager*.

product placement (1) Visibly featuring branded products or brand names in a movie or television program. (2) Paid verbal or visual brand exposure in entertainment programming.

promise A statement that tells you what good things will happen if you use the product.

promotional video network A company that uses either videos or satellite transmission to distribute programs and commercial messages.

proprietary packaging A package design that is patented to prevent any other brand from using it.

prospect A person who has not bought a brand but might be interested in it.

prospecting (1) Using data to identify prospective customer types. (2) Locating potential new customers (or prospects).

psychographics Measures that classify customers in terms of their attitudes, interests, and opinions as well as their lifestyle activities.

public relations (1) Communication activities that help an organization and its publics adapt mutually to each other. (2) A communication function used to promote mutual understanding between an organization and its various stakeholder groups.

public service announcement (PSA) Ads for nonprofit organizations that run on time and space donated by the media.

publicity See *brand publicity*.

puffery The use of hyperbole or exaggeration to promote a brand.

pull strategy The use of incentives to motivate end users to purchase a brand and thus pressure retailers to stock that brand.

pulsing A combination of flighting and continuous scheduling that provides a "floor" of media support throughout the year with periodic increases.

purposeful dialogue Communication that is mutually beneficial for the customer and the company.

push strategy The use of incentives to motivate the buying and reselling of products.

Q

qualified leads Prospects who seem most likely to buy because of some information known about them.

quintile analysis See *frequency distribution analysis*.

R

rate card A list of advertising space costs and discounts.

rating point 1 percent of a communication vehicle's coverage area that has been exposed to a broadcast program.

reach The percentage of an audience that has had the opportunity to be exposed to a media vehicle within a specified period.

reason why Support or proof points that explain why a product will provide the promised benefit.

rebate A cash refund.

recall A high level of awareness that involves bringing something back from memory.

receiver Anyone who is exposed to a message.

recency A measure of how long ago a customer purchased from a specific company.

recognition Identifying something and remembering that you saw or heard it before.

recourse Easy access to someone who can solve a problem.

reference group The associations and organizations with which people identify or to which they belong and which influence their attitudes and behaviors.

relationship metrics Output controls developed specifically for IMC programs to track the development of brand relationships.

relevance The extent to which a product or its message is pertinent and connects with a customer's personal interests.

reminder strategy A selling strategy that keeps a brand top-of-mind with the target.

reputation The esteem that a company or brand has in the eyes of its stakeholders.

respect Showing consideration.

response Something said or done in answer to a marketing communication message.

response list A list of people who have responded to related direct-marketing offers.

responsiveness Customer satisfaction following a customer-initiated company contact.

retailers Stores that sell products and services to consumers.

retainer An arrangement in which a client contracts to work with an agency for a year or more and pay that agency a certain amount.

return on investment (ROI) A ratio of income to spending.

rich media Media that feature audio or video formats.

rough layout Creative design stage in which the artist draws to the actual size of the ad. Headlines and subheads suggest the final type style; illustrations and photographs are sketched in; and body copy is simulated with lines.

S

sales lead A person or organization identified as being a prospect—someone able to benefit from the brand being sold.

sales literature Aids, such as videos, charts, catalogs, and forms designed to help the sales rep make the presentation.

sales promotion (1) A short-term, added-value offer designed to motivate an immediate response. (2) A tangible added value designed to motivate and accelerate a response.

sampling Offering prospects the opportunity to try a product before making a buying decision.

scanner data Point-of-purchase (also known as point-of-sale) information gathered at the retail level by chains that have frequent-buyer programs and by research companies such as ACNielsen Corporation and Information Resources Inc.

scanner market test A tracking of a household's purchases (also called *single-source test*).

search engine An internet tool that allows users to find help by typing in keywords.

segmenting Grouping customers or prospects according to common characteristics, needs, wants, or desires.

self-selection ("raise your hand") A method of segmenting prospects by motivating potential customers to respond in some way and therefore identify themselves as being interested in the brand.

sender See *source*.

share The percentage of persons using a radio or TV at a particular time who are tuned to a particular station.

share of wallet The percentage of a customer's spending in a product category for one particular brand.

share-of-voice spending A brand's portion of the total media spending in that brand's product category.

shipper displays Specially designed shipping cartons that when opened become display units complete with signage and a quantity of products ready for sale.

showings The basic units of sale for outdoor advertising.

signature A distinctive way of printing the brand name.

single-source test See *scanner market test*.

situation analysis An analysis of marketplace conditions.

skews Variations from the general population.

slogan A clever phrase that serves as a reminder of the brand, company image, or campaign theme; a memorability device.

slotting allowance A one-time, up-front fee for agreeing to stock a product.

slotting fee An up-front payment made in exchange for guaranteed shelf space.

social class How people in a society are ranked by such factors as family history, occupation, education, and income level.

social marketing The use of marketing to address societal problems.

society People who live together and organize their lives as a community.

solution selling Helping customers solve problems or take advantage of opportunities (also called *enterprise selling*).

source The initiator of a message (also called *sender*).

source credibility The extent to which a message sender is believable.

spam Unsolicited e-mail whose purpose is to sell a product or service.

specialties Items given free to customers and other stakeholders to help keep a brand's name top-of-mind.

split run A process in which a marketer places one ad in one half of a magazine's circulation and a different ad in the other half.

sponsorship Financial support of an organization, person, or activity in exchange for brand publicity and association.

spot buys Purchases of TV time only in certain markets by regional or national companies.

standard advertising unit (SAU) A set of predetermined spaces that are constant in size in every newspaper that has adopted SAU standards.

standardization strategy An international MC strategy in which the same basic brand message is used in all countries (also called *global strategy*).

stimulus-response theory See *conditioned learning theory*.

store brand A brand used exclusively by one chain of stores for a line of products made to the store's specification; also known as a house brand or private label.

storyboard A series of key visuals and accompanying dialogue that explain a TV commercial.

strategic business unit (SBU) A product, brand, or geographical division that operates as an individual business within a company.

strategic consistency The consistency that results when messages differ but all of them contain certain core elements.

strategic redundancy Saying the same thing in several different ways.

strategies Ideas for how to accomplish objectives.

style The general look or feel of an MC message.

subliminal advertising Messages that are received subconsciously, below a person's perceptual threshold, causing a desired response.

subscriber lists Lists of subscribers to magazines.

supplement insert An insert that is preprinted by an advertiser and enclosed with a newspaper.

support The reason or proof points on which a claim, benefit, or proposition rests.

support argument Information that strengthens the credibility of a message.

sweepstakes A form of sales promotion that offers prizes based on a chance drawing of entrants' names.

SWOT analysis A structured evaluation of internal strengths and weaknesses and external opportunities and threats that can help or hurt a brand.

synergy An interaction of individual parts that makes the "whole" greater than the sum of its parts.

T

tabloid A newspaper whose page size is half that of broadsheets.

tachistoscope A device that exposes a brand message briefly to test participants so that researchers can measure how long it takes for a certain message or elements to be communicated.

tactics Specific actions that must be taken to execute a strategy.

tag line Text at the end of the printed piece that provides either a call to action (such as instructions on how to respond) or a slogan.

target audience A group that has significant potential to respond positively to a brand message.

targeted GRPs (TGRPs) The number of gross rating points delivered against the targeted audience.

targeted reach The portion of a communication vehicle's audience that is in a brand's target market.

targeting Analyzing, evaluating, and prioritizing the market segments deemed most profitable to pursue.

teaser campaign A series of messages that carry no brand identification but are designed to create curiosity.

telemarketing The practice of using the telephone to deliver a brand message designed to create a sale or sales lead.

telephony The technical name for the transmission of sound between two points.

test marketing A research design in which an MC campaign is run in two to four markets for anywhere from 3 to 12 months.

theater test A test in which people are invited to a local location for the purpose, they are told, of critiquing a TV program, but actually for the purpose of evaluating their response to a brand message.

third-party credibility The believability of people who are not affiliated with a brand and have nothing to gain or lose from its success or failure; they are more believable than company sources.

third-party endorsement An objective perspective presented by a reputable source who has no personal interest in the success or failure of the product being endorsed.

thumbnail sketch A small, very rough, rapidly produced drawing used to try out ideas.

tie-in promotion The linking of two products in advertising and in-store merchandising promotion, such as promoting movies and their characters in fast-food restaurants.

tip-ins Preprinted ads that are bound or glued into a magazine but are printed on heavier-stock paper than that used in the magazine itself.

toll-free numbers Phone numbers that companies use to make it possible for their customers to call them without paying a long-distance charge.

tone A general atmosphere or manner of expression.

tracking studies Periodic trend surveys that measure brand awareness, trial, repeat, and customer satisfaction with a brand and its competitors.

trade promotions Discounts and premiums offered to retailers in exchange for their promotional support.

trade show An event at which customers in a particular industry gather to attend training sessions and visit with suppliers and vendors to review their product offerings and innovations.

trademark Any element, words, or design that differentiates one brand from another.

traffic manager A person who tracks the progress of MC materials as they are being produced, keeps jobs on deadline, and engages outside special services (such as artist, photographers, and typographers) when needed.

trailers Commercials that run before movies.

typeface A set of letters and numbers with a particular or distinguishing design.

U

undeveloped markets Markets in which consumption patterns remain focused on basic needs.

unexpected touch point An unanticipated reference to a brand that is beyond the control or influence of the company.

unique selling proposition (USP) A selling strategy based on a product's most distinctive difference from competitive products.

universe A specified target profile within a geographical area.

up-selling Encouraging customers to buy a more expensive product than they had in mind.

V

value A perception of what something is worth in terms of quality and price.

values Enduring points of view that a certain way of thinking and behaving is preferable to a different way of thinking and behaving.

video news release (VNR) A television news release or package, produced by a company to feature a product or service and designed to run from 30 to 90 seconds on a news program.

virtual communities Groups that focus on certain online activities and whose members establish relationships with one another.

visualization Turning the message strategy into a visual.

W

warranty cards Cards that come with new products, particularly electronics and appliances, and ask buyers to give the company purchase information.

wholesalers Companies that specialize in moving goods from manufacturers to retailers.

word-of-mouth brand messages Personal communication between customers or other stakeholders about a brand.

Z

zero-based planning Determining objectives and strategies based on current brand and marketplace conditions, which are considered the zero points.

Endnotes

Chapter 1

[1]Mercedes Cardona, "Big Guns Predict Smaller Ad Role," *Advertising Age*, July 1, 2002, pp. 1, 19.

[2]Bradley Johnson, "Moving Sideways," *Advertising Age*, May 6, 2002, p. 4.

[3]Thomas Harris, "Viagra Keeps It Up," *MRP Update*, May 1999, p. 2.

[4]<www.home.att.net/fullerbrush/history>, February 14, 2003.

[5]Barton Weitz et al., *Selling* (Burr Ridge, Il: Irwin, 1995), p. 6.

[6]Laurie Freeman, "The House That Ivory Built," *Advertising Age*, August 20, 1987, pp. 1-14, 162-200.

[7] "CNN," *The Future of Brands: Twenty-five Visions,* ed. Rita Clifton and Esther Maughan (New York: New York University Press and Intergrand, 2000), p. 53.

[8]Vanessa O'Connell, "'You-Are-There' Advertising," *Wall Street Journal*, August 5, 2002, p. B1.

[9]Theresa Howard, "Gap Counts on Known, New Stars," *USA Today*, August 8, 2002, p. 2B.

[10] Regis McKenna, "Marketing Is Everything," *Harvard Business Review*, January-February 1992, p. 65.

[11]Anders Grnstedt, *The Consumer Century* (New York: Routledge, 2000), p. 148.

[12]Peter M. Senge, *The Fifth Discipline: The Art and Practice of the Learning Organization* (New York: Doubleday Currency, 1990), p. 24.

Chapter 2

[1]Alice Cuneo, "Riney Pronounces 30-Second Ad Dead," *Advertising Age*, June 17, 2002, p. 16.

[2]Tobi Elkin, "Branding Big Blue," *Advertising Age*, February 20, 2000, pp. 42, 44.

[3]Jon Steel, *Truth, Lies, and Advertising* (New York: Wiley), p. xv.

[4]Lisa Fortini Campbell, *The Consumer Insight Workbook* (Chicago: Copy Workshop, 1992), p. 11.

[5]Claire Atkinson, "Integration Still a Pipe Dream for Many," *Advertising Age*, March 10, 2003, p. 1.

[6]Jack Myers, "Defining Media Brand Equity and Its Value for Measuring Advertising Effectiveness," *The Advertiser*, October-November 1999, p. 60.

[7]From AOL Time Warner's *Global Marketing Solutions* website home page, <www.aoltimewarner/companies/global_marketing>, March 2003.

[8]Matthew Rose et al., *Wall Street Journal*, July 18, 2002, p. 1A.

[9]*Advertising Age Fact Pack* (Chicago: Crain Communications, September 9, 2002), pp. 8, 10.

[10]Marshall Loeb, "Jack Welch Lets Fly on Budgets, Bonuses, and Buddy Boards," *Fortune*, May 29, 1995, p. 145.

[11]"Integrating Multiple Channels," *Chain Store Age*, August 2, 2001, p. 24A.

[12]*Advertising Age Fact Pack*, p. 8.

[13]Deborah Spake, Giles D'Souza, Tammy Crutchfield, and Robert Morgan, "Advertising Agency Compensation: An Agency Theory Explanation," *Journal of Advertising* 28, no. 3 (Fall 1999), pp. 53-72.

[14]"Mini Marketing Chief Proves Them Wrong," *Automotive News*, January 13, 2003.

[15]Stuart Elliott, "Advertising Shift Compensation Method," *New York Times*, June 11, 1998, p. D3.

[16]Michael Hammer and James Champy, *Reengineering the Corporation* (New York: HarperCollins, 1993), p. 167.

[17]David Prensky, John A. McCarty, and James Lucas, "Integrated Marketing Communication: An Organizational Perspective," in *Integrated Communication: Synergy of Persuasive Voices*, ed. Esther Thorson and Jeri Moore (Mahwah, NJ: Erlbaum, 1996), pp. 167-84.

[18]Bradley Johnson, "Moving Sideways," *Advertising Age*, May 6, 2002, p. 4.

[19]Cara B. Dipasquale, "How to Play the Game," *Advertising Age*, January 28, 2002, p. 25.

[20]Ibid.

[21]"IBM 'Plays to Win' with New Push," *Advertising Age*, April 15, 2002, p. 9.

[22]Philip Geier Jr., "Beyond the New Horizon," *IAA Perspectives*, August 1999, p. 2.

[23]David Prensky, John A. McCarty, and James Lucas, "Vertical Integration and Advertising Agency Participation in Integrated Marketing Communications Programs," AMA Summer Marketing Educator's Conference, Washington, DC, 1993.

Chapter 3

[1]Tom Duncan and Sandra Moriarty, *Driving Brand Value: Using Integrated Marketing to Manage Profitable Stakeholder Relationships* (New York: McGraw-Hill, 1997), p. 16.

[2]Rita Clifton and Esther Maughan, eds., *The Future of Brands: Twenty-five Visions* (New York: New York University Press and Interbrand, 2000), p. vii.

[3]Stan Gelsi, "Detroit's Model Year," *Brandweek*, January 1, 1996, pp. 19-23.

[4]Jeff Smith, "Brand Metrics: Your Key to Measuring Return on Brand Investment," <www.marketingprofs.com>, April 5, 2002.

[5]Dr. James G. Barnes, "What Drives Customer Satisfaction," *CRM-forum.com*, April 10, 2001.

[6]Daniel Morel, letter to the editor, *Advertising Age*, July 29, 2002, p. 14.

[7]Michael Dunn, "Slowdown Uncovers a Better Brand Plan," *Marketing News*, July 16, 2001, p. 21.

[8]Peter H. Farquhar, "Managing Brand Equity," *Journal of Advertising Research*, August-September 1990, p. RC-7.

[9]Jean-Noël Kapferer, *Strategic Brand Management: New Approaches to Creating and Evaluating Brand Equity* (New York: Free Press, 1994), p. 16.

[10]Hayes Roth, "Wielding a Brand Name," *Latin CEO*, August 2001, p. 64.

[11]Al Ries and Jack Trout, *Positioning: The Battle for Your Mind* (New York: McGraw-Hill, 1981).

[12]Bruce Orwall, "Wishing upon a Logo," *Wall Street Journal*, February 28, 2003, p. B1.

[13]Amy Goldwasser, "Something Stylish, Something Blue," *Business 2.0*, February 2002, p. 94; and the JetBlue website, <www.JetBlue.com>, January 2002.

[14]Theo Francis, "What's in a Name? Plenty for Mutual Funds," *Wall Street Journal*, March 14, 2003, p. C1. This is a report on a study done by P. Raghavendra Rau, Michael Cooper, and Huseyin Gulen.

[15]Kevin Keller, *Strategic Brand Management* (Upper Saddle River, NJ: Prentice-Hall, 1998), p. 138.

[16]Giep Franzen and Freek Holzhauer, *Brands: Signs, Names and Brands* (Amsterdam: BBDO Europe, 1989), p. 39.

[17]Regis McKenna, *Relationship Marketing* (Reading, MA: Addison-Wesley, 1991), p. 4.

[18]"To Fix Coca-Cola, Daft Sets Out to Get Relationships Right," *Wall Street Journal*, June 23, 2000, p. A1.

[19]"Customer Satisfaction: The Fundamental Basis of Business Survival," a white paper by Siebel eBusiness, February 2001, p. 5.

[20]Quoted in Peter Jordan, "Zero Defections," *Enterprise* magazine, 1995, p. 29.

[21]Arthur Middleton Hughes, "The Real Truth about Supermarkets—and Customers," *DM News*, October 3, 1994, p. 40.

[22]Scott Hensley, "Pfizer Hawks Discount-Drug Card," *Wall Street Journal*, September 17, 2002, p. D4.

[23]Richard Cross and Janet Smith, *Customer Bonding: Pathway to Lasting Customer Loyalty* (Lincolnwood, IL: NTC, 1994), pp. 54-55.

[24]Ruth Stevens, "It's Time to Return Meaning to CRM," *iMarketing News*, November 20, 2000, p. 16.

[25]Melind Nykamp and Carla McEachern, quoted in *The New Rules of Marketing* newsletter, published by Seklemian/Newell, October 2000, p. 1.

[26]Charlie Dawson, "Get in Touch with Your Emotional Side," *Customer Loyalty Today*, March 2000, pp. 16-17.

[27]Ronald Henkoff, "Service Is Everybody's Business," *Fortune*, June 27, 1994, p. 52.

[28]Kathy Boccella, "Study: Grocery Employees Steal More Than Customers Do," *Denver Post*, March 27, 1994, p. 71.

[29]Floyd Norris, "According to the Q Ratio, the End Is Near," *International Herald Tribune*, May 29, 1996, p. 19.

[30]From the Mercer Future of Brand-Building Survey, discussed in Andrew Pierce and Eric Almquist, "Brand Building May Face a Test," *Advertising Age*, April 9, 2001, p. 22.

[31]David A. Aaker, *Managing Brand Equity: Capitalizing on the Value of a Brand Name* (New York: Free Press, 1991), p. 39.

[32]Stephanie Clifford, "The Grill of Their Dreams," *Business 2.0*, February 2002, p. 96.

Chapter 4

[1]Patrick Jackson, *pr reporter* newsletter, January 23, 1995.

[2]Stephen Manes, "Baby, What'd I Say?" *Forbes*, November 1, 1999, p. 410.

[3]Tom Williams, "US West Revamps Customer Service," *Telephony*, February 12, 1995, p. 7; Julia King, "US West's Failed Restructuring Spells IS Overhaul," *Computerworld*, February 17, 1995, p. 6.

[4]Tom Duncan and Sandra Moriarty, *Driving Brand Value: Using Integrated Marketing to Manager Profitable Shareholder Relationships* (New York: McGraw-Hill, 1997), p. 6.

[5]Greg Burns, "McDonald's: Now, It's Just Another Burger Joint," *Business Week*, March 17, 1997, p. 38.

[6]Ricardo Baca, "Film Fans Learn to Be Patient," *Denver Post*, January 17, 2003, p. F1.

[7]Aimee Picchi and Kim Chipman, "Battle Shifts Theme of Ads," *Bloomberg News*, *Daily Camera*, March 21, 2003, p. E1.

[8]Jon Steel, *Truth, Lies and Advertising* (New York, Wiley, 1998), p. xv.

[9]Ibid.

[10]Patricia Odell, "Olay's Dial-Up Program to Deliver 250,000 Samples," *Direct Newsline*, April 17, 2003.

[11]Nick Wingfield, "Are You Satisfied?" *Wall Street Journal*, September 16, 2002, p. 17.

[12]Jeffrey Pfeffer, "The Face of Your Business," *Business 2.0*, December 2002/January 2003, p. 58.

[13]Roger Hallowell, Leonard A. Schlesinger, and Jeffrey Zornitsky, "Internal Service Quality, Customer and Job Satisfaction: Linkages and Implications for Management," *Human Resource Planning*, 19, no. 2 (1996), pp. 20-32.

[14]Jason Riley, "How Companies Handle Customer-Initiated Brand Contacts," *IMC Research Journal* (2001), p. 6.

[15]Jay Finegan, "Survival of the Smartest," *Inc.*, December 1993, p. 88.

[16]Catharine P. Taylor, "Getting Personal," *Adweek*, IQ special edition, November 4, 2002, pp. IQ 1-2.

[17]Earl Naumann, *Creating Customer Value* (Cincinnati: Thompson Executive Press, 1995), p. 82.

[18]Howard Luck Gossage, *The Book of Gossage*, ed. Bruce Bendinger (Chicago: Copy Workshop, 1995).

[19]Kristine Kirby Webster, *MarketingProfs.com*, September 17, 2002, <www.marketingprofs.com>.

Chapter 5

[1]Naomi Klein, *No Logo* (New York: Picador USA, 2002).

[2]Adapted from Richard P. Coleman and Lee P. Rainwater, *Social Standing in America: New Dimensions of Class* (New York: Basic Books, 1978).

[3]Dean Young and Denis Lebrun, "Blondie," *Denver Post*, April 21, 2003, p. 5F.

[4]Michael Solomon, *Consumer Behavior: Buying, Having, and Being*, 5th ed. (Upper Saddle River, NJ: Prentice-Hall, 2002).

[5]Lawrence F. Feick and Linda L. Price, "The Market Maven," *Managing*, July 1985, p. 10.

[6]Michael L. Ray, "Communication and the Hierarchy of Effects," in *New Models for Mass Communication Research,* ed. P. Clarke (Beverly Hills, CA: Sage, 1973), pp. 147-75; Robert C. Lavidge and Gary A. Steiner, "A Model for Predictive Measurements of Advertising Effectiveness," *Journal of Marketing* (October 1961), pp. 59-62.

[7]Bittar, Christine, "Abs and Ads, " *Brandweek,* May 5, 2003, p. 3.

[8]David L. Loudon and Albert J. Della Bitta, *Consumer Behavior: Concepts and Applications,* 3rd ed. (New York: McGraw-Hill, 1988), p. 532. Loudon and Della Bitta adapted this list from Martin Fishbein and Icek Ajzen, *Belief, Attitude and Behavior: An Introduction to Theory and Research* (Reading, MA: Addison-Wesley, 1975), p. 610.

[9]Ibid., Loudon and Bitta.

[10]Ivan L. Preston, "The Association Model of the Advertising Communication Process," *Journal of Advertising* 1, no. 2 (1982), pp. 3-15; Ivan L. Preston and Esther Thorson, "Challenges to the Use of Hierarchy Models in Predicting Advertising Effectiveness," in *Proceedings of the 1983 Convention of the American Academy of Advertising,* ed. Donald W. Jugenheimer (Lawrence, KS: American Academy of Advertising, 1983).

[11]Joseph Pereira, "Classic Roller Skates Return as Safety Fears Dull Blades," *Wall Street Journal,* October 24, 1997, p. B1.

[12]Adam Shell, "Brand Loyalty? Fuggedaboutit!" *Adweek,* May 12, 1997, p. 40.

[13]Michael Solomon, *Customer Behavior: Buying, Having, and Being* (Boston: Allyn and Bacon, 1992), p. 15.

[14]David W. Stewart and David H. Furse, *Effective Television Advertising* (Lexington, MA: Lexington Books, 1986).

[15]Kevin J. Clancy and Robert S. Shulman, *Marketing Revolution* (New York: HarperBusiness, 1993).

[16]B. Joseph Pine II and James H. Gilmore, *The Experience Economy: Work Is Theatre and Every Business a Stage* (Boston: Harvard Business School Press, 1999), p. 11.

[17]Mark Dolliver, "Value Your Own Savvy as a Customer," *Adweek,* May 19, 1997, p. 18.

[18]Loudon and Della Bitta, *Consumer Behavior.*

[19]Esther Thorson, "Likability: 10 Years of Academic Research," paper presented at the Eighth Annual ARF Copy Research Workshop, New York, September 11, 1991.

[20]"Who Do You Believe?" *Marketing Tools,* October 1996, p. 33.

[21]Sharon Shavitt, Pamela M. Lowrey, and James E. Haefner, *Public Attitudes toward Advertising: More Favorable Than You Might Think* (Urbana: Cummings Center for Advertising Studies, University of Illinois, 1997).

[22]John Deighton, "Features of Good Integration: Two Cases and Some Generalizations," in *Integrated Communication: Synergy of Persuasive Voices,* ed. Esther Thorson and Jeri Moore (Mahwah, NJ: Erlbaum, 1996), pp. 78.

[23]Lisa Fortini-Campbell, *Hitting the Sweet Spot: The Customer Insight Workbook* (Chicago: Copy Workshop, 1992), p. 7.

Chapter 6

[1]Tom Duncan and Sandra Moriarty, *Driving Brand Value: Using Integrated Marketing to Manage Profitable Stakeholder Relationships* (New York: McGraw-Hill, 1997), pp. 148-68.

[2]Allan J. Magrath, *How to Achieve Zero-Defect Marketing* (New York: American Management Association, 1993), p. 14.

[3]Gerry Khermouch, "Mondavi Seeks ID above Wine Glut," *Brandweek,* September 11, 1995, p. 14.

[4]Sybil Stershic, "Internal Marketing: Getting Employees to Be Customer-Focused," AMA Marketing Workshop, Oak Brook, IL, Fall 1999.

[5]Rance Crain, "No Mystery If the Ad Flops: 'Reality Check' Was Missing," *Advertising Age*, April 7, 2003, p. 18.

[6]Anders Gronstedt, "Integrated Communications at America's Leading TQM Corporations" (Ph.D. diss., University of Wisconsin-Madison, 1994).

[7]"Employees Can Create Loyalty," *Tampa Tribune*, May 7, 1999, p. 5.

[8]Mike Gilliland, "CEO Admits Mistake, Changes Store Policy," *Boulder Daily Camera*, March 14, 2000, p. 6A.

[9]Tom Duncan and Steve Everett, "Client Perceptions of Integrated Marketing Communications," *Journal of Advertising Research* 33 (1993), pp. 30-39; Clarke Caywood, Don Schultz, and Paul Wang, *A Survey of Consumer Goods Manufacturers* (New York: American Association of Advertising Agencies, 1993).

Chapter 7

[1]Don Peppers and Martha Rogers, *The One to One Future: Building Relationships One Customer at a Time* (New York: Currency Doubleday, 1993).

[2]Author experience when he was director of marketing communications for Eckrich Processed Meats.

[3]Kaj Storbacka, "Segmentation Based on Customer Profitability: Retrospective Analysis of Retail Bank Customer Bases," in *Contemporary Knowledge of Relationship Marketing*, ed. Atul Parvatiyar and Jagdish Sheth (Atlanta: Center for Relationship Marketing; Emory University, 1996), p. 32.

[4]William Taylor, "Permission Marketing," *Fast Company*, April 1998, p. 47.

[5]Tina Furuki, "Why Ask Y?" *American Advertising*, Winter 2000, pp. 11-14.

[6]"The Hearts of New-Car Buyers," *American Demographics*, August 1991, p. 14.

[7]Andrew Tilin, "Will the Kids Buy It?" *Business 2.0*, May 2003, pp. 94-100.

[8]Robert Berner, "Now Even Toddlers Are Dressing to the Nines," *Wall Street Journal*, May 27, 1997, p. B1.

[9]Dave Carpenter, "Businesses Tune In to Teens," *Associated Press*, November 11, 2000, reporting on a study done by Teenage Research Unlimited, Northbrook, IL.

[10]Eduardo Porter, "Buying Power of Hispanics Is Set to Soar," *Wall Street Journal*, April 18, 2003, p. B1.

[11]Leon E. Wynter, "Blacks and Hispanics Gain Spending Clout," *Wall Street Journal*, September 3, 1997, p. B1.

[12]Stephanie Capparell, "Ed Boyd Tore Down Race Barriers to Build a Market for Pepsi," *Wall Street Journal*, August 29, 1997, p. B1.

[13]Keith L. Alexander, "Communications Study Finds Ad Bias," *USA Today*, January 14, 1999, p. 1B.

[14]Jacques Horovitz and Nirmalya Kumar, "Getting Close to the Customer," *Financial Times*, February 2, 1996, p. 13.

[15]"Senior Spending," *American Advertising*, Winter 2000, p. 13.

[16]Phil Kotler and Gary Armstrong, *Principles of Marketing* (Upper Saddle River, NJ: Prentice-Hall, 1999), p. 215.

[17]"What's in Store?" *Direct* 4, no. 12 (December 1992), p. 26.

Chapter 8

[1]John O'Connor and Eamonn Galvin, *Marketing and Information Technology* (London: Pitman, 1997), p. 273.

[2]I. Linton, *Database Marketing: Know What Your Customer Wants* (London: Pitman, 1995).

[3]O'Connor and Galvin, *Marketing and Information Technology*, p. 79.

[4]Ron Kahan, *DM News*, January 13, 1997, p. 1.

[5]Jim Emerson, "Levi Strauss in the Early Stages of Shift to Database Marketing," *DM News*, December 7, 1992, p. 1.

[6]Ira Sager, "The Great Equalizer," *Business Week, Special Issue, The Information Revolution* (New York: Business Week, 1994), p. 104.

[7]"DMA: Over 90% of B2Bers Use Databases," *DM News*, January 31, 1994, p. 10.

[8]John Coe, "The Decay Rate of Business Databases—a Surprise," *DM News*, February 14, 1994, p. 25.

[9]Annette Kissinger, "You Say London, I Say Londres," *Marketing Tools*, May 1997, pp. 12-14.

[10]Tito Tezinde et al., "Getting Permission, Factors Affecting Permission Marketing," *Journal of Interactive Marketing*, Autumn 2002, p. 30.

[11]Risa Bauman, "Making Play Pay," *Direct* 5, no. 4 (April 1993), p. 29.

[12]Nancy Wong, "First Major Post-9/11 Survey Finds Consumers Demanding Companies Do More to Protect Privacy; Public Wants Company Privacy Policies to Be Independently Verified," *Harris Interactive*, February 20, 2002.

[13]Center for Democracy in Technology, April 2003, <www.cdt.org/legislation>.

[14]"Market Makers," *The Economist*, March 14, 1998, p. 68.

[15]Presentation by Martin E. Abrams to the Direct Marketing Association Educators' Conference, San Francisco, 1996.

[16]Kristen Meador, "The Role of Privacy as a Market Differentiator in the Consumer Marketplace," *IMC Research Journal*, 2003, p. 19 (from Kim Sheehan and Mariea Grubbs Hoy, "Dimensions of Privacy Concern among Online Consumers," *Journal of Public Policy and Marketing*, Spring 2000).

[17]Kim Cleland, "Few Wed Marketing, Communications," *Advertising Age*, February 27, 1995, p. 10.

[18]Jennifer Dejong, "Smart Marketing," *Computerworld*, February 7, 1994, p. 118.

[19]Brent Keltner and David Finegold, "Adding Value in Banking: Human Resource Innovations for Service Firms," *Sloan Management Review* (Fall 1996), p. 63.

[20]Diane Luckow, "Better Selling through Technology: Companies of All Sizes Are Using Database Marketing to Boost Sales through Old-Fashioned Personal Service," *Profit* 13, no. 4 (January 1995), sec. 1, p. 43.

[21]Keltner and Finegold, "Adding Value in Banking," p. 63.

Chapter 9

[1]"A Tip of the Cap to Kaplan Thaler," *Wall Street Journal*, house ad, November 14, 2002.

[2]"Penelope Cruz Can't Contain Herself in Coca-Cola Promotion," *Denver Post*, January 17, 2003, p. 3F.

[3]Bob St. Julian, "Put Away the Brief and Get Creative," *B&T Marketing & Media*, November 8, 2002, <www.bandt.com.au/articles/4f/0c01254f.asp>.

[4]Michael McCarthy, "Hummer H2 Makes Impression despite SUV Backlash," *USA Today*, December 27, 2002, p. 9A.

[5]Adapted from Sandra Moriarty, "The First Step in Creative Strategy: Creating Customer-Focused Objectives" (paper presented at the annual conference of the Academy of Advertising, Jacksonville, FL, March 2002).

[6]Stefano Hatfield, "Granger in Effect," *Creativity Magazine*, October 7, 2002, <www.adcritic.com/news/creativity/detil/?=36238>.

[7]"Diamonds in the Data," *one.a magazine* 5, no. 4 (Spring 2002), pp. 8-9.

[8]Lisa Fortini-Campbell, *The Consumer Insight Handbook* (Chicago: Copy Workshop, 1992), p. 19.

[9]Kelly Pate, "Former N.Y. Ad Man Is Sold on Denver," *Denver Post*, October 4, 2002, p. C1.

[10]Ibid.

[11]Bob Garfield, "Britney Bowl," *Advertising Age*, February 4, 2002, p. 34.

[12]Hatfield, "Granger in Effect"; Stefano Hatfield, "Sunshine Supermen," *Creativity Magazine*, April 1, 2002, <www.adcritic.com/news/creativity/detail/?q=35188>.

[13]"Planning Brief: The New York Times," *one.a magazine* 5, no. 4 (Spring 2002), p. 13.

[14]Stuart Elliott, "Sex Sells, with a Wink and a Nudge," *New York Times Direct*, April 10, 2003, NYTDirect@nytimes.com.

[15]Terry Kattleman, "Lwall Power," *Creativity Magazine*, September 7, 2002, <www.adcritic.com/news/creativity/detil/?q=36239>.

[16]Ann-Christine Diaz, "Kash Sree—Part of Wieden+Kennedy's 'Tag' Team—Moves to the Midwest," *Creativity Magazine*, July 29, 2002, <www.adcritic.com/news/creativity/details/?q-=35583>.

[17]"A Tip of the Cap to Kaplan Thaler," *Wall Street Journal*, house ad, November 14, 2002.

[18]"The Art of Empathy," *one.a magazine* 5, no. 2 (Fall 2001), pp. 8-9.

[19]Edward De Bono, *Serious Creativity: Using the Power of Lateral Thinking to Create New Ideas* (New York: HarperBusiness, 1992).

[20]Edward De Bono, *Six Thinking Hats* (New York: Little, Brown, 1986).

[21]Roger Von Oech, *A Whack on the Side of the Head: How You Can Be More Creative* (New York: Warner Books, 1998).

[22]"The Art of Empathy."

[23]Bruce Bendinger, *The Copy Workshop Workbook* (Chicago: Copy Workshop, 1993), pp. 170-74.

[24]Hatfield, "Granger in Effect."

[25]David Ogilvy, *Ogilvy on Advertising* (New York: Random House, 1985), pp. 17-18.

[26]John Eighmey, "Safety Net Failed in Super Bowl Flap," *Advertising Age*, February 15, 1999, p. 24.

[27]Hatfield, "Granger in Effect."

Chapter 10

[1]Bob St. Julian, "Put Away the Brief and Get Creative," *B&T Marketing & Media*, November 8, 2002, <www.bandt.com.au/articles/4f/0c01254f.asp>.

[2]Gary McWilliams, "Gateway Barks Right Up Apple's Tree in New Ad Campaign," *Wall Street Journal*, August 26, 2002, p. B1.

[3]James Surowiecki, "The Power of the Prize," *The New Yorker*, June 18 and 25 (double issue), p. 67.

[4]Stefano Hatfield, "Sunshine Supermen," April 1, 2002, *Creativity Magazine*, <www.adcritic.com/news/creativity/detail/?q=35188>.

[5]Laurel Wentz, "Anti-Tobacco Campaign Wins Media Grand Prix," *AdAge.com*, June 20, 2001, <www.adage.com/cannes2001/cn01_0620_03.shtml>.

[6]Sandra Moriarty, *Creative Advertising*, 2nd ed. (Englewood Cliffs, NJ: Prentice-Hall, 1991), p. 172.

[7]This story was recounted by advertising professor Dick Weltz in an e-mail to the Adforum listserv, January 19, 2003.

[8]Martha Irvine, "Media Feasting on 'Yo, Yo, Yo' diet," *Denver Post*, November 13, 2002, p. 5A.

[9]Stuart Elliott, "Selling Haircuts with Humor," April 22, 2003, *NYTimes.com*.

[10]Diane Scarponi, "GE Unplugs 'Good Things' Slogan," *Denver Post,* January 17, 2003, p. 2C.
[11]Murray Raphel, "Ad Techniques: Off with the Head," *Bank Marketing,* February 1988, pp. 54-55.
[12]Stefano Hatfield, "Granger in Effect," *Creativity Magazine,* October 7, 2002, <www.adcritic.com/news/creativity/detil/?=36238>.
[13]Paul C. Judge, "Has Your Company Found Its Voice?" *Fast Company,* August 2001, pp. 40-42
[14]Steve Morse, "Song Strikes Paydirt via Super Bowl Ad," *Denver Post,* February 4, 2003, p. 6F.
[15]Stuart Elliott, "Procter & Gamble's Hit Song," March 4, 2003, *NYTimes.com.*
[16]Joshua Levine, "Zap-Proof Advertising," *Forbes,* September 22, 1997, pp. 146-50.
[17]Karen Lewicki, "Minding the Gap," *Juked.com,* June, 6, 2002.
[18]"Best Reason for Even TiVo Users to Watch a Commercial," *Time,* January 6, 2003, p. 142.
[19]Charles Goldsmith, "Adding Special to Effects," *Wall Street Journal,* February 26, 2003, p. B1.
[20]"Spotlight: Special-Effects Editing," *one.a magazine* 5, no. 4 (Spring 2002), p. 23.
[21]Paul Tulenko, "Design Web Page Basically," *Boulder Daily Camera,* February 26, 2000, p. 6D.
[22]Stephen H. Wildstrom, "Untangle These Web Sites, Please," *Business Week,* August 30, 1999, p. 18.
[23]Bob Tedeschi, "Web Merchants Go Multimedia," *New York Times,* March 13, 2000, <www.nytimes.com/library/tech/00/03/cyber/commerce/13commerce.html>.
[24]Clint Swett, "E-Mail Response May Come Now, Later or Not at All," *Business Plus,* February 6, 2000, p. 15.
[25]Kim Sheehan and Caitlin Doherty, "Re-Weaving the Web: Integrating Print and Online Communications," *Journal of Interactive Marketing* 15, no. 2 (Spring 2001), p. 47.
[26]Tom Duncan and Sandra Moriarty, *Driving Brand Value: Using Integrated Marketing to Manage Profitable Shareholder Relationships* (New York: McGraw-Hill, 1997), p. 69-94.

Chapter 11

[1]Brian Steinberg and Suzanne Vranica, "Martha Stewart Firm Needs Space," *Wall Street Journal,* June 4, 2003, p. B4.
[2]Jennifer Waters, "Martha Stewart: The Woman, the Brand," *CBSMarketWatch.com,* June 4, 2003.
[3]Jonathan Bond and Richard Kirshenbaum, *Under the Radar* (New York: Wiley, 1998).
[4]Tom Duncan and Sandra Moriarty, *Driving Brand Value: Using Integrated Marketing to Manage Profitable Stakeholder Relationships* (New York: McGraw-Hill, 1997), pp. 102-03.
[5]Keith Hammonds, "Brand Aid," *Fast Company,* February 2003, p. 46.
[6]*Hispanic Newspaper and Magazine Network,* www.allied-media.com, July 2003
[7]Television Advertising Bureau, as cited on TVBasics website, July 2000.
[8]Radio Advertising Bureau, <www.rab.com>, June 2000.
[9]*TV Dimensions '98* (Media Dynamics, 1998), p. 335.
[10]Richard Siklos, "Will the Nielsen Spin-Off Be a Hit?" *Business Week,* July 20, 1998, pp. 66-67.
[11]Richard Hendersen, "Over One Million Sold," *Brandweek,* November 6, 2000, special advertising section, p. 6.
[12]Author interview with Amy Hume, Leo Burnett media department, September 2000.
[13]Kyle Pope, "In Battle for TV Ads, Cable Is Now the Enemy," *Wall Street Journal,* May 6, 1998, p. B1.
[14]Rachel Zoll, "Up on the Roof," *Boulder Sunday Camera,* June 14, 1998, p. 1B.
[15]Cara Beardi, "From Elevators to Gas Stations, Ads Multiplying," *Advertising Age,* November 13, 2000, p. 40.
[16]Erin White, "Advertisers Hope Fragrant Posters Are Nothing to Sniff At," *Wall Street Journal,* October 10, 2002, p. B1.
[17]Ricardo Baca, "Captive Audiences Bite Bullet, Accept Pre-Movie Advertising," *Denver Post,* September 19, 2002, p. F1.
[18]Scot Hume, "Consumers Pan Ads on Video Movies," *Advertising Age,* November 13, 2000, p. 40.
[19]Suzanne Vranica, "Marketing at the Movies," *Wall Street Journal,* September 5, 2002, p. B1.
[20]Kevin B. Tynan, *Multi-Channel Marketing: Maximizing Market Share with an Integrated Marketing Strategy* (Chicago: Probus, 1994), pp. 91-98.
[21]Rebecca Gardyn, "Moving Targets," *American Demographics,* October 2000, <www.americandemographics.com>.
[22]T. L. Stanley, "Place-Based Media," *Brandweek,* May 11, 1998, pp. 34-35.
[23]Stefano Hatfield, "Granger in Effect," *Creativity Magazine,* October 7, 2002, <www.adcritic.com/news/creativity/detil/?=36238>.

Chapter 12

[1]<www.nytimes.ecommerce>, March 25, 2002.
[2]Michael Liedtke, "After the 'Stupid Money,'" *Daily Camera,* February 1, 2003, p. 1E.
[3]"Business and the Internet," *The Economist,* June 26, 1999, p. 17.
[4]Stephen Warley, "Surviving the Digital Spotlight," from SpyTV's "In the Spotlight," February 27, 2003.
[5]David W. Moore, "Americans Say Internet Makes Their Lives Better," Gallup News Service, February 23, 2000, <www.gallup.com/poll/releases/pr000223.asp>.
[6]"The Net Only Gets Better for Business," *Business 2.0,* May 2003, p. 84.

[7]John Bissell, "Brave New World, Same Old Formula," *Brandweek,* November 18, 2002, p. 36.

[8]Steve Fioretti and Bob D'Acquisto, "Advertising Takes a Ride on the Wireless Wave," *iMarketing News,* August 21, 2000, p. 19.

[9]"US Adults Prefer E-mail to Post and Telephone," *NUA.net,* January 18, 2000, <www.nua.net/surveys/?f=VS&art_id=905355531&rel=true>.

[10]Jim Sterne, "In Praise of E-Mail," *Inc. Tech 2000,* September 15, 2000, p. 149.

[11]<www.Internetnews.com/iar/article.php/1564761>, January 6, 2003.

[12]Peter Lewis, "Pickets Halt Car Dealer's 'Spam,'" *Boulder Daily Camera,* May 9, 1998, p. 5B.

[13]Mylene Mangalindan, "Cut the Spam, Direct Marketers Say," *Wall Street Journal,* February 25, 2003, p. D4.

[14]Lisa Bertagnoli, "E-Marketing Tricky in Europe," *Marketing News,* July 16, 2001, p. 19.

[15]Bill McCloskey, "Rich Email: Part 1," *ClickZ Network,* February 24, 2000, <http://gt.clickz.com/cgi-bin/gt/sb/rm/rm.html?article=1357>.

[16]Sterne, "In Praise of E-Mail."

[17]McCloskey, "Rich Email: Part 1."

[18]Cara DiPasquale "E-Mail Effective for Customer Retention, Sales," *AdAge.com,* April 3, 2002.

[19]"Email—Most Effective Online Marketing Tool," *Los Angeles Times,* January 27, 2000, <www.nua.net/surveys/?f=VS&art_id=905355553&rel=true>; and Sterne, "In Praise of E-Mail."

[20]Sterne, "In Praise of E-Mail," p. 152.

[21]Susan Stellin, "Online Customer Service Found Lacking," *New York Times,* <www.newyorktimes.com>, January 3, 2002.

[22]Nat Ives, "Marketers Shift Tactics on Web Ads," *New York Times,* nytimes.com, February 11, 2003.

[23]James Daly, "Editor's Note: Service First," *Business 2.0,* June 27, 2000, p. 5.

[24]<www.the-dma.org/cgi/dispensenewsstand/article>, 2002.

[25]Keith Regan, "Era of E-Commerce Profits Underway," *E-Commerce Times,* <www.ecomercetimes.com>, June 20, 2001.

[26]Rachel Brand and Steve Cauk, "Super Bowl of Shopping," *Rocky Mountain News,* November 30, 2002, p. 1C.

[27]Regan, "Era of E-Commerce Profits Underway."

[28]<www.nua.ie.surveys>, June 20, 2001.

[29]Martin Lindstrom, "Morphing Offline into Online," *ClickZ Network,* August 26, 1999, <http://gt.clickz.com/cgi-bin/gt/wi/bm/bm.html?article=679>.

[30]Nick Wingfielde, "A Question of Trust," *Wall Street Journal,* citing a study done by Princeton Survey Research Associates, September 16, 2002, p. R6.

[31]NPD press release, February 7, 2000, <www.npd.com/corp/press/press_000207.htm>.

[32]Martin Lindstrom, "Rat Race Scurry," *ClickZ Network,* December 2, 1999, <http://gt.clickz.com/cgi-bin/>.

[33]Martin Lindstrom, "Dot-Com Branding Dilemma," *ClickZ Network,* February 24, 2000, <http://gt.clickz.com/cgi-bin/gt/wi/bm/bm.html?article=1356>; and Suein L. Hwang, "The Dot-Com Blur: Venture Capitalists Discover Marketing," *Wall Street Journal,* February 16, 2000, p. A16.

[34]Mukul Pandya, "A Good Brand Is Hard to Buy," *Wall Street Journal,* June 9, 2000, p. A18.

[35]"DoubleClick Cuts More than 120 Employees," *Boulder Daily Camera,* December 6, 2000, p. 5D.

[36]Lori Enos, interview with Shirley Choy-Marshall, director of marketing for HPShopping.com, *E-Commerce Times,* July 26, 2001.

[37]Louis Whitman, "Dotcoms Shaping Up," *BrandEra Times,* April 25, 2000, <www.brandera.com>.

[38]Barb Palser, "Attack of the Killer Ads," *American Journalism Review,* March 2000, p. 64.

[39]Jeffrey Graham, "Internet Advertising Best Practices: Five Rules to Brand By," *ClickZ Network,* October 25, 2000.

[40]Terry Lefton, "Blocking Those internet Ads," from *Industry Standard,* reprinted in *Boulder Daily Camera: Business Plus,* April 23, 2001, p. 12.

[41]Suein Hwang and Mylene Mangalindan, "Yahoo's Grand Vision for Web Advertising Takes Some Hard Hits," *Wall Street Journal,* September 1, 2000, p. A1.

[42]Chan-Hoan Cho and John Leckenby, "The Effectiveness of Banner Advertising: Involvement and Click-Through" (paper presented at the Association for Education in Journalism and Mass Communication conference, August 2000).

[43]Marc Langheinrich, Atsuyoshi Nakamura, Naoki Abe, Tomonari Kamba, Yoshiyuki Koseki, *Unintrusive Customization Techniques for Web Advertising,* <www8.org/w8-papers/2bcustomizing/unintrusive/unintrusive.html>.

[44]"Banners on the Decline," *CyberAtlas,* April 22, 1999, <http://cyberatlas.internet.com/big_picture/demographics/article/0,1323,5941_154461,00.html>.

[45]Clare Saliba, interview with Gerry Sweeney, VP e-Visa, *E-Commerce Times,* August 3, 2001.

[46]Bob Walker, "System for Measuring Clicks Is under Assault," *New York Times* <www.newyorktimes.com>, August 27, 2001.

[47]Tom McNichol, "The New Privacy Wars," *USA Weekend,* May 16, 1996, pp. 16–17; Ellyn E. Spragins and Mary Hager, "Naked before the World," *Newsweek,* June 30, 1997, p. 84.

[48]Susannah Fox, "Trust and Privacy Online; Why Americans Want to Rewrite the Rules," The Pew Internet and American Life Project, online posting, <www.pewinternet.org>, 2000.

[49]Michael Pastore, "Per Capita Online Spending Drops," *InternetNews.com*, January 3, 2000, <www.internetnews.com/ec-news/print/0,1089,4_272011,00.html>.

[50]Laurel Fortin, "Online Privacy Targeted in U.S.," *BrandEra Times*, May 31, 2000, <www.brandera.com>.

[51]D. Ian Hopper, "Privacy Group Breaks Ties with Amazon.com," *Boulder Daily Camera*, September 14, 2000, p. 3A.

[52]Jeri Clausing, "Self-Regulation of Internet Companies Is Poor," *New York Times*, June 5, 1998.

[53]Jeri Clausing, "On Eve of Privacy Conference, Trade Groups Jockey for Position," *New York Times*, June 23, 1998.

[54]Ibid.

[55]Moore, "Americans Say Internet Makes Their Lives Better."

[56]Sim D'Hertefelt, "Trust and the Perception of Security," *Interactionarchitect*, January 3, 2000, <www.interactionarchitect.com/research/report20000103shd.htm>.

[57]<www.forrester.com/ER/Press/Release/0,1769,177,FF.html>; "Forrester Technographics® Finds Online Consumers Fearful of Privacy Violations," Forrester Research press release, October 27, 1999.

Chapter 13

[1]Mark Goldstein, speech at University of Colorado IMC Program, November 8, 2000.

[2]Ed Chambliss, team leader, Phelps Group, June 2003 (personal interview).

[3]Jon Fine, "Cross-Media Catches Fire," *Advertising Age*, October 23, 2000, p. S2.

[4]Cathy Frisinger, "Legions Love Lizzie," *Daytona Beach New-Journal*, April 30, 2003, p. 6D.

[5]Thomas Harris, "A Radical Proposal," *Thomas L. Harris ViewsLetter*, March 2003, p. 2.

[6]Stuart Elliott, "A Convergence of TV Tastes," *New York Times*, April 21, 2003, <www.nytimes.com/2003/-4/21/business/media/21ADCO.html>.

[7]Sandra E. Moriarty, "Explorations into the Commercial Encounter," *Proceedings of the 1991 Conference of the American Academy of Advertising*, ed. Rebecca Holman; and Sandra E. Moriarty and Shu-Ling Everett, "Commercial Breaks: A Viewing Behavior Study," *Journalism Quarterly* 71, no. 2 (Summer 1994), pp. 346-55.

[8]*TV Dimensions '98* (Media Dynamics, 1998), p. 480.

[9]Stuart Elliott, "Advertisers Decide It's Time for 'Reality,'" *New York Times*, February 14, 2003, <www.nytimes.com/2003/02/04/business/media/14ADCO.html>.

[10]Goldstein, speech.

[11]Warren St. John, "Why TiVo Owners Can't Shut Up," *New York Times*, April 20, 2003, <www.nytimes.com/2003/04/20/fashion/20TIVO.html?th=&p>.

[12]John Battelle, "Is TiVo NeXT?" *Business 2.0*, May 2003, p. 60.

[13]Michele Hatty, "Exclusive Lord of the Rings Poster," *USA Weekend*, December 13-15, 2002, p. 8.

[14]Michael White, personal correspondence with the author, March 17, 1993.

Chapter 14

[1]*The Art of Sales Promotion, Promotion* (New York: Sibel/Mohr, 1981).

[2]"Different Tools for Different Strategies," *Promotional Sense* 3, no. 1 (Spring 1998), p. 2.

[3]Adapted from *The Art of Sales Promotion, Promotion*.

[4]Michelle Slatalla, "Online Shopper: A Path to Redemption (Limited Time Offer)," *New York Times*, June 21, 2001, <www.newyorktimes.com>.

[5]"The Test Bait," *Brandweek*, March 30, 1998, p. 27.

[6]Sally Beatty, "Block That Spry!" *Wall Street Journal*, December 16, 2002, p. B1.

[7]Ann Mack, "Choose Me," *Brandweek*, April 10, 2000, p. 106.

[8]Peter Breen, "Promotion Trends 2000," <www.promomagazine.com/content/report/2000>.

[9]Quoted ibid.

[10]"The Fellowship of New Line," *PROMO*, November 1, 2001, <www.industryclick.com>.

[11]Richard Barlow, "The Net Upends Tenets of Loyalty Marketing," *Advertising Age*, April 17, 2000, p. 46.

[12]Dennis L. Duffy, "Effective Design and Use of Loyalty Marketing and Frequency Marketing Programs," American Marketing Association Fall Workshop, Oak Brook, IL, 1999.

[13]Mike Capizzi, "Insulating the Brand," *Colloquy* 11, no. 2 (2003), p. 2.

[14]Kusum L. Ailawadi, Donald R. Lehmann, and Scott A. Neslin, "Market Response to a Major Policy Change in the Marketing Mix: Learning from Procter & Gamble's Value Pricing Strategy," *Journal of Marketing* 65, no. 1 (January 2001), pp. 44-61.

[15]Larry Light, "At the Center of It All Is the Brand," *Advertising Age*, March 29, 1993, p. 22.

[16]Ibid.

[17]Kate MacArthur, "Fracas Hits the Fountain," *Advertising Age*, May 29, 2000, p. 46.

[18]"Firm Studies New Features for Packaging," *Boulder Daily Camera*, February 12, 2001, p. 13A.

[19]Sarah Ellison, "Smell of Success: Suave Copies Hot Scents to Boost Sales," *Wall Street Journal*, November 14, 2002, pp. B1, B3.

Chapter 15

[1]Jack Neff, "Coupons Get Clipped" *Advertising Age*, November 5, 2001, p. 47.

[2]"The Comeback," special supplement report in *PROMO Magazine*, April 2003, p. S2.

[3]Jane Applegate, "'Visual Merchandising' Sets Mood," *The Denver Post*, April 26, 1998, p. 7-I.

[4]"A. C. Nielson Research Reveals Cheese Sales Skyrocket with In-Store Promotions," *POPAI News*, Marketplace 1990, p. 19.

[5]*The Point of Purchase Advertising Industry Fact Book*, 2000, p. 51.

[6]Website of POPAI, "Competitive Media Facts, July 2000.

[7]Mark Schmann, "The 2002 Megabrand Report," *Advertising Age*, July 24, 2002, AdAge.com.

[8]Betsy Spethman, "Wake Up and Smell the Co-Marketing," *PROMO Magazine*, August 1, 1998.

Chapter 16

[1]Charles Futrell, *Fundamentals of Selling* (Burr Ridge, IL: Irwin/McGraw-Hill, 1999), p. 5.

[2]Barton Weitz, Stephen Castleberry, and John Tanner, *Selling* (Burr Ridge, IL: Irwin/McGraw-Hill, 1995), p. 386.

[3]"Marketers Prefer CRM to Mass Media Advertising," research brief, <www.Reveries.com>, June 3, 2002.

[4]Bernaud Liautaud with Mark Hammond, *e-Business Intelligence* (New York: McGraw-Hill, 2001), p. 150.

[5]Bill Herr, "Bridging the Gap between Marketing and Sales," *A&M Review*, April 1996, p. 24.

[6]Martin Evertt, "It's No Fluke," *Sales & Marketing Management*, April 1994.

[7]Jim Obermayer, "Power Plays: Sales Leads Are Why You Exhibit" (paper presented at Exhibition Conference, Baltimore, MD, October 4-8, 1999).

[8]"Promising Long-Term Leads Are Too Often Lost through Impatience," *Promotional Sense* 3, no. 1 (Spring 1998), p. 2.

[9]Andy Cohen, "Sales Strikes Out on Campus," *Sales & Marketing Management*, November 1997, p. 13.

Chapter 17

[1]Regis McKenna, *Relationship Marketing* (Reading, MA: Addison-Wesley, 1991), p. 2.

[2]Fraser P. Seitel, *The Practice of Public Relations,* 7th ed. (Upper Saddle River, NJ: Prentice-Hall, 1998), p. 5.

[3]Adapted from Scott Cutlip, Allen Center, and Glen Broom, *Effective Public Relations* (Englewood Cliffs, NJ: Prentice-Hall, 1985), p. 4.

[4]"2001 Public Relations Industry Revenue Documentation and Rankings Fact Sheet," Council of Public Relations Firms, n.d.

[5]Quoted in Thomas L. Harris, *Value-Added Public Relations: The Secret Weapon of Integrated Marketing* (Lincolnwood, IL: NTC, 1998).

[6]Thomas L. Harris, *The Marketer's Guide to Public Relations: How Today's Top Companies Are Using the New PR to Gain a Competitive Edge* (New York: Wiley, 1991), p. 9.

[7]Richard Rotman, "Why Can't They Get Along?" *Brandera.com*, May 30, 2000.

[8]Sandra E. Moriarty, "PR and IMC: The Benefits of Integration," *Public Relations Quarterly* 39, no. 3 (Fall 1994), p. 41.

[9]David Bank, "Bay Networks' Results to Trail Forecasts," *Wall Street Journal*, March 18, 1998, p. B4.

[10]Sandra E. Moriarty, "The Big Idea: Creativity in Public Relations," in *The Handbook of Strategic Public Relations and Integrated Communications*, ed. Clarke L. Caywood (New York: McGraw-Hill, 1997), pp. 554-63.

[11]Paul A. Holmes, "Guerrilla Marketing: The Word on the Street," *Reputation Management* 6, no. 3 (March 2000), pp. 30-37.

[12]Steve Jarvis, "How the Internet Is Changing Fundamentals of Publicity," *Marketing News*, July 17, 2000, p. 6.

[13]"20/20 Vision," *Reputation Management* 6, no. 2 (February 2000), p. 40.

[14]"RepBriefs: By the Numbers," *Reputation Management* 5, no. 3 (May-June 1999), p. 12.

[15]Roger Haywood, "Media Relations," in *Strategic Public Relations*, ed. Norman A. Hart (London: Macmillan Business Press, 1995), pp. 178-79.

[16]Seitel, *The Practice of Public Relations*, p. 283.

[17]Haywood, pp. 178-79.

[18]"Next to Godliness," *Reputation Management* 6, no. 3 (March 2000), p. 17.

[19]Paul A. Holmes, "Promise Keepers," *Reputation Management* 6, no. 3 (March 2000), p. 4.

[20]"RepBriefs: By the Numbers," *Reputation Management* 6, no. 2 (February 2000), p. 18.

[21]"From Gay-Bashing Ministers to Striking Umps, Agency Names Top PR Blunders of 1999," *Inside PR*, January 3, 2000, p. 10.

[22]"Reputation Watch: Shell," *Reputation Management* 6, no. 3 (March 2000), p. 11.

[23]Thomas L. Harris, "Brand Maintenance," *Reputation Management* 6, no. 2 (February 2000), pp. 28-29.

[24]Thomas Harris/Impulse Research, "Corporate Communications Spending and Reputations of Fortune 500 Companies" (Los Angeles: Impulse Research Corp., June 4, 1999), p. 17.

[25]"An 'Invisible Giant' Awakens," *Reputation Management* 5, no. 2 (March-April 1999), pp. 68-70.

[26]Tom Duncan and Sandra Moriarty, "A Process for Managing Brand Relationships," *Academy Monograph* (New York: PRSA Counselors Academy, 2000), pp. 11-12.

[27]James Collins and Jerry Porras, *Built to Last* (New York: Harper Business, 1994), p. 69.

[28]Tom Duncan and Sandra Moriarty, *Driving Brand Value: Using Integrated Marketing to Manage Profitable Stakeholder Relationships* (New York: McGraw-Hill, 1997), pp. 126-47.

[29]Craig Smith, "The New Corporate Philosophy," *Harvard Business Review*, May-June 1994, p. 48.

[30]Koten, p. 149.

[31]Bill Goodwill, "Cause Marketing Pros and Cons," *Broadcast Café Newsletter*, October 1999, <www.psaresearch.com/CRMFEATURE.html>.

[32]Carol Cone, "Cause Branding in the 21st Century," *KG Independent Sector*, <www.independentsector.org/mission_market/cone.htm>.

[33]Paul A. Holmes, "With Friends like These . . .," *Reputation Management* 6, no. 7 (July-August 2000), p. 12.

[34]Dave Carpenter, "McDonald's Unveils New Game, but Stock Hits 10-Year Low," *Associated Press State and Local Wire*, March 6, 2003, <web.lexis-nexis.com/universe/document>.

[35]Roger Slavens, "AK Steel Campaign Bring Home the Point about New Coatings," *BtoB*, June 9, 2003, p. 18.

[36]Terrie Williams, "Putting Relationships Back into Public Relations" (Vernon C. Schranz Distinguished Lectureship in Public Relations, Muncie, IN: Ball State University, 1996).

Chapter 18

[1]*DMA Statistical Fact Book 1999* (New York: DMA, 2000), p. 3.

[2]Ibid, p. 287.

[3]Dawn Anfuso, "Integrated P.S. Campaign Wins Honors," *imedia connection.com*, November 11, 2002; Beth Viveiros, "Pushing the Envelope: Flight of Fancy," *Direct Marketing Business Intelligence Report*, <www.directmag.com>, June 16, 2003.

[4]Richard Levely, "On the Record: List Leaders of the Pack," *Directmag.com*, October 2000.

[5]Edward Nash, "The Roots of Direct Marketing," *Direct Marketing*, February 1995, pp. 38-40.

[6]Rick Brooks, "Post Office Plan Could Produce More Junk Mail," *Wall Street Journal*, April 3, 2003, p. B1.

[7]Melissa Campanelli, "Direct Mail Stays a Strong DM Vehicle, Study Finds," *DM News*, June 9, 2003, p. 2

[8]*DMA Statistical Fact Book 1999*, p. 72.

[9]Ibid., p. 193.

[10]Ibid., p. 37.

[11]Brain Steinberg et al., " 'Do Not Call' Registry Is Pushing Telemarketers to Plan New Pitches," *Wall Street Journal*, July 2, 2003, p. 1A; Matt Richtel, "Limits to Be Set on Telemarketing," *New York Times*, June 20, 2003.

[12]"About the ATA," <www.ataconnect.org/about.htm>, July 2, 2003.

[13]*Bob Coen's Insider's Report*, McCann-Erickson Worldwide website, June 2000, <www.mccann.com>.

[14]Charles Fishman, "This Is a Marketing Revolution," *Fast Company*, May 1999, p. 207.

[15]Scott Hovanyetz, "Speaker: Telemarketing Will Thrive," *DM News*, June 9, 2003, p. 2.

[16]<www.infomercial-production-marketing-company.com>, June 2003.

[17]Paul Niemann, "Infomercials," *Inventors' Digest Online*, <www.inventorsdigest.com/magazine>, June 17, 2003.

[18]<www.infomercial-production-marketing-company.com>, June 2003.

[19]"As a Promotional Tactic, Re-creation Continues to Impress—and Produce Results," *Promotional Sense* 2, no. 4 (Winter 1997), p. 2.

[20]Ernan Roman, *Integrated Direct Marketing* (Lincolnwood, IL: NTC, 1995), p. 46.

[21]Kristen Meador, "The Role of Privacy as a Market Differentiator in the Consumer Marketplace," *IMC Research Journal*, 2003, p. 17-22.

Chapter 19

[1]"PMA Announces Formation of Event Marketing Council . . ." (press release, Promotional Marketing Association, March 13, 2003), <www.pmalink.org/about/press_releases>.

[2]"The Comeback," *PROMO Magazine*, special supplement report, April 2003, p. S9, <www.pmalink.org.

[3]Quoted in Melanie Warner, "Can Tupperware Keep a Lid on the Web?" *Fortune*, January 12, 1998, p. 144.

[4]Joseph Pine II and James Gilmore, *The Experience Economy: Work Is Theatre and Every Business a Stage* (Boston: Harvard Business School Press, 1999).

[5]Melinda Fulmer, "Tricks of the Trade Shows," *Los Angeles Times,* February 19, 1997, p. D1.

[6]COMDEX press release, January 26, 1998.

[7]"Private Trade Shows," *Promotional Sense* 3, no. 1 (Spring 1998), p. 2.

[8]Jim Obermayer, "Power Play: Sales Leads Are Why You Exhibit" (presentation at Exhibitor Show, Baltimore, Fall 1999).

[9]"The Comeback," p. S8.

[10]David Sweet, "Bowing to TV, IOC Bars Web Use of Audio, Video from Olympics," *Wall Street Journal,* August 2, 2000, p. B1.

[11]Stephanie Zschunke, "Cause Marketing: Lost and Found," *Reputation Management,* February 2000, p. 22.

[12]Daniel Shannon, "Doing Well by Doing Good: Special Report on Cause Marketing," *PROMO Magazine,* February 1996, pp. 29-38.

[13]Kay Harmsen, "Experiential Event Marketing: Building Brand Relationships That Last," *IMC Research Journal,* Spring 2001, pp. 19-26.

[14]Kurt Miller, "Beyond ROI: Using Measurement to Improve Event Marketing Performance" (corporate handout, Jack Morton Worldwide, Boston, n.d.).

[15]"Alsop to Sprint: Drop Dead," *Fortune,* July 24, 2000, p. 31.

[16]"Consumers Eager to Know Values That Guide Business Decision," *Marketing News,* November 6, 1995, p. 5.

[17]Thomas Knect, Ralf Keszinski, and Felix A. Weber, "Making Profits after the Sale," *McKinsey Quarterly* 4 (1993), pp. 79-86.

[18]*Wall Street Journal,* January 19, 2000, p. B1.

[19]Bob Parks, "Where the Customer Service Rep Is King," *Business 2.0,* June 2003, p. 70.

[20]Ibid.

[21]Jennifer Beauprez, "Customer Service on Slippery Slope," *The Denver Post,* November 25, 2001, p. 25A.

[22]Erika Stutzman, "Online Customer Service," *Boulder Daily Camera,* October 3, 2000, p. B1.

[23]Stephanie Paterik, "Sheraton Plans to Pay Guests for Bad Service," *Wall Street Journal,* September 6, 2002, p. B1.

[24]Ron Lieber, " 'Operator, I Demand an Automated Menu,' " *Wall Street Journal,* July 30, 2002, p. D1.

[25]Jeffrey Pfeffer, "The Face of Your Business," *Business 2.0,* December 2002–January 2003, p. 58.

[26]Author's personal experience as brand manager at Jeno's.

[27]Christian Gronroos, *Service Management and Marketing* (Lanham, MD: Lexington Books, 1990), p. 47; A. Parasuraman, V. A. Zeithaml, and L. L. Berry, "A Conceptual Model of Service Quality and Its Implications for Future Research," *Journal of Marketing,* Fall 1985, p. 47.

[28]Mike Cote, "Can't Get No Satisfaction," *Boulder Daily Camera,* February 25, 2001, p. F1.

[29]Dana James "Just Do It: Customer Feedback Ineffective without Action," *Marketing News,* October 28, 2002, p. 43.

[30]Charles Weiser, "Championing the Customer," *Harvard Business Review,* November-December 1995, p. 113

[31]Lovelock, *Product Plus,* p. 214.

Chapter 20

[1]David Bauder, "CNN Pulls Two Ads on Global Warming," *Boulder Daily Camera,* October 5, 1997, p. 14a.

[2]Sean MacBride, *Many Voices, One World: Communication and Society* (New York: Unipub [UNESCO], 1980).

[3]Sharon Shavitt, Paula Lowrey, and James Haefner, "Public Attitudes toward Advertising, More Favorable Than You Might Think," *Journal of Advertising Research* 34, no. 4 (1998), pp. 7-22.

[4]Quoted in David Ogilvy, *Ogilvy on Advertising* (New York: Crown, 1983).

[5]<www.nytimes.com/2003/07/10/opinion/10THU2.html?th>.

[6]Yuminko Ono, "Magazines Spar with Television over Drug Ads," *Wall Street Journal,* October 10, 1997, p. B8.

[7]Herbert J. Rotfeld, "Power and Limitations of Media Clearance Practices and Advertising Self-Regulation," *Journal of Public Policy and Marketing* 11, no. 1 (Spring 1992), p. 93.

[8]Simon Beck, "World Gangs Up on US 'Culture,' " *South China Morning Post,* July 5, 1998, p. 12.

[9]Tyler Cowen, "French Kiss-Off: How Protectionism Has Hurt French Films," *Reason* 30, no. 3 (July 1998), p. 40.

[10]Suzanne Vranica, "Patient Channel to Blast Ads at Bedridden," *Wall Street Journal,* September 26, 2002, p. B1.

[11]Karen Uhlenhuth, "Ads, Consumer Images Bombard Kids," *Boulder Daily Camera,* October 9, 2001, p. 1D.

[12]Roy Fox, "Hucksters Hook Captive Yungsters," *Mizzou,* Summer 2002, pp. 23-27.

[13]Jim Drinkard, "Lobbyists Trying to Sway Younger Minds," *USA Today,* June 23, 1998, p. 7A.

[14]Lisa Sarkis Neaville, "Molding Young Minds: Firms Spend Big to Get Views into Public Schools," *Plastics News,* October 30, 1995, p. 1.

[15]"U.S. FTC: Consumers Lose Billions Annually to Fraud, FTC Chairman Tells Senate Subcommittee," *M2 Presswire,* February 6, 1998.

[16]Ryan Morgan, "No-Call List's First Year: Success," *Boulder Daily Camera,* July 3, 2003, p. 3B.

[17]James R. Schiffman, "After Uptown, Are Some Niches Out?" *Wall Street Journal,* January 22, 1990, pp. B1, B8.

[18]Alan Farnham, "Biggest Business Goofs of 1991," *Fortune,* January 13, 1992, pp. 80-83.

[19]"Love Is Playing with Fire," *Forbes*, November 3, 1997, p. 39.

[20]David B. Menkes, "Hazardous Drugs in Developing Countries: The Market May Be Healthier Than the People," *British Medical Journal* 315, no. 7122 (December 13, 1997), p. 1557.

[21]"First Mad Cows, Now Mad about Pigeons," *Inside PR* 2, no. 39 (July 22, 1996).

[22]Cecil Adams, "The Straight Dope," *Chicago Reader*, 1999 <www.chicagoreader.com>.

[23]Joel Saegert, "Why Marketing Should Quit Giving Subliminal Advertising the Benefit of the Doubt," *Psychology and Marketing*, 1987, pp. 107-20; Myron Gable, Henry T. Wilkins, Lynn Harris, and Richard Feinberg, "An Evaluation of Subliminally Embedded Sexual Stimuli in Graphics," *Journal of Advertising* 16, no. 1 (1987), pp. 26-31.

[24]Adam Liptak, "Maine Suits Swirl on Hebrew National Umbrella Ads," *New York Times*, February 6, 2003, <www.nytimes.com/2003/02/06/national/06UMBR.html>.

[25]Chris Adams, "Looser Lips for Food and Drug Companies?" *Wall Street Journal*, September 17, 2002, p. A4.

[26]Theresa Agovino, "Prescription Marketing Efforts Raise Eyebrows," *Boulder Daily Camera*, August 3, 2002, p. 4E.

[27]Thomas Burton, "Reining in Drug Advertising," *Wall Street Journal*, March 13, 2002, p. B1.

[28]"5 to 4 Supreme Court Decision Supports Free Commercial Speech," a commentary on *Thompson v. Western States Medical Center* and the decision by the U.S. Supreme Court on April 29, 2002, Vitamin Lawyer, <www.lifespirit.org/thompwest.html>.

[29]"FTC Policy Statement regarding Advertising Substantiation," issued March 11, 1983, from the FTC website <www.ftc.gov/bcp/guides/ad3subst.htm>, July 1, 2003.

[30]"FTC Policy Statement on Deception," issued October 14, 1983, from the FTC website <www.ftc.gov/bcp/policystmt/ad-decept.htm>, July 1, 2003.

[31]Daniel Golden and Suzanne Vranica, "Duracell's Duck Ad Will Carry Disclaimer," *Wall Street Journal*, February 7, 2002, p. B7; Jack Neff, "Duracell Agrees to Modify Robo-War Duck Ad," *AdAge.com*, February 6, 2002, <www.adage.com/news.cms?newsid=33981>.

[32]Vanessa O'Connell, "Marketers Increasingly Dispute Health Claims of Rivals' Products," *Wall Street Journal*, April 4, 2002, p. B1.

[33]Frank J. Giliberti, "Ads and Marketing Materials Can Lead to Liability," *Marketing Management*, Winter 1999, p. 53.

[34]Diane Richard, "Local Advertisers Turn to Arbitration to Resolve Disputes over Ads," *Minneapolis-St. Paul City Business* 15, no. 9 (August 1, 1997), p. 1.

[35]Paul Bloom, Gregory Gundlach, and Joseph Cannon, "Slotting Allowances and Fees: Schools of Thought and the Views of Practicing Managers," *Journal of Marketing*, April 2000, p. 92.

[36]Matthew Benjamin, "A World of Fakes: Counterfeit Goods Threaten Firms, Consumers, and National Security," <www.usnews.com/usnews/issue/030714/misc/14counterfeit.htm>, July 14, 2003.

[37]"Guidelines against Bait Advertising," <www.ftc.gov/bcp/guides/baitads-gd-htm>, from the FTC website, July 13, 2003.

[38]Herbert J. Rotfeld, "Power and Limitations of Media Clearance Practices and Advertising Self-Regulation," *Journal of Public Policy and Marketing* 11, no. 1 (Spring 1992), p. 90.

[39]Steve Pasternack and Sandra H. Utz, "Newspapers' Policies on Rejection of Ads for Products and Services," *Journalism Quarterly* 65 (Fall 1988), pp. 695-701.

[40]Herbert J. Rotfeld, Kathleen T. Lacher, and Michael S. LaTour, "Newspapers' Standards for Acceptable Advertising," *Journal of Advertising Research*, September-October 1996, pp. 37-48.

[41]Herbert J. Rotfeld and Patrick R. Parsons, "Self-Regulation and Magazine Advertising," *Journal of Advertising* 18, no. 4 (Winter 1989) pp. 33-40.

[42]U.S. Federal Trade Commission, docket no. 9268, agreement containing consent order to cease and desist, 1995, <www.ftc.gov/os>.

[43]David A. Weinstein, "Overlooking or Foregoing Federal Registration of a Trademark Can be a Costly Mistake," *Review 01*, 2001, November, p. 5.

[44]Sheila Calamba, "Group Targets 36 Products It Says Have 'Misleading' Labels; Several General Mills Cereals, Snacks on the List," *Minneapolis Star Tribune*, August 3, 1995, p. 1D.

[45]"Smoking Guns: PR/Marketing's Role in a Healthier America," *PR News* 53, no. 21 (April 21, 1997).

[46]Susan Okie, "Thai Condom Campaign Cuts HIV Infections," *Washington Post*, March 3, 1998, p. Z5.

[47]Courtney Kane, "A Federal Agency Starts a Paid Campaign Today to Influence Young People to Stay Away from Drugs," *New York Times*, July 9, 1998, p. D3.

Chapter 21

[1]Gabriel Kahn, "Still Going for Gold," *Wall Street Journal*, January 28, 2003, p. B1.

[2]Philip Cateora, *International Marketing* (Homewood, IL: Irwin, 1993), p. vii.

[3]Warren Keegan, *Global Marketing Management*, 6th ed. (Upper Saddle River, NJ: Prentice Hall, 1999), pp. 8-9.

[4]Ibid., p. 9.

[5]Ibid., p. 6.

[6]*2002 Fact Pack: A Handy Guide to the Advertising Business* (New York: Advertising Age, 2002).

[7]Marieke de Mooij, *Global Marketing and Advertising: Understanding Cultural Paradoxes* (Thousand Oaks, CA: Sage, 1998), p. 43.

[8]Sak Onkvisit and John Shaw, "Standardized International Advertising: Some Research Issues and Implications," *Journal of Marketing Research* 39, no. 6 (1999), pp. 19-24; and Frenkel Ter Hofstede, Jan-Benedict Steenkamp, and Michel Wedel, "International Market Segmentation Based on Consumer-Product Relations," *Journal of Marketing Research* 36, no. 1 (1999), pp. 1-17.

[9]John Quelch and Edward Hoff, "Customizing Global Marketing," *Harvard Business Review*, May–June 1986, pp. 59-68.

[10]Jee Young Lee and Trina Sego, "Culture in Advertising on the World Wide Web: Executional Elements of South Korean and U.S. Banner Advertisements," *Proceedings of the 2000 Conference of the American Academy of Advertising,* ed. Mary Alice Shaver (East Lansing: Michigan State University, 2000), p. 198; Gordon Miracle, Beate Bluhm, Juergen Bluhm, Yung Kyun Choi, and Hairong Li, "The Relationship between Cultural Variables and the Amount and Type of Information in Korean and German Television Commercials," in *Proceedings of the 1998 Conference of the American Academy of Advertising,* ed. Darrel D. Muehling (Pullman: Washington State University, 1998), pp. 9-15; and Jyotika Ramaprasad and Kazumi Hasegawa, "An Analysis of Japanese Television Commercials," *Journalism Quarterly,* 67 (Fall 1990), pp. 1025-33.

[11]Edward Hall, *Beyond Culture* (New York: Anchor Press-Doubleday, 1976).

[12]Augustine Ihator, "Understand the Cultural Patterns of the World—An Imperative in Implementing Strategic International PR Programs," *Public Relations Quarterly,* Winter 2000, pp. 38-44.

[13]Geert H. Hofstede, *Culture's Consequences: International Differences in Work-Related Values* (Beverly Hills, CA: Sage, 1980); *Cultures and Organizations: Software of the Mind* (New York: McGraw-Hill, 1991); "The Cultural Relativity of Organization Practices and Theories," *Journal of International Business Studies* 14, no. 2 (1983), pp. 75-89.

[14]Ihator, "Understand the Cultural Patterns of the World."

[15]Alan Shao, Mary Anne Raymond, and Charles Taylor, "Shifting Advertising Appeals in Taiwan," *Journal of Advertising Research,* November–December 1999, pp. 61-69.

[16]W. C. Gudykunst and S. Ting-Toomey, *Culture and Interpersonal Communication* (Newbury Park, CA: Sage, 1988); and B. C. Deng, "The Influence of Individualism-Collectivism on Conflict Management Style: A Cross-Culture Comparison between Taiwanese and U.S. Business Employees" (master's thesis, Sacramento: California State University, 1992).

[17]Frank Rose, "Think Globally, Script Locally," *Fortune,* November 8, 1999, p. 160.

[18]Grant McCracken, "Culture and Consumption: A Theoretical Account of the Structure and Movement of the Cultural Meaning of Consumer Goods," *Journal of Consumer Research* 13 (1986), pp. 71-84.

[19]M. Rokeach, *The Nature of Human Values* (New York: Free Press, 1973), p. 5.

[20]Hong Cheng and Kara Chan, "One Country, Two Systems: Cultural Values Reflected in Chinese and Hong Kong Television Commercials," *Proceedings of the 2000 Conference of the American Academy of Advertising,* p. 110.

[21]Young Sook Moon and George R. Franke, "Cultural Influences on Agency Practitioners' Ethical Perceptions: A Comparison of Korea and the U.S.," *Journal of Advertising* 29, no. 1 (Spring 2000), pp. 51-65.

[22]T. J. Knutson, R. Komolsevin, P. Chatiketu, and V. Smith, "Rhetorical Sensitivity and Willingness to Communicate: A Comparison of Thai and U.S. American Samples with Implications for Intercultural Communication Effectiveness" (paper presented at the annual conference of the International Communication Association, Acapulco, Mexico, June 2000).

[23]"Brad Pitt Car Ad an Insult to Asians, Says Malaysia," *Straits Times Interaction,* January 16, 2003, <www.straitstimes.asia1.com.sg>.

[24]Noelle Knox and Theresa Howard, "Anti-War Protesters Take Aim at American Brands," *USA Today,* April 4, 2003, p. B1.

[25]These are compiled from Subhash Jain, *International Marketing Management,* 3rd ed. (Boston: PWS-Kent, 1990), pp. 227-28.

[26]de Mooij, *Global Marketing and Advertising,* p. 56.

[27]Bob Coen, "Universal McCann's Insider's Report," <www.mccann.com>, presentation to investment analysts at Universal McCann's headquarters in New York, June 17, 2003.

[28]Rose, "Think Globally, Script Locally," p. 160.

[29]Leslie Chang and Peter Wonacott, "Cracking China's Market," *Wall Street Journal,* January 9, 2003, p. B1.

[30]Tom Duncan, "A Mother's a Mother," *Marketing and Media Decisions,* May 1990, p. 120.

[31]Elissa Moses, *The $100 Billion Allowance: Accessing the Global Teen Market* (New York: Wiley, 2000).

[32]Quoted in Brett Pulley and Andrew Tanzer, "Summer's Gemstone," *Forbes,* February 21, 2000, pp. 107-11.

[33]Theodore Levitt, "The Globalization of Markets," *Harvard Business Review,* May–June 1983, pp. 92-102.

[34]Marilyn Roberts, "2000 International Advertising Pre-Conference: The Global Best Practices Roundtable," *Proceedings of the 2000 Conference of the American Academy of Advertising*, pp. 239-41; Onkvisit and Shaw, "Standardized International Advertising."

[35]Jiafei Yin, "International Advertising Strategies in China," p. 30.

[36]"Global Internet Statistics (by Language)," June 2000, <www.glreach.com/globstats/index.php3>.

[37]Susan H. C. Tai, "Advertising in Asia: Localize or Regionalize?" *International Journal of Advertising* 16, no. 1 (1997), pp. 48-61.

[38]Robert Hite and Cynthia Fraser, "International Advertising Strategies of Multinational Corporations," *Journal of Advertising Research* 28, no. 4 (1988), pp. 9-17.

[39]Yin, "International Advertising Strategies in China," pp. 25-35.

[40]Stephen Gould, Dawn Lerman, and Andreas Green, "Agency Perceptions and Practices on Global IMC," *Journal of Advertising Research* 39, no. 1 (1999), pp. 7-20.

[41]Kate Maddox, "Microsoft Extends 'Agility' Campaign," *BtoB*, June 9, 2003, p. 19.

[42]Andreas Grein and Stephen Gould, "Globally Integrated Marketing Communications," *Journal of Marketing Communications* 2 (1996), pp. 141-58.

[43]Erin White and Sarah Ellison, "Unilever Ads Offer a Tribute to Dirt," *Wall Street Journal*, June 2, 2003, p. B3.

Chapter 22

[1]John Gaffney, "The Buzz Must Go On," *Business 2.0*, February 2002, p. 49.

[2]Ibid.

[3]David Bell, "Bozell's Bell Paints Active Future for 4A's," *Advertising Age*, April 7, 1997, p. 26.

[4]Laura Petrecca, "Agencies Urged to Show the Worth of Their Work," *Advertising Age*, April 14, 1997, pp. 3, 54.

[5]Information taken from the Advertising and Marketing Effectiveness (AME) award-winning brief for Buitoni by the McCann-Erickson Italiana office in Milan, Italy.

[6]Jane M. Von Bergen, "Her Job Is Monitoring Every Cable Infomercial," *Philadelphia Inquirer*, February 16, 2003, p. A1.

[7]Tobi Elkin, "TiVo Introduces Service to Measure Audience Data," *Advertising Age*, June 21, 2003, p. 8.

[8]Quoted from Richard M. Restak, *Brainscapes* (New York: Hyperion,1995), by David Wolfe in "What Your Customers Can't Say," *American Demographics*, February 1998, p. 24.

[9]Priscilla LaBarbare and Joel Tucciarone, "GSR Reconsidered: A Behavior-Based Approach to Evaluating and Improving the Sales Potency of Advertising," *Journal of Advertising Research*, September-October 1995, p. 35.

[10]Karl Weiss, "Internet Research: Harnessing the Power of the Internet with Online Data Reporting," *Alert 38*, no. 6 (June 2000), pp. 1-3.

[11]Ibid.

[12]Geneva J. King, "Today's Marketing Data Research Companies: The News You Need, When You Need It," *Online Newsletter*, July 7, 2000.

[13]Adapted from Phil Levine and Bill Ahlhauser, "Internet Interviewing—Pro," *Marketing Research*, Summer 1999, p. 35.

[14]Dale Kulp and Rick Hunter, "Internet Interviewing—Con," *Marketing Research*, Summer 1999, p. 36.

[15]Tom Duncan and Sandra Moriarty, *Driving Brand Value: Using Integrated Marketing to Manage Profitable Stakeholder Relationships* (New York: McGraw-Hill, 1997), pp. 261-278.

[16]Jeff Smith, comments on the MarketingProfs.com listserv, April 5, 2002.

[17]Ibid.

[18]Duncan and Moriarty, *Driving Brand Value*, pp. 262-63.

[19]Thomas O. Jones and W. Earl Sasser, Jr., "Why Satisfied Customers Defect," *Harvard Business Review*, November-December 1995, pp. 88-99.

[20]Gregory H. Watson, *Strategic Benchmarking* (New York: Wiley, 1993), p. 10.

[21]Anders Gronstedt and Anders Hogstrom, "Benchmarking Public Relations: The Volvo Story," *The Strategist*, Fall 1998, p. 10.

Photo Credits

p. 2: The Image Bank/Getty Images. p. 4 Ex. 1-1: Courtesy AFLAC, Inc. p. 7 Ex. 1-2: Reprinted with permission of the AAF. p. 8 Ex. 1-3: Courtesy Netaid. p. 9 Ex. 1-4: Courtesy Volkswagen of America; Agency: Arnold Worldwide. p. 10 Ex. 1-5: Courtesy Sears, Roebuck & Co. p. 11 Ex. 1-6: www.dell.com. Courtesy Dell Computer. p. 11 Ex. 1-7: www.businessweek.com. Courtesy Business Week. Copyright The McGraw-Hill Companies, by permission. p. 12 Ex. 1-9: © Michael J. Hruby. p. 13 Ex. 1-10: Reprinted with Permission of Callard & Bowser-Suchard, Inc. p. 14 Ex. 1-11: AP Photo/Peter Lennihan. p. 15 Ex. 1-12: Photo by Chris Stanford/Getty Images. p. 16 Ex. 1-13: Courtesy Southwest Airlines. p. 17 Ex. 1-14: Courtesy CNN. p. 18 Ex. 1-15: ©Laszlo Regos. p. 19 Ex. 1-16: Copyright 2002 Amazon.com®, Inc. All Rights Reserved. p. 20 Ex. 1-17: ©M. Hruby. p. 23 Ex. 1-18: Courtesy FedEx Corporation. p. 24 Ex. 1-19: Ad developed for EDS by Rehak Advertising Creative Services. p. 24 Ex. 1-20: Courtesy AFLAC, Inc. p. 28: Courtesy The Engine Room/San Francisco. p. 30 Ex. 2-1: Courtesy The Phelps Group. p. 32 Ex. 2-2: Courtesy National Fluid Milk Processor Promotion Board; Agency: Bozell Worldwide. p. 33 Ex. 2-3: Photo Courtesy Mall of America. p. 38 Ex. 2-4: Courtesy Clorox Canada; Agency: Palmer Jarvis DDB/Toronto. p. 41 Ex. 2-5: Courtesy Poppe Tyson. p. 42 Ex. 2-6: Courtesy Golin/Harris. p. 43 Ex. 2-7: With permission of Landor. p. 45 Ex. 2-9: Copyright 2003, USA TODAY. Reprinted with permission. p. 46 Ex. 2-10: Courtesy Canadian Magazine Publishers; Agency: One Company/Toronto. p. 48 Ex. 2-11: Courtesy Spicer's Paper. p. 49 Ex. 2-12: Courtesy W.L. Gore & Associates, Inc. p. 52 Ex. 2-13: Courtesy IBM Corporation. p. 58 Ex. 2-15: Courtesy Siebel. p. 63 Ex. 2-16: Courtesy General Motors Corporation. p. 66: Courtesy of Steven Bonini. p. 68 Ex. 3-1: © Michael J. Hruby p. 72 Ex. 3-2a: Courtesy University of Notre Dame. p. 72 Ex. 3-2b: Courtesy Massachusetts Institute of Technology. p. 72 Ex. 3-2c: Courtesy Bryn Mawr College. p. 72 Ex. 3-2d: Courtesy St. Olaf College. p. 73 Ex. 3-3: Courtesy Land Rover North America. p. 74 Ex. 3-4: HALLS is a registered trademark of Cadbury Ireland Ltd. ©2000 Warner-Lambert Co. p. 75 Ex. 3-5: Artwork provided courtesy of the United States Marine Corps. p. 77 Ex. 3-6: Courtesy JetBlue Airways. p. 80 Ex. 3-7: Courtesy H & R Block®. p. 81 Ex. 3-8: ©Monster 2003. www.monster.com. Used with permission. p. 81 Ex. 3-9a: ©The Procter & Gamble Company. Used with permission. p. 81 Ex. 3-9b: Courtesy Saturn Corporation. p. 81 Ex. 3-9c: BIC trademark and logo are registered trademarks of BIC Corporation and are reproduced with permission. p. 82 Ex. 3-10: Craftsman is used by permission of Sears Brands, LLC. p. 83 Ex. 3-11: Kellogg's Corn Flakes, Kellogg's Raisin Bran, Froot Loops, Mini-Wheats, Corn Pops, and Special K are trademarks of Kellogg Company. ©2003 Kellogg Co. p. 86 Ex. 3-12: TRUSTe, Web Site Privacy Certification. Used by permission. p. 87 Ex. 3-13: Reprinted with permission of AchieveGlobal. p. 88 Ex. 3-14: EdwardJones® is a registered trademark of Edward Jones/St. Louis, Missouri. p. 89 Ex. 3-15: Courtesy of Broilmaster Premium Gas Grills, a Division of Empire Comfort Systems, Inc. p. 95 Ex. 3-16: Courtesy Cushman & Wakefield Worldwide. p. 96 Ex. 3-17: Reproduced by permission of W.L. Gore & Associates, Inc. GORE-TEX is a registered Trademark of W.L. Gore & Associates. p. 97 Ex.3-18: ® St. Paul Fire and Marine Insurance Company, St. Paul, MN. p. 102: Courtesy InfoCision

Management Corporation. p. 104 Ex. 4-1: Courtesy McCann-Erickson Dublin Ltd. And Unilever/HB Ice Cream. p. 105 Ex. 4-2: Courtesy McCann-Erickson Dublin Ltd. And Unilever/HB Ice Cream. p. 108 Ex. 4-3: Courtesy Dunkin Donuts. p. 109 Ex. 4-4: "Transamerica," the Transamerica Pyramid building, and the Transamerica Pyramid logo are federally registered trademarks and service marks owned by Transamerica Corporation, a member of the AEGON Group. All rights reserved. Reprinted with permission. p. 111 Ex. 4-5: Courtesy Apple Computer. p. 112 Ex. 4-6: ©2001 Susan G. Holtz. p. 113 Ex. 4-7: Courtesy Spanish Broadcasting System. p. 114 Ex. 4-8: AP Photo/Kathy Willens. p. 115 Ex. 4-9: Courtesy Novell, Inc. p. 118 Ex. 4-10: Courtesy Gateway, Inc. p. 120 Ex. 4-11: Courtesy Virgin Atlantic Cargo. p. 121 Ex. 4-12: Photodisc Green/Getty Images. p. 123 Ex. 4-13: Courtesy FM Global. p. 125 Ex. 4-14: Courtesy of Texas Instruments, Incorporated. p. 127 Ex. 4-15: Courtesy Target Corporation. p. 130: Client: The Ritz-Carlton; Agency: Sawyer Riley Compton/Atlanta; Account Team: Alison Simmons & Andrea Brook; Creative Director: Bart Cleveland; Writer: Al Jackson; Photographer: Jim Erickson. p. 132 Ex. 5-1: AP Photo/Lynne Sladky. p. 135 Ex. 5-2: ©1998 BASF Corporation. p. 137 Ex. 5-3: Courtesy Hallmark Cards, Inc.; Agency: Leo Burnett/Toronto. p. 140 Ex. 5-4: Courtesy Swiss Army Brands. p. 142 Ex. 5-5: Courtesy Sunkist Growers. p. 143 Ex. 5-6: Courtesy MasterFoods USA. p. 145 Ex. 5-7: Courtesy Candies. p. 147 Ex. 5-8: Courtesy Clif Bar, Inc.; Agency: Wongdoody/Los Angeles. p. 148 Ex. 5-9: Courtesy Dunkin Donuts. p. 153 Ex. 5-10: TABASCO®, the TABASCO® diamond logo and the TABASCO® bottle design are trademarks exclusively of McIlhenny Co., Avery Island, LA. 70513. p. 154 Ex. 5-11: Courtesy Taxi/Toronto. p. 156 Ex. 5-12: Courtesy McCann-Erickson Southwest and Parkinson Coalition of Houston. p. 158 Ex. 5-13: Courtesy Kroger Company. p. 161 Ex. 5-14: Created by Rainey Kelly Campbell Roalfe/Y&R. p. 163 Ex. 5-15: Courtesy General Mills. p. 166: Courtesy GMC Envoy and McCann Relationship Marketing. p. 168 Ex. 6-1: Courtesy GMC Envoy and McCann Relationship Marketing. p. 170 Ex. 6-2: Courtesy GMC Envoy and McCann Relationship Marketing. p. 171 Ex. 6-3: Courtesy GMC Envoy and McCann Relationship Marketing. p. 172 Ex. 6-4: Courtesy Motorola. p. 176 Ex. 6-5: Courtesy Nike. p. 176 Ex. 6-6: Courtesy Shell Oil. p. 180 Ex. 6-7: Courtesy robertmondavi.com. p. 180 Ex. 6-8: Lands' End® Direct Merchants. p. 182 Ex. 6-9: Courtesy Periscope Marketing Communications. p. 185 Ex. 6-10: Courtesy Snapple-Beverage Corporation. p. 186 Ex. 6-11: Courtesy Canadian Egg Marketing Agency. p. 187 Ex. 6-12: Courtesy GMC Envoy and McCann Relationship Marketing. p. 190 Ex. 6-13: Courtesy Greteman Group; Copywriter: Todd Gimlin & Deanna Harms; Designer: Craig Tomson & James Strange; Art Director: Sonia Greteman. p. 196 Ex. 6-14: Courtesy Duracell. p. 198 Ex. 6-15: Courtesy Talisma Corporation. p. 201 Ex. 6-16: Courtesy Hewlett-Packard. p. 203 Ex. 6-17: Courtesy World Wildlife Fund 2003. PSA campaign. p. 206: ©1999 Jockey International, Inc. World Rights Reserved. p. 209 Ex. 7-1: Courtesy Holden Ltd. and McCann-Erickson/Melbourne. p. 210 Ex. 7-2: Courtesy Holden Ltd. and McCann-Erickson/Melbourne. p. 212 Ex. 7-3: Coricidin® is a registered trademark of Schering-Plough HealthCare Products, Inc. p. 215 Ex. 7-4: ©2002 The Great Indoors. p. 217 Ex. 7-5: ©2001. Susan G. Holtz. p. 219 Ex. 7-6: Courtesy Fox

Brand Index

Name Index

Subject Index